WHO IS MY NEIGHBOR?

WHO IS MY NEIGHBOR?

ENCYCLOPEDIA OF NATURAL RELATIONS

*Extensive index of universally acknowledged
norms among all human societies,
now largely forgotten in the West.*

—— 2nd, ed. ——

Western Front Books
Lake Buchanan, Texas, United States

Western Front Books
12407 N Mopac Expy #250
Austin, TX 78758

ISBN #s:
978-1959666516 (paperback)
978-1959666394 (hardcover)

Printed in the United States of America

"*Modern man is scandalized by what was commonplace in traditional society. The most radical book of our time would be a compendium of old proverbs.*"
— Nicolás Gómez Dávila

"*In half a lifetime, many have seen their God dethroned, their heroes defiled, their culture polluted, their values assaulted, their country invaded, and themselves demonized as extremists and bigots for holding on to beliefs held for generations.*"
— Pat Buchanan

CONTENTS

PREFACE TO THE SECOND EDITION

The second edition of *Who Is My Neighbor?* builds upon the first and marks more than a decade of research and study. This is not a work of quote-mining but of exhaustive, time-consuming, yet enjoyable labor in personal, public, and university libraries; in books, documents, articles, essays, speeches, and even manuscript fragments. In order to provide the best and widest scholarship, we have consulted authors, publishers, professors, translators, and other authorities beyond our expertise. The result is a second edition expanded over sixty percent from the original.

We have striven to create a proper work of scholarly and historical reference. Thus, this volume also has been reformatted alphabetically and dual-column for easier reference use and leisurely perusal. In-line citations can be checked with a full bibliography at the end of the book. There, readers will also find helpful indices outlining author, date or era, theme, and more. These allow quick reference searching – a far improvement over the first edition.

Who Is My Neighbor? should, thus, be viewed and read as a compendium of human thought upon a given topic. We have striven as much as possible to put forth the voice of others rather than ourselves, except for slight contextual notes and an introduction to the heart and spirit behind the project. However, it must be stressed that we neither assert nor assume that each source collected here expresses, say, modern sentiments concerning race, nation, or ethnic identity. This is a work of reference. As such, each source must be weighed within the context of its own times and era.

The one theme that unites our encyclopedia, as explained in the Introduction, is Natural Relations: "Natural social relations, or natural affections, are those which we find among humans at nearly all times and places – that humans have preferences and prejudices in favor of their own people, in nearness by nature and place, and in likeness to themselves; and that they tend to form particular social orders, with duties, loyalties, and bonds around these shared natural affinities." Keep this in your mind as you read!

– The Editors, January 2025

INTRODUCTION

The British statesman Edmund Burke once noted, "When ancient opinions and rules of life are taken away, the loss cannot possibly be estimated." It seems that we live in that time when ancient opinions and rules of life have been taken away and we are not estimating but experiencing the loss in real time. The reactionary Nicolás Gómez Dávila, remarking on such times, said that, "Modern man is scandalized by what was commonplace in traditional society. The most radical book of our time would be a compendium of old proverbs." A compendium of old proverbs, truths, and wisdom that were once commonplace in traditional society is just what is needed right now. You hold such a book in your hands.

One of the myths of modernity was that some bad people out there were trying to hide the bad past from us, so that we all might remain historically ignorant and fall prey to tyranny. According to liberals, leftists, and radicals, we are supposed to learn from the past in order to avoid the wickedness of our ancestors. We study history so we can escape it. But why must this be? This idea seems to come from people who hate their ancestors, or who, at any rate, want us to hate ours. Why not study the past in order to embrace it? While the saying is true that, those who are ignorant of the past are doomed to repeat it, it is equally true that those who do know the past are able to recover and preserve it. Those who are ignorant of the past are not free to carry it on but are doomed both to repeat the bad and to not repeat the good, but only rediscover it, perhaps, after long suffering and groping.

George Orwell said, "The most effective way to destroy people is to deny and obliterate their own understanding of their history." Indeed, these same learned classes who beg us to escape our history are in effect keeping people from the means to resist those forces dissolving them. For, if a people were to know their past; if they were to know their heritage and remember their ancestors, and what the now-torn-down statues meant and what their great men did, and why their grandfathers suffered and bled, and what their forbearers wrought and achieved; then their descendants today might imitate them. They might aspire and combine; they might strengthen and arise to free and rule themselves once more. If a people ever found the blueprints, they might rebuild the ruins.

Some time ago the West lost, or conveniently misplaced, its blueprint in the way of things. This Way was a long known set of experiences concerning how the world operates and how to be human in it. Cut off from those old paths, the modern mind is free to imagine whatever it pleases about these once-given truths. With such freedom comes uncertainty of truth, skepticism of knowledge claims, and confusion about personal and collective identity. The freedom to imagine new sorts of nations, ethnicities, and genders is all of a piece. It's all a "social construct" that can be deconstructed and reformulated.

This way of thinking is to misdirect our political and social life from one that is objective and formalized to one that is subjective and relativistic. The formerly strong structures which guided our experience of being in the world are now best described by Yeats who said "all that is solid melts into air" and "the best lack all conviction." In other words, it is an attack on objective truth itself.

C.S. Lewis' *The Abolition Of Man* argued against this pluralist, subjective view of life where truth lies within oneself and thus nothing is really true or real. He claimed that all humans have known some things to be universally true, that is, to correspond to reality or the way of things, apart from place, perspective, and condition. This natural Way he called the natural law or the Tao. Once known to all humans, this law is denied by modern people who replace it with new, abstract ideas of Theory or Right. More recently, late modernity replaces it with nothing but perceived reality and selfhood.

To prove this natural Way and lead us back to it, the appendix of Lewis' book contains an index of universally acknowledged norms among all human societies. In that appendix Lewis said, "The idea of collecting independent testimonies presupposes that 'civilizations' have arisen in the world independently of one another; or even that humanity has had several independent emergences on this planet. The biology and anthropology involved in such an assumption are extremely doubtful. It is by no means certain that there has ever (in the sense required) been more than one civilization in all history. It is at least arguable that every civilization we find has been derived from another civilization and, in the last resort, from a single centre—'carried' like an infectious disease or like the Apostolical succession." Common sentiments as expressions of a natural law reveal continuity of core truths among all peoples. This continuity tethers us to reality amid the morally storm-tossed modern era.

Lewis' illustrations of the Tao then commence with certain themes such as the "Law of General Beneficence" which shows, from Ancient Egyptians and Jews to the Chinese and Europeans, a universal ethic of doing good or at least not doing harm to other humans. After this law follow, in order, the Law of Special Beneficence; Duties to Parents, Elders, and Ancestors; Duties to Children and Posterity; the Law of Justice; the Law of Good Faith and Veracity; the Law of Mercy; and the Law of Magnanimity. The list could be multiplied, but the point is that, regardless of what the passing moment says, there are some truths or values that are real no matter how many people today shout to the contrary. Our present work picks up just one of the themes in Lewis' and continues it more exhaustively in an area particularly under attack in our time: natural social relations.

Natural social relations, or natural affections, are those which we find among humans at nearly all times and places – that humans have preferences and prejudices in favor of their own people, in nearness by nature and place, and in likeness to themselves; and that they tend to form particular social orders, with duties, loyalties, and bonds around these shared natural affinities. Here are the selections on this topic that Lewis himself recorded in the appendix to *The Abolition Of Man*:

2. The Law of Special Beneficence

'It is upon the trunk that a gentleman works. When that is firmly set up, the Way grows. And surely proper behaviour to parents and elder brothers is the trunk of goodness.' (Ancient Chinese. Analects, i. 2)

'Brothers shall fight and be each others' bane.' (Old Norse. Account of the Evil Age before the World's end, Volospá 45)

'Has he insulted his elder sister?' (Babylonian. List of Sins. ERE v. 446)

'You will see them take care of their kindred [and] the children of their friends...never reproaching them in the least.' (Redskin. Le Jeune, quoted ERE v. 437)

'Love thy wife studiously. Gladden her heart all thy life long.' (Ancient Egyptian. ERE v. 481)

'Nothing can ever change the claims of kinship for a right thinking man.' (Anglo-Saxon. Beowulf, 2600)

'Did not Socrates love his own children, though he did so as a free man and as one not forgetting that the gods have the first claim on our friendship?' (Greek, Epictetus, iii. 24)

'Natural affection is a thing right and according to Nature.' (Greek. Ibid. 1. xi)

'I ought not to be unfeeling like a statue but should fulfil both my natural and artificial relations, as a worshipper, a son, a brother, a father, and a citizen.' (Greek. Ibid. III. ii)

'This first I rede thee: be blameless to thy kindred. Take no vengeance even though they do thee wrong.' (Old Norse. Sigdrifumál, 22)

'Is it only the sons of Atreus who love their wives? For every good man, who is right-minded, loves and cherishes his own.' (Greek. Homer, Iliad, ix. 340)

'The union and fellowship of men will be best preserved if each receives from us the more kindness in proportion as he is more closely connected with us.' (Roman. Cicero. De Off. 1. xvi)

'Part of us is claimed by our country, part by our parents, part by our friends.' (Roman. Ibid. 1. vii)

'If a ruler...compassed the salvation of the whole state, surely you would call him Good? The Master said, It would no longer be a matter of "Good". He would without doubt be a Divine Sage.' (Ancient Chinese. Analects, vi. 28)

'Has it escaped you that, in the eyes of gods and good men, your native land deserves from you more honour, worship, and reverence than your mother and father and all your ancestors? That you should give a softer answer to its anger than to a father's anger? That if you cannot persuade it to alter its mind you must obey it in all quietness, whether it binds you or beats you or sends you to a war where you may get wounds or death?' (Greek. Plato, Crito, 51, a, b)

'If any provide not for his own, and specially for those of his own house, he hath denied the faith.' (Christian. 1 Timothy 5:8)

'Put them in mind to obey magistrates.'...'I exhort that prayers be made for kings and all that are in authority.' (Christian. Titus 3:1 and 1 Timothy 2:1, 2)"

3. Duties to Parents, Elders, Ancestors

'Your father is an image of the Lord of Creation, your mother an image of the Earth. For him who fails to honour them, every work of piety is in vain. This is the first duty.' (Hindu. Janet, i. 9)

'Has he despised Father and Mother?' (Babylonian. List of Sins. ERE v. 446)

'I was a staff by my Father's side...I went in and out at his command.' (Ancient Egyptian. Confession of the Righteous Soul. ERE v. 481)

"Honour thy Father and thy Mother.' (Ancient Jewish. Exodus 20:12)

'To care for parents.' (Greek. List of duties in Epictetus, 111. vii)

'Children, old men, the poor, and the sick, should be considered as the lords of the atmosphere.' (Hindu. Janet, i. 8)

'Rise up before the hoary head and honour the old man.' (Ancient Jewish. Leviticus 19:32)

'I tended the old man, I gave him my staff.' (Ancient Egyptian. ERE v. 481)

'You will see them take care...of old men.' (Redskin. Le Jeune, quoted ERE v. 437)

'I have not taken away the oblations of the blessed dead.' (Ancient Egyptian. Confession of the Righteous Soul. ERE v. 478)

'When proper respect towards the dead is shown at the end and continued after they are far away, the moral force (tê) of a people has reached its highest point.' (Ancient Chinese. Analects, i. 9)

4. Duties to Children and Posterity

'Children, the old, the poor, etc. should be considered as lords of the atmosphere.' (Hindu. Janet, i. 8)

'To marry and to beget children.' (Greek. List of duties. Epictetus, 111. vii)

'Can you conceive an Epicurean commonwealth?...What will happen? Whence is the population to be kept up? Who will educate them? Who will be Director of Adolescents? Who will be Director of Physical Training? What will be taught?' (Greek. Ibid.)

'Nature produces a special love of offspring' and 'To live according to Nature is the su-

preme good.' (Roman. Cicero, De Off. 1. iv, and De Legibus, 1. xxi)

"The second of these achievements is no less glorious than the first; for while the first did good on one occasion, the second will continue to benefit the state for ever.' (Roman. Cicero. De Off. 1. xxii)

'Great reverence is owed to a child.' (Roman. Juvenal, xiv. 47)

'The Master said, Respect the young.' (Ancient Chinese. Analects, ix. 22)

'The killing of the women and more especially of the young boys and girls who are to go to make up the future strength of the people, is the saddest part...and we feel it very sorely.' (Redskin. Account of the Battle of Wounded Knee. ERE v. 432)

'Natural affection is a thing right and according to Nature,' is one of the above quotes. It captures perfectly the theme of this anthology. In the introduction to his appendix, Lewis stated that his list was not exhaustive but reflected what was readily available to one "who is not a professional historian." We intend, humbly, to pick up where Lewis left off, following the theme of the above-quoted example. For indeed, these natural affections have been espoused by all humans, at all times, and in all places, religions, and social conditions. They are right, according to Nature. However, some people in the modern age have increasingly been warring against these natural passions as part of a larger war against Nature itself, and thus against Nature's God.

Contrary to mankind's common understanding of natural social relations, the idea of unnatural or artificial relations are those which encourage us to imagine utopias of abstract ideals like Humanity, Equality, or Right in place of empirical human experience. Artificial relations call us to spread our affections, loyalties, and duties upon all people everywhere equally and without distinction; to subvert the common sentiments of mankind in exchange for the ravings of a few mad philosophers. The fact that Lewis compiled examples of human sanity on this topic proves the existence of their insane antagonist contrary. Take a look at these contrasting opinions for example:

"And Moses returned unto the Lord, and said, Oh, this people have sinned a great sin, and have made them gods of gold. Yet now, if thou wilt forgive their sin; and if not, blot me, I pray thee, out of thy book which thou hast written." – Exodus 32:31-32

"For I could wish that I myself were accursed and cut off from Christ for the sake of my brothers, my kinsmen according to the flesh." – Romans 9:3

"Honor thy father and mother; which is the first commandment with promise; That it may be well with thee, and thou mayest live long on the earth." – Ephesians 6:2-3

"Even the natural differences within species, like racial differences....can and must be done away with historically." – Karl Marx, Collected Works V:103

"The nationalities of the peoples associating themselves in accordance with the principle of community will be compelled to mingle with each other as a result of this association and thereby to dissolve themselves." – Friedrich Engels, The Principles of Communism

"The aim of socialism is not only to abolish the present division of mankind into small states and end all national isolation; not only to bring the nations closer together, but to merge them...." – Vladimir Lenin, The Rights of Nations to Self Determination

The first three show a natural love of people and place. The second three show the dissolution of natural particularity for fancy theories. The first three are based on common human sentiment shared by the mass of humanity throughout history. The latter three are unique formulas developed recently in history, which had at their time of development no basis for human experience. Indeed, prior to the middle-to-late 1700s, one is hard-pressed to find any example of artificial social relations outside of high abstractions such as Plato's *Republic*, which argued for a proto-communism where all wives, children, and property were held in common. In Plato's thought-experiment, the particular attachments of humans to their near relations (each man's love for his particular wife, child, and so on) were to be dissolved through lies, propaganda, and breeding programs. Even Plato knew that natural relations cannot be altered without serious effort. Thus, no one seriously tried this until the modern era.

However, the past ~250 years of Western history has been an unfurling experiment to scientifically excise from humans their natural affections and natural social relations – their very natures – so that a new universal Humanity, a global nation, and a borderless government can arise. Talk of this first began with theories of a fake "state of nature" where humans supposedly existed prior to social obligations to family, people, or place. Then, political theory imported that individualist blank slate state-of-nature into real society via a classless, genderless, religionless order – with no duties due others but many Rights (mostly bread and circuses) due oneself. Society was going to be built, not on superstitions of myth and magic, tradition and theology, community and authority, but upon Reason and Theory. Peace, Progress, and Love were prophesied. A new age was dawning. Bliss it was to be alive, but to be young was very heaven, said Wordsworth. Unendingly, modern philosophers have waxed poetic on the blessings to be experienced when archaic human divisions (natural relations) were to be overcome with Freedom and Light. John Lennon's *Imagine* sums up the idea.

Imagine there's no heaven It's easy if you try No hell below us Above us, only sky Imagine all the people Living for today

Imagine there's no countries It isn't hard to do Nothing to kill or die for And no religion too Imagine all the people Living life in peace

Imagine no possessions I wonder if you can No need for greed or hunger A brotherhood of man Imagine all the people Sharing all the world

To understand artificial relations, all you need to do is imagine – because that is where they exist, in the imagination. *Imagine* there are no gods or genders. *Imagine* there are no borders or cultures. *Imagine* there are no possessions, no ethnicities, no families, no particularity. *Imagine* there are no blood-and-soil loyalties that stir the human soul. Then, we will achieve world peace!

Lennon's song would have made a fine anthem for the ancient Land of the Lotus Eaters, where Odysseus' men ate a magic herb and *forgot their homeward journey back to their families, friends, and fatherland.* Odyseeus' men forgot their mission in life. All their passions drained from them: courage, loyalty, will. Eat the herb and you will enjoy a blissful, peopleless, placeless utopia. That same herb is being force-fed to people today, especially white European peoples. You will eat the herb. You will forget your people and home. You will love everyone and no one. This sounds similar to the World Economic Forum's saying today that "you will own nothing, eat bugs, and be happy." You cannot love a homeland and fight for it, or a woman and fight for her, or a religion and its gods, or a piece of land as emplacement, if you have none of these to begin with. Do you see? We can eliminate greed and war, not by regenerating the heart but by removing its objects.

Another literary example of this phenomenon is the rabbits in *Watership Down* who thought they were in a comfortable paradise with no worries, but who in reality were kept well-fed in safe cages for slaughter at the pleasure of their owner. It is a metaphor of the age of prophesied harmony and peace which has instead produced the bloodiest several centuries (roughly the 19th-20th, even now into the 21st) in human history. Communism's vision of a classless society began, not by ameliorating, but by liquidating the classes – a hundred million or so. Women's liberation requires the slaughter of the unborn and evisceration of the family – hundreds of millions globally. Lennon's "brotherhood of Man" harmonizes all the small races and cultures of mankind through homogenization – every nation affected. Only through eliminating half the population, preventing the other half from coming to life, upending the family, and altering nations can we reach the idealist vision. As Chesterton said, in order to become humane, Man must cease being human.

This may come off as a bit Orwellian, overdone, and therefore outdated. Softer, more "winsome" iterations of the theory of artificial relations have come about in recent decades. Instead of liquidating ethnic peoples through conquest or colonization, more soothing voices call for inviting all nations into western countries. Instead of the Iron Fist, we have the Open Society. Instead of genocidal warlords, we have welcoming schoolmarms in well-lit offices writing policies about Diversity, Inclusion, and Equality. Isn't that N.I.C.E.? But the effect upon western peoples is little different in the end.

Even so-called "conservative" leaders today speak of "having more in common with someone of unlike skin color but similar ideology than their blood-kinfolk next door." Their pithy proverbs turn natural human passions on their head: love the far, fear the near. America is a nation of immigrants, they say, a propositional nation, a civic national project that transcends any one particular people or place – one where GDP, Israel's safety, and free trade comprise those core propositions. America for them is an imperial cash cow dispensing goodies and democracy to the teeming hordes. Yet, defending one particular people and way of life was written into the America's Declaration of Independence as a key purpose of government. For the founders, governments existed to secure the being of a people. However, instead of defending the rights of a collective people to its life and liberty, today's politically "conservative" element devotes itself to ideals as abstract and immaterial as any leveler, abolitionist, or revolutionary in history. The very last constituency or cause on the minds of these politicians is that of the American people, much less the middle American.

Not to be outdone, conservative Christians have also arisen calling parishioners to escape worldly politics where ideals destroy nature and to join the otherworldly church where grace destroys nature. Not a few supposed traditionally-minded Christian leaders speak of the church as replacing natural ties of family, kin, and people. "The bonds that unite Christians are stronger than blood," says one minister. "Our true family is not the natural family...the new family is the church," quoths another. One clergymen wordsmith is fond of saying that "the gospel makes men free and free men make free markets." Others laud mass immigration for "bringing the mission field to us." Do not ask why no Christian prior to some 19th c. unitarians spoke this way. Do not ask why the gospel has been around for 2,000 years and free markets only 200. Do not inquire how, having failed to evangelize their own nation, American Christians imagine they will succeed with dozens more. The eschatological drip is too good. These men are not radical revolutionaries but self-styled bearers of confessional tradition. They write books hallowing the dead for their piety but would excommunicate them for their politics. Indeed, the saying is true that they honor the prophets but are sons of those who stoned them.

However, contrary to unending propaganda of artificial relations, whether from madmen or from ministers, we have not forgotten ourselves; we have not risen above nature but have found it. A Great Remembering is happening in our age. The term "hiraeth" carries a deep desire for a time, land, people, country once possessed but lost; a hearkening back to a place we've never been but know existed. Hiraeth impels us to look back and remember. Natural relations get at the heart of that thing lost for which we yearn.

And indeed we yearn, for we are tired of the unnaturalness of our forced condition. We have grown restless in our forgetting. We have tasted every lotus leaf that cosmopolitanism has offered us for a few generations, and our appetite is not sated. We find ourselves as waking from a dream of longing for something discarded, stumbling through the halls of an empty house filled with images of our ancestors. We have looked them in full in the face and have seen a light in their eyes reflected back in our own. Rudyard Kipling wrote a poem, sometimes called *When The Saxon Began To Hate*. He might as well have entitled it *When The Saxon Began To Wake*. For, we are now full of sober remembrance and our voices are even and low, our eyes level and straight; what was not suddenly bred, will not swiftly abate.

"In a revolutionary epoch," says Russell Kirk, "sometimes men taste every novelty, sicken of them all, and return to ancient principles so long disused that they seem refreshingly hearty when they are rediscovered." We seek to discover those ancient principles, the ancient paths – the Tao, as Lewis called it – and bring ourselves into conformity to it and experience hearty revitalization in our time. "Does not nature teach...?" asked the apostle. We believe that it does and hope this humble work helps you, the reader, and those around you (your neighbor) to learn from it.

A

John Abernathy

"Another obligation to the practice of brotherly kindness and charity arises from the object of it, our brethren and neighbors, their condition, and the relation we stand in to them. We are all brethren, derive our being from one origin, and partake of the same common nature, and are liable to the same frailties, indigence, and vicissitudes. 'God has made men of one blood to dwell on all the face of the earth.' And through his providence, which fixes the 'bounds of their habitations,' and as Moses expresses it, has 'divided the earth among them,' appoints a diversity of stations for them, so that 'the rich and the poor meet together,' they ought to 'remember that the Lord is the maker of them all.' This consideration ought to unite their affections and engage their mutual help. How unnatural is discord, or even indifference, among children of the same family?...If he has distinguished some children of his house from others by his bounty, it is not that he would have others in more afflicted circumstances abandoned to perish, but...that the abundance of some might supply the want of others.

"The common kindred among men, and their proximity of blood, is an argument which nature strongly urges in favour of the needy. Thus the prophet expresses the exercise of compassion to the indigent, 'that thou hide not thyself from thine own flesh,' and thereby strongly enforces the acts of mercy there mentioned, dealing bread to the hungry, and clothing to the naked. But the Christian religion has superadded special obligations to those general ones which the common ties of humanity lay upon us, by establishing a new and intimate relation among the disciples of Christ." – *Sermons on Various Subjects*, vol. 2, pgs. 236-238

Adamantius

"Wherever the Hellenic and Ionic race has been kept pure, we see proper tall men of fairly broad and straight build, neatly made, of fairly light skin and blond; the flesh is rather firm, the limbs straight, the extremities well made. The head is of middling size, and moves very easily; the neck is strong, the hair somewhat fair, and soft, and a little curly; the face is rectangular, the lips narrow, the nose straight, and the eyes bright, piercing, and full of light; for of all nations the Greek has the fairest eyes." – quoted in *Günther*, pg. 157

John Adams

"I would, therefore, beg leave to propose to appoint a consul without loss of time to reside at Nantes, and to him consign all vessels from the United States. I think it should be an American, some merchant of known character, abilities, and industry, who would consent to serve his country for moderate emoluments. Such persons are to be found in great numbers in the United States. There are many applications from French gentlemen. But I think that from a want of knowledge of our language, our laws, customs, and even the humors of our people, for even these must be considered, they never would be able to give satisfaction or to do justice. Besides, if it is an honor, a profit, or only an opportunity to travel and see the world for improvement, I think the native Americans have a right to expect it; and further, that the public have a right to expect that whatever advantages are honestly to be made in this way should return sometime or other to America, together with the knowledge and experience gained at the same time." – In a letter to the President of Congress, written from Paris, 29th June, 1780, *The Works of John Adams*, vol. 7, pg. 209

"Our country has but lately been a dependent one, and our people, although enlightened and virtuous, have had their minds and hearts habitually filled with all the passions of a dependent and subordinate people; that is to say, with fear, with diffidence, and distrust of themselves, with admiration of foreigners, &c. Now, I say, that it is one of the most necessary and one of the most difficult branches of the policy of congress to eradicate from the American mind every remaining fibre of this fear and self-diffidence on one hand, and of this excessive admiration of foreigners on the other." – In a letter to the President of Congress, written from Paris, 5th September, 1783, *The Works of John Adams*, vol. 8, pg. 144

—JOHN ADAMS—

"...if a love of science and letters, and a wish to patronize every rational effort to encourage schools, colleges, universities, academies, and every institution for propagating knowledge, virtue, and religion among all classes of the people, not only for their benign influence on the happiness of life in all its stages and classes and of society in all its forms, but as the only means of preserving our constitution from its natural enemies, the spirit of sophistry, the spirit of party, the spirit of intrigue, profligacy, and corruption, and the pestilence of foreign influence, which is the angel of destruction to elective governments...can enable me in any degree to comply with your wishes, it shall be my strenuous endeavor that this sagacious injunction of the two Houses shall not be without effect." – In his inaugural speech to both Houses

of Congress, 4th March, 1797; *A Compilation of the Messages and Papers of the President, 1789-1908*, pg. 231

"It must not be permitted to be doubted, whether the people of the United States will support the government established by their voluntary consent, and appointed by their free choice; or whether, by surrendering themselves to the direction of foreign and domestic factions, in opposition to their own government, they will forfeit the honorable station they have hitherto maintained." – In his speech to both Houses of Congress on 16th May, 1797; *The Addresses and Messages of the Presidents of the United States*, pg. 48

"Republics are always divided in opinion, concerning forms of governments, and plans and details of administration. These divisions are generally harmless, often salutary, and seldom very hurtful, except when foreign nations interfere, and by their arts and agents excite and ferment them into parties and factions. Such interference and influence must be resisted and exterminated, or it will end in America, as it did anciently in Greece, and in our own time in Europe, in our total destruction as a republican government and independent power." – In his address to the citizens of Baltimore, and Baltimore County, Maryland, of 2nd May, 1798; *The Works of John Adams*, vol. 9, pg. 104

"If you have no attachments or exclusive friendship for any foreign nation, you possess the genuine character of true Americans." – In his address to the Inhabitants of Arlington and Sandgate, Vermont, 25th June,1798; *The Works of John Adams*, vol. 9, pg. 113

"At the time when we were inquiring for an agent to conduct the affairs of the United States before the commissioners at Philadelphia, Mr. Cooper wrote to me a solicitation for that appointment, and Dr. Priestley wrote me a letter strongly recommending him. Both made apologies for his reputation as a democrat, and gave intimation of a reformation. I wondered that either could think it possible that the people of the United States could be satisfied or contented to intrust interests of such magnitude to an Englishman, or any other foreigner. I wondered that either should think it compatible with my duty, to prefer a stranger to the great number of able natives, who wished for this trust.

"Having long possessed evidence the most satisfactory to my mind, that Collot is a pernicious and malicious intriguer, I have been always ready and willing to execute the alien law upon him. We are now about to enter on a negotiation with France, but this is no objection against expelling from this Country such an alien as he is. On the contrary, it is more necessary to remove such an instrument of mischief from among our people, for his whole time will be employed in exciting corrupt divisions, whether he can succeed or not. As to Letombe, if you can prove 'that he paid the bribes ordered by the French Minister, Adet',or any thing like it, he ought to be sent away too. But perhaps it would be better to signify that it is expected that he go, than to order him out at first by proclamation. There is a respect due to public commissions, which I should wish to preserve as far as may be consistent with safety. The alien law, I fear, will upon trial be found inadequate to the object intended, but I am willing to try it in the case of Collot." – In a letter to T. Pickering, Secretary of State, written from Quincy, 13th August1799; *The Works of John Adams*, vol. 9, pgs. 13-14

"...relative to the consulate of Madeira. If there is a necessity of removing Mr. John Marsden Pintard, a native American and an old consul, why should we appoint a foreigner in his stead? Among the number of applications for consulates, cannot we find an American capable and worthy of the trust? Mr. Lamar is a partner in a respectable house, but it is said to be an English, or rather a Scotch house. Why should we take the bread out of the mouths of our own children and give it to strangers? We do so much of this in the army, navy, and especially in the consulships abroad, that it frequently gives me great anxiety." – In a letter to J. Marshall, Secretary of State, written from Quincy, 14th August,1800; *The Works of John Adams*, vol. 9, pg. 77

This is the foundation of the military academy at West Point:
"I am very much pleased with your plan for executing the existing laws for the instruction of the artillerists and engineers...I wish you may easily find teachers. What think you of Captain Barron for one? Every one speaks well of Mr.

Bureau de Pusy. But I have an invincible aversion to the appointment of foreigners, if it can be avoided. It mortifies the honest pride of our officers, and damps their ardor and ambition. I had rather appoint the teachers, and form the schools, and take time to consider of an engineer." – In a letter to S. Dexter, Secretary of War, written from Quincy, 25th July, 1800; *The Works of John Adams*, vol. 9, pg. 36

"My worthy fellow-citizens! Our form of government, inestimable as it is, exposes us, more than any other, to the insidious intrigues and pestilent influence of foreign nations. Nothing but our inflexible neutrality can preserve us." – In "letter XII" of his correspondence originally published in the Boston Patriot in 1809; *The Works of John Adams*, vol. 9, pg. 154

"'Foreign meddlers,' as you properly denominate them, have a strange, a mysterious influence in this country. Is there no pride in American bosoms? Can their hearts endure that Callender, Duane, Cooper, and Lyon, should be the most influential men in the country, all foreigners and all degraded characters? ...The plan of our worthy friends, John Rutledge, relative to the admission of strangers to the privileges of citizens, as you explain it, was certainly prudent. Americans will find that their own experience will coincide with the experience of all other nations, and foreigners must be received with caution, or they will destroy all confidence in government." – In a letter to Christopher Gadsden, written from Quincy, Mass., 16th April, 1801; *The Works of John Adams*, vol. 9, pg. 584

"The foundation of national morality must be laid in private families....How is it possible that children can have any just sense of the sacred obligations of morality or religion if, from their earliest infancy, they learn their mothers live in habitual infidelity to their fathers, and their fathers in as constant infidelity to their mothers?" – Diary, June 2, 1778; *The Works of John Adams*, vol. 3, pg. 171

"Nature, which has established in the universe a chain of being and universal order, descending from archangels to microscopic animalcules, has ordained that no two objects shall be perfectly alike, and no two creatures perfectly equal. Although, among men, all are subject by nature to equal laws of morality, and in society have a right to equal laws for their government, yet no two men are perfectly equal in person, property, understanding, activity, and virtue, or ever can be made so by any power less than that which created them." – *Discourses on Davila; The Works of John Adams*, vol. 6, pg. 285

"That all men are born to equal rights is clear. Every being has a right to his own, as moral, as sacred, as any other has. This is as indubitable as a moral government in the universe. But to teach that all mean are born with equal powers and faculties, to equal influence in society, to equal property and advantages through life, is as gross a fraud, as glaring an imposition on the credibility of the people, as ever was practiced by monks, by Druids, by Brahmins, by priests of the immortal Lama, or by the self-styled philosophers of the French Revolution. For honor's sake, Mr. Taylor, for truth and virtue's sake, let American philosophers and politicians despise it." – Letter to John Taylor; *The Works of John Adams*, vol. 6, pg. 454

"The men are independent. But a physical inequality, an intellectual inequality, of the most serious kind, is established unchangeably by the Author of nature; and society has a right to establish any other inequalities it may judge necessary for its own good." – *The Works of John Adams*, vol. 1, pg. 462

"Is there not something extremely fallacious, in the common-place images of mother country and children colonies? Are we the children of Great-Britain, any more than the cities of London, Exeter and Bath? Are we not brethren and fellow subjects, with those in Britain, only under a somewhat different method of legislation, and a totally different method of taxation?" – *Papers of John Adams*, vol. 1, September 1755–October 1773, pgs. 123–28.

"I am old enough to remember the war of 1745, and its end; the war of 1755, and its close; the war of 1775, and its termination; the war of 1812, and its pacification. Every one of these wars has been followed by a general distress; embarrassment on commerce, destruction of manufacturers, fall of the price of produce and of lands, similar to those we feel at the present day, and all produced by the same causes. I have wondered that so much experience has not taught us more caution. The British merchants and manufacturers, immediately after the peace, disgorged again us all their stores of merchandise and manufacturers, not only without profit, but at certain loss for a time, with the express purpose of annihilating all our manufacturers, and ruining all our manufactories." – Letter to William Richmond, 1819; Charles F. Adams, John Adams, 10:384

"The Spirit of Commerce, Madam, which even insinuates itself into Families, and influences holy Matrimony, and thereby corrupts the Morals of Families as well as destroys their Happiness, it is much to be feared is incompatible with that purity of Heart, and Greatness of soul which is necessary for an happy Republic." – Letter to Mercy Otis Warren, 1776; *The Declaration of Independence in Historical Context*, pg. 437

John Quincy Adams

"...the Declaration of Independence announced the One People, assuming their station among the powers of the earth, as a civilized, religious, and Christian people,—acknowledging themselves bound by the obligations, and claiming the rights to which they were entitled by the laws of Nature and of Nature's God.

"They had formed a subordinate portion of an European Christian nation, in the condition of Colonies. The laws of social intercourse between sovereign communities constitute the laws of nations, all derived from three sources:—the laws of nature, or in other words the dictates of justice; usages, sanctioned by custom; and treaties, or national covenants. Superadded to these the Christian nations, between themselves, admit, with various latitudes of interpretation, and little consistency of practice, the laws of humanity and mutual benevolence taught in the gospel of Christ. The European Colonies in America had all been settled by Christian nations; and the first of them, settled before the reformation of Luther, had sought their justification for taking possession of lands inhabited by men of another race, in a grant of authority from the successor of Saint Peter at Rome, for converting the natives of the country to the Christian code of religion and morals.

After the reformation, the kings of England, substituting themselves in the place of the Roman Pontiff, as heads of the Church, granted charters for the same benebolent purposes; and as these colonial establishments successively arose, worldly purposes, the spirit of adventure, and religious persecution took their place, together with the conversion of the heathen, among the motives for the European establishments in this Western Hemisphere. Hence had arisen among the colonizing nations, a customary law, under which the commerce of all colonial settlements was confined exclusively to the metropolis or mother country. The Declaration of Independence cast off all the shackles of this dependency. The United States of America were no longer Colonies. They were an independent Nation of Christians, recognizing the general principles of the European law of nations." – *An Oration Delivered Before the Inhabitants of the Town of Newburyport, at Their Request, on the Sixty-first Anniversary of the Declaration of Independence*, July 4th, 1837, pg. 17

Sam Adams

"All persons born in the British American Colonies are, by the laws of God and nature and by the common law of England, exclusive of all charters from the Crown, well entitled, and by acts of the British Parliament are declared to be entitled, to all the natural, essential, inherent, and inseparable rights, liberties, and privileges of subjects born in Great Britain or within the realm." – *The Rights of the Colonists*, quoted by Peabody in *American Patriotism: Speeches, Letters and Other Papers*, pg. 35

Claudius Aelianus (Aelian)

"They affirm likewise that Alexander [the Great] Son of Philip was of a neglectful handsomeness: For his hair curled naturally, and was yellow." – *Claudius Aelianus His Various History*, pg. 226

"Of hair yellow, locks a little curling... skin delicate, complexion like roses" – *Claudius Aelianus His Various History*, pg. 213 [1]

Aeschylus

"And Cypris, you who are the first mother of our race, defend us who are sprung from your blood. We come to you, crying out in prayers for your divine ears." – *Seven Against Thebes*, 128

"First of all, their well organized right wing advanced in order. Then the entire force moved up, and, as it did, we all could hear a mighty cry:
　'You offspring of the Greeks, come on!
Free your native home! Free your wives, your children, the temples of your father's gods, the burial places of your ancestors! The time has come to fight for all of these!'"
– *Persians*, Johnston trans.

Ah me, how sudden have the storms of Fate,
Beyond all thought, all apprehension, burst
On my devoted head! O Fortune, Fortune!
With what relentless fury hath thy hand
Hurl'd desolation on the Persian race!
Woe unsupportable! The torturing thought
Of our lost youth comes rushing on my mind,
And sinks me to the ground. O Jove, that
Had died with those brave men that died in fight.
– *Persians*

Remains to think what honour best may greet
My lord, the majesty of Argos, home.
What day beams fairer on a woman's eyes
Than this, whereon she flings the portal wide,
To hail her lord, heaven-shielded,
　home from war?
This to my husband, that he tarry not,
But turn the city's longing into joy!
Yea, let him come, and coming may he find
A wife no other than he left her, true
And faithful as a watch-dog to his home,
His foemen's foe, in all her duties leal,
Trusty to keep for ten long years unmarred
The store whereon he set his master-seal.
Be steel deep-dyed, before ye look to see
Ill joy, ill fame, from other wight, in me!
– *Agamemnon*

O land of Argos, fatherland of mine!
To thee at last, beneath the tenth year's sun,
My feet return; the bark of my emprise,
Tho' one by one hope's anchors broke away,
Held by the last, and now rides safely here.

1　Describing Aspasia, a priestess and concubine of Cypress the Younger (400s b.c.)

Long, long my soul despaired to win, in death,
Its longed-for rest within our Argive land:
And now all hail, O earth, and hail to thee,
New-risen sun! and hail our country's God,
High-ruling Zeus, and thou, the Pythian lord,
Whose arrows smote us once-smite
   thou no more!
Was not thy wrath wreaked full upon our heads,
O king Apollo, by Scamander's side?
Turn thou, be turned, be saviour, healer, now
And hail, all gods who rule the street and mart
And Hermes hail! my patron and my pride,
Herald of heaven, and lord of heralds here!
And Heroes, ye who sped us on our way–
To one and all I cry, Receive again
With grace such Argives as the spear has spared.
– *Agamemnon*

Story of Ahikar

"Son, as a tree is enjoyable to see for its fruit
and branches, and the mountains are wooded
with the cedars, in the same way are enjoyable
to see man and wife and son and brother and
kinsman and friend, and all families.

"Son, one who hath not wife or son or
brother or kinsman or friend is in the long
years despised, and is like unto a tree that is in
the crossways, and all who pass by it pluck off
her leaves and break down her branches." –
*Pseudepigrapha of the Old Testament and the New
Testament*, pg. 733

Henry Ainsworth

"As many families compact together in one
tribe; many tribes in one nation or kingdom;
many kingdoms in one Empire; & these managed by one or by many; by Princes, Senators,
Judges, kings or Kaefers, as God shall dispose,
and the public states see best." – *Annotations
Upon the Five Bookes of Moses, the Booke of the
Psalmes, and the Song of Songs*, pg. 308

Alcman

The 7th century BC Spartan poet Alcman
described his beloved:

"to whom hath been shown the gift of the
sweet Muses at the hands of one that is right
happy among maidens, to wit the flaxen-haired
Megalostrata." – Fragment 130

"Aye, she sings like a very swan beside the
yellow streams of Xanthus, and she that cometh
next to that knot of yellow hair…" – Fragment
1, *Lyra Graeca 1*

Christopher Alexander

"…we believe that independent regions are the
natural receptacles for language, culture, customs, economy, and laws and that each region
should be separate and independent enough to
maintain the strength and vigor of its culture.

"…human cultures within a city can only
flourish when they are at least partly separated
from neighboring cultures…We are suggesting
here that the same argument also applies to
regions—that the regions of the earth must also
keep their distance and their dignity in order to
survive as cultures." – *A Pattern Language*, pg. 13

"Unless the present-day great nations have
their power greatly decentralized, the beautiful
and differentiated languages, cultures, customs,
and ways of life of the earth's people, vital to
the health of the planet, will vanish. In short,
we believe that independent regions are the natural receptacles for language, culture, customs,
economy, and laws and that each region should
be separate and independent enough to maintain the strength and vigor of each culture." –
"Independent Regions," in *A Pattern Language*,
pg. 13

"The homogeneous and undifferentiated
character of modem cities kills all variety of
life styles and arrests the growth of individual
character." – *A Pattern Language*, pg. 43

"Many of the people who live in metropolitan
areas have a weak character. In fact, metropolitan areas seem almost marked by the fact
that the people in them have markedly weak
character, compared with the character which
develops in simpler and more rugged situations.
This weakness of character is the counterpart
of another, far more visible feature of metropolitan areas: the homogeneity and lack of variety
among the people who live there. Of course,
weakness of character and lack of variety, are
simply two sides of the same coin: a condition
in which people have relatively undifferentiated
selves." – *A Pattern Language*, pg. 45

"It seems then, that the metropolis creates weak
character in two almost opposite ways; first,

because people are exposed to a chaos of values; second, because they cling to the superficial uniformity common to all these values. A nondescript mixture of values 'Will tend to produce nondescript people.' ...

"Maslow has pointed out that the process of self actualisation can only start after other needs, like the need for food and love, and security, have already been satisfied. [*Motivation and Personality*, pgs. 84–89.] Now the greater the mixture of kinds of persons in a local urban area, and the more unpredictable the strangers near your house, the more afraid and insecure you will become. In Los Angeles and New York this has reached the stage where people are constantly locking doors and windows, and where a mother does not feel safe sending her fifteen year old daughter to the corner mailbox. People are afraid when they are surrounded by the unfamiliar; the unfamiliar is dangerous. But so long as this fear is an unsolved problem, it will override the rest of their lives. Self-actualisation will only be able to happen when this fear is overcome; and that in turn, can only happen, when people are in familiar territory, among people of their own kind, whose habits and ways they know, and whom they trust." – *A Pattern Language*, pg. 48

Alexander III of Russia (Alexander Alexandrovich)

To his son Nicholas:
"You shall have to take from my shoulders the heavy burden of national authority and bear it to the grave, as I and our ancestors have done. I give you the kingdom entrusted to me by God. I received it thirteen years ago from my bleeding father.... From the height of the throne of your grandfather carried out many important reforms, directed to the good of the Russian people. As a reward for this, he received a bomb and death from Russian revolutionaries.... On the tragic day the question stood before me: which path was I to follow? Was it the one toward which I was being urged by so-called progressive society, infected with the liberal ideas of the West, or was it the one recommended by my own convictions, by my highest, sacred duty as sovereign, by my own conscious? I chose my path. The liberals called it reactionary. I was interested only in the good of my people, and the greatness of Russia. I

strove to give it internal and external peace, that the state might freely and calmly develop, becoming strong, rich and prosperous in an orderly way. Autocracy has created Russia's historical individuality. If autocracy falls, God forbid, Russia will collapse with it. The fall of the time-honored Russian government will inaugurate as era of civil strife and bloody internecine wars. I adjure you to love everything that serves the good, the honor, and the dignity of Russia. Guard autocracy, remembering at the same time that you bear the responsibility for the fate of your subjects before the throne of the Most High. May faith in God and in the sanctity of your royal duty be the foundation of your life. Be firm and courageous, and never show any weakness. Listen to everyone—there is nothing shameful in that—but hearken only to yourself and to your own conscience. In foreign policy, preserve an independent position. Remember—Russia has no friends. They fear our vastness. Avoid war. In domestic policy, first and foremost protect the Church. She has often saved Russian in times of misfortune. Strengthen the family, for it is the foundation of any state." – *The Royal Passion-Bearers*, pg. 7

Richard Allestree

"God in his wisdom discerning that Equality of Conditions would breed confusion in the world, has ordered several states, design'd some to Poverty, others to Riches; only annexing to the rich the care of the poor; yet that rather as an advantage, then a burden, a seed of more wealth both temporal." – *The Gentleman's Calling*, pg. 61

"He knoweth whether he shall go who remembreth whence he came." – *The Government Of The Thoughts*, pg. 3

Ahmad ibn Muhammad al-Maqqari

"Not only were the different independent [Muslim] chieftains at that time waging unrelenting war against each other, but they would not unfrequently avail themselves of the arms of the Christians to attack and destroy their own countrymen and brothers in religion.... The Christians, perceiving the state of corruption into which the Moslems had fallen, rejoiced extremely; for, at that time, very few men of virtue and principle were to be found amongst the Moslems, the generality of whom began to drink wine and commit all manner of excesses. The rulers of Andalusia thought of nothing else than purchasing singing-women and slaves, listening to their music, and passing their time in revelry and mirth, spending in dissipation and frivolous pastimes the treasures of the state, and oppressing their subjects with all manner of taxes and exactions, that they might send costly presents to Alfonso [VI], and induce him to serve their ambitious projects…. [In short,] the entire society was corrupted, and the body of Islam, deprived alike of life and soul, became a mere corpse." – al-Maqqari, vol 2, Appendix C, pgs. xxvii-xxviii

David Althoen

"Ever since the two terms [gens, natio] began to take on the general meaning of 'nation' during Romans times, they have been almost identical in meaning. The origins of the terms help clarify the early subtle difference in their meanings. The term 'gens', for example, originally meant 'clan', but soon expanded to include such meanings as 'family', 'descendants', and also 'race', 'nation', and 'people'. During the height of the Roman empire, the term 'gens' was mainly used in the plural in its meaning of 'nations' or 'peoples' and primarily signified any foreign peoples – in opposition to the populus Romanus. The term 'natio' had similar origins. In the very early Roman period it meant 'birth', and in the common language it came to mean 'litter' when referring to a brood of animals born to the same mother. It was in this sense that it expanded to its meaning close to 'nation', signifying those individuals born in the same place with a common ancestor. By the 1st century AD the meaning of 'natio' had become very similar to that of 'gens'. In the language of the Roman Church the term 'nationes' served, as did 'gentes' to translate 'the pagan nations', in opposition to the 'people of God' . . . By the 8th century Isidor of Seville's influential 'Etymology' was claiming that 'natio' and 'gens' were synonyms. This merging of meaning continued well into the early modern period….

"An examination of the subtle differences between 'gens' and 'natio' shows that 'natio' carried the more narrow, restrictive meaning – closer to the meaning of 'tribe'. 'Natio' referred to a nation or people who trace their descent to one ancestor, and who lived on the land where their mythological origins began, while 'gens' re-ferred to the larger sense of 'people' or 'nation' – independent of homeland or common ancestor . . . Tacitus spoke of all the Germans as one 'gens', and then broke them up into their various nationes, and Cicero chose the term 'natio' when emphasizing common descent….

"By no means, however, did all writers understand such a difference or consistently maintained clarity in their terminology . . . Moreover, there was no hierarchy understood when the terms 'natio' and 'gens' were used together; rather, the terms were usually used together for the rhetorical effect." – Natione Polonus and the Narod Szlachecki: Two Myths of National Identity and Noble Solidarity, pgs. 500-502

Johannes Althusius

"God distributed his gifts unevenly among men. He did not give all things to one person, but some to one and some to others, so that you have need for my gifts, and I for yours. And so was born, as it were, the need for communicating necessary and useful things, which communication was not possible except in social and political life. God therefore willed that each need the service and aid of others in order that friendship would bind all together, and no one would consider another to be valueless…Every one therefore needs the experience and contributions of others, and no one lives to himself alone." – Politica 1:26-27

"It is inborn to the more powerful and prudent to dominate and rule weaker men, just as it is also considered inborn for inferiors to submit. So in man the soul dominates the body, and the mind the appetites…Thus, the pride and high spirits of man should be restrained by sure reins of reason, law, and imperium less he throw himself precipitously into ruin." – Politica 1.38

"The members of a community are private and diverse associations of families and collegia, not the individual members of private associations. These persons, by their coming together, now become not spouses, kinsmen, and colleagues, but citizens of the same community. Thus passing from the private symbiotic relationship, they unite in the one body of a community. Differing from citizens, however, are foreigners, outsiders, aliens, and strangers whose duty it is to mind their own business, make no strange inquiries, not even to be curious in a foreign common-wealth, but to adapt themselves, as far as good conscience permits, to the customs of the place and city where they live in order that they may not be a scandal to others...." – *Politica*, 5.10-11

"The rights [jura] of the city, its privileges, statues, and benefits, which make the city great and celebrated, are also communicated by the citizens. They are shared with the people in the suburbs, outposts, and surrounding villages, but not with travelers and foreigners. For citizens enjoy the same laws (leges), the same religion, and the same language, speech, judgment under the law, discipline, customs, money, measures, weights, and so forth. They enjoy these not in such manner that each is like himself alone, but that all are like each other." – *Politica* 6.39

"Concord is fostered and protected by fairness (aequabilitas) when right, liberty, and honor are extended to each citizen according to the order and distinction of his worth and status. For it behooves the citizen to live by fair and suitable right with his neighbor, displaying neither ar-rogance nor servility, and thus to will whatever is tranquil and honest in the city. Contrary to this fairness is equality [aequalitas], by which in-dividual citizens are leveled among themselves in all those things I have discussed. From this arises the most certain disorder and disturbance of matters." – *Politica* 6.47

"Members [of a realm] are many cities, provinc-es, and regions agreeing among themselves on a single body constituted by mutual union and communication. Individual persons from these group members are called natives, inhabitants of the realm, and sons and daughters of the realm. They are to be distinguished from for-eigners and strangers, who have no claim upon the right or the realm. – *Politica*, 9.5

"Depopulation of a city and realm is under-stood to be among the more severe punish-ments." – *Politica*, 9.9

"The third right is the maintenance of a language, and of the same idiom of it, in the territory. The use of speech is truly necessary for men in social life, for without it no society can endure, nor can the communion of right." – *Politica* 9.16

—Johannes Althusius—

"Then, as the customs of regions often express diverse interests and discernments, so persons born in these regions hold diverse patterns in their customs. Accordingly, they are unable to come together at the same time without some antipathy toward each other, which when once aroused tends to stir up sedition, subversion, and damage to the life of the commonwealth." – *Politica*, 23.14

"It cannot be denied that provinces are con-stituted from villages and cities, and common-wealths and realms from provinces. Therefore, just as the cause by its nature precedes the effect and is more perceptible, and just as the simple or primary precedes in order what has been composed or derived from it, so also villages, cities, and provinces precede realms and are prior to them. For this is the order and progres-sion of nature, that the conjugal relationship, or the domestic association of man and wife, is called the beginning and foundation of human society. From it are then produced the associ-ations of various blood relations and in-laws. From them in turn come the sodalities and collegia, out of the union of which arises the composite body that we call a village, town, or city…It is necessary, therefore, that the doctrine of the symbiotic life of families, kinship associations, collegia, cities, and provinces precede the doctrine of the realm or universal symbiotic association that arises from the former associations and is composed of them." – *Politica*, 39.84

Alvíssmál

Thy good-will now shall I quickly get,
And win the marriage word;
I long to have, and I would not lack,
This snow-white maid for mine.
– *Poetic Edda, The Ballad of Alvis*, pg. 186

Ambrose of Milan

"We ought to love God first, then our parents, then our children, and lastly those of our household." – quoted in Aquinas' *Summa*, Part 2, Q 26, a 9, obj 3

Amenemope

Do not carry off the landmark at the
    boundaries of the arable land,
Nor disturb the position of the measuring-cord;
Be not greedy after a cubit of land,
Nor encroach upon the boundaries of a widow.
    … (vii 15)

Guard against encroaching upon the
    boundaries of the fields,
Lest a terror carry thee off. (viii 10)
One satisfies god with the will of the Lord,
Who determines the boundaries
    of the arable land.
– *Instruction of Amen-em-opet*, quoted in *The Ancient Near Eastern Texts Relating to the Old Testament*, pg. 422

Fisher Ames

"I have as loyal and respectful opinion as possible of the sincerity in folly of our rulers. But surely it exceeds all my credulity and candor on that head, to suppose even they can contemplate a republican form as practicable, honest, or free if applied when it is so manifestly inapplicable to the government of one third of God's earth. It could not, I think, even maintain forms; and as to principles, the otters

would as soon obey and give them effect, as the Gallo-Hispano-Indian omnium gatherum of savages and adventurers, whose pure morals are expected to sustain and glorify our republic."
– In a letter on the Purchase of Louisiana to Thomas Dwight, from Dedham, Mass.; *Works of Fisher Ames: Memoir*, pg. 329

"The Salus Reipublicae[2] so plainly requires the power of expelling or refusing admission to aliens, and the rebel Irish and negroes of the West Indies so much augment the danger, that reason, one would think, was disregarded by the Jacobins, too much even to be perverted."
– In a letter to Christopher Gore on the Alien Law; *Works of Fisher Ames*, vol. 2, pg. 1,304

— ANCIENT GRECO-ROMANS —

"As some principles of equity and justice remain in the hearts of men, the consent of the nations is as it were the voice of nature, or the testimony of that equity which is engraven on the hearts of men, and which they can never obliterate." – John Calvin, Commentary On Habakkuk 2:6, *Twelve Minor Prophets*, pg. 92

"The Most certain mark of goodness is the general conviction of all humanity…The general and perpetual vote of mankind is as the judgment of God Himself, since what all men at all times have come to believe must have been taught to them by Nature, and since God is nature's author, her voice is merely His instrument." – Richard Hooker, *Divine Law And Human Nature: Book 1 of Hooker's Law, A Modernization*, pg. 35

John Calvin and Richard Hooker point us to the profound truth of the existence of innate principles of equity (fairness) and justice that reside within the hearts of all humans. Calvin argues that when nations collectively agree on something, it can be seen as the voice of nature or a testimony of the inherent sense of justice in human beings. According to Calvin, these innate principles are so deeply ingrained that they cannot be erased or destroyed. In essence, when there is a consensus among nations, it reflects a fundamental, natural sense of justice that is present within all humans.

Richard Hooker similarly highlights the significance of a shared consensus among human-

---

2   The conservation of the State.

ity. He asserts that the general conviction of all humans is a reliable indicator of goodness. The "general and perpetual vote of mankind" refers to the collective beliefs and values held by people across different cultures and times. Hooker believes that this shared understanding is akin to God's judgment because it is derived from the teachings of nature. Since God is considered the author of nature, Hooker argues that nature's voice serves as an instrument of divine wisdom. In other words, the collective beliefs of humanity reflect the inherent goodness and wisdom of God, as expressed through nature.

When we find a common theme celebrated and cherished among all peoples, it should be taken as indication of its probable goodness and naturalness. The most celebrated themes of Greco-Roman life and values can be found on the Shield of Achilles which depicts common Greek life in the Bronze Age period. Homer's Iliad tells each detail forged upon the work: two cities, one with a wedding, another with a battle; farmers and countryside, gods and the river ocean. The Greek conception of a "hero" was one who, among other things, represented his nation or people. Achilles' bearing the scenes of everyday Greek life, therefore, places symbolic imagery of the quotidian at the forefront of this famous epic. It is perhaps more ironic, since Achilles gave up these things to pursue glory and a short life in war. Hence, the Iliad sings of the "rage of Achilles" that burned Troy and his own life. However, some have suggested that Achilles redeems himself upon his repentance at Priam's visit.

Virgil several hundred years after Homer would pick up this shield imagery when Aeneas received his own shield depicting the future history of Rome and its greatness. Aeneas carried this upon his shoulder, signifying his individual actions today are bound to and done on behalf of future posterity. Collective and generational duties were paramount for Romans. In the words of Thomas Macaulay, "For Romans in Rome's quarrel spared neither land nor gold, Nor son nor wife, nor limb nor life, in the brave days of old. Then none was for a party; then all were for the state; Then the great man helped the poor, and the poor man loved the great. Then lands were fairly portioned; then spoils were fairly sold: The Romans were like brothers in the brave days of old." For the ancient world, then, the things for which men fought, the places from which they came, the ideals they carried on their shoulders were those of their people, their gods, and their common lives together.

Achilles and Aeneas were not the only model men of the ancient world. Many of Homer's other main characters celebrated the heroism, valor, and sense of duty displayed by the characters in his works. Hector, Prince of Troy, was the quintessential western man seeking glory while also defending his home, hearth, family and gods. Although his body was bruised by the dust of a battlefield, Hector displayed manly virtues untarnished by the sands of time. He hugged his wife and kissed his child, then rallied his men to slaughter their foes. The only other character in the ancient world with such a wide character is King David of the Bible. These and other epic heroes highlight the importance of loyalty to one's homeland, family, and traditions, as well as respect for the gods and the natural order.

Indeed, many non-epic poetical Ancient Greek writers and philosophers often celebrated the love of people, place, and tradition through their works. Hesiod was a Greek poet who lived around the 8th century BC. In his works, such as Works and Days and Theogony, he emphasized the importance of hard work, traditional values, and the divine order of the cosmos. His writings also expressed a deep appreciation for the rural landscape and agricultural life, as well as the interconnectedness of people and their environment.

As the "Father of History," Herodotus documented in extended and respectful detail the stories and customs of various people, places, and life-ways in his work The Histories. He showed appreciation for the numerous cultures in the ancient world while promoting the significance of learning from history and preserving traditions. One cannot read Herodotus' documentary-length excursus into ancient ethnic peoples without getting the sense of honor both he and the people themselves had for particularity of ancient peoplehood, norms, social order, and more.

The playwright Sophocles, famous for his tragedies like Oedipus Rex and Antigone, often explored themes of human nature, family, and the importance of adhering both to natural laws and the traditions of one's people. His works frequently emphasized the consequences of going against the natural order and divine law. For instance, in Antigone the king issues an edict that contradicts the higher divine law. Antigone must choose between obeying the king's law and breaking natural order or disobeying the will of the gods and the natural way of things in order to obey the king. She chooses well – human order must reflect divine and natural order – but suffers for it.

Lastly, as a comic playwright, Aristophanes used humor and satire in his works like *The Frogs*, *Lysistrata*, and *The Clouds* to critique innovative mores and promote traditional values. His plays often focused on the importance of community, patriotism, and honoring the gods.

These are just a few examples of ancient Greek writers whose works promoted the love of people, place, and tradition. Behind the voluminous writings of the ancient Greeks lies the backdrop of a hard, consistent natural and divine order to which humans must adapt themselves. The themes in writing often portray humans – and even the gods – interacting with this Reality and the consequences of adhering to or violating it. The literary contributions of Greek writers continue to be celebrated for their exploration of human nature, society, and the role of tradition in shaping the world.

Ancient Roman writers, much like the Greeks before them, often promulgated the love of people, place, and tradition in their works. Virgil's works, mentioned above, extol the virtues of Rome, its people, and its founding myth, encouraging readers to appreciate the greatness of Rome's city and traditions. *The Eclogues* and *The Georgics*, also express admiration for rural life and the importance of living in harmony with the land and its folk-ways. Rural, agrarian, settled life for the Romans was a superior, noble manner of living; the only true form of freedom and uncorrupted power a man could and should aim to achieve in this life. To own land, to be productive, to have a family – these are not new or trending reactionary movements of the late modern world waxing nostalgic for an imaginary past. Rather, these sentiments are deep-seated ancient passions experienced by our ancestors for thousands of years. The Romans honored Cincinnatus. Americans honor George Washington.

Another Roman who felt like Virgil was Cicero, a renowned Roman statesman, philosopher, and orator who wrote extensively on politics, ethics, and rhetoric. In his works, Cicero often stressed the importance of Roman values, such as justice, wisdom, and duty to one's country, emphasizing the need to preserve and uphold these Roman virtues. During the decline of the Old Rome and the rise of the new empire, Cicero stood as one of many voices to call Romans back to their ancient ways and traditions, to the rational and natural virtues that made them a great people.

As a historian, Livy documented Rome's history from its foundation to the Augustan age in his work *Ab Urbe Condita (From the Founding of the City)*. Livy's writing aimed to inspire patriotism and love for Rome and its traditions, often highlighting the moral values that shaped Roman society. The Roman poet Ovid is best known for his work *Metamorphoses*, a collection of mythological stories that emphasize the importance of love and the transformative power of human emotion. While Ovid's work was not overtly patriotic, it showcased Roman values and beliefs by drawing on the myths and legends of the ancient world.

Pliny the Elder was a Roman author, naturalist, and philosopher who wrote *Naturalis Historia (Natural History)*, an extensive encyclopedic work that covered a wide range of subjects, including geography, history, and culture. Pliny's work sought to preserve knowledge about the natural world, as well as human customs and traditions, for future generations. Horace, a Roman poet and philosopher, wrote various works, including *Odes*, *Satires*, and *Epistles*. These works often explore themes of love, friendship, and the importance of living a virtuous life. Horace also expressed admiration for Roman values and traditions, promoting the idea that living in accordance with these principles leads to a fulfilling life.

Everywhere one looks patriotism, love of people, honor of the gods, and fidelity to one's country is to be found in the works of the Greco-Roman writers. So common are these themes, that they serve not as a special pericope or genre but are woven into the epics, the myths, the poetry, the histories, philosophies, traditions, habits, architecture, paintings, even the coins of the ancient world!

Lancelot Andrewes

"There are but three things that are motives to love. 1. Beauty. 2. Nearness of nature, or kindred. And 3. Benefits." – *The Pattern of Catechistical Doctrine at Large*, pg. 78

"In the ordering of our Love...we are to respect the conjunction by nature or grace in the duties of Love which we freely perform...We owe not so much to those persons with whom we have no such Conjunction. Thus, we should prefer a faithful man before an infidel, because in the one there is only the image of God by nature, in the other it is both by creation and regeneration…And among the faithful, we should rather do good to those of our own country, than to Strangers, because beside the bonds of Religion, there is also a second bond of proximity and cohabitation, and among them to our acquaintance before those that are unknown to us, because we have an easier entrance unto them to do them good by persuasion, etc. And among such, to our kindred and alliance before others…because we are joined and bound together as soon as we are born, and this bond cannot be dissolved as long as we live." – *The Pattern of Catechistical Doctrine at Large*, pgs. 320-321

"If it be demanded, 'Why did not God make all men excellent alike, and fit to be Superiors?' Answer: God made men of finite natures, and therefore of such condition, that one should need the help of another: for which end the woman also was made to be an helper to man. Besides, seeing men grow in wisdom and abilities for several performances according to their finite capacities, industry, and education, necessarily it follows, that 'as stars differ each from other in glory,' so one man doth excel another." – *The Pattern of Catechistical Doctrine at Large*, pg. 321

Helen Andrews

"Imagine there's no countries—it was the mantra first of the hippies, now of the globalist Davoisie. Their humanitarian universalism argues that a person who limits his loyalties to a single nation will only become narrow-minded and chauvinistic. It is a kindly sounding creed, but it simply does not work well in practice. Paradoxically, allowing everyone to be partial works out better for humanity. Steve Jobs was a family-obsessed psychological basket case haunted by themes of inheritance and lineage. Tim Cook's office contains photos of only two people, Bobby Kennedy and Martin Luther King, and when he dies, he plans to leave his personal fortune to charity—Jobs's total opposite. But which one has done more for the world?" – *Boomers*, pg. 79

David W. Anthony

"When you look in the mirror you see not just your face but a museum. Although your face, in one sense, is your own, it is composed of a collage of features you have inherited from your parents, grandparents, great-grandparents, and so on. The lips and eyes that either bother or please you are not yours alone but are also features of your ancestors, long dead perhaps as individuals but still very much alive as fragments in you. Even complex qualities such as your sense of balance, musical abilities, shyness in crowds, or susceptibility to sickness have been lived before. We carry the past around with us all the time, and not just in our bodies. It lives also in our customs, including the way we speak. The past is a set of invisible lenses we wear constantly, and through these we perceive the world and the world perceives us. We stand always on the shoulders of our ancestors, whether or not we look down to acknowledge them." – *The Horse, The Wheel, And Language*, pg. 3

Thabiti Anyabwile

"I'm going to argue that the vast majority of Black, Brown, and Yellow folks who don't know the Lord who live in predominantly Black, Brown, and Yellow neighborhoods, especially if they're poor neighborhoods, are not going to come in within earshot of the Gospel. So our missional concern, the way Paul did, longing for his kinsmen according to the flesh, to come to know Christ, is a godly, biblical missional concern. That's necessary if we want to see our families and our neighborhoods evangelized. Because given the way we are self-segregating, which is happening, not just ecclesiologically, in terms of membership in churches, but it's happening, missiologically, in terms of who we go to with the gospel. If we just ride that wave, we'll be riding that wave away from our people, taking the Gospel with us, and that is not a win for team Jesus…

"Being in ethnic-specific contexts (in Church) is not only permissible, it's actually quite necessary for a lot of Christians to receive the comfort and discipleship that's needed." – *Why Ethnic-Specific Churches are Still Important: An Interview with Pastor Thabiti Anyabwile and Dr. Alexander Jun*, SOLA Network, January 25, 2021

Apollonius of Perga

"...the son of Leto [Apollo], his golden locks flowed in clusters as he moved..." – *Argonautica*, pg. 149

Thomas Aquinas

These sections show a cosmic hierarchical order of reason from God to angels to humans to animals and plants, influencing human order itself:

"Forasmuch as some intellectual creatures are higher than others, as we have shown; the lower intellectual nature must needs be governed by the higher... Wherefore the higher spirits are called both angels, inasmuch as they direct the lower spirits, by message as it were, for angels are called messengers; and ministers, forasmuch as by their operation they execute, even in corporeal things, the order of divine providence: because a minister is like an animate instrument according to the Philosopher. This is what is said (Ps. 103:4): Who makest thy angels spirits: and thy ministers a burning fire." – *Summa Contra Gentiles*, pgs. 197-198

"There is also a desire in man as a rational being capable of regulating things beneath him: and he pursues this desire in the occupations of the active and civic life. The chief object of this desire is that man's entire life be regulated in accord with reason, to wit, that he may live according to virtue: because the end of every virtuous man in all his actions is the good of his own virtue, that of the brave man, for instance, that he may act bravely. Now this desire will then be wholly fulfilled: because the reason will be right vigorous, being enlightened with the very light of God lest it stray from righteousness." – *Summa Contra Gentiles*, vol. 3, pgs.148–149

"Since it belongs to divine providence that order be preserved in the world; and suitable order consists in a proportionate descent from the highest to the lowest, it is meet that divine providence should reach the most distant things according to a certain proportion. This proportion consists in this—that just as the highest creatures are subject to God and governed by Him, so the lower creatures are subject to and governed by the higher. Now of all creatures the highest is the intellectual, as was proved above. Therefore the very nature of divine providence demands that the remaining creatures be ruled by rational creatures.

"Accordingly those things which have the larger share of the power of divine providence, are the executors of divine providence in regard to those whose share is smaller. Now intellectual creatures have a greater share thereof than others: because, while providence requires disposition of order which is effected by the cognitive faculty, and execution which is the work of the operative power, rational creatures have a share of both powers, whereas other creatures have only the latter. Therefore all other creatures are ruled, under divine providence, by rational creatures." – *Summa Contra Gentiles*, pgs. 195-196

"In the same way, we find order among men. For those who excel in intelligence, are naturally rulers; whereas those who are less intelligent, but strong in body, seem made by nature for service, as Aristotle says in his *Politics*. The statement of Solomon (Prov. 11:29) is in agreement with this: The fool shall serve the wise; as also the words of Exodus (18:21, 22): Provide out of all the people wise men such as fear God … who may judge the people at all times. . .

"And just as in the works of one man there is disorder through the intellect being obsequious to the sensual faculty; while the sensual faculty, through indisposition of the body, is drawn to the movement of the body, as instanced in those who limp: so too, in human government disorder results from a man being set in authority, not on account of his excelling in intelligence, but because he has usurped the government by bodily force, or has been appointed to rule through motives of sensual affection. Nor does Solomon omit to mention this disorder, for he says (Eccles. 10:5, 6): There is an evil that I have seen under the sun, as it were by an error proceeding from the face of the prince; a fool set in high dignity. Now divine providence does not exclude a disorder of this kind: for it results, by God's permission, from the fault of the inferior agents; even as we have said of other evils. Nor is the natural order wholly perverted by such a disorder: for the government of fools is weak, unless it be strengthened by the counsels of the wise. Hence it is said (Prov. 20:18): Designs are strengthened by counsels: and wars are to be arranged by governments; and (24:5, 6): A wise man is strong, and a knowing man, stout and valiant: because war is managed by due ordering, and there shall be safety when there are many counsels. And since the counsellor rules him who receives his counsel, and, in a sense, governs him, it is said (Prov. 17:2) that a wise servant shall rule over foolish sons. It is therefore evident that divine providence imposes order on all things, and thus the Apostle says truly (Rom. 13:1) that the things which are of God are well ordered." – *Summa Contra Gentiles*, pgs. 206-207

"The divine law is a rule of divine providence for the governance of men. Now, it belongs to divine providence to keep all things subject to it within the bounds of right order: so that, to wit, each thing be in its place and degree. Accordingly, the divine law directs men to one another in such wise that each one remains in his own order: which is for men to be at peace with one another, for peace among men is nothing else but rightly ordered harmony, as Augustine says.

"Besides. Whenever a number of things are subordinate to one, they ought to be harmoniously ordered to one another: else they would hinder one another in the prosecution of the common end: thus, an army is harmoniously ordered to victory which is the end of the commander-in-chief. Now, every man is ordered to God by the divine law. Therefore it behooved the divine law to establish an ordered harmony, which is peace, among men, lest they be a hindrance to one another.

"Hence it is said in the psalm: Who hath placed peace in thy borders: and our Lord said (Jo. 16:33): These things I have spoken to you, that in me you may have peace.

"Now ordered harmony is observed among men when to everyone is given his due: and this belongs to justice. Wherefore it is said (Isa. 32:17): The work of justice shall be peace. Therefore it behooved the divine law to give precepts of justice, that everyone might give others their due, and refrain from doing them wrong.

"Among men our greatest debt is to our parents. Wherefore the first of the legal precepts (Exod. 20:12–17) that order us to our neighbour is: Honour thy father and thy mother, whereby we are to understand that each one is commanded to give their due both to his parents and to others, according to Rom. 13:7: Render to all men their dues.—The next place is given

to the precepts that forbid wrong-doing to one's neighbour: to harm him by deed either in his own person, for it is said: Thou shalt not kill; or in a person united to him, for it is said: Thou shalt not commit adultery; or in external things, for it is said: Thou shalt not steal. We are also forbidden to wrong our neighbour by word: for it is written: Thou shalt not bear false witness against thy neighbour. And since God is judge also of hearts, we are forbidden to injure our neighbour in thought, by coveting his wife or his goods." – *Summa Contra Gentiles*, pgs. 125-126

"From what has been said it may be seen that the things prescribed by the divine law are right not only because they are prescribed by law, but also by their very nature. For the divine law subjects the human mind to God, and all the rest of man, to reason. Now, the natural order demands that the inferior be subject to the superior. Therefore the precepts of the divine law are in themselves right by nature." – *Summa Contra Gentiles*, pgs.127-128

"Nor does the weakness of the female sex prejudice the perfection of those who will rise again, because that is not a weakness in default of nature, but intended by nature. Moreover this very distinction in nature by extending to all things, will serve as a proof of nature's perfection, and as an indication of divine wisdom disposing all things in order." – *Summa Contra Gentiles*, pg. 301

"If the citizens themselves devote their lives to matters of trade, the way will be open to many vices...It is better, therefore, that the supplies of food be furnished to the city from its own fields than that it be wholly dependent on trade...The pursuit of trade is, also, entirely opposed to military activity. For tradesmen, whilst they seek their leisure, do not hard work, and whilst they enjoy all pleasures, grow soft in spirit and their bodies are weakened and rendered unsuited to military labors...Consequently, the perfect city will make a moderate use of merchants." – *On the Governance of Rulers*, in Routledge Library Editions, pg. 53

"God holds first place, for He is supremely excellent, and is for us the first principle of being and government. In the second place, the principles of our being and government are our parents and our country, that have given us birth and nourishment. Consequently man is debtor chiefly to his parents and his country, after God. Wherefore just as it belongs to religion to give worship to God, so does it belong to piety, in the second place, to give worship to one's parents and one's country. The worship due to our parents includes the worship given to all our kindred, since our kinsfolk are those who descend from the same parents, according to the Philosopher (*Ethic.* viii. 12). The worship given to our country includes homage to all our fellow-citizens and to all the friends of our country. Therefore piety extends chiefly to these." – *Summa Theologica*, II-II q.101 a.1 resp.

— THOMAS AQUINAS —

"In what concerns nature we should love our kinsmen most, . . . and we are more closely bound to provide them with the necessities of life." – *Summa Theologica*, 2.2, 26

"Accordingly the first kind of likeness causes love of friendship or well-being. For the very fact that two men are alike, having, as it were, one form, makes them to be, in a manner, one in that form: thus two men are one thing in species of humanity; and two white men are one thing in whiteness. Hence the affections of one tend to the other, as being one with him; and he wishes good to him as to himself. But the second kind of likeness causes love concu-piscence, or friendship founded on usefulness or pleasure: because whatever is in potentiality, as such, has the desire for its act; and it takes pleasure in its realization, if it be a sentient and cognitive being." – *Summa Theologica*, I-II q.27 a.3 resp.

"Equality is the cause of equality in mutual love. Yet between those who are unequal there can be a greater love than between equals; although there be not an equal response: for a father naturally loves his son more than a brother loves his brother; although the son does not love his father as much as he is loved by him.

"The cause of inequality could be on the part of God; not indeed that He would punish some and reward others, but that He would exalt some above others; so that the beauty of order would the more shine forth among men. Inequality might also arise on the part of nature as above described, without any defect of nature." – *Summa Theologica*, I q.96 a.3 ad 2

Inequality is natural and for the common good:
"But a man is the master of a free subject, by directing him either towards his proper welfare, or to the common good. Such a kind of mastership would have existed in the state of innocence between man and man, for two reasons.

"First, because man is naturally a social being, and so in the state of innocence he would have led a social life. Now a social life cannot exist among a number of people unless under the presidency of one to look after the common good; for many, as such, seek many things, whereas one attends only to one. Wherefore the Philosopher[3] says, in the beginning of the *Politics*, that wherever many things are directed to one, we shall always find one at the head directing them.

"Secondly, if one man surpassed another in knowledge and virtue, this would not have been fitting unless these gifts conduced to the benefit of others, according to 1 Peter 4:10, 'As every man hath received grace, ministering the same one to another.' Wherefore Augustine says (De Civ. Dei xix, 14): 'Just men command not by the love of domineering, but by the service of counsel': and (De Civ. Dei xix, 15): 'The natural order of things requires this; and thus did God make man.'" – *Summa Theologica*, I q.96 a.4 resp.

---

3   When Aquinas and others write "the Philosopher" they typically refer to Aristotle.

"The general principles of the natural law cannot be applied to all men in the same way on account of the great variety of human affairs: and hence arises the diversity of positive laws among various people." – *Summa Theologica*, I-II q.95 a.2 ad 3

"We must hold that, properly speaking, a man is not a friend to himself, but something more than a friend, since friendship implies union, for Dionysius says (Div Nom iv) that love is a unitive force, whereas a man is one with himself which is more than being united to another. Hence, just as unity is the principle of union, so the love with which a man loves himself is the form and root of friendship. For if we have friendship with others it is because we do unto them as we do unto ourselves, hence we read in *Ethic*. ix. 4.8 that 'the origin of friendly relations with others lies in our relations to ourselves.'" – *Summa Theologica*, II-II q.25 a.4 resp.

"Wherefore, since they know not themselves aright, they do not love themselves aright, but love that they think themselves to be. But the good know themselves truly, and therefore truly love themselves." – *Summa Theologica*, II-II q.25 a.7 resp.

"One's obligation to love a person is proportionate to the gravity of the sin one commits in acting against that love. Now it is a more grievous sin to act against the love of certain neighbors, than against the love of others. Hence the commandment (Leviticus 10:9), 'He that curseth his father or mother, dying let him die,' which does not apply to those who cursed others than the above. Therefore we ought to love some neighbors more than others." – *Summa Theologica*, II-II q.26 a.6 s.c.

"It would seem that we ought to love those who are better more than those who are more closely united to us… [But] It is written (1 Timothy 5:8): 'If any man have not care of his own and especially of those of his house, he hath denied the faith, and is worse than an infidel.' Now the inward affection of charity ought to correspond to the outward effect. Therefore charity regards those who are nearer to us before those who are better." – *Summa Theologica*, II-II q.26 a.7 s.c.

"A thing is loved more in two ways: first because it has the character of a more excellent good, secondly by reason of a closer connection." – *Summa Theologica*, II-II q.26 a.12 resp.

"The friendship of kindred is more stable, since it is more natural, and preponderates over others in matters touching nature: consequently we are more beholden to them in the providing of necessaries." – *Summa Theologica*, II-II q.26 a.8 ad 1

"On the other hand, the intensity of love is measured with regard to the man who loves, and accordingly man loves those who are more closely united to him, with more intense affection as to the good he wishes for them, than he loves those who are better as to the greater good he wishes for them.

"Again a further difference must be observed here: for some neighbours are connected with us by their natural origin, a connection which cannot be severed, since that origin makes them to be what they are. But the goodness of virtue, wherein some are close to God, can come and go, increase and decrease, as was shown above (Q. XXIV., AA. 4, 10, 11). Hence it is possible for one, out of charity, to wish this man who is more closely united to one, to be better than another, and so reach a higher degree of happiness.

"Moreover there is yet another reason for which, out of charity, we love more those who are more nearly connected with us, since we love them in more ways. For, towards those who are not connected with us we have no other friendship than charity, whereas for those who are connected with us, we have certain other friendships, according to the way in which they are connected. Now since the good on which every other friendship of the virtuous is based, is directed, as to its end, to the good on which charity is based, it follows that charity commands each act of another friendship, even as the art which is about the end commands the art which is about the means. Consequently this very act of loving someone because he is akin or connected with us, or because he is a fellow-countryman or for any like reason that is referable to the end of charity, can be commanded by charity, so that, out of charity both eliciting and commanding, we love in more ways those who are more nearly connected with us." – *Summa Theologica*, II-II q.26 a.7 resp.

"We ought out of charity to love those who are more closely united to us more, both because our love for them is more intense, and because there are more reasons for loving them. Now intensity of love arises from the union of lover and beloved: and therefore we should measure the love of different persons according to the different kinds of union, so that a man is more loved in matters touching that particular union in respect of which he is loved. And, again, in comparing love to love we should compare one union with another. Accordingly we must say that friendship among blood relations is based upon their connection by natural origin, the friendship of fellow-citizens on their civic fellowship, and the friendship of those who are fighting side by side on the comradeship of battle. Wherefore in matters pertaining to nature we should love our kindred most, in matters concerning relations between citizens, we should prefer our fellow-citizens, and on the battlefield our fellow-soldiers." – *Summa Theologica*, II-II q.26 a.8 s.c.

"We have unequal love for certain persons in two ways: first, through our loving some and not loving others. As regards beneficence we are bound to observe this inequality, because we cannot do good to all." – *Summa Theologica*, II-II q.26 a.6 ad 1

"It would seem that the order of charity does not endure in heaven...On the contrary, Nature is not done away, but perfected, by glory. Now the order of charity given above is derived from nature: since all things naturally love themselves more than others. Therefore this order of charity will endure in heaven." – *Summa Theologica*, II-II q.26 a.13 obj. 2

"I answer that, According to the Philosopher (*Ethic.* iii, 11, 12) 'all friendship is based on some kind of fellowship.' And since friendship is a knot or union, it follows that the fellowship which is the cause of friendship is called 'a tie.' Wherefore in respect of any kind of a fellowship certain persons are denominated as though they were tied together: thus we speak of fellow-citizens who are connected by a common political life, of fellow-soldiers who are connected by the common business of soldiering, and in the same way those who are connected by the fellowship of nature are said to be tied

by blood [consanguinei]. Hence in the above definition 'tie' is included as being the genus of consanguinity; the 'persons descending from the same common ancestor,' who are thus tied together are the subject of this tie. while 'carnal procreation' is mentioned as being its origin.

"Reply to Objection 1. An active force is not received into an instrument in the same degree of perfection as it has in the principal agent. And since every moved mover is an instrument, it follows that the power of the first mover in a particular genus when drawn out through many mediate movers fails at length, and reaches something that is moved and not a mover. But the power of a begetter moves not only as to that which belongs to the species, but also as to that which belongs to the individual, by reason of which the child is like the parent even in accidentals and not only in the specific nature. And yet this individual power of the father is not so perfect in the son as it was in the father, and still less so in the grandson, and thus it goes on failing: so that at length it ceases and can go no further. Since then consanguinity results from this power being communicated to many through being conveyed to them from one person by procreation, it destroys itself by little and little, as Isidore says (*Etym.* ix). Consequently in defining consanguinity we must not take a remote common ancestor but the nearest, whose power still remains in those who are descended from him.

"Reply to Objection 2. It is clear from what has been said that blood relations agree not only in the specific nature but also in that power peculiar to the individual which is conveyed from one to many: the result being that sometimes the child is not only like his father, but also his grandfather or his remote ancestors (*De Gener. Anim.* iv, 3).

"Reply to Objection 3. Likeness depends more on form whereby a thing is actually, than on matter whereby a thing is potentially: for instance, charcoal has more in common with fire than with the tree from which the wood was cut. In like manner food already transformed by the nutritive power into the substance of the person fed has more in common with the subject nourished than with that from which the nourishment was taken. The argument however would hold according to the opinion of those who asserted that the whole nature of a thing is from its matter and that all forms are accidents: which is false. Reply to Objection 4. It is the blood that is proximately changed into the semen, as proved in *De Gener. Anim.* i, 18. Hence the tie contracted by carnal procreation is more fittingly called blood-relationship than flesh-relationship. That sometimes one relation is called the flesh of another, is because the blood which is transformed into the man's seed or into the menstrual fluid is potentially flesh and bone.

"I answer that, Consanguinity as stated (Article 1) is a certain propinquity based on the natural communication by the act of procreation whereby nature is propagated. Wherefore according to the Philosopher (*Ethic.* viii, 12) this communication is threefold. One corresponds to the relationship between cause and effect, and this is the consanguinity of father to son, wherefore he says that 'parents love their children as being a part of themselves.' Another corresponds to the relation of effect to cause, and this is the consanguinity of son to father, wherefore he says that 'children love their parents as being themselves something which owes its existence to them.' The third corresponds to the mutual relation between things that come from the same cause, as brothers, 'who are born of the same parents,' as he again says (*Ethic.* viii, 12). And since the movement of a point makes a line, and since a father by procreation may be said to descend to his son, hence it is that corresponding to these three relationships there are three lines of consanguinity, namely the 'descending' line corresponding to the first relationship, the 'ascending' line corresponding to the second, and the 'collateral' line corresponding to the third. Since however the movement of propagation does not rest in one term but continues beyond, the result is that one can point to the father's father and to the son's son, and so on, and according to the various steps we take we find various degrees in one line. And seeing that the degrees of a thing are parts of that thing, there cannot be degrees of propinquity where there is no propinquity. Consequently identity and too great a distance do away with degrees of consanguinity; since no man is kin to himself any more than he is like himself: for which reason there is no degree of consanguinity where there is but one person, but only when one person is compared to another.

"Nevertheless there are different ways of counting the degrees in various lines. For the degree of consanguinity in the ascending and descending line is contracted from the fact that And so the relation between all men as originating from Adam is not proximate in the same way that an ethnic kins-fellow is, or ethnic kinsfolk are; in whom a special bond owed the reverence of piety exists. one of the parties whose consanguinity is in question, is descended from the other. Wherefore according to the canonical as well as the legal reckoning, the person who occupies the first place, whether in the ascending or in the descending line, is distant from a certain one, say Peter, in the first degree—for instance father and son; while the one who occupies the second place in either direction is distant in the second degree, for instance grandfather, grandson and so on. But the consanguinity that exists between persons who are in collateral lines is contracted not through one being descended from the other, but through both being descended from one: wherefore the degrees of consanguinity in this line must be reckoned in relation to the one principle whence it arises. Here, however, the canonical and legal reckonings differ: for the legal reckoning takes into account the descent from the common stock on both sides, whereas the canonical reckoning takes into account only one, that namely on which the greater number of degrees are found. Hence according to the legal reckoning brother and sister, or two brothers, are related in the second degree, because each is separated from the common stock by one degree; and in like manner the children of two brothers are distant from one another in the fourth degree. But according to the canonical reckoning, two brothers are related in the first degree, since neither is distant more than one degree from the common stock: but the children of one brother are distant in the second degree from the other brother, because they are at that distance from the common stock. Hence, according to the canonical reckoning, by whatever degree a person is distant from some higher degree, by so much and never by less is he distant from each person descending from that degree, because 'the cause of a thing being so is yet more so.' Wherefore although the other descendants from the common stock be related to some person on account of his being descended from the common stock, these descendants of the other branch cannot be more nearly related to him than he is to the common stock. Sometimes, however, a person is more distantly related to a descendant from the common stock, than he himself is to the common stock, because this other person may be more distantly related to the common stock than he is: and consanguinity must be reckoned according to the more distant degree." – *Summa Theologica*, Suppliment, Q.54

"A city which must engage in much trade in order to supply its needs also has to put up with the continuous presence of foreigners. But association with foreigners, according to Aristotle's *Politics*, is particularly harmful to civic customs. For it is inevitable that strangers, brought up under other laws and customs, will in many cases act as citizens are not wont to act and thus, since the citizens are drawn by their example to act likewise, their own civic life is upset." – *De Regno*, ch. 3, 138

"The import of the commandment is mutual love; thus he says: 'love one another.' It is of the very nature of friendship that is not imperceptible; otherwise, it would not be friendship, but merely good-will. For a true and firm friendship the friends need a mutual love for each other; for this duplication makes it true and firm. Our Lord, wanting there to be perfect friendship among his faithful and disciples, gave them this command of mutual love: 'Whoever fears the Lord directs his friendship aright' (Sir. 6:17)." – *Commentary on John*, pg. 42

"But here it might be asked whether it is lawful to love one more than another. To answer this, it should be noted that love can be called greater or less in two ways. In one way, from the standpoint of the object; in another, from the intensity of the act. For to love someone is to will good to him. Accordingly, one can love one person more than another, either because he wills him a greater good, which is the object of love, or because he more intensely wills him a good, i.e., with a more intense love. Therefore, with respect to the first, we ought to love everyone equally, because we ought to wish the good of eternal life to everyone; but with respect to the second, it is not necessary that we love all equally, because since the intensity of an act results from the principle of the action, and the principle of the action is union and similarity, we ought to love in a higher degree and more

intensely those who are more like us and more closely united to us." – *Commentary on Galatians*, ch. 6, lect. 2

"Since marriage is affected by way of a contract, it comes under the ordinance of positive law like other contracts. Consequently according to law (cap. Tua, De sponsal. impub.) it is determined that marriage may not be contracted before the age of discretion when each party is capable of sufficient deliberation about marriage, and of mutual fulfillment of the marriage debt, and that marriages otherwise contracted are void. Now for the most part this age is the fourteenth year in males and the twelfth year in women: but since the ordinances of positive law are consequent upon what happens in the majority of cases, if anyone reach the required perfection before the aforesaid age, so that nature and reason are sufficiently developed to supply the lack of age, the marriage is not annulled. Wherefore if the parties who marry before the age of puberty have marital intercourse before the aforesaid age, their marriage is none the less perpetually indissoluble." – *Summa Theologica, Supplementum* q.58 a.5 resp.

"[137] It seems that self-sufficiency is also safer [for a city], for the import of supplies and the access of merchants can easily be prevented whether owing to wars or to the many hazards of the sea, and thus the city may be overcome through lack of food.

[138] Moreover, this first method of supply is more conducive to the preservation of civic life. A city which must engage in much trade in order to supply its needs also has to put up with the continuous presence of foreigners. But intercourse with foreigners, according to Aristotle's Politics [V, 3: 1303a 27; VII, 6: 1327a 13-15], is particularly harmful to civic customs. For it is inevitable that strangers, brought up under other laws and customs, will in many cases act as the citizens are not wont to act and thus, since the citizens are drawn by their example to act likewise, their own civic life is upset.

[139] Again, if the citizens themselves devote their life to matters of trade, the way will be opened to many vices. Since the foremost tendency of tradesmen is to make money, greed is awakened in the hearts of the citizens through the pursuit of trade. The result is that everything in the city will become venal; good

faith will be destroyed and the way opened to all kinds of trickery; each one will work only for his own profit, despising the public good; the cultivation of virtue will fail since honour, virtue's reward, will be bestowed upon the rich. Thus, in such a city, civic life will necessarily be corrupted." – *De Regno*, part 2

"…equality does not belong to the essence of an image; for, as Augustine says (ibid.): Where there is an image there is not necessarily equality, as we see in a person's image reflected in a glass. Yet this is of the essence of a perfect image; for in a perfect image nothing is wanting that is to be found in that of which it is a copy. Now it is manifest that in man there is some likeness to God, copied from God as from an exemplar; yet this likeness is not one of equality, for such an exemplar infinitely excels its copy. Therefore there is in man a likeness to God; not, indeed, a perfect likeness, but imperfect. And Scripture implies the same when it says that man was made to God's likeness; for the preposition to signifies a certain approach, as of something at a distance…" – *Summa Theologica*, I q.93 a.1 resp.

"We may speak of God's image in two ways. First, we may consider in it that in which the image chiefly consists, that is, the intellectual nature…Secondly, we may consider the image of God in man as regards its accidental qualities, so far as to observe in man a certain imitation of God, consisting in the fact that man proceeds from man, as God from God; and also in the fact that the whole human soul is in the whole body, and again, in every part, as God is in regard to the whole world…" – *Summa Theologica*, I q.93 a.3 resp.

"Since man is said to be to the image of God by reason of his intellectual nature, he is the most perfectly like God according to that in which he can best imitate God in his intellectual nature. Now the intellectual nature imitates God chiefly in this, that God understands and loves Himself. Wherefore we see that the image of God is in man in three ways. First, inasmuch as man possesses a natural aptitude for understanding and loving God; and this aptitude consists in the very nature of the mind, which is common to all men. Secondly, inasmuch as man actually and habitually knows and loves God, though

imperfectly; and this image consists in the conformity of grace. Thirdly, inasmuch as man knows and loves God perfectly; and this image consists in the likeness of glory. Wherefore on the words, The light of Thy countenance, O Lord, is signed upon us (Ps. 4:7), the gloss distinguishes a threefold image, of creation, of re-creation, and of likeness. The first is found in all men, the second only in the just, the third only in the blessed." – *Summa Theologica*, I q.93 a.4 resp.

Aristeas

"[The king] approved this guest, and said to the next, 'What is the value of the family?' He replied, 'If we think that we are afflicted by adverse circumstances, and suffer as they do, the great strength of the family bond is manifest, and when that trouble is over, glory and success will be ours in the eyes of such folk, for cooperation when given with goodwill is of itself indestructible in the face of everything; with prosperity, there is no further need of their help, except that you must pray God to bestow every blessing.'" – *The Old Testament pseudepigrapha and the New Testament*, pg. 28

Aelius Aristides

Rome practiced universal citizenship around the time its empire was in steady collapse:

"Most noteworthy and most praiseworthy of all is the grandeur of your conception of citizenship. There is nothing on earth like it. You have divided all of the people of the empire – and when I say that, I mean the whole world – into two classes; and all the more cultured, virtuous, and able ones everywhere you have made into citizens and nationals of Rome … Neither the sea nor any distance on land shuts a man out from citizenship. Asia and Europe are in this respect not separate. Everything lies open to everybody; and no one fit for office or responsibility is considered an alien. Rome has never said 'No more room!'

"No one is a foreigner who deserves to hold an office or is worthy of trust. Rather, there is here a common 'world democracy' under the rule of one man, the best ruler and director … You have divided humanity into Romans and non-Romans, … and because you have divided people in this manner, in every city throughout the empire there are many who share citizenship with you, no less than they share citizenship with their fellow natives. And some of these Roman citizens have not even seen this city [Rome]!" – *Orations*, pg. 393

Aristophanes

"Your pure notes rise through the thick leaves of the yew-tree right up to the throne of Zeus, where Phoebus listens to you, Phoebus with his golden hair..." – *Birds* 222

Aristotle

"The family is the association established by nature for the supply of men's everyday wants...But when several families are united, and the association aims at something more than the supply of daily needs, the first society to be formed is the village. And the most natural form of the village appears to be that of a colony from the family, composed of the children and grandchildren, who are said to be suckled 'with the same milk.' And this is the reason why Hellenic states were originally governed by kings; because the Hellenes were under royal rule before they came together...Every family is ruled by the eldest, and therefore in the colonies of the family the kingly form of government prevailed because they were of the same blood. As Homer says: 'Each one gives law to his children and to his wives.'" – *Politics*, bk. 1

"When several villages are united in a single complete community, large enough to be nearly or quite self-sufficing, the state comes into existence, originating in the bare needs of life, and continuing in existence for the sake of a good life. And therefore, if the earlier forms of society are natural, so is the state, for it is the end of them, and the nature of a thing is its end. For what each thing is when fully developed, we call its nature, whether we are speaking of a man, a horse, or a family. Besides, the final cause and end of a thing is the best, and to be self-sufficing is the end and the best. Hence it is evident that the state is a creation of nature, and that man is by nature a political animal. And he who by nature and not by mere accident is without a state, is either a bad man or above humanity." – *Politics*, bk. 1

"In the first place there must be a union of those who cannot exist without each other; namely, of male and female, that the race may continue (and this is a union which is formed, not of deliberate purpose, but because, in common with other animals and with plants, mankind have a natural desire to leave behind them an image of themselves), and of natural ruler and subject, that both may be preserved." – *Politics*, bk. 1

"Yet it is clear that if the process of unification [making all things in common, as in Plato's *Republic*. i.e., Communalism] advances beyond a certain point, the city will not be a city at all for a state essentially consists of a multitude of persons, and if its unification is carried beyond a certain point, city will be reduced to family and family to individual, for we should pronounce the family to be a more complete unity than the city, and the single person than the family; so that even if any lawgiver were able to unify the state, he must not do so, for he will destroy it in the process." – *Politics*, bk. 2

"A city [polis] is not a community sharing a location and for the sake of not committing injustice against each other and conducting trade...the city is the community [koinonia] in living well both of households and families for the sake of a complete and self-sufficient life." – *Politics*, bk. 3.9

"The best political community is formed by citizens of the middle class, and that those states are likely to be well-administered in which the middle class is large, and stronger if possible than both the other classes, or at any rate than either singly; for the addition of the middle class turns the scale, and prevents either of the extremes from being dominant. Great then is the good fortune of a state in which the citizens have a moderate and sufficient property; for where some possess much, and the others nothing, there may arise an extreme democracy, or a pure oligarchy; or a tyranny may grow out of either extreme – either out of the most rampant democracy, or out of an oligarchy; but it is not so likely to arise out of the middle constitutions and those akin to them." – *Politics*, bk. 4

"Another cause of revolution is difference of races which do not at once acquire a common spirit; for a state is not the growth of a day, any more than it grows out of a multitude brought together by accident. Hence the reception of strangers in colonies, either at the time of their foundation or afterwards, has generally produced revolution…" – *Politics*, bk. 5

"It is a habit of tyrants never to like anyone who has a spirit of dignity and independence. The tyrant claims a monopoly of such qualities for himself; he feels that anybody who asserts a rival dignity, or acts with independence, is threatening his own superiority and the despotic power of his tyranny; he hates him accordingly as a subverter of his own authority. It is also a habit of tyrants to prefer the company of aliens to that of citizens at table and in society; citizens, they feel, are enemies, but aliens will offer no opposition." – *Politics*, bk. 5

"The guard of a [legitimate] king is composed of citizens: that of a tyrant is composed of foreigners." – *Politics*, bk. 5

"Heterogeneity of stocks may lead to faction – at any rate until they have had time to assimilate. A city cannot be constituted from any chance collection of people, or in any chance period of time. Most of the cities which have admitted settlers, either at the time of their foundation or later, have been troubled by faction. For example, the Achaeans joined with settlers from Troezen in founding Sybaris, but expelled them when their own numbers increased; and this involved their city in a curse. At Thurii the Sybarites quarreled with the other settlers who had joined them in its colonization; they demanded special privileges, on the ground that they were the owners of the territory, and were driven out of the colony. At Byzantium the later settlers were detected in a conspiracy against the original colonists, and were expelled by force; and a similar expulsion befell the exiles from Chios who were admitted to Antissa by the original colonists. At Zancle, on the other hand, the original colonists were themselves expelled by the Samians whom they admitted. At Apollonia, on the Black Sea, factional conflict was caused by the introduction of new settlers; at Syracuse the conferring of civic rights on aliens and mercenaries, at the end of the period of the tyrants, led to sedition and civil war; and at Amphipolis the original

citizens, after admitting Chalcidian colonists, were nearly all expelled by the colonists they had admitted." – *Politics*, bk. 5

"Other measures which are also useful in constructing this last and most extreme type of democracy are measures like those introduced by Cleisthenes at Athens, when he sought to advance the cause of democracy, or those which were taken by the founders of popular government at Cyrene. A number of new tribes and clans should be instituted by the side of the old; private cults should be reduced in number and conducted at common centers; and every contrivance should be employed to make all the citizens mix, as much as they possibly can, and to break down their old loyalties. All the measures adopted by tyrants may equally be regarded as congenial to democracy. We may cite as examples the license allowed to slaves (which, up to a point, may be advantageous as well as congenial), the license permitted to women and children, and the policy of conniving at the practice of 'living as you like.' There is much to assist a constitution of this sort, for most people find more pleasure in living without discipline than they find in a life of temperance." – *Politics*, bk. 6

— ARISTOTLE —

"The Good of man must be the end of the science of Politics. For even though it be the case that the Good is the same for the individual and for the state, nevertheless, the good of the state is manifestly a greater and more perfect good, both to attain and to preserve. To secure the good of one person only is better than nothing; but to secure the good of a nation or a state is a nobler and more divine achievement. This then being its aim, our investigation is in a sense the study of Politics." – *Ethics*, bk. 7

"...are chiefly a question of friends...Therefore justice and friendship are the same thing, or close to it...We spend our days with family, relations, and pals, children, parents, or wife, and our personal acts of justice are directed toward friends are up to us, while just behavior directed toward others is established by law and not up to us." – *Ethics*, bk. 7

"Friendship is concerned with the same objects as those which are the sphere of justice. For in every partnership we find mutual rights of some sort, and also friendly feeling: one notes that shipmates and fellow-soldiers speak of each other as 'my friend,' and so in fact do the partners in any joint undertaking. But their friendship is limited to the extent of their association in their common business, for so also are their mutual rights as associates. Again, the proverb says 'Friends' goods are common property,' and this is correct, since community is the essence of friendship. Brothers have all things in common, and so do members of a comradeship; other friends hold special possessions in common, more or fewer in different cases, inasmuch as friendships vary in degree.

"The claims of justice also differ in different relationships. The mutual rights of parents and children are not the same as those between brothers; the obligations of members of a comradeship are not the same as those of fellow-citizens; and similarly with the other forms of friendship. Injustice therefore also is differently constituted in each of these relationships: wrong is increasingly serious in proportion as it is done to a nearer friend. For example, it is more shocking to defraud a comrade of money than a fellow-citizen; or to refuse aid to a brother than to do so to a stranger; or to strike one's father than to strike anybody else. Similarly it is natural that the claims of justice also should increase with the nearness of the friendship, since friendship and justice exist between the same persons and are co-extensive in range." – *Ethics*, bk. 8.1

"Golden-haired far-darter, son of Zeus." – *Rhetoric*, bk. 3.8

"Pray thee, bid the red haired Critias do what his father commands him." – *Rhetoric*, bk. 1.15

On Friendship as a prerequisite for state cohesion:

"We may even in our travels [hear] how near and dear every man is to every other. Friendship seems also to hold states together, and lawgivers to care more for it than for justice; for unanimity seems to be something like friendship, and this they aim at most of all, and expel faction as their worst enemy; and when men are friends they have no need of justice, while when they are just they need friendship as well, and the truest form of justice is thought to be a friendly quality." – *Ethics*, 8.1

"That we should not make the same return to every one, nor give a father the preference in everything, as one does not sacrifice everything to Zeus, is plain enough; but since we ought to render different things to parents, brothers, comrades, and benefactors, we ought to render to each class what is appropriate and becoming. And it would be thought that in the matter of food we should help our parents before all others, since we owe our own nourishment to them, and it is more honourable to help in this respect the authors of our being even before ourselves; and honour too one should give to one's parents as one does to the gods, but not any and every honour; for that matter one should not give the same honour to one's father and one's mother, nor again should one give them the honour due to a philosopher or to a general, but the honour due to a father, or again to a mother. To kinsmen, too, and fellow-tribesmen and fellow-citizens and to every other class one should always try to assign what is appropriate, and to compare the claims of each class with respect to nearness of relation and to virtue or usefulness." – *Ethics*, 9.2

John Arrowsmith

"Consent in Religion is wont to tie the fastest knots of mutual accord, but there are no greater animosities than those that arise from diversity of professions." – *A Chain Of Principles*, pg. 91

Paul S. Ash

"The ancient Israelites were concerned with boundaries. The beginning of Genesis recounts how light was separated from darkness (Gen 1:3–4), land from sea (Gen 1:9–10), upper waters from lower waters (Gen 1:6, 7) and so on. The Israelites also sought to establish cultural and religious boundaries to maintain their uniqueness...Likewise, dietary laws, sabbath laws and the like all worked to build boundaries and borders of various types.

"As part of this effort to create borders, the Bible established specific geographical boundaries for different groups: first for all the postdiluvian peoples and later for the Israelites themselves. For example, Genesis 10 records how Noah's sons occupied specific geographic areas of the known world...

"Central to the Pentateuch is the promise of land to the children of Israel...The allocated land is at first only loosely defined. As the biblical story progresses, however, it becomes more delimited, culminating in the border descriptions in the book of Joshua. The descriptions of the borders of the Promised Land fall into three categories: loose geographical definitions, definitions based on ethnic groups occupying it and definitions using the term Canaan...

"Several times the Promised Land is described, not in geographical terms per se, but in ethnic terms, that is, as the land of various groups of peoples all loosely labeled as either Canaanites or Amorites. Genesis 15:19–21, for instance, after giving the boundaries mentioned above, notes that the land was occupied by certain ethnic groups, including the Canaanites, Amorites and Jebusites. According to Genesis 10:15–19, these groups occupied a territory extending from Sidon in the north to roughly Gerar or Gaza in the south, and from the Mediterranean Sea in the west to the region of Sodom and Gomorrah in the east, roughly the Dead Sea. Although the land is not specifically called Canaan here, it is called the land of the Canaanites. This area does not describe quite the same region, then, as Genesis 15. The extension to the north is considerably shortened." – Borders. In T. D. Alexander & D. W. Baker (Eds.), *Dictionary of the Old Testament: Pentateuch*, pgs. 101-102

Joseph C. Atkinson

"The Semitic understanding in this area [anthropology] is radically different from our own modern understanding, particularly in the West. We have lost the profound sense of corporateness which is the mainspring of Semitic thought. Consequently, if we limit ourselves to modern categories, it will be impossible to understand the Hebraic concept of the human person or of the covenantal design of history. It is necessary to go beyond modern conceptualization, which sees the person in atomistic terms, and begin wrestling with the Hebraic principle of corporate personality and understanding of the soul (nephesh). Surprisingly, this Semitic understanding of the person pervades both the Old and the New Testaments and maintains a positive tension between, on the one hand, the value of the personal/subjective element, and, on the other, the recognition that each person is formed by, and is determined by, a prior corporate reality (the family, tribe, and/or nation). These two realities are inextricably linked and cannot be divided. This Semitic understanding, which always maintains both the personal and the corporate, is foundational for the New Testament's worldview. Consequently, in the new covenant in Christ, both the corporate and personal dimensions co-exist and never collapse into one another. In the New Testament's understanding of the Church, one finds personal salvation, but it is always found in terms of belonging to the corporate body of the Church. In household baptisms, there is personal response on the part of the head of the family, but this response also profoundly affects all who are a part of that family so that baptism becomes a familial reality (cf. Acts 16). The myth of the autonomous, self-determining individual does not function within the anthropology of either the Old or the New Testament. Rather, both the constitutive personal and corporate dimensions of the person are safeguarded." – *Biblical & Theological Foundations of the Family*, pg. 8

Augustine of Hippo

"Now he is a man of just and holy life who forms an unprejudiced estimate of things, and keeps his affections also under strict control, so that he neither loves what he ought not to love, nor fails to love what he ought to love, nor loves that more which ought to be loved less, nor loves that equally which ought to be loved either less or more, nor loves that less or more which ought to be loved equally. No sinner is to be loved as a sinner; and every man is to be loved as a man for God's sake; but God is to be loved for His own sake. And if God is to be loved more than any man, each man ought to love God more than himself. Likewise we ought to love another man better than our own body, because all things are to be loved in reference to God, and another man can have fellowship with us in the enjoyment of God, whereas our body cannot; for the body only lives through the soul, and it is by the soul that we enjoy God.

"Further, all men are to be loved equally. But since you cannot do good to all, you are to pay special regard to those who, by the accidents of time, or place, or circumstance, are brought into closer connection with you. For, suppose that you had a great deal of some commodity, and felt bound to give it away to somebody who had none, and that it could not be given to more than one person; if two persons presented themselves, neither of whom had either from need or relationship a greater claim upon you than the other, you could do nothing fairer than choose by lot to which you would give what could not be given to both. Just so among men: since you cannot consult for the good of them all, you must take the matter as decided for you by a sort of lot, according as each man happens for the time being to be more closely connected with you." – *On Christian Doctrine* in *St. Augustine's City of God and Christian Doctrine*, pg. 530

"And so also the Apostle Paul teaches when he says: 'For this, Thou shalt not commit adultery, Thou shalt not kill, Thou shalt not steal, Thou shalt not bear false witness, Thou shalt not covet; and if there be any other commandment, it is briefly comprehended in this saying, namely, Thou shalt love thy neighbor as thyself. Love worketh no ill to his neighbor.' Whoever then supposes that the apostle did not embrace every man in this precept, is compelled to admit, what

— AGUSTINE OF HIPPO —

is at once most absurd and most pernicious, that the apostle thought it no sin, if a man were not a Christian or were an enemy, to commit adultery with his wife, or to kill him, or to covet his goods. And as nobody but a fool would say this, it is clear that every man is to be considered our neighbor, because we are to work no ill to any man.

"But now, if every one to whom we ought to show, or who ought to show to us, the offices of mercy is by right called a neighbor, it is manifest that the command to love our neighbor embraces the holy angels also, seeing that so great offices of mercy have been performed by them on our behalf, as may easily be shown by turning the attention to many passages of Holy Scripture. And on this ground even God Himself, our Lord, desired to be called our neighbor." – *On Christian Doctrine* in *St. Augustine's City of God and Christian Doctrine*, pg. 531

"And hence it happened that even Holy Scripture, which brings a remedy for the terrible diseases of the human will, being at first set forth in one language, by means of which it could at the fit season be disseminated through the whole world, was interpreted into various tongues, and spread far and wide, and thus be-

came known to the nations for their salvation."
– *On Christian Doctrine*, in *St. Augustine's City of God and Christian Doctrine*, pg. 536

"Among the convenient and necessary arrangements of men with men are to be reckoned whatever differences they choose to make in bodily dress and ornament for the purpose of distinguishing sex or rank; and the countless varieties of signs without which human intercourse either could not be carried on at all, or would be carried on at great inconvenience; and the arrangements as to weights and measures, and the stamping and weighing of coins, which are peculiar to each state and people, and other things of the same kind. Now these, if they were not devices of men, would not be different in different nations, and could not be changed among particular nations at the discretion of their respective sovereigns. This whole class of human arrangements, which are of convenience for the necessary intercourse of life, the Christian is not by any means to neglect, but on the contrary should pay a sufficient degree of attention to them, and keep them in memory."
– *On Christian Doctrine* in *St. Augustine's City of God and Christian Doctrine*, pg. 548

"Now that this is a prophecy of the New Testament, to which pertain not only the remnant of that one nation of which it is elsewhere said, 'For though the number of the children of Israel be as the sand of the sea, yet a remnant of them shall be saved,' but also the other nations which were promised to their fathers and our fathers; and that there is here a promise of that washing of regeneration which, as we see, is now imparted to all nations, no one who looks into the matter can doubt. And that saying of the apostle, when he is commending the grace of the New Testament and its excellence in comparison with the Old, 'Ye are our epistle … written not with ink, but with the Spirit of the living God; not in tables of stone, but in fleshy tables of the heart,' has an evident reference to this place where the prophet says, 'A new heart also will I give you, and a new spirit will I put within you; and I will take away the stony heart out of your flesh, and I will give you an heart of flesh.' Now the heart of flesh from which the apostle's expression, 'the fleshy tables of the heart,' is drawn, the prophet intended to point out as distinguished from the stony heart by the

possession of sentient life; and by sentient he understood intelligent life. And thus the spiritual Israel is made up, not of one nation, but of all the nations which were promised to the fathers in their seed, that is, in Christ." – *On Christian Doctrine* in *St. Augustine's City of God and Christian Doctrine*, pgs. 570-571

"Nor did I know the true, inner justice which does not base its judgments on custom, but on the supremely right law of the omnipotent God, by which moral patterns of various places and times are determined according to those places and, since it is the same everywhere and always, not differing in different places and at different times. By its standards Abraham and Isaac and Jacob and Moses and David, and all who are praised by the mouth of God, were just. But they were adjudged evil by the inexperienced who judge 'by man's tribunal,' measuring all the behavior of mankind by their own moral standard. Just as if one….saw in one and the same house something being handled by a slave which is not customarily touched by the butler, or something being done behind the stable which is prohibited in the dining room, and became indignant on the pretext that it is one home and one family and that equal rights are not granted to all people in every place!

"These are the kind of people who become indignant when they hear that something was permitted to just men in times past which is not permitted to just men now, and at the fact that God commanded certain people to do one thing, and other people, for a temporal reason, to do something else, both observing the same justice. For, in one man, and on one day, and in one house, they may see that one thing is suitable to one member, another to another, and that something which was permissible up to now becomes illicit an hour hence, that something permitted or prescribed in one spot is prohibited and punished in a nearby place. But, is justice variable and mutable? Rather, the times over which it rules do not follow the same courses, for they are temporal. Men, whose life on earth is short, their sense not being able to fit together the reason of former times and other peoples which they know not with those which they have experienced, may easily see in one body, or day, or house, what is fitting to a certain member, or at a certain time and for what parts and persons. In one instance they feel offense, in this other they are compliant." – *Confessions*, pgs. 61-62

"Thus, O Lord, thus I pray Thee: let it spring up, Thou whose way it is to give joy and ability, let 'truth' spring up 'out of the earth,' and let 'justice look down from heaven,' and 'Let there be lights made in the firmament.' Let us break bread for the hungry and bring the poor man who has no shelter into our house; let us clothe the naked man and despise not the relatives of our flesh." – *Confessions*, pg. 464

"And, just as there is one thing in his soul which rules by virtue of the act of deliberation, and there is another which is made subject so that it may obey, so, also, there was also made for man, corporeally, woman—who had, indeed, a nature equal in mental capacity of rational intelligence, but made subject, by virtue of the sex of her body, to the male sex in the same way that the appetite for action is made subject, in order to conceive by the rational mind the skill of acting rightly." – *Confessions*, pg. 452

"The Catholic Church has been foretold, not as to be in any particular quarter of the world, as certain schisms are, but in the whole universe by bearing fruit and growing so as to attain even unto the very Ethiopians, to wit, the remotest and foulest of mankind." – *Exposition of Psalm 72*, pg. 459

"Difference of race or condition or sex is indeed taken away by the unity of faith, but it remains imbedded in our mortal interactions, and in the journey of this life the apostles themselves teach that it is to be respected, and they even proposed living in accord with the racial differences between Jews and Greeks as a wholesome rule. For we observe in the unity of faith that there are no such distinctions. Yet within the orders of this life they persist. So we walk this path in a way that the name and doctrine of God will not be blasphemed. It is not out of fear or anger that we wish to avoid offense to others but also on account of conscience, so that we may do these things not in mere profession, as if for the eyes of men, but with a pure love toward God." – *Epistle to the Galatians* on 3:28-29, pg. 49

"We ourselves can recognize in ourselves an image of God, in the sense of an image of the Trinity. Of course, it is merely an image and, in fact, a very remote one. There is no question of identity nor of co-eternity nor, in one word, of consubstantiality with Him. Nevertheless, it is an image which by nature is nearer to God than anything else in all creation, and one that by transforming grace can be perfected into a still closer resemblance." – *The City of God*, bks. VIII–XVI, pg. 228

"And therefore God created only one single man, not, certainly, that he might be a solitary, bereft of all society, but that by this means the unity of society and the bond of concord might be more effectually commended to him, men being bound together not only by similarity of nature, but by family affection." – *The City of God*, bks. VIII–XVI, pgs. 228-229

"In general, custom has great power both in provoking and preventing the play of human passion. In this matter, custom keeps concupiscence in bounds and, therefore, any detraction from or destruction of custom is branded as criminal. Thus, unjust as it is to encroach, out of greed, on another's property, it is still more wicked to transgress, out of lust, the limits of established morals." – *The City of God*, bks. VIII–XVI, pg. 453

"It is true that our ancestors had a religious regard for kinship and, being afraid that it might be lessened and lost in the course of successive generations, they tried to hold on to it by the bond of marriage and, as it were, to call it back before it got too far away. So it was that, when the world was fully populated and there was no more marrying of sisters or half-sisters, people still preferred to marry within their own clan... it is socially right to multiply and distribute relationships of love and wrong to have one person needlessly monopolizing two relationships which could be distributed to two persons and thus increase the community of kinship... The union of male and female is, then, so far as mortal living goes, the seed-bed, so to speak, from which a city must grow." – *The City of God*, bks. VIII–XVI, pg. 454

"Certain [pagan, nonchristian] philosophers, it is true, did get a glimpse of the truth amid the fog of their own fallacies and did try to build it up to solid conviction and persuasiveness by means of carefully worked-out argumentation—such truths, for example, as God's creation of the world, His providential governance of it, the excellence of virtue, of patriotism, of loyalty in friendship, of good works and all other things pertaining to morality. They saw these things even when they did not know to what final end, or how, they were to be referred. But in the City of God these truths are found in the words of the Prophets—God's words, even though spoken by men. And they were not driven into her people's heads amid the tumult of twisting and turning argumentation, but simply delivered to them. And those who heard them trembled, for they knew that if they despised them they were despising not the wisdom of man, but the word of God." – *The City of God*, bks. XVII–XXII, pg. 153

"The peace, then, of the body lies in the ordered equilibrium of all its parts; the peace of the irrational soul, in the balanced adjustment of its appetites; the peace of the reasoning soul, in the harmonious correspondence of conduct and conviction; the peace of body and soul taken together, in the well-ordered life and health of the living whole. Peace between a mortal man and his Maker consists in ordered obedience, guided by faith, under God's eternal law; peace between man and man consists in regulated fellowship. The peace of a home lies in the ordered harmony of authority and obedience between the members of a family living together. The peace of the political community is an ordered harmony of authority and obedience between citizens. The peace of the heavenly City lies in a perfectly ordered and harmonious communion of those who find their joy in God and in one another in God. Peace, in its final sense, is the calm that comes of order. Order is an arrangement of like and unlike things whereby each of them is disposed in its proper place." – *The City of God*, bks. XVII–XXII, pg. 217

"Meanwhile, God teaches him [man] two chief commandments, the love of God and the love of neighbor. In these precepts man finds three beings to love, namely, God, himself, and his fellow man, and knows that he is not wrong in loving himself so long as he loves God. As a result, he must help his neighbor (whom he is obliged to love as himself) to love God. Thus, he must help his wife, children, servants, and all others whom he can influence. He must wish, moreover, to be similarly helped by his fellow man, in case he himself needs such assistance. Out of all this love he will arrive at peace, as much as in him lies, with every man—at that human peace which is regulated fellowship. Right order here means, first, that he harm no one, and, second, that he help whomever he can. His fundamental duty is to look out for his own home, for both by natural and human law he has easier and readier access to their requirements.

"St. Paul says: 'But if any does not take care of his own, and especially of his household, he has denied the faith and is worse than an unbeliever.' From this care arises that peace of the home which lies in the harmonious interplay of authority and obedience among those who live there. For, those who have the care of the others give the orders—a man to his wife, parents to their children, masters to their servants. And those who are cared for must obey—wives their husband, children their parents, servants their masters. In the home of a religious man, however, of a man living by faith and as yet a wayfarer from the heavenly City, those who command serve those whom they appear to rule—because, of course, they do not command out of lust to domineer, but out of a sense of duty—not out of pride like princes but out of solicitude like parents." – *The City of God*, bks. XVII–XXII, pg. 222

"This heavenly city, then, while it sojourns on earth, calls citizens out of all nations, and gathers together a society of pilgrims of all languages, not scrupling about diversities in the manners, laws, and institutions whereby earthly peace is secured and maintained, but recognizing that, however various these are, they all tend to one and the same end of earthly peace. It therefore is so far from rescinding and abolishing these diversities, that it even preserves and adopts them, so long only as no hindrance to the worship of the one supreme and true God is thus introduced." – *The City of God*, bks. XVII–XXII, pg. 228

"After the city comes the world community. This is the third stage in the hierarchy of human associations. First, we have the home; then the city; finally, the globe. And, of course, as with the perils of the ocean, the bigger the community, the fuller it is of misfortunes.

"The first misfortune is the lack of communication resulting from language differences. Take two men who meet and find that some common need calls on them to remain together rather than to part company. Neither knows the language of the other. As far as intercommunication goes, these two, both men, are worse off than two dumb animals, even of different kinds. For all its identity in both, their human nature is of no social help, so long as the language barrier makes it impossible for them to tell each other what they are thinking about. That is why a man is more at home with his dog than with a foreigner." – *The City of God*, bks. XVII–XXII, pgs. 205-206

"The same account which is given of monstrous births in individual cases can be given of monstrous races. For God, the Creator of all, knows where and when each thing ought to be, or to have been created, because He sees the similarities and diversities which can contribute to the beauty of the whole. But he who cannot see the whole is offended by the deformity of the part, because he is blind to that which balances it, and to which it belongs. We know that men are born with more than four fingers on their hands or toes on their feet: this is a smaller matter; but far from us be the folly of supposing that the Creator mistook the number of a man's fingers, though we cannot account for the difference. And so in cases where the divergence from the rule is greater. He whose works no man justly finds fault with, knows what He has done. At Hippo-Diarrhytus there is a man whose hands are crescent-shaped, and have only two fingers each, and his feet similarly formed. If there were a race like him, it would be added to the history of the curious and wonderful. Shall we therefore deny that this man is descended from that one man who was first created? As for the Androgyni, or Hermaphrodites, as they are called, though they are rare, yet from time to time there appears persons of sex so doubtful, that it remains uncertain from which sex they take their name; though it is customary to give them a masculine name, as the more worthy. For no one ever called them Hermaphroditesses. Some years ago, quite within my own memory, a man was born in the East, double in his upper, but single in his lower half — having two heads, two chests, four hands, but one body and two feet like an ordinary man; and he lived so long

that many had an opportunity of seeing him. But who could enumerate all the human births that have differed widely from their ascertained parents? As, therefore, no one will deny that these are all descended from that one man, so all the races which are reported to have diverged in bodily appearance from the usual course which nature generally or almost universally preserves, if they are embraced in that definition of man as rational and mortal animals, unquestionably trace their pedigree to that one first father of all. We are supposing these stories about various races who differ from one another and from us to be true; but possibly they are not: for if we were not aware that apes, and monkeys, and sphinxes are not men, but beasts, those historians would possibly describe them as races of men, and flaunt with impunity their false and vainglorious discoveries. But supposing they are men of whom these marvels are recorded, what if God has seen fit to create some races in this way, that we might not suppose that the monstrous births which appear among ourselves are the failures of that wisdom whereby He fashions the human nature, as we speak of the failure of a less perfect workman? Accordingly, it ought not to seem absurd to us, that as in individual races there are monstrous births, so in the whole race there are monstrous races. Wherefore, to conclude this question cautiously and guardedly, either these things which have been told of some races have no existence at all; or if they do exist, they are not human races; or if they are human, they are descended from Adam." – *City Of God*, Book IX, pgs. 314-315

"Since every man is a part of the human race, and human nature is something social and possesses the capacity for friendship as a great and natural good, for this reason God wished to create all men from one, so that they might be held together in their society, not only by the similarity of race, but also by the bond of blood relationship. And so it is that the first natural tie of human society is man and wife. Even these God did not create separately and join them as if strangers, but He made the one from the other, indicating also the power of union in the side from where she was drawn and formed. They are joined to each other side by side who walk together and observe together where they are walking. A consequence is the union of society in the children who are the only worthy fruit, not of the joining of male and female, but of sexual intercourse. For there could have been in both sexes, even without such intercourse, a kind of friendly and genuine union of the one ruling and the other obeying." – *On The Good Of Marriage*, from *Treatises on Marriage and Other Subjects*, pg. 9

"...what food is to the health of man, intercourse is to the health of the race." – *On The Good Of Marriage*, from *Treatises on Marriage and Other Subjects*, pg. 32

"Since of His bounty He has granted to things which are born in time that each thing should beget offspring of its own substance, see how impious it is to say that He did not beget what He is, when man, by His gift, begets what he is, that is, man, not of another nature but of the same as his own, although He does not beget the Father of His Son which is Himself. These terms indicate analogy not nature, and, therefore, when applied to something they have a relative sense, sometimes identical, sometimes different. They have a meaning of identity, of course, when brother is compared to brother, friend to friend, neighbor to neighbor, kindred to kindred, and other like cases which could be drawn out to infinity if one wished to run through all of them. In these cases this one is to that one what that one is to this one. But they are different in comparisons of father to son, son to father, father-in-law to son-in-law, son-in-law to father-in-law, master to slave, slave to master: in these this one is not to that one what that one is to this one, although both are men. This comparison of diverse objects is not made in terms of their nature, since, as you notice, what one of the pair is to the other is not in the formula of this one is to that one as that one is to this one, because one is the father, the other the son; or one the father-in-law, the other the son-in-law; or one the master, the other the slave. But, if you notice what each one is to himself or in himself, one is the same as the other because one is man as the other is. Consequently, your Prudence understands the illogical contention of those from whose error the Lord has delivered you, which states that the nature of God the Father must be different from the nature of God the Son, because one is the Father, the other the Son, and therefore the Father did not beget what He is Himself, since

He did not beget the Father of the Son which He is Himself. Anyone can see that those terms do not denote their natures in themselves, but the Person of each toward the other." – *Augustine's Letters*, (165-203), Letter 170, pg. 64

"...although those in whom He dwells possess Him in proportion to the diversity of their own capacity, some more, some less, He builds up all of them by the grace of His goodness as His most beloved temple!" – *Augustine's Letters*, (165-203), Letter 187, pg. 236

"The case of strangers is different from the case of persons bound to us by any tie; the case of believers is not the same as that of unbelievers; the case of parents toward children differs from that of children toward parents; and, finally, the case of husband and wife (which is the one especially considered in the present circumstances) differs from the others, and the married woman has no right to say: 'I do what I please with my own property,' since she does not belong to herself, but to her head, that is, her husband. For 'after this manner,' as the Apostle Peter says, 'certain holy women who trusted in God adorned themselves, being in subjection to their own husbands; as Sara obeyed Abraham, calling him lord, whose daughters' he says 'you are,' and he was speaking to Christian, not to Jewish, women." – *Augustine's Letters*, (204-270), Letter 262, pg. 265

"If, however, your own wealth contains some of your family's property—in the management of which it is neither right nor proper for you to be involved—it should indeed be handed over to your mother and the members of your household. If you have decided to distribute such possessions to the poor that you may be perfect, the poverty of your own should hold first place with you..." – *Augustine's Letters*, (204-270), Letter 243, pg. 226

"But although in this life, because of the common faith itself, all who believe in one are one according to the words of the apostle, 'For ye are all one in Christ Jesus;' even thus we are one, not in order to our believing, but because we do believe. What, then, is meant by the words, 'That they all may be one, that the world may believe'? This, doubtless, that the 'all' are themselves the believing world. For those who shall be one are not of one class, and the world that is thereafter to believe on this very ground that these shall be one, of another; since it is perfectly certain that He says, 'That they all may be one,' of those of whom He had said before, 'Neither pray I for these alone, but for those also who shall believe on me through their word,' immediately adding as He does, 'That they all may be one.' And this 'all,' what is it but the world; not certainly that which is hostile, but that which is believing? For you see here that He who had said, 'I pray not for the world,' now prayeth for the world that it may believe. For there is a world whereof it is written, 'That we might not be condemned with this world.' For that world He prayeth not, for He is fully aware to what it is predestinated. And there is a world whereof it is written, 'For the Son of man came not to condemn the world, but that the world through Him might be saved;' and hence the apostle also says, 'God was in Christ, reconciling the world unto Himself.' For this world it is that He prayeth, in saying, 'That the world may believe that Thou hast sent me.' For through this faith the world is reconciled unto God when it believes in the Christ whom God has sent. How, then, are we to understand Him when He says, 'That they also may be one in us, that the world may believe that Thou hast sent me,' but just in this way, that He did not assign the cause of the world believing to the fact that those others are one, as if it believed on the ground that it saw them to be one; for the world itself here consisteth of all who by their own believing become one; but in His prayer He said, 'That the world may believe,' just as in His prayer He also said, 'That they all may be one;' and still further in the same prayer, 'That they also may be one in us.' For the words, 'they all may be one,' are equivalent to 'the world may believe,' since it is by believing that they become one, perfectly one; that is, those who, although one by nature, had ceased to be so by their mutual dissensions." – *Tractates on the Gospel According to Saint John, Nicene and Post-Nicene Fathers*, vol. 7, pg. 409

"Finally, not merely do like customs produce mutual friendship between souls, but in each individual soul as well like actions and virtues, without which there can be no constancy, are a mark of the happy life." – *On Genesis*, pg. 185

"And again, in another place, I said: 'But, in truth, man is not to be loved by man as brothers according to the flesh are loved, or sons or spouses or certain relatives or neighbors or fellow citizens; for love such as this is, indeed, temporal. For we would not have any such relationships as are connected with birth and death if our nature, by abiding in the precepts and image of God, had not been relegated to this corruption,' I certainly disapprove of this view….There would have been relatives and kindred even if no one had sinned and no one had died." – *The Retractions*, pg. 56

"By sin Adam lost the image of God according to which he was made… [I do not mean] as though no image remained in him, but that it was so deformed that there was need for re-formation." – *The Retractions*, pg. 169

"For in that eternal kingdom to which He has vouchsafed to call His disciples, to whom He also gives the name of brothers, there are no temporal relationships of this sort. For 'there is neither Jew nor Greek, there is neither bond nor free, there is neither male nor female; but Christ is all, and in all.' And the Lord Himself says: 'For in the resurrection they neither marry, nor are given in marriage, but are as the angels of God in heaven.' Hence it is necessary that whoever wishes here and now to aim after the life of that kingdom, should hate not the persons themselves, but those temporal relationships by which this life of ours, which is transitory and is comprised in being born and dying, is upheld; because he who does not hate them, does not yet love that life where there is no condition of being born and dying, which unites parties in earthly wedlock." – *Sermon On The Mount, The Works of Aurelius Augustine*, pg. 32

Augustine responds by analogy to those who say we cannot believe anything that is unseen:
"If this faith in human affairs is removed, who will not mark how great will be their disorder and what dreadful confusion will follow? For, who will be cherished by anyone in mutual charity, since love itself is invisible, if what I do not see I ought not to believe? Friendship, then, will wholly perish, since it rests upon nothing more than mutual love. What of this will one be able to receive from another, if it shall be believed that nothing of it can be shown?

Furthermore, when friendship perishes, neither the bonds of marriage nor of relationship and affinity will be retained in the mind, because in these, also, there surely is a friendly spirit of harmony. Then a husband and wife will not be able to have mutual affection, since they do not believe that there is any love, inasmuch as love cannot be seen. Nor will they desire to have children, for they do not believe that the children will return their love. And, if children should be born and grow up, the parents themselves will love their own much less, and they will not see love for themselves in their children's hearts because love is invisible—if things unseen are believed, not by praiseworthy faith but by blameworthy rashness." – *De Fide Rerum Quae Non Videntur*, pg. 87

"For, I ask, if what is not known need not be believed, how are children to be subject to their parents? And how are they to love with mutual affection those whom they do not believe to be their own parents? For this cannot in any way be known through reason, but is believed of the father on the authority of the mother; but, as to the mother herself, it is not she, for the most part, that is believed, but midwives, nurses, and servants. For cannot she from whom a son can be stolen and another substituted, having been deceived herself, deceive others? Yet we believe, and we believe without any doubt, what we admit we cannot know. For who would not see that, unless this were so, filial devotion, the most sacred bond of the human race, would be violated by a most grievous sin of pride? For who, no matter how crazy he were, should think one ought to be blamed for fulfilling his duties to those whom he believed to be his parents, even though they were not? Who, on the other hand, has not judged that man deserving of exile who, perhaps, loved his real parents very little, lest he might love counterfeit parents? Many examples can be cited which show that absolutely nothing would remain intact in human society if we should determine to believe only what we can grasp by perception." – *The Advantage of Believing, Fathers Of The Church*, vol. 2. pg. 426

"'Let us love, because He first loved us.' For how should we love, except He had first loved us? By loving we became friends: but He loved us as enemies, that we might be made friends. He first loved us, and gave us the gift of loving Him. We did not yet love Him: by loving we are made beautiful. If a man deformed and ill-featured love a beautiful woman, what shall he do? Or what shall a woman do, if, being deformed and ill-featured and black-complexioned, she love a beautiful man? By loving can she become beautiful? Can he by loving become handsome? He loves a beautiful woman, and when he sees himself in a mirror, he is ashamed to lift up his face to her his lovely one of whom he is enamored. What shall he do that he may be beautiful? Does he wait for good looks to come? Nay rather, by waiting old age is added to him, and makes him uglier. There is nothing then to do, there is no way to advise him, but only that he should restrain himself, and not presume to love unequally: or if perchance he does love her, and wishes to take her to wife, in her let him love chastity, not the face of flesh." – *Ten Homilies on the First Epistle of John*, vol. 11, pg. 1214

"If anyone fails to honor his parents, is there anyone he will spare?" – quoted in *Exodus, Leviticus, Numbers, Deuteronomy*, ed. Joseph T. Lienhard, *Ancient Christian Commentary on Scripture*, 3:106

"'God hath set the members, each one of them, in the body, as He would;' that neither the whole be an eye, nor the whole hearing, nor the whole smelling: and, whatever else there is, it hath its own property, although it have health equally with all. Thus because life eternal itself shall be alike to all, an equal penny was assigned to all; but, because in that life eternal itself the lights of merits shall shine with a distinction, there are many mansions in the house of the Father: and, by this means, in the penny not unlike, one lives not longer than another; but in the many mansions, one is honoured with greater brightness than another." – *Seventeen Short Treatises*, pg. 327. 1 Corinthians 12:18

Marcus Aurelius

"From Sextus, [I learned] a benevolent disposition, and the example of a family governed in a fatherly manner, and the idea of living conformably to nature; and gravity without affectation, and to look carefully after the interests of friends, and to tolerate ignorant persons, and those who form opinions without consideration: he had the power of readily accommodating himself to all, so that intercourse with him was more agreeable than any flattery; and at the same time he was most highly venerated by those who associated with him: and he had the faculty both of discovering and ordering, in an intelligent and methodical way, the principles necessary for life; and he never showed anger or any other passion, but was entirely free from passion, and also most affectionate; and he could express approbation without noisy display, and he possessed much knowledge without ostentation." – *Meditations*, bk. 1

— MARCUS AURELIUS —

"To the gods I am indebted for having good grandfathers, good parents, a good sister, good teachers, good associates, good kinsmen and friends, nearly everything good." – *Meditations*, bk. 1

"...a man should hold on to the opinion not of all, but of those only who confessedly live according to nature." – *Meditations*, bk. 3

"...comes from a member of the same tribe, a kinsman, and a fellow (one with whom life is shared), even when such a fellow is ignorant of that which accords with his nature. But I am not [ignorant], and therefore I treat him kindly and justly in accordance with the natural law of fellowship." – *Meditations*, bk. 3

Lawrence Auster

"The entire Western world is at present under the grip of the modern liberal ideology that targets every normal and familiar aspect of human life, and our entire historical way of being as a society. The key to this liberal ideology is the belief in tolerance or non-discrimination as the ruling principle of society, the principle to which all other principles must yield. We see this belief at work in every area of modern life. The principle of non-discrimination must, if followed consistently, destroy every human society and institution." – *A Real Islam Policy for America*

"This is the ubiquitous yet unacknowledged horror of modern liberalism, that it takes the ordinary, differentiated nature of the world, which all human beings have always recognized, and makes it impossible for people to discuss it, because under liberalism anyone who notes these distinctions and says that they matter has done an evil thing and must be banished from society, or at least be barred from a mainstream career." – *A Real Islam Policy for America*

"But to return to main question, I know that by explicitly expressing my concern about the white race and its survival, I make many people uncomfortable, even those who happen to share that concern, and they feel a need to distance themselves from me. I'll just say this: whether or not one is comfortable expressing it explicitly, without a certain degree of race consciousness on the part of whites, there is not going to be a turnaround on immigration (or indeed, on any other anti-white policy today). The reason for this is simple yet hard to understand: The West's policy of openness to non-white immigration (and to other anti-white policies) is itself driven primarily by the conviction that it's wrong to care about our own race. Therefore the only way that that policy can be turned around is by the opposite understanding, that there's nothing wrong with caring about our own race. This is true even for those immigration restrictionists who really do not care about race, who only care about the effect on the economy, or the environment, or population, or whatever. As long as they refuse to confront the underlying moral conviction that drives the West's suicidal openness to the Other, the West will continue in that openness. I cannot emphasize enough the importance of understanding this." – *What is European America*

"European-Americans must rediscover and reassert the racial and civilizational identity they have lost, must once again believe in themselves and assert their own consciousness as a people. To do this, they must squarely confront the double standard which says that a concern for the survival of a collective white identity is illegitimate and hateful, while a concern for the collective survival of other identities, such as a Jewish identity, is moral and admirable." – *Our Borders, Ourselves*, ch. 14

"Not ... the act of standing up for themselves make[s] whites contemptible in the eyes of nonwhites but ... giving away their country and peoplehood without a fight. When whites begin to assert their own [collective] existence and their desire to preserve it, not in a hateful way but in a calm, intelligent and firm way, then non-whites will begin to see whites, not as the oppressor figures of anti-racist demonology, nor as cowardly saps, but as human beings who have the same basic concerns for their culture and peoplehood that minorities have for theirs." – *Our Borders, Ourselves*, ch. 14

"The Christian belief in a common humanity under God should not tempt us to weaken or eliminate national borders. The division of mankind into distinct nations provides indispensable human needs, including stable social settings and systems of shared habit and culture. Equally importantly, national boundaries keep human hatred at bay. Common sense tells us that humanity tends to certain vices, and we should therefore not gratuitously remove the obstacles that impede those vices. It tells us that to adopt unconditional love as a political principle and to erase all boundaries on human behavior is to license unlimited aggression. But the liberal fundamentalists, having rejected the doctrine of man's innate sinfulness and even the cautions of ordinary common sense, cannot grasp those obvious facts. They condemn racism while fanatically spreading the very conditions of unassimilable diversity that increase racial conflict. They have no qualms about the effects of immigration on the host society because they regard openness to immigration as a religious obligation not as political choice governed by prudence." – *Our Borders, Ourselves*, ch. 11

B

Thomas Babington

Standing on a bridge against an invading army:
> Then out spake brave Horatius,
> The Captain of the gate:
> "To every man upon this earth
> Death cometh soon or late.
> And how can man die better
> Than facing fearful odds
> For the ashes of his fathers
> And the temples of his gods,
> And for the tender mother
> Who dandled him to rest,
> And for the wife who nurses
> His baby at her breast,
> And for the holy maidens
> Who feed the eternal flame,—
> To save them from false Sextus
> That wrought the deed of shame?"
> – *Horatius at the Bridge* [4]

Bacchylides

"All-powerful Hera drove these daughters in fear from the lovely halls... while still virgins, they entered the sanctuary of the purple-belted goddess, and said that their father far surpassed in wealth the golden-haired consort of holy, widely powerful Zeus." – *Ode*, 11.45

"Golden-haired Apollo still loves the state of Syracuse and honors Hieron, the city's lawful ruler." – *Ode*, 4

"Once in [spacious] Sparta the golden-haired Lacedaemonian women [sang] ... such a song ... when bold-hearted [Idas] led ... Marpessa, the maiden with lovely [cheeks], fleeing ... of death ... Poseidon, the lord of the sea ... and to him horses [swift as the wind] to well-built Pleuron, the son of [Ares] with golden shield ..." – *Odes*, 20, *Dithyrambs*, 6

Joyce Baldwin

"The future ministry of the coming prophet is described in terms of bridging the generation gap. The fifth commandment implied that the home was essentially the school of the community. There, in a 'world in miniature', authority and submission, love and loyalty, obedience and trust could be learned as nowhere else and, with the word of God as guide in the home, society could be changed. The dread alternative constituted Malachi's last word, God's curse (Heb. ḥērem). Connected with the idea of holiness the word 'curse' represents the taboo which set apart for destruction any person interfering with whatever had been vowed to the deity and was therefore 'holy', excluded from secular use (Josh. 7:11–15). The cities and population of Canaan which had belonged to other gods were also put under the curse and were to be utterly exterminated (Deut. 13:12–18; 20:16f.). This harsh fate later became associated with the terror of final judgment, to be set free from which was the height of blessing (Zech. 14:11; Rev. 22:3)." – verse 4:6. Tyndale Old Testament Commentaries. *Haggai, Zechariah and Malachi: An Introduction and Commentary*, vol. 28, pgs. 276–277.

Paul M. Barford

"The complex processes initiated by the Slav expansion and subsequent demographic and ethnic consolidation culminated in the formation of tribal groups, which later coalesced to create states which form the framework of the ethnic make-up of modern Eastern Europe ...

"Most early modern rulers . . . seemed to have recognized . . . the importance of imposing some form of unity and promoting a 'national feeling' among the people of their realms in order to discourage moves towards decentraliza-

---

4   The famous poem captures this pietas/pater/patria concept beautifully.

tion. In other words, like a giant roller the state was to level out any local irregularities. These developments may have been imposed by force, encouraged by imposing a common ideology of some form (and propaganda), or may have developed naturally. These factors may have involved a common religion, linguistic unity, the invention of shared ideals and traditions, a common enemy of the establishment of a unified material culture." – *The Early Slavs*, pg. 144

Albert Barnes

"[Gal 3:28] does not mean that all are on a level in regard to talents, comforts, or wealth; but it means only that all people are on a level 'in regard to religion.' This is the sole point under discussion; and the interpretation should be limited to this. It is not a fact that people are on a level in all things, nor is it a fact that the gospel designs to break down all the distinctions of society. Paul means to teach that no man has any preference or advantage in the kingdom of God because he is a rich man, or becaise he is of elevated rank; no one is under any disadvantage because he is poor, or because he is ignorant, or a slave... The essential idea is, that they are on a level, and that they are admitted to the favour of God without respect to their external condition in society. I do not see any evidence in this passage that the Christian religion designed to abolish slavery, any more than I do in the following phrase, 'there is neither male nor female,' that it was intended to abolish the distinction of the sexes; nor do I see in this passage any evidence that there should not be proper respect shown by the servant to the master, though both of them are Christians, any more that there is in the follow phrase, that suitable respect should not be shown in the intercourse [human relations] with the sexes."– *Commentary on Gal 3:28*, pg. 400

"The words 'his own,' refer to those who are naturally dependent on him, whether living in his own immediate family or not. There may be many distant relatives naturally dependent on our aid, besides those who live in our own house.

"And specially for those of his own house – 'kindred.' The word 'house,' or 'household,' better expresses the sense than the word 'kin-dred.' The meaning is, those who live in his own family. They would naturally have higher claims on him than those who did not. They would commonly be his nearer relatives, and the fact, from whatever cause, that they constituted his own family, would lay the foundation for a strong claim upon him. He who neglected his own immediate family would be more guilty than he who neglected a more remote relative.

"He hath denied the faith – By his conduct, perhaps, not openly. He may be still a professor of religion and do this; but he will show that he is imbued with none of the spirit of religion, and is a stranger to its real nature. The meaning is, that he would, by such an act, have practically renounced Christianity, since it enjoins this duty on all." – *Commentary on 1 Timothy 5:8*, pg. 220

Craig Bartholomew

"Chapters 15-21 [of Judges] have a vested interest in boundaries, a topic that anthropologists have long attended to. Even where a detailed list of towns in a tribal territory is lacking, the boundaries are emphasized. Clearly the boundaries portrayed in Joshua are intended to be understood as geographical. They provide the tribes with social cohesions as well as responsibility for full occupation of their part of the land. The boundaries are both separating and unifying. Israel is the one people of God in the land, and this the boundaries are not absolute but permeable; when necessary, for example, the tribes cooperate in clearing the land of Canaanites (Judges 1:3-7)." – *Where Mortals Dwell: A Christian View of Place for Today*, pg. 126

"Genesis 1 presents the earth as a potential place for humans; it is depicted as an ideal home...Genesis 2 becomes far more placially specific with its focus on Eden as the garden in which Adam and Eve are to dwell. As Von Rad notes of J's [5] account of creation, 'It is altogether a much smaller area with which the narrator deals—not even the 'earth,' but the world that lies at man's own doorstep—garden, rivers, trees, language, animals, and woman.'

"...the move from Genesis 1 to 2, rather than indicating a juxtaposition of two unrelated sources, involves a movement of progressive implacement culminating in the planting of Eden as the specific place in which the earth-

---

5 "J" is the term used for one of the hypothetical authors of Genesis in the theory of multiple authors.

lings Adam and Eve will dwell. It is important to note just how illuminating place is at this point. Genesis 1 presents the world as a potential place for human habitation, but the nature of Adam and Eve as embodied earthlings means that the human story itself must begin in a specific place, in this case Eden. As Casey notes, 'Implacement itself, being concretely placed, is intrinsically particular.'

"The Hebrew word for humankind in 1:26-28, namely 'ādām, already creates the closest connection between humankind and the earth, with its association with 'ădāmâ (= cultivable ground). True, the word used for the earth as a whole in Genesis 1 is 'ereṣ; in 2:7, however, Yahweh Elohim forms 'ādām out of the 'ădāmâ, and in Eden it is out of the 'ădāmâ that Yahweh Elohim causes trees to grow which are aesthetically pleasing and nutritionally satisfying. Throughout 2:5-3:24 'ădāmâ is used for Eden and 'ereṣ does not occur. 'Earthling' is therefore an apt description of human beings, since it points clearly to the embodied nature of human being. Hiebert notes, 'Not only does 'ādām cultivate 'ădāmâ, he is fashioned by God out of the land he farms.' This link between 'ādām and 'ădāmâ alerts us to the fact that human embodiment and place are deeply interwoven and in practice inseparable.

"The creaturely embodiment of human beings makes placement unavoidable. Embodied human life implies specific place, and the ordering of the content of Genesis 2 after that of chapter 1 exemplifies this. Human habitation can never straddle the whole earth; it is of necessity specific, and in Genesis 2 that means the garden which God plants, namely Eden. Place names begin to accumulate in Genesis 2—Eden, Pishon, Havilah, Gihon, Tigris, and Assyria—and this again indicates the differentiation toward a specific place: 'Place-names embody this complex collective concreteness despite their considerable brevity." – Genesis 1-2 commentary. *Where Mortals Dwell: A Christian View of Place for Today*, pgs. 46-47.

"Cain's punishment thus includes the radical displacement of a vagrant as well as the more holistic punishment of separation from family and from God. Cain is condemned to permanent displacement." – Genesis 4 commentary. *Where Mortals Dwell: A Christian View of Place for Today*, pg. 59.

"Because of his precipitate action in murdering an Egyptian, Moses is forced to flee into the desert and settle in Midian. The geographical location of Midian is uncertain, possibly because the Midianites were nomads. Moses is well received by the Midianites, finds a wife, and settles with them; among the Midianites he finds temporary implacement, as the name of his son, Gershom, indicates. Although Gershom is probably derived from grš (drive, cast out), the narrator relates it to 'stranger' (gēr) and 'there' (šām). As J. Durham notes, Gershom evokes Moses's 'most complete integration into his Midianite family. . . . Moses, who had been all his life a stranger there [in Egypt], was here a stranger no longer. . . . Moses has come to a people who not only worship the God of the fathers, but are free to do so. Thus he is at home, because this God is his God.' Moses's new occupation reconnects him placially with his ancestors." – Exodus 2 commentary. *Where Mortals Dwell: A Christian View of Place for Today*

"Wisdom can and does lead to emplacement and placid flourishing. Proverbs climaxes in chapter 31 with the Song of the Valiant Woman, who embodies holistic implacement. In the history of interpretation readers have struggled with this passage because her activities appear so worldly, but this is precisely the point: it is in and through her rich emplacement that she manifests wisdom…She is the quintessential homemakers, who creatively attends to food and clothing. The woman's scope of action encompasses the entire creation: Both land and sea provide resources for her house as she brings goods from near and far…As wisdom builds and supplies her house, so also the capable wife builds and fills her house with good. In sum, the Proverbs 31 woman is a marvelous example of…housewifery." – *Where Mortals Dwell: A Christian View of Place for Today*, pg. 142

Basil the Great

"It is more advantageous for someone who, because of a lack of intelligence, does not have it naturally in himself to be self-ruling, to become the possession of someone else, so that he can be set aright by the reason of his master. He is similar to a chariot that has a driver and a ship that has a pilot sitting at the helm. On account of this, Jacob was the lord of Esau by the blessing of their father, so that the senseless one, even against his will, would be helped by the sensible one, since the former did not have his mind as a proper guardian. And, 'Canaan will be a household slave to his brothers' (Genesis 9:25–27), since he is ignorant of virtue and has a father, Ham, who lacks understanding. Here, then, there are slaves in these ways. They are free, however, who escape poverty or war, and who need not the guardianship of others." – *On the Holy Spirit*, pgs. 87-88

"Did you snatch away the means of your inferiors, maltreat the poor, cover with disgrace by reproaches, blackmail, make false accusations, tamper with other's marriages, swear falsely, change your ancestral boundaries, attack the possessions of orphans, oppress widows, prefer the present pleasure to the blessings in the promises?" – *Exegetical Homilies*, Psalm 27, pgs. 350-358.

"Let me pass over the deceitfulness and trickery of the octopus (whose character Basil was using as an image of wicked men), which assumes on every occasion the color of the rock to which it fastens itself. As a result, many of the fish swimming unwarily fall upon the octopus as upon a rock, I suppose, and become an easy prey for the cunning fellow. Such in character are those men who always fawn upon the ruling powers and adapt themselves to the needs of every occasion, not continuing always in the same principles, but easily changing into different persons, who honor self-control with the chaste, but incontinence with the incontinent, and alter their opinions to please everyone. It is not easy to avoid nor to guard against harm from them because the evil they have fostered in themselves is hidden under a pretext of profound friendship. Such characters the Lord calls ravenous wolves which show themselves in sheep's clothing. Avoid inconstancy and fickleness, pursue truth, sincerity, simplicity. The serpent is subtle, and for that reason has been condemned to crawl. The just man is without pretense, such as was Jacob. Therefore, 'The Lord maketh men of one manner to dwell in a house.' So in this great sea, which stretcheth wide its arms: 'there are creeping things without number: Creatures little and great.' Nevertheless, there is a certain wisdom among them and an orderly arrangement. Not only are we able to bring charges against the fish, but there is also some-

thing worthy of imitation in them. How is it that all of the different species of fishes, having been allotted a place suitable for them, do not intrude upon one another, but stay within their own bounds? No surveyor apportioned the dwellings among them; they were not surrounded with walls nor divided by boundaries; but what was useful for each was definitely and spontaneously settled. This bay gives sustenance to certain kinds of fish and that one, to other kinds; and those that teem here are scarce elsewhere. No mountain extending upward with sharp peaks separates them; no river cuts off the means of crossing; but there is a certain law of nature which allots the habitat to each kind equally and justly according to its need.

"We, however, are not such. Why? Because we pass beyond the ancient bounds which our fathers set. We cut off a part of the land amiss; we join house to house and field to field, so that we may take something of our neighbor's. The cetaceans know the habitats assigned them by nature. They have taken the sea beyond the inhabited regions, that part free from islands, in which there is no continent confronting them on the opposite side, because, since neither desire of inquiry nor any necessity persuades the sailors to venture on it, it is not navigated. The cetaceans which occupy that sea, in size like

— BASIL THE GREAT —

the mightiest mountains, as they who have seen them say, remain within their own boundaries and do not injure the islands nor the seaboard cities. So then, each kind abides in the parts of the sea assigned to it, as if in certain cities or villages or ancient countries." – *Exegetical Homilies*, pgs. 110-111

Frederic Bastiat

"Let us banish from political economy all expressions borrowed from the military vocabulary: to fight on equal terms, conquer, crush, choke off, be defeated, invasion, tribute. What do these terms signify? Squeeze them, and nothing comes out. Or rather, what comes out is absurd errors and harmful preconceptions. Such expressions are inimical to international co-operation, hinder the formation of a peaceful, ecumenical, and indissoluble union of the peoples of the world, and retard the progress of mankind." – *Economic Sophisms*, pg. 271

"If the emperor Nicholas should venture to send 200,000 Muscovites, I sincerely believe that the best thing we could do would be to receive them well, to give them a taste of the sweetness of our wines, to show them our stores, our museums, the happiness of our people, the mildness and quality of our penal laws, after which we should say to them: Return as quickly as possible to your steppes and tell your brothers what you have seen." – *America Asleep*, pg. 57

Voddie Baucham

"In August 2006, I stood on African soil for the first time. It was an amazing two weeks.

"One Sunday, I was scheduled to preach at Evangel Baptist Church, pastored by Dr. Grave Singogo. When I arrived at the church, a spry eighty-seven-year-old man approached me. He was Pastor Singogo's father. He introduced himself, shook my hand, gave me a giant African smile, then a hug. Then he asked me, 'Is this your first time in Africa?' I said yes.

"Somehow, his smile got even bigger. He raised his left hand (his right never stopped shaking mine), grabbed my face, kissed me, and exclaimed, 'Son, welcome home!'

"I completely lost it. There I stood in the dirt parking lot of a church I had never been to before, and I just started sobbing.

"When I finally got myself together, I greeted more brethren, then found my way to my seat. As the service began, I was overcome with emotion once again. I thought about Papa Singogo's greeting and how much it had meant to me. I thought about how much my father, who had died four months before my trip, would have loved to be there with me." – *Fault Lines*, pg. 227

Herman Bavinck

"The term [tradition] can even be further expanded to include all those rich and multifarious bonds that link succeeding generations to preceding ones. In this sense, no family, no generation, no society, no people, no art, and no science can exist without tradition. Tradition is the means by which all the treasures and possession of our ancestors are transmitted to the present and the future." – *Reformed Dogmatics*, vol. 1. pg. 492

"In that community, which Christ has purchased and gathered from all nations, languages, and tongues (Rev. 5:9; etc.), all nations, Israel included, maintain their place and calling (Matt. 8:11; Rom. 11:25; Rev. 21:24; 22:2). And all those nations–each in accordance with its own distinct national character–bring into the new Jerusalem all they have received from God in the way of glory and honor (Rev. 21:24, 26)." – *Reformed Dogmatics*, vol. 4, pg. 720

"The entire organization of the nation was along patriarchal lines, arranged in terms of the principle of genealogical descent. The twelve tribes, among whom Judah was preeminent, were divided into clans, the clans into extended families, and these extended families into households. Each of those groups had its own head, representative, or prince, an all these heads or princes together formed the 'members of the assembly.' When they gathered, the 'congregation' of Israel was gathered." – *The Christian Family*, ch. 4

"The history of the human race did not begin atomistically, with a group of isolated individuals, but organically, with a marriage and a family. From the very beginning all those relationships were embedded in seed form within that family, relationships which would later arise among people in the most splendid manner. The disparity, which we presently observe everywhere in human society, is in principle and in essence not a result of sin, as many people thought in earlier and later times, but it existed from the very beginning, even before sin entered the world. Such disparity was willed by God for all his creatures and rests upon his good pleasure.

"Within the first family, the distinctions between man and woman, parents and children, brothers and sisters, were already present, and along with them was supplied in seed form all those relationships of authority and obedience, coordination and subordination, parity and fraternity, which now in various expressions and concrete ways still govern the social life of human beings. Even as one star differs in brightness from another star; even as all physical bodies are not the same, but can be distinuished as a human body or an animal or a fish or a bird; even as in the state of glory there will be a diversity of gifts and strengths and various degrees of blessedness; so too the human race has unfolded on earth according to God's will, in an endless diversity of persons and powers, relationships and capacities, talents and gifts, possessions and goods. From that first family have come clans and tribes and nations, and among those nations a rich group association has developed, which we generally refer to as society." – *The Christian Family*, ch. 9

"Nature teaches this distinction, and no science or philosophy is needed to acquaint oneself with this. Man and woman differ in physical structure and physical strength, in psychological nature and psychological strength; thereby they naturally enjoy different rights and are called to different duties." – *The Christian Family*, ch. 3

Richard Baxter

"It is a matter of very great importance, what teachers you choose, in order to your salvation. In this the free grace of God much differs some from others: for, as poor heathens and infidels have none [ie., no teachers] that know more, than what the book of nature teaches (if so much); so in the several nations of Christians, it is hard for the people to have any, but such as the sword of the magistrate forces on them,

or the stream of their country's custom recommends to them...

"In a nation where true religion is in credit, and hath the magistrate's countenance, or the major vote, some graceless men may join with better, in preaching and defending the purity of doctrine, and holiness of life: and they may be very serviceable to the church herein; especially in expounding and disputing for the truth." – *The Practical Works of the Rev. Richard Baxter*, vol. 2, pg. 146. [6]

"'Delight in your relations and family duties and mercies.' If you love the company and converse of your parents, or children, or wives, or kindred as you ought, you will find more pleasure in discoursing with them about holy things or honest business, than in foolish sports. But adulterers that love not their wives, and unnatural parents and children that love not one another, and ungodly masters of families, that love not their duty, are put to seek their sport abroad." – *The Practical Works of the Rev. Richard Baxter*, vol. 3, pg. 625

"The constituting consent or contract of ancestors obliges all their posterity, if they will have any of the protection or other benefit of government, to stand to the constitution; else governments should be so unsettled and mutable, as to be incapable of their proper end." – *The Practical Works of the Rev. Richard Baxter*, vol. 6, pg. 25

Baxter argues that Christians should love all men the same, but then qualifies that this only refers to a spiritual and "rational" love, and that practically we must show a "sensitive" preferential love to ourselves and our family over others:

"Quest. iv. 'Must I love every one as much as myself in degree, or only some?'

"Answ. You must love every one impartially as yourself, according to his goodness; and you must wish well to every one as to yourself; but you must love no man complacentially so much as yourself, who is not or seemeth not to have as much loveliness, that is, as much goodness, or as much of God, as yourself.

"Quest. v. 'Must I love any one more than myself?'

"Answ. Yes, every one that is and appeareth

---

6   Baxter is saying that a Christian nation produces a culture or set of customs that teaches righteousness. In it, false converts may come about, sure. But they may be of service to purity of doctrine, holiness of life, and promoting truth.

better than yourself. Your sensitive love to another cannot be as much as to yourself; and your beneficence (care, provision, generosity) must be most to yourself, because God in nature and his laws hath so appointed it; and your benevolence (kindness, compassion) to yourself and to others must be alike: but your rational estimation, and love or complacence (with the honour and praise attending it) must be more to every one that is better than yourself; for that which is best is most amiable, and that which hath most of God.

— RICHARD BAXTER —

"Quest. vi. 'Will it not then follow, that I must love another man's wife and children better than mine own, when they are really better?'

"Answ. Yes, no doubt; but it is only with that rational estimative love. But there is besides a love to wife and children, which is in some measure sensitive, which you are not obliged to give to others: and rationally they are more amiable to you, in their particular relations and respects, though others are more amiable in other respects: and besides, though you value and rationally love another more, yet the expressions must not be the same; for those must follow the relation according to God's command. You may not cohabit or embrace, nor maintain and provide for others as your own, even when you rationally love them more: the common good requires this order in the expressive part, as well as God's command." – *The Practical Works of the Rev. Richard Baxter*, vol. 6, pgs. 429-430 [7]

"Where God hath prescribed you some particular Good work or way of service, you must prefer that before another which is greater in its self. This is explicatory or limiting of Dir. 8. The reason is because God knoweth best what is pleasing to him, and Obedience is better than Sacrifice. You must not neglect the necessary maintenance of Wife and Children, under pretense of doing a work of piety or greater good: because God hath prescribed you this order of your duty, that you begin at home (though not to stop there) Another Minister may have a greater or more needy flock; but yet you must first do good in your own, and not step without a call into his charge. If God have called you to serve him in a low and mean imployment, he will better accept you in that work, than if you undertook the work of another mans place, to do him greater service." – *A Christian Directory*, part 1, ch. 3, §. 19. Direct. 16., *The Practical Works*, pg. 114

C.E.W. Bean

"The most beautiful, happy place for Australians to live in, with our sort of homes, and our sort of towns and cities, and our sort of games and occupations, and our sort of families, and our sort of marriages and laws, and our idea of fair trials—but how about other nations? How [about] if they were to say: 'No; you have got to make homes to suit us there, too. We are going to come in and set up our sort of ideas about work and play; our sort of schools to make all the population into our sort of people.' We Australians are firmly and definitely determined that that shall not happen." – in Cochrane, *Best We Forget*, pg. 24

Colette Beaune

"Nations are particularistic; Christianity is universal. One might have expected that Christianity itself would have tempered the growth of nationalism. But this did not happen. Most European nations in the Middle Ages had little difficulty projecting their sense of nationhood in religious terms. This was especially true with France, which emerged into nationhood particularly early." – *The Birth of an Ideology*, pg. 1

"What was the France of the late Middle Ages?

---

7   Baxter says that God's command and the common good require particularity of loves and preferential provision.

What were the sources of the 'incomprehensible and natural love' its inhabitants held for it? It was the awareness its people had of being a particular human community, unique in its origins and history, a people who imagined themselves linked to this specific valued land for all time. Its difference was imagined to be superiority, for it was willingly xenophobic. In order to see itself as good, it had to project an evil outside itself. The English played this role. French national sentiment was both ethnic and territorial; it rose from a conjunction of a given people and a given countryside." – *The Birth of an Ideology*, pg. 4-5

Bob Becking

"The language is traditional and the imagery specifically Israelite. The picture is simple, concrete, and surprisingly individualistic. The undisturbed cultivation of the vine is the preeminent sign of national and private security. There was a tradition, reflected in Gen 9:20–27, and perhaps by the Nazirites (Numbers 6) and the Rechabites (Jeremiah 35), that viewed the vine, or at least its product wine, with disfavor. Otherwise the vine was highly regarded (in one agricultural passage it is secondary to cereals [Deut 8:8]), and a man's pride in his vineyard provided a beautiful image of Yahweh's relationship to Israel (Isaiah 5)." – *Yale Anchor Bible: Micah*, vol. 24E, pg. 408

Bede

"I formerly, at your request, most readily sent to you the *Ecclesiastical History of the English Nation*, which I had lately published, for you to read and judge; and I now send it again to be transcribed, and more fully studied at your leisure. And I rejoice greatly at the sincerity and zeal, with which you not only diligently give ear to hear the words of Holy Scripture, but also industriously take care to become acquainted with the actions and sayings of former men of renown, especially of our own nation. For if history relates good things of good men, the attentive hearer is excited to imitate that which is good; or if it recounts evil things of wicked persons, none the less the conscientious and devout hearer or reader, shunning that which is hurtful and wrong, is the more earnestly

fired to perform those things which he knows to be good, and worthy of the service of God. And as you have carefully marked this, you are desirous that the said history should be more fully made known to yourself, and to those over whom the Divine Authority has appointed you governor, from your great regard to the common good. But to the end that I may remove all occasion of doubting what I have written, both from yourself and other readers or hearers of this history, I will take care briefly to show you from what authors I chiefly learned the same." – *Ecclesiastical History of the English People*, bk. I, ch. 1, pg. 1

"It is reported, that some merchants, having just arrived at Rome on a certain day, exposed many things for sale in the marketplace, and abundance of people resorted thither to buy: Gregory himself went with the rest, and, among other things, some boys were set to sale, their bodies white, their countenances beautiful, and their hair very fine. Having viewed them, he asked, as is said, from what country or nation they were brought? and was told, from the island of Britain, whose inhabitants were of such personal appearance." – *Ecclesiastical History of the English People*, Book II, ch. 1, pg. 64

"He therefore again asked, what was the name of that nation? and was answered, that they were called Angles. 'Right', said he, for they have an Angelic face, and it becomes such to be co-heirs with the Angels in heaven. 'What is the name', proceeded he, 'of the province from which they are brought?' It was replied, that the natives of that province were called Deiri. 'Truly are they De ira',[8] said he, 'withdrawn from wrath, and called to the mercy of Christ. How is the king of that province called?' They told him his name was Ælla: and he, alluding to the name said, "Hallelujah, the praise of God the Creator must be sung in those parts." – *Ecclesiastical History of the English People*, bk. II, ch. 1, pg. 64

Menachem Begin

"Our glorious fathers, we have a message for you: We have returned to the place from whence we came. The people of Israel lives, and will live in its homeland in Eretz Israel for

---

8   "De ira" Latin for "of anger."

generations upon generations. Glorious fathers, we are back and we will not budge from here. ... Israel and Judea are reborn, carried by the judges of Israel from the four corners of the earth. Our sons have returned. We have liberated all Western Eretz Israel. We have redeemed Jerusalem and united it into one city for generations." – Israeli prime minister, upon burial of ancient forefathers in newly established state of Israel, David K. Shipler, *Israel Buries Bones of Ancient Warriors, New York Times*, May 12, 1982

Hilaire Belloc

"The prime factor of unity in any society, large or small, is for all the members of that society to hold the same philosophy, to put human affairs in the same order of importance, and to agree on the prime matters of right and wrong and of public worship." – *The Crisis Of Civilization*, pg. 69

"The Barbarian is very certain that the exact reproduction in line or colour of a thing seen is beneath him, and that a drunken blur for line, a green sky, a red tree and a purple cow for colour, are the mark of a great painting.

"The Barbarian hopes – and that is the very mark, of him – that he can have his cake and eat it too. He will consume what civilization has slowly produced after generations of selection and effort, but he will not be at the pains to replace such goods, nor indeed has he a comprehension of the virtue that has brought them into being. Discipline seems to him irrational, on which account he is for ever marveling that civilization should have offended him with priests and soldiers.

"The Barbarian wonders what strange meaning may lurk in that ancient and solemn truth, 'Sine Auctoritate nulla vita.'

"In a word, the Barbarian is discoverable everywhere in this that he cannot make' that he can befog or destroy, but that he cannot sustain; and of every Barbarian in the decline of peril of every civilization exactly that has been true.

"We sit by and watch the barbarian. We tolerate him in the long stretches of peace, we are not afraid. We are tickled by his irreverence; his comic inversion of our old servitudes, and

our fixed creed refreshes us–we laugh. But as we laugh we are watched by large and awful faces from beyond, and on those faces there are no smiles.

"We permit our jaded intellects to play with drugs of novelty for the fresh sensation they arouse, though we know well there is no good in them, but only wasting at the last.

"Yet there is one real interest in watching the Barbarian and one that is profitable.

"The real interest of watching the Barbarian is not the amusement derivable from his antics, but the prime doubt whether he will succeed or no, where he will flourish. He is, I repeat, not an agent, but merely a symptom, yet he should be watched as a symptom. It is not he in his impotence that can discover the power to disintegrate the great and ancient body of Christendom, but if we come to see him triumphant we may be certain that that body, from causes much vaster than such as he could control, is furnishing him with sustenance and forming for him a congenial soil – and that is as much as to say that we are dying." – *This And That*, pgs. 226-227

Johann Bengel

"Faith does not set aside natural duties, but perfects and strengthens them. ἀπίστου, (an infidel) whom even nature teaches this, although he has never embraced the faith." – *1 Timothy 5:8*, pg. 273

Josiah Henry Benton

"That no person or persons hereafter shall be admitted to live and inhabit within the Government of New Plymouth without the leave and liking of the Governor or two of the Assistants at least." – Josiah Henry Benton, *Warning Out In New England*, pg. 30 [9]

Beowulf

"...in a man of worth the claims of kinship cannot be denied." – *Beowulf*, (2600), pg. 173

Louis Berkhof

"…usually distinguish between the image of God in a restricted, and the image of God in a

---

[9] 1636 Plymouth Colony statute showing that the magistrate had discretionary power relating to whether a stranger could stay in a community.

more comprehensive sense. The former consists in the spiritual qualities with which man was created, namely, true knowledge, righteousness and holiness. That these belong to the image of God, follows from Eph. 4:24 and Col. 3:10. The image of God in the more comprehensive sense of the word is found in the fact that man is a spiritual being, rational, moral, and immortal, in the body, not as a material substance, but as the organ of the soul, and in his dominion over the lower creation. Notice that Scripture links up this dominion immediately with man's creation in the image of God, Gen. 1:26. It is only in virtue of the image of God in this broader sense that man, even after he has lost the image of God in the restricted sense, consisting in true knowledge, righteousness, and holiness, can still be called the image-bearer of God, Gen. 9:6; 1 Cor. 11:7; 15:49; Jas. 3:9." – *Manual of Christian Doctrine*, pgs. 129-130

G.C. Berkouwer

"Thus, in delimiting the image of God in the broader sense, we meet various anthropological differentiations and descriptions against the background of the earlier distinction between man's essence and nature. A Kuyper, Jr., even says that theologians, using philosophical modes of approach, realized that the essence of man is something other than his nature, and only then realized that the image of God in the wider sense is revealed in man's essence; so that the restoration of the original image in the saved man refers only and exclusively to his nature, which 'is once again, after being unholy, made holy'. Kuyper's idea here could also be expressed in terms of a distinction between imago essentialis and imago existentialis, the latter referring to existence, to the manner of being, the quality of being." – *Man: The Image of God*, pg. 40

Isaiah Berlin

"Nationalism is not resurgent; it never died. Neither did racism. They are the most important movements in the world today." – *Two Concepts of Nationalism*, pg. 3

Bruce Berman, Dickson Eyoh, & Will Kymlicka

"It is, thus, the durability of kinship as the most fundamental unit of social trust that ultimately grounds the vitality of ethnicity as the idiom of political identity and competition in post-colonial Africa." – *Ethnicity And Democracy in Africa*, pg. 11

Wendell Berry

"...a man who knows that the world is not given by his fathers, but borrowed from his children; who has undertaken to cherish it and do it no damage, not because he is duty-bound, but because he loves the world and loves his children." – *The Unforeseen Wilderness: Kentucky's Red River Gorge*, pg. 26

"A community is not merely a condition of physical proximity, no matter how admirable the layout of the shopping center and the streets, no matter if we demolish the horizontal slums and replace them with vertical ones. A community is the mental and spiritual condition of knowing that the place is shared, and that the people who share the place define and limit the possibilities of each other's lives. It is the knowledge that people have of each other, their concern for each other, their trust in each other, the freedom with which they come and go among themselves.

"Now it has become urgent that the sense of community should include the world, that it should come to be a realization that all men ultimately share the same place, the same nature, and the same destiny. But this most necessary feeling that the world is a neighborhood cannot, I think, be expected to grow among the crowds of strangers that fill the cities. If it is to be hoped for at all, it is to be hoped for among the people who have had the experience of being involved responsibly and knowingly, and at some expense of their feelings and means, in the lives of their neighbors.

"Against a long-standing fashion of antipathy, I will venture to suggest that the best model we have of a community is still the small country town of our agricultural past. I do not mean that this was ever a perfect community, or that it did not have serious faults, or that it can be realistically thought of as a possibility that is still before us. But with its balance of variety and coherence, it is still more suggestive of the possibility of community, of neighborhood, than anything else we have experienced. Whatever may be said against it, it did bring into the condition and the possibility of neighborliness a number of people who varied a good deal in occupation, income, education, and often in opinion.

"Different sorts of people, different kinds of experience and levels of education were in constant touch with each other, and were taught and disciplined by each other. Knowledge of neighbors was encouraged and cultivated, by the natural curiosity that produced either gossip or understanding, and also by the caution and interest of business dealings. A merchant or banker in one of those towns, dealing constantly with the problem of whom to credit, would in a lifetime gather up an authoritative knowledge of literally thousands of people. He gained from his business, in addition to his living, a profound and various experience of other men.

"Though it was not inevitable, it was certainly possible in such a community for the life of a merchant or lawyer or teacher or doctor to be inspired and disciplined and even ennobled by a precise sense of its relation to other lives, its place among them, its usefulness and duty to them. Those places did not have the dead look of modern suburban towns in which the people live but do not work. The population was reasonably stable. People expected to remain in the same place all their lives, and often they did.

"In those communities it was always at least possible that charity could be personal, and that possibility enforced the likelihood that it would be. A man whose neighbor was hungry would give him something to eat because it was the natural thing to do. He knew who his neighbor was. And he felt, without needing to be told by a sociologist, that the condition of his neighbor was a reflection on him. Because he knew his neighbor it was possible for him to care about him, or be his friend, or love him.

"But the ideal community would include not just the living; it would include the unborn. It would be aware, with a clarity and concern which the best of us have hardly imagined, that the living cannot think or speak or act without changing the lives of those who will live after them. There would be a language, not yet spoken in any of our public places, to manifest and convey that awareness—a language that would

live upon the realization that no man can act purely on his own behalf, not only because it is not desirable that he should do so, but because it is in reality not possible. And it would include the place, the land, itself. For man is not merely 'in' the world. He is, he must realize and learn to say or be doomed, part of it. The earth he is made of he bears in trust." – *The Long-Legged House*, pgs. 63-65

"Science speaks properly a language of abstraction and abstract categories when it is properly trying to sort out and put in order the things it knows. But it often assumes improperly that it has said—or known—enough when it has spoken of 'the cell' or 'the organism,' 'the genome' or 'the ecosystem' and given the correct scientific classification and name. Carried too far, this is a language of false specification and pretentious exactitude, never escaping either abstraction or the cold-heartedness of abstraction.

"The giveaway is that even scientists do not speak of their loved ones in categorical terms as 'a woman,' 'a man,' 'a child,' or 'a case' Affection requires us to break out of the abstractions, the categories, and confront the creature itself in its life in its place. The importance of this for Mr. Wilson's (and my) cause of conservation can hardly be overstated. For things cannot survive as categories but only as individual creatures living uniquely where they live.

"We know enough of our own history by now to be aware that people exploit what they have merely concluded to be of value, but they defend what they love. To defend what we love we need a particularizing language, for we love what we particularly know. The abstract, 'objective,' impersonal, dispassionate language of science can, in fact, hmelp us to know certain things, and to know some things with certainty. It can help us, for instance, to know the value of species and of species diversity. But it cannot replace, and it cannot become, the language of familiarity, reverence, and affection by which things of value ultimately are protected.

"The abstractions of science are too readily assimilable to the abstractions of industry and commerce, which see everything as interchangeable with or replaceable by something else. There is a kind of egalitarianism which holds that any two things equal in price are equal in value, and that nothing is better than anything that may profitably or fashionably replace it.

Forest = field = parking lot; if the price of alteration is right, then there is no point in quibbling over differences. One place is as good as another, one use is as good as another, one life is as good as another—if the price is right. Thus political sentimentality metamorphoses into commercial indifference or aggression. This is the industrial doctrine of the interchangeability of parts, and we apply it to places, to creatures, and to our fellow humans as if it were the law of the world, using all the while a sort of middling language, imitated from the sciences, that cannot speak of heaven or earth, but only of concepts. This is a rhetoric of nowhere, which forbids a passionate interest in, let alone a love of, anything in particular.

— WENDELL BERRY —

"Directly opposed to this reduction or abstraction of things is the idea of the preciousness of individual lives and places. This does not come from science, but from our cultural and religious traditions. It is not derived, and it is not derivable, from any notion of egalitarianism. If all are equal, none can be precious. (And perhaps it is necessary to stop here to say that this ancient delight in the individuality of creatures is not the same thing as what we now mean by 'individualism.' It is the opposite. Individualism, in present practice, refers to the supposed 'right' of an individual to act alone, in disregard of other individuals.)" – *Life Is A Miracle: An Essay Against Modern Superstition*, pgs. 40-41

"A culture is not a collection of relics or ornaments, but a practical necessity, and its corruption invokes calamity. A healthy culture is a communal order of memory, insight, value, work, conviviality, reverence, aspiration. It reveals the human necessities and the human limits. It clarifies our inescapable bonds to the earth and to each other. It assures that the necessary restraints are observed, that the necessary work is done, and that it is done well. A healthy farm culture can be based only upon familiarity and can grow only among a people soundly established upon the land; it nourishes and safeguards a human intelligence of the earth that no amount of technology can satisfactorily replace. The growth of such a culture was once a strong possibility in the farm communities of this country." – *The Unsettling Of America*, pg. 73

"To forsake all others [in marriage] does not mean—because it cannot mean to ignore or neglect all others, to hide or be hidden from all others, or to desire or love no others. To live in marriage is a responsible way to live in sexuality, as to live in a household is a responsible way to live in the world. One cannot enact or fulfill one's love for womankind or mankind, or even for all the women or men to whom one is attracted. If one is to have the power and delight of one's sexuality, then the generality of instinct must be resolved in a responsible relationship to a particular person. Similarly, one cannot live in the world; that is, one cannot become, in the easy, generalizing sense with which the phrase is commonly used, a 'world citizen.' There can be no such thing as a 'global village.' No matter how much one may love the world as a whole, one can live fully in it only by living responsibly in some small part of it. Where we live and who we live there with define the terms of our relationship to the world and to humanity. We thus come again to the paradox that one can become whole only by the responsible acceptance of one's partiality." – *The Unsettling Of America*, pg. 182

"Husbandry pertains first to the household; it connects the farm to the household. It is an art wedded to the art of housewifery. To husband is to use with care, to keep, to save, to make last, to conserve…Husbandry is the name of all the practices that sustain life by connecting us conservingly to our places and our world; it is the art of keeping tied all the strands in the living network that sustains us." – *Way of Ignorance*, pgs. 127

"Today, local economies are being destroyed by the 'pluralistic,' displaced, global economy, which has no respect for what works in a locality. The global economy is built on the principle that one place can be exploited, even destroyed, for the sake of another place." – *The Art of Place: Interview with Wendell Berry*, 1992; *Conversations with Wendell Berry*, pgs. 50-51

"The issue here really is not whether international trade shall be free but whether or not it makes any sense for a country — or, for that matter, a region — to destroy its own capacity to produce its own food. How can a government, entrusted with the safety and health of its people, conscientiously barter away in the name of an economic idea that people's ability to feed itself? And if people lose their ability to feed themselves, how can they be said to be free?" – *Sex, Economy, Freedom & Community*, pg. 29

Jean-Marc Berthoud

"So we see that God is the creator of nations, clans and families of which humanity is made up. Humanity is not simply an amorphous multitude of individuals arbitrarily juxtaposed next to each other, but it is ordained by God into nations, clans and families. A clan is the extension of a family. The clans come together in a larger entity which is the tribe. A nation is a community of families, clans and tribes claiming a common origin. Family comes first; it is this which is the founding institution of all societies. Then the family develops into a clan. This one grows by alliances or by conquest to become a tribe, and finally, the alliances of clans and tribes give birth to the nation. Empires arise from the destruction of nations by a dominant entity." – *Le Règne Terrestre de Dieu*, pg. 157

Bhagavad-Gita

Thus, by Arjuna prayed, (O Bharata!)
Between the hosts that heavenly Charioteer
Drove the bright car, reining its milk-white steeds
Where Bhishma led, and Drona, and their Lords.
"See!" spake he to Arjuna, "where they stand,
Thy kindred of the Kurus:" and the Prince
Marked on each hand the kinsmen of his house,
Grandsires and sires, uncles and
    brothers and sons,
Cousins and sons-in-law and nephews, mixed
With friends and honoured elders;

some this side,
Some that side ranged: and, seeing
    those opposed,

Such kith grown enemies – Arjuna's heart
Melted with pity, while he uttered this:
Arjuna. Krishna! as I behold, come here to shed
Their common blood, yon concourse of our kin,
My members fail, my tongue dries in my mouth,
A shudder thrills my body, and my hair
Bristles with horror; from my weak hand slips
Gandiv, the goodly bow; a fever burns
My skin to parching; hardly may I stand;
The life within me seems to swim and faint;
Nothing do I foresee save woe and wail!
It is not good, O Keshav! nought of good
Can spring from mutual slaughter! Lo, I hate
Triumph and domination, wealth and ease,
Thus sadly won! Aho! what victory
Can bring delight, Govinda! what rich spoils
Could profit; what rule recompense; what span
Of life itself seem sweet, bought with such blood?
Seeing that these stand here, ready to die,
For whose sake life was fair,
    and pleasure pleased,
And power grew precious:– grandsires, sires,
    and sons,
Brothers, and fathers-in-law, and sons-in-law,
Elders and friends! Shall I deal death on these
Even though they seek to slay us? Not one blow,
O Madhusudan! will I strike to gain
The rule of all Three Worlds; then,
    how much less
To seize an earthly kingdom! Killing these
Must breed but anguish, Krishna! If they be
Guilty, we shall grow guilty by their deaths;
Their sins will light on us, if we shall slay
Those sons of Dhritirashtra, and our kin;
What peace could come of that, O Madhava?
For if indeed, blinded by lust and wrath,

These cannot see, or will not see, the sin
Of kingly lines o'erthrown and kinsmen slain,
How should not we, who see, shun such a crime-
We who perceive the guilt and feel the shame-
O thou Delight of Men, Janardana?
By overthrow of houses perisheth
Their sweet continuous household piety,
And – rites neglected, piety extinct –
Enters impiety upon that home;
Its women grow unwomaned,
    whence there spring
Mad passions, and the mingling-up of castes,

Sending a Hell-ward road that family,
And whoso wrought its doom by wicked wrath.
Nay, and the souls of honoured ancestors
Fall from their place of peace, being bereft
Of funeral-cakes and the wan death-water.
So teach our holy hymns. Thus, if we slay
Kinsfolk and friends for love of earthly power,
Ahovat! what an evil fault it were!
Better I deem it, if my kinsmen strike,
To face them weaponless, and bare my breast
To shaft and spear, than answer blow with blow.
So speaking, in the face of those two hosts,
Arjuna sank upon his chariot-seat,
And let fall bow and arrows, sick at heart.
– *The Bhagavad Gita*, pgs. 14-16

"With the destruction of the family, the spiritual traditions of the family perish forever; when spiritual values are destroyed, then unrighteousness predominates the entire society."
– *The Bhagavad-Gita*: ch. 1, v. 39

— The Bible —

Genesis

"So God created man in his own image, in the image of God he created him; male and female he created them. And God blessed them. And God said to them, 'Be fruitful and multiply and fill the earth and subdue it, and have dominion over the fish of the sea and over the birds of the heavens and over every living thing that moves on the earth.'" – 1:17-18

"The sons of Japheth were Gomer and Magog and Madai and Javan and Tubal and Meshech and Tiras. The sons of Gomer were Ashkenaz and Riphath and Togarmah. The sons of Javan were Elishah and Tarshish, Kittim and Dodanim. From these the coastlands of the nations were separated into their lands, every one according to his language, according to their families, into their nations." – 10:2-5

God set boundaries in place, confused languages and created tribes, and separated peoples from one another:
"These are the families of the sons of Noah, according to their genealogies, by their nations; and out of these the nations were separated on the earth after the flood." – 10:32

"'Come, let Us go down and there confuse their language, so that they will not understand one another's speech.' So the Lord scattered them abroad from there over the face of the whole earth; and they stopped building the city. Therefore its name was called Babel, because there the Lord confused the language of the whole earth; and from there the Lord scattered them abroad over the face of the whole earth." – 11:7-9

"And I will make of you a great nation, and I will bless you and make your name great, so that you will be a blessing. I will bless those who bless you, and him who dishonors you I will curse, and in you all the families of the earth shall be blessed." – 12:2-3

"Then the Lord said to him, 'Know for certain that for four hundred years your descendants will be strangers in a country not their own and that they will be enslaved and mistreated there.'" – 15:13 [10]

"And Abraham said unto his eldest servant of his house, that ruled over all that he had, 'Put, I pray thee, thy hand under my thigh: And I will make thee swear by the Lord, the God of heaven, and the God of the earth, that thou shalt not take a wife unto my son of the daughters of the Canaanites, among whom I dwell: But thou shalt go unto my country, and to my kindred, and take a wife unto my son Isaac.'" – 24:2-4

Exodus

"This day shall be for you a memorial day, and you shall keep it as a feast to the Lord; throughout your generations, as a statute forever, you shall keep it as a feast." – 12:14

"'Now therefore, if you will indeed obey my voice and keep my covenant, you shall be my treasured possession among all peoples, for all the earth is mine; and you shall be to me a kingdom of priests and a holy nation.' These are the words that you shall speak to the people of Israel." – 19:5-6

---

10 Even after 400 years the descendants of Jacob's family were strangers, not Egyptians.

"You shall make no covenant with them, nor with their gods." – 23:32

"Take care, lest you make a covenant with the inhabitants of the land to which you go, lest it become a snare in your midst. You shall tear down their altars and break their pillars and cut down their Asherim (for you shall worship no other god, for the LORD, whose name is Jealous, is a jealous God), lest you make a covenant with the inhabitants of the land, and when they whore after their gods and sacrifice to their gods and you are invited, you eat of his sacrifice, and you take of their daughters for your sons, and their daughters whore after their gods and make your sons whore after their gods." – 34:12-16

Leviticus

"You shall treat the stranger who sojourns with you as the native among you, and you shall love him as yourself, for you were strangers in the land of Egypt: I am the LORD your God." – 19:34

"There shall no stranger eat of the holy thing: a sojourner of the priest, or an hired servant, shall not eat of the holy thing…

If the priest's daughter also be married unto a stranger, she may not eat of an offering of the holy things…

Neither from a stranger's hand shall ye offer the bread of your God of any of these; because their corruption is in them, and blemishes be in them: they shall not be accepted for you." – 22:10, 12, 25

"As for your male and female slaves whom you may have: you may buy male and female slaves from among the nations that are around you. You may also buy from among the strangers who sojourn with you and their clans that are with you, who have been born in your land, and they may be your property. You may bequeath them to your sons after you to inherit as a possession forever. You may make slaves of them, but over your brothers the people of Israel you shall not rule, one over another ruthlessly." – 25:44-46

Numbers

"Every man of the children of Israel shall pitch by his own standard, with the ensign of their father's house: far off about the tabernacle of the congregation shall they pitch." – 2:2

"And behold, one of the people of Israel came and brought a Midianite woman to his family, in the sight of Moses and in the sight of the whole congregation of the people of Israel, while they were weeping in the entrance of the tent of meeting. When Phinehas the son of Eleazar, son of Aaron the priest, saw it, he rose and left the congregation and took a spear in his hand and went after the man of Israel into the chamber and pierced both of them, the man of Israel and the woman through her belly. Thus the plague on the people of Israel was stopped." – 25:6-8

"We will not return to our homes until each of the people of Israel has gained his inheritance." – 32:18

"And if they be married to any of the sons of the other tribes of the children of Israel, then shall their inheritance be taken from the inheritance of our fathers, and shall be put to the inheritance of the tribe whereunto they are received: so shall it be taken from the lot of our inheritance. This is the thing which the Lord doth command concerning the daughters of Zelophehad, saying, Let them marry to whom they think best; only to the family of the tribe of their father shall they marry. So shall not the inheritance of the children of Israel remove from tribe to tribe: for every one of the children of Israel shall keep himself to the inheritance of the tribe of his fathers. And every daughter, that possesseth an inheritance in any tribe of the children of Israel, shall be wife unto one of the family of the tribe of her father, that the children of Israel may enjoy every man the inheritance of his fathers. Neither shall the inheritance remove from one tribe to another tribe; but every one of the tribes of the children of Israel shall keep himself to his own inheritance." – 36:3, 6-9

Deuteronomy

"For ask now of the days that are past, which were before you, since the day that God created man on the earth, and ask from one end of heaven to the other, whether such a great thing as this has ever happened or was ever heard of. Did any people ever hear the voice of a god speaking out of the midst of the fire, as you have heard, and still live? Or has any god ever attempted to go and take a nation for himself from the midst of another nation..." – 4:32-34 [11]

"When the Lord your God brings you into the land that you are entering to take possession of it, and clears away many nations before you, the Hittites, the Girgashites, the Amorites, the Canaanites, the Perizzites, the Hivites, and the Jebusites, seven nations more numerous and mightier than you, and when the Lord your God gives them over to you, and you defeat them, then you must devote them to complete destruction. You shall make no covenant with them and show no mercy to them. You shall not intermarry with them, giving your daughters to their sons or taking their daughters for your sons." – 7:1-3

"You shall not move your neighbor's landmark, which the men of old have set, in the inheritance that you will hold in the land that the Lord your God is giving you to possess." – 19:14

"If a man have two wives, one beloved, and another hated, and they have born him children, both the beloved and the hated; and if the firstborn son be hers that was hated: Then it shall be, when he maketh his sons to inherit that which he hath, that he may not make the son of the beloved firstborn before the son of the hated, which is indeed the firstborn: But he shall acknowledge the son of the hated for the firstborn, by giving him a double portion of all that he hath: for he is the beginning of his strength; the right of the firstborn is his." – 21:15-17

"He that is wounded in the stones, or hath his privy member cut off, shall not enter into the congregation of the LORD. A bastard shall not enter into the congregation of the LORD; even to his tenth generation shall he not enter into the congregation of the LORD." – 23:1-2 [12]

"'Cursed be anyone who moves his neighbor's landmark.' And all the people shall say, 'Amen.'" – 27:17

"Thy sons and thy daughters shall be given unto another people, and thine eyes shall look, and fail with longing for them all the day long: and there shall be no might in thine hand. The fruit of thy land, and all thy labours, shall a nation which thou knowest not eat up; and thou shalt be only oppressed and crushed always: So that thou shalt be mad for the sight of thine eyes which thou shalt see...The Lord shall bring thee...unto a nation which neither thou nor thy fathers have known." – 28:32-36

"Remember the days of old; consider the years of many generations; ask your father, and he will show you, your elders, and they will tell you." – 32:7

"When the Most High gave the nations their inheritance, when He separated the sons of man, He set the boundaries of the peoples according to the number of the sons of Israel." – 32:8

Joshua

"Then the people of Reuben, the people of Gad, and the half-tribe of Manasseh said in answer to the heads of the families of Israel, 'The Mighty One, God, the LORD! The Mighty One, God, the LORD!' He knows; and let Israel itself know! If it was in rebellion or in breach of faith against the Lord, do not spare us today for building an altar to turn away from following the Lord. Or if we did so to offer burnt offerings or grain offerings or peace offerings on it, may the Lord himself take vengeance. No, but we did it from fear that in time to come your children might say to our children, 'What have you to do with the Lord, the God of Israel? For the Lord has made the Jordan a boundary between us and you, you people of Reuben and people of Gad. You have no portion in the Lord.' So your children might make our children cease to worship the Lord. Therefore we said, 'Let us now build an altar, not for burnt offering, nor for sacrifice, but to be a witness between us and you, and between our generations after us, that we do perform the service of the Lord in his presence with our burnt offerings and sacrifices and peace offerings, so your children will not say to our children in time to come, "You have no portion in the Lord."' And we thought, 'If

---

11   Nation within a nation. A nation is not its borders, its ideas, its laws, merely. A nation is its people.
12   Bastards (no connection to the past) and Eunuchs (no connection to the future) not allowed in the assembly.

this should be said to us or to our descendants in time to come, we should say, 'Behold, the copy of the altar of the Lord, which our fathers made, not for burnt offerings, nor for sacrifice, but to be a witness between us and you.'" – 22:21-28 [13]

"And if it is evil in your eyes to serve the Lord, choose this day whom you will serve, whether the gods your fathers served in the region beyond the River, or the gods of the Amorites in whose land you dwell. But as for me and my house, we will serve the Lord." – 24:15

Judges

"Is there not a woman among the daughters of your kinsmen, or among all our people, that you must go to take a wife from the uncircumcised Philistines?" – 14:3

2 Chronicles

"Solomon took a census of all the foreigners residing in Israel, after the census his father David had taken; and they were found to be 153,600. He assigned 70,000 of them to be carriers and 80,000 to be stonecutters in the hills, with 3,600 foremen over them to keep the people working." – 2:17-18 [14]

Nehemiah

"So in the lowest parts of the space behind the wall, in open places, I stationed the people by their clans, with their swords, their spears, and their bows. And I looked and arose and said to the nobles and to the officials and to the rest of the people, 'Do not be afraid of them. Remember the Lord, who is great and awesome, and fight for your brothers, your sons, your daughters, your wives, and your homes.'" – 4:13-14

"Then those of Israelite lineage separated themselves from all foreigners; and they stood and confessed their sins and the iniquities of their fathers." – 9:2

"In those days also I saw the Jews who had married women of Ashdod, Ammon, and Moab. And half of their children spoke the language of Ashdod, and they could not speak the language of Judah, but only the language of each people. And I confronted them and cursed them and beat some of them and pulled out their hair. And I made them take an oath in the name of God, saying, 'You shall not give your daughters to their sons, or take their daughters for your sons or for yourselves. Did not Solomon king of Israel sin on account of such women? Among the many nations there was no king like him, and he was beloved by his God, and God made him king over all Israel. Nevertheless, foreign women made even him to sin.'" – 13:23-26

Job

"He makes nations great, and he destroys them; he enlarges nations, and leads them away. He takes away understanding from the chiefs of the people of the earth and makes them wander in a trackless waste. They grope in the dark without light, and he makes them stagger like a drunken man." – 12:23–25

"Some move landmarks; they seize flocks and pasture them." – 24:2

Psalms

"Ask of me, and I will make the nations your heritage, and the ends of the earth your possession."– 2:8

"The wicked shall return to Sheol, all the nations that forget God." – 9:17

"All the ends of the earth shall remember and turn to the Lord, and all the families of the nations shall worship before you." – 22:27

"For kingship belongs to the Lord, and he rules over the nations." – 22:28

"Blessed is the nation whose God is the Lord, the people whom he has chosen as his heritage!" – 33:12

"Be still, and know that I am God. I will be exalted among the nations, I will be exalted in the earth!" – 46:10

---

13   A monument serves as a marker, a symbol of national unity.

14   How did Solomon perform this count if there were not border controls in place and immigrants were not kept track of?

By the waters of Babylon,
   there we sat down and wept,
   when we remembered Zion.
On the willows there
   we hung up our lyres.
For there our captors
   required of us songs,
and our tormentors, mirth, saying,
   "Sing us one of the songs of Zion!"

How shall we sing the Lord's song
   in a foreign land?
If I forget you, O Jerusalem,
   let my right hand forget its skill!
Let my tongue stick to the roof of my mouth,
   if I do not remember you,
if I do not set Jerusalem
   above my highest joy!

Remember, O Lord, against the Edomites
   the day of Jerusalem,
how they said, "Lay it bare, lay it bare,
   down to its foundations!"
O daughter of Babylon, doomed to be destroyed,
   blessed shall he be who repays you
   with what you have done to us!
Blessed shall he be who takes your little ones
   and dashes them against the rock! – 137

Proverbs

"A good man leaves an inheritance to his children's children, but the sinner's wealth is laid up for the righteous." – 13:22

"Righteousness exalts a nation, but sin is a reproach to any people." – 14:34

"A friend loves at all times, and a brother is born for adversity." – 17:17

"Wisdom is before him that hath understanding; but the eyes of a fool are in the ends of the earth." – 17:24

"Do not move the ancient landmark that your fathers have set." – 22:28

"Do not move an ancient landmark or enter the fields of the fatherless, for their Redeemer is strong; he will plead their cause against you." – 23:10-11

There are those who curse their fathers
   and do not bless their mothers.
There are those who are clean in their own eyes
   but are not washed of their filth.
There are those—how lofty are their eyes,
   how high their eyelids lift!
There are those whose teeth are swords,
   whose fangs are knives,
to devour the poor from off the earth,
   the needy from among mankind...
The eye that mocks a father
   and scorns to obey a mother
will be picked out by the ravens of the valley.
 – 30:12-14, 17

An excellent wife who can find?
 She is far more precious than jewels.
The heart of her husband trusts in her,
 and he will have no lack of gain.
She does him good, and not harm,
all the days of her life.
She seeks wool and flax,
 and works with willing hands.
She is like the ships of the merchant;
 she brings her food from afar.
She rises while it is yet night
 and provides food for her household
 and portions for her maidens.
She considers a field and buys it;
 with the fruit of her hands she
  plants a vineyard.
She dresses herself with strength
 and makes her arms strong.
She perceives that her merchandise
 is profitable.
 Her lamp does not go out at night.
She puts her hands to the distaff,
 and her hands hold the spindle.
She opens her hand to the poor
 and reaches out her hands to the needy.
She is not afraid of snow for her household,
 for all her household are clothed in scarlet.
She makes bed coverings for herself;
 her clothing is fine linen and purple.
Her husband is known in the gates
 when he sits among the elders of the land.
She makes linen garments and sells them;
 she delivers sashes to the merchant.
Strength and dignity are her clothing,
 and she laughs at the time to come.
She opens her mouth with wisdom,
 and the teaching of kindness is on her tongue.
She looks well to the ways of her household

and does not eat the bread of idleness.
Her children rise up and call her blessed;
  her husband also, and he praises her:
"Many women have done excellently,
  but you surpass them all."
Charm is deceitful, and beauty is vain,
  but a woman who fears the Lord
  is to be praised.
Give her of the fruit of her hands,
  and let her works praise her in the gates. – 31

Isaiah

"Is not this the fast that I choose: to loose the bonds of wickedness, to undo the straps of the yoke, to let the oppressed go free, and to break every yoke? Is it not to share your bread with the hungry and bring the homeless poor into your house; when you see the naked, to cover him, and not to hide yourself from your own flesh?"
– 58:6-7

"Arise, shine, for your light has come, and the glory of the Lord has risen upon you....And nations shall come to your light, and kings to the brightness of your rising....because the abundance of the sea shall be turned to you, the wealth of the nations shall come to you.... Your gates shall be open continually; day and night they shall not be shut, that people may bring to you the wealth of the nations, with their kings led in procession. For the nation and kingdom that will not serve you shall perish; those nations shall be utterly laid waste."
– 60:1-12

Jeremiah

"Therefore, behold, the days come, saith the Lord, that it shall no more be said, 'The Lord liveth, that brought up the children of Israel out of the land of Egypt; But, The Lord liveth, that brought up the children of Israel from the land of the north, and from all the lands whither he had driven them: and I will bring them again into their land that I gave unto their fathers.'" – 16:14-15

"And I will set up shepherds over them which shall feed them: and they shall fear no more, nor be dismayed, neither shall they be lacking, saith the Lord. Behold, the days come, saith the Lord, that I will raise unto David a

righteous Branch, and a King shall reign and prosper, and shall execute judgment and justice in the earth. In his days Judah shall be saved, and Israel shall dwell safely: and this is his name whereby he shall be called, THE LORD OUR RIGHTEOUSNESS. Therefore, behold, the days come, saith the Lord, that they shall no more say, The Lord liveth, which brought up the children of Israel out of the land of Egypt; But, The Lord liveth, which brought up and which led the seed of the house of Israel out of the north country, and from all countries whither I had driven them; and they shall dwell in their own land." – 23:4-8

"Build houses and live in them; plant gardens and eat their produce. Take wives and become the fathers of sons and daughters, and take wives for your sons and give your daughters to husbands, that they may bear sons and daughters; multiply there and do not decrease." – 29:5-6

Lamentations

"Our inheritance is turned to strangers, our houses to aliens." – 5:2

Ezekiel

One argument against abortion is that value and dignity belong to every child. A more powerful argument against abortion is that every child belongs to God:
  "You took your sons and your daughters, whom you had borne to me, and these you sacrificed to them to be devoured." – 16:20

"As a shepherd seeketh out his flock in the day that he is among his sheep that are scattered; so will I seek out my sheep, and will deliver them out of all places where they have been scattered in the cloudy and dark day. And I will bring them out from the people, and gather them from the countries, and will bring them to their own land, and feed them upon the mountains of Israel by the rivers, and in all the inhabited places of the country. I will feed them in a good pasture, and upon the high mountains of Israel shall their fold be: there shall they lie in a good fold, and in a fat pasture shall they feed upon the mountains of Israel." – 34:12-14

"And say unto them, 'Thus saith the Lord God;

Behold, I will take the children of Israel from among the heathen, whither they be gone, and will gather them on every side, and bring them into their own land: And I will make them one nation in the land upon the mountains of Israel; and one king shall be king to them all: and they shall be no more two nations, neither shall they be divided into two kingdoms any more at all: Neither shall they defile themselves any more with their idols, nor with their detestable things, nor with any of their transgressions: but I will save them out of all their dwelling places, wherein they have sinned, and will cleanse them: so shall they be my people, and I will be their God.'" – 37:21–23

Daniel

"And the fourth kingdom shall be strong as iron: forasmuch as iron breaketh in pieces and subdueth all things: and as iron that breaketh all these, shall it break in pieces and bruise. And whereas thou sawest the feet and toes, part of potters' clay, and part of iron, the kingdom shall be divided; but there shall be in it of the strength of the iron, forasmuch as thou sawest the iron mixed with miry clay. And as the toes of the feet were part of iron, and part of clay, so the kingdom shall be partly strong, and partly broken. And whereas thou sawest iron mixed with miry clay, they shall mingle themselves with the seed of men: but they shall not cleave one to another, even as iron is not mixed with clay." – 2:40-43 [15]

Micah

"He shall judge between many peoples, and shall decide disputes for strong nations far away; and they shall beat their swords into plowshares, and their spears into pruning hooks; nation shall not lift up sword against nation, neither shall they learn war anymore; but they shall sit every man under his vine and under his fig tree, and no one shall make them afraid, for the mouth of the Lord of hosts has spoken." – 4:3-4

Malachi

"A son honors his father, and a servant his master." – 1:6

"He will turn the hearts of the fathers back to their children and the hearts of the children to their fathers, so that I will not come and strike the land with complete destruction." – 4:6

Ecclesiasticus

"If children live honestly, and have wherewithal, they shall cover the baseness of their parents. But children, being haughty, through disdain and want of nurture do stain the nobility of their kindred." – 22:9-10

"All human beings are from the ground, and Adam was created of the dust. In the fullness of his knowledge the Lord distinguished them and appointed their different ways; some of them he made holy and brought near to himself; but some of them he cursed and brought low, and he turned them out of their place. Like clay in the hand of the potter for all his ways are as he pleases so are human beings in the hand of him who made them, to give to them as he decides. Good is the opposite of evil, and life the opposite of death; so the sinner is the opposite of the godly." – 33:10-14

"Do not make fun of the ignorant lest your ancestors be dishonored." – 8:4

"Every living thing loves its like, and every person his neighbor. All flesh gathers together according to kind, and a man will stick with the one like him." – 13:15-16

"My son, keep the flower of thine age sound; and give not thy strength to strangers. When thou hast gotten a fruitful possession through all the field, sow it with thine own seed, trusting in the goodness of thy stock. So thy race which thou leavest shall be magnified, having the confidence of their good descent." – 26:19-21

"Birds will settle with the ones like them, and truth will return to those who practice it." – 27:9

"The one who disciplines his son will benefit by him, and he will boast about him among acquaintances. The one who teaches his son will make his enemy jealous, and he will rejoice over

---

15 The kingdom is multi-ethnic and therefore it breaks apart. Referring to Rome, the Bible says that the reason it would fall was due to not being unified as a people.

him before his friends. His father died, and it is like he had not died, for he has left after him one who is like him. During his life he saw and rejoiced, and at his end he was not grieved. He has left behind an avenger against enemies and one who repays kindness to friends." – 30:2-6

"You lay your flanks beside women, and you were brought into subjection by your body. You put disgrace in your honor, and you profaned your seed, making wrath come upon your children." – 47:19-21a

Tobit

"Thou knowest, Lord, that I am pure from all sin with man, And that I never polluted my name, nor the name of my father, in the land of my captivity: I am the only daughter of my father, neither hath he any child to be his heir, neither any near kinsman, nor any son of his alive, to whom I may keep myself for a wife: my seven husbands are already dead; and why should I live? but if it please not thee that I should die, command some regard to be had of me, and pity taken of me, that I hear no more reproach." – 3:14-15

"Beware of all whoredom, my son, and chiefly take a wife of the seed of thy fathers, and take not a strange woman to wife, which is not of thy father's tribe: for we are the children of the prophets, Noah, Abraham, Isaac, and Jacob: remember, my son, that our fathers from the beginning, even that they all married wives of their own kindred, and were blessed in their children, and their seed shall inherit the land. Now therefore, my son, love thy brethren, and despise not in thy heart thy brethren, the sons and daughters of thy people, in not taking a wife of them: for in pride is destruction and much trouble, and in lewdness is decay and great want: for lewdness is the mother of famine." – 4:12-13

1 Maccabees

"Now when Judas and his brethren saw that miseries were multiplied, and that the forces did encamp themselves in their borders: for they knew how the king had given commandment to destroy the people, and utterly abolish them; And they said every man to his neighbor: Let us raise up the low condition of our people, and let us fight for our people, and our sanctuary. Then was the congregation gathered together, that they might be ready for battle, and that they might pray, and ask mercy and compassion. Now Jerusalem lay void as a wilderness, there was none of her children that went in or out: the sanctuary also was trodden down, and aliens kept the strong hold; the heathen had their habitation in that place; and joy was taken from Jacob, and the pipe with the harp ceased. Wherefore the Israelites assembled themselves together, and came to Maspha, over against Jerusalem; for in Maspha was the place where they prayed aforetime in Israel." – 3:42-46

"It also happened that seven brothers were arrested together with their mother. The king tortured them with whips and scourges in an attempt to force them to eat pork, in violation of the law of God. One of the brothers, acting as a spokesman for the others, said, 'What do you expect to achieve by questioning us? We are prepared to die rather than transgress the laws of our ancestors.'" – 7:1-2

Matthew

"Go ye therefore, and disciple all the nations, baptizing them in the name of the Father, and of the Son, and of the Holy Ghost: Teaching them to observe all things whatsoever I have commanded you: and, lo, I am with you always, even unto the end of the world. Amen." – 28:19-20 [16]

μαθητεύσατε πάντα τὰ ἔθνη – 28:19, NA28

Luke

"I tell you, my friends, do not fear those who kill the body, and after that have nothing more that they can do." – 12:4

John

"Greater love has no one than this, that a man lay down his life for his friends." – 15:13

---

16   In the Greek "them" refers to "nations" and not individual disciples. Thus, Jesus is commanding to teach the nations, baptizing (putting them under the influence of) the Name. And teaching the nations to observe all things He commanded.

"You are my friends if you do what I command you." – 15:14

Acts

"Now there were dwelling in Jerusalem Jews, devout men, from every nation under heaven. And when this sound occurred, the multitude came together, and were confused, because everyone heard them speak in his own language. Then they were all amazed and marveled, saying to one another, 'Look, are not all these who speak Galileans? And how is it that we hear, each in our own dialect in which we were born?'" – 2:5-8 [17]

"The same dealt subtilly with our kindred, and evil entreated our fathers, so that they cast out their young children, to the end they might not live." – 24:19

"He made from one man every nation of mankind to live on all the face of the earth, having determined their appointed times and the boundaries of their habitation." – 17:26

Romans

"For those whom he foreknew he also predestined to be conformed to the image of his Son, in order that he might be the firstborn among many brothers. And those whom he predestined he also called, and those whom he called he also justified, and those whom he justified he also glorified." – 8:29-30

1 Corinthians

"Now there are varieties of gifts, but the same Spirit; and there are varieties of service, but the same Lord; and there are varieties of activities, but it is the same God who empowers them all in everyone. To each is given the manifestation of the Spirit for the common good. For to one is given through the Spirit the utterance of wisdom, and to another the utterance of knowledge according to the same Spirit, to another faith by the same Spirit, to another gifts of healing by the one Spirit, to another the working of miracles, to another prophecy, to another the ability to distinguish between spirits, to another various kinds of tongues, to another the interpretation of tongues. All these are empowered by one and the same Spirit, who apportions to each one individually as he wills.

"For just as the body is one and has many members, and all the members of the body, though many, are one body, so it is with Christ. For in one Spirit we were all baptized into one body—Jews or Greeks, slaves or free—and all were made to drink of one Spirit.

"For the body does not consist of one member but of many. If the foot should say, 'Because I am not a hand, I do not belong to the body,' that would not make it any less a part of the body. And if the ear should say, 'Because I am not an eye, I do not belong to the body,' that would not make it any less a part of the body. If the whole body were an eye, where would be the sense of hearing? If the whole body were an ear, where would be the sense of smell? But as it is, God arranged the members in the body, each one of them, as he chose. If all were a single member, where would the body be? As it is, there are many parts, yet one body.

"The eye cannot say to the hand, 'I have no need of you,' nor again the head to the feet, 'I have no need of you.' On the contrary, the parts of the body that seem to be weaker are indispensable, and on those parts of the body that we think less honorable we bestow the greater honor, and our unpresentable parts are treated with greater modesty, which our more presentable parts do not require. But God has so composed the body, giving greater honor to the part that lacked it, that there may be no division in the body, but that the members may have the same care for one another. If one member suffers, all suffer together; if one member is honored, all rejoice together.

"Now you are the body of Christ and individually members of it. And God has appointed in the church first apostles, second prophets, third teachers, then miracles, then gifts of healing, helping, administrating, and various kinds of tongues. Are all apostles? Are all prophets? Are all teachers? Do all work miracles? Do all possess gifts of healing? Do all speak with tongues? Do all interpret? But earnestly desire the higher gifts." – 12:4-31

---

17 The gospel goes out, the church begins, and the nations are not blended into one. Rather, they are preserved as the gospel recognizes and moves within them and their languages.

"But all things should be done decently and in order." – 14:40

"God gives it a body as he has chosen, and to each kind of seed its own body. For not all flesh is the same, but there is one kind for humans, another for animals, another for birds, and another for fish. There are heavenly bodies and earthly bodies, but the glory of the heavenly is of one kind, and the glory of the earthly is of another. There is one glory of the sun, and another glory of the moon, and another glory of the stars; for star differs from star in glory." – 15:38-41 [18]

"So is it with the resurrection of the dead. What is sown is perishable; what is raised is imperishable. It is sown in dishonor; it is raised in glory. It is sown in weakness; it is raised in power. It is sown a natural body; it is raised a spiritual body. If there is a natural body, there is also a spiritual body. Thus it is written, 'The first man Adam became a living being'; the last Adam became a life-giving spirit. But it is not the spiritual that is first but the natural, and then the spiritual. The first man was from the earth, a man of dust; the second man is from heaven. As was the man of dust, so also are those who are of the dust, and as is the man of heaven, so also are those who are of heaven. Just as we have borne the image of the man of dust, we shall also bear the image of the man of heaven." – 15:42-49

2 Corinthians

"And we all, with unveiled face, beholding the glory of the Lord, are being transformed into the same image from one degree of glory to another. For this comes from the Lord who is the Spirit." – 3:18

Ephesians

"For this reason I bow my knees before the Father, from whom every family in heaven and on earth is named." – 3:14

Colossians

"...seeing that you have put off the old self with its practices and have put on the new self, which is being renewed in knowledge after the image of its creator. Here there is not Greek and Jew, circumcised and uncircumcised, barbarian, Scythian, slave, free; but Christ is all, and in all." – 3:9-11

Timothy

"If any provide not for his own, and specially for those of his own house, he hath denied the faith." – I Timothy 5:8

"This know also, that in the last days perilous times shall come. For men shall be lovers of their own selves, covetous, boasters, proud, blasphemers, disobedient to parents, unthankful, unholy, without natural affection, trucebreakers, false accusers, incontinent, fierce, despisers of those that are good." – II Timothy 3:1-3

Revelation

"And they sang a new song, saying, 'Worthy are you to take the scroll and to open its seals, for you were slain, and by your blood you ransomed people for God from every tribe and language and people and nation...'" – 5:9

"After this I looked, and behold, a great multitude that no one could number, from every nation, from all tribes and peoples and languages, standing before the throne and before the Lamb, clothed in white robes, with palm branches in their hands..." – 7:9

"She gave birth to a male child, one who is to rule all the nations with a rod of iron..." – 12:5

"Then I saw another angel flying directly overhead, with an eternal gospel to proclaim to those who dwell on earth, to every nation and tribe and language and people." – 14:6

"And they sing the song of Moses, the servant of God, and the song of the Lamb, saying, 'Great and amazing are your deeds, O Lord God the Almighty! Just and true are your ways, O King of the nations! Who will not fear, O Lord, and glorify your name? For you alone are holy. All nations will come and worship you, for your righteous acts have been revealed.'" – 15:3-4

---

18   God created variety, diversity, and inequality in nature. See the Bible Commentary section.

"And I saw no temple in the city, for its temple is the Lord God the Almighty and the Lamb. And the city has no need of sun or moon to shine on it, for the glory of God gives it light, and its lamp is the Lamb. By its light will the nations walk, and the kings of the earth will bring their glory into it, and its gates will never be shut by day – and there will be no night there. They will bring into it the glory and the honor of the nations." – 21:24-26

"Through the middle of the street of the city; also, on either side of the river, the tree of life with its twelve kinds of fruit, yielding its fruit each month. The leaves of the tree were for the healing of the nations." – 22:2

Bion of Smyrna

"The beauteous Adonis lieth low in the hills, his thigh pierced with the tusk, the white with the white, and Cypris is sore vexed at the gentle passing of his breath; for the red blood drips down his snow-white flesh, and the eyes beneath his brow wax dim; the rose departs from his lip, and the kiss that Cypris shall never have so again, that kiss dies upon it and is gone. Cypris is fain enough now of the kiss of the dead; but Adonis, he knows not that she hath kissed him." – *Lament for Adonis, The Greek Bucolic Poets*, pg. 387

Black's Law Dictionary

A nation as it is defined in Scripture is precisely the same way it is defined in the Sixth Edition of Black's Law Dictionary:

"A people, or aggregation of men, existing in the form of an organized jural society, usually inhabiting a distinct portion of the earth, speaking the same language, using the same customs, possessing historic continuity, and distinguished from other like groups by their racial origin and characteristics, and generally, but not necessarily, living under the same government and sovereignty." – *Handbook of American Constitutional Law*, pg. 15

James Blaine

"Protection . . . is based on the controlling principle, that competition at home will always prevent monopoly on the part of the capitalist, assure good wages to the laborer, and defend the consumer against the evils of extortion. The competition of home producers will . . . rapidly reduce the price to the consumer." – *Twenty Years*, 1:211–12

"And in a Republic especially, in any government that maintains itself, the unit of order and administration is in the family. The emigrants that come to us from the British Isles, from Germany, from Denmark, from France, from Spain, from Italy, come here with the idea of the family as engraven on their minds and in their customs and in their habits as we have it. The Asiatic cannot go on with our population and make a homogeneous element. The idea of comparing European immigration with an immigration that has no regard for family, that does not recognize the relation of the husband and wife, that does not have in the slightest degree the ennobling and the civilizing influences of the hearthstone or the fireside! Why, when gentlemen talk loosely about emigration from European states as contrasted with that, they certainly are forgetting history and forgetting themselves." – Senator from Mass., speech in debate held before the Senate on Feb. 13-15, 1879; *Great Debates in American History* part 2, pg. 247

Thom Blair

"The family is the primary setting for many biblical narratives. The main events of the stories of Genesis, for example, relate to the family—including Adam and Eve (Gen 3–4), Noah and his family (Gen 6–9), Abraham and Sarah (Gen 12–23), Isaac and Rebekah (Gen 24–26), and Jacob with his 4 wives and 12 sons (Gen 27–50). In the flood story, God preserved mankind through Noah and his family (Gen 6–9). Later, God's plan for the salvation of mankind involved choosing Abraham and his family for special blessing (Gen 12:1–3).

"Throughout the OT, the family is a central concern. Many laws are focused on regulating and protecting family interests (e.g., Deut 21:15–17; 25:5–10). Other laws were designed to protect those who were outside the traditional family structure and so lacked the protection and support provided by the family (Exod 22:22–23; Deut 24:17). The people of Israel were commanded to pass down these laws within the family, instructing their own children and grandchildren (Deut 6:1–2). In Proverbs 1–9, the instruction in wise living is framed as family teaching, lessons from a father to his son.

"The family had a similar function in the Graeco-Roman world as the basic unit of social organization. Some sections of Paul's letters are commonly known as 'household codes' because they contained ethical instructions directed at different members of the household—such as husbands, wives, children, and slaves (Col 3:18–4:1; Eph 5:22–6:9).

"Jesus' incarnation means that he was part of a human family…Jesus highlights the importance of families by explaining who God is and who he himself is in terms of a familial relationship—God is the Father and Jesus is the Son of God (John 10:22–39).

"Family property and cultural values were passed on from father to son. The command in Deut 6 that Israelites should teach God's law to their children literally says they should teach their sons (bēn) and the sons of their sons (Deut 6:2)…Inclusion in a people group or a family is also expressed in terms of being descended from a common ancestor. For example, Israelites are referred to as לְאָרְשֵׁי יֶנֶב (benê yiśrā'ēl, 'sons of Israel')." – Family. *Lexham Theological Workbook*

William Blake

And did those feet in ancient time
Walk upon England's mountains green?
And was the holy Lamb of God
On England's pleasant pastures seen?

And did the Countenance Divine
Shine forth upon our clouded hills?
And was Jerusalem builded here
Among these dark Satanic Mills?

...

I will not cease from Mental Fight,
Nor shall my Sword sleep in my hand:
Till we have built Jerusalem
In England's green & pleasant Land.
– *Jerusalem* (lines 1-8, 13-16) [19]

Albert Taylor Bledsoe

"To give to all men equal power where the majority is ignorant and depraved, would be indeed to establish equality, but not liberty.... it would be to establish the most odious despotism on earth–the reign of ignorance, passion, prejudice, and brutality." – *Cotton Is King*, pg. 335

Daniel I. Block

"To adopt the lifestyle and the religious commitments of a Canaanite is to render oneself a Canaanite and thus provoke the ire of Yahweh." – *NIV Application Commentary, Deuteronomy*, Deut. 7:3, pg. 302

Mary Whitlock Blundell

In the Greek world:

"respect for friends could be ranked alongside reverence for gods, parents, and law. In other words, it was amogst the most powerful moral imperatives of Greek like. When Hesiod predicts the total moral degeneracy in which the iron age will culminate, he envisages the breakdown of the bonds of philia between parent and child, guest and host, friend and friend, brother and brother." – *Helping Friends and Harming Enemies: a Study in Sophocles and Greek Ethics*, pg. 31

Darrell L. Bock

"Does he love others by being a neighbor to them regardless of their origin? Talbert paraphrases the lawyer's question this way: 'How can I spot others who belong to God's people so that I can love them?'... Jesus' answer to the lawyers real question is, 'Do not worry about spotting God's people first, just be a neighbor to all, as this Samaritan was.'" – Luke, *Baker Exegetical Commentary on the New Testament*, pg. 1452 [20]

"Household instruction following the three-pair pattern of husband-wife, parents-children, master-slave was commonly known for centuries on either side of the New Testament. It was considered to be a normal topic for paraenetic or preceptorial advice in the first century...

---

19   Also known as "And did those feet in ancient time," is a short poem that serves as the preface to his epic poem "Milton." The poem celebrates England's mythic past and future potential.

20   Indicating that the primary issue was spiritual favoritism, which no longer remains.

"In the Greco-Roman world, the duties of children toward their parents included love, honor, providing for them in old age, burying them, and venerating them after death. All these activities were part of pietas, the virtue that lay 'at the core of the Romans' ideal of family relations' and that involved the heartfelt fulfillment of one's duty toward the gods, country, and family. A person's highest moral duty, said Cicero, was first to one's country and then to one's parents, 'for their services have laid us under the heaviest obligation.'" – with Frank Thielman. Ephesians, *Baker Exegetical Commentary on the New Testament*, pg. 396

"Another practical issue is the personal, compassionate meeting of basic needs, not the mere throwing of money at a problem in the hopes it will fix itself. The Samaritan not only provides resources but personally undertakes to make sure that others who become a part of the process are aware that he wants the victim brought back to health. Care is left in the hands of those who will responsibly complete the task… Neighbors are people with a heart that does more than pump blood. It [their heart] sees, feels, and serves." – *NIV Application Commentary, Luke*, pgs. 452-453

István Bocskay

"It should be demanded that every man who loves his country and fatherland stand up for his nation and hasten against our common enemy… We owe it to our dear country and nation . . . to rise all together and live or die together." [21] – quoted in *From Hunyadi to Rakoczi: War and Society in Late Medieval and Early Modern Hungary*, pg. 283

Loraine Boettner

"Apart from this election of individuals to life, there has been what we may call a national election, or a divine predestination of nations and communities to a knowledge of true religion and to the external privileges of the Gospel. God undoubtedly does choose some nations to receive much greater spiritual and temporal blessings than others. This form of election has been well illustrated in the Jewish nation, in certain European nations and communities, and in America. The contrast is very striking when we compare these with other nations such as China, Japan, India, etc." – *The Reformed Doctrine of Predestination*, pg. 41

Dietrich Bonhoeffer

"We teach according to Scripture that God the Lord commanded man before the fall to be fruitful, to hold dominion, and to work; that God created man as male and female; that man gets his food from nature by means of his lordship over nature and the service of his labor; that man cannot live in isolation but only through the community. All this the creatureliness ordered for man.

"Every order which is not commanded by God's commandment, being thus defined and sanctified by God's law, must again and again fall to the devil. Thus God keeps man alive through his life-creating word in these orders and gives him in them life and salvation through Christ (Ap. XVI). The orders do not have any value in themselves, but only live from Christ, the Word. Yet this means that they exist as orders of preservation only for the sake of Christ's future and for the sake of the new creation. This is, then, their ultimate and deepest meaning and their limitation: that man may and should live in them until redemption. The orders are valid orders of God; therefore they are not indifferent matters, but they are also not final orders of God. The orders of preservation have the unconditional value of being divine institutions, and their transgression makes us enemies of God and closes access to the Christ. At the same time, however, they are cancelled and overcome from Christ and his future.

"As such orders have been established for us marriage, family, nation, property [labor, economy], vocation, worldly authority. Man cannot evade any one of these orders, and none of them can be changed or transformed into another.

"The question whether race belongs to the orders of creation is discussed much today. Based on Holy Scripture and the confession it is to be answered this way: Race, unlike marriage or worldly authority or nation, does not belong to the orders of life with which God's commandment has charged man. It belongs to the orders of nature to which all life, even outside of man-

---

21 Followers of Istvan had this saying as their banner.

kind, is necessarily subjected (cf. the 'laws of the seasons,' Ap. XVI, 6). In this sense, the reality of race, as all orders of nature, may be counted among the divinae ordinationes in the broader sense. Holy Scripture, in what it says about our flesh, attests to what is true in the modern ideas on race, namely, that the inner life is bound to the form of our corporeity. The church's doctrine concerning race cannot go beyond this. In particular, it must reject all attempts to place the natural phenomenon of race on the same level as the institutional orders that are grounded in a direct divine commandment to man. ...

"Christ is sent as the Redeemer of the whole world. This is why he commissions the church to bring the gospel to all nations. As it carries out this commission, it enters into the forms and structures of the nations of their time. It can live among a multitude of nations as the one church regardless of political boundaries. It can be a national church within the boundaries of a realm regardless of ethnicity. It can be church within a certain ethnicity while transcending political boundaries. It can be church within a certain ethnicity without transcending political boundaries, but within the boundaries of this ethnicity. Its external form is not subject to duress, but is determined by the only rule, namely, 'by all means to gain some' [1 Cor. 9:22]. This is why it becomes a Jew to the Jews, a Greek to the Greeks, a Chinese to the Chinese, a German to the Germans. The manner and extent of such entering into time can be determined only based on the commission of the church. The proclamation of the church always remains the alien grain of seed that is planted in the ground. Where the content of a specific time becomes the content of the proclamation the gospel is betrayed, because it is no longer said to the time, but absorbed by it.

"The proclamation of the message concerning Christ is equally accessible and equally inaccessible for all nations. This proclamation is always good news and offense at the same time. God's Holy Spirit alone works faith in man. He alone creates the fellowship of confessing rightly. The fellowship of such confessing is never coextensive with the boundaries of a certain ethnicity.

"The church of Christ never floats above the nations. It lives in the nations. The nations are not the church. Yet the members of a specific nation, who are at the same time members of the church living in this nation, are inextricably connected to both. They participate in the glory and guilt of their nation and in the promise and guilt of their church.

"We reject the false doctrine, in whatever form it may appear, concerning a naturally Christian soul of certain individuals, nations, or races.

"We reject the false doctrine that the existence of the nation is a presupposition for the existence of the church, or that the existence of the church is a presupposition for the life of a nation.

"The church can live even where there is no nation, for 'where two or three are gathered in my name, there I am in the midst of them' [Matt. 18:20].

"A nation can live and have a grand history, even where there is no church. Nations live within the natural world and have incurred the law of death that reigns over all creation. This is why a nation as a whole cannot be redeemed, for redemption is always God's act upon an individual. However, the church, grateful to God, always lays hold of the assistance offered to it in the ethnicity or other natural orders for the execution of its commission.

"We reject the false doctrine that the church belongs to the nation, or that it exists for the nation. The church does not belong to the nation, but to Christ. He alone is its Lord. Only in intrepid obedience to him it truly serves the nation in which it lives. It exists for every member of the nation, to gain him for the congregation of Jesus.

"We oppose the teaching that it belongs to the essence of the church to be a national church ['Volkskirche']. The church is free to be national church, so long as this form is a means to carry out its commission." – *The Bethel Confession, Dietrich Bonhoeffer Works* vol. 12, pgs. 411-413

George Borjas

"The decline in immigrant economic performance can be attributed to a single factor, the changing national origin mix of the immigrant population. Put differently, the United States would not have witnessed a decline in the relative economic performance of immigrants if the ethnic mix of immigrants had not changed." – *Heaven's Door*, pg. 45

"The relative decline in the skills and economic performance of immigrants in the post-1965 period is striking and irrefutable. A question remains: why did this decline occur? A great deal of evidence points to a single—and disturbing—culprit: the changing national origin mix of the immigrant population. Between the 1960s and the 1990s, the United States experienced a historic shift in the national origin mix of its immigrant population, away from the 'traditional' Western European source countries and toward developing countries. It turns out that there are huge differences in the skills of immigrants who belong to different ethnic groups, with immigrants who originate in developing countries typically having a much harder time in the U.S. labor market." – *Heaven's Door*, pg. 39

"The available evidence suggests that the skills of the children of immigrants are affected not only by the skills of their parents, but also by measures of the group's ethnic capital, such as the mean education or wage of the ethnic group in the parental generation. In fact, the impact of ethnic capital on social mobility may account for half of the persistence in ethnic skill differentials across generations. Because the children of particular ethnic groups tend to follow in the group's footsteps, ethnic capital effectively lowers the flame under the melting pot from a full boil to a slow simmer. In a sense, ethnic capital makes it hard to escape the economic fate implied by one's ethnic background." – *Heaven's Door*, pg. 14

"Although some participants in the immigration debate claim that these gains from immigration are large, the facts are quite different: all of the available estimates suggest that the annual net gain is astoundingly small, less than .1 percent of GDP. In the late 1990s, this amounted to a net gain of less than $10 billion a year for the entire native population, or less than $30 per person.

"Immigration, however, does more than just increase the total income accruing to natives. Immigration also induces a substantial redistribution of wealth, away from workers who compete with immigrants and toward employers and other users of immigrant services. Workers lose because immigrants drag wages down. Employers gain because immigrants drag wages down. These wealth transfers may be in the tens of billions of dollars per year." – *Heaven's Door*, pg. 12

"Remarkably, the size of the native economic pie did not change much after immigration increased the number of workers by more than 15 percent. But the split of the pie certainly changed, giving far less to workers and much more to employers." – *Immigration Debate*

Eugene Borza

"I once wondered whether Macedon was Europe's earliest national state … the Macedonians were an ethnic group derived from their predecessors, the Makedones, and defined in historical times by their service to their king … In this sense they were a people, or ethos, with a common set of loyalties and a shared historical experience." – *In the Shadow of Olympus*, pgs. 281-282.

G. Johannes Botterweck

"…nokrî means 'unfamilial,' i.e., standing outside the family. Someone outside a family has not only no emotional and social ties with that family but also no legal ties. When a person is excluded from a family, all such ties are lost…

"For a third group of texts, the OT itself provides definitions: 'a nokrî, [someone] who is not of your people Israel and comes from a distant land' (1 K. 8:41); and 'someone nokrî, [someone] who is not your brother' (Dt. 17:15)—in other words, a 'foreigner.'…

"…isolation from foreigners or xenophobia does not appear in Israel during the monarchy but is first documented in the period of early Judaism, when the people were living under foreign domination and were concerned for their identity…" – Foreigner. *Theological Dictionary of the Old Testament*, vol. 9, pgs. 425-427

C.R. Boxer

"When the protectionist measures adopted by neighboring countries from the time of Colbert onwards effectively stimulated the consumption of their own manufactured goods at the expense of Dutch exports, the Dutch industrialists could not fall back on an increased internal demand, nor was it possible to greatly increase their sales in the tropical dependencies. Moreover, the Dutch industries had originally been primarily finishing industries for the products of other countries. … but in course of time these countries made sufficient technical progress to undertake these finishing processes themselves." – *The Dutch Seaborne Empire 1600-1800*, pg. 288

Mel Bradford

"Let us have no foolishness, indeed. Equality as a moral or political imperative, pursued as an end in itself—Equality, with the capital 'E'—is the antonym of every legitimate conservative principle. Contrary to most Liberals, new and old, it is nothing less than sophistry to distinguish between equality of opportunity (equal starts in the 'race of life') and equality of condition (equal results). For only those who are equal can take equal advantage of a given circumstance." – *Better Guide Than Reason*, pg. 29

"But behind the cult of equality …is an even more sinister power, the uniformitarian hatred of providential distinctions which will stop at nothing less than what Eric Voegelin calls 'a reconstitution of being': a nihilistic impulse which is at bottom both frightened and vain in its rejection of a given contingency and in its arrogation of a godlike authority to annul that dependency." – *Better Guide Than Reason*, pg. 31

Chad Brand

"FAMILY A group of persons united by the ties of marriage, blood, or adoption, enabling interaction between members of the household in their respective social roles. God has ordained the family as the foundational institution of human society.

"Within the ethnic 'people' (am) of Israel descended from Jacob were three levels of family relationships. One was the tribe (shevet or mateh) comprising the descendants of one of Jacob's sons. Within the tribe were the 'clans' (mishpachah), and within the clan were the family units, which were the basic units of Israel's social structure. They were typically referred to as 'the father's house' (בא תיב; Josh. 7:16-18). This unit would be similar to what we mean by 'family,' but it was usually larger than our 'nuclear family,' including three or four generations of sons and their wives and children, who lived on the same land under the leadership of the family patriarch or 'head.' The group of elders who judged at the gate of a town (e.g., Deut. 21:19) probably comprised all the local 'heads.' The perception and value of the two-generation 'nuclear family' may be inferred from repeated references to the parent-child relationship. ...

"New Testament: As the family is the basic unit in society and in OT Israel, it was also essential to the life and growth of the early church. The apostolic missionaries sent by Jesus were to focus on households (Matt. 10:11-14), early worship consisted in part of 'break[ing] bread from house to house' (Acts 2:36; see also 5:42; 12:12; 20:20), and later churches met regularly in homes (Rom. 16:23; 1 Cor. 16:19; Col. 4:15). Conversions even sometimes happened by household (Acts 10:24, 33, 44; 16:15, 31-34; 18:8; 1 Cor. 1:16). The family also served as a proving ground for church leaders, who should exhibit marital faithfulness, hospitality, competent household management, including wise parenting skills, and having wives 'worthy of respect.' (1 Tim. 3:2-13; Titus 1:6-9)." – Family. *Holman Illustrated Bible Dictionary*, pgs. 556-557

Jan Bremmer

"In Homer's time the individual did not yet know of the will as an ethical factor, nor did he distinguish between what was inside and outside himself as we do. When referring to themselves, the early Greeks, like other Indo-European peoples, did not primarily consider themselves to be independent individuals but rather members of a group." – *The Early Greek Concept of the Soul*, pg. 67

Peter Brimelow

"Let us start with a definition. What is a 'nation state'? It is the political expression of a nation. And what is a 'nation'? It is an ethno-cultural community — an interlacing of ethnicity and culture.

"In recent years there has been a tendency to emphasize the cultural part of the equation, particularly in the U.S. But this is to miss a critical point. The word 'nation' is derived from the Latin nescare, to be born. It intrinsically implies a link by blood. A nation in a real sense is an extended family. The merging process by which all nations are created is not merely cultural, but to a considerable extent biological, through intermarriage...

"The second difficulty hampering American

discourse is perceptual. Americans are used to being told that they are a 'nation of immigrants.' They therefore tend to assume that they cannot share a common ethnic heritage. But even on its own term, this is false — at least, it was false until the great wave of Third World immigration unleashed by the 1965 Immigration Act. At the time of the American Revolution, the white population in the U.S. was 60 percent English, 80 percent British, 98 percent Protestant. As late as 1980, it was estimated that the U.S. population would still have been about half its then-current level if there had been no immigration at all after 1790. And in 1980, nearly 90 percent of the American population was European, the great bulk of it closely related, from the British Isles, Germany and Italy...

"It also brings me to my third conclusion: immigration is potentially much more of a threat to public order than we realize...But introducing diverse populations strikes at the nation-state's Achilles heel: its need for homogeneity. In fact, on the analysis I have presented here, the very concept of a multicultural and multiracial nation is suspect. In essence, it is a contradiction in terms. Of course, nations do contain contradictions, particularly given time to digest them — and American immigration history, incidentally, has been marked by many such pauses for digestion. But mostly, multicultural and multiracial polities are not nations: they are states, empires. And they are not democratic." – *Does the Nation-State Exist*

"The free market necessarily exists within a social framework. And it can function only if the institutions in that framework are appropriate. For example, a defined system of private property is now widely agreed to be one essential precondition. Economists have a word for these preconditions: the 'metamarket.' Some degree of ethnic and cultural coherence may be among them. Thus immigration may be a metamarket issue." – *Time to Rethink Immigraion*

Geoffrey W. Bromiley

"Cultural anthropology has provided us information and insight into the ancient (and sometimes primitive) conceptions of the relationship between the living and the dead. These conceptions of the relationship can range from abject fear to reverential awe. Many cultures have

'deified' their human ancestors; and at least one known culture has the category of 'ancestor' among the deities (the Hittite 'former deities')...

"The OT's seeming preoccupation with the earlier generations has a historicolegal basis, viz., the covenantal relationship between Yahweh and His people. The corporate nature of the covenant community is expressed in terms of solidarity within a given generation as well as a oneness with previous generations. One's ancestors were not to be worshiped, but they were not to be forgotten either. It is Yahweh, the God of Abraham, Isaac, and Jacob, the God of one's ancestors/forefathers, with whom each contemporary generation must be personally and covenantally related." – Ancestor. *The International Standard Bible Encyclopedia*, vol. 1, pg. 122

Rupert Brooke

If I should die, think only this of me:
That there's some corner of a foreign field
That is for ever England. There shall be
In that rich earth a richer dust concealed;
A dust whom England bore,
    shaped, made aware,
Gave, once, her flowers to love,
    her ways to roam,
A body of England's, breathing English air,
Washed by the rivers, blest by suns of home.
 – *The Soldier* (lines 1-8)

"Stands the Church clock at ten to three?
And is there honey still for tea?
...
And laughs the immortal river still
Under the mill, under the mill?
Say, is there Beauty yet to find?
And Certainty? and Quiet kind?
Deep meadows yet, for to forget
The lies, and truths, and pain?... oh! yet
Stands the Church clock at ten to three?
And is there honey still for tea?"
 – *The Old Vicarage, Grantchester* (lines 167-184)

William P. Brown

"The new age is described as 'great and terrible,' and yet the final note is one of redemption rather than destruction: Elijah will reconcile parents and their children to each other. The day of the Lord is first and foremost a healing of the wounds within family and community.

"It is no accident that the Old Testament begins with a family history full of strife and conflict: Adam's blame of Eve, Cain's murder of Abel, the squabbles between Abraham and Sarah, the rivalry and deception among the later generations. It is out of this conflicted and sordid background that Israel comes into being. Some would say it is the history of a dysfunctional family. It is no coincidence then that the Old Testament ends with Malachi's vision of absolute reconciliation within the family. In the end, the book of Malachi looks forward to that day when peace and unity will break out, beginning with the family..." – Malachi 4:6. *Westminster Bible Companion*, pg. 205

Rogers Brubaker

"Citizenship in a nation-state is inevitably bound up with nationhood and national identity, membership of the state with membership of the nation. Proposals to redefine the legal criteria of citizenship raise large and ideologically charged questions of nationhood and national belonging. Debates about citizenship...are debates about what it means to belong to the nation-state. The politics of citizenship today is first and foremost a politics of nationhood... The central question is not 'who gets what?' but rather 'who is what?'" – *Citizenship and Nationhood in France and Germany*, pg. 182

F.F. Bruce

"God, having created the whole race of human beings, has given them the whole earth for their dwelling place, allotting appropriate living space to each nation. Another interpretation, favored by Dibelius, is that God has appointed the habitable zones of the earth for the human family to live in. But the divine allocation of national territories has biblical authority, the locus classicus being Deut. 32:8:

"When the Most High gave to the nations their inheritance, when he separated the sons of men, he fixed the bounds of the peoples according to the number of the sons of God."

"According to the Genesis account, the earth was formed and furnished to be a home for humanity before humanity itself was brought into being to occupy it; the tenses of the Greek verbs here similarly suggest that 'the determination of man's home preceded his creation,

in the Divine plan.' And part of the forming and furnishing of this home consisted in the regulation of the 'allotted seasons,' by which, after the analogy of the Lystran speech (14:17), we are probably to understand the seasons of the year by whose sequence annual provision is made for the supply of food." – *The Book of Acts*, pg. 337

Walter Brueggemann

"The ecumenical and political reality of this text affirms that all nations derive their historical existence from the life-giving power of God and are called to be responsive to him:

"And he made from one every nation of men to live on all the face of the earth, having determined allotted periods and the boundaries of their habitation, that they should seek God, in the hope that they might feel after him and find him. Yet he is not far from each one of us, for 'In him we live and move and have our being.' (Acts 17:26-28).

"No nation or people is given ground or reason for being other than this one God who has formed all creatures. The multiplication of nations is here regarded as a fulfillment of creation (cf. v. 32). The nations are indeed blessed, being fruitful and multiplying. In the map of chapter 10, the well-being promised and envisioned in chapter 1 becomes visible." – Genesis. *Interpretation: A Bible Commentary for Teaching and Preaching*, pgs. 93-94

Emil Brunner

"Jesus Christ is the true Imago Dei, which man regains when through faith he is 'in Jesus Christ.' Faith in Jesus is therefore the restauratio imaginis [restoration of the image], because he restores to us that existence in the Word of God which we had lost through sin. When man enters into the love of God revealed in Christ he becomes truly human. True human existence is existence in the love of God." – *Doctrine of Creation*, pg. 58

"It is evident that our thought will become terribly muddled if the two ideas of the Imago Dei—the 'formal' and 'structural' one of the Old Testament, and the 'material' one of the New Testament—are either confused with one another or treated as identical. The result will be: either that we must deny that the sinner possesses the quality of humanity at all; or, that which makes him a human being must be severed from the Imago Dei; or, the loss of the Imago in the material sense must be regarded merely as an obscuring or a partial corruption of the Imago, which lessens the heinousness of sin." – *Doctrine of Creation*, pg. 59

William Jennings Bryan

"Good fortune has had more to do with such success as I may have achieved than any efforts of my own.... Opportunity comes independently of one's own efforts; and his preparedness to meet opportunity is due, as I shall show, largely to others.... I have been wonderfully fortunate in the opportunities that have come to me....

"To begin the story of my good fortune. I was born in the greatest of all ages. No golden ages of the past offered any such opportunity for large service and, therefore, for the enjoyment that comes from consciousness that one has been helpful.

"I was born a member of the greatest of all the races—the Caucasian Race, and had mingled in my veins the blood of English, Irish, and Scotch. One has only to consider the limitations upon one's opportunities imposed by race to understand the incalculable benefit of having the way opened between the child and the stars.

"I was born a citizen of the greatest of all lands. So far as my power to prevent was concerned, I might have been born in the darkest of the continents and among the most backward of earth's peoples. It was a gift of priceless value to see the light in beloved America, and to live under the greatest of the republics of history.

"And I was equally fortunate, I shall show, in my family environment. [My ancestors] were honest, industrious, Christian, moral, religious people—not a black sheep in the flock.... The environment in which my youth was spent was as ideal as any that I know." – *The Memoirs of William Jennings Bryan*, vol. 10, pgs. 9-10

Pat Buchanan

"To hear men endlessly recite this mindless mantra, 'Our diversity is our strength,' when tribal, ethnic, and religious diversity is tearing nations to pieces, is to recall Orwell: Only an intellectual could make a statement like that. No ordinary man could be such a fool." – *Suicide of a Superpower*, pg. 237

"Ethnomasochism, the taking of pleasure in the dispossession of one's own ethnic group, is a disease of the heart that never afflicted the America of Andrew Jackson, Theodore Roosevelt, or Dwight Eisenhower. It comes out of what James Burnham called an 'ideology of Western suicide,' a belief system that provides a morphine drip for people who have come to accept the inevitability of their departure from history." – *Suicide of a Superpower*, pg. 134

"To ethnonationalists, their countrymen are not equal to all others, but superior in rights. Many may nod at Thomas Jefferson's line that 'All men are created equal,' but they no more practice that in their own nations than did Jefferson in his....Europe is rejecting, resisting, recoiling from 'diversity,' the multiracial, multicultural, multiethnic and multilingual future." – *Is Liberalism a Dying Faith?*

"We may deny the existence of ethnonationalism, detest it, condemn it. But this creator and destroyer of empires and nations is a force infinitely more powerful than globalism, for it engages the heart. Men will die for it. Religion, race, culture and tribe are the four horsemen of the coming apocalypse." – *Suicide of a Superpower*, pg. 328

"The colonists were WASP supremacists. Without moral qualms, they drove the Indians over the mountains and established a society of white and Christian men and women along with African slaves. Catholics were unwelcome. Priests were put back on the boats that brought them. Virginia had been named for the 'Virgin Queen' Elizabeth, who was determined to complete the work of her father, Henry VIII, who sought to end religious diversity in England by eradicating Catholicism. America was largely settled by colonists from the British Isles. Nearly two centuries after Jamestown and Plymouth Rock, when Washington took his oath as president, the thirteen states were 99 percent Protestant. In 1790, U.S. citizenship was opened up for 'free white persons' of 'moral character.' No others need apply." –*Suicide of a Superpower*, pg. 232

"Once Europe went out to convert, colonize and Christianize the world. Now the grandchildren of the colonized peoples come to Europe to demand their share of their inheritance from a West besotted with guilt over its past sins that cannot say 'No!'" – *Alone Perhaps, But Is Trump Right?*

"When the faith dies, the culture dies, the civilization dies, the people die. That is the progression. And as the faith that gave birth to the West is dying in the West, peoples of European descent from the steppes of Russia to the coast of California have begun to die out, as the Third World treks north to claim the estate. The last decade provided corroborating if not conclusive proof that we are in the Indian summer of our civilization." – *Suicide Of A Superpower*, pg. VIII

"Our intellectual, cultural, and political elites are today engaged in one of the most audacious and ambitious experiments in history. They are trying to transform a Western Christian republic into an egalitarian democracy made up of all the tribes, races, creeds, and cultures of planet Earth. They have dethroned our God, purged our cradle faith from public life, and repudiated the Judeo-Christian moral code by which previous generations sought to live..." – *Suicide Of A Superpower*, pg. 400

"Nationalism is an idea whose time has come again. Those 'old ties of blood, and race, and sectarianism' do seem everywhere ascendant. But that is a reality we must recognize and deal with. Deploring it will not make it go away." – *Is Russia An Enemy?*

"History teaches that multiethnic states are held together either by an authoritarian regime or a dominant ethnocultural core, or they are ever at risk of disintegration in ethnic conflict...

"In democracies it is an ethnocultural core that holds the county together....

"Intellectuals deceive themselves if they believe the new trinity of their faith—democracy, equality, and diversity—can replace the old idea of what it meant to be a Briton, what it meant to be an Englishman." – *Day of Reckoning*, pgs. 184-185

"It is the belief of this author and the premise of this book that America is indeed coming apart, decomposing, and that the likelihood of her survival as one nation through mid-century is improbable—and impossible if America continues on her current course. For we are on a path to national suicide." – *Day of Reckoning*, pg. 7

"As Rome passed away, so the West is passing away, from the same causes and in much the same way. What the Danube and Rhine were to Rome, the Rio Grande and Mediterranean are to America and Europe, the frontiers of a civilization no longer defended." – *State of Emergency*, pg. 2

"Patriotism is the soul of a nation. When it dies, when a nation loses the love and loyalty of its people, the nation dies and begins to decompose.

"Patriotism is not nation-worship, such as we saw in Europe in the 1930s. It is not that spirit of nationalism that must denigrate or dominate other nations. It is a passionate attachment to one's own country—its land, its people, its past, its heroes, literature, language, traditions, culture, and customs." – *State of Emergency*, pg. 139

— PAT BUCHANAN —

"Hierarchies are as natural as they are essential. As history demonstrates, all peoples, cultures, and civilizations are not equal. Some have achieved greatness often, others never. All lifestyles are not equal. All religions are not equal. All ideas are not equal. Indeed, what is true martyrdom but that most eloquent and compelling of all testimonies that all ideas are not equal." – *Death of the West*, pg. 63

"From 1869 to 1900, GDP quadrupled. Budget surpluses ran for 27 straight years. The U.S. debt was cut two-thirds to 7 percent of GDP. Commodity prices fell 58 percent. America's population doubled, but real wages rose 53 percent. Economic growth averaged 4 percent a year. And the United States, which began this era with half of Britain's production, ended it with twice Britain's production. Under Warren Harding, Cal Coolidge, and the Fordney-Mc-Cumber Tariff, GDP growth between 1922 and 1927 hit 7 percent, an all-time record." – *Tariffs Made America Great*

"Once a nation is hooked on the cheap goods that are the narcotic free trade provides, it is rarely able to break free. The loss of its economic independence is followed by the loss of its political independence, the loss of its greatness and, ultimately, the loss of its national identity." – *Tariffs Made America Great*

"America's elites are slaves to the ideas of nineteenth-century scribblers, none of whom ever built a nation. Our industrial base is shrinking and Middle America's standard of living is no longer rising, because we forgot how America became a mighty industrial power and we embraced the myth that it was free trade that made us great. To challenge this myth–now an article of faith in both parties–is to be treated as imbecilic or immoral. Yet, the lie must be exposed, for more is being sacrificed on the altar of this Moloch than the jobs of our workers and the standard of living of our people…

"Both parties have collaborated in the sellout. In embracing free trade, Democrats betrayed their workers. In worshiping this golden calf, Republicans turned their back on their history, tradition, and greatest men. Most do not even know it, but they elaborate today what their wisest leaders used to ridicule as the utopian nonsense of the idiot savants of the Paris salons." – *Great Betrayal*, pgs. 16-17

"Free trade is a myth. It envisions a future that will never exist and assumes an ideal world that does not exist. True believers, however, will never be dissuaded. To them, free trade is not an economic theory or policy option, it is revealed truth about how the world should work, and it is held to the heart with a devotion that is almost religious. In its economic determinism, its utopianism, and its hold on the imagination, free-trade theory is first cousin to socialism and Marxism." – *Great Betrayal*, pg. 44

"One irritant in the discussion over trade policy is the penchant for free trade proponents to devolve all arguments to micro-level concerns. 'What is prudence in the conduct of every private family,' wrote Adam Smith, 'can scarce be folly in that of a great kingdom.' To equate the decisions of a 'private family' with those of a 'great kingdom' is absurd. A great nation can and will prudently borrow from itself–as America did in two world wars–and go into debt for generations. No family can do that. Families are natural friends, while nations are rivals, antagonists, and often mortal enemies. To compare a family's dependence on a grocer or gas station to a nation's dependence on imported food or OPEC oil is folly for a leader and suicidal for a country." – *Great Betrayal*, p. 45

"The winners in a world of free trade and floating exchange rates are regimes whose central bankers manipulate currency values for national benefit, and a global corporate elite that can shift production from one country to another and calls no country home. Losers are the rooted people, the conservative people tied by the bonds of family, memory, and neighborhood to one community and one country." – *Great Betrayal*, pg. 57

"Free-trade ideology is thus a product of a shift in perspective, from a God-centered universe to a man-centered one. It finds its intellectual roots in the minds of men, most of whom were pacifists and atheists and looked to the end of empires and nations in a brave new world in which the buying and selling of earthly goods would bring mankind as close to paradise as these Utopians believed was possible. It is remarkable that Godly men and women celebrate such dogmas and such dogmatists!" – *Great Betrayal*, pg. 201

"What is wrong with the Global Economy is what is wrong with our politics: it is rooted in the myth of Economic Man. It elevates economics above all. But man does not live by bread alone. In a true nation many things are place on a higher altar than maximum efficiency or a maximum variety of consumer goods. Once, conservatives understood that." – *Great Betrayal*, pg. 287

"What do we mean by 'economic nationalism'? We mean tax and trade policies that put America before the Global Economy, and the well-being of our own people before what is best for 'mankind.' Trade is not an end in itself; it is the means to an end, to a more just society and more self-reliant nation. Our trade and tax policies should be designed to strengthen U.S. sovereignty and independence and should manifest a bias toward domestic, rather than foreign, commerce. For, as von Mises said, peaceful commerce binds people together, and Americans should rely more on one another." – *Great Betrayal*, pg. 288.

William F. Buckley

"Democracy's finest bloom is seen only in its natural habitat, the culturally homogeneous community. There, democracy induces harmony. Harmony (not freedom) is democracy's finest flower. Even a politically unstable society of limited personal freedom can be harmonious if governed democratically, if only because the majority understand themselves to be living in the house that they themselves built... The point remains: the claims that are made in behalf of democracy, the showpiece of the Liberal ideology, are illusory, for the attributes imputed to it are wholly extrinsic to democracy itself." – *Up From Liberalism*, pgs. 125-126

Thomas Bulfinch

On patriotism, duty, and sacrifice:
"The principal stay and support of (ancient Troy's) throne was his son Hector, one of the noblest characters painted by heathen antiquity. He felt, from the first, a presentiment of the fall of his country, but still persevered in his heroic resistance [to Greek invasion], yet by no means justified the wrong which brought this danger upon her. He was united in marriage with Andromache, and as a husband and father his character was not less admirable than as a warrior." – *Bulfinch's Mythology*

Henry Bullinger

"Now touching the country wherein every one is born and brought up; every man doth well esteem of it, love it, and wish to advance it; every man doth deck it with his virtue and prowess; every one doth help it with all sorts of benefits, stoutly defending it, and valiantly fighting for it, if need be, to save it from violent robbers. What is, I pray yon, more to be delighted in, than the good platform of a well ordered city, wherein there is (as one did say) the church well grounded; wherein God is rightly worshipped; and wherein the word of God in faith and charity is duly obeyed, so far forth as it pleaseth God to give the gift of grace; wherein also the magistrate doth defend good discipline and upright laws; wherein the citizens are obedient and at unity among themselves, having their assemblies for true religion and matters of justice; wherein they use to have honest meetings in the church, in the court, and places of common exercise; wherein they apply themselves to virtue and the study of learning, seeking an honest living by such sciences as man's life hath need of, by tillage, by merchandise, and other handy occupations; wherein children are honestly trained up, parents recompensed for their pains, the poor maintained of alms, and strangers harboured in their distress? There are therefore in this commonweal virgins, married women, children, old men, matrons, widows, and fatherless children. If any (by the naughty disposition of nature) transgress the laws, they are worthily punished; the guiltless are defended; peace, justice, and civility doth flourish, and is upheld. Now what is he, that can abide to behold such a commonweal, the country where he is born and bred up, to be troubled, vexed, torn, and pulled in pieces, either by seditious citizens or foreign enemies? In civil seditions and foreign wars all virtue and honesty is utterly overthrown, virgins defiled, matrons uncivilly dealt withal, old men derided, and religion destroyed. Wherefore the valiant captain Joab, being ready to fight against the Syrians in defence of his country, speaketh to his brother Abisai, saying: 'If the Syrians be stronger than I, then shalt thou help me; but if the sons of Ammon be too strong for thee, then will I come and aid thee. Be courageous therefore, and let us fight lustily for our people, and for the cities of our God: and let the Lord do the thing that is good in his own eyes.' Moreover Judas Machabeus, a man among the Israelites worthily esteemed, and a famous warrior, and singularly affected toward his country, encouraging his soldiers and countrymen against their enemies, said: 'They come upon us wrongfully in hope of their force, to spoil and make havoc of us, with our wives and children; but we fight for our lives and liberty of our laws, and the Lord will destroy them before our faces.' The people also among themselves, exhorting one another, do cry out and say: 'Let us take this affliction from our people, and let us fight for our nation and our religion.'

"Let not any man make an objection here, and say: 'Tush, these are works pertaining to the law, which we, that are of the church of Christ, have nothing to do withal.' For the apostle Paul, speaking to the Hebrews, as concerning christian faith, doth say: 'These through faith did subdue kingdoms, wrought righteousness, were valiant in fight, and turned to flight the armies of aliants.' Now, since our faith is all one, and the very same with theirs, it is lawful for us, as well as for them, in a rightful quarrel by war to defend our country and religion, our virgins and old men, our wives and children, our liberty and possessions. They are flatly unnatural to their country and countrymen, and do transgress this fifth commandment, whosoever do (under the pretense of religion) forsake their country afflicted with war, not endeavouring to deliver it from barbarous soldiers and foreign nations, even by offering their lives to the push and prick of present death for the safeguard thereof. St John saith: 'By this we know his love, because he gave his life for us; and we ought to give our lives for the brethren.' The hired soldiers, who fight unlawful battles for pay of wages, and sell their bodies for greediness of money, shall judge the men that leave their country in peril and danger. For the one put loss of life and limbs in adventure for gain of a few odd crowns; whereas the other dainty fools and effeminate hearts will not hazard the loss of a limb for their religion, magistrates, wives, children, and all their possessions. What, I beseech you, shall those traitors to their country say in that day, wherein the Lord shall reward the lovers and the unnatural traitors of their country and countrymen; when before their eyes they shall see the Gentiles to excel them in virtue and love to their country-people? Publii Decii, the father and the son, gave their lives freely for the safeguard of the commonweal, and died willingly for the love of

their country. Codrus, the natural and loving king of the Athenians, when he understood by the oracle of Apollo that Athens could not be saved but by the king's death, and that therefore the enemies had given commandment that no man should wound the king; this Codrus laid aside his kinglike furniture, and, clothing himself in base apparel, rushed into the thickest of his enemies, and found the means by egging to provoke one of them perforce to kill him. The two brethren, called Phileni, chose rather to lengthen their country with a mile of ground than to prolong their lives with many days; and therefore did they suffer themselves to be buried alive. But what suffer we for the health and safeguard of our country? Hierocles saith: 'Our country is as it were a certain other god, and our first and chiefest parent.' Wherefore he, that first called our country by the name of patria, did not unadvisedly give it that name, but called it so in respect of the thing which it was indeed; for patria, 'our country,' is derived of pater, 'a father,' and hath his ending or termination in the feminine gender, thereby declaring, that it taketh the name of both the parents. And this reason doth covertly lead us to think that our country, which is but one, ought to be reverenced and loved as well as both our parents, jointly knitting them together, to make them equal in honor.

"Furthermore, we must make our earnest prayer for the safeguard of our country. Babylon was not the country of the Jews; but yet, for because the Jews for their sins were banished by God to Babylon for the space of seventy years, Babylon was counted to them instead of their country. And therefore saith the prophet Jeremy: 'Build up houses, and dwell therein; plant gardens, and eat the fruit thereof; marry wives, and beget sons and daughters, and give them in marriage, that they may get children. Seek the peace of that city to which I do carry you, and pray to the Lord for it; because your peace and safeguard is joined to the peace thereof.' Traitors to their country therefore sin exceedingly, whom the laws of the realm do command their foul offence to be hanged and quartered." – *The Decades of Henry Bullinger: The First and Second Decades.* (T. Harding, Ed.) pgs. 275-279

John Bunyan

"I have been in his family, and have observed him both at home and abroad; and I know what I say of him is the truth. His house is as empty of religion, as the white of an egg is of savour.... Thus say the common people that know him, "A saint abroad, and a devil at home." – *The Pilgrim's Progress, Works* vol. 3, pg. 122

Jacob Burckhardt

"It was regarded as the most sorrowful misfortune conceivable for a polis to become barbarian, be it by sudden overthrow or by gradual penetration by foreigners. Greek cities subject to the Persian Empire fell into this category, as when Ephesus was being overrun by foreigners in about 408 B.C., when Persians quartered there and Lydians rapidly infiltrated, until Lysander appeared and by redirecting commerce, establishing shipyards, and other measures, again assured predominance to Greek life. ... From here it was but a short step to the glorifications of the barbarians. This was in part motivated by a longing for inchoate conditions of life, a longing found at times in the late and highly refined periods of every culture, and it is significant that one expects to find such conditions in lands far away. At that time it was fashionable to single out the primitive people in Homer and Aeschylus, like the glorious Hippemolgoi, the law-abiding Scythians, or the Abioi, a fabulous tribe of the north and the most just of all peoples, for even in early antiquity men knew the central portions of the world so well that they sought goodness and happiness on its margins. Such notions gradually turned into rationalizations. The barbarians were supposed to have profound religious insight; in the temple of Asclepius in Aegium a Sidonian contended in the presence of Pausanias that the Phoenicians understood divine matter better than the Greeks did. Whereas formerly the fabulous Hyperboreans had been credited with prodigious piety, now barbarians in general were praised for their piety, in contrast to the growing godlessness of the Greeks. Finally, the barbarians were considered to be morally superior; the late Greek thought of his own nation much as Machiavelli did of the Italians. And the inevitable conclusion was that if the barbarians were departed, the Greeks had corrupted them." – *History of Greek Culture*, pgs. 121-122

Edmund Burke

"A nation is not an idea only of local extent, and individual momentary aggregation; but it is an idea of continuity, which extends in time as well as in numbers and in space. And this is a choice not of one day, or one set of people, not a tumultuary and giddy choice; it is a deliberate election of ages and of generations; it is a constitution made by what is ten thousand times better than choice, it is made by the peculiar circumstances, occasions, tempers, dispositions, and moral, civil, and social habitudes of the people which disclose themselves only in a long space of time. Nor is prescription of government formed upon blind, unmeaning prejudices—for man is a most unwise and a most wise being. The individual is foolish; the multitude, for the moment, is foolish, when they act without deliberation; but the species is wise, and, when time is given to it, as a species it always acts right." – speech in the House of Commons, 7th May 1782; *The Works of Edmund Burke* vol. 10, pg. 97

"The happiness...found by virtue in all [social] conditions...[is] the true moral equality of mankind, and not in that monstrous fiction, which, by inspiring false ideas and vain expectations into men destined to travel in the obscure walk of laborious life, serves only to aggravate and embitter that real inequality, which it never can remove; and which the order of civil life establishes as much for the benefit of those whom it must leave in an humbled state, as those whom it is able to exalt to a condition more splendid, but not more happy." – *Reflections on the Revolution in France, Works*, pg. 38

"The blood of man should never be shed but to redeem the blood of man. It is well shed for our family, for our friends, for our God, for our country, for our kind. The rest is vanity; the rest is crime." – *Reflections on the Revolution in France*; quoted in *A Genius Reconsidered*, pg. 202

"You will observe, that from Magna Carta to the Declaration of Right, it has been the uniform policy of our constitution to claim and assert our liberties, as an entailed inheritance derived to us from our forefathers, and to be transmitted to our posterity; as an estate specially belonging to the people of this kingdom without any reference whatever to any other more general or prior right. By this means our constitution preserves a unity in so great a diversity of its parts. We have an inheritable crown; an inheritable peerage; and a House of Commons and a people inheriting privileges, franchises, and liberties, from a long line of ancestors.

"This policy appears to me to be the result of profound reflection; or rather the happy effect of following nature, which is wisdom without reflection, and above it. A spirit of innovation is generally the result of a selfish temper and confined views. People will not look forward to posterity, who never look backward to their ancestors. Besides, the people of England well know, that the idea of inheritance furnishes a sure principle of conservation, and a sure principle of transmission; without at all excluding a principle of improvement. It leaves acquisition free; but it secures what it acquires. Whatever advantages are obtained by a state proceeding on these maxims, are locked fast as in a sort of family settlement; grasped as in a kind of mortmain for ever. By a constitutional policy, working after the pattern of nature, we receive, we hold, we transmit our government and our privileges, in the same manner in which we enjoy and transmit our property and our lives. The institutions of policy, the goods of fortune, the gifts of Providence, are handed down, to us, and from us, in the same course and order. Our political system is placed in a just correspondence and symmetry with the order of the world, and with the mode of existence decreed to a permanent body composed of transitory parts; wherein, by the disposition of a stupendous wisdom, moulding together the great mysterious incorporation of the human race, the whole, at one time, is never old, or middle-aged, or young, but in a condition of unchangeable constancy, moves on through the varied tenour of perpetual decay, fall, renovation, and progression. Thus, by preserving the method of nature in the conduct of the state, in what we improve we are never wholly new; in what we retain we are never wholly obsolete. By adhering in this manner and on those principles to our forefathers, we are guided not by the superstition of antiquarians, but by the spirit of philosophic analogy. In this choice of inheri-

tance we have given to our frame of polity the image of a relation in blood; binding up the constitution of our country with our dearest domestic ties; adopting our fundamental laws into the bosom of our family affections; keeping inseparable, and cherishing with the warmth of all their combined and mutually reflected charities, our state, our hearths, our sepulchers, and our altars.

— Edmund Burke —

"Through the same plan of a conformity to nature in our artificial institutions, and by calling in the aid of her unerring and powerful instincts to fortify the fallible and feeble contrivances of our reason, we have derived several other, and those no small, benefits from considering our liberties in the light of an inheritance. Always acting as if in the presence of canonized forefathers, the spirit of freedom, leading in itself to misrule and excess, is tempered with an awful gravity. This idea of a liberal descent inspires us with a sense of habitual native dignity which prevents that upstart insolence almost inevitably adhering to and disgracing those who are the first acquirers of any distinction. By this means our liberty becomes a noble freedom.

"It carries an imposing and majestic aspect. It has a pedigree and illustrating ancestors. It has its bearings and its ensigns armorial. It has its gallery of portraits, its monumental inscriptions, its records, evidences, and titles. We procure reverence to our civil institutions on the principle upon which nature teaches us to revere individual men: on account of their age and on account of those from whom they are descended. All your sophisters cannot produce anything better adapted to preserve a rational and manly freedom than the course that we have pursued, who have chosen our nature rather than our speculations, our breasts rather than our inventions, for the great conservatories and magazines of our rights and privileges." – *Reflections on the Revolution in France*, pgs. 34-35

"We are not the converts of Rousseau; we are not the disciples of Voltaire; Helvetius has made no progress amongst us. Atheists are not our preachers; madmen are not our lawgivers. We know that we have made no discoveries, and we think that no discoveries are to be made in morality, nor many in the great principles of government, nor in the ideas of liberty, which were understood long before we were born, altogether as well as they will be after the grace has heaped its mold upon our presumption and the silent tomb shall have imposed its law on our pert loquacity. In England we have not yet been completely embowelled of our natural entrails; we still feel within us, and we cherish and cultivate, those inbred sentiments which are the faithful guardians, the active monitors of our duty, the true supporters of all liberal and manly morals. We have not been drawn and trussed, in order that we may be filled, like stuffed birds in a museum, with chaff and rags and paltry blurred shreds of paper about the rights of men. We preserve the whole of our feelings still native and entire, unsophisticated by pedantry and infidelity. We have real hearts of flesh and blood beating in our bosoms. We fear God; we look up with awe to kings, with affection to parliaments, with duty to magistrates, with reverence to priests, and with respect to nobility. Why? Because when such ideas are brought before our minds, it is natural to be so affected; because all other feelings are false and spurious and tend to corrupt our minds, to vitiate our primary morals, to render us unfit for rational liberty." – *Reflections On The Revolution In France*, pg. 87

"There ought to be a system of manners in every nation which a well-formed mind would be disposed to relish. To make us love our country, our country ought to be lovely." – *Reflections On The Revolution In France*, pg. 100

"Dark and inscrutable are the ways by which we come into the world. The instincts which give rise to this mysterious process of nature are not of our making. But out of physical causes, unknown to us, perhaps unknowable, arise moral duties, which, as we are able perfectly to comprehend, we are bound indispensably to perform. Parents may not be consenting to their moral relation; but consenting or not, they are bound to a long train of burdensome duties towards those with whom they have never made a convention of any sort. Children are not consenting to their relation, but their relation, without their actual consent, binds them to its duties; or rather it implies their consent because the presumed consent of every rational creature is in unison with the predisposed order of things. Men come in that manner into a community with the social state of their parents, endowed with all the benefits, loaded with all the duties of their situation. If the social ties and ligaments, spun out of those physical relations which are the elements of the commonwealth, in most cases begin, and always continue, independently of our will, so without any stipulation, on our part, are we bound by that relation called our country, which comprehends (as it has been well said) 'all the charities of all.' Nor are we left without powerful instincts to make this duty as dear and grateful to us, as it is awful and coercive. Our country is not a thing of mere physical locality. It consists, in a great measure, in the antient order into which we are born. We may have the same geographical situation, but another country; as we may have the same country in another soil. The place that determines our duty to our country is a social, civil relation." – *An Appeal from the New to the Old Whigs August, Select Specimens of English Prose*, pg. 603

"A nation is not only an idea of local extent, and individual momentary aggregation, but it is an idea of continuity, which extends in time as well as in numbers and in space. And this is a choice not of one day, or of one set of people, not a tumultuary and giddy choice. It is a deliberate election of ages and of generations. It is a constitution made by what is ten thousand times better than choice: It is made by the peculiar circumstances, occasions, tempers, dispositions, and moral, civil and social habitudes of the people, which disclose themselves only in a long space of time." – Speech before the House of Commons, May 7, 1782

Gilbert Burnet

Burnet's catechism asks,
  "Question: But who is your neighbor?
  Answer: Every man, of what Nation or Religion soever he may happen to be.
  Question: Must you love all these alike?
  Answer: NO. I must make a difference, according to the Degree of their worth, and of the Image of God that I see in them; and according to the Relation God has placed me in to them."
– *Exposition of the Church Catechism*, pg. 105

James Burnham

"What distinguishes the globalist abstractions from genuine internationalist ideas is precisely their divorce from technical, social and historical realities. There are three billion plus human beings now living on the face of the earth, but there is no Humanity: that is to say, actual human beings, though they may share a metaphysical and theological identity, do not in point of fact have common psychological, social and historical traits that link them into an operative social grouping that we may name 'Humanity.' In real life men are joined on a much less than universal scale into a variety of groupings—family, community, church, business, club, party, etc.—which on the political scale reach the maximum significant limit in the nation." – *The War We Are In*, pg. 138

"Selectivity is a built-in feature of conservatism... conservatives are tribal—let us not pretend on this score...Conservatives are not indifferent to family, home, neighborhood, party, community, church, school, country, to all the interlinked ties that form man's existential context. They do not, like rationalists, dismiss these ties as prejudice and superstition, but find the meaning of human life in and with and through them. At heart (and the heart, too, has its reasons) even the most sophisticated conservatives are peasants, Norman Rockwell types." – quoted by Sam Francis in *Burnham Agonistes*, Chronicles, 2017

Robert Burns

"My dear, my native soil! For whom my warmest wish to Heav'n is sent, Long may thy hardy sons of rustic toil Be blest with health, and peace, and sweet content."
– *The Cotter's Saturday Night, Works*, pg. 26

Paul Bushkovitch

"Two methods are most common: to project into the past the modern forms of national consciousness (the approach of all nineteenth-century writers), or to despair at the distortion introduced by that approach and then deny the existence of any national consciousness in Russia at all before the eighteenth century. Neither position need be taken, however. Russians of the sixteenth and seventeenth century had a defined national consciousness, even if it did not take the same form as the national consciousness of Pushkin, Alexander III, or Lenin."
– *Harvard Ukrainian Studies*, pg. 355

Prescott Bush

"I never was a free trader. I never felt that we could abolish tariffs and do away with all protective devices, because we would have been flooded with imports which would have hurt our economy, hurt our defense posture, and I felt that these things had to be done gradually, selectively." – Interview, September 26, 1966, *Columbia University Oral History Project; Trade Policy Outlook Past as Prologue*, pg. 6

H.L. Dudley Buxton

"Long before Hellenic civilization had developed the inhabitants of the Greek world appear.... similar generally the inhabitants of that area today." – *The Inhabitants*, pg. 111

Lord Byron

"I can't but say it is an awkward sight To see one's native land receding through The growing waters; it unman's one quite, Especially when life is rather new." – *Don Juan*, pg. 43

"Yon Sun that sets upon the sea We follow in his flight; Farewell awhile to him and thee, My native land–Good Night!" – *Childe Harold's Pilgrimage, Poetical Works*, pg. 18

The isles of Greece! the isles of Greece
    Where burning Sappho loved and sung,
  Where grew the arts of war and peace,
    Where Delos rose, and Phoebus sprung!
  Eternal summer gilds them yet,
  But all, except their sun, is set.
  The Scian and the Teian muse,

The hero's harp, the lover's lute,
Have found the fame your shores refuse:
    Their place of birth alone is mute
To sounds which echo further west
Than your sires' 'Islands of the Blest'.
The mountains look on Marathon—
    And Marathon looks on the sea;
And musing there an hour alone,
    I dream'd that Greece might still be free;
For standing on the Persians' grave,
I could not deem myself a slave.
A king sate on the rocky brow
    Which looks o'er sea-born Salamis;
And ships, by thousands, lay below,
    And men in nations;—all were his!
He counted them at break of day—
And when the sun set, where were they?
And where are they? and where art thou,
    My country? On thy voiceless shore
The heroic lay is tuneless now—
    The heroic bosom beats no more!
And must thy lyre, so long divine,
Degenerate into hands like mine?
'Tis something in the dearth of fame,
    Though link'd among a fetter'd race,
To feel at least a patriot's shame,
    Even as I sing, suffuse my face;
For what is left the poet here?
For Greeks a blush—for Greece a tear.
Must we but weep o'er days more blest?
    Must we but blush?—Our fathers bled.
Earth! render back from out thy breast
    A remnant of our Spartan dead!
Of the three hundred grant but three,
To make a new Thermopylae!
What, silent still? and silent all?
    Ah! no;—the voices of the dead
Sound like a distant torrent's fall,
    And answer, 'Let one living head,
But one, arise,—we come, we come!'
'Tis but the living who are dumb.
In vain—in vain: strike other chords;
    Fill high the cup with Samian wine!
Leave battles to the Turkish hordes,
    And shed the blood of Scio's vine:
Hark! rising to the ignoble call—
How answers each bold Bacchanal!
You have the Pyrrhic dance as yet;
    Where is the Pyrrhic phalanx gone?
Of two such lessons, why forget
    The nobler and the manlier one?
You have the letters Cadmus gave—
Think ye he meant them for a slave?

Fill high the bowl with Samian wine!
    We will not think of themes like these!
It made Anacreon's song divine:
    He served—but served Polycrates—
A tyrant; but our masters then
Were still, at least, our countrymen.
The tyrant of the Chersonese
    Was freedom's best and bravest friend;
That tyrant was Miltiades!
    O that the present hour would lend
Another despot of the kind!
Such chains as his were sure to bind.
Fill high the bowl with Samian wine!
    On Suli's rock, and Parga's shore,
Exists the remnant of a line
    Such as the Doric mothers bore;
And there, perhaps, some seed is sown,
The Heracleidan blood might own.
Trust not for freedom to the Franks—
    They have a king who buys and sells;
In native swords and native ranks
    The only hope of courage dwells:
But Turkish force and Latin fraud
Would break your shield, however broad.
Fill high the bowl with Samian wine!
    Our virgins dance beneath the shade—
I see their glorious black eyes shine;
    But gazing on each glowing maid,
My own the burning tear-drop laves,
To think such breasts must suckle slaves.
Place me on Sunium's marbled steep,
    Where nothing, save the waves and I,
May hear our mutual murmurs sweep;
    There, swan-like, let me sing and die:
A land of slaves shall ne'er be mine—
Dash down yon cup of Samian wine!
– *The Isles of Greece*

C

Edward Cahill

"Its Foundation and Nature. Patriotism is a branch or subdivision of Piety. Piety is the virtue which inclines one to render due honour and service to those that are the source of one's being, and the agents or authors of one's upbringing and education. Now, since God is the primary source of man's being and of all the good he has, the first duties of piety are towards God. These duties, however, by reason of their transcendent excellence, are usually classed apart, under the special name of Religion, and the term Piety is confined to one's obligations towards those that are the secondary or immediate source of one's being and education. Principal among these are one's parents and the country or civil society amid which one was born and brought up. [22]

"Obligations of piety extend in due proportion, directly or indirectly, to parents, relatives, fellow-countrymen, and to all persons closely connected with these.... Patriotism may be defined as the virtue which inclines one to love and serve the country to which one belongs. The existence of the strong natural instinct which we have already described, and which God has implanted so deeply in the human heart, goes far to show that man is bound by the natural law to love and serve the civil society with which he is naturally identified, just as he is bound to love and, when necessary, to assist his parents and his own immediate family. Besides the ties of origin upon which the virtue of Patriotism primarily rests, there are other kindred relations between a citizen and his country to which St. Thomas frequently refers, in connexion with the civic virtues (Virtutes Politicae), which latter he identifies, at least partially, with the virtue of Patriotism. His doctrine is briefly this: The part tends instinctively to seek the good of the whole to which it naturally belongs, rather than its own. This tendency, which belongs to all creatures, points unmistakably, in the case of rational beings, to a dictate of the natural law, and hence it may be taken as the guide in determining the citizen's duty of service to his country. For, within certain limitations, the country or State may be compared to the human body, and the citizens or members of the State to the parts or members of that body. In other words the State is, or may be, a natural whole of which citizens or members are the parts..." – *The Framework of a Christian State*, pgs. 485-486

"Our Divine Lord Himself, who possessed all virtues in perfection, must have had in His human soul the virtue of Piety in all its fullness. Consequently, just as He had an intense filial affection for His Blessed Mother and for His foster-father, St. Joseph, and just as He must have loved in a special way His cousins, who are called in the Gospel history the 'Brothers of the Lord,' so also there can be no doubt that, in accordance with reasonable human tendencies, He esteemed in a special way the land of His birth and the home of His race, and that He cherished with a peculiar love the Jewish nation, in whose bosom He was born and grew to manhood. He burst into tears on one occasion when, seeing the beauty and grandeur of the city of His people, He thought of the awful fate that would overtake it. 'Seeing the city, He wept over it. ... "For the days shall come upon thee," He cried, "and thy enemies shall cast a trench round about thee, and compass thee round, and straiten thee on every side, and beat thee flat to the ground, and shall not leave in thee a stone upon a stone."'

"One may say, indeed, that our Divine Lord's special grief for the obstinacy and consequent destruction of the people of Jerusalem may be partially or principally explained by the fact

---

22   Cahill proceeds to quote Aquinas to this effect.

that He saw in Jerusalem a type of the human soul hardened in sin; but it is also reasonable to hold that in the words and incidents here referred to, He gives expression to a special love for the Jewish nation, founded upon natural human ties, a type of love which He wishes not to be destroyed, but elevated and sanctified by the addition of supernatural motives.

"Hence, when St. Paul says that in the Church there is neither 'Gentile nor Jew...Barbarian or Scythian, bond or free, but Christ, all in all'...he does not imply that the Church wishes to abolish or ignore the natural ties which bind individuals to their own country, no more than she would wish to abolish family ties or distinction of sex, or even reasonable distinctions of class, all of which are necessary for the good of the human race. He means rather, that just as the Church, while consecrating and upholding domestic ties and obligations, nevertheless, receives equally into her fold the members of every family, so also she receives and cherishes impartially the citizens of all nations, for all are equally dear to her Founder. She receives all into her fold, and binds together the members of the various nationalities into a single brotherhood, realizing the ideal of the Brotherhood of Man in the only way it can ever be realized on earth." – *The Framework of a Christian State*, pgs. 57-58

Calgacus

"Children and kin are by the law of nature each man's dearest possessions...but we shall fight as men untamed, men who have never fallen from freedom, not as returning penitents: let us show them at the very first encounter what manner of men Caledonia holds in reserve for her cause in her far places. On, then, into action and, as you go, think of those who went before you and of those that shall come after.

"Or do you imagine that the Romans have as much courage in war as wantonness in peace? It is our dissensions and feuds that bring them fame: their enemy's mistake becomes their army's glory. That army, gathered from races widely separate, is held together only by success, and will melt away with defeat: unless you suppose that Gauls and Germans, and even—to their shame be it spoken—many of the tribes of Britain, who lend their blood to an alien tyranny, of which they have been enemies for

more years than slaves, are attached to Rome by loyalty and liking. Fear and panic are sorry bonds of love: put these away, and they who have ceased to fear will begin to hate...Here you have a general and an army; on the other side lies tribute, labour in the mines, and all the other pangs of slavery. You have it in your power to perpetuate your sufferings for ever or to avenge them to-day upon this field: therefore, before you go into action, think upon your ancestors and upon your children." – excerpt from Calgacus' speech as recorded by Tacitus in *Agricola*, pgs. 223-225

John C. Calhoun

"What is that constitution of our nature, which, while it impels man to associate with his kind, renders it impossible for society to exist without government?

"The answer will be found in the fact (not less incontestable than either of the others) that, while man is created for the social state, and is accordingly so formed as to feel what affects others, as well as what affects himself, he is, at the same time, so constituted as to feel more intensely what affects him directly, than what affects him indirectly though others; or, to express it differently, he is so constituted, that his direct or individual affections are stronger than his sympathetic or social feelings....If reversed — if their feelings and affections were stronger for others than for themselves, or even as strong, the necessary result would seem to be, that all individuality would be lost; and boundless and remediless disorder and confusion would ensue. For each, at the same moment, intensely participating in all the conflicting emotions of those around him, would, of course, forget himself and all that concerned him immediately, in his officious intermeddling with the affairs of all others; which, from his limited reason and faculties, he could neither properly understand nor manage. Such a state of things would, as far as we can see, lead to endless disorder and confusion, not less destructive to our race than a state of anarchy. It would, besides, be remediless — for government would be impossible; or, if it could by possibility exist, its object would be reversed." – *Disquisition On Government* – *John C. Calhoun Selected Writings and Speeches*, pgs. 2-4

"I know further, sir, that we have never dreamt

of incorporating into our Union any but the Caucasian race–the free white race. To incorporate Mexico, would be the very first instance of the kind of incorporating an Indian race; for more than half of the Mexicans are Indians, and the other is composed chiefly of mixed tribes. I protest against such a union as that! Ours, sir, is the Government of a white race."– *Speech on the War With Mexico, The Papers of John C. Calhoun* vol. 25, pg. 64

— JOHN C. CALHOUN —

"Liberty, then, when forced on a people unfit for it, would, instead of a blessing, be a curse; as it would, in its reaction, lead directly to anarchy — the greatest of all curses. No people, indeed, can long enjoy more liberty than that to which their situation and advanced intelligence and morals fairly entitle them. If more than this be allowed, they must soon fall into confusion and disorder — to be followed, if not by anarchy and despotism, by a change to a form of government more simple and absolute; and, therefore, better suited to their condition. And hence, although it may be true, that a people may not have as much liberty as they are fairly entitled to, and are capable of enjoying — yet the reverse is questionably true — that no people can long possess more than they are fairly entitled to…

"It follows, from what has been stated, that it is a great and dangerous error to suppose that all people are equally entitled to liberty. It is a reward to be earned, not a blessing to be gratuitously lavished on all alike — a reward

reserved for the intelligent, the patriotic, the virtuous and deserving — and not a boon to be bestowed on a people too ignorant, degraded and vicious, to be capable either of appreciating or of enjoying it. Nor is it any disparagement to liberty, that such is, and ought to be the case. On the contrary, its greatest praise — its proudest distinction is, that an all-wise Providence has reserved it, as the noblest and highest reward for the development of our faculties, moral and intellectual. A reward more appropriate than liberty could not be conferred on the deserving — nor a punishment inflicted on the undeserving more just, than to be subject to lawless and despotic rule. This dispensation seems to be the result of some fixed law — and every effort to disturb or defeat it, by attempting to elevate a people in the scale of liberty, above the point to which they are entitled to rise, must ever prove abortive, and end in disappointment. The progress of a people rising from a lower to a higher point in the scale of liberty, is necessarily slow — and by attempting to precipitate, we either retard, or permanently defeat it." – *Disquisition On Government – John C. Calhoun Selected Writings and Speeches*, pgs. 31-32

"[Man's] natural state is, the social and political — the one for which his Creator made him, and the only one in which he can preserve and perfect his race." – *Disquisition On Government – John C. Calhoun Selected Writings and Speeches*, pg. 33

"The human race is not comprehended in a single society or community. The limited reason and faculties of man, the great diversity of language, customs, pursuits, situation and complexion, and the difficulty of intercourse, with various other causes, have, by their operation, formed a great many separate communities, acting independently of each other. Between these there is the same tendency to conflict — and from the same constitution of our nature — as between men individually; and even stronger — because the sympathetic or social feelings are not so strong between different communities, as between individuals of the same community. So powerful, indeed, is this tendency, that it has led to almost incessant wars between contiguous communities for plunder and conquest, or to avenge injuries, real or supposed." – *Disquisition On Government – John C. Calhoun Selected Writings and Speeches*, pg. 6

"Taking the proposition literally (it is in that sense it is understood), there is not a word of truth in it. It begins with 'all men are born,' which is utterly untrue. Men are not born. Infants are born. They grow to be men. And concludes with asserting that they are born 'free and equal,' which is not less false. They are not born free. While infants they are incapable of freedom, being destitute alike of the capacity of thinking and acting, without which there can be no freedom. Besides, they are necessarily born subject to their parents, and remain so among all people, savage and civilized, until the development of their intellect and physical capacity enables them to take care of themselves. They grow to all the freedom of which the condition in which they were born permits, by growing to be men. Nor is it less false that they are born 'equal.' They are not so in any sense in which it can be regarded; and thus, as I have asserted, there is not a word of truth in the whole proposition, as expressed and generally understood." – *Speech on the Oregon Bill – Works of John C. Calhoun*, vol. 4, pg. 507

"It follows from all this that the quantum of power on the part of the government, and of liberty on that of individuals, instead of being equal in all cases, must necessarily be very unequal among different people, according to their different conditions. For just in proportion as a people are ignorant, stupid, debased, corrupt, exposed to violence within and danger from without, the power necessary for government to possess, in order to preserve society against anarchy and destruction becomes greater and greater, and individual liberty less and less, until the lowest condition is reached, when absolute and despotic power becomes necessary on the part of the government, and individual liberty extinct." – *Speech on the Oregon Bill – Works of John C. Calhoun*, vol. 4, pg. 511

"Instead, then, of all men having the same right to liberty and equality, as is claimed by those who hold that they are all born free and equal, liberty is the noble and highest reward bestowed on mental and moral development, combined with favorable circumstances. Instead, then, of liberty and equality being born with man; instead of all men and all classes and descriptions being equally entitled to them, they are high

prizes to be won, and are in their most perfect state, not only the highest reward that can be bestowed on our race, but the most difficult to be won—and when won, the most difficult to be preserved." – *Speech on the Oregon Bill – Works of John C. Calhoun*, vol. 4, pg. 511

"If we trace it back, we shall find the proposition differently expressed in the Declaration of Independence. That asserts that 'all men are created equal.' The form of expression, though less dangerous, is not less erroneous. All men are not created. According to the Bible, only two, a man and a woman, ever were, and of these one was pronounced subordinate to the other. All others have come into the world by being born, and in no sense, as I have shown, either free or equal." – *Speech on the Oregon Bill – Works of John C. Calhoun*, vol. 4, pg. 508

"We cannot…be indifferent to dangers from abroad, unless,…[Congress] is prepared to indulge in the phantom of eternal peace, which seemed to possess the dream of some of its members." – quoted in Meriwether, *The Papers of John C. Calhoun*, 1:348-49. [23]

John Calvin

"If ignorance of God is to be looked for anywhere, surely one is most likely to find an example of it among the more backward folk and those more remote from civilization. Yet there is, as the eminent pagan says, no nation [gens] so barbarous [i.e., 'animalistic'], no people so savage, that they have not a deep-seated conviction that there is a God. And they who in other aspects of life seem least to differ from brutes [i.e., 'wild beasts'] still continue to retain some seed of religion." – *Institutes of the Christian Religion*, 1.1.3, pg. 44

"Now, since Christ has shown in the parable of the Samaritan that the term 'neighbor' includes even the most remote person [Luke 10:36], we are not expected to limit the precept of love to those in close relationships. I do not deny that the more closely a man is linked to us, the more intimate obligation we have to assist him. It is the common habit of mankind that the more closely men are bound together by the ties of kinship, of acquaintanceship, or of neighbor-

23 Speaking in defense of the Tariff of 1826

hood, the more responsibilities for one another they share. This does not offend God; for his providence, as it were, leads us to it. But I say: we ought to embrace the whole human race without exception in a single feeling of love; here there is no distinction between barbarian and Greek, worthy and unworthy, friend and enemy, since all should be contemplated in God, not in themselves." – *Institutes of the Christian Religion*, 2.8.55, pg. 418

"There is no piety towards God, when a person can thus lay aside the feelings of humanity. Would faith, which makes us the sons of God, render us worse than brute beasts? Such inhumanity, therefore, is open contempt of God, and denying of the faith.

"Not content with this, Paul heightens the criminality of their conduct, by saying, that he who forgets his own is worse than an infidel. This is true for two reasons. First, the further advanced any one is in the knowledge of God, the less is he excused; and therefore, they who shut their eyes against the clear light of God are worse than infidels. Secondly, this is a kind of duty which nature itself teaches; for they are (st-orgai phusikai) natural affections. And if, by the mere guidance of nature, infidels are so prone to love their own, what must we think of those who are not moved by any such feeling? Do they not go even beyond the ungodly in brutality?" – *Commentary on 1 Timothy* 5:8, pg. 127

"By language, we know, not only words, but also feelings are communicated. Language is the expression of the mind, as it is commonly said, and it is therefore the bond of society. Had there been no language, in what would men differ from brute beasts? One would barbarously treat another; there would indeed be no humanity among them. As then language conciliates men one towards another, the Prophet, in order to terrify the Jews, says that that nation would be barbarous, for there would be no communication made with it by means of a language." – *Commentary on Jeremiah* 5:15, pg. 286

"Lo, I will bring a nation upon you from far, O house of Israel, saith the Lord: it is a mighty nation, it is an ancient nation, a nation whose language thou knowest not, neither understandest what they say." – *Sermon on Jeremiah* 5:15

"Now, we see, as in a camp, every troop and band hath his appointed place, so men are placed upon earth, that every people may be content with their bounds, and that among these people every particular person may have his mansion. But though ambition have, oftentimes raged, and many, being incensed with wicked lust, have passed their bounds, yet the lust of men hath never brought to pass, but that God hath governed all events from out of his holy sanctuary. For though men, by raging upon earth, do seem to assault heaven, that they may overthrow God's providence, yet they are enforced, whether they will or no, rather to establish the same. Therefore, let us know that the world is so turned over through divers tumults, that God doth at length bring all things unto the end which he hath appointed." – *Commentary on Acts* 17:26, pg. 165

"For when he saith that the times were ordained before by him, he doth testify that he had determined, before men were created, what their condition and estate should be. When we see divers changes in the world; when we see realms come to ruin, lands altered, cities destroyed, nations laid waste, we foolishly imagine that either fate or fortune beareth the swing in these matters; but God doth testify in this place by the mouth of Paul, that it was appointed before in his counsel how long he would have the state of every people to continue, and within what bounds he would have them contained. But and if he have appointed them a certain time and appointed the bounds of countries, undoubtedly he hath also set in order the whole course of their life." – *Commentary on Acts* 17:26, pg. 165

"Political and outward order is widely different from spiritual government." – *Commentary on Matthew* 19:7, pg. 382

"Now, although all mankind had been formed for the worship of God, and therefore sincere religion ought everywhere to have reigned; yet since the greater part had prostituted itself, either to an entire contempt of God, or to depraved superstitions; it was fitting that the small portion which God had adopted, by special privilege, to himself, should remain separate from others. It was, therefore, base ingratitude in the posterity of Seth, to mingle themselves with the children of Cain, and with other profane races; because they voluntarily deprived themselves of the inestimable grace of God. For it was an intolerable profanation, to pervert, and to confound, the order appointed by God. It seems at first sight frivolous, that the sons of God should be so severely condemned, for having chosen for themselves beautiful wives from the daughters of men. But we must know first, that it is not a light crime to violate a distinction established by the Lord.

"That ancient figment, concerning the intercourse of angels with women, is abundantly refuted by its own absurdity; and it is surprising that learned men should formerly have been fascinated by ravings so gross and prodigious. The opinion also of the Chaldean paraphrase is frigid; namely, that promiscuous marriages between the sons of nobles, and the daughters of plebeians, is condemned. Moses, then, does not distinguish the sons of God from the daughters of men, because they were of dissimilar nature, or of different origin; but because they were the sons of God by adoption, whom he had set apart for himself; while the rest remained in their original condition." – *Commentary on Genesis 6:1, in Commentaries vol. 1, pg. 238*

"Regarding our eternal salvation it is true that one must not distinguish between man and woman, or between king and a shepherd, or between a German and a Frenchman. Regarding policy however, we have what St. Paul declares here; for our Lord Jesus Christ did not come to mix up nature, or to abolish what belongs to the preservation of decency and peace among us.... Regarding the kingdom of God (which is spiritual) there is no distinction or difference between man and woman, servant and master, poor and rich, great and small. Nevertheless, there does have to be some order among us, and Jesus Christ did not mean to eliminate it, as some flighty and scatterbrained dreamers [believe]." – *Sermon on 1 Corinthians 11:2-3, in Calvin's Political Theology, pg. 165*

"All are not created on equal terms ... This God has testified, not only in the case of single individuals; He has also given a specimen of it in the whole posterity of Abraham, to make it plain that the future condition of each nation was entirely at His disposal." – *Institutes, vol. 2, Book 3.21.5, pg. 289*

"It may seem that Abram was unjust to the Egyptians, in suspecting evil of them, from whom he had yet received no injury. And, since charity truly is not suspicious; he may appear to deal unfairly, in not only charging them with lust, but also in suspecting them of murder. I answer, that the holy man did, not without reason, fear for himself from that nation, concerning which he had heard many unfavorable reports. And already he had, in other places, experienced so much of the wickedness of men, that he might justly apprehend everything from the profane despisers of God. He does not however pronounce anything absolutely concerning the Egyptians; but, wishing to bring his wife to his own opinion, he gives her timely warning of what might happen. *And God, while he commands us to abstain from malicious and sinister judgments, yet allows to be on our guard against unknown persons; and this may take place without any injury to the brethren.* Yet I do not deny that this trepidation of Abram exceeded all bounds and that an unreasonable anxiety caused him to involve himself in another fault, as we have already stated. Although Abram had sinned by fearing too much and too soon, yet the event teaches, that he had not feared without cause: for his wife was taken from him and brought to the king." – *Commentary on Genesis 12:11-13, pg. 361*

"The sweetness of their native soil holds nearly all men bound to itself." – *Commentary on Genesis 12:1, pg. 343*

"Delightful to every one is his native soil, and it is also delightful to dwell among one's own people . . . all his relatives and the nation from which he sprang." – *Commentary on Jeremiah 9:2, pg. 459*

"Among men, in proportion to the closeness of the tie that mutually binds us, some have stronger claims than others." – *Commentary on Matthew 10:37, pg. 471*

"...There is a twofold government in man...the one which, placed in the soul or inward man, relates to eternal life, [but] we are here called to say something of the other, which pertains only to civil institutions and the external regulation of manners... [F]rantic and barbarous men are furiously endeavouring to overturn the order established by God, and, on the other, the flatterers of princes, extolling their power without measure, hesitate not to oppose it to the government of God. Unless we meet both extremes, the purity of the faith will perish. We may add, that it in no small degree concerns us to know how kindly God has here consulted for the human race, that pious zeal may the more strongly urge us to testify our gratitude. And first, before entering on the subject itself, it is necessary to attend to the distinction which we formerly laid down (Book 3 ch. 19 sec. 16, et supra, ch. 10), lest, as often happens to many, we imprudently confound these two things, the nature of which is altogether different.

"For some, on hearing that liberty is promised in the gospel, a liberty which acknowledges no king and no magistrate among men, but looks to Christ alone, think that they can receive no benefit from their liberty so long as they see any power placed over them. Accordingly, they think that nothing will be safe until the whole world is changed into a new form, when there will be neither courts, nor laws, nor magistrates, nor anything of the kind to interfere, as they suppose, with their liberty. But he who knows to distinguish between the body and the soul, between the present fleeting life and that which is future and eternal, will have no difficulty in understanding that the spiritual kingdom of Christ and civil government are things very widely separated.

"Seeing, therefore, it is a Jewish vanity to seek and include the kingdom of Christ under the elements of this world, let us, considering, as Scripture clearly teaches, that the blessings which we derive from Christ are spiritual, remember to confine the liberty which is promised and offered to us in him within its proper limits. For why is it that the very same apostle who bids us 'stand fast in the liberty wherewith Christ hath made us free, and be not again entangled with the yoke of bondage' (Gal. 5:1), in another passage forbids slaves to be solicitous about their state (1 Cor. 7:21), unless it be that spiritual liberty is perfectly compatible with civil servitude? In this sense the following passages are to be understood: 'There is neither Jew nor Greek, there is neither bond nor free, there is neither male nor female' (Gal. 3:28). Again, 'There is neither Greek nor Jew, circumcision nor uncircumcision, barbarian, Scythian, bond nor free: but Christ is all and in all' (Col. 3:11).

It is thus intimated, that it matters not what your condition is among men, nor under what laws you live, since in them the kingdom of Christ does not at all consist." – *Institutes*, Book 4, ch. 20, pg. 1168

"Every one who goes beyond the limits of his calling provokes the wrath of God against himself by his rashness. Let every one therefore be satisfied with his lot, and learn not to aim at anything higher, but, on the contrary, to remain in his own rank in which God has placed him. If God stretch out his hand, and lift us up higher, we ought to go forward; but no one ought to take it on himself, or to strive for it from his own choice. And even those who are raised to a higher rank of honor ought to conduct themselves humbly and submissively, not with any pretended modesty, but with minds so thoroughly depressed that nothing can lift them up." – *Commentary on Isaiah* 14.13, pg. 443

"Let us learn that where there is an accepted custom, and it is a good and decent one, we must accept it. And whoever tries to change it is surely the enemy of the common good, and should be held in abomination." – *Sermon on 1 Corinthians* 11:11-16

"Let us perceive that there are wicked nations; let us examine their vices in order to keep ourselves from (learning) them. The French, for example, are more corrupt in their attire than the other nations. Why? Because they have always had the folly of having to dress the body now this way, or the neck now that way – there is no style they have not seen fit to try, and God has condemned them and had them in derision, because of this mad curiosity which they have always had. And it is more in sway today than ever.

"Thus it is true that all the world must be completely corrupt, and everything in it is topsy-turvy now. Yet, be that as it may, we must still take note of the particular vices of the nations, so that we may know how to keep ourselves from them." – *Sermon on 1 Corinthians* 11:11-16, pgs. 55-59

"The inhabitants of Crete, of whom he speaks with such sharpness were undoubtedly very wicked. The Apostle, who is wont to reprove mildly those who deserved to be treated with extreme severity, would never have spoken so harshly of the Cretans, if he had not been moved by very strong reasons. What term more reproachful than these opprobrious epithets can be imagined; that they were 'lazy, devoted to the belly, destitute of truth, evil beasts?' Nor are these vices charged against one or a few persons, but he condemns the whole nation." – *Commentary on Titus* 1:12, pg. 302

—John Calvin—

"Here a question arises, Is perpetual servitude so displeasing to God, that it ought not to be deemed lawful? To this the answer is easy – Abraham and other fathers had servants or slaves according to the common and prevailing custom, and it was not deemed wrong in them. Before the Law was given, there was nothing to forbid one who had servants or maids to exercise power over them through life; and then the Law, mentioned here, was not given indiscriminately and generally, but it was a peculiar privilege in favor of the chosen people. Hence it is without reason that any one infers that it is not lawful to exercise power over servants and maids; for, on the contrary, we may reason thus, That since God permitted the fathers to remain servants and maids, it is a thing lawful; and further, as God permitted the Jews also, under the Law, to bear rule over aliens, and to keep them perpetually as servants, it follows that this cannot be disapproved. And still a clearer evidence may be adduced; for since the Gentiles have been called to the hope of salvation, no change has in this respect been made. For the

Apostles did not constrain masters to liberate their servants, but only exhorted them to use kindness towards them, and to treat them humanely as their fellow-servants. (Ephesians 6:9; Colossians 4:1) If, then, servitude were unlawful, the Apostles would have never tolerated it; but they would have boldly denounced such a profane practice had it been so. Now, as they commanded masters only to be humane towards their servants, and not to treat them violently and reproachfully, it follows that what was not denied was permitted, that is, to retain their own servants. We also see that Paul sent back Onesimus to Philemon. (Philemon 1:12) Philemon was not only one of the faithful, but a pastor of the Church. He ought, then, to have been an example to others. His servant had fled away from him; Paul sent him back, and commended him to his master, and besought his master to forgive his theft. We hence see that the thing in itself is not unlawful.

"Our servitudes have been abolished, that is, that miserable condition when one had no right of his own, but when the master had power over life and death; that custom has ceased, and the abolition cannot be blamed. Some superstition might have been at the beginning; and I certainly think that the commencement of the change arose from superstition. It is, however, by no means to be wished that there should be slaves among us, as there were formerly among all nations, and as there are now among barbarians. The Spaniards know what servitude is, for they are near neighbors to the Africans and the Turks; and then those they take in war they sell; and as one evil proceeds from another, so they retain miserable men as slaves throughout life. But as no necessity constrains us, our condition, as I have said, is better, that is, in having hired servants and not slaves; for those called servants at this day are only hired servants.

"When heathens commended humanity and kindness towards servants, they said, Let them not be treated as servants, but as those who are hired. So also Cicero said. (Off. 1) he distinguished between servants and such as were hired, he calls the first slaves, that is, those who were under the power of another, and those hired servants who undertook to work for hire, as the case is with us.

"But as I have already said, the practice among the chosen people was peculiar. For it was the Lord's will that those whom he had redeemed should remain free and enjoy in this respect the benefits of freedom. That there might then be a memorial of God's favor among the people of Israel, it was the Lord's will that servitude among them should be temporary, even for six years only. And as the law had been disregarded, Zedekiah exhorted the people to set free their servants. But there is no doubt but that God at the same time made it known, that external enemies justly exercised cruelty towards the people, because they themselves shewed no commiseration towards their own brethren. For when they ruled over their servants according to their own wantonness, they in vain complained of the Chaldeans or of the Assyrians, they in vain proclaimed that they were unjustly oppressed, or that the people of God were harassed by the violence of a tyrannical power; for the first originators of cruelty were themselves, and not the Chaldeans or the Assyrians. It was then on this account that Zedekiah was induced to call the people together, and that by a public act all the servants were set free." – *Commentary on Jeremiah 34:8-17, pgs. 282-284*

"In external respects, there is diversity of condition among those with whom, through His agency God enters covenant. But Paul asserts that God's covenant must not be assessed like this as if it contradicted itself or varied on account of the differences in men. As (sicuti [or 'in the same way']) Christ formerly reconciled God to the Jews in making a covenant, so now He is the Mediator of the Gentiles." – *Commentary in Galatians 3:20, pg. 63*

"Since Isaiah reckons this confusion among the curses of God, and declares that, when the distinction of ranks is laid aside, it is a terrible display of the vengeance of God, we ought to conclude, on the other hand, how much God is pleased with regular government and the good order of society, and also how great a privilege it is to have it preserved among us; for when it is taken away, the life of man differs little from the sustenance of cattle and of beasts of prey." – *Commentary on Isaiah 24:2, pg. 167*

"Meanwhile, the political distinction of ranks is not to be repudiated, for natural reason itself dictates this in order to take away confusion." – *Commentary on Numbers 3:5, pg. 221*

"It is the Lord's peculiar work to divide people into their respective ranks, distinguishing one from another, as seemeth good to him, all men being on a level by nature." – *Commentary on Psalm 87*

"Now we know for what end God would have rank and dignity to exist among men, and that is, that there might be something like a bridle to restrain the waywardness of the multitude." – *Commentary on Hosea, lect. 26, pg. 346*

"Certainly, if there is any quarter where it may be supposed that God is unknown, the most likely for such an instance to exist is among the dullest tribes farthest removed from civilisation. But, as a heathen tells us, there is no nation so barbarous, no race so brutish, as not to be imbued with the conviction that there is a God. Even those who, in other respects, seem to differ least from the lower animals, constantly retain some sense of religion; so thoroughly has this common conviction possessed the mind, so firmly is it stamped on the breasts of all men." – *Institutes of the Christian Religion, 3.1, pg. 44*

"It seems, indeed, very likely, that after having been degraded and scattered through so many disasters, they were not able to retain any certain distinction as to their tribes; for a census could not have been made at that time, nor did there exist a regular government, which was necessary to preserve an order of this kind; and they dwelt scattered and in disorder; and having been worn out by adversities, they were no doubt less attentive to the records of their kindred. But though you may not grant these things to me, yet it cannot be denied but that a danger of this kind was connected with such disturbed state of things." – *Commentary on Romans 2:17, pg. 102*

"For although God's glory shines forth in the outer man, yet there is no doubt that the proper seat of his [God's] image is in the soul... although the primary seat of the divine image was in the mind and heart, or in the soul and its powers, yet there was no part of man, not even the body itself, in which some sparks did not glow...The integrity with which Adam was endowed is expressed by this word [image or likeness of God], when he had full possession of right understanding, when he had his affections kept within the bounds of reason, all his senses tempered in right order, and he truly referred his excellence to exceptional gifts bestowed upon him by his Maker." – *Institutes Of The Christian Religion*, I.15.3

"The true nature of the image of God is to be derived from what Scripture says of its renewal through Christ. Nevertheless, it seems that we do not have a full definition of 'image' if we do not see more plainly those faculties in which man excels, and in which he ought to be thought the reflection of God's glory. That, indeed, can be nowhere better recognized than from the restoration of his corrupted nature. There is no doubt that Adam, when he fell from his state, was by this defection alienated from God. Therefore, even though we grant that God's image was not totally annihilated and destroyed in him, yet it was so corrupted that whatever remains is frightful deformity. Consequently, the beginning of our recovery of salvation is in that restoration which we obtain through Christ, who also is called the Second Adam for the reason that he restores us to true and complete integrity. For even though Paul, contrasting the life-giving spirit that the believers receive from Christ with the living soul in which Adam was created [1 Cor. 15:45], commends the richer measure of grace in regeneration, yet he does not remove that other principal point, that the end of regeneration is that Christ should reform us to God's image. Therefore elsewhere he teaches that 'the new man is renewed … according to the image of his Creator' [Col. 3:10 pg.]. With this agrees the saying, 'Put on the new man, who has been created according to God' [Eph. 4:24, Vg.].

"Now we are to see what Paul chiefly comprehends under this renewal. In the first place he posits knowledge, then pure righteousness and holiness. From this we infer that, to begin with, God's image was visible in the light of the mind, in the uprightness of the heart, and in the soundness of all the parts. For although I confess that these forms of speaking are synecdoches, yet this principle cannot be overthrown, that what was primary in the renewing of God's image also held the highest place in the creation itself. To the same pertains what he teaches elsewhere, that 'we … with unveiled face beholding the glory of Christ are being transformed into his very image' [2 Cor. 3:18]. Now we see how

Christ is the most perfect image of God; if we are conformed to it, we are so restored that with true piety, righteousness, purity, and intelligence we bear God's image." – *Institutes Of The Christian Religion*, I.15.4

"But here Scripture helps in the best way when it teaches that we are not to consider that men merit of themselves but to look upon the image of God in all men, to which we owe all honor and love. However, it is among members of the household of faith that this same image is more carefully to be noted [Gal. 6:10], in so far as it has been renewed and restored through the Spirit of Christ." – *Institutes Of The Christian Religion*, III.8.6

"Although charity (as being 'the bond of perfectness,' Col. 3:14) contains the sum of the Second Table, still, mutual obligation does not prevent either parents or others, who are in authority, from retaining their proper position. Nay, human society cannot be maintained in its integrity, unless children modestly submit themselves to their parents, and unless those, who are set over others by God's ordinance, are even reverently honoured.

"…children are laid under obligation by natural reason itself…

"If any should object that there are many ungodly and wicked fathers whom their children cannot regard with honour without destroying the distinction between good and evil, the reply is easy, that the perpetual law of nature is not subverted by the sins of men.

"The natural sense itself dictates to us that we should obey rulers. If servants obey not their masters, the society of the human race is subverted altogether. It is not, therefore, the least essential part of righteousness that the people should willingly submit themselves to the command of magistrates, and that servants should obey their masters; and, consequently, it would be very absurd if it were omitted in the Law of God." – *Exodus 20, Calvin's Commentaries*

Luís Vaz de Camões

The feats of Arms, and famed heroick Host,
from occidental Lusitanian strand,
who o'er the waters ne'er by seaman crost,
fared beyond the Taprobane-land,
forceful in perils and in battle-post,

with more than promised force of mortal hand;
and in the regions of a distant race
rear'd a new throne so haught in Pride of Place
And, eke, the Kings of mem'ory
   grand and glorious,
who hied them Holy Faith and Reign to spread,
converting, conquering, and in lands notorious,
Africk and Asia, devastation made;
nor less the Lieges who
   by deeds memorious brake
from the doom that binds the vulgar dead;
my song would sound o'er Earth's
   extremest part
were mine the genius, mine the Poet's art.
– Opening, *The Lusiads*

The Canons of the Apostles

In the eighty-second of these canons, we read:

"We do not allow slaves to be advanced to
the order of the clergy without the will of their
masters, to the injury of those who possess
them; for such things produce the overthrow of
houses. But when a slave is seen to be worthy,
who may be chosen for that degree, as our
Onesimus was, and the masters shall have consented, and given liberty, and dismissed them
from their houses, it may be done." – *Nicene and
Post-Nicene Fathers, Second Series*, ed. Schaff [24]

"Let the slaves work five days; but on the
Sabbath day and the Lord's day let them have
leisure to go to church for instruction in piety.
We have said that the Sabbath is on account of
the creation, and the Lord's day of the resurrection. Let slaves rest from their work all the great
week, and that which follows it…"

"Let not one of the godly pray with an
heretic, no, not in the house. For what fellowship has light with darkness? Let Christians,
whether men or women, who have connections
with slaves, either leave them off, or let them be
rejected (referring to slaves of sin)."

"And if any one be a slave, let him be asked
who is his master. If he be slave to one of the
faithful, let his master be asked if he can give
him a good character. If he cannot, let him be
rejected, until he show himself to be worthy
to his master. But if he does give him a good
character, let him be admitted. But if he be

household slave to an heathen, let him be
taught to please his master, that the word be not
blasphemed." – The Constitutions Through
Hippolytus. *The Ante-Nicene Fathers The Writings
of the Fathers Down to A. D. 325*, pgs. 495-496 [25]

The Canons Of Dort

"God created man good, and after his own
image, in true righteousness and holiness…" –
Canons of Dort, Third and Fourth Heads of Doctrine,
art. 1

Tucker Carlson

"Q: If I achieve one thing in life, what should it
be?

"A: Now it tells you a lot about modern
America, that that is even a question. No person, certainly no man, in the last 15,000 years,
would have asked 'What should I achieve in
life?'. There is really only one objective in life:
and that is reproduction. Pass on your genes so
you don't become extinct.

"They are called 'children' and then one
hopes they make and have 'grandchildren' and
that makes you the 'patriarch of the clan' and
gives meaning to your life." – *Ask Tucker: Reproduction & Keeping the Passion Alive*

Thomas Carlyle

"Many Irishmen talk of dying, etc., for Ireland,
and I really believe almost every Irishman now
alive longs in his way for an opportunity to do
the dear old country some good. Opportunities
of at once usefully and conspicuously 'dying'
for countries are not frequent, and, truly, the
rarer they are the better; but the opportunity
of usefully if inconspicuously living for one's
country, this was never denied to any man. Before 'dying' for your country, think my friends,
in how many quiet strenuous ways you might
beneficially live for it.

"Every patriotic Irishman (that is, by hypothesis, almost every Irishman now alive),
who would so fain make the dear old country
a present of his whole life and self, why does
he not for example – directly after reading this,
and choosing a feasible spot – at least, plant
one tree? That were a small act of self devotion,

---

24   Eleven church councils discussed and regulated slavery but never condemned it nor sought, in any way, to abolish the institution.

25   See 1 Peter 3, where the Christian wife of an unbeliever is given similar instruction.

small, but feasible. Him such tree will never shelter. Hardly any mortal but could manage that – hardly any mortal, if he were serious in it, but could plant and nourish into growth one tree. Eight million trees before the present generation run out, that were an indubitable acquisition for Ireland, for it is one of the barest, raggedest countries now known; far too ragged a country with patches of beautiful park and fine cultivation like shreds of bright scarlet on a beggar's clouted coat – a country that stands decidedly in need of shelter, shade, and ornamental fringing, look at its landscape where you will. Once, as the old chroniclers write, 'a squirrel (by bending its course a little, and taking a longish leap here and there) could have run from Cape Clear to the Giant's Causeway without once touching the ground;' but now, eight million trees, and I rather conjecture eight times eight million would be very welcome in that part of the empire. Of fruit trees, though these too are possible enough, I do not yet insist, but trees – at least, trees.

"That eight million persons will be persuaded to plant each his tree we cannot expect just yet; but do thou, my friend, in silence go and plant thine – that thou canst do; one most small duty, but a real one, if among the smallest conceivable, and a duty which henceforth it will be a sweet possession for thee to have lying done. Ireland for the present is not to be accounted a pleasant landscape – vigorous corn, but thistles and docks equally vigorous; ulcers of reclaimable bog lying black, miry and abominable at intervals of a few miles; no tree shading you, nor fence that avails to turn cattle – most fences merely, as it were, soliciting the cattle to be so good as not come through – by no means a beautiful country just now? But it tells all men how beautiful it might be. Alas, it carries on it, as the surface of this earth ever does ineffaceably legible, the physiognomy of the people that have inhabited it; a people of hold breeches, dirty faces, ill-roofed huts – a people of impetuosity and of levity – of vehemence, impatience, imperfect, fitful industry, imperfect, fitful veracity. Oh Heaven! there lies the woe of woes, which is the root of all.

"'Trees of liberty,' though an Abbe wrote a book on them, and incalculable trouble otherwise was taken, have not succeeded well in these ages. Plant you your eight million trees of shade, shelter, ornament, fruit; that is a symbol much more likely to be prophetic. Each man's tree of industry will be, of a surely, his tree of liberty; and the sum of them, never doubt of it, will be Ireland's." – *Trees Of Liberty, From The Nation*, 1 December, 1849; also *The Living Age*, vol. 193, pg. 240

Taylor Carman

"In the forward to Heidegger's 'Being And Time' (trans. John Macquarrie, Harper, 2008), describing Heidegger's philosophy: 'Consider the example of the world itself. Things always only show up for us in the context of a world. But what is a world? What is its being? What makes a world a world? What does a world's 'worldhood' consist in? The only way to get clear about that question, let alone try to answer it, Heidegger insists, is to describe how we experience and understand our world by inhabiting it, by being–in it. A world is a world by being structured by norms, ways, means, purposes, and 'for-the-sakes-of,' which constitute the point of what we do. We inhabit a world not simply by confronting objects in perception and judgment, but by pursuing ends, participating in practices, occupying social roles, establishing at least presumptive identities. A world is not an object standing over against a subject; it is where we live our lives, the milieu in which we dwell.'" – *Being And Time*, pg. xix

Lewis Carroll

"'If everybody minded their own business,' the Duchess said in a hoarse growl, 'the world would go round a deal faster than it does.'" – *Alice's Adventures in Wonderland*, pg. 84

Jimmy Carter

"Jimmy Carter said today that the Federal Government should not take the initiative to change the 'ethnic purity' of some urban neighborhoods or the economic 'homogeneity' of well-to-do suburbs....'Any exclusion of a family because of race or ethnic background I would oppose very strongly and aggressively as President,' he said. 'But I think it's good to maintain the homogeneity of neighborhoods if they've been established that way.' ... 'If there is a neighborhood that's homogeneous and if a family of another ethnic group wanted to move in,' he said 'I would use the full resources of the Federal Government to enforce their right to do that.'... 'I have nothing against a community that's made up of people who are Polish or Czechoslovakian or French-Canadian, or black, who are trying to maintain the ethnic purity of their neighborhoods. This is a natural inclination on the part of people, and I made this statement in Milwaukee, where there has been over a period of 100 or 150 years a compatibility among neighborhoods, for the churches, the private clubs, the newspapers, restaurants, all designed to accommodate members of a particular ethnic group. I see nothing wrong with that as long as it's done freely.'... 'I would never, though, condone any sort of discrimination against, say, a black family, or any other family, from moving into that neighborhood. But I don't think government ought deliberately to try to break down an ethnically oriented community—deliberately by injecting into it a member of another race, This Is Contrary to the best interest of the community. It creates disharmony. It creates hatred.' ... 'the government ought not take as a major purpose the intrusion of alien groups into a neighborhood, simply to establish that intrusion.'" – *Carter Defends All-White Areas, New York Times*, April 7, 1976

John Cassian

"And the genealogy of Cain is given separately as follows: 'Cain begat Enoch, Enoch begat Cainan, Cainan begat Mahalaleel, Mahalaleel begat Methuselah, Methuselah begat Lamech, Lamech begat Jabal and Jubal.' And so the line which sprang from the seed of righteous Seth always mixed with its own kith and kin, and continued for a long while in the holiness of its fathers and ancestors, untouched by the blasphemies and the wickedness of an evil offspring, which had implanted in it a seed of sin as it were transmitted by its ancestors. As long then as there continued that separation of the lines between them, the seed of Seth, as it sprang from an excellent root, was by reason of its sanctity termed 'angels of God,' or as some copies have it 'sons of God;' and on the contrary the others by reason of their own and their fathers' wickedness and their earthly deeds were termed 'children of men.' Though then there was up to this time that holy and salutary

separation between them, yet after this the sons of Seth who were the sons of God saw the daughters of those who were born of the line of Cain, and inflamed with the desire for their beauty took to themselves from them wives who taught their husbands the wickedness of their fathers, and at once led them astray from their innate holiness and the single-mindedness of their forefathers. To whom this saying applies with sufficient accuracy: 'I have said: Ye are Gods, and ye are all the children of the Most High. But ye shall die like men, and fall like one of the princes;' who fell away from that true study of natural philosophy, handed down to them by their ancestors, which the first man who forthwith traced out the study of all nature, could clearly attain to, and transmit to his descendants sure grounds, inasmuch as he had seen the infancy of this world, while still as it were tender and throbbing and unorganized; and as there was in him not only such fulness of wisdom, but also the grace of prophecy given by the Divine inspiration, so that while he was still an untaught inhabitant of this world he gave names to all living creatures, and not only knew about the fury and poison of all kinds of beasts and serpents, but also distinguished between the virtues of plants and trees and the natures of stones, and the changes of seasons of which he had as yet no experience, so that he could well say: 'The Lord hath given me the true knowledge of the things that are, to know the disposition of the whole world, and the virtues of the elements, the beginning and the ending and the midst of times, the alterations of their courses and the changes of their seasons, the revolutions of the year and the disposition of the stars, the natures of living creatures and the rage of wild beasts, the force of winds, and the reasonings of men, the diversities of plants and the virtues of roots, and all such things as are hid and open I have learnt.' This knowledge then of all nature the seed of Seth received through successive generations, handed down from the fathers, so long as it remained separate from the wicked line, and as it had received it in holiness, so it made use of it to promote the glory of God and the needs of everyday life. But when it had been mingled with the evil generation, it drew aside at the suggestion of devils to profane and harmful uses what it had innocently learnt, and audaciously taught by it the curious arts of wizards and enchantments and magical superstitions, teaching its posterity to forsake the holy worship of the Divinity and to honour and worship either the elements or fire or the demons of the air.

"How it was then that this knowledge of curious arts of which we have spoken, did not perish in the deluge, but became known to the ages that followed, should, I think, be briefly explained, as the occasion of this discussion suggests, although the answer to the question raised scarcely requires it. And so, as ancient traditions tell us, Ham the son of Noah, who had been taught these superstitions and wicked and profane arts, as he knew that he could not possibly bring any handbook on these subjects into the ark, into which he was to enter with his good father and holy brothers, inscribed these nefarious arts and profane devices on plates of various metals which could not be destroyed by the flood of waters, and on hard rocks, and when the flood was over he hunted for them with the same inquisitiveness with which he had concealed them, and so transmitted to his descendants a seed-bed of profanity and perpetual sin. In this way then that common notion, according to which men believe that angels delivered to men enchantments and diverse arts, is in truth fulfilled. From these sons of Seth then and daughters of Cain, as we have said, there were born still worse children who became mighty hunters, violent and most fierce men who were termed giants by reason of the size of their bodies and their cruelty and wickedness. For these first began to harass their neighbours and to practise pillaging among men, getting their living rather by rapine than by being contented with the sweat and labour of toil, and their wickedness increased to such a pitch that the world could only be purified by the flood and deluge. So then when the sons of Seth at the instigation of their lust had transgressed that command which had been for a long while kept by a natural instinct from the beginning of the world, it was needful that it should afterwards be restored by the letter of the law: 'Thou shalt not give thy daughter to his son to wife, nor shalt thou take a wife of his daughters to thy son; for they shall seduce your hearts to depart from your God, and to follow their gods and serve them.'" – *Second Conference of Abbot Serenus; A Select Library*, vol. 11, pgs. 383-384

---

26 Berenice was queen of egypt.

Catullus

Diana's faith inbred we bear
Youths whole of heart and maidens fair,
Let boys no blemishes impair,
And girls of Dian sing!
O great Latonian progeny,
Of greatest Jove descendancy,
Whom mother bare 'neath olive-tree,
Deep in the Delian dell;
That of the mountains reign thou Queen
And forest ranges ever green,
And coppices by man unseen,
And rivers resonant.
Thou art Lucína, Juno hight
By mothers lien in painful plight,
Thou puissant Trivia and the Light
Bastard, yclept the Lune.
Thou goddess with thy monthly stage,
The yearly march doth mete and gauge
And rustic peasant's messuage,
Dost brim with best o' crops,
Be hailed by whatso name of grace,
Please thee and olden Romulus' race,
Thy wonted favour deign embrace,
And save with choicest aid.
– *Carmina*, poem 34

"Berenice's Hair, which, from her glorious head, Fulgent in brightness afar...the consecrate spoils shed by a blond-hued head" – *Carmina*. Quoted in *Acta Orientalia*, pg. 107 [26]

Catholic Encyclopedia

"Character is the expression of the personality of a human being. . . . A man's character is the resultant of two distinct classes of factors: the original or inherited elements of his being, and those which he has acquired. On the one hand, every human being starts with a certain nature or disposition—a native endowment of capacities for knowledge, and feelings, and tendencies towards volitions and action—which varies with each individual. This disposition is dependent in part on the structure of the bodily organism and especially of the nervous system which he has inherited; in part, perhaps, also on his soul which has been created. . . . The transmission from parent to offspring of hereditary dispositions, therefore, involves no conflict with the doctrine of the creation of each human soul." – Entry on "Character", *Catholic Encyclopedia 1908*

Joseph Chamberlain

"These qualifications (for office of imperial colonial secretary) are that, in the first place, I believe in the British race. I believe that the British race is the greatest of governing races that the world has ever seen ... and I believe that there are no limits to its future." – quoted in Julian Symons, *Buller's Campaign*, pg. 55

Chun-shu Chang

As early as the time of the Han, China's first enduring imperial dynasty, a popular song proclaimed:
"Within the Four Seas,
We all are brothers,
And none be taken as strangers!"
– *The Rise of the Chinese Empire*, pg. 263.

Ha Joon Chang

"The truth is that the free movement of goods, people, and money that developed under British hegemony between 1870 and 1913 – the first episode of globalization – was made possible, in large part, by military might, rather than market forces. Apart from Britain itself, the practitioners of free trade during this period were mostly weaker countries that had been forced into, rather than had voluntarily adopted, it as a result of colonial rule or 'unequal treaties' (like the Nanking Treaty), which, among other things, deprived them of the right to set tariffs and imposed externally determined low, flat-rate tariffs (3–5%) on them." – *Bad Samaritans*, pg. 24

Charles Chaput

"The word 'patriotism' comes from the Latin pater (father) and patria (homeland, native soil). As with any human father, the nation-state is not a little godling. It can never require our worship. It can never demand that we violate our religious identity and beliefs. But properly understood, patriotism is a virtue and a form of filial love. We're sons and daughters of the land of our birth. It's natural and deeply human to love our home and be faithful to the best qualities in our native land." – *Piety And Patriotism*

Cherokee Nation

"The land on which we stand we have received as an inheritance from our fathers, who possessed it from time immemorial, as a gift from our common Father in Heaven. They bequeathed it to us as their children, and we have sacredly kept it, as containing the remains of our beloved men. This right of inheritance we have never ceded nor ever forfeited. Permit us to ask what better right can the people have to a country than the right of inheritance and immemorial peaceable possession?" – Petition to Congress, December 1829. *Voices of a People's History of the United States*, pg. 107 [27]

G.K. Chesterton

"To one who loves his fatherland, for instance, our boasted indifference to the ethics of a national war is mere mysterious gibberism. It is like telling a man that a boy has committed murder, but that he need not mind because it is only his son. Here clearly the word 'love' is used unmeaningly. It is the essence of love to be sensitive, it is a part of its doom; and anyone who objects to the one must certainly get rid of the other. This sensitiveness, rising sometimes to an almost morbid sensitiveness, was the mark of all great lovers like Dante and all great patriots like Chatham. 'My country, right or wrong,' is a thing that no patriot would think of saying except in a desperate case. It is like saying, 'My mother, drunk or sober.' No doubt if a decent man's mother took to drink he would share her troubles to the last; but to talk as if he would be in a state of gay indifference as to whether his mother took to drink or not is certainly not the language of men who know the great mystery." – *The Defendant*, pg. 125

"Impartiality is a pompous name for indifference which is an elegant name for ignorance. Tolerance is the virtue of the man without convictions. Merely having an open mind is nothing. The object of opening the mind, as of opening the mouth, is to shut it again on something solid. Do not be so open-minded that your brains fall out." – *Puritan and Anglican*, reprinted in *The Chesterton Review*, vol.9, no. 4, pg. 305

"If you choose to lump all flowers together, lilies, and dahlias and tulips and chrysanthemums

---

27 They were appealing what would become the "trail of tears."

and call them daisies, you will find that you have spoiled the very fine word daisy." [It is barbaric and reactionary to destroy cultural distinctions between one thing and another; because it is like rubbing out all the lines of a fine drawing.] – *What's Wrong With the World*, pgs. 117-118

"The truth is that only men to whom the family is sacred will ever have a standard or status by which to criticize the state." – *The Everlasting Man*, pg. 167

"It is true that the historic Church has at once emphasised celibacy and emphasised the family; has at once (if one may put it so) been fiercely for having children and fiercely for not having children. It has kept them side by side like two strong colours, red and white, like the red and white upon the shield of St. George. It has always had a healthy hatred of pink. It hates that combination of two colours which is the feeble expedient of the philosophers. It hates that evolution of black into white which is tantamount to a dirty grey. In fact, the whole theory of the Church on virginity might be symbolized in the statement that white is a colour: not merely the absence of a colour. All that I am urging here can be expressed by saying that Christianity sought in most of these cases to keep two colours co-existent but pure. It is not a mixture like russet or purple; it is rather like a shot silk, for a shot silk is always at right angles, and is in the pattern of the cross." – *Orthodoxy*, in *Collected Works* vol. 1, pg. 301

"This is what makes Christendom at once so much more perplexing and so much more interesting than the Pagan empire; just as Amiens Cathedral is not better but more interesting than the Parthenon. If any one wants a modern proof of all this, let him consider the curious fact that, under Christianity, Europe (while remaining a unity) has broken up into individual nations. Patriotism is a perfect example of this deliberate balancing of one emphasis against another emphasis. The instinct of the Pagan empire would have said, 'You shall all be Roman citizens, and grow alike; let the German grow less slow and reverent; the Frenchmen less experimental and swift.' But the instinct of Christian Europe says, 'Let the German remain slow and reverent, that the Frenchman may the more safely be swift and experimental. We will

make an equipoise out of these excesses. The absurdity called Germany shall correct the insanity called France.'" – *Orthodoxy*, in *Collected Works* vol. 1, pg. 304

"My acceptance of the universe is not optimism, it is more like patriotism. It is a matter of primary loyalty. The world is not a lodging-house at Brighton, which we are to leave because it is miserable. It is the fortress of our family, with the flag flying on the turret, and the more miserable it is the less we should leave it. The point is not that this world is too sad to love or too glad not to love; the point is that when you do love a thing, its gladness is a reason for loving it, and its sadness a reason for loving it more. All optimistic thoughts about England and all pessimistic thoughts about her are alike reasons for the English patriot. Similarly, optimism and pessimism are alike arguments for the cosmic patriot. . . . People first paid honour to a spot and afterwards gained glory for it. Men did not love Rome because she was great. She was great because they had loved her." – *Orthodoxy*, in *Collected Works* vol. 1, pg. 270

— G.K. CHESTERTON —

"It is exactly because the Serbian feels like a Serbian, and the Montenegrin like a Montenegrin, it is precisely because the Bulgar is proud of Bulgaria and fighting for Bulgaria, that the Serbian can count on the Bulgar and the Montenegrin on the Serbian. Each can count on the other precisely because each knows that the other is acting on a fundamental and ineradicable human motive — patriotism. If they had all felt internationally solid, the Turk would have hammered them like eggshells; and especially if they had also felt proletarian.

"And as it is with cooperation and the nation, so it is with cooperation and the family. If nations are to act together, they must admit each other's nationality. And if we want to play at Happy Families (that delightful game), the first necessity is, despite Divorce Reports, to see that we have families of some kind. If the families are independent, they will cooperate; if they are 'solid' they will quarrel. For the chief lesson of the whole of this war is that free things can achieve a unity, but tied things cannot. The small nations came together, where the great empire had always been breaking up." – *The Patriotic Idea*, in *Collected Works* vol. 29, pg. 401

"I should very much like to know where in the whole of the New Testament the author finds this violent, unnatural, and immoral proposition. Christ did not have the same kind of regard for one person as for another. We are specifically told that there were certain persons whom He especially loved. It is most improbable that He thought of other nations as He thought of His own. The sight of His national city moved Him to tears, and the highest compliment he paid was, 'Behold an Israelite indeed.' The author has simply confused two entirely different things. Christ commanded us to have love for all men, but even if we had equal love for all men, to speak of having the same love for all men is merely bewildering nonsense. If we love a man at all, the impression he produces on us must be vitally different to the impression produced by another man whom we love. To speak of having the same kind of regard for both is about as sensible as asking a man whether he prefers chrysanthemums or billiards. Christ did not love humanity; He never said He loved humanity; He loved men. Neither He nor anyone else can love humanity; it is like loving a gigantic centipede. And the reason Tolstoians can even endure to think of an equally distributed affection is that their love of humanity is a logical love, a love into which they are coerced by their own theories, a love which would be an insult to a tom-cat." – *Varied Types*, pg. 142

"A strange coldness and unreality hangs about their [modern cosmopolitans] love for men.

If you ask them whether they love humanity, they will say, doubtless sincerely, that they do. But if you ask them, touching any of the classes that go to make up humanity, you will find that they hate them all. They hate kings, they hate priests, they hate soldiers, they hate sailors. They distrust men of science, they denounce the middle classes, they despair of working men, but they adore humanity. Only they always speak of humanity as if it were a curious foreign nation. They are dividing themselves more and more from men to exalt the strange race of mankind. They are ceasing to be human in the effort to be humane." – *The Patriotic Idea, The Collected Works of G.K. Chesterton*, vol. 20, pg. 597

"The man who loves his own children is much more universal, is much more fully in the general order, than the man who dandles the infant hippopotamus or puts the young crocodile in a perambulator. For in loving his own children he is doing something which is (if I may use the phrase) far more essentially hippopotamic than dandling hippopotami; he is doing as they do. It is the same with patriotism. A man who loves humanity and ignores patriotism is ignoring humanity. The man who loves his country may not happen to pay extravagant verbal compliments to humanity, but he is paying to it the greatest of compliments – imitation. The fundamental spiritual advantage of patriotism and such sentiments is this: that by means of it all things are loved adequately, because all things are loved individually. Cosmopolitanism gives us one country, and it is good; nationalism gives us a hundred countries, and every one of them is the best. Cosmopolitanism offers a positive, patriotism a chorus of superlatives. Patriotism begins the praise of the world at the nearest thing, instead of beginning it at the most distant, and thus it insures what is, perhaps, the most essential of all earthly considerations, that nothing upon earth shall go without its due appreciation." – *The Patriotic Idea, in The Collected Works of G.K. Chesterton*, vol. 20, pg. 597

"To the cosmopolitan, therefore, who professes to love humanity and hate local preference, we shall reply: 'How can you love humanity and hate anything so human?' If he replies that in his eyes local preference is a positive sin, is only human in the sense that wife-beating is human, we shall reply that in that case he has a code of morality so different from ours that the very use of the word 'sin' is almost useless between us. If he says that the thing is not positive sin, but is foolish and narrow, we shall reply that this is a matter of impression, and that to us it is his atmosphere which is narrow to the point of suffocation. And we shall pray for him, hoping that some day he will break out of the little stifling cell of the cosmopolitan world, and find himself in the open fields and infinite sky of England." – *The Patriotic Idea, The Collected Works of G.K. Chesterton*, vol. 20, pg. 598

"Sometimes the best business of an age is to resist some alien invasion; sometimes to preach practical self-control in a world too self-indulgent and diffused; sometimes to prevent the growth in the State of great new private enterprises that would poison or oppress it. Above all it may sometimes happen that the highest task of a thinking citizen may be to do the exact opposite of the work which the Radicals had to do. It may be his highest duty to cling on to every scrap of the past that he can find, if he feels that the ground is giving way beneath him and sinking into mere savagery and forgetfulness of all human culture." – *Appreciations and Criticisms of the Works of Charles Dickens*, pg. 163

"The internationalist and the imperialist are not only similar men, but even the same men. There is no country which the Imperialist may not claim to conquer in order to convert. There is no country which the Internationalist may not claim to convert in order to conquer. Whether it is called international law or imperial law, it is the very soul and essence of all lawlessness. Against all such amorphous anarchy stands that great and positive creation of Christendom, the nation, with its standards of liberty and loyalty, with its limits of reason and proportion." – *The Apostles of Compromise, The Illustrated London News*, October 5, 1918, pg. 392 (Also in *Collected Works* vol. 31, pg. 370)

"In all normal civilisations the trader existed and must exist. But in all normal civilisations the trader was the exception; certainly he was never the rule; and most certainly he was never the ruler. The predominance which he has gained in the modern world is the cause of all the disasters of the modern world." – *Reflections On A Rotten Apple, Collected Works*, vol. 3, pg. 497

"Whatever else is evil, the pride of a good mother in the beauty of her daughter is good. It is one of those adamantine tendernesses which are the touchstones of every age and race. If other things are against it, other things must go down…. With the red hair of one she-urchin in the gutter I will set fire to all modern civilization. Because a girl should have long hair, she should have clean hair; because she should have clean hair, she should not have an unclean home; because she should not have an unclean home, she should have a free and leisured mother; because she should have a free mother, she should not have an usurious landlord; because there should not be an usurious landlord, there should be a redistribution of property; because there should be a redistribution of property, there shall be a revolution. That little urchin with the gold-red hair, whom I have just watched toddling past my house, she shall not be lopped and lamed and altered; her hair shall not be cut short like a convict's; no, all the kingdoms of the earth shall be hacked about and mutilated to suit her. She is the human and sacred image; all around her the social fabric shall sway and split and fall; the pillars of society shall be shaken, and the roofs of ages come rushing down; and not one hair of her head shall be harmed." – *What's Wrong With The World*, pgs. 316-317

"It is obviously not common sense to say that good always results from the mere mixing of anything with anything, the mere pouring in of any wind through any window, the mere pouring of any fluid into any flood.

"Anyhow, some of us do disbelieve in that sort of unity. We do not think a picture will be a better picture because all the colours run, however freely and largely they run into each other. We do not believe that a dinner will always be a better dinner because all the liquors and liqueurs are successively poured into the soup; or that our taste and enjoyment will really be widened by mixing the coffee with the claret or the vermouth with the port. We believe in certain Enclosures, called 'courses,' or appropriate selections from the carte de vins, being actually interposed to prevent all these separate pleasures from flowing into each other. We do not believe that every tennis-court should be flooded to turn it into a swimming-bath, and people be forced to play tennis only in the water (that the two sports may be unified and made one); we should not hesitate to erect artificial Enclosures, in the form of walls and partitions, around baths, bath-rooms, swimming-pools, and similar things, lest this one delight should end in universal Deluge. We should not shrink even from marking out, on the grass or the ground, the severe and restricting limits of the tennis-court, discouraging enthusiasts from playing tennis all over the billiard-room and the progressive whist party, lest one good custom should corrupt the world, as the first Lord Tennyson observed.

"In short, we have a curious notion, firmly fixed in our heads, that Enclosures do play a highly practical and profitable part in the real life of this world; and that the mere destruction of them is not the destruction of mere negative taboos, but the destruction of positive creations, positive achievements, positive arts and pleasures of life. And in the same way we think that a mere philosophy of unification, of mixing sex with sex or nation with nation or style with style, is altogether a paltry, sterile, and provincial simplification; no more truly intellectual than the act of a baby in mixing all the paints in a paint-box or stirring five or six things together with a spoon." – *The Philosophy of Enclosures— And Openings, The Illustrated London News*, 12/15/1928, pg. 1122 (*Also Collected Works* vol. 34, pg. 647)

"And when he [George MacDonald] comes to be more carefully studied as a mystic, as I think he will be when people discover the possibility of collecting jewels scattered in a rather irregular setting, it will be found, I fancy, that he stands for a rather important turning-point in the history of Christendom, as representing the particular Christian nation of the Scots. As Protestants speak of the morning stars of the Reformation, we may be allowed to note such names here and there as morning stars of the Reunion.

"The spiritual colour of Scotland, like the local colour of so many Scottish moors, is a purple that in some lights can look like grey. The national character is in reality intensely romantic and passionate indeed, excessively and dangerously romantic and passionate. Its emotional torrent has only too often been turned towards revenge, or lust, or cruelty, or witchcraft. There is no drunkenness like Scotch drunkenness; it has in it the ancient shriek and the wild shrillness of the Maenads on the mountains. And

of course it is equally true on the good side, as in the great literature of the nation. Stopford Brooke and other critics have truly pointed out that a vivid sense of colour appears in the medieval Scottish poets before it really appears in any English poets. And it is absurd to be talking of the hard and shrewd sobriety of a national type that has made itself best known throughout the modern world by the prosaic literalism of *Treasure Island* and the humdrum realism of *Peter Pan*." – G.K. Chesterton, from the introduction to *George MacDonald and His Wife*, by Greville M. MacDonald, pg. 13

Chesterton defends saving Jordans Meeting House – an icon of the Quaker movement near his home in Beaconsfield – from the intrusion of road traffic following plans for a local road-widening scheme:

"I am most warmly in favour of the effort... which aims at preserving Jordans and its setting from the operation of this dull mania for driving ugly roads through places, and past places, to the disadvantage of those who still possess the intelligence to go to places. Jordans is not only a historic place; it is one of the few examples of such a place that has contrived to remain a place, and has not been turned by tourists into a totally different sort of place. It is a shrine of pilgrimage which does still to some extent exist for pilgrims, and not only for touts and trippers. The shrine is not one of my religion, but it is one of enormous significance in the history of my country. What many people will not understand is that what should remain sacred in such a place is the place; the approach, the surroundings, the background; not detached and dead objects that might be put in a museum. The effect of Stonehenge is the effect of Salisbury Plain. If you wire in Stonehenge like a beast at the zoo, you are really making it a fetish, and idolatrously worshipping the mere stones; instead of seeing the large vision of the beginnings of Britain. Anybody who would leave Jordans must leave it looking like Jordans. And Stonehenge marks only a dead religion. Whereas the other is historic in the living sense that its history is not ended, for no one knows what may come at last of that revival of a purer mysticism in spite of the storms of Puritanism; of the beginnings of a Reformation of the Reformation, and of the greatness of William Penn." – Chesterton to Mr. G. Langley Taylor, 15 July 1931

Of his English ancestors, Chesterton wrote that they believed:

"..as a solid and most sacred reality that there was a thing called England and a sentiment of patriotism which ought to be felt towards it." – *A Short History of England*, pg. 440

A light, a glimmer outlines
   the crest of the mountain walls,
Starlike it broadens and brightens,
   and day o'er the valley fails;
It waketh the prince to praise,
   and it waketh the fool to mirth,
And it waketh a man to his toil
   and his place on the ordered earth.

There are uplands cloudlet-shadowed
   and mountains thunder-browed,
There are wastes of wood untravelled,
   and leagues of land unploughed,
Swamp-worlds heavy with poison,
   worlds grey and chill,
And I go, a clearer and builder,
   the voice of the human will.
God has struck all into chaos,
   princes and priests down-hurled,
But He leaves the place of the toiler,
   the old estate of the world.
In a season of doubt and of wrangle,
   in the thick of a world's uproar,
With the new life dark in wrestle,
   with the ghost of a life that is o'er,
When the old Priest fades to a phantom,
   when the old King nods on his throne,
The old, old hand of Labour
   is mighty and holdeth its own.
Other leaders may rest upon words,
   wax proud, and neglect the hours,
But our work is real, and standeth,
   in leaf and in fruit and in flowers,
In roofs and farms and fences,
   in draining of mere and of fen,
In the endless going and coming
   in the homes of the children of men.
Through the blaze of the regal ages,
   through the wrack of the feudal strife,
We toiled unseen for ever
   at the roots of the racial life.
The earth brought forth in abundance
   at the stroke of the hind and the churl,
Till his roof was fired by the chieftain,
   his fields trodden down by the earl.
Stand to it silently, brothers,

and watch for the hour and the day.
We have tramped and toiled for the idle,
   we have sorrowed and starved for the gay;
We have hewn out the road for the
   passers through thicket and mountain high—
Stand to it bravely, brothers,
   for the day and the hour are nigh.
Sorry and weary it is,
   our terrible army of toil —
With swart limbs bent to the tool,
   and dark brows turned to the soil.
We look not to heaven, nor pray:
   we see not the stars overhead,
But we stamp our stern evangel
   on the face of the earth we tread.
Sorry and weary it is,
   our army of labour and pain —
Its words are vague and frantic,
   its hopes are dark and vain;
Yet laugh not aloud, ye mighty,
   nor triumph, nor pass ye on,
For the High God heareth for ever
   the voice of the work we have done;
He knows who have striven with Nature,
   and claimed and conquered the earth,
He knows who have stood to a manhood
   where work is the title of worth,
He knows who are feeding the nations,
   are working at eve and at morn.
And He knows who have sneered
   and been idle, and struck them,
   and laughed them to scorn.
The poet may look into Nature
   for mirrors of passion and pain,
For the breadth of an isolation,
   the nurse of a black disdain;
The painter may look into Nature
   for shaping of sky and of land,
For blending of glorious hues
   and visions of fairyland;
But we who are dwelling with her
   can bend to her breast and hear
The roar of the endless purpose
   that grappleth sphere to sphere.
Therefore I go at the dawn
   to my work with a mighty mirth,
For the law of the earth is labour
   and man is the dust of the earth.
– "The Song of Labour," *The Speaker*, 17 December 1892, pg. 742

Vincent Cheung

"When it comes to justification, and when it comes to being the children of Abraham and the sons of God, it does not matter whether you are Jew or non-Jew, slave or free, male or female. Before you come to Christ, one is not more disadvantaged than the other, for all are condemned according to the divine standard. When you come to Christ, one is not more welcomed than the other, for all must come through the faith that God gives. After you have come to Christ, one is not more privileged than the other, for all are sons of God in him.

"However, Paul is by no means saying, 'Christ has abolished all racial differences, all class disparities, and all gender distinctions.' Although the verse has been used as if it says this, or almost as if it says this, it is far...far from what the verse teaches. It cannot be used, for example, to refute alleged differences in the intelligence, disposition, and physiology between races, classes, and genders. Whether these differences exist is a separate question – this verse does not affirm or refute them, since it does not address them at all.

"Therefore, the verse cannot be used to refute racism, classism, and sexism outside of the context of this passage, unless where the relevance could be established by necessary inference from the verse. It cannot even be used as an appeal to non-Christians against racism, classism, and sexism, since the lack of distinction referred to here is based on the fact that believers are 'all one in Christ Jesus.'

"But unbelievers are not in Christ Jesus, so that believers are not one with them. However, from this verse a legitimate appeal may be made for unbelievers to convert, to become believers, so that they may become one with all believers in Christ, where spiritually speaking, there is this basis to end racism, classism, and sexism.

"Even among believers, many distinctions between these groups remain. For example, just because we are 'all one in Christ Jesus' does not mean that it is appropriate for a man to walk into a women's restroom in church, claiming that there is neither 'male nor female' in Christ. Once we wrest the verse out of its context, one may no longer arbitrarily limit its usage. In fact, we may respond to someone who uses this verse out of its context that according to his usage, the problem that he is trying to address no longer exists. That is, if in Christ there is neither male nor female in the sense that he understands it, that no gender distinction should remain, then the very idea of sexual discrimination also vanishes. If there is no sexual distinction, there can be no sexual discrimination, and this means that no one who uses the verse in this manner can say that there is such a thing as a victim of sexism. The person is discriminated against as an individual apart from his or her gender. Thus once the verse is used to address what it is not supposed to address, the problem that it is not supposed to address also disappears.

"The same applies to the application of this verse to racism and classism. A person's skin color does not change just because he becomes a Christian. And a person does not automatically possess more or less wealth or status just because he now believes in Christ. All such distinctions between individuals remain. A man is still a man, and a woman is still a woman. The Scripture even gives the two different instructions regarding their roles, and thus insisting on a sharp distinction between the genders, even when it addresses believers." – *Commentary on Galatians*, pgs. 97-98

David Chilton

"When God created Adam, He placed him into a land, and gave him dominion over it. Land is basic to dominion; therefore, salvation involves a restoration to land and property... A scattered, homeless people cannot have dominion." – *Paradise Restored*, pg. 49, 51

Peter Chrysologus

"Thus all nations are created a second time to salvation by that one and the same Power, which created them to being." – archbishop of Ravenna a.d. 433, Sermon 80, on Matthew, quoted by Aquinas in *Catena Aurea*, vol. 2, pg. 968

John Chrysostom

"For generally the children acquire the character of their parents, are formed in the mold of their parents' temperament, love the same things their parents love, talk in the same fashion, and work for the same ends." – *On Marriage and Family Life*, pg. 64

"[God has allowed] some good dispositions to exist naturally within us. For we are all naturally disposed to feel indignation along with those who are contemptuously treated, (whence it arises that we become the enemies of those who are injurious, though we ourselves may have suffered no part of the grievance,) and we sympathize in the pleasure of those who enjoy (mutual) assistance and protection; and we are overcome by the calamities of others, as well as by mutual tenderness. For although calamitous events may seem to induce a sort of contractedness of soul, we entertain nevertheless a common fondness for each other. And to this effect a certain wise man speaks significantly; Every animal loveth his like, and man his neighbour."
– *Homilies, Concerning the Statues*, pg. 226

Commenting on Genesis:

"'When they travelled from the east, they found open country in the land of Sennar and settled there.' Notice how the human race, instead of managing to keep to their own boundaries, always longs for more and reaches out for greater things. This is what the human race has lost in particular, not being prepared to recognize the limitations of their own condition but always lusting after more and entertaining ambitions beyond their capacity. In this regard, too, when people who chase after the things of the world acquire for themselves much wealth and status, they lose sight of their own nature, as it were, and aspire to such heights that they topple into the very depths. You could see this happening every day without others being any the wiser from the sight of it; instead, they pause for a while, but immediately lose all recollection of it and take the same road as the others and fall over the same precipice. This is exactly what you can see happening to these people in the present instance: 'When they travelled from the east, they found open country in the land of Sennar and settled there.' See how in gradual stages it teaches us the instability of their attitude: when they saw the open country (the text says), they packed up and left their previous dwelling and settled down there... Like an everlasting memorial, he says, I am setting in place for them such terrible punishment that would last forever and no length of time would suffice to bring them forgetfulness of it. In other words, since they abused their similarity of language, I intend them to come to their senses through their difference in language.... when the people in the present case, who had been dignified with similarity of language used the privilege given them for evil purposes, he put a stop to the impulse of their wickedness through difference in language. 'Let us confuse their speech,' he says, 'so that they will be unable to understand one another's language,' his purpose being that, just as similarity of language achieved their living together, so difference in language might cause dispersal among them. How could people lacking the same language and converse live in conformity with one another?... Dearly beloved, you have heard what gave rise to their dispersal and the conflict of tongues. Let us, I beseech you, avoid imitating them, and make proper use of advantages provided for us by God; let us have human nature in mind and keep our ambitions on the level that is proper for human beings, being mortal as we are." – *Homilies on Genesis 18–45*, Homily 30, vol. 82, pgs. 222-224

— JOHN CHRYSOSTOM —

"Moses, the blessed Moses, surpassed even those that love with human passion. How, and in what respect? First, in that he gave up the court, and the luxury, and the retinue, and the renown attending it, and chose rather to be with the Israelites. Yet is this not only what no one else would ever have done, but would have even been ashamed, were another to have discovered him, of being found to be a kinsman of men, who were not only slaves, but were looked upon as even execrable. Yet was he not only not ashamed of his kindred, but with all his spirit defended them, and exposed himself to perils for their sake." – *Commentary on Ephesians* 3:21, pg. 176

"Here on earth, indeed, families are the races sprung from one parent stock…" – *Commentary on Ephesians* 3:21, pg. 176

Of those accursed who turn from God: "Did they not trample kinship under foot, did they not forget their children, did they not forget the very God who created them?" – *Discourses Against Judaizing Christians*, pg. 58

"The three boys in Babylon, Daniel, and all the others who spent their days in captivity kept expecting to recover their own city and, after seventy years, to see the soil of their fatherland; they kept looking forward to living again under their ancestral laws. They had a clear pledge and promise that this would come to pass." – *Discourses Against Judaizing Christians*, pg. 98

"Remember the eunuch of the queen of Ethiopia. Being a man of a barbarous nation, occupied with numerous cares, and surrounded on all sides by manifold business, he was unable to understand that which he read." – *Four Discourses Of Chrysostom*, pg. 67

Speaking of Joseph's dreams:
    "he was to be the crown of the whole family, and the glory of all his race." – *Four Discourses Of Chrysostom*, pg. 105

"If any provide not for his own, and especially for those of his own house, that is, those who are nearly related to him, he is worse than an infidel. And so says Isaiah, the chief of the Prophets, You shall not overlook your kinsmen of your own seed. Isaiah 58:7 For if a man deserts those who are united by ties of kindred and affinity, how shall he be affectionate towards others? Will it not have the appearance of vainglory, when benefiting others he slights his own relations, and does not provide for them? And what will be said, if instructing others, he neglects his own, though he has greater facilities; and a higher obligation to benefit them? Will it not be said, These Christians are affectionate indeed, who neglect their own relatives? He is worse than an infidel. Wherefore? Because the latter, if he benefits not aliens, does not neglect

his near kindred. What is meant is this: The law of God and of nature is violated by him who provides not for his own family. But if he who provides not for them has denied the faith, and is worse than an infidel, where shall he be ranked who has injured his relatives? With whom shall he be placed? But how has he denied the faith? Even as it is said, They profess that they know God, but in works they deny Him. Titus 1:16 What has God, in whom they believe, commanded? Hide not yourself from your own flesh. Isaiah 58:7-9 How does he then believe who thus denies God? Let those consider this, who to spare their wealth neglect their kindred. It was the design of God, in uniting us by the ties of kindred, to afford us many opportunities of doing good to one another. When therefore you neglect a duty which infidels perform, have you not denied the faith? For it is not faith merely to profess belief, but to do works worthy of faith. And it is possible in each particular to believe and not to believe. For since he had spoken of luxury and self-indulgence, he says that it is not for this only that such a woman is punished, because she is luxurious, but because her luxury compels her to neglect her household. This he says with reason; for she that lives to the belly, perishes hereby also, as having denied the faith. But how is she worse than an infidel? Because it is not the same thing to neglect our kindred, as to neglect a stranger. How should it be? But the fault is greater here, to desert one known than one who is unknown to us, a friend than one who is not a friend." – *Homilies*, XIV on 1 Timothy 5:8, pg. 12

"…from the beginning, God tied the man to labour, not for the purpose of punishing or chastising, but for amendment and education… Let us not then despise labours; let us not despise work [exertion]; for before the kingdom of Heaven, we receive the greatest recompense from thence, while we gather pleasure from that circumstance; and not pleasure only, but what is greater than pleasure, the purest health. For in addition to their want of relish, many diseases also attack the rich; but the poor are freed from the hands of physicians; and if at times they do fall into a sickness, they recover themselves quickly, being far removed from all effeminacy, and having robust constitutions." – *Homilies, Concerning the Statues*, pg. 50

"Nothing is more powerful in forming good habits in the young than the love and reverence they have for their parents." – *Homily on Colossians*, 4:18

Winston Churchill

"I do not understand the squeamishness about the use of gas. I am strongly in favour of using poisonous gas against uncivilised tribes." – *War Office Memorandum*, *The Oxford Handbook of Genocide Studies*, pg. 357

"It is alarming and nauseating to see Mr. Gandhi, a seditious Middle Temple lawyer, now posing as a fakir of a type well known in the east, striding half naked up the steps of the viceregal palace, while he is still organising and conducting a campaign of civil disobedience, to parlay on equal terms with the representative of the Emperor-King." – Commenting on Gandhi's meeting with the Viceroy of India, 1931; *Churchill's Empire*, pg. 176

"[India is] a godless land of snobs and bores." – Letter to his mother, 1896; *Churchill's First War*, pg. 106

"I do not admit... that a great wrong has been done to the Red Indians of America, or the black people of Australia. I do not admit that a wrong has been done to these people by the fact that a stronger race, a higher grade race, a more worldly-wise race, to put it that way, has come in and taken their place." – to Palestine Royal Commission, 1937; *Churchill and Australia*, pg. 3

"This movement among the Jews is not new. From the days of Spartacus-Weishaupt to those of Karl Marx, and down to Trotsky (Russia), Bela Kun (Hungary), Rosa Luxembourg (Germany), and Emma Goldman (United States)... this worldwide conspiracy for the overthrow of civilisation and for the reconstitution of society on the basis of arrested development, of envious malevolence, and impossible equality, has been steadily growing. It has been the mainspring of every subversive movement during the 19th century; and now at last this band of extraordinary personalities from the underworld of the great cities of Europe and America have gripped the Russian people by the hair of their heads and have become practically the undisputed masters of that enormous empire." – writing on *Zionism versus Bolshevism* in the *Illustrated*. – *Sunday Herald*, February 8th, 1920

"We must never cease to proclaim in fearless tones the great principles of freedom and the rights of man which are the joint inheritance of the English-speaking world and which through Magna Carta, the Bill of Rights, the Habeas Corpus, trial by jury, and the English common law find their most famous expression in the American Declaration of Independence." – *Sinews of Peace* address delivered at Westminster College in Fulton, Missouri; *Churchill's "Iron Curtain" Speech Fifty Years Later*, pg. 5

"Our difficulties come from the mood of unwarrantable self-abasement into which we have been cast by a powerful section of our own intellectuals.... What have they to offer but a vague internationalism, a squalid materialism, and the promise of impossible utopias?" – The Royal Society of St George (1933); *Never Give In! Winston Churchill's Speeches*, pg. 84

William Church

"A survey of the relationship between the French monarchy and patriotic sentiment demonstrates that the latter fluctuated significantly according to the fortunes, policies, and repute of the monarchy itself. During the sixteenth century, French patriotism assumed the form of a broadly based idealization of many elements of the life of the nation, the monarchy included. But in the seventeenth century, as part of the massive swing towards absolutism, this sentiment was more and more centered in the crown, even in the person of the king. With the triumph of absolutism, both in theory and in fact, it was in the nature of things that the sovereign should symbolize the nation and become the focal point of patriotic sentiment. In the years of Louis XIV's reign, however, a revulsion began to be expressed toward the equation of patriotism with loyalty to the Bourbon dynasty, and the way was opened for the much more comprehensive views of the Enlightenment which grounded patriotism in the life of the people and eventually led to the massive, virile nationalism of the French Revolution." – *National Consciousness, History, and Political Culture in Early-Modern Europe*, pg. 45

Cicero

"Then, too, there are a great many degrees of closeness or remoteness in human society. To proceed beyond the universal bond of our common humanity, there is the closer one of belonging to the same people, tribe, and tongue, by which men are very closely bound together; it is a still closer relation to be citizens of the same city-state; for fellow-citizens have much in common—forum, temples, colonnades, streets, statutes laws. Courts, rights of suffrage, to say nothing of social and friendly circles and diverse business relations with many.

"But a sill closer social union exists between kindred. Starting with that infinite bond of union of the human race in general, the conception is now confined to a small and narrow circle. For since the reproductive instinct is by Nature's gift the common possession of all living creatures, the first bond of union is that between husband and wife; the next, that between parents and children; then we find one home, with everything in common. And this is the foundation of civil government, the nursery, as it were, of the state. Then follow the bonds between brothers and sisters, and next those of first and then of second cousins; and when they can no longer be sheltered under one roof, they go out into other homes, as into colonies. Then follow between these, in turn, marriages and connections by marriage, and from these again a new stock of relations; and from this propagation and after-growth states have their beginnings. The bonds of common blood hold men fast through good-will and affection; for it means much to share in common the same family traditions, the same forms of domestic worship, and the same ancestral tombs.

"But of all the bonds of fellowship, there is none more noble, none more powerful than when good men of congenial character are joined in intimate friendship; for really, if we discover in another that moral goodness on which I dwell so much, it attracts us and makes us friends to the one in whose character it seems to dwell. And while every virtue attracts us and makes us love those who seem to possess it, still justice and generosity do so most of all. Nothing, moreover, is more conducive to love and intimacy than compatibility of character in good men; for when two people have the same ideals and the same tastes, it is a natural consequence that each loves the other as himself;

and the result is, as Pythagoras requires of ideal friendship, that several are united in one.

"Another strong bond of fellowship is effected by mutual interchange of kind services; and as long as these kindnesses are mutual and acceptable, those between whom they are interchanged are united by the ties of an enduring intimacy.

"But when with a rational spirit you have surveyed the whole field, there is no social relation among them all more close, none more dear than that which links each one of us with our country." – De Officiis, pg. 57

"As for the foreigner or the resident alien, it is his duty to attend strictly to his own concerns, not to pry into other people's business, and under no condition to meddle in the politics of a country not his own." – De Officiis pg. 125

"MARCUS: I acknowledge that when I can escape for a few days, especially in this delectable season, I usually come here, on account of the beauty of the scenery, and the salubrity of the air; but these vacations occur not very often. There is one reason, however, why I am so fond of this Arpinum, which does not apply to you.
ATTICUS: Prithee, what reason is that?
MARCUS: Because, to confess the truth, it is my native place, and my brother's, for here indeed, descended from a very ancient race, we first saw the day. Here was our altar, here our ancestry, and here still remains many vestiges of our family. Besides, this villa which you behold in its present form, was originally constructed under my father's superintendence; for having very infirm health, he spent the later years of his life here, engaged in literary pursuits. At the time of my birth, my grandfather also lived here, and resided according to the olden custom, in that little villa, like another Curius on his Sabine farm. There is, therefore, an indiscribable sympathy which attaches me to the spot; it pervades my soul and sense with a peculiar fascination, whenever I reside here. Even the wisest Ulysses was not wholly exempt from a similar weakness, for Homer tells us that he renounced immortality, that he might once more re-visit his beloved Ithaca." – De Legibus, in The Treatises, pg. 428

"But, O Africanus [continued the apparition] that you may be more zealous in the defence of the Republic, rely upon this; that for all those who shall have saved, assisted, or aggrandized their country, a certain and destined place is reserved, where they shall enjoy an eternal felicity. For to the Supreme Governor of the universe, there is nothing on earth which is dearer, than those assemblies and societies of men who are connected by one common system of jurisprudence, and are considered as forming one state; the governors and preservers of these being sent from hence, hither also return." – *The Dream of Scipio*

David J. Clark

"Verse 4 describes the happy results of worldwide peace in terms of an agricultural society such as that in which Micah lived. The description is given in traditional language (see also 1 Kgs 4:25; Zech 3:10). For everyone to 'sit … under his vine and under his fig tree' (RSV) means that they will be able to live in peace and enjoy the results of their own labors. For people who know fig trees, it is not hard to imagine sitting under one, but it may seem more difficult to sit under a grapevine. What is probably meant here is a vine which has been allowed to grow up onto a trellis, that is, a structure of raised poles which the vines can grow on. Even though in Hebrew only one vine and one fig tree are mentioned, TEV gives the correct meaning when it speaks of vineyards and fig trees. In areas where these plants are unknown, it would be better to translate by a generic expression such as 'among his own fields and gardens' rather than substituting local produce such as coconuts or mangoes which were not known in Israel." – with Mundhenk, *A Translator's Handbook on the Book of Micah*, pg. 189

H.B. Clark

"But even the doctrine of equality is not applicable in every situation. So, though the general rule that the homeborn (native) and the stranger (foreigner) should be governed by 'one law,' yet it was expressly provided that a stranger should not 'eat of the passover' or 'enter into the congregation.'" – *Biblical Law*, pg. 31

Henry Clay

"What is the true nature of the evil of the existence of a portion of the African race in our population? It is not that there are some but that there are so many … who can never amalgamate with the great body of our population. [Repatriation to Africa would] rid our country of a useless and pernicious, if not dangerous portion of its population." – Speech to the American Colonization Society, 1827; *The Life and Public Services of Henry Clay, Down to 1848*, pg. 513

"The wants of man may be classed under three heads: food, raiment, and defense…"

"What is true of individuals is equally so of nations. The country, then, which relies upon foreign nations for either of those great essentials, is not, in fact, independent. Nor is it any consolation for our dependence upon other nations that they are also dependent upon us, even were it true…

"If the governing consideration were cheapness; if national independence were to weigh nothing; if honor nothing why not subsidize foreign powers to defend us? Why not hire Swiss or Hessian armies to protect us? Why not get our arms of all kinds, as we do, in part, the blankets and clothing of our soldiers, from abroad?" – *Speech on the Protection of Home Industry*, 1820; *The Papers of Henry Clay The Rising Statesman 1815–1820*, pg. 828

"Foreign commerce is the great source of foreign wars The eagerness with which we contend for every branch of it; the temptations which it offers, operating alike upon us and our foreign competitors, produce constant collisions." – *Speech on the Tariff*, 1820; Hopkins, Clay, 2:828

Clement of Alexandria

"Who are the two or three who gather in the name of Christ with the Lord in their midst? By three does he not mean husband, wife, and child?" – *Stromateis, Books One to Three*, pg. 298.

"The man who has produced of himself one like him has achieved fulfillment—even more when he sees the other having followed in his footsteps too, in other words, when he has established a child in the same natural place as the father." – *Stromateis, Books One to Three*, pg. 251.

"Our good Plato enunciated that an unmarried man should hand over the equivalent of a wife's upkeep into the public treasury, paying the appropriate costs to the authorities. If they do not marry or produce children, they will be playing their part in reducing the population and undermining the cities and the world they compose." – *Stromateis, Books One to Three*, pg. 252.

Richard Cobden

"...In the present day, commerce is the grand panacea, which, like a beneficent medical discovery, will serve to inoculate with the healthy and saving taste for civilization all the nations of the world. Not a bale of merchandise leaves our shores, but it bears the seeds of intelligent and fruitful thought to the members of some less enlightened community; not a merchant visits our seats of manufacturing industry, but he returns to his own country the missionary of freedom, peace, and good government – whilst our steam boats, that now visit every port of Europe, and our miraculous railroads, that are the talk of all nations, are the advertisements and vouchers for the value of our enlightened institutions." – Cited in Dawson, *Richard Cobden and Foreign Policy*, pg. 87

"I look farther; I see in the Free-trade principle that which shall act on the moral world as the principle of gravitation in the universe,—drawing men together, thrusting aside the antagonism of race, and creed, and language, and uniting us in the bonds of eternal peace. I have looked even farther. I have speculated, and probably dreamt, in the dim future—ay, a thousand years hence—I have speculated on what the effect of the triumph of this principle may be. I believe that the effect will be to change the face of the world, so as to introduce a system of government entirely distinct from that which now prevails. I believe that the desire and the motive for large and mighty empires; for gigantic armies and great navies—for those materials which are used for the destruction of life and the desolation of the rewards of labour—will die away; I believe that such things will cease to be necessary, or to be used, when man becomes one family, and freely exchanges the fruits of his labour with his brother man. I believe that, if we could be allowed to reappear on this sublunary scene, we should see, at a far distant period, the governing system of this world revert to something like the municipal system; and I believe that the speculative philosopher of a thousand years hence will date the greatest revolution that ever happened in the world's history from the triumph of the principle which we have met here to advocate." – *Free Trade*, pg. 229

Corneliu Zelea Codreanu

"There cannot be any people in this world, be they only a tribe of savages that, faced by a foreign invasion, would not consider with rending pain the predicament of its land. All peoples of the world, from history's beginnings to this day have defended the soil of their fatherland. The history of all peoples, as ours, is replete with battles in defense of its land. Would it be an anomaly, a state of illness of ours, the Romanian youth, that we stand to be counted in the defense of our menaced land? Or an anomaly if we did not defend it when we see it endangered? It would be an anomaly for us not to defend it, namely, not doing what all nations have done. Placing us in contradiction to the entire world and our entire history would be an anomaly and a state of illness. Why is it, I wonder, that all peoples have fought, fight and will always fight for the defense of their land? Land is a nation's basis for existence. The nation has its roots like those of a tree deep in the country's soil whence it derives its nourishment and life. There is no people that can live without land, as there is no tree which can live hanging in air. A nation which has no land of its own cannot live unless it settles on the land of another nation – on its very body, sapping its sustenance. There exist God-given laws which ordain the life of peoples. One of these laws is the territorial law. God gave each people a definite territory to live in, grow in and on which to develop and create its own culture." – *For My Legionaries*, pg. 62

"From this Legionary school a new man will have to emerge, a man with heroic qualities; a giant of our history to do battle and win over all the enemies of our Fatherland, his battle and victory having to extend even beyond the material world into the realm of invisible enemies, the powers of evil. Everything that our mind can imagine as more beautiful spiritually; everything the proudest that our race can produce, greater, more just, more powerful, wiser, purer, more diligent and more heroic, this is what the Legionary school must give us! A man in whom all the possibilities of human grandeur that are implanted by God in the blood of our people be developed to the maximum. This hero, the product of Legionary education, will also know how to elaborate programs; will also know how to solve the Jewish problem; will also know how to organize the state well; will also know how to convince other Romanians; and if not, he will know how to win, for that is why he is a hero. This hero, this Legionary of bravery, labour, and justice, with the powers God implanted in his soul, will lead our Fatherland on the road of its glory." – *For My Legionaries*, pg. 248

Colluthus

"And all the race of the gods hastened to do honour to the white-armed bride, own sister of Amphitrite: Zeus from Olympus and Poseidon from the sea. Out of the land of Melisseus from fragrant Helicon, Apollo came leading the clear-voiced choir of the Muses. On either side, fluttering with golden locks, the unshorn cluster of his hair was buffeted by the west wind." – *Rape of Helen*, quoted in *New Studies in Greek Poetry*, pg. 51

— Colonial Laws — and Constitutions

Concisely stated, the colonial laws of the 17th century reflect the original American project: English-Christian polities established for "us and for our posterity."

In the early colonization days, strangers were viewed with suspicion due to the fear of their possible indigence or hostile attitude towards the religious and secular government of the colony. New England colonies were particularly careful about admitting strangers and imposed heavy fines on those who brought or entertained them without permission. The cautious attitude towards strangers was maintained by Puritan settlements, and in the eighteenth century, Massachusetts passed several acts regulating immigration, practically excluding those who could not begin life in the colony without aid from the older settlers. Some colonies required newcomers to take an oath of allegiance or pay special taxes, while others prohibited them from owning land or holding public office.

In Virginia, for example, a law passed in 1670 required all incoming immigrants to take an oath of allegiance to the English monarch, and imposed special taxes on those who were not of English or Welsh descent. Similarly, in Massachusetts, a law passed in 1634 prohibited immigrants who were not members of the Puritan church from settling in the colony, and imposed a fine on those who did.

Other colonies, such as Maryland and Pennsylvania, were more welcoming to immigrants, with laws that encouraged settlement and offered land grants to newcomers. However, even in these colonies, there were still restrictions on the rights and privileges of strangers, and immigrants were often subject to suspicion and discrimination.

Between 1700 and 1750, a large number of Germans migrated to the middle states of America, raising concerns similar to those associated with contemporary immigration. The influx of foreigners into Pennsylvania was so significant that there was a risk of it turning into a foreign colony. In 1729, the Quaker province passed an anti-immigration act, a tax on all foreigners entering the colony, which was the most comprehensive anti-immigration act ever passed in America.

A fascinating aspect of colonial immigration is the transportation of convicts, which was suggested in some of the earliest tracts promoting English exploration and settlement in America. The idea was to transport indigent and criminal classes from the mother country to the new world to relieve the burden on the home country. The southern colonies' natural resources created a demand for servant labor and may have inspired the deportation of criminals to the new world.

As Sir Humphrey Gilbert, a 16th century MP and explorer for the crown, said, "We might inhabit some part of those countries and settle there such needy of our own which now trouble the Commonwealth, and through want, here at home are enforced to commit outrageous offences, whereby they are daily consumed by the gallows." It was against such ideas that the American colonists through the founding era wrote their immigration laws. They wanted not for America to be a dumping ground of every convict, criminal, insane, and slavish reject. Indeed, the great agents behind the transAtlantic slave trade were foreign investors and non-American merchantmen. Rather, the idea was to people the Americas with free, European, Christian men, and turn it, if not into the Puritan "City On A Hill," then at least into a land of manly freedom and ordered liberty.

Overall, the colonial laws of the 17th century regarding immigrants and strangers reflected a general mistrust of newcomers and a desire to maintain the social and cultural norms of the established colonial society.

———

Stephen Colwell

"No nation can attain . . . its maximum wealth which does not by its national policy furnish sources of employment for its whole population." – *Report on Iron and Steel*; pg. 292

Confucius

"What are the things which men consider right? Kindness in a father, filial piety in a son; gentleness in an elder brother, obedience in a younger; righteousness in a husband, submission in a wife; kindness in elders, deference in juniors; benevolence in a ruler, loyalty in a minister. These ten are things which men consider right." – *Ethics Of Confucius*, ch. 2

"Our bodies, to every hair and shred of skin, are received from our parents. We must not presume to injure or to wound them. This is the beginning of filial piety. When we have established our character by the practice of this filial course, so as to make our name famous in future ages and thereby glorify our parents, this is the end of filial piety." – *Ethics Of Confucius*, ch. 4

"The son derives his life from his parents and no greater gift could possibly be transmitted..." – *Ethics Of Confucius*, ch. 4

"The filial piety with which the superior man serves his parents may be transferred as loyalty to the ruler; the fraternal duty with which he serves his elder brother may be transferred as deference to elders; his regulation of his family may be transferred as good government in any official position." – *Hsiâo King, Ethics Of Confucius*, ch. 5

— CONFUCIUS —

"I have heard that relatives should not forget their relationship nor friends their friendship." – *Li King*, pg. 199

"He whom the superior man pronounces filial is he whom the people of the state praise, saying with admiration, 'Happy are the parents who have such a son as this!'" – *Li King*, pg. 119

"The superior man, going back to his ancient fathers and returning to the authors of his being, does not forget those to whom he owes his life; and therefore he calls forth all his reverence, gives full vent to his feelings, and exhausts his strength in discharging this service—as a tribute of gratitude to his parents he dares not but do his utmost." – *Li King*, as quoted in *Ethics Of Confucius*, ch. 5

"A competent provision was secured for the aged till their death, employment for the able-bodied, and the means of growing up to the young. They showed kindness and compassion to widows, orphans, childless men, and those who were disabled by disease; so that they were all sufficiently maintained. Men had their proper work and women their homes." – *Li King*, pg. 365

"I hate those who with their sharp tongues overthrow kingdoms and families." – *Analects*, pg. 843

"From them you learn the more immediate duty of serving one's father and the remoter one of serving one's prince." – *Analects*, pg. 830

"What does the 'Shu King' say of filial piety? 'You are filial, you discharge your fraternal duties. These qualities are displayed in government. This, then, also constitutes the exercise of government.'" – *Analects*, pg. 172

"This is meant by 'To rightly govern the state, it is necessary first to regulate one's own family.' One cannot instruct others who cannot instruct his own children. Without going beyond the family, the prince may learn all the lessons of statecraft, filial piety by which the sovereign is also served, fraternal submission by which older men and superiors are also served, kindness by which also the common people should be ministered unto." – *Great Learning, The Basic Thoughts*, pg. 172

"From the loving example of one family, love extends throughout the state; from its courtesy, courtesy extends throughout the state; while the ambition and perverse recklessness of one man may plunge the entire state into rebellion and disorder." – *Great Learning, The Basic Thoughts*, pg. 172

James Connolly

Some men, faint-hearted, ever seek
  Our programme to retouch,
  And will insist, whene'er they speak
  That we demand too much.
'Tis passing strange, yet I declare
  Such statements give me mirth,
  For our demands most moderate are,
  We only want the earth.
"Be moderate," the trimmers cry,
  Who dread the tyrants' thunder.
  "You ask too much and people fly
  From you aghast in wonder."
'Tis passing strange, for I declare
  Such statements give me mirth,
  For our demands most moderate are,
  We only want the earth.
Our masters all a godly crew,
  Whose hearts throb for the poor,
  Their sympathies assure us, too,
  If our demands were fewer.
Most generous souls! But please observe,

What they enjoy from birth
  Is all we ever had the nerve
  To ask, that is, the earth.
The labour "fakir" full of guile,
  Base doctrine every preaches,
  And whilst he bleeds the rank and file
  Tame moderation teaches.
Yet, in despite, we'll see the day
  When, with sword in its girth,
  Labour shall march in war array
  To realize its own, the earth.
For labour long, with sighs and tears,
  To its oppressors knelt.
  But never yet, to aught save fears,
  Did the heart of tyrant melt.
We need not kneel, our cause is high
  Of true men there's no dearth
  And our victorious rallying cry
  Shall be we want the earth!
– *We Only Want The Earth*

Calvin Coolidge

"We are confronted by the clamor of multitudes who desire the opportunity offered by American life, we must face the situation unflinchingly, determined to relinquish not one iota of our obligation to others, yet not be so sentimental as to overlook our obligations to ourselves...

"It is a duty our country owes itself to require of all those aliens who come here that they have a background not inconsistent with American institutions. Such a background might consist of a racial tradition or a national experience...Our country must cease to be regarded as a dumping ground. Which does not mean that it must deny the value of rich accretions drawn from the right kind of immigration...

"There are racial considerations too grave to be brushed aside for any sentimental reasons. Biological laws tell us that certain divergent people will not mix or blend. The Nordics propagate themselves successfully. With other races, the outcome shows deterioration on both sides. Quality of mind and body suggests that observance of ethnic law is as great a necessity to a nation as immigration law.

"We must remember that we have not only the present but the future to safeguard; our obligations extend even to generations yet unborn. The unassimilated alien child menaces our children, as the alien industrial worker, who has destruction rather than production in mind, menaces our industry. It is only when the alien adds vigor to our stock that he is wanted. The dead weight of alien accretion stifles national progress. But we have a hope that cannot be crushed; we have a background that we will not allow to be obliterated." – *Whose Country Is This*, in *Good Housekeeping*, February 1921

"American institutions rest solely on good citizenship. They were created by people who had a background of self-government. New arrivals should be limited to our capacity to absorb them into the ranks of good citizenship. America must be kept American. For this purpose, it is necessary to continue a policy of restricted immigration. It would lie well to make such immigration of a selective nature with some inspection at the source, and based either on a prior census or upon the record of naturalization. Either method would insure the admission of those with the largest capacity and best intention of becoming citizens. I am convinced that our present economic and social conditions warrant a limitation of those to be admitted. We should find additional safety in a law requiring the immediate registration of all aliens. Those who do not want to be partakers of the American spirit ought not to settle in America." – *First Message to Congress*, December 06, 1923

"Restricted immigration has been adopted by this administration chiefly for the purpose of maintaining American standards. It undoubtedly has a very great economic effect. We want the people who live in America, no matter what their origin, to be able to continue in the enjoyment of their present unprecedented advantages. This opportunity would certainly be destroyed by the tremendous influx of foreign peoples if immigration were not restricted. Unemployment would become a menace, and there would follow an almost certain reduction of wages with all the attendant distress and despair which are now suffered in so many parts of Europe. Our first duty is to our own people." – Speaking to a delegation of labor leaders on September 1, 1924; *Foundations of the Republic*, pg. 83

"It is true that we could, with profit, be less sectional and more national in our thought. It would be well if we could replace much that

is only a false and ignorant prejudice with a true and enlightened pride of race." – *Inaugural Address*, March 4, 1925; *Reports and Documents* vol. 8, pg. 223

James Fenimore Cooper

"Equality, in a social sense, may be divided into that of condition, and that of rights. Equality of condition is incompatible with civilization, and is found only to exist in those communities that are but slightly removed from the savage state. In practice, it can only mean a common misery. Equality of rights is a peculiar feature of democracies. These rights are properly divided into civil and political, though even these definitions are not to be taken as absolute, or as literally exact." – *On the Disadvantages of a Monarchy*; *The American Democrat*, pg. 39

John Cotton

"Inheritances are to descend naturally to the next of kin, according to the law of nature, delivered by God." – *An Abstract of the Laws of New England*, 1641, *Decisions of the Superior and Supreme Courts of New Hampshire*, pg. 462

Council of Agde

A.D. 506: "Concerning slaves of the Church, if any bishop shall reasonably have bestowed liberty freely upon well-deserving cases, it is pleasing that the liberty conferred should be cared for by his successors, with whatever the manumitter conferred on them in granting liberty; yet nevertheless we order him to give them the sum of twenty solidi and to set bounds to their lands, little vineyards, or house. Whatever was given above this the Church will revoke after the death of the manumitter. But little things, or things less useful to the Church, to pilgrims, or to the clergy, we permit to remain for their use, saving the right of the Church. The Church shall take care of freedmen legitimately freed by their masters if necessity demands it; but if any one presume to plunder them or to oppress them before the hearing of their case, he shall be prevented by the Church." – *Sacrorum Conciliorum Nova et Amplissima Collectio*, pgs. 280-281

Council of Aix-La-Chapelle

A.D. 816: "Because of the sin of the first man, the punishment of servitude was divinely appointed to the human race, so that to those whom He (the Almighty) saw to be unfit for freedom, he mercifully ordained slavery. And although original sin is remitted to all the faithful by the grace of baptism, nevertheless God, in equity, distributed life to men, constituting some slaves, and others masters, in order that the license of evil-doing by the slaves might be restrained by the power of their lords. There is no accepting of persons with God. For our only Lord sets forth His ordinance equally to the masters and to the slaves. Better a subject servitude than a proud liberty. For many are found freely serving God under flagitious masters, who, although they are subject to them in body, are far above them in mind." – quoted in *The Biblical World*, pg. 409

Council of Berghamstead

A.D. 697: "If anyone shall manumit his slave at the altar, let him be free, and capable to enjoy heirship and weregild, and it shall be lawful for him to go wherever he will, without restraint." – Hopkins, *A View Of Slavery*, pg. 112

Delegation to the Council of Constance

"...whether nation [natio] be understood as a people [gens] marked off from others by blood relationship and habit of unity or by peculiarities of language, the most sure and positive sign and essence of a nation [natio] is divine and human law ... or whether nation [natio] be understood, as it should be, as a territory equal to that of the French nation [natio]....

"Everyone knows that it matters not whether a nation obeys one prince only or several. Are there not many kingdoms in the Spanish nation that pay no tribute to the king of Castile, the chief ruler of Spain? But it does not follow that they are not parts of the Spanish nation. Are not Provence, Dauphiny, Savoy, Burgundy, Lorraine, and many other regions that have nothing to do with our adversary of France included nevertheless in the French or Gallican nation?" –quoted in Louis Loomis, *Nationality at the Council of Constance: An Anglo-FrenchDispute* in S. Thrupp [ed.], *Change in Medieval Society*, New York: Appleton, 1964, pgs. 279-296

Council of Epaone

A.D. 517: "If anyone shall kill his own slave without judicial authority, he shall expiate the effusion of blood by excommunication during two years." – Hopkins, *A View Of Slavery*, pg. 112

Council of Mâcon

A.D. 581: "Therefore, in this present Council, God being the author, we decree that no Christian from henceforth shall serve a Jew, but that any Christian may have license to redeem him, either for freedom or for slavery, twelve shillings being given for a good slave. For it is an impiety that those, whom Christ our Lord has redeemed with the shedding of His blood, should remain bound with the chains of His persecutors. In addition, if any Jew were unwilling to consent to our decree, it shall be lawful for the slave to dwell with Christians, wherever he chooses, so long as his Jewish master delays to come for his money." – Hopkins, *A View Of Slavery*, pg. 112

Council of Narbonne

A.D. 589: "Every man, whether free, or bound, Goth, Roman, Syrian, Greek, or Jew, shall abstain from work on the Lord's Day, neither shall he yoke the oxen, except necessity compels in harvest. Moreover, if any presume to act contrary, if he were a free man, he shall pay six shillings, as a fine to the treasurer of the city, and if he were a slave, he shall receive one hundred stripes." – Hopkins, *A View Of Slavery*, pg. 112

Council of Orléans

A.D. 511: "The slave, who has taken refuge in the Church for any transgression, if he has received the sacrament after the admission of his fault, shall be compelled to return immediately to the service of his master.

A.D. 541: "It shall not be allowed to the slaves of the Church or of the Priests, to take spoils or captives, for it is unjust that while their masters are sustaining the benefit of redemption, the excesses of the slaves should stain the discipline of the Church.

A.D. 549: "No bishop shall ordain any slave who has not received liberty from his master, nor even one who is already free, without the consent of him to whom he is either a slave or who is known to have enfranchised him." – quoted in *The Catholic Encyclopedia*

Council of Toledo

A.D. 589: "Since we are informed that in many cities the slaves of the churches, and of the Bishops, or of all the clergy, are wearied out with various vexatious burdens by the judges, or the public functionaries, this whole Council asks of the piety of our lord [the king] that he will prohibit such presumptuous doings from henceforth: so that the slaves of the aforesaid officers shall labor for their use, or for the Church." – Hopkins, *A View Of Slavery*, pg. 112

Council of Worms

A.D. 868:
28. "If any one shall kill his slave whatever he may have committed worthy of death, without the knowledge of the judges, he shall cleanse away the guilt of blood by a penance of two years, or by excommunication...

38. "If any one shall kill his own slave without the knowledge of the judges–a slave who has committed such thing as may be worthy of death–he shall emend the guilt of blood by excommunication or by a penance for two years.

39. "If any woman incensed by a fit of jealousy should beat her slave, so that within three days she [the slave] should die in torment, so that it be uncertain whether she killed her intentionally or by accident, she shall do lawful penance for five years, if it be by chance, but for seven years if she do it intentionally." – *Sacrorum Conciliorum*, pg. 285

Pierre Courthial

"In giving the Church a mission to the nations, Jesus does not diminish the importance of the individual... At stake is the salvation, well-being, and peace of the nations, that is, societies as God would have them. The Son of God must 'rule all nations' (Rev. 12:5). The nations must bow down before the Lord and come to walk in His light (Rev. 15:4; 21:24). These nations, with their cultures, traditions, and religions turned away from the God of Holy Scripture, are called to be converted to a sure salvation. This conversion of a nation does not happen apart from the individual lives of faithful Christians, but precisely through the influence of such lives. Moreover, each nation's conversion is to reflect the uniqueness of that nation." – *A New Day of Small Beginnings*, pgs. 111-112

William Cowper

England, with all thy faults, I love thee still
My Country! and, while yet a nook is left
Where English minds and manners
    may be found,
Shall be constrained to love thee.
 – *The Task*, pg. 43

Thomas Cranmer

"We condemn no other nations, nor prescribe any thing but to our own people only: For we think it convenient that every country should use such Ceremonies as they shall think best...as in men's ordinances it often chanceth diversely in divers countries." – *On Ceremonies*, in *1549 Book of Common Prayer*, pg. 17

Question. What is thy duty towards thy Neighbour?
"Answer. My duty towards my Neighbour is to love him as myself, and to do to all men as I would they should do unto me: To love, honour, and succour my father and mother: To honour and obey the Queen, and all that are put in authority under her: To submit myself to all my governors, teachers, spiritual pastors and masters: To order myself lowly and reverently to all my betters: To hurt nobody by word nor deed: To be true and just in all my dealing: To bear no malice nor hatred in my heart: To keep my hands from picking and stealing, and my tongue from evil-speaking, lying, and slandering: To keep my body in temperance, soberness, and chastity: Not to covet nor desire other men's goods; but to learn and labour truly to get mine own living, and to do my duty in that state of life, unto which it shall please God to call me." – *1928 Book of Common Prayer*

"Lord God almighty, we rejoice that you are the sovereign Lord who rules over all: may the nations of the world hear your voice and the peoples acknowledge you. Banish the darkness of sin and unbelief. Break down every barrier that stands in the way of the triumph of your Word and gospel and hasten the day when every knee shall bow and every tongue confess that Jesus Christ is Lord. We ask this in his name, and to his glory. Amen." – *1928 Book of Common Prayer*

"Bless all in authority over us; and so rule their hearts and strengthen their hands, that they may punish wickedness and vice, and maintain thy true religion and virtue." – *1928 Book of Common Prayer*

Martin Van Creveld

"Equality... is a dream. When we keep in mind the costs that dream demands, the contradictions to which it inevitably leads, and the horrendous amounts of blood that are so often shed in its name, we would be wise to ensure that the quest for it does not become a nightmare." – *Equality: The Impossible Quest*, ch. 11, pg. 325 (kindle)

Oliver Cromwell

"We are apt to boast that we are Englishmen," he noted, "and truly it is no shame to us that we are so; but it is a motive to us to do like Englishmen, and seek the real good of this nation, and the interest of it." – Cromwell's Speech to Parliament 25th January 1658, in *Nationalism Five Roads to Modernity*, pg. 76

Thomas Cromwell

"Where by dyvers sundrie old authentike histories and cronicles it is manifestly declared and expressed that this realme of Englond is an Impire, and so hath ben accepted in the worlde, governed by one supreme heede and King." – Act of Appeals. *Works of John Brimhall*, pg. 531

Form of Prayer For the Fifth Day of November:
  "We confess, it was thy mercy, thy mercy alone, that we were not then consumed. For our sins cried to heaven against us; and our iniquities justly called for vengeance upon us. But thou hast not dealt with us after our sins, nor rewarded us after our iniquities; nor given us over, as we deserved, to be a prey to our enemies; but didst in mercy delivered us from their malice, and preserved us from death

and destruction. Let the consideration of this thy goodness, O Lord, work in us true repentance, that iniquity may not be our ruine. And increase in us more and more a lively faith, and fruitful love in all holy obedience, that thou maist continue thy favour, with the light of thy Gospel to us and our posterity for evermore; and that for thy dear Son's sake, Jesus Christ our only Mediator and Advocate. Amen." – Act of Appeals. Referenced now in the *Book of Common Prayer* Texts of 1549, 1559, and 1662, pg. 653 [28]

"...it is manifestly declared and expressed that this realm of England is an empire...governed by one Supreme Head and King having the dignity and royal estate of the imperial Crown of the same, unto whom a body politic, compact of all sorts and degrees of people...be bounden and owe next to God a natural and humble obedience; he being also institute[d] and furnished by the goodness and sufferance of Almighty God with plenary, whole, and entire power, preeminence, authority, prerogative, and jurisdiction to render and yield justice and final determination to all...subjects within this his realm, in all causes, matters, debates, and contentions happening to occur, insurge, or begin with the limits thereof, without restraint or provocation to any foreign princes or potentates of the world." – Act Of Restraint 1553, quoted in *The Origins of the Western Legal Tradition*, pg. 296

Rebekah Curtis

"In early American history, suffrage rights were determined by states, most of which originally limited the franchise to property owners. This granted governance to those who were most invested in promoting a healthy community. Property owners literally 'had a stake' in the community that more transient people did not have. Their real connection to that community gave them incentive to vote in a way that considered the good of the community (including the members of their families) rather than their own immediate interests. They were more future- and investment-oriented than present- and spending-oriented. Limiting the franchise to property-owning heads of house-

---

28 Within three months of the Gunpowder Plot being discovered, an Act of Parliament was passed on January 21st 1606, to appoint 5th November in each year as a day of thanksgiving for 'the joyful day of deliverance'. – The Act remained in force until 1859.

holds effectively kept the nuclear family as the fundamental unit of society. Membership in a nuclear family was politically beneficial when political anchorage was located in the family's head. He would cast his family's vote for what would strengthen their community in the long term." – *Emancipated Surf, Touchestone Magazine*, 29.2 – March/April 2016

Cyprian

"If it is a source of joy and glory to men to have children like unto themselves – and it is more agreeable to have begotten an offspring then when the remaining progeny responds to the parent with like distinctive features – how much greater is the gladness of God the Father, when any one is so spiritually born that in his acts and praises the divine eminence of race [genus] is announced!" – *The Treatises of Cyprian*, in *Ante-Nicene Fathers*, edited by Roberts, 1886, pg. 495 [29]

Czech Nobility

Upon the death of Jan Hus, a Czech, at the hands of the Germans, the Czech barons (ultimately 452 signatories) strongly protested "the dishonor of our nationality and of the Bohemian land." They called the killers "patent enemies of our nationality [lingua]," who tended "to the indelible besmirching of our Bohemian and Moravian race [gens] and of the whole Slavic nationality [lingua]." In addition to their religious demands, the leaders of the brewing revolution requested, among other things (1419): that no foreigners were to be put in civil offices if capable Czechs were available; that the Czech language was to be used in judicial proceedings; and that Czechs were to have "first voice" everywhere in the realm. Assembling in Prague Castle in 1420, the Czech nobles issued a proclamation in which they described Emperor Zikmund as "a great and brutal enemy of the Czech kingdom and language." To their religious demands they added "the common weal of the kingdom and our Czech language." As late as 1469, long after the Hussite Wars ended, in response to a papal rejection of a Czech elected to the Bohemian crown, a call was issued

"to all faithful Czechs and Moravians, genuine lovers of God's truth and disciples of your own Czech language." The pope and his allies were blamed for wishing "to destroy, wipe out, and utterly suppress the Czech language"; he "inflames and incites all the nations and languages of the surrounding lands against us." – quoted in Kaminsky, *A History of the Hussite Revolution*, pg. 138

---

29 Cyprian's argument presupposes that it is proper and fitting for men to take such joy, and hence that it is improper and unfitting for men to neglect the value of lineal similitude or, worse, to positively value dissimilitude.

D

R.L. Dabney

"The duties of patriotism are not prominently urged in sacred Scripture. This we account for, not by supposing, with a certain sickly school of moralists, that this sentiment is selfish, narrow or inconsistent with the broadest philanthropy; but by the facts, that the obligations of the citizen are not directly religious, and that they are so natural as to require little inculcation. The Hebrew Scriptures do indeed say enough, as in the text, to justify an intense love of native land and its institutions. Civil government is God's ordinance, and if it be just, one of his greatest temporal blessings. The diversity of tongues, characters, races and interests among mankind forbids their union in one universal commonwealth. The aggregation of men into separate nations is therefore necessary; and the authority of the governments instituted over them, to maintain internal order and external defence against aggression, is of divine appointment. Hence, to sustain our government with heart and hand is not only made by God our privilege, but our duty. Our best way to advance the well-being of the [human] race is to advance that of the portion of our [human] race associated with us in the same society. He who extends his philanthropy so broadly as to refuse a special attachment to the interests of his own people, will probably make it so thin as to be of no account to any people. I therefore believe that there is nothing opposed to an enlightened Christianity in a warm patriotism for our particular country. This feeling is made up of several elements: a legitimate regard for our own welfare and worldly estate, interest in that of our families, and a wider benevolence towards our fellow citizens; together with an honest pride in the glories of our history, and in the justice of our institutions, with the attachments of local affection to the very scenery and soil of our native land." – *Sermon: The Christian Soldier, Discussions*, vol. 1, pg. 614

"The theistic scheme [of social order], then, traces civil government and the civic obligation to the will and act of God, our sovereign, moral ruler and proprietor, in that he from the first made social principles a constitutive part of our souls, and placed us under social relations that are as original and natural as our own persons. These relations were: first of the family, then of the clan, and, as men multiplied, of the commonwealth. It follows, thence, that social government in some form is as natural as man. If asked whence my obligation to obey my equal, or possible inferior, as civil magistrate, it answers; Because God wills me to do it. He has an infinite right. The advantages and conveniences of such an arrangement may illustrate and even reinforce the obligation; they do not originate it. Civil government is an ordinance of the Maker: magistrates receive place and power under His Providence. They are His ministers to man." – *Discussions on Civic Ethics, The Practical Philosophy*, pg. 375

"The right of suffrage and eligibility to office is not an inalienable natural franchise, but a function of responsibility entrusted to suitable classes of citizens as a trust." – *Discussions on Civic Ethics, The Practical Philosophy*, pg. 401

"The instrumentalities of the family are chosen and ordained of God as the most efficient of all means of grace—more truly and efficaciously means of saving grace than all the other ordinances of the church. To family piety are given the best promises of the gospel, under the new, as well as under the old dispensation." – *Parental Responsibilities* in *Discussions*, vol.1, pg. 693

"Nothing is more obnoxious to the principles of Jacobinism than what it denounces as 'caste.' It delights to use the word because it is freighted with bad associations derived from the stories

— R.L. Dabney —

we hear of the oppressive hereditary distinctions of the people of Hindostan. Of course there is a sense in which every just conscience reprehends inequalities of caste. This is, where they are made pretext for depriving an order or class of citizens of privileges which belong to them of right, and for whose exercise they are morally and intellectually qualified. But this is entirely a different thing from saying that all the different orders of persons in a state are naturally and morally entitled to all the same privileges, whether qualified or not, simply because they are men and adults. The Jacobin trick of sophistry is to confound these different propositions together; and when they denounce 'wicked caste,' the application they make of their denunciation includes not only oppressive inequalities, but every difference in the distribution of powers and privileges. Now, the Scripture[s] recognize and ordain such distribution; of, if the reader pleases, such distinctions of caste in the latter sense. Such is the stubborn fact. Thus, in the Hebrew commonwealth, the descendants of Levi were disfranchised of one privilege which belonged to all their brethren of the other tribes; and enfranchised with another privilege from which all their brethren were excluded. A Levite could not hold an inch of land in severalty. (Num. xviii. 22, 33) No member of another tribe, not even of the princely tribe of Judah, could perform even the lowest function in the tabernacle. (Heb. vii. 13, 14) These differences are nowhere grounded in any statement that the children of Levi were more or less intelligent and religious than their fellow-citizens. Another 'caste distinction' appears among the descendants of Levi himself. The sons of Aaron alone could offer sacrifices or incense in the sanctuary... Among the sons of Aaron another hereditary distinction presents itself. The individual who had the right of the first born took the high priesthood, with its superior prerogatives... This privilege was limited by a certain hereditary disqualification. He could only marry a virgin, and was forbidden to marry a widow, however virtuous and religious. A 'caste distinction' is also found among the bondmen, whose subjection was legalized by the constitution. A person of Hebrew blood could only be enslaved for six years. A person of foreign blood could be held in hereditary slavery, although born within the land of Israel as much as the other. It was also provided that the treatment of bondmen of Hebrew blood should be more lenient. A 'caste distinction' was also provided concerning the entrance of persons of foreign blood into the Hebrew state and church (Exodus xvii. 16; Deut xxiii. 3-8). The descendants of Amalek were forever inhibited. The descendants of Ammon and Moab were debarred to the tenth generation. The Egyptians and Edomites could be admitted at the third generation; the one, because their patriarch Esau was brother to Jacob, the other, because the Israelites had once lived in Egypt.

"Let the inference from these histories be clearly understood. It is not claimed that these caste distinctions established by God himself obligate us positively to establish similar distinctions in our day. But the fact that God once saw fit to establish them does prove that they cannot be essentially sinful. To assert that they are, impugns the righteousness of God. Whence it follows, in direct opposition to the Jacobin theory, that should suitable circumstances again arise such 'caste distinctions' may be righteous. It will be exclaimed that the New Testament reversed all this. We shall be reminded of Paul's famous declaration (Col. iii. 11): 'Where there is neither Jew nor Greek, circumcision nor uncircumcision, barbarian, Scythian, bond nor free, but Christ is all and in all'; or this (Gal. iii. 28): 'There is neither Jew nor Greek, there is neither bond nor free, there is neither male nor female, for ye are all one in Christ Jesus.' But before a literal and mechanical equality can be inferred from these, it must be settled what the Holy Spirit meant by being 'one in Christ,' and whether the parts which are combined to construct a component unity are not always unequal instead of equal. The latter is certainly the apostle's teaching when he compares the spiritual body to the animal body, with many members of dissimilar honor. The apostle himself demonstrates that he never designed the leveling sense to be put upon his words by proceeding after he had uttered them to subject women in one sense to an inequality by imposing upon them ecclesiastical subordination, and even a different dress, in the church. The Scriptures thus teach that all distinctions of caste are not unjust in the sense charged by the current theory." – *Anti-Biblical Theories of Rights, Pres. Quarterly.* pgs. 295-297

"I assert that it is incredible the American Congress of 1776 could have meant their proposition to be taken in the Jacobin sense; for they were British Whigs. Their perpetual claim was to the principles and franchises of the British Constitution, and no other. Their politics were formed by the teachings of John Hampden, Lord Fairfax, Algernon Sidney, Lord Somers, and the revolutionists of 1688. I should be loath to suppose those great men so stupid and ignorant of the history of their own country as not to understand the British rights, which they expressly say they are claiming." – *Civic Ethics, The Practical Philosophy,* pg. 887

"Instead of allowing to all human beings a specific equality and an absolute natural independence, these Scripture doctrines assume that there are orders of human beings naturally unequal in their inherited rights, as in their bodily and mental qualities; that God has not ordained any human being to this proud independence, but placed all in subordination under authority, the child under its mother, the mother under her husband, the husband under the ecclesiastical and civil magistrates, and these under the law, whose guardian and avenger is God himself." – *The Public Preaching of Women, Discussions,* vol. 2, pg. 107

"To meet the argument of these aspiring Am-

azons fairly, one must teach, with Moses, the Apostle Paul, John Hampden, Washington, George Mason, John C. Calhoun, and all that contemptible rabble of 'old fogies,' that political society is composed of 'superiors, inferiors, and equals'; that while all these bear an equitable moral relation to each other, they have very different natural rights and duties; that just government is not founded on the consent of the individuals governed, but on the ordinance of God, and hence a share in the ruling franchise is not a natural right at all, but a privilege to be bestowed according to a wise discretion on a limited class having qualification to use it for the good of the whole; that the integers out of which the State is constituted are not individuals, but families represented in their parental heads; that every human being is born under authority (parental and civic) instead of being born 'free' in the licentious sense that liberty is each one's privilege of doing what he chooses; that subordination, and not that license, is the natural state of all men; and that without such equitable distribution of different duties and rights among the classes naturally differing in condition, and subordination of some to others, and of all to the law, society is as impossible as is the existence of a house without distinction between the foundation-stone and the capstones" – *Women's Rights,* in *Southern Magazine,* pg. 326

"A hundred years ago French atheism gave the world the Jacobin theory of political rights. The Bible had been teaching mankind for three thousand years the great doctrine of men's moral equality before the universal Father, the great basis of all free, just, and truly republican forms of civil society. Atheism now travestied this true doctrine by her mortal heresy of the absolute equality of men, asserting that every human being is naturally and inalienably entitled to every right, power, and prerogative in civil society which is allowed to any man or any class. The Bible taught a liberty which consists in each man's unhindered privilege of having and doing just those things, and no others, to which he is rationally and morally entitled. Jacobinism taught the liberty of license—every man's natural right to indulge his own absolute will; and it set up this fiendish caricature as the object of sacred worship for mankind. Now, democratic Protestantism in these United

States has become so ignorant, so superficial and willful, that it confounds the true republicanism with this deadly heresy of Jacobinism. It has ceased to know a difference. Hence, when the atheistic doctrine begins to bear its natural fruits of license, insubordination, communism, and anarchy, this bastard democratic Protestantism does not know how to rebuke them. It has recognized the parents; how can it consistently condemn the children?" – *The Attractions of the Roman Catholic Church, Pres. Quarterly*, vol. 8, pg. 159

"Other active principles come in to limit and intensify the affection [of patriotism]: similarity of language, race, and modes of thought and feeling; common interests; the ties of a thousand proud associations of country and ancestors; the local associations of the familiar and beloved scenery, the plains, the mountains, the streams, the homes, the cemeteries, to which our hearts are knit by a thousand tender bonds of suggestion." – *The Practical Philosophy*, pg. 95

"Other instances of supposed loss of natural rights are alleged with more plausibility; as when a citizen is restrained by law from selling his corn out of the country, (a thing naturally moral per se) from some economic motive of public good; and yet the righteous citizen feels bound to obey. I reply: if the restriction of the government is not unjust, then there exists such a state of circumstances among the fellow citizens, that the sale of the corn out of the country, under those circumstances, would have been a natural breach of the law of righteousness and love towards them. So that, under the particular state of the case, the man's natural right to sell his corn had terminated. Natural rights may change with circumstances." – *Syllabus and Notes*, pg. 868

John Dagg

"As every individual of our race is born of depraved parents, and brings depravity with him into the world, we are led to conceive of it as propagated from parent to child. This accords with the representations of Scripture; 'Adam begat a son in his own likeness.' It accords also with analogies to which we are familiar. Plants and animals propagate their like; diseases are often hereditary, and peculiarities of temper

and mind by which parents were distinguished, often appear in their children." – *Manual Of Theology*, bk. 4, ch. 3, pg. 154

"There is a natural union between Adam and his descendants. He is their natural parent; and, because of this relation, they inherit a depraved nature. Our moral union with him renders our condemnation just, from the moment we possess separate existence, because of our personal depravity; and our natural union with him rendered it proper, that our condemnation should be included in the general sentence. There is a federal union between Adam and his descendants. We have before seen that a covenant, not in the common, but the Scripture sense of the term, was made with Adam. This covenant, this arrangement or constitution of things, made the future character and condition of his descendants dependent on his obedience. He was, in this respect, their federal head." – *Manual Of Theology*, bk. 4, ch. 3, pg. 165

"Nature is not something different from God operating." – *Manual Of Theology*, bk. 4, ch. 3, pg. 166

"Every individual of mankind is a neighbor to be loved; but, in the arrangements of society, peculiar relations arise, giving origin to peculiar obligations. No one ceases to be a neighbor; and the obligation to love every one as a neighbor does not cease; but, instead of unvarying benevolence to every human being, we have, according to the relations which spring up in society, the modifications of love corresponding to these relations—such as conjugal love, parental love, &c. And the outward forms of duty, in which these various modifications of love are expressed, vary according to the several relations, and become what are denominated social duties." – *Moral Science*, pg. 236

"The benefits of marriage are not confined to those who are at the head of the family. The children are shut up by it under the joint protection of their parents, and blessed with their united care. If piety and love regulate the household, the children are trained in the ways of virtue and religion, and are taught how to enrich themselves with wealth of character, and treasure laid up in heaven. Children born out of wedlock are usually thrown on the care of the mother, the weaker parent; and hence they have less than half of the means which legitimate children enjoy for support and education. They witness none of the sacred affection and tender sympathy which subsist between parents lawfully united in the conjugal relation; and they have few inducements to obey the command, 'Honor thy father and mother.' Such unfortunates enter on life under many disadvantages; yet, if surrounded by a society generally virtuous, they may have sufficient intercourse with well-regulated families to guard their morals. But if marriage were universally abolished, all the human race would be born in these sad circumstances. All would be without a well-regulated home for their childhood, and without the influence and example of well-regulated families in the vicinity. Brought into the world like the beasts of the field, they would be given up to animal appetites and passions, without the training necessary to develop and cultivate the moral powers.

"Another advantage of marriage consists in the provision which it makes for aged and infirm parents. Children who have been taught to honor their father and mother, take pleasure in sustaining them when old age comes, and in rendering their declining days happy. But were matrimony unknown, not only would helpless infants be left to perish for want of parental care, but aged and helpless parents would also be left to perish for want of filial affection and maintenance.

"Civil government was at first patriarchal; and, having derived its origin from family government, it is still indebted to family government for its most efficient support. When children have been taught to obey their parents, they are prepared to obey civil rulers; and virtue and order must prevail in a state which is composed of well-regulated families. But if family organizations were destroyed, the fences of morality would be broken down, and vice would overrun the community, spreading everywhere misery and desolation.

"Marriage, by producing family government, is an important means of preserving and perpetuating religion in the world. A well-regulated family is a garden enclosed, in which the young plants of piety may be nurtured. Here we find the examples of religious education, by which men are trained to moral greatness, and prepared to adorn, elevate, and bless the human race, and glorify God. Were marriage banished from the earth, religious education would cease; and human beings, herding together like the beasts, would be given up to beastly vices. If the natural tendencies of things were not counteracted by some divine interposition, the knowledge of God and the practice of virtue would soon become extinct in the world.

"As God's appointed means of propagating the human race, as his first institution for the benefit of the race, and as the source of many inestimable blessings, indispensable to the existence and happiness of society, marriage deserves to be honored by all; and its sanctity to be guarded from every encroachment. To incorrect views respecting the importance of this divine institution, and a want of reverence for it, much of the vice may be traced, that now degrades mankind, curses human society, and brings down the wrath of heaven, as formerly on sinful Sodom." – *Moral Science*, pgs. 240-242

"The first form of civil society was patriarchal. The father was the natural protector of his children. In the protection of the family, he was under obligation to employ his own strength, and had the right to command the aid of his children according to their strength. The employment of children in this service is manifestly alluded to in the words of Scripture: 'As arrows are in the hand of a mighty man, so are the children of the youth. Happy is the man that hath his quiver full of them; they shall not be ashamed, but they shall speak with the enemies in the gate.' This allusion takes us back to the early period in the history of mankind, when the family constituted the civil society, and the father was the civil governor.

"A second form of civil society embraced a tribe descended from one ancestor. After the death of the father, the oldest brother succeeded to his authority, and governed the family. Whole tribes remained through successive generations combined in one society under one government; and originally the authority to govern was transmitted by natural descent. But in various cases superior strength or superior skill prevailed over primogeniture, and elevated to authority a rival of the natural claimant. Alliances, conquests, or other causes frequently united two or more tribes under one government, and civil societies became enlarged into the nations which now divide the population of the globe.

"While the patriarchal form of civil society continued, the right of membership was determined by natural descent. The inheritance might be taken away by injustice; but, unless forfeited by crime, it was the right of every descendant from the patriarchal ancestor. It was the exclusive right of the descendants, and no alien could claim it. The present forms of civil society so far retain the patriarchal features, that membership is universally transmitted by descent, and in many nations men of an alien race are found who are not admitted to membership as children of the family.

"We have before proved it to be the will of God, that men should live in society; and we shall hereafter prove that civil government is an ordinance of God. But it cannot be proved that the whole human race should be united under one civil government; or that the boundaries or forms of the several governments are determined by the divine will, irrespective of human judgment and choice. The patriarchal features, being natural, exhibit the best claim to divine authority." – *Moral Science*, pgs. 279-280

"In every case, that form of government is best which is best adapted to the character of the people." – *Moral Science*, pg. 281

"The natural endowments of men, physical and intellectual, differ greatly; and the opportunities which his providence affords for obtaining enjoyment, are much greater to some men than to others. If human governments should attempt to make the rights of all men equal in extent, they would oppose the manifest will of the Creator; and any equalization which could be effected, would not continue a single day, unless the natural endowments of men were made equal." – *Moral Science*, pg. 285

"It is not necessary to the justice of social regulations, that they have the universal consent of those who are governed by them. Men are, for the most part, born into society previously organized; and they are bound by its regulations, before their consent can be asked. The poor man may never consent to the distribution of property, which denies him the use of his neighbor's wealth, but he is nevertheless bound to observe it. No man has a right to steal from his neighbor, because he has not yielded his formal consent to the existing distribution of property.

The social regulations under which each one is born, are to him the will of God, when they do not interfere with his duty to God. He is required to obey 'every ordinance of man for the Lord's sake,' whether he consents to the duty or not; and the requirement is approved by the moral judgments of men generally." – *Moral Science*, pg. 286

"Marriage is a divine institution, and the superiority of the husband in the conjugal relation, has been established by divine authority. In many ages and countries, husbands have tyrannized over their wives, and the female sex have been reduced to deplorable degradation; but Christianity has never attempted to relieve their sufferings, by teaching them insubordination to their husbands. So civil governments have often been oppressive, and the people have groaned under their intolerable burden; but the voice of Christianity to them, in the midst of their sufferings, has always been, 'Submit yourselves to every ordinance of man for the Lord's sake. Honor the king.' Whatever abuses of the matrimonial relation may have cursed the earth, it would be a still greater curse, if marriage were banished from human society. In like manner, the worst form of human government under which men have ever suffered, is better than total anarchy. Hence, even in oppressive governments, the rulers are 'powers ordained of God;' and hence, obedience has been required to the king, even when that king was Nero." – *Moral Science*, pg. 288

Dante

"...as life of happiness, which no one is able to attain by himself without the aid of someone else, since one has need of many things which no single individual is able to provide. Therefore the Philosopher says that man is by nature a social animal. And just as for his well-being an individual requires the domestic companionship provided by family, so for its well-being a household requires a community, for otherwise it would suffer many defects that would hinder happiness." – *Convivio*, pg. 155

"All men on whom the Higher Nature has stamped the love of truth should especially concern themselves in laboring for posterity, in order that future generations may be enriched by their efforts, as they themselves were made rich by the efforts of generations past." – *De Monarchia*, pg. 115

"Since it was the pleasure of the citizens of the most beautiful and famous daughter of Rome, Florence, to cast me out of her sweet bosom— where I was born and bred up to the pinnacle of my life, and where, with her good will, I desire with all my heart to rest my weary mind and to complete the span of time that is given to me—I have traveled like a stranger, almost like a beggar, through virtually all the regions to which this tongue of ours extends, displaying against my will the wound of fortune for which the wounded one is often unjustly accustomed to be held accountable. Truly I have been a ship without sail or rudder, brought to different ports, inlets, and shores by the dry wind that painful poverty blows." – *Convivio*, pg. 9

"Brother, the virtue of charity
   brings quiet to our wills, so we desire
   but what we have, and thirst for nothing else.
If we should feel a yearning to be higher,
   such a desire would strike disharmony
   against His will who knows, and wills us here.
That cannot catch these wheels,
   as you shall see:
   recall love's nature, recall that Heaven is
   to live in loving, necessarily.

For it is of the essence of this bliss
   to hold one's dwelling in the divine Will,
   who makes our single wills the same, and His,
So that, although we dwell from sill to sill
   throughout this kingdom, that is as we please,
   as it delights the King in whose desire
We find our own. In His will is our peace."
– *Paradiso*, pg. 29 [30]

Charles Darwin

"A tribe including many members who from possessing in a high degree the spirit of patriotism fidelity obedience courage and sympathy, always ready to aid one another, to sacrifice themselves for the common good, would be victorious over most other tribes." – *Origin of the Species*, pg. 537

Donald Davidson

I was not there, at Talladega,
   Horseshoe Bend, King's Mountain,
Not at Suwanee, Mobile, or Pensacola
In days when men were tall.
   I have not eaten
Acorns to still my hunger
   or followed the war-path
After a fiery leader tough as the hickory.
I have not heard the cry of the owl at night
With dreadful understanding. I have not seen
A friend plunge, furred with arrows,
   across his plough
Or heard the scream
   of a woman snatched from the hearth
By painted warriors.
   And when it was misty dawn
I was not by the ragged breastworks,
   priming my rifle,
Hearing the British drums beat. I have not sung
Old songs or danced old tunes.
   I have read a book.
I have loitered by graves. I have trod old floors,
Tiptoed through musty rooms
   and glanced at letters
Spread under glass and signed Yr Obt Servant,
And wistfully conned old platitudes in stone.
But shall I say the praise of men, bright honor,
The songs of my own race
   and the ways of fighters
Are something read in a book only, or graven
Only in stone and not in the hearts of men?
– *The Tall Men, in Poems*

Martin Davie

"The Trinity expresses God's fundamental nature as three persons in one unity, a family community. Many see in the Trinity a model for family relationships, with each person being unique, yet living and being in close spiritual and communal contact. The family is the basic unity of human life in creation. Men and women made in the image of God are set in creation as a family. It was not good for man to be alone, and humanity is to be fruitful and multiply (Gen. 1:28)." – *New Dictionary of Theology*, Second ed., pgs. 330–331

---

30   Dante is in the lowest sphere of Paradise, that of the inconstant moon – an allegory for those who did not fulfill their sacred vows – he asks his sister-in-law Piccarda whether she desires a higher place, to love more and see more and be held more dear. He is thinking in emulous terms: envy, not love, demands equality.

Samuel Davies

"What! shall we resign so extensive and flourishing a country—a land of plenty, and liberty—shall we tamely surrender it to a parcel of perfidious French, and savage Indians? Shall slavery here clank her chain, or tyranny rage with lawless fury?" – From a sermon preached during the French and Indian War, in *Memoir*, pg. 72

Thomas Osborne Davis

How bright will the day be–
   how radiant and blest
The dawning of Freedom
   and Peace in the west,
When the chain that foul treason
   around us had cast
Will be shattered and flung
   to the spoiler at last.
When that trumpet-toned voice
   will go forth, as before,
Till its echo resounds
   on earth's uttermost shore-
"No laws under Heaven
   will the Irishman own,
But the home hallowed laws
   of his country alone."
Then our national emblems
   aloft shall be seen,
The shamrock and harp
   on a banner of green;
And when free to the breezes
   that banner shall fly,
The wide world
   to enslave it again we defy!
The shameful distinction
   of class and of creed
Will be trampled to dust
   like a poisonous weed;
And the sweet flower of concord
   shall rise in its room,
Breathing Union and peace
   over bigotry's tomb.
The peasant no more
   shall be driven from the soil,
Nor robbed like a slave
   of the fruit of his toil;
But the right to his cot
   and his acres shall be,
As the lord's to his manor-hall,
   sacred and free!
The loom and the workshop,

now silent so long,
Will echo again
   with glad industry's song;
And comfort and smiling
   contentment be there,
Where our artisans languish
   in want and despair.
Let us pray for that day–
   let us manfully strive,
Nor cease while
   one true Irish heart is alive;
And shame on the sceptic
   who dreams we can fail,
Or the dastard whose heart
   for a moment could quail.
We have God on our side,
   who hath blessed the green isle,
And made it with beauty
   and verdure to smile
Who preserved us in bondage
   still faithful and true,
And gave us the spirit
   no chains could subdue.
We have him still to lead us
   our guide from the first,
Who despaired not when prospects
   were darkest and worst–
Whose fervour the cold hand
   of time cannot chill
Our true-hearted,
   high-minded Patriot still!
In that God we will trust–
   by that leader we'll stand,
United – unshrinking –
   bold heart, and brave hand,
And the Saxon shall quail
   at the voice of our zeal,
"O'Connell–the land of our love–
   and Repeal!"
– Irish national poem, *Spirit Of The Nation*,
pgs. 60-61

When all beside a vigil keep,
The West's asleep, the West's asleep—
Alas! and well may Erin weep,
When Connaught lies in slumber deep.
There lake and plain smile fair and free,
'Mid rocks—their guardian chivalry—
Sing oh! let man learn liberty
From crashing wind and lashing sea.

That chainless wave and lovely land
Freedom and Nationhood demand—

Be sure, the great God never planned,
For slumbering slaves, a home so grand.
And, long, a brave and haughty race
Honoured and sentinelled the place—
Sing oh! not even their sons' disgrace
Can quite destroy their glory's trace.

For often, in O'Connor's van,
To triumph dashed each Connaught clan—
And fleet as deer the Normans ran
Through Corlieu's Pass and Ardrahan.
And later times saw deeds as brave;
And glory guards Clanricarde's grave—
Sing oh! they died their land to save,
At Aughrim's slopes and Shannon's wave.

And if, when all a vigil keep,
The West's asleep, the West's asleep—
Alas! and well may Erin weep,
That Connaught lies in slumber deep.
But, hark! some voice like thunder spake:
"The West's awake! the West's awake!"—
"Sing oh! hurra! let England quake,
We'll watch till death for Erin's sake!"
— *The West's Asleep* [31]

Christopher Davis

"This is the meaning of Revelation 21:24 and
26: 'The kings of the earth will bring their
splendor into [God's kingdom]…. The glory
and honor of the nations will be brought into
it.' The Greek term translated 'nations' (ἔθνη,
ethnē) refers not to nation states, but to all the
various ethnic groups that make up the human
race. John is saying that the 'new heaven and
new earth' will include people 'from every tribe
and language and people and nation' (see Rev
5:9; 7:9). Each ethnic group will make its unique
contributions to the richness and beauty of
God's New Creation. The consummated kingdom of God will be a community based on the
best theology and best philosophy, the best city
planning and best social theory, the best science
and best technology. The 'new heaven and new
earth' will include the best art, the best architecture, and the best landscaping from every culture. We will enjoy the best music, the best drama, the best literature, and the best food from
every nation. Over time, we will learn every
language so that we may share with each of the
redeemed saints in his or her 'heart language.'

This will be necessary because there are aspects
of the glory of God that can only be communicated in Navaho or Hmong or Chibemba.
We will have minds that can understand and
retain the finer points of molecular biology and
quantum theory, so that we may grasp all the
wonders God wants to show us." – *College Press
NIV Commentary. Revelation*, pgs. 376-377

Christopher Dawson

"A civilization like that of China, in which the
patriarchal family remained the cornerstone
of society and the foundation of religion and
ethics, has preserved its cultural traditions for
more than 2,000 years without losing its vitality.
In the classical cultures of the Mediterranean
world, however, this was not the case. Here the
patriarchal family failed to adapt itself to the
urban conditions of the Hellenic civilization,
and consequently the whole culture lost its
stability. Conditions of life both in the Greek
city state and in the Roman Empire favoured
the man without a family who could devote
his whole energies to the duties and pleasures
of public life. Late marriages and small families
became the rule, and men satisfied their sexual
instincts by homosexuality or by relations with
slaves and prostitutes. This aversion to marriage and the deliberate restriction of the family
by the practice of infanticide and abortion was
undoubtedly the main cause of the decline of
ancient Greece, as Polybius pointed out in the
second century B.C. And the same factors were
equally powerful in the society of the Empire,
where the citizen class even in the provinces
was extraordinarily sterile and was recruited
not by natural increase, but by the constant
introduction of alien elements, above all from
the servile class. Thus the ancient world lost
its roots alike in the family and in the land and
became prematurely withered. The reconstitution of Western civilization was due to the
coming of Christianity and the re-establishment
of the family on a new basis." – *The Dynamics
Of World History*, pgs. 162-163

"It was literally Rome that killed Rome. The
great cosmopolitan city of gold and marble,
the successor of Alexandria and Antioch, had
nothing in common with the old capital of the
rural Latin state. It served no social function, it

---

31   In this poem "The West" refers to the Irish region of Connacht, and "Erin" refers to Ireland itself.

was an end in itself, and its population drawn from every nation under heaven existed mainly to draw their Government doles, and to attend the free spectacles with which the Government provided them. It was a vast useless burden on the back of the empire which broke at last under the increasing strain."– *The Dynamics Of World History*, pg. 72

"It is true that Europe was also a society of nations and that therefore the racial element, the bond of common blood, like the bond of common speech and common fatherland, played an important part in its development. But both civilization and nation are like chemical compounds which owe their very existence to their synthesis and any attempt to resolve them into their compound elements involves their destruction." – *Judgment of the Nations*, pg. 143

"Every form of education that mankind has known, from the savage tribe to the highest forms of culture, has always involved two elements–the element of technique and the element of tradition; and hitherto it has always been the second that has been more important. In the first place education teaches children how to do things–how to read and write, and even at a much more primitive level how to hunt and cook, and plant and build. But besides all these things, education has always meant the initiation of the young into the social and spiritual inheritance of the community: in other words education has meant the transmission of culture." – *Understanding Europe*, pg. 6

"An ideology in the modern sense of the word is very different from a faith, although it is intended to fulfill the same sociological function. It is the work of man, an instrument by which the conscious political will attempts to mold the social traditions to its purpose. But faith looks beyond the world of man and his works; it introduces man to a higher and more universal range of reality than the finite and temporal world to which the state and economic order belong. And thereby it introduces into human life an element of spiritual freedom which may have a creative and transforming influence on man's social culture and historical destiny as well as on his inner personal experience." – *Christopher Dawson: A Cultural Mind in the Age of the Great War*, pg. 391

"The process of secularization arises not from the loss of faith but from the loss of social interest in the world of faith. It begins the moment men feel that religion is irrelevant to the common way of life and that society as such has nothing to do with the truths of faith." – *Divinings*, pg. 406

"The beginnings of Western culture are to be found in the new spiritual community which arose from the ruins of the Roman Empire owing to the conversion of the Northern barbarians to the Christian faith. The Christian Church inherited the traditions of the Empire. It came to the barbarians as the bearer of a higher civilization, endowed with the prestige of Roman law and the authority of the Roman name. The breakdown of the political organization of the Roman Empire had left a great void which no heathen king or general could fill, and this void was filled by the Church as the teacher and law-giver of the new peoples. The Latin Fathers–Ambrose, Augustine, Leo and Gregory–were in a real sense the fathers of Western culture, since it was only in so far as the different peoples of the West were incorporated in the spiritual community of Christendom that they acquired a common culture. It is this, above all, that distinguishes the Western development from that of the other world civilizations. The great cultures of the ancient East, like China and India, were autochthonous growths which represent a continuous process of development in which religion and culture grew together from the same sociological roots and the same natural environment. But in the West it was not so. Primitive Europe outside the Mediterranean lands preserved no common center and no unified tradition of spiritual culture. The people of the North possessed no written literature, no cities, no stone architecture. They were, in short, 'barbarians'; and it was only by Christianity and the elements of higher culture transmitted to them by the Church that Western Europe acquired unity and form." – *Religion and the Rise of Western Culture*, pg. 26

"The Middle Ages were not the ages of faith in the sense of unquestioning submission to authority and blind obedience. They were ages of spiritual struggle and social change, in which the existing situation was continually being modified by the reforming energy and the intellectual activity that were generated by the contact between the living stream of Christian tradition and the youthful peoples of the west." – *Medieval Essays*, pg. 66

"Western civilization at the present day is passing through a crisis which is essentially different from anything that has been previously experienced. Other societies in the past have changed their social institutions or their religious beliefs under the influence of external forces or the slow development of internal growth. But none, like our own, has ever consciously faced the prospect of a fundamental alteration of the beliefs and institutions on which the whole fabric of social life rests ... Civilization is being uprooted from its foundations in nature and tradition and is being reconstituted in a new organization which is as artificial and mechanical as a modern factory." – *Desire and Deceit*, pg. 134

"If we condemn the principle of diversity or polarity in history and demand an abstract uniform civilization which will obviate the risk of wars and religious schisms, we are offending against life in the same way as though we condemned the differences of the sexes, as many heretics actually have done, because it leads to immorality." – *Judgment of the Nations*, pg. 119

Vox Day

"There are not two alternatives. Universalism is dead, because it only ever had appeal to a) white Anglo imperialists and b) Jewish globalists. Universalism can only hold lasting mass appeal in a homogeneous society where everyone is the same tribe; once the society becomes sufficiently heterogeneous, tribalism and identity politics will inevitably rise to the fore. This is the process we have witnessed in the post-1965 USA." – *Don't Resist the Truth*

Dead Sea Scrolls

"They shall love each man his brother as himself; they shall succour the poor, the needy, and the stranger. A man shall seek his brother's well-being and shall not sin against his near kin. They shall keep from fornication according to the statute. They shall rebuke each man his brother according to the commandment and shall bear no rancour from one day to the next." – *The Dead Sea scrolls in English*, pg. 102

Guido De Bres

"We believe that God created man out of the dust of the earth, and made and formed him after His own image and likeness, good, righteous, and holy, capable in all things to will agreeably to the will of God." – *Belgic Confession*, art. 14

Declaration Of The Rights Of Man

"The nation constitutes the principal source of all sovereignty. No assembly or individual may exercise a power that does not derive expressly from the nation."

Declaration of Arbroath

"...we know and from the chronicles and books of the ancients we find that among other famous nations our own, the Scots, has been graced with widespread renown.

"They journeyed from Greater Scythia by way of the Tyrrhenian Sea and the Pillars of Hercules, and dwelt for a long course of time in Spain among the most savage tribes, but nowhere could they be subdued by any race, however barbarous.

"Thence they came, twelve hundred years after the people of Israel crossed the Red Sea, to their home in the west where they still live today.

"The Britons they first drove out, the Picts they utterly destroyed, and, even though very often assailed by the Norwegians, the Danes and the English, they took possession of that home with many victories and untold efforts; and, as the historians of old time bear witness, they have held it free of all bondage ever since.

"In their kingdom there have reigned one hundred and thirteen kings of their own royal stock, the line unbroken a single foreigner.

"The high qualities and deserts of these people, were they not otherwise manifest, gain glory enough from this: that the King of kings and Lord of lords, our Lord Jesus Christ, after His Passion and Resurrection, called them, even though settled in the uttermost parts of the earth, almost the first to His most holy faith." – quoted in *Islands Of Destiny*, pg. 189

Charles de Gaulle

"We are above all a European people, racially White, of Greek and Latin culture, and of the Christian Faith...the Muslims, have you seen them...with their turbans and their djellabas? You can clearly see that they're not French!... Try to mix oil and vinegar. Shake the bottle. After a minute, they separate again. Arabs are Arabs, French are French. Do you think that French society can absorb 10 million Muslims, who tomorrow will be 20 million and the day after that 40 million? If we integrate, if all the Arabs and Berbers of Algeria were to be considered French, how would we stop them from coming to the metropole, where the standard of living is so much higher? My village would no longer be Colombey-les-Deux-Eglises, but Colombey-les-Deux-Mosquées." – Conversation between de Gaulle and Alain Peyrefitte, 5 March 1959; *The Politics of the Veil*, pgs. 61-62

"So far as I am concerned, I have always...felt what the nations that people [Europe] have in common. All of them being of the same white race, of the same Christian origin, sharing the same way of life, interconnected since time immemorial by countless relations of thought, art, science, politics, and trade, it is in conformity with their nature that they should come to form a whole, having its own character and organization in the middle of the world. It is by virtue of this essence of Europe that the Roman emperors reigned there, that Charlemagne, Charles V, and Napoleon attempted to bring it together, that Hitler sought to impose on it his crushing domination. But how can we fail to observe that none of these federators were able to force the countries they subdued to give up being themselves? On the contrary, arbitrary centralization always provoked, as a rebound, the virulence of nationalities. I therefore think that at present, no more than in other periods, Europe cannot be unified by the fusion of peoples; rather, it can and must result from their systematic rapprochement... My policy thus seeks the institution of the concert of European states... Nothing prevents us from thinking, that on that basis, and especially if someday they [the European states] should be the object of the same threat, this development might lead to their confederation." – de Gaulle, *Mémoires d'espoir*, pg. 137

Henri Delassus

"Men will tell you that love for the Church is incompatible with love of your country; that sooner or later you will have to choose between them, and that you can only remain a faithful member of the one by becoming an undutiful son to the other. I greatly desire to clear away this error, inasmuch as love of our country and love of the Church are, taken together, the most sacred feelings of the human heart, and were it possible for the one to be the enemy of the other, it would in my apprehension be the most terrible crisis that God has ever suffered to try His people here below; but it is nothing of the sort. A man's country is his Church in Time, as the Church is his country in Eternity; and if the orbit of one is more vast than that of the other, they have alike but one centre, and that is God; but one interest, which is justice; but one home, which is conscience; the same citizens, the souls and bodies of their children. It is true that the Church may be at variance with the Government of a country, but the Government is not the nation, much less the country.[32] Who among us ever imagined that his country is in the head or the heart of the men who govern it? Our country is the soil on which we were born, the blood and the hearth of our fathers, the love of our parents, the memories of our childhood, our traditions, our laws, our customs, our liberties, our history, and our religion. It is all that we believe, and all that we love, protected by those who were born at the same period of time and the same given place with ourselves, in heaven and earth. The Government is for us merely a means of preservation for these possessions in their right place and full security; and if, so far from fulfilling this mission, it betrays or dishonours it, we take refuge in the love of country for succour, hope, and consolation. When Nero governed the world, Rome existed in those who loved her, and her deserted Forum was the country of such as still possessed a country. If, then, the Government of any nation persecutes the Church, either that nation is Catholic or it is not. If it is Catholic, it is not the Church which attacks the country, but the country which is itself oppressed in one of its dearest, most holy rights–its religious Faith; and the Church, when defending itself by the words or the blood of its sons, is simultaneously defending an outraged, insulted country. If, on

---

32   [original footnote] "Country" fails wholly to reproduce the meaning of *patrie*, as Lacordaire uses it.

the contrary, the nation is not Catholic, it is true that the Church is not one of the component parts which make it what it is; but even then it is included in the natural right of all men to truth, grace, and eternal salvation; and the Church enduring persecution forwards two benefits to the country–one in the future, its conversion; the other present, namely, liberty of conscience." – quoted in *Henri Dominique Lacordaire, A Biographical Sketch* by H.L. Sidney Lear, pgs. 292-294

Patrick Deneen

"Family is the wellspring of the cultural habits and practices that foster the wisdom, judgment, and local knowledge by which humans flourish and thrive in common and rightly claim the primary role in the education and upbringing of a given community's children." – *Why Liberalism Failed*, pg. 80

"As naturally political and social creatures, people require a thick set of constitutive bonds in order to function as fully formed human beings. Shorn of the deepest ties to family (nuclear as well as extended), place, community, region, religion, and culture, and deeply shaped to believe that these forms of association are limits upon their autonomy, deracinated humans seek belonging and self-definition through the only legitimate form of organization remaining available to them: the state." – *Why Liberalism Failed*, pg. 60

John Denver

Almost heaven, West Virginia
Blue Ridge Mountains, Shenandoah River
Life is old there, older than the trees
Younger than the mountains, growin'
  like a breeze

Country roads, take me home
To the place where I belong
West Virginia, mountain momma
Take me home, country roads

All my memories gathered 'round her
Miner's lady stranger to blue water
Dark and dusty painted on the sky
Misty taste of moonshine, teardrop in my eye

Country roads, take me home
To the place I belong
West Virginia, mountain momma
Take me home, country roads

I hear her voice, in the mornin' hour
  she calls me
Radio reminds me of my home far away
And driving down the road I get a feeling
I should have been home yesterday, yesterday

Country roads, take me home
To the place where I belong
West Virginia, mountain momma
Take me home, country roads
 – *Take Me Home, Country Roads*

C.S. Dessain

"God 'from one man' caused every nation to dwell on the earth. The argument is from the unity of the human race. Each nation had its separate god from whom it claimed to originate. Since the human race originates from one man made by God, there is only one God. He has not merely arranged seasons, as in 14:16, and geographical boundaries. His Providence in history fixes the times of prosperity and the territorial limits of the nations..." – The Acts of the Apostles, *A Catholic Commentary on Holy Scripture*, pg. 1038

F. Roger Devlin

"Antiracism also resembles communism in its defiance of certain constant aspects of human nature. As communism ignored economic self-interest, antiracism is built upon ignoring or suppressing our tribal bonds. These are an extension of family bonds and serve the same evolutionary function, viz., helping weak individuals survive in an indifferent or hostile world. Building upon such natural affections, traditional moral thinking inculcated the virtue of patriotism, or loyalty to the tribe into which one has been born, a loyalty that was expected to extend to self-sacrifice where necessary. Antiracist ideology aims to persuade European-descended people (and them alone) that such loyalty is actually the most inexcusable of moral failings. The ideal antiracist is supposed to cultivate perfect indifference to his tribe, to the point of preferring other groups to his own when directed to do so. Even within our own dissident circles, I fear many fail to grasp just what a breathtaking revolution in moral thinking this represents. Perhaps only the shift from paganism to Christianity in the fourth century A.D. was comparable. It is a revolution being pushed on us by people conspicuous for both their own tribal loyalties and for carefully maintained historical grudges against us. It leaves Western man disarmed in a competitive world, and that is precisely its purpose." – Speech at the *Scandza Forum*, 24 May 2023

Ruaidh Ui Dhomhnaill

"We, though a small number, are on the side of right, as it seems to us, and the English, whose number is large, are on the side of robbery, in order to rob you of your native land and your means of living, and it is far easier for you to make a brave, stout, strong fight for your native land and your lives while you are your own masters and your weapons are in your hands than when you are put into prison and in chains after being robbed of your weapons and when your limbs are bound with hard, tough cords of hemp, after being broken and torn, some of you half dead after you are chained and taken in crowds on waggons and carts through the streets of the English towns through contempt and mockery of you. My blessing on you, true men; bear in your minds the firm resolution that you had when such insults and violence were offered to you (as was done to many of your race), that today is the day of battle which you have needed to make a vigorous fight in defence of your liberty by the strength of your arms and the courage of your hearts, while you have your bodies under your control and your weapons in your hands, as it is not a necessity that the English should be your conquerors. Have no dread or fear of the great number of the soldiers of London or of the strangeness of their weapons and arms, but put your hope and confidence in the God of glory. I am certain if you take into your minds what I say to you, that the English will be defeated and that victory will be with you." – *Red Hugh's Speech At Curlew Pass*, in *A Literary History of Ireland*, pg. 565

Michael Dibdin

"There can be no true friends without true enemies. Unless we hate what we are not, we cannot love what we are. These are the old truths we are painfully rediscovering after a century and more of sentimental cant. Those who deny them deny their family, their heritage, their culture, their birthright, their very selves! They will not lightly be forgiven." – *Dead Lagoon*, pg. 261

John Dickinson

"Where was there ever a confederacy of republics united as these states are…or, in which the people were so drawn together by religion, blood, language, manners, and customs?" – *Observations on the Constitution proposed by the Federal Convention; Pamphlets on the Constitution of the United States*, pg. 205

Didache

The oldest of the church orders was the first or second century *Didache*. In 4:10-11:

"You shall not command anything in your bitterness upon your bondman or maidservant who hope in the same God, lest they ever cease to fear God who is over both; for he comes not to call according to outward appearance, but to those the Spirit has prepared. And you, bondmen, shall be subject to your masters as to a type of God, in modesty and fear." – *The Teaching of the Twelve Apostles*, ed. Charles Taylor, pg. 126

Didascalia Apostolorum

Chapter 18:

"For they receive, forsooth, to administer for the nourishment of orphans and widows, from rich persons who keep men shut up in prison, or ill-treat their slaves, or behave with cruelty in their cities, or oppress the poor; or from the lewd, and those who abuse their bodies; or from evildoers…" From such, "redeem slaves and captives and prisoners, and those who are treated with violence…" – *Didascalia Apostolorum*, pg. 158

Everett Dirksen

"For years the United States has not benefitted reciprocally from its trade agreements. … A number of basic domestic industries have suffered grievously under unwisely 'liberalized' customs and tariff practices and ineptly administered trade agreements legislation.

Foreign-produced goods have prospered in our markets. But foreign markets have not reciprocally responded to our products of America's mines, farms, forests and industry...sweeping across-the-board reductions in duty being pursued by the United States in the Kennedy Round could have an even worse effect on the trade position of the United States in future years." – *Congressional Record*, March 20, 1967, pgs. 7,213-7,216

Benjamin Disraeli

"No man will treat with indifference the principle of race. It is the key to history, and why history is often so confused is that it has been written by men who are ignorant of this principle and all the knowledge it involves. As one who may become a statesman and assist in governing mankind, it is necessary that you should not be insensible to it; whether you encounter its influences in communities or in individuals, its qualities must ever be taken into account... Language and religion do not make a race – there is only one thing which makes a race, and that is blood." – *Endymion*, pg. 223

John Dix

"The mass of crime committed by Africans is greater in proportion to numbers, in the non slaveholding than in the slaveholding States; and as a rule the degree of comfort enjoyed by them is inferior. This is not an argument in favor of slavery; but it is an unanswerable argument in favor of rendering emancipation and colonization [to Africa] coextensive with each other." – Governor of NY, Speech to New York Colonization Society, 1830; *African Repository* vols. 6-7, pg. 164

Testamentum Domini

In addition to references to Christ freeing us from the yoke of slavery, bk 1, ch 1 contains:
"And also let him who cometh be asked if he be a slave or free; and if the slave of one who is faithful, and if also his master permit him, let him hear. But if his master be not faithful and do not permit him, let him be persuaded to permit him. And if [his master] say truly about him that he wisheth to become a Christian because he hateth his masters, let him be cast out. But if no cause be shewn of hatred of servitude, but [if]

he [really] wish to be a Christian, let him hear. But if his master be faithful and do not bear witness to him, let him be cast out. Similarly if [a woman] be the wife of a man, let the woman be taught to please her husband in the fear of God. But if both of them desire to serve purity in piety, they have a reward."

Bk 2, ch 1:
"If any be the slave of a heathen, he may only be baptized with his master's consent; let him be content that he is a Christian." – *The Testament of Our Lord*, pg. 116

Jack Donovan

"All of our life stories are a collection of highs and lows, of victories and defeats, of struggles and of overcoming. Without conflict, no life story is worth telling. Without conflict and struggle, the answer to the question 'What happened?' is 'Nothing.'" – *Becoming a Barbarian*, pg. 23

"Moral universalism is a philosophy for men who have surrendered. They have surrendered their land, their history, their women, their dignity and their identity. They've become impotent half-men who deserve to be victims and slaves. Moral universalism is a poisonous, emasculating philosophy for any man who adopts it." – *Becoming a Barbarian*, pg. 41
"...many seem determined to survive some ordeal only to rebuild the same civilization, incorporating the same egalitarian, universalist, trade-oriented values that will inevitably lead to the same end. If you rebuild the Mother of Exiles and light a lamp for all the huddled masses and wretched refuse of the world without regard for race, religion or tradition, you will end up with the same money-driven matriarchal mess of self-loving bonobos you currently see before you." – *Becoming a Barbarian*, pg. 71

"The only way to become barbarians today is to create that magical place inside the Empire, hollow out little pockets inside of it and become outsiders who undermine the Empire within its borders." – *Becoming a Barbarian*, pg. 74

"When one cannot escape modernity, one must secede spiritually and nurture a world within a world." – *Becoming a Barbarian*, pg. 74

"Giving everything to your own people, to your own tribe, means leaving nothing for strangers. You must harden your heart or be at the mercy of the many. This is not hate. This is selective love, and practiced indifference. Your heart is like your eyes. Everything is a blur until you focus." – *Becoming a Barbarian*, pg.101

"The love of a man who is willing to discriminate, to separate 'us' from 'them,' has far greater value than the cheap sentiment of the man who says he loves all mankind. The love of a man who loves everyone and anyone is spread so thin it is weak and meaningless, but the love of man who discriminates is concentrated, powerful and profound. It gives him direction and purpose." – *Becoming a Barbarian*

"The dissolution of difference and identity has become the one true religion of this new Empire of Nothing – this is their only dream for the future, their only final end, their heaven, their catholic caliphate of consumerism. The choice available to us is to embrace this dream of the dying, to let go and become men of the Empire and follow it into emptiness – or to become the new barbarians, the forefathers of future Empires, who fight and flourish around the dying giant as we build new worlds from its remains." – *Becoming a Barbarian*, pg.154

Thomas Doolittle

"Let the master of the family exercise his authority in the good government of his household.—He is to be the foreman in the worship of God in the family. Mr. Perkins writes thus: 'That the master of the family hath the proper government of the whole household, and he comes not to it by election, but by the ordinance of God, settled even in the order of nature; and by the light of nature hath the principality and sovereignty therein. He is pater-familiâs, 'the father and chief head of the family,' and ought therefore to bear the chief stroke, and to be the principal agent, director, and furtherer of the worship of God in his family, and to keep order, and to exercise discipline in his house.' Let him improve his authority in commanding and causing every one in his house, under his charge, to be present, and to attend upon God, in family prayer. God and nature have made him the head of all the rest; and the head is to govern, rule, direct, and influence the whole body. Let him also take care to purge his house from sin; and, to his utmost power, endeavour that none in his house live in gross sins, that there be no swearers, drunkards, and openly profane sinners under his roof." – *How May The Duty Of Daily Family Prayer Be Best Managed For The Spiritual Benefit Of Every One In The Family?*, in *Puritan Sermons*, vol. 2, pg. 237

Fyodor Dostoevsky

"And he who has no people has no God. You may be sure that all who cease to understand their own people and lose their connection with them at once lose to the same extent the faith of their fathers, and become atheistic or indifferent. I'm speaking the truth! This is a fact which will be realised. That's why all of you and all of us now are either beastly atheists or careless, dissolute imbeciles, and nothing more." – *The Possessed*, pg. 32

"Everyone belongs to all, and all belongs to everyone. All are slaves and equal in their slavery ... Slaves are bound to be equal. Without despotism there has never been either freedom or equality, but in the herd there is bound to be equality ... The moment you have family ties or love you have the desire for property. We will destroy that desire. We shall reduce everything to a common denominator: complete equality, complete obedience, complete loss of individuality." – *The Possessed*, pg. 391

"The more I love humanity in general the less I love man in particular. In my dreams, I often make plans for the service of humanity, and perhaps I might actually face crucifixion if it were suddenly necessary. Yet I am incapable of living in the same room with anyone for two days together. I know from experience. As soon as anyone is near me, his personality disturbs me and restricts my freedom. In twenty-four hours I begin to hate the best of men: one because he's too long over his dinner, another because he has a cold and keeps on blowing his nose. I become hostile to people the moment they come close to me. But it has always happened that the more I hate men individually the more I love humanity." – *The Brothers Karamazov*, pg. 48

Stephen A. Douglas

"I believe this government was made on the white basis. I believe it was made by white men for the benefit of white men and their posterity forever, and should be administered by white men and none others." – Douglas in debate with Lincoln, Sept 15, 1858; *Speeches and Writings 1832-1858*, vol. 10, pg. 598

"For one, I am opposed to negro citizenship in any form. I believe that this government was made on the white basis. I believe it was made by white men for the benefit of white men and their posterity forever, and I am in favor of confining the citizenship to white men—men of European birth and European descent, instead of conferring it upon negroes and Indians, and other inferior races." – Douglas in debate with Lincoln, Sept 15, 1858; *Speeches and Writings 1832-1858*, vol. 10, pg. 599

Vlad Dracul

"Because by no means do we want to leave unfinished what we began, but to follow this through to the end. Because we will not flee before their savagery, but stand by all of the Christians, and if he will kindly lend his ear to the prayers of his poor subjects and grants us victory over the Infidels, the Enemies of the Cross of Christ, it will be the greatest honor, benefit, and spiritual help for Your Majesty... and for all true Christians. Because we will not flee before their savagery, but by all means we will fight them. And if, God forbid, it ends badly for us, and our little country is lost, Your Majesty will not benefit from this either, because it will be a loss for all Christianity." – Letter to Hungarian king Matthias Corvinus; in *Dracula: Essays on the Life and Times of Vlad the Impaler*, pgs. 417-419

"Hungarians, you know that we are your neighbors and that both our countries are next to the Danube. You have probably heard by now that the Emperor of the Turks is waging a terrible war against us, with a large army. And if he conquers Dacia [Wallachia], you know very well that he will not sit still, but he will wage war against you, and your countrymen will suffer greatly at his hands. So, it is time now that you should give us assistance and defend yourselves as well by keeping their army as far as possible from your country; please don't let them spoil our country and ruin and conquer our people." – *Dracula: Essays on the Life and Times of Vlad the Impaler*, pg. 433

Michael Drayton

O Flood [i.e. river] in happy plight,
    which to this time remain'st,
As still along in state
    to Neptune's Court thou strain'st,
Revive thee with the thought
    of those forepasséd hours,
When the rough Wood-gods kept,
    in their delightful bowers,
On thy embroidered banks,
    when now this Country fill'd,
With villages, and by
    the labouring plowman till'd,
Was Forest, where the fir,
    arid spreading poplar grew.
O let me yet the thought of
    those past times renew,
When as that woody kind,
    in our umbrageous wild,
Whence every living thing
    save only they exil'd,
In this world of waste,
    the sovereign empire sway'd
– *The Forest*

John Dryden

"And nobler is a limited command, Given by the love of all your native land, Than a successive title, long and dark, Drawn from the mouldy rolls of Noah's Ark."
– *Absalom and Achitophel*, pg. 22

Charles Gavan Duffy

Joy! joy! the day is come at last,
    the day of hope and pride,
And see! our crackling bonfires
    light old Bann's rejoicing tide,
And gladsome bell, and bugle-horn
    from Newry's captured Towers,
Hark! how they tell the Saxon swine,
    this land is ours, is ours!

Come, trample down their robber rule,
    and smite its venal spawn,

Their foreign laws, their foreign church,
  their ermine and their lawn;
And all the specious fry of fraud
  that robbed us of our own,
And plant our ancient laws again,
  beneath our lineal throne.
– *The Muster of the North; The Spirit of the Nation*,
pg. 27

Archie Duncan

"Reliable narratives of the years 1309-14 tell of
Forfar Castle taken by a small laird Philip For-
rester of Platan, Linlithgow by William Bunnok
a husbandman, Dumbartonby Oliver a carpenter, and the way into Edinburgh and Roxburgh
shown by men of no social eminence; the
foundation of this war was a capacity to bypass
the reluctant traditional leaders of the 'community' and to appeal to and command the
opinion of the other social ranks in the 'nation'
... the rise of nationality in this sense reflects the
wide support and increased importance of the
freeholders and husbandmen." – *The Nation of
Scots*, pgs. 20-21

Félix Dupanloup

"The more a saint understands what he owes
God, the more he understands what he owes
to men... In the love of God, all noble loves
are found and elevated. And among the most
noble, that which God has consecrated and
which our Lord Himself felt, and which has
never ceased to beat in the hearts of saints, is
the love of country." – *Second eulogy of Joan of
Arc*, Cathedral of Sainte-Croix d'Orléans, 8
May 1869; quoted in *The Monitor*, 1879, pg. 39

Will Durant

"Utopias of equality are biologically doomed." –
Lessons Of History, ch. 3

"Nature ... has not read very carefully the
American Declaration of Independence or the
French Revolutionary Declaration of the Rights
of Man." – *Lessons Of History*, ch. 3

"We are all born unfree and unequal: subject
to our physical and psychological heredity, and
to the customs and traditions of our group;

diversely endowed in health and strength, in
mental capacity and qualities of character.
Nature loves differences as the necessary material of selection and evolution;[33] identical twins
differ in a hundred ways, and no two peas are
alike." – *Lessons Of History*, ch. 3

"Nature smiles at the union of freedom and
equality in our utopias. For freedom and equality are sworn and everlasting enemies, and when
one prevails the other dies. Leave men free, and
their natural inequalities will multiply almost
geometrically, as in England and America in
the nineteenth century under laissez-faire. To
check the growth of inequality, liberty must be
sacrificed, as in Russia after 1917." – *Lessons Of
History*, ch. 3

James Durham

"Nations now become the Lord's as formerly
they were Antichrist's, that is, they give now
the profession of purity by a publick acknowledgement as formerly they gave it to the beast;
now they reject him and take Christ in his
room, but the first was done nationally. Nations
become now the Lord's as they were not His
before; for, thus the opposition is to be understood also, but that was in respect of the complex body the generality of them; and if now
the phrase be, such a Nation is not the Lord's,
because the generality and complex body do
not publickly acknowledge Him, Then on the
contrary, a Nations becoming His, must import
His having His publick worship nationally
among them. Nations now are to become His,
and to be admitted to the Church under the
Gospel, as they were formerly secluded before
Christ came in the flesh, Ps. 147. ...

"This phrase, The Kingdoms of this world
are become the Kingdoms of our Lord's, is to
be understood with respect to the commission
given to the Apostles for calling in Nations
and Kingdoms, so that this is marked as the
fruit and success of that: but that commission, Matth. 28. Go, disciple all Nations, &c.
looketh to the body and generality of Nations,
it being a warrant to invit, disciple, and gather
in a whole Nation: and although sometimes in
the event, but some of Kingdoms and Nations
are gathered in; yet it cannot be said that upon
supposition that a whole Kingdom or Nation

---

33 Drivel about Darwinian Evolution notwithstanding, the point regarding differences in nature stands.

should yeeld, but they might be by this warrant received and admitted; even as by this warrant indefinitly the call and offer is made to all the Nation in common. And although not one should yeeld, yet this commission and warrant sheweth it is neither inconsistent with the Gospel to call a Nation, nor to admit them upon the former supposition. ...

"If it be all one to say, that Nations shall be the Lord's, and Nations shall be Church's, Then the Scripture doth assert nationall Churches in the dayes of the Gospel, not only as consistent with the Gospel's administration, but as an evident commendation of it..." – *Commentary on Revelation* 11:15-19, pgs. 511-516

John I. Durham

"Just as the relationship with Yahweh is the beginning of the covenant, so this relationship [i.e., between parents and children] is the beginning of society, the inevitable point of departure for every human relationship. The first relationship beyond the relationship with Yahweh, who according to the OT is the giver of life, is the relationship to father and to mother, who together are channels of Yahweh's gift of life. No other human relationship is so fundamental, and none is more important...." – *Exodus, Word Biblical Commentary*, 20:12, pg. 290.

Émile Durkheim

"There can be no society which does not feel the need of upholding and reaffirming at regular intervals the collective sentiments and the collective ideas which make its unity and its personality." – *Elementary Forms*, pg. XLIX

Timothy Dwight IV

"This, young Gentlemen, is the field in which you are to act. It is here described to you, that you may not be ignorant or regardless of that great whole, of which each of you is a part, and perhaps an important one. The period, in which your lot is cast, is possibly the happiest in the roll of time. It is true, you will scarcely live to enjoy the summit of American glory; but you now see the foundations of that glory laid. A scene like this is not unfolded in an instant. Innumerable are the events in the great system of Providence, which must advance the mighty design before it can be completed. Innumera-

ble must be the Actors in so vast a plot, and infinitely various the parts they act. Every event is necessary in the great system, and every character on the extended stage. Some part or other must belong to each of you, perhaps a capital one. You should by no means consider yourselves as members of a small neighbourhood, town or colony only, but as being concerned in laying the foundations of American greatness. Your wishes, your designs, your labors are not to be confined by the narrow bounds of the present age, but are to comprehend succeeding generations, and be pointed to immortality. You are to act, not like inhabitants of a village, nor like beings of an hour, but like citizens of a world (the new world; i.e., America), and like candidates for a name that shall survive the conflagration. These views will enlarge your minds, expand the grasp of your benevolence, ennoble all your conduct, and crown you with wreaths which cannot fade." – A valedictory address to the young gentlemen, who commenced Bachelors of Arts, at Yale College, July 25th. 1776. Dwight, Timothy, 1752-1817., Yale College, Class of 1776; *Fisher's National Magazine and Industrial Record*, vol. 1, pg. 327

E

F.R. Earp

"Friendship called forth the deepest feelings of the Greeks. In its highest form it was more honored than the love between opposite sexes; it was felt to be more profound, and, so far as the Greeks conceived romance, more romantic. Moreover the obligations of friendship were very real and binding, and were normally honored even by those whose friendship fell far short of romantic devotion. A man in danger could look to his friends for defense, a man in need could look to them for help in money; and in both cases seemed usually to have received what he asked. The refusal conferred a stigma." – *The Way of the Greeks*, pg. 31

Mary Eberstadt

"Family and faith are intricately connected, and each requires the other to reproduce. That's why times of family decline—like our own—are times of religious decline; and conversely, why times of religious flourishing are also times of family revival... Similarly, social science documents that across the world, the more religious you are, the more likely you are to have families of size; fertility and religiosity are tightly linked, any way the numbers are run." – Interview on *How the West Really Lost God*, *Catholic World Report*, Aug 5, 2013

Alfred Eckes

"It is important to note that free trade theory focuses on benefits to individuals and to world welfare, not to nations. Even if all the theoretical conditions prevail, nineteenth-century economists pointed out, individual nations may still lose. It is possible for free trade to maximize the wealth of individuals and the global community while it destroys the nation and its social stability." – *Opening America's Market: U. S. Foreign Trade Policy Since 1776*, pg. xviii

"Before World War I, protectionism apparently did not significantly harm U.S. economic growth or retard export expansion. Between 1870 and 1913, nations pursuing more protective policies (the United States and Germany) experienced higher domestic growth rates and more rapid export expansion than did free trade Great Britain. If, as economic theorists argue, free trade is more beneficial, it is striking that the single nation pursuing a free trade policy throughout this period exhibited annual real growth far below its chief commercial rivals." – *Opening America's Market: U. S. Foreign Trade Policy Since 1776*, pg. 50

William Edgar

"All things will be reconciled in heaven and on earth through the power of the cross of Christ (Col. 1:20). We will be members of the same family, bound together with unbreakable ties. Differences will remain. For every tongue shall confess that Christ is Lord (Rom. 14:11, Phil. 2:11). Christ has ransomed people from every tribe and language, people, and nation. (Rev. 5:9, 13:7, 14:6). These verses indicated that something of ethnic and social identity of different people will be preserved." – *Created and Creating; A Biblical Theology of Culture*, p. 225

James R. Edwards

On Luke 10:24 and following:
"But the Samaritan does what the priest and the Levite do not do: he makes contact with the man and is moved with compassion. ...

"For the lawyer, 'neighbor' is a noun. 'Neighbor' is an object to whom one owes duties – burdensome duties that the lawyer desires to avoid. For Jesus, 'Neighbor' is a verb, a way of behaving toward people in need that gives life both to giver and receiver...For Jesus, one does not have a neighbor; one is a neighbor, or better, becomes a neighbor. The parable does not require hearers to convert enemies into friends, to do everything for everyone, to solve the problems of the world. To be a neighbor is not a condition one inherits, in other words, but a choice one makes to render the tangible assistance one is able to render to those in need to it, and to render it irrespective of ethnic, religious, cultural, or racial differences." – *Pillar New Testament Commentary, The Gospel According To Luke*, pg. 618

Jonathan Edwards

"The law of nature and the law of divine revelation teach us to be united with those that we dwell with in the same country, to have a special affection for them, and makes us in many respects one body with them." – *Miscellanies*, no. 928, *Works*, vol. 20, pg. 171

"Before I dismiss this head of the degenerating of experiences, I would mention one thing more that tends to it; and that is, persons aiming in their experience to go beyond the rule of God's Word, i.e. aiming at that which is indeed, in some respect, beyond the rule. Thus some persons have endeavoured utterly to root out and abolish all natural affection, or any special affection or respect to their near relations, under a notion that no other love ought to be allowed but spiritual love, and all that other love is to be abolished as carnal, and that it becomes Christians to love none upon the account of any thing else but the image of God; and that therefore love should go out to one and another only in that proportion in which the image of God is seen in them. They might as well argue that a man ought utterly to disallow of, and endeavor to abolish, all love or appetite to his daily food, under a notion that it is a carnal appetite, and that no other appetite should be tolerated but spiritual appetites. Why should the saints strive after that, as a high attainment in holiness, which the apostle in Rom. i. 31. mentions as one instance wherein the heathen had got to the most horrid pass in wickedness, viz. being without natural affections? ... The Creator of the world has put them in us, for the good of mankind, and because He saw they would be needful for them, as they must be united in society in the present state, and are of great use when kept in their proper place; and

to endeavour totally to root them out, would be to reproach and oppose the wisdom of the Creator. Nor is the being of these natural inclinations, if well regulated, inconsistent with any part of our duty to God, or any argument of a sinful selfishness, any more than our natural abhorrence of pain, and the natural inclination to ease that was in the man Christ Jesus Himself.

"It is the duty of parents to be more concerned and to pray more for the salvation of their children, than for the children of their neighbors; as it is the duty of a minister to be more concerned for the salvation of the souls of his flock, and to pray more for them, than those of other congregations, because they are committed to his care. So our near friends are more committed to our care than others, and our near neighbors, than those that live at a great distance; and the people of our land and nation are more, in some sense, committed to our care than the people of China, and we ought to pray more for them, and to be more concerned that the kingdom of Christ should flourish among them, than in another country, where it would be as much, and no more, for the glory of God." – *A Narrative of Many Surprising Conversions*, pg. 292

Egyptian Church Order

"Concerning new persons who wish to be baptised, and concerning the occupations which they ought to leave off. New persons who are to be baptised in order that they may hear the word, shall be brought to the teachers before all the people come in; and they shall ask them for what reason they sought the Faith. And they who brought them shall be witness as to whether they are able to hear [the word]. And they shall examine them concerning their life, as to what they are; if they have a wife; or, if he was a slave, if his master allowed him to hear; and if his master was not witness for him, he shall go away: and if his master was an idolater, and they know not if there was permission of his master, that there be not scandal. And if he was a man who had a wife, or a woman who had a husband, they shall know if the man lives with his wife, and the wife with her husband. And if it was a man who did not live with a wife, he shall be instructed not to be a fornicator, but to marry according to law or to remain so. And if it was a man who had a devil, then he shall not hear the word of instruction." – *Texts and Studies: Contributions to Biblical and Patristic Literature*, pg. 180

Joseph von Eichendorff

"Es war, als hätt' der Himmel
Die Erde still geküsst,
Dass sie im Blütenschimmer
Von ihm nun träumen müsst."

Translation:
 "It was as if the heavens
 Had quietly kissed the earth,
 So that, in a shimmer of blossoms,
 She must now dream of him."
– *Moonlit Night* (Mondnacht, lines 1-4) [34]

"Die Luft ging durch die Felder,
Die Ähren wogten sacht,
Es rauschten leis' die Wälder,
So sternklar war die Nacht."

Translation:
 "The breeze swept through the fields,
 The ears of corn swayed gently,
 The woods whispered softly,
 So starry-clear was the night."
– *Moonlit Night* (lines 5-8)

"Schläft ein Lied in allen Dingen,
Die da träumen fort und fort,
Und die Welt hebt an zu singen,
Triffst du nur das Zauberwort."

Translation:
"A song sleeps in all things,
That dream on and on,
And the world begins to sing,
If only you find the magic word."
– *Wünschelrute* (The Divining Rod, lines 13-16)

George Eliot

"A human life, I think, should be well rooted in some spot of a native land, where it may get the love of tender kinship for the face of earth, for the labors men go forth to, for the sounds and accents that haunt it, for whatever will give that early home a familiar unmistakable difference amid the future widening of knowledge: a spot where the definiteness of early memories may be inwrought with affection, and—kindly acquaintance with all neighbors, even to the dogs and donkeys, may spread not by sentimental effort and reflection, but as a sweet habit of the blood. At five years old, mortals are not prepared to be citizens of the world, to be stimulated by abstract nouns, to soar above preference into impartiality; and that prejudice in favor of milk with which we blindly begin, is a type of the way body and soul must get nourished at least for a time. The best introduction to astronomy is to think of the nightly heavens as a little lot of stars belonging to one's own homestead." – *Daniel Deronda*, pg. 26

T.S. Eliot

"By far the most important channel of transmission of culture remains the family: and when family life fails to play its part, we must expect our culture to deteriorate.

 "Now the family is an institution of which nearly everybody speaks well: but it is advisable to remember that this is a term that may vary in extension. In the present age it means little more than the living members. Even of living members, it is a rare exception when an advertisement depicts a large family or three generations: the usual family on the hoardings consists of two parents and one or two young children.

 "What is held up for admiration is not devotion to a family, but personal affection between the members of it: and the smaller the family, the more easily can this personal affection be sentimentalised.

 "But when I speak of the family, I have in mind a bond which embraces a longer period of time than this: a piety towards the dead, however obscure, and a solicitude for the unborn, however remote. Unless this reverence for past and future is cultivated in the home, it can never be more than a verbal convention in the community." – *Notes Toward a Definition of Culture; Christianity and Culture*, pg. 116

"It is important that a man should feel himself to be, not merely a citizen of a particular nation, but a citizen of a particular part of his country, with local loyalties. These, like loyalty to class, arise out of loyalty to the family. Certainly, an

---

34 Eichendorff was a German poet and novelist known for his Romantic works that celebrate the beauty of the German countryside and the connection between nature and the human spirit.

individual may develop the warmest devotion to a place in which he was not born, and to a community with which he has no ancestral ties. But I think we should agree that there would be something artificial, something a little too conscious, about a community of people with strong local feeling, all of whom had come from somewhere else. I think we should say that we must wait for a generation or two for a loyalty which the inhabitants had inherited, and which was not the result of a conscious choice. On the whole, it would appear to be for the best that the great majority of human beings should go on living in the place in which they were born. Family, class and local loyalty all support each other; and if one of these decays, the others will suffer also." – *Notes Towards the Definition of Culture; Christianity and Culture*, pg. 125. [35]

— T.S. Eliot —

"For the health of the culture of Europe two conditions are required: that the culture of each country should be unique [our principle of Integrity], and that the different cultures should recognize their relationship to each other, so that each should be susceptible of influence from the others [our principle of Relationships]. And this is possible because there is a common element in European culture, an interrelated history of thought and feeling and behavior, an interchange of arts and of ideas [our principle of unity]." – *Christianity And Culture*, pg. 19

"It is in Christianity that our arts have developed; it is in Christianity that the laws of Europe—until recently—have been rooted. It is against a background of Christianity that all of our thought has significance. An individual European may not believe that the Christian faith is true, and yet what he says, and makes, and does will all spring out of his heritage of Christian culture and depend upon that culture for its meaning... I do not believe that culture of Europe could survive the complete disappearance of the Christian faith. And I am convinced of that, not merely because I am a Christian myself, but as a student of social biology. If Christianity goes, the whole culture goes." – *Christianity and Culture*, pg. 200

"Tradition is not solely, or even primarily, the maintenance of certain dogmatic beliefs; these beliefs have come to take their living form in the course of the formation of a tradition. What I mean by tradition involves all those habitual actions, habits and customs, from the most significant religious rite to our conventional way of greeting a stranger, which represent the blood kinship of 'the same people living in the same place'...

"You are hardly likely to develop tradition except where the bulk of the population is relatively so well off where it is that it has no incentive or pressure to move about. The population should be homogeneous; where two or more cultures exist in the same place they are likely either to be fiercely self-conscious or both to become adulterate. What is still more important is unity of religious background; and reasons of race and religion combine to make any large number of free-thinking Jews undesirable. There must be a proper balance between urban and rural, industrial and agricultural development. And a spirit of excessive tolerance is to be deprecated." – *After Strange Gods; A Symposium*, pg. 144

J.H. Elliott

"It took little time for the news of trouble to spread from one village to the next, especially as it was common practice in Catalonia for villages to ring their church bells whenever help was needed. The bells were ringing in all the

---

35   Elliot was born in the United States, but moved to England, where his ancestors were from, married, and renounced his American citizenship.

valleys from Sant Feliu to Tordera during the first week of May. The countryside stood armed and ready." – *The Revolt of the Catalans*, pg. 422

Mark C. Elliott

The proclamation of the rebels during the 19th century Taiping Rebellion in China:

"O you masses, listen to our words. It is our belief that the empire is China's empire, not the Manchu barbarian empire . . . Alas! Since the Ming's misrule, the Manchu availed themselves to the opportunity to throw China into confusion; they stole China's empire, appropriated China's food and clothing, and ravished China's sons and daughters . . . The Chinese have Chinese characteristics; but now the Manchus have ordered us to shave our hair around the head, leaving a long tail behind, thus making the Chinese appear like brute animals. The Chinese have Chinese dress; but now the Manchus have . . . discarded the robes . . . of former dynasties, in order to make the Chinese forget their origins . . . The Chinese have the Chinese language; but now the Manchus have introduced slang of the capital and changed the Chinese tones, desiring to deluge China with barbarian speech and barbarian expressions . . .

"We have carefully investigated the Manchus' Tartar origins and have found that their first ancestor was a crossbreed of a white fox and a red dog, from whom sprang this race of demons .... They established their own imperial throne and the wild fox ascended to occupy it [while] ... we Chinese ... fell into their treacherous plots, bore their insults, and obeyed their commands." – *The Manchu Way*, pgs. 23-24.

W.A. Elwell

"Foreigners or sojourners had certain rights but also certain limitations while in Israel. They could offer sacrifices (Lv 17:8; 22:18) but could not enter the sanctuary unless circumcised (Ez 44:9). They were allowed to participate in the three great Jewish festivals (Dt 16:11, 14) but could not eat the Passover meal unless circumcised (Ex 12:43, 48). Foreigners were not obliged to follow the Israelite religion, but shared in some of its benefits (Dt 14:29). They were not to work on the sabbath and the Day of Atonement (Ex 20:10; 23:12; Lv 16:29; Dt 5:14) and could be stoned for reviling or blaspheming God's name (Lv 24:16; Nm 15:30). Foreigners

were forbidden to eat blood (Lv 17:10, 12) but could eat animals that had died a natural death (Dt 14:21). Israel's code of sexual morality also applied to the foreigner (Lv 18:26). There were prohibitions against Israelite intermarriage with foreigners, but it was nevertheless a common occurrence (Gn 34:14; Ex 34:12, 16; Dt 7:3, 4; Jos 23:12).

"Civil rights were provided for foreigners by the Law of Moses (Ex 12:49; Lv 24:22), and they came under the same legal processes and penalties (Lv 20:2; 24:16, 22; Dt 1:16). They were to be treated politely (Ex 22:21; 23:9), loved as those under the love of God (Lv 19:34; Dt 10:18, 19), and treated generously if poor and receive the fruits of the harvest (Lv 19:10; 23:22; Dt 24:19–22). They could receive asylum in times of trouble (Nm 35:15; Jos 20:9). Foreign servants were to receive treatment equal to Hebrew servants (Dt 24:14). A foreigner could not take part in tribal deliberations or become a king (17:15). The prophet Ezekiel looked forward to the messianic age when the foreigner would share all the blessings of the land with God's own people (Ez 47:22, 23)." – Entry on "Foreigner" in *Baker Encyclopedia of the Bible*, vol. 1, pg. 807

"Generally, the bride left her parents when she married and went to live with her husband's clan, as Rebekah did (Gn 24:58, 59). The phrase 'to marry a wife' is from a root meaning to 'become master' (Dt 21:13), and the wife frequently treated her husband and referred to him as master..." – Entry on "Marriage, Marriage Customs" in *Baker Encyclopedia of the Bible*, vol. 2, pg. 1406

"Marriage within the clan or tribe was considered ideal, although marriage with another Israelite family was quite acceptable. Concern was often expressed, however, about marriage with foreigners, as this tended to dilute the strong links with the Hebrew heritage, and could endanger the religion of the covenant people if foreign wives introduced their family members and children to strange gods.

"When the Israelites settled in Canaan, many of them married Canaanite women, much to the consternation of those who desired to maintain the purity of the Hebrew religion (1 Kgs 11:4). Such intermarriage was prohibited under Mosaic law (Ex 34:15, 16; Dt 7:3, 4)...

The danger of intermarriage affecting the

purity of Hebrew religion was considered so great that in the postexilic period wholesale divorce was ordered where Jews had married foreign wives (Ezr 9:2; 10:3, 16, 17). The intent was that the faith should remain pure, even though homes and families were destroyed. Even in NT times, Paul denounced marriage with non-Christians (2 Cor 6:14, 15).

"It is difficult to estimate at what age young people married. A boy was considered to be a man by his middle teens, and late in Jewish tradition this transition was celebrated by the bar mitzvah, which generally occurred when the boy was 13. It seems most probable that Mahlon and Chilion were still quite young when they died (Ru 1:5, 9) from some unspecified illness. At the time of his death, Absalom was about 20, but he had been living in his own house for the previous five years, and may have been married (2 Sm 13:19). In point of fact there were possibly quite different average ages for the marriages of the sons of kings and for other people. Subsequently, minimum ages of 13 for boys and 12 for girls were set." – Entry on "Marriage, Marriage Customs" in *Baker Encyclopedia of the Bible*, vol. 2, pg. 1407

Ralph Waldo Emerson

"The duty to our fellow man the Slave: We are to assert his right in all companies. An amiable joyous race who for ages have not been permitted to unfold their natural powers we are to befriend I think it cannot be maintained by any candid person that the African race have ever occupied or do promise ever to occupy any very high place in the human family. Their present condition is the strongest proof that they cannot. The Irish cannot; the American Indian cannot; the Chinese cannot. Before the energy of the Caucasian race all the other races have quailed and done obeisance. Yet the colony at Liberia is somewhat. The black merchants are so fond of their lucrative occupations that it is with difficulty any of them can be prevailed upon to take office in the Colony. They dislike the trouble of it. Civilized arts are found to be as attractive to the wild negro as they are disagreeable to the wild Indian." – *Journals and Miscellaneous Notebooks*, vol. 12, pg. 152

Mihai Eminescu

"The fundamental principle is nationality within the boundaries of truth: the untrue does not become true, the ugly does not become beautiful, evil does not become good merely because it is a national characteristic." – *Nationalii si Cosmopolitii*, in *Opera Politice*, pgs. 614-615

Epictetus

"Our duties are in general measured by our social relationships. He is a father. One is called upon to take care of him, to give way to him in all things, to submit when he reviles or strikes you. 'But he is a bad father.' Did nature, then, bring you into relationship with a good father? No, but simply with a father. 'My brother does me wrong.' Very well, then, maintain the relation that you have toward him; and do not consider what he is doing, but what you will have to do, if your moral purpose is to be in harmony with nature. For no one will harm you without your consent; you will have been harmed only when you think you are harmed. In this way, therefore, you will discover what duty to expect of your neighbor, your citizen, your commanding officer, if you acquire the habit of looking at your social relations with them." – *Enchiridion*, pgs. 511-512

"Did not Socrates love his own children? But in a free spirit, as one who remembers that it was his first duty to be a friend to the gods." – *Enchiridion*, pg. 205

"…whatever is done in accordance with nature is rightly done." – *Enchiridion*, pg. 80

"The second field of study deals with duty; for I ought not to be unfeeling like a statue, but should maintain my relations, both natural and acquired, as a religious man, as a son, a brother, a father, a citizen." – *Enchiridion*, pg. 23

Desiderius Erasmus

"In living bodies, how all the various limbs harmonize, and mutually combine, for common defense against injury! What can be more heterogeneous, and unlike, than the body and the soul? and yet with what strong bonds nature has united them, is evident from the pang of separation. As life itself is nothing else but the concordant union of body and soul, so is health the harmonious cooperation of all the parts and functions of the body." – *Complaint Of Peace*, pg. 1

"...she [Nature] so distributed among various men different endowments of the mind and the body, that no individual should be so completely furnished with all of them, but that he should want the occasional assistance of the lowest orders, and even of those who are most moderately furnished with ability. Nor did she give the same talents either in kind or in degree to all, evidently meaning that the inequality of her gifts should be ultimately equalized by a reciprocal interchange of good offices and mutual assistance." – *Complaint Of Peace*, pg. 7

"Let kings once settle among themselves, how much and how far each ought to govern, and then let no marriage connection among them either extend or contract; let no treaty alter the limits once ascertained. Thus every one will endeavour to improve his allotted portion to the utmost of his power. All his efforts will be concentrated on one country, and he will endeavour to transmit it to his posterity in a rich and flourishing condition. The result will be, that when every one minds his own, all will thrive.... Moreover, let the king avoid traveling into foreign countries, let him never wish to pass the boundaries of his own dominions; but let him shew that he approves a proverbial saying, sanctioned by the wisdom of ages, frons occipitio prior est: by which was intimated, that nothing goes on well when conducted by secondaries and mercenaries only, and in the absence of the principal." – *Complaint Of Peace*, pg. 49

Anthony Esolen

"It is the essence of piety to honor your father and mother because they are yours and because they have given you a gift you can never recompense. This piety extends to the land of your birth, the 'rocks and rills,' the 'templed hills,' as the old patriotic anthem has it. The character of a nation is not to be found primarily in great political movements, and certainly not in an obsession with 'progress.' It is found in its land and weather, the kind of people who work

there, the music they sing, the places where they worship, the games they play, the food they raise; what they honor and love, and what they will shed their blood to save." – *Out of the Ashes*, pg. 64

"I have never met a single person who was happy that the school he attended, the church where he worshiped, or the old house where he grew up is now dust. It is natural for man to long for home. It is not natural for him to knock out its posts and feed its beams to termites." – *Nostalgia: Going Home in a Homeless World*, Introduction

"For just as we have nearly lost the capacity to weep a tear of gratitude at our nation's birthday, so have we lost the local geography of life. In every sense of the word, from the homestead to the town, from the state to the nation, from the distant past to the last lights darkening in the west, we do not honor our father and mother." – *Ten Way to Destroy the Imagination of Your Child*, pg. 121

"Remember that while we do want to raise children who are alienated from deep affection for their nation, their town, their heritage, their neighbors, and even their families, that does not mean that we want them to know how to do things for themselves." – *Ten Ways to Destroy the Imagination of Your Child*, pg. 75

"The very purpose of what is miscalled multiculturalism is to destroy culture, by teaching students to dismiss their own and patronize the rest. Hence the antidote to love of this place is not only a hatred of this place, but a phony engagement with any other place. Multiculturalism in this sense is like going a-whoring." – *Ten Ways to Destroy the Imagination of Your Child*, pg. 134

Euripides

Euripides wrote a play where two ladies discuss how they may obtain a special water that gives them the coveted "golden hair":
   "Chorus: I've heard these waters give your hair a golden glow.
   "Chorus: They nourish the whole country those waters..." – *Trojan Women*, Theodoridis trans., pgs. 6-7

"No Dionysus is here, no dances, no Bacchic worship and carrying his wand, no ecstatic noise of drums by the gushing springs of water, no fresh drops of wine. Nor on Mount Nysa can I join the Nymphs in singing the song 'Iacchos Iacchos' to Aphrodite, whom I swiftly pursued in company with white-footed Bacchants. Ah me, lord Dionysus, where are you faring without your companions, shaking your golden hair?" – *Cyclops*, pg. 83

"But, dear lady, take this coronal for your bright hair from a worshipful hand." – *Hyppolytus* 73, in *Euripides* with an English Trans.

"Phoebus' virgin-priestess, to whom the god with flaxen locks granted the gift of maidenhood?" – *The Trojan Women*, Coleridge trans., 239

"Never, never, Lady Artemis, golden-haired child of Zeus, may I endure that slavery." – *Phoenissae, Euripides* IV, pg. 108

"I came to his grave, an addition to my journey, and falling on it I wept for its desolation; then I opened the wine-skin which I am bringing to the guests, and poured a libation, and set myrtle-sprigs round the tomb. On the alter itself I saw a black-fleeced ram as an offering, and there was blood, not long poured out, and severed locks of yellow hair. And I wondered, child, who ever dared come to the the tomb; for it was no Argive at least. But perhaps your brother has somehow come secretly and on his return has done honor to his father's wretched grave. Go look to see if the color of the cut lock is the same as yours, putting it to your own hair; it is usual for those who have the same paternal blood to have a close resemblance in many features." – *Electra* 487, in *Medea Hippolytus*, pg. 95

"To requite him [Heracles] for all his labors in purging land and sea. If I were young and still powerful in body, I would have seized my spear and dabbled those flaxen locks of his with blood." – *Heracles* 233, in *The Plays*, pg. 179

"First he [Hercales] cleared the grove of Zeus of a lion, and put its skin upon his back, hiding his yellow hair in its fearful tawny gaping jaws." – *Heracles*

"Breast, cheek, and golden hair! ah, how grievous you have found Helen." – Iphigenia in *Aulis, The Plays*, vol. 2

F

Denis Fahey

"Our Lord Jesus Christ, in and through the Catholic Church, aims at showing forth to the world the resplendent qualities of the English, French, Irish, German, America, etc., members of Christ. Catholic saints are all convinced that the highest life is not their national life — in fact their lives are a striking proof of the contrary — but they all know and teach that any act of subordination of the legitimate interests of the nation of which they are members to those of any other nation would be a sin and a failure in their duty to the Supernatural Messias." – *The Rulers of Russia*, pgs. 77-78

Andrew Robert Fausset

"For I could wish that myself were accursed from Christ for—'in behalf of my brethren, my kinsmen according to the flesh'—In proportion as he felt himself severed from his nation, he seems to have realized all the more vividly their natural relationship. To explain away the wish here expressed, as too strong for any Christian to utter or conceive, some have rendered the opening words, 'I did wish,' referring it to his former unenlightened state; a sense of the words too tame to be endured: others unwarrantably soften the sense of the word 'accursed.' But our version gives the true import of the original; and if it be understood as the language rather of 'strong and indistinct emotions than of definite ideas' [Hodge], expressing passionately how he felt his whole being swallowed up in the salvation of his people, the difficulty will vanish, and we shall be reminded of the similar idea so nobly expressed by Moses (Ex 32:32)." – Romans 9:3, *Jamieson, Fausset, Brown, Commentary Critical and Explanatory on the Whole Bible*, vol. 2, pgs. 244-245.

Guillaume Faye

"Today, the mere idea of aristocracy is incompatible with the dominant ideology. But every people needs an aristocracy. It's an integral part of human nature and can't be dispensed with. The question then is not 'For or against aristocracy?' but 'What kind of aristocracy?'" – *Why We Fight*, pg. 80

"The present dominant values (xenophilia, cosmopolitanism, narcissistic individualism, humanitarianism, bourgeois economism, hedonism, homophilia, permissivenes, etc.) are actually anti-values – values of devirilising weakness, since they deplete a civilization's vital energies and weaken its defensive or affirmative capacities." – *Why We Fight*, pg. 258

"Aristotelian concept signifying 'friendship' — ethno-cultural consensus between members of the same City. For Aristotle, democracy is possible only within homogeneous ethnic groups, while despots have always reigned over highly fragmented societies.
   "A multi-ethnic society is thus necessarily anti-democratic and chaotic, for it lacks philia, this profound, flesh-and-blood fraternity of citizens. Tyrants and despots divide and rule, they want the City divided by ethnic rivalries. The indispensable condition for ensuring a people's sovereignty accordingly resides in its unity. Ethnic chaos prevents all philia from developing. A citizenry is formed on the basis of proximity — or it is not formed at all. The abstract, integrationist doctrines of the French Revolution envisage man as simply a 'man', a resident, a consumer. Civic spirit, like public safety, social harmony, and solidarity, is based not on education or persuasion alone, but on cultural unanimity — on common values, lifestyles, and innate behaviours." – *Why We Fight*, pg. 217

Gordon Fee

"Christian behavior be circumspect before the outsider and therefore at least be ethically equal to theirs—although obviously more is expected as well. Paul is not condemning unbelievers; on the contrary, he is saying that they do in fact take care of their own widows. To do less is therefore to be less than an unbeliever; it equals a denial of the faith, since it is to act worse than a person who makes no profession of faith." – *Understanding the Bible Commentary Series, 1 & 2 Timothy, Titus*, pg. 191, 5:3-8

Marcus Minucius Felix

"We distinguish between nations and tribes; to God this whole world is but one household." – *Apologetical Works and Octavius*, pg. 391

Johann Gottlieb Fichte

"Possible though this is, and to faith not difficult, and joyfully though one must resign one's self, once it is the unalterable will of God, to having an earthly fatherland no longer and to being serfs and exiles here below, nevertheless it is not the natural condition nor the rule of the universe; on the contrary, it is a rare exception. It is a gross misuse of religion, a misuse of which Christianity among other religions has frequently been guilty, to make a point of recommending, on principle and without regard to existing circumstances, such a withdrawal from the affairs of the state and the nation as the mark of a true religious disposition. In such a condition of things, if it is true and real and not merely the product of fitful religious zeal, temporal life loses all independent existence and becomes merely a forecourt of true life and a period of severe trial which is endured only out of obedience and resignation to the will of God. Then it is true that immortal souls, as many have imagined, are housed in earthly bodies, as in prisons, for their punishment. But on the other hand, in the regular order of things this earthly life itself is intended to be truly life, of which we may be glad and which we may enjoy in gratitude, while, of course, looking forward to a higher life. Although it is true that religion is, for one thing, the consolation of the unjustly oppressed slave, yet this above all is the mark of a religious disposition, viz., to fight against slavery and, as far as possible, to prevent religion from sinking into a mere consolation for captives. No doubt it suits the tyrant well to preach religious resignation and to bid those look to heaven to whom he allows not the smallest place on earth. But we for our part must be in less haste to adopt this view of religion that he recommends; and we must, if we can, prevent earth from being made into a hell in order to arouse a greater longing for heaven." – *Address To The German Nation*, pg. 131

"What man of noble mind is there who does not earnestly wish to relive his own life in a new and better way in his children and his children's children, and to continue to live on this earth, ennobled and perfected in their lives, long after he is dead? Does he not wish to snatch from the jaws of death the spirit, the mind, and the moral sense by virtue of which, perchance, he was in the days of his life a terror to wrongdoing and corruption, and by which he supported righteousness, aroused men from indolence, and lifted them out of their depression? Does he not wish to deposit these qualities, as his best legacy to posterity, in the souls of those he leaves behind, so that they too, in their turn, may some day hand them on again, increased and made more beautiful? What man of noble mind is there who does not want to scatter, by action or thought, a grain of seed for the unending progress in perfection of his race, to fling something new and unprecedented into time, that it may remain there and become the inexhaustible source of new creations? Does he not wish to pay for his place on this earth and the short span of time allotted to him with something that even here below will endure forever, so that he, the individual, although unnamed in history (for the thirst for posthumous fame is contemptible vanity), may yet in his own consciousness and his faith leave behind him unmistakable memories that he, too, was a dweller on the earth? What man of noble mind is there, I say, who does not want this?" – *Address To The German Nation*, pg. 132

"He who does not first regard himself as eternal has in him no love of any kind, and, moreover, cannot love a fatherland, a thing which for him does not exist. He who regards his invisible life as eternal, but not his visible life as similarly eternal, may perhaps have a heaven and therein, a fatherland, but here below he has no fatherland, for this, too, is regarded only in the image of eternity–eternity visible and made sensuous–and for this reason also he is unable to love his fatherland. If none has been handed down to such a man, he is to be pitied. But he to whom a fatherland has been handed down, and in whose soul heaven and earth, visible and invisible meet and mingle, and thus, and only thus, create a true and enduring heaven– such a man fights to the last drop of his blood to hand on the precious possession unimpaired to his posterity....Not the spirit of the peaceful citizen's love for the constitution and the laws, but the devouring flame of higher patriotism, which embraces the nation as the vesture of the eternal, for which the noble-minded man joyfully sacrifices himself....It is not that love of the citizen for the constitution; that love is quite unable to achieve this....The promise of a life here on earth extending beyond the period of life here on earth—that alone it is which can inspire men even unto death for the fatherland." – *Address To The German Nation*, pg. 137

—JOHANN GOTTLIEB FICHTE —

"Life merely as such, the mere continuance of changing existence, has in any case never had any value for him; he has wished for it only as the source of what is permanent. But this permanence is promised to him only by the continuous and independent existence of his nation. In order to save his nation he must be ready even to die that it may live, and that he may live in it the only life for which he has ever wished." – *Address To The German Nation*, pg. 136

Millard Fillmore

"But a duty laid upon an article which may be produced here stimulates the skill and industry of our own country to produce the same article, which is brought into the market in competition with the foreign article, and the importer is thus compelled to reduce his price to that at which the domestic article can be sold, thereby throwing a part of the duty upon the producer of the foreign article. The continuance of this process creates the skill and invites the capital which finally enable us to produce the article much cheaper than it could have been procured from abroad, thereby benefiting both the producer and the consumer at home. The consequence of this is that the artisan and the agriculturist are brought together, each affords a ready market for the produce of the other, the whole country becomes prosperous, and the ability to produce every necessary of life renders us independent in war as well as in peace. – *State of the Union Address*, 1850; *Congressional Record*, vol. 23, appendix, pg. 347

First Constitution of the Transvaal

"The nation desires to preserve its Dutch Reformed religion as established in 1618-1619 at the Synod of Dort. The nation does not desire to tolerate in its midst the Roman Church nor any other Protestant Church which rejects the core doctrines as outlined in the Heidelberg Catechism. No one apart from those who are members of the Dutch Reformed Church may hold a civil office." – *SA Argiefstukke Tvl* no. 3:382

David Hackett Fischer

"During the very long period from 1629 to 1775, the present area of the United States was settled by at least four large waves of English-speaking immigrants. The first was an exodus of Puritans from the east of England to Massachusetts during a period of 11 years from 1629 to 1640. The second was the migration of a small Royalist elite and large numbers of indentured servants from the south of England to Virginia (ca. 1642-75). The third was a movement from the North Midlands of England and Wales to the Delaware Valley (ca. 1675-1725). The fourth was a flow of English-speaking people from the borders of North Britain and northern Ireland to the Appalachian backcountry mostly during the half-century from 1718 to 1775.

"These four groups shared many qualities in common. All of them spoke the English language. Nearly all were British Protestants. Most lived under British laws and took pride in possessing British liberties. At the same time, they also differed from one another in many ways: in their religious denominations, social ranks, historical generations, and also in the British region whence they came. They carried across the Atlantic four different sets of British folkways which became the basis of regional cultures in the New World... They had different methods of doing much of the ordinary business of life. Most important for the political history of the US, they also had four different conceptions of order, power and freedom which became the cornerstones of a voluntary society in British America." – *Albion's Seed*, pg. 6

"The founders of Massachusetts and their descendants for many generations tended to cling to the cultural baggage which they had carried out of England. This mood of cultural conservatism created a curious paradox in colonial history. New settlements tended to remain remarkably old-fashioned in their folkways. They missed the new fads and customs that appeared in the mother country after they were planted. They tended to preserve cultural dynamics that existed in the hour of their birth. It was if they were caught in a twist of time and held in its coils while the rest of the world moved beyond them." – *Albion's Seed*, pg. 56-57

"So important was the idea of a covenanted family in Massachusetts that everyone was compelled by law to live in family groups. The provinces of Connecticut and Plymouth forbade any single person to 'live of himself.' These laws were enforced. In 1668 the court of Middlesex County systematically searched its towns for single persons and placed them in families. This custom was not invented in New England. It had long been practiced in East Anglia." – *Albion's Seed*, pg. 73

"Virginia speech ways were not invented in America. They derived from a family of regional dialects that had been spoken throughout the south and west of England during the 17th century... Virginia's building ways, like its speech ways, were not created de novo in the New World. They grew out of the vernacular architecture of southern England in a process that was guided by cultural purposes, environmental conditions and the inherited memory of an English past." – *Albion's Seed*, pg. 259

"The people of Virginia thought less of the biblical commandment to increase and multiply and replenish the earth which so obsessed the Puritans, and more of breeding stocks and bloodlines. Children of the elite were bred to one another in a manner not unlike dogs and horses... Six generations after settlement, Virginians still perceived the culture of England as a precious inheritance to be protected from change, and passed intact from one generation to the next. For a very long time, the Chesapeake colonists thought of themselves as Englishmen apart from England — cultural exiles in a distant land. They often referred to their nation as 'the mother country.'" – *Albion's Seed*, pg. 304-305

"The English Friends who founded West Jersey and Pennsylvania welcomed immigrants of different national origins but remained firmly in control of their colonies long enough to shape the character of the region. The proportion of Quakers in the Pennsylvania Assembly remained as high as 50% until 1773. For 80 years they wrote the laws, distributed the land, decided immigration policy and created institutions which still survive to the present day. Most important, the Quakers also established the rules of engagement among people of different ethnic groups." – *Albion's Seed*, pg. 433

"Many scholars call these people 'Scotch-Irish'. That expression is an Americanism, rarely used in Britain and much resented by the people to whom it was attached. "We're no Eerish bou Scoatch,' one of them was heard to say in Pennsylvania... 'We are a mixed people,' a border immigrant declared in America during the 18th century. So they were in many ways. They were mixed in their social rank, mixed in their religious denomination, and most profoundly mixed in their ancestry... But in another way, these immigrants were very similar to one another. No matter whether rich or poor, Anglican or Presbyterian, Saxon or Celt, they were all a border people. They shared a unique regional culture which was the product of a place in time." – *Albion's Seed*, pg. 618

Joseph Fitzmyer

"He it is who has fixed the dates of their epochs and the boundaries of their habitation; i.e., the regular periods in the history of nations and their set geographical boundaries. So God is close to human beings. The historic limitations set upon humanity, the times and places where they dwell, are all the object of divine determination." – *Anchor Yale Bible, The Acts of the Apostles: A New Translation with Introduction and Commentary*, vol. 31, pg. 609

"My kinsmen by descent. Lit., 'my relatives according to the flesh.' This added phrase explains further the sense in which Jews are Paul's 'brothers.' Kata sarka expresses the natural, human connection, as in 1:3; 4:1; 8:1; 9:5; 11:14; 1 Cor 10:8. Paul writes syngeneis, lit., 'relatives,' in the broad sense of tribesmen, members of the same background and culture." – Romans 9:3, *Anchor Yale Bible, Romans: A New Translation with Introduction and Commentary*, vol. 33, pg. 544

Valerius Flaccus

"Venus smiled upon the lovers, and Cupid with his pleadings roused Aeetes' daughter from the gloomy thoughts that vexed her; Cytherea clothes the girl with her own robe of saffron texture, and gives her her own twofold coronal and the jewels destined to burn upon another bride. Then did a new beauty inform her features, her yellow tresses received the tiring that was due to them, and she moved without a thought of ill." – *The Argonautica*, pg. 429

John Flavel

"Q. What relatives are directly and more especially concerned in this fifth commandment?

"A. All superiors and inferiors are concerned in it; especially, (1.) Political fathers and their children; that is, kings and subjects; Mark 11:10. Blessed be the kingdom of our father David, &c. (2.) Spiritual fathers, and their children; that is, ministers, and their people; 1 Corinthians 4:15. For though you have ten thousand instructors in Christ, yet have ye not many fathers, for in Christ Jesus have I begotten you through the gospel. (3.) Natural parents, and their children; Ephesians 6:1. Children, obey your parents in the Lord. (4.) All civil superiors and inferiors, as husbands and wives, masters and servants; Ephesians 5:22. Wives, submit yourselves unto your husbands, as unto the Lord. And Ephesians 6:5. Servants be obedient to them that are your masters, according to the flesh, &c." – *An Exposition of the Assembly's Shorter Catechism, Of the Fifth Commandment*

"My dear kinsman, my flesh, and my blood; my soul thirsteth for your salvation, and the salvation of your family. Shall you and I resolve with good Joshua, that whatever others do, 'we and our families will serve the Lord;' that we will walk as the redeemed by his blood, shewing forth his virtues and praises in the world? that as God hath made us one in name, and one in affection, so we may be one in Christ; that it may be said of us, as it was of Austin and Alippous long ago, that they were sanguine Christi conghttinati, glued together by the blood of Christ." – *The Fountain of Life Opened: Or, a Display of Christ in His Essential and Mediatorial Glory, Works*, vol. 1, pg. xviii

"Let us take heed that we withhold not our knowledge of Christ in unrighteousness from the people. O that our lips may disperse knowledge and feed many. Let us take heed of the napkin, remembering the day of account is at hand. Remember, I beseech you, the relations wherein you stand, and the obligations resulting thence: Remember, the great Shepherd gave himself for, and gave you to the flock; your time, your gifts are not yours, but God's…" – *The Fountain of Life Opened: Or, a Display of Christ in His Essential and Mediatorial Glory, Works*, vol. 1, pg. 41

Thomas Fleming

"The one essential insight of free-market economics is that human beings are more efficient at providing for their own needs than any set of other people could possibly be, no matter how enlightened." – *The Morality of Everyday Life*, pg. 18

"A Christian saint, if he had the power to do everyone good, would be obliged to exercise it, but such powers belong to the divine and not to the human. People make a very basic mistake when they assume that, even in principle, we have an obligation to act in such a way that 'everybody' (however defined) is better off. Most valuable resources are limited, and, in disposing of food and water, property and time, we must choose between one action and another, one person and another. If the greatest good to the greatest number were the goal, then I might be justified (as some utilitarians have argued) in killing one man to save the lives of millions, in accordance with the military maxim 'the sacrifice of few to save many.'" – *The Morality of Everyday Life*, pg. 20

"This is the Christian...response both to socialism and to internationalism: not an undifferentiated mass of the globe's peoples 'sharing all the wealth' without the benefit of a coercive state, but a pyramid of natural associations within which men and women inherit identities that shape their character and in which they cooperate for the common good." – *The Morality Of Everyday Life*, pg. 65

— THOMAS FLEMING —

"...man, as Aristotle said, is a zoon politikon, a creature framed to live in society, and if he thinks he can transcend the ordinary civilities of family, neighborhood, and nation, he may turn out to be that 'tribeless, lawless, hearthless man' denounced by Homer' (*Iliad* 9.63), who resembles an isolated checker on the game board (*Politics* 1253a)." – *The Morality Of Everyday Life*, pg. 163

"To delegitimize the rights of nations to defend their territory, leftists like to quote Paul's statement that in Christ, 'There is neither Jew nor Greek', as if Paul's intent was not to repress the quarrels that broke out between Gentile and Jewish Christians but to obliterate ethnic and cultural boundaries. The absurdity (and dishonesty) of such an interpretation is made clear in what follows: 'There is neither bond nor free, there is neither male nor female: for ye are all one in Christ Jesus.' Surely, no sane person would argue Paul, who more than once instructs slaves to obey their masters and runaway slaves to return, condemned slavery per se. Paul, who has been unfairly stigmatized as a misogynist, can hardly be accused of pursuing a feminist agenda." – *Family Tradition*

"The elimination of kinship as an essential part of the social network is fraught with consequences. Before the city or the state came into existence and before the invention of the 'individual,' men and women lived within families that were part of broader groups of kinfolk, such as clans and tribes. The Israel depicted in the Book of Judges is a network of villages belonging to tribal entities that are both territorial and, at least in principle, based on kinship. These villages are made up of compounds of extended families that acknowledge a broader social structure, a clan, that may or may not be coextensive with the village itself. These village clans are joined together into tribes. From what we can make out of ancient writers and the archaeological record, this structure was paralleled (not replicated) in archaic Greece, and similar patterns are found in medieval Europe, not only among primitive Germans and Scandinavians but also in France and Italy." – *Family Tradition*

"For most of the past hundred years, defenders of 'family values' have limited their attention to the so-called bourgeois or nuclear family, and some have even pretended that these isolated households of parents-cum-children are a human norm...In rough times, isolated households are incapable of defending themselves from predatory enemies, and in the conditions imposed by modern states, nuclear families cannot stand up against the legions of public school teachers, child-saving social workers, and children's rights advocates. Stripped of the protection offered by broader networks of kith and kin, the nuclear family cannot even protect its children from mass culture, much less the vast network of social agencies arrayed against it." – *Family Tradition*

"Kinship provides the institutional structures by which individuals and households are integrated into society. Once these ties of blood have been cut, there is only anarchy—and the despotism of absolute government." – *Family Tradition*

"Some leftists have pretended that Christians cannot restrict immigration into their country, even if they believe it is harmful to their nation's security and prosperity. They cite such statements as 'Thou shalt neither vex a stranger nor oppress him: for ye were strangers in the land of Egypt.' Like most proof texts taken out context, these sentences are open to misinterpretation. Did strangers possess the same rights as Jews? Apparently not. If a priest's daughter married a foreigner, she could not eat the holy food that priests and their families partook of. [Lev 22:10] Solomon did a census of the strangers in Israel and sent them off to do hard labor.

"A foreigner who approached the tabernacle was put to death [Num 21:51]. A Jew could charge interest on money loaned to a stranger but not to a Jew [Num 23:20], and the Jews' ethnic first cousins, the Edomites, only gained full rights after three generations of living with the children of Israel. [Num 23:10] Like most ancient peoples, the Israelites were intensely chauvinistic and xenophobic. By their own (albeit exaggerated) account in Joshua and Judges, they exterminated the gentile population of Canaan when they entered the Promised Land."

"These historical facts, though, are of little interest to the bone-headed Marxists who fill the pews of mega-churches and make a show of their do-gooding piety that cannot disguise their hatred of their neighbors and fellow citizens." – *Death Throes*

"Properly applied to immigration, this commandment (the 5th) tells us we have the right and duty to defend our parents, households, villages and countries against invasion. If there is a natural right to immigrate (as opposed to emigrate), it is strange that it was only discovered when immigration rights had been put on

the leftist agenda." – *Aliens and Strangers*

"The apparent contradiction in the Old Testament's approach to foreigners is easily resolved by a closer look at the words. The Hebrew language and the Law made a clear distinction between, on the one hand, sojourning immigrants who have been given permissionn to stay in the land and generously accorded the protection of the law (rendered in Greek as prosyletos and in Latin as advena), and, on the other foreigners who have not been given this legal status (in Greek allogenes and in Latin by alienigena). While the former are treated as potential or real converts to Judaism, the latter are unclean. An alien could not so much as touch the bread being offered to God, and if a priest's daughter married a foreigner, she could not eat the holy food that priests and their families partook of [Lev. 22:10, 12]. A foreigner who approached the tabernacle was put to death, and no bread could be offered to their God from a foreigner's hand 'because their corruption is in them.' [Lev 22:25]" – *The Reign of Love*, pgs. 28-29

"One-worldism is not even a Christian heresy but a post-Christian delusion. Free enterprise, tempered both by duties to family and community and by charity to others, is certainly consistent with the Christian moral order, but imperial globalism, dominated by a handful of world-controllers who make war on all distinctions of blood and affection is the economic Anti-Christ." – *The Reign of Love*, pg. 30

"Utopian projects run aground on a fundamental principle enunciated by Cicero: The family is the foundation of the city (principium urbis) the seed-bed of the commonwealth (seminarium rei publicae)....

"Cicero's view of the family was no an eccentric opinion. For Christians and Jews, the story of Adam and Eve has been a vivid confirmation of the family's status as a divinely established institution that stands at the beginning of human history, and political thinkers from Cicero to St. Thomas and even down to the 17th century were influenced by Aristotle's account of social evolution as an unfolding process that begins with the married couple and culminates in the commonwealth." – *The Reign of Love*, pg. 42

"But before liberals invented the individual and leftists invented the collective hive, ordinary people and philosophers understood very well that, while human persons were distinct, they inevitably existed in a familial and social context. Inevitably the liberation of the individual has meant the dismantling of fundamental social institutions from the family to the Church and the construction of vastly larger political mechanisms with coercive powers that an Alexander or a Nero never dreamed of possessing." – *The Reign of Love*, pg. 125

"Man is by nature a corporate being who belongs to a family, a tribe, or a religious brotherhood. It is only within a society, that family members, kinsmen, neighbors, and co-religionists can cooperate in protecting each other from the depredations of thugs, gang-leaders and the bureaucratic tyrants who administer the organs of the modern state. It is only as members of a certain kind of society that human beings can aspire to the moral dignity classical liberals have in mind when they use the term 'individual.'" – *The Reign of Love*, pg. 126

"The modern obsession with befriending the other' goes back at least as far as Montaigne's famous 'Essay on the Cannibals,' in which Latin American savages are depicted as superior to French Catholics. The wise and benevolent alien—whether Turk or Persian or Chinese—became a common theme in the Enlightenment, a generation or more before Rousseau infected the European imagination with his fantasy of the noble savage. But if we are taught to seek our highest friendships among exotic strangers, then we might think everyday friendships with relatives and neighbors to be humdrum affairs. On the other hand, perhaps only a culture that has rejected the local and provincial in favor of the universal and the bizarre could be taken in by tales of wise Turks and noble savages." – *The Reign of Love*, pg. 136

"For ancient Greeks and Roman, then, 'friendship' was a complex notion that might include kinship, an affectionate bond between men who respect each other, and a practical alliance for some agreed upon purpose. However complicated the idea(s), these connections—and not some rational abstraction like rights or justice—

were the foundation of social and political life." – *The Reign Of Love*, pg. 159

"The Jewish and thus the Christian notion of neighbor (in its moral, non-geographical sense) is not a universal term nor does it refer to someone who accidentally lives nearby: It is rather more precise and even restrictive. It is a moral bond, like brotherhood and friendship, and it does not extend to people trying to harm us or our children or to hypothetical strangers who may live a thousand miles away. If we live next door to an anti-Christian abortionist, he is not our neighbor in the Christian sense, while if someone living a Christian life across town, he (even if his views are heretical or he belongs to a Christian sect we happen to loathe), he has certain moral claims on our time, resources, and attention." – *The Reign of Love*, pg. 175

"We have, then, a stark contrast between the modern way of analyzing moral duties and the older way of looking at moral relations. On the one side stand the abstract and universal principles of right and wrong that each society advances as true, while on the other are arrayed the primary bonds of attachment that claim our loyalty. Since Descartes, Western man has tended to maximize the importance of abstract concepts of right(s), while ignoring or denigrating or condemning sub-rational loyalties... These abstractions have alienated ordinary men and women not only from the traditions of their ancestors but from the reality of human nature." – *The Reign of Love*, pg. 176

"A Christian's highest priority cannot be his own life, with all its affections and duties, but his loyalty and obedience to God. If he is willing to lose his life, he must also be willing to lose his family.

"However, short of martyrdom, he must fulfill every jot and tittle of the law, which prescribed 'Honor thy father and thy mother'

"The Law that Christ came to fulfill was rooted in the duties of kinship. In the Old Testament, the system of descent is patrilineal. A mother's family is thus not kin to her child. There appears secondarily to be some preference for endogamy, that is for marriage within the tribe or kindred. The practice is reflected in the commandment concerning the daughters of

Zelophehad [Num 36:6]: 'Let them marry whom they think best; only, they shall marry within the family of the tribe of their father.'

"That this practice was seen as desirable by the Hebrews can be seen in Judge 14:2, where Samson's parents lament the fact that their son wants to marry a Philistine woman: 'Is there not a woman among the daughters of kinsmen, or among all our people, that you must go to take a wife from the uncircumcised Philistines?' Ideally Samson's spouse would be a woman from his kinsmen (i.e., his patrilineage). If he did not want to marry one of them, his parents would have preferred any Israelite woman, rather than for their son to marry a foreigner." – *The Reign of Love*, pgs. 189-190

"Ancient Greeks were hardly unique in putting a high value on filial piety, familial solidarity, and the duties of kinship. These are moral tendencies so common, both in primitive societies and advanced civilizations, that they can be regarded as universal human traits." – *The Reign of Love*, pg. 200

"Educated liberals and conservatives, however, may find cold comfort in the realization that the art and literature they were brought up to admire–everything from the Parthenon to Euripides to Vergil and the Pantheon, Dante and the cathedrals of Tuscany, Shakespeare, Milton, and Christopher Wren–were created by retrograde societies that revered the ties of blood and feared divine wrath." – *The Reign of Love*, pg. 214

"Life is brief, but a kindred may go on for centuries. Our natural immortality begins in marriage which, in unniting two sexes and kindreds, is the foundation of the family, and if, as a people once believed, the basic function of marriage is to create heirs to whom property and staus is passed down, then systems of kinship extend the range of the marital functions." – *The Reign of Love*, pgs. 241-242

"The laws and customs that regulate inheritance can teach the observer two important lessons: First, their universality—despite the great diversity—is strong evidence for the overriding importance of kinship in human societies; and, second, the diversity of the specific arragements themselves provide insight into the natue of the socieities and their hierarchy of value." – *The Reign of Love*, pg. 245

"Family and kinship remained vital forces in maintaining the Roman social order, and the gradual infusion of Christian morality into legislation did little or nothing to loosen the ties of blood. The rules on incest were, in fact, more sharply drawn, the evidence of wills suggests that, of those Roman citizens, Christian or pagan, who possessed enough property to make wills a practical necessity, most continued to favor close relatives." – *The Reign of Love*, pg. 253

"The way we view a nation is inextricably linked with our conception of family and kindred. If cousins and great-grandparents mean little to us, we shall probably view the nation as nothing more than a set of laws and markets, 'a land of opportunity'; a place where (in the words of T.S. Eliot in 'The Rock')
    We all dwell together
    To make money from each other..."
– *The Reign of Love*, p. 279

"If we work for a large company, we may have little choice when told we must move from Huntsville, Alabama to Seattle, Washington, and the ruthless self-denial once demanded of professional military officers and missionaries is now expected of computer technicians and corporate executives. As we move, we lose not only our connection with a particular place but also with friends as we grow older, the whole concept of friendship, in an increasingly mobile society, gradually becomes foreign." – *The Reign Of Love*, pg. 92

"Friendship, more than philosophy and theology, is the driving force that urges Dante toward his salvation.

"Friendship was also the basis of Roman political life and the subject of one of Cicero's most popular essays, the De Amicitia, which partly formed Dante's views on the importance of friendship. ...

"If friendship is the moral foundation of Dante's and Cicero's universe, it is the individual that occupies the center stage in ours." – *The Reign Of Love*, pg. 95

"What Conservative one-worlders fail to see are two facts of life: First, that there is not now and has never been anything remotely resembling Free Trade. Someone always controls the market and our choice is whether to exercise that control here in the United States or turn it over to international regulators in the pay of trans-national corporations. Second, that the underlying ideology of Free Trade is based on the assumption that–to quote a former Wall Street Journal editor's observation to free-trader Peter Brimelow–'the nation state is finished.' The late Robert Bartley's approach to this question might have been torn from the pages of the Communist Manifesto, in which Marx and Engels predicted that the phase of the bourgeois nation state would lead ultimately to a process of globalization that would insure economic justice for poor nation states." – *City-States Rights*, Part I A

Ian Fletcher

"Xenophobia is not necessary for [deficit foreign trading] to be a bad thing, only bookkeeping. Americans are poorer simply because we own less and owe more. Our net worth is lower. The situation is unsustainable." – *Free Trade Doesn't Work: What Should Replace It and Why*, ch. 2

"Compared to the U.S., Japan's culture is indeed rather closed and insular. It may fairly be described as an ethnocentric, patriarchal, and conformist society, sometimes reminding observers of America in the 1950s. Yet its record of economic innovation has been strong. The Walkman was not created by some free spirit in a garage in Silicon Valley, but by Kozo Ohsone, manager of the tape recorder division of Sony. And innovations, such as commercially viable hybrid cars and flat panel TV, have continued to flow in the decades since then. Japan's corporate conformists are today generating more high-tech initial public offerings than the U.S. So whatever perfectly valid reasons one might have for objecting to that kind of culture, lack of economic creativity is not one." – *Free Trade Doesn't Work: What Should Replace It and Why*, ch. 3

"For more than a century, nationalist sentiments have been a basic driving force underlying East Asian economic growth." – *Free Trade Doesn't Work: What Should Replace It and Why*, ch. 6

"Economic history actually reveals that no major developed nation got that way by practicing free trade. Every single one did it by way of protectionism and industrial policy." – *Free Trade Doesn't Work: What Should Replace It and Why*, ch. 6

John Gould Fletcher

"We have a mental habit—not the least pernicious of all our habits—of regarding the savage races of mankind as rude and uncultivated, and of ourselves by contrast as 'civilized' and even 'progressive.' But a few hours of reading at anthropology suffices to dissipate the illusion that there are any races on the earth's surface so primitive as to lack all the elements of culture. Apart, perhaps, from the extinct Tasmanians, the nearly extinct Bushmen, and a few other interesting survivals here and there, man shows at the very outset of his career the elements of tribal confederation. This, like the later social organizations of the clan, the family, the city-state, and the religious brotherhood, is essentially a band of individuals held together by certain practices which, it is assumed, will be of mutual benefit to its members. The tribe lives and acts in common, and its actions are motivated by a complete knowledge, embodied in totemism and taboo, of what is permitted and what is forbidden. These taboos—religious, social, moral—are the unwritten but infrangible laws of the tribal community. They represent the unconscious demands of that community embodied in definite practice—and all the actions of the tribe must respond to them. Culture without such a system of taboos is not culture, and we cannot understand the early Greeks, the American Indians, or any other race of antiquity without understanding first of all the system of taboos and of licit and illicit practices from which they sprang and took their being. The fact that these taboos were unconsciously assumed before all else gave to the tribes practicing them the quality above all of balance..." – *I'll Take My Stand*, pgs. 99-100

Anthony Flood

"Aquinas's principle states that the greater the similitude, the greater the stability and permanency of the love. The greater the permanency of the love, the greater real union the lovers seek and likely obtain. Thus, a greater similitude prima facie effects a greater real union between friends. The ultimate rationale for this principle draws from the relation between unity and union. As unity is the principle of union, the closer two things are together naturally, the closer they can be through love. At the level of persons, the closer a relationship with another person comes to unity, the stronger it will be. Since self-love arises immediately from substantial unity, we can say that the more a lover's love for the beloved approaches one's own self-love (and vice versa), the greater the loving union between them will be. In other words, the most stable and permanent love relationship will be the one that approximates most each person's love of self. Moreover, friendships based on choice often affect a greater intensity of love relative to friendships based on nature. Marriage forms a union with the potential for the greatest stability and permanency based on nature and the greatest intensity based on choice. In short, marriage forms the greatest human union simplicite." – *The Metaphysical Foundations of Love*, pg. 35

Radu Florescu

Speaking of what motivated Vlad Dracul:
"Following the fall of Constantinople, he [Dracula], like many of his successors, considered himself the only truly independent patron and defender of Eastern Orthodoxy, centuries before Russia assumed this traditional mantle…. Beyond his country, however, was the much broader concept of a fatherland of European civilization that had to be defended from an alien creed. This mission he inherited from his mentor Hunyadi and the crusaders of old." – *Dracula: Prince of Many Faces*, pg. 241

— FOLK SAYINGS —

◊ Blood is thicker than water.
◊ The apple doesn't fall far from the tree.
◊ A leopard cannot change its spots.
◊ Birds of a feather flock together.
◊ Bloom where you're planted.
◊ You aren't required to set yourself on fire to keep others warm.
◊ The greatest kindness will not bind the ungrateful.

◊ The same law for both the lion and ox is oppression.
◊ You can drive out Nature with a pitchfork, yet she will hurry back.
◊ Good fences make good neighbors.
◊ Every tub sits on its own bottom.
◊ They that lay down with dogs get up with fleas.
◊ A lamb adopted by a wolf pack will never be the alpha.
◊ Home is where you go when you have no place else to go.
◊ A house divided against itself cannot stand.
◊ Be it ever so humble, there is no place like home.
◊ Charity begins at home.
◊ Children are a poor man's riches.
◊ Like Father, like son.
◊ An ounce of blood is worth more than a pound of friendship.
◊ Our ancestors dwell in the attics of our brains as they do in the spiraling chains of knowledge hidden in every cell of our bodies.
◊ Just because a cat has her kittens in the oven that doesn't make them biscuits.
◊ I'll scratch your back if you'll scratch mine.
◊ One hand washes the other.

————

John Fortescue

"What mechanic is there so inattentive to the advantage of his child, as not to instruct him in his trade while he is young, whereby he may afterwards gain a comfortable subsistence. So the carpenter teaches his son to handle the axe; the smith brings up his at the anvil; a person designed for the sacred office of the ministry is bred, in a liberal way, at school: so it becomes a king to have his son (who is to succeed him) instructed in the laws of his country whilst he is yet young." – *In Praise Of The Laws Of England, in Works*, pg. 392

"The Customs of England are of great Antiquity, received and approved by five several Nations successively. The realm of England was first inhabited by the Britons; afterwards it was ruled and civilized under the government of the Romans; then the Britons prevailed again; next, it was possessed by the Saxons, who changed the

name of Britain into England. After the Saxons, the Danes lorded it over us, and then the Saxons prevailed a second time; at last, the Normans came in, whose descendants obtain the kingdom at this day: and, during all that time, wherein those several nations and their kings prevailed, England has nevertheless been constantly governed by the same customs, as it is at present..."
– *In Praise Of The Laws Of England*, pg. 401

"But since, my good Chancellor, you have now performed what you undertook at first, and have fully persuaded me to apply myself to the study of the laws of my country, I will no longer detain you on this subject. But, I now earnestly desire, that you will proceed, as you have formerly begun with it, to instruct me in the principles, method and nature of the Law of England: which law, I am resolved, shall be ever dear to me, preferably to all other laws in the world, which it as far surpasses, as the morning star exceeds the other stars in glory and brightness."
– *In Praise Of The Laws Of England*, pgs. 441-442

Meyer Fortes

"The facts I have here described have long been familiar and have commonly been designated by such terms as kinship solidarity. What I wish to stress is the basic premise: kinship is binding; it creates inescapable moral claims and obligations. Diffuse as these claims and obligations appear to be, they are, nevertheless, correlated to morphological and institutional distinctions which put kinship proper on one side, and the complementary or coordinate spheres, notably those of affinity, locality, and polity on the other. An interesting test is found in the spillover I alluded to in passing which often leads to a fusion of kinship and locality in neighborhood relations. They may appear to blend inextricably, but it is always possible to separate them out. In an Ashanti brono (town quarter), neighbors who are not lineage kin, patrikin, or affines, but merely fellow citizens of a deceased, condole and mourn with the bereaved but are not under an obligation to contribute to the funeral expenses, nor have they a right to or a voice in the selection of an heir. Tallensi explain many ties of clanship between genealogically independent lineages, and especially ties of ritual collaboration, by invoking long lasting association through, 'dwelling together in the same place,' and the ensuing common interests in peace and in the maintenance of the social and ritual activities upon which the common well-being is believed to depend." – *Kinship and the Social Order: The Legacy of Lewis Henry Morgan*, ch. 8

Michael Foster

"The divisions between things are how God orders them all toward the ultimate goal of glorifying Him. A creation without distinctions is a world that is waste and void, formless and empty, chaotic and futile. Creation is not and should not be a homogeneous mass. It can only glorify God when everything is in its place—not when all things are mushed together.

"The importance of this is impossible to overestimate. To give an analogy, sharing in the common goal of winning a football game does not eliminate the distinctions between the players. Rather, it is why the team is divided into those positions in the first place. A team with eleven quarterbacks is not a 'very good' team.

"By the same token, sharing in the common goal of producing power does not eliminate the distinctions between the parts of an engine. Rather, this common purpose is why the engine has parts at all. If you were to melt everything down into an undifferentiated hunk of metal, it would no longer produce power. It would not be a 'very good' engine.

"This is true also of bodies (1 Cor. 12:14–26), both literal and symbolic. A man with a head only, and no torso or limbs, is hardly a 'very good' man. An army with everyone in command is an army with everyone in confusion. And a house with many heads cannot stand. Vertical divisions are not only as fitting as horizontal ones, but they are also as necessary and indispensable. It is good that all creatures are subordinated beneath their creator. And it is also good that some created things are subordinated beneath others.

"Modern evangelicals are quick to defend the importance of God dividing things horizontally. For instance, we ardently defend the goodness of individuality. Each of us by nature thinks of himself as a special snowflake. By the same token, we are happy enough that God created more than two hundred species of finches. But when it comes to acknowledging the significance of His vertical divisions, we are reluctant." – *It's Good To Be A Man*, ch. 4

— FOUNDING FATHERS —

The founding fathers carry on the ancient constitutions and rights, in the words of Patrick Henry, of their ancestors. They reflect at once the desire to lay hold of their English heritage while also preserving themselves from Parliamentary overreach. As one historian has written, "The United States began as a country of Englishmen who found themselves obliged to declare their independence from the motherland when they felt that their liberties as Englishmen were being infringed upon." The following quotation from the *Declaration of Independence* also reveals this to be true. Here we find "British rights and the ties of brotherhood, descent, kinship, and, indeed, consanguinity (shared blood) between the motherland and the colonies were inseparable in the Declaration."

Another significant example is George Washington's farewell address, which is a long and comprehensive speech that he delivered to the American people in 1796, at the end of his second term as President. In his address, Washington emphasized the importance of national unity, independence, and patriotism for the survival and prosperity of the nation. He warned against the dangers of political parties, sectionalism, and particularly foreign influence, and urged Americans to prioritize domestic, as opposed to international, concerns. Entangling alliances abroad would distract and split the nation, draining its resources of men and materials toward fruitless ventures.

Alexander Hamilton confirms Washington's sentiments when he argued that immigrants are likely to have attachments to their home countries and incompatible political beliefs, making it difficult for them to adopt American ideals. He stated (see below) that the influx of foreigners would lead to a heterogeneous compound, corrupt the national spirit, and introduce foreign propensities, complicating and confounding public opinion. Additionally, Hamilton warned that this policy could compromise the interests of the country, weaken the strength of the nation, and even aid an invader. Diversity, for the founding fathers, was not a strength but a source of discord, distraction, and national weakness.

———

John Frame

"The biblical teaching about the differences of supernatural gifts in the body of Christ (Rom. 12, 1 Cor. 12) suggests a similar way of looking at the natural gifts in the human race in general. No individual, no race, has all possible human abilities. And the 'lesser' abilities are just as necessary to the whole society as are the 'greater.' Indeed, those that are most widely acclaimed may be less valuable in the sight of God." – *Racism, Sexism, Marxism*

"It was God who placed human beings in families, so that our most intimate associations are generally those with which we are closest genetically. Usually we turn to our own cultural group to find spouses and close friends. There *is* a [higher] level of mutual understanding and appreciation within ethnic and culture groups than among them. With your own people, it is usually easier to let your hair down, to joke, to cry, even to worship. With people very different from yourself, you often feel that you are 'walking on eggs.' You are never quite sure when something you say or do will be found offensive, so you tend not to intrude too far into the emotional space of the other group. It is no accident that blacks refer to one another as 'soul brothers.' It is not that people outside one's ethnic group have no souls, but it sometimes seems like that. The outsiders seem stiff and formal, or their language of friendship seems incomprehensible. You do what you need to do, and then you run home to your home base.

"It is important to understand that it is this natural human phenomenon, rather than 'racism' in the objectionable senses discussed earlier, which results in much of the informal racial and cultural segregation in our society. Why is it, for example, that blacks and whites worship in separate churches? For the most part, I think it is not because white Christians hate black Christians, or vice versa. Nor is it because they bear continued grudges or believe in the superiority of their own group, though some of these motives may at times be present. Churches tend to belong predominantly to one race or another, because worship is one of those times in which it is important to understand one another on an intimate level. The church is like a family; indeed it is the family of God. Much of its ministry involves communication; and communication is almost always better within ethnic limits. Blacks and whites tend to speak different languages in worship, a difference evident in their choice of music and of preaching style.

"Much has been said about how Sunday at 11:00 A. M. is the 'most segregated hour of the week.' But can it be doubted that both blacks and whites prefer to worship with people of their own race? Would black Christians willingly give up their black churches to become, say, 20% minorities within white churches? Such 'integrated' churches might try hard to include gospel music and black-style preaching occasionally; but it would never be quite the same.

"The phenomenon is not limited to differences between whites and blacks. In the US, there are churches of people that are predominantly of Dutch ancestry, as well as German, Scandinavian, Korean, Chinese, Mexican, etc. Each of these ethnic churches are somewhat distinct in style and emphasis. In the general culture, as immigrants' families have learned English, these ethnic differences have become less important. But in the churches they persist, and they persist because many people want to keep them.

"But doesn't the gospel break down racial barriers, bringing people of every kindred, tongue, tribe, and nation into one great new family? Certainly it broke through the barriers between Jew and Gentile, so that the uncircumcised could have full fellowship with God in Christ. And surely the various ethnic groups within the church are to love one another and to accept one another as joint heirs of God's grace.

"On the other hand, there is no suggestion in the New Testament that every house church must have representation of both Jews and Gentiles. In many localities, such equality would have been unlikely. And as the church moves throughout the world, congregations are segregated by language differences. Nothing in Scripture suggests that this is wrong.

"I therefore defend 'freedom of association' within some limits. I don't believe that we are obligated to seek friends of all ethnic groups on an egalitarian basis. Nor do I believe that it is wrong for a church to be 90% Dutch, or 80% African American, or 95% Anglo." – *Racism, Sexism, Marxism*

"Scripture, as I read it, does not require societies, or even churches, to be integrated racially. Jews and Gentiles were brought together by God's grace into one body. They were expected to love one another and to accept one another as brothers in the faith. But the Jewish Christians continued to maintain a distinct culture, and house churches were not required to include members of both groups." – *Racism, Sexism, Marxism*

"What we see in Scripture, rather, is a kind of gradual development from family authority to something which we would tend to call a state." – *Toward A Theology Of The State*

"Yet he warrants the extension of that authority to extended families, tribes, nations. Yes, he warrants the popular selection of leaders to implement that authority (a selection into which, of course, he is always free to intervene, and over which he always exercises providential superintendence). Yes, that authority includes the power to use deadly force and to resolve disputes which cannot otherwise be resolved. In that sense, we may say with Paul in Rom 13:1 that 'the authorities that exist have been established by God.' But it is important to remember that the authority of the state is essentially a family authority, not something different." – *Toward A Theology Of The State*

"God claims families with a special zeal. He chose the process of childbearing as the means by which his son would enter the world and announced that fact at the beginning of redemption (Gen 3:15). He saved the family of Noah from the flood (6:18; 7:1, 13; 8:16ff.), and he gave to that family dominion over the earth and the right to avenge bloodshed (Gen 8:20-9:17). He called Abram, promising to bless his offspring, and to bless all nations through that offspring (Gen 12:7; 15:4f.). God commanded as a sign of the Abrahamic covenant an injury to the male organ of generation, and he commanded that that sign be applied to all of Abraham's family including the young children (17:9-27). Similarly, Israel, the family of Jacob, was to circumcise its males on the eighth day of their lives (Lev 12:3) to acknowledge God's claim upon all their seed. (Cf. also the consecration of the firstborn by ransom of his life, Exod 13:12.) Certainly, then, there is nothing strange about a family head professing faith in God on behalf of his household. 'Choose for yourselves this day whom you will serve,' said Joshua, 'but as for me and my household, we will serve the Lord'

(Josh 24:15).

"Household commitments, indeed household baptisms, are also found in the NT (Acts 2:39; 11:14; 16:15, 31; 18:8; 1 Cor 1:16). To me and others, these references are a strong argument in favor of infant baptism: surely first-century Jews would have understood these events as a continuation of the OT practice of claiming households for God and of administering the sign of the covenant to all those in the household. At any rate, God continues to call families. The importance of the family to God is not exhausted when the 'seed' of Gen 3:15 comes in Christ. Rather, Christ himself, now at the right hand of God the Father, continues to work through families to extend his kingdom throughout the earth (Matt 28:19ff.). And indeed, his goal is not only to rule families, but extended families, tribes, nations (Psalms 2; 72; 110; Matt 25:32; 28:19; Rom 4:17f.; Gal 3:8; Rev. 2:26; 12:5; 15:4; 20:3; 21:24ff.; 22:2).

"On my earlier account, states are family governments. If a family is to profess Christ as Lord, its government must do the same. If a tribe or nation is to profess Christ as Lord, its government, the state, must do the same. A non-Christian family-state should also profess its religious commitment. For there is no neutrality, for states any more than for individuals." – *Toward A Theology Of The State*

"In the modern world, then, each Christian IS a citizen of two nations: An earthly nation like France, England, or the U.S.A., and the heavenly nation (Eph 2:6; not of this world, John 18:36), the church. Though we belong entirely to Christ, we do not on that account renounce our citizenship in the earthly nations, any more than we leave our earthly families. Indeed, we seek to be good citizens, for those earthly nations themselves, and their rulers, received their authority from God (Rom 13:1-7)." – *Toward A Theology Of The State*

R.T. France

"The parable of the good Samaritan, however, is not primarily a call to universal benevolence; rather, it is a challenge to social and ethnic stereotyping." – *Teach The Text Commentary Series, Luke*, pg. 433

Sam Francis

"The late Roman Empire, the Byzantine Empire, the Ottoman Empire, and the dominions of the Habsburgs and the Romanovs, among others, all presided over a kind of rainbow coalition of nations and peoples, who for the most part managed to live happily because their secret compulsions to spill each other's blood were restrained by the overwhelming power of the despots and dynasties who ruled them. Political freedom relies on a shared political culture as much as on the oppositions and balances that social differentiation creates, and when the common culture disintegrates under the impact of mass migrations, only institutionalized force can hold the regime together." – *Ounces of Flesh*

"America First trade and immigration policies should recognize that we, as Americans, owe duties to ourselves and our compatriots before we owe anything to other peoples, and restrictions on immigration, free trade, and technology transfer should be debated and framed in terms of our national identity and interests, and not in terms of natural or human rights or the interests of a fictitious 'global community.' Immigration from countries and cultures that are incompatible with and indigestible to the Euro-American cultural core of the United States should be generally prohibited, current border controls should be rigorously enforced, illegal aliens already here should be rounded up and deported, and employers who hire them should be prosecuted and punished. As for immigrants from less backward countries, we should balance consideration of whatever gains they might bring to our economy with at least equal consideration of their long-term impact on our cultural identity (including our economic and scientific culture). Similar considerations should apply to trade policy; the basic test of free trade or specific restrictions on it should be their consequences for the American national interest, and not whether they promote global economic integration, help less advanced economies, or facilitate individual economic aspirations." – *The Phrase 'America First'*

"In foreign policy, the idea of putting America first involves a radical dismantling of the Cold War state. It means abrogating most of the mutual defense treaties of the 1950's, withdrawing most of the troops and military bases from Europe and Asia, and terminating almost all foreign aid. It also means that much or most of the national security and foreign policy bureaucracy—in the Pentagon, the State Department, the intelligence community, the U.S. Information Agency, the Agency for International Development, the Peace Corps, etc. —should be abolished or radically reduced in size and functions. Most of these agencies were established for explicitly Cold War purposes, and their continued existence at this point in their present form not only is useless and expensive but also provides a powerful pressure group for continuing globalist adventure and entanglement." – *The Phrase 'America First'*

"If a new nationalism is to flourish and endure, it must do more than offer a merely narrow, pragmatic, and largely economic definition of the national identity and the national interest. It will have to look to the historic norms of the American people and their culture to discover and articulate what America is and what it should be, and it will have to recognize that the American cultural identity involves a good bit more than merely economic growth and individual gratification." – *The Phrase 'America First'*

"The recognition of the significance of race does not imply or lead to 'hate' or domination of one race by another, but racial differentiation does imply social differentiation. The existence of significant biological differences between groups of human beings means there will be social differences between them: differences in educational and economic achievement, personal and political behavior, and social and cultural institutions. And if there is social differentiation between races, then competition and conflict between them is also likely, especially if they occupy the same territory. 'Hatred,' domination, and racial antagonism may therefore result, not as relationships to be desired or advocated, but as the consequence of the natural reality of racial differences and the effort to ignore or deny such differences." – *The Return of the Repressed*

"There are three general reasons why a revival of white racial consciousness and identity is needed.

"First, we now know enough about the bio-

logically grounded cognitive and behavioral differences between the races to be able to say with confidence that race deeply affects and shapes cultural life. Races with a lower level of cognitive capacity could have produced neither the modern West, with its scientific and technological achievements, nor the ancient West, with its vast political organization and sophisticated artistic and philosophical legacies. Nor is the inclinations of white Westerners to innovate, explore, expand, and conquer apparent among most non-white races, even if their cognitive capacities are greater than those of whites.

"Second, whites, like any race, should wish to survive and flourish simply for their own sake whatever their merits or flaws. Even this minimal rationale for racial survival is denied to whites today because of their constant demonization. And third, white racial consciousness is necessary simply as a means of self-protection. It is an integral component of the historic identity of America as a culture and a nation." – *The Return of the Repressed*

"The doctrine of equality is unimportant because no one save perhaps Pol Pot and Ben Wattenberg really believes in it, and no one, least of all those who profess it most loudly, is seriously motivated by it.… The real meaning of the doctrine of equality is that it serves as a political weapon." – *Beautiful Losers: Essays on the Failure of American Conservatism*, pg. 209

"In the universalist world-view, there is neither history nor race nor even species, neither specific cultures nor particular peoples nor meaningful boundaries. Therefore there are no concrete duties to race, nation, community, family, friend or neighbor and indeed no distinctions to be drawn between neighbor and stranger, friend and foe, mine and thine, us and them." – *Why Race Matters*

"The holidays, public anniversaries, flags, songs, statues, museums, symbols, and heroes that a people shares are fundamental to its identity and its existence as a people. What we are witnessing on the official level of public culture in the attacks on these traditional symbols and their displacement by the symbols of other races is the effective abolition of one people and the gradual creation of another." – *Why Race Matters*

— SAMUEL T. FRANCIS —

"'Tribal behavior' is what makes human beings human. Take it away from 'man' or 'humankind' and what you get is not 'pure man' or 'liberated man' but dehumanization, and from that, tyranny." – *Christmas and the National Question*, December 23, 2014

"Alexander the Great's solution of the Gordian Knot by simply slashing it to pieces with his sword is no less a racial trait of Aryans than the scientific achievements of Plato and Aristotle, Galileo and Newton, and hundreds of other scientists who were heirs of the ancient Aryans and who slashed through obscurantism and mythologies with their minds. Their descendants have cured diseases, shrunk distances, raised cities out of jungles and deserts, constructed technologies that replace and transcend human strength, restored lost languages, recovered forgotten histories, stared into the hearts of distant galaxies, and reached into the recesses of the atom. No other people has ever dreamed of these achievements, and insofar as other peoples even know such things are possible, it is because they have learned about them from European Man." – *Essential Writings on Race*, pg. 54

"America First trade and immigration policies should recognize that we, as Americans, owe duties to ourselves and our compatriots before we owe anything to other peoples, and restrictions on immigration, free trade, and technol-ogy transfer should be debated and framed in terms of our national identity and interests, and not in terms of natural or human rights or the interests of a fictitious 'global community.' Immigration from countries and cultures that are incompatible with and indigestible to the Euro-American cultural core of the United States should be generally prohibited, current border controls should be rigorously enforced, illegal aliens already here should be rounded up and deported, and employers who hire them should be prosecuted and punished. As for immigrants from less backward countries, we should balance consideration of whatever gains they might bring to our economy with at least equal consideration of their long-term impact on our cultural identity (including our economic and scientific culture). Similar considerations should apply to trade policy; the basic test of free trade or specific restrictions on it should be their consequences for the American national interest, and not whether they promote global economic integration, help less advanced economies, or facilitate individual economic aspirations." – *Phrase America First*

"Similarly, the mass corporation must seek to break down the differentiations that characterize the bourgeois order, the diversity that exists in a decentralized and localized society that is not united by mass communications, transportation, and markets. The corporation must promote the homogenization of society because of the nature of mass production and mass consumption. Mass production requires not only homogeneous goods and services, produced by the same molds and processes, but also homogeneous consumers, who cannot vary in their tastes, values, and patterns of consumption and who must consume if the planning of the corporations is to be effective. The comparatively compact and differentiated institutions of the bourgeois order sustain its heterogeneity and constrain the consumption of mass-produced goods and services. Managerial capitalism must therefore articulate and sponsor an ideology of cosmopolitanism that asserts universal identities, values, and loyalties, challenges the differentiations of the bourgeois order, and rationalizes the process of homogenization. In the cosmopolitan view of man, family, local community, religious sect, social class, sexual and racial identity, and moral character are at best subordinate considerations and are regarded as artificial, repressive, and obsolete barriers to the fulfillment of human potential. Cosmopolitanism thus rationalizes the adoption of the mass framework and collective disciplines that characterize the managerial regime and the homogenization of production and consumption through which the multinational organizations and economies of managerial capitalism operate." – *Leviathan And Its Enemies*, p. 33

"The environmentalist premises of liberalism also served to justify cosmopolitanism and to reject national, class, racial, and regional identities on which the bourgeois order relied to sustain its localized and particularized structure...Liberalism thus developed an 'allegiance mankind' that delegitimized and discredited bourgeois codes that affirmed particular social, biological, regional, and national identities...The general direction of liberal though has thus been internationalist and universalist in world affairs and egalitarian and homogenizing in domestic policy." – *Leviathan And Its Enemies*, pg. 211

Benjamin Franklin

"21. The importation of foreigners into a country that has as many inhabitants as the present employments and provisions for subsistence will bear, will be in the end no increase of people, unless the new comers have more industry and frugality than the natives, and then they will provide more subsistence, and increase in the country; but they will gradually eat the natives out. Nor is it necessary to bring in foreigners to fill up any occasional vacancy in a country for such vacancy (if the laws are good, see secs.14,16) will soon be filled by natural generation. Who can now find the vacancy made in Sweden, France, or other warlike nations, by a plague of heroism forty years ago; in France, by the expulsion of the Protestants; in England, by the settlement of her colonies; or in Guinea, by one hundred years' exportation of slaves, that has blackened half America? The thinness of inhabitants in Spain is owing to national pride and idleness, and other causes, rather than to the expulsion of the Moors, or to the making of new settlements.

"22. There is, in short, no bound to the prolific nature of plants or animals, but what is made by their crowding and interfering with each other's means of subsistence. Were the face of the earth vacant of other plants, it might be gradually sowed and over-spread with one kind only, as, for instance, with fennel; and were it empty of other inhabitants, it might in a few ages be replenished from one nation only, as, for instance, with Englishmen. Thus, there are supposed to be now upwards of one million English souls in North America (though it is thought scarce eighty thousand has been brought over sea), and yet perhaps there is not one the fewer in Britain, but rather many more, on account of the employment the colonies afford to manufacturers at home. This million doubling, suppose but once in twenty-five years, will in another century be more than the people of England, and the greatest number of Englishmen will be on this side the water. What an accession of power to the British empire by sea as well as land! What increase of trade and navigation! What numbers of ships and seamen! We have been here but little more than one hundred years, and yet the force of our privateers in the late war, united, was greater, both in men and guns, than that of the whole British navy in Queen Elizabeth's time. How important an affair then to Britain is the present treaty for settling the bounds between her colonies and the French, and how careful should she be to secure room enough, since on the room depends so much the increase of her people.

"23. In fine, a nation well regulated is like a polypus. Take away a limb, its place is soon supplied; cut it in two, and each deficient part shall speedily grow, out of the part remaining. Thus, if you have room and subsistence enough, as you may, by dividing, make ten polypuses out of one, you may of one make ten nations, equally populous and powerful, or rather increase a nation tenfold in numbers and strength. And since detachments of English from Britain, sent to America, will have their places at home so soon supplied and increase so largely here, why should the Palatine boors be suffered to swarm into our settlements, and, by herding together, establish their language and manners, to the exclusion of ours? Why should Pennsylvania, founded by the English, become a colony of aliens, who will shortly be so numerous as to Germanize us, instead of our Anglifying them, and will never adopt our language or customs any more than they can acquire our complexion?

"24. Which leads us to add one remark, that the number of purely white people in the world is proportionably very small. All Africa is black or tawny; Asia chiefly tawny; America (exclusive of the new comers) wholly so. And in Europe, the Spaniards, Italians, French, Russians, are generally of what we call a swarthy complexion; as are the Germans also, the Saxons only excepted, who, with the English, make the principal body of white people on the face of the earth. I could wish their numbers were increased. And while we are, as I may call it, scouring our planet, by clearing America of woods, and so making this side of our globe reflect a brighter light to the eyes of inhabitants of Mars or Venus, why should we, in the sight of superior beings, darken its people? Why increase the sons of Africa by planting them in America, where we have so fair an opportunity, by excluding all blacks and tawnys, of increasing the lovely white and red? But perhaps I am partial to the complexion of my country, for such kind of partiality is natural to mankind?" – *Observations Concerning the Increase of Mankind, Peopling of Countries, &c*, pgs. 223-224

"Those who come hither are generally the most stupid of their own nation, and, as ignorance is often attended with credulity when knavery would mislead it, and with suspicion when honesty would set it right; and as few of the English understand the German language, and so cannot address them either from the press or the pulpit, it is almost impossible to remove any prejudices they may entertain. Their clergy have very little influence on the people, who seem to take a pleasure in abusing and discharging the minister on every trivial occasion. Not being used to liberty, they know not how to make a modest use of it. And as Holben says of the young Hottentots, that they are not esteemed men until they have shown their manhood by beating their mothers, so these seem not to think themselves free, till they can feel their liberty in abusing and insulting their teachers. Thus they are under no restraint from ecclesiastical government; they behave, however, submissively enough at present to the civil government, which I wish they may continue to do, for I remember when they modestly declined intermeddling in our elections, but now they come in droves and carry all before them, except in one or two counties.

"Few of their children in the country know English. They import many books from Germany; and of the six printing-houses in the province, two are entirely German, two half German, half English, and but two entirely English. They have one German newspaper, and one half-German. Advertisements, intended to be general, are now printed in Dutch and English. The signs in our streets have inscriptions in both languages, and in some places only German. They begin of late to make all their bonds and other legal instruments in their own language, which (though I think it ought not to be) are allowed in our courts, where the German business so increases that there is continued need of interpreters; and I suppose in a few years they will also be necessary in the Assembly, to tell one-half our legislators what the other half say.

"In short, unless the stream of their importation could be turned from this to other colonies, as you very judiciously propose, they will soon so outnumber us that we will, in my opinion, be not able to preserve our language, and even our government will become precarious. The French, who watch all advantages, are now themselves making a German settlement, back of us, in the Illinois country, and by means of these Germans they may in time come to an understanding with ours; and, indeed, in the last war, our Germans showed a general disposition, that seemed to bode us no good. For, when the English, who were not Quakers, alarmed by the danger arising from the defenseless state of our country, entered unanimously into an association, and within this government, and the Lower Counties raised, armed, and disciplined near ten thousand men, the Germans, except a very few in proportion to their number, refused to engage in it, giving out, one amongst another, and even in print, that, if they were quiet, the French, should they take the country, would not molest them; at the time abusing the Philadelphians for fitting out privateers against the enemy, and representing the trouble, hazard, and expense of defending the province, as a greater inconvenience than any that might be expected from a change of government. Yet I am not for refusing to admit them entirely into our colonies. All that seems to me necessary is, to distribute them more equally, mix them with the English schools, where they are not too thickly settled, and take some care to prevent the practice, lately fallen into by some of the shipowners, of sweeping the German gaols to make up the number of their passengers. I say I am not against the admission of Germans in general, for they have their virtues. Their industry and frugality are exemplary. They are excellent husbandmen, and contribute greatly to the improvement of a country." – *Letter to Peter Collinson*, 9 May 1753

— BENJAMIN FRANKLIN —

"We may all remember the time when our mother country, as a mark of her parental tenderness, emptied her gaols into our habitations, for the BETTER 'peopling,' as she expressed it, 'of the colonies.' It is certain that no due returns have yet been made for these valuable consignments. We are therefore much in her debt on that account; and as she is of late clamorous for the payment of all we owe her, and some of our debts are of a kind not so easily discharged, I am for doing however what is in our power. It will show our good-will as to the rest. The felons she planted among us have produced such an amazing increase, that we are now enabled to make ample remittance in the same commodity. And since the wheel-barrow law is not found effectually to reform them, and many of our vessels are idle through her restraints on our trade, why should we not employ those vessels in transporting the felons to Britain?

"I was led into this thought by perusing the copy of a petition to Parliament, which fell lately by accident into my hands. It has no date, but I conjecture from some circumstances, that it must have been about the year 1767 or 1768. [It seems, if presented, it had no effect, since the act passed.]

"On second thoughts, I am of opinion, that besides employing our own vessels, as above proposed, every English ship arriving in our ports with goods for sale, should be obliged to give bond, before she is permitted to trade, engaging that she will carry back to Britain at least one felon for every fifty tons of her burthen. Thus we shall not only discharge sooner our debts, but furnish our old friends with the means of 'better peopling,' and with more expedition, their promising new colony of Botany Bay." – In an article *On Sending Felons to America* from the *Pennsylvania Gazette*, written in 1789; *Memoirs*, pgs. 444-445

"There is no doubt but that a body of sober, industrious, and ingenious artisans [English], men of honest and religious principles, such as you and your friends are described to be, would be a valuable acquisition to any country; and I am certain you would meet with a kind and friendly reception in Pennsylvania, and be put into possession of all the rights and privileges of free citizens; but neither that government nor any other in America that I know of has ever been at any public expense to augment the number of its inhabitants. All who are established there have come at their own charge. The country affords to strangers a good climate, fine, wholesome air, plenty of provisions, good laws, just and cheap government, with all the liberties, civil and religious, that reasonable men can wish for. These inducements are so great, and the number of people in all nations of Europe who wish to partake of them is so considerable, that if the States were to undertake transporting people at the expense of the public, no revenues that they have would be sufficient. Having therefore no orders or authority either from the Congress or the State of Pennsylvania to procure settlers or manufacturers by engaging to defray them [sic], I cannot enter into the contract proposed in your second article. The other articles would meet with no difficulty. Men are not forced there[36] into the public service, and a special law might

---

36 Editor's note in original: "he was writing from France".

easily be obtained to give you a property for seven years in the useful inventions you may introduce." – In his reply to Messrs. Henry Royle, Thomas Helt, Joseph Heathcote, John Rowbotham, and John Schofield, Manufacturers at Hatherton, near Stockport (England), writing from Passy (France); *The Works of Benjamin Franklin*, vol. 9, pg. 84

David Noel Freedman

"Founder of a family or people. Descendants viewed themselves as expressions of immediate or distant ancestors, and ancestors were considered present in the institutions and traditions of the family. The term used for 'ancestor' (Heb. אָב) is the word for 'father,' translated 'patriarch' in some passages and versions.

"Israel participated in its salvation and calling through God's gracious action toward Abraham, Isaac, and Jacob. Yahweh was 'God of the ancestors' (Deut. 1:11), and through them Israel was promised land (1:8; Gen. 28:13), many descendants (Deut. 13:17), and a blessing (Gen. 12:3). Because of his covenant oath with the ancestors, Yahweh delivered Israel from Egypt (Deut. 7:8; Exod. 2:24–25; 6:2–9) and would continue to be merciful toward them (Deut. 4:31). However, continued fulfillment of the promises rested on Israel's obedience to the Sinai covenant (Deut. 29:1 [MT 28:69]–30:20). The exilic prophet appealed to the ancestors to inspire hope for God's future deliverance (Isa. 51:1–3).

"The NT affirms that the story of salvation culminating with God's act in Christ had its beginning in the promises and election of the ancestors (Luke 1:46–55; Acts 13:15–41; Rom.

9; Gal. 3:15–16). Paul states that through the mystery of God's mercy, the election of Israel through the ancestors would not be revoked (Rom. 11:11–35)." – *Eerdmans Dictionary of the Bible*, Ancestor, pgs. 61-62

Milton Friedman

"It's a curious fact that capitalism developed and has really come to fruition in the English-speaking world. It hasn't really made the same progress even in Europe–certainly not in France, for instance. I don't know why this is so, but the fact has to be admitted." – *Why Liberalism Is Now Obsolete*, interview December 12, 1988

Francis Fukuyama

"...immigrants have been extremely important to the United States, but they have been valuable because the diversity has been harnessed to central American institutions... the more one is familiar with different cultures, the more one understands that they are not all created equal. An honest multiculturalist would recognise that some cultural traits are not helpful in the sustenance of a healthy democratic political system and capitalist economy. This should not be the grounds for barring certain peoples with cultures deemed unacceptable but, rather, grounds for the assertion of the positive aspects of American culture like the work ethic, sociability, and citizenship as immigrants move through the educational system." – *Trust The Social Virtues and the Creation of Prosperity*, pgs. 318-319

G

Christopher Gadsden

"God grant that the recollection of your ungrateful treatment may not deter truly firm, virtuous men from venturing their names to be held up to the public on such elections! I am not without my suspicions, that foreign meddlers must have had this deep political slyness in view.

"Many of our new-comers cajoled and imposed upon by emissaries from without, and egged on by a numerous or rather innumerable tribe of young law-followers amongst ourselves, especially in the circuits, have brought on a strange renversement in our State. Our old-standers and independent men of long well-tried patriotism, sound understanding, and good property, have now in general very little influence in our public matters. Our too easy admittance of strangers has entangled us in this evil, and when or where it will end, God only knows!

"But here, my dear Sir? I must confess my own credulity and shortsightedness, who was amongst the most zealous in that over-hasty and not sufficiently guarded step, which we now have good reason to lament as big with innumerable mischiefs. Our worthy deceased friend John Rutledge, looking farther, was for giving them every reasonable protection and encouragement, but for admitting only their sons born amongst us into such complete citizenship as to vote either at State or Congress elections; and when unsuccessful in this point, was then for extending the time to ten years at least. Had even this been carried, it would have given new-comers full time to look so deliberately about them, as greatly to have deterred and hindered all designing tamperers and deceivers in most of their infernal views and mischievous suggestions; and much better, in all probability, would this have been for the peace, safety, and lasting political security of both." – In a letter to John Adams, written from Charleston, 11th March, 1801; *Works Of John Adams*, vol. 9, pg. 322

Mahatma Gandhi

"My ambition is much higher than independence. Through the deliverance of India, I seek to deliver the so-called weaker races of the earth from the crushing heels of Western exploitation in which England is the greatest partner." Indeed, Gandhi believed that "India's coming into her own will mean every nation doing likewise." – quoted in Kramer, *Nationalism in Europe and America*, pg. 175.

James A. Garfield

"[I have] a strong feeling of repugnance when I think of the negro being made our political equal and I would be glad if they could be colonized, sent to heaven, or got rid of in any decent way." – Letter to Governor Jacob Dolson Cox; *Reconstruction in the South* vol. 80, pg. 294

Azar Gat

"...nationalism and ethnicity are closely associated; by and large, nationalism is one particular form of a broader phenomenon, that of political ethnicity; and ethnicity has always been highly political, ever since the emergence of the state and even before. By ethnicity I mean a population of shared kinship (real or perceived) and culture..." – *Nations: The Long History and Deep Roots of Political Ethnicity and Nationalism*, pg. 3

"...it is the continuous reproduction and reinterpretation by the members of a national community of the pattern of symbols, values, myths, memories and traditions that compose the distinctive heritage of nations." – *Nations*, pg. 26.

"The differences in gene frequency simply indicate that neighboring populations today lived separately from one another as far back as the Bronze and even the Stone Age."
– *Nations*, pg. 51

"Far from being a modern invention, Serbs, Croats, Bulgarians, Hungarians, and, to a lesser degree, Slovenes and Romanians crystallized as distinctive ethno-national political identities during their early histories in the Middle Ages."
– *Nations*, pg. 188

"...while there have been many national states without free government, free government has scarcely existed in the absence of a national community. ... once people, rather than being coerced by force, are given the freedom to express and enact their will, they almost invariably elect to live in their own national state. The people's will, once spoken, has been revealed to be unmistakably nationalistic." – *Nations*, pg. 249.

"...reflecting the post-1945 climate of ideas and normative atmosphere, modernists have lost sight of the ethno-national phenomenon's deep roots and have declared the nation and nationalism to be a pure socio-historical construct or artificially contrived. As a result, they misinterpret the ethno-national phenomenon's historical trajectory and either remain confounded by or turn a blind eye to its highly explosive potency, so evidently one of the strongest forces in human history.

"Nations and nationalism are not primordial. Nonetheless, they are rooted in primordial human sentiments of kin-culture affinity, solidarity and mutual cooperation, evolutionarily engraved in human nature. These attachments, permeating social life and extending beyond family to tribe and ethnos, became integral to politics when states emerged millennia ago. Ethnicity has always been political and politicised, ever since the beginning of politics, because people have always been heavily biased towards those they view as their kin-culture community." – *Roots of Nationalism*, pg. 31

Geoffrey of Monmouth

"Britain, the best of islands, is situated in the Western Ocean, between France and Ireland, being eight hundred miles long, and two hundred broad. It produces every thing that is useful to man, with a plenty that never fails." – *History Of The Kings Of Briton*, ch. 2, in *Six Old English Chronicles*, pg. 90

Edward Gibbon

"From the foot of the Alps to the extremity of Calabria, all the natives of Italy were born citizens of Rome. Their partial distinctions were obliterated, and they insensibly coalesced into one great nation, united by language, manners, and civil institutions . . . Virgil was a native of Mantua; Horace was inclined to doubt whether he should call himself an Apulian or a Lucanian: it was in Padua that an historian [Livy] was found worthy to record the majestic series of Roman victories. The patriot family of the Catos emerged from Tusculum; and the little town of Arpinum claimed the double honour of producing Marius and Cicero." – *The Decline and Fall of the Roman Empire*, pg. 41

"In the purer ages of the commonwealth, the use of arms was reserved for those ranks of citizens who had a country to love, a property to defend, and some share in enacting those laws, which it was their interest as well as duty to maintain. But in proportion as the public freedom was lost in extent of conquest, war was gradually improved into an art, and degraded into a trade." – *The Decline and Fall of the Roman Empire*, pg. 10

"I shall soon revisit the banks of the Lake of Lausanne, a country which I have known and loved from my early youth. Under a mild government, amidst a beauteous landscape, in a life of leisure and independence, and among a people of easy and elegant manners, I have enjoyed, and may again hope to enjoy, the varied pleasures of retirement and society. But I shall ever glory in the name and character of an Englishman: I am proud of my birth in a free and enlightened country; and the approbation of that country is the best and most honorable reward of my labors." – *The Decline and Fall of the Roman Empire*, pg. 444

George Gilder

"The different roles of men and women, the love that arises from them, the allegiance to one's own family, the worship of God, the possession and improvement of property, the production of wealth, the cultivation of excellence and beauty, the competitive masculine rituals of sport and play, the emergence of loyalty to kin and community, church and country, all are among the highest values of human life. Because they spring from human reality, they can be fulfilled in ordered freedom in a democratic society." – *Men and Marriage: Sexual Suicide*, pg. 164

John Gill

Speaking of Sarah:

"...though sixty five years of age, being ten years younger than her husband, see (Genesis 17:17), who was now seventy five years old, (Genesis 12:4) yet might still be a fair woman, having a good complexion and comely features, and having never bore children, and especially she would be reckoned so among the Egyptians, whose women were of a blackish, sallow, swarthy complexion... Abram knew that Sarai was a fair woman; but in the eyes of the Egyptians she was very fair, exceeding fair, they not being used to seeing very beautiful women." – *Commentary on Genesis* 12:11, 14, in *Exposition Of The Old Testament*, pg. 77

On Exodus 20:12, honor thy father, etc.,:

"though it may be extended to all ancestors in the ascending line, as father's father and mother, mother's father and mother and to all such who are in the room of parents, as step-fathers and step-mothers, guardians, nurses and to all superiors in dignity and office, to kings and governors, to masters, ministers, and magistrates; yet chiefly respects immediate parents, both father and mother, by showing filial affection for them, and reverence and esteem of them, and by yielding obedience to them, and giving them relief and assistance in all things in which they need it; and if honour, esteem, affection, obedience, and reverence are to be given to earthly parents, then much more to our Father which is in heaven." – *Commentary on Exodus* 20:12, in *Exposition Of The Old Testament*, pg. 451

"The Cretans are always liars: lying is a sin common to human nature, and appears in men as early, or earlier than any other; and all men are guilty of it, at one time or another; but all are not habitually liars, as it seems these Cretans were: lying was a governing vice among them; they were not only guilty of it in some particular instances, but always; ... it [lying] was a sin they were addicted to: some countries are distinguished by their vices; some for pride; some for levity, vanity, and inconstancy; some for boasting and bragging some for covetousness; some for idleness; some for effeminacy; some for hypocrisy and deceit; and others, as the Cretans, it seems, for lying; this was their national sin." – *Commentary on Titus* 1:12, in *Exposition Of The New Testament*, pg. 653

Nathan Glazer

"The fundamental challenge to the requirement that workforces should reflect availability is that the differences among ethnic and minority groups, and men and women, are real differences, deeply based, and that requiring any fixed proportions of one group or another to be hired or promoted inevitably means that employers must act as if these differences do not exist. . . . The most crucial point about the occupational distribution of ethnic groups in the United States is that this distribution is only in part— and probably for most of the protected groups in small part—owing to discrimination." – *Ethnic Dilemmas*, 1964–1982, pgs. 183, 187

John Bagot Glubb

"Every race on earth has distinctive characteristics. Some have been distinguished in philosophy, some in administration, some in romance, poetry or religion, some in their legal system. During the pre-eminence of each culture, its distinctive characteristics are carried by it far and wide across the world.

"If the same nation were to retain its domination indefinitely, its peculiar qualities would permanently characterise the whole human race. Under the system of empires each lasting for 250 years, the sovereign race has time to spread its particular virtues far and wide. Then, however, another people, with entirely different peculiarities, takes its place, and its virtues and accomplishments are likewise disseminated. By this system, each of the innumerable races of the world enjoys a period of greatness, during which its peculiar qualities are placed at the service of mankind." – *The Fate Of Empires*, pgs. 5-6

"One of the oft-repeated phenomena of great empires [in their period of decline] is the influx of foreigners to the capital city. Roman historians often complain of the number of Asians and Africans in Rome. Baghdad, in its prime in the ninth century, was international in its population—Persians, Turks, Arabs, Armenians, Egyptians, Africans and Greeks mingled in its streets.

"In London today, Cypriots, Greeks, Italians, Russians, Africans, Germans and Indians jostle one another on the buses and in the underground, so that it sometimes seems difficult to find any British. The same applies to New York, perhaps even more so. This problem does not consist in any inferiority of one race as compared with another, but simply in the differences between them.

"In the age of the first outburst and the subsequent Age of Conquests, the race is normally ethnically more or less homogeneous. This state of affairs facilitates a feeling of solidarity and comradeship. But in the Ages of Commerce and Affluence, every type of foreigner floods into the great city, the streets of which are reputed to be paved with gold. As, in most cases, this great city is also the capital of the empire, the cosmopolitan crowd at the seat of empire exercises a political influence greatly in excess of its relative numbers.

"Second- or third-generation foreign immigrants may appear outwardly to be entirely assimilated, but they often constitute a weakness in two directions. First, their basic human nature often differs from that of the original imperial stock. If the earlier imperial race was stubborn and slow-moving, the immigrants might come from more emotional races, thereby introducing cracks and schisms into the national policies, even if all were equally loyal.

"Second, while the nation is still affluent, all the diverse races may appear equally loyal. But in an acute emergency, the immigrants will often be less willing to sacrifice their lives and their property than will be the original descendants of the founder race.

"Third, the immigrants are liable to form communities of their own, protecting primarily their own interests, and only in the second

degree that of the nation as a whole.

"Fourth, many of the foreign immigrants will probably belong to races originally conquered by and absorbed into the empire. While the empire is enjoying its High Noon of prosperity, all these people are proud and glad to be imperial citizens. But when decline sets in, it is extraordinary how the memory of ancient wars, perhaps centuries before, is suddenly revived, and local or provincial movements appear demanding secession or independence. Some day this phenomenon will doubtless appear in the now apparently monolithic and authoritarian Soviet empire. It is amazing for how long such provincial sentiments can survive.

"Historical examples of this phenomenon are scarcely needed. The idle and captious Roman mob, with its endless appetite for free distributions of food—bread and games—is notorious, and utterly different from that stern Roman spirit which we associate with the wars of the early republic.

"In Baghdad, in the golden days of Harun al-Rashid, Arabs were a minority in the imperial capital. Istanbul, in the great days of Ottoman rule, was peopled by inhabitants remarkably few of whom were descendants of Turkish conquerors. In New York, descendants of the Pilgrim Fathers are few and far between.

"This interesting phenomenon is largely limited to great cities. The original conquering race is often to be found in relative purity in rural districts and on far frontiers. It is the wealth of the great cities which draws the immigrants. As, with the growth of industry, cities nowadays achieve an ever greater preponderance over the countryside, so will the influence of foreigners increasingly dominate old empires.

"Once more it may be emphasised that I do not wish to convey the impression that immigrants are inferior to older stocks. They are just different, and they thus tend to introduce cracks and divisions." – *The Fate Of Empires*, pgs. 13-14

"The people of the great nations of the past seem normally to have imagined that their pre-eminence would last for ever. Rome appeared to its citizens to be destined to be for all time the mistress of the world. The Abbasid Khalifs of Baghdad declared that God had appointed them to rule mankind until the day of judgement. Seventy years ago, many people in Britain believed that the empire would endure for ever. Although Hitler failed to achieve his objective, he declared that Germany would rule the world for a thousand years. That sentiments like these could be publicly expressed without evoking derision shows that, in all ages, the regular rise and fall of great nations has passed unperceived. The simplest statistics prove the steady rotation of one nation after another at regular intervals.

"The belief that their nation would rule the world forever, naturally encouraged the citizens of the leading nation of any period to attribute their pre-eminence to hereditary virtues. They carried in their blood, they believed, qualities which constituted them a race of supermen, an illusion which inclined them to the employment of cheap foreign labour (or slaves) to perform menial tasks and to engage foreign mercenaries to fight their battles or to sail their ships. These poorer peoples were only too happy to migrate to the wealthy cities of the empire, and thereby, as we have seen, to adulterate the close-knit, homogeneous character of the conquering race. The latter unconsciously assumed that they would always be the leaders of mankind, relaxed their energies, and spent an increasing part of their time in leisure, amusement or sport.

"In recent years, the idea has spread widely in the West that 'progress' will be automatic without effort, that everyone will continue to grow richer and richer and that every year will show a 'rise in the standard of living'. We have not drawn from history the obvious conclusion that material success is the result of courage, endurance and hard work—a conclusion nevertheless obvious from the history of the meteoric rise of our own ancestors. This self-assurance of its own superiority seems to go hand-in-hand with the luxury resulting from wealth, in undermining the character of the dominant race." – *The Fate Of Empires*, pgs. 16-17

Johann Wolfgang von Goethe

"The world is so empty if one thinks only of mountains, rivers and cities; but to know someone who thinks and feels with us, and who, though distant, is close to us in spirit, this makes the earth for us an inhabited garden."

"Der du von dem Himmel bist,
Alles Leid und Schmerzen stillest,

Den, der doppelt elend ist,
Doppelt mit Erquickung füllest,"

Translation:
  "You, who are from the heavens,
  Silencing all pain and sorrow,
  Filling the doubly wretched
  With double refreshment,"
– *Wanderer's Night Song* (Wandrers Nachtlied I, lines 1-4)

"Über allen Gipfeln
Ist Ruh,
In allen Wipfeln
Spürest du
Kaum einen Hauch;"

Translation:
  "Over all the peaks
  There is peace,
  In all the treetops
  You feel
  Hardly a breath;"
– *Wanderer's Night Song* (Wandrers Nachtlied II, lines 1-5)

"Die Vögelein schweigen im Walde.
Warte nur, balde
Ruhest du auch."

Translation:
  "The birds are silent in the forest.
  Just wait, soon
  You too will rest."
– *Wanderer's Night Song* (Wandrers Nachtlied II, lines 6-8)

Jonah Goldberg

"Certain quarters of the left assert that 'Zionism equals racism' and that Israelis are equivalent to Nazis. As invidious and problematic as those comparisons are, why aren't we hearing similar denunciations of groups ranging from the National Council of La Raza—that is, 'The Race'—to the radical Hispanic group MEChA, whose motto—'Por La Raza todo. Fuera de La Raza nada'—means 'For my race, everything. For other races, nothing'? Why is it that when a white man spouts such sentiments it's objectively fascist, but when a person of color says the same thing it's merely an expression of fashionable multiculturalism?" – *Liberal Fascism*, pg. 6

Samuel Gompers

"It must be clear to every thinking man and woman that while there is hardly a single reason for the admission of Asiatics, there are hundreds of good and strong reasons for their absolute exclusion." – *Meat Vs. Rice: American Manhood Against Asiatic Coolieism*, pg. 22

"We immediately realized that immigration is, in its fundamental aspects, a labor problem." – Vernon M. Briggs, Jr., *Mass Immigration and the National Interest*, pg. 79

Anna Andreyevna Gorenko

"In the terrible years of the Yezhov terror I spent seventeen months waiting in line outside the prison in Leningrad. One day somebody in the crowd identified me. Standing behind me was a woman, with lips blue from the cold, who had, of course, never heard me called by name before. Now she started out of the torpor common to us all and asked me in a whisper (everyone whispered there):
— Can you describe this?
And I said: I can.
Then something like a smile passed fleetingly over what had once been her face."
– *Requiem* (Introduction) [37]

"I know how the faces of the condemned
Suddenly take on a mild expression,
How the final horror takes hold,
And a separation that is terrible."
– *Requiem* (Part 3)

From "Poem Without a Hero":
"Here's your ticket, I'm handing it to you,
Here's a scarf and a handkerchief,
And this will be enough for you,
You'll return to me, you will return."
– *Requiem* (Part 1, sec. 10, lines 1-4)

"And memory, the brute, will not release
The shadows in the corners of my eyes
And the sky-blue tunic, and the breeze
From the Black Sea where the gull cries."
– *Requiem* (Part 1, sec. 1, lines 1-4)

Charles Gore

"There is a very specifically Anglican colour about our home religion, which we ought to have no desire to perpetuate in India. An Englishman, wherever he goes, is apt to identify his religion with his memories of home. We ought to identify our religion with the Christ of all nations. What we desire is to see an Indian Church arise with an Indian episcopate and an Indian spirit." – *The Churchman*, June 27, 1908, pg. 9

Paul Gottfried

"Catholic ethnics, as minorities, have generally positioned themselves to the left of majority populations. This tendency is even more dramatically apparent for American, Canadian, and European Jews, who combine strong nationalist feelings for their own group and for Israel with the advocacy of open borders, alternative lifestyles, and extreme pluralism for their host countries. This Jewish double standard, abundantly documented by cultural historian and clinical psychologist Kevin MacDonald, has aroused considerable controversy. But a double standard of the kind MacDonald notes exists outside of Jewish communities as well. Southern Italian immigrants vote overwhelmingly for center-left parties in Canada but give enthusiastic receptions to Italian right-wing politicians like Gianfranco Fini of the Alleanza Nazionale. Irish Catholics in England vote heavily for the Labour Party but give no indication of transferring these leftist attachments to the Irish Republic. Indeed many are devout, practicing Catholics, who, like Italian Canadians, live in patriarchal households with extended families. Such groups, though not oppressed by the majority populations, continue to view themselves as living in someone else's society. Their political efforts therefore go toward neutralizing the cultural and institutional particularities associated with the majority out-group." – *Multiculturalism and the Politics of Guilt*, pg. 41

"The notion of individuals defending their values and identities—while inhabiting an imaginary state of nature—does not seem to be

37 Anna Akhmatova was a Russian poet known for her deeply emotional works, often reflecting her love for her homeland and her connection to Russians during times of war and repression.

a convincing account of where we come from as human beings. ... Unlike the essentialist Right's reading of Aristotle or Burke, Libertarians understand freedom as a universally shared good to which everyone everywhere is entitled by virtue of being an individual. ... The classical conservative view of liberty flows from the legal implications of someone's standing in a particular society, held together by shared custom and distributed duties.

"From this view that obtained among opponents of the French Revolution there arose a concept of socially situated liberty, which stands in vivid contrast to the Libertarian idea of unfettered individual liberty. Libertarians are seen from the Right as promoting a leftist position, which presupposes the idea of universal equality and even universal citizenship. The doctrinaire [libertarians] scorned [by the Old Right] rejected the conservative notion of the social bond and were proclaiming principles that issued from the French Revolution." – *Revisions and Dissents*, pg. 29

"People have usually viewed themselves and been seen by others through their ethnic or national identities." – *Fascism*, pg. 155

Saxo Grammaticus

"Forasmuch as all other nations are wont to vaunt the glory of their achievements, and reap joy from the remembrance of their forefathers: Absalon, Chief Pontiff of the Danes, whose zeal ever burned high for the glorification of our land, and who would not suffer it to be defrauded of like renown and record, cast upon me, the least of his followers—since all the rest refused the task—the work of compiling into a chronicle the history of Denmark, and by the authority of his constant admonition spurred my weak faculty to enter on a labour too heavy for its strength. For who could write a record of the deeds of Denmark? It had but lately been admitted to the common faith: it still languished as strange to Latin as to religion. But now that the holy ritual brought also the command of the Latin tongue, men were as slothful now as they were unskilled before, and their sluggishness proved as faultful as that former neediness. Thus it came about that my lowliness, though perceiving itself too feeble for the aforesaid burden, yet chose rather to strain

beyond its strength than to resist his bidding; fearing that while our neighbours rejoiced and transmitted records of their deeds, the repute of our own people might appear not to possess any written chronicle, but rather to be sunk in oblivion and antiquity. Thus I, forced to put my shoulder, which was unused to the task, to a burden unfamiliar to all authors of preceding time, and dreading to slight his command, have obeyed more boldly than effectually, borrowing from the greatness of my admonisher that good heart which the weakness of my own wit denied me." – *The Danish History*, Book 1, Preface, pg. 1

Ulysses S. Grant

"For centuries England has relied on protection, has carried it to extremes and has obtained satisfactory results from it. There is no doubt that it is to this system that it owes its present strength. After two centuries, England has found it convenient to adopt free trade because it thinks that protection can no longer offer it anything. Very well then, gentlemen, my knowledge of our country leads me to believe that within 200 years, when America has gotten out of protection all that it can offer, it too will adopt free trade." – quoted in *Capitalism and Underdevelopment in Latin America* by AG Frank, pg. 56

Henry Grattan

"I am now to address a free people: ages have passed away, and this is the first moment in which you could be distinguished by that appellation.

"I have now spoken on the subject of your liberty so often, that I have nothing to add, and have only to admire by what heaven-directed steps you have proceeded until the whole faculty of the nation is braced up to the act of her own deliverance.

"I found Ireland on her knees, I watched over her with a paternal solicitude; I have traced her progress from injuries to arms, and from arms to liberty. Spirit of Swift! Spirit of Molyneux! Your genius has prevailed. Ireland is now a nation. In that new character I hail her, and bowing to her august presence, I say, Esto Perpetua!

"She is no longer a wretched colony, returning thanks to her governor for his rapine, and to her king for his oppression; nor is she now a squabbling, fretful sectary, perplexing her little wits, and firing her furious statutes with bigotry, sophistry, disabilities, and death, to transmit to posterity insignificance and war.

"You, with difficulties innumerable, with dangers not a few, have done what your ancestors wished, but could not accomplish; and what your posterity may preserve, but will never equal: you have moulded the jarring elements of your country into a nation. You had not the advantages which were common to other great countries; no monuments, no trophies, none of these outward and visible signs of greatness, such as inspire mankind and connect the ambition of the age which is coming on with the example of that going off, and form the descent and concatenation of glory: no; you have not had any great act recorded among all your misfortunes, nor have you one public tomb to assemble the crowd and spread to the living the language of integrity and freedom.

"Your historians did not supply the want of monuments; on the contrary, these narrators of your misfortunes, who should have felt for your wrongs, and have punished your oppressors with oppressions, natural scourges, the moral indignation of history, compromised with public villainy and trembled; they excited your violence, they suppressed your provocation, and wrote in the train which entrammelled their country. I am come to break that chain, and I congratulate my country, who, without any of the advantages I speak of, going forth, as it were, with nothing but a stone and a sling, and what oppression could not take away, the favour of Heaven, accomplished her own redemption and left you with nothing to add and everything to admire." – Speech to Irish Parliament, 16 April, 1782; *Galignani's Literary Gazette* vol. 17 1823, pg. 60

Jack P. Greene

"And touching the law of importation of Quakers, that it may be more strictly executed, and none transgressing to escape punishment,—It is hereby ordered, that the penalty to that law averred be in no case abated to less than twenty pounds." – *Settlements to Society, 1607-1763: A Documentary History of Colonial America*, pg. 176

Nathanael Greene

"I have no wish to see such a large proportion of important offices in the military department in the hands of foreigners...If foreigners are introduced, their command should not be very extensive, then the injury cannot be great, but even in this case it is an injury to America, for the multiplying foreign officers gives us no internal strength. A good nursery of officers, nursed by experience, firmly attached to the interest of the country, is a great security against foreign invaders. The only tie that we have upon foreigners, is the sentiment of honor, too slender for the happiness of a country to depend upon, –while officers created among the people are bound, not only by the ties of honor, but by that of interest and family connection. We, in many instances, see the power of British gold; let us not neglect to guard against its influence. I have no narrow prejudices upon this subject, neither have I any private differences with any of those gentlemen. My opinion is founded upon the general conduct of mankind." – In a letter among Washington's papers written on the 28th May 1777; *The Life of Nathanael Greene, Major-general in the Army of the Revolution*, vol. 1, pg. 417

Joel B. Green

On Luke 10:24 and following:

"In its context in Leviticus 19, love for the neighbor is love for fellow Israelites, though love for the other is extended to 'resident aliens' who embrace the covenant with Yawheh. As a consequence of the Hellenistic imperialism and Roman occupation, it could not be generally assumed in the first century of the Common Era that those dwelling among the people of Israel qualified as 'neighbors.' ...

"The care the Samaritan offers is not a model of moral obligation but of exaggerated action grounded in compassion that risks much more than could ever be required or expected." – *New International Commentary on the New Testament, Gospel of Luke*, pg. 761, 765

Pierre Grégoire

"Just as from lyres of diverse tones, if properly tuned, a sweet sound and pleasant harmony arise when low, medium, and high notes are united, so also the social unity of rulers and subjects in the state produces a sweet and pleasant harmony out of the rich, the poor, the workers, the farmers, and other kinds of persons. If agreement is thus achieved in society, a praiseworthy, happy, most durable, and almost divine concord is produced....But if all were truly equal, and each wished to rule others according to his own will, discord would easily arise, and by discord the dissolution of society. There would be no standard of virtue or merit, and it follows that equality itself would be the greatest inequality." – *De Republica*, quoted in *Social Philosophers*, pg. 404

Gregory of Nazianzus

"Do you also say, 'See, here is water, what does hinder me to be baptized?' Seize the opportunity; rejoice greatly in the blessing; and having spoken be baptized; and having been baptized be saved; and though you be an Ethiopian body, be made white in soul." – *Nicene And Post-Nicene Fathers*, Oration 40, pg. 369[38]

Gregory of Tours

"Now there was a rumour that the Huns intended to overrun Gaul. At that time there lived in the town of Tongres Aravatius, a bishop of the most excellent holiness, who devoted himself to fasting and vigil, and often, bathed with a rain of tears, besought God's mercy that He would not suffer this unbelieving race, ever unworthy of His grace, to penetrate into Gaul. But feeling in his heart that his prayer had not been granted through the sins of the people, he formed the design of visiting Rome, that he might be strengthened by the miraculous power of the apostle, and thereby better deserve to obtain that for which he made humble supplication to God." – *History Of The Franks*, vol. 2, pg. 44

"Now Clovis the king said to his people: 'I take it very-hard that these Arians hold part of the Gauls. Let us go with God's help and conquer them and bring the land under our control.' Since these words pleased all, he set his army in motion and made for Poitiers where Alaric was at that time. But since part of the host was passing through Touraine, he issued an edict out of respect to the blessed Martin that no one should take anything from that country except grass for fodder, and water. But one from the army found a poor man's hay and said:

'Did not the king order grass only to be taken, nothing else? And this,' said he, 'is grass. We shall not be transgressing his command if we take it.' And when he had done violence to the poor man and taken his hay by force, the deed came to the king. And quicker than speech the offender was slain by the sword, and the king said: 'And where shall our hope of victory be if we offend the blessed Martin? It would be better for the army to take nothing else from this country.' The king himself sent envoys to the blessed church saying: 'Go, and perhaps you will receive some omen of victory from the holy temple.' Then giving them gifts to set up in the holy place, he said: 'If thou, O Lord, art my helper, and hast determined to surrender this unbelieving nation, always striving against thee, into my hands, consent to reveal it propitiously at the entrance to the church of St. Martin, so that I may know that thou wilt deign to be favorable to thy servant.'" – *History Of The Franks*, vol. 2, pg. 45

— GREGORY OF TOURS —

"I am weary of relating the details of the civil wars that mightily plague the nation and kingdom of the Franks; and the worst of it is that we see in them the beginning of that time of woe which the Lord foretold: 'Father shall rise against son, son against father, brother against brother, kinsman against kinsman.' They should have been deterred by the examples of former kings who were slain by their enemies as soon as they were divided. How often has the

---

38   Gregory says that baptism transforms the soul in a way different than our physicality and does not destroy or flatten our physical natures.

very city of cities, the great capital of the whole earth, been laid low by civil war and again, when it ceased, has risen as if from the ground! Would that you too, O kings, were engaged in battles like those in which your fathers struggled, that the heathen terrified by your union might be crushed by your strength! Remember how Clovis won your great victories, how he slew opposing kings, crushed wicked peoples and subdued their lands, and left to you complete and unchallenged dominion over them!... Examine carefully the books of the ancients and you will see what civil wars beget. Read what Orosius writes of the Carthaginians, who says that after seven hundred years their city and country were ruined and adds: 'What preserved this city so long? Union. What destroyed it after such a period? Disunion.' Beware of disunion, beware of civil wars which destroy you and your people. What else is to be expected but that your army will fall and that you will be left without strength and be crushed and ruined by hostile peoples. And, king, if civil war gives you pleasure, govern that impulse which the apostle says is urgent within man, let the spirit struggle against the flesh and the vices fall before the virtues; and be free and serve your chief who is Christ, you who were once a fettered slave of the root of Evil." – *History Of The Franks*, vol. 2, pg. 105

The Brothers Grimm

"The outermost lines [of common heritage in stories] are coterminous with those of the great race which is commonly called Indo-Germanic, and the relationship draws itself in consistently narrowing circles round the settlements of the Germans ... it is my belief that the German stories do not belong to the northern and southern parts of our fatherland alone but that they are absolutely common property of the nearly related Dutch, English, and Scandinavians." – *German Folklore*, pg. 175

Steven Grosby

"In order for a nation to exist, in addition to the belief in the existence of a 'people,' there must also be a belief in the existence of a specific territory which is believed to be in some way 'appropriate for,' 'having a special affinity with,' or 'belonging to' only that people (Hertz 1945:

146–51; Dumont 1970: 108; Shils 1983: ix–xvi). In other words, and in contrast to an empire, one necessary characteristic of nationality is that its territory is delimited, in principle. On the other hand, in contrast to a patchwork of territorially distinct and smaller city-kingdoms, the existence of a nation presupposes a conception of a larger territory that is not only bounded, but is also perceived to be contiguous within those boundaries. Note here that I have begun to introduce elementary criteria to distinguish empire, nation and city-kingdom from one another.

"Did the ancient Israelites at some point in their history have a conception of 'all Israel' as being constituted by a bounded territory? We read in Numbers 34: 'And the Lord spake unto Moses, saying, Command the children of Israel, and say unto them, When ye come into the land of Canaan; (this is the land that shall fall unto you for an inheritance, even the land of Canaan with the coasts thereof:) Then your south quarter shall be from the wilderness of Zin along by the coast of Edom, and your south border shall be the outmost coast of the salt sea eastward: And your border shall turn from the south to the ascent of Akrabbim, and pass on to Zin: and the going forth thereof shall be from the south to Kadeshbarnea, and shall go on to Hazaraddar, and pass on to Azmon: And the border shall fetch a compass from Azmon unto the river of Egypt, and the goings out of it shall be at the sea. And as for the western border, ye shall even have the great sea for a border: this shall be your west border. And this shall be your north border: from the great sea ye shall point out for you mount Hor: From mount Hor ye shall point out your border unto the entrance of Hamath; and the goings forth of the border shall be to Zedad: And the border shall go on to Ziphron, and the goings out of it shall be at Hazarenan: this shall be your north border. And ye shall point out your east border from Hazarenan to Shepham: And the coast shall go down from Shepham to Riblah, on the east side of Ain; and the border shall descend, and shall reach unto the side of the sea of Chinnereth eastward: And the border shall go down to Jordan, and the goings out of it shall be at the salt sea: this shall be your land with the coasts thereof round about.'

"All that such a description of the territory of ancient Israel lacks is the degrees of latitude and longitude—a not insignificant point, viz., the importance of modern land-surveying techniques for designating the territory of the modern nation-state. (In this regard, recall the slogan of the 1840s in the United States, '54,40 and fight.') Nonetheless, what is decisive for our consideration of ancient Israel as a nation is the existence of an image of a bounded territory which was understood to be, at least in part, constitutive of Israel.

"At this point we can with confidence conclude that at a certain point in the history of ancient Israel: (1) there was a belief in the existence of a trans-clan/tribal people, namely, Israel; and (2) there was a belief in the existence of a trans-local territory, Israel. Note that the term 'Israel' applies both to the 'people' and to the 'land.' This terminological 'conflation' represents a 'conjoining' of a people to a land. This conjoining is a characteristic referent in the shared beliefs constitutive of nationality, ancient and modern: a people has its land and a land has its people." – *Biblical Ideas of Nationality*, pgs. 22-24

Hugo Grotius

"The conjunction with Spain brought a huge growth. But already at that time men with better insight predicted, with a certain amount of fear (since the rulers' resources had grown enormously), a change in the political conditions. This they based on the customs of the Spanish, which they had studied during their service with them in wars, and on their differences with themselves. For as long as they were joined as neighbouring peoples by equivalent origins and identical wishes, they interacted easily and in fraternal relationships. Between Spaniards and the Netherlanders, however, most things are different, and they collide the more sharply in those matters that they have in common. Both peoples had in all ages been distinguished for martial valour; except that the latter had lost the habit of it, while the former were kept vigorous by continuous discipline and rewards through campaigns in Italy and across the Ocean. But the Dutch, frugal indeed and willing to suffer hard labour in their zeal for profit, with this in view seek peace and trade, but not so as to put up with injury. No people is more abstinent with respect to others' possessions; their own they defend stoutly. For this

reason, in their little corner of the world there are cities exceedingly numerous and strengthened, originally near the sea and the rivers; later everywhere, strengthened by a multitude of newcomers and progeny. And thus, after the furies from Scandinavia had been driven off, they survived for eight centuries unconquered by foreign arms and unplundered.

"Possession of Spain, after under various conquerors it had drawn much from their customs, at length returned to the Goths. Old and new writers describe those to us as of undaunted spirit in the face of trials and dangers, ever since they mixed their character of origin with that of their dwellings; eager – uncertain whether more for glory than for wealth, so arrogant as to be contemptuous of others, respectful, however, of things sacred and fairly loyal in return for benefits, but so passionate for revenge and wild in victory that against an enemy nothing is shameful, nothing forbidden. With the Lowlanders, this is all just the other way round: they are a people of innocent craftiness and furthermore in customs, as in position, a blend of Germany and France: not free of the faults of both, not without their virtues. You will neither easily fool, nor rashly insult them. That they have never been second to the Spanish in religious devotion is shown by the fact that ever since the time they took up Christianity, they have collectively resisted the pressure of Norman violence to change their creed. Not infected by any condemned error until our times, they attached so much value to their faith that it was necessary to prescribe a limit to the possessions of ministers of the gospel. Generally, for both peoples honouring and admiring princes was innate. But the Dutch think laws superior, under which pretext there was often disorder. The people of Castile love to be ruled even a bit more strictly than the other peoples of Spain, and yet the liberty that they demand for themselves, however great or small it be, they do not tolerate in others. Hence a very great danger, with the attention of princes divided as if over two realms: the Dutch were not able to tolerate anyone superior in influence, nor the Spaniards any equal." – *Annals of the War in the Low Countries*, pg. 135

"...the nature and culture of the English and the Dutch are quite different: just as willingly as the English [Angli] resign themselves to servitude,

so vehemently do they compensate this humility by brutality once they have reached a high position. Lowlanders [Belgae] command and obey moderately, and no nation [gens] is more strongly attached to its leaders or turns against them with greater anger if the respect gets lost."
– *Annals of the War in the Low Countries*, pg. 95

Wayne Grudem

"Prior to 1965, the United States had much more effective control over who would be allowed to enter the nation as an immigrant. Priority was rightfully given to those people who would most clearly bring benefit to American society as well as to their spouses and their immediate minor children. But under pressure from President Lyndon Johnson, Congress passed the Hart-Celler Act of 1965. It established a new system by which citizens of the United States could sponsor not only a spouse and immediate children for immigration, but also all of their brothers and sisters as well as their parents who are living in other countries."
– *Politics According to the Bible*, pg. 965

"Illegal immigrants are living in constant disobedience of Paul's command, 'Let every person be subject to the governing authorities' (Rom. 13:1). It is not just that they have broken the laws of the United States by entering the country illegally, but they also continue living in the country in an undocumented status without the legal permission of the United States. They can hardly be subject to the governing authorities when those authorities do not even have a record that they exist. In this way, the continuing presence of a growing illegal minority that is invisible to the entire legal record-keeping system of the society is a destructive force in the society itself—one that will increasingly bring negative consequences to the respect for law and the legal fabric of the nation. It therefore astounds me that anyone in either party, whether Democrat or Republican, would oppose having Congress and the President take the necessary steps to complete a secure and impenetrable border fence immediately." – *Politics According to the Bible*, pg. 960

"It seems to me inexcusable that Congress has delayed so long in simply authorizing and clearing the way to build a secure fence that would effectively stop something like 99% of illegal immigration from Mexico. The United States as a nation must get control of its borders, as all strong nations throughout history have done. As long as the borders are ineffective, we have no control and no ability to keep criminals, terrorists, and others who would harm our nation from entering." – *Politics According to the Bible*, pg. 960

Francis Grund

"I consider the domestic virtue of the Americans as the principal source of all their other qualities. It acts as a promoter of industry, as a stimulus to enterprise, and as the most powerful restrainer of public vice. It reduces life to its simplest elements, and makes happiness less dependent on precarious circumstances; it ensures the proper education of children, and acts, by the force of example, on the morals of the rising generation; in short, it does more for the preservation of peace and good order, than all the laws enacted for that purpose; and is a better guarantee for the permanency of the American government, than any written instrument, the Constitution itself not excepted." – *The Americans in Their Moral, Social, and Political Relations*, vol. 1, pg. 171

H

Ernest van den Haag

"One need not believe that one's own ethnic group, or any ethnic group, is superior to others...in order to wish one's country to continue to be made up of the same ethnic strains in the same proportions as before. And, conversely, the wish not to see one's country overrun by groups one regards as alien need not be based on feelings of superiority or 'racism'... the wish to preserve one's identity and the identity of one's nation requires no justification...any more than the wish to have one's own children, and to continue one's family through them need be justified or rationalized by a belief that they are superior to the children of others." – *More Immigration?*; *National Review*, September 21, 1965, pgs. 821-822

Jürgen Habermas

"Even if [a liberal democratic] community is grounded in the universalist principles of a democratic constitutional state, it still forms a collective identity, in the sense that it interprets and realizes these principles in light of its own history and in the context of its own particular form of life." – *The Postnational Constellation*, pg. 107

J.B.S. Haldane

"...just as there is a best size for every animal, so the same is true for every human institution. In the Greek type of democracy all the citizens could listen to a series of orators and vote directly on question of legislation. Hence their philosophers held that a small city was the largest possible democratic state." – *On Being the Right Size*, *The World of Mathematics*, vol, 2, pgs. 962-967

Fitz-Greene Halleck

"They love their land, because it is their own, And scorn to give aught other reason why; Would shake hands with a king upon his throne, And think it kindness to his majesty." – *Connecticut, Poems*, pg. 123

"Strangers no more, a kindred 'pride of place,' Pride in the gift of country and of name, Speaks in your eye and step— Ye tread your native land, And your high thoughts are on her glory's day, The solemn sabbath of the week of battle, Whose tempests bowed to earth Here foeman's banner here." – *Saratoga, Poems*, pg. 94-95

Thomas Hall

"In the last dayes, men shall be so vile, that no bonds of Nature can bind them, and no wonder, for they that are blasphemers of God, disobedient to Parents, ingrateful to Benefactors, must needs at last come to that height of inhumanity and brutishness, as to be without Naturall Affection. They shall not only be without Humane affection, which is a love to men, as they are men, or Christian affection, which is a love to good men, because they are good; but they shell be without Naturall affection toward those, to whom they are bound by the bond of consanguinity and affinity, and by a special instinct of Nature, to shew a tender love and respect unto. These are those innate and tender affections, which are planted in our Nature by the God of Nature, towards those to whom we are conjoyned by the bond of Nature. Such is that naturall affection, which is between Parents and their children, Husand and Wife, Brother and Brother, Kindred and Country, a Governour and his Family. There is no Nation so base and barbarous, but there are some sparkles of this Naturall affection towards their own. Yea, the very bruit beasts we see, are very tender over their young. The very Lionesse, the Beare, the Tygre, the Eagle, the Hen, yea the Bitch will rise up in judgment against those unnaturall Parents that provide not for their own. Men love their Riches, they love their Houses, they love their Horses, yet their Dogs; but not with that naturall affection, as they love their children....

"Now is not this unnaturall sin, the sin of our Age?...'Twas the glory of the Primitive times, that there were so loving and unanimous, that their enemies could say, Ecce quam se mutue diligunt. Behold how these Christians love one another! but now we may say, Ecce quam se mutuo dilacerent! Behold how they tortue and teare one another in words and deedes?...Such men are worse than Heathens, let me profess the faith in words, yet if in their deeds they deny it, and be not careful in a prudentiall, providentiall way, to provide for their owne, they are worse than Infidels in this respects; for they by the light of Nature know, that 'tis their duty to provide for their own, and though they be barbarous, yet are they not so barbarous, as to cast off naturall affection to them. God will surely visit for such sins.

"Lastly, whereas there is planted in us a naturall affection to the Land of our Nativity, insomuch that Heathens have been prodigall of their lives, for the good of their Country, yet how many are there among us, that by destructive course, seek the ruin of their Mother that bare them, and the land that nurse them? True, we must love our Parents, love our children, love our friends, and neighbours, but the public good must be preferred before them all.

"This then informs us of their follow, who plead for a Stoicall Apostacy, commending the want of naturall affections as a point of perfection, which the Lord condemns as a great imperfection; accounting that for a Vertue which the Apostle reckons for a great Vice. So that to banish them out of man, is to banish man out of man, and to make him a stock, rather than a Stoick. The Affections are not sinful, per se, and in themselves, but only by Accident, when they are misplaced and set upon wrong objects, or not kept to their just proportion, so that they neither exceed, nor come short of their measure." – (writing on 2 Tim. 3:3), *A Practical and Polemical Commentary Or, Exposition Upon the Third and Fourth Chapters of the Latter Epistle of Saint Paul to Timothy*, pg. 76

Hamðismál, Poetic Edda

ᛖᛁᚾᛖᛏᛋᛁᚱ ᛗᛖᛗ ᛗᚲ ᚬᚱᚦᛁᚾ
ᛖᛗᛈ ᚬᛖᚲ ᛁ ᚺᚬᚱᛏᛁ
ᚠᛚᛏᛏᛁᚾ ᚠᛏ ᚠᚱᛋᛏᚾᛚᛚ
ᛖᛗᛈ ᚠᚢᚱᚠ ᚠᛏ ᚲᚾᛁᛖᛏᛁ
ᚾᚠᚦᛁᚾ ᚠᛏ ᛏᛁᚱᛋᚠ ᛖᛗᛈ ᛏᛁᚦᚱ
ᚠᛏ ᛚᚠᚾᚠᛁ ᚦᚠ ᛗᚱ ᛁᚾ
ᚲᚾᛁᛖᛏᛖᚲᛋᚦᚠ ᚲᛏᛗᚱ ᚾᛈ
ᚾᚠᚷ ᚾᚠᚱᛗᚠᚾ

Lonely I am become, as the asp-tree
　in the forest,
of kindred bereft, as the fir of branches;
of joy deprived, as is the tree of foliage,
when the branch-spoiler comes
　in the warm day.
– *The Ballad of Hamðir*, trans. by Benjamin Thorpe, st. 5

Lonely am I as the forest aspen,
Of kindred bare as the fir of its boughs,
My joys are all lost as the leaves of the tree
When the scather of twigs from
　the warm day turns
– *The Lay of Hamdir*, pg. 547

Alexander Hamilton

"It is a known fact in human nature, that its affections are commonly weak in proportion to the distance of diffusiveness of the object." – *Federalist #17*, in *The Constitution of the United States of America and Other Writings of the Founding Fathers*, pg. 206

"To render the people of this country as homogeneous as possible, must tend as much as any other circumstance to the permanency of their union and prosperity." – In his first draft of Washington's speech to Congress; *The Works of Alexander Hamilton*, edited by Henry Cabot Lodge, *Collector's Federal Edition*, 1904, vol. 8, pg. 217

"Particular attachment to any foreign nation is an exotic sentiment which, where it exists, must derogate from the exclusive affection due to our own country." – *The Works of Alexander Hamilton*, edited by Henry Cabot Lodge, *Collector's Federal Edition*, 1904, vol. 7, pg. 148

"The information which the address of the convention contains ought to serve as an instructive lesson to the people of this country. It ought to teach us not to overrate foreign friendships, and to be upon our guard against foreign attachments. The former will generally be found hollow and delusive; the latter will have a natural tendency to lead us aside from our own true interest, and to make us the dupes of foreign influence. Both serve to introduce a principle of action which in its effects, if the expression may be allowed, is anti-national. Foreign influence is truly the Grecian horse to a republic. We cannot be too careful to exclude its entrance. Nor ought we to imagine that it can only make its approaches in the gross form of direct bribery. It is then most dangerous when it comes under the patronage of our passions, under the auspices of national prejudice and partiality." – In an article from the *Gazette of the United States*, "Pacificus," No. VI; *The Works of Alexander Hamilton*. pg. 360

— ALEXANDER HAMILTON —

"The next most exceptionable feature in the message, is the proposal to abolish all restriction on naturalization, arising from a previous residence. In this the President is not more at variance with the concurrent maxims of all commentators on popular governments, than he is with himself. The 'Notes on Virginia' are in direct contradiction to the message, and furnish us with strong reasons against the policy now recommended. The passage alluded to is here presented. Speaking of the population[1]

of America, Mr. Jefferson says: 'Here I will beg leave to propose a doubt. The present desire of America, is to produce rapid population, by as great importations of foreigners as possible. But is this founded in good policy? Are there no inconveniences to be thrown into the scale, against the advantage expected from a multiplication of numbers, by the importation of foreigners? It is for the happiness of those united in society, to harmonize as much as possible, in matters which they must of necessity transact together. Civil government being the sole object of forming societies, its administration must be conducted by common consent. Every species of government has its specific principles. Ours, perhaps, are more peculiar than those of any other in the universe. It is a composition of the freest principles of the English Constitution, with others, derived from natural right and reason. To these, nothing can be more opposed than the maxims of absolute monarchies. Yet from such, we are to expect the greatest number of emigrants. They will bring with them the principles of the governments they leave, imbibed in their early youth; or if able to throw them off, it will be in exchange for an unbounded licentiousness, passing as is usual, from one extreme to another. It would be a miracle were they to stop precisely at the point of temperate liberty. Their principles with their language, they will transmit to their children. In proportion to their numbers, they will share with us in the legislation. They will infuse into it their spirit, warp and bias its direction, and render it a heterogeneous, incoherent, distracted mass. I may appeal to experience, during the present contest, for a verification of these conjectures; but if they be not certain in event, are they not possible, are they not probable? Is it not safer to wait with patience for the attainment of any degree of population desired or expected? May not our government be more homogeneous, more peaceable, more durable? Suppose twenty millions of republican Americans, thrown all of a sudden into France, what would be the condition of that kingdom? If it would be more turbulent, less happy, less strong, we may believe that the addition of half a million of foreigners, to our present numbers, would produce a similar effect here.' Thus wrote Mr. Jefferson in 1781.–Behold the reverse of the medal. The message of the President contains the following sentiments: 'A denial of citizenship under a residence of fourteen years, is a denial to a great proportion of those who ask it, and controls a policy pursued from their first settlement, by many of these States, and still believed of consequence to their prosperity. And shall we refuse to the unhappy fugitives from distress, that hospitality which the savages of the wilderness extended to our fathers arriving in this land? Shall oppressed humanity find no asylum on this globe? Might not the general character and capabilities of a citizen, be safely communicated to every one manifesting a bona-fide purpose of embarking his life and fortune permanently with us?'

"But if gratitude can be allowed to form an excuse for inconsistency in a public character–in the man of the people–a strong plea of this sort may be urged in behalf of our President. It is certain, that had the late election been decided entirely by native citizens, had foreign auxiliaries been rejected on both sides, the man who ostentatiously vaunts that the doors of public honor and confidence have been burst open to him, would not now have been at the head of the American nation. Such a proof, then, of virtuous discernment in the oppressed fugitives had an imperious claim on him to a grateful return, and, without supposing any very uncommon share of selflove, would naturally be a strong reason for a revolution in his opinions.

"The pathetic and plaintive exclamations by which the sentiment is enforced might be liable to much criticism, if we are to consider it in any other light than as a flourish of rhetoric. It might be asked in return, Does the right to asylum or hospitality carry with it the right to suffrage and sovereignty? And what, indeed, was the courteous reception which was given to our forefathers by the savages of the wilderness? When did these humane and philanthropic savages exercise the policy of incorporating strangers among themselves on their first arrival in this country? When did they admit them into their huts, to make part of their families? and when did they distinguish them by making them their sachems? Our histories and traditions have been more than apocryphal, if any thing like this kind and gentle treatment was really lavished by the much-belied savages upon our thankless forefathers. But the remark obtrudes itself. Had it all been true, prudence requires us to trace the history further and ask

what has become of the nations of savages who exercised this policy, and who now occupies the territory which they then inhabited? Perhaps a lesson is here taught which ought not to be despised.

"But we may venture to ask, What does the President really mean by insinuating that we treat aliens coming to this country with inhospitality? Do we not permit them quietly to land on our shores? Do we not protect them, equally with our own citizens, in their persons and reputation, in the acquisition and enjoyment of property? Are not our courts of justice open for them to seek redress of injuries? and are they not permitted peaceably to return to their own country whenever they please, and to carry with them all their effects? What, then, means this worse than idle declamation?

"The impolicy of admitting foreigners to an immediate and unreserved participation in the right of suffrage, or in the sovereignty of a republic, is as much a received axiom as anything in the science of politics, and is verified by the experience of all ages. Among other instances, it is known that hardly any thing contributed more to the downfall of Rome than her precipitate communication of the privileges of citizenship to the inhabitants of Italy at large. And how terribly was Syracuse scourged by perpetual seditions, when, after the overthrow of the tyrants, a great number of foreigners were suddenly admitted to the rights of citizenship? Not only does ancient, but modern, and even domestic, story furnish evidence of what may be expected from the dispositions of foreigners when they get too early a footing in a country. Who wields the sceptre of France, and has erected a despotism on the ruins of her former government? A foreigner. Who rules the councils of our own ill-fated, unhappy country? and who stimulates persecution on the heads of its citizens for daring to maintain an opinion, and for daring to exercise the rights of suffrage? A foreigner! Where, then, is the virtuous pride that once distinguished Americans? where the indignant spirit, which, in defence of principle, hazarded a revolution to attain that independence now insidiously attacked?" – In the seventh of his papers entitled *Examination of Jefferson's Message to Congress of December 7th, 1801*; *The Works of Alexander Hamilton*, edited by Henry Cabot Lodge, *Collector's Federal Edition*, vol. 8, pgs. 284–288

"Resuming the subject of our last paper, we proceed to trace still further the consequences that must result from a too unqualified admission of foreigners to an equal participation in our civil and political rights. The safety of a republic depends essentially on the energy of a common national sentiment; on a uniformity of principles and habits; on the exemption of the citizens from foreign bias, and prejudice; and on that love of country which will almost invariably be found to be closely connected with birth, education, and family.

"The opinion advanced in the Notes on Virginia is undoubtedly correct, that foreigners will generally be apt to bring with them attachments to the persons they have left behind; to the country of their nativity, and to its particular customs and manners. They will also entertain opinions on government congenial with those under which they have lived, or if they should be led hither from a preference to ours, how extremely unlikely is it that they will bring with them that temperate love of liberty, so essential to real republicanism? There may as to particular individuals, and at particular times, be occasional exceptions to these remarks, yet such is the general rule. The influx of foreigners must, therefore, tend to produce a heterogeneous compound; to change and corrupt the national spirit; to complicate and confound public opinion; to introduce foreign propensities. In the composition of society, the harmony of the ingredients is all important, and whatever tends to a discordant intermixture must have an injurious tendency...

"The United States have already felt the evils of incorporating a large number of foreigners into their national mass; by promoting in different classes different predilections in favor of particular foreign nations, and antipathies against others, it has served very much to divide the community and to distract our councils. It has been often likely to compromise the interests of our own country in favor of another.

"The permanent effect of such a policy will be, that in times of great public danger there will be always a numerous body of men, of whom there may be just grounds of distrust; the suspicion alone will weaken the strength of the nation, but their force may be actually employed in assisting an invader. To admit foreigners indiscriminately to the rights of citizens the moment they put foot in our country would be nothing less than to admit the Grecian horse into the citadel of our liberty and sovereignty." – In his *Examinations of Jefferson's Message to Congress of December 7th, 1801*; *The Works of Alexander Hamilton*, edited by Henry Cabot Lodge, *Collector's Federal Edition*, vol. 8, pgs. 288–291

"In the recommendation to admit indiscriminately foreign emigrants to the privileges of American citizens, on their first entrance into our country, there is an attempt to break down every pale which has been erected for the preservation of a national spirit and a national character, and to let in the most powerful means of perverting and corrupting both the one and the other." – *Examinations of Jefferson's Message to Congress of December 7th, 1801*; *The Works of Alexander Hamilton*, edited by Henry Cabot Lodge, *Collector's Federal Edition*, vol. 8, pg. 292

"There are certain social principles in human nature from which we may draw the most solid conclusions with respect to the conduct of individuals and of communities. We love our families more than our neighbors; we love our neighbors more than our countrymen in general. The human affections, like the solar heat, lose their intensity as they depart from the center and become languid in proportion to the expansion of the circle on which they act." – Alexander Hamilton, *Speech to the New York Convention, June 24, 1788*; *The Political Writings of Alexander Hamilton*: vol. 1, 1769–1789, pg. 370

"The wealth…independence, and security of a Country, appear to be materially connected with the prosperity of manufactures. Every nation…ought to endeavor to possess within itself all the essentials of national supply. These compromise the means of subsistence, habitation, clothing, and defense." – *Report on Manufactures*

"There are some who maintain that trade will regulate itself, [but] this is one of those speculative paradoxes . . . rejected by every man acquainted with commercial history." – *The Continentalist*, No. V, pg. 170

Victor P. Hamilton

"The OT never mandates an ideal age range for marriage.... In Egypt girls were married between the ages of twelve and fourteen, and young men between fourteen and twenty. In Greece girls were usually between fourteen and twenty, and men usually between twenty and thirty. In Rome, at the time of Augustus, the legal minimum age for girls was twelve, and for boys fourteen. The Talmud recommends marriage for girls at the age of puberty, which would be twelve or thirteen (*Yebam.* 62b). Males are encouraged to marry between fourteen and eighteen." – *Anchor Yale Bible Dictionary*, "Marriage (OT and ANE)", 4:563

"...failure to honor appropriately one's progenitors opens the door to violating other relationships...

"The most interesting thing about Lev. 19:3 is its coupling of commandments 5 and 4: 'Each of you must respect his mother and father [v. 3a], and you must observe my Sabbaths [v. 3b].' All this after 'Be holy [v. 2].' Holiness? Where does it shine forth? In how a person treats one's parents and how one treats the Sabbath. As Milgrom (2000b: 1608) says, 'The fact that this one verse combines a quintessentially ethical commandment with a quintessentially cultic one is proof that . . . both ethics and ritual are of equal value.' ...

"The fifth commandment is addressed primarily to an adult son rather than to a school-age son. The son who is to honor his folks is also the person who is to give his slaves the seventh day off, not commit adultery, nor cast his eyes on his neighbor's wife. For that reason, it is possible that honoring one's parents includes not only while the parent is alive, but showing the necessary respect after the parent's death (Brichto 1973: 31).

"The consequence of honoring one's parents is that the days (and years) of the commandment keeper will 'long endure.' The verb for 'long endure' is 'ārak (Hiphil). This is its only occurrence in Exodus, but in Deuteronomy it appears, apart from its use in the Decalogue (5:16), ten times. Eight times it is used positively to refer to the promise of long life for obedience (4:40; 5:33; 6:2; 11:9; 17:20; 22:7; 25:15; 32:47). Twice it is used negatively to refer to the loss of long life for disobedience (4:26; 30:18).

"There is a very interesting use of this verb in one of the Servant Songs of Isaiah: 'He will see his offspring and prolong ['ārak, Hiphil] his days' (Isa. 53:10).... 'long life,' such as Deuteronomy holds out for the faithful, may not be re-stricted exclusively to the life of the individual, but may refer to realities continuing beyond the lifetime of the devotee." – *Exodus: An Exegetical Commentary*, 20:12, pgs. 341-342

Peter Hammond

"As we look at Old Testament history, an important observation is that once Israel had conquered the Promised Land, God nowhere sanctions further expansion. Israel, of course, fought defensive wars to protect its territory, but God never ordained that Israel become an empire like her neighbors in the Middle East such as the Egyptians, Medes, Babylonians and Persians.

"When Solomon attempted to build an empire, God judged him for, among other things, taking to himself foreign wives, a common diplomatic practice among would-be empire builders.

"A reasonable conclusion from both the Bible and secular history is that the nation is the upper limit of human organization ordained by God. All multinational empires eventually die, even mighty Greece and Rome." – *The Christian Case for Intra-Racial Marriage*

"If I should tell them that it is because I believe that people should ideally marry within their race, most Africans would agree with me. In fact, most Africans that I know oppose marriage outside of their tribe. Not merely outside of their race. Are all the Zulus, Matabele, Nuba, Moru, Bemba, Dinka and Nuer Christians racists?...We know of many passages, such as in Nehemiah and Ezra, which forbid marrying nations around them, but no verses condemning those who teach that one should ideally marry within ones race....

"The Bible tells us of Jacob's twin brother, Esau, who took Hittite wives: 'and they were a grief of mind to Isaac and Rebecca' Genesis 26:34-35. 'Then Isaac called Jacob and blessed him and charged him and said to him, 'You shall not take a wife from the daughters of Canaan.' Genesis 28:1. The Law of God declares: 'Nor shall you make marriages with them. You shall not give your daughter to their son, nor take their daughter for your son.' Deuteronomy 7:3

"In his great prayer of National Repentance, Ezra warned against mixed marriages (Ezra

9:2-6, 12,13-14). Intermarrying with the nations around them, Ezra describes as 'our great guilt… our iniquities…' Similarly Nehemiah denounced intermarriage with other nations (Nehemiah 13:24-30).

"All these passages are well known and often taught and quoted in African churches that we minister amongst. We also study the great Creeds and Councils of the Church. Which Creed, Council or Confession of the Christian Church condemns those who teach that marriage should be within ones race? African women have expressed their strong opposition to mixed marriages. They feel devalued by incessant media promotion of black men with white women. Black women see it as an attack on their worth – that they are 'not good enough for our own men…'

"…the multiculturalists of America and the New World Order have now invented a new standard for Christianity. A standard completely unknown by Christians of previous centuries. Indeed almost two millenniums of church history. By your standard, Christians such as Augustine, Patrick, Athanasius, Luther, Tyndale, Calvin, Zwingli, Whitefield, Jonathan Edwards, Andrew Murray and Charles Spurgeon would be condemned for not holding to your new standard, which just coincidentally happens to be the standard avidly promoted by Marxists and the secular media in the world today.

"We are not teaching anything different from Dr. R.J. Rushdoony, or Professor Francis Nigel Lee, Robert Lewis Dabney, the Chief of Staff to Stonewall Jackson and General Robert Lee, would similarly be damned by your standards. Indeed, so too would most of the Christians of the last 20 centuries and certainly most of the Christians alive in Africa today, would fall under your condemnation by these Marxist standards of the New World Order.

"The Frankfurt School advocated breaking every tie of blood, soil, family, race and nation. Certainly their Marxist disciples have been so busy and effective in doing so that the secularisation, paganisation and Islamisation of Europe is far advanced. The United States of America is also facing tremendous social and moral upheavals. Multiculturalism and guilt manipulation have played a major role in this revolution." – *A response to Joel McDurmon*

Hammurabi

"If a seignior, upon adopting a boy, seeks out his father and mother when he had taken him, that foster child may return to his father's house." – *Ancient Near Eastern Texts Relating to the Old Testament*, pg. 174

"If the [adopted] son of a chamberlain or the [adopted] son of a votary has said to his foster father or his foster mother, 'You are not my father,' 'You are not my mother,' they shall cut out his tongue.

"If the [adopted] son of a chamberlain or the [adopted] son of a votary found out his parentage and came to hate his foster father and his foster mother and so has gone off to his paternal home, they shall pluck out his eye." – Code Of Hammurabi, *Ancient Near Eastern Texts Relating to the Old Testament*, pgs. 192-193

Walter Hampel

"Every nation must have a collective memory if it is to survive. Memory is the core of its history. Even though no living Americans have personal memory of President George Washington, we still remember him as our first president. Without a national memory, we would soon forget what it means to be American." – *The Morning And Evening Sacrifice, Ashland Theological Journal*, vol. 34, (2002), pg. 1

Warren G. Harding

"I believe in the protection of American industry and it is our purpose to prosper America first. … The privileges of the American market to the foreign producer are offered too cheaply today, and the effect on much of our own productivity is the destruction of our self-reliance, which is the foundation of the independence and good fortune of our people. … imports should pay their fair share of our cost of government." – *Address to a Joint Session of Congress*, April 12, 1921; Johnson and Porter, *National Party Platforms*, pg. 235

"One who values American prosperity and … American standards of wage[s] and living can have no sympathy with the proposal that easy entry and the flood of imports will cheapen our cost of living. It is more likely to destroy our capacity to buy." – *Address to a Joint Session of Congress*, April 12, 1921; Johnson and Porter, *National Party Platforms*, pg. 235

Benjamin Harrison

"A general process of wage reduction can not be contemplated by any patriotic citizen without the gravest apprehension. It may be ... possible for the American manufacturer to compete successfully with his foreign rival in many branches of production without the defense of protective duties if the pay rolls are equalized; but ... the distress of our working people when it is attained ... [is] not pleasant to contemplate." – *Address to Congress*, December 6, 1892; Richardson, *Messages*, 12:5746

Adrian Hastings

"What has to be asserted counter to modernism is not any kind of primordialism – a claim that every nation existent today, and just those nations, all existed in embryo a thousand or fifteen hundred years ago – but, rather, a finely constructed analysis of why some ethnicities do become nations while others do not. The defining origin of the nation, like that of every other great reality of modern western experience, whether it be the university, the bureaucratic state of individualism, needs to be located in an age a good deal further back than most modernist historians feel safe to handle, that of the shaping of medieval society.

"I will argue that ethnicities naturally turn into nations or integral elements within nations at the point when their specific vernacular moves from an oral to written usage to the extent that it is being regularly employed for the production of a literature, and particularly for the translation of the Bible. Once an ethnicity's vernacular becomes a language with an extensive living literature of its own, the Rubicon on the road to nationhood appears to have been crossed. If it fails to pass that point – and most spoken vernaculars do fail that hurdle – then transformation to nationhood is almost certain never to take place." – *The Construction of Nationhood*, pg. 11

"[The Venerable Bede] takes it for granted that this whole medley of peoples and kingdoms has become a single nation, 'gens Anglorum,' the people of the English, and he regularly uses the name 'English' to include not only Northumbrians and other Angles, but Saxons and Jutes." – *The Construction of Nationhood*, pgs. 36-37

"Once a Christian history has been constructed for a nation from the baptism of a first king and on through great deliverances, a history of a people's faith and divine providence, once the Bible is meditated upon in one's own language with all the immediacy this could bring, once one's own church is fully independent of any other and identified in extent with that of the nation, the more it seems easy to do the final step and claim to be a chosen people, a holy nation, with some special divine mission to fulfill. The Old Testament provided the paradigm. Nation after nation applied it to themselves, reinforcing their identity in the process." – *The Construction of Nationhood*, pg. 196

Stanley Hauerwas

"Tradition is a function and a product of community. So all ethics, even non-Christian ethics, make sense only when embodied in sets of social practices that constitute a community. Such communities support a sense of right and wrong. Yet most modern ethics begin from the Enlightenment presupposition of the isolated, heroic self, the allegedly rational individual who stands alone and decides and chooses. The goal of this ethic is to detach the individual from his or her tradition, parents, stories, community, and history, and thereby allow him or her to stand alone, to decide, to choose, and to act alone. It is an ethic of great value in our type of society because the corporation needs workers who are suitably detached from communities other than their place of work, people who are willing to move at the beck and call of the corporation. Growing up, becoming a mature, functioning adult is thus defined as becoming someone who has no communal, traditionalist, familial impediments." – *Resident Aliens*, pgs. 102-103

F.A. Hayek

"There is no reason why, in a society which has reached the general level of wealth ours has, the first kind of security should not be guaranteed to all without endangering general freedom;

that is: some minimum of food, shelter and clothing, sufficient to preserve health. Nor is there any reason why the state should not help to organize a comprehensive system of social insurance in providing for those common hazards of life against which few can make adequate provision." – *Road To Serfdom*, pg. 148

"To modern man the belief that all law governing human action is the product of legislation appears so obvious that the contention that law is older than law-making has almost the character of a paradox. Yet there can be no doubt that law existed for ages before it occurred to man that he could make or alter it." – *Law, Legislation, Liberty*, pg.73

"It would be no exaggeration to say that social theory begins with—and has an object only because of—the discovery that there exist orderly structures which are the product of the action of many men but are not the result of human design." – *Law, Legislation, and Liberty*, pg. 37

"We understand one another and get along with one another, are able to act successfully on our plans, because, most of the time, members of our civilization conform to unconscious patterns of conduct, show a regularity in their actions that is not the result of commands or coercion, often not even of any conscious adherence to known rules, but of firmly established habits and traditions. The general observance of these conventions is a necessary condition of the orderliness of the world in which we live, of our being able to find our way in it, though we do not know their significance and may not even be consciously aware of their existence. In some instances it would be necessary, for the smooth running of society, to secure a similar uniformity by coercion, if such conventions or rules were not observed often enough. Coercion, then, may sometimes be avoidable only because voluntary conformity exists, which means that voluntary conformity may be a condition of a beneficial working of freedom." – *Constitution of Liberty*, pg. 123

"There is an advantage in obedience to such rules not being enforced by coercion-not only because coercion as such is bad, but because it is in fact often desirable that rules should be observed only in most instances, and that the

individual should be able to transgress them when it seems to him worthwhile to incur the odium which this will cause. It is also important that the strength of the social pressure and of the force of habit which insure their observance is variable." – *Constitution of Liberty*, pg. 123

— F.A. HAYEK —

"We all know that in the pursuit of our individual aims we are not likely to be successful unless we lay down for ourselves some general rules to which we adhere without re-examining their justification in every particular instance. Whether it is the problem of how to order our day, or of doing disagreeable but necessary tasks at once, or of refraining from certain stimulants, or of suppressing certain impulses, we frequently find it necessary to make such practices an unconscious habit because we know that without this the rational grounds which make such behavior desirable would not be sufficiently effective to balance temporary desires and to make us do what we should wish to do from a long-run point of view. Though it sounds paradoxical that in order to make us act rationally we should often find it necessary to be guided by habit rather than reflection–or, in other words, that to prevent ourselves from making the wrong decision we should deliberately reduce the range of choice before us–we all know that this is in practice necessary to make us effective in achieving our long-range aims.

"The same considerations apply even more where the consequences of our conduct that we want to avoid are not direct effects on ourselves but effects on other people–these are not so immediately visible to us–and where the aim must be that we should adjust our actions to the actions and expectations of others so that we avoid doing them unnecessary harm. In this field it is not only unlikely that any individual should succeed in rationally constructing rules which would be more effective for their purpose than those which have been gradually evolved; even if he did they could not really serve their purpose unless they were observed by all. We have thus no choice but to submit to rules whose rationale we often do not understand, and to do so irrespective of whether we can see that anything important depends on their being observed in the particular instance. Though the rules of morals are instrumental in the sense that they mostly assist in the achievement of other human values, since we only rarely can know what depends on their being followed in the particular instance, to observe them must be regarded as a value in itself, a sort of intermediate end which we must pursue without questioning its justification in the particular case." – *Freedom, Reason, and Tradition. Ethics*, vol. 68, No. 4 (Jul., 1958), pg. 236

"A familiar instance of how a firmly established tradition assists frictionless human intercourse is the manner in which in the Anglo-Saxon countries a general familiarity with the rules of parliamentary procedure facilitates all proceedings of groups of men. To one who comes from another milieu it is a source of constant wonder how, as a result of this, a committee of schoolboys in England or the United States is generally more effective than many a group of grave and learned scholars in Germanic or Latin countries. Many similar examples could be given of how the general adherence to rules, which often may be far from rational and whose reasons those who submit to them are far from understanding, assists the effective collaboration of men. The often ridiculed propensity of Englishmen to form a queue at any bus station, which is of course merely the result of the unquestioned acceptance of the rule 'first come, first served,' is a humbler instance of the same trait. Much of the difference between Anglo-Saxon manners and the more formal, courtly etiquette of the Continent is probably due to the fact that the former have spontaneously developed to smooth intercourse in ordinary life rather than from the organized ceremonial of a hierarchic society." – *Freedom, Reason, and Tradition*, pg. 236

Carlton J.H. Hayes

"Nationalism, in its historic and simplest sense, is patriotism applied to one's nationality. As such it is a common cultural phenomenon, and one compatible with Catholic tradition and precept. For patriotism is a love of one's country, a prime expression of that sense of loyalty which holds men together in groups and without which men could not be the gregarious creatures that by nature they are.

"Men have always lived in groups. Apparently it is a part of God's plan that they should. And one of the things which have enabled them to live in groups has been the loyalty – the patriotism – which God has implanted in their very nature. This loyalty, this patriotism – this 'love of country' – involves a triple affection. It embraces an affection for familiar places, an affection for familiar persons, and an affection for familiar ideas. One's 'country' connotes all three of these: the land itself, the persons on it, and the traditions associated with it. One's 'native land' – the terra patria, la patrie, das Vaterland – is an extension of hearth and home. It is the soil that has given life to one's forefathers and holds their tombs, and which in turn nurtures one's children and grandchildren. It is a link between generations, between families and friends, between common experience of the past and that of the present and future. It is the earthly means, at once familiar and sacred, of establishing and maintaining a community or group life.

"The right use of patriotism is a precept of the natural law and a Christian duty. Such has been the invariable teaching of the Catholic Church and the Roman Pontiffs. In the words of Pope Leo XIII: 'The natural law enjoins us to love devotedly and to defend the country in which we had birth and in which we were reared, so that every good citizen hesitates not to face death for his native land.' And Pope Pius XI has added that patriotism is 'the stimulus of so many virtues and of so many noble acts of heroism when kept within the bounds of the law of Christ.'

"This, too, has invariably been a reservation

which the Catholic Church and the Roman Pontiffs have made to their inculcation of patriotism. Duties to our compatriots must not blind us, the Church constantly proclaims, to our paramount duties to God, or to the duties of justice and charity which we owe to mankind at large. Christ Himself instructed us at the beginning 'to render unto Cæsar the things that are Cæsar's, and to God the things that are God's.' Pope Pius XI reminds us in the present age that 'love of country becomes merely an occasion for, and an added incentive to, grave injustice, when true love of country is debased to the condition of an extreme nationalism, when we forget that all men are our brothers and members of the same great human family, that other nations have an equal right with us both to life and to prosperity, that it is never lawful nor even wise to dissociate morality from the affairs of practical life, that, in the last analysis, it is 'justice which exalteth a nation, but sin maketh nations miserable.'

"If one group of human beings is naturally and divinely held together by patriotism, then other groups are similarly held together by a like patriotism, and what one esteems for one's self, one must not deny to others. This is natural justice, re-enforced and ennobled for Christians by the Christ – given law of charity. As Pope Benedict XV says: 'There is nothing that Christ recommended more frequently and more insistently to His disciples than the precept of mutual charity, and that because it embraces all others; Christ called it the new precept, His commandment, and He wished to make it a characteristic mark of Christians, by which they would be distinguished from the rest of mankind... The Gospel does not contain one law of charity for individuals and another law, different from the first, for cities and peoples.'

"Patriotism, in its true and basic sense, is a Christian virtue. This is not to say, however, that patriotism must be, or always has been, synonymous with nationalism. Nationalism is but one form of patriotism. Nationalism is patriotism applied to a nationality, and if it is true patriotism (in the Christian sense) that is applied to nationality, then the resulting nationalism is compatible with Christian ethics."
– *Patriotism, Nationalism, And The Brotherhood Of Man*, in Pamphlet 19-36 of the *Catholic Association for International Peace*, pgs. 6-8

Robert Hayne

"Their first principle of action is to leave their own affairs, and neglect their own duties, to regulate the affairs and the duties of others. Theirs is the task to feed the hungry and clothe the naked, of other lands, whilst they thrust the naked, famished, and shivering beggar from their own doors; to instruct the heathen, while their own children want the bread of life. When this spirit infuses itself into the bosom of a statesman (if one so possessed can be called a statesman), it converts him at once into a visionary enthusiast. Then it is that he indulges in golden dreams of national greatness and prosperity. He discovers that 'liberty is power'; and not content with vast schemes of improvement at home, which it would bankrupt the treasury of the world to execute, he flies to foreign lands, to fulfill obligations to 'the human race,' by inculcating the principles of 'political and religious liberty,' and promoting the 'general welfare' of the whole human race." – *Speech on Foot Resolution 1830*; *American Eloquence*, vol. 2, pg. 564

Yoram Hazony

"The overwhelming dominance of a single, cohesive nationality, bound together by indissoluble bonds of mutual loyalty, is in fact the only basis for domestic peace within a free state...What is needed for the establishment of a stable and free state is a majority nation whose cultural dominance is plain and unquestioned, and against which resistance appears to be futile. Such a majority nation is strong enough not to fear challenges from national minorities, and so is able to grant them rights and liberties without damaging the internal integrity of the state. Similarly, the national minorities that stand against such a national majority are themselves largely reluctant to engage in confrontations that they know they cannot win. For the most part, they therefore assimilate themselves into the system of expectations established by the constitutional and religious culture of the majority nation, learning its language and resorting to violence only on rare occasions. This has been the case in the most successful national states such as Britain, America, France, and other countries in Europe, in addition to national states such as Australia, Japan, Korea, Thailand, Turkey, India, and Israel.

In each case, the overwhelming dominance of a single majority nation has produced states that are dramatically more stable, prosperous, and tolerant than neighboring states that have not been constituted as national states.

"Where the state is not constituted as a national state, precisely the opposite happens: The various nations or tribes that have been forcibly thrown together, having no common language or religion and no history of collaboration against common enemies, cannot form bonds of mutual loyalty, and so cannot become a nation. They battle for power until one national or tribal group does eventually seize control of the government. But because the population remains internally divided along national and tribal lines, this seizure of power does nothing to alter the fundamental unsoundness of the state. What prevents utter ruin are the bonds of mutual loyalty that unite the national or tribal group that has seized the government, and the iron hand of its leadership, which keeps all others afraid. In this way, the non-national state inevitably tilts toward a despotic regime, and finally, once the despotism of the state can no longer be held in place, dissolution. Not only Syria and Iraq, but states such as the Soviet Union, Yugoslavia, Czechoslovakia, Lebanon, Yemen, Sudan, Nigeria, and Congo, all of which were multinational entities claiming some kind of neutrality among the various nations under their aegis, exploded into civil war or simply collapsed." – *The Virtue Of Nationalism*, ch. 16, pg. 106

"The state of Iraq attained its independence from imperial Britain in 1932 as a consequence of boundaries drawn in negotiation with France. There had never in history been an "Iraqi" nation prior to this, but the British, ignoring national and religious boundaries, nonetheless asserted that such a nation could be created by forcing together Kurdish, Assyrian, Sunni Arab, and Shia Arab tribes, among others—peoples sharing neither language nor religion, nor a prior history of united action. They were called a nation and given a written constitution, a flag, and the right to send ambassadors the world over, as well as various other symbols of a national state. All these things were done with the aim of establishing that this new state of Iraq was in fact a national state in the same way that England or France

or America is a national state. However, there was no truth in any of this. In reality, Sunni Arabs were the dominant tribal group, holding the state together through the ruthless oppression of the much larger population of Shiite Arabs. The large Kurdish population never accepted Arab rule. The poison gassing in 1988 of Kurds in Halabja by the Sunnis in Iraq is only the best-known example of the unspeakable brutality that the Sunni Arab regime felt it needed to exercise in order to maintain the integrity of the state. The American attempt to save the country by forcibly reconstituting it as a Western democracy, complete with a new written constitution guaranteeing individual liberties in 2005, quickly ended in failure and a terrible civil war.

"A similar fate has befallen Syria, which was established as an independent state by the French in 1946. There had never in history been a 'Syrian' nation prior to this, the name itself having been invented by the Greeks to describe this geographic region. Yet contrary to the evident facts, the Alawite, Druze, Kurd, Assyrian Christian, and Sunni Arab tribes in this arbitrarily drawn territory were declared a nation. The result has been that this mass of violently opposed groups lived through two decades of chronic instability and state oppression until the Alawites, a non-Muslim nationality or tribe with a religion and historic identity of its own, were finally able to seize power. Establishing a minority alignment together with Christians and Druze, they imposed a reign of terror on the majority Sunni Arab population, up to and including the famous destruction of the Sunni city of Hama by the Alawites. In the present decade, the Alawites have continued to prevent the establishment of a Sunni Arab regime at a cost of half a million deaths and the displacement of perhaps half the population of the country." – *The Virtue Of Nationalism*, ch. 16, pg. 104

"Human reason is capable of arriving at virtually any conclusion, and has never in history been able to arrive at a single political truth that all can agree upon. Thus the importance of national freedom, which permits each nation to develop its own unique purposes, traditions, and institutions that may be tested through painstaking trial and error over centuries. This conception of the need for a diversity of nations, each pursuing the truth according to its own understanding, is not intended to deny that there are principles of government and morals that are best. What is denied is that these principles are known to anyone who will but exercise reason to try and get to them." – *The Virtue Of Nationalism*, pg. 80

"My own background allows me some insight into the subject. I have been a Jewish nationalist, a Zionist, all my life. Like most Israelis, I inherited this political outlook from my parents and grandparents. My family came to Jewish Palestine in the 1920s and early 1930s with the aim of establishing an independent Jewish state there. They succeeded, and I have lived most of my life in a country that was established by nationalists, and has been governed largely by nationalists to this day. Over the years, I have known a great many nationalists, including public figures and intellectuals both from Israel and from other countries. And while not everyone among them has been to my taste, on the whole these are people I deeply admire—for their loyalty and courage, their good sense, and their moral decency. Among them, nationalism is not some unfathomable political illness that periodically takes over countries for no good reason and to no good end, as many in America and Britain seem to think these days. It is instead a familiar political theory on which they were raised, a theory of how the political world should be ordered.

"What is this nationalist political theory about?

"The nationalism I grew up with is a principled standpoint that regards the world as governed best when nations are able to chart their own independent course, cultivating their own traditions and pursuing their own interests without interference. This is opposed to imperialism, which seeks to bring peace and prosperity to the world by uniting mankind, as much as possible, under a single political regime. I do not suppose that the case for nationalism is unequivocal. Considerations can be mustered in favor of each of these theories. But what cannot be done without obfuscation is to avoid choosing between the two positions: Either you support, in principle, the ideal of an international government or regime that imposes its will on subject nations when its officials regard this as necessary; or you believe that nations should

be free to set their own course in the absence of such an international government or regime." – *The Virtue Of Nationalism*, Introduction, pgs. 9-10

"...a conservative political theory begins with the understanding that individuals are born into families, tribes, and nations to which they are bound by mutual loyalty. This means that a conservative recognizes the nation is an ineliminable reality. Political reality, as the conservative sees it, is full of competing nations, each of which consists of a number of tribes tied to one another by bonds of mutual loyalty. Each nation and tribe is engaged in a constant competition with its neighbors, allying or warring with them as circumstances dictate. Each nation and tribe possesses a unique cultural inheritance carrying forward certain traditional institutions, which can include its language, religion, laws, and the forms of its government and economic life." – *Conservatism: A Rediscovery*, pg.133

"By a nation, then, we mean a number of tribes with a shared heritage, usually including a common language, law, or religious tradition, and a past history of joining together against common enemies and to pursue common endeavors— characteristics that permit tribes united in this way to recognize themselves as a nation distinct from the other nations that are their neighbors. By a national state, we mean a nation whose disparate tribes have come together under a single standing government, independent of all other governments.

"The liberal paradigm is blind to the nation. Nothing like the nation is to be found in the premises of Enlightenment liberal political theory. In the rationalist political tracts of the Enlightenment, the term 'nation' (or 'people') is merely a collective name for the individuals who live under the state. On this view, the nation comes into existence with the establishment of the state and is dissolved when the state is dissolved. This is another way of saying that the nation has no real existence of its own. There are only individuals and the state that rules over them.

"Thus we find that instructors in political theory (whether in high school civics classes or at the university level) avoid discussing the nation, as well as those characteristics of the nation that explain its behavior in the political world. Instead, they discuss the political world using only concepts such as the individual, freedom, equality, government, and consent, which appear in the premises of Enlightenment liberal political theory, and additional terms such as rights that permit liberal premises to be elaborated in greater detail. But such instruction is powerless to explain many of the most basic phenomena of political life. It has no resources to describe the rivalry among nations and their ceaseless quest for honor, their pursuit of internal unity and cohesion, their struggle to maintain their own language, religion, and political traditions, or their insistence on the inviolability of their laws and borders. And indeed, entire generations of political and intellectual figures have been educated in such a way as to leave them blind to the importance of these things—or else to see them as 'primitive' phenomena that will disappear from the world as reason and liberalism take hold.

"This blindness to the real existence of the nation as something distinct from the individual or the state stands behind almost all of the great policy disasters of the last generation." – *Conservatism: A Rediscovery*, pg. 135

"This inability [of liberals] to see tribe and nation as central in political affairs is reflected in debates on immigration as well. Viewed through the lens of Enlightenment liberalism, immigrants and prospective immigrants are indistinguishable from the native individuals of a given country. They are perfectly free and equal, just as the natives are. Nothing in the liberal paradigm justifies depriving them of their freedom of movement into a given country, or their freedom to compete with native individuals for employment and other resources. From a strict, free-trade perspective, preventing immigrants from arriving in the country and selling their labor is just another market distortion introduced by the national and tribal loyalties of the natives, which, again, leads to reduced freedom and to economic inefficiency.

"But national and tribal loyalties are powerful and real, and tribes and nations compete with their neighbors when they feel strong enough to do so. As soon as national and tribal competition is seen as having a real existence, it is obvious that the adoption of immigrant communities into a new nation can only be successful if the immigrants are sufficiently weak, and therefore willing to assimilate themselves

into the language, laws, and traditions of their adopted nation. Where immigrant communities are too large and internally cohesive, they resist such dissolution and begin to compete with the native population. This can result in open hatred, domestic tension, and violence." – *Conservatism: A Rediscovery*, pg. 137

"Most conservatives are empiricists. They are open to experience. And the experience of the last generation *seems to* point to rigid free-market purism as an unrealistic and dangerous policy. I say 'seems to' because I'm not myself ready to draw sweeping conclusions yet. But I know for sure that I'm not interested in hearing yet again the 'deductive' arguments from first principles about freedom that you recite from Locke, Mises, Rand, Nozick, and Friedman. I grew up reading these writers and was mostly sympathetic. But deductive arguments won't help us understand what's gone wrong over the last 25 years. So like many conservatives I know, I'm reading books that emphasize an empirical approach to national economies.

"[He quotes some books and then says] … Some of this material is compelling and some of it is not. But what these books have in common is that they try to understand from experience–not deductively–what actually works to strengthen a national economy and what doesn't. I don't see it as surprising that conservatives want to learn in response to policies that have gone badly wrong. What is surprising to me is that market deductivists such as yourself are not responding to the arguments in these and similar books.

"If the economic nationalists are wrong, then why not cite their arguments directly and then challenge them head on? I believe that many conservatives right now are open to hearing powerful, empirically based refutations of the economic-nationalist case. I know I am. But just reciting dogma drawn from Locke, Mises, Rand, and Nozick is pointless. It just makes it seem as though you're not actually familiar with the historical-empiricist economic critique of market purism that's winning over many conservatives right now. That's what's going on." – X (Twitter) post

"The order of national states offers the greatest possibility of collective self-determination; that it inculcates an aversion to the conquest of foreign nations and opens the door to a tolerance of diverse ways of life; and that it establishes a life of astonishingly productive competition among nations as each strives to attain the maximal development of its abilities and those of its individual members. In addition, I find that the powerful mutual loyalties that are at the heart of the national state give us the only known foundation for the development of free institutions and individual liberties. These and other considerations suggest that a world of independent national states is the best political order to which we can aspire." – *Virtue Of Nationalism*, pg. 14

"Consider the policy of 'free trade.' For an entire generation, democratic nations have sought a regime of free business transactions with China as a way of securing an unlimited supply of inexpensive labor for their industries — policy that reached its climax in 2001 with the entry of China into the World Trade Organization. These policies were supported not only by the desire of private individuals (and, by extension, corporations owned by private individuals) to exercise their freedom in order to earn higher profits. They were also promoted by governments, media, and academics committed to the liberal theory that there should be no state-imposed barriers preventing individuals and corporations from freely buying whatever they want at the lowest price and selling whatever they want to the highest bidder.

"This is a policy couched entirely in terms of the individual, the state, and the individual's presumptive freedom to do whatever he and his trading partners consent to do without state interference. It is blind to the nation, and to the bonds of mutual loyalty that bind nations and tribes together. Indeed, to the extent that bonds of national loyalty are even mentioned in discussions of free trade, they are described as irrational 'market distortions' that may cause inefficiencies and make life more expensive—and therefore presumably less free. An 'ideal world' is said to be one in which such distortions are eliminated in order to maximize the freedom of the individual. In other words, an ideal world is imagined to be one in which the effects of national and tribal loyalties are suppressed.

"In light of this ideal, national loyalty was suppressed as a significant factor in policymaking. American and European industrialists were encouraged to move manufacturing to China and other Asian countries, even as millions of Chinese were invited to attend Western universities to study engineering and the sciences. These expressions of individual and corporate freedom had two crucial consequences: First, the Chinese economy grew rapidly, both in absolute size and in its technical capacities in numerous fields, until it began to challenge American and European dominance of the world economy. Second, more expensive American and European workers lost their livelihood. For years, liberals in America and Europe cheered these developments, emphasizing that free trade was lifting hundreds of millions of individuals in China out of poverty, that Enlightenment ideas were striking root in China and transforming it into a liberal democracy, and that Western workers who had lost their jobs would have new and better employment as private corporations reinvested their enlarged profits.

"But these claims were made by political and academic figures who had been blinded by the liberal paradigm, and so were unable to understand the political world in terms of nations, their rivalries, their cohesion, and their dissolution. Incredible, but true: They were unable to see that massive, sustained industrial growth and gains in scientific expertise would transform a hostile, authoritarian China into a fearsome new enemy. Nor did they recognize that abandoning America's manufacturing capabilities would lead workers to regard themselves as betrayed by the business leaders who had transferred their jobs to China, and by the liberal governments that had encouraged this, bursting the bonds of mutual loyalty that had made America a cohesive and internally powerful nation. Yet this is what happened. Western liberals, who see the political world in terms of the freedom of the individual and cannot see the nation as having a real existence in the political sphere, inadvertently succeeded in immensely strengthening the Chinese nation at the expense of the American nation." – *Conservatism*, pgs. 135-136

Seamus Heaney

"Between my finger and my thumb
The squat pen rests; snug as a gun."
– *Digging* (lines 1-2) [39]

"The cold smell of potato mould,
    the squelch and slap
Of soggy peat, the curt cuts of an edge
Through living roots awaken in my head."
– *Digging* (lines 25-27)

"The pockets of our greatcoats full of barley...
No kitchens on the run, no striking camp...
We moved quick and sudden in our own country."
– *Requiem for the Croppies* (lines 1, 3-4)

"We have no prairies
To slice a big sun at evening—
Everywhere the eye concedes to
Encroaching horizon,"
– *Bogland* (lines 1-4)

"Out here in Jutland
In the old man-killing parishes
I will feel lost,
Unhappy and at home."
– *The Tollund Man* (lines 41-44)

Hebrew Literature (Fragments)

"So that they should turn aside from the paths
of righteousness, And remove the landmark
which the forefathers had set in their inheritance:
    So as to make cleave unto them
    The curses of His covenant,
    To deliver them to the sword
    That avengeth with the vengeance
        of the covenant."
– quoted by Charles, R. H., *Pseudepigrapha of the
Old Testament*, pgs. 801-802

John Hector St. John de Crèvecœur

"...whence came all these people? They are
a mixture of English, Scotch, Irish, French,
Dutch, Germans, and Swedes... What, then, is
the American, this new man? He is either a European
or the descendant of a European; hence
that strange mixture of blood, which you will
find in no other country. I could point out to
you a family whose grandfather was an Englishman,
whose wife was Dutch, whose son married
a French woman, and whose present four sons
have now four wives of different nations. He
is an American, who, leaving behind him all
his ancient prejudices and manners, receives
new ones from the new mode of life he has
embraced, the new government he obeys, and
the new rank he holds. . . . The Americans were
once scattered all over Europe; here they are
incorporated into one of the finest systems of
population which has ever appeared." – *Letters
from an American Farmer*, pg. 54

G.W.F. Hegel

"A Nation is moral – virtuous – vigorous –
while it is engaged in realizing its grand objects,
and defends its work against external violence
during the process of giving to its purposes an
objective existence. The contradiction between
its potential, subjective being – its inner aim
and life – and its actual being is removed; it has
attained full reality, has itself objectively present
to it. But this having been attained, the activity
displayed by the Spirit of the people in question
is no longer needed; it has its desire. The Nation
can still accomplish much in war and peace
at home and abroad; but the living substantial
soul itself may be said to have ceased its activity.
The essential, supreme interest has consequently
vanished from its life, for interest is
present only where there is opposition. The nation
lives the same kind of life as the individual
when passing from maturity to old age – in the
enjoyment of itself – in the satisfaction of being
exactly what it desired and was able to attain
... In order that a truly universal interest may
arise, the Spirit of a People must advance to
the adoption of some new purpose; but whence
can this new purpose originate? It would be a
higher, more comprehensive conception of itself
– a transcending of its principle – but this very
act would involve a principle of a new order, a
new National Spirit." – *The Philosophy of History*,
pg. 77

"It is not our concern to become acquainted
with the land occupied by nations as an external
locale, but with the natural type of the locality,
as intimately connected with the type and

---

39   A Nobel Prize-winning poet, Heaney often explored themes of Irish identity, history, and rural life.

character of the people which is the offspring of such a soil." – *The Philosophy Of History*, pg. 83

"With respect to the diversity of races of mankind it must be remembered first of all that the purely historical question, whether all these races sprang from a single pair of human beings or from several, is of no concern whatever to us in philosophy. Importance was attached to this question because it was believed that by assuming descent from several couples, the mental and spiritual superiority of one race over another could be explained, indeed, it was hoped to prove that human beings are by nature so differently endowed with mental or spiritual capacities that some can be dominated like animals. But descent affords no ground for granting or denying freedom to human beings. Man is implicitly rational; herein lies the possibility of equal justice for all men and the futility of a rigid distinction between races which have rights and those which have none. The difference between the races of mankind is...a difference which, in the first instance, concerns the natural soul. As such, the difference is connected with the geographical differences of those parts of the world where human beings are gathered together in masses" – *The Philosophy Of Mind*, pg. 41

"Nature is the element of inequality. Yet the objective right of particularity of spirit, contained in the idea itself, does not in the civic community supersede the inequality set up by nature. On the contrary, it produces inequality out of spirit and exalts it to an inequality of talents, wealth, and intellectual and moral education. To oppose to the objective right a demand for equality is a move of the empty understanding, which takes its own abstraction and mandate to be real and reasonable. In the sphere of particularity the universal images itself, forming with the particular merely a relative identity. The particular thus retains both the natural and the capricious particularity, and also a remnant of the state of nature. It is the reason immanent in the system of human wants and their activities, which fashions this system into an organic whole, of which the differences are members." – *Philosophy of Right*, pg. 105

"The ignorant man is not free, because what confronts him is an alien world, something

outside him and in the offing, on which he depends, without his having made this foreign world for himself and therefore without being at home in it by himself as in something his own. The impulse of curiosity, the pressure for knowledge, from the lowers level up to the highest run of philosophical insight arises only from the struggle to cancel this situation of unfreedom and to make the world one's own in one's ideas and thought." – *Lectures On Fine Art, Aesthetics*, vol. 1, pg. 98

Johann Heidegger

"The love of one's self establishes the rule of love of one's neighbor." – *Ethicae Christianae Elementa*

Martin Heidegger

"What seems natural to us is probably just something familiar in a long tradition that has forgotten the unfamiliar source from which it arose. And yet this unfamiliar source once struck man as strange and caused him to think and to wonder." – *Being And Time; Heidegger on Art and Art Works*, pg. 115

"Sciences are ways of Being in which Dasein comports itself towards entities which it need not be itself. But to Dasein, Being in a world is something that belongs essentially. Thus Dasein's understanding of Being pertains with equal primordiality both to an understanding of something like a 'world', and to the understanding of the Being of those entities which become accessible within the world. So whenever an ontology takes for its theme entities whose character of Being is other than that of Dasein, it has its own foundation and motivation in Dasein's own ontical structure, in which a pre-ontological understanding of Being is comprised as a definite characteristic." – *Being And Time*, pg. 33

Heidelberg Catechism

The fifth commandment requires:
    "that I show honor, love, and faithfulness to my father and mother and to all who are set in authority over me; that I submit myself with respectful obedience to all their careful instruction and discipline; and that I also bear patiently their failures, since it is God's will to govern us by their hand." – *Answer 104*

Heinrich Heine

"Ich weiß nicht, was soll es bedeuten,
Dass ich so traurig bin;
Ein Märchen aus alten Zeiten,
Das kommt mir nicht aus dem Sinn."

Translation:
 "I don't know what it could mean,
 That I am so sad;
 A fairy tale from old times,
 That I cannot get out of my mind."
 – *Die Lorelei* (*The Lorelei*, lines 1-4) [40]

"Im wunderschönen Monat Mai,
Als alle Knospen sprangen,
Da ist in meinem Herzen
Die Liebe aufgegangen."

Translation:
 "In the beautiful month of May,
 When all the buds were bursting,
 That is when in my heart
 Love began to bloom."
 – *Im wunderschönen Monat Mai* (*In the Beautiful Month of May*, lines 1-4)

"Leise zieht durch mein Gemüt
Liebliches Geläute.
Klinge, kleines Frühlingslied,
Kling hinaus ins Weite."

Translation:
 "Softly through my mind
 Lovely chimes are ringing.
 Ring, little springtime song,
 Ring out into the distance."
 – *Leise zieht durch mein Gemüt* (*Softly Through My Mind*, lines 1-4)

Helmold of Bosau

"Many nations [naciones] are seated about this sea. The Danes and the Swedes, whom we call Northmen, occupy the northern coast and all the islands it contains. Along the southern shore dwell the Slavic nations [naciones] of whom, reckoning from the east, the Russians [Ruci] are the first, then the Poles who on the north have the Prussians, on the south the Bohemians and those who are called Moravi-ans and the Carinthians and the Sorbs." – *The Chronicles of the Slavs*, quoted in *Nations: The Long History*, pg. 183

Alexander Henderson

"Secondly, that it is no marvail if that Nation stand to the defence of their Reformation. Had the Lord been pleased to blesse us with the like at the time of our Reformation we would not have been so unwise as to make exchange of it with Prelacy, we would have forsaken all things rather then have forsaken it. It is more strange that any should have been found amongst them at any time to speak or to do against their own Church: 'But after you have with your reason and minde made a generall survey of all societies, there is none more grave, more dear, then that which each one of us hath with his Countrey; Parents are dear, Children, Friends, familiars are dear; But our native Countrey alone taketh all these within her compasse, for which what good man would doubt to die, could his death serve her for good? So much the more detestable is their barbarity, who have with all kinde of wickednesse rent asunder their native Countrey, and both are and have been exercised in overturning her from the very foundation' (Cicero, *De Officiis* 1.57). If a Patriote spoke so of his Countrey, a Citizen so of his Republike, what should the Christian born, baptized, and bred in Scotland think and say, if he have been borne there not only to this mortall, but to that immortall and everlasting life: No children on earth have better reason to say, Wee are not ashamed of our Mother, and it were to be wished that the saying were reciprocally true." – *Preface to Alexander Henderson, The Government and Order of the Church of Scotland*

Matthew Henry

"The ancient church, the medieval exegesis, and the interpreters of the early modern period almost uniformly interpret πάντα τὰ ἔθνη in the universal sense of 'all nations.' In John Chrysostom and other interpreters influenced by him there is even the assertion that Christ did not mention the Jews and Peter because he forgave them: 'He does not mention what has happened, and he does not reprove Peter for his

---

40   Heine was a prominent German poet and journalist. His poetry often reflects his love for his homeland, even as he critiques various aspects of German society.

denial.' If on occasion the meaning 'Gentiles' is in the foreground, it is usually not exclusively in the sense that the Jews are thereby excluded. Only infrequently and especially in polemical texts is that not the case.

"Today opinions are divided on this question. The majority of exegetes interpret πάντα τὰ ἔθνη universally as 'all nations,' a large minority as 'all Gentiles....'

"What is the principal intention of this commission; to disciple all nations? Matheteusate—'Admit them disciples; do your utmost to make the nations Christian nations;' not, 'Go to the nations, and denounce the judgments of God against them, as Jonah against Nineveh, and as the other Old-Testament prophets' (though they had reason enough to expect it for their wickedness), 'but go, and disciple them.' Christ the Mediator is setting up a kingdom in the world, bring the nations to be his subjects; setting up a school, bring the nations to be his scholars; raising an army for the carrying on of the war against the powers of darkness, enlist the nations of the earth under his banner. The work which the apostles had to do, was, to set up the Christian religion in all places, and it was honourable work; the achievements of the mighty heroes of the world were nothing to it. They conquered the nations for themselves, and made them miserable; the apostles conquered them for Christ, and made them happy."– *Complete Bible Commentary*, on Matthew 21-28

"He hath determined the times before appointed, and the bounds of their habitation. The sovereignty of God's disposal concerning us: he hath determined every event, horisas, the matter is fixed; the disposals of Providence are incontestable and must not be disputed, unchangeable and cannot be altered...He has also determined and appointed the bounds of our habitation. He that appointed the earth to be a habitation for the children of men has appointed to the children of men a distinction of habitations upon the earth, has instituted such a thing as property, to which he has set bounds to keep us from trespassing one upon another. The particular habitations in which our lot is cast, the place of our nativity and of our settlement, are of God's determining and appointing, which is a reason why we should accommodate ourselves to the habitations we are in, and make the best of that which is." – *Complete Bible Commentary*, Acts 17:26

"Note, It is the will of God that mutual love and affection, converse and communion, should be kept up among relations. Those that are of kin to each other should, as much as they can, be acquainted with each other; and the bonds of nature should be improved for the strengthening of the bonds of Christian communion. Every one must know his place and keep in it; they were not allowed to fix where they pleased, nor to remove when they pleased, but God quarters them, with a charge to abide in their quarters. Note, It is God that appoints us the bounds of our habitation, and to him we must refer ourselves. He shall choose our inheritance for us (Ps. xlvii. 4), and in his choice we must acquiesce, and not love to flit, nor be as the bird that wanders from her nest. Every tribe had its standard, flag, or ensign, and it should seem every family had some particular ensign of their father's house, which was carried as with us the colours of each troop or company in a regiment are. These were of use for the distinction of tribes and families, and the gathering and keeping of them together, in allusion to which the preaching of the gospel is said to lift up an ensign, to which the Gentiles shall seek, and by which they shall pitch, Isa. xi. 10, 12. Note, God is the God of order, and not of confusion." – *Commentary on Numbers* ch. 2:1-2, pg. 112

"Every tribe had a captain, a prince, or commander-in-chief, whom God himself nominated, the same that had been appointed to number them, ch. i. 5. Our being all the children of one Adam is so far from justifying the levellers, and taking away the distinction of place and honour, that even among the children of the same Abraham, the same Jacob, the same Judah, God himself appointed that one should be captain of all the rest. There are powers ordained of God, and those to whom honour and fear are due and must be paid." – *Commentary on Numbers* 2:3-34, pg. 114

"See the mischief of marrying with strangers. When men once became akin to Tobiah, they soon became sworn to him. A sinful love leads to a sinful league." – *Commentary on Nehemiah* 6, pg. 71

"He tells them the charge his master had given him, to fetch a wife for his son from among his kindred, with the reason of it, v.37,38. The highest degrees of divine affection must not divest us of natural affection." – *Commentary on Genesis 24:29-53, pg. 134*

— MATTHEW HENRY —

"Direction is given what should be done if a servant died by his master's correction. This servant must not be an Israelite, but a Gentile slave, as the negroes to our planters." – *Commentary on Exodus 21:12-21*

"That they might purchase bondmen of the heathen nations that were round about them, or of those strangers that sojourned among them (except of those seven nations that were to be destroyed); and might claim a dominion over them, and entail them upon their families as an inheritance, for the year of jubilee should give no discharge to them, v. 44, 46. Thus in our English plantations the negroes only are used as slaves; how much to the credit of Christianity I shall not say." – *Commentary on Leviticus 25:39-55, pg. 467*

"Japheth has the blessing of the earth beneath: God shall enlarge Japheth, enlarge his seed, enlarge his border. Japheth's prosperity peopled all Europe, a great part of Asia, and perhaps America." – *Commentary on Genesis 9, pg. 24*

"The temper of some nations is more inclined to some vices than others. The Cretans were too generally such as here described, slothful and ill-natured, false, and perfidious, as the Apostle himself vouches." – *Commentary on Titus 1:12, Comprehensive Commentary, pg. 1360*

"Paul was a Hebrew of the Hebrews. We ought to be in a special manner concerned for the spiritual good of our relations, our brethren and kinsmen. To them we lie under special engagements, and we have more opportunity of doing good to them; and concerning them, and our usefulness to them, we must in a special manner give account." – *Commentary on Romans 9, pg. 218*

"The times are perilous when men will not be held by the bonds either of nature or common honesty, when they are without natural affection, and truce-breakers, v. 3. There is a natural affection due to all. Wherever there is the human nature, there should be humanity towards those of the same nature, but especially between relations. Times are perilous when children are disobedient to their parents (v. 2.) and when parents are without natural affection to their children, v. 3. See what a corruption of nature sin is, how it deprives men even of that which nature has implanted in them for the support of their own kind; for the natural affection of parents to their children is that which contributes very much to the keeping up of mankind upon the earth. And those who will not be bound by natural affection, no marvel that they will not be bound by the most solemn leagues and covenants." – *Commentary on 2 Timothy 3, pg. 391*

Patrick Henry

"This virtue, morality, and religion is the armor, my friend, and this alone, that renders us invincible. These are the tactics we should study. If we lose them, we are conquered, fallen indeed... so long as our manners and principles remain sound, there is no danger. But believing as I do that these are in danger, that infidelity in its broadest sense, under the name of philosophy, is fast spreading, and that everything that ought to be dear to man is covertly but successfully assailed, I feel the value of those men amongst us who hold out to the world the idea, that our continent is to exhibit an originality of character; and that instead of that imitation and inferiority, which the countries of the old world have been in the habit of exacting from the new, we shall maintain that high ground upon which nature has placed us, and that Europe will alike cease to rule us and give us modes of thinking." – In a letter to Archibald Blair, written from Red Hill, Charlotte, 8th January 1799; *Patrick Henry* By Moses Coit Tyler, pg. 365

Frank Herbert

"Jessica stared out into the sunlight. She had heard what she had heard in Stilgar's voice— the unspoken offer of more than his countenance. Did he need a wife? She realized she could step into that place with him. It would be one way to end conflict over tribal leadership—female properly aligned with male. But what of Paul then? Who could tell yet what rules of parenthood prevailed here? And what of the unborn daughter she had carried these few weeks? What of a dead Duke's daughter? And she permitted herself to face fully the significance of this other child growing within her, to see her own motives in permitting the conception. She knew what it was—she had succumbed to that profound drive shared by all creatures who are faced with death—the drive to seek immortality through progeny. The fertility drive of the species had overpowered them." – *Dune*, pg. 359

Johann Gottfried Herder

"The most natural state is, therefore, one nation, an extended family with one national character. This it retains for ages and develops most naturally if the leaders come from the people.... Nothing, therefore, is more manifestly contrary to the purposes of political government than the unnatural enlargement of states, the wild mixing of various races and nationalities under one scepter. A human scepter is far too weak and slender for such incongruous parts to be engrafted upon it. Such states are but patched up contraptions, fragile machines,... and their component parts are connected by mechanical contrivances instead of bonds of sentiment.... It would only be the curse of fate that would condemn to immortality these forced unions, these lifeless monstrosities. But history shows sufficiently that the instruments of human pride are formed of clay, and like all clay, they will dissolve or crumble to pieces." – *Ideas for a Philosophy of the History of Mankind; Herder on Social and Political Culture,* pg. 324

Felicia Hemans

Fair land! of chivalry the old domain,
Land of the vine and olive, lovely Spain!
Though not for thee with classic shores to vie
In charms that fix th' enthusiast's pensive eye;
Yet hast thou scenes of beauty richly fraught
With all that wakes the glow of lofty thought.
– *The Abencerrage, Works*, vol. 2, pg. 18

Herodotus

The Athenians explain to the Spartans why they will not make a pact with Persia but will join in with the Spartans to fight:

"For there are many great reasons why we should not do this, even if we so desired; first and foremost, the burning and destruction of the adornments and temples of our gods, whom we are constrained to avenge to the utmost rather than make pacts with the perpetrator of these things, and next the kinship of all Greeks in blood and speech, and the shrines of gods and the sacrifices that we have in common, and the likeness of our way of life, to all of which it would not befit the Athenians to be false." – *The Histories*, pg. 163

"The Bhudini are a large and powerful nation: they all have deep blue eyes, and bright red hair." – *Histories*, pg. 125

Trevor Herriot

An ornithologist says of his drawings and writings of birds that:

"...each story, argument, species profile, and drawing was conceived within a longing to reclaim the original spirit of grassland that survives yet in its birds. Beneath that longing lie the deeper human wish we all share: to find out how we might belong to a place, to find a way home." – *Grass, Sky, Song: Promise And Peril In World Of Grassland Birds*, pg. 4 [41]

---

41 Bird-watching requires one be settled in a place, familiar with the variation of the ordinary, attentive to the particular.

Theodor Herzl

"With a flag people are led—perhaps even to the Promised Land. For a flag men live and die." – *The Jewish State: An Attempt at a Modern Solution of the Jewish Question*

Hesiod

"And from Ithaca the sacred might of Odysseus, Laërtes' son, who knew many-fashioned wiles, sought her to wife. He never sent gifts for the sake of the neat-ankled maid, for he knew in his heart that golden-haired Menelaus would win, since he was greatest of the Achaeans in possessions and was ever sending messages to horse-taming Castor and prize-winning Polydeuces." – *Catalogues*, fragment 68

"But golden-haired Demeter sat there apart from all the blessed gods and stayed, wasting with yearning for her deep-bosomed daughter." – *Homeric Hymns*, pg. 311

"So said the bright-eyed goddess and swiftly got up into the car with victory." – *Homeric Hymns*, pg. 245

"And blue-eyed Athene went thence to great Olympus." – *Homeric Hymns*, pg. 253

"And golden-haired Dionysus made brown-haired Ariadne, the daughter of Minos, his buxom wife..." – *Homeric Hymns*, pg. 149

"I will sing of stately Aphrodite, gold-crowned and beautiful, whose dominion is the walled cities of all sea-set Cyprus. There the moist breath of the western wind wafted her over the waves of the loud-moaning sea in soft foam, and there the gold-filleted Hours welcomed her joyously. They clothed her with heavenly garments: on her head they put a fine, well-wrought crown of gold, and in her pierced ears they hung ornaments of orichalc and precious gold, and adorned her with golden necklaces over her soft neck and snow-white breasts, jewels which the gold-filleted Hours wear themselves whenever they go to their father's house to join the lovely dances of the gods. And when they had fully decked her, they brought her to the gods, who welcomed her when they saw her, giving her their hands. Each one of them prayed that he might lead her home to be his wedded wife, so greatly were they amazed at the beauty of violet-crowned Cytherea." – *Homeric Hymns*, pg. 427

"And again she bore a third, the evil-minded Hydra of Lerna, whom the goddess, white-armed Hera nourished, being angry beyond measure with the mighty Heracles." ... "Also he came to the bed of all-nourishing Demeter, and she bare white-armed Persephone whom Aidoneus carried off from her mother; but wise Zeus gave her to him." – *Homeric Hymns*, pg. 103

Moses Hess

"After an estrangement of twenty years, I am back with my people. I have come to be one of them again, to participate in the celebration of the holy days, to share the memories and hopes of the nation, to take part in the spiritual and intellectual warfare going on within the House of Israel, on the one hand, and between our people and the surrounding civilized nations, on the other...

"The Jew in exile who denies his nationality will never earn the respect of the nations among whom he dwells." – *Rome and Jerusalem: The Last Nationality Question*, pg. 43

Richard Hess

"She identifies herself as 'black but beautiful' (Song 1:5). The word for 'black' (šĕḥôrâ) elsewhere describes the color of hair (Lev. 13:31, 37; Song 5:11), of a horse (in contrast with the white, red, and dappled ones that were approved; Zech. 6:2, 6), and of skin during an illness (Job 30:30). It identifies a color, not a race, and here it is caused by the sun. The blackness of the skin is explained in Song 1:6, but in v. 5 it is contrasted with the beauty that she claims...

"The blackness of her skin may contrast with the fairness of the complexion of her maidens, though we are not told this. However, it serves as a mark of the female that selects her in contrast to others...

"The female here identifies her form, contrasting her dark skin with her beauty. This is compared to dark tents that, like her skin and form, cover the inhabitant. The woman's 'tent' is exotic like those of Qedar, and it is magnificent like that of Solomon.

"It furthers the brothers' hostility in their act of placing their sister in the vineyard, where they know she will lose her fair complexion under the angry sun...

"Thus the female's own body has not been cared for as would be appropriate for someone seeking love. She has not devoted herself to her physical appearance because her domestic tasks have not permitted it. Worse than that, they have actively contributed to a skin condition other than what she might have wanted...

"The darkness of the skin forms a badge of her social condition in which her past may not measure up to the expectations of class before the maidens of Jerusalem." – *Baker Commentary on the Old Testament Wisdom and Psalms*, Song Of Songs 1:6, pgs. 64-69

Theodore Hiebert

"Like his father (Adam), he (Cain) is an errant farmer, transgressing a divine command (2:16-17; 4:7). The result of disobedience is the same for both (Adam and Cain): the relationship between farmer and soil is imperiled. For Adam the ground is cursed and yields its produce only to great labor (3:17-19); for Cain the ground refuses to produce at all (4:12)." – Genesis 4 commentary. *Yahwist's Landscape: Nature and Religion in Early Israel*, pg. 40 [42]

Hierocles of Alexandria

"After the discourse on the gods, it is most reasonable to take up how one should behave toward one's country. For it is, as it were, a kind of second god, or, by Zeus, a first and greater parent; indeed, he who gave its name to the thing [i.e., πατρίς, that is, 'fatherland'] did not do so ineptly, since he modeled it on father [πατήρ] but produced it in the feminine, so that, like a mixture, it should acquire both a paternal and a maternal [dignity]. This reasoning, indeed, suggests that we honor our country, which is one, on a par with our two parents, so as in fact to prefer our country to either one of those who bore us, and not even to honor the two together more than it, but rather to hold them in equal respect. But there is also another argument, which exhorts us to honor our country more than both our parents together, and not only more than them, but also more than our wife

together with them, and our children and our friends and, in a word, more than all other things, apart from the gods." – *Elements*, pg. 69

"A discussion of marriage is most necessary. For our entire race is naturally disposed to community, and the first and most elementary of the communities is that in accord with marriage. For there would not be cities if there were not households, and the household of an unmarried man is in truth only half complete, but that of a man who is married is complete and full." – *Elements*, pg. 73

Hilary of Poitiers

"These are not our own conjectures which we offer, nor do we falsely put together any of these things in order to deceive the ears of our hearers by perverting the meaning of words; but holding fast the form of sound teaching we know and preach the things which are true. For the Apostle shews that this unity of the faithful arises from the nature of the sacraments when he writes to the Galatians, For as many of you as were baptized into Christ did put on Christ. There is neither Jew nor Greek, there is neither bond nor free, there is neither male nor female; for ye are all one in Christ Jesus. That these are one amid so great diversities of race, condition, sex,—is it from an agreement of will or from the unity of the sacrament, since these have one baptism and have all put on one Christ? What, therefore, will a concord of minds avail here when they are one in that they have put on one Christ through the nature of one baptism?" – *On The Trinity*, bk. 8; *A Select Library*, pg. 139

D.H. Hill

"The Latin poet has beautifully said that they who change their sky do not change their minds. The emigrant from his natal soil carries with him his old opinions, his old sentiments, and his old habits. In selecting a place for his residence in the land of his adoption, he seeks some hill or vale which resembles the spot on which stands the dear old homestead far away. The new edifice is made as near alike as may be to the paternal building. His garden, his vineyard, his orchard, his grounds are fashioned after the models so fondly cherished in

---

42   The curse of Adam and of Cain is the same: displacement, wandering, unsettlement.

his memory. His style of living, his mode of thought, his habits, his manners, his passions, and his prejudices will all be unchanged. The accents that first struck his childish ear will still be heard with delight, and most joyfully will he meet some countryman from that loved land, with whom he may converse in his sacred native tongue. And still more grateful will it be to him to find a colony of his own people, where familiar tones will ever greet him, and where the worship and customs of his fathers will ever be preserved. And in fact it is just because men do not change their minds with their sky that these colonies so frequently dot the surface of this mighty Republic.

"To us there is something beautiful in this love for home and home associations, this clinging to the language, the religion, and the customs transmitted from generation to generation; and we never pass such a settlement from the Old World without the feeling that they who venerate the traditions of the past will respect the laws of the present, and that they whose hearts go out toward those of their own blood and tongue are the better prepared thereby to exercise benevolence toward all mankind. He who does not love his own family better than the whole of the rest of the world, who does not love his own land better than all the countries on earth, is so far from being a Christian and patriot, that he is a monster utterly unworthy of trust and confidence. The Apostle Paul pronounces him to be worse than an infidel. So strong was sectional love in the great apostle himself that he could wish himself accursed from Christ for the sake of his brethren, his kinsmen according to the flesh. Moses, the heaven-appointed leader of Israel, who talked with God face to face, as a man talketh with his friend, went even beyond Paul in his devotion to his people, and did actually offer the request which Paul expressed his willingness to offer:

"Yet now, if thou wilt forgive their sin; and if not, blot me, I pray thee, out of thy book, which thou hast written.

"Among the sweet psalms of David, the man after God's own heart, and constituting a part of the sacred canon of Scripture, is the touching lament of the captive at Babylon as the representative of the true-hearted Israelite, invoking a fearful curse upon himself if ever found wanting in love to his native land. 'If I forget thee, Je-rusalem, let my right hand forget her cunning. If I do not remember thee, let my tongue cleave to the roof of my mouth; if I prefer not Jerusalem above my chief joy.' Jeremiah, the holy prophet who was sanctified ere he was born, represents himself as weeping day and night for the miseries of his people. Nehemiah, while a member of the household of the king of Babylon, and occupying toward him the confidential relation of cup-bearer, had no relish for the enjoyments of that most luxurious city when he heard the sad news from his native land. So profound was his grief that the imperious monarch noticed it, and was offended. 'Wherefore, the king said unto me, 'Why is thy countenance sad, seeing thou art not sick? This is nothing else but sorrow of heart.' Then I was very sore afraid, and said unto the king, 'Let the king live forever: why should not my countenance be sad when the city, the place of my fathers' sepulchers lieth waste, and the gates thereof are consumed by fire?'

"With all these holy men of old, love to their own nation was a part of their religion, nor did they understand that modern philanthropy which consists in going to the uttermost parts of the earth to seek objects of its beneficence, while squalor, ignorance, sin and misery are all around it at home. One of this school, whose name is a household word throughout the civilized world, visited every abode of wretchedness in Europe, but left his own son to become a maniac through neglect and cruelty. On the contrary, our Saviour spent his energies and his activities in Judea and Galilee. His life of labor, privation, and suffering passed away among his own people. His last instructions to his disciples were to begin their ministry at Jerusalem, the capital of his native country. His example hallows the sweet charities which begin at home, and sheds a fragrance around that holy feeling which burns in the bosom of the patriot for the land we love." – *The Land We Love*, vol. 1, pg. 1

Bonaventure Hinwood

"Consequently at the same time as acknowledging the diversity and singularity of races, the Church rejects, equally with the racist assertions of radical racial superiority and inferiority, the tendency towards a depreciation and leveling of races found at the opposite extreme. It does this in the confidence that Christianity, grounded in reality and truth, is able to harmonize the affirmation of the radical unity of mankind with the recognition of racial diversity…There can therefore be no better way of combatting racism and racial discrimination, than by a sane and realistic acknowledgement of the facts of race and of historical and cultural inequalities." – *Race*, pg. 103

"That racial differences are not only somatic but also psychic, not only material in their influence but also spiritual, is among the facts of race which are readily accepted in the Church, and regarded as fundamental by catholic writers, because of the integral unity of the human person." – *Race*, pg. 105

"Pope Pius XII, speaking of the human composite, emphasized the perfect union of soul and body … In virtue of this integral wholeness he pointed out the value, but also the unfathomableness, of the transmission of a treasure of material and spiritual riches in a hereditary group, perpetuating the same physical and spiritual type from generation to generation. There is no denying the material substratum of this transmission, since, on account of the intimate union of soul and body, even the most spiritual activities depend on the body. Hence heredity is worthy of high esteem, even from the supernatural viewpoint." – *Race*, pg. 105-106

"For the community of blood between people, whether in families or in larger collectivities, brings with it duties and responsibilities, because, granted that the formal element of human societies is of the psychic and moral order, nevertheless heredity is its material foundation, which merits great respect and must not be injured. So it is that whatever can be said about heredity in a restricted sphere can also be applied in a modified way to the vast groups which constitute the races of mankind. Nevertheless, like his successor, Pope John XXIII, Pope Pius XII did not stop at the merely negative point of censuring the injury of the hereditary racial factors, but gave his blessing to all wise and moderate regulations and efforts aimed at the evolution and flourishing of the potentialities and powers that spring up from the hidden sources of life of the different races. All this had already been foreshadowed in Pope Pius XI's encyclical against racism, when he ranked race among the fundamental values of human

society in the order of the world as designed and created by God. This he would hardly have done had he considered race a superficial and incidental matter of little or no import, simply a 'question of colour' as some would put it." – *Race*, pg. 106

"…the Church recognizes a real diversity among the races of men, in virtue of which each race has something which is peculiar and native to it, and which Popes Pius XII and John XXIII call 'innate potentialities' or 'innate dispositions.' It is by no means surprising, therefore, to find numerous explicit testimonies to this racial diversity, which some authors even go so far as to compare with the differences existing between the two sexes." – *Race*, pg. 107

"Taking as his basis the principles that a race is something good in the order or creation, and that mankind is enriched by a diversity of races, Folliet reasons as follows. Since being and goodness are convertible, race, like any other human factor not inherently vitiated by error or evil, being a positive good, has the right to existence and identity… Since mankind has a right not to be mutilated by the violent destruction of any race, it is licit for a person even to lay down his life for the conservation of his race." – *Race*, pg. 111

"…because nature in producing its effects does not operate aimlessly and by chance, but rather gives concrete form to and reflects the pattern of things in the mind of the supreme Architect, it must therefore be admitted that ethnic groups, 'solidarities of similarity,' have their own inherent purpose. The consciousness and will of the individual gravitate naturally in the first place towards the ethnic group to which he belongs. The innate human tendency towards solidarity aroused and stimulated by this consciousness gives rise to that communal aspiration, which is the psychic prerequisite for the existence of any social life and any society." – *Race*, pg. 112

"For each race has the right to peaceful expansion, by multiplying itself through procreation, by promoting the purity of its blood and its physical vigour, and by cultivating its psychic potentialities, in all of which the civil authorities should cooperate. Whence the members of a race have a responsibility towards their racial heritage." – *Race*, pg. 114

Hippocrates of Kos

"The Scythians are a ruddy race because of the cold, not through any fierceness in the sun's heat. It is the cold that burns their white skin and turns it ruddy." – *De Aere Aquis Et Locis*, pg. 20

Hippolytus of Rome

Chapter 16 repeats the section about concubine slaves from Apostolic Church-Order above, and in chapter 15:

"Those who are newly brought forward to hear the Word shall first be brought before the teachers at the house, before all the people enter. Then they will be questioned concerning the reason that they have come forward to the faith. Those who bring them will bear witness concerning them as to whether they are able to hear.

"They shall be questioned concerning their life and occupation, marriage status, and whether they are slave or free. If they are the slaves of any of the faithful, and if their masters permit them, they may hear the Word. If their masters do not bear witness that they are good, let them be rejected. If their masters are pagans, teach them to please their masters, so that there will be no blasphemy." – *Canons of Hippolytus*, quoted in *Thriving in Babylon*, pg. 371 [43]

Hittite Laws

"168: If anyone violates the boundary of a field and takes 1 furrow off [the neighbor's field], the owner of the field shall cut one gipeššar of field [from the other's field] and take it for himself. He who violated the boundary, shall give 1 sheep, 10 loaves [and] 1 jug of strong beer and resanctify the field.

"169: If anyone buys a field and then violates the boundary, he shall take a sacrificial loaf, break it for the Sun-god and say: 'Thou hast planted my balance in the ground.' Thus he shall say; [whether it is] the Sun-god [or] the Storm-god, does not make any difference." – quoted in *The Ancient Near Eastern Texts Relating to the Old Testament*, pg. 195

Eric Hobsbawm

"While governments were plainly engaged in conscious and deliberate ideological engineering, it would be a mistake to see these exercises as pure manipulation from above. They were, indeed, most successful when they could build on already present unofficial nationalist sentiments, whether of demotic xenophobia or chauvinism . . . or, more likely, in nationalism among the middle and lower middle classes." – *Nations and Nationalism Since 1780*, pg. 92

Archibald Alexander Hodge

"Millenarian missionaries have a style of their own. Their theory affects their work in the way of making them seek exclusively, or chiefly, the conversion of individual souls. The true and efficient missionary method is, to aim directly, indeed, at soul winning, but at the same time to plant Christian institutions in heathen lands, which will, in time, develop according to the genius of nationalities. English missionaries can never hope to convert the world directly by units." – *Princetoniana*, pgs. 238-239

Charles Hodge

"Whether the slaves of this country may be safely admitted to the enjoyments of personal liberty, is a matter of dispute; but that they can not, consistently with the public welfare, be entrusted with the exercise of political power, is on all hands admitted." – *Slavery*, pg. 502

"If the fact that the master and slave belong to different races, precludes the possibility of their living together on equal terms, the inference is, not that the one has a right to oppress the other, but that they should separate. Whether this should be done by dividing the land between them and giving rise to distinct communities, or by the removal of the inferior class on just and wise conditions, it is not for us to say. We have undertaken only to express an opinion as to the manner in which the Bible directs those, who look to it for guidance, to treat this difficult subject, and not to trace out a plan to provide for ulterior results. It is for this reason, we have said nothing of African colonization, though

---

43 These Canons have a curious provision for a confessor who is a slave (and therefore incapable of receiving ordination); such a one is "a presbyter for the congregation," even though he does not receive "the insignia of the presbyterate."

we regard it as one of the noblest enterprises of modern benevolence." – *Slavery*, pg. 511

"Under the old dispensation it [slavery] was expressly permitted by divine command, and under the New Testament is nowhere forbidden or denounced, but on the contrary, acknowledged to be consistent with the Christian character and profession (that is, consistent with justice, mercy, holiness, love to God and love to man), to declare it to be a heinous crime, is a direct impeachment of the word of God. We, therefore, felt it incumbent upon us to prove, that the sacred Scriptures are not in conflict with the first principles of morals; that what they sanction is not the blackest and basest of all offences in the sight of God." – *Slavery*, pg. 503

"This is a law of our being…Members of the same nation have a feeling for each other which they have not for foreigners. Members of the same tribe or class in a community are bound together by a still closer tie." – *The Unity of the Church*, pg. 24

"It cannot be denied that there is a great difference in men in this respect. Some are morose, irritable, and unsocial in their dispositions, others are directly the reverse … They may be born with these distinctive traits of character, and such traits beyond doubt are in numerous cases innate and often hereditary … It is admitted that nations as well as tribes and families, have their distinctive characteristics, and that these characteristics are not only physical and mental, but also social and moral. Some tribes are treacherous and cruel. Some are mild and confiding. Some are addicted to gain, others to war. Some are sensual, some intellectual. We instinctively judge of each according to its character; we like or dislike, approve or disapprove, without asking ourselves any questions as to the origin of these distinguishing characteristics. And if we do raise that question, although we are forced to answer it by admitting that these dispositions are innate and hereditary, and that they are not self-acquired by the individual whose character they constitute, we nevertheless, and none the less, approve or condemn them according to their nature. This is instinctive and necessary, and therefore the correct, judgment of the mind. …

"The Irish people have always been remark-

— CHARLES HODGE —

able for their fidelity; the English for honesty; the Germans for truthfulness. These national traits, as revealed in individuals, are not the effect of self-discipline. They are innate, hereditary dispositions, as obviously as the physical, mental, or emotional peculiarities by which one people is distinguished from another. And yet by the common judgment of men this fact in no degree detracts from the moral character of these dispositions." – *Systematic Theology*, vol. 2, ch. 5, sec. 6, pg. 112

"[The] differences between the Caucasian, Mongolian, and Negro races, which is known to have been as distinctly marked two or three thousand years before Christ as it is now. … [T]hese varieties of race are not the effect of the blind operation of physical causes, but by those cause as intelligently guided by God for the accomplishment of some wise purpose. … So God fashions the different races of men in their peculiarities to suit them to the regions which they inhabit." – *Systematic Theology*, vol. 2, ch. 1, sec. 3, pg. 39

"Paul had two classes of brethren; those who were with him the children of God in Christ; these he calls brethren in the Lord, Philip, i. 14, holy brethren, &c. The others were those who belonged to the family of Abraham. These he calls brethren after the flesh, that is, in virtue of natural descent from the same parent. Philemon he addresses as his brother, both in the flesh and in the Lord. The Bible recognizes the validity and rightness of all the constitutional principles and impulses of our nature. It therefore approves of parental and filial affection, and, as is plain from this and other passages, of peculiar love for the people of our own race and country." – *Commentary* on Romans 9:4, pg. 298

James Hoffmeier

"Were ancient territorial borders taken seriously and was national sovereignty recognized? The answer is emphatically yes...Nowhere in the Old Testament is there any sense that a nation had to accept immigrants, nor was being received as an alien a right." – *The Immigration Crisis*, pg. 32, pg. 156

Anthony Hoekema

"In this way human beings reflect God, who exists not as a solitary being but as a being in fellowship—a fellowship that is described at a later stage of divine revelation as that between the Father, the Son, and the Holy Spirit. From the fact that God blessed human beings and gave them a mandate (v. 28), we may infer that humans also resemble God in that they are persons, responsible beings, who can be addressed by God and who are ultimately responsible to God as their Creator and Ruler. As God is here revealed as a person (later in the history of revelation this is expanded to three persons) who is able to make decisions and to rule, so man is a person who is likewise able to make decisions and to rule." – *Created in God's Image*, pg. 14

"The fact that the new self is said to be progressively renewed after the image of its Creator implies that man through his fall into sin has so corrupted the original image that it must be restored in the process of redemption." – (Commenting on Colossians 3:9-10) *Created in God's Image*, pg. 26

"...to be faithful to the biblical evidence, our understanding of the image of God must include these two senses: (1) The image of God as such is an unlosable aspect of man, a part of his essence and existence, something that man cannot lose without ceasing to be man. (2) The image of God, however, must also be understood as that likeness to God which was perverted when man fell into sin, and is being restored and renewed in the process of sanctification." – *Created in God's Image*, pg. 32

Elias B. Holmes

"I am for my country, any way and always, right or wrong. In all time, under all circumstances, in prosperity or in adversity, in peace or in war, in every aspect which ingenuity can invent or imagination can conceive, I am for my country, right or wrong. Sir, I am for my children, right or wrong. My duty impels me to chide and rebuke them when wrong; but to be for them, and feel for them, and to act for their prosperity, happiness and protection, where right or wrong, is a feeling interwoven with the very ligaments of my nature. Sir, in this same sense I am for my country, right or wrong; freely reproving her public functionaries when wrong, and holding up their constitutional aggressions and their legislative oppressions to the just judgment of the people." – *Speech On The Mexican War*, delivered in the House of Representatives of the U.S., June 18, 1846; *History of Congress Biographical and Political; Comprising Memoirs of Members of the Congress of the United States*, vol. 1, pg. 460

Homer

"Are the sons of Atreus the only men in the world who love their wives? Any man of common right feeling will love and cherish her who is his own, as I this woman, with my whole heart, though she was but a fruitling of my spear." – *Iliad*, Butler trans., pg. 135

"I am Odysseus, son of Laertes, known to the world for every kind of craft —my fame has reached the skies. Sunny Ithaca is my home. Atop her stands our seamark, Mount Neriton's leafy ridges shimmering in the wind. Around her a ring of islands circle side-by-side, Dulichion, Same, wooded Zacynthus too, but mine lies low and away, the farthest out to sea, rearing into the western dusk while the others face the east and breaking day. Mine is a rugged land but good for raising sons — and I myself, I know no sweeter sight on earth than a man's own native country. True enough, Calypso the lustrous goddess tried to hold me back, deep in her arching caverns, craving me for a husband. So did Circe, holding me just as warmly in her halls, the bewitching queen of Aeaea keen to have me too. But they never won the heart inside me, never. So nothing is as sweet as a man's own country, his own parents, even though he's settled down in some luxurious house, off in a foreign land and far from those who bore him." – *Odyssey*, Fagles trans., pg. 212

"Those of them who tasted the sweetest fruit of the lotus had no desire to return to report news but preferred to stay with those geniuses to taste the lotus, forgetting the homeland." – *Odyssey*, Murray trans., pg. 82

"Without a sign, his sword the brave man draws, and asks no omen, but his country's cause." – *Iliad*, Pope trans., pg. 230

"For he lay in idleness among the ships in wrath because of the fair-haired girl Briseïs." – *Iliad*, Murray trans., pg. 101

"As she spoke Athena touched him with her wand and covered him with wrinkles, took away all his yellow hair, and withered the flesh over his whole body; she bleared his eyes, which were naturally very fine ones; she changed his clothes and threw an old rag of a wrap about him, and a tunic, tattered, filthy, and begrimed with smoke; she also gave him an undressed deer skin as an outer garment, and furnished him with a staff and a wallet all in holes, with a twisted thong for him to sling it over his shoulder." – *Odyssey*, Butler trans., pg. 169

— HOMER —

"And now would the king of men, Aeneas, have perished, had not the daughter of Zeus, Aphrodite, been quick to mark, even his mother, that conceived him to Anchises as he tended his kine. About her dear son she flung her white arms, and before him she spread a fold of her bright garment to be a shelter against missiles, lest any of the Danaans with swift horses might hurl a spear of bronze into his breast and take away his life." – *Iliad*, Murray trans., pg. 217

"But goodly Alexander did don about his shoulders his beautiful armour, even he, the lord of fair-haired Helen." – *Iliad*, Murray trans., pg. 141

"...when fair-haired Demeter amid the driving blasts of wind separates the grain from the chaff..." – *Iliad*, Murray trans., pg. 231

"For I, too, being their ally, was numbered among them on the day when the Amazons came, the peers of men. Howbeit not even they were as many as are the bright-eyed Achaeans." – *Iliad*, Murray trans., pg. 131

"Let her gather the older women on the Acropolis, at bright-eyed (blue) Athena's shrine: unlock the doors of the sacred temple, and lay on the knees of golden-haired Athena." – *Iliad*, Kline trans., pg. 125
"Theano took the robe, laid it on golden-haired Athena's knees.." – *Iliad*, Kline trans., pg. 130

"Athena came down from heaven: She stood behind him [Achilles] and held him back by his long yellow hair. No other man saw her but Achilles alone." – *Iliad*, Johnston's trans., 1.190

"Men say that you [Achilles] are son to noble Peleus [grandson of Zeus], and that your mother is Thetis, fair-haired daughter of the sea." – *Iliad*, Butler trans., pg. 313

"Achilles then bethought him of another matter. He went and cut off the yellow lock which he had let grow." – *Iliad*, Butler trans., pg. 355

"Our people who saw it, when they carried fair-haired Rhadamanthus to visit Tityus" – *Odyssey*, Murray trans., pg. 255

"Show me the way to town, and give me some

rags to throw over me, perhaps whatever wrapped the clothes you brought. And may the gods grant you all your heart's desire, a husband and a home, and mutual harmony, in all its beauty. Since nothing is finer or better than when a man and a woman of one heart and mind stay together, a joy to their friends, a sorrow to their enemies: their own reputation of the very highest…Now Nausicaa of the white arms had another idea…'" – *Odyssey*, Kline trans., pg. 170

"This I heard from fair-haired Calypso, and she said that she herself had heard it from the messenger Hermes." – *Odyssey*, Murray trans., pg. 464

Homer describes how Athena made Penelope, the wife of Odysseus, even more beautiful than she was normally:
    "Meanwhile the goddess, bright-eyed Athene, had another idea. She shed sweet sleep over Penelope, so that she leaned back, her limbs relaxed, and fell asleep on her couch. Then the lovely goddess endowed her with immortal gifts, so the Achaeans would wonder at her. First she cleansed her lovely face with beauty itself, am-brosial beauty such as Cythereia of the lovely crown anoints herself with when she joins with the Graces in their sweet dance. She made her taller and statelier too, and whiter of skin than new-cut ivory. As the lovely goddess left, the white-armed maids came from the hall, chatter-ing together." – *Odyssey*, Kline trans., pg. 480
"…ambrosial loveliness that Aphrodite wears when she goes dancing with the Graces, while as for her complexion it was whiter than sawn ivory." – *Odyssey*, Butler trans., pg. 229

"On this Athena came close up to him and said, 'Son of Arceisius—pray to the blue-eyed dam-sel, and to Zeus her father.'" – *Odyssey*, Butler trans., pg. 305

Richard Hooker

Affirming social inequality as part of the created order:
    "Without Order there is no living in public Society, because the want thereof is the mother of confusion, whereupon division of necessity followeth; and out of division destruction…

If things and persons be ordered, this doth imply that they are distinguished by degrees: for Order is a gradual disposition. The whole world consisting of parts so many, so different, is by this only thing upheld; he which framed them, hath set them in order. The very Deity itself both keepeth and requireth for ever this to be kept as a Law, that wheresoever there is a coagmentation of many, the lowest be knit unto the highest by that which being interjacent may cause each to cleave to the other, so all continue one. This order of things and persons in public Societies is the work of Policy, and the proper instrument hereof in every degree is Power." – *Laws of Ecclesiastical Polity*, Book VIII, pg. 390

Herbert Hoover

"The unit of American life is the family and the home. Through it vibrates every hope of the future. It is the economic unit as well as the moral and spiritual unit. But it is more than this. It is the beginning of self-government. It is the throne of our highest ideals. It is the center of the spiritual energy of our people." – *The Challenge to Liberty*, 1934; *Herbert Hoover As Secretary of Commerce*, pg. 228

"Thousands of villages and towns would be deprived of their employment. Their schools, churches and skills would be greatly deci-mated." – Herbert Hoover, October 24, 1953, *Post-Presidential Papers*, HCH. [44]

Hans-Hermann Hoppe

"In a covenant founded for the purpose of protecting family and kin, there can be no tolerance toward those habitually promoting lifestyles incompatible with this goal. They— the advocates of alternative, non-family and kin-centered lifestyles such as, for instance, individual hedonism, parasitism, nature-envi-ronment worship, homosexuality, or commu-nism—will have to be physically removed from society, too, if one is to maintain a libertarian order." – *Democracy*, pg. 218

"[Libertarian leader Ludwig von Mises] grew up in a multinational state and was painfully aware of the antiliberal results of majority rule in ethnically mixed territories. Rather than

44 Predicting the consequences of throwing open U. S. markets in the post-WWII period

majority rule, to Mises 'democracy' meant literally 'self-determination, self-government, self-rule,' and accordingly, a democratic government was an essentially voluntary membership organization in that it recognized each of its constituents' unrestricted right to secession." – *Democracy*, pg. 79

"The ideal of the left- or 'modal'- libertarians, as Murray referred to them, of 'live and let live as long as you don't aggress against anyone else,' that sounds so appealing to adolescents in rebellion against parental authority and any social convention and control, may be sufficient for people living far apart and dealing and trading with each other only indirectly and from afar.

"But it is decidedly insufficient when it comes to people living in close proximity to each other, as neighbors and cohabitants of the same community. The peaceful cohabitation of neighbors and of people in regular direct contact with each other on some territory requires also a commonality of culture: of language, religion, custom, and convention.

"There can be peaceful co-existence of different cultures on distant, physically separated territories, but multiculturalism, cultural heterogeneity, cannot exist in one and the same place and territory without leading to diminishing social trust, increased conflict, and ultimately the destruction of anything resembling a libertarian social order." – *Getting Libertairianism Right*

Horace

Grant to our sons unblemish'd ways;
Grant to our sires an age of peace;
Grant to our nation power and praise,
And large increase.
Faith, Honour, ancient Modesty,
And Peace and Virtue, spite of scorn,
Come back to earth; and Plenty, see,
With teeming horn. – *Odes*, pg. 128

"Fortune keeps a smiling face, at Rome let Samos be praised, and Chios and Rhodes— though far away! And you—whatever hour God has given for your weal, take it with grateful hand, nor put off joys from year to year; so that, in whatever place you have been, you may say that you have lived happily. For if 'tis reason and wisdom that take away cares, and not a site commanding a wide expanse of sea, they change their clime, not their mind, who rush across the sea. Tis a busy idleness that is our bane; with yachts and cars we seek to make life happy. What you are seeking is here; it is at Ulubrae, if there fail you not a mind well balanced." – *Epistles*, pg. 325

"Fortunate the man who, free from cares,
 like men of old still works
His father's fields with his own oxen,
 encumbered by no debt.
No solider he, aroused by bugle's blare,
 nor does he fear the angry sea.
The Forum he avoids and lofty doors
 of powerful citizens.

"And so, to daughters of the vine
when they are come of age,
he weds tall poplars;
in sheltered vallyes sees
his wandering herds of lowing cattle;
or with his sickle prunes
the useless growth
and grafts more fruitful shoots;
or stores pressed honey in clean jars;
or shears his helpless sheep.

"When Autumn raises in the fields
its head with fruit so richly crowned,
with what delight he plucks the pears
he grafted and grapes
that challenge any purple dye...
He loves to lie beneath an ancient ilex tree,
or deep in grass too lush to leave,
as all the while the water glides
between high banks,
and birds are moaning in the woods,
and leaves speak out
against the flowing stream,
and every sound invites to easy sleep.

"But when the thunder of Jove's
winter season musters the rains and snows,
with all his dogs on every side
he drives wild boar into his ring of nets,
or stretches wide-meshed toils
on twigs he's smoothed
to trap the greedy thrushes,
and hunts the timid hare and crane
migrating to his snare – delicious prey.
Amid these pleasures who
would not forget the miseries
brought on by love?

"But if chaste wife were there
to play her part and make the home
and children sweet,
like Sabine women,
or like sun-scorched wife
of busy farmer in Apulia,
she'd heap the sacred hearth
with seasoned logs to wait
her weary husband's coming,
shutting the lusty flock
in wattle pens and milking swollen udders,
decanting this year's wine
from its sweet cask,
and setting out a meal unbought.

"Then oysters from the Lucrine Lake
would hold no charm for me,
nor turbot, not the parrot-wrasse,
if storms of thunder rumbling in the East
should drive them into our Italian sea.
No guinea fowl from Africa
nor heathcock from Ionia
would then go down my throat
so tastily as the choice olives
picked from richest branches of my trees,
or sorrel leaf that loves our meadowlands,
or mallows so digestible for invalids,
or lamb killed on the holy day of Treminus,
or kid snatched from the wolf.
At such a feast what pleasure it would give
to see the full-fed sheep all hurry home,
to see the weary oxen drag on sluggish necks
their plough with share upturned,
while houseborn slaves,
the rich hive's swarm,
stand by the hearth around its smiling god." –
Beatus Ille, Epodes, pgs. 4-5

A.E. Housman

"Loveliest of trees, the cherry now
Is hung with bloom along the bough,
And stands about the woodland ride
Wearing white for Eastertide."
– *A Shropshire Lad II: Loveliest of Trees, the Cherry Now* (lines 1-4) [45]

"Clay lies still, but blood's a rover;
Breath's a ware that will not keep.
Up, lad; when the journey's over
There'll be time enough to sleep."
– *A Shropshire Lad IV: Reveille* (lines 13-16)

"Into my heart an air that kills
From yon far country blows:
What are those blue remembered hills,
What spires, what farms are those?
That is the land of lost content,
I see it shining plain,
The happy highways where I went
And cannot come again."
– *A Shropshire Lad XL: Into My Heart an Air That Kills* (lines 1-8)

Hávamál

A son is better, though late he be born,
And his father to death have fared;
Memory-stones seldom stand by the road
Save when kinsman honors his kin.
– *Poetic Edda, The Ballad of the High One*, pg. 72

Give praise to the day at evening,
    to a woman on her pyre,
To a weapon which is tried,
    to a maid at wed lock,
To ice when it is crossed,
    to ale that is drunk.
...
In a brother's slayer, if thou meet him abroad,
In a half-burned house, in a horse full swift–
One leg is hurt and the horse is useless–
None had ever such faith as to trust in them all.
– *Poetic Edda, The Ballad of the High One*, pg. 45

Billing's daughter I found on her bed,
In slumber bright as the sun;
Empty appeared an earl's estate
Without that form so fair.
– *Poetic Edda, The Ballad of the High One*, pg. 48

Rodney Howard-Browne

"Bonded by blood, history and heritage, Americans were never united by a political ideology, not even by the concept of democracy. 'Democracy wastes, exhausts, and murders itself,' John Adams wrote in a letter to John Taylor in 1814. Even Thomas Jefferson, the most 'democratic' of the Founding Fathers, possessed doubts about this system of government. 'A democracy,' he wrote to Isaac Tiffany in 1816, 'is the only pure republic, but impracticable beyond the limits of a town.' James Madison, the author of the Constitution, was consider-

---

45   A.E. Housman's collection "A Shropshire Lad" is filled with poems that express nostalgia and longing for the English countryside. Here are some quotations from the collection that showcase these themes:

ably more guarded in his opinion of this system of government. In The Federalist No.10, he maintained: 'Democracies have been spectacles of turbulence and contention; have ever been incompatible with personal security or the rights of property; and have in general been as short in their lives as they have been violent in the death.' Alexander Hamilton, the most undemocratic of the Founding Fathers, wrote: 'The ancient democracies, in which the people themselves deliberated, never possessed one feature of good government. Their very nature was tyranny.'

"Recognizing that the United States was an organic entity, a unique blend of Western Europeans within an Anglo-American model, legislation was enacted to safeguard the racial and ethnic composition of the country as it existed at the turn of the twentieth century. Such laws culminated in the Immigration Act of 1924, which limited immigration by a quota system. The number of newcomers was now limited to 2 percent of each nationality who lived in the country not in 1924 but in 1890. The reliance of this legislation on the ethnic composition of America before the turn of the century guaranteed that the majority of new arrivals in the future would be from Northern Europe. ...

"America was a nation because of its lack of diversity. Its organic nature stemmed from its very tribalism, the fact that the people who inhabited the country shared a common heritage, a common history, and a common faith." – *The Killing of Uncle Sam*, pgs. xviii-xx

John Howting

"One cannot achieve the supernatural virtues at the expense of the natural ones. And the supernatural virtues are much more difficult to exercise. Men need to practice the natural ones before attempting the supernatural ones. God introduced men to an 'eye for an eye' before He told them to 'turn the other cheek.' Christianity teaches that charity is a supernatural virtue. But Christianity also teaches that charity begins at home. If one cannot be pious, how can one be charitable? Piety is not a part of charity, but piety is anterior to charity." – *Protectionism as a Path to Piety*

"As creatures, we owe everything to the Creator. Therefore, nothing can be more just than honoring God the Father, giving Him what He is due. But it stands to reason that the man who cannot honor his father on earth will struggle to honor his Father in heaven. There is something in this earthly order that directs man to the heights." – *Protectionism*

"We are born into an hierarchical structure: family, folk, fatherland. To live piously is to accept one's place in this structure, which entails favoring the near over the far. This includes favoring one's family and countrymen over foreigners. Favoring the far-off over the nearby is impious. Thus, importing foreign workers to do the work that one's neighbors could do is impious. Exporting work to foreign lands that could be done by one's neighbors is impious. We owe something to our father simply because he is our father, and to our fatherland simply because it is our fatherland." – *Protectionism*

"Exalting the science of economics over the natural order and our obligations to it is impious. Science does not change the fact that we were born into our communities, to our fathers, and to our fatherlands. It is impious and unjust to revolt against this order." – *Protectionism*

R. Kent Hughes

"Practically, Paul was saying that they were not living in Athens as a result of some cosmic accident. Rather, God had structured their lives in order to attract them to him. Great truths about God led to the truth about themselves: they were specially created by God, and he was seeking a personal relationship with them." – *Acts (ESV Edition): The Church Afire*

"God's plan for preserving the family calls for keeping the fifth commandment...

"If we analyze the Ten Commandments this way, then the second table of the law would begin with the fifth commandment. This is significant. In telling us how to treat one another, God starts with our families. Loving our neighbor starts at home...

"The relationship between parent and child is the first and primary relationship, the beginning of all human society. Under ordinary circumstances, the first people a child knows are his parents. God intends the family to be our first hospital, first school, first government, first church. If we do not respect authority at home, we will not respect it anywhere. Charity really does begin at home!...

"The expression 'live long in the land' is a Hebrew phrase for the fullness of God's blessing. It means to have an abundant life. This is confirmed by the New Testament, which says, '"Honor your father and mother" . . . that it may go well with you and that you may enjoy long life on the earth' (Eph. 6:2, 3). Anyone who wants to live long and prosper should honor his mother and father....

"When God tells us to respect our parents, he is telling us to respect anyone who has legitimate authority over us." – with Ryken, *Exodus: Saved for God's Glory (Preaching the Word)*, 20:12, pgs. 908-912

"The inevitable fact is, with the rhythm of generations a dramatic reversal comes to us all. We who once held our helpless children in our arms and nursed them and provided for their every need will one day be held in their arms as they nurse us at the end of our lives. This responsibility will come to us all. And when we sons and daughters do this, we are only making 'some return to [our] parents.' We will be living out the fifth commandment. We will be 'show[ing] godliness to [our] own household.' We will not have God's approval without such loving family care—'for this is pleasing in the sight of God.'

"The negative expression of our filial responsibility is meant to shock us: 'But if anyone does not provide for his relatives, and especially for members of his household, he has denied the faith and is worse than an unbeliever' (v. 8). This is a scathing judgment—almost all pagans in Roman times did take care of their parents. To do less than an unbeliever denies the faith because it is an act worse than a person who makes no profession of faith." – *Preach The Word Commentary, 1-2 Timothy and Titus: To Guard the Deposit*, pg. 186. 1 Tim 5:3-8

Victor Hugo

"The author of this book, who regrets the necessity of mentioning himself, has been absent from Paris for many years. Paris has been transformed since he quitted it. A new city has arisen, which is, after a fashion, unknown to him. There is no need for him to say that he loves Paris: Paris is his mind's natal city. In consequence of demolitions and reconstructions, the Paris of his youth, that Paris which he bore away religiously in his memory, is now a Paris of days gone by. He must be permitted to speak of that Paris as though it still existed. It is possible that when the author conducts his readers to a spot and says, 'In such a street there stands such and such a house,' neither street nor house will any longer exist in that locality. Readers may verify the facts if they care to take the trouble. For his own part, he is unacquainted with the new Paris, and he writes with the old Paris before his eyes in an illusion which is precious to him. It is a delight to him to dream that there still lingers behind him something of that which he beheld when he was in his own country, and that all has not vanished. So long as you go and come in your native land, you imagine that those streets are a matter of indifference to you; that those windows, those roofs, and those doors are nothing to you; that those walls are strangers to you; that those trees are merely the first encountered haphazard; that those houses, which you do not enter, are useless to you; that the pavements which you tread are merely stones. Later on, when you are no longer there, you perceive that the streets are dear to you; that you miss those roofs, those doors; and that those walls are necessary to you, those trees are well beloved by you; that you entered those houses which you never entered, every day, and that you have left a part of your heart, of your blood, of your soul, in those pavements. All those places which you no longer behold, which you may never behold again, perchance, and whose memory you have cherished, take on a melancholy charm, recur to your mind with the melancholy of an apparition, make the holy land visible to you, and are, so to speak, the very form of France, and you love them; and you call them up as they are, as they were, and you persist in this, and you will submit to no change: for you are attached to the figure of your fatherland as to the face of your mother." – *Les Misérables*, pg. 317

Johan Huizinga

"The word natio has always remained much more current than patria. Actually it had changed very little in connotation since classical times. Closely linked with natus and natura, it vaguely indicated a larger context than gens or populus, but without being any fixed distinction between the three terms. The Vulgate used gentes, populos, and nationes interchangeably for the nations of the Old Testament, and that biblical usage determined the significance of natio for the time being." – *Men and Ideas*, pgs. 106-107

"Gradually, over a period of a good six centuries, Latin Christendom arranged itself in a number of kingdoms corresponding, though still very roughly, to national lines . . . France, England, and Scotland, the three Scandinavian kingdoms, Aragon, Castile, and Portugal, Sicily, Hungary, and Poland had all of them taken their places as units of Latin Christendom by around 1150." – *Men and Ideas*, pgs. 103-105

Emperor Huizong of Song

With people gone, the flower city is desolate;
My spring dreams go around the Tartar sands.
Where is my homeland?
How can I bear to listen to the barbarian flute
Playing to the end of "The Plum Blossom"?
– *Charming Eyes*, pg. 294

Cordell Hull

"Unhampered trade dovetailed with peace; high tariffs, trade barriers, and unfair economic competition, with war." – *Memoirs*, pg.81

Ernest R. Hull

"The bodily gifts of nature are . . . unequally distributed; and hence a huge difference of quality in the composition of the brain, nerves, sensitive organs and the rest. And since all our functionings in life have to be carried on through this conjoint instrument called the body, it follows that men come into existence with an immense initial difference of mental and even moral capacity, according to the qualities of these different organs. ... Hence there is no difficulty in acknowledging the fact that some people are born stupid, others clever, some weak and others strong, some sluggish . . . others vivacious and active. . . . Even in the moral order there are some who are almost literally born angels in the flesh, while others are painfully prone to anger, sloth, gluttony." – *The Formation of Character*, pg. 96

David Hume

"The practice of the world goes farther in teaching us the degrees of our duty, than the subtle philosophy, which was ever yet invented." – *A Treatise of Human Nature*, pg. 569

"In every situation or incident, there are many particular and seemingly minute circumstances, which the man of greatest talent is, at first, apt to overlook, though on them the justness of his conclusions, and consequently the prudence of his conduct, entirely depend. Not to mention, that, to a young beginner, the general observations and maxims occur not always on the proper occasions, nor can be immediately applied with due calmness and distinction. The truth is, an unexperienced reasoner could be no reasoner at all, were he absolutely unexperienced; and when we assign that character to any one, we mean it only in a comparative sense, and suppose him possessed of experience, in a smaller and more imperfect degree.
   "Custom, then, is the great guide of human life. It is that principle alone which renders our experience useful to us, and makes us expect, for the future, a similar train of events with those which have appeared in the past. Without the influence of custom, we should be entirely ignorant of every matter of fact beyond what is immediately present to the memory and senses. We should never know how to adjust means to ends, or to employ our natural powers in the production of any effect." – *An Inquiry Concerning Human Understanding*, pg. 46

"Enormous monarchies are, probably, destructive to human nature; in their progress, in their continuance, and even in their downfall, which never can be very distant from their establishment." – *Essays, Moral, Political and Literary*, vol. 1, pg. 326

"Enormous cities are ... destructive to society, beget vice and disorder of all kinds, starve the remoter provinces, and even starve themselves, by the prices to which they raise all provision." – *Essays, Moral, Political and Literary*, pg. 380

"I am apt to suspect the negroes, and in general all the other species of men (for there are four or five different kinds) to be naturally inferior to the whites. There never was a civilized nation of any other complexion than white, nor even any individual eminent either in action or speculation. ... Not to mention our colonies, there are Negroe slaves dispersed all over EUROPE, of which none ever discovered any symptom of ingenuity; tho' low people, without education, will start up amongst us, and distinguish themselves in every profession." – *On National Characters; Political Essays*, pg. 86

"All small states naturally produce equality of fortune, because they afford no opportunities of great increase; but small commonwealths much more, by that division of power and authority which is essential to them." – *Essays, Moral, Political and Literary*, pg. 381

"Where each man had his little house and field to himself, and each county had its capital, free and independent; what a happy situation of mankind!" – *Essays, Moral, Political and Literary*, pg. 380

"Where a number of men are united into one political body, the occasions of their intercourse must be so frequent, for defense, commerce, and government, that, together with the same speech or language, they must acquire a resemblance in their manners, and have a common or national character, as well as a personal one, peculiar to each individual." – *Of National Characters, Political Essays*, pg. 82

"To tamper, therefore, in this affair, or try experiments merely upon the credit of supposed argument and philosophy, can never be part of a wise magistrate, who will bear a reverence to what carries the marks of age; and though he may attempt some improvements for the public good, yet will he adjust his innovations, as much as possible, to the ancient fabric, and preserve entire the chief pillars and supports of the constitution." – *Idea of a Perfect Commonwealth; Theory and Practice in the Philosophy of David Hume*, pg. 224

"There is no such passion in human minds, as the love of mankind, merely as such, independent of personal qualities, of services, or of relation to ourself. 'Tis true, there is no human, and indeed no sensible, creature, whose happiness or misery does not, in some measure, affect us, when brought near to us, and represented in lively colours: But this proceeds merely from

sympathy, and is no proof of such an universal affection to mankind..." – *Treatise on Human Nature*, pg. 645

— DAVID HUME —

"Nature has preserve'd a great resemblance among all human creatures, and that we never remark any passion or principle in others, of which, in some degree or other, we may not find a parallel in ourselves...There is a very remarkable resemblance, which preserves itself amidst all their variety; and this resemblance must very much contribute to make us enter into the sentiments of others, and embrace them with facility and pleasure. Accordingly we find, that where, beside the general resemblance of our natures, there is any peculiar similarity in our manners, or character, or country, or language, it facilitates the sympathy. The stronger the relation is betwixt ourselves and any object, the more easily does the imagination make the transition, and convey to the related idea the vivacity of conception, with which we always form the idea of our own person." – *Treatise Concerning Human Nature*, pg. 318

"Historians, and even common sense, may inform us, that, however specious these ideas of perfect equality may seem, they are really, at bottom, impracticable; and were they not so, would be extremely pernicious to human society. Render possessions ever so equal, men's different degrees of art, care, and industry will immediately break that equality. Or if you check these virtues, you reduce society to the most extreme indigence; and instead of preventing want and beggary in a few, render it unavoidable to the whole community. The most rigorous inquisition too is requisite to watch every inequality on its first appearance; and the most severe jurisdiction, to punish and redress it. But besides, that so much authority must soon degenerate into tyranny, and be exerted with great partialities; who can possibly be possessed of it, in such a situation as is here supposed? Perfect equality of possessions, destroying all subordination, weakens extremely the authority of magistracy, and must reduce all power nearly to a level, as well as property.

"We may conclude, therefore, that in order to establish laws for the regulation of property, we must be acquainted with the nature and situation of man; must reject appearances, which may be false, though specious; and must search for those rules, which are, on the whole, most useful and beneficial." – *An Enquiry Concerning the Principles of Morals; Readings in Political Philosophy Theory and Applications*, pg. 749

George Humphrey

"We were protectionists by history and had been living under a greatly lowered schedule of tariffs in a false sense of security because the world was not in competition. That has changed now and the great wave of world competition from plants we had built for other nations was going to bring vast unemployment to our country" – Cabinet meeting on August 6, 1954.[46]; cited in Eckes, *Opening America's Market: U.S. Foreign Trade Policy Since 1776*, pg. 168

Samuel Huntington

"The most obvious, most salient, and most powerful cause of the global religious resurgence is precisely what was supposed to cause the death of religion: the processes of social, economic, and cultural modernization that swept across the world in the second half of the twentieth century. Longstanding sources of identity and systems of authority are disrupted. People move from the countryside into the city, become separated from their roots, and take

new jobs or no job. They interact with large numbers of strangers and are exposed to new sets of relationships. They need new sources of identity, new forms of stable community, and new sets of moral precepts to provide them with a sense of meaning and purpose."—*The Clash of Civilizations*, pg. 97

"More broadly, the religious resurgence throughout the world is a reaction against secularism, moral relativism, and self-indulgence, and a reaffirmation of the values of order, discipline, work, mutual help, and human solidarity." – *The Clash of Civilizations*, pg. 98

"Spurred by modernization, global politics is being reconfigured along cultural lines. Peoples and countries with similar cultures are coming together. Peoples and countries with different cultures are coming apart. Alignments defined by ideology and superpower relations are giving way to alignments defined by culture and civilization. Political boundaries increasingly are redrawn to coincide with cultural ones: ethnic, religious, and civilizational. Cultural communities are replacing Cold War blocs, and the fault lines between civilizations are becoming the central lines of conflict in global politics." – *The Clash of Civilizations*, pg. 125

"First, everyone has multiple identities which may compete with or reinforce each other: kinship, occupational, cultural, institutional, territorial, educational, partisan, ideological, and others...In the contemporary world, cultural identification is dramatically increasing in importance compared to other dimensions of identity...The increased salience of cultural identity at lower levels may well reinforce its salience at higher levels." – *The Clash of Civilizations*, pg. 128

"The increased salience of cultural identity is in large part the result of social-economic modernization at the individual level, where dislocation and alienation create the need for more meaningful identities, and at the societal level, where the enhanced capabilities and power of non-Western societies stimulate the revitalization of indigenous identities and culture. Third, identity at any level—personal, tribal, racial, civilizational—can only be defined in relation

---

46 Eisenhower's Treasury Secretary

to an 'other,' a different person, tribe, race, or civilization." – *The Clash of Civilizations*, pg. 129

"A multicultural America will, in time, become a multi-creedal America, with groups with different cultures espousing distinctive political values and principles rooted in their particular cultures." – *Who Are We?*, pg. 340

"People can with relative ease change their political ideologies... A nation defined only by political ideology is a fragile nation." – *Who Are We?*, pg. 338

"Historically the substance of American identity has involved four key components: race, ethnicity, culture (most notably language and religion), and ideology. The racial and ethnic Americas are no more. Cultural America is under siege. And as the Soviet experience illustrates, ideology is a weak glue to hold together people otherwise lacking racial, ethnic, and cultural sources of community. Reasons could exist, as Robert Kaplan observed, why 'America, more than any other nation, may have been born to die.'" – *Who Are We?*, pg. 12

János Hunyadi

"We have addressed Your Holiness with complete faith, with the conviction that we shall obtain not only promises, but real help. Your holiness, however, encouraging us rather than giving us support, wishes the postponement of the campaign and anticipates a delay in the assistance. But when our old enemy has gained new powers as a result of its latest victories over Christianity and is gathering great forces at our borders, it is useful for us to take up arms, so that an attack does not find us unprepared ... The war has been decided, the army has been gathered, the orders have been given. Power is always greater when used in attack rather than in defense, and the outcome of the war smiles more favorably upon the one who pursues the enemy in its own land. Besides, it is not certain that next year we will be able to gather the same army and that it will be as enthusiastic. We are prepared to do everything to defend our country from impending danger. Our descendants will glorify our victory, as well as our death in battle. We and our brave comrades have endan-

gered our lives for the well-being of Christianity, and it would be appropriate for the Holy Father to offer financial help for the gathering of a supporting army." – Letter dated Sept 8, 1448; *Hunyadi: Defender of Christendom*, pg. 168 [47]

Jan Hus

"According to every law, including the law of God, and the natural order of things, Czechs in the kingdom of Bohemia should be preferred in the offices of the Czech kingdom. This is the way it is for the French in the French kingdom and for the Germans in German lands. Therefore a Czech should have authority over his own subordinates as should a German." – *Jan Hus: Religious Reform and Social Revolution in Bohemia*, pg. 96

Andrew Hussey

"In 1933 the French colonial authorities banned the Islamic reformers from preaching in the mosques of Algiers and Constantine, preferring the more traditional and politically naïve forms of Islam. The inevitable result was growing anger among the Muslim masses. In 1936 the mood was caught in the words of Shayk Ben Badis, who declared: '...this Algerian nation is not France, cannot be France, and does not want to be France ... [but] has its culture, its traditions and its characteristics, good or bad, like every other nation of the earth.'" – *The French Intifada*, pg. 243

"Islamist forces which have been rallying in the northern part of the country. The French had little choice but to attack as the Islamists ratcheted up their provocations against France and threatened to set off an insurgency in the southern part of Algeria, which shares a border with Mali. Publicly, the Algerians are furious about what seems to be another neo-colonialist war being fought in their back yard. Secretly, they welcome and support the French. The risk is that the Islamists destabilize the whole region, from Morocco and Algeria to Tunisia, and take the war across the Mediterranean. They are armed with high-grade weapons from the wreckage of Libya and they have a plan to bring the Afghan wars to Europe. My contacts in British and French counter-terrorism

---

47   Hunyadi was a general and governor of the kingdom of Hungary from 1446 to 1452, who led battles against the Turks.

and intelligence have been worrying over the intervention in Mali for months. Their biggest fear is the blowback in France. In North Africa their fears were confirmed in the days after the first French air strikes, when an Islamist group launched a deadly assault on a BP gas plant in eastern Algeria on 16 January 2013, killing foreign hostages. Immediately France's conflict in Mali took on a new, dangerous global dimension.

"Back in the banlieues little has yet changed. There is a lot of anger and a lot of young men willing to turn themselves into soldiers for God. Most importantly, the rioters, wreckers, even the killers of the banlieues are not looking for reform or revolution. They are looking for revenge. Their rage is often expressed symbolically: appropriating the language of the intifada, which was originally a spontaneous and legitimate uprising against oppression; speaking Arabic slang; waving the Algerian flag; provocatively wearing the veil. These are all acts directed at subverting the French Republic. For many French people, for all these reasons, the banlieues represent 'otherness' – the otherness of exclusion, of the repressed, of the fearful and despised. Until this ceases to be the case, the unacknowledged civil war between France and its disturbed suburbs – one of the banlieues – their identification with Palestine, their hatred of France – reveal the struggle to be part of the 'long war', just like those caught up in the conflicts in Iraq and Afghanistan. It is a short journey from symbolic revolt to real action in the minds of those who are so bitterly disenchanted with and excluded from French 'civilization'.

"In the nineteenth century, Charles Baudelaire wrote of Paris being haunted by its past, by 'ghosts in daylight'. In the early twenty-first century, the ghosts of colonial and anti-colonial assassins continue to be visible in the daylight of the banlieues. It may be that what France needs is not hard-headed political solutions or even psychiatry, but an exorcist." – *The French Intifada*, pgs. 373-374

Hyndluljóð

Now let us down from our saddles leap,
And talk of the race of the heroes twain;
The men who were born of the gods above,
We must guard, for the hero young to have,
His father's wealth, the fruits of his race.
…
Tell to me now the ancient names,
And the races of all that were born of old:
Who are of the Skjoldungs,
    who of the Skilfings,
Who of the Othlings, who of the Ylfings,
Who are the free-born, who are the high-born,
The noblest of men that in Mithgarth dwell?

– *Poetic Edda, The Poem of Hyndla*, pg. 220

I

Ivan Ilyin

"How is Christian culture even possible today when the cultural elite runs away from Christianity and tries to lead along the uneducated or half-educated masses with them? How is Christian culture possible when Christianity has still not found a true and creative reconcilement and cooperation with the great secular powers that inspire people these days, that is, with science, art, the economy, and politics? Especially when a strange and frightening revolt is occurring in the human soul against faith and Christianity, that same bestial and unbridled instinct preached by Nietzsche. And especially when the first historical force that arose against this reality – nationalism – has not yet been accepted by Christianity and has not itself understood its Christian roots!" – *Foundations of Christian Culture*, ch. 2

John Kells Ingram

Who fears to speak of Ninety-Eight ?
  Who blushes at the name?
  When cowards mock the patriots' fate,
  Who hangs his head for shame ?
  He's all a knave, or half a slave,
  Who slights his country thus;
  But a true man, like you, man,
  Will fill your glass with us.
We drink the memory of the brave,
  The faithful and the few
  Some lie far off beyond the wave,
  Some sleep in Ireland, too;
  All, all are gone but still lives on
  The fame of those who died;
  All true men, like you, men,
  Remember them with pride.
Some on the shores of distant lands
  Their weary hearts have laid,
  And by the stranger's heedless hands
  Their lonely graves were made,

But, though their clay be far away
  Beyond the Atlantic foam
  In true men, like you, men,
  Their spirit's still at home.
The dust of some is Irish earth;
  Among their own they rest;
  And the same land that gave them birth
  Has caught them to her breast;
  And we will pray that from their clay
  Full many a race may start
  Of true men, like you, men,
  To act as brave a part.
They rose in dark and evil days
  To right their native land;
  They kindled here a living blaze
  That nothing shall withstand.
  Alas! that might can vanquish Right
  They fell and pass'd away;
  But true men, like you, men,
  Are plenty here to-day.
Then here's their memory-may it be
  For us a guiding light,
  To cheer our strife for liberty,
  And teach us to unite.
  Through good and ill, be Ireland's still,
  Though sad as theirs your fate;
  And true men be you, men,
  Like those of Ninety-Eight.
– "The Memory of the Dead," Irish national poem, *Spirit Of The Nation*, pgs. 48-50

T. Robert Ingram

"The movement toward integration is a denial of Christ. It is part of an effort to create one society in which there are no distinctions or differences. . . . For it is not the races only that must disappear and be brought into conformity with the requirements of a world-state: so with the sexes, so with parents and children, so with nations, states, tribes, and empires. All must go and be swallowed up in the maw of the great monad, theologically familiar to students of oriental mysticism as religion, and to traditional Christianity as Satan." – *Essays on Segregation*, pgs. 13-14

"Nonetheless, the Holy Ghost and the Apostles agreed that any policy which would result in destruction of the Jewish community or the Gentile community to establish a new single so-called Christian community in and of this world was tempting God, a denial of the sufficiency of the Cross of Christ and an abandonment of faith. The whole family of Christ had to include Jewish and Gentile members. The Christian fellowship superseded the old ties, but did not eliminate them." – *Essays on Segregation*, pg. 82

Irenaeus

"…when the spirit here blended with the soul is united to [God's] handiwork, the man is rendered spiritual and perfect because of the outpouring of the Spirit, and this is he who was made in the image and likeness of God. But if the Spirit be wanting to the soul, he who is such is indeed of an animal nature, and being left carnal, shall be an imperfect being, possessing indeed the image [of God] in his formation (in plasmate), but not receiving the similitude through the Spirit; and thus is this being imperfect." – *Against Heresies*, bk. 5, ch. 6

"And then, again, this Word was manifested when the Word of God was made man, assimilating Himself to man, and man to Himself, so that by means of his resemblance to the Son, man might become precious to the Father. For in times long past, it was said that man was created after the image of God, but it was not [actually] shown; for the Word was as yet invisible, after whose image man was created. Wherefore also he did easily lose the similitude. When, however, the Word of God became flesh, He confirmed both these: for He both showed forth the image truly, since He became Himself what was His image; and He re-established the similitude after a sure manner, by assimilating man to the invisible Father through means of the visible Word." – *Against Heresies*, bk. 5, ch. 16

"Earthly rule, therefore, has been appointed by God for the benefit of nations, and not by the devil, who is never at rest at all, nay, who does not love to see even nations conducting themselves after a quiet manner, so that under the fear of human rule, men may not eat each other up like fishes; but that, by means of the establishment of laws, they may keep down an excess of wickedness among the nations." – *Against Heresies*, pg. 460

"…the creation is suited to [the wants of] man; for man was not made for its sake, but creation for the sake of man. Those nations however, who did not of themselves raise up their eyes unto heaven, nor returned thanks to their Maker, nor wished to behold the light of truth, but who were like blind mice concealed in the depths of ignorance, the word justly reckons 'as waste water from a sink, and as the turning-weight of a balance—in fact, as nothing;' so far useful and serviceable to the just, as stubble conduces towards the growth of the wheat, and its straw, by means of combustion, serves for working gold." – *Against Heresies*, pg. 471

Isidore of Seville

"What the law of nations is [Quid sit ius gentium]. The law of nations concerns the occupation of territory, building, fortification, wars, captivities, enslavements, the right of return, treaties of peace, truces, the pledge not to molest embassies, the prohibition of marriages between different races. And it is called the 'law of nations' [ius gentium] because nearly all nations [gentes] use it." – *Etymologies*, pg. 118

"The languages of nations [De linguis gentium]. The diversity of languages arose with the building of the Tower after the Flood, for before the pride of that Tower divided human society, so that there arose a diversity of meaningful sounds, there was one language for all nations, which is called Hebrew. The patriarchs and prophets used this language not only in their speech, but also in the sacred writings. But at the outset there were as many languages as there were nations, and then more nations than languages, because many nations sprang from one language stock. The term 'languages' [lingua] is used in this context for the words that are made by the tongue [lingua], according to the figure of speech by which the thing that produces is named after the thing that is produced. Thus we will say 'mouth' for 'words,' as we speak of the letters we form as 'a hand.'" – *Etymologies*, pg. 191

"The names of nations [De gentium vocabulis].

   "1. A nation [gens] is a number of people sharing a single origin, or distinguished from another nation [natio] in accordance with its own grouping, as the 'nations' of Greece or of Asia Minor. From this comes the term 'shared heritage' [gentilitas]. The word gens is also so called on account of the generations [generatio] of families, that is from 'begetting' [gignere, ppl. genitus], as the term 'nation' [natio] comes from 'being born' [nasci, ppl. natus].

   "2. Now, of the nations into which the earth is divided, fifteen are from Japheth, thirty-one from Ham, and twenty-seven from Shem, which adds up to seventy-three – or rather, as a proper accounting shows, seventy-two. And there are an equal number of languages, which arose across the lands and, as they increased, filled the provinces and islands." – *Etymologies*, pg. 192

"People's faces and coloring, the size of their bodies, and their various temperaments correspond to various climates. Hence we find that the Romans are serious, the Greeks easy-going, the Africans changeable, and the Gauls fierce in nature and rather sharp in wit, because the character of the climate makes them so." – *Etymologies*, pg. 198

"Exile [exul], because one is 'outside his native soil' [extra solum suum], as if sent beyond his soil, or wandering outside his soil, for those who go outside their soil are said to 'be in exile' [exulare]. Banished [extorris], because one is 'outside his own land' [extra terram suam], as if the term were exterris but properly speaking one is banished when driven out by force and ejected from his native soil with terror [terror]. Also extorris, driven 'from one's own land' [ex terra sua]. Banished [extorris], 'outside the land' [extra terram], or 'beyond one's frontier' [extra terminos suos], because one is frightened [exterrere]. Expeller [exterminator], not the one who is commonly said ἀφα- νισθῆναι ('to be destroyed'), but the one who casts out and expels someone from the boundaries [terminus] of a city. Expelled [exterminatus], because such a one is driven out 'beyond his boundaries' [extra terminos]." – *Etymologies*, pg. 218

"A city properly so called is one that has been founded not by newcomers but by those native to its soil. Therefore communities [urbs] founded by their own citizens [civis] are named cities [civitas], not colonies. On the other hand, a colony [colonia] is what is filled by new inhabitants [cultor) when there are no indigenous people. Hence also a 'colony' is so called from the tilling [cultus, ppl. of colere] of a field. A free town is one that, while remaining in the status of a city, obtains from the sovereign some legal right to a greater or lesser obligation. It is called 'free town' [municipium] from 'official functions' [munia], that is 'obligations,' because they yield only these functions, that is, as the owed tributes or services [munus]. The most notorious court cases and those involving a person's freedom, as well as those which proceed from the sovereign, are not conducted there; these belong to the jurisdiction of the city [civitas]." – *Etymologies*, pg. 306

— ISIDORE OF SEVILLE —

"Every realm in this world is procured in wars and extended by victories. A victory [victoria] is so called because it is attained by 'force' [vis], that is, 'strength' [virtus]. This is the law of nations, to expel 'force by force' [vim vi], for a victory acquired by guile is wicked. A sure victory is either the killing or the complete despoiling of the enemy, or both." – *Etymologies*, pg. 360

"Nationalities are distinguished by their costume just as they differ in their languages. The Persians cover their arms and legs with drawings and their heads with a turban. The Alani are distinguished by their pointed hats. The Scotti raise the hackles with their ugly dress, as well as with their barking tongues. The Alemanni are clothed in their woolen cloaks [sagum], the Indians in linen. The Persians wear jewels, the Chinese wear silk, and the Armenians wear quivers. It is not simply in clothing but in physical appearance also that some groups of people lay claim to features peculiar to themselves as marks to distinguish them, so that we see the curls [cirrus, perhaps 'topknot'] of the Germans, the mustaches and goatees of the Goths, the tattoos of the Britons. The Jews circumcise the foreskin, the Arabs pierce their ears, the Getae with their uncovered heads are blond, the Albanians shine with their white hair. The Moors have bodies black as night, while the skin of the Gauls is white. Without their horses, the Alani are idle. Nor should we omit the Picts [Pictus], whose name is taken from their bodies, because an artisan, with the tiny point of a pin and the juice squeezed from a native plant, tricks them out with scars to serve as identifying marks, and their nobility are distinguished by their tattooed [pictus] limbs." – *Etymologies*, pg. 386

"...a people is a multitude stemming from one origin or distinguished from another people by its proper ties." – quoted in *The Barbarian North in Medieval Imagination*, pg. 13

Jean Baptiste-Claude Isoard

"The man who lives in a time when the spirit of the tradition reigns is one link in a chain that links many generations. He lives in each of them. He feels that his own life was already prepared for him in the lives of those who preceded him, and that it will continue to live still much longer in those who come after him." – *Oeuvres Pastorales*, quoted in *Human Dignity And The Common Good*, pg. 191

J

Andrew Jackson

"We have been too long subject to the policy of the British merchants. We need to become more Americanized and instead of feeding the paupers and laborers of Europe....feed our own, or in a short time...we shall be rendered paupers ourselves. It is my opinion...that a careful and judicious tariff is much wanted." – Letter to Dr. Coleman, April 26, 1824; *Congressional Globe*, April 6, 1872, pg. 192

"A careful Tariff is much wanted to pay our national debt, and afford us the means of that defense within ourselves on which the safety and liberty of the country depend." – Bassett, *Jackson*, 3:249-51

Anthony Jacob

"The traditional Boer is a man whose happiness is complete when he is sitting on the stop of his farmhouse, miles from his nearest neighbour, with his pipe and coffee and Bible and family, gazing out upon his land extending across the veld to infinity. He is the lord of all he surveys, the world's last baron. World organisations meet with his contempt, and world opinion leaves him unmoved. His way of life is the way of life he wants, and that is the way it is going to be. The world can either like it or lump it. Without interfering with anyone else, he will fight against any odds – as he always has done – to be the master in his own house. Nor must it be forgotten that while it is an easy matter to throw a man out of an office or overthrow a caste of civil servants, it is anything but easy to dispossess those with their feet planted firmly on the soil and whose Government acts for them instead of acting against them." – *White Man: Think Again!*, pg. 80

John Angell James

"He who created you is best qualified to declare the intention of his own acts, and you may safely, as you should humbly allow him to fix your position, and make known your duties." – *Female Piety*, pg. 73

"A community is not likely to be overthrown where woman fulfills her mission; for by the power of her noble heart over the hearts of others, she will raise it from its ruins, and restore it again to prosperity and joy. Here, then, beyond the circle of wedded life, as well as within it, is no doubt part of woman's mission, and an important one it is. Her field is social life, her object is social happiness, her reward is social gratitude and respect." – *Female Piety*, pg. 84

"We may pause for a moment, to observe how constantly and completely Christianity is the parent of order, and the enemy of indecorum of every kind." – *Female Piety*, pg. 79

John Jay

"Providence has been pleased to give this one connected country to one united people, a people descended from the same ancestors, speaking the same language, professing the same religion, attached to the same principles of government, very similar in their manners and customs, without which a common and free government would be impossible." – *Federalist #2*, in *The Constitution of the United States of America and Other Writings of the Founding Fathers*, pg. 130

"Permit me to hint whether it would not be wise and reasonable to provide a strong check to the admission of foreigners into the administration of our national government, and to declare expressly that the command-in-chief of the American army shall not be given to nor devolve on any but a natural born citizen." – In a letter to George Washington, written from New York, 25th July, 1787; *Congressional Record*, vol. 113, 1967, pg. 13,170

"It certainly is chiefly owing to institutions, laws, and principles of policy and government, originally derived to us as British colonists, that, with the favour of Heaven, the people of this country are what they are." – In a letter to Robert Goodloe Harper, written from New York 19th January, 1796; *The Life of J. Jay*, with Selections from *His Correspondence and Miscellaneous Papers*, vol. 2, pgs. 262-263

David Lyle Jeffrey

"While most of the exegesis of this parable is moral theology, reflecting the tropological or moral force of the text, the allegorical sense of the text is an added dimension that struck early Christian interpreters as a characteristic register for further contemplation of the believer. On this level, the parable reveals itself as essentially christological, broadly hinting at Christ's full soteriological identity, his own saving ministry to a sin-wounded world. For Origen, as for Ambrose and Augustine after him, we can see in the poor traveler, descending from Jerusalem, the viso pacis, toward Jericho, a city identified with the sin of the world, a kind of everyman figure, embodying in his descent from divine intention the universal journey into the fallen world of the first Adam. On this reading the robbers are the demonic assaults and depredations of sin, which indeed leave us bereft of substance and half dead. The priest and Levite are figures for the law and the prophets, or for the establishments of religiosity, which do not minister to our condition. Christ is the good Samaritan, the one regarded as outcast by these religiously proper persons and institutions but who actually seeks and saves the lost at his own expense. The pandocheion or inn is like the church, which receives the wounded first Adam for whom the Second Adam, Christ, alone as made saving provision. This Christ, moreover, will return to his church and restore all accounts one day (Origen, *Homilies* on Luke 34; Ambrose, *Exposition* of Luke 7.73-74; Augustine, Sermon 179.A7-8). At this level, the parable of the good Samaritan is not only an explicit guide

to loving our neighbor as ourselves but also tacitly and more deeply an insight into the history of human salvation as the early church saw it revealed in scripture and fulfilled in the ministry of Christ." – *Brazos Theological Commentary on the Bible, Luke*, pg. 269

James S. Jeffers

The Greco-Roman World of the NT Era:
"Roman law made the minimum marriage age twelve for girls, fourteen for boys. The age of first marriage for free Roman girls normally was twelve to eighteen. Men married for the first time as late as thirty, but in Roman culture a five-year difference between man and woman seems to have been most common among both free persons and slaves. The age of first marriage for Jewish girls probably also was between twelve and eighteen." – *The Greco-Roman world of the New Testament era: Exploring the background of early Christianity*, pg. 238

Thomas Jefferson

"The present desire of America is to produce rapid population by as great importations of foreigners as possible... But are there no inconveniences to be thrown into the scale against the advantage expected from a multiplication of numbers by the importation of foreigners? It is for the happiness of those united in society to harmonize as much as possible in matters which they must of necessity transact together. Civil government being the sole object of forming societies, its administration must be conducted by common consent. Every species of government has its specific principles. Ours perhaps are more peculiar than those of any other in the universe. It is a composition of the freest principles of the English constitution, with others derived from natural right and natural reason. To these nothing can be more opposed than the maxims of absolute monarchies. Yet, from such, we are to expect the greatest number of emigrants. They will bring with them the principles of the governments they leave, imbibed in their early youth; or, if able to throw them off, it will be in exchange for an unbounded licentiousness, passing, as is usual, from one extreme to another. It would be a miracle were they to stop precisely at the point of temperate liberty. These principles, with their language, they will transmit to their children. In proportion to their numbers, they will share with us the legislation. They will infuse into it their spirit, warp and bias its direction, and render it a heterogeneous, incoherent, distracted mass... May not our government be more homogeneous, more peaceable, more durable? Suppose 20 millions of republican Americans thrown all of a sudden into France, what would be the condition of that kingdom? If it would be more turbulent, less happy, less strong, we may believe that the addition of half a million of foreigners to our present numbers would produce a similar effect here. If they come of themselves they are entitled to all of the rights of citizenship; but I doubt the expediency of inviting them by extraordinary encouragements. I mean not that these doubts should be extended to the importation of useful artificers. The policy of that measure depends on very different considerations. Spare no expense in obtaining them. They will after a while go to the plough and the hoe; but, in the mean time, they will teach us something we do not know. It is not so in agriculture. The indifferent state of that among us does not proceed from a want of knowledge merely; it is from our having such quantities of land to waste as we please. In Europe the object is to make the most of their land, labor being abundant; here it is to make the most of our labor, land being abundant." – *Notes on the State of Virginia*, pgs. 89-91

"Are not the fine mixtures of red and white, the expressions of every passion by greater or less suffusions of colour in the one [whites], preferable to that eternal monotony, which reigns in the countenances, that immovable veil of black, which covers all the emotions of the other race?" – *Notes on the State of Virginia*, pgs. 144-145

"To our reproach it must be said, that though for a century and a half we have had under our eyes the races of black and of red men, they have never yet been viewed by us as subjects of natural history. I advance it therefore as a suspicion only, that the blacks, whether originally a distinct race, or made distinct by time and circumstances, are inferior to the whites in the endowments both of body and mind. It is not against experience to suppose, that different species of the same genus, or varieties of the same species, may possess different qualifications." – *Notes on the State of Virginia*, pg. 150

— THOMAS JEFFERSON —

"Although as to other foreigners it is thought better to discourage their settling together in large masses, wherein, as in our German settlements, they preserve for a long time their own languages, habits, and principles of government, and that they should distribute themselves sparsely among the natives for quicker amalgamation, yet English emigrants are without this inconvenience." – Letter to George Fowler, Sept. 12, 1817; *The Writings of Thomas Jefferson* vol. 7, pg. 65

"Be it enacted by the General Assembly, that all white persons born within the territory of this commonwealth and all who have resided therein two years next before the passing of this act ... shall be deemed citizens of this commonwealth ...

"And all others not being citizens of any of the United States of America shall be deemed aliens. ... The free white inhabitants of every of the states, parties to the American confederation, paupers, vagabonds, and fugitives from justice excepted, shall be entitled to all rights, privileges, and immunities of free citizens in this commonwealth..." – *A Bill Declaring Who Shall Be Deemer Citizens or this Commonwealth; The Papers of Thomas Jefferson*, vol. 2, pg. 476

"I agree with you that there is a natural aristocracy among men. The grounds of this are virtue and talents...The natural aristocracy I consider as the most precious gift of nature for the instruction, the trusts, and government of society. And indeed it would have been inconsistent in creation to have formed man for the social state, and not to have provided virtue and wisdom enough to manage the concerns of the society not even say that that form of government is the best which provides the most effectually for a pure selection of these natural aristoi into the offices of government? – Letter to John Adams, Oct. 28, 1813; *Political Writings*, Cambridge Texts, pg. 187

"The papers from the free people of color in Grenada...I apprehend it will be best to take no notice of. They are parties in a domestic quarrel, which, I think, we should leave to be settled among themselves. Nor should I think it desirable, were it justifiable, to draw a body of sixty thousand free blacks and mulattoes into our country." – in a letter to Washington; *The Papers of Thomas Jefferson*, vol. 20, April 1791 to August 1791, pg. 558

"But they have wished a monopoly of commerce and influence with us; and they have in fact obtained it. When we take notice that theirs is the workship to which we go for all we want; that with them centre either immediately or ultimately all the labors of our hands and lands; that to them belongs, either openly or secretly, the great mass of our navigation; that even the factorage of their affairs here, is kept to themselves by fictitious citizenships; that these foreign and false citizens now constitute the great body of what are called our merchants, fill our seaports, are planted in every little town and district of the interior country, sway everything in the former places, by their own votes, and those of their dependents, in the latter, by their insinuations and the in fluence of their ledgers; that they are advancing rapidly to a monopoly of our banks and public funds, and thereby placing our public finances under their control; that they have in their alliance the most influencial characters in and out of office; when they have shown that by all these bearings on the different branches of the government, they can force it to proceed in whatever direction they dictate, and bend the interests of this country entirely to the will of another; when all this, I say, is attended to, it is impossible for us to say we stand on independent ground, impossible for a free mind not to

see and to groan under the bondage in which it is bound. If anything after this could excite surprise, it would be that they have been able so far to throw dust in the eyes of our own citizens, as to fix on those who wish merely to recover self-government the charge of serving one foreign influence because they resist submission to another. But they possess our printing presses, a powerful engine in their government of us. At this very moment they would have drawn us into a war on the side of England, had it not been for the failure of her bank. Such was their open and loud cry, and that of their gazettes, till this event. After plunging us into all the broils of the European nations, there would remain but one act to close our tragedy, that is, to break up our Union; and even this they have ventured seriously and solemnly to propose and maintain by arguments in a Connecticut paper. I have been happy, however, in believing from the stifling of this effort, that that dose was found too strong, and excited as much repugnance there as it did horror in other parts of our country, and that whatever follies we may be led into as to foreign nations, we shall never give up our Union, the last anchor of our hope, and that alone which is to prevent this heavenly country from becoming an arena of gladiators. Much as I abhor war, and view it as the greatest scourge of mankind, and anxiously as I wish to keep out of the broils of Europe, I would yet go with my brethren into these, rather than separate from them. But I hope we may still keep clear of them, notwithstanding our present thraldom, and that time may be given us to reflect on the awful crisis we have passed through, and to find some means of shielding ourselves in future from foreign influence, political, commercial, or in whatever other form it may be attempted. I can scarcely withhold myself from joining in the wish of Silas Deane, that there were an ocean of fire between us and the old world." – In a letter to Elbridge Gerry written from Philadelphia, May 1797; *The Life of Thomas Jefferson*, pg. 353

"The same question to ourselves would recur here also, as did in the first case: should we be willing to have such a colony in contact with us? However our present interests may restrain us within our own limits, it is impossible not to look forward to distant times, when our rapid multiplication will expand itself beyond those limits, & cover the whole northern, if not the southern continent, with a people speaking the same language, governed in similar forms, & by similar laws; nor can we contemplate with satisfaction either blot or mixture on that surface." – In a letter to James Monroe (then Governor of Virginia) from Washington, 24 November, 1801; *Correspondence*, pg. 420

"Nor have We been wanting in attentions to our Brittish brethren. We have warned them from time to time of attempts by their legislature to extend an unwarrantable jurisdiction over us. We have reminded them of the circumstances of our emigration and settlement here. We have appealed to their native justice and magnanimity, and we have conjured them by the ties of our common kindred to disavow these usurpations, which, would inevitably interrupt our connections and correspondence. They too have been deaf to the voice of justice and of consanguinity. We must, therefore, acquiesce in the necessity, which denounces our Separation, and hold them, as we hold the rest of mankind, Enemies in War, in Peace Friends."– *U.S. Declaration of Independence* [48]

"The prohibiting duties we lay on all articles of foreign manufacture which prudence requires us to establish at home, with the patriotic determination of every good citizen to use no foreign article which can be made within ourselves, without regard to difference of price, secures us against a relapse into foreign dependancy." – Letter to Jean-Baptiste Say, 1815; *Congressional Record*, vol. 91. Part 4, May 26, pg. 4,996

"He...who is now against domestic manufacture, must be for reducing either to dependence on that foreign nation, or to be clothes in skins, and to live like wild beasts in dens and caverns. I am not of these; experience has now taught me that manufacturers are now as necessary to our independence as to our comfort; and if those who quote me as of a different opinion, will keep pace with me in purchasing nothing foreign where an equivalent domestic fabric can be obtained, without regard to difference of price, it will not be our fault if we do not soon have a supply at home equal to our demand, and wrest that weapon of distress from the hand which has wielded it...

"For in so complicated a science as political economy, no one axiom can be laid down as wise and expedient for all times and circumstances, and for their contraries inattention to this is what has called for this explanation, which reflection would have rendered unnecessary with the candid, while nothing will do it with those who use the former opinion [free trade] only as a stalking horse to cover their disloyal propensities to keep us in eternal vassalage to a foreign and unfriendly people." – Letter to Benjamin Austin, 1816; The Congressional Globe, June 1844, vol. 13, pg. 743

"Our commerce on the ocean and in other countries must be paid for by frequent war." – Letter to John Jay, 1785; Boyd, Jefferson, 8:427, 633

Jerome

"How then, says Helvidius, do you make out that they were called the Lord's brethren who were not his brethren? I will show how that is. In Holy Scripture there are four kinds of brethren— by nature, race, kindred, love. . . . As to race, all Jews are called brethren of one another, as in Deuteronomy, Deuteronomy 15:12: 'If your brother, an Hebrew man, or an Hebrew woman, be sold unto you, and serve you six years; then in the seventh year you shall let him go free from you.' And in the same book, Deuteronomy 17:15: 'You shall in anywise set him king over you, whom the Lord your God shall choose: one from among your brethren shall you set king over you; you may not put a foreigner over you, which is not your brother.' And again, Deuteronomy 22:1: 'You shall not see your brother's ox or his sheep go astray, and hide yourself from them: you shall surely bring them again unto your brother. And if your brother be not near unto you, or if you know him not, then you shall bring it home to your house, and it shall be with you until your brother seek after it, and you shall restore it to him again.' And the Apostle Paul says, Romans 9:3-4: 'I could wish that I myself were anathema from Christ for my brethren's sake, my kinsmen according to the flesh: who are Israelites.' Moreover they are called brethren by kindred who are of one family, that is πατρία, which corresponds to the Latin paternitas, because

---

48 The signers appealed to common brotherhood, kindred, and consanguinity in their protest of injustice.

from a single root a numerous progeny proceeds. In Genesis 13:8, 11 we read: 'And Abram said unto Lot, Let there be no strife, I pray you, between me and you, and between my herdmen and your herdmen; for we are brethren. And again, So Lot chose him all the plain of Jordan, and Lot journeyed east: and they separated each from his brother.' Certainly Lot was not Abraham's brother, but the son of Abraham's brother Aram. For Terah begot Abraham and Nahor and Aram: and Aram begot Lot. Again we read, Genesis 12:4: 'And Abram was seventy and five years old when he departed out of Haran. And Abram took Sarai his wife, and Lot his brother's son.' But if you still doubt whether a nephew can be called a son, let me give you an instance. Genesis 14:14: 'And when Abram heard that his brother was taken captive, he led forth his trained men, born in his house, three hundred and eighteen.' And after describing the night attack and the slaughter, he adds: 'And he brought back all the goods, and also brought again his brother Lot.' Let this suffice by way of proof of my assertion." – *Against Helvidius*, in *Selected Writings*, by Schaff, pg. 434 [49]

Samuel Johnson

"To be happy at home is the ultimate result of all ambition, the end to which every enterprise and labour tends." – *The Rambler*, No.68

Garett Jones

"If the next hundred years is at all like the last hundred—or the last five hundred—we can predict that year after year of massive immigration from the world's poorest countries into the I-7, the world's most innovative nations, would eventually tend to have effects like these:

"The quality of government would fall; corruption would rise.

"Social conflict would increase—and so would the risk of civil war.

"Trust—and probably trustworthiness—toward strangers would decline.

"Support would rise for higher minimum wages and laws making it harder to fire workers.

"Innovation would decline overall, and since new innovations eventually spread across the entire planet, the entire planet would eventually lose out.

"The final result of this kind of decades-long immigration wave: average incomes in the I-7 would be lower than if that massive wave of immigration had never happened, and there would be a world of slower, more sluggish growth in new science, new technology." – *The Culture Transplant*, pgs. 157-158

"[The] difference in per capita income today between Western Europe and sub-Saharan Africa is . . . a factor of 13.3. This income difference is usually attributed to the post-1500 slave trade, colonialism, and post-independence factors in sub-Saharan Africa. [But in Comin, Easterly, and Gong's simple model] 78 percent of the . . . difference in income today between sub-Saharan Africa and Western Europe . . . is associated with the technology differences in 1500 AD." – *The Culture Transplant*, pgs. 50-51

"If the only thing you knew about each nation on the planet was the fraction of that nation with ancestors of European descent, and you did the best job you could trying to predict average modern income per person using just that one fact, you'd be able to predict two-thirds of all global income differences." – *The Culture Transplant*, pg. 39

"Because immigration, to a large degree, creates a culture transplant, making the places that migrants go a lot like the places they left. And for good and for ill, those culture transplants shape a nation's future prosperity." – *The Culture Transplant*, pg. xi

"When immigrants move to a place with different institutions, overwhelmingly their cultural values change gradually, if ever, but rarely within two generations." – *The Culture Transplant*, pg. 6

---

49 Jerome, in his *Against Helvidius*, writes a reply to Helvidius's assertion that Mary did not perpetually remain a virgin. As Helvidius argues that Scripture speaks of "brothers" of Jesus, implying that Mary was no longer a virgin after giving birth to Jesus, Jerome counters by specifying the different way in which that term can be taken. One need not agree with Jerome's arguments for Mary's perpetual virginity to endorse his argumentation for the biblical support of racial brotherhood.. While many may not have an issue with the use of the word "brother" to denote membership in an extended family (such as Lot and Abraham), it is but a natural extension of this same principle to say that national and racial kinsmen are likewise "brothers": that they are part of a real, hereditary, biological grouping, and that it is fitting to assign moral duties of nearness unto these groupings – that we ought to love our kinsmen with a higher love than foreigners.

"The message from these rough ancestry measures is consistent: average trust levels in ancestral homelands explain about half the differences in average trust levels across these different groups of hyphenated Americans." – *The Culture Transplant*, pg. 15

"People from high-trust societies pass on about half of their high-trust attitudes to their descendants, and people from low-trust societies pass on about half of their low-trust attitudes. On average, hyphenated-Americans appear to get about half of their attitudes toward trust from the land that comes before the hyphen." – *The Culture Transplant*, pg. 14

"Whether you looked at the amount a person saved, whether the person saved at all, or how much the person's wealth had increased over the years, the children of migrants made financial choices that looked quite a bit like the financial choices of people in the country where their parents had been born…Two independent sets of scholars coming to the same conclusion: an immigrant's country of origin really does help predict the frugality of the children of immigrants. Based on what we know so far, it's reasonable to believe that migrants import a substantial portion of their views toward frugality, toward giving thought for the financial morrow, toward whether they act like Aesop's patient ant or like his shortsighted grasshopper. And for a nation as a whole, more frugality means more saving and therefore more investment. It also means a larger stock of funds to push into venture capital, into research and development, and even into college education— all forms of investment, all ways to raise future incomes. Attitudes toward the future are, to a great extent, just a cultural attitude, not a matter of right or wrong. And migrants can, to a great extent, transplant those cultural attitudes from one nation to another." – *The Culture Transplant*, pgs. 20-21

"Exceptions bend but don't break this general rule: ancestral homes help predict county incomes and county productivity. Fulford finds that a little more than half—56 percent—of county's modern productivity looks like it's transmitted from the old country to the new county." – *The Culture Transplant*, pg. 140

"How much do fourth-generation immigrants conform to the views of the average American on the proper role of government?

"A mere 38 percent by Giavazzi's estimates. That's actually less than in the second generation! He found that the second generation closed 43 percent of the government attitude gap between the old country and the average American. Overall, that low level of conformity is a bad sign, unless you think most immigrants come from countries with better political attitudes than Americans currently have. If it turned out that most of America's immigrants came from prosperous, market-friendly Singapore, I'd be open to that argument—but in reality we should probably be skeptical about claims that the last few generations of immigrants, on average, came from countries with better views on economic policy." – *The Culture Transplant*, pg. 146

James Jordan

"The Christ to come would be the final World Emperor, and His non-political Church would be the true world empire, embracing and transforming every nation without dominating or destroying any of them." – *Through News Eyes*, pg. 250

"In giving His great commission to His disciples, the Lord Jesus Christ spoke in terms not of individuals, nor yet of families, but of nations: 'All authority has been give to Me in heaven and on earth. Go therefore and make disciples of all the nations, baptizing them in the name of the Father and of the Son and of the Holy Spirit, teaching them to observe all things that I have commanded you: and, I am with you always, even to the end of the age' (Matthew 28:18-20).

"Nations are made up of people, and it is people who are baptized and taught; yet Jesus says that the goal of all this baptizing and teaching is that the nations as such be discipled. This has always been the view of the church. There were Christian nations and non-Christian nations. Christian nations were nations that (1) recognized the sanctity of the visible or institutional church, and (2) lived by Christian moral values. Non-Christian nations were nations that did not recognize the church and did not live by Christian values…

"…the Bible is concerned with nations far

more than with states. States or governments come and go, but the peoples to whom God has apportioned the earth abide from generation to generation. As Christians, we must think primarily in terms of nations and peoples and only secondarily in terms of states or governments." – *Christendom and the Nations*, pg. 1

"Many Christians are used to thinking that the nations are a result of a curse by which God scattered people at the Tower of Babel. No so. The curse of Babel came because the people rejected God's plan of diversified nations. God had to come down and force them to do what He intended for them. Notice that it is in Genesis 9 that we have listed the seventy nations of the world. The story of Babel is not recorded until Genesis 11." – *Christendom and the Nations*, pg. 5

"The states of modern Europe are actually composed of several nations each. In recent years, these small nations have become insistent that they be allowed cultural diversity, and some have even demanded independence. This seems strange to us, because we are used to thinking of France, Spain, and Great Britain as single, unified nations, but they are not. In each case, the most powerful nation in these countries has conquered and subdued the others. This state-imposed unity is falling apart today, however." – *Christendom and the Nations*, pg. 12

"When God created the world, He established many distinct lands. Humanity was put in the land of Eden, but there were rivers that flowed out of Eden to other lands, such as Havilah and Cush. As men multiplied and spread, they would move to these other lands and form new nations. While this gives us a picture of diversity, it also gives us a picture of unity.

"Genesis 2:10 says, 'Now a river went out of Eden to water the Garden, and from there it parted and became four riverheads.' The following verses describe how these rivers spread out to the 'four corners of the earth' in order to water all the lands. What we want to see here is that the water flowing from Eden to the whole world is the basic symbol of international unity." – Genesis. *The Bible And The Nations*, pg. 14

"Many Christians are used to thinking that the nations are a result of a curse by which God scattered people at the Tower of Babel. Not so. The curse of Babel came because the people rejected God's plan of diversified nations. God had to come down and force them to do what He intended for them. Notice that it is in Genesis 10 that we have listed the seventy nations of the world. The story of the Tower of Babel is not recorded until Genesis 11." – *The Bible And The Nations*, pg. 5. Genesis 10-11

"A couple of centuries after the Assyrians took away the people of Northern Israel, the Babylonians under Nebuchadnezzar carried off the people of Judah into captivity. The books of Daniel and Ezekiel describe this captivity. "Now, what was going on here? It was the policy of these ancient empires to move whole populations of people from place to place, scattering them, so as to destroy national unity. The central planners of these empires wanted to break up all local ties and allegiances and make people loyal only to the central state, that is, to the imperial court and bureaucracy." – Daniel. *The Bible And The Nations*, pg. 11

Alexander Jun

When asked by an interviewer how Asian-American Christians find confidence:

"I think that people are more comfortable now, increasingly with pastors. [They have] feelings of inadequacy because they know they're not in a Korean language and Korean culture, context. And then feelings of inadequacy of being ethnically a minority in white spaces. Finding others sort of [leads] to a greater sense of solidarity, that you're not alone. I don't know if that necessarily leads to confidence, but it certainly leads to knowing that God sees us. God sees you and you see others who are in the same situation. And there's a strange sort of comfort that comes from knowing that you're not alone. And I think if nothing else, you feel like the denomination is for you. And that's part of the goal of KALI.[50] To know that you belong. But I think a big part of before we get into service and leadership, you have to want to be there. And so part of our role is just finding a place for people to feel like they belong.

"And I don't know if others are like this, but I certainly am. When I go to some new situation.

---

50 The PCA's Korean American Leadership Initiative.

I look and I see, oh, there's another Korean American. Let me go talk to this person, right. And you start counting noses. Oh, that person looks Korean, that person's Asian. Let me go talk to them. And we're just leaning into that and being intentional to say, hey, guess what, there's a space for you, Korean Americans, Asian Americans to gather together, and we used to do one event during the General Assembly. Now we're doing it every day, every night, there will always be a place for you. So we have Airbnb, and it's, we're going to call it the KALI house. And people are welcome to come over and stay as a respite for the business of assembly business, or just to be there and make new networks and friendships and ministry partnerships." – *The Journey and Value of Asian American Churches: An Interview with Dr. Alexander Jun*, *SOLA Network*, September 22, 2022

Carl Jung

"Our souls as well as our bodies are composed of individual elements which were all already present in the ranks of our ancestors. The 'newness' in the individual psyche is an endlessly varied recombination of age-old components. Body and soul therefore have an intensely historical character and find no proper place in what is new, in things that have just come into being. That is to say, our ancestral components are only partly at home in such things. We are very far from having finished completely with the Middle Ages, classical antiquity, and primitivity, as our modern psyches pretend.

"Nevertheless, we have plunged down a cataract of progress which sweeps us on into the future with ever wilder violence the farther it takes us from our roots. Once the past has been breached, it is usually annihilated, and there is no stopping the forward motion. But it is precisely the loss of connection with the past, our uprootedness, which has given rise to the 'discontents' of civilization and to such a flurry and haste that we live more in the future and its chimerical promises of a golden age than in the present, with which our whole evolutionary background has not yet caught up. We rush impetuously into novelty, driven by a mounting sense of insufficiency, dissatisfaction, and restlessness. We no longer live on what we have, but on promises, no longer in the light of the present day, but in the darkness of the future, which, we expect, will at last bring the proper sunrise. We refuse to recognize that everything better is purchased at the price of something worse; that, for example, the hope of greater freedom is canceled out by increased enslavement to the state, not to speak of the terrible perils to which the most brilliant discoveries of science expose us. The less we understand of what our fathers and forefathers sought, the less we understand ourselves, and thus we help with all our might to rob the individual of his roots and his guiding instincts, so that he becomes a particle in the mass, ruled only by what Nietzsche called the spirit of gravity.

"Reforms by advances, that is, by new methods or gadgets, are of course impressive at first, but in the long run they are dubious and in any case dearly paid for. They by no means increase the contentment or happiness of people on the whole. Mostly, they are deceptive sweetenings of existence, like speedier communications which unpleasantly accelerate the tempo of life and leave us with less time than ever before. Omnis festinatio ex parte diaboli est; all haste is of the devil, as the old masters used to say.

"Reforms by retrogressions, on the other hand, are as a rule less expensive and in addition more lasting, for they return to the simpler, tried and tested ways of the past and make the sparsest use of newspapers, radio, television, and all supposedly timesaving innovations...

"In the Tower at Bollingen it is as if one lived in many centuries simultaneously. The place will outlive me, and in its location and style it points backward to things of long ago. There is very little about it to suggest the present. If a man of the sixteenth century were to move into the house, only the kerosene lamp and the matches would be new to him; otherwise, he would know his way about without difficulty. There is nothing to disturb the dead, neither electric light nor telephone. Moreover, my ancestors' souls are sustained by the atmosphere of the house, since I answer for them the questions that their lives once left behind. I carve out rough answers as best I can. I have even drawn them on the walls. It is as if a silent, greater family, stretching down the centuries, were peopling the house. There I live in my second personality and see life in the round, as something forever coming into being and passing on." – *Memories, Dreams, Reflections*, pgs. 235-237

Ernst Jünger

"After fourteen days I was lying on the feather mattress of a hospital train. Once again a German landscape flitted by me, tinged this time with the first dyes of autumn, and once again, as on that time at Heidelberg, I was gripped by the sad and proud feeling of being more closely bound to my country because of the blood shed for her greatness. Why should I conceal that tears smarted in my eyes when I thought of the end of the enterprise in which I had borne my share ? I had set out to the war gaily enough, thinking we were to hold a festival on which all the pride of youth was lavished, and I had thought little, once I was in the thick of it, about the ideal that I had to stand for. Now I looked back: four years of development in the midst of a generation predestined to death, spent in caves, smoke-filled trenches, and shell-illumined wastes; years enlivened only by the pleasures of a mercenary, and nights of guard after guard in an endless perspective; in short, a monotonous calendar full of hardships and privation, divided by the red-letter days of battles. And almost without any thought of mine, the idea of the Fatherland had been distilled from all these afflictions in a clearer and brighter essence. That was the final winnings in a game on which so often all had been staked: the nation was no longer for me an empty thought veiled in symbols; and how could it have been otherwise when I had seen so many die for its sake, and been schooled myself to stake my life for its credit every minute, day and night, without a thought? And so, strange as it may sound, I learned from this very four years' schooling in force and in all the fantastic extravagance of material warfare that life has no depth of meaning except when it is pledged for an ideal, and that there are ideals in comparison with which the life of an individual and even of a people has no weight. And though the aim for which I fought as an individual, as an atom in the whole body of the army, was not to be achieved, though material force cast us, apparently, to the earth, yet we learned once and for all to stand for a cause and if necessary to fall as befitted men.

"Hardened as scarcely another generation ever was in fire and flame, we could go into life as though from the anvil; into friendship, love, politics, professions, into all that destiny had in store. It is not every generation that is so favoured.

"And if it be objected that we belong to a time of crude force our answer is: We stood with our feet in mud and blood, yet our faces were turned to things of exalted worth. And not one of that countless number who fell in our attacks fell for nothing. Each one fulfilled his own resolve. For to every one may be applied the saying from St. John that Dostoievski put in front of his greatest novel: 'Verily, verily, I say unto you, except a corn of wheat fall into the ground and die, it abideth alone: but if it die, it bringeth forth much fruit.'

"To-day we cannot understand the martyrs who threw themselves into the arena in a transport that lifted them even before their deaths beyond humanity, beyond every phase of pain and fear. Their faith no longer exercises a compelling force. When once it is no longer possible to understand how a man gives his life for his country—and the time will come —then all is over with that faith also, and the idea of the Fatherland is dead; and then, perhaps, we shall be envied, as we envy the saints their inward and irresistible strength. For all these great and solemn ideas bloom from a feeling that dwells in the blood and that cannot be forced. In the cold light of reason everything alike is a matter of expedience and sinks to the paltry and mean. It was our luck to live in the invisible rays of a feeling that filled the heart, and of this inestimable treasure we can never be deprived." – *Storm of Steel*, pgs. 315-317

Justinian

"The law of nature is that law which nature teaches to all animals. For this law does not belong exclusively to the human race, but belongs to all animals, whether of the earth, the air, or the water. Hence comes the union of the male and female, which we term matrimony; hence the procreation and bringing up of children. We see, indeed, that all the other animals besides men are considered as having knowledge of this law." – *Institutes* 1.2, *Natural Law Reader*, pg. 91

K

Kamose

"Let me understand what this strength of mine is for! [One] prince is in Avaris, another is in Ethiopia, and [here] I sit associated with an Asiatic and a Negro! Each man has his slice of this Egypt, dividing up the land with me. I cannot pass by him as far as Memphis, the waters of Egypt, [but], behold, he has Hermopolis. No man can settle down, being despoiled by the imposts of the Asiatics. I will grapple with him, that I may cut open his belly! My wish is to save Egypt and to smite the Asiatics!" – pharaoh, king of Thebes, 18th century b.c., quoted in *Ancient Near Eastern Texts Relating to the Old Testament*, pg. 132.[51]

Gjergj Kastrioti (Skanderbeg)

"The two most important things in a man's life, are first to adore God by faithfully serving him, and second to give our lives and to shed our blood for our country's preservation and safety." – as quoted in Raymond Ibrahim, *The Defenders of the West: The Christian Heroes Who Stood Against Islam*, pg. 268

"Although we lived together as a family, as it were, in one and the same course of life, although we ate at one and the same table and though we did in a manner breathe jointly with one and the same soul, nevertheless, neither they [Hamza and other Albanian confidants] nor any man alive ever heard me mention my country—except during the war with Hungary. Neither was there any man that heard me use any speech, or utter any word at any time, which might reveal me to be a Christian or a free man, until such time as I saw and perceived

that I might freely do so and without fear of danger. ... [Even so] I still lived in the hope that you should one day see me as I am now..."
"It was not I that put arms in your hands. I found you ready in arms. I found you everywhere bearing the signs of liberty in your hearts, in your faces, in your swords, and in your lances. And, as most loyal teachers and guardians ordained by my father, you have put the scepter in my hands with no less faith and diligence than as if you had kept and preserved it especially for me even unto this day. And you have brought me by your effort and careful care into my ancestral possession [of Croya] without shedding any [Albanian] blood." – *Scanderbeg*, pgs. 2-5 [52]

"Let us levy and muster our soldiers. And let us make known unto all ages to come that we are men worthy of a Christian Nation." – *Scanderbeg*, pg. 13

On his deathbed, speaking to his comrades-in-arms:
"The two most important things in a man's life, he offered, are first to "adore God" by faithfully serving him, and second, "to give our lives and to shed our blood for our country's preservation and safety..."
"Before my soul departs from my body and before I leave you, there is one thing of which I find it necessary to admonish you and to plead with you: until now, during my lifetime, you have endured all suffering for the safety and dignity of our Christian religion and our country. By these means you have won the favor, honor and admiration of all the princes of Christendom. Even hereafter, when I am dead and gone, let that be the only and the whole desire of your

---

51 The saying recounts the localist retaliation of the Hyksos invasion. As found on the Carnarvon Tablet.
52 Skanderberg was an Albanian lord and military commander who had been taken captive by Ottomans, feigned loyalty to them for a time, but returned to his people and land to free them from Muslim attack and rule. He spoke often of being motivated by loyalty to his people, place, and religion.

hearts. All things, I can assure you, will fall out happily for you as long as you continue steadfastly united and as long as you put the public and common good above personal interest...."
– Scanderbeg, pgs. 86-87

Leon R. Kass

Commenting on Genesis 11 and the Tower of Babel episode:

"The House of the Foundation of Heaven and Earth thus sought to link the city with the cosmos, and to bring the city into line with the heavenly powers that be, or to bring the powers that be into line with the goals of the city. In more ways than one, the towered city is, in principle, 'cosmopolis.' ...

"To make a name for oneself is, most radically, to 'make that which requires a name.' To make a new name for oneself is to remake the meaning of one's life so that it deserves a new name... At once makers and made, the founders of Babel aspire to nothing less than self-recreation – through the arts and crafts, customs and mores of their city... The children of man remake themselves and, thus, their name, in every respect taking the place of God." – The Beginning of Wisdom: Reading Genesis, pgs. 230-231

Patrick Kavanagh

"The bicycles go by in twos and threes–
There's a dance in Billy Brennan's barn tonight,
And there's the half-talk code of mysteries
And the wink-and-elbow language of delight."
– Inniskeen Road: July Evening (lines 1-4) [53]

"My father played the melodeon
Outside at our gate;
There were stars in the morning east
And they danced to his music."
– A Christmas Childhood (lines 1-4)

"Clay is the word
   and clay is the flesh
Where the potato-gatherers
   like mechanised scarecrows move
Along the side-fall of the hill –
   Maguire and his men."
– The Great Hunger (lines 1-3)

"My hills hoard the bright shillings of March
While the sun searches in every pocket.
They are my Alps and I have
   climbed the Matterhorn
With a sheaf of hay for three perishing calves."
– Shancoduff (lines 1-4)

John Keats

"Here will I sit and wait, while to my ear
From yonder grove of brooding blackbird sings,
And tell me where is he who knows not tears
When piped to in these pleasant minstrelries.
How many idle flitting phantasies
Have danced before me ere their thin array
Fled like the moonbeam's watery white,
And left me on the green hill's side at morn
Wandering alone, and weeping silently!"
 – Ode to a Nightingale (lines 62-70)

"Season of mists and mellow fruitfulness,
Close bosom-friend of the maturing sun;
Conspiring with him how to load and bless
With fruit the vines that round
   the thatch-eves run;
To bend with apples the moss'd cottage-trees,
And fill all fruit with ripeness to the core;
To swell the gourd, and plump the hazel shells
With a sweet kernel; to set budding more,
And still more, later flowers for the bees,
Until they think warm days will never cease,
For summer has o'er-brimm'd
   their clammy cells."
 – To Autumn (lines 1-11)

"Where are the songs of Spring?
   Ay, where are they?
Think not of them, thou hast thy music too,—
While barred clouds bloom the soft-dying day,
And touch the stubble-plains with rosy hue;
Then in a wailful choir the small gnats mourn
Among the river sallows, borne aloft
Or sinking as the light wind lives or dies;
And full-grown lambs loud bleat
   from hilly bourn;
Hedge-crickets sing; and now with treble soft
The red-breast whistles from a garden-croft;
And gathering swallows twitter in the skies."
 – To Autumn (lines 23-33)

---

53 Kavanagh's poetry exalts the beauty of the Irish countryside and the everyday lives of its people. His works often express a love for the authenticity of rural life.

Bartholomäus Keckermann

"Concerning the duty towards the whole community, there are these principles:

1. You should pursue with ardent love the whole community, that is, the country in which you were born, or in which you are a citizen, or finally in which you are well off, as one to which God and nature have bound you. However, if there are faults and deficiencies in your country, you should seriously wish and strive to correct them as much as you can, not excuse or augment them.
2. Every private good must be subordinated to the good of the republic or country.
3. You should strive to preserve the language and idiom of your country, if it is intact; or if it lacks something, you should cultivate it by all means, as language is the bond that connects people in a country and the ornament by which they are adorned among foreigners.
4. Do not rashly condemn or change the customs received in your country unless they are completely absurd.
5. Retain the dress customary in your country; for with the change of dress, customs often change too."

– *The System of Political Discipline*

Craig S. Keener

"God demonstrates his majesty by 'separating' both time and space (Gen 1:4, 7), but he also 'separated' peoples (Gen 10:5, 32; Deut 32:8). God arranged the cosmos (Ps 74:16–17; Wis 7:17–19) but also the nations. Psalm 74:17 declares God's sovereignty over both seasons and boundaries. The focus is more likely primarily on the nations than on nature here. Yet Luke is already preparing for Paul's peroratio here by his use of ὁρίσας (and a similar sounding noun, which facilitates a wordplay here): God determines both times and nations and therefore has the sovereign right to determine Jesus as judge of humanity (Acts 17:31, the only other use of ὁρίζω in this context and one of only six uses in Luke-Acts; cf. Rom 1:4; Heb 4:7).

"Luke more often speaks of 'seasons' in God's dealings with humanity, culminating in the end time (1:7; 3:20; cf. 14:16; 17:31) and including his plan for the nations and their crossing national boundaries (Luke 21:24). Thus the idea may involve the appointed periods of various nations emphasized in Daniel (Dan 2:37–45; 8:19–26; 11:2–45). Given the apocalyptic notion of pre-destined eras, likely shared by Luke (Acts 1:7), this language probably applies to the appointed durations of nations, such as the rise and fall of Assyria, Babylon, the Hellenistic empire, and ultimately Rome. Josephus uses the accuracy of such prophecies to argue for God's sovereignty (Ant. 10.280); their accuracy regarding empires reveals God's authority over history....Genesis follows the creation of humanity with a dispersion of peoples to various locations (Gen 10:5, 10–12, 18–20, 30–32; 11:9, 31), however, and pre-Christian Jewish tradition also emphasizes God's ordaining political boundaries among peoples...Most important, Daniel (Dan 2:21) affirms that God both removes and establishes kings and is sovereign over the times and epochs (i.e., the periods allotted to various kingdoms)." – *Acts: An Exegetical Commentary*, vol. 3, 15:1-23:35

John Kekes

"...there is a universal and objective standard that can be appealed to when evaluating all values ... but there [are also] secondary values—the particular traditional forms in which primary values are interpreted in some context ... particular societies also go beyond general moral requirements by developing and maintaining a framework of traditions that safeguards both the primary and secondary values recognized in that context." – *Case For Conservatism*, pgs. 32, 58-59

Tim Keller

"Science can't prove that all people are equal. That's an act of faith." – quoted in *The Moral Universe of Timothy Keller, The Atlantic*, December 5, 2019

William "Pig Iron" Kelley

"A people who cannot supply their own demand for iron and steel, but purchase it from foreigners beyond seas, are not independent;... they are politically dependent." – *Congressional Globe*, January 11, 1870, p. 369

Willmoore Kendall

"The Framers...did not so much as mention the topic of equality in the new instrument of government—not even in the Preamble, where, remember, they pause to list the purposes (a more perfect union, the blessings of liberty, justice, etc.) for which We the people ordain and establish the Constitution, and, where, if nowhere else, one might expect them to recall that first proposition of the Declaration, under which and for which, remember, they had just fought a great war." – *Contra Mundum*, pgs. 351-352

John Maynard Keynes

"We must hold to Free Trade, in its widest interpretation, as an inflexible dogma, to which no exception is admitted, wherever the decision rests with us. We must hold to this even where we receive no reciprocity of treatment and even in those rare cases where by infringing it we could in fact obtain a direct economic advantage. We should hold to Free Trade as a principle of international morals, and not merely as a doctrine of economic advantage." – *Against the Tide*, pg. 189

"Defense of free trade theory is, I submit, the result of pure intellectual error, due to a complete misunderstanding of the theory of equilibrium in international trade – an error which it is worthwhile to extirpate if one can, because it is shared, I fancy, by a multitude of less eminent free traders. Does he [Beveridge] believe that it makes no difference to the amount of employment in this country if I decide to buy a British car instead of an American car?" – *The Collected Writings Of John Maynard Keynes*, vol. 20, pg. 508

"I am no longer a free trader... to the extent of believing... in abandoning any industry which is unable for the time being to hold its own." – *The Collected Writings Of John Maynard Keynes*, vol. 20, pg. 379

King Edward IV

"Lord, I commit my spirit to Thee. O Lord, thou knoweth how happy it were for me to be with thee. Yet for thy chosen sake, send me life and health, that I may truly serve Thee. O, my Lord God, blesse thy people, and serve thine in-heritance. O Lord God, save thy chosen people of England. O my Lord God, defend this realme from papistry, and maintain thy true religion, that I and my no less that to our parents people may praise thy holy Name, for thy Sonne, Jesus Christ's sake." – quoted by Cranmer in *Eclesiatical Biography Connected With The History Of Religion In England*, pg. 200

Rufus King

"Principles more and more national appear in every quarter of the Union, strong marks of displeasure on the subject of foreign influence and foreign interferences in our affairs are likewise seen in the different News Papers; so that I think it will be soon perceived that we are neither Greeks nor Trojans, but truly Americans." – In a letter to General Pinckney, written from London, January 20th, 1797; *The Life and Correspondence of Rufus King: 1795-1799*, pg. 134

"In case the Rebellion is suppressed...thousands of the fugitives will seek an asylum in our Country. Their principles and habits would be pernicious to the order and industry of our people, and I cannot persuade myself that the Malcontents of any character or country will ever become useful citizens of ours. It is my duty seasonably to apprize you of the probability of this Emigration; but it belongs to others to decide what the safety and welfare of the Country may require to be done, should it actually take place." – In a letter to the Secretary of State (No. 78) written from London, England, June 14th, 1798; *The Life and Correspondence of Rufus King: 1795-1799*, pg. 637

"As I have intimated to you would probably be the case, I perceive that numbers of the disaffected will be expelled and that they will be disposed to plant themselves among us. It was the practice of the Emigrants from Scotland to bring with them Certificates from the religious Societies to which they belonged, of their honesty, sobriety, and generally of their good Character! Why should we not require some such Document from all Emigrants, and it would be well to add to the Testimonial that the person to whom it was granted was not expelled from his Country and had not been convicted of any crime. I am, I confess, very anxious upon this subject. The contrast between New England and some other Parts of the U. S. is in my view a powerful admonition to us to observe greater caution in the admission of Foreigners among us. If from the emigrations of past time we have suffered inconvenience and our true national character has been disfigured, what are we to expect from the Emigrants of the present Day?" – In a letter to Col. Pickering, written from London, England, July 19th, 1798; *The Life and Correspondence of Rufus King: 1795-1799*, vol. 2, pg. 371

Rudyard Kipling

Land of our Birth, we pledge to thee
Our love and toil in the years to be;
When we are grown and take our place
As men and women with our race.
Father in Heaven who lovest all,
Oh, help Thy children when they call;
That they may build from age to age
An undefiled heritage.
Teach us to bear the yoke in youth,
With steadfastness and careful truth;
That, in our time, Thy Grace may give
The Truth whereby the Nations live.

...

Land of our Birth, our faith, our pride,
For whose dear sake our fathers died;
Oh, Motherland, we pledge to thee
Head, heart and hand through the years to be!
– *Children's Song*

Now, this is the cup the White Men drink
When they go to right a wrong,
And that is the cup of the old world's hate–
Cruel and strained and strong.
We have drunk that cup—and a bitter,
   bitter cup
And tossed the dregs away.
But well for the world when the
   White Men drink
To the dawn of the White Man's day!
Now, this is the road that the
   White Men tread
When they go to clean a land–
Iron underfoot and levin overhead
And the deep on either hand.
We have trod that road—
   and a wet and windy road
Our chosen star for guide.
Oh, well for the world when the
   White Men tread

Their highway side by side!
Now, this is the faith that the
   White Men hold
When they build their homes afar–
"Freedom for ourselves and
   freedom for our sons
And, failing freedom, War."
We have proved our faith—
   bear witness to our faith,
Dear souls of freemen slain!
Oh, well for the world when the
   White Men join
To prove their faith again!
– *A Song of the White Men*

The Stranger within my gate,
He may be true or kind,
But he does not talk my talk–
I cannot feel his mind.
I see the face and the eyes and the mouth,
But not the soul behind.
The men of my own stock
They may do ill or well,
But they tell the lies I am wonted to.
They are used to the lies I tell,
And we do not need interpreters
When we go to buy and sell.
The Stranger within my gates,
He may be evil or good,
But I cannot tell what powers control
What reasons sway his mood;
Nor when the Gods of his far-off land
Shall repossess his blood.
The men of my own stock,
Bitter bad they may be,
But, at least, they hear the things I hear,
And see the things I see;
And whatever I think of them and their likes
They think of the likes of me.
This was my father's belief
And this is also mine:
Let the corn be all one sheaf–
And the grapes be all one vine,
Ere our children's teeth are set on edge
By bitter bread and wine.
– *The Stranger*

It was not part of their blood,
 It came to them very late,
 With long arrears to make good,
 When the Saxon began to hate.
They were not easily moved,
 They were icy — willing to wait

— RUDYARD KIPLING —

Till every count should be proved,
 Ere the Saxon began to hate.
Their voices were even and low.
 Their eyes were level and straight.
There was neither sign nor show
 When the Saxon began to hate.
It was not preached to the crowd.
 It was not taught by the state.
No man spoke it aloud
 When the Saxon began to hate.
It was not suddenly bred.
 It will not swiftly abate.
 Through the chilled years ahead,
 When Time shall count from the date
 That the Saxon began to hate.
– *Wrath of the Awakened Saxon*

"You belong with your people.
A true man like a true horse
runs with his breed."
 – *Mahbub Ali, Kim*

Patriarch Kirill

"The most fundamental conflict of our present era is the clash between the liberal model of civilization on the one hand and national cultural and religious identity on the other." – *Religious Faith As The Source of Social Norms*

"The real problem lies elsewhere, in the absence of barriers in today's world to protect nations' spiritual health, and their religious and historical identity, from the expansion of alien, destructive social and cultural factors, from the new way of life that is arising and taking shape outside of any tradition under the influence of today's post-industrial world. At the basis of this lifestyle are liberal ideas, combining pagan anthropocentrism – which entered European culture through the Renaissance – Protestant theology and Jewish philosophical thought. By the end of the Enlightenment these ideas had shaped themselves into a certain set of liberal principles. The French Revolution marked the culmination of this spiritual and ideological revolution, based on the rejection of the normative significance of tradition. Where did this revolution start? It began with the Reformation and with the reformers' rejection of the normative significance of tradition in the field of Christian dogma. In Protestantism, tradition ceased being a criterion of truth, to be replaced by the believer's personal understanding of the Scriptures and personal religious experience. Protestantism is in essence a liberal reading of Christianity." – *Religious Faith As The Source of Social Norms*

"Another sensitive topic is that of Church and nation. Unfortunately, in this area, very one-sided affirmations are presented as the teaching of the Church. Some seek to deny the very concept of Christian patriotism and the right of Christians to national identity. Others effectively degrade the Orthodox faith to the role of one attribute of traditional national identity. It is therefore vital for the Church to show how, based on the word of God and Tradition, national and universal principles blend harmoniously with Christian life." – *Religious Faith As The Source of Social Norms*

"The rapid development of communications and mass media in modern times has radically changed not only the face of the world, but also the structure of inter-personal, inter-ethnic and inter-state relations. In today's world almost all the boundaries that formerly separated national cultures have come tumbling down. Today people move with unprecedented ease right around the globe, freely choosing to live and work anywhere in the world. This is producing enormous cultural and ethnic displacements, the full consequences of which we have not yet fully grasped. The era of mono-ethnic and mo-no-confessional states is gradually disappearing before our very eyes." – *Religious Faith As The Source of Social Norms*

"Personal ethics do indeed lie at the very heart of Christian morality. The Christian message is aimed in the first place at the individual person, seeking to elicit a personal spiritual experience and response which will open the way to the transfiguration of his or her soul. Nonetheless, these salvation-bringing changes in our inner worlds take place, not in isolation from the external environment, not in special laboratory conditions, but in real and living contact with the people around us, in the first instance in our families, then with our colleagues at work, with society and ultimately, with the institutions of state. It is not possible to be a Christian inside the walls of one's own home, in one's family circle or in the solitude of one's cell and to cease to be Christian when teaching at university or in school, standing in front of a television camera, voting in Parliament or undertaking a scientific experiment. Christian motivation must be present in everything that constitutes the believer's sphere of vital interests. A believer cannot exclude his professional life or scientific interests, his political, economic or social activities, his work in the media and the like from this spiritual and moral context. Religious belief encompasses everything a believer is or does. The religious way of life is the mode of existence in the world of people whose choices are motivated and determined by their religious principles." – *Religious Faith As The Source of Social Norms*

"What we are facing today is a new post-industrial way of life, based on personal freedom from any conventions and restrictions, other than the limitations imposed by law. How should we handle this theologically? The concept of liberalism rests on the idea of liberating human beings from all that is understood as limiting their desires and their rights. Asserting the absolute value of the individual, the liberal standard takes individual freedom as the goal and means of human existence...

"However, on the other side of this borderline begins the region of sly, diabolic and destructive falsehood. When the Apostle Paul calls us to freedom, he is speaking of man's destiny to be free in Christ: that is, liberated from the shackles of sin. Man finds his true freedom in being liberated from sin, from the dark powers of instinct and of evil hanging over him....

"The liberal idea does not call for any freeing from sin, because the very concept of sin is absent in liberalism. Man is allowed to behave sinfully, providing he remains within the law of the land and does not violate the freedom of another person. In other words liberal doctrine releases man's potential for sin. A free person is entitled to reject everything that binds him and prevents him from adopting his sinful 'me'. In all this he is entirely independent of anyone but himself. In this respect, the liberal idea is diametrically opposed to Christianity, and may be justly labelled anti-Christian.

"The problem we are considering is considerably complicated by the fact that modern liberalism has long outgrown the baby clothes of the philosophical emancipation of the human individual. It has continued its forward march into all spheres of human life, including economics, politics, law, religion, social relations and the organization of society. From this liberal idea stems the generally accepted understanding of civil liberties, democratic institutions, the market economy, free competition, freedom of speech, freedom of conscience – all that is included in the concept of modern civilization'" – *Religious Faith As The Source of Social Norms*

"Multiculturalism has no future, because it implies different cultures mixing, different cultures and religions poured together and shaken vigorously to create a kind of cocktail. That would be impossible because of deep-rooted traditions. If multiculturalism implies weakening people's connection to their religion and traditions, it automatically makes them victims of discrimination and forces them to be defensive; so this very approach contains a dangerous source of division, and I mean the fundamental division of the brother-against-brother kind." – RT Interview, *Western laws now clash with moral nature of man*

"What's happening in the Western countries is that, for the first time in human history, legislation is at odds with the moral nature of human beings... This moral nature, created by God, served as a foundation for the legislation which is designed. Laws defined moral values in legal terms, telling us what's good and what's bad. We know that stealing is bad and helping people is good, and laws define what stealing is and what the suitable punishment for it is. Now, for the first time in human history, the law allows something that doesn't correspond to our moral nature. The law contradicts it." – RT Interview, *Western laws now clash with moral nature of man*

Russell Kirk

"The only true forms of equality are equality at the Last Judgment and equality before a just court of law; all other attempts at leveling must lead, at best, to social stagnation." – *The Portable Conservative Reader*, pg. xvii

"In the affairs of nations, the American conservative feels that his country ought to set an example to the world, but ought not to try to remake the world in its image. It is a law of politics, as well as of biology, that every living thing loves above all else—even above its own life—its distinct identity, which sets it off from all other things. The conservative does not aspire to domination of the world, nor does he relish the prospect of a world reduced to a single pattern of government and civilization." – *Concise Guide to Conservatism*, pg. 5

"Modern society urgently needs true community: and true community is a world away from collectivism. Real community is governed by love and charity, not by compulsion. Through churches, voluntary associations, local governments, and a variety of institutions, conservatives strive to keep community healthy. Conservatives are not selfish, but public-spirited. They know that collectivism means the end of real community, substituting uniformity for variety and force for willing cooperation.

"Variety and diversity are the characteristics of a high civilization. Uniformity and absolute equality are the death of all real vigor and freedom in existence. Conservatives resist with impartial strength the uniformity of a tyrant or an oligarchy, and the uniformity of what Tocqueville called 'democratic despotism.'" – *Concise Guide to Conservatism*, pg. 4

Gerhard Kittel

"God intervenes to re-establish the order imposed by Him. Similarly, in Dt. 32:8 the division of the world into nations is a divine order and not a punishment for human sin: 'When the most High divided to the nations their inheritance, when he separated the sons of Adam, he set the bounds of the people according to the number (of the sons of God) ...' The LXX makes the final subsidiary clause into the main clause: ὅτε διεμέριζεν ὁ ὕψιστος ἔθνη, ὡς διέσπειρεν υἱοὺς Ἀδάμ, ἔστησεν ὅρια ἐθνῶν κατὰ ἀριθμὸν ἀγγέλων θεοῦ." – "Nation" in *Theological Dictionary Of The New Testament*, vol. 2, pg. 367

"...it remains true that Hebrew evidences a tendency for goy to describe a people in terms of its political and territorial affiliation, and so to approximate much more closely to our modern term 'nation.' 'am, conversely, always retains a strong emphasis on the element of consanguinity as the basis of union into a people." – "Nation" in *Theological Dictionary Of The Old Testament*, vol. 2, pg. 427

"Since the OT does not contain any ordered or consistent doctrine of nationhood, we find that there is no precise definition of what constitutes a goy. Instead, we find that the three major aspects of race, government, and territory all contribute features of their own toward a comprehensive picture. The element of common racial origin, with its basis in consanguinity, plays an important part in the structure of a goy, even though it is more strongly expressed in the OT by the terms 'am and mishpachah." – "Nation" in *Theological Dictionary Of The Old Testament*, vol. 2, pg. 428

Ludwig Klages

"The man of instinct is devoted to his homeland. In this feeling for the homeland is rooted all art, nobility, and race. Only the man without a homeland can break with his past. The noble man attaches himself completely to the historical fortunes of his tribe. He will never repudiate his youth; he will never abandon his home." – *Rhythmen Und Runen*, pg. 246; quoted in *Cosmogonic Reflections*, pg. 10

John Knox

"Give me Scotland, or I die." – quoted in *Collected Prayers*, Preface

"We have expedient, so truly and briefly as we can, to commit to writing the causes moving us to take the sword of just defense against those that most unjustly seek our destruction. And in this Confession we shall faithfully declare what moved us to put our hands to the Reformation of Religion; how we have proceeded in the same; what we have asked and what we presently require of the sacred authority...that our brethren, natural Scotsmen, of whatever religion they be, may have occasion to examine themselves, who seek nothing but Christ Jesus and his glorious evangel to be preached; his holy Sacraments to be truly ministered; superstition, tyranny, and idolatry to be suppressed in this Realm; and finally the liberty of this our native country to remain free from the bondage and tyranny of strangers." – *Works*, vol. I, pg. 298

Complaining to the Scottish Lords about the Queen:
"And farther, that same time did thrust in upon the heads of the inhabitants of the said town proves and belies, against all order of election; as lately, in this last month of September, she had down in the towns of Edinburgh and Jedburgh, and diverse other places, in manifest oppression of our liberties. Last of all, declaring her evil mind toward the Nobility, community, and whole nation, has brought in strangers, and daily pretends to bring in greater force of the same; pretending a manifest conquest of our native land and country, as the deed itself declares: in so far as she having brought in the said strangers...has placed and planted her said strangers in one of the principal towns and ports of the realm, sending continually for greater forces, (intending) thereby to suppress the commonweal and liberty of our native country, and to make us and our posterity slaves to strangers forever." – *Works*, vol. I, pg. 445

"For your subjects, yea your brethren are oppressed, their bodies and souls held in bondage and God speaketh to your consciences, unless ye be dead with the blind world, that ye ought to hasard your own lives, be it against kings or emperors for their deliverance, for only for that cause are ye called. Ye are princes of the people, not by birth, but by reason of your office and duty which is to deliver your subjects and brethren from all violence and oppression to the uttermost of your power." – *Works*, vol. I, pg. 272

"To bridle the fury and rage of princes in free kingdoms and realms appertains to the nobility, sworn and born counsellors of the same, and also to the barons and people whose votes and consent are required in all great and weighty matters of the commonwealth." – *Works*, vol. I, pg. 830

"We [i.e. the Congregation] wrote to the Queen Regent saying, 'If we do not have the Word truly preached and the holy sacraments ministered to us, we will revolt from our accustomed obedience.'" – *Works*, vol. I, pg. 326

"The occasion of this disputation and conclusion, was a certain disorder and tyranny that was attempted by the Pope's governors, who began to make innovations in the country against the laws that were before established, alleging themselves not to be subject to such laws, by reason that they were not instituted by the people, but by the Pope, who was King of that country; and therefore they, having full commission and authority of the Pope, might alter and change statutes and ordinances of the country, without all consent of the people." – *Works*, vol. II, pg. 132

"The office of the civil magistrate is not only to purge the church of God from all superstitions and set it at liberty from bondage and tyranny, but also to provide how it may abide in the same purity to the posterities following." – *Works*, vol. II, pg. 208

"That subjects not only may but also ought to withstand and resist their princes whensoever they do anything expressly repugnant to God, his law or holy ordinance." – *Works*, vol. II, pg. 450

"Against this their usurped tyranny, the learned and the people opposed themselves openly: and when that all reasons which the Pope's governors could allege were heard and confuted, the Pope himself was feign to take up the matter, and to promise to keep not only the liberty of the people, but also that he should neither abrogate any law or statute, neither yet make any new law without their own consent. And, therefore, my Lord (said he), my vote and conscience is, that princes are not only bound to keep laws and promises to their subjects, but also, that in case they fail, they justly may be deposed; for the band betwix the Prince and the people is reciprocal." – *Works*, vol. II, pg. 459

"God hath placed kings to punish vice and maintain virtue. They should therefore admit no worship of God, but that which is commanded in Scriptures. For God, because of idolatry, hath destroyed many kingdoms." – *Works*, vol. III, pg. 26

"Why the Pope and his kingdom do hate and persecute us, is that we affirm that no power on earth is above the power of the civil ruler, that every soul, be he Pope or Cardinal, ought to be subject to the higher powers. With Tertullian we affirm that the Emperor and every Prince within his own dominions hath his whole authority of God, and is inferior but to God only." – *Works*, vol. IV, pg. 324

"This precept requireth not only that the king himself should keep God's laws and statutes, but that also he, as the chief ruler, should provide that God's true religion should be kept by the people, which, by God, was given to his charge. The reformation of religion, together with the punishment of false teachers, is within the power and duty of the civil magistrate." – *Works*, vol. IV, pg. 487

"It is lawful to God's prophets and preachers of Christ Jesus to appeal from the sentence of the visible church to the knowledge of the temporal Magistrates, who, by God's laws, are bound to hear their causes, and defend them from tyranny." – *Works*, vol. IV, pg. 472

"The punishment of idolatry, blasphemy and other sins that touch the majesty of God doth not appertain only to kings and chief rulers, but to the whole body of the people, and to every member of them according to his vocation, and according to his opportunity." – *Works*, vol. IV, pg. 501

"I feel a sob and a groan, willing that Christ Jesus might openly be preached in my native country, although it should be with the loss of my wretched life." – in a letter to his sister in Edinburgh, April 16, 1558, *Select Practical Writings*, pg. 346

"To promote a woman to bear rule, superiority, dominion, or empire above any realm, nation, or city, is repugnant to nature; contumely to God, a thing most contrary to his revealed will and approved ordinance; and finally, it is the subversion of good order, of all equity and justice." – *The First Blast*, pg. 5

—JOHN KNOX—

"WE, Noblemen, Barons, Knights, Gentlemen, Citizens, Burgesses, Ministers of the Gospel, and Commons of all sorts, in the kingdoms of Scotland, England, and Ireland, by the providence of GOD living under one King, and being of one reformed religion, having before our eyes the glory of GOD, and the advancement of the kingdom of our Lord and Saviour JESUS CHRIST, the honour and happiness of the King's Majesty and his posterity, and the true publick liberty, safety, and peace of the kingdoms, wherein every one's private condition is included..." – *The Solemn League & Covenant*, referenced in *The Covenanted Reformation*, pg. 287

E. Christian Kopff

"The normal, healthy person loves his country as he loves his family, not because either fits into a theory, but because they are his own. If one's son fails an examination, or one's country loses a battle, one does not abandon him or repudiate it. Most Americans know what Stephen Decatur meant when he made his famous toast: 'Our country, right or wrong.' Just as they know what kind of man deserts his wife and children and flatters brutal dictators for self-advancement... 'You must not think that living according to your country's way of life is slavery,' says Aristotle; 'It is salvation.' This is a truth [postmodern deconstructionists] do no understand. The mystery of tradition — that one must be happily rooted in family, in nation, in religion, in culture in order to rise above them — is lost on critical theorists...The truest critique for [such people] are the words John Steinbeck gave to the Chicano warrior Emilio Zapata. 'You have no wife, no woman. You have no farm, no land. You have no love. To destroy, that is your love.'

"The modern ideologue has turned his back on his family, community, and nation to revel in the destruction of the cultural traditions that are built on them. They are totalitarians, despite all their chatter of ridding the world of 'totalizing language.' The great enemy of the anti traditional ideologues of the twentieth century has been the United States. Now as in the past, the American way of life — the life really lived by traditional Americans — represents a profound commitment to the political, ethical, and religious ideals that developed out of ancient Greece, Rome, and Israel, the traditions that formed Europe. Those traditions live on in the memory and actions of our libraries and homes. The key that opens those treasuries to young people is as close as a teacher's enthusiasm or a parent's love." – *The Devil Knows Latin*, pgs. 133-135

A.J. Köstenberger

"Ancient perceptions of nationhood were largely a function of the following factors (D. I. Block, in NIDOTTE, pgs. 967-970): ethnicity and language; territory; religion; kingship; and history. Israel's history can be understood in this context. The ancient Hebrews exhibited a strong sense of ethnic cohesion. This cohesion was reinforced by Israel's call to be distinct from the surrounding nations (e.g. Lev. 20:24, 26). God's promise of territory to Abraham followed from that of his descendants becoming a great nation (Gen. 12:1-3). In the Promised Land, the Israelites would experience fullness of life, prosperity and security." – "Nation" in *New Dictionary of Biblical Theology*, T. D. Alexander & B. S. Rosner (Eds.), pg. 676

Ronald L. Koteskey

"...the minimum legal age for marriage has, until recently, been 12 to 14 years of age. In older cultures girls could be married earlier than boys, reflecting differences in the rate of maturation. The minimum legal age for marriage among the ancient Hebrews was at the end of the twelfth year for girls and at the end of the thirteenth year for boys. The Talmud states that persons were expected to be married by age 18. If not married by age 20, some considered their singleness a sign that the wrath of God was upon them...

"Roman girls also were often betrothed during their childhood...Husbands were actively sought when Roman girls reached their thirteenth year; girls not married by age 19 were considered 'old maids.' In these early cultures the choice of a marriage partner was considered too serious a decision to be made by a teenager in an emotional state, and so such decisions were made by the parents and nearly always accepted by the children.

"During the Middle Ages in England parents could betroth their children as early as seven years of age. This contract could be broken until the child was 10 without any penalty, but if broken between 10 and 12 years of age, a fine was levied on the parent, and if broken after 12, both parent and child could be fined. During the Renaissance, betrothals often occurred when the girl was 3 or 4 years of age, with marriage at 12, the legal marriageable age in most of Europe. Most parents considered it a mild disgrace to have a daughter unmarried or unbetrothed by age 16 or 17.

"Early marriages were also the rule in England during the seventeenth and eighteenth centuries. Any boy of 14 and girl of 12 who wished could be married without their parents' consent and at little expense..." – *Growing up Too Late, Too Soon*. Christianity Today, 25(5), 328.

Paul Earl Kragt

"Deuteronomy's absolute insistence on cultural exclusivity. The alien who presumably is amenable to becoming a member of Israelite society–this one is to be treated with respect, empathy. But towards alien cultures themselves there is to be maintained an absolute rejection, else elements of those cultures will come to contaminate and pollute the God-given and wholesome Israelite way of life. There is no modernistic interest in 'learning from other cultures' and no interest in a hypothetical pluralistic amalgamation of miscellaneous cultures.

"Israelite culture would be considered as being complete and self-sustaining already. And God-given; not ever in process of becoming, ever susceptible to cumulative improvement.

"And it must be granted philosophically, it seems to me, that while in general cultures may in fact learn or may adapt, it is even more essential to the continuation of any living human culture that it be able to protect itself, as necessary, from outside influences and forces that might be fundamentally harmful, to shield itself from modification by (potentially deleterious) foreign machination. Because Deuteronomy is most interested in the integrity of one unique entity, the singular and live socio-religious culture of the future Israel, a demand for continued and uncontaminated cultural integrity is stated in absolute terms. No other strange cultures may co-exist in this land." – *Deuteronomy: A Concise Theological Commentary*, 7:3, pg. 62

Léon Krier

"We are told that our works should express the spirit of our age but the best works of the past has always proved the contrary. To transmit a perennial message and value, our work has to transcend the particularities of its age of creation." – *The Architecture of Community*, pg. 73

James Howard Kunstler

"Chronological connectivity lends meaning and dignity to our little lives. It charges the present with a vivid validation of our own aliveness. It puts us in touch with the ages and with the eternities, suggesting that we are part of a larger and more significant organism. It even suggests that the larger organism we are part of cares about us, and that, in turn, we should respect

ourselves and our fellow creatures and all those who will follow us in time, as those preceding us respected those who followed them. In short, chronological connectivity puts us in touch with the holy….

"The buildings our predecessors constructed paid homage to history in their design, including elegant solutions to age-old problems posed by the cycles of weather and light, and they paid respect to the future in the sheer expectation that they would endure through the lifetimes of the people who built them. They therefore embodied a sense of chronological connectivity, one of the fundamental patterns of the universe: an understanding that time is a defining dimension of existence—particularly the existence of living things, such as human beings, who miraculously pass into life and then inevitably pass out of it." – *Home From Nowhere, The Atlantic*, September iss., 1996

Ralph Milan Kundera

"The first step in liquidating a people is to erase its memory. Destroy its books, its culture, its history. Then have someone write new books, manufacture a new culture, invent a new history. Before long the nation will begin to forget what it is and what it was." – *The Book of Laughter and Forgetting*, pg. 218

"The struggle of man against power is the struggle of memory against forgetting." – *The Book of Laughter and Forgetting*, pg. 3

James Kurth

"The Enlightenment, especially in its French version, has been especially committed to the idea of universality, and with it a disdain for the particularities of time, place, culture, and religion. Indeed, the Enlightenment worldview does not take either the classical culture or the Christian religion seriously (its French version actively despises Christianity); it holds that religious or cultural traditions provide no good reason to exclude anyone from immigrating to an enlightened society. Similarly, the Enlightenment thinker has not traditionally taken the Muslim culture or the Islamic religion seriously, but rather has tended to assume that a Muslim who is exposed to or immigrates to an enlightened society will eventually give up the Islamic faith and become an enlightened, universal individual like everyone else. Thus, what the Enlightenment tradition takes seriously is the imperative of universalism. Accordingly, the indiscriminate admission of immigrants, including Muslim immigrants, into Western nations has not only been permitted by this particular, and peculiar, Western tradition; it has been seen as its fulfillment." – *Family and Civilization*, pg. 307

Abraham Kuyper

"Barely touching upon this idea, ladies and gentlemen, let us take a quick glance at the struggle to be waged in the political arena. There, too, the uniformity of modern life is raging. A uniform constitution has to be adopted in all European states, a uniform structure of government in every region and every city. Uniform the model by which the life of Javanese and Hollander has to be tailored; uniform the pattern on which all education must be organized. Uniformity, in a word, is the shibboleth that recurs in the debates on all the burning issues of our time. Well then, right here everyone belonging to the Christian-Historical school rises in principial opposition, for this school strives toward the unity that is in Christ precisely through the free unfolding of historically developed life. Far from wanting to inject the virus of reaction into the bloodstream of our national life, this school's opposition to the existing state of affairs aims only to maintain the unique life-form of our people against the lethal uniformity of our age. It loves 'Freedom and Development.' 'Progress and Refinement' is its watchword when it girds itself for battle against the tyrannies sanctioned by a false uniformity that buries freedom in voluntary slavery and, by severing the root, renders all developmental growth impossible. Accordingly, it is weak when, repristinating, it would substitute the forms of the past for the uniformity of the modern state, but irresistible when it argues the case for the rights of its own form against the blandishments of a false uniformity... It has the obligation to maintain not an arbitrary but a historical autonomy—an autonomy bound to the laws of life itself—for persons, cities, and regions against an all-homogenizing centralism. It has the calling to oppose with vigor the attempts to structure our colonies by the standards of life at home, should there be people who would introduce the experiments of

revolution also among the Javanese and Madurese people. Its slogan has to be: by Javanese or European, a distinct form of government for a distinct way of life. Nor must it anxiously cling to the existing system of culture if it is evident that life's vitalities have totally outgrown that form. On the contrary, following Sinai's laws and practicing justice with integrity, I should not exact the treasure from but rather introduce the Gospel to the peoples of the Indonesian archipelago, not to make them 'Dutch' but to make them Javanese Christians in whose domestic and social life a spiritual life will flow according to its own character and form." – *A Centennial Reader*, pgs. 40-41

"The Javanese are a different race than us; they live in a different region; they stand on a wholly different level of development; they are created differently in their inner life; they have a wholly different past behind them; and they have grown up in wholly different ideas. To expect of them that they should find the fitting expression of their faith in our Confession and in our Catechism is therefore absurd.

"Now this is not something special for the Javanese, but stems from a general rule. The men are not all alike among whom the Church occurs. They differ according to origin, race, country, region, history, construction, mood and soul, and they do not always remain the same, but undergo various stages of development. Now the Gospel will not objectively remain outside their reach, but subjectively be appropriated by them, and the fruit thereof will come to confession and expression, the result may not be the same for all nations and times. The objective truth remains the same, but the matter in appropriation, application and confession must be different, as the color of the light varies according to the glass in which it is collected. He who has traveled and came into contact with Christians in different parts of the world of distinct races, countries and traditions cannot be blind for the sober fact of this reality. It is evident to him. He observes it everywhere." – *Common Grace*, vol. 3, ch. 20, sec. 5

"The fact that now for the first time the actual history of our human race gets underway is expressed in the prophecy that the Holy Spirit placed on Noah's lips. It led him to sketch out the lines along which the history of the world would unfold, in his full blessing for Shem, his partial blessing for Japheth, and his curse on Ham. Within that prophecy lay embedded the concise program of all of world history; the disappointing experience with blacks, the enduring significance of the Jews and Muslims as Shem's offspring, and the great significance Japheth has currently achieved, provide us to this day with the key for explaining world history…

"Whoever ignores or underestimates this powerful act of God's grace, and thereby also his common grace, distorts his view on life, ends up with a false dualism, and easily runs the risk of allowing his Christian religion to deviate from the Reformed track, that is, from the correct track." – *Common Grace*, vol. 1, pg. 110

"And thus we see the fact that Noah had only three sons absolutely does not by itself preclude the possibility that the world of humanity became divided into nine or even more groups or races. It remains striking in this context that from of old the more direct descendants of Shem and Japheth have dominated the history of our human race, and that Ham's descendants never could achieve significance, whereas the other races outside the main groups, with the exception of the Mongols, either languish or disappear." – *Common Grace*, vol. 1, pg. 358

"And thus my final lecture is rapidly drawing to its end. But before I close, I feel nevertheless that one question continues to press for an answer, which accordingly I shall not refuse to face, the question namely, at what I am aiming in the end: at the abandonment of the doctrine of election … Our generation turns a deaf ear to Election [God's order], but grows madly enthusiastic over Selection [encompassing everything from evolution to democracy, liberalism, imagination, and license] … The problem concerns the fundamental question: Whence are the differences? Why is not all alike? Whence is it that one thing exists in one state, another in another? There is no life without differentiation without inequality. The perception of difference, the very source of our human consciousness, the causative principles of all that exists, and grows and develops, in short, the mainspring of all life and thought … Whence are those differences? Whence is the dissimilarity, the heterogeneity of existence, of genesis, and consciousness? To put it concretely, if you were a plant, would you rather be a rose than a mushroom; if insect, butterfly rather than spider; if bird, eagle rather than owl; if a higher vertebrate, a lion rather than a hyena; and again, being a man, richer than poorer, talented rather than dull-minded, of Aryan race rather than Hottentot or Kaffir? Between all these there is differentiation, wide differentiation. Everywhere then differences, differences between one thing and the other; and that too, such differences involve in almost every instance, preference … This is the one supreme question in the vegetable and animal kingdom, among men, in all social life and it is by means of the theory of Selection that our present age attempts to solve this problem of problems …

"Now the blade of grass is not conscious of this, and the spider goes on entrapping the fly, the tiger killing the stag, and in those cases the weaker being does not account to itself for its misery. But we men are clearly conscious of these differences, and by us therefore the question cannot be evaded, whether the theory of Selection be a solution calculated to reconcile the weaker, the less richly endowed creature, with its existence. It will be acknowledged that in itself this theory can but incite to a more furious struggle, with a lasciate ogni speranza, voi che'ntrate[54] for the weaker being. Against the ordinance of faith that the weaker shall succumb to the stronger, according to the system of election, no struggle can avail …

"For this is precisely the high significance of the doctrine of Election that, in this dogma, as long as three centuries ago, Calvinism dared to face this same all-dominating problem, solving it, however, not in the sense of a blind selection stirring in unconscious cells, but honoring the sovereign choice of Him Who created all things visible and invisible. The determination of our own persons, whether one is to be born as girl or boy, rich or poor, dull or clever, white or colored, or even as Abel or Cain, is the most tremendous predestination conceivable in heaven or on earth; and still we see it taking place before our eyes every day, and we ourselves are subject to it in our entire personality; our existence, our very nature, our position in life being entirely dependent on it. This all embracing predestination … all-dominating election. Election in creation, election in providence,

---

54   Latin for 'abandon all hope, ye who enter' from Dante's *Inferno*.

and so election also to eternal life; election in the realm of grace as well as in the realm of nature ... all Christians hold election as we do, in honor, both in creation and in providence; and that Calvinism deviates from the other Christian confessions in this respect only, that, seeking unity and placing the glory God above all things, it dares to extend the mystery of Election to spiritual life, and to the hope for all life to come?" – *Lectures on Calvinism*, pgs. 268-269

"A traveller from the old European Continent, disembarking on the shore of this New World, feels as the Psalmist says, that 'his thoughts crowd upon him like a multitude'. Compared with the eddying waters of your new stream of life, the old stream in which he was moving seems almost frostbound and dull; and here, on American ground, for the first time, he realizes

— ABRAHAM KUYPER —

how so many divine potencies, which were hidden away in the bosom of mankind from our very creation, but which our old world was incapable of developing, are now beginning to disclose their inward splendour, thus promising a still richer store of surprises for the Future.

"You would not, however, ask me to forget the superiority which, in many respects, the Old World may still claim, in your eyes, as well as in mine. Old Europe remains even now the bearer of a longer historical past, and therefore stands before us as a tree rooted more deeply, hiding between its leaves some more matured fruits of life. You are yet in your Springtide,—we are passing through our Fall;—and has not the harvest of Autumn an enchantment of its own?

"But, though, on the other hand, I fully acknowledge the advantage you possess in the fact, that (to use another simile) the train of life travels with you so immeasureably faster than with us,—leaving us miles and miles behind,—still we both feel that the life in Old Europe is not some thing separate from life here; it is one and the same current of human existence that flows through both Continents.

"By virtue of our common origin, you may call us bone of your bone,—we feel that you are flesh of our flesh, and although you are outstripping us in the most discouraging way, you will never forget that the historic cradle of your wondrous youth stood in our old Europe, and was most gently rocked in my once mighty Fatherland.

"Moreover, besides this common parentage, there is another factor which, in the face of even a wider difference, would continue to unite your interests and ours. Far more precious to us than even the development of human life, is the crown which ennobles it, and this noble crown of life for you and for me rests in the Christian name. That crown is our common heritage. It was not from Greece or Rome that the regeneration of human life came forth;—that mighty metamorphosis dates from Bethlehem and Golgotha; and if the Reformation, in a still more special sense, claims the love of our hearts, it is because it has dispelled the clouds of sacerdotalism, and has unveiled again to fullest view the glories of the Cross. But, in deadly opposition to this Christian element, against the very Christian name, and against its salutiferous influence in every sphere of life, the storm of Modernism has now arisen with violent intensity." – *Calvinism: Six Lectures*, pgs. 1-3

"No flower exudes a fragrance other than that of its own kind, whether it is a rose, a daisy, or a lily; and no precious stone sparkles except in accordance with the special name it bears, whether a diamond, a ruby, or a jasper. So also no human beings live under the sun without belonging to their own country and their own people, be it Russian, Spanish, Belgian, or whatever other nation you might name. It is no different with us. We too are not just human beings, but come from the province of Zeeland, Friesland, or North or South Holland. But together we are people of the Netherlands, and as such, we are proud of our country and thank our God that the love of our native soil dwells innately in our lives. We also love the House of Orange-Nassau, and we continue to grow in our national history. No blow would destroy our national conscience more than if our existence as a people were destroyed and the Netherlands were to disappear from the ensemble of free European states." – *Two-fold Fatherland* in *On the Church*, pg. 286

"The drive toward unity in God's revelation is so powerful that every false theory of political unity has hung its banner from the standard of Christianity. Even the theme song of the communists and the revolutionary slogan of 'equality, liberty, and fraternity' were taken from Scripture with seeming legitimacy. But people have failed to see that the unity of the human family may only be looked for in its origin and destiny, never in the developmental phases it passes through on its way. All humanity stems from one ancestor, but from its very beginning it was destined to be sent forth in a variety of directions along different roads. If humanity at Babel's tower tries to unite itself to be a single people forever, the Lord disturbs that undertaking and scatters the peoples over the ends of the earth. The founding of empires, however frequently attempted thereafter, is just as frequently frustrated, and humanity's division into nations and peoples, tribes and races, clans, and families goes on its age-old way. Yet just as it was one in origin, so for all its diversity and dispersion its ideal unity for the future still holds in the promised Messiah, the head of humanity, who is coming. That unity, however,

is not based on the sameness of model but on the oneness of a body in which every member retains its own place. Not like a drop of water in a stream or piece of gravel in a pit but like branches grafted into the one vine, the members of the human race must find their unity in Christ. In the unity of the kingdom of God diversity is not lost but all the more sharply defined. On the great day of Pentecost the Holy Spirit did not speak in one uniform language; instead, everyone heard the Spirit proclaiming the mighty works of God in his own tongue. Though the wall of separation has been demolished by Christ, the lines of distinction have not been abolished. Someday, before the throne of the Lamb, doxologies will be sung to him who conquered, not by a uniform mass of people but by a humanity diversified in peoples and tribes, in nations and tongues [Rev. 5:9]." – From a speech entitled *Uniformity: The Curse of Modern Life* (April 22, 1869), in *Centennial Reader*, pg. 35

"...it is impossible to supply a handbook for Christian political theory that is valid for all nations and all times. The Christian statesman cannot placidly accept such neglect of the differences among nations and the changing times. Each nation, he finds, has its own character, and in the course of time he finds a perpetual fluctuation of circumstance." – *The Ordinances Of God*, quoted in *Natural Law* by VanDrunen, pg. 285

L

Jean-Baptiste Henri Lacordaire

"The love of country is, with the love of Church, the holiest sentiment in the heart of man." – quoted in *Henri Dominique Lacordaire, A Biographical Sketch* by H.L. Sidney Lear, pg. 292

Lactantius

"Under the teaching of Socrates, it did not escape Plato that the strength of justice consists in equity, if, indeed, all are born in an equal condition. 'Therefore,' he said, 'let them have nothing private and personal, but that all may be equal, which the system of justice desires, let them possess all things in common.' This can be taken, as long as it seems to be money that is under discussion. And this, itself, I was able to show in many ways how impossible and how unjust it is. [Socrates said,] 'Marriages also ought to be common,' meaning that many men, as though dogs, might come upon the same woman, and that he, of course, might obtain the prize who has overcome with his strength; or, if they are patient, as philosophers, they may wait and go in turn as if to a house of ill-repute. Marvelous equity of Plato! But where is the virtue of chastity? Where conjugal faith? If you remove these, all justice is taken away.

"But the same man said that the states would be happy if either philosophers would rule or if kings would become philosophers. Would you give the ruling power to this man so just, in truth, so fair, who would have taken away their goods from some, who would have bestowed on others possessions not their own, who would have prostituted the virtue of women, things which not only no king ever did, but not even any tyrant? What reason, therefore, for this most base advice did he offer? 'In this way,' he said, 'the state will be in concord and bound with the chains of a mutual love, if all are the husbands and fathers and wives and children of all.' What a confusion of humankind this is! How can charity be preserved where there is nothing certain which may be loved? What man may love a woman or what woman a man unless they have lived always together, unless a devoted mind and faith kept by and for one another has built up individual charity? This virtue does not have place in that promiscuous pleasure. Likewise, if all are the children of all, who will be able to love sons as his own, since either he does not know his own or he is doubtful of them? Who will bring honor to his father, as it were, since he does not know of whom he has been born? From this it happens that, not only does he take another for his father, but he may even hold his father as a stranger. Because a wife may be common, why cannot a son be so? But it must needs be that he be conceived from one. Therefore, the idea of community perishes for that one through nature herself as the reclaimer. There remains, then, that it is only for the reason of concord that he wishes that wives be common. But there is no more vehement cause of discord than the seeking of one woman by many husbands. If Plato could not be advised of this by reason, surely he could by the examples both of the dumb animals which fight most bitterly on account of this, and also of men who have always waged most severe wars among themselves for the same reason.

"It remains that that community of wives holds nothing else but adultery and lusts, for the complete uprooting of which virtue is especially necessary. Therefore, he does not find that concord which he sought, because he did not see whence it comes. He who wishes to make men equal, then, ought to withdraw not matrimony, not wealth, but arrogance, pride, boastfulness, so that those powerful and elated men may know that they are the equals of even the most beggarly. For when insolence and iniquity are removed from wealth, it will make no difference whether some are rich and some are poor, since their spirits will be equal, and nothing besides the religion of God can affect this. He thought that he had discovered justice when he was turning it over absolutely, because community ought to be not of fragile things but of minds. For if justice is the mother of all virtues, when those single ones are taken away, she herself is subverted. Plato put frugality before all things, but surely there is no frugality where nothing of one's own property is had. He advocated abstinence, if only there were nothing of another's from which to abstain. He presented temperance, and he offered chastity, virtues which are very great in both sexes; he upheld reverence, shame, modesty, if things can begin to be honorable and legitimate which are accustomed to be judged wicked and base. Thus, while he wishes to give virtue to all, from all he takes it away.

"For ownership of things contains the matter of virtues and vices, but community holds nothing other than the license of vices. Nothing else can be said of the men who have many wives than that they are wanton and prodigal. Likewise, the women who are possessed by many, are, to be sure, not adulteresses, since there is no certain matrimony, but it is necessary that they be prostitutes and harlots. He reduced human life, therefore, to a likeness, I will not say of dumb animals, but of beasts and cattle. For almost all the birds make and form equal marriages and they defend their nests as though nuptial chambers with unified feeling, and they love their offspring because they are certainly their own, and they drive out any others if you should slip them into the nest. But a 'wise' man, against the custom of men and against nature, chose for himself more foolish things to imitate, and because he saw that in other animals the functions and duties of males and females were not different, he thought it was necessary also for women to engage in military service, to take part in public businesses, to hold magistracies, and to undertake commands. So he assigned to them arms and horses. The consequence is that spinning and weaving and the feeding of infants would belong to men. Nor did he see that the things he said were impossible, and for this reason, that up to now upon the earth no race so foolish nor one so wise ever existed which lived in this manner." – *The Divine Institutes*, vol. 49, pgs. 223-226

George Eldon Ladd

"John is using conventional human language to describe the universality of the knowledge of God in the eternal order. In the divine consummation, the redeemed will consist of peoples from every nation and tribe and people and tongue (7:9) who will not lose their national identity. John's language means no more than the statements of the prophets: 'and many peoples shall come and say: "Come, let us go up to the mountain of the Lord, to the house of the God of Jacob"' (Isa. 2:3); 'and nations shall come to your light, and kings to the brightness of your rising' (Isa. 60:3). This is the affirmation of the universality of the knowledge of God." – on Revelation 21:24, *A Commentary on the Revelation of John*, pg. 284

Louis L'Amour

"We are all of us, it has been said, the children of immigrants and foreigners—even the American Indian, although he arrived here a little earlier. What a man is and what he becomes is in part due to his heritage, and the men and women who came west did not emerge suddenly from limbo. Behind them were ancestors, families, and former lives. Yet even as the domestic cattle of Europe evolved into the wild longhorns of Texas, so the American pioneer had the characteristics of a distinctive type.

"Physically and psychologically, the pioneers' need for change had begun in the old countries with their decision to migrate. In most cases their decisions were personal, ordered by no one else. Even when migration was ordered or forced, the people who survived were characterized by physical strength, the capacity to endure, and not uncommonly, a rebellious nature.

"History is not made only by kings and parliaments, presidents, wars, and generals. It is the story of people, of their love, honor, faith, hope and suffering; of birth and death, of hunger, thirst and cold, of loneliness and sorrow. In writing my stories I have found myself looking back again and again to origins, to find and clearly see the ancestors of the pioneers.

"Some time ago, I decided to tell the story of the American frontier through the eyes of three families —fictional families, but with true and factual experiences. The names I chose were Sackett, Chantry, and Talon. There is a real Sackett family my research revealed, which derives from the Isle of Ely, in Cambridgeshire, England. For historical accuracy I decided to bring my fictional Sacketts from the same area.

"Cambridgeshire is fen-county—low, boggy land partially covered with water, and the fen-men were men of independent mind, as are my fictional Sacketts. They were also hunters and fishermen, which was important, though few of those who first landed in America had any idea of how to survive. In a land teeming with game, with edible wild plants, many were starving in the midst of plenty, and had to learn hunting and fishing from the Indians.

"Story by story, generation by generation, these families are moving westward. When the journeys are ended and the forty-odd books are completed, the reader should have a fairly true sense of what happened on the American frontier." – *Sackett's Land*, Preface

— LOUIS L'AMOUR —

". . . some of the great families of the world were founded with nothing but a sword and a strong right arm." – *Sackett's Land*, pg. 29

"What a man is and what he becomes is in part due to his heritage. . . ." – *Sackett's Land*, pg. v

"A boy should know his pa—he needs some-body to look up to. A boy or a girl, they learn how to be a man or a woman by watching their folks." – *Conagher*, pgs. 64-65

"Pa told us we held the land in trust. We were free to use it so long as it was kept in shape for the generations following after, for our sons and yours." – *Ride the Dark Trail*, pg. 36

"They had been warm shelters, and when does a man leave a place he has lived without some regret? For each time some part of him is left behind." – *Jubal Sackett*, pg. 211

"We had come a far piece into a strange land, a trail lit by lonely campfires and by gunfire, and the wishing we did by day and by night. Now we rode back to plant roots in the land, and with luck, to leave sons to carry on a more peaceful life, in what we hoped would be a more peaceful world." – *The Sky-Liners*, pg. 188

Johann Peter Lange

"The question, how the Gentiles are to be received into the Church, is not yet answered, though the unconditioned reception of believ-ers is found in the appointment, that nations, as nations, are to be christianized....that they are to be marked out as Christians by bap-tism…" – *A commentary on the Holy Scriptures: Matthew*, pg. 557

"If then the kings of the earth, and the nations bring their glory and their treasures into her, and if none shall ever enter into her that is not written in the book of life, it follows that these kings, and these nations, are written in the book of life. And so perhaps some light may be thrown on one of the darkest mysteries of redemption." – on Revelation 21:24, *A commen-tary on the Holy Scriptures: Revelation*, pg. 388

Julien Langella

"Multiculturalism, a weapon of mass subver-sion, is indispensable to the good order of a consumer society: without identity, without fixed landmarks, men who are empty inside, so they try to fill this void with material goods." – *Catholic and Identitarian*, pg. 83

"For capitalism to attain a new stage in its evo-lution, humanity must adopt a way of life more compliant with the standards of an economy in perpetual motion. Hence the necessity to fash-ion a new man: without attachments, transfer-able at any moment according to a company's need for human resources or business opportu-nities." – *Catholic and Identitarian*, pgs. 85-86

"We will not actually stop the migrant hurricane without calling free trade into question. In effect, global interdependence subjects people to foreign demand in order to satisfy their vital needs. It is a system against nature that lets the fox into the hen house. Here's how. Saint Thomas Aquinas writes, 'a city that needs a multitude of goods to survive must necessarily maintain contact with foreigners. Social life is disrupted. … Therefore, it is preferable for a city to receive its food from its own territory than to be fully exposed to trading.'" – *Catholic and Identtitarian*, pgs. 153-154

"A human community cannot live separated from its Creator, from Whom it receives all life, nor can it live without ethno-cultural homogeneity, a sine qua non for social peace and common well-being. This is why multicultural societies, sinking ever more each day into violence, are doomed to perish. Finally, a nation disappears — simply put — when the people it embodies ceases to exist, carried away by hate for their God and progressively replaced by a foreign population." – *Catholic and Identitarian*, pg. 19

"Through immigration, they have robbed us of our country. Through a tyranny of guilt, they have taken our collective pride. Through pacifist moralism, they have stifled our physical courage. Through manipulative advertisement, they have atrophied our free-agency. Through the systematic deconstruction of all authority, they have broken our mental equilibrium. Through skepticism erected as the ultimate standard, they have removed faith from us. Finally, through globalism and the call to miscegenation, they attempt to dissolve our identity. Our land, our self-esteem, our strength of character, our critical mind, our standards, our sense of the sacred: all of that must we reconquer. The ideal of reconquest is the healthy response to the problems of Europe." – *Catholic and Identitarian*, pgs. 241-242

"The pathological refusal to name the enemy – that's true fear. We no longer name the enemy because we incorrectly interpret Christ's commandment to love.

"In the Latin text of the Gospels, as the German thinker Carl Schmitt points out, 'Love your enemies' comes from diligite inimicos vestros, and not diligite hostes vestros; there is no reference here to loving a political enemy. And in the thousand-year war between Christianity and Islam, it would not have occurred to any Christian that it was necessary to love the Saracens or the Turks and to deliver Europe to Islam instead of defending her. An enemy in the political sense of the term does not imply personal hatred, so it is only in the sphere of private life that loving one's enemy makes sense." – *Catholic and Identitarian*, pgs. 202-203

"Mass immigration is a cancer. It ruins us and makes us live our own lives in fear. It is a profound injustice: the face of our country is mutilated and our people despised. Immigration such as we know it is like locking a man up in a dark room with a pack of hungry wolves. It's a collective kidnapping. It's murder. They're killing us." – *Catholic and Identitarian*, pg. 182

"An identity is a subtle alchemy of blood, soil, and Heaven. You cannot remove a part of it without distorting and weakening the whole." – *Catholic and Identitarian*, pg. 173

"Creativity does not belong to the nomadic man; it cannot hatch in a relativistic and libertarian time period. Creativity is the privilege of the rooted, sedentary culture, which sees itself as a link in a very ancient tradition. There, where things do not change, man is all the more inclined to forge works that time wishes to conserve in order to pass them down to our descendants. It is in periods of stability and social order that one creates the most, not in troubled times where everything is questioned in permanent insecurity, where fear of the future discourages any initiative, including starting a family." – *Catholic and Identitarian*, pgs. 156-157

"We must cherish and transmit the identity of our homeland, this little corner of Creation which belongs to us to love as a child loves his mother and with the protective tenderness of a mother for her child. It is like Christ's metaphor of the hen and her chicks, which expresses so well the nature of His love. In the relationship with our homeland we are both chicks, as inheritors of a multi-thousand year history which is above and beyond us, and we are hens to the degree that all our deeds shape the face of the country that we pass down to our children." – *Catholic and Identitarian*, pg. 145

"To justify laxity on migration, some take Jewish history as a model, invoking the Old Testament and the sufferings of the Hebrews in exile, or the flight of the Holy Family into Egypt. They derive an argument from this to defend the virtue of hospitality in all circumstances. This cheap exegesis is done in bad faith. It forgets that the Hebrews then returned home and did not lose sight of a land that had been promised to them..." – *Catholic and Identitarian*, pg.136

"We must pay attention to political extrapolations of this parable, used by certain people to justify mass immigration. Let us recall that after caring for the foreigner, the Samaritan leaves the foreigner. He doesn't bring him back to his home so that he can move in, eat the family's food and sleep in his daughter's bed. Once he is back on his feet, the way-laid inhabitant of Jerusalem certainly went back home to his country. Caring for strangers has its limits: firstly, we must consider the peace and security of our own, to whom our duties are greater than for others; and secondly, the stranger already has a homeland where he has more reason to flourish than elsewhere."

"To refuse this limit imposed upon human nature is the mark of an extreme pride, comparable to the builders of Babel. Only our Father can simultaneously love every creature on the earth with the same intensity. Individuals, families, peoples and civilizations — we are all the preferred ones of God. But this perfect love is out of man's reach; he will always remain an imperfect creature. If we want to help the whole world, we end up systematically neglecting our brothers." – *Catholic and Identitarian*, pg. 39

"The Jewish example helps us understand that, in the history of salvation, the Trinitarian God gives a fundamental place to nations. This stands out during Pentecost: 'devout men, out of every nation under heaven … were bewildered, because each one heard [the apostles] speaking in his own language' (Acts 2:5–6). This is the sign that the salvation of man passes through cultures, rootedness, identities." – *Catholic and Identitarian*, pg. 29

"The aim is to convince men of good will that Christian charity and struggle for identity are not contradictory. To defend one's identity is first and foremost to love one's people, that is to say one's extended family. Is this not the meaning of the fourth commandment 'Honor your father and your mother' (Deuteronomy 5:16)? Wanting to preserve one's identity simply means to refuse to disappear: to prefer genuine diversity, guaranteed by mutually respected borders, rather than the uniformity imposed by globalism and consumerism. To defend one's identity is to prefer life over death." – *Catholic and Identitarian*, pg. 11

"As for the flight of the Holy Family into Egypt, it concludes with their return to Israel after the angel of the Lord appeared to Saint Joseph: 'Rise, take the child and his mother, and go to the land of Israel, for those who sought the child's life are dead' (Matthew 2:20). In the Bible, hospitality is only temporary; it is a lesser evil to endure while awaiting the return home — the one and only way out of a crisis for the Hebrew people." – *Catholic and Identitarian*, pg. 136

"In the face of migrant flows, which destabilize the world and impoverish the countries that migrants are leaving, we must respond with a policy of rootedness. Europe must be at the forefront of this movement. Chosen by Providence to spread the Good News and civilization across the world, Europe bears a destiny. This isn't about imperialist pride or a desire for power; it's about assuming the talents we've received from Heaven." – *Catholic and Identitarian*, pg. 147

Lao Tzu

"A man has his place among other men in the world; he is a member, while he lives, of the body of humanity. And as he has his place in society, so also he has his special duties to discharge, according to his position, and his relation to others." – *The Texts of Taoism*. bk. IV: *Zăn Kien Shih*

What [Tâo's] skillful planter plants
Can never be uptorn;
What his skillful arms enfold,
From him can ne'er be borne.
Sons shall bring in lengthening line,
Sacrifices to his shrine.
Tâo when nursed within one's self,
His vigour will make true
And where the family it rules

What riches will accrue!
The neighbourhood where it prevails
In thriving will abound;
And when 'tis seen throughout the state,
Good fortune will be found.
Employ it the kingdom o'er,
And men thrive all around.
– *The Texts of Taoism, The Tao Teh King*

Philip Larkin

"That Whitsun, I was late getting away:
    Not till about
One—twenty on the sunlit Saturday
Did my three-quarters-empty train pull out,
All windows down, all cushions hot, all sense
Of being in a hurry gone."
– *The Whitsun Weddings* (lines 1-6)

"A hothouse flashed uniquely: hedges dipped
And rose: and now and then a smell of grass
Displaced the reek of buttoned carriage-cloth
Until the next town, new and nondescript,
Approached with acres of dismantled cars."
– *The Whitsun Weddings* (lines 18-22)

"Once I am sure there's nothing going on
I step inside, letting the door thud shut.
Another church: matting, seats, and stone,
And little books; sprawlings of flowers, cut
For Sunday, brownish now;
    some brass and stuff
Up at the holy end; the small neat organ;"
– *Church Going* (lines 1-6)

"A serious house on serious earth it is,
In whose blent air all our compulsions meet,
Are recognized, and robed as destinies.
And that much never can be obsolete,
Since someone will forever be surprising
A hunger in himself to be more serious,"
– *Church Going* (lines 41-46)

Christopher Lasch

"My study of the family suggested ... that the
capacity for loyalty is stretched too thin when it
tries to attach itself to the hypothetical solidarity of the whole human race. It needs to attach
itself to specific people and places, not to an
abstract ideal of universal human rights. We
love particular men and women, not humanity
in general. The dream of universal brotherhood, because it rests on the sentimental fiction

that men and women are all the same, cannot
survive the discovery that they are not. This
sentimental fiction arises, I think, when we take
our own personal experience of love of ethical
responsibility and say: 'because I feel this for
one or a few people, and because this feeling is
good, I must feel the same way toward everyone, I must act on the same basis toward the
entire human race as a collective whole.' Once
people have taken this stand, and especially
if they try to convert it into public policy, all
rational limits of common sense or self-interest
are thrown out the window. Ultimately, this
obligation must be imposed by political force,
since no one can actually love the whole human race. What starts, then, as a personal sense
of compassion and responsibility for individuals ends as a collectivized ethics which compels
men to love the foreigner (not just the individual foreigner, but all foreigners) more than their
own." – *The True and Only Heaven: Progress and
Its Critics*, pg. 36

James Laurens

"The Congress have I think very wisely resolved against employing any more foreigners unless they are forced to it by the special
contracts of their embassadors, or very pointed
recommendations." – from a letter to his father,
of 25th March, 1778; recorded in *The Writings
of George Washington*, collected and edited by
Worthington Chauncey Ford, Letter-Press Ed.,
1889, vol. 6, pg. 448

Learned Divines

"A perpetual possession; for they shall not be
bought out at the year of Jubilee, though they
were Proselytes, or converts to the Jewish religion; for the difference betwixt an Israelite and
one of another nation, and the preeminence
of the one above the other, was a privilege of
pedigree from Abraham, Isaac, and Jacob, and
not of profession, though he that forsook his
religion, was not worthy to enjoy this privilege;
and he that sincerely embraced this religion,
(though an alien in nation and nature from the
Israelites) no doubt had a more easy bondage
than another bondman... When their masters
die, their children shall inherit the masterly
power over them, and they shall abide in bondage as long as they live." – *The English Annotations on the Whole Bible*, ch. 25, pg. 362

Francis Nigel Lee

"I don't believe [racial integration] is what the Bible teaches. Even though we may have transgressed the boundaries of nationhood and of peoplehood, it seems to me that God did create man of one blood in order that he may dwell as different nations throughout the world. But after the fall, when sinful man cosmopolitanly – meaning by that, with a desire to obliterate separate nationhood, with a desire to build a sort of United Nations organization under the Tower of Babel...attempted to resist developing peoplehood...[God confused the tongues of men]...because men had said, 'Let us build a city and a tower which will stretch up to heaven lest we be scattered'... Pentecost sanctified the legitimacy of separate nationality rather than saying this is something we should outgrow... In fact, even in the new earth to come, after the Second Coming of Christ, we are told that the nations of them which are saved shall walk in the light of the heavenly Jerusalem, and the kings of the earth shall bring the glory and the honor—the cultural treasures—of the nations into it... But nowhere in Scripture are any indications to be found that such peoples should ever be amalgamated into one huge nation.

"In another fourteen years, the future looks bleak for White Christians everywhere. In 1900, Europe possessed two-thirds of the world's Christians. By 2025, that number will fall below 20% — with most Christians living in the Third World of Latin America, Africa, and Southeast Asia. Then, nearly 75% of the world's Catholics will be Non-Western Mestizos or Black Africans. Right now, Nigeria has the world's largest Catholic Theological School. India has more Christians than most Western nations. And Jesus is more and more being portrayed with a dark skin. By 2050, more than 80% of Catholics in the U.S. will be of Non-Western origins. Only a fraction of Anglicans will be English. Lutherans, Presbyterians and other mainstream denominations will find their chief centres of growth in Africa, Asia and Latin America — often syncretistically absorbing large quantities of Pre-Christian Paganism as revived Voo-dooism and increasing ancestor-worship. This 'Christianity' rapidly degenerates into an immigrationistic, prolific and socialistic jungle-religion." – *Christian-Afrikaners*, pg. 87

G.A. Lee

"Kin, Kinsfolk, Kinsman These terms most frequently translate Heb. ʾāḥ. Although ʾāḥ is usually rendered 'brother,' it can also denote a nephew (Gen. 13:8; 14:14, 16; 29:12, 15), a more distant relative (Ruth 3:2; 4:3), any relative at all (Gen. 16:12; 1 Ch. 9:6, 9, 13), or one descended, according to tradition, from a common ancestor (1 K. 12:24; 1 Ch. 7:5; 2 Ch. 28:8; Jer. 7:15; 29:16)...

"Kindred This is another vague term for relatives. In Gen. 12:1 the progression from country to kindred (Heb. môleḏet ‹ yālaḏ, 'bear [children]') to father's house sets the limits of the term. Thus môleḏet does not mean the immediate family (father's house) or just a countryman, but, as G. Wenham (Leviticus [NICOT, 1979], pg. 257) suggested 'patrilineage' or 'extended family' (cf. also môleḏet in Gen. 24:4 and ʾāḥ in v 27)...

"The three NT Greek words denoting kinship are all based on syn, 'with,' + génos, 'race, stock.' Gk. syngenḗs in Mk. 6:4 seems to designate distant relatives (note the progression country-kin-house). It may have the same meaning in Luke, especially in 21:16, where the progression is parents—brothers—kinsmen—friends (note also the links with 'neighbor' in 1:58, 'acquaintances' in 24:4, and 'friends, brothers, and neighbors' in 14:12; cf. Acts 10:24)." – *The International Standard Bible Encyclopedia*, "Kin; Kins(wo)man; Kinsfolk," ed. Geoffrey W Bromiley, Revised (Wm. B. Eerdmans, 1979–1988), 18.

Ryszard Legutko

"Socialist and communist have always embraced the notion of community to a larger extent than liberals, whom they accused of individualism and falsified human nature. However, while emphasizing the role of community, they sternly and ruthlessly criticized — just as liberals did — existing communities with long traditions, and after seizing power, brutally destroyed. Villages were treated with particular aversion because they were seen as the mainstay of tradition. Marx and Engels contemptuously wrote about the 'idiocy' of rural life, and their successors did everything to destroy rural communities, which they regarded as strongholds of conservatism and bigotry. The communist regimes systematically did their best to wipe out rural culture while at the same time seemingly defended the peasants as victims of exploitation. The Communists also effectively destroyed working class communities, even though in its official program with the Party proclaimed itself to be the strongest-ever champion of the working class, which is honored by calling on it to become a history-making liberator of humanity." – *Demon In Democracy*, pg. 93

"The conservatives, who, in principle, should oppose the socialists and liberal democrats, quite sincerely argue that they, too, are open, pluralistic, tolerant, and inclusive, dedicated to the entitlements of individuals and groups, non-discriminatory and even supportive of the claims of feminists and homosexual activists. All in all, the liberal democrats, the socialists, and the conservatives are unanimous in their condemnations: they condemn racism, sexism, homophobia, discrimination, intolerance, and all the other sins listed in the liberal-democratic catechism while also participating in an unimaginable stretching of the meaning of these concepts and depriving them of any explanatory power. All thoughts and all modes of linguistic expression are moving within the circle of the same clichés, slogans, spells, ideas, and arguments. All are involved in the grand design of which those who think and speak are not the authors but with whose authorship they deeply identify, or – in case of doubt – from which they do not find the strength or reasons enough to distance themselves." – *Demon In Democracy*, pg. 66

"The portrayal of liberal democracy as a realization of the eternal desire for freedom is very popular, almost verging on a platitude, especially in recent decades. This picture is false. First, liberalism was certainly not the only orientation expressing desire for freedom, nor was it particularly consistent in this devotion. The supporters of republicanism, conservatism, romanticism, Christianity, and many other movements also demanded freedom, and did a lot to advance its cause. If freedom as we understand it in Western civilization is not only an abstract of value, but has a concrete shape well grounded in institutions, social practices, and mental habits, then the contribution of liberalism is one of many, far from decisive. It is hard to imagine freedom without classical philosophy and of the heritage of antiquity, without Christianity and scholasti-

cism, without different traditions in the philosophy law and political and social practices, without ancient and modern republicanism, without strong anthropology and ethics of virtues and duties, without Anglo-Saxon and continental conservatism or many other components of the entire Western civilization." – *Demon In Democracy*, pg. 45

"[In a Liberal-Democracy] Not only should the state and the economy be liberal and democratic, but the entire society as well, including ethics and mores, family, churches, schools, universities, community organizations, culture, and human sentiments and aspirations. The people, structures, thoughts that exist outside the liberal-democratic pattern are deemed outdated, backward-looking, useless, but at the same time extremely dangerous as preserving the remnants of old authoritarianisms. Some may still be tolerated for some time, but as anyone with a minimum of intelligence is believed to know, sooner of later they will end up in the dustbin of history. Their continued existence will most likely threaten the liberal-democratic progress and therefore they should be treated with the harshness they deserve.

"Once one sends one's opponents to the dustbin of history, any debate with them becomes superfluous. Why waste time, they think, arguing with someone whom the march of history condemned to nothingness and oblivion? Why should anyone seriously enter into a debate with the opponent who represents what is historically indefensible and what will sooner or later perish? People who are not liberal democrats are to be condemned, laughed at, and repelled, not debated. Debating with them is like debating with alchemists or geocentrists. Again, an analogy with Communism immediately comes to one's mind. The opponents of Communism were at best enemies to be crushed, or laughingstocks to be humiliated: how else could any reasonable soul react to such anachronistic dangerous ravings or a deluded mind?" – *Demon In Democracy*, pg. 21

Peter Leithart

"Genesis 1 says we are created in the image of a God who speaks of Himself in the plural, a God who can not only say 'I' but 'we'. We are created as social beings, entangled with the lives of others and with the things of the world in such profound ways that it's often difficult to know where one ends and another begins. A woman loses her husband of fifty years and feels that she's lost part of herself. A burglar empties a home, and the owners feel raped. People get attached to places – to rocks, trees, soil, topography – and feel disoriented when they move to a new place." – *The Baptized Body*, pg. 58

"The church does not transform the rich diversity of humanity into a boring uniformity; it brings each historical community to its completion in Christ. Chinese churches will be different from Indian and Nigerian churches, but each church will represent the fulfillment of the peoples. In Christ, incorporated into his body by his Spirit, Chinese, Indian, Nigerian, and all other cultures will reach their richest fulfillment." – *Revelation 12-22*, pgs. 345-346

Mikhail Lermontov

"The vision spread before him was
A paradise of stillness, peace:
The vale was slumbering like a child,
Its breast heaving with gentle sighs;
The mountain stream, transparent, bright,
Like silver snakes, wound through the grass."
– *Demon* (Canto I, lines 163-168) [55]

"The day was clear and the air was so transparent that the most distant peaks of the Caucasus seemed quite near. The snow was dazzlingly white, and the sky was such a deep blue that my eyes ached as they gazed upon it." – *A Hero of Our Time* (Part 3, "Bela")

"Their customs are still strange to me, but their morals are beyond reproach. I have met people of deep religious conviction, people with a profound sense of justice, and, above all, a fidelity which nothing can shake. I have encountered rough, unlettered men, strong in their simple faith, proud of their honesty, and living according to their own code of honor." – *A Hero of Our Time* (Part 2, "Maxim Maximych")

C.S. Lewis

"The demand for equality has two sources; one of them is among the noblest, the other is the basest, of human emotions. The noble source is the desire for fair play. But the other source is the hatred of superiority. At the present moment it would be very unrealistic to overlook the importance of the latter. There is in all men a tendency (only corrigible by good training from without and persistent moral effort from within) to resent the existence of what is stronger, subtler or better than themselves. In uncorrected and brutal men this hardens into an implacable and disinterested hatred for every kind of excellence. The vocabulary of a period tells tales. There is reason to be alarmed at the immense vogue today of such words as 'highbrow', 'up-stage', 'old school tie', 'academic', 'smug', and 'complacent'. These words, as used today, are sores: one feels the poison throbbing in them...

"Equality (outside mathematics) is a purely social conception. It applies to man as a political and economic animal. It has no place in the world of the mind. Beauty is not democratic—she reveals herself more to the few than to the many, more to the persistent and disciplined seekers than to the careless. Virtue is not democratic—she is achieved by those who pursue her more hotly than most men. Truth is not democratic—she demands special talents and special industry in those to whom she gives her favors. Political democracy is doomed if it tries to extend its demand for equality into these higher spheres. Ethical, intellectual, or aesthetic democracy is death." – *Present Concerns*, pgs. 33-34

"The first and fatal charm of national repentance is, therefore, the encouragement it gives us to turn from the bitter task of repenting of our own sins to the congenial one of bewailing—but, first, of denouncing—the conduct of others...

"A group of such young penitents will say, 'Let us repent our national sins': what they mean is 'Let us attribute to our neighbor (even our Christian neighbor) in the Cabinet, whenever we disagree with him, every abominable motive that Satan can suggest to our fancy." – *Dangers of National Repentance, God In The Dock*, pg. 206

---

55 Lermontov's works, including his poem "Demon" and novel "A Hero of Our Time," reveal his love and admiration for the Russian land and its people.

"Men fail so often to repent their real sins that the occasional repentance of an imaginary sin might appear almost desirable." – *Dangers of National Repentance, God In The Dock*, pg. 206

"The communal sins which they should be told to repent are those of their own age and class— its contempt for the uneducated, its readiness to suspect evil, its self-righteous provocations of public obloquy, its breaches of the Fifth Commandment. Of these sins I have heard nothing among them. Till I do, I must think their candour towards the national enemy a rather inexpensive virtue." – *Dangers of National Repentance, God In The Dock*, pg. 206

"As to the business about being 'rooted' or 'at home everywhere,' I wonder are they really the opposite, or are they the same thing? I mean, don't you enjoy the Alps more precisely because you began by first learning to love in an intimate and homely way our own hills and woods [in Ireland]? While the mere globe-trotter starting not from a home feeling but from guide books feels equally at home everywhere only in the sense that he is really at home nowhere? It is just like the difference between vague general philanthropy (which is all balls) and learning first to love your own friends and neighbors which makes you more, not less, able to love the next stranger who comes along. If a man loveth not his brother whom he hath seen–etc. In other words, doesn't one get to the universal (either in people or in inanimate nature) through the individual?–not by going off into a mere generalised mash." – *Collected Letters*, vol. 1, pg. 702

"Tolkien once remarked to me that the feeling about home must have been quite different in the days when the family had fed on the produce of the same few miles of country for six generations, and that perhaps this was why they saw nymphs in the fountains and dryads in the wood – they were not mistaken for there was in a sense a real (not metaphorical) connection between them and the countryside. What had been earth and air and later corn, and later still bread, really was in them. We of course who live on a standardised international diet (you may have had Canadian flour, English meat, Scotch oatmeal, African oranges, and Aus-

tralian wine to day) are really artificial beings and have no connection (save in sentiment) with any place on earth. We are synthetic men, uprooted. The strength of the hills is not ours." – *Collected Letters*, vol. 1, pg. 689

"I think love for one's country means chiefly love for people who have a good deal in common with oneself (language, clothes, institutions) and is in that way like love of one's family or school: or like love (in a strange place) for anyone who once lived in one's home town. The familiar is in itself a ground for affection. And it is good: because any natural help towards our spiritual duty of loving is good and God seems to build our higher loves round our merely natural impulses – sex, maternity, kinship, old acquaintance, etc. And in a less degree there are similar grounds for loving other nations – historical links and debts for literature etc. (hence we all reverence the ancient Greeks)." – *Collected Letters*, vol. 3, pg. 119

"Equality is a quantitative term and therefore love often knows nothing of it. Authority exercised with humility and obedience accepted with delight are the very lines along which our spirits live. Even in the life of the affections, much more in the Body of Christ, we step outside that world which says 'I am as good as you.' It is like turning from a march to a dance. It is like taking off our clothes. We become, as Chesterton said, taller when we bow; we become lowlier when we instruct. It delights me that there should be moments in the services of my own Church when the priest stands and I kneel. As democracy becomes more complete in the outer world and opportunities for reverence are successfully removed, the refreshment, the cleansing, and invigorating returns to inequality, which the Church offers us, become more and more necessary." – *The Weight of Glory*, pg. 170

"First [regarding patriotism], there is love of home, of the place we grew up in or the places, perhaps many, which have been our homes; and of all places fairly near these and fairly like them; love of old acquaintances, of familiar sights, sounds and smells. Note that at its largest this is, for us, a love of England, Wales, Scotland, or Ulster. Only foreigners and politicians talk about 'Britain.' ... With this love for the place there goes a love for the way of life; for beer and tea and open fires, trains with compartments in them and an unarmed police force and all the rest of it; for the local dialect and (a shade less) for our native language. As Chesterton says, a man's reasons for not wanting his country to be ruled by foreigners are very like his reasons for not wanting his house to be burned down; because he 'could not even begin' to enumerate all the things he would miss." – *Four Loves*, pg. 41

— C.S. Lewis —

"It would be hard to find any legitimate point of view from which this feeling could be condemned. As the family offers us the first step beyond self-love, so this offers us the first step beyond family selfishness. Of course it is not pure charity; it involves love of our neighbours in the local, not of our Neighbour, in the Dominical, sense. But those who do not love the fellow-villagers or fellow-townsmen whom they have seen are not likely to have got very far towards loving 'Man' whom they have not. All natural affections, including this, can become rivals to spiritual love: but they can also be preparatory imitations of it, training (so to speak) of the spiritual muscles which Grace may later put to a higher service; as women nurse dolls in childhood and later nurse children. There may come an occasion for renouncing this love; pluck out your right eye. But you need to have an eye first: a creature which had none ... would be very ill employed in meditation on that severe text." – *The Four Loves*, pgs. 41-42

"Friendship is unnecessary, like philosophy, like art ... It has no survival value; rather it is one of those things which give value to survival." – *The Four Loves*, pg. 103
"A duty to our own kin, because they are our own kin, is a part of traditional morality. But side by side with it in the Tao, and limiting it, lie the inflexible demands of justice, and the rule that, in the long run, all men are our brothers... "What purport to be new systems or ideologies, all consist of fragments of the Tao itself, arbitrarily wrenched from their context in the whole and then swollen to madness in their isolation...If my duty to my parents is a superstition, then so is my duty to posterity. If justice is a superstition, then so is my duty to my country or my race." – *The Abolition Of Man*, pg. 76

"Shasta was not at all interested in anything that lay south of his home because he had once or twice been to the village with Arsheesh and he knew that there was nothing very interesting there. In the village he only met other men who were just like his father—men with long, dirty robes, and wooden shoes turned up at the toe, and turbans on their heads, and beards, talking to one another very slowly about things that sounded dull. But he was very interested in everything that lay to the North because no one ever went that way and he was never allowed to go there himself. When he was sitting out of doors mending the nets, and all alone, he would often look eagerly to the North. One could see nothing but a grassy slope running up to a level ridge and beyond that the sky with perhaps a few birds in it. ...
"Two men of the South are discussing the price of the sale of young 'Shasta':
"This boy is manifestly no son of yours, for your cheek is as dark as mine but the boy is fair and white like the accursed but beautiful barbarians who inhabit the remote North." – Excerpts from *The Horse And His Boy*

The main characters of the story decide to escape North to Narnia:
"Oh hurrah!" said Shasta. "Then we'll go North. I've been longing to go to the North all my life."
"Of course you have," said the Horse. "That's because of the blood that's in you. I'm sure you're true Northern stock. But not too loud. I should think they'd be asleep soon now." ...

"Narnia and the North," exclaimed the Horse (Bree). – Excerpts from *The Horse And His Boy*

Shasta is walking in the crowded streets of Tashbaan and sees Narnians for the first time in his life:

"It was quite unlike any other party they had seen that day. The crier who went before it shouting 'Way, way!' was the only Calormene in it. And there was no litter; everyone was on foot. There were about half a dozen men and Shasta had never seen anyone like them before. For one thing, they were all as fair-skinned as himself, and most of them had fair hair. And they were not dressed like men of Calormen. Most of them had legs bare to the knee. Their tunics were of fine, bright, hardy colors—woodland green, or gay yellow, or fresh blue. Instead of turbans they wore steel or silver caps, some of them set with jewels, and one with little wings on each side. A few were bare-headed. The swords at their sides were long and straight, not curved like Calormene scimitars. And instead of being grave and mysterious like most Calormenes, they walked with a swing and let their arms and shoulders go free, and chatted and laughed. One was whistling. You could see that they were ready to be friends with anyone who was friendly and didn't give a fig for anyone who wasn't. Shasta thought he had never seen anything so lovely in his life." – Excerpts from *The Horse And His Boy*

Shasta is taken in by the Narnians while in the Calormene city of Tashbaan:

"Meanwhile the people in that cool airy room were very interesting. Besides the Faun there were two Dwarfs (a kind of creature he had never seen before) and a very large Raven. The rest were all humans; grown-ups, but young, and all of them, both men and women, had nicer faces and voices than most Calormenes. And soon Shasta found himself taking an interest in the conversation. 'Now, Madam,' the King was saying to Queen Susan (the lady who had kissed Shasta). 'What think you? We have been in this city fully three weeks. Have you yet settled in your mind whether you will marry this dark-faced lover of yours, this Prince Rabadash, or no?' The lady shook her head. 'No, brother,' she said, 'not for all the jewels in Tashbaan.'" – Excerpts from *The Horse And His Boy*

In *The Last Battle*, King Tirian and his unicorn are looking on at the destruction of Narnia's Talking Trees:

"The first thing that struck the King and the Unicorn was that about half the people in the crowd were not Talking Beasts but Men. The next thing was that these men were not the fair-haired men of Narnia: they were dark, bearded men from Calormene, that great and cruel country that lies beyond Archenland across the desert to the south. There was no reason, of course, why one should not meet a Calormene or two in Narnia – a merchant or an ambassador – for there was peace between Narnia and Calormen in those days. But Tirian could not understand why there were so many of them: nor why they were cutting down a Narnian forest. He grasped his sword tighter and rolled his cloak round his left arm. They came quickly down among the men. ...

"After slaying the Caloremes and freeing a horse, the King asks:

"Master Horse," said Tirian as he hastily cut its traces, "how came these aliens to enslave you? Is Narnia conquered? Has there been a battle?" – Excerpts from *The Last Battle*

Library of Ashurbanipal

"Friendship is for the day of trouble, posterity for the future." – *Archaeology and The Bible*, pgs. 407-408.

Abraham Lincoln

When asked what his goal was in waging war against the South:

"I would save the Union. I would save it the shortest way under the Constitution. The sooner the national authority can be restored; the nearer the Union will be 'the Union as it was.' If there be those who would not save the Union, unless they could at the same time save slavery, I do not agree with them. If there be those who would not save the Union unless they could at the same time destroy slavery, I do not agree with them. My paramount object in this struggle is to save the Union, and is not either to save or to destroy slavery. If I could save the Union without freeing any slave I would do it, and if I could save it by freeing all the slaves I would do it; and if I could save it by freeing some and leaving others alone I would also do

that. What I do about slavery, and the colored race, I do because I believe it helps to save the Union; and what I forbear, I forbear because I do not believe it would help to save the Union. I shall do less whenever I shall believe what I am doing hurts the cause, and I shall do more whenever I shall believe doing more will help the cause. I shall try to correct errors when shown to be errors; and I shall adopt new views so fast as they shall appear to be true views."
– Letter to Horace Greely, editor of the *New York Tribune*, Executive Mansion, Washington, August 22, 1862; *Collected Works*, vol. 5, pg. 388

— ABRAHAM LINCOLN —

"But Judge Douglas is especially horrified at the thought of the mixing blood by the white and black races: agreed for once–a thousand times agreed. There are white men enough to marry all the white women, and black men enough to marry all the black women; and so let them be married. On this point we fully agree with the Judge; and when he shall show that his policy is better adapted to prevent amalgamation than ours we shall drop ours, and adopt his. Let us see. In 1850 there were in the United States, 405,751, mulattoes. Very few of these are the off-spring of whites and free blacks; nearly all have sprung from black slaves and white masters. A separation of the races is the only perfect pre-ventive of amalgamation but as an immediate

separation is impossible the next best thing is to keep them apart where they are not already together. If white and black people never get together in Kansas, they will never mix blood in Kansas. That is at least one self-evident truth... The proportion of free mulattoes to free blacks– the only colored classes in the free states–is much greater in the slave than in the free states. It is worthy of note too, that among the free states those which make the colored man the nearest to equal the white, have, proportion-ably the fewest mulattoes the least of amalgama-tion. In New Hampshire, the State which goes farthest towards equality between the races, there are just 184 Mulattoes while there are in Virginia–how many do you think? 79,775, being 23,126 more than in all the free States togeth-er... Judge Douglas is delighted to have them decided to be slaves, and not human enough to have a hearing, even if they were free, and thus description left subject to the forced concubi-nage of their masters, and liable to become the mothers of mulattoes in spite of themselves–the very state of case that produces nine tenths of all the mulattoes–all the mixing of blood in the nation...

"I have said that the separation of the races is the only perfect preventive of amalgamation. I have no right to say all the members of the Republican party are in favor of this, nor to say that as a party they are in favor of it. There is nothing in their platform directly on the subject. But I can say a very large proportion of its members are for it, and that the chief plank in their platform–opposition to the spread of slavery–is most favorable to that separation.

"Such separation, if ever effected at all, must be effected by colonization; and no political party, as such, is now doing anything directly for colonization. Party operations at present only favor or retard colonization incidentally. The enterprise is a difficult one; but 'when there is a will there is a way;' and what colonization needs most is a hearty will. Will springs from the two elements of moral sense and self-inter-est. Let us be brought to believe it is morally right, and, at the same time, favorable to, or, at least, not against, our interest, to transfer the African to his native clime, and we shall find a way to do it, however great the task may be."
– speech in Springfield, Illinois, June 26, 1857; *Collected Works Of Abraham Lincoln*, vol. 2, pgs. 408-409

"I will say then that I am not, nor ever have been in favor of bringing about in anyway the social and political equality of the white and black races–that I am not nor ever have been in favor of making voters or jurors of negroes, nor of qualifying them to hold office, nor to intermarry with white people; and I will say in addition to this that there is a physical difference between the white and black races which I believe will forever forbid the two races living together on terms of social and political equality. And inasmuch as they cannot so live, while they do remain together there must be the position of superior and inferior, and I as much as any other man am in favor of having the superior position assigned to the white race. I say upon this occasion I do not perceive that because the white man is to have the superior position the negro should be denied everything." – fourth debate with Douglas, Charleston, Sept 18, 1858; Collected Works of Abraham Lincoln, vol. 1, pg. 636 [56]

"If all earthly power were given me, I should not know what to do, as to the existing institution. My first impulse would be to free all the slaves, and send them to Liberia,—to their own native land…[But] Free them, and make them politically and socially, our equals? My own feelings will not admit of this; and if mine would, we well know that those of the great mass of white people will not.… A universal feeling, whether well or ill founded, can not be safely disregarded. We can not, then, make them equals."– Collected Works of Abraham Lincoln, vol. 2, 255-56

"Let it not be said I am contending for the establishment of political and social equality between the whites and blacks. I have already said the contrary. I am not now combating the argument of NECESSITY, arising from the fact that the blacks are already amongst us; but I am combating what is set up as MORAL argument for allowing them to be taken where they have never yet been–arguing against the EXTENSION of a bad thing, which where it already exists, we must of necessity, manage as we best can." – The Collected Works Of Abraham Lincoln, vol.2, pg. 266

"In the course of his reply, Senator Douglas remarked, in sub-stance, that he had always considered this government was made for the white people and not for the negroes. Why, in point of mere fact, I think so too." – The Collected Works Of Abraham Lincoln, vol.2, pg. 281
"I think the authors of that notable instrument intended to include all men, but they did not intend to declare all men equal in all respects. They did not mean to say all were equal in color, size, intellect, moral developments, or social capacity. They defined with tolerable distinctness, in what respects they did consider all men created equal—equal in 'certain inalienable rights, among which are life, liberty, and the pursuit of happiness.' This they said, and this They meant." – Speech on the Dred Scott Decision, Sept 16, 1859; Writings And Speeches, 1859-1865, vol. 2, pg. 32

"Now I say to you, my fellow citizen, that in my opinion, the signers of the Declaration of Independence had no reference to the Negro whatever. One great evidence is to be found in the fact that at the time every one of the thirteen colonies was a slaveholding colony, every signer of the Declaration representing a slaveholding constituency, and not one of them emancipated his slaves, much less offered citizenship to them when they signed the Declaration. If they intended to declare the Negro was equal of the white man, they were bound that day and hour to have put the Negroes on an equality with themselves." – October 16, 1858 debate in Peoria, IL with Douglas; Life and Works of Abraham Lincoln, vol. 4, pg. 243

"I can conceive of no greater calamity than the assimilation of the Negro into our social and political life as our equal... We can never attain the ideal union our fathers dreamed, with millions of an alien, inferior race among us, whose assimilation is neither possible nor desirable."
– After signing the Emancipation Proclamation; Congressional Record Proceedings and Debates of the Congress, vol. 116, part 4, pg. 5,582

"Give us a protective tariff and we will have the greatest nation on earth." – 1844; quoted in Day of Reckoning, pg. 191

"Abandonment of the protective policy by the American Government must result in the

---

56   It is significant that Lincoln espouses this opinion three days after Douglas' remarks quoted elsewhere in this book, in broader context of which Douglas accused Lincoln of claiming blacks equal to whites.

increase of both useless labor and idleness and …must produce want and ruin among our people." – Fragments of Notes regarding a Tariff Discussion, 3 August 1846 – 6 December 1847; Rutgers, vol. 1, pg. 95

"The Tariff is the cheaper System, while by the direct-tax system the land must be literally covered with assessors and collectors going forth like swarms of Egyptian locusts. By the tariff system the whole revenue is paid by the consumers of foreign goods….By this system the man who contents himself to live upon the product of his own country pays nothing at all." – *Resolutions At A Whig Meeting*, 1843; *Speeches & Letters of Abraham Lincoln, 1832-1865*, pg. 17

Charles Lindbergh

"We won the war in a military sense; but in a broader sense it seems to me we lost it, for our Western civilization is less respected and secure than it was before. In order to defeat Germany and Japan we supported the still greater menaces of Russia and China – which now confront us in a nuclear-weapon era. Poland was not saved … Much of our Western culture was destroyed. We lost the genetic heredity formed through aeons in many million lives … It is alarmingly possible that World War II marks the beginning of our Western civilization's breakdown, as it already marks the breakdown of the greatest empire ever built by man." – *Costs of War*, pg. xviii

Friedrich List

"The nation must sacrifice and give up a measure of material property in order to gain culture, skill, and powers of united production; it must sacrifice some present advantages in order to insure to itself future ones." – *National System*, pg. 117

"But politics demands, in the interests of each separate nation, guarantees for its independence and continued existence, special regulations to help its progress in culture, prosperity, and power, to build its society into a perfectly complete and harmoniously developed body politic, self-contained and independent." – quoted in Hirst, *Life of Friedrich List*, pg. 291

"We have already observed that the fortunes or misfortunes of individuals are dependent upon the maintenance of the independence and progress of the whole nation." – *Natural System*, pg. 33

"Finally, a nation should not regard the progress of industries from a purely economic point of view. Manufactures become a very important part of the nation's political and cultural heritage." – *Natural System*, pg. 39

"Following these examples every responsible government should strive to remove those obstacles that hinder the progress of civilization and should stimulate the growth of those economic forces that a nation carries in its bosom." – *Natural System*, pgs. 41-42

"Individuals owe to a nation their culture, their language, their opportunity to work, and the safety of their property. Above all they depend on the state in their relations with people in other countries. They share in the nation's glory and in its misfortunes; they share in its memories of the past and its hopes for the future; they share its wealth and its poverty. From the nation they draw the benefits of civilization, enlightenment, progress, and social and political institutions, as well as advances in the arts and sciences. If a nation declines, the individual shares in the disastrous consequences of its fall. 'So it is right and proper that the individual should be prepared to sacrifice his own interests for the benefit of the nation to which he belongs.'" – *Natural System*, pg. 30

"In the argument before adverted to, as in every other when international freedom of trade is the subject of discussion, we meet with a misconception which has been the parent of much error, occasioned by the misuse of the term 'freedom.' Freedom of trade is spoken of in the same terms as religious freedom and municipal freedom. Hence the friends and advocates of freedom feel themselves especially bound to defend freedom in all its forms. And thus the term 'free trade' has become popular without drawing the necessary distinction between freedom of internal trade within the State and freedom of trade between separate nations, notwithstanding that these two in their nature and operation are as distinct as the heaven is from the earth. For while restrictions on the internal trade of a state are compatible in only very few cases with the liberty of individual citizens, in the case of international trade the highest degree of individual liberty may consist with a high degree of protective policy. Indeed, it is even possible that the greatest freedom of international trade may result in national servitude, as we hope hereafter to show from the case of Poland." – *National System*, pg. 9

Liutprand of Cremona

Arguing in 968 against the Byzantine claim to southern Italy, asserted that:

"the race and language of the inhabitants [gens incola et lingua] makes it clear that that land is part of the kingdom of Italy." – Liudprand of Cremona, Legatio 7; ed. Albert Bauer and Reinhold Rau, *Quellen zur Geschichte der sächsischen Kaiserzeit, Ausgewählte Quellen zur deutschen Geschichte des Mittelalter*s 8, rev. ed., 530.

Livy

A woman betrayed Rome to the enemy, and the enemy killed her because traitors of their own people are despised even by the enemy:

"The last to attack Rome were the Sabines, and this war was by far the gravest of all, for passion and greed were not their motives, nor did they parade war before they made it. To their prudence they even added deception. Spurius Tarpeius commanded the Roman citadel. This man's maiden daughter was bribed with gold by Tatius to admit armed men into the fortress: she happened at that time to have gone outside the walls to fetch water for a sacrifice. Once within, they threw their shields upon her and killed her so, whether to make it appear that the citadel had been taken by assault, or to set an example, that no one might anywhere keep faith with a traitor. There is also a legend that because most of the Sabines wore heavy golden bracelets on their left arms and magnificent jewelled rings, she had stipulated for what they had on their left arms, and that they had therefore heaped their shields upon her, instead of gifts of gold. Some say that, in virtue of the compact that they should give her what they wore on their arms, she flatly demanded their shields and, her treachery being perceived, forfeited her life to the bargain she herself had struck." – *History of Rome*, bk. 1.11.

— LIVY —

"One has but to think of what the populace was like in those early days (just after Rome's last king, Superbus) – a rabble of aliens, mostly runaways and refugees – and to ask what would have happened if they had suddenly found themselves protected from all authority by inviolable sanctuary, and enjoying complete freedom of action, if not full political rights. In such circumstances, unrestrained by the power of the throne, they would, no doubt, have set sail on the stormy sea of democratic politics, swayed by the gusts of popular eloquence and quarreling for power with the governing class of a city which did not even belong to them, before any real sense of community had time to grow. That sense – the only true patriotism – comes slowly and springs from the heart: it is founded upon respect for family and love of the soil. Premature liberty of this kind would have been a disaster: we should have been torn to pieces by petty squabbles before we had ever reached a political maturity, which, as things were, was made possible by long quiet years under monarchical government; for it was that government which, as it were, nursed our strength and enabled us ultimately to produce sound fruit from liberty, as only a politically adult nation can." – *Early History of Rome*, Penguin, pg. 105

"It is your duty,' he said, 'to recover your country not by gold but by the sword. You will be fighting with all you love before your eyes: the temples of the gods, your wives and children, the soil of your native land scarred with the ravages of war, and everything which honor and truth call upon you to defend, or recover, or avenge." – *Early History Of Rome*, Penguin, pg. 549

Henry Cabot Lodge

"The question of immigration—and I am only about to repeat what has been often said—is perhaps the greatest of fundamental sovereign rights. If a country cannot say who shall come into the country, it has ceased to be a sovereign country; it has become a subject country." – Speech to the Senate, April 14, 1924; *Congressional Record*, vol. 65, pg. 6,305

"Merely to live without actually breaking the laws does not constitute good citizenship, except in the narrow sense of contrast to those who openly or covertly violate the laws which they have helped to make. The word 'good' as applied to citizenship, means something more positive and affirmative than mere passive obedience to statutes, if it has any meaning at all. The good citizen, if he would deserve the title, must be one who performs his duties to the State, and who in due proportion serves his country… A man may not be a bad citizen—he may pay his taxes and commit no statutory offenses; but, if he gives no service to his country, nor any help to the community in which he lives, he cannot properly be called a good citizen." – *Good Citizenship*, 1902; *A Frontier Town And Other Essays*, pg. 33

"I am a Senator of the United States. My first allegiance as an American is to the great nation founded, built up, preserved by heroic sacrifices and untold treasure. My first loyalty is that bright flag in which the stars glitter and to which we bare our heads in homage as it floats above our soldiers and our sailors and the sight of which dims our eyes and chokes our throats when we see it in a foreign land.

"But I am also a senator from Massachusetts, and that last word touches the chords of memory with tender hand and moves the heart of all to whom it speaks of home. I was born and bred in Massachusetts. I love every inch of the old State, from the rocks of Essex and the glittering sands of the Cape to the fair valley of the Connecticut and the wooded Berkshire Hills.

Here my people have lived before me since the days of the Massachusetts Bay Company. They lie at rest in the graveyards of Essex, on Boston Common, beneath the shadow of Park Street Church. Here I have lived all my life. Here my dead are buried. Here I hope and pray my children and my children's children will always live and serve the state in peace or war as best they may.

"To this love I add the deep gratitude I feel to the people of Massachusetts for the confidence they have so long reposed in me. No matter what the future may have in store, that gratitude which comes from my heart can never be either chilled or lessened. To be Senator from Massachusetts has been the pride of my life. I have put aside great offices, for to me no public place, except one to which I never aspired, has seemed equal to that which I held, and there was assuredly none which could so engage my affections.

"…Every tradition of our great State is dear to me, every page of her history is to me a household word. To her service I have given the best years of my life and the best that was in me to give. I hope that I have not been an altogether unprofitable servant. I have given my all; no man can give more. Others may well serve her with greater ability than I. I fervently hope that there will be many such others in the days to come, when her light will still shine before men as it now shines with steady radiance in the pages of history. Others may easily serve her better than I in those days yet to be, but of this I am sure: that no one can ever serve her with a greater love or deeper loyalty." – *Speech at Symphony Hall*, 1911; *Henry Cabot Lodge By Charles Grenfill Washburn*, pgs. 50-51

"An American I was born, an American I have remained all my life. I can never be anything else but an American, and I must think of the United States first, and when I think of the United States first in an arrangement like this I am thinking of what is best for the world, for if the United States fails, the best hopes of mankind fail with it… Internationalism, illustrated by the Bolshevik and by the men to whom all countries are alike provided they can make money out of them, is to me repulsive. National I must remain, and in that way I like all other Americans can render the amplest service to the world. The United States is the world's best hope, but if you fetter her in the interests and quarrels of other nations, if you tangle her in the intrigues of Europe, you will destroy her power for good and endanger her very existence." – *Address on the Proposed League of Nations*, 1919; pg. 57

"The nation which does not cherish and guard all that stands for the great deeds of the past will have a present and a future barren of aught that posterity will care to recall." – *A Fighting Frigate*, pg. 23

Henry Wadsworth Longfellow

"Sweet the memory is to me
Of a land beyond the sea,
Where the waves and mountains meet." –
Amalfi, *Twenty Poems*, pg. 26

Ye who believe in affection that hopes,
   and endures, and is patient,
Ye who believe in the beauty
   and strength of woman's devotion,
List to the mournful tradition
   still sung by the pines of the forest;
List to a Tale of Love in Acadie,
   home of the happy.
...
Then came the laborers home from the field,
   and serenely the sun sank
Down to his rest, and twilight prevailed.
   Anon from the belfry
Softly the Angelus sounded,
   and over the roofs of the village
Columns of pale blue smoke,
   like clouds of incense ascending,
Rose from a hundred hearths,
   the homes of peace and contentment.
Thus dwelt together in love
   these simple Acadian farmers,—
Dwelt in the love of God and of man.
   Alike were they free from
Fear, that reigns with the tyrant,
   and envy, the vice of republics.
Neither locks had they to their doors,
   nor bars to their windows;
But their dwellings were open as day
   and the hearts of their owners;
There the richest was poor,
   and the poorest lived in abundance.
– *Evangeline*, *Poems*, pg. 165

Russell Long

"If we trade away American jobs and farmers' incomes for some vague concept of a 'new international order,' the American people will demand from their elected representatives a new order of their own, which puts their jobs, their security, and their incomes above the priorities of those who dealt them a bad deal." – *Congressional Record*-House, May 4, 2000, p. 6,827; also in Eckes, *Opening America's Market U.S. Foreign Trade Policy Since 1776*

Tremper Longman

"She is not happy with her darker than normal skin, so the disjunctive ("but") makes sense. In the next verse, she will complain that her brothers forced her to work their vineyard, where she was exposed to the scorching heat of the sun. Her discomfort is accentuated by her comment that the other women not look at her…Different cultures at different times either esteem or denigrate a tan. Her reaction invites us to suggest that the text assumes a culture where a deep, dark tan or burn is not attractive. Perhaps in the culture at the time the effects of the sun indicated that she was a laborer or lower class woman. In spite of some ambiguities, the text is clear about two matters: (1) the woman considers her dark skin unattractive, and (2) her dark skin is not her natural skin color but rather the result of a tan. Besides being an indicator of class…the woman's darkness may also be part of the opposition that we frequently see in the Song between the city and the country. Here the contrast would be between the pale city girls (the daughters of Jerusalem) and the dark girl, who is burned while laboring in the country… Verse 6 makes it clear that the woman finds her scorched complexion unattractive." – *Song of Songs*, *New International Commentary on the Old Testament*, pg. 486

Chas Lotter

"My country, right or wrong
This is my land my home,
I yearn not
For that strange unfamiliar place called Europe
I am an African
A white African."
 – *A Handful Of Hard Men*, pg. 19

"People talk
Of the gulf between our races
Which must be crossed
To mend these times of ours.
What gulf? By now
The community must be rare
Where families have not mourned."
– *Echoes of an African War*, pg. 117

"When the war drums rolled
   and the dark clouds gathered.
Through the smoke as it rose
   from the burning huts.
A brotherly band of hard dangerous men
Who held the fire in our hands
And the storm in our souls."
– *Echoes of an African War*, pg. 164

H.P. Lovecraft

"Only a damn fool can expect the people of
one tradition to feel at ease when their country
is flooded with hordes of foreigners who —
whether equal, superior, or inferior biologically
— are so antipodal in physical, emotional, and
intellectual makeup that harmonious coales-
cence is virtually impossible. Such an immigration is death to all endurable existence, and
pollution and decay to all art and culture. To
permit or encourage it is suicide." – from a letter
written September 27, 1926; *Selected Letters*, vol.
2, pg. 71

"…In my opinion the paramount things of
existence are those mental & imaginative landmarks—language, culture, traditions, perspectives, instinctive responses to environmental
stimuli, etc.—which give to mankind the illusion of significance & direction in the cosmic
drift. Race & civilisation are more important,
according to this point of view, than concrete
political or economic status; so that the weakening of any racial culture by political division is
to be regarded as an unqualified evil—justifiable
only by the most extreme provocation. Greece
suffered from lack of unity—Athens & Sparta,
Syracuse & Thebes, etc., etc., being all separate
city-states which acted together only under the
most exceptional circumstances. They managed
to stand unitedly against Persia, but could not
do it against Rome. Rome itself, on the other
hand, was always admirably united—hence
stood firm against all comers till dissolved by

internal decay. The English civilisation has
so far stood up successfully on both sides, &
with good luck can probably continue to do so;
but whenever an external menace appears one
wishes that a coordinated defence by Britain
& America were firmly guaranteed instead
of merely probable. In addition, the state of
culture in America would have been greatly
improved by continued solidarity with Great
Britain. It is unlikely that the vulgar financial
& quantitative ideals of the American majority
today would have been quite so paramount
had the region remained true to its rightful
sovereign—nor would the spirit of lawlessness
have been so general & deep-seated. Some
foreigners would have entered, but probably
not in such vast quantities; & the machinery
of assimilation would have been better. The
policy of inviting 'oppressed' races is fatal to national welfare, since these elements are almost
always biologically inferior & therefore unfit to
uphold the institutions established by elements
of greater stamina. When a race or group is
oppressed, it is usually because of its own
inherent inferiority–& we do not want a nation
of inferior cringers on the soil settled by sturdy
Englishmen. I think the 'melting pot' delusion
is about played out, & doubt if any immigrants
of non-Nordic stock will ever be welcomed on
a large scale again. To fancy that the posterity
of Slavs, Jews, & Latins can approximate the
instinctive emotional life of sturdy, fighting
Teutono-Celtic peoples is to subscribe to a fatal
fallacy…" – from a letter written February 26,
1932; *Selected Letters: 1932-1934*, pg. 19

"The village rings with ribald foreign cries;
Around the wine-shops loaf with bleary eyes
A vicious crew, that mock the name of 'man'
Yet dare to call themselves 'American'.
New-England's ships no longer ride the sea;
Once prosp'rous ports are sunk in poverty.
The rotting wharves as ruins tell the tale
Of days when Yankees mann'd the swelling sail.
The Indies yield no more their cargoes rare;
The sooty mill's New-England's present care:
The noisy mill, by foreign peasants run,
Supplants the glorious shipping that hath gone.
In arid fields, the kine no longer low;
The soil knows not the furrow of the plough;
The rolling meadows all neglected lie,
Fleck'd here and there by some foul alien's sty.
The school no more contains the busy class;

The walls are down, the ruins chok'd with grass.
Within the gate-post swallows build their nests;
Upon the hill, the gentle master rests.
The mossy lane with briers is o'ergrown;
The bound'ry walls are shapeless heaps of stone,
And thm' the mourning trees the winds
   in sorrow moan.
Whence comes this devastation of the land,
This awful blow of the Almighty's hand?
Where is New-England, that our fathers knew,
Where pious men in rugged virtue grew?
Where law and order rul'd the rustic realm,
And honour stood unconquer'd at the helm?
Gone! with the noble race that gave it life,
And given o'er to foreign crime and strife.
The Saxon yeoman made New-England great,
And when he leaves, he leaves it to foul fate.
No baser tribe can take his honour'd place,
And with like virtues old New-England grace.
This pow'r lies lock'd within
   the noble British race!"
– *New England Fallen*

Rich Lowry

"Would America be the same if its people spoke Russian, the language of a country that has never effectively supported property rights, the rule of law, or limited government, rather than English? Would democracy have emerged if Americans read the Koran instead of the Bible?" – *The Case For Nationalism*, pg. 18

"Nationalism, or at least national feeling, isn't new or manufactured but quite old and entirely natural. It isn't based on hatred, instead on love: our affection for home and our own people. It is caught up in culture, in the language, manners, and rituals that set off any given country from another. It is an elemental force that can't be effaced without government coercion, and even then has proved impossible to wipe out. Empires and totalitarian ideologies have failed to eradicate it." – *The Case for Nationalism*, pg. 32

"National loyalty gives everyone in society a common interest that is deeper than any specific power struggle. It transcends tribe and sect. It establishes the parameters within which a discrete people and its government can arrive at something approximating the social contract imagined by philosophers such as John Locke. It renders a society, as Roger Scruton puts it, in

the first-person plural 'we.' Only on this basis is it possible to create citizens with equal rights and reciprocal obligations, living together under the rule of law. This arrangement, in turn, makes possible the social trust that lubricates everyday life and the market economy." – *The Case for Nationalism*, pg. 47

"Contrary to the claims of antinationalists, it wasn't simply ideas that mattered in establishing the American project…Culture, and the people who embodied and delineated it, mattered as much or more. . . . Nations aren't mere intellectual constructs but accretions of history and culture." – *The Case For Nationalism*, pg. 101

"America is not a nation of immigrants, as we are constantly told, at least it wasn't at the crucial outset; it was a nation of settlers who came here with a specific mission and whose religio-cultural attributes and commitments have helped define our national identity to this day. Contrary to the claims of anti-nationalists, it wasn't simply ideas that mattered in establishing the American project. Culture, and the people who embodied and delineated it, mattered as much or more. This point is worth dwelling on at length because it is so often dismissed or poorly understood. Nations aren't mere intellectual constructs but accretions of history and culture, usually shaped over the long term by their beginnings." – *The Case for Nationalism*, pg. 102

Thomas Clarke Luby

"In a word, we do not hesitate to say, that Emancipation has done more harm than good. To benefit Ireland, it should never have been separated from the national cause. It and Ireland's independence should have sunk or swam together; and it should have been won by the sword!

"Finally, if, on the one hand, Emancipation has deprived the Irish people of those from whom, considering their talents and acquirements, they might justly claim help and guidance in a struggle for independence; on the other hand, let us guard against exaggerating the importance of the loss. The commercial classes would, in any case, be liable to corrupting influences. In all countries, in times of perilous crisis, they have too often been found wanting in public virtue. The extinction of patriotism in the professional classes, however, is a more serious loss. Yet, even this is far from being ruinous. The most hasty glance will perceive, that there are good men (more than enough, thank Heaven) to fill up these gaps in the host of patriotism. There are this moment, in Ireland, thousands of brave and intelligent young men, with life before them and still undebased by the sordid worldliness which here, even more than in other lands, besets the successful man. These young men, with thoughts freshened and souls alive with faith and eager patriotism, have all the essential qualities which fit men to form the rallying points of a people in the hour of danger…In spite, then, of any and all untoward issues of the past, our confidence in the national cause should remain rooted and strong. Let the people only strive, with might and main, to develop and rouse to vigorous life all the intelligence, energy, and virtue they have amongst themselves – let them do this, and they will soon find substitutes within their own ranks, for the corrupt and craven classes that have abandoned the cause of their country. To this end, we say, let the people toil day and night. This is what is chiefly requisite, in order to make Ireland an independent nation!" – '82 and '29, From the first issue of The Irish People, November 28, 1863

John Lukacs

"This writer, an historian, has no Anglo Saxon blood in his veins, and he professes no blind admiration for some mythical virtues of the Anglo-Saxon race and its peoples. He must, however, insist on the obvious matter . . . that the English speaking character of the United States must not be taken for granted…The still extant freedoms of Americans—of all Americans—are inseparable from their English speaking roots…the freedoms guaranteed by the Constitution—and the consequent prosperity and relative stability of the country flowing therefrom—were not abstract liberties but English liberties, dependent on practical as well as sentimental attachments and habits of English laws." – Immigration and Migration—A Historical Perspective, American Immigration Control Foundation, pg. 21

Lucian

"Then one of them might proceed to question me like this: 'Suppose, Lycinus, that an Ethiopian who had never been abroad in his life, nor seen other men like us, were to state categorically in an Ethiopian assembly that there did not exist on earth any white or yellow men–nothing but blacks–, would his statement be accepted? or would some Ethiopian elder remark, How do you know, my confident friend? you have never been in foreign parts, nor had any experience of other nations.' Shall I tell him the old man's question was justified? what do you advise, my counsel?" – Works, pg. 58

Luo Guanzhong

"We three, Liu Bei, Guan Yu, and Zhang Fei, though of different families, swear brotherhood and mutual help to one end. From now on, we will aid each other in difficulty and rescue each other in danger. We will serve the country and protect the people. We ask not the same day of birth but we are willing to die at the same time. May Heaven, the all-powerful, and Earth, the ever bountiful, read our hearts! If we break our oath or betray each other's trust, may Heaven and man smite us!" – Oath of the Peach Garden, The Three Kingdoms. ch. 1[57]

Martin Luther

"I was born for my Germans, and will serve them." – The Life of Luther From His Own Writings, pg. 104

"I also boast that Japheth, Noah's firstborn son, is my true, natural ancestor and his wife (whoever she may have been) is my true, natural ancestress; for as Moses informs us in Genesis 10, he is the progenitor of all of us Gentiles. Thus Shem, the second son of Noah, and all of his descendants have no grounds to boast over against his older brother Japheth because of their birth. Indeed, if birth is to play a role, then Japheth as the oldest son and the true heir has reason for boasting over against Shem, his younger brother, and Shem's descendants, whether these be called Jews or Ishmaelites or Edomites." – On The Jews, in The Annotated Luther, pg. 465

---

57   This story is written in the 1300's a.d., but the tale depicts a more ancient period, circa 200's a.d.

"A person who wants to live in a certain city and enjoy its privileges should know and observe its laws, no matter whether he believes in them or is at heart a rogue or scoundrel." – *Small Catechism, in A Daily Prayer Catechism*, pg. 9

"False love is that which seeks its own as a man loves money, possessions, honor and women taken outside of marriage and against God's command. Natural love is that between father and child, brother and sister, friend and relatives." – *A Sermon On The Marriage Estate, Annotated Luther*, pg. 25

"...each town should support its own poor and should not allow strange beggars to come in, whatever they may call themselves, pilgrims or mendicant monks. Every town could feed its own poor; and if it were too small, the people in the neighbouring villages should be called upon to contribute. As it is, they have to support many knaves and vagabonds under the name of beggars..." – *Address To The Nobility Of The German Nation*

"In this commandment belongs a further statement regarding all kinds of obedience to persons in authority who have to command and to govern. For all authority flows and is propagated from the authority of parents. For where a father is unable alone to educate his [rebellious and irritable] child, he employs a schoolmaster to instruct him; if he be too weak, he enlists the aid of his friends and neighbors; if he departs this life, he delegates and confers his authority and government upon others who are appointed for the purpose. Likewise, he must have domestics, man-servants and maid-servants, under himself for the management of the household, so that all whom we call masters are in the place of parents and must derive their power and authority to govern from them. Hence also they are all called fathers in the Scriptures, as those who in their government perform the functions of a father, and should have a paternal heart toward their subordinates. As also from antiquity the Romans and other nations called the masters and mistresses of the household patres- et matres familiae that is, housefathers and housemothers. So also they called their national rulers and overlords patres patriae, that is fathers of the entire country, for a great shame to us who would be Christians

—Martin Luther—

that we do not likewise call them so, or, at least do not esteem and honor them as such....

"The same also is to be said of obedience to civil government, which (as we have said) is all embraced in the estate of fatherhood and extends farthest of all relations. For here the father is not one of a single family, but of as many people as he has tenants, citizens, or subjects. For through them, as through our parents, God gives to us food, house and home, protection and security. Therefore since they bear such name and title with all honor as their highest dignity, it is our duty to honor them and to esteem them great as the dearest treasure and the most precious jewel upon earth....

"Thus we have two kinds of fathers presented in this commandment, fathers in blood and fathers in office, or those to whom belongs the care of the family, and those to whom belongs the care of the country. Besides these there are yet spiritual fathers; not like those in the Papacy, who have indeed had themselves called thus, but have performed no function of the paternal office. For those only are called spiritual fathers who govern and guide us by the Word of God; as St. Paul boasts his fatherhood 1 Cor. 4, 15, where he says: In Christ Jesus I have begotten you through the Gospel. Now, since they are fathers they are entitled to their honor, even above all others." – *The Larger Catechism, 4th Commandment*

"I, the German prophet seek salvation and blessedness not for myself but for the Germans." – quoted in *The Impact of the Reformation*, pg. 70

"Every German should on this account rue having been born a German and being called a German....Just as we thought we had achieved independence, we became the slaves of the craftiest of tyrants; we have the name, title, and coats of arms of the empire, but the pope has the wealth, power, the courts, and the laws. Thus the pope devours the fruit and we play with the peels." – *Works*, vol. 47, pg. 22 [58]

"It was Paul through whom this prophecy was fulfilled. He almost unaided taught the Gospel doctrine to the posterity of Japheth. He says: 'From Jerusalem, and round about even unto Illyricum, I have fully preached the Gospel of Christ' (Rom 15, 19). Almost all of Asia, with the exception of the oriental peoples, together with Europe, belongs to the posterity of Japheth." – *Commentary on Genesis*, pg. 185 [59]

"Whenever I read these names, I think of the wretched state of the human race. Even though we have the most excellent gift of reason, we are nevertheless so overwhelmed by misfortunes that we are ignorant not only of our own origin and the lineal descent of our ancestors but even of God Himself, our Creator." – *Commentary on Genesis*, pg. 207

"Oh ye unhappy men, who are now leagued with the Pope at Augsburg! your posterity will have eternal cause to blush at your names, and hear with shame, that their forefathers acted thus. Oh disgraceful Diet! such as was never held before, nor ever shall be, in all future time; an eternal blot on every prince, on the whole empire collectively, and one which has degraded the Germans before God and the whole world! What will the Turk and his whole empire exclaim, when they hear of such untold enormities in our country? What will the Tatar and the Muscovite exclaim? Who under the sun, will in future esteem the Germans, or regard us in any respect as honest men, when they hear that we have submitted to be made such fools and blockheads by the Pope and his maskers. . . . Truly, every German might

well lament, that he was born on this polluted soil, or that he bears the name of German...I will, according to the duty of a faithful teacher, warn my beloved countrymen against their danger, and their ruin. . . . I seek not my own, but your welfare and salvation." – Dr. Martin Luther's Warning to His Dear German People, in *The Life of Luther with Notices and Extracts of His Popular Writings*, pg. 147

"What, there is to be no serf because Christ has redeemed us all? What is this? This means that Christian liberty is turned into liberty of the flesh. Did not Abraham and other patriarchs and prophets own serfs? Read what St. Paul has to say about servants, who at that time were all in bondage. Therefore this article is directly opposed to the Gospel and it is rapacious, for everyone who is a bondman to remove himself from his master. A bondman can very well be a Christian and have Christian freedom, just as a prisoner or sick person can be a Christian, but yet is not free. This article proposes to free all men, and turn the spiritual kingdom of Christ into a worldly one, which is impossible. For a worldly kingdom cannot exist where there is no class distinction, where some are free, some are prisoners, some are masters, and some are vassals, etc. As St. Paul says in Gal. 3:28, that in Christ both master and vassal are one." – Admonishment to Peace on the *12 Articles of the Swabian Farmers*, *Works*, vol. 46, pg. 39

"Let us now consider the matters which should be treated in the councils, and with which popes, cardinals, bishops, and all learned men should occupy themselves day and night, if they love Christ and His Church. But if they do not do so, the people at large and the temporal powers must do so..." – *Address To The Nobility*, in *First Principles*, pg. 70

"Let me talk German, for I am being misunderstood by the people." – at the *Diet of Worms*, *Here I Stand*, pg. 116

"I think also that the common law and the usage of the country should be preferred to the law of the empire and that the law of the empire should only be used in cases of necessity. And would to God, that, as each land has its own

---

58 In the preface to the *Book of Concord*, Luther describes his nation, "Germany, our most beloved fatherland."

59 Luther presupposes that certain peoples reside in certain lands collectively and are united by common ancestry.

peculiar character and nature, they could all be governed by their own simple laws, just as they were governed before the law of the empire was devised, and as many are governed even now!"
– *Address To The Nobility*, in *First Principles*, pg. 81

Andrew Nelson Lytle

"If you don't know who you are, or where you come from, you will find yourself at a disadvantage. The ordered slums of suburbia are made for the confusion of the spirit. Those who live in units called homes or estates—both words do violence to the language—don't know who they are. For the profound stress between the union that is flesh and the spirit, they have been forced to exchange the appetites. Each business promotion uproots the family. Children become wayfarers. Few are given any vision of the Divine. They perforce become secular men, half men, who inhabit what is left of Christendom....If we dismiss the past as dead and not as a country of the living which our eyes are unable to see, as we cannot see a foreign country but know it is there, then we are likely to become servile. Living as we will be in a lesser sense of ourselves, lacking that fuller knowledge which only the living past can give, it will be so easy to submit to pressure and receive what is already ours as a boon from authority." *A Wake for the Living*, pg. 3

M

Alasdair MacIntyre

"A crucial turning point in that earlier history occurred when men and women of good will turned aside from the task of shoring up the Roman imperium and ceased to identify the continuation of civility and moral community with the maintenance of that imperium. What they set themselves to achieve instead—often not recognising fully what they were doing—was the construction of new forms of community within which the moral life could be sustained so that both morality and civility might survive the coming ages of barbarism and darkness. If my account of our moral condition is correct, we ought to conclude that for some time now we too have reached that turning point. What matters at this stage is the construction of local forms of community within which civility and the intellectual and moral life can be sustained through the new dark ages which are already upon us. And if the tradition of the virtues was able to survive the horrors of the last dark ages, we are not entirely without grounds for hope. This time however the barbarians are not waiting beyond the frontiers; they have already been governing us for quite some time. And it is our lack of consciousness of this that constitutes part of our predicament. We are waiting not for a Godot, but for another—doubtless very different—St. Benedict." – *After Virtue*, pg. 244-245, 263

Diarmaid MacCulloch

"Repeatedly the Bible has come to mean salvation to a particular people or cultural grouping by saving not merely their souls, but their language, and hence their very identity. So it was, for example, for the people of Wales, through the Bible published for the first time in good literary Welsh by the Protestant Bishop William Morgan in 1588. Morgan's Bible preserved the special character of Welsh culture in the face of the superior resources and colonial self-confidence of the English, and it also ensured, against all likelihood in the early Reformation, that the religious expression of the Welsh became overwhelmingly Protestant. So it was too for Koreans at the end of the nineteenth century, when the Korean Bible translation revived their alphabet and became a symbol of their national pride, sustaining them through Japanese repression and paving the way for the extraordinary success of Christianity in Korea over the last half-century. And one of the reasons for the obstinate survival and now huge revival of Orthodox Christianity has been a story (largely unknown in the Christian West) of biblical translation, undertaken by the Russian Orthodox Church for an astonishing variety of language groups in Eastern Europe and the area of the former Soviet Union." – *Christianity The First Three Thousand Years*, pg. 6

J. Gresham Machen

"… one thing is perfectly plain—whether or not liberals are Christians, it is at any rate perfectly clear that liberalism is not Christianity. And that being the case, it is highly undesirable that liberalism and Christianity should continue to be propagated within the bounds of the same organization. A separation between the two parties in the Church is the crying need of the hour… The modern liberal doctrine is that all men everywhere, no matter what their race or creed, are brothers." – *Christianity and Liberalism*, pg. 135

"Many ties—ties of blood, of citizenship, of ethical aims, of humanitarian endeavor—unite us to those who have abandoned the gospel. We trust that those ties may never be weakened, and that ultimately they may serve some purpose in the propagation of the Christian faith." – *Christianity and Liberalism*, pg. 44

"In the presence of this apparent collapse of free democracy, any descendant of the liberty-loving races of mankind may well stand dismayed; and to those liberty-loving races no doubt most of my hearers tonight belong. I am of the Anglo-Saxon race; many of you belong to a race whose part in the history of human freedom is if anything still more glorious; and as we all contemplate the struggle of our fathers in the winning of that freedom which their descendants seem now to be so willing to give up, we are impressed anew with the fact that it is far easier to destroy than to create." – *The Necessity of the Christian School*, pg. 289

"There, in that glorious round spread out before you, that land of Europe, humanity has put forth its best. There it has struggled; there it has fallen; there it has looked upward to God. The history of the race seems to pass before you in an instant of time, concentrated in that fairest of all the lands of the earth. You think of the great men whose memories you love, the men who have struggled there in those countries below you, who have struggled for light and freedom, struggled for beauty, struggled above all for God's Word. And then you think of the present and its decadence and its slavery, and you desire to weep. It is a pathetic thing to contemplate the history of mankind." – *Mountains and Why We Love Them*

"It is true some of them are 'sticklers' for the civil rights of negroes – it always makes me intensely angry to hear people talking glibly about equal civil rights of negroes when in many parts of the South those equal rights would mean that every legislator and every judge would be a savage of a type and the white men would be more unsafe in parts of this country than in the most parts of the world where at least the protection of his home government is to some extent with him." – Letter to his mother, October 5, 1913

"These chapters are also interesting because they attest the attachment of Paul to the Jewish people. Where is there a nobler expression of patriotism than Rom. 9:1-5?...Paul did not advocate the destruction of the identity of his people. He believed that even the natural Israel had a part to play on the stage of history." – *The New Testament*, pg. 118

"Very different is this Christian conception of brotherhood from the liberal doctrine of the 'brotherhood of man.' The modern liberal doctrine is that all men everywhere, no matter what their race or creed, are brothers. ...

"We are not dealing here with delicate personal questions; we are not presuming to say whether such and such an individual man is a Christian or not. God only can decide such questions; no man can say with assurance whether the attitude of certain individual 'liberals' toward Christ is saving faith or not. But one thing is perfectly plain – whether or not liberals are Christians, it is at any rate perfectly clear that liberalism is not Christianity. And that being the case, it is highly undesirable that liberalism and Christianity should continue to be propagated within the bounds of the same organization. A separation between the two parties in the Church is the crying need of the hour." – *Christianity and Liberalism*, pgs. 157-160

John MacArthur

"God is not only the sovereign ruler of the universe but also the controller of the affairs and destinies of men and nations. Paul declares that He made from one (Adam) every nation of mankind to live on all the face of the earth. That statement was a blow to the national pride of the Greeks, who scornfully referred to non-Greeks as 'barbarians.' All men are equal, because all were created by God. He determined their appointed times; the rise and fall of nations and empires are in His hands (cf. Dan. 2:36ff.; Luke 21:24). God also set the boundaries of their habitation, placing certain nations in specific geographical locations (Deut. 32:8) and determining the extent of their conquests (cf. Isa. 10:12–15)." – *The MacArthur New Testament Commentary*, Acts 13-28, pg. 140

"The family has the primary responsibility for its own widows. A widow's relatives must first learn to practice piety in regard to their own family. The adverb proton (first) means first in time or priority. Piety, or godliness, begins in one's own family, since the family is the context in which genuine godliness is manifested (cf. 3:4, 5, 12; 5:8).

"Supporting widows is not only a mark of godliness, but of obedience. Believers are commanded to make some return to their parents.

They owe a debt to those who brought them into the world, clothed them, fed them, housed them, supported them, and loved and nurtured them. Caring for a mother in the time of her need is but a small return for all she has done. This, Paul writes, is acceptable in the sight of God (cf. Ex. 20:12). The phrase carries a heavy responsibility, since it makes it obvious that this is a matter of priority for every child of God. No one can ever question what God requires in this area.

"The principle that children must support their parents was generally accepted even in the pagan world. William Barclay writes a very interesting section on this historical perspective:

"It was Greek law from the time of Solon that sons and daughters were, not only morally, but also legally bound to support their parents. Anyone who refused that duty lost his civil rights. Aeschines, the Athenian orator, says in one of his speeches: 'And whom did our law-giver (Solon) condemn to silence in the Assembly of the people? And where does he make this clear? 'Let there be,' he says, 'a scrutiny of public speakers, in case there be any speaker in the Assembly of the people who is a striker of his father or mother, or who neglects to maintain them or to give them a home.' Demosthenes says: 'I regard the man who neglects his parents as unbelieving in and hateful to the gods, as well as to men.' Philo, writing of the commandment to honour parents, says: 'When old storks become unable to fly, they remain in their nests and are fed by their children, who go to endless exertions to provide their food because of their piety.' To Philo it was clear that even the animal creation acknowledged its obligations to aged parents, and how much more must men? Aristotle in the Nichomachean Ethics lays it down: 'It would be thought in the matter of food we should help our parents before all others, since we owe our nourishment to them, and it is more honourable to help in this respect the authors of our being, even before ourselves.' As Aristotle saw it, a man must himself starve before he would see his parents starve. Plato in The Laws has the same conviction of the debt that is owed parents: 'Next comes the honour of loving parents, to whom, as is meet, we have to pay the first and greatest and oldest of debts, considering that all which a man has belongs to those who gave him birth and brought him up, and that he must do all

that he can to minister to them; first, in his property; secondly, in his person; and thirdly, in his soul; paying the debts due to them for their care and travail which they bestowed upon him of old in the days of his infancy, and which he is now able to pay back to them, when they are old and in the extremity of their need.'" – *The MacArthur New Testament Commentary*, 1 Timothy 5:3-8, pgs. 309-311

"His generosity knew no bounds. He cared for the injured stranger the way most people care for themselves. That is the kind of limitless love that it takes to earn one's way into God's kingdom. The scribe did not like love like that... The idea is that only by continuously, perfectly loving God and every neighbor on every occasion – even his worst enemy – could the scribe satisfy the first and second commandments and obtain eternal life. Obviously, Christ's point is that neither the scribe nor anyone else is capable of such love." – *The MacArthur New Testament Commentary*, Luke 6-10, pg. 543

John Macpherson

"We have in Acts 6 an account of the election of seven men to supply a want that had been made subject of complaint. It is usual to call the men there spoken of the first deacons. We should, however, remember that even though we may be convinced that they were the precursors of our deacons, and that their office is practically identical with the diaconate, yet this name is not given them in Scripture. To prevent misunderstanding, we shall give them their simple scriptural designation, and speak of them as 'the seven.' A complaint had been made to the Apostles by that portion of the membership of the church at Jerusalem which was not purely Hebrew—the Greek or Hellenist section,—that the poor, and widows, and orphans, belonging to the purely Hebrew membership, were being attended to better, and were being more liberally aided, than the similar classes among themselves. The Apostles listened to their complaint, found apparently that there was some ground for it, and suggested means for remedying the evil. The work was not such as the Apostles, already fully occupied with the ministry of the word, felt it their duty to undertake. The members of the church, therefore, were called upon to elect of their own number seven men, who would have the confidence of all, for their uprightness and true Christian principle. The number was in this particular instance fixed at seven, probably because it was considered that the needs of the Jerusalem Church of that time could best be served by such a staff. Superstition stereotyped the number of deacons in all churches at seven; and in after ages, in churches of great dimensions, where the Presbyterate was very large, the diaconate was strictly limited to this original number. The names of all the seven are given, and it is certainly striking to observe that all the names are Greek. This of itself, however, is no proof that all bearing those names were Greeks; for in the Apostolate we have Andrew and Philip, most undoubted Hebrews, bearing Greek names. Yet when we put side by side these two facts,—the complaint coming from the Greeks, and the appointment of men all bearing Greek names as office-bearers to endeavour the removal of that which occasioned the complaint,—the conviction becomes very strong that these men, for the most part at least, not only bore Greek names, but belonged to the Greek section of the church at Jerusalem. This being so, it may further be concluded with good probability that the seven became members of a board, as specially representing that portion of the church out of which they themselves sprang, and that their presence on the board secured for it the confidence of the Greeks." – *John Macpherson Commentary*, Presbyterianism, pgs. 91-92

Niccolo Machiavelli

"Sparta, as I said, was governed by a king and a senate of limited size. It was able to sustain itself for such a long time because it had few inhabitants and access to participation had been taken away from those who came there to live, and once the laws of Lycurgus, the observance of which removed all causes for strife, were adopted to good effect, the Spartans were able to live in unity over a long period of time...But there were two principal causes for this unity: first, the fact that Sparta had few inhabitants and could therefore be governed by few men; second, the fact that by not accepting foreigners into their republic, they did not have the opportunity either to become corrupt or to grow to such an extent that the city became an intolerable burden for the few who governed it." – *Discourses*, pg. 35

"In considering, therefore, why all the peoples of ancient times were greater lovers of liberty than those of our own day, I believe this arises from the same cause that today makes men less strong, which I believe lies in the difference between our education and that of antiquity, based upon the difference between our religion and that of antiquity. For, while our religion has shown us truth and the true path, it also makes us place a lower value on worldly honour, whereas the pagans, who greatly valued honour and considered it the highest good, were more ferocious in their actions. This can be seen in many of their customs, beginning with the magnificence of their sacrifices as compared to the modesty of our own, in which there is some pomp that is more delicate than magnificent but no bold or ferocious action. In their rites neither pomp nor magnificence was lacking in the ceremonies, but there was, in addition, the act of sacrifice full of blood and cruelty, and the slaughter of a great number of animals, a spectacle which inspired awe and rendered the men who witnessed it equally awesome. Besides this, ancient religion beatified only men fully possessed of worldly glory, such as the leaders of armies and the rulers of republics. Our religion has more often glorified humble and contemplative men rather than active ones. Moreover, our religion has defined supreme good as humility, abjection, and contempt of worldly things; ancient religion located it in greatness of mind, strength of body, and in all the other things apt to make men the strongest. And if our religion requires that you have inner strength, it wants you to have the capacity to endure suffering more than to undertake brave deeds. This way of living seems, therefore, to have give it over to be plundered by wicked men, who are easily able to dominate it, since in order to go to paradise, most men think more about enduring their pains than about avenging them. Although it appears that the world has become soft and heaven has been disarmed, without a doubt this arises more from the cowardice of men who have interpreted our religion according to an ideal of freedom from earthly toil and not according to one of exceptional ability. For if they would consider how our religion permits us to exalt and defend our native land, they would see that it also wants us to love and honour it and to prepare ourselves in such a way that we can defend it." – *Discourses*, pgs. 158-159

"The other cause for war is when an entire people with all its families leaves a place, driven either by famine or by war, and goes to seek out a new location and a new province, not to rule over it as those above do but, rather, to possess it, even the private property, and to drive out or murder its ancient inhabitants. This kind of war is extremely cruel and frightful. It is about this type of war that Sallust speaks at the end of his history of Jugurtha, when he declares that once Jugurtha was defeated, the movement of the Gauls who were coming into Italy began to be felt; he then states that with all other peoples, the Romans fought only about who was to be in command, while with the Gauls they always fought for their safety. Accordingly, for a prince or a republic that attacks a province, it is sufficient to destroy only those who are in command, but populations such as these need to destroy everyone since they wish to live off the resources that supported others. The Romans waged three of these extremely dangerous wars. The first occurred during the occupation of Rome, when the city was captured by those Gauls who had taken Lombardy from the Etruscans, as was mentioned above, and made it their territory; Livy sets forth two reasons for this invasion: first, as was mentioned above, the Gauls were attracted by the sweetness of the fruits and wines of Italy, which were lacking in France; secondly, the kingdom of Gaul was so overpopulated with men that it could no longer support them, and the rulers of those places decided that it was necessary for part of them to seek new land, Once they had made this decision, they elected as captains of the people who had to leave Bellovesus and Sicovesus, two kings of the Gauls; Bellovesus came into Italy and Sicovesus went on to Spain. It was Bellovesus' passage into Italy that brought about the occupation of Lombardy and, as a result, the first war that the Gauls waged against Rome. Then came the war that the Gauls waged after the First Carthaginian War, when between Piombino and Pisa the Romans killed more than 200,000 Gauls. The third war occurred when the Teutones and the Cimbri came into Italy: having defeated several Roman armies, they were destroyed by Marius. The Romans, therefore, won these three extremely dangerous wars. Nor was only minor ability required to win them, because it can be seen later on that once Roman ability grew faint and their arms lost their ancient valour, their empire was destroyed by similar peoples, such as the Goths, the Vandals, and other like tribes who occupied the entire Western empire.

"Peoples such as these leave their own lands, as was mentioned above, driven out by necessity, and this necessity arises either from famine or from a war and the oppression they have experienced in their own country, which has compelled them to seek new homelands. Such peoples come in great numbers, and then they violently enter the lands of others, murder the inhabitants, take possession of their property, create a new kingdom, and change the very name of the province, just as Moses did and as those other peoples did when they occupied the Roman empire. Accordingly, these new names, which exist in Italy and in other provinces, arise from nothing other than the fact that they have been named in this way by the new occupants... Such peoples as these are, therefore, extremely formidable, since they are driven by extreme necessity, and if they do not encounter good armies, they will never be stopped. But when peoples who are compelled to abandon their homeland are not numerous, they are not as dangerous as those we have discussed, because they cannot employ such violence and are obliged to occupy some location with cunning and, once it has been occupied, to maintain themselves there by means of allies and confederations." – *Discourses*, pgs. 172-175

"It does not seem beside the point to discuss somewhere in these discourses how dangerous a thing it is to believe those who have been driven from their native land, since those who rule states must deal with such matters everyday, and since this idea can be demonstrated with a memorable example cited by Livy in his histories, even though it was outside the scope of his topic. When Alexander the Great passed through Asia with his army, his brother-in-law and uncle Alexander of Epirus came into Italy with his troops, summoned by the exiled Lucanians, who gave him hope that with their help he could occupy that entire country. Whereupon, based upon their word and in that hope, he entered Italy and was killed by them once their fellow-citizens promised them they could return home if they murdered him. One must consider, therefore, how vain are both the word and promises of those who find themselves deprived of their homeland. Accordingly, with respect to their word, it must be assumed that any time they can return to their native land by any other means than with your assistance, they will abandon you and draw near to others, notwithstanding whatever promises they have made to you. As for their vain promises and hopes, their desire to return home is so intense that they naturally believe many things which are false, and to them they add many things with guile, so that between the things they believe and the things they say they believe to fill you with hope, they fill you up with so much hope that if you rely upon it, you either incur expenses or undertake an enterprise in which you are ruined." – *Discourses*, pg. 240

— NICCOLO MACHIAVELLI —

"I say, then, that in hereditary states accustomed to the rule of their prince's family, there are far fewer difficulties in maintaining them than in new states, for it is sufficient simply not to break ancient customs, and then to suit one's actions to unexpected events. In this way, if such a prince is of ordinary ability he will always maintain his state, unless some extraordinary and inordinate force should deprive him of it, and although it may be taken away from him, he will regain it at the slightest mistake of the usurper." – *The Prince*, ch. 2 pgs. 7-8 [60]

"Anyone who becomes master of a city accustomed to living in liberty and does not destroy it may expect to be destroyed by it, because such a city always has as a refuge in any rebellion the name of liberty and its ancient institutions, neither of which is ever forgotten either because of the passing of time or because of the bestowal of benefits. And it matters very little what one does or foresees, since if one does not separate or scatter the inhabitants, they will not forget that name or those institutions... But in republics, greater vitality, greater hatred, and greater desire for revenge exist. The memory of ancient liberty does not and cannot allow them to rest, so that the most secure course is either to wipe them out or to go to live there." – *The Prince*, ch. 5, pgs. 19-20 [61]

On the use of "auxiliaries" – foreign soldiers to fight a nation's battles:
"In order to oppose his neighbours, the Emperor of Constantinople brought ten thousand Turkish troops into Greece: when the war was over they did not want to leave, and this was the beginning of Greek servitude under the infidel. Anyone, therefore, who wishes to be unable to win should make use of these soldiers, for they are much more dangerous than mercenary troops. With them ruin is assured, for they are completely united and completely under the command of others. Whereas, after they have been victorious mercenaries require more time and a better opportunity if they are to injure you, for they are not a single body of men and they have been brought together and paid by you. Any third party whom you might make their commander cannot immediately seize enough authority to harm you. In short, with mercenaries the greatest danger is their reluctance to fight; with auxiliaries, their military virtue. A wise prince has always avoided these soldiers and has turned to his own troops. He has preferred to lose with his own troops rather than to win with those of others, judging that to be no true victory which has been gained by means of foreign troops." – *The Prince*, ch. 13, pgs. 49-50 [62]

---

60 Conserving ancient customs of a people makes for peaceful, easy rule.

61 A common people with a shared past and memory are not easily mastered, *unless they are scattered*.

62 Bringing in foreign troops may win a nation a battle, but it costs them dearly as the troops do not leave but end up ruling over the nation they had aided.

"And if, as I said, it was necessary for the people of Israel to be enslaved in Egypt to make known the virtue of Moses, and it was necessary for the Persians to be oppressed by the Medes to make known the greatness of spirit in Cyrus, and it was necessary for the Athenians to be scattered to make known the excellence of Theseus, then at present, to make known the virtue of an Italian spirit, it was necessary for Italy to be reduced to her present conditions, and that she be more enslaved than the Hebrews, more servile than the Persians, and more scattered than the Athenians: without a leader, without order, beaten, despoiled, ripped apart, overrun, and having suffered every sort of ruin.

"And even though, before now, some glimmer of light may have shown itself in a single individual, so that it was possible to believe that God had ordained him for Italy's redemption, yet afterwards it was seen how, at the height of his deeds, he was rejected by Fortune. Now Italy, left as if lifeless, awaits the man who may heal her wounds and put an end to the plundering of Lombardy, the extortions in the Kingdom of Naples and in Tuscany, and who can cure her of those sores that have been festering for so long. Look how she now prays to God to send someone to redeem her from these barbaric cruelties and insults. See how ready and willing she is to follow a banner, provided that someone picks it up.

"This opportunity, therefore, must not be allowed to pass by, so that Italy may behold her redeemer after so long a time. Nor can I express with what love he will be received in all those territories that have suffered through these foreign floods; with what thirst for revenge, with what stubborn loyalty, with what devotion, with what tears! What doors will be closed to him? What people will deny him their obedience? What envy could oppose him? What Italian could deny him homage? This barbarian dominion stinks in everyone's nostrils! Therefore, may Your Illustrious House take up this task with the spirit and the hope with which just enterprises are begun, so that under your banner this country may be ennobled, and under your auspices those words of Petrarch may come true: Virtue will seize arms Against frenzy, and the battle will be brief: For ancient valour Is not yet dead in Italian hearts." – *The Prince*, ch. 26, pgs. 87-90

James Madison

"It is no doubt very desirable that we should hold out as many inducements as possible for the worthy part of mankind to come and settle amongst us, and throw their fortunes into a common lot with ours. But why is this desirable? Not merely to swell the catalogue of people. No, sir, it is to increase the wealth and strength of the community; and those who acquire the rights of citizenship, without adding to the strength or wealth of the community are not the people we are in want of." – *Congressional Register*, III, 212, *Speech on the Naturalization Act of 1790; The Writings of James Madison: 1787-1790*, pg. 437

"I do not wish that any man should acquire the privilege of citizenship, but such as would be a real addition to the wealth or strength of the United States." – *Congressional Register*, III, 212, *Speech on the Naturalization Act of 1790; The Writings of James Madison: 1787-1790*, pg. 437

"To be consistent with existing and probably unalterable prejudices in the U.S. freed blacks ought to be permanently removed beyond the region occupied by or allotted to a White population." – Letter to Robert J. Evans, June 15, 1819; *The Writings of James Madison: 1769-1783*, ch. 15, doc. 65

"The intrusion of obnoxious aliens through other States, merit[s] attention. [This] subject has, on several occasions, been mentioned in Congress, but, I believe, no committee has ever reported a remedy for the abuse. A uniform rule of naturalization ought certainly to be recommended to the States." – Letter from James Madison to Edmund Randolph, Aug. 27, 1782; *The Writings of James Madison: 1769-1783*, pg. 226

"Our kind reception of emigrants is very proper, but it is dictated more by benevolent than by interested considerations, tho some of them seem to be very far from regarding the obligations as lying on their side. According to the general laws of Europe, no emigrant ceases to be a subject. With this double aspect, I believe it cannot be doubted that naturalized Citizens among us have found it more easy than native ones to practice certain frauds. I have been led to think it worthy of consideration whether our law of naturalization might not be so varied as to communicate the rights of Citizens by degrees, and in that way, preclude or abridge the abuses committed by naturalized merchants particularly Ship owners. The restrictions would be felt it is true by meritorious individuals, of whom I could name some & you doubtless more, but this always happens in precautionary regulations for the general good." – letter to Richard Peters, 22nd February, 1819; *The Writings of James Madison: 1808-1819*, pg. 424

"Without entering into a detailed view of the subject, it may be remarked, that every prudent nation will wish to be independent of other nations, for the necessary articles of food, of raiment, and of defense; and particular considerations applicable to the U.S. seem to strengthen the motives to this independence." – Letter to Dominick Lynch Jr., 1817; *The Writings of James Madison: 1808-1819*, pg. 393

Magdeburg Confession

"Just as the Church is an ordinance of God, in which God wants there to be an order of teachers and of learners, so also politics and economy are truly ordinances of God in which He likewise wants there to be an order of superiors and order of inferiors who are ruled by laws and precepts that agree with reason and are not at variance with the Word, and obey them, not only because of wrath or fear of the punishment which threatens from their rulers, but also because of conscience, that is, fear of the wrath and judgment of God.

"For God has armed these his ordinances and powers with fear of both wrath and punishment, divine and human, and they both hold their respective power. And He has distinguished one power from another in His Word, so that He has attributed to each of them its own object and task, and likewise to each its own method of punishment. And although He does not desire the powers to be mixed up with each other, nonetheless He desires them to help each other in turn, so that in the end they all may agree and everything in its own place and way principally may promote true knowledge of God and His Glory and their eternal salvation, or, when it does not attain this ultimate goal, may at least bring about a secondary sort of well-being, that men may live peacefully,

uprightly, not unfruitful in this civil manner of life." – *Tyranny and Resistance*, pg. 121

Apollon Maykov

"Stand firm! … and you withstood,
Holy Rus, all the Lord sent you –
All the blood and burden,
Slaughter and pain.
A heavy hammer has forged you
Into one people –
    the pounding lasted for centuries.
But you know that God, out of love,
Punished you,
    and by that you are unbreakable."
– 'Uprazdnennyi Monastyr'; *Roots Of Nationalism*, pg. 164

Joseph de Maistre

"Now, there is no such thing as 'man' in this world. In my life I have seen Frenchmen, Italians, Russians, and so on. I even know, thanks to Montesquieu, that one can be Persian. But as for man, I declare I've never encountered him." – *Considerations on France*, pg. xxiii

"A constitution that is made for all nations is made for none... [such a constitution is] a pure abstraction, an academic exercise of the mind, according to some hypothetical ideal, that should be addressed to man, in whatever imaginary realm he inhabits." – *Considerations on France*, pg. 80

"No nation can give itself liberty if it is not already free, for human influence extends only as far as existing rights have developed...There never existed a free nation which did not have seeds of liberty as old as itself in its natural constitution. Nor has any nation ever successfully attempted to develop, by its fundamental written laws, rights other than those which existed in its natural constitution." – *Essay on the Generative Principle of Political Constitutions and other Human Institutions*, in *Considerations on France*; pg. 50

"Until now nations were killed by conquest, that is by invasion: But here an important question arises; can a nation not die on its own soil, without resettlement or invasion, by allowing the flies of decomposition to corrupt to the very core those original and constituent principles which make it what it is." – Quoted by Philippe Ploncard d'Assac in *Le nationalisme français*, pg. 26

"Human reason reduced to its own resources is perfectly worthless, not only for creating but also for preserving any political or religious association, because it only produces disputes, and, to conduct himself well, man needs not problems but beliefs. His cradle should be surrounded by dogmas, and when his reason is awakened, it should find all his opinions ready-made, at least all those relating to his conduct. Nothing is so important to him as prejudices, Let us not take this word in a bad sense. It does not necessarily mean false ideas, but only, in the strict sense of the word, opinions adopted before any examination. Now these sorts of opinions are man's greatest need, the true elements of his happiness, and the Palladium of empires. Without them, there can be neither worship, nor morality, nor government. There must be a state religion just as there is a state policy; or, rather, religious and political dogmas must be merged and mingled together to form a complete common or national reason strong enough to repress the aberrations of individual reason, which of its nature is the mortal enemy of any association whatever because it produces only divergent opinions.

"All known nations have been happy and powerful to the extent that they have more faithfully obeyed this national reason, which is nothing other than the annihilation of individual dogmas and the absolute and general reign of national dogmas, that is to say, of useful prejudices. Let each man call upon his individual reason in the matter of religion, and immediately you will see the birth of an anarchy of belief or the annihilation of religious sovereignty. Likewise, if each man makes himself judge of the principles of government, you will at once see the birth of civil anarchy or the annihilation of political sovereignty. Government is a true religion: it has its dogmas, its mysteries, and its ministers. To annihilate it or submit it to the discussion of each individual is the same thing; it lives only through national reason, that is to say through political faith, which is a creed. Man's first need is that his nascent reason be curbed under this double yoke, that it be abased and lose itself in the national reason, so that it changes its individual existence into another common existence, just as a river that flows into

the ocean always continues to exist in the mass of water, but without a name and without a distinct reality." – *Against Rousseau: On the State of Nature and On the Sovereignty of the People*, pgs. 87-88

Sir Thomas Mallory

"Yet some men say in many parts of England that King Arthur is not dead, but had by the will of our Lord Jesu into another place. And men say that he shall come again, and he shall win the Holy Cross." – *Le Morte d'Arthur*, pg. 481

Basil Manly, Sr.

Suggested that since God appointed them to a state of perpetual slavery, they had no natural right to freedom.

"Whatever may have been the motives of men engaged in their transportation, God has overruled it for good. ... All will depend on the question, 'Is liberty of person given to all?' God gives power to some and bondage to others. Only God can be held accountable for the differences in social condition and inequalities of human capacity. To quarrel with this will be to waste our rage upon a dispensation as old as nature." – as quoted in *Report on Slavery and Racism in the History of the Southern Baptist Theological Seminary*, pg. 15

Martin Manser

"Humanity is created in the image or likeness of God. This image of God, given in creation, was damaged in the fall, but may be restored through Jesus Christ...

"Paul implies that the divine image is associated in the first place with men. Although Paul at points seems to imply that the image of God is especially associated with males, he does not imply that this involves male supremacy: 1Co 11:7, 11-12." – *Dictionary of Bible Themes: The Accessible and Comprehensive Tool for Topical Studies*, "Image Of God", 5023

Michael Mann

"Well, in spite of what everyone says, I personally and the British people are a very traditional people...Every human being needs to have roots. They need to know where they come from. Look at the way the Americans spend endless dollars on genealogical tables. We all need to know where we come from. A Muslim said to me the other day, 'If you don't know where you come from, how can you know who you are or where you're going?' And in that sense we need tradition. That sense of continuity and a sense of being here not just for ourselves but because of those who have gone before and for those who are then to follow after. And tradition reinforces this very strongly. It's part of a moving tapestry." – Church of England Bishop of Dudley and Dean of Windsor, from an interview on *In The Highest Tradition*, BBC, Episode 1

Constance Markievicz

"This Society is likely to be a means the most powerful for the promotion of a great end. What end? The Rights of Man in Ireland, the greatest happiness of the greatest number in this island, the inherent and indefeasible claims of every free nation to rest in this nation …
The greatest happiness of the greatest number – on the rock of this principle let this Society rest; by this let it judge and determine every political question, and whatever is necessary for this end let it not be accounted hazardous, but rather our interest, our duty, our glory and our common religion. The Rights of Man are the Rights of God, and to vindicate the one is to maintain the other. We must be free in order to serve Him whose service is perfect freedom." – Wolfe Tone's *Ideals of Democracy; The "Irish Rebellion of 1798," with Numerous Historical Sketches, Etc*, pg. 156

Justin Martyr

"Christians are not distinguished from the rest of mankind by either country, speech, or customs; the fact is, they nowhere settle in cities of their own; they use no peculiar language; they cultivate no eccentric mode of life. Certainly, this creed of theirs is no discovery due to some fancy or speculation of inquisitive men; nor do they, as some do, champion a doctrine of human origin. Yet while they dwell in both Greek and non-Greek cities, as each one's lot was cast, and conform to the customs of the country in dress, food, and mode of life in general, the whole tenor of their way of living stamps it as worthy of admiration and admit-

tedly extraordinary." – *The Didache, The Epistle of Barnabas, The Epistles and the Martyrdom of St. Polycarp, The Fragments of Papias and The Epistle to Diognetus*, pgs. 138-139

Karl Marx

"National differences and antagonisms are already tending to disappear more and more as the bourgeoisie develops, as free trade becomes more general, as the world market grows in size and importance, as manufacturing conditions and the resulting conditions of life become more uniform." – *Communist Manifesto*, pg. 39

"The Protective system in these days is conservative, while the Free Trade system works destructively. It breaks up old nationalities and carries antagonism of proletariat and bourgeoisie to the uttermost point. In a word, the Free Trade system hastens the Social Revolution. In this revolutionary sense alone, gentlemen, I am in favor of Free Trade." – *Free Trade*, pg. 42

"Owing to the constantly increasing concentration of leaseholds, Ireland constantly sends her own surplus to the English labor market, and thus forces down wages and lowers the material and moral position of the English working class." – cited in Carchedi, *Behind the Crisis*, pg. 213

La Marseillaise

Let's go children of the fatherland,
The day of glory has arrived!

Ralph P. Martin

"Hebrews 11. Ancestors are sometimes held up as figures deserving reverence and emulation (e.g., 2 Tim 1:3). Abraham, Isaac and Jacob are treated with particularly high regard (Barn. 8.4; cf. Ign. Phld. 9.1). In Hebrews 11 the author 'brings before his audience a long series of exemplary witnesses to an enduring faith,' who act upon God's promises even though the fulfillment of those promises is not in sight (Lane, 315; cf. Heb 11:2, presbyteroi, 'ancestors')…
   "Acts 7. Stephen's speech contains another major catalogue of revered ancestors. The speech provides the framework for several allusions to Abraham (Acts 7:2–8, 16–17, 32) in which he appears as the recipient of promises

by which his descendants benefit." – *Dictionary of the Later New Testament and its Developments*, pg. 40

— Massachusetts Laws — (Modern Era)

What marks the modern era is the explosion of material on the themes of this anthology. Attempts to explain this phenomenon run into the hundreds of volumes. It is likely due to a combination of the emergence of nation-states and the discovery of the new world and, with it, the realization that Europeans constitute a global minority of people on the earth. The attempt to define each nationality, and to do so in the face of untold millions of other people in "new" worlds, likely played an important role in fostering thought and discussion on peoplehood. This is the popular interpretation by nationalists and universalists alike. But it should be noted that hierarchical structures and notions of social differences were in place before and only enhanced by these discoveries and explorations.

Another large factor recognized by all scholars is the effects of modernity itself: the vast changes in communication, industrialization, and popular government. Industrialization, to take but one facet, motivated the mass of peasants, hitherto ignored by political powers, to stuff into cities where the governing classes had to confront them almost daily. However, these changes did not produce a change in natural or national sentiment, but, as mentioned above, only built upon and enhanced them in ways both new and familiar with old ways of life. The confrontation of the populace accelerated their sense of peoplehood, bringing it to the forefront of political deliberation and cultural urban expression. Simply put, there are fewer mass demonstrations when the people live dispersed among the countryside, but "the people" had still existed. Indeed, it is the countryside where patriotic sentiment is bred and expropriated by popular cultural art. Modernity ushered in changes such as the mass gathering of the people, and therefore a bloom of national consciousness arose; but the people and their self-consciousness existed a priori to city-centered developments.

Because of the wide range of people and topics, in what follows we will only intersperse what commentary is needed to aid contextual reading throughout. The first selection is taken from American colonial laws. The largest theme is one of foreign exclusion in the interest of communal settlement, peace, and order.

Mass., General Court

During King Philip's War (1675-1678), the Massachusetts General Court identified the sins of the colony, called for a general humiliation and repentance before God. They repented, in part, of not zealously keeping Quakers from entering.

"This court taking into consideration the great wars, combustions and divisions, which are this day in Europe, and that the same are observed to be raised and fomented chiefly by the secret underminings and solicitations of those of the Jesuitical order, men brought up and devoted to the religion and court of Rome, which hath occasioned divers states to expel them their territories, for prevention whereof among ourselves:

"It is ordered and enacted by authority of this court, that no Jesuit, or spiritual or ecclesiastical person (as they are termed) ordained by the authority of the pope or see of Rome, shall henceforth at any time repair to, or come within this jurisdiction: and if any person shall give just cause of suspicion, that he is one of such society or order, he shall be brought before some of the magistrates, and if he cannot free himself of such suspicion, he shall be committed to prison, or bound over to the next court of assistants, to be tried and proceeded with, by banishment or otherwise as the court shall see cause.

"And if any person so banished, be taken the second time within this jurisdiction, upon lawful trial and conviction, he shall be put to death. Provided this law shall not extend to any such Jesuit, spiritual or ecclesiastical person, as shall be cast upon our shores by shipwreck or other accident, so as he continue no longer than till he may have opportunity of passage for his departure; nor to any such as shall come in company with any messenger hither upon public occasions, or merchant, or master of any ship belonging to any place, not in enmity with the state of England, or ourselves, so as they depart again with the same messenger, master or merchant, and behave themselves inoffensively during their abode here." – *Massachusetts General Court, The Charters and General Laws of the Colony and Province of Massachusetts Bay*, pg. 129

Boston, MA

"Whereas sundry inhabitants in this town have not so well attended to former orders made for the securing the town from charge by sojourners, inmates, hired servants, journeymen, or other persons that come for help in physick [medical treatment?] or chyrurgery [surgery?], whereby no little damage hath already, and much more may accrue to the town. For the prevention whereof it is therefore ordered, that whosoever of our inhabitants shall henceforth receive any such persons before named into their houses or employments without liberty granted from the select men, shall pay twenty shillings for the first week, and so from week to week, twenty shillings, so long as they retain them, and shall bear all the charge that may accrue to the town by every such sojourner, journeyman, hired servt., inmate, &c., received or employed as aforesaid. Provided, always, that if any person so receiving any shall, within fifteen days, give sufficient security unto the select men that the town may be secured from all charges that may arise by any person received, and that the persons so received be not of notorious evil life and manners, their fine above said shall be remitted or abated according to the discretion of the select men. And it is further ordered that if after bond given by any, they give such orderly notice to the select men that the town may be fully cleared of such person or persons so received according to law, then their bonds shall be given in again." – *Warning Out In New England*, pgs. 25, 26.

Woburn, MA

In 1648 a stranger was admitted an inhabitant of Woburn and permitted to buy land for his convenience:

"provided he unsettle not any inhabitant and bring testimony of his peaceable behaviour which is not in the least measure questioned." – *Warning Out In New England*, pg. 26.

Lancaster, MA

"[F]or the better preserving of the purity [of] religion and ourselves from the infection of error [we are] not to distribute allotments and to receive into the plantation as inhabitants any excommunicate or otherwise profane and scandalous (known so to be) nor any notoriously erring against the doctrine and discipline of the churches and the state and government of this Commonweale." – *Warning Out In New England*, pg. 33.

Medfield, MA

"We shall all of us in the said town faithfully endeavor that only such be received to our society & township as we may have sufficient satisfaction in, that they are honest, peaceable, & free from scandal and erroneous opinions." – Cited in Benton, *Warning Out In New England*, pg. 34.

Salem, MA

In 1670 a person was appointed and instructed:

"...to go from house to house about the town, once a month, to inquire what strangers are come, or have privily thrust themselves into town and to give notice to the Selectmen in being, from time to time, and he shall have the fines for his pains or such reasonable satisfaction as is meet." – *Warning Out In New England*, pg. 36.

Massachusetts Bay, MA

"Whereas we are credibly informed that great mischiefs and outrages have been wrought in other plantations in America by commanders, and soldiers of several qualities, and other strangers issuing out of other parts, usurping power of government over them, plundering of their estates, taking up arms, and making great divisions amongst the inhabitants where they have come, to prevent the like mischief in this jurisdiction, this court doth order, and it is hereby enacted, that henceforward all strangers, of what quality soever, above the age of sixteen years, arriving here in any ports or parts of this jurisdiction in any ship or vessel, shall immediately be brought before the governor, deputy governor, or two other magistrates, by the master or mate of the said ships or vessels, upon the penalty of twenty pounds; for default thereof, there to give an account of their occasions and business in this country, whereby satisfaction may-be given to this commonwealth, and order taken with such strangers as the said governor, deputy governor, two assistants, or the next county court shall see meet; and that the law for entertaining of strangers be strictly put in execution, and this order to be posted up upon the several meetinghouses doors, or posts, or other public places in the port towns of this jurisdiction. And it is ordered, that the captain of the castle shall make known this order to every ship or vessel as it passeth by, and the constables of every port town shall endeavor to do the like to such ships or vessels before they land their passengers; and that a true record be kept of all the names of such strangers, and their qualities, by the clerks of the writs, who shall have the names given them by the said governor or magistrates, to be returned to the next immediate sessions of the General Court. This to continue and be in force till the next session." – *Warning Out In New England*, pg. 47

General Laws of Massachusetts

In its section on Strangers, *The Book of the General Laws and Liberties Concerning the Inhabitants of the Massachusetts*, published in 1648, forbids allowing a stranger admission without the allowance of the magistrate. Fines were to be imposed for violating this law:

"It is ordered by this Court and the Authority thereof; that no town or person shall receive any stranger resorting hither with intent to reside in this Jurisdiction, nor shall allow any lot or habitation to any, or entertain any such above three weeks, except such person shall have allowance under the hand of some one Magistrate, upon pain of every town that shall give, or sell any lot or habitation to any not so licensed such fine to the country as that county court shall impose, not exceeding fifty pounds, nor less then ten pounds. And of every person receiving any such for longer time then is here expressed or allowed, in some special cases as before, or in case of entertainment of friends resorting from other parts of this Country in amity with us, shall forfeit as aforesaid, not exceeding twenty pounds, nor less then four pounds: and for every month after so offending, shall forfeit as aforesaid not exceeding ten pounds, nor less then forty shillings. Also, that all Constables shall inform the Courts of newcomers which they know to be admitted without licence, from time to time." – *Charters and General Laws*, pgs. 191-192

———

Peter Van Mastricht

"The order of this love is such that, because God is to be cherished with love first and most highly, thus he is the formal reason as it were of love for neighbor. Then closest after God, we love ourselves with that love that aims at true blessedness, for by loving God with a love of union, we immediately love ourselves with the highest love that aims at our spiritual blessedness; and we love others as it were secondarily, as we want them to be partakers with us of the same good. Among men, although no one is to be excluded from our love, yet the same degree of love is not to be observed toward all. Indeed, with regard to the good that we ought to will for our neighbor, there is no inequality, because we ought to will the highest good for each neighbor, as we do for ourselves; nor with regard to the affection of willing or wishing that good ought there be any inequality of intensity and remission. But with regard to the exercise and effects of this affection, an inequality of frequency, order, and extension occurs, as the concurrence of circumstances makes the operation of love necessary. For (1) we ought to elicit more frequently the act itself of charity toward those in whom the reasons and causes of love more frequently come before us. (2) An order ought to be observed according to the occasion that is offered, and the proportion of acts to their objects. (3) There ought to be an extension to more or nobler effects, according to their necessity, and the worthiness of the things loved. See Ames, Cases of Conscience (bk. 5, ch. 7, q. 4). Now, with these points introduced generally, among men those are to be loved more than others who draw nearer to God, and in God to ourselves (Gal. 6:10). Consequently, with other things being equal, believers should be loved more than unbelievers; blood relatives, other things being equal, more than strangers; and among blood relatives, those who are more closely conjoined to us than those who are so more distantly, but that according to the nature of the conjunction by which they draw near to us: if the conjunction with someone is physical, physical things are owed more to him; if spiritual, more so spiritual things; that is, if an act of charity that regards both cannot be exercised equally toward both at the same time." – *Theoretical-Practical Theology*, 2.3.2

Victor Harold Matthews

"Blood kinship played an important role in the determination of personal identity and the distribution of power in the villages of early Israel. No blood relationship was taken for granted. However, despite the fact that members of households, clans, villages and tribes in early Israel may have been physically related, the critical requirement for membership was not kinship but covenant (Meyers 1988, 127). The Israelites were not just households with the same biological parents but households with the same sociological experience and a shared legal commitment to one another. As a result, their understanding of membership in a covenantal community placed social obligations on them to uphold the honor of their individual households while also providing support to the larger community and sustaining the needs of a set of protected classes…

"In ancient Israel there existed a patrilineal, segmentary lineage system in which each of its households (bêt ʾābôt) belonged to a lineage (mišpāḥâ). These lineages, in which membership and inheritance were based on the father, made up a clan. The clans formed several phratries, and the phratries made up the tribe. Its lineages were also, once the Israelites entered Canaan, described as localized, having their own designated territories (Josh 13-19). These social groupings are not necessarily evolutionary. They all continued to exist and served as the basis of personal identity even after the monarchy was established…

"The bêt ʾābôt, the Israelite households, were part of a remarkably sophisticated political system for distributing power. The Bible describes early Israel's political system in terms of kinship ties, as with many traditional societies. One place in which these patterns of kinship in the Bible are preserved is in genealogies (Edelman; Wilson). Linear genealogies, such as the one that begins with the creation of Adam, have a clear end point (Noah and the flood), and their intent is to bridge a gap between major events in the narrative. Vertical genealogies trace the descendants of a single family (Esau in Gen 36:1–5, 9–43), and they focus on establishing legitimacy for membership in the family or tribe (Gen 46:8–27). Genealogies describe not only blood relationships but also economic relationships, social status, financial worth and the power that a household can exercise in the community as a whole (Malina, 25–93). To understand a genealogy it is necessary to understand the particular social system it reflects and the language that it uses…

"The weight of evidence indicates male dominance was the rule and patriarchal lineage and inheritance systems were the norm in the ancient Near East. One of the clearest indications of this situation is found in the mandated devotion of a woman to worship the personal or household god of her male partner. Thus, initially, a woman would worship the god of her father, and then, once her marriage contract had been arranged and she had officially joined the new household of her husband, she would transfer her allegiance and her worship to the god of her husband (van der Toorn 1995, 1–2). This practice is echoed in the story of Rebekah's betrothal to Isaac and her quick decision to leave her father's household once the marriage contract was concluded (Gen 24:50–60)." – *Dictionary of the Old Testament: Pentateuch. Family Relationships.* In T. D. Alexander & D. W. Baker (Eds.), pgs. 291–293

Giuseppe Mazzini

"Our country is our home, the home which God has given us, placing therein a numerous family which we love and are loved by, and with which we have a more intimate and quicker communion of feeling and thought than with others." – Quoted in Lloyd Kramer, *Nationalism in Europe and America: Politics, Cultures, and Identities Since 1775,* pg. 106

"God has given you your country as cradle, and humanity as mother; you cannot rightly love your brethren of the cradle if you love not the common mother." – *Life and Writings of Joseph Mazzini; The World's Great Speeches,* Fourth Enlarged (1999) Ed., pg. 101

"A Country is not a mere territory: the particular territory is only its foundation. The Country is the idea which rises upon that foundation; it is the sentiment of love, the sense of fellowship which binds together all the sons of that territory. So long as a single one of your brothers is not represented by his own vote in the development of the national life–so long as a single one vegetates uneducated among the educated–so long as a single one able and willing to work languishes in poverty for want of work–you have not got a Country such as it ought to be, the Country of all and for all." – *For Love of Country An Essay on Patriotism and Nationalism*, pg. 149

"Without Country you have neither name, token, voice, nor rights, no admission as brothers into the fellowship of the Peoples. You are the bastards of Humanity. Soldiers without a banner, Israelites among the nations, you will find neither faith, nor protection; none will be sureties for you. Do not beguile yourselves with the hope of emancipation from unjust social conditions if you do not first conquer a Country for yourselves; where there is no Country there is no common agreement to which you can appeal; the egoism of self-interest rules alone, and he who has the upper hand keeps it, since there is no common safeguard for the interests of all." – *For Love of Country: An Essay on Patriotism and Nationalism*, pg. 149

Daniel McCarthy

"The idea that economic nationalism is not compatible with free-market economics is absurd. The history of America from the founding to the New Deal belies the idea that nationalist economics is bad for business or growth. Its virtue is that it is good for labor and political stability as well. From growth, a contented middle class, and moderate political culture flow a strong country and stronger families and citizens. In the early decades of the twenty-first century, when nations and supranational institutions are in turmoil, those benefits are of existential significance." – *New Conservative Agenda*

"Free trade is a clear and simple rule, and the economic theory of which it is a part is elegant and logical. But it is only a partial truth. The value of the middle class has to be weighed in political terms, not merely economic ones, and national security has a strategic logic all its own that springs from different and darker assumptions about human nature than the hopeful logic of economic efficiency. To reduce public policy to a single dimension, as free-trade ideologues do, is foolish and dangerous. Yet it is attractive because it provides definite answers to difficult questions, even if those answers are

less than complete." – *Case For Trump's Tariffs*

John McCone

"The problem of foreign competition with American business was a problem that was going to grow rapidly in the future. The costs of production abroad of competitive products were shockingly lower than costs in the U.S., mostly as a result of cheaper labor costs." – Discussion of 409th Meeting of the National Security Council, June 4, 1959, vol. 16 (1990), document 971, DDC [63]

Wilfred McClay

"It [his book] means to offer to American readers, young and old alike, an accurate, responsible, coherent, persuasive, and inspiring narrative account of their own country – an account that will inform and deepen their sense of the land they inhabit and equip them for the privileges and responsibilities of citizenship. 'Citizenship' here encompasses something larger than the civics-class meaning. It means a vivid and enduring sense of one's full membership in one of the greatest enterprises in human history: the astonishing, perilous, and immensely consequential story of one's own country. Let me emphasize the term story. Professional historical writing has, for a great many years now, been resistant to the idea of history as narrative. Some historians have even hoped that history could be made into a science. But this approach seems unlikely ever to succeed, if for no other reason than that it fails to take into account the ways we need stories to speak to the fullness of our humanity and help us orient ourselves in the world. The impulse to write history and organize our world around stories is intrinsic to us as human beings. We are, at our core, remembering and story-making creatures, and stories are one of the chief ways we find meaning in the flow of events. What we call 'history' and 'literature' are merely the refinement and intensification of that basic human impulse, that need. The word need is not an exaggeration. For the human animal, meaning is not luxury; it is a necessity. Without it, we perish. Historical consciousness is to civilized society what memory is to individual identity. Without memory, and without the stories by which our memories are carried

---

63 McCone is a former CIA Director

forward, we cannot say who, or what, we are. Without them, our life and thought dissolve into a meaningless, unrelated rush of events. Without them, we cannot do the most human of things: we cannot learn, use language, pass on knowledge, raise children, establish rules of conduct, engage in science, or dwell harmoniously in society. Without them, we cannot govern ourselves. Nor can we have a sense of the future as a time we know will come, because we remember that other tomorrows also have come and gone. A culture without memory will necessarily be barbarous and easily tyrannized, even if it is technologically advanced. The incessant waves of daily events will occupy all our attention and defeat all our efforts to connect past, present, and future, thereby diverting us from an understanding of the human things that unfold in time, including the paths of our own lives…As individuals, as communities, as countries: we are nothing more than flotsam and jetsam without the stories in which we find our lives' meaning. These are stories of which we are already a part, whether we know it or not. They are the basis of our common life, the webs of meaning in which our shared identities are suspended." – *The Land We Love*, Introduction

James McKeown

"God is cast in the roles of Creator and 'supreme landlord' in the Pentateuch. The land owes its existence to him, and he creates its inhabitants, continually monitoring and supervising their behavior. He allocates land to people…Conversely, he removes people from land when they do not behave in a worthy manner…

"Land and people are portrayed in a close interdependent relationship. This is initiated when God, having already commanded the ground to bring forth vegetation, uses the soil ('ădāmâ) as the material for the creation of humankind ('ādām)… [T]hat the man is made from clay, elevates the ground while reminding human beings of their innate vulnerability; not only do they come from the ground, but when they die they return to it as mere dust (Gen 3:19). The close relationship that humans have with the ground means that they are obliged to care for it and enabled to reap its benefits (Gen 2:16), but it also means that anything adverse that affects the ground/land strikes deeply at

the very basis of their existence…

"The relationship between land and its inhabitants is contingent on good relations between humans and God. When humans are alienated from God there are significant repercussions, because God uses the land to punish his recalcitrant subjects…As a result, the ground is cursed (Gen 3:17–19), thorns and thistles make the ground more difficult to cultivate and less productive (cf. Gen 5:29), human beings must still work the soil but the benefits they receive are greatly reduced (Gen 3:19, 23), and the harmony established at creation is replaced by alienation culminating in the expulsion of the human beings from the idyllic surroundings of the garden of Eden (Gen 3:24)….The final crime in the primeval narratives is that of the tower builders whose insubordination results in them being scattered over all the earth.

"In these early stories fertile land is a gift from God and a sign of his blessing while infertility (famine) may be a consequence of divine displeasure. While later famines in the Pentateuch are not explicitly described as punishment from God, they clearly imply the absence of blessing and suggest that the lands so afflicted are not blessed with divine favor (Gen 12:10; 26:1). Fertile soil and secure boundaries, however, are evidence of divine favor and blessing (Gen 26:12–33)…" – *Dictionary of the Old Testament Pentateuch*, "Land, Fertility, Famine". In T. D. Alexander & D. W. Baker (Eds.), pgs. 487-491

Scot McKnight

"Equality is not traditional; hierarchicalism is traditional. The more equality they affirm the less traditional they become and the more tension they create with equality. Holding both in the same hand is a sleight of the hand." – *The (so-called) "Traditional" Argument is not Traditional, Christianity Today*

William McKinley

"What these other countries want is a free and open market with the United States. . . wherever we have tried reciprocity or low duties we have always been the Loser." – *Debate over the McKinley Tariff*, 1980; *Reciprocity with Canada*, pg. 2,836

"The things we can not make for ourselves or produce for ourselves we must buy elsewhere, and therefore we want no tax upon them; but it is economy for our people to buy from each other the things we can produce among ourselves and for ourselves; and if the foreign producer wants to enjoy any part of this market, he must be subject to the terms we shall fix in the interest of our own countrymen. That is the principle of protection. That is the doctrine of patriotism. That is the principle of our country first and our countrymen first. That is the principle of home and family. That is the doctrine of true Americanism ...

"We have free trade among ourselves throughout our forty-four States and the several Territories. That is because we are one family, one country. We have one standard of citizenship, one flag, one Constitution, one Nation, one destiny. That is why we have free trade among ourselves. Our relations with the nations outside are necessarily different from our relations among ourselves. They are a separate organism – a distinct and independent political society organized to work out their own destiny. They are our commercial rivals. We deny to those foreign nations trade with us upon the same terms we enjoy among ourselves. The foreign producer is not entitled to equality with us in this market. He pays no taxes; he is not amenable to our laws; he performs no civil or military duties; he is exempt from State, county, and municipal taxes; he contributes nothing primarily to the support of the Government or its progress and prosperity. Upon what principle, I pray you, should he enjoy equal privileges and profits in our markets with our producers, our laborers, our taxpayers? ...

"Free trade gives to the foreign producer equal privileges with us. Upon what principle of fair play should he have them? It invites the product of his cheaper labor to this market to destroy the domestic product representing our higher and better-paid labor. It destroys our factories or reduces our labor to the level of his. It increases foreign production but diminishes home production. It will kindle fires in the furnaces of England, and extinguish the fires in our own. It will close the iron mines of the great Northwest, and leave untenanted the coal and coke regions of the East. It will do all this with unerring certainty, unless the standard of American labor shall be pulled down to the plane and condition of foreign labor: one or the other is inevitable. In any event it destroys the dignity and independence of American labor, diminishes its pay and employment, decreases its capacity to buy the products of the farm and the commodities of the merchant. We can not have free trade in this country without having free-trade conditions." – Campaign Speech, August 2, 1892; *Speeches and Addresses*, pgs. 594-595

John McClintock

"Adult Age, or that at which marriage may be contracted or religious vows made. The canonists agree that men may contract marriage at fourteen years of age, and women at twelve. Until the contracting parties are each twenty-one years of age, no marriage can be legally contracted without the consent of the parents or guardians of the party which is a minor." – with James Strong. *Cyclopædia of Biblical, Theological, and Ecclesiastical Literature*, Marriage, vol. 1, pg. 102

Thomas M'Crie

"The whole tenor of the declarations, promises, and predictions of the Old Testament, lead to the conclusion that Christianity shall be owned, countenanced, and supported in a national way. God addresses the nations in a collective capacity, reproves them for their idolatry, and calls them to his worship (Isa. 34:1; 41:1, 21-29). He proposes Christ, as his anointed servant, to them (Isa. 42:1); declares that he has given him the nations for his inheritance, and that he shall inherit them all (Ps. 2:8; 82:8; Isa. 52:15; 55:5). Christ addresses himself, not only to individuals, but to whole islands (Isa. 44:1); nations join themselves to him (Isa. 2:2; Micah 4:1-2; Zech. 2:11; 8:20-22), bless themselves, and glory in him (Jer. 4:2); all nations and dominions serve him (Dan. 7:14, 27). They consecrate all things in them, and employ them in his service (Isa. 60:6-12; Zech. 14:20-21); he owns these nations as his, and blesses them, while he breaks in pieces and wastes others (Ps. 33:12; 145:15; Isa. 19:25; Ps. 2:9, 12; Isa. 60:12). [64]" – *Brief View of the Evidence for the Exercise of Civil Authority About Religion, in Statement Of The Difference* etc., pgs. 136-137

---

64 [Footnote in original] The force of the argument arising from these and similar predictions, is such that Mr. Edward Williams, although an Independent, acknowledges that they imply a national profession and establishment of Christianity. In answer to the objection, 'If the above prophecies refer to national conversions, does not that lead to national churches?'

Grady McWhiney

"Change, historians are wont to believe, is the stuff of history; but the stuff of society, if cultural anthropologists are to be credited, is resistance to change, or at least resistance to the changing of fundamental patterns of life's rhythms, rituals, and belief-structures. To be more precise, cultural conservatism is the tendency to continue to think and behave in customary, socially conditioned, and familiar ways unless wars, conquest, technology, interaction with alien groups, or other forces necessitate change; and it is the tendency to retain or revert to those norms in modified form despite the forces of change.

"The principle is, of course, most readily apparent when one observes relatively primitive societies, but it can be equally operative among more advanced peoples. In eastern Europe, successions of regimes have been trying for a thousand years and more to impose a viable political hegemony over the scores of ethnic and national groups in the area, invariably in vain. Present Communist regimes, for all their ruthlessness and their modern technology have been unable to homogenize even such small, multiethnic countries as Czechoslovakia and Yugoslavia, as were Hapsburgs, Jagiellonians, Ottomans, and Romanovs before them. As for the West, Eugen Weber has demonstrated that in France, that epitome of nineteenth-century nationalism, nearly half of the population, six decades after the Revolution, still not only read no French but did not even speak it. And modern Spain offers a striking example of the retention of identity by such groups as the Basques, Catalonians, Murcians, Andalucians, and Castilians, even though the kingdom has been politically unified for nearly five centuries. If cultural conservatism could be so potent in a Europe that had experienced absolutism, the scientific revolution, the Enlightenment, the French Revolution, and the industrial revolution, it seems likely that it would have been even stronger in an isolated colonial America." – *Cracker Culture: Celtic Ways in the Old South*, pg. xlii

"At the end of the eighteenth century Alexander Campbell offered an explanation for the Celtic commitment to hospitality. This Scot believed that Celts would remain hospitable just as long as they remained Celts – that is, only so long as there was a recognizable Celtic personality: 'A natural warmth of temper, a strong tincture of family pride, a love of shew and pleasure, and a thirst almost insatiable for distinction; Inflexible, and ever in extremes, his soul glows fervently in friendship, or rages in unextinguishable hatred. A perfect savage in his desires and aversions, he knows no bounds to his resentment, no limits to his love; and he rarely turns his back either on a friend or a foe.' Campbell claimed that such people still could be found – 'in the woods of America,' in the 'mountains of Wales,' in 'the highlands of Scotland-but not in many other places. 'The more remote from the busy world, and the more ignorant of the comforts of civil society as established in great cities, and other parts that have imbibed the spirit of trade or commerce, the more do the affections which indicate innocent hilarity, equanimity, and all the amiable qualities of uncontaminated respect for sincerity, truth, strict honour, and a due observance of whatever is fit, just, and right, diffuse their influence over even the most trivial occurrence of domestic intercourse. Hence, the hospitality we so much admire among a rude and simple people, such as the Welsh peasantry, or those of the highlands of Scotland [is rapidly vanishing.']" – *Cracker Culture: Celtic Ways in the Old South*, pg. 103

John Médaille

"Economic actors, producers, and consumers are 'produced' and socialized within the confines of the family; without the family there will be no next generation, and hence no future, for the economists to worry about. Therefore, it is the family that is the basic economic unit as well as the basic social unit. Modern economics tends to ignore the role of the family completely to focus on the individual. However, the individual, by himself, is sterile and not a self-sustaining entity." – *Toward a Truly Free Market*, pg. 39

---

he replies, 'That a national establishment, if well ordered, appears more agreeable to the prophetic passages we have been considering than the antipaedobaptist plan; nay, more agreeable to the general tenor of revelation.'

Gilbert Meilaender

"It is surely natural for husband and wife to desire a child of 'their own.' We recognize the importance of this natural desire precisely because we find human meaning and personal significance in the biological bond that unites generations. Were human nature simply freedom, simply will and choice, such a feeling would be inexplicable, such a desire irrational... We can and should recognize the human significance of the biological bond. It is significant in at least three ways. First, because we are not just free spirits but also animals, we need to know ourselves as embodied creatures who occupy a fixed place in the generations of humankind. Lines of kinship and descent locate and identify us, and, unless we learn to accept such a limit on our freedom, we remain alienated from our shared human nature. Such alienation is, at least in part, overcome as we learn to keep the commandment that calls upon us to honor our father and mother...To learn to affirm and give thanks for our place in lines of kinship and descent is to begin to learn how to give thanks for the mysterious gift of life. We learn to accept and rejoice in our limits, our creatureliness, and we learn gradually to relinquish the secret longing to be more than that. And we learn that before we can love everyone we must accept the hard task of learning to love someone — that is, to love those given to us in the close tie of kinship." – *Bioethics: A Primer for Christians*, pgs. 12-13

Juan Vázquez de Mella

"Who has ever seen 'the individual', if not defined by his family, his region, his profession, his language, his inheritance, his faith?" – *Spanish Carlism and Polish Nationalism*, pg. 31

Phillip Melanchthon

"It is wanton and violent that they do not want to be bondmen. They are citing Scripture, that Christ has freed them. This pertains to spiritual freedom: that we are assured that through Him our sins have been forgiven without our own doing, and that henceforth we may look to God's blessings, that we may beseech Him and be hopeful; that Christ poured out the Holy Spirit on those who believe in Him so that they may oppose Satan and not fall under his power like the godless whose hearts he has in his power. He forces them to commit murder, adultery, etc. Therefore, Christian freedom is of the heart, it cannot be seen with the eye. Outwardly a Christian submits joyfully and patiently to all worldly and social order and makes personal use of it. He can be a bondman or a subject, he can avail himself of the Saxon or Roman law regarding the division of goods. These things do not, however, influence the faith, indeed, the Gospel demands that such worldly order be maintained for the sake of peace. Paulus writes in his letter to the Ephesians 6:5,6,7: 'You slaves, obey your masters with fear and trembling, with a willing heart, as serving Christ, not merely with outward show of service to curry favor with men, but as slaves of Christ, do wholeheartedly the will of God.' And in Colossians 3:22, he writes: 'Slaves, give entire obedience to your earthly masters. . . Whoever does wrong, will receive what he has done wrong.' Joseph too was a slave in Egypt for a long time, as well as many other saints. Therefore, the farmer's demands have no basis, indeed, it seems necessary that these wild, insolent people as the Germans are, should have less freedom than they have now." – *Statement Against the Farmers' Articles, in Lehre und Wehre* vol. 2, pgs. 33-46

The opening of the Augsburg Confession states that the emperor and princes met in part to protect the people against the Turk (Muslim):

"Most Invincible Emperor, Caesar Augustus, Most Clement Lord: Inasmuch as Your Imperial Majesty has summoned a Diet of the Empire here at Augsburg to deliberate concerning measures against the Turk, that most atrocious, hereditary, and ancient enemy of the Christian name and religion, in what way, namely, effectually to withstand his furor and assaults by strong and lasting military provision." – *Augsburg Confession, in Documents of the Reformation*, pg. 56

Menander

"The bad son does not understand that if his father dies, it is not good for the sons: the head [of the family] no longer lives for them. Love and honor your father, because he gave himself to you." – *The Old Testament pseudepigrapha and the New Testament*, pg. 598.

Mencius

"I have heard of men using the doctrines of our great land to change barbarians, but I have never yet heard of any being changed by barbarians." – *The Chinese Classics*, trans. James Legge, bk. 3, pt. I, ch. 4

"Hence there is this saying: 'Some labour with their minds and some with their muscles. They who labour with their minds, govern others; they who labour with their muscles are governed by others. They who are governed by others, support them; they who govern others, are supported by them.' This is a principle universally recognized." – *The Chinese Classics*, trans. James Legge, bk. 3. pt. 1, ch. 4

"Mencius replied, 'With a territory which is only a hundred li square, it is possible to attain to the royal dignity. If Your Majesty will indeed dispense a benevolent government to the people, being sparing in the use of punishments and fines, and making the taxes and levies light, so causing that the fields shall be ploughed deep, and the weeding of them be carefully attended to, and that the strong-bodied, during their days of leisure, shall cultivate their filial piety, fraternal respectfulness, sincerity, and truthfulness, serving thereby, at home, their fathers and elder brothers, and, abroad, their elders and superiors, you will then have a people who can be employed, with sticks which they have prepared, to oppose the strong mail and sharp weapons of the troops of Qin and Chu. The rulers of those States rob their people of their time, so that they cannot plough and weed their fields, in order to support their parents. Their parents suffer from cold and hunger. Brothers, wives, and children are separated and scattered abroad. Those rulers, as it were, drive their people into pit-falls, or drown them. Your Majesty will go to punish them. In such a case, who will oppose your Majesty? In accordance with this is the saying, "The benevolent has no enemy." I beg your Majesty not to doubt what I say.'" – *The Chinese Classics*, trans. James Legge, ch. 1

Mesopotamian Laws

"Be it enacted forever and for all future days: If a son say to his father, 'You are not my father,'

he [the father] can cut off his [the son's] locks, make him a slave and sell him for money. If a son say to his mother, 'You are not my mother,' she can cut off his locks, turn him out of town, or (at least) drive him away from home, deprive him of citizenship and of inheritance, but his liberty he loses not. If a father say to his son, 'You are not my son,' the latter has to leave house and field and he loses everything. If a mother say to her son, 'You are not my son,' he shall leave house and furniture. If a wife be unfaithful to her husband and then says, 'You are not my husband,' let her be thrown into the river. If a husband say to his wife, 'You are not my wife,' he shall as a fine pay one half mana of silver. If some one hires a servant and the latter dies or is rendered useless otherwise (e.g. by flight, rebellion, or sickness) he shall give to the owner as daily wages ten qa of grain a day." – *Some Babylonian Laws* quoted in Robert Francis Harper *Assyrian and Babylonian Literature*, pgs. 445-447

Tryggve Mettinger

"...the proper concept of this divine ownership appears to be that every Israelite was to regard his holding as deriving from God himself... There existed the consciousness of an intrinsic equality among the Hebrews before God... which was expressed...by each head of a family holding his land as from God." – *Solomonic State Officials*, pg. 109

— THE MIDDLE AGES —

The Middle Ages as an epoch spans a wide timeframe and a broad cultural-geographic area. We draw special attention to the *Song Of Roland*, which deserves reading in full to experience the intense French nationalist spirit that flared up in opposition to the invading Muslims. Its passions resound in the calls to crusades in the following centuries, which serve to forge a European consciousness. Modern historians argue that this, among other developments elsewhere, demonstrates a sense of nationalism extant prior to the modern period (see Azar Gat, *Nations: The Long History and Deep Roots of Political Ethnicity and Nationalism*.)

The *Poetic Edda* further north depicts clannish Norsemen bluntly exhibiting familiar themes common to mankind: brother-loyalty, family bonds, defense of place, national legends whose memory unites posterity, and the like. Some of these views are too casually mentioned to make for reference material. The same is true for many ethnic developments during this period, which are not recounted but are recorded in works such as Anthony D. Smith's *Nationalism: Theory, Ideology, History*. They are interwoven throughout the time period, like marbled meat, and treatment of them is found in national histories. It is at Aquinas and those following where we begin to see an open and scholarly political, theological, and philosophical account of natural social order.

Sir Alfred Milner

"I have emphasized the importance of the racial bond. From my point of view this is fundamental. It is the British race which built the Empire and it is the undivided British race which can alone uphold it…deeper, stronger, more primordial than…material ties is the bond of common blood, a common language, common history and traditions." – quoted in A. M. Gollin, *Proconsul in Politics*, pg. 123.

John Milton

"Consider what Nation it is whereof ye are, and whereof ye are the governours: a Nation not slow and dull, but of a quick, ingenious, and piercing spirit, acute to invent, suttle and sinewy to discours, not beneath the reach of any point the highest that human capacity can soar to."
– *Areopagitica*

John Stuart Mill

"The third essential condition of stability in political society, is a strong and active principle of cohesion among the members of the same community or state. We need scarcely say that we do not mean nationality, in the vulgar sense of the term; a senseless antipathy to foreigners; indifference to the general welfare of the human race, or an unjust preference of the supposed interests of our own country; a cherishing of bad peculiarities because they are national, or a refusal to adopt what has been found good by other countries. We mean a principle of sympathy, not of hostility; of union, not of separation. We mean a feeling of common interest among those who live under the same government, and are contained within the same natural or historical boundaries. We mean, that one part of the community do not consider themselves as foreigners with regard to another part; that they set a value on their connection—feel that they are one people, that their lot is cast together, that evil to any of their fellow-countrymen is evil to themselves, and do not desire selfishly to free themselves from their share of any common inconvenience by severing the connection. How strong this feeling was in those ancient commonwealths which attained any durable greatness, every one knows. How happily Rome, in spite of all her tyranny, succeeded in establishing the feeling of a common country among the provinces of her vast and divided empire, will appear when any one who has given due attention to the subject shall take the trouble to point it out. In modern times the countries which have had that feeling in the strongest degree have been the most powerful countries: England, France, and, in proportion to their territory and resources, Holland and Switzerland; while England in her connection with Ireland is one of the most signal examples of the consequences of its absence. Every Italian knows why Italy is under a foreign yoke; every German knows what maintains despotism in the Austrian empire; the evils of Spain flow as much from the absence of nationality among the Spaniards themselves, as from the presence of it in their relations with foreigners: while the completest illustration of all is afforded by the republics of South America, where the parts of one and the same state adhere so slightly together, that no sooner does any province think itself aggrieved by the general government than it proclaims itself a separate nation." – *System Of Logic*, pgs. 561-562

"Free institutions are next to impossible in a country made up of different nationalities. Among a people without fellow-feeling, especially if they read and speak different languages, the united public opinion, necessary to the working of representative government, cannot exist…For the preceding reasons, it is in general a necessary condition of free institutions that the boundaries of governments should coincide in the main with those of nationalities." – *Considerations On Representative Government*, pg. 296

"...a portion of mankind may be said to constitute a Nationality if they are united amongst themselves by common sympathies, which do not exist between them and any others—which make them co-operate with each other more willingly than with other people, desire to be under the same government, and desire that it should be government by themselves or a portion of themselves exclusively." – cited in Jusdanis, *Necessary Nation*, pg. 20

"The economical advantages of commerce are surpassed in importance by those of its effects which are intellectual and moral. It is hardly possible to overrate the value, in the present low state of human improvement, of placing human beings in contact with persons dissimilar to themselves, and with modes of thought and action unlike those with which they are familiar. Commerce is now what war once was, the principal source of this contact...

"It may be said without exaggeration that the great extent and rapid increase of international trade, in being the principal guarantee of the peace of the world, is the great permanent security for the uninterrupted progress of the ideas, the institutions, and the character of the human race." – *Principles of Political Economy*, pgs. 351-352

Patrick D. Miller

"It is in the commandment regarding the honor of parents that the community hears that its life is in a gifted place, 'the land that the Lord your God is giving you.' This order of space is marked not so much by substantive freedom as it is by substantive goodness." – *Way Of The Lord*, pg. 62

"What the commandments do, therefore, is to chart the moral topography of the Christian life, a topography that, because of the other images and metaphors I have called upon is found to be diverse and detailed, a map that takes one in many directions and charts windy paths, straight and highly visible routes, places to settle in, hills to be climbed, home territory and foreign territory, and the like...The Commandments create a structure in which one is at home." – *Way Of The Lord*, pg. 49

"Implacement itself, being concretely placed, is intrinsically particular...Place names embody this complex collective concreteness despite their considerable brevity." – *Getting Back Into Place*, ed. by Edward Casey, pg. 23

Ludwig von Mises

"In order to grasp the meaning of this liberal program we need to imagine a world order in which liberalism is supreme....In this liberal world... there are no trade barriers' men can live and work where they want. Frontiers are drawn on the maps but they do not hinder the migrations of men and shipping of commodities. In such a world it makes no difference where the frontiers of a country are drawn. Nobody has a special material interest in enlarging the territory of the state in which he lives; nobody suffers loss if a part of this area is separated from the state. It is also immaterial whether all parts of the state's territory are in direct geographical connection, or whether they are separated by a piece of land belonging to another state. It is of no economic importance whether the country has a frontage on the ocean or not. In such a world the people of every village or district could decide by plebiscite to which state they wanted to belong. There would be no more wars because there would be no incentive for aggression. War would not pay. Armies and navies would be superfluous. Policemen would suffice for the fight against crime. In such a world the state is not a metaphysical entity but simply the producer of security and peace.

"The reality in which we have to live differs very much from this perfect world of ideal liberalism. But this is due only to the fact that men have rejected liberalism for statism." – *Omnipotent Government*, pgs. 91-92

"Any stoppage in these trade relations would involve serious economic losses for Europe as well as for the colonies and would sharply depress the standard of living of great masses of people. ... Ought the well-being of Europe and, at the same time, that of the colonies as well to be allowed to decline further in order to give the natives a chance to determine their own destinies, when this would lead, in any event, not to their freedom, but merely to a change of masters?

"This is the consideration that must be decisive in judging questions of colonial policy. European officials, troops, and police must remain in these areas, as far as their presence is necessary in order to maintain the legal and political conditions required to insure the participation of the colonial territories in international trade." – *Liberalism*, pgs. 127-128

Margaret Mitchell

"Half of Atlanta was kin to or claimed kin with Melanie and India. The ramifications of cousins, double cousins, cousins-in-law and kissing cousins were so intricate and involved that no one but a born Georgian could ever unravel them...They had always been a clannish tribe, presenting an unbroken phalanx of overlapping shields to the world in time of stress, no matter what their private opinions of the conduct of individual kinsmen might be." – *Gone With the Wind*

Hugh M'Neile

"But his [St. Paul] assurance as a Christian did not supersede his patriotism as a Jew; for in the very passage which follows that glorious expression of his assurance, we find that although triumphing as a believer in Jesus, he had a heaviness and sorrow in his heart on account of his own dear nation. He saw that the church of God – although it would truly inviolably preserved to the end, by its great Creator, Redeemer, and Sanctifier, the Living and Triune Jehovah – was yet about to emigrate, and no longer to prove conservator of his nation; and he had so much nationalism in his religion that while he repeats his triumph as a Christian, he weeps as a Jew. Nay, higher still. The Lord Jesus knew full well, that the Church of God was safe, that the gates of hell could not prevail against His Church; and His bosom glowed with the most unlimited philosophy: yet while He rejoiced in spirit, because the will of His Father was about to be accomplished, He forgot not that the tears of his patriotism dropped over the tomb of Jerusalem." – Sermon: *Nationalism in Religion*, Delivered – 08 May, 1839

James Monroe

"Satisfied I am, whatever may be the abstract doctrine in favor of unrestricted commerce, provided all nations would concur in it and it was not liable to be interrupted by war, which has never occurred and can not be expected, that there are other strong reasons applicable to our situation and relations with other countries which impose on us the obligation to cherish and sustain our manufactures." – *State of the Union Address*, 1822; Richardson, Messages, 2:760-61

Michel de Montaigne

"To undertake to recast so great a mass, to change the foundations of so great a structure, that is the job for those who wipe out a picture in order to clean it, who want to reform defects of detail by universal confusion and cure illnesses by death, 'who desire not so much to change as to overthrow everything' [Cicero]. The world is ill-fitted to cure itself; is so impatient of its affliction that it aims only at getting rid of it, without considering the cost. We see by a thousand examples that it usually cures itself to its own disadvantage. Riddance from a present evil is not cure, unless there is an all-around improvement in condition.

"The surgeon's aim is not to kill the diseased flesh; that is only the road to his cure. He looks beyond, to make the natural flesh grow again, and restore the part to its proper condition. Whoever proposes merely to remove what is biting him falls short, for good does not necessarily succeed evil; another evil may succeed it, and a worse one, as happened to Caesar's slayers, who cast the Republic into such a state that they had reason to repent of having meddled with it. To many others since, right down to our times, the same thing has happened. The French, my contemporaries, could tell you a thing of two about it. All great changes shake the state and overthrow it into disorder." – *Of Vanity, The Essays of Montaigne*, pgs. 731-732

Montesquieu

"Commerce is never subjected to greater restrictions than in free nations, and never subjected to less ones than in those under despotic government." – *Spirit of the Laws*, pg. 284

Gouverneur Morris

"If we examine the various Countries and Climates of the Earth, we shall perceive the patriot Passion to be coextensive with the human Race. He feels it who basks on the burning Sand of Libya, and he who shivers on the frozen Shores of Lapland. The sedentary Belgian, the wandering Tatar, the sprightly Frenchman, the sober Spaniard, the proud Briton and obsequious Italian are all imbued with the Love of their Country. Nay in those alpine Regions where the Perseverance of helvetian Industry forces with Pain a scanty Subsistence from the rugged Soil, this Love seems to gather Strength from Circumstances, which would damp or extinguish it, if Reason were the Rule of Passion.

"This strong Passion swells the ingenuous Heart from early Youth till we bend over the Grave. Men of ardent Temper and Affections feel it for their adopted Country; but who ever forgot his own? If there be a Wretch preeminently foul, whose Soul is beyond all Measure and Degree polluted, it is that Wretch who can see with Indifference the Ruin of his Country. But if among the countless Myriads of Mankind there be one solitary Individual who can wish for that Ruin, or who can malign his native Soil, "the Motions of his Soul are dark as Erebus and his Affections black as Hell. Let no such man be trusted." – *Oration on Patriotism; To Secure the Blessings of Liberty: Selected Writings*, oration 27

"The Love of our Country is a primal Sense—the fair Impression of that Hand which form'd the human Heart. And with the characteristic Simplicity of creative Wisdom it is intimately blended with and strengthened by every other virtuous and honorable Sentiment. It is interwoven with the Bonds of connubial Tenderness, hallowed by the pious Sense of filial Duty, endear'd by the Charities of parental affection, nourished by the social Habits of Life, animated by the Fellowships of Youth, confirmed by the Amities of Age, and consecrated by the Mysteries of Religion. In the complex Idea of our Country is included Parents Wives Children Companions Friends, the Usages we respect, the manners we approve, the Language we speak, the Laws we love, and the Religion we venerate. Such (is) the Principle Scope and Extent of the patriot Passion." – *Oration on Patriotism; To Secure the Blessings of Liberty: Selected Writings*, oration 27

— GOUVERNEUR MORRIS —

James Madison taking notes of Morris' speech at the Constitutional Convention said:

"...the lesson we are taught is that we should be governed as much by our reason, and as little by our feelings, as possible. What is the language of reason on this subject? That we should not be polite at the expense of prudence...He ran over the privileges which emigrants would enjoy among us, though they should be deprived of that of being eligible to the great offices of Government; observing that they exceeded the privileges allowed to foreigners in any part of the world; and said that, as every Society from a great Nation down to a Club had the right of declaring the conditions on which new members should be admitted, there could be no room for complaint." – Constitutional Convention debate held on 9 August 1787; *Compilation of Senate Election Cases from 1789 to 1885*, pg. xi

Henry Morris

"The so-called race question has certainly been one of the most important issues of our time. The same is true for the issue of nationalism versus internationalism. The existence of distinctive races and nations and languages is obviously a fact of modern life, in spite of the efforts of many modern sociologists and politicians to break down all racial and national barriers. The problems created by these issues often seem almost insurmountable.

"The true origin of the world's various races and nations, and the events associated with it, must be clearly understood and placed in right perspective before these problems can ever be adequately resolved. The Genesis record gives us the only fully reliable account of these matters, and it is thus urgently important that we understand and believe what it says.

"In the world today there seem to be several major 'races' (three to six or more, depending on the particular system of classification), perhaps 150 or so nations of some significance, and well over 3,000 tribal languages and dialects. Yet this diversity of peoples and tongues must have come from a common ancestor, because all of these are human, capable of physical interrelationships, capable of learning and education, and even capable of spiritual fellowship with the Creator, through faith in Christ. The origin of races and nations is still a mystery to most scientists, determined as they are to explain man and his cultures in an evolutionary framework. There are numerous contradictory theories on these matters among anthropologists and ethnologists, but the only fully reliable record of the true origin of races, nations, and languages is found here in Genesis 9 through 11.

"Although the 'sons of Noah' have been referred to several times throughout the Flood narrative, they are here actually once again identified by name. Although, when listed, their names are usually given in the order 'Shem, Ham, and Japheth' (Genesis 5:32; 6:10; 7:13; 9:18), it is not certain as to what chronological order actually applies to them. In any case, it was from these three, and their wives, that 'the whole earth was overspread.' Scripture is quite explicit in teaching that all men now living in the world are descended from Noah through his three sons (see also Genesis 10:32; Acts 17:26). All the physical characteristics of the different nations and tribes must, therefore, have been present in the genetic constitutions of these six people who came through the Flood in the Ark. Somehow, by the regular mechanisms of genetics — variation, recombination — all the various groups of nations and tribes must have developed from this beginning." – *The Genesis Record*, pgs. 232-233

"According to Acts 17:26, God has a specific time and place and purpose for each nation throughout the ages. Although each race and nation were to contribute to the corporate life of mankind as a whole, the overriding purpose of every national entity was 'that they should seek the Lord' (Acts 17:27). The basic outline of the function of each of the three major streams of nations is given in the remarkable prophecy of Noah in Genesis 9:25-27." – *The Genesis Record*, pg. 237

"Mankind thus had three fundamental types of duties to perform as God's steward over the world: (1) spiritual — receiving, preserving, and teaching the knowledge of the word of God; (2) intellectual — expanding and teaching the knowledge of the world of God; and (3) physical — providing the material means for man's bodily needs and comforts, thus enabling him to fulfill his intellectual and spiritual functions more effectively. These three duties correspond, in fact, to the tripartite nature of man: spirit, soul, and body.

"Every person has, to some degree, all three capacities, but in each person one usually dominates. That is, some people are dominated by physical considerations, some by intellectual, some by spiritual. The same generalization applies to nations: some have historically been primarily motivated by religious considerations, some by philosophical and scientific thinking, others by materialistic (or so-called practical) pursuits.

"It is therefore very significant that these first three progenitors of all modern nations were recognized by their father to have characteristics representing these three emphases. Shem was mainly motivated by spiritual considerations, Japheth by intellectual, and Ham by physical; and the same would be true (in a very general way, of course) of the nations descending from them, by reasons of both genetic inheritance and parental example.

"Each was regarded as God's servant — Shem in spiritual service and Japheth in intellectual service. Ham, responsible for physical service, was thus a 'servant of servants,' serving both Shem and Japheth, who were also servants. He would provide the physical means (food, clothing, shelter, weapons, machinery, transportation, technological inventions, and equipment of all kinds) which would enable his brothers to carry out their spiritual and mental responsibilities toward mankind and toward God. In this way, Ham also would be serving God." – *The Genesis Record*, pgs. 239-240

Iolo Morganwg

"First Hu the Mighty who first conducted the Nation of the Cymmry to the Island of Britain, and they came from the Summer Country otherwise called Defrobani, where now Constantinople is, and they came over the Hazy Sea into the Island of Britain and to Llydaw (where they remained). The second was Prydian Son of Aedd the Great who first instituted Government and social compact in the Island of Britain, before which time there was no regular order, excepting what might take place of free Courtesy nor any Law but that of Superior force. The third was Dyvnwal Moelmud who first reduced to order the Laws and Injunctions and Rights and Immunities of the Nation and Country." – *Triodd Ynys Prydain*, *(Welsh Triads)*, in *The Gentleman's Magazine*, pg. 498

Justin Morrill

"I am for ruling America for the benefit, first, of Americans, and, for the 'rest of mankind' afterwards." – *Debate over the Walker Tariff; Congressional Globe*, February 5, 1857 (app., pg. 226)

"A reciprocity treaty . . . is a modern invention, which, like the Trojan horse, hides in its belly all of its sinister and miscreated forces." – *Reciprocity Treaties, So Called; Reciprocity with Canada*, pg. 1,895

"There is a transcendental philosophy of free trade, with devotees as ardent as any of those who preach the millennium. . . . Free trade abjures patriotism and boasts of cosmopolitism. It regards the labor of our own people with no more favor than that of the barbarian on the Danube or the cooly on the Ganges." – *Congressional Globe*, February 5, 1857 (app., pg. 226)

Leon Morris

"He [Paul] describes the Jews first as my brothers, a term he generally uses of Christians (indeed, this is the only place where he uses the term of the Jews). But he is still within the same community as other Jews, and we should note that he is speaking here of what is true 'according to the flesh'. He prefaces this expression with 'my kinsmen', a way of referring to his fellow-countrymen. There were ties that bound Paul to his nation, and while he came to see his relationships in Christ as much more significant than these, that did not give him license to forget the race to which he belonged." – Romans 9:3, *The Epistle to the Romans, The Pillar New Testament Commentary*, pgs. 347-348

"Diversity is no accidental attribute of the body. It is of its very essence. No one member is to be equated with the body. It takes many members to make up one body...Therefore individual members cannot contract out...The whole discussion is placed on the highest level, for the members are not in the body haphazardly; God has arranged them, or better, 'put' them (jb). It is not only a matter of arrangement; God created the parts to make a body like this. Every one of them brings out the point that God's care does not extend only to the more important and spectacular. His oversight and creativity extend to every member of the body. He made them all just as he wanted them to be ('just as he willed')...

"The action of God is directed to the prevention of division (the word used in 1:10 of the dissensions that caused factions in the Corinthian church). In his perfect blending of the parts in the human body God provided against dissension. On the contrary (the strong adversative alla), it is his plan that the members have equal concern for each other. Equal (to auto, 'the same') guards against partiality. In the body all the members without distinction work for the good of the whole. No special care is lavished on one member to the detriment of other members." – *Tyndale New Testament Commentary, 1 Corinthians*, vol. 7, pg. 169-171. 1 Corinthians 15:14-25 [65]

Morkinskinna

"King Magnus established his rule as far as his father's power had extended, and he subdued the land without a battle and with the consent and agreement of all the people, rich and poor. They all desired rather to be free under King Magnus than to suffer the tyranny of the Danes any longer." – *Morkinskinna: The Earliest Icelandic Chronicle*, pg. 100

---

65   God created diversity in order to stave off division.

Diana Muir Appelbaum

"Christians inspired by the Reformation to read or hear the Bible found a 'developed model' of nationhood, beginning with an expansive description of a world arranged into 'kindreds, tongues, lands, and nations' Genesis 10:20. This association of nations with kin, language, and territory is part of a biblical discourse that reflects many of the desiderata identified by later scholars as characteristic of nations. The biblical world is imagined as composed of rightfully sovereign and equal nations. God put the borders of the nations (Deuteronomy 32:8), and generally played an active role in human history, allotting territories to specific peoples." – *Biblical Nationalism and the Sixteenth Century States*

"Several aspects of the Bible appear to prefigure modern nationalism, including rituals in which every farmer recites the national history when carrying his first fruits to the national temple, and the mandate to study Israel's history and law and teach them to one's children (Deuteronomy 26:1-11; 11:19). Furthermore, the right of the people of Israel to assemble as a body or to be represented by elders with authority to take actions including entering a covenant, renewing a covenant, instituting a monarchy against the advice of God, and placing Josiah on the throne (2 Kings 21:24) deploy fundamental assumptions of nationalism." – *Biblical Nationalism and the Sixteenth Century States*

"But [John] Foxe would have had in mind the establishment of Protestant states in the Swiss cantons and Germanies, Sweden (1531), Denmark (1536), and Scotland (1560). Protestantism in each of these states was driven by specific factors along a unique path. What they shared was a new conviction that the model of the Godly life, for whole societies as for individuals, must be sought and would be found in the unmediated text of the Bible. Some lands experienced the Reformation primarily as a top-down royal programme, some as popular revolutions, others as a reform movement harnessed by magnates. What the several sixteenth-century 'New Israels' had in common was the power of the biblical narrative of nationhood to generate mass political participation because the Bible not only provided both a lexicon and a discourse of nationhood, it provided those ideas with unmatched authority as the word of God." – *Biblical Nationalism and the Sixteenth Century States*

"The Church of England read the Bible aloud, in English, in sequence, and in its entirety; every respectable person in England, literate or not, heard every word of the Bible on annual and triennial cycles. But the discourse of nationhood not only merged from the Bible as it was read aloud, and discussed in sermons; it was heard, memorized, and recited in the words of the 1549 Book of Common Prayer which assumes that the world is composed of 'nations.' With the exception of Mary's five-year reign, everyone who grew up in England from 1549 on learned much of that book by heart, and, with it, the understanding that the world is naturally divided into nations." – *Biblical Nationalism and the Sixteenth Century States*

"The emergence of Protestant nations in sixteenth-century Europe was driven by the sudden rediscovery of biblical nationalism, a political model that did not separate the religious from the political. Biblical nationalism was new because pre-Reformation Europeans encountered the Hebrew Bible through paraphrases and abridgments. Full-text Bibles revealed a programmatic nationalism backed by unmatched authority as the word of God to readers primed by Reformation theology to seek models in the Bible for the reform of their own societies. Sixteenth-century biblical nationalism was the unintended side effect of a Reformation intended to save souls." – *Biblical Nationalism and the Sixteenth Century States*

Jerry Z. Muller

"Americans generally belittle the role of ethnic nationalism in politics. But … it corresponds to some enduring propensities of the human spirit, it is galvanized by modernization, and in one form or another, it will drive global politics for generations to come. Once ethnic nationalism has captured the imagination of groups in a multiethnic society, ethnic disaggregation or partition is often the least bad answer." – *Us and Them*

"The creation of ethnonational states across Europe, a consequence of two world wars and ethnic cleansing, was a precondition of stability, unity and peace. With no ethnic rivals inside their national homes, European peoples had what they had fought for, and were now prepared to live in peace with their neighbors.

"As a result of this massive process of ethnic unmixing, the ethnonationalist ideal was largely realized: for the most part, each nation in Europe had its own state, and each state was made up almost exclusively of a single ethnic nationality. During the Cold War, the few exceptions to this rule included Czechoslovakia, the Soviet Union, and Yugoslavia. But these countries' subsequent fate only demonstrated the ongoing vitality of ethnonationalism." – *Us and Them*

"In short, ethnonationalism has played a more profound and lasting role in modern history than is commonly understood, and the processes that led to the dominance of the ethnonational state and the separation of ethnic groups in Europe are likely to reoccur elsewhere." –*Us and Them*

"The ethnonationalist view has traditionally dominated through much of Europe and has held its own even in the United States until recently. For substantial stretches of U.S. history, it was believed that only the people of English origin, or those who were Protestant, or white, or hailed from northern Europe were real Americans." – *Us and Them*

"One could argue that Europe has been so harmonious since World War II not because of the failure of ethnic nationalism but because of its success, which removed some of the greatest sources of conflict both within and between countries. The fact that ethnic and state boundaries now largely coincide has meant that there are fewer disputes over borders or expatriate communities, leading to the most stable territorial configuration in European history." – *Us and Them*

Robert Mundell

"The United States can't keep a completely open system if the rest of the world is less open. The United States may have to take a leaf out of the book of Japan, China, and Germany, and have protectionism inside the system." – Interview, *Forbes*, May 26, 2013

Andrew Murray

"You have heard how in the South African Republic not many years ago the war of liberty was fought. After three years of oppression by the English the people [Boers] said they would endure it no longer, and so they gathered together to fight for their liberty. They knew how weak they were, as compared with the English power, but they said, 'We must have our liberty.' They bound themselves together to fight for it, and when that vow had been made, they went to their homes to prepare for the struggle. Such a thrill of enthusiasm passed through that country that in many cases women, when their husbands might have been allowed to stay at home, said to them: 'No, go, even though you have not been commanded.' And there were mothers who, when one son was called out to the front, said: 'No, take two, three.' Every man and woman was ready to die. It was in very deed 'Our country first, before everything.' And even so, friends, must it be with you if you want this wonderful Kingdom of God to take possession of you." – *The Master's Indwelling*, pg. 67

"Suppose away in South Africa there is a woman whose husband has gone on a long journey into the interior. He is to be away for months from all posts. The wife is anxious to receive news. In weeks she has had no letter or tidings from him. One day, as she stands in her door, there comes a great, savage Kafir. He is frightful in appearance, and carries his spears and shield. The woman is alarmed and rushes into the house and closes the door. He comes and knocks at the door, and she is in terror. She sends her servant, who comes back and says, 'The man says he must see you.' She goes, all affrighted. He takes out an old newspaper. He has come a month's journey on foot from her husband, and inside the dirty newspaper is a letter from her husband, telling her of his welfare. How that wife delights in that letter! She forgets the face that has terrified her. And now as weeks are passing away again, how she begins to long for that ugly Kafir messenger! After long waiting he comes again, and this time she rushes out to meet him because he is the messenger that comes from her beloved husband, and she knows that with all his repelling exterior, he is the bearer of a message of love. Beloved, have you learned to look at tribulation, and vexation, and disappointment, as the dark, savage-looking messenger with a spear in his hand, that comes straight from Jesus?" – *The Master's Indwelling*, pgs. 173-174

"I do not know whether you have ever noticed what a part difficulties play in our natural life. They call out man's powers as nothing else can. They strengthen and ennoble character. We are told that one reason of the superiority of the Northern nations, like Holland and Scotland, in strength of will and purpose, over those of the sunny South, as Italy and Spain, is that the climate of the latter has been too beautiful, and the life it encourages too easy and relaxing—the difficulties the former had to contend with have been their greatest boon; how all nature has been so arranged by God that in sowing and reaping, as in seeking coal or gold, nothing is found without labour and effort. What is education but a daily developing and disciplining of the mind by new difficulties presented to the pupil to overcome? The moment a lesson has become easy, the pupil is moved on to one that is higher and more difficult. With the race and the individual, it is in the meeting and the mastering of difficulties that our highest attainments are found." – *The Ministry of Intercession*, pg. 47

"Now, just as in a human family there is one central relation on which all the rest depend,— that of the father to all the members of this little whole,—so is there in the universe one supreme position, which is the support of all the rest, and which, in the interest of all beings, must be above all others preserved intact—that of God." – *Holy in Christ*, pg. 296

Douglas Murray

"The only culture that couldn't be celebrated was the culture that had allowed all the other cultures to be celebrated... In order to become multicultural, countries found that they had to do themselves down, particularly focusing on their negatives. Thus the states that had been so open and liberal that they had allowed and encouraged large-scale migration were portrayed as countries which were uniquely racist. And while any and all other cultures in the world

could be celebrated within Europe, to celebrate even the good things about Europe within Europe became suspect. The multicultural era was one of European self-abnegation where the host society appeared to stand back from itself and hoped that it would not be noticed other than as some form of benign convener. It was for this reason, among others, that the celebrated American political philosopher, Samuel Huntington, wrote in his last book, 'Multiculturalism is in its essence anti-European civilisation. It is basically an anti-Western ideology.'" – *The Strange Death Of Europe*, pgs. 101-102

"Putting tens of millions of people with their own sets of ideas and contradictions into a continent with its own set of ideas and contradictions is bound to have consequences. The presumption of those who believed in integration is that in time everybody who arrives will become like Europeans, a presumption made less likely by the fact that so many Europeans are unsure whether they want to be Europeans. A culture of self-doubt and self-distrust is uniquely unlikely to persuade others to adopt its own stance. Meantime it is possible that many – at least – of the incomers will either hold fast to their own certainties or even, quite plausibly, attract Europeans in the generations to come with these certainties. It is also plausible that many of those who come will enjoy the lifestyle, will take part in the aspirations and the fruits of the economic uplift so long as it continues, and yet despise or disdain the culture into which they have come. They may use it – as President Erdoğan so memorably said of democracy – like a bus, and get off whenever it has taken them to their desired destination." – *The Strange Death Of Europe*, pgs. 225-226

"We sometimes behave as though we had the certainties of our ancestors, yet we have none of them, and none of their consolations. Even the bleakest philosophers of nineteenth-century Germany look plagued with certainty and consolation beside their descendants today. Today German philosophy, like the philosophy of the rest of the continent, has been ravaged not just by doubt (as it should be) but by decades of deconstruction. It has pulled itself and everything else apart, without having any notion of how to put anything – let alone itself – back together again. Instead of being inspired by the spirit of truth and the search for the great questions, the continent's philosophers have instead become entranced by how to avoid questions. Their deconstruction not only of ideas but of language has led to a concerted effort never to get beyond the tools of philosophy. Indeed, avoidance of the great issues sometimes seems to have become the sole business of philosophy. In its place is an obsession with the difficulties of language and a distrust of all fixed things. The desire to question everything in order never to get anywhere appears to be the point, perhaps in order to defang both words and ideas for fear of where both might lead." – *The Strange Death Of Europe*, pgs. 223-224

"Among the sins that Europeans are now accused of having spread around the world is the sin that constitutes the founding sin of America: slavery, and through slavery, racism. To say that American presidents have been apologising for these for decades is an understatement. The country fought and won a civil war over the issue nearly two centuries ago. Nevertheless, on a visit to Uganda in 1998 President Clinton made yet another fulsome apology for the slave trade. If he or anyone among his advisors thought that this would put the matter to rest, they could not have been more wrong. Despite slavery having involved at least as many people at the Ugandan end of the chain as at the American end, the idea that people of European descent alone should feel continuous guilt for the actions of their forebears is now embedded, and helpful to everyone other than those of the guilty nation. In the last couple of decades, as the situation for American blacks has slowly improved, the rhetoric of shame has only increased. America has had black Secretaries of State of both parties, black Supreme Court Justices and a black President, but even in Barack Obama's second term there were ever louder demands for 'reparations' to be paid to all black Americans. Indeed, the argument got more mainstream than it had in generations. As though to prove that nothing can ever truly be done to alleviate the sins of the past, during the sixth year of Obama's presidency it became mainstream thinking to believe that the actions of the ancestors of many white Americans should cause their descendants to give most black Americans a cash settlement for acts carried out centuries earlier. The question

of reparations to other ethnic groups who had suffered historic wrongs did not become part of the ensuing debate. Only Europeans and their descendants remember guilt. So only Europeans and their descendants have continuously to atone for it.

"In America, as in Australia, such a constant drumbeat of guilt changes a people's natural feelings about their own past. It transforms feelings of patriotism into shame or at the very least into deeply mixed emotions, and troubling effects result from this. A country that believes it has never done any wrong is a country that could do wrong at any time. But a country that believes it has only done wrong, or done such a terrible, unalleviated amount of wrong in the past, is likely to become a country that is inclined to doubt its ability to ever do any good in the future. It makes a country nervous about itself whatever the wisdom of its actions. Embedding the idea of original sin in a nation is the best possible way to breed self-doubt. National original sin suggests you can do little by way of good because you were rotten from the start." – *The Strange Death Of Europe*, pgs. 168-169

John Murray

"The use of the term 'brethren' bespeaks the bond of affection which united the apostle to his kinsmen. 'According to the flesh' is added to show that those for whom he had concern were not contemplated as brethren in the Lord... but it also expresses what is implicit in the term 'kinsmen' and supplies an additional index to the bond of love created by this natural, genetic relationship." – commentary on Romans 9, *The Epistle to the Romans*

N

Judith Nagata

Speaking of the various religions and ethnicities that make up Malaysia:

"When it was necessary for a Malay to differentiate himself from a Muslim Javanese or Acehnese, the usual resort would be to that of a separate bangsa, that is, all those descended from a different (putative) social line."
While the concept:

"...also has overtones of shared culture, this is secondary in the emic view to the solidarity acquired through common descent or origin." – *In Defense of Ethnic Boundaries: The Changing Myths and Charters of Malay Identity*, in C. Keyes (ed.), *Ethnic Change*, citations from pgs. 97, 99

National Synod of 1888

"The Dutch Reformed Church is the Church of our Fathers and the Church of the nation which founded this republic. Our founding fathers conceived a republic with an own national church along with a national state: for the people and through the people." – *Handelinge van die Algemene Kerkvergadering* 1888, pg. 91

Watchman Nee

"A Chinese may be born America and be unable to speak Chinese at all, but he is a Chinese for all that, because he was born a Chinese. It is birth that counts. So I am a sinner not of my behaviour but of my heredity, my parentage. I am not a sinner because I sin, but I sin because I come of the wrong stock. I sin because I am a sinner." – *The Normal Christian Life*, 1957

Nikolay Nekrasov

Where is that Russia, which, knowing not
The deadly strife of parties, grew,

Which, under the wise rule of law,
Was calm, and strong, and free and true?
– *Who is Happy in Russia?* (Part 1, Scene 3) [66]

Yet courage! Open, sacred source
Of good! Flow, cleansing river, flow!
And grant the people's sorely tried
And weary heart the strength to bear
Its heavy load of woe!
– *Who is Happy in Russia?* (Part 4, Scene 2)

O Russian women! You are strong
In patience, and in hope profound!
In days of storm and terror black,
When woe beset our native land,
You did not falter, nor look back,
But took your burden in your hand.
– *Russian Women* (st. 1)

O women of our native land,
In life's rough path, by fate oppressed,
Like shadows passing o'er the sand,
You glide, and suffer, and are blessed.
– *Russian Women* (st. 6)

Nennius

"Be it known to your charity, that being dull in intellect and rude of speech, I have presumed to deliver these things in the Latin tongue, not trusting to my own learning, which is little or none at all, but partly from traditions of our ancestors, partly from writings and monuments of the ancient inhabitants of Britain, partly from the annals of the Romans, and the chronicles of the sacred fathers, Isidore, Hieronymus, Prosper, Eusebius, and from the histories of the Scots and Saxons, although our enemies, not following my own inclinations, but, to the best of my ability, obeying the commands of my seniors; I have lispingly put together this history from various sources, and have endeav-

---

66   Nekrasov was a Russian poet known for his works focusing on the struggles and resilience of the Russian people.

oured, from shame, to deliver down to posterity the few remaining ears of corn about past transactions, that they might not be trodden under foot, seeing that an ample crop has been snatched away already by the hostile reapers of foreign nations. For many things have been in my way, and I, to this day, have hardly been able to understand, even superficially, as was necessary, the sayings of other men; much less was I able in my own strength, but like a barbarian, have I murdered and defiled the language of others. But I bore about with me an inward wound, and I was indignant, that the name of my own people, formerly famous and distinguished, should sink into oblivion, and like smoke be dissipated. But since, however, I had rather myself be the historian of the Britons than nobody, although so many are to be found who might much more satisfactorily discharge the labour thus imposed on me; I humbly entreat my readers, whose ears I may offend by the inelegance of my words, that they will fulfill the wish of my seniors, and grant me the easy task of listening with candour to my history. For zealous efforts very often fail: but bold enthusiasm, were it in its power, would not suffer me to fail. May, therefore, candour be shown where the inelegance of my words is insufficient, and may the truth of this history, which my rustic tongue has ventured, as a kind of plough, to trace out in furrows, lose none of its influence from that cause, in the ears of my hearers. For it is better to drink a wholesome draught of truth from a humble vessel, than poison mixed with honey from a golden goblet." – *Historia Britto-num*, in *Six Old English Chronicles*, pg. 383

Netherland Songs

Oh what has happened to us,
That we in our youth
Had to serve voluntarily
For the fatherland.
In the distance I see something approaching.
It is death that comes closer.
Singing and crying will make no difference.
It is for the imperial crown.
It is for the Emperor Napoleon.
In the dark grave
I will bow for him.
Oh pale dead, please release me!
I rather want to fight myself free

Than to die in such slavery!
– quoted by Bart Verheijen in *Roots Of Nationalism*, pgs. 315-316 [67]

Goodbye, my love. I have to leave you.
Cry for me because this will be my end.
It is my destiny,
    lamenting won't change a thing.
It is for the country that I must fight.
Please stop crying; it is the law.
We will rather fight to be free,
    than embrace this slavery.

Ah, listen, my love, Heaven knows my pain,
How it grieves me to leave you behind.
But alas, my dear, I have no choice,
This call of duty cannot be denied.
It's the law that commands, even unto death,
What can we do, this is the fate we face.

The cold winds blow, Heaven hears my cry,
My cheeks chilled as I marched on.
The sound of war makes my heart ache,
As I part from you, my beloved, in sorrow.
Tears roll down my face in pain,
But I must go, the call is strong.

Do not cry, my love, and say in despair,
That all hope is lost, that I will never return.
Maybe Heaven will take pity on us,
And spare me from the grip of death.
Perhaps this war will soon be over,
And I will return to your arms again.

Heaven alone knows
    where my fate will take me,
As I march with a heavy heart.
But if I do not return to you,
And fall upon some distant field,
Remember me, as I fall for our freedom,
Stay true, my love, and let time heal.

Ah, tell me, Heaven, will I see you again?
Will I hold you once more in my arms?
Or will I perish on foreign soil,
Struck down by the sword in a far-off land?
The news may come to you, full of grief,
That I have fallen, so far from your side.

But stay strong, my love, and be brave,
Even if I cannot return to you.
I leave with your love in my heart,

---

67   Many such songs were sung in resistance to French imperialism under Napoleon.

To fight for freedom, to do my part.
Whether I live or die, my dearest,
My heart will forever belong to you.

Farewell, dear love, and take comfort in this,
Even though my fate is uncertain.
I fight for our land, for freedom's cause,
And pray that one day we'll meet again.
If Heaven wills it, I shall return,
But if I fall, remember me with pride.

– *Sad Farewell of a Requisitioned Soldier to His Beloved – Bind us, where fate brings us*, an anti-conscription song, spring 1811. Translated from the original Dutch. Archives Nationales (aN), *Police des livres imprimés* (1810-14), quoted by Bart Verheijen in *Roots Of Nationalism*, pg. 317

New Plymouth Laws

"Whereas it hath been an ancient and wholesome order bearing date March the seventh 1636 that no person coming from other parts be allowed an inhabitant of this jurisdiction but by the approbation of the governor and two of the magistrates at least and that many persons contrary to this order of court are crept into some townships of this jurisdiction which are and may be a great disturbance of our more peaceable proceedings, be it enacted by the court and the authority thereof that if any such person or persons shall be found that hath not doth not or will not apply and approve themselves so as to procure the approbation of the governor and two of the assistants that such be inquired after, and if any such persons shall be found that either they depart the government or else that the court take some such course therein as shall be thought meet." – *Compact, Charter and Laws of Colony of New Plymouth*, pgs. 57, 119

Robert Nisbet

"There is the upthrust of ethnicity … the 'unmeltable ethnics' … with its only too clear implications for the American myth of the melting pot, yes, but also for the political bond itself which, after all, has justified itself during the past century or more largely on its capacity to divert tribal loyalties from ancient tribalistic unities and to reunify these loyalties in the political community. We might have learned a general lesson from the profound change of black militants and intellectuals shortly after the civil rights revolution commenced in the late 1950s: a change of orientation or mission from the once hallowed 'integration' to something far more nationalistic, so far as blacks were concerned, and more pluralistic in thrust for the America. Conceivably we could have sensed something coming even earlier from the renascence of the Jewish community … Ethnicity is, along with the family, locality, and religion, among the most ancient and powerful of bonds for mankind. Only the political illusion could have caused us to forget this fact. We are relearning it today." – *Twilight of Authority*, pgs. 9-10

"Man's alienation from man must lead in time to man's alienation from God. The loss of the sense of visible community in Christ will be followed by the loss of the sense of the invisible. The decline of community in the modern world has as its inevitable religious consequence the creation of masses of helpless, bewildered individuals who are unable to find solace in Christianity regarded merely as creed. The stress upon the individual, at the expense of the churchly community, has led remorselessly to the isolation of the individual, to the shattering of the man-God relationship, and to the atomization of personality." – *The Quest For Community*, pg. 11

"The historic triumph of secularism and individualism has presented a set of problems that looms large in contemporary thought. The modern release of the individual from traditional ties of class, religion, and kinship has made him free; but, on the testimony of innumerable works in our age, this freedom is accompanied not by the sense of creative release but by the sense of disenchantment and alienation. The alienation of man from historic moral certitudes has been followed by the sense of man's alienation from his fellow man." – *The Quest For Community*, pg. 7

"The alleged disorganization of the modern family is, in fact, simply an erosion of its natural authority, the consequence, in considerable part, of the absorption of its functions by other bodies, chiefly the state." – *The Quest For Community*, pg. xxvii

Mark Noll

"The great influence of the King James Version in American history came precisely because it was so widely available; because precisely its words, and what the words communicated, had entered so deeply into the consciousness of so many Americans, and particularly of otherwise voiceless Americans." – *In The Beginning Was The Word*, pgs. 122-123.

Novalis

"...Assiduously this powerful peace-creating organization [the Catholic Church] sought to make all men sharers in this beautiful faith and sent their colleagues into all parts of the world to proclaim everywhere the Gospel of Life and to make the Kingdom of Heaven the only kingdom on this earth. With good cause the wise Head of the Church [the Pope] countered insolent excrescences of human talents at the expense of the sacred sense, as well as untimely, dangerous discoveries in the area of knowledge. Thus he prevented bold thinkers from asserting publicly that the earth was an insignificant planet, for he realized that humans, together with respect for their dwelling place and their earthly homeland, would also lose respect for their heavenly home and for their race, would prefer circumscribed knowledge to infinite faith, and would become accustomed to scorning everything great and worthy of wonder and look upon these as dead legalisms. ...

"Such were the fine essential characteristics of the truly Catholic or truly Christian times. For this splendid kingdom mankind was not ripe, not developed enough. It was a first love, which died away amid the press of business life, whose memory was crowded out by selfish cares, and whose bond – afterwards cried down as imposture and illusion and judged in the light of subsequent experiences – was sundered forever by a large proportion of Europeans. This great inner cleavage, which was attended by destructive wars, was a noteworthy sign of the harmfulness of culture to the sense for the Invisible, or at least of the temporary harmfulness of the culture of a certain stage. Annihilated that immortal sense cannot be, but it can be troubled, lamed, crowded out by other senses. Protracted intercourse of human beings decreases their affections, their belief in their race, and accustoms them to devoting their entire aim and endeavor solely to the means of wellbeing. Their needs and the devices for the satisfaction of their needs become more complex; and the greedy man requires so much time to get to know them and to acquire skills in them, that no time is left for the quiet composure of the spirit, for attentive observation of the inner world. ...

"All that is specialized unto itself has its own measure of ability; only the capacity of the race is infinite. All projects must fail which are not projects fully consonant with all the natural inclinations of the race...." – *Novalis, Christendom or Europe?*

O

Samuel Gyasi Obeng and Efurosibina Adegbija

"In sub-Saharan Africa, there is a strong emotional attachment to language and ethnicity. Language is seen as the storehouse of ethnicity: each ethnic group expresses and identifies itself by the language it speaks, and its cultural paraphernalia is shaped by its language. Sameness of language and ethnicity creates a bond of acceptance and provides a basis for togetherness, for identity, for separateness, for solidarity, and for brotherhood and kinship." – *Handbook of Language and Ethnic Identity*, pg. 353

Jerzy Ochmański

"The Lithuanian nation was formed during the thirteenth and fourteenth centuries, when the early feudal Lithuanian state came into being . . . The Lithuanian ethnic group, divided among a number of 'lands,' i.e, tribal territories . . . had long shared a common agricultural culture and been closely related linguistically; from the ninth to the eleventh centuries it had also been united culturally. Joined under one ruler, this group gradually started to lose its tribal diversity and to develop a common national consciousness." – *Harvard Ukrainian Studies*, pg. 300

Oera Linda

"Frya was white, like snow in the red of dawn, and the blue of her eyes was more beautiful than the rainbow.

Beautiful Frya! Like rays of the sun at noon shone her hair, fine as spiders' webs."
– Oera Linda Foundation, 3rd Ed., pg. 25 [68]

"(The Twisklanders were banished and fugitive children of Frya, but they stole their wives from the Tartars. The Tartars are a brown Finda's folk, thus named because they provoke — or 'tarta' — all nations to battle. They are all riders and robbers. This is how the Twisklanders have become so bloodthirsty.)

The Twisklanders who had committed this crime called themselves Frees or Franks. My brother said there were red, brown- and white-haired among them.

Those with red or brown hair bleached their hair white with chalk or lime water, but as their faces remained brown, it made them even more ugly."
– Oera Linda Foundation, 3rd Ed., pg. *120*

Páll Eggert Ólason

"It has arisen before Jón Sigurðsson that Bishop Jón Arason was the last Icelander to fight against rulers and a monarch for the country's national rights, the last men to show, not only in word, but also in deed, with life and [death] ... that he valued his people, his land, his tongue, and his church, above all." – *Menn og menntir siðskiptaaldarinnar á Íslandi* v. 1

Domhnall Ó Néill

"Lest the sharp-toothed and viperous calumny of the English and their untrue representations should to any degree excite your mind against us and the defenders of our right, which God forbid, and so that there may be no ground for what is not well known and is falsely presented to kindle your displeasure, for our defence we pour into your ears with mighty outcry by means of this letter an entirely true account of our origin and our form of government, if government it can be called, and also of the cruel wrongs that have been wrought inhumanly on us and our forefathers by some kings of England, their evil

---

68   The veracity of this manuscript is disputed, but it nevertheless represents uncontested Frisian sentiments of the period.

ministers and English barons born in Ireland, wrongs that are continued still; and this we do in order that you may be able to approach the subject and see in which party's loud assertion the truth bears company. And thus being carefully and sufficiently informed so far as the nature of the case demands, your judgment, like a naked blade, may smite or correct the fault of the party that is in the wrong.

"Know then, most Holy Father, that since the time when our early ancestors, the three sons of Milesius or Micelius of Spain, by God's will came into Ireland (then destitute of all inhabitants) with a fleet of thirty ships from Cantabria, a city of Spain standing on the bank of the river Ebro or Hiberus (from which we take the name we bear), 3,500 years and more have passed, and of those descended from these men 136 kings without admixture of alien blood assumed the monarchical rule over all Ireland down to king Legarius, from whom I, Donald, have derived my descent in a straight line. It was in days that our chief apostle and patron St. Patrick, sent us at the inspiration of the Holy Ghost by your predecessor Celestine in the year 432 taught the truths of the Catholic faith with the fullest success to our fathers...

"And although for so long a time those kings with their own power had stoutly defended against tyrants and kings of divers countries the inheritance that God had given them and had always kept their birthright of freedom unimpaired, yet at last, in the year of the Lord 1155, at the false and wicked representation of King Henry of England, under whom and perhaps by whom St. Thomas of Canterbury, as you know, in that very year suffered death for justice and defence of the church, Pope Adrian, your predecessor, an Englishman not so much by birth as by feeling and character, did in fact, but unfairly, confer upon that same Henry (whom for his said offence he should rather have deprived of his own kingdom) this lordship of ours by a certain form of words, the course of justice entirely disregarded and the moral vision of that great pontiff blinded, alas! by his English proclivities. And thus, without fault of ours and without reasonable cause, he stripped us of our royal honour and gave us over to be rent by teeth more cruel than any beast's; and those of us that escaped half-alive and woefully from the deadly teeth of crafty foxes and greedy wolves were thrown by violence into a gulf of doleful slavery.

"For, from the time when in consequence of that grant the English iniquitously but with some show of religion entered within the limits of our kingdom, they have striven with all their might and with every treacherous artifice in their power, to wipe our nation out entirely and utterly to extirpate it. By base and deceitful craftiness they have prevailed against us so far that, with no authority from a superior, they have driven us by force from the spacious places where we dwelt and from the inheritance of our fathers; they have compelled us to seek mountains, woods, bogs, barren tracts and even caverns in the rocks to save our lives, and for a long time back to make our dwellings there like beasts. Yet even in such places as these they harass us continually and endeavour all they can to expel us from them and seek unduly to usurp to themselves every place we occupy, mendaciously asserting in their blind madness that there is to be no free abode for us in Ireland but that all the land is entirely theirs by right...

"Therefore, on account of the aforesaid wrongs and infinite other wrongs which cannot easily be comprehended by the wit of man and yet again on account of the injustice of the kings of England and their wicked ministers and the constant treachery of the English of mixed race, who, by the ordinance of the Roman curia, were bound to rule our nation with justice and moderation and have set themselves wickedly to destroy it; and in order to shake off the hard and intolerable yoke of their slavery and to recover our native liberty, which for a time through them we lost, we are compelled to wage deadly war with them, aforesaid, preferring under stress of necessity to put ourselves like men to the trial of war in defence of our right, rather than to bear like women their atrocious outrages." – *Remonstrance of the Irish Chiefs to Pope John XXII, in Robert the Bruce's Irish Wars, pg. 179*

Niall Mór O'Neill

1. "That the Lord Chancellor, Lord Treasurer, Lord Admiral, the Council of State, the Justices of the laws, Queen's Attorney, Queen's Serjeant, and all other officers appertaining to the Council and law of Ireland, be Irishmen.
2. That all principal governments of Ireland, as Connaught, Munster, &c., be governed by Irish noblemen.

3. That the Master of Ordnance, and half the soldiers with their officers resident in Ireland, be Irishmen.
4. That no Irishman's heirs shall lose their lands for the faults of their ancestors.
5. That O'Neill, O'Donnell, and the Earl of Desmond, with all their partakers, may peaceably enjoy all lands and privileges that did appertain to their predecessors 200 years past.
6. That all Irishmen, of what quality they be, may freely travel in foreign countries for their better experience, without making any of the Queen's officers acquainted withal."

– *War Aims* (1599), quoted in *A Treatise on Northern Ireland*, pg. 160

Sybiline Oracles

"…nor does neighbor move the boundaries of neighbor…" – Charlesworth, *Old Testament*, vol. 1, pg. 36

Origen

On how we should approach inequality in the world:

"…in created things there may appear to be nothing unrighteous or accidental, but that all things may be shown to be in conformity with the law of equity and righteousness. How, then, so great a variety of things, and so great a diversity, can be understood to be altogether just and righteous, I am sure no human power or language can explain, unless as prostrate supplicants we pray to the Word, and Wisdom, and Righteousness Himself, who is the only-begotten Son of God, and who, pouring Himself by His graces into our senses, may deign to illuminate what is dark, to lay open what is concealed, and to reveal what is secret; if, indeed, we should be found either to seek, or ask, or knock so worthily as to deserve to receive when we ask, or to find when we seek, or to have it opened to us when we knock. Not relying, then, on our own powers, but on the help of that Wisdom which made all things, and of that Righteousness which we believe to be in all His creatures, although we are in the meantime unable to declare it, yet, trusting in His mercy, we shall endeavour to examine and inquire how that great variety and diversity in the world may appear to be consistent with all righteousness and reason. I mean, of course,

merely reason in general; for it would be a mark of ignorance either to seek, or of folly to give, a special reason for each individual case." – *Anti-Nicene, Writings Of Origen, First Principles*, pg. 130

"Now God, who deemed it just to arrange His creatures according to their merit, brought down these different understandings into the harmony of one world, that He might adorn, as it were, one dwelling, in which there ought to be not only vessels of gold and silver, but also of wood and clay (and some indeed to honour, and others to dishonour), with those different vessels, or souls, or understandings. And these are the causes, in my opinion, why that world presents the aspect of diversity, while Divine Providence continues to regulate each individual according to the variety of his movements, or of his feelings and purpose. On which account the Creator will neither appear to be unjust in distributing (for the causes already mentioned) to every one according to his merits; nor will the happiness or unhappiness of each one's birth, or whatever be the condition that falls to his lot, be deemed accidental; nor will different creators, or souls of different natures, be believed to exist." – *Anti-Nicene, Writings Of Origen, First Principles*, pg. 133

"Certain beings are called earthly, and among them, i.e., among men, there is no small difference; for some of them are Barbarians, others Greeks; and of the Barbarians some are savage and fierce, and others of a milder disposition. And certain of them live under laws that have been thoroughly approved; others, again, under laws of a more common or severe kind; while some, again, possess customs of an inhuman and savage character, rather than laws. And certain of them, from the hour of their birth, are reduced to humiliation and subjection, and brought up as slaves, being placed under the dominion either of masters, or princes, or tyrants. Others, again, are brought up in a manner more consonant with freedom and reason: some with sound bodies, some with bodies diseased from their early years; some defective in vision, others in hearing and speech; some born in that condition, others deprived of the use of their senses immediately after birth, or at least undergoing such misfortune on reaching manhood. And why should I repeat and enumerate all the horrors of human misery, from which some have been free, and in which others have been involved, when each one can weigh and consider them for himself? There are also certain invisible powers to which earthly things have been entrusted for administration; and amongst them no small difference must be believed to exist, as is also found to be the case among men. The Apostle Paul indeed intimates that there are certain lower powers, and that among them, in like manner, must undoubtedly be sought a ground of diversity. Regarding dumb animals, and birds, and those creatures which live in the waters, it seems superfluous to inquire; since it is certain that these ought to be regarded not as of primary, but of subordinate rank." – *Anti-Nicene, Writings Of Origen, First Principles*, pg. 290

"When He in the beginning created those beings which He desired to create, i.e., rational natures, He had no other reason for creating them than on account of Himself, i.e., His own goodness. As He Himself, then, was the cause of the existence of those things which were to be created, in whom there was neither any variation nor change, nor want of power, He created all whom He made equal and alike, because there was in Himself no reason for producing variety and diversity. But since those rational creatures themselves, as we have frequently shown, and will yet show in the proper place, were endowed with the power of free-will, this freedom of will incited each one either to progress by imitation of God, or reduced him to failure through negligence. And this, as we have already stated, is the cause of the diversity among rational creatures, deriving its origin not from the will or judgment of the Creator, but from the freedom of the individual will. Now God, who deemed it just to arrange His creatures according to their merit, brought down these different understandings into the harmony of one world, that He might adorn, as it were, one dwelling, in which there ought to be not only vessels of gold and silver, but also of wood and clay (and some indeed to honour, and others to dishonour), with those different vessels, or souls, or understandings. And these are the causes, in my opinion, why that world presents the aspect of diversity, while Divine Providence continues to regulate each individual according to the variety of his movements, or of his feelings and purpose. On which account the Creator will neither appear to be unjust in distributing (for the causes already mentioned) to every one according to his merits; nor will the happiness or unhappiness of each one's birth, or whatever be the condition that falls to his lot, be deemed accidental; nor will different creators, or souls of different natures, be believed to exist." – *Anti-Nicene, Writings Of Origen, First Principles*, pg. 292

"The Bride [in Song Of Songs] knows that the daughters of the former people impute this to her, and that because of it they call her black, as one who has not been enlightened by the patriarchs' teaching. She answers their objections thus: 'I am indeed black, O daughters of Jerusalem, in that I cannot claim descent from famous men, neither have I received the enlightenment of Moses' Law. But I have my own beauty, all the same. For in me too there is that primal thing, the Image of God wherein I was created; and, coming now to the Word of God, I have received my beauty. Because of my dark colouring you may compare me to the tents of Cedar and the curtains of Solomon; but even Cedar was descended from Ismael, being born his second son, and Ismael was not without a share in the divine blessing. You liken me even to the curtains of Solomon, which are none other than the curtains of the tabernacle of God-indeed I am surprised, O daughters of Jerusalem, that you should want to reproach me with the blackness of my hue. How have you come to forget what is written in your Law, as to what Mary suffered who spoke against Moses because he had taken a black Ethiopian to wife? How is it that you do not recognize the true fulfilment of that type in me? I am that Ethiopian. I am black indeed by reason of my lowly origin; but I am beautiful through penitence and faith...' It can be said also of each individual soul that turns to repentance after many sins, that she is black by reason of the sins, but beautiful through her repentance and the fruits of her repentance. And finally, because she who now says: 'I am black and beautiful' has not remained in her blackness to the end, the daughters of Jerusalem say later on concerning her: Who is this that cometh up, having been made white, and leaning upon her Nephew?" – *Commentary on Song Of Songs*, pg. 92

"And it is commonly said among the whole of

the Ethiopian race, in which there is a certain natural blackness inherited by all, that in those parts the sun burns with fiercer rays, and that bodies that have once been scorched and darkened, transmit a congenital stain to their posterity. But the reverse is the case with the blackness of the soul; for the soul is scorched, not by being looked at by the sun, but by being looked down upon. Its blackness, therefore, is acquired not through birth, but through neglect; and, since it comes through sloth, it is repelled and driven away by means of industry...

"And lastly, as I said just now, this same person who is now called black, is mentioned towards the end of this Song as coming up, having been made white, and leaning on her Nephew. She became black, then, because she went down; but, once she begins to come up and to lean upon her Nephew, to cleave to Him and suffer nothing whatever to separate her from Him, then she will be made white and fair; and, when all her blackness has been cast away, she will shine with the enveloping radiance of the true Light." – *Commentary on Song Of Songs,* pgs. 107-109

— ORIGEN —

"Justice...keeps inviolate the rights common to our neighbour, and our kindred, and observes fairness, and benevolence, and goodness." – *Anti-Nicene, Against Celsus,* pg. 186

"According to the trustworthiness of scripture, no Egyptian was free. For 'Pharao reduced the people to slavery to himself' nor did he leave anyone free within the borders of the Egyptians, but freedom was taken away in all the land of Egypt. And perhaps for this reason it is written: 'I am the Lord your God who brought you out of the land of Egypt, out of the house of bondage.' Egypt, therefore, became the house of bondage and, what is more unfortunate, of voluntary bondage.

"For although it is related of the Hebrews that they were reduced to bondage, and that, freedom having been snatched away, they bore the yoke of tyranny, nevertheless they are said to have been brought to this state 'violently.' For it is written: 'The Egyptians abhored the children of Israel and with might the Egyptians violently oppressed the sons of Israel and afflicted their life with hard works in mud and brick, and with all the works which were in the plains, in all of which they reduced them to bondage by force.' Notice carefully, therefore, how the Hebrews are recorded to have been reduced to bondage 'violently.' There was a natural freedom in them which was not wrenched away from them easily or by some deception, but by force.

"But Pharao easily reduced the Egyptian people to bondage to himself, nor is it written that he did this by force. For the Egyptians are prone to a degenerate life and quickly sink to every slavery of the vices. Look at the origin of the race and you will discover that their father Cham, who had laughed at his father's nakedness, deserved a judgment of this kind, that his son Chanaan should be a servant to his brothers, in which case the condition of bondage would prove the wickedness of his conduct. Not without merit, therefore, does the discolored posterity imitate the ignobility of the race.

"But the Hebrews, even if they be reduced to bondage, even if they suffer tyranny from the Egyptians, suffer 'violently' and by necessity. For this reason, therefore, they are freed 'from the house of bondage' and recalled to the original freedom which they had lost against their will. For it is even provided for in the divine laws that if perhaps someone buy a Hebrew servant, he may not possess him in perpetual bondage, but he may serve him for six years but in the seventh year he may depart free. Nothing like this is proposed concerning the Egyptians. Nowhere does the divine Law entertain concern for Egyptian freedom, because they had lost it willingly. It leaves them to the eternal yoke of their condition and to perpetual bondage." – *Homilies on Genesis and Exodus; The Fathers of the Church*, vol. 71, pgs. 214–215

"What I mean will be clear from the following comments. Because the sower has in himself both ancestral and kindred principles, when his own principle prevails and is brought to birth, what is born is like the sower. But when the principle of the sower's brother, or father, or uncle—sometimes even of his grandfather—[prevails], consequently those who are born are like one or the other of these.

"It is also possible to see the principle of the wife, or the wife's father, or brother, or grandfather prevailing in the course of the agitation in the mingling when all the seeds are shaken together until one of the generative principles prevails." – *Commentary on the Gospel According to John*, pg. 213

William F. Orr

"Christ exists as a body, the parts of which are all the Christians. The one Spirit is related to this as the effective force which, in the act of baptism, brings this body to experiential reality. Diversity of race and social class does not prevent incorporation into one body, but conversely the unity of the body does not eliminate the differences among the parts. Jews are still Jews and Greeks are still Greeks, but they are related together in a common society—and again Paul stresses that it is the one Spirit which produces this." – with James Arthur Walther, *Anchor Yale Bible Commentary. I Corinthians: a new translation, introduction, with a study of the life of Paul, notes, and commentary*, vol. 32, pg. 285. 1 Corinthians 15:18-28.

Ovid

"King Minos, while the fair wind moved their ship, was laying waste the land of Megara. He gathered a great army round the walls built by Alcathous, where reigned in splendor King Nisus—mighty and renowned in war—upon the center of whose hoary head a lock of purple hair was growing.—Its proved virtue gave protection to his throne.

"Six times the horns of rising Phoebe grew, and still the changing fortune of the war was in suspense; so, Victory day by day between them hovered on uncertain wings. Within that city was a regal tower on tuneful walls; where once Apollo laid his golden harp; and in the throbbing stone the sounds remained. And there, in times of peace the daughter of king Nisus loved to mount the walls and strike the sounding stone with pebbles: so, when the war began, she often viewed the dreadful contest from that height; until, so long the hostile camp remained, she had become acquainted with the names, and knew the habits, horses and the arms of many a chief, and could discern the signs of their Cydonean quivers. More than all, the features of King Minos were engraved upon the tablets of her mind. And when he wore his helmet, crested with gay plumes, she deemed it glorious; when he held his shield shining with gold, no other seemed so grand; and when he poised to hurl the tough spear home, she praised his skill and strength; and when he bent his curving bow with arrow on the cord, she pictured him as Phoebus taking aim,—but when, arrayed in purple, and upon the back of his white war horse, proudly decked with richly broidered housings, he reined in the nervous steed, and took his helmet off, showing his fearless features, then the maid, daughter of Nisus, could control herself no longer; and a frenzy seized her mind. She called the javelin happy which he touched, and blessed were the reins within his hand. She had an impulse to direct her steps, a tender virgin, through the hostile ranks, or cast her body from the topmost towers into the Gnossian camp. She had a wild desire to open to the enemy the heavy brass-bound gates, or anything that Minos could desire.

"And as she sat beholding the white tents, she cried, 'Alas! Should I rejoice or grieve to see this war? I grieve that Minos is the enemy of her who loves him; but unless the war had brought him, how could he be known to me? But should he take me for a hostage? That might end the war—a pledge of peace, he might keep me for his companion. O, supreme of mankind! she who bore you must have been as beautiful as you are; ample cause for Jove to lose his heart. O, happy hour! If moving upon wings through yielding air, I could alight within the hostile camp in front of Minos, and declare to him my name and passion! Then would I implore what dowry he could wish, and would provide whatever he might ask, except alone the city of my father. Perish all my secret hopes before one act of mine should offer treason to accomplish it. And yet, the kindness of a conqueror has often proved a blessing, manifest to those who were defeated. Certainly the war he carries on is justified by his slain son. He is a mighty king, thrice strengthened in his cause. Undoubtedly we shall be conquered, and, if such a fate awaits our city, why should he by force instead of my consuming love, prevail to open the strong gates? Without delay and dreadful slaughter, it is best for him to conquer and decide this savage war. Ah, Minos, how I fear the bitter fate should any warrior hurl his cruel spear and pierce you by mischance, for surely none can be so hardened to transfix your breast with purpose known. Oh, let her love prevail to open for his army the great gates. Only the thought of it, has filled her soul; she is determined to deliver up her country as a dowry with herself, and so decide the war!

'But what avails this idle talk. A guard surrounds the gates, my father keeps the keys, and he alone is my obstruction, and the innocent account of my despair. Would to the Gods I had no father! Is not man the God of his own fortune, though his idle prayers avail not to compel his destiny? Another woman crazed with passionate desires, which now inflame me, would not hesitate, but with a fierce abandon would destroy whatever checked her passion. Who is there with love to equal mine? I dare to go through flames and swords; but swords and flames are not now needed, for I only need my royal father's lock of purple hair. More precious than fine gold, it has a power to give my heart all that it may desire.'

"While Scylla said this, night that heals our cares came on, and she grew bolder in the dark. And now it is the late and silent hour when slumber takes possession of the breast. Out-wearied with the cares of busy day; then as her father slept, with stealthy tread she entered his abode, and there despoiled, and clipped his fatal lock of purple hair. Concealing in her bosom the sad prize of crime degenerate, she at once went forth a gate unguarded, and with shameless haste sped through the hostile army to the tent of Minos, whom, astonished, she addressed: 'Only my love has led me to this deed. The daughter of King Nisus, I am called the maiden Scylla. Unto you I come and offer up a power that will prevail against my

country, and I stipulate no recompense except yourself. Take then this purple hair, a token of my love.—Deem it not lightly as a lock of hair held idly forth to you; it is in truth my father's life.' And as she spoke she held out in her guilty hand the prize, and begged him to accept it with her love. Shocked at the thought of such a heinous crime, Minos refused, and said, 'O wicked thing! Despised abomination of our time! May all the Gods forever banish you from their wide universe, and may the land and the deep ocean be denied to you! So great a monster shall not be allowed to desecrate the sacred Isle of Crete, where Jupiter was born.'

"So Minos spoke. Nevertheless he conquered Megara, (so aided by the damsel's wicked deed) and as a just and mighty king imposed his own conditions on the vanquished land. He ordered his great fleet to tarry not; the hawsers were let loose, and the long oars quickly propelled his brazen-pointed ships.—When Scylla saw them launching forth, observed them sailing on the mighty deep, she called with vain entreaties; but at last, aware the prince ignored her and refused to recompense her wickedness, enraged, and raving, she held up her impious hands, her long hair streaming on the wind,—and said: 'Oh, wherefore have you flown, and left behind the author of your glory. Oh, wretch! wretch to whom I offered up my native land, and sacrificed my father! Where have you now flown, ungrateful man whose victory is both my crime and virtue? And the gift presented to you, and my passion, have these not moved you? All my love and hope in you alone! Forsaken by my prince, shall I return to my defeated land? If never ruined it would shut its walls against me.—Shall I seek my father's face whom I delivered to all-conquering arms? My fellow-citizens despise my name; my friends and neighbors hate me; I have shut the world against me, only in the hope that Crete would surely welcome me;—and now, he has forbidden me.'" – *Metamorphoses*, bk. 8

The pleasures of the fam'd Elysian field
Can no such rapture to a stranger yield.
No wonder Venus, bless'd with such a mien,
And such a person, reigns of beauty queen;
Her golden hair disheveled, crisp and long,
In easy curls around her shoulders hung;
– *Art Of Love*, pg. 355

I only wish to find
A faithful mistress, beautiful and kind;
No woman yet my settled passion moves,
One I have seen whom most my soul approves;
Of stature low, cast in a lovely mould,
Healthful and young, with hair more
   bright than gold;

Her looks are fresh, her countenance demure,
Her eyes, tho' killing, look like crystal pure [69]
– *Art Of Love*, pg. 248

— Ovid —

But still her image dwelt within my breast,
Too excellent to be in verse expressed.
Her head is round, and flaxen is her hair,
Her eye-brows darker, but her forehead fair;
Straight is her nose; her eyes like
   emeralds bright; [70]
Her well-made cheeks are lovely red and white;
Short is her mouth, her lips are made to kiss,
Rosy and full, and prodigal of bliss;
Her teeth like ivory are, well-sized and even,
And to her breath ethereal sweets are given;
Her hands are snowy white, and
   small her waist,
And what is yet untold is sure the best.
– *Art Of Love*, pg. 249

Ovid's Metamorphoses, where Medea asks why

she loved Jason, offspring of the gods:
  "Why did I take more pleasure than I should
in your blonde hair, and your comeliness, and
the lying favours of your tongue?" – *The Heroides*

Ovid writes of a man who prays his "ivory girl"
be made a real woman and his wife:
  "If you can grant all things, you gods, I wish
as a bride to have…" and not daring to say "the
girl of ivory" he said "one like my ivory girl." –
The Metamorphoses, Kline trans., pg. 270

Ovid writes of Atalanta who is most beautiful
of women, for whom men compete in deadly
races:
  "The race gave her a beauty of its own. The
breeze blew the streaming feathers on her
speeding sandals behind her, and her hair was
thrown back from her ivory shoulders. Ribbons
with embroidered edges fluttered at her knees,
and a blush spread over the girlish whiteness
of her body, just as when a red awning over a
white courtyard stains it with borrowed shadows." – *The Metamorphoses*, Kline trans., pg. 277

Describing the beauty of the upper man-portion
of a centaur:
  "His beard was beginning to show; a beard
the colour of gold; and a golden mane fell from
his shoulders half way down his flanks. He had
a liveliness of expression that was pleasing; his
neck and shoulders, chest and hands, and all
his human parts, you would praise as almost
sculpted by an artist." – *The Metamorphoses*,
Kline trans., pg. 323

Describing that Rome made a statue of the hero
Aesculapius:
  "His cult centre was Epidaurus where there
was a statue of the god with a golden beard." –
The Metamorphoses, Kline trans., pg. 430

"But though her father promised her desire, her
loveliness prevailed against their will; for, Phoebus when he saw her waxed distraught, and
filled with wonder his sick fancy raised delusive
hopes, and his own oracles deceived him.—
As the stubble in the field flares up, or as the
stacked wheat is consumed by flames, enkindled
from a spark or torch the chance pedestrian

---

69 green, blue, sparkling
70 green

may neglect at dawn; so was the bosom of the god consumed, and so desire flamed in his stricken heart. He saw her bright hair waving on her neck;—'How beautiful if properly arranged!' He saw her eyes like stars of sparkling fire, her lips for kissing sweetest, and her hands and fingers and her arms; her shoulders white as ivory;—and whatever was not seen more beautiful must be." – *Ovid's Metamorphoses, Apollo sees Daphne*, Brookes More trans., pg. 24

"While Titania is bathing there, in her accustomed place, Cadmus's grandson, free of his share of the labour, strays with aimless steps through the strange wood, and enters the sacred grove. So the fates would have it. As soon as he reaches the cave mouth dampened by the fountain, the naked nymphs, seeing a man's face, beat at their breasts and filling the whole wood with their sudden outcry, crowd round Diana to hide her with their bodies. But the goddess stood head and shoulders above all the others. Diana's face, seen there, while she herself was naked, was the colour of clouds stained by the opposing shafts of sun, or Aurora's brightness." – *The Metamorphoses*, Kline trans., pg. 85

Frank Lawrence Owsley

"The term 'folk' has for its primary meaning a group of kindred people, forming a tribe or nation; a people bound together by ties of race, language, religion, custom, tradition, and history. Such a common tie we call folkways. A folk thus possesses a sense of solidarity and is quite different from a conglomerate mass of people. It has most if not all of the characteristics of nationalism. Indeed, it may be contended with much force that there can be no true nationalism where the population does not constitute a folk. The Southern people, according to these several characteristics, were a genuine folk long before the Civil War...

"The greatest single factor, perhaps, in developing the Southern population into a genuine American folk was the common national origin of the bulk of the people. With the exception of the large French element in Louisiana the Southern people prior to 1860 were predominantly British, being a mixture of English and Scotch, with here and there a dash of German, French, or Irish. As a rule they were more English than Scotch in blood, but in physical

appearance they probably resembled the Scotch more than they did the English or even the other Americans except in the lower part of the Midwest where so many Southern folk had settled. The English and Scotch temperaments were blended in the Southerners. They usually had the steady, easygoing nature of the English combined with an underlying Gaelic temper and humor. Fat or lean, blond or brunet, the Southern type could be discerned by travelers from abroad and from other parts of America. Appearance, the indefinable qualities of personality, and their manners and customs, particularly their distinctive speech, set them apart from the inhabitants of the other sections of the United States, and in this way strengthened their sense of kinship.

"Southern folkways were in part the folkways of rural England, Scotland, and North Ireland of the sixteenth and seventeenth centuries, modified by the impact of the New World environment; and in part they were an indigenous growth of the South." – *Plain Folk of the Old South*, pgs. 90-91

"But after the military surrender at Appomattox there ensued a peace unique in history. There was no generosity. For ten years the South, already ruined by the loss of nearly $2,000,000,000 invested in slaves, with its lands worthless, its cattle and stock gone, its houses burned, was turned over to the three millions of former slaves, some of whom could still remember the taste of human flesh and the bulk of them hardly three generations removed from cannibalism. These half-savage blacks were armed. Their passions were roused against their former masters by savage political leaders like Thaddeus Stevens, who advocated the confiscation of all Southern lands for the benefit of the negroes, and the extermination, if need be, of the Southern white population; and like Charles Sumner, whose chief regret had been that his skin was not black. Not only were the blacks armed; they were upheld and incited by garrisons of Northern soldiers, by Freedman's Bureau officials, and by Northern ministers of the gospel, and at length they were given the ballot while their former masters were disarmed and, to a large extent, disfranchised. For ten years ex-slaves, led by carpetbaggers and scalawags, continued the pillages of war, combing the South for anything left by the invading armies, levying taxes, selling empires of plantations under the auction hammer, dragooning the Southern population, and visiting upon them the ultimate humiliations.

"After the South had been conquered by war and humiliated and impoverished by peace, there appeared still to remain something which made the South different–something intangible, incomprehensible, in the realm of the spirit. That too must be invaded and destroyed; so there commenced a second war of conquest, the conquest of the Southern mind, calculated to remake every Southern opinion, to impose the Northern way of life and thought upon the South, write 'error' across the pages of Southern history which were out of keeping with the Northern legend, and set the rising and unborn generations upon stools of everlasting repentance." – *I'll Take My Stand*, pgs. 62-63

— Frank Lawrence Owsley —

"Complex though the factors were which finally caused war, they all grew out of two fundamental differences which existed between the two sections: the North was commercial and industrial, and the South was agrarian. The fundamental and passionate ideal for which the South stood and fell was the ideal of an agrarian society. All else, good and bad, revolved around this ideal—the old and accepted manner of life for which Egypt, Greece, Rome, England, and France had stood. History and literature, profane and sacred, twined their tendrils about the cottage and the villa, not the factory.

"When America was settled, the tradition of the soil found hospitable root-bed in the Southern colonies, where climate and land combined to multiply the richness of an agrarian economy. All who came to Virginia, Maryland, the Carolinas and Georgia were not gentlemen; in fact, only a few were of the gentry. Most of them were of the yeomanry, and they were from rural England with centuries of country and farm lore and folk memory. Each word, name, sound, had grown from the soil and had behind it sweet memory, stirring adventure, and ofttimes stark tragedy. Thoughts, words, ideas, concepts, life itself, grew from the soil. The environment all pointed toward an endless enjoyment of the fruits of the soil. Jefferson, not visualizing the industrial revolution which whipped up the multiplication of populations and tore their roots from the soil, dreamed of America, free from England, as a boundless Utopia of farms taking a thousand generations to fill.

"Men so loved their life upon the soil that they sought out in literature and history peoples who had lived a similar life, so that they might justify and further stimulate their own concepts of life and perhaps set a high goal for themselves among the great nations which had sprung from the land. The people whom they loved most in the ancient world were the Greeks and the Romans of the early republic. The Greeks did not appeal to them as did the Romans, for they were too inclined to neglect their farms and turn to the sea and to handicraft. But the even-poised and leisurely life of the Greeks, their oratory, their philosophy, their art—especially their architecture— appealed to the South. The Greek tradition became partly grafted upon the Anglo-Saxon and Scotch tradition of life. However, it was the Romans of the early republic, before land speculators and corn laws had driven men from the soil to the city slums, who appealed most powerfully to the South. These Romans were brave, sometimes crude, but open and without guile—unlike the Greeks. They reeked of the soil, of the plow and the spade; they had wrestled with virgin soil and forests; they could build log houses and were closer to many Southerners than even the English gentleman in his moss-covered stone house. It was Cincinnatus, whose hands were rough with guiding the plow, rather than Cato, who wrote about Roman agriculture and lived in a villa, whom Southerners admired the most, though they read and admired Cato as a fine gentleman with liberal ideas about tenants and slaves and a thorough knowledge and love of the soil. The Gracchi appealed to Southerners because the Gracchi were lovers of the soil and died in the attempt to restore the yeomanry to the land.

"With the environment of the New World and the traditions of the Old, the South thus became the seat of an agrarian civilization which had strength and promise for a future greatness second to none. The life of the South was leisurely and unhurried for the planter, the yeoman, or the landless tenant. It was a way of life, not a routine of planting and reaping merely for gain. Washington, who rode daily over his farms and counted his horses, cattle, plows, and bushels of corn as carefully as a merchant takes stock of his supplies, inhaled the smell of ripe corn after a rain, nursed his bluegrass sod and shade trees with his own hands, and, when in the field as a soldier or in the city as President of the United States, was homesick at the smell of fresh-plowed earth. He kept vigil with his sick horses and dogs, not as a capitalist who guards his investments, but as one who watches over his friends.

"The system of society which developed in the South, then, was close to the soil. It might be organized about the plantation with its wide fields and its slaves and self-sufficiency, or it might center around a small farm, ranging from a fifty-acre to a five-hundred-acre tract, tilled by the owner, undriven by competition, supplied with corn by his own toil and with

meat from his own pen or from the fields and forests. The amusements might be the fine balls and house parties of the planter or the three-day break-down dances which David Crockett loved, or horse races, foot races, cock and dog fights, boxing, wrestling, shooting, fighting, log-rolling, house raising, or corn-shucking. It might be crude or genteel, but it everywhere was fundamentally alike and natural. The houses were homes, where families lived sufficient and complete within themselves, working together and fighting together. And when death came, they were buried in their own lonely peaceful graveyards, to await doomsday together." – *I'll Take My Stand*, pgs. 69-72

P

Thomas Paine

"'Tis not the affair of a City, a County, a Province, or a Kingdom; but of a Continent — of at least one-eighth part of the habitable Globe. 'Tis not the concern of a day, a year, or an age; posterity are virtually involved in the contest, and will be more or less affected even to the end of time, by the proceedings now. Now is the seed-time of Continental union, faith and honour." – *Common Sense*

B.M. Palmer

"By natural expansion, the Family grows into the tribe, and the principles of law are carried out under an administration that is strictly patriarchal. Tribes diverge, and are then consolidated into nations; and as society becomes more complex, its diversified interests are controlled by an authority which is more remote and kingly."

"But in the whole development, it is simply the law of the household expanding itself through all the ramifications of the commonwealth; and a true statesmanship must glean its great and essential principles from the subordination first established in the Family. The nearer a government is confirmed to this ideal, in the distribution of power and in the combination of influences by which society shall be controlled, the more perfect it will be, both in its conception and administration." – *The Family in its Civil and Churchly Aspects*; pg. 175

"It is difficult to see how the cumulative evidence could be stronger than it is – all the more valuable because so incidental – that God designed the Family to be the radix of the Church. It holds through all the dispensations, and will continue to the end of time." – *The Family in its Civil and Churchly Aspects*; pgs. 208-209

"I have said to them – and to their credit be it testified, the proposition has generally been accepted as the council of wisdom – if you are to be a historic people, you must work out your own destiny upon your own foundation. You gain nothing by a parasitic clinging to the White race; and immeasurably less, by trying to jostle them out of place. If you have no power of development from within, you lack the first quality of a historic race, and must, sooner or later, go to the wall.... Were I a black man, I should plead a pure Black race, as, being a White man I claim it for the White race; and should only ask the opportunity for it to work out its mission.... The true policy of both races is, that they shall stand apart in their own social grade, in their own schools, in their own ecclesiastical organizations, under their own teachers and guides: but with all the kindness and helpful co-operation to which the old relations between the races, and their present dependence on each other would naturally predispose." – As quoted by Morton Howison Smith in *Brotherhood and Race*, pgs. 213-214

Pamphilus of Caesarea

"'Honor your father and mother, that it may be well with you' is sufficient without any spiritual interpretation, and that it is necessary for those who observe it, especially since Paul also has confirmed that command by repeating it in the same words." – *Apology For Origen*, in *Ante-Nicene Fathers*: Tertullian, etc., pg. 368

Constantin Pancu

"Following years of frightful battles the world celebrates peace among men; the wise leaders in all civilized countries endeavor, to do away with war by establishing a law to guarantee a peaceful existence in the future. But lo, from the East one hears voices of hatred which indicate the attempt of our enemies to rip us apart through discord and misunderstandings among us. From Russia, ruled by the darkness of erroneous teachings, we are urged to battle and fire and to kill our brothers of like blood. From Hungary, which weeps over her former grandeur, one hears the same urgings. The enemies in the East have united with those in the West to disturb our peace so they can invade us. The foreigners beyond our borders try to pass the cup of poison among us, through the aliens living in the bosom of our country. They dare state that they prod us forward in the name of peace, justice and liberty, and in the name of the workers. Their word is a lie, their urgings a killing poison for: They say they want peace, but they themselves destroy it, killing the most worthy; Demand freedom, but by death threats, oblige people to submit to them; Wish brotherhood, while they sow hatred, injustice, and licentiousness within nations. Moreover, they say they want the abolishment of capital earned by the sweat of one's brow.

"They tell us they do not want war, but they war. They demand the army be abolished, but they arm themselves. They urge us to discard the tricolor flag, while in its stead they hoist the red flag of hatred. Do not lend any credence to their manifestoes and urgings just as you did not believe that of the enemy when you were fighting at Oituz, Marasti and Marasesti. The duty of every good Romanian is to see to it that in the future, too, the seed of dissension the enemy endeavors to throw among us does not take root. Perfect the Work you began by your labor and your honor. Your enemies are the indolence, hatred and dishonor that rule across the borders, that threaten us as well. Beware! Keep clean your soul, do not forget that our salvation is work, unity and honor.

"Brother soldiers, With faith in God, you have broken the enemy's power. With your weapons you have carved for eternity the country's borders. With your blood you have perfected and sealed your sacrifice. That is why you must not allow foreign and lawless bands to destroy that which you perfected. Continue to hold your love of country and faith in your King. You took an oath to defend with your blood to the last drop the fatherland's borders. Guard them attentively against the evil intentions of the enemy, for that is what our parents and ancestors did.

"Brother peasants, The God of our parents took mercy on our suffering and gave us as bountiful a year as was rarely seen. Be grateful to the good Lord, through your labor and your faith. Renew your working powers, gather assiduously the yield of the land. Rest assured that the land from the Tisa, the Danube, and the Black Sea, was entirely won by you. Keep it in sacredness, defend its riches through your labor and your love.

"Brother Romas, It is in you that the hopes and strength of this country lie. You are also the happiness of tomorrow. Do not gather for yourselves curses, but blessings. The enemy is attacking at the Dniester and at the Tisa. He also tries to disrupt the inner peace of our country. Our deliverance is in labor, honor, love of country and faith in God. Be careful, call onto the righteous path also those who straying have crossed over to those without a people and without a faith. United around the throne and under the shadow of the tricolor banner stand watch for the peace of the country. Tell the foreigners and foreign-lovers who try to disturb us, that around us a national guard has formed that watches, that will fight those wishing to sow among us discord. Romanians everywhere, workers, craftsmen, soldiers and peasants, be worthy of our ancestors and of the call of these times in which we live." – quoted by Corneliu Zelea Codreanu, in *For My Legionnaires*, 1919

Papyrus Harris I

"The Land of Egypt was abandoned, and every man was master of himself. For many years there was no leader who could speak for the others. The central government expired, petty officials and chieftains took over the whole country. Any man, great or small, could kill his neighbor. In the calamity and void that followed came a Syrian, a foreigner who imposed himself on the whole country and the people formed gangs to rob one another. They treated gods no better than men." – quoted in *A History Of Western Society*, pg. 34

Frederic Passy

"Some day all barriers will fall; someday mankind, constantly united by continuous transactions, will form just one workshop, one market, and one family. . . . And this is . . . the grandeur, the truth, the nobility, I might almost say the holiness of the free-trade doctrine; by the prosaic but effective pressure of interest it tends to make justice and harmony prevails in the world." – cited in Silberner, *Problem of War*, pg. 105

Pádraic H. Pearse

"Now I think that one may speak of a national soul and of a national mind, and distinguish one from the other, and that this is not merely figurative speaking ... But I believe that there is really a spiritual tradition which is the soul of Ireland, the thing which makes Ireland a living nation, and that there is such a spiritual tradition corresponding to every true nationality. This spiritual thing is distinct from the intellectual facts in which chiefly it makes its revelation, and it is distinct from them in a way analogous to that in which a man's soul is distinct from his mind. Like other spiritual things, it is independent of the material, whereas the mind is to a large extent dependent upon the material. ...

"If nationality be regarded as the sum of the facts, spiritual and intellectual, which mark off one nation from another, and freedom as the condition which allows those facts full scope and development, it will be seen that both the spiritual and intellectual fact, nationality, and the physical condition, freedom, enter into a proper definition of independence or nationhood. Freedom is a condition which can be lost and won and lost again; nationality is a life which, if once lost, can never be recovered. A nation is a stubborn thing, very hard to kill; but a dead nation does not come back to life, any more than a dead man. There will never again be a Ligurian nation, nor an Aztec nation, nor a Cornish nation.

"Irish nationality is an ancient spiritual tradition, and the Irish nation could not die as long as that tradition lived in the heart of one faithful man or woman. But had the last repositor of the Gaelic tradition, the last unconquered Gael, died, the Irish nation was no more. Any free state that might thereafter be erected in Ireland, whatever it might call itself, would certainly not be the historic Irish nation." — *The Spiritual Nation, Political Writings and Speeches*, pgs. 300-304

"And I assert the sovereignty and the sanctity

of the nations, which are the people embodied and organised. The nation is a natural division, as natural as the family, and as inevitable. That is one reason why a nation is holy and why an empire is not holy. A nation is knit together by natural ties, ties mystic and spiritual, and ties human and kindly; an empire is at best held together by ties of mutual interest, and at worst by brute force. The nation is the family in large; an empire is a commercial corporation in large. The nation is of God; the empire is of man—if it be not of the devil." — *The Sovereign People, Political Writings and Speeches*, pg. 343

Richard Pervo

"The verse opens with a compressed assertion of the unity of the human race grounded in a common origin from God. Representatives of the philosophical tradition had protested against the division of humankind into Greeks and barbarians. Luke applied this concept to the division between Jews and gentiles, overcome by the miraculous action of God rather than from acquiescence to the political ramifications of an intellectual argument, but Paul does not point that out on this occasion. The creation of humankind is described without reference to Genesis or to any mythic account, but Christian readers will take it as a summary of Genesis. Greek tradition also viewed [a] god as the parent of the human race. A reason for creating humanity—inhabitation of the whole world—evokes Gen 1:28.

"The chief difficulty in v. 26b is the meanings of καιροί and ὁροθεσίαι ('times' and 'boundaries'). The former could refer to the seasons of the year and is often taken as such. That would correspond to 14:17, but the address is not speaking of proofs of God from nature, and the participle προστεταγμένους ('arranged') does not suit that sense. Another understanding, although not consonant with the traditional argument, which contends that the divine hand is apparent in the structure of the universe, is 'historical periods,' as in Luke 24:3 (cf. Acts 1:7; 3:20). In this context, ὁροθεσίαι would apply to political boundaries. The underlying notion would be that countries rise and fall in political power and dominance. The vicissitudes of history are elements of God's plan for the human race." – *Pervo, R. I. Acts: a commentary on the Book of Acts.* (H. W. Attridge, Ed.), pgs. 435-436

Walker Percy

"The self sees itself as a sovereign and individual consciousness, liberated by education from the traditional bonds of religion, by democracy from the structures of class, by technology from the drudgery of poverty, and by self-knowledge from the tyranny of the unconscious—and therefore free to pursue its own destiny without God." – *Lost in the Cosmos: The Last Self-Help Book*, Preface

William Perkins

"The whole [political] body is not the hand, nor the foot, nor the eye, but the hand one part, the foot another, and the eye another; and howsoever in the body one part is linked to another, yet there is a distinction betwixt the members.... In every society one person should be above or under another; not making all equal, as though the body should be all head and nothing else; but even in degree and order, he [God] hath set a distinction, that one should be above another." – quoted in Alden T. Vaughan, *The Puritan Tradition in America*, 1620-1730, pg. 135

"If any demand, what these churches of Galatia are? I answer, that they were a people of Asia the Less. And though they were famous churches in the days of the apostle, yet now the country is under the dominion of the Turk. This shows what God might have done to us in England long ago for the contempt of the gospel. This again shows what desolation will befall us unless we repent, and bring forth better fruits of the gospel." – *Commentary on Galatians* 1:2, *Works*, vol. 2, pg. 20

Heinrich Pesch

Germanic-Christian society was 'rooted in nature itself,' because it:

"...was based on the family, which bound: people together on the basis of reciprocal rights and obligations. As such, it turns out to be the basis of the physical, intellectual, and the moral existence of the human race, and the basic cell of all natural social life. It was the historical starting point for all socio-organic structures in the natural order, up to and including the state, and it will always continue to be that, as well as the stable foundation for happiness and well-being." – *Lehrbuch der Nationalokonomie*, translated and edited by Rupert J. Ederer, vol. I, bk. 1, pg. 193

"The need to provide food, clothing and shelter for a number of persons in a common economy naturally inclines the family to settle down in a stable situation; and it leads to the establishment of a home which, in turn, binds it solidly to the homeland, the fatherland. ...

"Wherever a nation, like the nomads of former times or the Indians of America did not have the ambition to take root in native soil and build houses for their families, it was insignificant in the pages of history. With the establishment of a home, you get the beginning of culture, and with domesticity, civilization begins." – *Lehrbuch der Nationalokonomie*, translated and edited by Rupert J. Ederer, vol. I, bk. 1, pg. 194

"We may not permit the acquisitive interest of those who own capital to dominate in the governance of economic life. The highest purpose of the national community organized in the form of a political state is the welfare of the entire nation...

"...the fulfillment of the economic purpose remains the highest and ultimate task of the national economic process. The private economy must fall in line with the national economy, and not make the latter subordinate to it." – *Lehrbuch der Nationaloekonomie*, pg. 161

David G. Peterson

"A sense of racial superiority can only be overcome by recognising the unity of the human race in terms of its origin and God's purpose in creating us. Yet the next clause – and he marked out their appointed times in history and the boundaries of their lands – indicates that, in the plan of God, there are specific destinies for races and nations. The Greek (horisas prostetagmenous kairous kai tas horothesias tēs katoikias autōn) may be more literally translated 'having determined their appointed times and the boundaries of their dwelling-places...' The boundaries of their lands seems to be a reference to the various areas in which the races live (cf. Dt. 32:8) and so it could be argued that the preceding expression refers to the periods in history when those regions are dominated by particular races. Thus, there is a collective responsibility and privilege shared by humanity as a whole in God's creation. Yet God has also ordained special times and places for nations within that overarching purpose. Both truths must be held in tension when applying biblical teaching to situations in our world today." – *Pillar New Testament Commentary, The Acts of the Apostles*, Acts 17:26, pg. 468

Istvan Petroczy

"Our eyes are full of tears when watching the sorrowful nightfall of our decaying dear fatherland and nation . . . Oh, Hungary! Hungary! Your empire comprised twelve countries . . . now you can mourn for twelve lost possessions, and you are driven back to only certain parts even of the twelfth . . . Understand, true Hungarians, make yourselves believe that the Germans hate the whole Hungarian nation indiscretion religion is [without any religious distinction] . . . The archbishops and the prelates have been deprived of their property, the chamberlains – although left in their offices – have become subservient to the Germans . . . In the frontier castles the Hungarians get neither payment, nor respect . . . The Germans use every means they can to get hold of, unheard of . . . [new kinds of taxes] to put the poor Hungarian nation's body and soul on the butcher's block and cut it into pieces . . . If, therefore, there is any Hungarian sensitivity, or any drop of Hungarian blood in you, my beloved nation, wake up, and love your brethren." – cited in Laszlo Benczedi, *Hungarian National Consciousness as Reflected in the Anti-Habsburg and Anti-Ottoman Struggles of the Late Seventeenth Century, Harvard Ukrainian Studies*, 10 (3 – 4) (1986), pg. 430

Jordan Peterson

"Raising young children is demanding and exhausting. Because of this, it's easy for a parent to make a mistake. Insomnia, hunger, the aftermath of an argument, a hangover, a bad day at work—any of these things singly can make a person unreasonable, while in combination they can produce someone dangerous. Under such circumstances, it is necessary to have someone else around, to observe, and step in, and discuss. This will make it less likely that a whiny provocative child and her fed-up cranky parent will excite each other to the point of

no return. Parents should come in pairs so the father of a newborn can watch the new mother so she won't get worn out and do something desperate after hearing her colicky baby wail from eleven in the evening until five in the morning for thirty nights in a row. I am not saying we should be mean to single mothers, many of whom struggle impossibly and courageously—and a proportion of whom have had to escape, singly, from a brutal relationship—but that doesn't mean we should pretend that all family forms are equally viable. They're not. Period." – *12 Rules*, pg. 142

"In the West, we have been withdrawing from our tradition, religion, and even nation-centered cultures, partly to decrease the danger of group conflict. But we are increasingly falling prey to the desperation of meaninglessness, and that is no improvement at all." – *12 Rules*, pg. 32

Michael Boro Petrovich

"Most of the people of Eastern Europe achieved a sense of identity and some political expression of that identity in medieval times, long before the Age of Nationalism . . . Religion in Eastern Europe served a nation-building role and it acted as a surrogate state for people who had lost political independence . . . The Church has been literally militantly involved in movements for ethnic survival and wars for national independence in Eastern Europe from medieval times to the present." – *Religion and Ethnicity in Eastern Europe* (1980), reprinted in Hutchinson and Smith (eds.), *Nationalism*, vol. iv, 1356-1381, citations from 1359, 1361, 1367.

Peter The Great

"Warriors! Here came the hour that should decide the fate of the Fatherland. And so you should not think that you are fighting for Peter, but for the State, handed to Peter, for your kind, for the Fatherland, for our Orthodox faith and the Church... And know of Peter that he does not care about his life but only that Russia lives in bliss and glory for your well-being." – quoted in Buturlin D. P. Military история Russian campaigns in the eighteenth century. SPb., 1821. CH 1. T. 3. C. 52. In English: *Main Concepts Of Russian Politics*, pg. 12

Philo of Alexandria

"In the fifth commandment on honouring parents we have a suggestion of many necessary laws drawn up to deal with the relations of old to young, rulers to subjects, benefactors to benefited, slaves to masters. For parents belong to the superior class of the above-mentioned pairs, that which comprises seniors, rulers, benefactors and masters, while children occupy the lower position with juniors, subjects, receivers of benefits and slaves. And there are many other instructions given, to the young on courtesy to the old, to the old on taking care of the young, to subjects on obeying their rulers, to rulers on promoting the welfare of their subjects, to recipients of benefits on requiting them with gratitude, to those who have given of their own initiative on not seeking to get repayment as though it were a debt, to servants on rendering an affectionate loyalty to their masters, to masters on showing the gentleness and kindness by which inequality is equalized." – from his *On The Decalogue*, in *Reading Philo*, pg. 193

"For to whom else will they show kindness if they despise the closest of their kinsfolk who have bestowed upon them the greatest boons, some of them far exceeding any possibility of repayment? For how could the begotten beget in his turn those whose seed he is, since nature has bestowed on parents in relation to their children an estate of a special kind which cannot be subject to the law of exchange?" – from his *On The Decalogue, The Wisdom Instructions in the Book of Tobit*, pg. 60.[71]

"Parents, in my opinion, are to their children what God is to the world, since just as He achieved existence for the non-existent, so they in imitation of His power, as far as they are capable, immortalize the race. And a father and mother deserve honour, not only on this account, but for many other reasons. For in the judgement of those who take account of virtue, seniors are placed above juniors, teachers above pupils, benefactors above beneficiaries, rulers above subjects, and masters above servants. Now parents are assigned a place in the higher of these two orders, for they are seniors and instructors and benefactors and rulers and masters: sons and daughters are placed in the lower order, for they are juniors and learners and recipients of benefits and subjects and servants." – *Works of Philo, Special Laws*, pg. 589

"One who pays respect to an aged man or woman who is not of his kin may be regarded as having remembrance of his father and mother. He looks to them as prototypes and stands in awe of those who bear their image." – *Works of Philo, Special Laws*, pg. 591

Dares Phrygius

"Dares the Phrygian, who wrote this history, says that he did military service until the capture of Troy and saw the people listed below either during times of truce or while he was fighting. As for Castor and Pollux, he learned from the Trojans what they were like and how they looked: they were twins, blond haired, large eyed, fair complexioned, and well built with trim bodies. Helen resembled Castor and Pollux. She was beautiful, ingenuous, and charming. Her legs were the best; her mouth the cutest. There was a beauty-mark between her eyebrows... Alexander was fair, tall, and brave. His eyes were very beautiful, his hair soft and blond, his mouth charming, and his voice pleasant. He was swift, and eager to take command...Andromache was bright-eyed and fair, with a tall and beautiful body. She was modest, wise, chaste, and charming. Cassandra was of moderate stature, round-mouthed, and auburn-haired. Her eyes flashed. She knew the future. Polyxena was fair, tall, and beautiful. Her neck was slender, her eyes lovely her hair blond and long, her body well-proportioned, her fingers tapering, her legs straight, and her feet the best. Surpassing all the others in beauty, she remained a completely ingenuous and kind-hearted woman. Agamemnon was blond, large, and powerful. He was eloquent, wise, and noble, a man richly endowed...Patroclus was handsome and powerfully built. His eyes were gray. He was modest, dependable, wise, a man richly endowed... Protesilaus was fair-skinned, and dignified. He was swift, self-confident, even rash...Briseis was beautiful. She was small and blond, with soft yellow hair. Her eyebrows were joined above her lovely eyes. Her body was well-proportioned. She was charming, friendly, modest, ingenuous, and pious." – *History of the Fall of Troy*

---

71   He speaks here if those who disobey the fifth commandment.

Benedict Pictet

"What are the general precepts of ethics?

Answer: We must love all those who are connected to us by some bond: our parents, our in-laws, our kinsmen, our fatherland, and so on, especially those who deserve our gratitude."
– *Marrow of Christian Ethics*, translated by Michael Hunter, pg. 11

"Must we love all men equally?"

"Answer: By No means! Charity is different from brotherly love (2 Pet. 1:7; Heb. 13:1; 1 Thess. 4:9; Pet. 1:22; 2:17). We are allowed to love the members of the household of faith more than we love others. Those whom God loves more than He loves others (e.g., believers) we are allowed to love more than we love others. We are also allo329wed to love those who are connected to us by the bond of blood more than we love others."
– *Marrow of Christian Ethics*, translated by Michael Hunter, pg. 99

Charles Pinckney

"In South Carolina we consider all white persons born in the same, or adopted according to law, to be citizens, and entitled, as such, to all the privileges of a citizen, where not disabled by something personal to themselves. Their privileges vary according to their sex and situation. Females are wholly excluded from a right to vote, or to office, and are confined to their proper sphere; but all males born in the State, or in the United States, after a certain residence in that State, or adopted according to law, are equal, except clergymen, who, on account of their office, are excluded from the Legislature. At the age of eighteen they are all enrolled into the militia, and serve as the defenders of their country. At twenty-one they are, from our general suffrage law, qualified to vote, to serve on juries, and to be eligible to the Legislature, and all offices except two, which require greater age. They have a right to sue, and are liable to be sued; to take a freehold, and hold property: They are all entitled to the trial by jury, and intermarry at any age. This, and this alone, is called a citizen there; and nothing less than this can, in my opinion, constitute a citizen of the United." – *Speech on the admission of Missouri; Abridgment of the Debates of Congress, from 1789 to 1856*: Nov. 13, 1820-April 14, 1824, pg.109

Pindar

A woman is killed by Apollo because she abandoned her husband, doing so because "she loved what was distant":

"[Cheiron's] mother, the daughter of Phlegyas with his fine horses, before she could bring him to term with the help of Eleithuia who attends on childbirth, was stricken by the golden arrows of Artemis in her bedroom and descended to the house of Hades, by the skills of Apollo. The anger of the children of Zeus is not in vain. But she made light of Apollo, in the error of her mind, and consented to another marriage without her father's knowledge, although she had before lain with Phoebus of the unshorn hair, and was bearing within her the pure seed of the god. She did not wait for the marriage-feast to come, nor for the full-voiced cry of the hymenaeal chorus, such things as unmarried girls her own age love to murmur in evening songs to their companion. Instead, she was in love with what was distant; many others have felt that passion. There is a worthless tribe among men which dishonors what is at home and looks far away, hunting down empty air with hopes that cannot be fulfilled. Such was the strong infatuation that the spirit of lovely-robed Coronis had caught. For she lay in the bed of a stranger who came from Arcadia; but she did not elude the watcher." – *Pythian*, bk. 2, poem 3

"And once the golden-haired, bright-eyed goddess [Athena] made Diomedes an immortal god." – *Nemean X*

"But to us, Apollo, splendid in your golden hair, grant in your own contests" – *Odes*

"The golden-haired god [Apollo] sent gentle-minded Eleithuia and the Fates to help her." – *Olympian Odes*

"...beloved of the gold-haired god, Apollo, in fulness of heart" – *Odes*

"Son of Alexibias, the fair-haired Graces flare about you. Aiakos wears the wreath luxuriant with flowers, the gift of the fair-haired Graces." – *Pythian Odes*

"Thereafter they were the high lords of the fair-haired Danaans..." – *Odes*

"...man-conquering Eriphyle became the most powerful of the golden-haired Danaans." – *Nemean Odes*

Pío Baroja y Nessi

"Great states, great captains, great kings, great gods, leave me cold. They are all for peoples who dwell on vast plains which are crossed by might rivers, for the Egyptians, for the Chinese, for the Hindus, for the Germans, for the French. We Europeans who are of the region of the Pyrenees and the Alps, love small states, small rivers, and small gods, whom we may address familiarly." – *Youth And Egolatry*, pg. 58

Plato

"Has a philosopher like you failed to discover that our country is more to be valued and higher and holier far than mother or father or any ancestor, and more to be regarded in the eyes of the gods and of men of understanding? also to be soothed, and gently and reverently entreated when angry, even more than a father, and if not persuaded, obeyed? And when we are punished by her, whether with imprisonment or stripes, the punishment is to be endured in silence; and if she leads us to wounds or death in battle, thither we follow as is right; neither may anyone yield or retreat or leave his rank, but whether in battle or in a court of law, or in any other place, he must do what his city and his country order him; or he must change their view of what is just: and if he may do no violence to his father or mother, much less may he do violence to his country." – *Crito, Dialogues*, pg. 152

"There is an element of friendship in the community of race, language, and laws, and in common temples and rites of worship; but colonies which are of this homogeneous sort are apt to kick against any laws or any form of constitution differing from that which they had at home..." – *Laws*, pg. 227

"...to these duty enjoins that the debtor should pay back the first and greatest of debts, the most primary of all dues, and that he should acknowledge that all that he owns and has belongs to those who begot and reared him." – *Laws*, pg. 287

"As regards duties to children, relations, friends and citizens, and those of service done to strangers for Heaven's sake, and of social intercourse with all those classes—by fulfilling which a man should brighten his own life and order it as the law enjoins—the sequel of the laws themselves, partly by persuasion and partly (when men's habits defy persuasion) by forcible and just chastisement, will render our State, with the concurrence of the gods, a blessed State and a prosperous." – *Laws*, from *Plato with an English Translation*, pg. 301

"By paying honor and reverence to his kinsfolk, and all who share in the worship of the tribal gods and are sprung from the same blood, a man will, in proportion to his piety, secure the goodwill of the gods of Birth to bless his own begetting of children. Moreover, a man will find his friends and companions kindly disposed, in regard to life's intercourse, if he sets higher than they do the value and importance of the services he receives from them, while counting the favors he confers on them as of less value than they are deemed by his companions and friends themselves. In relation to his State and fellow-citizens that man is by far the best who, in preference to a victory at Olympia or in any other contest of war or peace, would choose to have a victorious reputation for service to his native laws, as being the one man above all others who has served them with distinction throughout his life." – *Laws*, pg. 331

"And may I not observe with equal propriety that the Hellenic race is all united together by ties of blood and friendship, and alien and strange to the barbarians?...Consider then, I said, when that which we have acknowledged to be discord occurs, and a city is divided, if both parties destroy the lands and burn the houses of one another, how wicked does the strife appear! No true lover of his country would bring himself to tear in pieces his own nurse and mother: There might be reason in the conqueror depriving the conquered of their harvest, but still they would have the idea of peace in their hearts and would not mean to go on fighting for ever...

"And as they are Hellenes themselves they will not devastate Hellas, nor will they burn houses, not even suppose that the whole population of a city–men, women, and children–are equally their enemies, for they know that the guilt of war is always confined to a few persons and that the many are their friends. And for all these reasons they will be unwilling to waste their lands and raze their houses; their enmity to them will only last until the many innocent sufferers have compelled the guilty few to give satisfaction?" – *Republic*, pg. 258

— PLATO —

"Do you think it right that Hellenes should enslave Hellenic States, or allow others to enslave them, if they can help? Should not their custom be to spare them, considering the danger which there is that the whole race may one day fall under the yoke of the barbarians? To spare them is infinitely better. Then no Hellene should be owned by them as a slave; that is a rule which they will observe and advise the other Hellenes to observe. Certainly, he said; they will in this way be united against the barbarians and will keep their hands off one another." – *Republic*, pg. 257

"Do you know, I said, that governments vary as the dispositions of men vary, and that there must be as many of the one as there are of the other? For we cannot suppose that States are made of 'oak and rock,' but out of the human natures which are in them, and which in a figure turn the scale and draw other things after them?" – *Republic*, pg. 311

"Cities find colonization in some respects easier if the colonists are one race, which like a swarm of bees is sent out from a single country, either when friends leave friends, owing to some pressure of population or other similar necessity, or when a portion of a state is driven by factions to emigrate. And there have been whole cities which have taken flight when utterly conquered by a superior power in war. This, however, which is in one way an advantage to the colonist or legislator, in another point of view creates a difficulty. There is an element of friendship in the community of race, and language, and laws, and in common temples and rites of worship; but colonies which are of this homogeneous sort are apt to kick against any laws or any form of constitution differing from that which they had at home; and although the badness of their own laws may have been the cause of the factions which prevailed among them, yet from the force of habit they would fain preserve the very customs which were their ruin, and the leader of the colony, who is their legislator, finds them troublesome and rebellious." – *The Dialogues of Plato*, Jowett trans., pg. 90

"Well, try it this way, I went on: suppose some one tinged your golden locks with white lead, would they then be or appear to be white?" – *Lysis* 217d, English Trans., pg. 53

Pliny the Elder

Describes how women could die their hair blonde or black. Commentary by John Bostock said the blonde "tint" was the most desirable:

"Lysimachia imparts a blonde tint to the hair, and the hypericon, otherwise called 'corisson,' makes it black...[The blonde tint is] the most highly esteemed among the Romans of all colours of the hair." – *Natural History*, pg. 214

Joseph Plummer

"There is always one nonnegotiable element in any plan to secure global domination: sovereign nations (truly independent nations) cannot be tolerated. Why? Because global domination is about centralizing all power into the would-be rulers' hands. Independent nations impede this consolidation and disturb the proper chain of command. This seems straightforward enough, but, since it's rarely boiled down to its simplest form, it's worth repeating: to rule the world, you must first destroy national sovereignty. You must consolidate and control the real levers of power, regardless of the different forms of government that appear in each country." – *Tragedy and Hope 101*, pg. 51

Plutarch

Theseus turned Athens into a democracy by permitting the entry of people from all nations, yet not without some measure of assimilating order:

"Farther yet designing to enlarge his city, he invited all strangers to come and enjoy equal privileges with the natives, and it is said that the common form, Come hither all ye people, was the words that Theseus proclaimed when he thus set up a commonwealth, in a manner, for all nations. Yet he did not suffer his state, by the promiscuous multitude that flowed in, to be turned into confusion and be left without any order or degree, but was the first that divided the Commonwealth into three distinct ranks, the noblemen, the husbandmen, and artificers. To the nobility he committed the care of religion, the choice of magistrates, the teaching and dispensing of the laws, and interpretation and direction in all sacred matters; the whole city being, as it were, reduced to an exact equality, the nobles excelling the rest in honor, the husbandmen in profit, and the artificers in number. And that Theseus was the first, who, as Aristotle says, out of an inclination to popular government, parted with the regal power, Homer also seems to testify, in his catalogue of the ships, where he gives the name of People to the Athenians only." – *Lives*, pg. 24

"He [Lycurgus] filled Lacedæmon all through with proofs and examples of good conduct; with the constant sight of which from their youth up, the people would hardly fail to be gradually formed and advanced in virtue. And this was the reason why he forbade them to travel abroad, and go about acquainting themselves with foreign rules of morality, the habits of ill-educated people, and different views of government. Withal he banished from Lacedæmon all strangers who could not give a very good reason for their coming thither; not because he was afraid lest they should inform themselves of and imitate his manner of government (as Thucydides says), or learn any thing to their good; but rather lest they should introduce something contrary to good manners. With strange people, strange words must be admitted; these novelties produce novelties in thought; and on these follow views and feelings whose discordant character destroys the harmony of the state. He was as careful to save his city from the infection of foreign bad habits, as men usually are to prevent the introduction of a pestilence." – *Lives*, pg. 120

"But of all [of Numa's] measures the most commended was his distribution of the people by their trades into companies or guilds; for as the city consisted, or rather did not consist of, but was divided into, two different tribes, the diversity between which could not be effaced and in the mean time prevented all unity and caused perpetual tumult and illblood, reflecting how hard substances that do not readily mix when in the lump may, by being beaten into powder, in that minute form be combined, he resolved to divide the whole population into a number of small divisions, and thus hoped, by introducing other distinctions, to obliterate the original and great distinction, which would be lost among the smaller. So, distinguishing the whole people by the several arts and trades, he formed the companies of musicians, goldsmiths, carpenters, dyers, shoemakers, skinners, braziers, and potters; and all other handicraftsmen he composed and reduced into a single company, appointing every one their proper courts, councils, and religious observances. In this manner all factious distinctions began, for the first time, to pass out of use, no person any longer being either thought of or spoken of under the notion of a Sabine or a Roman, a Romulian or a Tatian; and the new division became a source of general harmony and intermixture." – *Lives*, pgs. 151-152

"They say, therefore, that Solon, coming to Cræsus at his request, was in the same condition as an inland man when first he goes to see the sea; for as he fancies every river he meets with to be the ocean, so Solon, as he passed through the court, and saw a great many nobles richly dressed, and proudly attended with a multitude of guards and footboys, thought every one had been the king, till he was brought to Cræsus, who was decked with every possible rarity and curiosity, in ornaments of jewels, purple, and gold, that could make a grand and gorgeous spectacle of him. Now when Solon came before him, and seemed not at all surprised, nor gave Crœsus those compliments he expected, but showed himself to all discerning eyes to be a man that despised the gaudiness and petty ostentation of it, he commanded them to open all his treasure houses, and carry him to see his sumptuous furniture and luxuries, though he did not wish it; Solon could judge of him well enough by the first sight of him; and, when he returned from viewing all, Crœsus asked him if ever he had known a happier man than he. And when Solon answered that he had known one Tellus, a fellow-citizen of his own, and told him that this Tellus had been an honest man, had had good children, a competent estate, and died bravely in battle for his country, Crœsus took him for an ill-bred fellow and a fool, for not measuring happiness by the abundance of gold and silver, and preferring the life and death of a private and mean man before so much power and empire." – *Lives*, pgs. 195-196

"Cæsar [probably Augustus] once, seeing some wealthy strangers at Rome, carrying up and down with them in their arms and bosoms young puppy-dogs and monkeys, embracing and making much of them, took occasion not unnaturally to ask whether the women in their country were not used to bear children; by that prince-like reprimand gravely reflecting upon persons who spend and lavish upon brute beasts that affection and kindness which nature has implanted in us to be bestowed on those of our own kind. With like reason may we blame those who misuse that love of inquiry and observation which nature has implanted in our souls, by expending it on objects unworthy of the attention either of their eyes or their ears, while they disregard such as are excellent in themselves, and would do them good." – *Lives*, pg. 318

"Now, at his [Caesar's] love of danger his men were not astonished, knowing his ambition; but that he should undergo toils beyond his body's apparent power of endurance amazed them, because he was of a spare habit, had a soft and white skin, suffered from distemper in the head, and was subject to epileptic fits, a trouble which first attacked him, we are told, in Corduba." – *Lives*, pg. 483

"Apelles, however, did not reproduce his (Alexander's) complexion, but made it too dark and swarthy. Whereas he (Alexander) was of a fair colour, as they say." – *Lives*, pg. 231

Edgar Allen Poe

"The self-same Saxon current animates the British and the American heart."
– *The Poets and Poetry of America* (Text-02), the *Boston Miscellany of Literature and Fashion* (Boston, MA), vol. II, November 1842, pgs. 218-221

Matthew Poole

"But if any provide not for his own, and specially for those of his own house: here is a manifest distinction between his own, idiwn, and his own household, oikeiwn, they are distinguished by terms in the Greek, and as to the care which men and women ought to extend to them. By his own he means his relations, all of a man's family or stock; by his own household, he seemeth to mean those who cohabit with him. The apostle saith that he who is careless of providing for the former, (so far as he is able), but especially for the latter, hath denied the Christian faith, that is, in the practice of it, though in words he professeth it; he liveth not up to the rule of the gospel, which directeth other things." – *Commentary on 1 Timothy* 5:8, pg. 784

"Iure naturae servitus poena peccati gravioris."
[72] – *Synopsis Criticorum*, Genesis 9

Alexander Pope

"The stoic husband was the glorious thing . The man had courage, was a sage, ' tis true, And lov'd his country."
– Epilogue to *Rowe's Jane Shore*

Pope Benedict XVI

"Europe seems to have become empty inside, paralyzed almost, in a certain sense, by a crisis in her circulatory system ... which undermines her life. But we want to treat this with transplants which can only end in abolishing her identity. Along with her decreasing spiritual strength, is the fact that, ethnically speaking, Europe appears to be endangered." – *Europe, Its Foundations, Today And Tomorrow*, pg. 25

---

72   Latin for: "Slavery to the law of nature is the penalty of a graver sin."

"Countries should keep vigilant to preserve and develop their own culture, never letting it be absorbed by others or drown in a dull uniformity."– *Serving National Identity*, speech at Lourdes, 14 September 2008.

Pope John Paul II

"By receiving and inheriting faith and the values and elements that make up the culture of your society and the history of your nation, each one of you is spiritually endowed in your individual humanity.... We must do everything we can to accept this spiritual inheritance, to confirm it, maintain it and increase it." – *Dilecti Amici*

"If we ask where patriotism appears in the Decalogue, the reply comes without hesitation: it is covered by the Fourth Commandment, which obliges us to honor our father and mother." – *Memory and Identity: Conversations at the Dawn of a Millennium*, pg. 65

"Catholic social doctrine speaks of 'natural societies,' indicating that both the family and the nation have a particular bond with human nature, which has a social dimension. Every society's formation takes place in and through the family: of this there can be no doubt. Yet something similar could also be said about the nation. The cultural and historical identity of any society is preserved and nourished by all that is contained within this concept of nation." – *Memory and Identity: Conversations at the Dawn of a Millennium*, pg. 67

"The mystery of the Incarnation, the foundation of the Church, belongs to the theology of nation." – *Memory and Identity: Conversations at the Dawn of a Millennium*, pg. 71

"Patriotism, as love for the homeland, recognizes in all other nations the same rights that the patriot claims for his own land and it forms therefore a path toward an ordered societal love." – *Memory and Identity: Conversations at the Dawn of a Millennium*, pg. 72

"The Gospel gave a new meaning to the concept of native land ... The inheritance we receive from Christ orients the patrimony of human native lands and cultures towards the eternal homeland." – *Memory and Identity: Personal Reflections*, pgs. 68-69

— Pope John Paul II —

"Yet it still seems that nation and native land, like the family, are permanent realities ... 'natural' societies, indicating that both the family and the nation have a particular bond with human nature, which has a social dimension. ... The cultural and historical identity of any society is preserved and nourished by all that is contained within this concept of 'nation.'" – *Memory and Identity: Personal Reflections*, pg. 60

"The primordial right of man is to live in his homeland." But this right "only becomes effective if you get the factors driving emigration under control." – *Speech to the 4th World Congress on Migration*, 1998.

Pope John XXIII

"'The Church of Jesus Christ,' as Our Predecessor Pius XII observed with such penetration, 'is the repository of His wisdom; she is certainly too wise to discourage or belittle those peculiarities and differences which mark out one nation from another. It is quite legitimate for nations to treat those differences as a sacred inheritance and guard them at all costs. The Church aims at unity, a unity determined and kept alive by that supernatural love which should be actuating everybody; she does not aim at a uniformity which would only be external in its effects and would cramp the natural tendencies of the nations concerned. Every nation has its own genius, its own qualities, springing from the hidden roots of its being. The wise development, the encouragement within limits, of that genius, those qualities, does no harm; and if a nation cares to take precautions, to lay down rules, for that end, it has the Church's approval. She is mother enough to befriend such projects with her prayers.'" – *Mater et Magistra*, pg. 181

Pope Leo XIII

"Nature did not form society in order that man should seek in it his last end, but in order that in it and through it he should find suitable aids whereby to attain to his own perfection." – *Sapientiae Christianae*

"...even nations and empires themselves cannot long remain unharmed, since, when Christian institutions and morality decline, the main foundation of human society goes together with them. Force alone will remain to preserve public tranquillity and order. But force is very feeble when the bulwark of religion has been removed, and, being more apt to beget slavery than obedience, it bears within itself the germs of ever-increasing troubles." – *Sapientiae Christianae*

"Now, if the natural law enjoins us to love devotedly and to defend the country in which we had birth, and in which we were brought up, so that every good citizen hesitates not to face death for his native land, very much more is it the urgent duty of Christians to be ever quickened by like feelings toward the Church. For the Church is the holy City of the living God, born of God Himself, and by Him built up and established. Upon this earth, indeed, she accomplishes her pilgrimage, but by instructing and guiding men she summons them to eternal happiness. We are bound, then, to love dearly the country whence we have received the means of enjoyment this mortal life affords, but we have a much more urgent obligation to love, with ardent love, the Church to which we owe the life of the soul, a life that will endure forever. For fitting it is to prefer the good of the soul to the well-being of the body, inasmuch as duties toward God are of a far more hallowed character than those toward men." – *Sapientiae Christianae*

"Moreover, if we would judge aright, the supernatural love for the Church and the natural love of our own country proceed from the same eternal principle, since God Himself is their Author and originating Cause. Consequently, it follows that between the duties they respectively enjoin, neither can come into collision with the other. We can, certainly, and should love ourselves, bear ourselves kindly toward our fellow men, nourish affection for the State and the governing powers; but at the same time we can and must cherish toward the Church a feeling of filial piety, and love God with the deepest love of which we are capable." – *Sapientiae Christianae*

"Hallowed, therefore, in the minds of Christians is the very idea of public authority, in which they recognize some likeness and symbol as it were of the Divine Majesty, even when it is exercised by one unworthy. A just and due reverence to the laws abides in them, not from force and threats, but from a consciousness of duty; 'for God hath not given us the spirit of fear.'" – *Sapientiae Christianae*

"From God has the duty been assigned to the Church not only to interpose resistance, if at any time the State rule should run counter to religion, but, further, to make a strong endeavor that the power of the Gospel may pervade the law and institutions of the nations. And inasmuch as the destiny of the State depends mainly on the disposition of those who are at the head of affairs, it follows that the Church cannot give countenance or favor to those whom she knows to be imbued with a spirit of hostility to her; who refuse openly to respect her rights; who make it their aim and purpose to tear asunder the alliance that should, by the very nature of things, connect the interests of religion with those of the State. On the contrary, she is (as she is bound to be) the upholder of those who are themselves imbued with the right way of thinking as to the relations between Church and State, and who strive to make them work in perfect accord for the common good." – *Sapientiae Christianae*

"The Church alike and the State, doubtless, both possess individual sovereignty; hence, in the carrying out of public affairs, neither obeys the other within the limits to which each is restricted by its constitution. It does not hence follow, however, that Church and State are in any manner severed, and still less antagonistic, Nature, in fact, has given us not only physical existence, but moral life likewise." – *Sapientiae Christianae*

"But although all citizens, without exception, can and ought to contribute to that common good in which individuals share so advantageously to themselves, yet it should not be supposed that all can contribute in the like way and to the same extent. No matter what changes may occur in forms of government, there will ever be differences and inequalities of condition in the State. Society cannot exist or be conceived of without them." – *Rerum Novarum*

"No human law can abolish the natural and original right of marriage, nor in any way limit the chief and principal purpose of marriage ordained by God's authority from the beginning: 'Increase and multiply.' Hence we have the family, the 'society' of a man's house – a society very small, one must admit, but none the less a true society, and one older than any State. Consequently, it has rights and duties peculiar to itself which are quite independent of the State." – *Rerum Novarum*

"It is a most sacred law of nature that a father should provide food and all necessaries for those whom he has begotten; and, similarly, it is natural that he should wish that his children, who carry on, so to speak, and continue his personality, should be by him provided with all that is needful to enable them to keep themselves decently from want and misery amid the uncertainties of this mortal life. Now, in no other way can a father effect this except by the ownership of productive property, which he can transmit to his children by inheritance. A family, no less than a State, is, as We have said, a true society, governed by an authority peculiar to itself, that is to say, by the authority of the father." – *Rerum Novarum*

"The contention, then, that the civil government should at its option intrude into and exercise intimate control over the family and the household is a great and pernicious error... In like manner, if within the precincts of the household there occur grave disturbance of mutual rights, public authority should intervene to force each party to yield to the other its proper due; for this is not to deprive citizens of their rights, but justly and properly to safeguard and

strengthen them. But the rulers of the commonwealth must go no further; here, nature bids them stop. Paternal authority can be neither abolished nor absorbed by the State; for it has the same source as human life itself. 'The child belongs to the father,' and is, as it were, the continuation of the father's personality; and speaking strictly, the child takes its place in civil society, not of its own right, but in its quality as member of the family in which it is born. And for the very reason that 'the child belongs to the father' it is, as St. Thomas Aquinas says, 'before it attains the use of free will, under the power and the charge of its parents.' The socialists, therefore, in setting aside the parent and setting up a State supervision, act against natural justice, and destroy the structure of the home." – *Rerum Novarum*

"Of these duties, the following bind the proletarian and the worker: fully and faithfully to perform the work which has been freely and equitably agreed upon; never to injure the property, nor to outrage the person, of an employer; never to resort to violence in defending their own cause, nor to engage in riot or disorder; and to have nothing to do with men of evil principles, who work upon the people with artful promises of great results, and excite foolish hopes which usually end in useless regrets and grievous loss. The following duties bind the wealthy owner and the employer: not to look upon their work people as their bondsmen, but to respect in every man his dignity as a person ennobled by Christian character. They are reminded that, according to natural reason and Christian philosophy, working for gain is creditable, not shameful, to a man, since it enables him to earn an honorable livelihood; but to misuse men as though they were things in the pursuit of gain, or to value them solely for their physical powers – that is truly shameful and inhuman. Again justice demands that, in dealing with the working man, religion and the good of his soul must be kept in mind. Hence, the employer is bound to see that the worker has time for his religious duties; that he be not exposed to corrupting influences and dangerous occasions; and that he be not led away to neglect his home and family, or to squander his earnings. Furthermore, the employer must never tax his work people beyond their strength, or employ them in work unsuited to their sex and age. His great and principal duty is to give every one what is just." – *Rerum Novarum*

"Let the working man and the employer make free agreements, and in particular let them agree freely as to the wages; nevertheless, there underlies a dictate of natural justice more imperious and ancient than any bargain between man and man, namely, that wages ought not to be insufficient to support a frugal and well-behaved wage-earner. If through necessity or fear of a worse evil the workman accept harder conditions because an employer or contractor will afford him no better, he is made the victim of force and injustice." – *Rerum Novarum*

— Pope Leo XIII —

"The consciousness of his own weakness urges man to call in aid from without. We read in the pages of holy Writ: 'It is better that two should be together than one; for they have the advantage of their society. If one fall he shall be supported by the other. Woe to him that is alone, for when he falleth he hath none to lift him up.' And further: 'A brother that is helped by his brother is like a strong city.' It is this natural impulse which binds men together in civil society; and it is likewise this which leads them to join together in associations which are, it is true, lesser and not independent societies, but, nevertheless, real societies." – *Rerum Novarum*

"The fact that God has given the earth for the use and enjoyment of the whole human race can in no way be a bar to the owning of private property. For God has granted the earth to mankind in general, not in the sense that all without distinction can deal with it as they like, but rather that no part of it was assigned to any one in particular, and that the limits of private possession have been left to be fixed by man's own industry, and by the laws of individual races. Moreover, the earth, even though apportioned among private owners, ceases not thereby to minister to the needs of all, inasmuch as there is not one who does not sustain life from what the land produces. Those who do not possess the soil contribute their labor; hence, it may truly be said that all human subsistence is derived either from labor on one's own land, or from some toil, some calling, which is paid for either in the produce of the land itself, or in that which is exchanged for what the land brings forth." – *Rerum Novarum*

"Man's natural instinct moves him to live in civil society, for he cannot, if dwelling apart, provide himself with the necessary requirements of life, nor procure the means of developing his mental and moral faculties. Hence, it is divinely ordained that he should lead his life–be it family, or civil–with his fellow men, amongst whom alone his several wants can be adequately supplied. But, as no society can hold together unless some one be over all, directing all to strive earnestly for the common good, every body politic must have a ruling authority, and this authority, no less than society itself, has its source in nature, and has, consequently, God for its Author." – *Immortale Dei*

"They, therefore, who rule should rule with evenhanded justice, not as masters, but rather as fathers, for the rule of God over man is most just, and is tempered always with a father's kindness. Government should, moreover, be administered for the well-being of the citizens, because they who govern others possess authority solely for the welfare of the State. Furthermore, the civil power must not be subservient to the advantage of any one individual or of some few persons, inasmuch as it was established for the common good of all." – *Immortale Dei*

"...civil society, established for the common welfare, should not only safeguard the well-being of the community, but have also at heart the interests of its individual members, in such mode as not in any way to hinder, but in every manner to render as easy as may be, the possession of that highest and unchangeable good for which all should seek. Wherefore, for this purpose, care must especially be taken to preserve unharmed and unimpeded the religion whereof the practice is the link connecting man with God." – *Immortale Dei*

Pope Paul VI

"In His gracious goodness, God has seen to it that what He had revealed for the salvation of all nations would abide perpetually in its full integrity and be handed on to all generations. Therefore Christ the Lord, in whom the full revelation of the supreme God is brought to completion (see 2 Cor. 1:20; 3:13; 4:6), commissioned the Apostles to preach to all men that Gospel which is the source of all saving truth and moral teaching, and to impart to them heavenly gifts." – *Dei Verbum*

"It follows that though there are many nations there is but one people of God, which takes its citizens from every race, making them citizens of a kingdom which is of a heavenly rather than of an earthly nature. All the faithful, scattered though they be throughout the world, are in communion with each other in the Holy Spirit, and so, he who dwells in Rome knows that the people of India are his members. Since the kingdom of Christ is not of this world the Church or people of God in establishing that kingdom takes nothing away from the temporal welfare of any people. On the contrary it fosters and takes to itself, insofar as they are good, the ability, riches and customs in which the genius of each people expresses itself. Taking them to itself it purifies, strengthens, elevates and ennobles them." – *Lumen Gentium*

Pope Pius X

"Yes, your country is worthy not only of love but of predilection, whose sacred name awakens in your minds the dearest memories and thrills all the fibers of your soul, this common land which has been your cradle and to which the bonds of blood and that other more noble community of affections and traditions attach you." – *Principles for Peace*, pg. 121

Pope Pius XI

"While it is true that the race or the people, the State or a particular form of government, the representatives of the civil power, or other fundamental elements of human society have an essential and honorable place in the natural order, nevertheless, if anyone detaches them from this scale of earthly values and exalts them as the supreme norm and standard of all things, even of religious values, deifying them with idolatrous worship, he perverts and falsifies the order of things created and constituted by God, and is far from true faith in God and from a conception of life in conformity therewith … our God is the personal God, transcendent, almighty, infinitely perfect, One in the Trinity of Persons and Three in the Unity of the Divine Essence, Creator of the Universe, Lord, King and ultimate purpose of the history of the world, Who does not suffer and can never suffer any other divinity beside Him … only superficial minds can fall into the error of speaking of a national God of a national religion, of foolishly attempting to restrict within the narrow confines of a single race, that God, Who is the Creator of the world, the King and Lawgiver of all peoples, before Whose greatness the nations are as small as drops of water in a bucket." – *Mit Brennender Sorge*

"Whoever exalts race, or the people, or the State, or a particular form of State, or the depositories of power, or any other fundamental value of the human community – however necessary and honorable be their function in worldly things – whoever raises these notions above their standard value and divinizes them to an idolatrous level, distorts and perverts an order of the world planned and created by God; he is far from the true faith in God and from the concept of life which that faith upholds." – *Mit Brennender Sorge*

"Faith in Christ cannot maintain itself pure and unalloyed without the support of faith in the Church, 'the pillar and ground of the truth' (1 Tim. iii. 15); for Christ Himself, God eternally blessed, raised this pillar of the Faith. His command to hear the Church (Matt. xviii. 15), to welcome in the words and commands of the Church His own words and His own commands (Luke x. 16), is addressed to all men, of all times and of all countries. The Church founded by the Redeemer is one, the same for all races and all nations. Beneath her dome, as beneath the vault of heaven, there is but one country for all nations and tongues; there is room for the development of every quality, advantage, task and vocation which God the Creator and Savior has allotted to individuals as well as to ethnical communities. The Church's maternal heart is big enough to see in the God-appointed development of individual characteristics and gifts, more than a mere danger of divergency. She rejoices at the spiritual superiorities among individuals and nations. In their successes she sees with maternal joy and pride fruits of education and progress, which she can only bless and encourage, whenever she can conscientiously do so." – *Mit Brennender Sorge*

"No one would think of preventing young Germans establishing a true ethnical community in a noble love of freedom and loyalty to their country. What We object to is the voluntary and systematic antagonism raised between national education and religious duty. ...He who sings hymns of loyalty to this terrestrial country should not, for that reason, become unfaithful to God and His Church, or a deserter and traitor to His heavenly country....You are often told about the human deficiencies which mar the history of the Church: why ignore the exploits which fill her history, the saints she begot, the blessing that came upon Western civilization from the union between that Church and your people?" – *Mit Brennender Sorge*

Pope Pius XII

"And the nations, despite a difference of development due to diverse conditions of life and of culture, are not destined to break the unity of the human race, but rather to enrich and embellish it by the sharing of their own peculiar gifts and by that reciprocal interchange of goods which can be possible and efficacious only when a mutual love and a lively sense of charity unite all the sons of the same Father and all those redeemed by the same Divine Blood." – *Summi Pontificatus*, 43

"The Church of Christ, the faithful depository of the teaching of Divine Wisdom, cannot and does not think of deprecating or disdaining the particular characteristics which each people, with jealous and intelligible pride, cherishes and

retains as a precious heritage. Her aim is a supernatural union in all-embracing love, deeply felt and practiced, and not the unity which is exclusively external and superficial and by that very fact weak." – *Summi Pontificatus*, 44

"The Church hails with joy and follows with her maternal blessing every method of guidance and care which aims at a wise and orderly evolution of particular forces and tendencies having their origin in the individual character of each race, provided that they are not opposed to the duties incumbent on men from their unity of origin and common destiny." – *Summi Pontificatus*, 45

"Nor is there any fear lest the consciousness of universal brotherhood aroused by the teaching of Christianity, and the spirit which it inspires, be in contrast with love of traditions or the glories of one's fatherland, or impede the progress of prosperity or legitimate interests. For that same Christianity teaches that in the exercise of charity we must follow a God-given order, yielding the place of honor in our affections and good works to those who are bound to us by special ties. Nay, the Divine Master Himself gave an example of this preference for His Own country and fatherland, as He wept over the coming destruction of the Holy City. But legitimate and well-ordered love of our native country should not make us close our eyes to the all-embracing nature of Christian Charity, which calls for consideration of others and of their interests in the pacifying light of love." – *Summi Pontificatus*, 49

"The charge laid by God on parents to provide for the material and spiritual good of their offspring and to procure for them a suitable training saturated with the true spirit of religion, cannot be wrested from them without grave violation of their rights.

"Undoubtedly, that formation should aim as well at the preparation of youth to fulfill with intelligent understanding and pride those offices of a noble patriotism which give to one's earthly fatherland all due measure of love, self-devotion and service. But, on the other hand, a formation which forgot or, worse still, deliberately neglected to direct the eyes and hearts of youth to the heavenly country would be an injustice to youth, an injustice against the inalienable duties and rights of the Christian family and an excess to which a check must be opposed, in the interests even of the people and of the State itself." – *Summi Pontificatus, 66-67*

"A disposition, in fact, of the divinely sanctioned natural order divides the human race into social groups, nations or States, which are mutually independent in organization and in the direction of their internal life. But for all that, the human race is bound together by reciprocal ties, moral and juridical, into a great commonwealth directed to the good of all nations and ruled by special laws which protect its unity and promote its prosperity." – *Summi Pontificatus, 72*

"Catholic doctrine urges Catholics to nourish a profound and sincere love towards their homeland….We proclaim that the Christian does not cede and cannot cede to anyone the true love and fidelity toward his earthly homeland." – *Ad Apostolorum Principis*

Pope Urban II

"Oh race of the Franks, we learn that in some of your provinces no one can venture on the road by day or by night without injury or attack by highwaymen, and no one is secure even at home. Let us then re-enact the law of our ancestors known as the Truce of God. And now that you have promised to maintain the peace among yourselves you are obligated to succour your brethren in the East, menaced by an accursed race, utterly alienated from God. The Holy Sepulchre of our Lord is polluted by the filthiness of an unclean nation. Recall the greatness of Charlemagne. O most valiant soldiers, descendants of invincible ancestors, be not degenerate. Let all hatred depart from among you, all quarrels end, all wars cease. Start upon the road to the Holy Sepulchre to wrest that land from the wicked race and subject it to yourselves." – preaching to knights, lords, etc. to embark on the crusades in 1095. Quoted in Bainton, *Christian Attitudes Toward War and Peace*, pg. 111

Stanley E. Porter

"Here Paul expresses the terrible implications of not caring for one's own: It amounts to a denial of Christianity and an action and attitude worse than that of an unbeliever…. Contrasted with οἰκείων by means of the emphasis provided by καὶ μάλιστα, τῶν ἰδίων refers to the larger family relationship and corresponds to the reference to 'grandchildren' (ἔκγονα) in v. 4. Similarly, plural οἰκείων (Gal. 6:10; Eph. 2:19; 1 Tim. 5:8) has the meaning here 'members of the household' in the sense of 'his immediate family.'" – *The Pastoral Epistles: A Commentary on the Greek Text*, pgs. 220-221

John Poynet

"And men ought to have more respect to their country, than to their prince: to the commonwealth, than to any one person. For the country and commonwealth is a degree above the king. Next unto God, men ought to love their country, and the whole commonwealth before any member of it: as kings and princes (be they ever so great) are but members: and commonwealths may withstand well enough and flourish, albeit there be no kings, but to the contrary, without a commonwealth there can be no king." – *A Shorte Treatise Of Politike Power*, quoted in *The Genevan Reformation and the American Founding*, pg. 184

Vern Poythress

"See, people are trying to get unity between cultures in all kinds of false and counterfeit ways. And that won't work, of course. Although, they may do some temporary good here and there. But what the vision of the Bible is, is these diverse nations and peoples and individuals all praising God and all contributing to that gigantic chorus of praise which is richer than any one voice." – *Interview, Reformed Forum, Christ the Center* [73]

Presbyterian Joint Address

"We cannot condemn a man, in one breath, as unfaithful to the most solemn earthly interests, his country and his race, and commend him in the next as a loyal and faithful servant of his God. If we distrust his patriotism, our confidence is apt to be very measured in his piety." – *Joint Address of the First General Assembly of the Presbyterian Church in the Confederate States of America*, pg. 52

---

[73] c.f. Poythress on Babel

Guillaume Groen Van Prinsterer

"Just as all truth rests upon the truth that is from God, so the common foundation of all rights and duties lies in the sovereignty of God. When that sovereignty is denied or (what amounts to the same thing) banished to heaven because His kingdom is not of this world, what becomes then of the fountain of authority, of law, of every sacred and dutiful relation in state, society and family? What sanction remains for the distinctions of rank and station in life? What reason can there be that I obey another's commands, that the one is needy, the other rich? All this is custom, routine, abuse, injustice, oppression. Eliminate God, and it can no longer be denied that all men are, in the revolutionary sense of the words, free and equal. State and society disintegrate, for there is a principle of dissolution at work that does not cease to operate until all further division is frustrated by that indivisible unit, that isolated human being, the individual—a term of the Revolution – naively expressive of its all-destructive character."
Unbelief and Revolution, lect. 9, quoted in *Selected Studies*, pg. 28

"All people are equal. This is not true; equality is, much like the common liberty, unachievable. The people are not free. In fact, by virtue of the nature and society, they are placed in various relations which entail either authority or submission. A proposed liberty which destroys these relations would lead to a licentiousness which in itself would make true liberty impossible and arbitrariness and coercion inevitable. The people are not equal. In fact, in terms of the abilities of body and spirit, in the tendencies of character, in eagerness, in courage, and in perseverance, deviations exist whereby providence has established the differences in class, position, rank, and financial abilities. In this, the organic growth and health of society is manifested. If you attempt to erase the outcomes of these inequalities, there will only arise new inequalities. Do you know what was meant by earlier generations when they mentioned 'equality'? That everyone was equal before the law and that there was no respecter of persons when it came to applying the law—all while remaining in harmony with the variety of ranks that made up a given society and provided the foundations of each state. Men even regarded these inequalities as things that cannot be

missed and which are in everyone's interest. People thought that there ought to be differences in terms of property and pleasure on earth, and that the abundance of the rich was necessary for the wealth of the middle class, whereas the wealth of the middle class, in turn, was a guarantee against the impoverishment of the laborers' class. They were also convinced that the rights with regard to and influence on the organization of the state were to stand in relation to these inequalities of rank and financial abilities and that through these means alone the stability and durability of those institutions desirable for both the strong and the weak could be guaranteed.

"They were especially aware of the fact that for the difficult art of governance, special knowledge and talents were required and that not everyone was equipped thereunto. Moreover, that it was in the interest of all to be governed by the most able. Especially with regard to this aspect, the general opinion has now changed. Everyone must now be equal in terms of the governing of the state. This is embodied in the ideal of universal franchise." – *Liberty, Equality, Fraternity: A Refutation of Liberalism*

"Historians, in forsaking Christianity, abandon the very notion of a personal God, and along with history's religious character. The true soul and drive of many historical figures are thereby completely ignored, and historical events and achievements are exclusively explained by means of secondary causes. An example can be taken from the writings of someone who is not an enemy of Christianity by any stretch of the imagination. Europe has Christianity to thank for its supremacy over other parts of the world. Before it became civilized by virtue of the gospel, large parts of the continent remained uncultivated and were roamed by barbarian hordes. Yet how is this European supremacy explained by [the German historian] Heeren? What does he regard as the main cause of this spiritual and moral primacy? 'Europe had a distinct indigenous character as white nations,' he writes. The white nations are probably endowed with higher aptitudes, but in order to maintain a view in which the main reason for our advancement is sought in our physical traits, he often regards as European the origin of things which must much rather be sought in Asia. Europe has been civilized by Asia: the Greek civilization was largely eastern; the arts and sciences had, forgotten

in Europe, flourished under the Arabs. And, as long as the dominance of Christianity was not appreciated, the people of the East would have been able to build a dominant civilization. Europe has been shaped by the gospel – our supremacy and civilization would have been lost, if it had not found fruitful soil in our part of the world. It would have been more reasonable had Heeren, in appreciating our racial characteristics, not concealed the impact of Christianity."
– *Proeve over de middelen waardoor de waarheid wordt gekend en gestaafd* (1858), pg. 49. Translated by Adi Schlebusch

Nicholas Pringle

"My own experience is; The first 25 years after the war we spent building a family and their security, it then became obvious that the politicians had taken over our lives. Today in my doltage, I have many, many misgivings on how matters have turned out. Problems seem to be resolved, by more and more legislation, instead of action at the source. Our women today have been conned into going out to work, and they are still required to do most of the chores as before, except the education of children. They no longer seem to have the skills of cooking, how to discipline children, resulting in junk food (no time for cooking) over-viewing of T.V and computers. The families are no longer as close as we were. We notice on our many trips to the old battlefields how close the Italian families are. The children of today are ill dressed, scruffy, and unable to communicate. Not their fault. What many veterans abhor, is the acceptance of homosexuality as the norm. It goes against our Christian teachings, and in our youth it was a serious offence. We went to war to defend our beloved country, our families and our faith." – letter from WWII British soldier, John Clarke MBE, The Monte Cassino Veterans Association, in *The Unknown Warriors*, pg. 16

[After WWII was over]...
"We settled in my home village of Marston Green. Of course we had a motor-cycle, then a side car as the children came along, then a car when we had 3 children. When the Health Service started, and the Common Market life was satisfactory, everything looked hopeful, but things got worse. I think it was in the early '80's' the rot set in. We started to lose all our industry,

profit and money became the only aim in life.
"Immigration became a big problem to the 'man in the street'. Charles [the WWII British veteran and husband of the woman writing the letter] often said that his years in the Army and especially his friends lives, were wasted. He said 'They stole seven years of my life and what for?' He felt that all the values of a decent, law abiding, peaceful life were disappearing, he got quite bitter about it sometimes. It is now 18 years since I lost him and as I look around parts of Birmingham today you would never know you were in England. He would have hated it ...
"Some of the things today that I and a lot of my veteran friends disagree with are same sex marriages, school girl mothers, rubbish TV programmes, so called celebrities, and most of all, unlimited immigration. I am very unhappy about the way this country is being transformed. I go nowhere after dark, I don't even answer my doorbell then. My husband used to say he wouldn't want to come back to this world, and that was before 1988, I fear it is much worse now.
"Thank you for giving me this opportunity to give you my views. I am sorry it sounds so miserable for I usually have a smile on my face. I lead a full life and have lots of good friends and family and make the best of things. It is hidden inside me that I worry about my grandchildren's future." – letter from Mrs. M. Moulds, wife of Charles Moulds, WWII British soldier, in *The Unknown Warriors*, pgs. 18-19

"I was 15 years old when the war started, 21 when it finished and I really remember England as a 'green and pleasant land', but not any more. I was born and brought up in Essex, near Epping Forest, and recall being able to walk and have picnics there without fear for our safety, but I wouldn't dream of doing it now on my visit there. I think England is now crime ridden. Far too many immigrants who come to this country cause trouble and have no wish to integrate, but only grumble about our way of life. We have many incidents here in Lowestoft of our own yobs and slobs causing harrasment to home owners and the police seem powerless to stop them or are disinterested in their antics. There is no discipline at home or in schools and teenagers appear to roam the streets at all hours putting many people in fear of their lives. Oh for the England our soldiers fought for and loved, but I fear it has all gone wrong and it's too late to do anything about it. I can only say I am glad I am at the end of my life and not the beginning, but I have real worries for my granddaughter and great granddaughter as to how they will survive. One of the worst things we ever did was to join the Common Market in my opinion." – letter from "A very disgruntled Englishwoman" in *The Unknown Warriors*, pg. 28

"I found it very difficult to readjust to civilian life. Firstly civilians and I were a world apart, they had no idea of our experiences. Work was very difficult to explain. I married soon after my demob. I managed to sustain myself, wife and child through great hardship for many years but it was a struggle.

"I am now retired and in my 80's. It is very sad to see this country being run and taken over by foreigners who have no right or business to be here at all. Successive governments have literally 'sold us up the river'. Being an Englishman it is galling to feel that I and thousands of dead and living service personnel feel badly let down whilst this country is pandering to the so called refugees and immigrants who take advantage of benefits, which we have earned and paid for in our taxes.

"Our children are not taught our true history or our Christian heritage, which is being withered away. It is disappointing that we have a government of 'wimps and twits' (I could use stronger language). Many of my age group and many younger people I have talked to are very angry that all we fought for is being whittled down to accommodate people, who have their own country and customs, and who come here to tell us what to do. It is time to call a halt before there is serious civil unrest on a large scale." – letter from D.G. Hull, former WWII British soldier, in *The Unknown Warriors*, pgs. 36-37

"I served in the Army, in the D.L.I (Durham Light Infantry) for about 4 years. I was overseas for 3 1/2 years in Italy and Austria. Upon demob I served a further 4 years in the T.A (REME). The dumbing down of public opinion continues into most debates involving race and ethnic religions. These subjects are not for discussion by ordinary people. Government ministers, police chiefs, community leaders, and race relation overlords seem to be the sole arbiters of these subjects. Anyone disagreeing

with their 'overview' is immediately classed as 'rabble rousing', 'Little Englanders' or racist and very definitely not politically correct. Our British culture is draining away at an ever increasing pace and we are almost forbidden to make any comment.

"It is time to be completely pragmatic and acknowledge that too many of our politicians of all parties are corrupt beyond redemption. Not only have the norms of decency diminished, but sadly, also the nurtured probity and inherent patriotism, once expected of all M.P.s. Like most of my generation I fail to understand what motivates the current leader of the Conservative party. Hug a hooded 'mugger'! Forget you once fought for your country and change your perspective to accommodate the madness that this leader espouses! New Labour 'sold' the British people the idea of a 'sleaze' free government based on the principles and honesty. Sadly we have known only liars, incompetents, and self aggrandizing charlatans, at the head of the nation's affairs.

"So far as I can recall no-one voted for or requested ethnic or cultural changes to our society, so who precisely benefits by allowing hundreds of thousands (or even millions) of people, about who we know nothing to enter our country. Why do our political elite insist in thwarting the will of the majority of voters by recommending ever closer union. What is demonstrated is a traitorous desire to permit foreigners to have a say in how Britain is governed. It is even suggested that this would be in our best interests. Never in the history of our island has it been less than traitorous to suggest that foreigners govern us." – letter from Mr. V. Turner, former WWII British soldier, in *The Unknown Warriors*, pgs. 33-34

Emberson Edward Proper

"For a period of several years, beginning with 1656, the records of the Massachusetts Bay Colony, and indeed of all of the New England Colonies, except Rhode Island, are filled with legislation designed to prevent the coming of the Quakers and the spread of their 'accursed tenets.' Whippings, imprisonment, banishment, and in a few instances capital punishment, were the order of the day. To what extent these various laws restricted the immigration of this sect, it is, of course, impossible to ascertain. That they were not prohibitive, and consequently did not meet the expectations of the authorities, is painfully evident; for, in spite of the severe penalties, members of that sect continued to come ... There can be but little doubt, however, that many Quakers were deterred from immigrating to these inhospitable shores; while, judging from the throngs that afterward poured into Pennsylvania and the Jerseys, it is fair to presume that, had they received a welcome to the New England Colonies ... a very considerable number would have found homes in that section." – *Colonial Immigration Laws*, pg. 25.

"The charter of the Massachusetts Bay Company contained no direct or implied reference to Catholics, and nearly a quarter of a century passed before laws aimed at their exclusion were passed; though it is very probable that none of that persuasion were permitted to live in either of the Massachusetts Colonies. The order giving magistrates full authority over the admission of immigrants, could easily be made to exclude all persons professing obedience to the Church of Rome. The French Catholics had made settlements in the valley of the St. Lawrence and on the shores of Nova Scotia long before the establishment of permanent colonies in New England; and ten years before the landing of the Pilgrims, the Jesuits had made their way to the French settlements. From that time until the American Revolution, this strange sect, largely because of their influence over the Indians, became the terror of the frontier settlers, and their presence in any of the colonies was an occasion for alarm and distrust." – *Colonial Immigration Laws*, pgs. 25, 26.

"It seems a fair inference, from the writings of the founders of the Massachusetts Bay Colony, and from a careful study of their early government, that it was their aim to found a state based on the Scriptures, interpreted strictly according to their own ideas. Accordingly, it seemed wise and even essential that all persons differing in matters of faith and worship should be prohibited from settling amongst them." – *Colonial Immigration Laws*, pg. 22.

Iain Provan

"The passage itself makes clear, however, that this darkness (lit., "blackness") of skin is not something with which she has been born, but a coloring that has come about as a result of exposure to the sun. The situation is somewhat like that in Job 30:30, where Job's skin grows black (šḥr, as in Song 1:5–6) as a result of the heat of a fever. We should also note Job 30:28, where it is said that Job goes about "blackened" (qdr), but not by the sun (implying that "blackening" by the sun is a fairly normal phenomenon)..."

"There is no evidence in the text, then, that the female speaker is racially distinguishable from those who observe her. It is simply that her life has been lived outdoors, and she has consequently been scorched by the sun, which has "gazed" at her (Heb. šzp, as in Job 20:9; 28:7) long before humans ever stared at her. This is why she is dissimilar from these other women who have lived (we deduce) a more secluded life." – *NIV Application Commentary*, *Ecclesiastes, Song of Songs*, 1:6, pgs. 410-411

Alexander Pushkin

On the beauty of the Russian landscape:
"But ever lovelier are the woods,
In autumn, when the silent grief
Of nature clothes each lonely leaf."
– *Eugene Onegin* (ch. 2, st. 27) [74]

On Russian culture:
"In winter all was gaiety
And stir: the neighbours, driving by,
Would halt, and in a trice the hall
Resounded with a festival,
With French and Russian songs, and talk,
And the bold mazurka's call."
– *Eugene Onegin* (ch. 1, st. 16) [75]

On Russian history:
"Peter's epoch he admires:
Of Catherine's times he has no doubt;
But most he loves the present hours,
And, like the age, hates retrospection:
He laughs at all that came before,
Sighs for the future, but at present
He lives, he loves, he drinks and jests."
– *Eugene Onegin* (ch. 1, st. 45)

---

74 a novel in verse that touches upon various aspects of Russian life, including the landscape, culture, and history.
75 This quote captures the festive atmosphere and social gatherings that were a significant part of Russian culture during the 19th century, with music, dancing, and conversations in both French and Russian.

R

A. Philip Randolph

"We favor reducing [immigration] to nothing… shutting out the Germans…Italians…Hindus… Chinese…and even the Negroes from the West Indies. The country is suffering from immigration indigestion…excessive immigration is against the masses of all races and nationalities in the country." – quoted in Patrick J. Buchanan, *State of Emergency*, pg. 233

NY Times (editorial on the Immigration Act of 1924):

"It is both natural and wise that the American race wishes to preserve its unity and does not wish to see its present blend greatly changed [because it] prefers immigrants who will be easily absorbed and…it strenuously objects to the formation of alien colonies here [and not because it] adheres to silly notions of 'superior' and 'inferior' races." – quoted in Patrick J. Buchanan, *State of Emergency*, pg. 234

John Crowe Ransom

"It is out of fashion in these days to look backward rather than forward. About the only American given to it is some unreconstructed Southerner, who persists in his regard for a certain terrain, a certain history, and a certain way of living." – *I'll Take My Stand*, pg. 1

"Memories of the past are attended with a certain pain called nostalgia. It is hardly a technical term in our sociology or our psychiatry, but it might well be. Nostalgia is a kind of growing-pain, psychically speaking. It occurs to our sorrow when we have decided that it is time for us, marching to some magnificent destiny, to abandon an old home, an old provincial setting, or an old way of living to which we had become habituated. It is the complaint of human nature in its vegetative aspect, when it is plucked up by the roots from the place of its origin and transplanted in foreign soil, or even left dangling in the air. And it must be nothing else but nostalgia, the instinctive objection to being transplanted, that chiefly prevents the deracinaton of human communities and their complete geographical dispersion as the casualties of an insatiable wanderlust.

"Deracination in our Western life is the strange discipline which individuals turn upon themselves, enticed by the blandishments of such fine words as Progressive, Liberal, and Forward-looking. The progressivist says in effect: Do not allow yourself to feel homesick; form no such powerful attachments that you will feel a pain in cutting them loose; prepare your spirit to be always on the move. According to this gospel, there is no rest for the weary, not even in heaven." – *I'll Take My Stand*, pg. 7

John Randolph of Roanoke

"Anarchy is the chrysalis state of despotism; and to that state have the measures of this government long tended, amidst the professions, such as we have heard in France and seen the effects of, of Liberty, Equality, Fraternity." – Richmond Enquirer, April 1, 1815; *John Randolph of Roanoke, 1773-1833, A Biography*, pg. 418

"John Randolph, in speaking of the disposition of the Virginians, very freely cautioned us against disobliging or offending any person of note in the Colony …; for says he, either by blood or marriage, we are almost all related, and so connected in our interests, that whoever of a stranger presumes to offend any one of us will infallibly find an enemy of the whole. Nor, right or wrong, do we forsake him, till by one means or other his ruin is accomplished." – As recalled by an English immigrant named George Fisher, quoted in David Hackett Fischer's *Albion's Seed*, pg. 224

Daniel Raymond

"It is the duty of the legislator to find employment for all the people, and if he cannot find them employment in agriculture and commerce, he must set them to manufacturing. It is his duty to take special care that no other nation interferes with their industry. He is not to permit one half of the nation to remain idle and hungry, in order that the other half may buy goods where they may be had the cheapest" – *Political Economy*, 2:230-33

"Legislators, however, are not permitted to take such limited, short-sighted views of things– they move in a higher sphere–they are traitors to their high trust, if they do not look to the future, as well as the present–they are in one sense, (though, in a very humble one,) the vicegerents of God on earth...."

"The true policy of every wise legislator is, to consider the nation immortal, and to legislate for it, as though it was to exist forever; but unfortunately, most legislators act as though they thought the nation as short lived as themselves; and, instead of adopting a policy, which looks prospectively to future generations and centuries, they adopt one which look only to themselves, and the present race; and, too frequently, on which looks only to the interests of some particular individuals, or classes, in the community, instead of the the interests of the nation." – cited in Giles, *Thoughts on Political Economy; Political Miscellanies*, iss. 1, pg. 53

— REFORMERS —

The reformers drew upon biblical and classical instruction to inform their understanding of human relations. In short, their education included the foregoing material. The charges combated by the reformers from the side of Rome was that they disrupted social order, and from the side of the anabaptists or nonconformists that they did not go far enough in envisioning a new community. Their collective response has developed into a doctrine commonly known as "two kingdom theology." The reformers were not entirely unified in their conception of the gospel and society, but all recognize a "natural order of things" that the gospel does not fundamentally revolutionize.

Essentially, the two kingdoms are the visible and the invisible, the earthly and the heavenly, realms; and Christ's rule as King of kings and Lord of lords is over both kingdoms. The visible includes everything that is visible: both pastoral ministry and public magistrates, both visible church and earthly civic life. The invisible consists of the heavenly life, the eternal church. This includes the worship of God and the salvation of the soul. Thus, the church dwells both partly in the visible kingdom and partly in the invisible kingdom. Tension exists among reformed thinkers concerning how to balance this duality.

Notably, the reformed position avoids two errors: the one is the tendency to flatten everything into one kingdom, applying the politics of heaven to the political life of earth. In this view, Christ rules over all and does so in the same way.

All (should or ought to) belong to the same one kingdom, share in same ways, life, laws, means, authorities. For instance, the "political" authority in heaven is religious, therefore the political authority on earth should also be religious. Or again, in Christ there are no male and female, Greek and Jew; so on earth there should be no gender differences or no nationalities. Christ tells his (religious) disciples to be good Samaritans and care for strangers, therefore our (civil) national politics should welcome millions of immigrants and legislate extensive welfare systems. This is a flattening of heaven and earth into a religio-politics, including moral denunciations of skeptics as unChristian or "on the wrong side of Jesus." Politics, in this view, are an extension of the gospel, because the polis is an extension of heaven.

The first error is to make a complete overlap between the two kingdoms. The second error makes a complete separation of the two kingdoms with no overlap. In this second view, the earthly church and the civil society actually constitute two separate political societies. The two kingdoms are not the visible and the invisible, with Christ ruling over them both. Rather, the two kingdoms are the civil realm and the church, with Christ ruling over the church only. The civil realm is left to itself as a secular world, presumably governed by the "god of this world," the devil. Thus, society must always be viewed as other, pagan, hostile, antithetical, persecutory, etc. The church – both eternal in heaven and temporal on earth – is a separate, distinct, sovereign, and political society that stands apart from secular civil society altogether, often in "prophetic denunciation" or "moral witness" to its decline. Meanwhile, the church builds its own social life in every aspect and begins to fill the roles of the secular realm. The church is not merely a place to worship God, hear the Word, and receive the sacraments, but the locus of one's physical and social life as a new society of friends and relations, civil authority and political adjudication, natural and temporal identity. "We are not citizens of any country but of heaven." It is as though one moved to a new country, one without geography or customs; a global country where all people are one.

In contrast to these the reformers recognized that the church exists both temporally and eternally. Temporally, the church exists in the visible kingdom where natural laws adhere; such as filial loyalty, social duties and rights, peoplehood, language, customs, civil authority and national boundaries. The church also exists in the invisible kingdom governed by spiritual laws that concern worship, salvation, holiness, etc. The two have some overlap, such as morality and righteousness. But this overlap does not destroy the distinction. As Calvin said:

"Regarding our eternal salvation it is true that one must not distinguish between man and woman, or between king and a shepherd, or between a German and a Frenchman. Regarding policy however, we have what St. Paul declares here; for our Lord Jesus Christ did not come to mix up nature, or to abolish what belongs to the preservation of decency and peace among us...Regarding the kingdom of God (which is spiritual) there is no distinction or difference between man and woman, servant and master, poor and rich, great and small. Nevertheless, there does have to be some order among us, and Jesus Christ did not mean to eliminate it, as some flighty and scatterbrained dreamers believe."

– Calvin, sermon on 1 Cor. 11:2-3

Regino of Prüm

"...the various nations and peoples are distinguished from each other by descent, customs, language and laws." – quoted in *The Barbarian North in Medieval Imagination*, pg. 12

Ernest Renan

"A nation is a soul, a spiritual principle. Two things, which in truth are but one, constitute this soul or spiritual principle. One lies in the past, one in the present. One is the possession in common of a rich legacy of memories; the other is present-day consent, the desire to live together, the will to perpetuate the value of the heritage that one has received in an undivided form. Man, Gentlemen, does not improvise. The nation, like the individual, is the culmination of a long past of endeavors, sacrifice, and devotion. Of all cults, that of the ancestors is the most legitimate, for the ancestors have made us what we are. A heroic past, great men, glory (by which I understand genuine glory), this is the social capital upon which one bases a national idea. To have common glories in the past and to have a common will in the present; to have performed great deeds together, to wish to perform still more – these are the essential conditions for being a people. One loves in proportion to the sacrifices to which one has consented, and in proportion to the ills that one has suffered. One loves the house that one has built and that one has handed down. The Spartan song – 'We are what you were; we will be what you are' – is, in its simplicity, the abridged hymn of every patrie [fatherland]." – *What is a Nation?*, Sorbonne, March 11th, 1882

R.R. Reno

"Globalization is associated with economic and cultural changes that are dissolving inherited forms of solidarity—the nation foremost, but local communities, as well, and even the family. This dissolution encourages an atomistic individualism, which in turn makes all of us more vulnerable to domination and control. By my reading of the signs of the times, the dangers of dissolved solidarity in the West are far more dire than our present upsurges of ethnocentrism and nationalism. It is atomized societies that are susceptible to demagogues—not societies that enjoy strong social bonds and organic communal solidarity. Islamic extremism thrives where traditional Muslim societies are disintegrated by the pressures of globalization." – *Nationalism is Not Xenophobia*

"The fall of man left every civilization, every era under the law of entropy, which is why renewing shared loves and unifying loyalties is one of the primary arts of leadership." – *Return of the Strong Gods*, pg. 15

"The strong god of the nation draws us out of our 'little worlds.' Our shared loves—love of our land, our history, our founding myths, our warriors and heroes—raise us to a higher vantage point. We see our private interest as part of a larger whole, the 'we' that calls upon our freedom to serve the body politic with intelligence and loyalty. As Aristotle recognized, this loyalty is intrinsically fulfilling, for it satisfies the human desire for transcendence." – *Return Of The Strong Gods*, pg. 155

"A man who cannot affirm the border between male and female will find it difficult to defend a border between nations. Those who shrink from the strong god of truth are sure to see danger rather than blessing in the strong god of patriotism." – *Return of the Strong Gods*, pg. 193

"The United States is a place to which countless people have actively chosen to come. Immigration plays a central role in our history. But consent does not supersede love, and we should never let ourselves be bewitched by liberal theories into thinking that reasoned defenses for a system of government give life to a people. The ceremony by which immigrants become citizens is called naturalization. It ascribes paternity. We do not consent to our parents. Our paternity is not the consequence of reasoned assent. The same holds for our political and cultural inheritance, whether bestowed at birth or acquired later in what is best understood as civic adoption. The 'we' is never confected out of shared choices. It is always a gift conferred by shared loves. The objects of our loves in a real sense choose us, not we them." – *Return of the Strong Gods*, pg. 193

"Trump is undoubtedly a populist, as are antiestablishment politicians in Europe. At one of his campaign rallies he said, 'Our country is being run by very stupid people.' As a description of native intelligence and expertise, this is implausible. But it resonated as an attack on the political establishment. It was, in truth, a generous attack. It encouraged voters to adopt the forgiving view that they were being betrayed out of incompetence, not deliberately by Western elites who would sell them out to the win-win promises of the open economy, open culture, and open borders–promises that in reality mean only they win." – *Return of the Strong Gods*, pg. 167

"When talking to a smart graduate student in Cambridge, Massachusetts, doing work in social policy, I was not surprised to discover that he could not formulate a reason to give preference to an unemployed worker in Ohio over someone in Senegal who wants to migrate to the United States. More and more voters in the West sense this strange inability among our leadership class to affirm their loyalty to the people they lead. And so voters suspect, correctly, that those who lead are not willing to protect them from economic competition or cultural displacement. Their leaders will not do what leaders are supposed to do, which is to protect and preserve the realm, to sustain and build up our shared home." – *Return of the Strong Gods*, pg. 164

"Open borders are an emblem of the open society. Immigration policy over the past few decades has exposed middle-class workers to wage competition and has disrupted settled patterns of cultural transmission. The preference for open borders among elites, often unspoken but almost always strongly felt, exposes their profound refusal to shelter those whom they lead." – *Return of the Strong Gods*, pg. 157

"A society lives on answers, not merely questions; convictions, not simply opinions. The political and cultural crisis of the West today is the result of our refusal—perhaps incapacity—to honor the strong gods that stiffen the spine and inspire loyalty. We are subjected to the increasingly shrill insistence that 'critical questioning' is the highest good and 'diversity is our strength.' We are told that every motif of weakening, dispersion, and disenchantment serves the common good because it forestalls the return of Hitler.

"But we are not living in 1945. Our societies are not threatened by paramilitary organizations devoted to powerful ideologies. We do not face a totalitarian adversary with world-conquering ambitions. Insofar as there are totalitarian temptations in the West, they arise from the embattled postwar consensus, which is becoming increasingly punitive in the face of political populism and its rebellion against the dogmas of openness. Our problems are the opposite of those faced by the men who went to war to defeat Hitler. We are imperiled by a spiritual vacuum and the apathy it brings. The political culture of the West has become politically inert, winnowed down to technocratic management of private utilities and personal freedoms. Our danger is a dissolving society, not a closed one; the therapeutic personality, not the authoritarian one." – *Return of the Strong Gods*, ch. 3, pg. 119

Republican Party Platform, 1896

"We renew and emphasize our allegiance to the policy of protection, as the bulwark of American industrial independence, and the foundation of American development and prosperity." – *The North American Review*, vol. 194, pg. 179

Susan Reynolds

"There is no foundation at all for the belief, common among students of modern nationalism, that the word natio was seldom used in the Middle Ages except to describe the nationes into which university students were divided. Its use was much more widely than that, and often as a synonym for gens . . . Like a gens or natio, a populus was thought of as community of custom, descent, and government – a people." – *Kingdoms and Communities in Western Europe*, pgs. 255-256

"In the nineteenth century, as in the middle ages, the groups which medieval writers called gentes, nationes, or populi were actually thought of as units of common biological descent . . . as well as of common culture." – *Kingdoms and Communities in Western Europe*, pg. 254

"A kingdom was never thought of merely as the territory which happened to be ruled by a king. It comprised and corresponded to a 'people' (gens, natio, populus) . . . So much was this taken for granted that learned writers seldom argued about this directly when they discussed political subjects: they merely made remarks which suggested that it was an unreasoned premise of their political arguments . . . The trouble about all this [modern theorizing about the nation] for the medieval historian is not that the idea of the permanent and objective real nation is foreign to the middle ages, as so many historians of nationalism assume, but that it closely resembles the medieval idea of the kingdom." – *Kingdoms and Communities in Western Europe*, pgs. 251-252

Greg Richards

"Economists think mercantilism can never work...But it depends on a key assumption: that capital is fixed. Ricardo's example was that the British should raise sheep and the French should make wine, and they should trade these goods with each other. The example was based on climate, the ultimate in fixed capital.

"With capital mobile, as it is now, mercantilism works. By forcing a trading partner to move its assets, technology, know-how, intellectual property, and R&D to the mercantilist country in order to participate in its market, a country can build itself up at the expense of its trading partner." – *Trade War*

Herman Ridderbos

"It is not said here (I Cor. 11) 'in the Lord' marriage has received another destiny than it had by virtue of creation, it is said however, that in the Lord the principle of reciprocity, mutual dependence, and service to one another in love, applies, and comes into effect in a new way. For in Christ the husband does not have an advantage over the wife (Gal. 3:28). The distinction that exists between them by virtue of creation is not abolished, any more that than between Jews and Greeks; to be in Christ therefore does not therefore mean natural equality.... The revelation of Christ does not abrogate the natural and present life, but makes it recognized and practiced, from the viewpoint of Christ, exactly in its divine significance." – *Paul: An Outline of His Theology*, pgs. 307, 315

John M. Riddle

"He made provision for them in two ways. Firstly in 'the times before appointed'. The word 'times' (kairos) is translated 'seasons' in Acts 14.17, and refers to Genesis 8.22). Secondly, by apportioning appropriate 'living space' to each nation. See Deuteronomy 32.8: 'When the Most High divided to the nations their inheritance, when he separated the sons of Adam, he set the bounds of the people according to the number of the children of Israel.' The 'unknown God' had made all these arrangements in order that men and women 'should seek the Lord, if haply (indeed) they might feel after him and find him'. Compare Romans 1.19-20. He made it possible for men and women to know Him, and with this in mind He did not keep at a distance from them. Tragically, they did not seek the Lord, and the long years of human history had been 'times of…ignorance' (v.30). Men and women did not know that He was not far from them (v.27) – see Isaiah 55.6 – and that their day to day life came from Him (v.28)." – *The Acts of the Apostles*

Rígsþula

A son had Mothir, in silk they wrapped him,
With water they sprinkled him, Jarl he was;
Blond was his hair, and bright his cheeks,
Grim as a snake's were his glowing eyes.
– *Poetic Edda, The Song of Rig*, pg. 212

Rainer Maria Rilke

"Wer, wenn ich schriee, hörte mich
    denn aus der Engel
Ordnungen? Und gesetzt selbst, es nähme
einer mich plötzlich ans Herz: ich
    verginge von seinem
stärkeren Dasein."

Translation:
"Who, if I cried out, would hear me
    among the angelic orders?
And even if one of them suddenly
pressed me against his heart, I would
    be consumed in that
overwhelming existence."
– *The Duino Elegies*, First Elegy (*Duineser Elegien*, lines 1-4) [76]

"Und wir, die an steigendes Glück
denken, empfangen es nur, weil wir lieben."

Translation:
"And we, who think of happiness ascending,
only receive it because we love."
– *The Duino Elegies*, Tenth Elegy (lines 69-70)

"Ein Gott vermags. Wie aber, sag mir, soll
ein Mann ihm folgen durch die schmale Leier?
Sein Sinn ist Zwiespalt."

Translation:
"A god can do it. But tell me, how
can a man follow him through the narrow lyre?

His mind is divided."
– *Sonnets to Orpheus* (*Sonette an Orpheus*, Part I, Sonnet 1, lines 1-3)

Arthur Rimbaud

"Plus léger qu'un bouchon j'ai dansé sur les flots
Qu'on appelle rouleurs éternels de victimes,
Dix nuits, sans regretter l'œil niais des falots!"

Translation:
  "The Flemish wheat,
    the English cotton in their tow.
  As all that clamor died along
    with my bargemen,
  The River let me sail at will
    upon its flow."
– *Le Bateau ivre* (*The Drunken Boat* translation by Milos Maricic, lines 7-9) [77]

"Je m'en allais, les poings dans
    mes poches crevées;
Mon paletot aussi devenait idéal;
J'allais sous le ciel, Muse! et j'étais ton féal;
Oh! là là! que d'amours splendides j'ai rêvées!"

"Mon unique culotte avait un large trou.
— Petit-Poucet rêveur, j'égrenais dans ma course
Des rimes. Mon auberge était
    à la Grande-Ourse.
— Mes étoiles au ciel avaient
    un doux frou-frou."

Translation:
  I went off, fists thrust into my pockets,
    all tattered;
  My jacket suddenly transformed for the better;
  Beneath the sky, I went, O Muse,
    becoming your debtor;
  Oh! What joy! What splendid loves
    I dreamed as your steward!

  My only trouser had a big hole;
  I dreamt of Tom Thumb
    and picked my rhymes from the road:
  The Great Bear became my abode
  And my stars in the sky whispered
    into my soul.
– *Ma Bohème* (*My Bohemia* translation by David Paley, lines 1-8)

---

76 Rilke was an Austrian-born German-language poet who is considered one of the greatest poets of the 20th century.

77 Although Rimbaud's poetry is often characterized by its rebellious and innovative nature, his work also reflects a deep love for his native country, its landscapes, and its people.

"Et je m'écoutais vivre,
   et que le vent froid tombe
Aux bondés lacets, — c'est un joli nid,
   ma chambre,
Où l'on rêve de houx verts
   et de soleils d'ambre."
– *Ma Bohème* (lines 17-19)

Julian Pitt-Rivers

"Neighbors are thought to have particular rights and obligations towards one another. Borrowing and lending, passing embers, help in situations of emergency, discretion regarding what they may have chanced to discover, compose the obligations in which neighbors are forced by their proximity..." – *The People of the Sierra*, pg. 137

"A system of thought that takes the individual as its starting-point and assumes that he is motivated by self-interest, faces a difficulty in confronting the examples of behaviour that is not so motivated...the majority of the world's cultures do not share the individualism of the modern West and have no need to explain what appears to them evident: that the self is not the individual self alone, but includes, according to circumstances, those with whom the self is conceived as solidary in the first place, his kin." – *The Character of Kinship*, pg. 90

Alastair Roberts

"Mass immigration, in the form it is practiced in the liberal West, is a profoundly socially destructive force, antagonistic to historic modes of life. It fractures the foundations of society upon which our liberal institutions and freedoms are built, as I argued in my recent post. It is less a matter of welcoming the stranger into our society as a guest and much more typically a matter of a host people being steadily dispossessed of their land by a liberal polity to which all are slowly subjected as an ever more atomized and amorphous mass of people. Without becoming an inhospitable people, we need to be a lot more resistant to such developments." – *President Trump's Executive Order*

"Both Dr Leibhart and Dr Heimburger press that Hauerwasian question of the identity of the 'us': do we instinctively identify with our nations, or do we think the Church as our primary peoplehood? This question is an important one, but in the context of the present debate, we need to be very careful about how it is deployed. For irrespective of what our first community is as Christians, it is precisely as settled nations and peoples that we must establish immigration policies. Having a robust understanding of the senses in which we can and do speak of an American or a British peoplehood, for instance—as things that constitute us as a 'we' with our compatriots—is necessary for any cogent Christian approach to politics...."

"It is by no means obvious what it means to focus upon the Church as the true 'we' when it comes to thinking about our nation's immigration policies. Perhaps because of its greater concreteness, people would be much more alert to the confusion that could be caused by applying the same logic to the family. Although other members of Christ's body could be spoken of as our primary family, we still clearly recognize the 'we' of the natural family that exists, the obligations that it places upon us, and the ways that a 'we' of the body of Christ can inform and relativize its relations without radically denying, displacing, or intruding upon them. Jesus himself condemned those who appealed to loyalty to God in a way that undermined their natural duties to family (Mark 7:9-13)." – *Welcoming the Stranger*

"The biblical vision of charity 'begins at home', with those who are our immediate neighbours, and with the principled extension of our places to others–or the creation of new shared places–in a manner that preserves and develops their character as specific refractions of universal human goods. Although this extension is and should be transformative, the particular is never abandoned for the universal, however. Scripture emphasizes the household (1 Timothy 5:8) and the church (Galatians 6:10) as the sites of our primary responsibility to our neighbours, responsibilities that take priority over any to those outside these most immediate spheres. We should not extend ourselves beyond these realms in any manner that would compromise our primary neighbourly duties. Nor should we thoughtlessly open up our places to those who would undermine or attack them. Here prudence requires of us a more discriminating approach to the welcoming of displaced persons." – *Welcoming the Stranger*

"The 'charity' of a guilt-ridden people can be characterized by a 'self'-lessness, a handing over or abnegation of the self in futile attempts at atonement for themselves. This self-lessness of Europe is perhaps nowhere more clearly on display than in our abandonment of cultural identity for multiculturalism. British identity, it is meekly suggested, is located in virtues such as tolerance, diversity, respect, and equality, the bare formalities that delineate a realm surrendered to largely unopposed contestation. A society that has lost its self will spinelessly accommodate itself to the demands of the unreasonable, seeking to appease them through compliance." – *Refugee Crisis*

"Leibniz articulates liberalism's viewpoint, 'I am indifferent to that which constitutes a German or a Frenchman because I will only the good of all mankind.'

"Although participating in a common life and having a place are universal human goods, these can only be realized in the particular yet variegated forms of specific societies, through which they are refracted. Liberalism's undervaluation of particularity encourages it to think in terms of abstract right-bearers and of mere space. The paradigmatic person of liberalism is a displaced one: the universal human subject. As one might expect, the result of the liberal vision has often been the breaking down of particular communities and places into interchangeable territories, rendering all increasingly 'placeless', both in the social, historical, and material order." – *Refugee Crisis*

"Cosmopolitans tend to be post-nationalist supporters of the market state. A market state is a neoliberal entity, which typically maximizes the market choices and autonomy of all persons within it, whether citizens or not. The borders of such a state are largely open and function on little more than an administrative level. Individual opportunity, unrestricted choice, and validated autonomy are core values and, consequently, freedom of movement between nations is prized. The ideal citizen of a market state is a deracinated universal subject, belonging both everywhere and nowhere, all differences reduced to a level of indifference. For the citizen of the market state, the most important matter is the expansion of the conditions for autonomous self-realization and the market that

sustains that. The market state neither excites nor demands much in the way of loyalty. The economy and the technocratic structures that secure a realm of radical and relatively unconstrained possibility for the individual are the primary political structures. Progressive values that affirm all individuals in their autonomous choices are sacred.

"By contrast, provincial persons typically favour the nation as the political entity (they also have extremely strong attachments to their regions, towns, and neighbourhoods). The borders of the nation protect and project specific communal identities that exceed and enfold individuals within them. Such nations privilege and prioritize some identities over others. They emphasize cultural, historic, ethnic, religious, familial, locational, and social forms of belonging over autonomy. The intergenerational continuities of family and people, tradition, institution, history, and heritage are central to the shared life. Individual choice, autonomy, and agency are curtailed and subordinated to communal belonging." – *Brexit and the Moral Vision of Nationhood*

"The indiscriminate welcoming of migrant populations can attenuate place for everyone. Although this may serve the interests of capitalists and governments who stand to benefit from a mobile, dependent, and biddable workforce and a population with little internal solidarity, this is at heavy cost to the wellbeing of the people within such groups. The persons who bear the heaviest burden of this loss of place are typically the poorest within society." – *Refugee Crisis*

"The repeated failure of multiculturalism has exposed the unwelcome truth that, although persons can be displaced and populations atomized, they cannot so easily be homogenized. In our values, behavioural traits, and cultural tendencies, etc. we are products and bearers of histories and identities much greater than our own. Experience has repeatedly demonstrated that, intentionally or not, people tend to take their cultural habits with them." – *Brexit and the Moral Vision of Nationhood*

"The study of anthropology reveals the profound diversity of cultures, and the divergence of human peoples. Much as it fails to account for the differences between the sexes, the anthropology of neoliberalism, formed around the fungible, transactional, and detached individual fails to account for the varying 'viscosities' of populations and the significant differences and peculiar affinities between cultures and ethnicities. For instance, immigrants from any of the countries which are largely constituted by the diaspora of the British peoples—the USA, Canada, Australia, New Zealand—typically have a far more natural affinity with and instinct for our country and culture than persons from most other countries, and not merely on account of shared ethnicity and language. Britain's less committed relationship to Europe has arisen in no small measure from the strength of its bonds with such countries in the Anglosphere." – *Brexit and the Moral Vision of Nationhood*

"No human being should be regarded as any more my neighbour than any other. Those who subscribe to such universalized ethics will often be deeply morally engaged with the well-being of completely unrelated persons or creatures, in many cases pointedly siding with other groups against their own group of origin. For the cosmopolitan, the state exists to ensure universal human rights and the equality of all persons within the area it administrates.

"By contrast, the ethics of more provincial persons are the ethics of filial love. This love is necessarily particularized, committed to particular people, places, and things over others—and even to the exclusion of others in some cases. Loving one party doesn't mean you have to hate or be indifferent to others. But it does require that you commit to and prioritize the good and well-being of that party over all others. The particularity of love for one's family does not prevent one from showing hospitality to the stranger—nor deny the existence of a moral duty towards them—but a person who treats all people exactly as they treat their spouse and family will be seen to have betrayed their kin." – *Brexit and the Moral Vision of Nationhood*

"Patriotism does not accord value to its country because it has been persuaded that its country is objectively better than all other countries, but rather because filial love is absolutizing. The lover typically knows that the person, people, or place that they love is deeply flawed and far from ideal, but for them there is no other that

could take the place of that object. Even the flaws of the objects of our love can be loved, simply because they play a part in making the object of our love what it is." – *Brexit and the Moral Vision of Nationhood*

"It is often presumed that persons are essentially blank slates, that old cultures can be shed and new cultures assumed with ease, and that persons and their communities are radically plastic and adaptable to new situations. The reality is not nearly so simple.

"There is rich diversity within the families of humanity and a surprising tenacity of the character of peoples and their cultures over time. For a great many millennia, human peoples have adapted to very different situations, to different climates, geographies, environmental challenges, diets, forms of subsistence (e.g. to agriculture or hunting and gathering), modes of settlement, civilization, and social conditions. Peoples and their various cultures have developed over millennia of adaptation, development, and exchange.

"The peculiar climactic, geographical, environmental, dietary, civilizational, historical, cultural, religious, and ideological forces that our peoples have both adapted to and developed have all left their subtle traces upon us and exerted a selective and moulding effect upon us. Some of these have been known to us for some time, while certain other forms of human biodiversity are only gradually becoming clear through advancements in the field of genetics: within the genes of each one of us are exciting clues to stories of migration, settlement, invasion, adaptation, and exchange." – *Brexit and the Moral Vision of Nationhood*

"In order to love one's neighbour and fellow countryman, you must prioritize their interests over those of outsiders, without thereby being indifferent to the outsider. In order truly to love one's country, one must prioritize seeking its well-being over that of others, and value it more highly than and favour it over other countries." – *Brexit and the Moral Vision of Nationhood*

"The ethics of universal benevolence, equality, and altruism directly conflicts with the ethics of filial love. Radical departicularization of our ethical stance is fundamental to universalized ethics, yet this is necessarily the rejection of the ethics of filial love. For the advocate of universalized ethics, the ethics of filial love reeks of bigotry, injustice, inequality, and hatred." – *Brexit and the Moral Vision of Nationhood*

"...ethnicity is almost invariably at least implicitly a constitutive fact for national identity for those who think in terms of the ethics of filial love, even though many of them may be embarrassed about admitting the fact. In this belief they should not be presumed to exclude those of other ethnicities from such an identity nor be judged to assert sole title to our shared national ecosystem. They are generally recognizing and seeking to protect the peculiar and remarkable bond that has been formed between the long settled ethnic groupings to which they belong in the family of human peoples to the land in which they have been the constant recognizable presence for millennia." – *Brexit and the Moral Vision of Nationhood*

"This notion of nationhood does not absolutely exclude newcomers at all. However, as the nation is formed by common objects of love, faithfulness to past labour and sacrifice, and labour and sacrifice of our own, truly becoming a part of the nation requires a deep commitment and submission to an intergenerational moral project. The love, faithfulness, sacrifice, and labour that are required of the member of the people can take many different forms, as the national project is a variegated and complex one. Resistance to immigration is most pronounced where incoming groups have proved ambivalent or hostile to the moral project of the nation, which is why the immigration of certain Muslim populations has provoked particular concerns.

    "Once the logic of this notion of nationhood is appreciated, it can be recognized that it is not founded upon any antipathy towards different cultures as such, nor to persons from them. Rather, it is driven by the concern to protect and extend the nation as a unique and particular moral project, and to oppose those who would, by their ambivalence or hostility, undermine or compromise it." – *Brexit and the Moral Vision of Nationhood*

"For an alternative vision of peoplehood, by contrast, the state exists to adumbrate and protect the particular and substantial realities of a defined and formed people, a people that has persisted and developed through time. Such a people is differentiated from other peoples, and borders typically serve to control admixtures of people. Borders are existential for the nation, not purely administrative. Borders are that which protect the 'we' of the nation, a 'we' that represents much more than an agglomeration of individuals, but a uniquely constituted and formed people in their specifically differentiated identities and variegated relations." – *Brexit and the Moral Vision of Nationhood*

Clemens Romanus

The only reference to slavery in the Apostoic Church-Ordinance is that a man with a concubine should:

    "leave off that course, and let him marry according to the law; but if he will not, let him be cast out... But a concubine of one, if she is a slave, if she have brought up her children, and is with him alone, let her hear [the word]. If she hath not, let her be rejected." – *The Apostolical Constitutions*, pg. 48

Franklin Roosevelt

"No tariff duty should be lowered to a point where our natural industries would be injured." – Speech, October 25, 1932; cited in Eckes, *Opening America's Market: U.S. Foreign Trade Policy Since 1776*, pg. 142

Teddy Roosevelt

"I don't go so far as to think that the only good Indians are the dead Indians, but I believe nine out of ten are, and I shouldn't inquire too closely into the health of the tenth." – Speech January 1886; *Theodore Roosevelt and the Art of American Power*, pg. 67

"It is sometimes announced that part of the peace agreement must be a league of nations, which will avert all war for the future, and put a stop to the need of this nation preparing its own strength for its own defense. Many of the adherents of this idea grandiloquently assert that they intend to supplant nationalism by internationalism. In deciding upon proposals of this nature it behooves our people to remember that competitive rhetoric is a poor substitute for the habit of resolutely looking facts in the face.

"Nothing in the world can alter facts. Patriotism stands in national matters as love of family does in private life. Nationalism corresponds to the love a man bears for his wife and children. Internationalism corresponds to the feeling he has for his neighbors generally. The sound nationalist is the only type of really helpful internationalist, precisely as in private relations it is the man who is most devoted to his own wife and children who is apt, in the long run, to be the most satisfactory neighbor. To substitute internationalism for nationalism means to do away with patriotism, and is as vicious and as profoundly demoralizing as to put promiscuous devotion to all other persons in the place of steadfast devotion to a man's own family. Either effort means the atrophy of robust morality. The man who loves other countries as much as his own stands on a level with the man who loves other women as much as he loves his own wife. One is as worthless a creature as the other. The professional pacifist and the professional internationalist are equally undesirable citizens. The American pacifist has in actual fact shown himself to be the tool and ally of the German militarist. The professional internationalist is a man who, under a pretense of diffuse attachment for everybody hides the fact that in reality he is incapable of doing his duty by anybody.

"We Americans should abhor all wrong-doing to other nations. We ought always to act fairly and generously by other nations. But we must remember that our first duty is to be loyal and patriotic citizens of our own nation, of America. These two facts should always be in our minds in dealing with any proposal for a league of nations. By all means let us be loyal to great ideals. But let us remember that, unless we show common sense in action, loyalty in speech will amount to considerably less than nothing." – *The Terms Of Peace*, Address at Lafayette Day exercises, Aldermanic Chambers, New York City, Sept. 6, 1918; *The Great Adventure*, pgs. 371-372

"There is no room in this country for hyphenated Americanism...The one absolutely certain way of bringing this nation to ruin, of preventing all possibility of its continuing to be a nation at all, would be to permit it to become a tangle of squabbling nationalities." – Address to the Knights of Columbus, *Americanism*, 1915; *Americanization*, pg. 42

— TEDDY ROOSEVELT —

"America is a Nation and not a mosaic of nationalities. The various nationalities that come here are not to remain separate, but to blend into the one American nationality — the nationality of Washington and Lincoln, of Muhlenberg and Sheridan. Therefore, we must have but one language, the English language. Every immigrant who comes here should be required within five years to learn English or to leave the country, for hereafter every immigrant should be treated as a future fellow citizen and not merely as a labor unit. English should be the only language taught or used in the primary schools. We should provide by law so that after a reasonable interval every newspaper in this country should be published in English. A square deal for all Americans means relentless attack on all men in this country who are not straight-out Americans and nothing else." – Statement to the *Kansas City Star*, 1918, pgs. 143-144

"The immigrant cannot possibly remain what he was, or continue to be a member of the Old-World society. If he tries to retain his old language, in a few generations it becomes a barbarous jargon; if he tries to retain his old customs and ways of life, in a few generations he becomes an uncouth boor." – *True Americanism*, 1894; *History of the American Nation* vol. 9, pg. 2,624

"Here is your country. Cherish these natural wonders, cherish the natural resources, cherish the history and romance as a sacred heritage, for your children and your children's children. Do not let selfish men or greedy interests skin your country of its beauty, its riches or its romance."
– Statement to wilderness advocate John Muir while looking over the Yosemite Valley; *Congressional Record*, vol. 160, part 2, pg. 2,544

"American and Indian, Boer and Zulu, Cossack and Tartar, New Zealander and Maori—in each case the victor, horrible though many of his deeds are, has laid deep the foundations for the future greatness of a mighty people. The consequences of struggles for territory between civilized nations seem small by comparison. Looked at from the standpoint of the ages, it is of little moment whether Lorraine is part of Germany or of France, whether the northern Adriatic cities pay homage to Austrian Kaiser or Italian King; but it is of incalculable importance that America, Australia, and Siberia should pass out of the hands of their red, black, and yellow aboriginal owners, and become the heritage of the dominant world races." – *The Winning of The West*, vol. III, 1894

"Thank God I am not a free trader. Pernicious indulgence in the doctrine of free trade seems inevitably to produce fatty degeneration of the moral fibre" – Morison, *Theodore Roosevelt*, 1:504

"Our first duty is to see that the protection granted by the tariff in every case where it is needed is maintained, and that reciprocity be sought for so far as it can safely be done without injury to our home industries…. [Duties] must never be reduced below the point that will cover the difference between the labor cost here and abroad. The well-being of the wage-worker is a prime consideration of our entire policy of economic legislation."
Like his predecessor, Roosevelt also recognized that foreign customers must sell in the U.S. market in order to continue buying American products. He proposed: "…arranging our tariff as to enable us to take from them those products which we can use without harm to our own industries and labor, or the use of which will be of marked benefit to us." – *First Annual Message*, December 3, 1901; Richardson, *Messages*, 13:6403

"The phenomenal growth of our export trade emphasizes the urgency of the need for wider markets and for a liberal policy in dealing with foreign nations. … Their ability to purchase our products should as far as possible be secured by so arranging our tariff as to enable us to take from them those products which we can use without harm to our own industries and labor, or the use of which will be of marked benefit to us." – *First Annual Message*, December 3, 1901; Richardson, *Messages*, 13:6403

"Our present immigration laws are unsatisfactory. We need every honest and efficient immigrant fitted to become an American citizen, every immigrant who comes here to stay, who brings here a strong body, a stout heart, a good head, and a resolute purpose to do his duty well in every way and to bring up his children as law-abiding and God-fearing members of the community. But there should be a comprehensive law enacted with the object of working a threefold improvement over our present system. First, we should aim to exclude absolutely not only all persons who are known to be believers in anarchistic principles or members of anarchistic societies, but also all persons who are of a low moral tendency or of unsavory reputation. This means that we should require a more thorough system of inspection abroad and a more rigid system of examination at our immigration ports, the former being especially necessary." – *First Annual Message*, December 3, 1901; Richardson, *Messages*, 13:6403

"The second object of a proper immigration law ought to be to secure by a careful and not merely perfunctory educational test some intelligent capacity to appreciate American institutions and act sanely as American citizens. This would not keep out all anarchists, for many of them belong to the intelligent criminal class. But it would do what is also in point, that is, tend to decrease the sum of ignorance, so potent in producing the envy, suspicion, malignant passion, and hatred of order, out of which anarchistic sentiment inevitably springs. Finally, all persons should be excluded who are below a certain standard of economic fitness to enter our industrial field as competitors with American labor. There should be proper proof of personal capacity to earn an American living and enough money to insure a decent start under American conditions. This would stop the influx of cheap labor, and the resulting competition which gives rise to so much of bitterness in American industrial life; and it would dry up the springs of the pestilential social conditions in our great cities, where anarchistic organizations have their greatest possibility of growth." – *First Annual Message*, December 3, 1901; Richardson, *Messages*, 13:6403

"The question of what tariff is best for our people is primarily one of expediency, to be determined not on abstract academic grounds, but in the light of experience." – *American Economist*, February 17, 1905, *Tariff League Bulletin*

Wilhelm Röpke

"Mass man is individualistic because of the loosening of the social fabric and the disintegration of community. One of the least well understood aspects of the process of enmassment is that it detaches the individual from his natural social fabric and leaves him to his own resources. . . . [Individualism] also became one of the most corrosive of spiritual acids, dissolving the organic structure of society and thereby contributing to the formation of mass society and mass democracy." – *Humane Economy*, pg. 70

"The market economy is no exception to the rule. Indeed, its advocates, in so far as they are at all intellectually fastidious, have always recognized that the sphere of the market, of competition, of the system where supply and demand move prices and thereby govern production, may be regarded and defended only as part of a wider general order encompassing ethics, law, the natural conditions of life and happiness, the state, politics, and power. Society as a whole cannot be ruled by the laws of supply and demand, and the state is more than a sort of business company, as has been the conviction of the best conservative opinion since the time of Burke. Individuals who compete on the market and there pursue their own advantage stand all the more in need of the social and moral bonds of community, without which competition degenerates most grievously. As we have said before, the market is not everything. It must find its place in a higher order of things. It must be firmly contained within an all-embracing order of society." – *Humane Economy*, pgs. 90-91

"Ownership illustrates the fact that the market economy is a form of economic order belonging to a particular philosophy of life and to a particular social and moral universe...

"In all honesty, we have to admit that the market economy has a bourgeois foundation. This needs to be stressed all the more because the romantic and socialist reaction against everything bourgeois has, for generations past, been astonishingly successful in turning this concept into a parody of itself from which it is very difficult to get away. The market economy, and with it social and political freedom, can thrive only as a part and under the protection of a bourgeois system. This implies the existence of a society in which certain fundamentals are respected and color the whole network of social relationships: individual effort and responsibility, absolute norms and values, independence based on ownership, prudence and daring, calculating and saving, responsibility for planning one's own life, proper coherence with the community, family feeling, a sense of tradition and the succession of generations combined with an open-minded view of the present and the future, proper tension between individual and community, firm moral discipline, respect for the value of money, the courage to grapple on one's own with life and its uncertainties, a sense of the natural order of things, and a firm scale of values." – *Humane Economy*, pg. 98

"An uncommonly impressive and at the same time repulsive symbol of such a race of all for everything is to be found in the spectacle that memorable day, more than half a century ago, when a part of the territory of the present state of Oklahoma (the land had been taken from the Indians) was thrown open to settlers. They were waiting at the border, and at the shot of a pistol they all rushed forward from this completely equal starting line to compete for the best plots of land. Surely it must be obvious to everyone that nothing could be more unwise or dangerous than to turn society into such a continual race. Even if the production of goods could so be maximized, it would not be worth the price. Men would be incessantly on the move; culture, happiness, and nerves would be destroyed by an unending to and fro and up and down from place to place, from profession to profession, from one social class to another, from 'shirt sleeves' to a fortune of millions and back to 'shirt sleeves.' No, the deeper — we might say here the conservative — meaning of decentrism is that it behooves us to bethink ourselves of the indispensable conditions for a sound and happy society. These are a certain stratification of society, respect for natural developments, a modicum of variety and of horizontal and vertical social articulation, family traditions, personal inclinations, and inherited wealth. From this point of view, it is, for example, by no means foolish if a country's townships or districts try to preserve their character to some extent by not immediately granting every newcomer the same rights as are enjoyed by the original inhabitants." – *Humane Economy*, pg. 232

Edward Alsworth Ross

"I am not of those who consider humanity and forget the nation, who pity the living but not the unborn. To me, those who are to come after us stretch forth beseeching hands as well as the masses on the other side of the globe. Nor do I regard America as something to be spent quickly and cheerfully for the benefit of pent-up millions in the backward lands. What if we become crowded without their ceasing to be so? I regard it as a nation whose future may be of unspeakable value to the rest of mankind, provided that the easier conditions of life here be made permanent by high standards of living, institutions and ideals, which finally may be appropriated by all men. We could have helped the Chinese a little by letting their surplus millions swarm in upon us a generation ago; but we have helped them infinitely more by protecting our standards and having something worth their copying when the time came." – *The Old World in the New*, Preface

Murray Rothbard

"An egalitarian society can only hope to achieve its goals by totalitarian methods of coercion; and, even here, we all believe and hope the human spirit of individual man will rise up and thwart any such attempts to achieve an ant-heap world." – *Egalitarianism*, pg. 8

"The great fact of individual difference and variability (that is, inequality) is evident from the long record of human experience; hence, the general recognition of the antihuman nature of a world of coerced uniformity. Socially and economically, this variability manifests itself in the universal division of labor, and in the 'Iron Law of Oligarchy' — the insight that, in every organization or activity, a few (generally the most able and/or the most interested) will end up as leaders, with the mass of the membership filling the ranks of the followers. In both cases, the same phenomenon is at work — outstanding success or leadership in any given activity is attained by what Jefferson called a 'natural aristocracy' — those who are best attuned to that activity.

"The age-old record of inequality seems to indicate that this variability and diversity is rooted in the biological nature of man. But it is precisely such a conclusion about biology and human nature that is the most galling of all possible irritants to our egalitarians. Even egalitarians would be hard put to deny the historical record, but their answer is that 'culture' has been to blame; and since they obviously hold that culture is a pure act of the will, then the goal of changing the culture and inculcating society with equality seems to be attainable. In this area, the egalitarians slough off any pretense to scientific caution; they are scarcely content with acknowledging biology and culture as mutually interacting influences. Biology must be read out of court quickly and totally." – *Egalitarianism*, pgs. 8-9

"Since egalitarians start with the a priori axiom that all people and hence all groups of people, are equal, it there follows for them that any and all group differences in status, prestige, or authority in society must be the result of unjust oppression and irrational discrimination." – *Egalitarianism*, pg. 10

"Women are another recently discovered 'oppressed class,' and the fact that political delegates have habitually been far more than 50 percent male is now held to be an evident sign of their oppression. Delegates to political conventions come from the ranks of party activists, and since women have not been nearly as politically active as men, their numbers have understandably been low. But, faced with this argument, the widening forces of 'women's liberation' in America again revert to the talismanic argument about 'brainwashing' by our 'culture.' For the women's liberationists can hardly deny the fact that every culture and civilization in history, from the simplest to the most complex, has been dominated by males. (In desperation, the liberationists have lately been countering with fantasies about the mighty Amazonian empire.) Their reply, once again, is that from time immemorial a male-dominated culture has brainwashed oppressed females to confine themselves to nurture, home, and the domestic hearth. The task of the liberationists is to effect a revolution in the female condition by sheer will, by the 'raising of consciousness.' If most women continue to cleave to domestic concerns, this only reveals the 'false consciousness' that must be extirpated.

"Of course, one neglected reply is that if, indeed, men have succeeded in dominating every culture, then this in itself is a demonstration of male 'superiority'; for if all genders are equal, how is it that male domination emerged in every case?" – *Egalitarianism*, pg. 12

"The genetic basis for inequality of intelligence has also become increasingly evident, despite the emotional abuse heaped upon such studies by fellow scientists as well as the lay public. Studies of identical twins raised in contrasting environments have been among the ways that this conclusion has been reached; and Professor Richard Herrnstein has recently estimated that 80 percent of the variability in human intelligence is genetic in origin. Herrnstein concludes that any political attempts to provide environmental equality for all citizens will only intensify the degree of socioeconomic differences caused by genetic variability." – *Egalitarianism*, pgs. 16-17

"The egalitarian revolt against biological reality (inequality), as significant as it is, is only a subset of a deeper revolt: against the ontological structure of reality itself, against the 'very organization of nature'; against the universe as such. At the heart of the egalitarian left is the pathological belief that there is no structure of reality; that all the world is a tabula rasa that can be changed at any moment in any desired direction by the mere exercise of human will—in short, that reality can be instantly transformed by the mere wish or whim of human beings…

"Egalitarians, however intelligent as individuals, deny the very basis of human intelligence and of human reason: the identification of the ontological structure of reality, of the laws of human nature, and the universe. In so doing, the egalitarians are acting as terribly spoiled children, denying the structure of reality on behalf of the rapid materialization of their own absurd fantasies. Not only spoiled but also highly dangerous; for the power of ideas is such that the egalitarians have a fair chance of destroying the very universe that they wish to deny and transcend, and to bring that universe crashing around all of our ears. Since their methodology and their goals deny the very structure of humanity and of the universe, the egalitarians are profoundly antihuman; and, therefore, their ideology and their activities may be set down as profoundly evil as well. Egalitarians do not have ethics on their side unless one can maintain that the destruction of civilization, and even of the human race itself, may be crowned with the laurel wreath of a high and laudable morality." – *Egalitarianism*, pg. 19

"The nation, of course, is not the same thing as the state, a difference that earlier libertarians, such as Ludwig von Mises and Albert Jay Nock understood full well. Contemporary libertarians often assume, mistakenly, that individuals are bound to each other only by the nexus of market exchange. They forget that everyone is born into a family, a language, and a culture. Every person is born into one or several overlapping communities, usually including an ethnic group, with specific values, cultures, religious beliefs, and traditions. He is generally born into a country; he is always born into a specific time and place, meaning neighborhood and land area." – *Nations by Consent*

"The question of open borders, or free immigration, has become an accelerating problem for classical liberals. This is first, because the welfare state increasingly subsidizes immigrants to enter and receive permanent assistance, and second, because cultural boundaries have become increasingly swamped. I began to rethink my views on immigration when, as the Soviet Union collapsed, it became clear that ethnic Russians had been encouraged to flood into Estonia and Latvia in order to destroy the cultures and languages of these peoples. Previously, it had been easy to dismiss as unrealistic Jean Raspail's anti-immigration novel *The Camp of the Saints*, in which virtually the entire population of India decides to move, in small boats, into France, and the French, infected by liberal ideology, cannot summon the will to prevent economic and cultural national destruction. As cultural and welfare-state problems have intensified, it became impossible to dismiss Raspail's concerns any longer." – *Nations by Consent*

Jean Jacques Rousseau

"Liberty, not being a fruit of all climates, is not within the reach of all peoples. The more this principle, laid down by Montesquieu, is considered, the more its truth is felt; the more it is combated, the more chance is given to confirm it by new proofs." – *Social Contract*, pg. 51

"The virtue of its citizens, their patriotic zeal, the particular form that national institutions can give to their spirit, that is the only rampart always ready to defend it, and which no army could breach. If you arrange things such that a Pole could never become a Russian, then I can assure you that Russia will never subjugate Poland." – *Considerations on the Government of Poland and on its Proposed Reformation; Rousseau: The Social Contract and Other Later Political Writings*, pg. 172

Edmon L. Rowell, Jr.

"A 'foreigner' or 'resident alien' residing among a people or in a land not his or her own (Heb. gēr, usually translated 'stranger' or 'alien').

"The sojourner prototype was Abraham (Gen. 12:10; 23:4; cf. Heb. 11:9). The continuing sojourner/alien status of Abraham's progeny is recalled for perpetuity in the credo of Deut. 26:5–10. When Israel became established as a nation and a people, remembrance of Israel's past alien status justified laws regarding fair treatment of the alien among them (Exod. 22:21 [MT 20]; 23:9; Lev. 19:34; Deut. 10:19). Officially aliens in Israel enjoyed equal status with regard to worship (Num. 9:14; 15:15–16), sabbath rest (Exod. 23:12; Deut. 5:14), and, with widows and orphans, protective care (Exod. 22:21–24 [20–23]; Deut. 24:17, 19–20; cf. Mal. 3:5). This may have been especially or only true for the circumcised alien (Exod. 12:48–49). Alien legis-

lation includes an early example of the so-called great commandment: 'You shall love the alien as yourself, for you were aliens in the land of Egypt' (Lev. 19:34).

"Of course, in everyday life the alien in Israel did not always enjoy equal or even fair treatment. In fact, Heb. gēr may stem from Akk. gārû, 'enemy' or 'opponent.'" – "Sojourner" in *Eerdmans Dictionary of the Bible*, D. N. Freedman, A. C. Myers, & A. B. Beck (Eds.), pg. 1235

H. Rondel Rumburg

"Salvation changes fallen men's standing with God but it does not and can not change men's earthly physiognomy. Not only does the Bible identify the beginnings of races, languages, and nations prior to Christ's redemption, but it also reveals that these distinctions are maintained after redemption. There are many texts which evidence this truth (some examples are Rev. 7:9; 5:9; 11:9; 14:6; 20:3,8). Christ Jesus maintained this distinction for He sent His disciples to the lost sheep of the house of Israel, and later sent Paul to the Gentiles. The distinction is maintained in the person of Christ, for He is the same race or nationality in eternity as He was during His incarnation. The New Jerusalem was let down out of heaven upon the new earth (Rev. 21:1-3) 'And the nations (ethne) of them which are saved shall walk in the light of it; And the Kings of the earth do bring their glory and honor into it.... And they shall bring the glory and the honor of the Nations (ton ethnon) into it' (Rev. 21:24, 26) 'The nations of them which are saved shall walk in the light of it' show that the distinction is maintained or perpetuated into eternity. God was the one who divided the lands, languages, races, and nations (Gen. 10:5; Dt. 32:8; Acts 17:26). God condemned those who would remove these distinctions (Dt. 7:3; Ezra 9:10; Neh. 9:2; 13:3, 23ff [see Neh. 9-13]. What of those who reject the distinctions God made relative to the races? His Word bears out the results in the passages just mentioned and others (Jud. 6:5-7; Num. 5:1-9; Dt. 7:1-6). Abraham and Isaac forbade that their sons should marry Canaanites (Gen. 24; 27). Some would say that the point is Canaanites were unbelievers. Is that the only factor? Esau's rebellion was seen in his miscegenation (Gen. 25-28). Is Esau considered a believer? Was Esau, an unbeliever marrying unbelievers?

Then what was the factor in his wrongdoing? The Lord did not even teach the amalgamation of fabrics, seeds, creatures, etc. (Lev. 19:19). Certainly, God cannot be charged with racism when He made Israel a chosen nation.... Modern men have so perverted language that racism is a word without a proper denotation and its connotations match the meaning given by the user of the word at that moment in time. Today's men find it an inconvenience to submit to God's standards, and thus man lives in a world of flux. Therefore men reject God's order." – *One Blood, Many Races*, pgs. 40-42

Benjamin Rush

"He [the ideal student] must be taught to love his fellow creatures in every part of the world, but he must cherish with a more intense and peculiar affection, the citizens of Pennsylvania and of the United States. I do not wish to see our youth educated with a single prejudice against any nation or country; but we impose a task upon human nature, repugnant alike to reason, revelation and the ordinary dimensions of the human heart, when we require him to embrace, with equal affection, the whole family of mankind." – A plan for the establishment of public schools and the diffusion of knowledge in Pennsylvania; in *American Educational Thought Essays* from 1640-1940, pg. 65

Bertrand Russell

"The society of experts will control propaganda and education. It will teach loyalty to the world government, and make nationalism high treason. The government, being an oligarchy, will instill submissiveness into the great bulk of the population...It is possible that it may invent ingenious ways of concealing its own power, leaving the forms of democracy intact, and allowing the plutocrats or politicians to imagine that they are cleverly controlling these forms...whatever the outward forms may be, all real power will come to be concentrated in the hands of those who understand the art of scientific manipulation." – *The Scientific Outlook*, pg. 175

James C. Russell

"Recent scientific research has affirmed a genetic component to many individual personality traits such as traditionalism, alienation, and aggressiveness. Genetic factors are now claimed to account for approximately 50 percent of the individual differences in religious attitudes...

"A common feature among the Germanic peoples is 'the development of a concept of collective security. This was closely related to two Germanic institutions: The family and kin group on the one hand and personal lordship on the other.' ...

"The traditional Indo-European religions in their early stages exhibited characteristics which may be expected of a pastoral, nomadic, warrior people who conquered agrarian peoples. The Indo-Europeans 'had a patriarchal social organization.'

"Given the significant role of the warrior in Indo-European societies, it is not surprising that the warrior ideology is 'perhaps the most distinctive feature of the Indo-European worldview.'

"Indo-European society, as far as we can judge, was agnatic and ethno-centric, its basic unit being the patriarchal, patrilinear, and essentially patrilocal extended family. Kindred was the foundation of its concentric structure, grouping the families in clans ...

"Ethnic solidarity became especially manifest in contrast with outsiders. Inside his group, with his kith and kin, the Indo-European is safe; outside lurk the dangers. Inside his family, his clan, his tribe, he enjoys all the rights and privileges that pertain to free members" – *The Germanization Of Early Medieval Christianity*, pgs. 14, 43, 58, 59, 115

John Ruskin

"If there be any one point insisted on throughout my works more frequently than another, that one point is the impossibility of Equality. My continual aim has been to show the eternal superiority of some men to others, sometimes even of one man to all others; and to show also the advisability of appointing such persons or person to guide, to lead, or on occasion even to compel and subdue, their inferiors, according to their own better knowledge and wiser will." – *Unto This Last*, pg. 102

"Inequalities of wealth, justly established, benefit the nation in the course of their establishment; and, nobly used, aid it yet more by their existence." – *Unto This Last*, pg. 46

R.J. Rushdoony

"It is phariseeism to send money abroad to care for the needy, an impersonal act, and to neglect the personal and responsible act at home.
To help someone close by means a continual involvement, back-aches and heart-aches, but this is what any work involves." – *God's Plan for Victory: The Meaning of Postmillennialism*, ch. 3.[78]

"Norman Mailer has pointed out that the modern outsider to God and law find his hero in the Negro, whom he sees as a 'natural and social adventurer sworn against respectability, conformity, dullness, and emotional timidity.' The modern 'white Negro' is a man who imagines the Negro to be the ideal man, a natural anarchist and nihilist, and therefore a social hero. Moreover, to gain the acceptance of the Negro, irrespective of his Character, is to gain a victory against law and standards in the name of equality.

"There is indication already of another 'civil rights' offensive as a next step after the Negro: 'the Homosexual may be partly replacing the Negro as an object of liberal solicitude and the prime test of liberal tolerance.' If there is no God and no divinely ordained law, then not only does perversion have equal rights with morality, but actually truer rights, because Christian morality is seen as an imposition on and a dehumanization of man, whereas perversion is an act of liberty and autonomy for this school of thought.

"In any case, the goal is, whether directly or slowly, total destruction of Christian civilization. Some have called for ... a long period of chaos and revolution, of anarchy, racial amalgamation, and the total destruction of civilization." – *Roots of Reconstruction*, pg, 618

"The demand of humanism (and of its child, socialism) is for a universal ethics. In universal ethics we are told that, even as the family gave way to the tribe, and the tribe to the nation, so the nation must give way to a one-world order. All men must treat all other men equally. Partiality to our family, nation, or race, represents a lower morality, we are told, and must be replaced by a 'higher' morality of a universal ethics." – *Roots of Reconstruction*, pg. 574

"The only logical conclusion of the present concept of civil rights is communism. It demands 'full equality.' And where does equality stop? Economic, political, cultural, racial, personal, and every other kind of equality is demanded....

'Full equality' means that no differences can be tolerated with respect to race, color, creed, economics and all things else. This means the planned destruction of the very elements of society who have made our civilization." – *Roots of Reconstruction*, pg. 581

"These laws forbid the blurring of God-ordained distinctions. The nature and direction of sin is to blur and finally erase all the God-ordained boundaries ... God's laws are case laws. If vegetable seeds are not to be mingled, nor an ass and a horse crossbred, then in the human realm it follows that the confusion of God-ordained boundaries is even more serious." – *Commentary on Leviticus*, pg. 230

"[The] Bible makes clear that God does not permit us to despise heredity and background. That God does not permit immediate integration of all peoples. For example, in Deuteronomy 23:2-3 the Amalekites and the Moabites were banned from the congregation to the tenth generation, because of their background and spiritual and moral degeneracy. The Edomites, verses 7-8 of Deuteronomy 23, were barred till the third generation. And yet at the same time the hatred of an Edomite was declared to be a sin in front of God. Thus these people could not be detested, or despised or hated, but they could not be brought immediately into the congregation, they had to worship separately in some cases to the tenth generation, and others to the third generation. So that they have a background of segregated worship and of character for so many generation before they could be integrated with the Congregation of Israel. And this is a part of Gods law." – *Tents of Shem*, audio lecture

---

78 Rushdoony here is speaking about the duties of the church to take care of their own. The principle of universalism do not apply even within the church.

"Because the Bible is a land-based book, and our faith tied to the earth as the Lord's (Ps. 24:1), the question is not an academic one. For modern man, land has become a commodity and an investment, not essentially a faith inheritance. Our modern outlook thus warps our perspective. For this reason, our federal government thinks nothing of allowing in as immigrants an increasing number of people who are religiously and racially hostile to us. They see no relationship between faith and land. As a result, the United States and the Western world have embarked on a suicidal course. They reject the concept of Christendom and embrace instead the humanistic 'family of man,' and thus immigration policies in the U.S. and Europe are based on myths and illusions of a destructive nature. Because neither land nor inheritance is now seen from the perspective of faith, we have problems in these spheres. The modern state sees itself as the primary owner, and hence eminent domain is basic to its life, and it therefore views itself as the primary heir with death taxes. Both a tax on the land and death taxes are anti-Biblical.

"A disregard for ties to the land has been one of the most destructive forces of the twentieth century. In Africa, artificial nations were created after World War II without regard for the fact that they encompassed rival warring tribes. Artificial unions such as Yugoslavia were created after World War I, bringing together differing peoples and religious groups. All such efforts have simply created chaos and conflict. The rationalistic planners of our time are Hegelians: for them, the rational is the real, and their rational ideas become a Procrustean bed on which humanity is tortured." – *Numbers: Commentaries on the Pentateuch*, pg. 62

"If Negroes are only 'white men with black skins, nothing more, nothing less,' then, conversely, white men are only Negroes with white skins, nothing more, nothing less. This means that all cultural differences, hereditary predispositions, and historical traditions are irrelevant and meaningless. It means, in other words, that history is meaningless. And how can one be an historian if it is his purpose to deny history?

"The white man has behind him centuries of Christian culture, and the discipline and selective breeding this faith requires. Although the white man may reject this faith and subject himself instead to the requirements of humanism, he is still a product of this Christian past. The Negro is a product of a radically different past, and his heredity has been governed by radically different considerations...

"If you and I have our histories abstracted from us, and our heredities as well, and all our cultural conditioning and responses, we are no longer men, no longer human beings, but an abstract and theoretical concept of man. No real history of us can then be written. Stampp's Negroes are thus neither black men nor white men: they are an abstraction, but an abstraction to illustrate the devil in Stampp's humanistic morality play." – *Biblical Philosophy of History*, pgs. 112-114

"The equalitarians end up by asserting, as in Orwell's Animal Farm, that some animals are more 'equal', than others! Whether it is the peasants of Russia, or the Negroes of America, the most rebellious and angry people, the most disillusioned members of equalitarian society, are those who have been 'made equal' by acts of state. They know that they have been defrauded, and their impulse becomes revolutionary." – *Roots of Reconstruction*, pg. 697

"Our Lord states emphatically then He has other sheep which are not of this fold – not of Judea – [but] all over the world. These He shall bring in so that they will be one flock and one shepherd under Himself. Now, the translation of the Bible is faulty at this point in almost every version because the translators are scholars and not Shepherds and where sheep are concerned a fold is a small group. A portion of the flock which is the sum total. A flock can number hundreds or thousands. A fold is a small group that a boy or some elderly man is leading around in the hills. Now, this clearly sets forth the premise that the Church is much more than one racial or national group. Other sheep I have he says. The basic premise of unity is not in the common origin of the members but in Jesus Christ. There is no evil in a Church that is German, Italian, or Jewish in its membership. The evil begins when the Church is limited to such a group. The membership of the Church is not defined by the people but by Jesus Christ. Very early there were those who attempted to limit the Church in terms of Judaic antecedents and these groups perished. Since then many like Nationalistic definitions have been current and their failures are notable. This tells us that the danger to the Church is greater than the hireling, the false shepherds, the wolves, the thieves and the robbers. The dangers exist and include all Christians who want to place their limitations on what is not theirs because they are Christ's property – not His overlords. Thus, the otherwise devout believer can become as dangerous as these alien threats if he tries to erect his prejudices as barriers not of Christ's making." – *Enemies Inside & Outside the Church*

[Rushdoony] "Yes. Well, we live in a world in which no one preaches against envy, neither in the church or out of the church. It is regarded as altogether natural to be envious.

[Scott] Well, it is promoted. It is encouraged, but it is true that you don't hear sermons about. I don't really know what the church today sermonizes against. Once we... when we really come to it, all sins seem to have shriveled down to racism. Beyond that there is no sin.

[Rushdoony] Yes. That is very good. That is about the only sin that is left. And that is an odd thing to choose as a sin, because one of the characteristics of people all over the world has been a preference for their own. People prefer their own families. They prefer their own nationality or their own race, which is entirely legitimate as long as they don't abuse and mistreat others. I believe that the world has seen more racism in this century than ever before precisely because we are trying to equalize everything and we are trying to obscure the differences and say they don't exist. And when you do that, you are going to create a situation where there will be a bootlegged and resentful recognition of differences." – *From the Easy Chair, Envy*

"Man is now defined as humanity rather than the individual, and this great one, humanity, to be truly a unity, must exist as one in the state. In this picture, any assertion of individuality, local or national independence, or the reality of races, is viewed with hostility and as a sign of mental sickness; it is an assertion of plurality which challenges the reality and unity of the universal. It is a 'sick' shattering of the great oneness of being. But, since differences and distinctions are basic to all description and definition, meaning disappears as this universal triumphs." – *The One and the Many* pg. 17

Q. "How does this apply to illegal aliens?
A. "Well, first of all they have broken the law. And justice to everyone requires that the law be upheld. So if they are illegal aliens they should be deported. Now that's justice because it's comparable to breaking and entering into a man's house." – *Justice and World Law*

"The Presbyterian Guardian this year shows signs of outdoing the UPUSA Presbyterian Life in its social gospel preaching. The racist articles of C. Herbert Oliver are examples of this. There are two kinds of racism. First, there is the exaltation of one race above others as inherently virtuous, divine, great, or the like. Second, there is the exaltation of humanity as a race and a demand that we identify ourselves with all men as one people. Oliver is of this second type. He asks us so to exalt humanity, and states, 'The truly secure personality has identified with all creation and with God through Christ.'

"These two forms of racism are both to be rejected as well as their legal safeguards. The first form demands legalized segregation; the second form of racism demands legalized integration. Both deny Christian liberty and the right of free association. ...

"Oliver reads the Scriptures and the Reformation in terms of 'an insistence on the value of the individual,' 'the doctrine of the intrinsic worth of the individual,' and similar statements, and regards the French Revolution with approval. This is rather the Enlightenment faith and 19th Century religious liberalism, not the Reformation faith in the sovereignty of God and justification by faith.

"The test of the Reformed faith is theocentric, in terms of the sovereignty of God and the infallible Word. The test of modernistic faith is always drawn from humanitarian ethics, and the current test is race, not Jesus Christ.

"Unfortunately, The Presbyterian Guardian has of late been busy citing one or another of the humanitarian and liberal shibboleths as 'tests' rather than the Word and the Confession. Was it for this that Machen fought?" – a letter submitted in *The Presbyterian Guardian*, see *Morton Smith in Bibliography*, pg. 131

"A contrary development is increasingly in evidence in the Western world, and especially in the United States, is the development by systematic indoctrination of a bad conscience. The political cultivation of guilt is a central means to power, for guilty men are slaves; their conscience is in bondage, and hence they are easily made objects of control. Guilt is thus systematically taught for purposes of control...Tragically, this politics of guilt is aided, not only by the apostate clergy of the left, but also by ostensibly conservative clergymen." – *The Politics of Guilt and Pity*, pg. 20

— R.J. RUSHDOONY —

"Wherever false responsibility is promoted, an ugly strategy of power is present." – *The Politics of Guilt and Pity*, pg. 45

"Systematic propaganda has taught the Christian that he has a 'guilty past' with reference to the Jew. The reality is that the relationship has had all the diversity of tension and peace, good and evil, on both sides as exists between all conflicting groups, and very often the Jew has been the offended and also the offender. Very often too, because Christians, as witness Cromwell, have had erroneous views concerning biblical prophecy, they have assumed a respectful and reverent attitude towards the Jew. And, paradoxically, we are assured by the same theologians that the Jews are innocent of Christ's blood, even as Christians are declared guilty of the deaths of Jews who died centuries ago! Such teaching is simply the political cultivation of guilt. Christ came to free men from sin, guilt and shame, whereas the political theologians would bind men's consciences." – *The Politics of*

Guilt and Pity, pg. 20

"Americans are repeatedly assured that American history is a long account of guilt, towards Indians, Negroes, minority groups, labor, Mexico, and, ultimately, all the world as well for refusing to enter the League of Nations. This is defective history and perverse politics. Its purpose is the cultivation of guilt in order to produce a submissive populace." – *The Politics of Guilt and Pity*, pg. 20

"The more a civilization advances, the deeper will its sense of sin become, because the increase of prosperity and cultural advantages will only increase the masochistic desire to pay for progress, which the individuals unconsciously believe requires atonement before enjoyment. As a result, the very liberating forces of civilization themselves call into existence the forces of enslavement. The citizens of the civilization progressively demand political enslavement as their masochistic price for advancement. As a result, the most ruthless totalitarian enslavement is invited, and the culture uses its material liberation to forge a new slavery." – *The Politics of Guilt and Pity*, pg. 12

"Men remain feeling guilty, for a false sense of guilt has no cure save the truth, and this is not forthcoming. Since the citizens are now guilt-ridden because of their education and political indoctrination, they are more amenable to robbery, and even murder. If the white man feels guilty towards the Negro, he is less capable of defending himself against the Negroes who turn into a revolutionary rabble, bent on theft and murder. The state finds it easier to rob men when men feel guilty for what they are and have, and the state drones on and on about the needs of the poor of the nation and of the world." – *Politics of Guilt and Pity*, pg. 46

"We must render honor and justice to all men wherever due, but we have a particular responsibility to care for our own. This means first of all our families. . . . Biblical conduct is regulated by relationship, and to subvert this is to lead directly into welfare economics and socialism. If a man must exercise towards all men the same care, oversight, and charity he does towards his own family, then an impossible burden is placed on him. . . . Every system of 'universal' ethics is at one and the same time a system of universal slavery." – *The Politics of Guilt and Pity*, pg. 248 Referencing Leviticus 18:1-30 and 20:22-24:

"As the last statement declares, God identifies Himself as the God who separates His people from other peoples: this is a basic part of salvation. The religious and moral separation of the believer is thus a basic aspect of biblical law. Even as segregation from disease is necessary to avoid contagion, so separation from religious and moral evil is necessary to the preservation of true order.

"Segregation or separation is thus a basic principle of Biblical law with respect to religion and morality. Every attempt to destroy this principle is an effort to reduce society to its lowest common denominator. Toleration is the excuse under which this leveling is undertaken, but the concept of toleration conceals a radical intolerance. In the name of toleration, the believer is asked to associate on a common level of total acceptance with the atheist, the pervert, the criminal, and the adherents of other religions as though no differences existed." – *The Institutes of Biblical Law*, pg. 294

"God, by the way, does not despise the idea of a nation, contrary to some liberals today. When he says 'I will make of thee a great nation' it is because the idea of a nation is a good one, it's a Godly one." – *Eschatology of Covenant Man*

"Unequal yoking plainly means mixed marriages between believers and unbelievers is clearly forbidden. But Deuteronomy 22:10 not only forbids unequal yoking by inference, and as a case law, but also unequal yoking generally. This means that an unequal marriage between believers or between unbelievers is wrong. Man was created in the image of God (Gen. 1:26), and woman is the reflected image of God in man, and from man (1 Cor. 11:1-12; Gen. 2:18, 21-23). 'Helpmeet' means a reflection or a mirror, an image of man, indicating that a woman must have something religiously and culturally in common with her husband. The burden of the law is thus against inter-religious, inter-racial, and inter-cultural marriages, in that they normally go against the very community which marriage is designed to establish.

"Unequal yoking means more than marriage. In society at large it means the enforced integration of various elements which are not congenial. Unequal yoking is in no realm productive

of harmony; rather, it aggravates the differences and delays the growth of the different elements toward a Christian harmony and association… Cross-cultural marriages are thus normally a failure… A man can identify character within his culture, but he cannot do more than identify the general character of another culture." – *Institutes of Biblical Law*, pg. 257

With Otto Scott on the inevitability of tribalism:
[Murray] "If what we are saying is that, you know, we have got a group of tribes here on earth that can't seem to get along. You know, if we are all created by God why can't we live together in harmony? Are we inherently tribal?
[Scott] Yes.
[Rushdoony] Yes, the family, the clan or tribe, that is still basic in most of the world and it is a pattern that reasserts itself in time even in areas that become very cosmopolitan, because when you make life too impersonal, people rebel against that.
[Rushdoony] Otto, you wanted to say something about Tribalism.
[Scott] Yes. There is an effort to deny that there are tribes. There is even an effort to deny that there are nationalities or people as such, that there are… that there are Celts, that there are Saxons, Anglo Saxons that… that there are Mêlées, that there are Germans or French or Spaniards. There is an effort to say that all cultural differences are on the surface, are trivial and unimportant and that everybody basically is the same, which comes very close to arguing that everyone is an integer, like a number that you can shuffle back and forth and that we are not real personalities, we don't represent separate cultures or individual cultures even.
[Rushdoony] Well, I think Tribalism is as natural to people as is the family. There is an instinctive drawing together with those who are close to you as against the outsider. I know that although it has been 19 years since we lived in Los Angeles, the various parts were like villages. And each had its character and you had an opinion about people who came from another area, not that it was hostile, but that you figured they were of a particular character. There are counties in California where if you are an outsider you are a really cut out of things, because they have generations of having shared a common background. And this you can find all over the country.

[Scott] Of course.

[Rushdoony] We cannot destroy it. It is something that is basic to people. They want to feel common ties." – *War*

"The problem, of course, is that now we have a great deal of illegal immigration. We have immigration laws that no longer follow the older pattern and concentrate on European countries. We allow many, many peoples in who have nothing in common with us, who are Moslems or members of other religions and it appears that there is an effort to break the Christian heritage and character of the United States." – *Immigration*

"As we view men and nations, we must recognize three things or else we warp our thinking. First, to quote Joseph Parker who, more than a century ago, so powerfully expressed this point, and I quote, 'All nations are not equally honored.' Now that's a fact of history. Nothing can eliminate the fact of differences. If we resist God's predestinating purpose, we fall into a variety of humanistic answers ... because some people, as they look to the difference between people, they refuse to say, 'God has ordained all things.'" – *Calling vs. Presumption*

"Democracy make[s] every man forget his ancestors ... it hides his descendants and separates his contemporaries from him; it throws him back forever upon himself alone and threatens in the end to confine him entirely within the solitude of his own heart.

"What had characterized Americans previously and continued to govern many years was not individualism but a sense of destiny as God's chosen people, with faith in their calling, not only in terms of the personal covenant of grace and as a church covenant ... but also as a civil covenant, a called people of God as a civil order, surrounded by the notable and marvelous tokens of His providence." – *This Independent Republic*, pg. 85

"Equality as it is often championed today is a rationalistic and scientific abstraction, a concept best promulgated in French revolutionary thought. Basic to this concept of equality is a utopianism, a desire to end history and an intolerance for the very human fact of problems and tensions. – *This Independent Republic*, pg. 80

"In this Christian pattern, the integrity of differences was recognized. In the New Testament, there is neither segregation nor integration. Jewish converts organized Jewish churches, and Gentiles their own congregations, without barring one another. Each was to develop in terms of his history and tradition within the framework of Christ's body. Community, not uniformity, was the emphasis." – *This Independent Republic*, pg. 80

"Non-Christian individualism and democracy erode societal forms, ties, and institutions, and finally leave only the lonely and atomistic individual before the power of the democratic state, which then destroys that individual." – *This Independent Republic*, pg. 84

"It is a serious error and a form of antinomianism to limit the application of the law to individuals. The law applies to men and to society. There is an essential link between the faith and the character of men, and the social order they live in. It is their faith, their character, that creates or alters in one direction or another, their social order. To assume that a society can be just when the people are not is a modern heresy. One of the worst titles of this century by Reinhold Niebuhr, was a book titled *Moral Man and Immoral Society*. Well, that's nonsense. If men are moral, they will soon create a moral society. If immoral, they will create an immoral society. This heresy of seeing a difference between men and their society, gives an independent life and character to a civil government and a society apart from the people in it, and no state has an independent life. It isn't something that floats out there in space with a character, apart from the people, but this illusion is essential to the errors of the U.S. State Department and millions of Americans. They assume that the United States, its Constitution, and its laws have an independent character from the people. But this is nonsense. The Constitution has always been interpreted in terms of the character of the people, and if we have a bad character, we have a bad Constitution as it has been interpreted. Its meaning is varied, and legally, the Constitution is to be interpreted by the most recent decisions of the Supreme Court. Some people believe these people who hold to this heresy that all that is necessary is to allow the unlimited immigration of aliens, of non-Christian peoples into the United States, and to ensure them of equal rights, and they will become what the Americans of 1800 were, or of 1900. And the same illusion marks Europe. In Europe, they believe that because the country has a character, everyone who comes in will soon pick up that character. So, all the blacks and Arabs that are in France will become Frenchmen. That's an illusion. They don't have the same faith, therefore they're not going to give the same character to society." – *Third Commandment*

"This is a very interesting point because there is a verse that is used in St. John with respect to ecumenicism and the assertion of one worldism. In this verse, our Lord says, 'Other sheep have I which are not of this fold,' and he declares that them also he is calling that there may be one-fold, one shepherd, it reads. Actually, it should read one flock, one shepherd. Now, what's the difference here? The translators, by and large, have been ignorant of the meaning of the words, because they're not sheep men. You can have a fold of sheep which is a part of a larger flock. If we are all to be one-fold, then we are all to be in one church and in one world government, but if we are many folds in one flock, then our Lord is saying there are to be many groups, many peoples, many nations, but not in one-fold, in one flock. In other words, our unity is in Christ, not in our organizations. Today, all attempts at unity are to make men one in organization, not in Christ, and the two are radically different." – *Virgin Birth and Property*

Russian Orthodox Church

"In the contemporary world, the notion of 'nation' is used in two meanings, as an ethnic community and the aggregate citizens of a particular state. Relationships between church and nation should be viewed in the context of both meanings of this word.

"In the Old Testament, the terms 'am and goy are used to denote 'a people'. In the Hebrew Bible, each term is given a quite concrete meaning, the former denoting God's chosen people of Israel, the latter in its plural form goyim the Gentiles. In the Greek Bible (Septuagint), the first term was rendered by the term laos (people) or demos (a nation as a political entity), while the second by the term ethnos (nation, in plural ethne, meaning 'heathens'). ...

"The universal nature of the Church, however, does not mean that Christians should have no right to national identity and national self-expressions. On the contrary, the Church unites in herself the universal with the national. Thus, the Orthodox Church, though universal, consists of many Autocephalous National Churches. Orthodox Christians, aware of being citizens of the heavenly homeland, should not forget about their earthly homeland. The Lord Jesus Christ Himself, the Divine Founder of the Church, had no shelter on earth (Mt. 8:20) and pointed that the teaching He brought was not local or national in nature: 'the hour cometh, when ye shall neither in this mountain, nor yet at Jerusalem, worship the Father' (Jn. 4:21). Nevertheless, He identified Himself with the people to whom He belonged by birth. Talking to the Samaritan woman, He stressed His belonging to the Jewish nation: 'Ye worship ye know what: we know what we worship: for salvation is of the Jews' (Jn. 4:22). Jesus was a loyal subject of the Roman Empire and paid taxes in favour of Caesar (Mt. 22-16-21). St. Paul, in his letters teaching on the supranational nature of the Church of Christ, did not forget that by birth he was 'an Hebrew of the Hebrews' (Phil. 3:5), though a Roman by citizenship (Acts 22:25-29).

"The cultural distinctions of particular nations are expressed in the liturgical and other church art, especially in the peculiarities of Christian order of life. All this creates national Christian cultures.

"Among saints venerated by the Orthodox Church, many became famous for the love of their earthly homeland and faithfulness to it. Russian hagiographic sources praise the holy Prince Michael of Tver who 'gave his life for his fatherland', comparing his feat to the martyrdom of the holy protomartyr Dimitrius of Thessaloniki: 'The good lover of his fatherland said about his native city of Thessaloniki, "O Lord, if you ruin this city, I will perish together with it, but if you save it, I will also be saved"'.

"In all times the Church has called upon her children to love their homeland on earth and not to spare their lives to protect it if it was threatened. The Russian Church on many occasions gave her blessing to the people for them to take part in liberation wars. Thus, in 1380, the venerable Sergius the abbot and miracle-maker of Radonezh blessed the Russian troops headed by the holy Prince Dimitry Donskoy before their battle with the Tartar-Mongol invaders. In 1612, St. Hermogen, Patriarch of Moscow and All Russia, gave blessing upon the irregulars in their struggle with the Polish invaders. In 1813, during the war with the French aggressors, St. Philaret of Moscow said to his flock: 'If you avoid dying for the honour and freedom of the Fatherland, you will die a criminal or a slave; die for the faith and the Fatherland and you will be granted life and a crown in heaven'.

"The holy righteous John of Kronstadt wrote this about love of one's earthly homeland: 'Love the earthly homeland... it has raised, distinguished, honoured and equipped you with everything; but have special love for the heavenly homeland... that homeland is incomparably more precious that this one, because it is holy, righteous and incorruptible. The priceless blood of the Son of God has earned that homeland for you. But in order to be members of that homeland, you should respect and love its laws, just as you are obliged to respect and really respect the laws of the earthly homeland'.

"Christian patriotism may be expressed at the same time with regard to a nation as an ethnic community and as a community of its citizens. The Orthodox Christian is called to love his fatherland, which has a territorial dimension, and his brothers by blood who live everywhere in the world. This love is one of the ways of fulfilling God's commandment of love to one's neighbour which includes love to one's family, fellow-tribesmen and fellow-citizens.

"The patriotism of the Orthodox Christian should be active. It is manifested when he defends his fatherland against an enemy, works for the good of the motherland, cares for the good order of people's life through, among other things, participation in the affairs of government. The Christian is called to preserve and develop national culture and people's self-awareness.

"When a nation, civil or ethnic, represents fully or predominantly a monoconfessional Orthodox community, it can in a certain sense be regarded as the one community of faith — an Orthodox nation.

"At the same time, national sentiments can cause such sinful phenomena as aggressive nationalism, xenophobia, national exclusiveness and inter-ethnic enmity. At their extremes, these phenomena often lead to the restriction of the rights of individuals and nations, wars and other manifestations of violence.

"It is contrary to Orthodox ethics to divide nations into the best and the worst and to belittle any ethnic or civic nation. Even more contrary to Orthodoxy are the teachings which put the nation in the place of God or reduce faith to one of the aspects of national self-awareness.

"Opposing these sinful phenomena, the Orthodox Church carries out the mission of reconciliation between hostile nations and their representatives. Thus, in inter-ethnic conflicts, she does not identify herself with any side, except for cases when one of the sides commit evident aggression or injustice." – *The Basis of the Social Concept, Church And Nation*, pgs. 6-9

"Throughout her millennium-long history the Russian Orthodox Church educated the faithful in the spirit of patriotism and love of peace. Patriotism is manifested in the concern for the historical heritage of the Fatherland, in active civil position by sharing the joys and hardships of her people, in zealous and conscientious work and in concern for the moral state of society and for the preservation of nature.

"The religio-ideological neutrality of the state does not contradict the Christian idea of the Church's calling in society. The Church, however, should point out to the state that it is inadmissible to propagate such convictions or actions which may result in total control over a person's life, convictions and relations with other people, as well as erosion in personal, family or public morality, insult of religious feelings, damage to the cultural and spiritual identity of the people and threats to the sacred gift of life. In implementing her social, charitable, educational and other socially significant projects, the Church may rely on the support and assistance of the state. She also has the right to expect that state, in building its relations with religious bodies, will take into account the number of their followers and the place the occupy in forming the historical, cultural and spiritual image of the people and their civic stand." – *The Basis of the Social Concept, Church and State*, pgs. 15,19

"An even more inexorable factor of migration was the spread of hedonistic quasi-religion, which captured not only the elite, but also the widest masses of citizens in countries with a high standard of living. A sign of time is the refusal to continue the race for the sake of the most carefree, self-satisfied and secured personal existence. Popularization of the ideology of child-free, the cult of childless and family-free life for its own sake, leads to a reduction in the population in the most seemingly prosperous societies." – *Economy in the Context of Globalization – Orthodox Ethical View*

"A concomitant phenomenon of globalization is becoming a permanent migration crisis, accompanied by a sharp cultural conflict between immigrants and citizens of host countries. And in this case, the openness of borders does not lead to a rapprochement and unification, but to the separation and bitterness of people." – *Economy in the Context of Globalization – Orthodox Ethical View*

"Another way of artificially raising the standard of living is 'living on loan'. Without having the desired material values in the real world today, a person seeks to get them from tomorrow, to consume what is not yet created, to spend what is not earned – in the hope that tomorrow he will be able to earn and repay a debt. We see that in the modern economy, like a snowball, the size of borrowing is growing, not only personal, but also corporate and government. It becomes more and more aggressive, more and more attractive pictures are drawn by advertisements calling for a live loan. Borrowed loans increase, maturity dates are postponed – when the possibilities to borrow from tomorrow are exhausted, they start borrowing from the day after tomorrow. Whole countries and nations plunged into debt.

"The business of lending expectations, often illusory, becomes more profitable than the production of tangible goods. In this connection, it is necessary to remember the moral doubtfulness of the situation when money 'makes' new money without the use of human labor. The declaration of the credit sphere as the main engine of the economy, its predominance over the real economic sector comes into conflict with the revealed moral principles condemning usury.

"If earlier the impossibility of repaying the taken debt threatened with bankruptcy to one borrower, then in the context of globalization, an exaggerated 'financial bubble' threatens the bankruptcy of all humanity. The interdependence between people and countries has become so great that for the greed and carelessness of some will have to pay everyone. The Orthodox Church recalls that financial activities of this kind are fraught with severe economic and moral risks; calls on governments to develop measures to limit uncontrolled growing borrowings, and on all Orthodox Christians to develop economic relations that restore the link between wealth and labor, consumption and creation." – *Economy in the Context of Globalization – Orthodox Ethical View*

"In the context of globalization, the transnational elite has grown significantly stronger, able to evade the social mission, in particular, by transferring funds abroad to offshore zones, exert political pressure on governments, and not obey public demands. We see that national governments are increasingly losing their self-reliance, less and less dependent on the will of their own peoples and more and more on the will of transnational elites. These elites themselves are not constituted in the legal space, and therefore they are not accountable to either nations or national governments, turning into a shadow regulator of socio-economic processes. The greed of the shadow rulers of the global economy leads to the fact that the thinnest layer of the 'chosen ones' becomes richer and at the same time more and more free from responsibility." – *Economy in the Context of Globalization – Orthodox Ethical View*

"The most important socio-psychological phenomenon associated with globalization has become the widespread distribution of the cult of consumption. Thanks to modern means of communication, an excessively high standard of living, inherent only to a narrow elite circle of people and inaccessible to the overwhelming majority, is advertised as a social landmark for the whole society. Hedonism turns into a kind of civil religion, defining people's behavior, excusing immoral acts, forcing to devote all mental strength and precious time to just one consumer race. The main criterion of social success, the main measure of values is the volume of material goods consumed. Consumption is seen as the only meaning of life, abolishing care for the salvation of the soul and even the fate of future generations." – *Economy in the Context of Globalization – Orthodox Ethical View*

"In modern life, globalization not only removes obstacles to communication and knowledge of the truth, but also removes barriers to the spread of sin and vice. The rapprochement of people in space is accompanied by their spiritual separation from each other and from God, aggravation of property inequality, increased competition, and increasing mutual misunderstanding. A process designed to unite leads to even greater separation." – *Economy in the Context of Globalization – Orthodox Ethical View*

"Globalization – the involvement of the peoples and states of the Earth in a single economic, cultural, informational, political processes – has become the main distinguishing feature of the new era... Therefore, an understanding of the opportunities and the threats that globalization brings to the world is impossible without understanding its economic background.

"The Christian conscience cannot remain indifferent to phenomena of such magnitude as globalization, which radically change the face of the world... The core of the economy should not be the multiplication of temptations, but the transformation of the world and man through labor and creativity." – *Economy in the Context of Globalization – Orthodox Ethical View*

"Attempts by indigenous people of the rich countries to stop the migration flow are futile, because they come in conflict with greed of their own elites who are interested in the low-wage workforce. But an even more inexorable factor driving migration was the spread of hedonic quasi-religion capturing not only elite, but also the broad masses of people in countries with high living standards. Renunciation of procreation for the most careless, smug and personal existence becomes [the sign] of the times. The popularization of the ideology of child-free, the cult of childless and without family life for themselves lead to a reduction in the population in the most seemingly prosperous societies.

"We must not forget that the commandment to all the descendants of Adam and Eve, said: 'Fill the earth and subdue it.' ... Anyone who does not want to continue his race will inevitably have to give way to the ground for those who prefer having children over material well-being." – *Economy in the Context of Globalization – Orthodox Ethical View*

Samuel Rutherford

"Deut. 17:15 demands that for the purposes of governance God's people are to 'choose one from amongst their brethren' only and...the fifth commandment layeth obedience to the king on us no less than to our parents..." – *Lex Rex*: Q.III, pg. 4

S

Jerry D. Salyer

"Nowhere does Lewis say that my duty to my country or my nation is a superstition. To the contrary, he asserts that 'duty to our own kin' is very much 'a part of the traditional morality.' What 'respectable' Lewis boosters carefully ignore, time and again, is that the passage implies that every obligation of natural law demands recognition...With all due respect to neo-pagan theorist Alain de Benoist, there really is a human nature, which is precisely how we can know that the leveling of ethnic and national identities via globalism is monstrous....

"Why do few intelligent people take seriously the p.c. 'family values' conservatism that has appropriated Lewis as its corporate mascot? Because there is not an argument against 'irrational' loyalty to nation, tribe, and clan that cannot be effortlessly redirected against 'irrational' loyalty to the nuclear family itself." – *After Strange Gods*

"Perhaps the most bitter irony of our time lies in the fact that celebrity apologists who purport to defend an incarnational religion have joined the chorus of those who deny the importance of flesh and blood. The bloodless creed such gurus peddle is a cold, ineffectual abstraction, one which the great Christian teachers of yesteryear would find alien.

"If we are serious about combating the neopagan temptation, we need to remember our ancestors–spiritual as well as biological." – *After Strange Gods*

"Neopaganism appeals to those who find revolting the injustices of egalitarian multiculturalism, a regime too often treated as sacrosanct by Southern Baptist theologians and Catholic pundits alike. To check neopaganism's spread, we must emphasize that the Christian tradition does indeed transcend political correctness." – *After Strange Gods*

"If 'white American' is a meaningful expression–and it surely is–then so, too is WASP, Scots-Irish, Hoosier, Cajun, Sooner, Midwesterner, Southerner, Yankee, Irish, Italian, and all the other interconnected and often overlapping terms denoting all the other British-rooted and European-rooted identities that reside at the heart of the American story. Subsidiarity is a concept that should be applied to blood and soil no less than to economics and political structures, and Vance does us all a service by highlighting this." – *Silcon Hillbilly*

"There is no argument for denying significance to ethnicity or nationality that does not ultimately translate into an attack upon the natural family itself. Either organic and historical bonds matter or they don't." – *Books in Brief*

Salic Law

"...the illustrious nation of the Franks, chosen by God, valorous in arms, constant in peace, profound in wisdom, noble in body, spotless in purity, handsome without equal, intrepid, quick and fierce, newly converted to the Catholic faith, and free of heresy." – quoted in *The Cultural Foundations of Nations*, pg. 98

Paul Samuelson

"After World War I, laws were passed severely limiting immigration. Only a trickle of immigrants has been admitted since then.... By keeping supply down, immigration policy tends to keep wages high. Let us underline this basic principle: Limitation in the supply of any grade of labor relative to all other productive factors can be expected to raise its wage rate; an increase in supply will, other things being equal, tend to depress wage rates." – *Economics*, pg. 538

Sappho

I have a daughter, golden,
Beautiful, like a flower –
Kleis, my love –
And I would not exchange her for
All the riches of Lydia…
– Fragments, Kline trans.

Robert Sarah

"Civilized man is fundamentally an heir, he receives a history, a culture, a language, a name, a family. This is what distinguishes him from the barbarian. To refuse to be inscribed within a network of dependence, heritage, and filiation condemns us to go back naked into the jungle of a competitive economy left to its own devices. Because he refuses to acknowledge himself as an heir, man is condemned to the hell of liberal globalization in which individual interests confront one another without any law to govern them besides profit at any price." – *Cardinal Sarah's Cri de Coeur: The Catholic Church Has Lost Its Sense of the Sacred*, Interview with *Nation Catholic Register*

"Men do not resemble one another. Nature, too, is multifariously rich, because he ordained it so. Our Father thought that his children could be enriched by their differences. Today globalization is contrary to the divine plan. It tends to make humanity uniform. Globalization means cutting man off from his roots, from his religion, from his culture, history, customs, and ancestors. He becomes stateless, without a country, without a land. He is at home everywhere and nowhere." – *The Day is Now Far Spent*, pg. 242

"The standardization of ways of life is the cancer of the postmodern world. Men become unwitting members of a great planetary herd, that does not think, does not protest, and allows itself to be guided toward a future that does not belong to it.

"Individual isolation and the degradation of persons, who are doomed to be no more than elements lost in the mass of consumers, are the two most horrible children of capitalism.

"God's creature is deadened. He places his heart as a burnt offering on the altar of artificial happiness. He no longer knows the taste of true joys. He is an animal that eats, drinks, revels, and enjoys. The critical sense has become a ghost from the past.

"Globalized humanity, without borders, is a hell." – *The Day is Now Far Spent*, pg. 276

"The Church cannot cooperate with this new form of slavery that has come of mass migration. If the West continues on this disastrous course, there is a great risk that, with declining births, it will disappear, invaded by foreigners, as Rome was invaded by the barbarians. I speak as an African; my country is mostly Muslim. I think I know the reality of which I speak." – *The Church Is Plunged Into The Darkness Of Good Friday*, Interview with *Culture à Valeurs Actuelles*

"[Poland] is free to tell Europe that each was created by God to be placed in a particular place, with its culture, its traditions, its history. The current drive toward globalizing the world by doing away with nations is pure madness. The Jewish people endured exile, but God brought them back to their country. Christ fled from Herod and into Egypt, but he returned to his country upon the death of Herod. Each should live in his own country. Like a tree, each to his own soil, his place where he flourishes perfectly. It would be better to help people to flourish in their own cultures, than to encourage them to come to a Europe filled with decadence. It is a false exegesis that uses the Word of God to celebrate migration. God never wanted this tearing away." – *The Church Is Plunged Into The Darkness Of Good Friday*, Interview with *Culture à Valeurs Actuelles*

"When I went to Poland, a country which is often criticized, I encouraged the faithful to affirm their identity as they had done over the centuries. My message was simple: You are first Poles, Catholics, and only afterwards Europeans. You should not sacrifice the two first types of identity on the altar of a nationless, technocratic Europe. The Brussels Commission thinks of nothing except the construction of a free market in the service of great financial powers." – *The Church Is Plunged Into The Darkness Of Good Friday*, Interview with *Culture à Valeurs Actuelles*

"In what manner is it possible to remove the rights of the nation to distinguish between a political or religious refugee, who must flee from his homeland, and the economic migrant, who wants to change his address without adapting himself, identifying with, and accepting the culture of the country in which he will live?" – *The Church Is Plunged Into The Darkness Of Good Friday*, Interview with *Culture à Valeurs Actuelles*

Arthur M. Schlesinger Jr.

"Ethnic and racial conflict, it seems evident, will now replace the conflict of ideologies as the explosive issue of our times." – *The Disuniting of America*, pg. 10

"The hostility of one tribe for another is among the most instinctive human reactions.... Mass migrations have produced mass antagonisms since the beginning of time." – *The Disuniting Of America*, pg. 12

"The language of the new nation, its laws, its institutions, it political ideas, its literature, its customs, its precepts, its prayers, primarily derived from Britain." – *The Disuniting Of America*, pg. 34

Eckhard J. Schnabel

"Paul asserts that the human race was created by God to inhabit the earth in all its diversity. God 'determined' not only the existence of human beings but also the conditions of their existence... 'Boundaries of the land' refers to the inhabitable zones of the earth...The 'boundaries of their lands' are the political boundaries between places where people live – whether cities, regions provinces, or continents...Paul argues that cities, countries, and empires rise and fall during the course of history, both in terms of their political power and in terms of their political boundaries. The God whom Paul proclaims is the Creator of the world and of the human race, and He is the Lord of the history of the human race." – *Zondervan Exegetical Commentary on the New Testament* on Acts 17:26

Friedrich Schiller

"Mit der Glocke schwingendem Tritte,
Das Schifflein fliegt vorüber,
Die Welle zittert, der Nachen zittert,
Vorüber fliegt das Glück.
Greif' in die Ruder, die Segel schwellen,

Nur Mut! schon landest du glücklich wieder,
Und sicher traget dich einst das Schifflein
Durch jeden Sturm zum Port."

Translation:
  "With the swinging step of the bell,
  The little ship flies past,
  The wave trembles, the skiff trembles,
  Happiness flies past.
  Seize the oars, the sails swell,
  Take courage! Soon you'll land happily again,
  And one day the little ship will carry you
  Safely through every storm to port."
– *The Song of the Bell (Das Lied von der Glocke, lines 243-250)* [79]

"Freude, schöner Götterfunken,
Tochter aus Elysium,
Wir betreten feuertrunken,
Himmlische, dein Heiligtum!"

Translation:
  "Joy, beautiful spark of the gods,
  Daughter from Elysium,
  We enter, drunk with fire,
  Heavenly one, your sanctuary!"
– *Ode to Joy (An die Freude, lines 25-26)*

"Alle Menschen werden Brüder,
Wo dein sanfter Flügel weilt."

Translation:
  "All people become brothers,
  Where your gentle wing rests."
– *Ode to Joy (lines 25-26)*

Herbert Schlossberg

"When the provision of paternal security replaces the provision of justice as the function of the state, the state stops providing justice. The ersatz parent ceases executing judgment against those who violate the law, and the nation begins losing the benefits of justice. Those who are concerned about the chaos into which the criminal justice system has fallen should consider what the state's function has become. Because the state can only be a bad imitation of a father, as a dancing bear act is of a ballerina, the protection of this Leviathan of a father turns out to be a bear hug..." – *Idols for Destruction*, pg. 184

79 Schiller was a prominent German poet, philosopher, and playwright.

"Rulers who wish to attach the loyalty of the citizens unconditionally to the state apparatus do everything in their power to detach them from intermediate loyalties. They are abetted by one of the delusions of libertarianism, which often unwittingly aids the state in this aim…In asserting total autonomy in those ways, the individualist sets the stage for his complete loss of liberty, for there is nothing to protect him from the idol state, which is only too happy to assist in the destruction of intermediate institutions." – *Idols for Destruction*, pg. 212

"One of the chief errors in Ayn Rand's philosophy is her idea that the altruism of social democracy is the opposite of individual egoism. Seeing the destruction wrought by the former, she argues for the latter. But collectivism and egoism are both derived from immanence, both can live only when the limitations of transcendent law are overthrown, both are symptoms of the same disease. If it is lawful for the individual to do as he pleases, why should it not be lawful for the commissar to do as he pleases? If there is nothing to restrain one lawfully, then there is nothing to restrain the other." – *Idols for Destruction*, pg. 267

James V. Schall

"A culture is a complex composition of the manners, rites, language, laws, ideas, and customs of a people. These sources describe what a given people hold to be true, or at least valid. How they act to one another, how they build things, how and what they punish and reward, how they think of birth and death—all these make up the outlines of a given culture." – *15 Lies at the Basis of Our Culture*

Joseph Schumpeter

"It may be the case also with societies that are not primitive provided they are not too differentiated and do not harbor any serious problems. Switzerland is the best example. There is so little to quarrel about in a world of peasants which, excepting hotels and banks, contains no great capitalist industry, and the problems of public policy are so simple and so stable that an overwhelming majority can be expected to understand them and to agree about them." – *Capitalism, Socialism and Democracy*, pg. 267 [80]

"English workmen are well organized and as a rule responsibly led. An experienced bureaucracy of irreproachable cultural and moral standards could be trusted to assimilate the new elements required for an extension of the sphere of the state. The unrivaled integrity of the English politician and the presence of a ruling class that is uniquely able and civilized make many things easy that would be impossible elsewhere. In particular this ruling group unites in the most workable proportions adherence to formal tradition with extreme adaptability to new principles, situations and persons. It wants to rule but it is quite ready to rule on behalf of changing interests. It manages industrial England as well as it managed agrarian England, protectionist England as well as free trade England. And it possesses an altogether unrivaled talent for appropriating not only the programs of oppositions but also their brains. It assimilated Disraeli who elsewhere would have become another Lassalle." – *Capitalism, Socialism and Democracy*, pg. 229

"Take Sweden for an instance. Like her art, her science, her politics, her social institutions and much besides, her socialism and her socialists owe their distinction not to any peculiar features of principle or intention, but to the stuff the Swedish nation is made of and to its exceptionally well-balanced social structure. That is why it is so absurd for other nations to try to copy Swedish examples; the only effective way of doing so would be to import the Swedes and to put them in charge. The Swedes being the people they are and their social structure being what it is, we shall have no difficulty in understanding the two outstanding characteristics of their socialism. The socialist party, almost always ably and conscientiously led, grew slowly in response to a very normal social process, without any attempt to push ahead of normal development and to antagonize for the sake of antagonizing. Hence its rise to political power produced no convulsions. Responsible office came naturally to its leaders who were able to meet the leaders of other parties on terms of equality and largely on common ground: to this day, though a communist group has of course developed, the differences in current politics reduce to such questions as whether a few million kroner more or less should be spent on some social purpose accepted by all. And within the

80 Schumpeter is writing about the canton system in Switzerland which cannot be exported to other nations

party, the antagonism between intellectuals and labor men only shows under the microscope precisely because, owing to the level of both, there is no great cultural gulf between them and because, the Swedish social organism producing a relatively smaller supply of unemployable intellectuals than do other social organisms, exasperated and exasperating intellectuals are not as numerous as they are elsewhere." – *Capitalism, Socialism, and Democracy*, pg. 325

Philip Schaff

"KIN'DRED, in the O. T. the translation of the terms signifying—(1) 'clan,' persons belonging to a common stock, Gen. 12:1; 24:4, 7, 38, 40, 41; (2) 'birth,' and so 'off-spring,' as Gen. 31:3; 43:7; Esth. 8:6; (3) 'knowledge,' one known by relationship, Ruth 3:2; (4) 'redemption,' from the duty of a near relation to redeem, Eze. 11:15; comp. Ruth 4:6; (5) 'brother,' 1 Chron. 12:29; (6) the immediate family. Gen. 10:31." – *A Dictionary of the Bible*, pg. 496

Thomas R. Schreiner

"The kings of the nations will also bring their glory into the city (cf. Ps. 72:10). As Isaiah 60:5 says, 'The wealth of the nations shall come to [Jerusalem]' (cf. Ps. 68:29), while Isaiah 60:11 declares, 'People [will] bring to you the wealth of the nations.' It seems John is saying that every good and beautiful thing from the old creation will be in the new creation. Nothing of beauty will be lost. Instead, it will be present in a perfected and incorruptible way." – on Revelation 21:24, In I. M. Duguid, J. M. Hamilton Jr., & J. Sklar (Eds.), *ESV Exposition Commentary, Hebrews–Revelation*, vol. XII, pg. 745

Otto Scott

"It is very interesting that the first effort to restrict immigration in a overall sense was in, I believe, around 1921. Although the... they were very strict before that. You had to have a clean police record. You had to be healthy. You had to have a job. You had to have a skill of some sort or you had to have relatives who were responsible. But in 1921 on the basis of the most recent census, they tried to restrict immigration proportionately to the proportions of the population, so many from each European country according to the proportion of

their descendants here. And that made sense, because it would not disrupt society and it was attacked viciously by the liberal press as prejudicial and racial. And this as interesting because it was almost to say that the critics wanted to change the racial composition of the country in the name of anti racism." – in *Immigration*, an online discussion

Scottish Confession of Faith

"The Estates of Scotland, with the inhabitants of the same, professing Christ Jesus' holy evangel: to their natural countrymen, and unto all other realms and nations, professing the same Lord Jesus with them, wish grace, mercy, and peace from God the Father of our Lord Jesus Christ, with the spirit of righteous judgment..." – quoted in *Wesley's Revision of the Shorter Catechism*, pg. 97

"[The] kirk is Catholic, that is, universal, because it contains the elect of all ages, all realms, nations, and tongues, be they of the Jews, or be they of the Gentiles; who have communion and society with God the Father, and with his Son Christ Jesus, through the sanctification of his Holy Spirit..." – quoted in *Wesley's Revision of the Shorter Catechism*, pg. 113

"We confess and acknowledge empires, kingdoms, dominions and cities to be ordained by God. We further confess that such persons as are placed in authority are to be loved, feared and holden in most reverent estimation, because they are lieutenants of God. Such as resist the Supreme Power do resist God's ordinance and cannot be guiltless." – quoted in *Wesley's Revision of the Shorter Catechism*, pg. 125

Walter Scott

"My foot is on my native heath, and my name is MacGregor" – *Rob Roy*, pg. 246

Breathes there the man, with soul so dead,
Who never to himself hath said,
This is my own, my native land!
Whose heart hath ne'er within him burn'd,
As home his footsteps he hath turn'd
From wandering on a foreign strand!
If such there breathe, go, mark him well;
For him no Minstrel raptures swell;
High though his titles, proud his name,

Boundless his wealth as wish can claim;
Despite those titles, power, and pelf,
The wretch, concentred all in self,
Living, shall forfeit fair renown,
And, doubly dying, shall go down
To the vile dust, from whence he sprung,
Unwept, unhonour'd, and unsung...

Breathes there the man with soul so dead,
Who never to himself hath said,
This is my own, my native land!
Whose heart hath ne'er within him burn'd,
As home his footsteps he hath turn'd,
From wandering on a foreign strand!...
O Caledonia! stern and wild,
Meet nurse for a poetic child!
Land of brown heath and shaggy wood,
Land of the mountain and the flood,
Land of my sires! what mortal hand
Can e'er untie the filial band,
That knits me to thy rugged strand!
Still, as I view each well-known scene,
Think what is now, and what hath been,
Seems as, to me, of all bereft,
Sole friends thy woods and streams were left;
And thus I love them better still,
Even in extremity of ill.
– *The Lay of the Last Minstrel*

"The eagerness with which the Scottish people meet, communicate, and to the extent of their power assist each other, although it is often objected to us as a prejudice and narrowness of sentiment, seems on the contrary to arise from a most justifiable and honorable feeling patriotism, combined with a conviction ... that the habits and principles of the nation are a sort of guarantee for the character of the individual." – *The Wisdom of Sir Walter*, pg. 197

Roger Scruton

"This repudiation is the result of a peculiar frame of mind that has arisen throughout the Western world since the second world war, and which is particularly prevalent among the intellectual and political élites. No adequate word exists for this attitude, though its symptoms are instantly recognised: namely, the disposition, in any conflict, to side with 'them' against 'us', and the felt need to denigrate the customs, culture and institutions that are identifiably 'ours'. Being the opposite of xenophobia I propose to call this state of mind oikophobia, by which I mean (stretching the Greek a little) the repudiation of inheritance and home. Oikophobia is a stage through which the adolescent mind normally passes. But it is a stage in which some people—intellectuals especially—tend to become arrested. As George Orwell pointed out, intellectuals on the Left are especially prone to it, and this has often made them willing agents of foreign powers... The oik (short for oikophobe) is, in his own eyes, a defender of enlightened universalism against local chauvinism. And it is the rise of the oik that has led to the growing crisis of legitimacy in the nation states of Europe. For we are seeing a massive expansion of the legislative burden on the people of Europe, and a relentless assault on the only loyalties that would enable them voluntarily to bear it. The explosive effect of this has already been felt in Holland and France. It will be felt soon everywhere, and the result may not be what the oiks expect." – *The Need For Nations*, pgs. 36-38

"Internationalists, by contrast, wish to break down the distinctions between people; they do not feel at home in any city since they are aliens in all. They see the world as one vast system in which everyone is equally a customer, a consumer, a creature of wants and needs. They are happy to transplant people from place to place, to abolish local attachments, to shift boundaries and customs in accordance with the inexorable tide of political need or economic progress." – *How to Think Seriously about the Planet*, pg. 321

"In free association with their neighbours, the 'nation' means simply the historical identity and continuing allegiance that unites them in the body politic. It is the first-person plural of settlement. Sentiments of national identity may be inflamed by war, civil agitation and ideology, and this inflammation admits of many degrees. But in their normal form these sentiments are not just peaceful in themselves, but a form of peace between neighbours." – *How to Be a Conservative*, pg. 32

"It is not an arbitrary cultural imperialism that leads us to value Greek philosophy and literature, the Hebrew Bible, Roman law, and the medieval epics and romances, and to teach these things in our schools. They are ours, in just the way that the legal order and the political institutions are ours: they form part of what made us, and convey the message that it is right to be what we are." – *How To Be A Conservative*, pg. 91

"Many environmentalists will acknowledge that local loyalties and local concerns must be given a proper place in our decision-making, if we are to counter the adverse effects of the global economy. Hence the oft-repeated slogan: 'Think globally, act locally.' However, they will tend to baulk at the suggestion that local loyalty should be seen in national terms, rather than as the small-scale expression of a humane universalism. Yet there is a very good reason for emphasizing nationality. For nations are communities with a political shape. They are predisposed to assert their sovereignty, by translating the common sentiment of belonging into collective decisions and self-imposed laws. Nationality is a form of territorial attachment, but it is also a proto-legislative arrangement." – *How To Be A Conservative*, pg. 95

"Indeed, it is only at the local level that it is realistic to hope for improvement. For there is no evidence that global political institutions have done anything to limit the damage – on the contrary, by encouraging communication around the world, and by eroding national sovereignty and legislative barriers, they have fed into the global entropy and weakened the only true sources of resistance to it. I know many environmentalists who agree with me that the WTO and the World Bank are potential threats to the environment, not merely by breaking down self-sufficient and self-reproducing peasant economies, but also by eroding national sovereignty wherever this places an obstacle before the goal of free trade. Many also seem to agree with me that traditional communities deserve protection from sudden and externally engineered change, not merely for the sake of their sustainable economies, but also because of the values and loyalties that constitute the sum of their social capital." – *How To Be A Conservative*, pg. 96

"Take away borders, and people begin to identify themselves not by territory and law, but by tribe, race or religion. Nationality is composed of land, together with the narrative of its possession." – *Confessions of a Heretic*, pg. 59

"...religion is not simply a matter of believing a few abstract metaphysical propositions that stand shaking and vulnerable before the advance of modern science. Religion is a way of life, involving customs and ceremonies that validate what matters to us, and which reinforce the attachments by which we live. It is both a faith and a form of membership, in which the destiny of the individual is bound up with that of a community." – *Our Church*, pg. 6

"Liberal laws are the triumph of political order, but only when the people have the social knowledge to understand and obey them... Liberalism only makes sense in the context that conservatism defends." – *Conservatism: An Invitation to the Great Tradition*, pg. 55

"The market economy presupposes honest people who wish to reach deals honestly through agreement. Hence, it must always be backed up by the moral and legal strictures which issue from our shared fund of sympathy." – *Conservatism: An Invitation to the Great Tradition*, pg. 42

"Just as prices in a market condense into themselves information that is otherwise dispersed throughout contemporary society, so do laws condense information that is dispersed over a society's past. From this thought it is a small step to reconstructing Burke's celebrated defence of custom, tradition and 'prejudice' against the 'rationalism' of the French Revolutionaries. To put Burke's point in a modern idiom: the knowledge that we need in the unforeseeable circumstances of human life is neither derived from nor contained in the experience of a single person, nor can it be deduced a priori from universal laws. This knowledge is bequeathed to us by customs, institutions and habits of thought that have shaped themselves over generations, through the trials and errors of people many of whom have perished in the course of acquiring it. Such is the knowledge contained in the common law, which is a social bequest that could never be adequately replaced by a doctrine, a plan or a constitution, however entrenched that constitution may be in a vision of individual rights." – *Fools, Frauds and Firebrands*, pg. 57

"Common law for old England was 'a familiar companion, an unspoken background to daily dealings, an impartial observer who can be called upon at any time to bear witness, to give judgement and to bring peace. ... It was the root cause of the law abidingness of the English, and their ability to live side by side as strangers in a condition of trust. All communities depend upon trust: but in few communities does trust extend beyond the family; in almost none does it embrace the stranger, while conceding his right to remain a stranger, and to go about his business undisturbed." – *England: An Elegy*, pgs. 10-11

— ROGER SCRUTON —

"In families, people often get together to discuss matters of shared concern. There'll be many opinions, conflicting councils, and even factions. But in a happy family everyone will accept to be bound by the final decision, even if they disagree with it. That is because they have a shared investment in staying together. Something is more important to all of them then their own opinion, and that is the family, the thing whose welfare and future they have come together to discuss. To put it another way: the family is part of their identity; it is the thing that does not change, as their several opinions alter and conflict. A shared identity takes the sting from disagreement. It is what makes opposition, and therefore rational discussion, possible; and is the foundation of any way of life in which compromise, rather than dictatorship, is the norm.

"The same is true in politics...Opposition, disagreement, the free expression of dissent and the rule of compromise all presuppose a shared identity. There has to be a first person plural, a 'we', if the many individuals are to stay together, accepting each other's opinions and desires, regardless of disagreements... The nation-state, as we now conceive it, is the byproduct of human neighborliness, shaped by an 'invisible hand' from the countless agreements between people who speak the same language and live side-by-side. The results from compromises established after many conflicts, and expresses a slowly forming agreement among name were supposed to grant each other space and to protect that space as common territory...

"All of the kind that follows automatically from the ties of affection, kinship and love. To prevent this result would require so great an interference in the spontaneous practices of gift and cooperation, as to threaten the very fabric of society...

"Unless and until people identify themselves with the country, its territory and its cultural inheritance – in something like the way people identify themselves with the family – the politics of compromise will not emerge." – *Scruton, Conservative Texts: An Anthology, Introduction*

"Family and friendship define the unchosen obligations from which our obligation to the state is formed. Hence there is no conservative outlook on the state which does not involve, at some point, the acceptance of social differentiation, of the kind that follows automatically from the ties of affection, kinship and love. To prevent this result would require so great an interference in the spontaneous practices of gift and cooperation, as to threaten the very fabric of society." – quoted in *The Sociology of Politics: Political Ideologies and Movements*, 1998, pg. 151

"To put the point more simply, the ordinary American regards the flag as sacred, and therefore as capable of desecration. Someone who desecrates what I hold to be sacred is attacking me, in the deepest part of my being. For those things are sacred to me that represent, in heightened form, the identity and obligations that define my place on earth. As Durkheim pointed out, sacred things are 'set apart and forbidden'. Only the initiated can make full use of them, and the use is carefully hedged by taboos. Sacred things define what we are, and to expose them to profanation is to bring them down from the transcendental to the empirical sphere – to deprive them of their permanence and 'aura', and therefore to expose both them and us to destruction.

"Things become sacred when sacrifices on behalf of the community have been distilled in them, as the sacrifices of generations of soldiers, sailors and airmen are distilled in the American flag. And sacred things are invitations to sacrifice, as is the flag in time of war. Sacred things create bridges across generations: they tell us that the dead and the unborn are present among us, and that their 'real presence' lives in each of us, and each of us in it. The decline of religion has deprived us of sacred things. But it has not deprived us of the need for them. Nor has it deprived us of the acute sense of desecration we feel, when facetious images intrude at the places once occupied by these visitors from the transcendental.

"Flags represent ancient claims and loyalties, and owe their power to what they mean, rather than to what they look like. The American... is an image that owes its power to its use; and this is something that it shares with the icons of saints in the Eastern Church, and with the sacred vessels that embellish every altar. The American flag has retained its aura, even now when it hangs from a million suburban porches. That is why people are always burning it." – *Confessions of a Heretic*, pgs. 119-120

"Who should we blame for this? Some point their finger at the free marketeers, saying that their philosophy is one that endorses big business, whatever big business might do. But that, I think, would be a mistake. The free market, as defended by Mises and Hayek, is simply an instance of the kind of conservative problem-solving that I have been advocating in this article. The Burkean argument for a partnership across generations is an argument of the same kind, which asks us to recognise that consensual solutions may sometimes require that we consult the interests of the unborn and the dead. What has gone wrong, it seems to me, is not the attachment of conservatives to the market, but the failure to see what a real market solution requires: namely the retreat of the state and its projects from every decision in which local aims and loyalties are at stake. It is surely time for conservative politicians to recognise

that, with really big issues, you need to think small." – *Confessions of a Heretic*, pg. 162

"The strange superstition has arisen in the Western world that we can start all over again, remaking human nature, human society, and the possibilities of happiness; as though the knowledge and experience of our ancestors were now entirely irrelevant." – *Gentle Regrets*

John Seldon

Speaking of the development of human society after the Noahic Flood:

"...no man should invade the Bounds of his Brother, nor should they wrong one another; because it would of necessitie occasion Discords and deadly Wars among them ...

"After this, Exchanges, Buying, and selling came in fashion; and besides Weights and Measures, they appointed Judges of Covenants and Contracts, and added Bounds or Limits to Fields and Pastures.

"So at length came in private Dominions or Possessions; which (whether by virtue only of a preceding universal dominion of a single person, as in Adam; or of som universal and common interest in Things, as betwixt Noah and his Sons) happened first by the Donation, Assignment, or some other Grant of those whom it concerned, either to Princes, or Communities representing a single person, or to any others whomsoever, as particular Lords." ...

"But in this division of Bounds and Territories, there intervened, as it were, a consent of the whole bodie or universalitie of mankinde (by the mediation of something like a compact, which might binde their posteritie) for quitting of the common interest or ancient right in those things that were made over thus by distribution to particular Proprietors; in the same manner as when Partners or Co-heirs do share between themselves any portions of those things which they hold in common." ...

"Nor can it otherwise bee conceived in the case of Partners or Co-heirs (such as all men seem to have been in the State of Communitie) how those things which com not under division, should not continue common, as before. Therefore (I suppose) it must bee yielded, that som such Compact or Covenant was passed in the very first beginnings of private Dominion or possession, and that it was in full force and virtue transmitted to posteritie by the Fathers, who had the power of distributing possessions…

"So that wee may conclude no less concerning distribution by Assignment, then touching Seisure by occupation of things relinquish it at pleasure, that a general compact or Agreement was made or ratified, either expressly in words, or implicitly by custom." – *Mare Clausum*, Book 1, ch. IV, pg. 17-23

Seneca the Younger

"Judging by what you write me, and by what I hear. I am forming a good opinion regarding your future. You do not run hither and thither and distract yourself by changing your abode; for such restlessness is the sign of a disordered spirit. The primary indication, to my thinking, of a well-ordered mind is a man's ability to remain in one place and linger in his own company. Be careful, however, lest this reading of many authors and books of every sort may tend to make you discursive and unsteady. You must linger among a limited number of master-thinkers, and digest their works, if you would derive ideas which shall win firm hold in your mind. Everywhere means nowhere. When a person spends all his time in foreign travel, he ends by having many acquaintances, but no friends. And the same thing must hold true of men who seek intimate acquaintance with no single author, but visit them all in a hasty and hurried manner. Food does no good and is not assimilated into the body if it leaves the stomach as soon as it is eaten; nothing hinders a cure so much as frequent change of medicine; no wound will heal when one salve is tried after another; a plant which is often moved can never grow strong. I believe nothing so efficacious that it can be helpful while it is being shifted about. And in reading of many books is distraction." – *Epistles*, pg. 7

Horatio Seymour

"There is in history a power to lift a people up and make them great and prosperous. The story of a nation's achievements excites that patriotic pride which is a great element in vigor, boldness and heroism. He who studies with care the jurisprudence of the Old Testament will see that this feeling of reverence for forefathers and devotion to country is made the substance of positive law in the command that men should honor their fathers and mothers. But sacred poetry is filled with appeals to these sentiments, and the narratives of the Bible abound with proofs of the great truth that the days of those who fear them shall be long upon the land which God hath given them. All history, ancient and modern, proves that national greatness springs in no small degree from pride in their histories, and from the patriotism cherished by their traditions and animated by their examples…

"You will find that all history, all jurisprudence, all just reasonings, force us to the conclusion that not only does a Divine command, but that reason and justice call upon us all to honor our ancestors, and that there is a great practical truth which concerns the welfare and the power of all communities in the words of the inspired penman: 'Honor thy father and thy mother that thy days may be long in the land which the Lord thy God giveth thee.'" – Governor of New York, "Centennial Address" July 4, 1876, entitled *The Future Of The Human Race; Addresses, Historical and Patriotic*, pg. 381

William Shakespeare

O nation miserable!
With an untitled tyrant, bloody-sceptred,
When shalt thou see thy wholesome days again,
Since that the truest issue of thy throne
By his own interdiction stands accursed,
And does blaspheme his breed? – *Macbeth*

This royal throne of kings, this scepter'd isle,
This earth of majesty, this seat of Mars,
This blessed plot, this earth,
    this realm, this England,
This nurse, this teeming womb of royal kings,
. . .
This land of such dear souls, this dear dear land
– John of Gaunt, Duke of Lancaster, *Richard II*

On, on, you noblest English.
Whose blood is fet from fathers of war-proof,
Fathers that, like so many Alexanders,
Have in these parts from morn till even fought
. . .
And you, good yeoman,
Whose limbs were made in England,
    show us here
The mettle of your pasture; let us swear
That you are worth your breeding;
    which I doubt not;

For there is none of you so mean and base,
That hath not noble lustre in your eyes.
– *Henry V*

— WILLIAM SHAKESPEARE —

From fairest creatures we desire increase,
That thereby beauty's rose might never die,
But as the riper should by time decease,
His tender heir might bear his memory:
But thou contracted to thine own bright eyes,
Feed'st thy light's flame
    with self-substantial fuel,
Making a famine where abundance lies,
Thy self thy foe, to thy sweet self too cruel:
Thou that art now the world's fresh ornament,
And only herald to the gaudy spring,
Within thine own bud buriest thy content,
And, tender churl, mak'st waste in niggarding:
    Pity the world, or else this glutton be,
    To eat the world's due, by the grave and thee.
– *Sonnet 1*

When forty winters shall besiege thy brow,
And dig deep trenches in thy beauty's field,
Thy youth's proud livery so gazed on now,
Will be a totter'd weed of small worth held:
Then being asked, where all thy beauty lies,
Where all the treasure of thy lusty days;
To say, within thine own deep sunken eyes,
Were an all-eating shame, and thriftless praise.
How much more praise

deserv'd thy beauty's use,
If thou couldst answer 'This fair child of mine
Shall sum my count, and make my old excuse,'
Proving his beauty by succession thine!
    This were to be new made when thou art old,
    And see thy blood warm when thou feel'st it
cold.
– *Sonnet 2*

Look in thy glass and tell the face thou viewest
Now is the time that face should form another;
Whose fresh repair if now thou not renewest,
Thou dost beguile the world,
    unbless some mother.
For where is she so fair whose uneared womb
Disdains the tillage of thy husbandry?
Or who is he so fond will be the tomb
Of his self-love, to stop posterity?
Thou art thy mother's glass and she in thee
Calls back the lovely April of her prime;
So thou through windows of thine age shalt see,
Despite of wrinkles, this thy golden time.
    But if thou live, remembered not to be,
    Die single and thine image dies with thee.
– *Sonnet 3*

Unthrifty loveliness, why dost thou spend
Upon thy self thy beauty's legacy?
Nature's bequest gives nothing, but doth lend,
And being frank she lends to those are free:
Then, beauteous niggard, why dost thou abuse
The bounteous largess given thee to give?
Profitless usurer, why dost thou use
So great a sum of sums, yet canst not live?
For having traffic with thy self alone,
Thou of thy self thy sweet self dost deceive:
Then how when nature calls thee to be gone,
What acceptable audit canst thou leave?
    Thy unused beauty must be tombed with thee,
    Which, used, lives th' executor to be.
– *Sonnet 4*

Then let not winter's ragged hand deface,
In thee thy summer, ere thou be distilled:
Make sweet some vial; treasure thou some place
With beauty's treasure ere it be self-killed.
That use is not forbidden usury,
Which happies those that pay the willing loan;
That's for thy self to breed another thee,
Or ten times happier, be it ten for one;
Ten times thy self were happier than thou art,
If ten of thine ten times refigured thee:
Then what could death do

if thou shouldst depart,
Leaving thee living in posterity?
  Be not self-willed, for thou art much too fair
  To be death's conquest and make worms thine
heir.
— *Sonnet 6*

Lo! in the orient when the gracious light
Lifts up his burning head, each under eye
Doth homage to his new-appearing sight,
Serving with looks his sacred majesty;
And having climbed the steep-up heavenly hill,
Resembling strong youth in his middle age,
Yet mortal looks adore his beauty still,
Attending on his golden pilgrimage:
But when from highmost pitch, with weary car,
Like feeble age, he reeleth from the day,
The eyes, 'fore duteous, now converted are
From his low tract, and look another way:
  So thou, thyself outgoing in thy noon
  Unlooked on diest unless thou get a son.
— *Sonnet 7*

By law of nature thou art bound to breed,
That thine may live,
  when thou thyself art dead;
And so in spite of death though dost survive,
In that thy likeness still is left alive.
— *Venus And Adonis*

Fulton J. Sheen

"The revolt of the modern child against his
parents is a miniature of the revolt of the
modern world against the memory of 1900 years
of Christian culture and the great Hebrew,
Grecian and Roman cultures which preceded
them. Any respect for that tradition is called
'reactionary,' with the result that the modern
soul has developed a commentator mentality
which judges yesterday by today, and today by
tomorrow. Nothing is more tragic in an individual who once was wise than to lose his memory,
and nothing is more tragic to a civilization than
the loss of its tradition.." – *Peace Of The Soul*,
pg. 9

Thomas Shepard

"Would you have this state in time to degenerate
into tyranny?...be gentle and open the door to
all comers that may cut our throats in time; and
if being come they do offend, threaten them and

fine them, but use no sword against them. You
fathers of the country, be not offended; this I
speak not to disparage any, the practice speaks
otherwise; I only forewarn; I hope the Lord has
prepared better days and mercies for us; I am
sure he will, if what means we have we preserve,
and what we preserve, we through grace, shall
improve." – *The Parable of the Ten Virgins*, pg. 250

Victoria Sherrow

"Hair dyes were popular in ancient Rome, and
historians have found more than 100 different
recipes that the Romans used for bleaching or
dying hair. Light hair became fashionable after
Greek culture reached Italy and the Roman
legionnaires began bringing back fair-haired
slaves from Gaul. Women, and some men,
applied bleaching agents to their hair and then
exposed it to the sun to achieve a golden or red
color. Wealthier people could afford to sprinkle
actual gold dust on their hair to create a blond
look, as did the ancient Phoenicians. Another
way to achieve a lighter shade was to cover the
hair with flower pollen and the crushed petals
of yellow-colored flowers. When harsh bleaching agents caused hair loss, Roman women
resorted to wigs made from the hair of blond
slaves." – *Encyclopedia of Hair: A Cultural History*, pg. 154

Samuel Shortridge

"What the American people want is a tariff that
protects . . . American-raised, American-mined,
American-manufactured products and American men and women from competition with
like foreign products raised, mined, or manufactured by cheap foreign labor. . . . The free-trade
theory has cursed America. The protective theory has blessed America. If the free-trade theory
were now put into operation, it would bankrupt
America." – *Debate over Tariff Act of 1930*; cited
in Eckes, *Opening America's Market: U.S. Foreign
Trade Policy Since 1776*, pg. 31

Empress Michiko Shōda

Waka poems, written for the "seijin no hi" cere-
mony of Crown Prince Naruhito:
  "On the threshold of his twenties,
    childhood left behind,
  A serene crystal heart, he will then go forth

On the wide, straight path
  of glorious ancestors.
He stands there, virile Prince, son of mine."

A short poem written to commemorate the end
of the Second World War:
  "You depart,
on which sea, which land
I know not.
The noble souls
guardians of the nation
remain invisible."

– Seoto (瀬音, *The Sound Current*), translated
into French and then English, published in
Dominuq Venner's *A Handbook For Dissidents*,
Amsterdam, 2021, pgs. 88-89

Richard Sibbes

"'Houses' we take for the persons that are in
it, and persons that are ordered, or else it is a
confusion, and not a house. It is a company
of those that are voluntary. They come not by
chance into our house, those that are members
of our society; but there is an order. There is a
governor in a house, and some that are under
government, and there is a voluntary conjunction and combination. So the church is a
voluntary company of people that is orderly,
some to teach, and some to be instructed; and
thereupon it is called a house." – *The Complete
Works of Richard Sibbes*, vol. 2, pg. 226

"And as this is true of the church in general,
so it is true of particular families, that are little
churches. There is rest and happiness in them.
God blesseth all under the roof of a godly man.
Whosoever comes under that shadow comes
for a blessing, or for further hardening. We see
in the current of Scripture ordinarily that when
God converted any one man, he converted his
whole family. 'Salvation is this day come to
thy house,' saith Christ to Zaccheus, Luke 19:9.
When salvation came to his heart, it came to
his house; all was the better for it. So the jailor,
when he believed, he and his whole house were
baptized, Acts 16:33. When God blesseth the
governor once, then it is supposed all the house
comes under the covenant of grace. Abraham
and his house were blessed, Gen. 22:17." – *The
Complete Works of Richard Sibbes*, vol. 2, pg. 354 [81]

"Again, where true hatred and indignation is,
there the nearer the ill is to us, the more we hate
it, &c. As we hate it in itself, so we hate it the
more, the nearer it is to us. As a toad or any
venomous thing, the nearer it is to us, we loathe
and abhor it the more, so certainly, whosoever
hates and abhorreth sin as sin (as it is a hateful
thing to a renewed soul), so he hateth sin more
in himself than in others, because it is nearest
in his own bosom. Every man hates a snake
more in his bosom than afar off, because it is
more likely to do him harm there. Therefore
those that flatter their own corruptions, and are
violent against others, as Judah against Tamar,
'She shall be burned, bring her forth and burn
her,' when himself had gotten her with child,
Gen. 38:24. So many are severe in punishing of
others, as if they were wondrous zealous; but
what are they in their own breast? Do they reform sin in their own hearts and lives? He that
truly hates sin, he hateth his own sin more than
others, because it is near him.

"And so, in proportion, he that hates sin
truly will hate it in his own family, children
and servants, more than in others abroad. It
was a great fault in David, that he cockered
up (indulged) Adonijah, and others in his own
house, whilst he was more strict abroad. Can
men think to redress and hate sin in the commonwealth, and yet suffer it in their families?
True hatred is most conversant in its strength
near hand. Those who suffer debauchery and
profaneness in their families, and never check
it in their children and servants, they hate not
sin. Whatsoever countenance they may take
upon them, of reformation abroad, it cometh
out of by-respects, and not out of true hatred."
– *The Complete Works of Richard Sibbes*, vol. 2,
pgs. 370-371

"God 'knows our souls in adversity, Ps. 31:7;
so should we do the souls of others, if they be
knit to us in any bond of kindred, or nature,
or neighbourhood, or the like. That bond
should provoke us; for bonds are as the veins
and arteries to derive comfort. All bonds are to
derive good, whether bonds of neighbourhood,
or acquaintance, &c. A man should think with
himself, I have this bond to do my neighbour
good. It is God's providence that I should be
acquainted with him, and do that to him that
I cannot do to a stranger. Let us consider all

---

81   Covenantal Patriarchy.

bonds, and let this work upon us: let us consider their grievance is a bond to tie us." – *The Complete Works of Richard Sibbes*, vol. 3, pg. 69

Algernon Sidney

"...as the Christian law exempts no man from the duty he owes to his father, master, or the magistrate, it does not make him more a slave than he was before, nor deprive him of any natural or civil right." – *Discourses Concerning Government*, vol. 2, pg. 90

"A nation, and most especially one that is powerful, cannot recede from its own right, as a private man from the knowledge of his own weakness and inability to defend himself, must come under the protection of a greater power than his own. The strength of a nation is not in the magistrate, but the strength of the magistrate is in the nation. The wisdom, industry and valour of a prince may add to the glory and greatness of a nation, but the foundation and substance will always be in itself." – *Discourses Concerning Government*, vol. 2, pg. 339

"Changes therefore are unavoidable, and the wit of man can go no farther than to institute such, as in relation to the forces, manners, nature, religion or interests of a people and their neighbours, are suitable and adequate to what is seen, or apprehended to be seen: And he who would oblige all nations at all times to take the same course, would prove as foolish as a physician who should apply the same medicine to all distempers, or an architect that would build the same kind of house for all persons, without considering their estates, dignities, the number of their children or servants, the time or climate in which they live, and many other circumstances; or, which is, if possible, more sottish, a general who should obstinately resolve always to make war in the same way, and to draw up his army in the same form, without examining the nature, number, and strength of his own and his enemies' forces, or the advantages and disadvantages of the ground. But as there may be some universal rules in physick, architecture and military discipline, from which men ought never to depart; so there are some in politicks also which ought always to be observed: and wise legislators adhering to them only, will be ready to change all others as occasion may

require, in order to the public good."– *Discourses Concerning Government*, vol. 1, pg. 244

Henryk Sienkiewicz

A description of a random Roman market at the time of its decline and fall:

"In truth, the local element [native Romans] was well-nigh lost in that crowd, composed of all races and nations. There appeared Ethiopians, gigantic light-haired people from the distant north, Britons, Gauls, Germans, sloping-eyed dwellers of Lericum; people from the Euphrates and from the Indus, with beards dyed brick color; Syrians from the banks of the Orontes, with black and mild eyes; dwellers in the deserts of Arabia, dried up as a bone; Jews, with their flat breasts; Egyptians, with the eternal, indifferent smile on their faces; Numidians and Africans; Greeks from Hellas, who equally with the Romans commanded the city, but commanded through science, art, wisdom, and deceit; Greeks from the islands, from Asia Minor, from Egypt, from Italy, from Narbonic Gaul." – *Quo Vadis*, pg. 15

Larry Siedentop

"The ancient citizen saw himself as defending the land of his ancestors, who were also his gods. His ancestors were inseparable from the ground of the city. To lose that ground was to lose the gods of the family. Indeed, the loss of the city meant that the gods had already abandoned it. That is why, whenever a new city was about to be founded, the first public rite involved its members digging a trench to receive soil carried from their previous city, representing the soil in which their ancestors had been buried. Citizens could then still say this was the land of their ancestors, terra patria.

"The foundation of a city was not the construction of a few houses, but the assertion of a hereditary religious identity, 'patriotism'. When defending his city, the ancient citizen was therefore defending the very core of his identity. Religion, family and territory were inseparable, a combination which turned ancient patriotism into an overwhelming passion. The enslavement that often followed the unsuccessful defence of a city merely confirmed a truly dreadful anterior fact: the loss of identity that necessarily accompanied the loss of domestic gods.

"Everything that was important to him– his ancestors, his worship, his moral life, his pride and property– depended upon the survival and well-being of the city. That is why devotion to the 'sacred fatherland' was deemed the supreme virtue. In devoting himself to the city before everything else, the citizen was serving his gods. No abstract principle of justice could give him pause. Piety and patriotism were one and the same thing.

"For the Greeks, to be without patriotism, to be anything less than an active citizen, was to be an 'idiot'. That, indeed, is what the word originally meant, referring to anyone who retreated from the life of the city. So it is no accident that exile was the most severe punishment the citizen of a polis could suffer. It was worse than death, or rather it was a living death." – *Inventing the Individual: The Origins of Western Liberalism*, pgs. 24-25

Moisés Silva

"The OT teaching about the family is embodied in the first chapters of the TORAH. The CREATION of God was in a world-order and in a family-order. In the OT, family relationships are concentric: husband and wife form the nucleus of the circle, the children lie in the next circle, then the grandparents, cousins, and the like…

"The OT often uses the common Semitic term for 'house' (Heb. bayit H1074) with reference to the household or family (cf. Ruth 4:11 [NIV, 'home']; 1 Chr. 13:14; 2 Chr. 35:5, 12; Ps. 68:6). The most frequently occurring term for this concept, however, is mišpāhâ H5476 (e.g., Exod. 12:21). This noun, though applicable to the family, actually embraces the whole range of meanings from 'clan' (10:5) through 'species' (8:19) to 'consanguinity' (24:38; cf. NRSV, 'kindred')…

"The initial statement of the relationship of man and woman in the Scripture is given in the narrative of the creation account. In the section that begins the creation of the world-order (the creation ordinances, Gen. 2:4-5:1), the form of human family life is set forth. The unity of male and female in the MARRIAGE bond is set down on two levels, the fulfillment of man's need for companionship and the sexual relationship for the procreation of the race (2:18; 3:20; 4:1-2). There is no question throughout the rest of the Bible that the monogamy of the

Garden of Eden is the situation to be considered 'normal' because it is the ordained law of marriage (Mk. 10:6-9). This relationship was not to supersede the relationship to God (Deut. 13:6-10; Matt. 19:29; Lk. 14:26) nor was it binding upon either party when separated by death (Matt. 22:30 and Mk. 12:25, on the analogy of many OT passages).

"This complete reliance upon the monogamous law-order was an inherent part of the Israelite worldview and from that source has continued to be a mark of Western civilization. Regardless of all evolutionary and psycho-analytic theories of explanation, the monogamous, lifelong relationship is that which is the nature of human beings." – "Family" in *Zondervan Encyclopedia of the Bible*, vol. 2: D-G, pgs. 1979-1980

Silius Italicus

Fabius reprimands his son for being angry with Rome:
"Now take this from your aged father, son, don't doubt it, and keep it eternally fixed in your heart: it is an unspeakable crime to be angry at your country. Mortal men take no more disgusting fault to the ghosts below. Thus our ancestors have taught us." – *Punica*, pg. 124

Hannibal is supposedly approaching Rome to invade it during the second Punic war:
"But in any event the dutiful crowd of surviving senators indeed entered into their offices by lot. Fabius swiftly surveyed all these matters and called out to the astonished men: 'Trust me, there is no reason left for delay. Let us hurry, so the enemy's effort to enter our fortified walls will be in vain. Sitting still nourishes harsh Fortune among terrified people, and adverse circumstances increase in fear. Go quickly, young men, seize your weapons from the temples. Hurry and strip your atriums bare and fit out the shields that you captured in combat. We are enough to defend our country, if fear takes nothing away from our number for battle. We should be afraid of horrible devastation on the open battlefield. But naked Moors agile at leaping will never smash our walls.'" – Fabius' speech, in *Punica*, pg. 174

Two members of Carthage's senate debate resisting Rome in the second Punic war:
"But Hanno piles on Libya's defeat and the

first war's conflagration, and he forbids us to endure struggles once more in liberty's name. Let him put aside his swells of fear and, unwarlike woman that he is, keep his sobbing spirit inside his house's walls. For our part, we will go against the enemy. We've resolved to push our masters far from the Byrsa, founded by the Tyrians, even if Jupiter is unfair to us. But if the Fates resist us, and Mars has departed from a Carthage already doomed, I would rather die than hand you over, my famous homeland, to be a slave forever. I will see the Underworld as a free man. For what is Fabius ordering, by the gods! 'Shed your armor right now and come down from Saguntum's captured citadel. Next, let your hand-picked band of soldiers burn up heaps of shields, set fire to the ships, and hold off from the entire sea.' Oh gods, if Carthage has never deserved to suffer such things, keep this unspeakable shame far from us and keep our leader's hands free!" – Gesto's speech, in *Punica*, pg. 33

During the second Punic War, a man dies and loses his beauty:

"Death robbed Cinyps of his beauty, a Stygian hue spread over his snow-white skin spoiling the comeliness of his form, while his ambrosial locks were disordered…" – *Punica*, pg. 165

Charles Simeon

"There is a love of benevolence, a love of beneficence, and a love of complacency, if we may so speak: the two former must be exercised toward all: the last may fitly be reserved for those who alone possess the dispositions worthy of it. Such a preference God himself authorizes, when he says, "Do good unto all men, but especially unto them who are of the household of faith." – *Horae Homileticae*, vol. 11, pg. 162

Ivan Sirko

Turkish Sultan Mehmed IV sent a letter to the Zaporozhian Cossack Christians to surrender to his foreign rule. The Cossacks sent a famous reply, showing their hatred of imperial power and love of freedom and fraternity.

"Sultan Mehmed IV to the Zaporozhian Cossacks: As the Sultan; son of Muhammad; brother of the sun and moon; grandson and viceroy of God; ruler of the kingdoms of Macedonia, Babylon, Jerusalem, Upper and Lower Egypt; emperor of emperors; sovereign of sovereigns; extraordinary knight, never defeated; steadfast guardian of the tomb of Jesus Christ; trustee chosen by God Himself; the hope and comfort of Muslims; confounder and great defender of Christians – I command you, the Zaporogian Cossacks, to submit to me voluntarily and without any resistance, and to desist from troubling me with your attacks." – Turkish Sultan Mehmed IV, quoted in *The Orientalists*, pg. 171

"Zaporozhian Cossacks to the Turkish Sultan!

"O sultan, Turkish devil and damned devil's kith and kin, secretary to Lucifer himself. What the devil kind of knight are thou, that canst not slay a hedgehog with your naked arse? The devil s***s, and your army eats. Thou shalt not, thou son of a whore, make subjects of Christian sons. We have no fear of your army; by land and by sea we will battle with thee. F*** thy mother.

"Thou Babylonian scullion, Macedonian wheelwright, brewer of Jerusalem, goat-f***er of Alexandria, swineherd of Greater and Lesser Egypt, pig of Armenia, Podolian thief, catamite of Tartary, hangman of Kamyanets, and fool of all the world and underworld, an idiot before God, grandson of the Serpent, and the crick in our d**k. Pig's snout, mare's arse, slaughterhouse cur, un*****ened brow. S***w thine own mother!

"So the Zaporozhians declare, you lowlife. You won't even be herding pigs for the Christians. Now we'll conclude, for we don't know the date and don't own a calendar; the moon's in the sky, the year with the Lord. The day's the same over here as it is over there; for this kiss our arse!" – "Reply Of The Cossacks" by Koshovyi otaman Ivan Sirko, with the whole Zaporozhian Host. – quoted in *The Orientalists*, pg. 171

Jean Charles Léonard de Sismondi

"Every day must convince us more that the ancients understood liberty, and the conditions of free governments, infinitely better than we do. They, at least, did not fall into similar errors; they gave, to sustain their republics, not phrases, but a spirit of life. They taught all the citizens to make a religion of the love of country, instead of considering their country as only a mercantile partnership, where profit and loss are calculated, and from whence a man endeavours to retire when the balance is not favourable. They encompassed the majesty of the people with veneration, but the people was to them the whole of the nation, with every class of citizens, all its interests, all its recollections, all its hopes, and all its glory....They wished their senate to be the unchangeable representative of the spirit of conservatism, always the same in republics. They wished it to be in some sort immortal, and they avoided with care all those crises which could change its spirit....The spirit of conservatism, the spirit of duration, belongs to antiquity of race. The patricians, in possession of the past, in imagination seized on the future; they identified themselves with their ancestors, and with their descendants; they were deeply moved at any suspicion cast on their forefathers, by any danger which threatened their most distant posterity. The republics of antiquity seized on this precious feeling, they fixed it on the eternal city, as each affectionately called his country; they were eager to adorn their senate with noble and historical distinctions. But they did not wish any citizen to think himself great in himself: he must derive it all from his country." – *Philosophy of Government*, pgs. 411-413

Thomas H. Skinner

"It has been said that Christianity is against Patriotism: It removes the walls of partition between the different nations; makes the world one brotherhood; and thus leaves no place for the love of country, which is a sectarian and selfish sentiment, and is consistent with enmity to mankind. ...

"The Gospel indeed proclaims peace and good-will to the world: It seeks to make all men in reference to earth, pilgrims and strangers, to unite them in one holy and happy fellowship, and to subject them to new and celestial relationships, strong and lasting as eternity, and embracing in their wide scope, the entire universe of the good, both on earth and in heaven. But the reasoning which would hence infer any inconsistency in the spirit of the Gospel, with the highest degrees of devotion to the welfare of our country, would make Christianity subversive of the foundations of society, and opposed

not to nationality only, but to the continuance of the human race: For if the love of country be excluded by the predominance of that heavenly-mindedness which the Gospel inculcates, so are the love of neighborhood, and the love of domestic relations, and all the endearments of friendship, and all local attachments, and the pursuits of business, and labors for a household provision, and whatever else is necessary to the continued existence of man in this world. ...

"A Philanthropy which has no particular localities, no definite spheres of labor, no fixedness of regards, no specific tasks, no preferences, no individual or vicinal trials and pleasures, is a mere abstraction; why then may not the love of country consist with, nay, be a modification of the love of Man! Nothing is more manifest than that the same Law of Nature, which unites us in different degrees of affection, with different portions and individuals of our kind, must originate a peculiar love of country, in every unperverted heart; and therefore to make the spirit of Christianity opposed to patriotism is to make it unnatural." – *Love Of Country*, A sermon preached Dec. 12, 1850 at Bleecker Street Church, NY

Adam Smith

"Some foreign nation [may restrain] by high duties or prohibitions the importation of some of our manufacturers into their country. Revenge in this case naturally dictates retaliation, and that we should impose the like duties and prohibitions upon the importation of some or all of their manufactures into ours...." – *Wealth of Nations*, pg.300

"There may [also] be good policy in retaliation of this kind when there is a probability that they (tariffs) will procure the repeal of the high duties or prohibitions complained of. The recovery of a great foreign market will generally more than compensate for the transitory inconveniency of paying dearer during a short time for some sort of goods." – *Wealth of Nations*, pg. 301

"But the great object of the political economy of every country, is to increase the riches and power of that country. It ought, therefore, to give no preference nor superior encouragement to the foreign trade of consumption above the

—ADAM SMITH—

home-trade, nor to the carrying trade above either of the other two. It ought neither to force nor to allure into either of those two channels, a greater share of the capital of the country than what would naturally flow into them of its own accord." – *Wealth of Nations*, pg. 467

"We do not love our country merely as a part of the great society of mankind: we love it for its own sake, and independently of any such consideration. That wisdom which contrived the system of human affections, as well as that of every other part of nature, seems to have judged that the interest of the great society of mankind would be best promoted by directing the principal attention of each individual to that particular portion of it, which was most within the sphere both of his abilities and of his understanding." – *Theory of Moral Sentiments*, pg. 231

"The state or sovereignty in which we have been born and educated, and under the protection of which we continue to live, is, in ordinary cases, the greatest society upon whose happiness or misery, our good or bad conduct can have much influence. It is accordingly, by nature, most strongly recommended to us. Not only we ourselves, but all the objects of our kindest affections, our children, our parents, our relations, our friends, our benefactors, all those whom we naturally love and revere the most, are commonly comprehended within it; and their prosperity and safety depend in some measure upon its prosperity and safety. It is by

nature, therefore, endeared to us, not only by all our selfish, but by all our private benevolent affections. Upon account of our own connection with it, its prosperity and glory seem to reflect some sort of honor upon ourselves. When we compare it with other societies of the same kind, we are proud of its superiority, and mortified in some degree, if it appears in any respect below them. All the illustrious characters which it has produced in former times (for against those of our own times envy may sometimes prejudice us a little), its warriors, its statesmen, its poets, its philosophers, and men of letters of all kinds; we are disposed to view with the most partial admiration, and to rank them (sometimes most unjustly) above those of all other nations. The patriot who lays down his life for the safety, or even for the vain-glory of this society, appears to act with the most exact propriety." – *Essays*, pg. 202

Anthony D. Smith

"Investing 'our' homeland with special qualities, and regarding it with reverence and awe, as the birthplace of the nation or the resting-place of its heroes and ancestors, is to continue in secular form the premodern practice of hallowing historic places and marking off sacred ancestral territories." – *The 'Sacred' Dimension of Nationalism* in *Millennium: Journal of International Studies*, vol. 29, No. 3, 2000.

"Nationalisms may be secular, or better secularizing, but they retain many 'religious' features—sacred texts, prophets, priests, liturgies, rites, and ceremonies—as well as specific ethno-religious motifs." – *Chosen Peoples*, pg. 14

"Perhaps the central question in our understanding of nationalism is the role of the past in the creation of the present...For nationalists themselves, the role of the past is clear and unproblematic. The nation was always there, indeed it is part of the natural order, even when it was submerged in the hearts of its members." – *Role of Nationalism* (no page numbers)

"All this points to the importance of social memory; as the example of the relationship between modern and ancient Greeks shows, ethnicities are constituted, not by lines of physical descent, but by the sense of continuity, shared memory and collective destiny, i. e. by lines of cultural affinity embodied in myths, memories, symbols and values retained by a given cultural unit of population." – *Nationalism and Modernism*

"...nations require ethnic cores if they are to survive. If they lack one, they must 're-invent' one. That means discovering a suitable and convincing past which can be reconstructed and represented to members and outsiders. The first European nations were constructed around strong, cohesive ethnic cores, and their states were able to incorporate, even acculturate, neighbouring ethnie. Many later states in Eastern Europe and the Middle East were designed expressly to fit such ethnic cores, in Poland, Rumania, Greece, Turkey, Iran and Iraq, despite the fact that they often had significant ethnic minorities. Colonial rulers in south-east Asia and sub-Saharan Africa had a similar ethnic model in mind; but here it proved much harder to select the ethnie which could provide the socio-cultural base of the new colonial state. In south-east Asia, the new 'plural society' that evolved soon tended to favour a dominant ethnie, as in Burma and Indonesia, with ensuing secessionist tendencies in outlying ethnic communities like the Karen and Achinese. In Africa, dominant ethnie have emerged in a few states like Kenya and Zimbabwe, but in most the ethnic balance is too even or too complex to allow any one ethnie to furnish the basis of the state. The result is that African states are likely to face serious problems in trying to create 'territorial nations' without the benefit of ethnic cores and a common historical mythology." – *Ethnic Origins of Nations*, pg. 12

Ian Douglas Smith

"In the lives of most nations there comes a moment when a stand has to be made for principles, whatever the consequences. This moment has come to Rhodesia.

"I call upon all of you in this historic hour to support me and my government in the struggle in which we are engaged. I believe that we are a courageous people and history has cast us in a heroic role. To us has been given the privilege of being the first Western nation in the last two decades to have the determination and fortitude to say: 'So far and no further.'

"We may be a small country but we are a determined people who have been called upon to play a role of worldwide significance. We Rhodesians have rejected ... appeasement and surrender.

"We have struck a blow for the preservation of justice, civilisation and Christianity—and in the spirit of this we have thus assumed our sovereign independence." – Rhodesian Prime Minister, Unilaterally Declaring Independence From Britain; *A Handful Of Hard Men*, pg. 19

Julia Smith

"...central to Latin and the various local languages of the early Middle Ages were words that denoted in undifferentiated fashion a group whose members shared one or more of the following: putative descent from a common ancestor; common cultural attributes; organization into a single polity . . . Writing between 906 and 913, Regino of Prum echoed a millennium-long tradition and encapsulated the assumptions inherent in this vocabulary when he declared: 'the various nations and peoples are distinguished from each other by descent, customs, language and laws.'" – *Europe After Rome*, pg. 261

Morton Smith

"It should be noted that this segregation of Abraham's seed was done by God ultimately for the purpose of preserving their religious purity, yet it was accomplished by means of a racial or ethnic segregation." – *The Racial Problem Facing America*, *The Presbyterian Guardian*, pg. 126

"Paul's doctrine of the unity of the church should not be construed as teaching that the church should forget or erase the God-given distinctions. Rather, she should recognize them and develop them in their particular gifts." – *The Racial Problem Facing America*, *The Presbyterian Guardian*, pg. 127

"The present writer feels that it would have been far better had separate churches never been established for the white and Negro races in the South following the War between the States. Before the war the slaves worshipped with their masters in the same churches. After the war, however, under the influence of Northern white leaders, the Negroes established separate congregations and went their separate way.

"Now, we are faced with pressure from Northern whites and blacks to abolish a custom and pattern that has become fixed over the past century." – *The Racial Problem Facing America, The Presbyterian Guardian*, pg.127

"Again, if diversity is God's revealed way for mankind, one wonders about any program that advocates the intermarriage of the diverse races in a way which will eradicate the differences that God has established." – *The Racial Problem Facing America, The Presbyterian Guardian*, pg. 127

"If from this we may conclude that ethnic pluriformity is the revealed will of God for the human race in its present situation, it is highly questionable whether the Christian can have part in any program that would seek to erase all ethnic distinctions. That such distinctions may be crossed over by individuals may be granted, but it is at least questionable whether a program designed to wipe out such differences on a mass scale should be endorsed by the Christian. It is this line of argument that the average Christian segregationist uses to back his view. He fears that the real goal of the integrationist is the intermarriage of the races, and therefore the breakdown of the distinctions between them. Many who would be willing to integrate at various lesser levels refuse to do so, simply because they feel that such will inevitably lead to intermarriage of the races, which they consider to be morally wrong. . . .

"The mass mixing of the races with the intent to erase racial boundaries he does consider to be wrong, and on the basis of this, he would oppose the mixing of the two races in this way. Let it be acknowledged that a sin in this area against the Negro race has been perpetrated by godless white men, both past and present, but this does not justify the adoption of a policy of mass mixing of the races. Rather, the Bible seems to teach that God has established and thus revealed his will for the human race now to be that of ethnic pluriformity, and thus any scheme of mass integration leading to mass mixing of the races is decidedly unscriptural." – *The Racial Problem Facing America, The Presbyterian Guardian*, pg. 124

"It is rather striking to see that the very verse used by the integrationist as supporting his posi-

tion also speaks of the diversity of peoples. The verse reads: 'And He made of one every nation of men to dwell on all the face of the earth, having determined their appointed seasons, and the bounds of their habitation' (Acts 17:26). Notice that the verse not only teaches the basic unity of the human race, but it also speaks of the diversity of mankind in different nations and groups, whose bounds have been set by God. Granting that this may be speaking primarily of the national distinctions as being under God's sovereign control, one who believes in God's sovereignty over the history of the world must also grant that racial distinctions have arisen under his plan and control." – *The Presbyterian Guardian*, pg. 125

Samuel Francis Smith

My country tis of thee,
Sweet land of liberty,
Of thee I sing.
Land where my fathers died!
Land of the Pilgrim's pride!
From every mountain side,
Let freedom ring!
My native country, thee,
Land of the noble free,
Thy name I love.

Reed Smoot

"This Government should have no apology to make for reserving America for Americans. That has been our traditional policy ever since the United States became a nation. We have refused to participate in the political intrigues of Europe, and we will not compromise the independence of this country for the privilege of serving as schoolmaster for the world. In economics as in politics, the policy of this Government is, 'America first.' The Republican Party will not stand by and see economic experimenters fritter away our national heritage." – *Congressional Record*, June 12, 1930 (pg. 10,560)

Joseph Sobran

"There are two possible basic attitudes toward social reality. One of these, as I say, has many names, but I will call, it, for convenience, Nativism: a prejudice in favor of the native, the normal, and so forth, reaching an extreme in lynchings and pogroms. Its most ghastly form was German National Socialism.

"The other attitude I am forced, for lack of a better word–or any word at all–to call Alienism: a prejudice in favor of the alien, the marginal, the dispossesed, the eccentric, reaching an extreme in the attempt to 'build a new society' by destroying the basic institutions of the native. The most terrible fulfillment of this principle is Communism.

"It would be natural to assume that Nativism would be more destructive, because native forces would seem to be better situated in most cases to destroy the alien than alien forces to destroy the native. But for some reason history hasn't worked out that way. What is plain, at any rate, is that Alienism is far from a marginal force. It offers malcontents of all sorts an ideology or gnosis that enables them to interpret normal life maliciously as a crude though somewhat disguised struggle between oppressors and victims." – Pensees

Sobieslaw II

The Duke Sobieslaw II of Bohemia defined the rights of the Germans resident in Prague around 1177. His charter based their distinctiveness on the fact that:

"...just as the Germans are different from the Bohemians [Czechs] by nation, so they should be distinct from the Bohemians in their law and custom." – Herbert Helbig and Lorenz Weinrich, eds., *Urkunden und erzählende Quellen zur deutschen Ostsiedlung im Mittelalter, Ausgewählte Quellen zur deutschen Geschichte des Mittelalters* 26, 2 vol, no. 93, pgs. 352–56.

Social Welfare Forum

"Of the population of the state of New York about one-third are of foreign birth, and from that one-third about two-thirds of the paupers supported at the expense of the state are derived. This fact alone will show the evil to which we have alluded to be a serious one. It repeats itself in various degrees of intensity in our maritime states, and, to a certain extent, in all the states of our union. While we gladly throw open our territory, and extend the protection of our institutions to emigrants from foreign countries that are able and willing to earn their own support, we cannot and ought not to relieve the old countries of Europe from the care of their dependent population.

"Certain propositions regarding the duty of the nations to their dependent population seem to be clear:

"First. A Nation is a moral organism which owes certain duties to its members, and to which its members owe certain duties in return. The bond between government and subject is a reciprocal one. Therefore, every citizen or subject is bound to maintain by his property, and defend by his life, the government, which extends to him its protection; and, on the other hand, by the common practice of civilized peoples, the government assumes the care of its subjects when they are unable to care for themselves.

"Second. This obligation of a nation towards its dependent classes cannot be transferred to another without that other's consent. Commercial nations recognize this principle in their provisions through the consular system for the care of ship-wrecked, discharged, or disabled seamen. The foreign consuls of civilized nations provide for their maintenance, and return to their homes.

"Third. It is clearly an offense against the comity of nations for any government, national or municipal, to throw the burden of caring for its dependent population upon any foreign country. But it has been proved beyond all question, that both foreign municipalities and foreign nations have provided at the public expense for the transportation of considerable numbers of their pauper class to the United States. It is beyond all question that paupers and criminals in considerable numbers have been sent to the United States by their relatives.

"Fourth. A nation becomes bound to support a foreign born pauper only through his naturalization. Naturalization involves a reciprocal contract. The naturalized party repudiates his allegiance to the country in which he was born, and takes upon himself all the obligations of a citizen. He becomes bound to pay taxes according to his ability, and if necessary to serve in the army or navy against domestic or foreign enemies: but an alien is free from a large measure of these obligations, and the state, on its part, comes under no obligation to maintain him, if he becomes dependent. The American sailor or resident living in England, who becomes a pauper, appeals naturally and rightfully to his own consul for protection and aid. There is no reason in the nature of the case, why we should maintain paupers who are subjects of Great Britain or Germany, who are landed upon our shores in a dependent condition or in such a state of mental or bodily health that they must necessarily become dependent. We are no more bound, apart from the general law of humanity, to maintain such persons, than we are to pay the interest on the English national debt, or furnish conscripts for the German army. The question arises how shall this transference of the pauper population of the old countries of Europe to our shores be stopped." – *The Social Welfare Forum Official Proceedings [of The] Annual Meeting, 1885*, pgs. 171-172

"In the year 1636 Plymouth Colony, and a year later Massachusetts Bay, enacted laws to the effect that no town or person should receive any stranger with intent to entertain such person more than three weeks without the consent of the authorities. The purpose of these laws, it is said, was to prevent the coming of individuals who might further political strife or become an economic burden. Then, as now, the fear of foreign radicals and paupers was abroad in the land ..." – *National Conference on Social Welfare, The Social Welfare Forum: Official Proceedings of The Annual Forum, 1922*, pg. 458.

Aleksandr Solzhenitsyn

"Before the camps, I regarded the existence of nationality as something that shouldn't be noticed—nationality did not really exist, only humanity. But in the camps one learns: if you belong to a successful nation you are protected and you survive. If you are part of universal humanity—too bad for you." – *Nobel Lecture*, 1970

"And literature conveys irrefutable condensed experience in yet another invaluable direction; namely, from generation to generation. Thus it becomes the living memory of the nation. Thus it preserves and kindles within itself the flame of her spent history, in a form which is safe from deformation and slander. In this way literature, together with language, protects the soul of the nation.

"(In recent times it has been fashionable to talk of the levelling of nations, of the disappearance of different races in the melting-pot of contemporary civilization. I do not agree with this opinion, but its discussion remains another question. Here it is merely fitting to say that the disappearance of nations would have impoverished us no less than if all men had become alike, with one personality and one face. Nations are the wealth of mankind, its collective personalities; the very least of them wears its own special colours and bears within itself a special facet of divine intention.)

"But woe to that nation whose literature is disturbed by the intervention of power. Because that is not just a violation against 'freedom of print', it is the closing down of the heart of the nation, a slashing to pieces of its memory. The nation ceases to be mindful of itself, it is deprived of its spiritual unity, and despite a supposedly common language, compatriots suddenly cease to understand one another. Silent generations grow old and die without ever having talked about themselves, either to each other or to their descendants. When writers such as Achmatova and Zamjatin – interred alive throughout their lives – are condemned to create in silence until they die, never hearing the echo of their written words, then that is not only their personal tragedy, but a sorrow to the whole nation, a danger to the whole nation.

"In some cases moreover – when as a result of such a silence the whole of history ceases to be understood in its entirety – it is a danger to the whole of mankind." – *Nobel Prize Acceptance Speech* in 1970

Solomon

"I considered in my heart that I was full of righteousness, for I had prospered and had many children." – *The Old Testament Pseudepigrapha and the New Testament*, pg. 651.[82]

"I am very dark, but lovely, O daughters of Jerusalem, like the tents of Kedar, like the curtains of Solomon. Do not gaze at me because I am dark, because the sun has looked upon me. My mother's sons were angry with me; they made me keeper of the vineyards, but my own vineyard I have not kept!" – *Song of Songs* [83]

---

82 Included here due to extra-canonicity.

83 "dark, but lovely" – See commentary section on this verse.

Sophocles

"If I nurture rebels within my household there'll be many more rebels outside it. The man who's good at managing the affairs of his own household will be worthy also of being the ruler of his nation. Whereas he who violates the laws of the gods and his city, or wants to command its leaders, will never gain my respect.

"We must obey those whom the city has ordained to be its leaders. We should obey them, unquestioningly, in all things, minor or great, those we agree with and those we oppose. I believe such a man would govern well and he'd also be an obedient servant; and he'd stay at his post even in the hurricane of war, honourably, bravely defending his country.

"There's no worse evil than anarchy.

"Anarchy destroys nations, my son.

"Anarchy destroys homes."

– *Antigone*, lines 660-70

Thomas Sowell

"Slavery was an evil of greater scope and magnitude than most people imagine and, as a result, its place in history is radically different from the way it is usually portrayed. Mention slavery and immediately the image that arises is that of Africans and their descendants enslaved by Europeans and their descendants in the Southern United States—or, at most, Africans enslaved by Europeans in the Western Hemisphere. No other historic horror is so narrowly construed. No one thinks of war, famine, or decimating epidemics in such localized terms. These are afflictions that have been suffered by the entire human race, all over the planet—and so was slavery. Had slavery been limited to one race in one country during three centuries, its tragedies would not have been one-tenth the magnitude that they were in fact.

"Why this provincial view of a worldwide evil? Often it is those who are most critical of a 'Eurocentric' view of the world who are most Eurocentric when it comes to the evils and failings of the human race. Why would anyone wish to arbitrarily understate an evil that plagued mankind for thousands of years, unless it was not this evil itself that was the real concern, but rather the present-day uses of that historic evil? Clearly, the ability to score ideological points against American society

or Western civilization, or to induce guilt and thereby extract benefits from the white population today, are greatly enhanced by making enslavement appear to be a peculiarly American, or a peculiarly white, crime." – *Black Rednecks and White Liberals*, pg. 171

"People tend to sort themselves out, not only in their residential patterns but also in their social interactions. Twentieth-century Japanese immigrants to Brazil not only settled in Japanese enclaves, most Okinawan immigrants in Brazil married other Okinawans, rather than marrying Japanese from other parts of Japan, much less marrying members of the Brazilian population at large.

"It was much the same story among German immigrants in nineteenth-century New York, where most Bavarians married other Bavarians, and most Prussians married other Prussians. Among the Irish immigrants as well, most nineteenth-century marriages that took place in New York's Irish enclaves were marriages between people from the same county in Ireland.

"In the Australian city of Griffith, in the years from 1920 to 1933, 90 percent of Italian men who had emigrated from Venice and gotten married in Australia married Italian women who had also emigrated from Venice. Another five percent married Italian women from other parts of Italy, the same percentage as married 'British-Australian' women.

"However striking these patterns may be statistically, they are not patterns that most people are made aware of by seeing them with the naked eye, as is the case with differences between black neighborhoods and white neighborhoods in the United States. As a result, black-white residential separations have been seen and treated as if they were unique, as well as being inconsistent with prevailing background assumptions of equal or random outcomes in the absence of discriminatory impositions.

"History shows that there have in fact been discriminatory impositions of residential patterns, at various times and places, not only as regards blacks in the United States, but also many other groups in countries around the world.

"Sorting has been as common within black neighborhoods as within other neighborhoods around the world. Back in the 1930s, the research of noted black scholar E. Franklin Fra-

zier showed clear patterns of residential clustering of people with different ways of life within
the black community in Chicago.

"After dividing that community into seven
zones, Professor Frazier showed empirically
that the proportion of adults to children varied
greatly from one zone to another, as did the
ratio of males to females, and the percentage of
mulattoes in the population was several times
higher in one zone than in another.

"Moreover, these were not simply isolated
differences. They were differences reflecting
different socioeconomic levels and differences in
family stability and behavioral standards. De-
linquency rates within Chicago's black community ranged from more than 40 percent in some
neighborhoods to under 2 percent in others.

In nineteenth-century Detroit, black home-
owners lived clustered together and separate
from black renters. Similar residential differentiation took place in Cleveland's black community. A history of Harlem pointed out occupational differences among people who returned home
from work and got off at different subway stops
in Harlem.

"Mid-twentieth-century data showed income
distribution among blacks in the country as a
whole to be slightly more unequal than among
whites. So did later data. A 1966 study indicated that among the more than 4 million black
American families at that time, just 5.2 thousand families produced all the black physicians,
dentists, lawyers and academic doctorates in the
country. Despite how exceptional such occupations and achievements were among blacks at
that time, these particular families averaged 2.25
individuals each in those categories. That is,
every four such families averaged nine individuals at these levels.

"Awareness of such social differences was
both widespread and often acute within the
black population. There is a whole literature on
exclusive black elites, including such books as
Aristocrats of Color by Willard B. Gatewood, *Our
Kind of People* by Lawrence Otis Graham, and
Certain People by Stephen Birmingham.

"Particular upscale neighborhoods within
mid-twentieth-century Harlem were known as
'Strivers' Row' and 'Sugar Hill.' A luxury apart-
ment building at 409 Edgecombe Avenue was so
widely known as a residence of the black elite
that it was said to be sufficient to get into a taxi
in Harlem and say simply '409' for the driver to

know where to take you.

"Similar patterns existed in Chicago. There
had long been a small black community in
Chicago in the nineteenth century, before the
great migrations of blacks from the South in the
twentieth century led to severalfold increases in
the number of blacks in that city. Those blacks
born and bred in nineteenth-century Chicago,
and living as small enclaves of blacks in an
overwhelmingly white population, had over
time assimilated culturally to the norms of the
surrounding society, as other groups have in
similar circumstances.

"The later massive migrations of Southern
blacks to Chicago in the twentieth century
created acute polarization within the black community there. The Chicago Defender, a black
newspaper, was highly critical of the newcomers
for behavior that gave blacks in general a bad
name. So were other blacks from the pre-ex-
isting black community there and in other
Northern cities, where both the existing black
residents and the local black press denounced
the new arrivals from the South as vulgar, row-
dy, unwashed and criminal." – *Discrimination
and Disparities*, ch. 3, pgs. 37-39

— THOMAS SOWELL —

"People who would never walk through a
particular neighborhood at night, or perhaps
not even in broad daylight, may nevertheless be
indignant at banks that engage in 'redlining'—
that is, putting a whole neighborhood off-limits
as a place to invest their depositors' money.

The observers' own 'redlining' in their choices of where to walk may never be seen by them as a different example of the same principle. ...

"Where there are real differences between groups, with potentially dire consequences, such as murder rates several times higher in one group than in another, (generalized discrimination) may be carried to the point of 'redlining' a whole neighborhood or group, even when a majority of the group avoided are not guilty of the behavior feared.

"Even in a high-crime neighborhood, for example, most people are not necessarily criminals. But the costs of sorting the local population individually can be prohibitively high. Therefore decisions are likely to be made through a cruder decision-making process, relying on empirically based generalizations...

"One of the consequences of such situations is that a law-abiding majority in a high-crime neighborhood can end up paying a high price for the presence of a criminal minority living in their midst. Some businesses will not deliver their products—whether pizzas or furniture—to high-crime neighborhoods, rather than risk bodily harm, including death, to their drivers.

"Taxi drivers may avoid taking passengers to such neighborhoods for the same reason, even when these are black taxi drivers refusing to go into black high-crime neighborhoods, especially at night. Supermarket chains and other businesses often avoid locating local stores in such neighborhoods, for similar reasons." – *Discrimination And Disparities*, ch. 2, pg. 23

"There has been a particularly tragic consequence of the quest for cosmic justice for young black Americans. Just as some parents make the mistake of talking around small children as if they cannot hear or understand, so those promoting a vision of cosmic injustices as the cause of all the problems of black Americans have failed to understand the consequences of this vision for young blacks who do not yet have either the personal experience or the maturity to weigh those words against reality. The net result in many ghetto schools has been the development of an attitude of hostility to learning or to conforming to ordinary standards of behavior in society. Worse, those young black students who do wish to get an education, to speak correct English, and to behave in ways compatible with getting along with others, are accused

of 'acting white'—betraying the race—and are subject to both social pressures and outright intimidation and violence." – *Quest for Cosmic Justice*, pg. 41

"The most obvious fact about the history of racial and ethnic groups is how different they have been-and still are." – *Economics and Politics of Race*, pg. 244

"Back in nineteenth-century America, for example, when there were many immigrants from Europe in the workforce, some groups brought their mutual antagonisms in Europe with them to America. To have a workforce including both Irish Protestants and Irish Catholics working together at that time was to risk distracting frictions and even violence, with negative effects on productivity. In other words, a workforce consisting exclusively of either group might be more efficient than a workforce consisting of both." – *Discrimination and Disparities*, pg. 33

"Neither sweeping attacks on immigrants in general nor sweeping defenses of immigrants in general make any sense, because there are no immigrants in general. Instead, there are very different behavior patterns— in education, employment and crimes, for example— among immigrants from different countries and cultures." – *Discrimination and Disparities*, pg. 206

"Verbal virtuosity can blur such distinctions and produce such wonderful-sounding generalities as judging each person as an individual, or declaring all cultures equally valid or valuable in some elusive and unverifiable sense. In this world of words, much controversy is based on assertions and counter-assertions, rather than on hard facts about such things as the educational levels, welfare state dependency, automobile accident rates, or crime rates of particular groups from particular countries or cultures. Rhetoric, visions and catchwords often serve as substitutes for such basic information. – *Discrimination and Disparities*, pgs. 206-207

"Despite wide disparities among immigrant groups from different countries and cultures, empirical facts about such differences are seldom part of public debates about immigration policies. The very attempt to discuss such issues in factual terms has been treated as morally unworthy. Any concerns about a need to preserve a domestic culture that has produced a level of prosperity, order and freedom seldom found in some other cultures risks being dismissed as phobias or racism. It is as if the only morally legitimate way to discuss immigration issues is in terms of the prevailing social vision, based on the seemingly invincible fallacy of assuming a sameness of developed capabilities among both peoples and cultures." – *Discrimination and Disparities*, pgs. 208

Oswald Spengler

"In place of a type-true people, born of and grown on the soil, there is a new sort of nomad, cohering unstably in fluid masses, the parasitical city dweller, traditionless, utterly matter-of-fact, religionless, clever, unfruitful, deeply contemptuous of the countryman and especially that highest form of countryman, the country gentleman. This is a very great stride towards the inorganic, towards the end — what does it signify?" – *The Decline of the West: Form and Actuality*, pg. 25

"But conjure away the phantom [of the abstract idea of a universal 'Mankind'], break the magic circle, and at once there emerges an astonishing wealth of actual forms—the Living with all its immense fullness, depth and movement—hitherto veiled by a catchword, a dry as dust scheme, and a set of personal 'ideals.' I see, in place of that empty figment of one linear history which can only be kept up by shutting one's eyes to the overwhelming multitude of the facts, the drama of a number of mighty Cultures, each springing with primitive strength from the soil of a mother region to which it remains firmly bound throughout its whole life-cycle; each stamping its material, its mankind, in its own image; each having its own idea, its own passions, its own life, will and feeling, its own death. Here indeed are colours, lights, movements, that no intellectual eye has yet discovered. Here the Cultures, peoples, languages, truths, gods, landscapes bloom and age as the oaks and the stone-pines, the blossoms, twigs and leaves—but there is no aging 'Mankind.' Each Culture has its own new possibilities of self-expression which arise, ripen, decay, and never return. There is not one sculpture,

one painting, one mathematics, one physics, but many, each in its deepest essence different from the others, each limited in duration and self-contained, just as species of plant has its peculiar blossom or fruit, its special type of growth and decline." – *The Decline of the West: Form and Actuality*, pg. 17

"...every individual being that has any sort of importance recapitulates, of intrinsic necessity, all the epochs of the Culture to which it belongs. In each one of us, at that decisive moment when he begins to know that he is an ego, the inner life wakens just where and just how that of the Culture wakened long ago. Each of us men of the West, in his child's day-dreams and child's play, lives again its Gothic — the cathedrals, the castles, the hero-sagas, the crusader's 'Dieu le veult,' the soul's oath of young Parzival. Every young Greek had his Homeric age and his Marathon...Connected with this is the spiritual relation of grandfather and grandson, a relation which produces in the mind of primitive peoples the conviction that the soul of the grandfather returns in the grandson, and has originated the widespread custom of giving the grandson the grandfather's name, which by its mystic spell binds his soul afresh to the corporeal world."
– *The Decline of the West: Form and Actuality*, pg. 105

"From the maternal care the way leads to the paternal, and there we meet with the highest of all the time-symbols that have come into existence within a Culture, the State. The meaning of the child to the mother is the future, the continuation, namely, of her own life, and mother-love is, as it were, a welding of two discontinuous individual existences. Likewise, the meaning of the state to the man is comradeship in arms for the protection of hearth and home, wife and child, and for the insurance for the whole people of its future and its efficacy. The state is the inward form of a nation, its 'form' in the athletic sense, and history, in the high meaning, is the State conceived as kinesis and not as kinema. The Woman as Mother is, and the Man as Warrior and Politician makes, History." – *The Decline of the West: Form and Actuality*, pg. 137

"And then, when Being is sufficiently uprooted

and Waking Being sufficiently strained, there suddenly emerges into the bright light of history a phenomenon that has long been preparing itself underground and now steps forward to make an end of the drama — the sterility of civilized man. This is not something that can be grasped as a plain matter of Causality (as modern science naturally enough has tried to grasp it); it is to be understood as an essentially metaphysical turn towards death. The last man of the world city no longer wants to live — he may cling to life as an individual, but as a type, as an aggregate, no, for it is a characteristic of this collective existence that it eliminates the terror of death. That which strikes the true peasant with a deep and inexplicable fear, the notion that the family and the name may be extinguished, has now lost its meaning. The continuance of the blood relation in the visible world is no longer a duty of the blood, and the destiny of being the last of the line is no longer felt as a doom.

"Children do not happen, not because children have become impossible, but principally because intelligence at the peak of intensity can no longer find any reason for their existence. Let the reader try to merge himself in the soul of the peasant. He has sat on his glebe from primeval times, or has fastened his clutch in it, to adhere to it with his blood. He is rooted in it as the descendant of his forbears and as the forbear of future descendants. His house, his property, means, here, not the temporary connection of person and thing for a brief span of years, but an enduring and inward union of eternal land and eternal blood. It is only from this mystical conviction of settlement that the great epochs of the cycle — procreation, birth, and death — derive that metaphysical element of wonder which condenses in the symbolism of custom and religion that all landbound people possess. For the 'last men' all this is past and gone. Intelligence and sterility are allied in old families, old peoples, and old Cultures, not merely because in each microcosm the over-strained and fettered animal element is eating up the plant element, but also because the waking consciousness assumes that being is normally regulated by causality. That which the man of intelligence, most significantly and characteristically, labels as 'natural impulse' or 'life force,' he not only knows, but also values, causally, giving it the place amongst his other needs that his judgment assigns to it. When the

— OSWALD SPENGLER —

ordinary thought of a highly cultivated people begins to regard 'having children' as a question of pro's and con's, the great turning point has come. For Nature knows nothing of pro and con. Everywhere, wherever life is actual, reigns an inward organic logic, an 'it,' a drive, that is utterly independent of waking being, with its causal linkages, and indeed not even observed by it. The abundant proliferation of primitive peoples is a natural phenomenon, which is not even thought about, still less judged as to its utility or the reverse. When reasons have to be put forward at all in a question of life, life itself has become questionable. At that point begins prudent limitation of the number of births.

"In the Classical world the practice was deplored by Polybius as the ruin of Greece, and yet even at his date it had long been established in the great cities; in subsequent Roman times it became appallingly general. At first explained by the economic misery of the times, very soon it ceased to explain itself at all. And at that point, too, in Buddhist India as in Babylon, in Rome as in our own cities, a man's choice of the woman who is to be, not mother of his children as amongst peasants and primitives, but his own 'companion for life,' becomes a problem of mentalities. The Ibsen marriage appears, the 'higher spiritual affinity' in which both parties are 'free' — free, that is, as intelligences, free from the plantlike urge of the blood to continue itself, and it becomes possible for a Shaw to say 'that unless Woman repudiates her womanliness, her duty to her husband, to her children, to society, to the law, and to everyone but herself, she cannot emancipate herself.' The primary woman, the peasant woman, is mother. The whole vocation towards which she has yearned from childhood is included in that one word. But now emerges the Ibsen woman, the comrade, the heroine of a whole megalopolitan literature from Northern drama to Parisian novel. Instead of children, she has soul conflicts; marriage is a craft art for the achievement of 'mutual understanding.' It is all the same whether the case against children is the American lady's who would not miss a season for anything, or the Parisienne's who fears that her lover would leave her, or an Ibsen heroine's who 'belongs to herself' — they all belong to themselves and they are all unfruitful. The same fact, in conjunction with the same arguments, is to be found in the Alexandrian, in the Roman, and, as a matter of course, in every other civilized society — and conspicuously in that in which Buddha grew up. And in Hellenism and in the nineteenth century, as in the times of Lao Tzu and the Charvaka doctrine, there is an ethic for childless intelligences, and a literature about the inner conflicts of Nora and Nana. The 'quiverful,' which was still an honorable enough spectacle in the days of Werther, becomes something rather provincial. The father of many children is for the great city a subject for caricature; Ibsen did not fail to note it, and presented it in his Loves Comedy.

"At this level all Civilizations enter upon a stage, which lasts for centuries, of appalling depopulation. The whole pyramid of cultural man vanishes. It crumbles from the summit, first the world cities, then the provincial farms, and finally the land itself, whose best blood has incontinently poured into the towns, merely to bolster them up awhile. At the last, only the primitive blood remains, alive, but robbed of its strongest and most promising elements." – *The Decline of the West: Form and Actuality*, pgs. 156-158

"Every Culture possesses a proper conception of home and fatherland, which is hard to comprehend, scarcely to be expressed in words, full of dark metaphysical relations, but nevertheless unmistakable in its tendency. The Classical home-feeling which tied the individual corporally and Euclidean-ly to the Polis is the very antithesis of that enigmatic 'Heimweh' of

the Northerner which has something musical, soaring and unearthly in it. Classical man felt as 'Home' just what he could see from the Acropolis of his native city. Where the horizon of Athens ended, the alien, the hostile, the 'fatherland' of another began. Even the Roman of late Republican times understood by 'patria' nothing but Urbs Roma, not even Latium, still less Italy. The Classical world, as it matured, dissolved itself into a large number of point-patriæ, and the need of bodily separation between them took the form of hatreds far more intense than any hatred that there was of the Barbarian. And it is therefore the most convincing of all evidences of the victory of the Magian world-feeling that Caracalla in 212 A.D. granted Roman citizenship to all provincials. For this grant simply abolished the ancient, statuesque, idea of the citizen. There was now a Realm and consequently a new kind of membership. The Roman notion of an army, too, underwent a significant change. In genuinely Classical times there had been no Roman Army in the sense in which we speak of the Prussian Army, but only 'armies,' that is, definite formations (as we say) created as corps, limited and visibly present bodies, by the appointment of a Legatus to command—an exercitus Scipionis, Crassi for instance—but never an exercitus Romanus. It was Caracalla, the same who abolished the idea of 'civis Romanus' by decree and wiped out the Roman civic deities by making all alien deities equivalent to them, who created the un-Classical and Magian idea of an Imperial Army, something manifested in the separate legions. These now meant something, whereas in Classical times they meant nothing, but simply were. The old 'fides exercituum' is replaced by 'fides exercitus' in the inscriptions and, instead of individual bodily conceived deities special to each legion and ritually honoured by its Legatus, we have a spiritual principle common to all.

So also, and in the same sense, the 'fatherland'-feeling undergoes a change of meaning for Eastern men—and not merely Christians—in Apollinian man, so long as he retained any effective remnant at all of his proper world-feeling, regarded 'home' in the genuinely corporeal sense as the ground on which his city was built—a conception that recalls the 'unity of place' of Attic tragedy and statuary. But to Magian man, to Christians, Persians,

Jews, 'Greeks,' Manichæans, Nestorians and Mohammedans, it means nothing that has any connexion with geographical actualities. And for ourselves it means an impalpable unity of nature, speech, climate, habits and history—not earth but 'country,' not point-like presence but historic past and future, not a unit made up of men, houses and gods but an idea, the idea that takes shape in the restless wanderings, the deep loneliness, and that ancient German impulse towards the South which has been the ruin of our best, from the Saxon Emperors to Hölderlin and Nietzsche.

"The bent of the Faustian Culture, therefore, was overpoweringly towards extension, political, economic or spiritual. It overrode all geographical material bounds. It sought— any practical object, merely for the Symbol's own sake—to reach North Pole and South Pole. It ended by transforming the entire surface of the globe into a single colonial and economic system. Every thinker from Meister Eckhardt to Kant willed to subject the 'phenomenal' world to the asserted domination of the cognizing ego, and every leader from Otto the Great to Napoleon did it. The genuine object of their ambitions was the boundless, alike for the great Franks and Hohenstaufen with their world-monarchies, for Gregory VII and Innocent III, for the Spanish Habsburgs 'on whose empire the sun never set,' and for the Imperialism of to-day on behalf of which the World-War was fought and will continue to be fought for many a long day. Classical man, for inward reasons, could not be a conqueror, notwithstanding Alexander's romantic expedition—for we can discern enough of the inner hesitations and unwillingnesses of his companions not to need to explain it as an 'exception proving the rule.' The never-stilled desire to be liberated from the binding element, to range far and free, which is the essence of the fancy-creatures of the North—the dwarfs, elves and imps—is utterly unknown to the Dryads and Oreads of Greece. Greek daughter-cities were planted by the hundred along the rim of the Mediterranean, but not one of them made the slightest real attempt to conquer and penetrate the hinter lands. To settle far from the coast would have meant to lose sight of 'home,' while to settle in loneliness—the ideal life of the trapper and prairie-man of America as it had been of Icelandic saga-heroes long before—was

something entirely beyond the possibilities of Classical mankind. Dramas like that of the emigration to America—man by man, each on his own account, driven by deep promptings to loneliness—or the Spanish Conquest, or the Californian gold-rush, dramas of uncontrollable longings for freedom, solitude, immense independence, and of giant-like contempt of all limitations whatsoever upon the homefeeling— these dramas are Faustian and only Faustian. No other Culture, not even the Chinese, knows them...

"If, in fine, we look at it all together the expansion of the Copernican world-picture into that aspect of stellar space that we possess to-day; the development of Columbus's discovery into a worldwide command of the earth's surface by the West; the perspective of oil painting and of tragedy-scene; the sublimed home-feeling; the passion of our Civilization for swift transit, the conquest of the air, the exploration of the Polar regions and the climbing of almost impossible mountain-peaks—we see, emerging everywhere the prime symbol of the Faustian soul, Limitless Space. And those specially (in form, uniquely) Western creations of the soul-myth called 'Will,' 'Force' and 'Deed' must be regarded as derivatives of this prime-symbol."
– *The Decline of the West: Form and Actuality*, pgs. 552-553

"There is always one nonnegotiable element in any plan to secure global domination: sovereign nations (truly independent nations) cannot be tolerated. Why? Because global domination is about centralizing all power into the would-be rulers' hands. Independent nations impede this consolidation and disturb the proper chain of command. This seems straightforward enough, but, since it's rarely boiled down to its simplest form, it's worth repeating: to rule the world, you must first destroy national sovereignty. You must consolidate and control the real levers of power, regardless of the different forms of government that appear in each country." – *The Decline of the West: Form and Actuality*

Robert Elliott Speer

"This spirit of nationalism is inevitable and it is invaluable. It is not in conflict with the ideal of a united humanity. It is essential to its realisation. The same God Who made of one blood all nations of men, assigned them also their racial and national character and destinies to the end of a perfected humanity. The development of state consciousness, state conscience, state ambition, state duty, is a development in the will of God for man, and the true world citizenship will recognise this and build the unity of mankind, not upon any speculative theory of humanity, nor upon any sand-heap of individual units, but upon corporate nationalities such as God has always dealt with and built upon in human history. He used a nation to prepare the salvation of the world, and He has always wrought His purposes through racial movements. His men were men of their nations, and His judgments were judgments of nations of men…

"Now this problem of the nations is the inevitable problem of the Churches also. For the aim of foreign missions is to plant Christianity indigenously in the life of each nation, to domesticate it there and let it grow up and out in the forms of life appropriate to it in the new environment to which it has been naturalised, to which, indeed, it has not needed to be naturalised so far as it has been presented in its true character of the universal life and faith of man. So far as we succeed in carrying out this aim, we build up in each nation, or we are witnesses to a building up by God of Churches rooted in the life of each separate nation, each one made up of its nation's people, subject to its distinctive character and participating in its national mission and destiny. Our very fundamental ideal in foreign missions involves the creation of the national problem, the problem of the relation of national Churches or of Churches which are to become national."
– *Christianity And The Nations, Duff Lectures*, pgs. 118-120

"Our ideal is to establish in each land a native Church that shall be of the soil, rooted in the tradition and life of the people, fitted to its customs and institutions, sharing its character and participating in its mission, yes, defining and inspiring that mission as it can do only when it is a truly national Church subject to no alien bondage. In such a Church Christianity will, of course, surrender nothing that is essential and universal. She enters into no compromise. She simply domesticates herself in a new home which she has been long in finding, and from the new roots which she sinks into humanity expands that interpretation of the life of God in man and nourishes that hope of man's future

in God, which can only be perfected as all the peoples bring their glory and honour into the final temple of humanity." – *Christianity And The Nations, Duff Lectures*, pg. 122

R.C. Sproul

"Other theologians argue that image and likeness are really synonyms in this verse, so we cannot make a neat distinction between the two. They—including most traditional Protestant theologians—explain the situation this way: There is a wider sense in which man is the image of God (imago essentialis), and also a narrow or particular sense (imago conformitas). In the wider sense, man simply is the image of God, and since that is what man is by definition, it cannot be changed or lost. As long as man is man, he is the image of God.

"In the narrow sense, however, man images God's holiness and righteousness. Man, therefore, stopped imaging God at the Fall. He lost his conformity to God's image. We are still the image of God, but we are distorting that image. If other people look at us to see what God is like, they will get the wrong idea, because we image Him imperfectly. Only in Jesus Christ do we see a man who is the perfect image of God in both senses." – *Tabletalk Magazine, August 1990: Parables: Kernels of Truth*, 40.

Charles Spurgeon

"Piety must begin at home as well as charity. Conversion should begin with those who are nearest to us in ties of relationship. I stir you up, not to be attempting missionary labors for India, not to be casting eyes of pity across to Africa, not to be occupied so much with tears for popish and heathen lands, as for your own children, your own flesh and blood, your own neighbors, your own acquaintance. Lift up your cry to heaven for them, and then afterwards you shall preach among the nations."

"Andrew goes to Cappadocia in his after-life, but he begins with his brother (Peter); and you shall labor where you please in years to come, but first of all your own household, first of all those who are under your own shadow must receive your guardian care. Be wise in this thing; use the ability you have, and use it amongst those who are near at hand." – *Words of Counsel for Christian Workers, in Men Of The New Testament*, pg. 69

"When the patriot mother tears her son from her bosom and cries, 'Go, my firstborn, to your country's wars, there go and fight until your country's flag is safe, and the hearths and homes of your native land are secure,' there is something in it, for she can look forward to the bloody spectacle of her son's mangled body, and yet love her country more than her own child. Here is heroism indeed; but God spared not His own Son, His only begotten Son, but freely delivered Him up for us all. 'God commendeth his love toward us, in that, while we were yet sinners, Christ died for us.'" – sermon entitled *Expiation*, in *Sermons* vol. 10, pg. 109

"Christianity does not come into a nation to break up its arrangements, or to break down its fabric. All that is good in human society it preserves and establishes. It snaps no ties of the family; it dislocates no bonds of the body politic." – sermon entitled *To Those Who Are Angry With Their Godly Friends*, in *Metropolitan* vol. 32, pg. 383

"What business have foreigners to plot against the government, or to intermeddle with the politics of a country in which they have no citizenship? An Englishman in New York had best be without a tongue just now, if he should criticize the courage of the generals, the accuracy of their dispatches, or the genius of the President, he might meet with rather rough usage. He will be injudicious, indeed, if he cannot leave America to the Americans." – sermon entitled *Citizenship in Heaven*, *Metropolitan* vol. 2, pg. 591

Preaching on Psalm 76:3:

"The writer of this song of triumph gloried as a patriot in the defeat of his country's foes, he did better, he triumphed as a believer in Jehovah in the victories which were worked by the power of the Lord his God. I have sometimes wished that we English Christians blended in ourselves a little more of the two characters of patriots and believers. I am persuaded that if our poets had been holy and devout men, and at the same time bold patriots, like David, they would not have lacked subjects for the most glorious national hymns. The events of English history are not less stirring than the annals of Judah and Israel. What a theme for a master singer would be the defeat of the proud Spanish Armada, or the frustration of Rome's knavish tricks on November the fifth, or the gallant fights of Oliver and his valiant Ironsides, or the landing of William III, and the overthrow of the hopes of the enemies of the Gospel!

— Charles Spurgeon —

"Our national minstrelsy has never been so devout as it should be, and we are poor in holy national song as compared to the Hebrews, may the taste of coming ages improve in this respect. Let us, in the events which occur in our own time, see the hand of God, and if we cannot write psalms and hymns, yet at any rate let us feel the spirit of glowing thanksgiving to that God who has bid the ocean gird our native isle, and thus protected her with a better guard than gates of brass or triple steel. Blessed be the Lord our God, who till now has held the shield of omnipotence over this land, and made it the citadel of liberty, the refuge of the oppressed, and the stronghold of the Gospel of Christ." – sermon entitled *The Arrows Of The Broken Bow In Zion*, in *Spurgeons' Sermons* vol. 14, pg. 27

"A Christian has nothing to lose by death. You say he has to lose his friends. I am not so sure of that. Many of you have many more friends in heaven than on earth; some Christians have more dearly beloved ones above than below. You often count your family circle, but do you do as that little girl of whom Wordsworth speaks, when she said, 'Master, we are seven.' Some of them were dead and gone to heaven, but she would have it that they were all brothers and sisters still. Oh! how many brothers and sisters we have up stairs in the upper room in our Father's house; how many dear ones, linked with us in the ties of relationship, for they are as much our relations now as they were then! Though in the resurrection they neither marry nor are given in marriage, yet in that great world, who has said that the ties of affection shall be severed, so that we shall not even there claim kindred with one another, as well as kindred with Jesus Christ?" – sermon entitled *The Death of the Christian*, in *The New Park Street Pulpit Sermons*, vol. 1, pg. 327

Dumitru Staniloae

"There are various kinds of nationalism. One kind can be a fall into sinfulness – and this is very often what happens; yet anti-nationalism is a more serious fall into sin, being contrary not only to the Christian way of community life, but also to nature. Like anything genuine, salvific belief in the nation as opposed to nationalism need not lead to our destruction if developed in accord with faith. Though not in itself redemptive, it is not destructive. What saves us is faith, the Christian spirit we infuse into national aspiration. Nationalism of itself can neither save nor destroy. But in practice all nationalism is either redemptive or destructive, according to whether or not it is animated by Christian faith." – *Ortodoxie și Românism*, pg. 104

Statius

"Thereon was embossed work of images: all golden, a winged youth holds the snake-tressed Gorgon's severed head, and even upon the moment – so it seems – leaps up into the wandering breeze; she almost moves her heavy eyes and drooping head, and even grows pale in the living gold." – *Thebaid*, pg. 381[84]

"Just so might Pallas and Phoebus' sterner sister glide down together from high heaven, terrible alike in armour and in looks, and with golden hair braided on their heads, bringing their maiden company, from Cynthus she and she from Aracynthus; they wouldst thou never learn by long gazing, even had thine eyes leave to gaze, which had the greater beauty, which the greater charm, or which had more of Jove..." – *Thebaid*, pg. 411

Percy Reginald Stephensen

"Australian literature, like that of any other country, is an expression of the life of all the people, and not only of university cliques, who make a living by following foreign fashions, and taking in one another's washing. The main body of Australian literature has therefore been built up, and will continue to be built up, by writers with that non-academic, professional outlook, whose first aim is to supply reading-matter to please the average or ordinary Australian readers of books. These professional writers are unique among workers in our community. They have no benefit of governmental protection for their industry by tariffs, subsidies, or anything of that kind. They have no Arbitration Court awards or Basic Wage. They must write books which can be commercially published, and sold in large quantities, to yield an income from royalties on those sales; or, if that fails, they must starve, or go into exile, or cease writing books...

"The active fostering of the Australian national spirit, by means of its expression in a living literature, has in these ways devolved chiefly upon writers who have not been colonially conditioned, or otherwise handicapped, by a university training. The development of a national spirit, on which the survival of any community depends, is instinctive in the life of the people. It should be encouraged in every possible way at Australian Universities...

"Books are the repositories of knowledge and the messengers of ideas. There is no substitute for books. A nation which does not produce enough books to proclaim and define its existence on a civilised level cannot compel respect, no matter how many bales of wool it might export...

"Writers who can convey that atmosphere of self-confidence to the Australian people will take rank as nation-builders. The others — the disparagers, the pessimists, the colonial imitators of faraway fashions — having no roots in our soil, will fade away, and no one will be sorry to see them disappear." – *Colonialism In Our Literature; The Bulletin* (Sydney, NSW) 16 June 1962, pgs. 27-29

---

84   Loeb Classic Library notes this passage: "Gold is naturally pale"

Hendrik G. Stoker

"A state which binds a group of individuals who don't share the inherent bond of blood and culture, is fundamentally no unity. The creation-principle demands an intrinsic unity as the most intimate embodiment of any extrinsic unity." – *The Philosophy of the Creation-Principle: Foundations of a Calvinist Philosophy*

Snorri Sturluson

Norse Mythology, the creation of man develops into two lines: those mixed with giants are "dark" and represent Night; and those mixed with the gods (Allfather) are "bright" and represent Day:

"Then said Gangleri: 'Much indeed they had accomplished then, methinks, when earth and heaven were made, and the sun and the constellations of heaven were fixed, and division was made of days; now whence come the men that people the world?' And Hárr answered: 'When the sons of Borr were walking along the sea-strand, they found two trees, and took up the trees and shaped men of them: the first gave them spirit and life; the second, wit and feeling; the third, form, speech, hearing, and sight. They gave them clothing and names: the male was called Askr, and the female Embla, and of them was mankind begotten, which received a dwelling-place under Midgard. Next they made for themselves in the middle of the world a city which is called Ásgard; men call it Troy. There dwelt the gods and their kindred; and many tidings and tales of it have come to pass both on earth and aloft. There is one abode called Hlidskjálf, and when Allfather sat in the high-seat there, he looked out over the whole world and saw every man's acts, and knew all things which he saw. His wife was called Frigg daughter of Fjörgvinn; and of their blood is come that kindred which we call the races of the Æsir, that have peopled the Elder Ásgard, and those kingdoms which pertain to it; and that is a divine race. For this reason must he be called Allfather: because he is father of all the gods and of men, and of all that was fulfilled of him and of his might. The Earth was his daughter and his wife; on her he begot the first son, which is Ása-Thor: strength and prowess attend him, wherewith he overcomes all living things.

"Nörfi or Narfi is the name of a giant that dwelt in Jötunheim: he had a daughter called Night; she was swarthy and dark, as befitted her race. She was given to the man named Naglfari; their son was Audr. Afterward she was wedded to him that was called Annarr; Jörd was their daughter. Last of all Dayspring had her, and he was of the race of the Æsir; their son was Day: he was radiant and fair after his father. Then Allfather took Night, and Day her son, and gave to them two horses and two chariots, and sent them up into the heavens, to ride round about the earth every two half-days. Night rides before with the horse named Frosty-Mane, and on each morning he bedews the earth with the foam from his bit. The horse that Day has is called Sheen-Mane, and he illumines all the air and the earth from his mane." – *Prose Edda*, "Gylfaginning", *The Beguiling of Gylfa*, pg. 222

"Each one singly is called man; it is twain if they are two; three are a thorp; four are a group; a band is five men; if there are six, it is a squad; seven complete a crew; eight men make a panel; nine are 'good fellows;' ten are a gang; eleven form an embassy; it is a dozen if twelve go together; thirteen. are a crowd; fourteen are an expedition; it is a gathering, when fifteen meet; sixteen make a garrison; seventeen are a congregation; to him who meets eighteen, they seem enemies enough. He who has nineteen men has a company; twenty men are a posse; thirty are a squadron; forty, a community; fifty are a shire; sixty are an assembly; seventy are a line; eighty are a people; one hundred is a host.

"Beside these there are those terms which men prefix to the names of men: we call such terms epithets of possession, or true terms, or surnames. It is an epithet of possession when one names a thing by its true name, and calls him whom one desires to periphrase Owner of that thing; or Father or Grandfather of that which was named; Grandsire is a third epithet. Moreover, a son is also called Heir, Heritor, Bairn, Child and Boy, Inheritor. A blood-kinsman is called Brother, Twin, Germane, Consanguine; a relation is also called Nephew, Kinsman, Kin, Kith, Friend, Kin-Stave, Descendant, Family-Prop, Family-Stem, Kin-Branch, Family-Bough, Offshoot, Offspring, Head-Tree, Scion. Kinsmen by marriage are further called Sib-folk, Minglers of Blood. A friend is called Counsel-Mate, Counsel-Giver, Adviser, Secret-Sharer, Converser, Bench-Fellow, Fondling, Seat-Mate; bench-fellow also means Cabin-Mate. A foe is called Adversary, Shooter Against One, Hater,

Attacker, Scather, Slayer, Hard Presser, Pursuer, Overbearer."

"These are simple terms for women in skald ship: Wife and Bride and Matron are those women who are given to a man. Those who walk in pomp and fine array are called Dame and Lady. They who are witty of speech are called Women of Wisdom. They who are gentle are called Girls; they who are of high countenance are called Proud and Haughty Ones. She who is of noble mind is called Gentlewoman; she who is richest, Lady. She who is bashful, as young -maids are, or those women who are modest, is called Lass. The woman whose husband has departed from the land is called Stay-at-Home.

"That woman whose husband is slain is called War-Widow: Widow is the term for her whose husband has died of sick ness. Maid means, first, every woman, and then carlines that are old. Then there are those terms for women which are libellous: one may find them in songs, though they be not ill writing. Those women who have one husband in common are called Concubines. A son's wife is termed Daughter-in-law; the husband's mother is called Mother-in-law. A woman may also be called Mother, Grand mother, Great-Grandmother; a Mother is called Dam. Woman is further called Daughter, Bairn, and Child. She is also called Sister, Lady, and Maiden. Woman is also called Bed-Fellow, Speech-Mate, and Secret-Sharer of her husband; and that is an epithet of possession." – *Prose Edda, Snorri, The Poesy of Skalds*, pg. 235

Thou wast not, Fródi,
Full in wisdom,
Thou friend of men,
When thou boughtest the maidens:
Didst choose for strength
And outward seeming;
But of their kindred
Didst not inquire.
– *Prose Edda*, "Skáldskaparmál", *The Poesy of Skalds*, pg. 164

Suetonius

To increase population, Augustus pays Romans to have babies:

"Having thus regulated the city and its concerns, he augmented the population of Italy by planting in it no less than twenty-eight colonies, and greatly improved it by public works, and a beneficial application of the revenues. In rights and privileges, he rendered it in a measure equal to the city itself, by inventing a new kind of suffrage, which the principal officers and magistrates of the colonies might take at home, and forward under seal to the city, against the time of the elections. To increase the number of persons of condition, and of children among the lower ranks, he granted the petitions of all those who requested the honour of doing military service on horseback as knights, provided their demands were seconded by the recommendation of the town in which they lived; and when he visited the several districts of Italy, he distributed a thousand sesterces a head to such of the lower class as presented him with sons or daughters." – *The Twelve Caesars*, pg. 109

"He had clear, bright eyes, in which he liked to have it thought that there was a kind of divine power, and it greatly pleased him, whenever he looked keenly at anyone, if he let his face fall as if before the radiance of the sun; but in his old age he could not see very well with his left eye. His teeth were wide apart, small, and ill-kept; his hair was slightly curly and inclining to golden; his eyebrows met. His ears were of moderate size, and his nose projected a little at the top and then bent slightly inward. His complexion was between dark and fair. He was short of stature (although Julius Marathus, his freedman and keeper of his records, says that he was five feet and nine inches in height), but this was concealed by the fine proportion and symmetry of his figure, and was noticeable only by comparison with some taller person standing beside him." – *Lives Of The Caesars, Life of Augustus*, pgs. 83-85

"He was about the average height, his body marked with spots and malodorous, his hair light blond, his features regular rather than attractive, his eyes blue and somewhat weak, his neck over thick, his belly prominent, and his legs very slender. His health was good, for though indulging in every kind of riotous excess, he was ill but three times in all during the fourteen years of his reign, and even then not enough to give up wine or any of his usual habits. He was utterly shameless in the care of his person and in his dress, always having his hair arranged in tiers of curls, and during the trip to Greece also letting it grow long and hang down behind; and he often appeared in public in a dining-robe, with a handkerchief bound about his neck, ungirt and unshod." – *Suetonius, Life of Nero*, Rolfe trans., pg. 181

Suger

"France is 'our land' . . . the mother of us all, of the king and of the commoner. The land gives us life and everything associated with it. We are all born French of France, all 'from the same womb,' part of one and the same flesh, protected by this earth and sky. We all owe it therefore our love and support." – quoted in *The Birth of an Ideology*, pgs. 308-309

Andrew Sullivan

"The truth is that liberal democracy is hard, counter-intuitive, complicated and requires self-restraint, reason, and toleration at levels most humans are incapable of. That's why it is such a rare and fleeting exception in the world today and all but non-existent for the vast majority of human history." – *Why Is Wokeness Winning?*

The Sydney Morning Herald

"The love of country is a passion inherent in the breast of man, whether civilized or savage, whether born in the luxurious regions of the tropics, or amid the frosts and snows of the most inhospitable of arctic climes. The place, the society, the institutions, the customs, which first occupied our infant thoughts, and interested our budding affections, and formed our habits and our tastes, however distant the land in which our after years may be passed, or however lengthened the period of our expatriation, can never be erased from the tablet of the heart. For the existence of this passion we are not accountable: it is part of our nature, as closely interwoven into the human system as hope and fear, joy and sorrow, hunger and thirst; but for its government we are not less responsible than for that of any other of our passions. It is good or evil in proportion as we encourage it to be generous or permit it to be contracted. If subordinated to that universal love of the species which forms the cardinal virtue of Christian ethics, the love of country is an ennobling virtue: for it carries man beyond himself, and teaches him to sympathize with the great family of the earth. But if in loving our country we shut out from our affections all other portions of the world's household, the passion becomes nothing but a modification of inordinate selfishness: we love our country merely because it coincides with our own tastes and predilections, and ministers to our individual enjoyments; whilst other countries, because the selfish principle derives from them no perceptible advantage, are regarded with indifference or dislike...

"There is some danger of a species of national bigotry springing up in the Australias; and we can assign to it no more descriptive name than the one placed at the head of this article — AUSTRALIANISM. That our native youth should love the land of their birth above all other lands, is perfectly natural; that they should love it with a stricter exclusiveness because they have no opportunity of comparing it with other lands, is also natural; but that they should bind up their national sympathies within the limits of their own soil, and permit their national predilections to be poisoned by feelings of envy, jealousy, or mistrust towards all other classes of their fellow-subjects, is not only perfectly unnatural, but most unjust, absurd, and monstrous. Australianism of this sort would be even worse than any nationality which can divide English, Scotch, and Irish; for the Australians are even more closely allied by the ties of blood to native Britons, than the three kingdoms are to each other. The Australians are the sons, the brothers, the husbands, the wives, of Britons born; and, moreover, the British parents, brothers, wives, and husbands, are themselves Australians — though not by birth, by adoption. We are therefore all united by civil ties, as well as by those of consanguinity. We have not only one ancestry, one language, one complexion, one Sovereign — but one country, one home. In Australia, whether by birth or by choice matters not, the lot of all of us is cast. In her prosperity we have an equal interest. We all subsist upon the fruits of her soil — we are all concerned in the freedom of her institutions, in the equity of her laws, in the wisdom and justice of her government...

"Wherever, whensoever, or by whomsoever this novel species of nationality may be exhibited, we trust it will be scouted by all true Britons, whether born in England, Ireland, Scotland, or Australia." – *The Sydney Morning Herald* (Sydney, NSW), Monday 14 November 1842, pg. 2

T

Tacitus

Commenting upon the breeding and subsequent appearance of the Germans:

"Personally I associate myself with the opinions of those who hold that in the peoples of Germany there has been given to the world a race untainted by intermarriage with other races, a peculiar people and pure, like no one but themselves; whence it comes that their physique, in spite of their vast numbers, is identical: fierce blue eyes, red hair, tall frames, powerful only spasmodically, and impatient at the same time of labour and hard work, and by no means habituated to bearing thirst and heat; to cold and hunger, thanks to the climate and the soil, they are accustomed." – *Germania*, pgs. 269-271

"They carry with them into battle certain figures and images taken from their sacred groves, what most stimulates their courage is, that their squadrons or battalions, instead of being formed by chance or by a fortuitous gathering, are composed of families and clans." – *The Agricola and Germany of Tacitus: And the Dialogue on Oratory*, pg. 92

Jean Talon

"During the peak of immigration in the 1660s, most colonists came alone, two-thirds were male, and most were either very young or very old and had little experience with agriculture. The situation became so serious that in 1667 Jean Talon, Québec's senior economic official, begged Versailles not to send children, those over forty, or any 'idiot, cripples, chronically ill person or wayward sons under arrest' because 'they are a burden to the land.'" – *American Nations*, pg. 40

Nicholas Nassim Taleb

"Is it possible to be both ethical and universalist? In theory, yes, but, sadly, not in practice. For whenever the 'we' becomes too large a club, things degrade, and each one starts fighting for his own interest. The abstract is way too abstract for us. This is the main reason I advocate political systems that start with the municipality, and work their way up, rather than the reverse, which has failed with larger states. Being somewhat tribal is not a bad thing – and we have to work in a fractal way in the organized harmonious relations between tribes rather than merge all tribes in one large soup. In that sense, an American-style federalist is the ideal system.

"This scale transformation from the particular to the general is behind my skepticism about unfettered globalization and large centralized multiethnic states...Putting Shiites, Christians, and Sunnies in one pot and asking them to sing 'Kumbaya' around the campfire while holding hands in the name of unity and fraternity of mankind has failed. Blaming people for being sectarian – instead of making the best of such a natural tendency – is one of the stupidities of interventionists. Separate tribes for administrative purposes, or just put markers somewhere, and they suddenly become friendly to one another. The Levant has suffered (and keeps suffering) from Western (usually Anglo-Saxon) Arabists enamored with their subject, with no skin in the game in the place, who somehow have a vicious mission to destroy local indigenous cultures and languages, and separate the Levant from its Mediterranean roots.

"But we don't have to go very far to get the importance of scaling. You know instinctively that people get along better as neighbors than roommates.

"When you think about this, it is obvious, even trite, from the well-known behavior of crowds in the 'anonymity' of big cities compared to groups in small villages. I spend some time in my ancestral village, where it feels like a family. People attend others' funerals, help out, and care about the neighbor, even if they hate his dog. There is no way you can get the same cohesion in a larger city when the 'other' is a theoretical entity, and our behavior toward him or her is governed by some general ethical rule, not someone in flesh and blood. We get it easily when seen that way, but fail to generalize that ethics is something fundamentally local." – *Skin In The Game*, pgs. 59-60

Tao Qian

Since youth out of tune with the vulgar world,
My nature instinctively loves hills
    and mountains
By mishap I fell into the dusty net,
Once gone, thirteen years went by.
The caged bird longs for its grove of old,
The pond's fish thinks of its former depths.
Clearing land at the edge of the southern wilds,
Guarding simplicity, I returned to my farm.
The homestead amounts to ten-odd mou,
With a thatched hut of eight or nine bays.
Elms and willows shade the rear eaves,
Peach and plum line up in front of the hall.
In a haze lie the distant villages,
Indistinct is the smoke above the houses.
A dog barks somewhere in the deep alley,
A cock crows from atop the mulberry tree.
My home is unsoiled by worldly dust,
Within empty rooms I have peace to spare.
For long I have lived within a cage,
And now I may return to nature.
– *Returning to Live on the Farm*, No. 1, pgs. 122-123

Charles Taylor

"To know who you are is to be oriented in moral space, a space in which questions arise about what is good or bad, what is worth doing and what not, what has meaning and importance for you and what is trivial and secondary. I feel myself drawn here to use a spatial metaphor; but I believe this to be more than personal predilection. There are signs that the link with spatial orientation lies very deep in the human psyche." – *Sources Of The Self*, pg. 28

Janusz Tazbir

"Up to the sixteenth century the Polish nation was still conceived as a community inhabiting the same territory and embracing population groups sharing the same customs, history, and language. It was only late in that century that substantial changes in the national consciousness among the nobility came about..." – *Harvard Ukrainian Studies*, pgs. 316-317

Lord Tennyson

"I have felt with my native land,
    I am one with my kind,
I embrace the purpose of God,
    and the doom assign'd." – *Maud*

Then spake Sir Bedivere:
"And care not thou for dreams from him,
    but rise—
I hear the steps of Modred in the west,
And with him many of thy people, and knights
Once thine, whom thou hast loved,
    but grosser grown
Than heathen, spitting at their vows and thee.
Right well in heart they know thee for the King.
Arise, go forth and conquer as of old."

Then spake King Arthur to Sir Bedivere:
"Far other is this battle in the west
Whereto we move, than when
    we strove in youth,
And brake the petty kings,
    and fought with Rome,
Or thrust the heathen from the Roman wall,
And shook him thro' the north.
    Ill doom is mine
To war against my people and my knights.
The king who fights his people fights himself."
– *Idylls of the King; The Passing of Arthur*

Tertullian

"Purity is the flower of virtue. It does honor to the body and is an ornament of both sexes. It preserves blood untainted and guarantees parentage." – *On Purity*, pg. 53

"...the soul is seminally placed in man, by human agency, and its seed from the very beginning is uniform, as is that of the soul also, to the race of man...

"The soul is sown in the womb at the same time as the body [is formed], and it receives likewise along with it its sex...

"...the seminations of the two substances [body and soul] are inseparable in point of time, and their effusion is also one and the same, in consequence of which a community of gender is secured to them; so that the course of nature, whatever that be, shall draw the line [for the distinct sexes]..." – A Treatise on the Soul, pg. 497

The soul and body of the race and gender of man are created at the same time.

"The particular character of a posterity is shown by the original founders of the race— mortal beings [come] from mortals, earthly ones from earthly; step after step comes in due relation—marriage, conception, birth—country, settlements, kingdoms, all give the clearest proofs." – To the Heathen, in Ante-Nicene Christian Library vol. XI, pg. 494

The soul as tied to the flesh, each influencing the other; there being one stock but many variations, by environment and by nature:

"Here, then, we may offer our conclusion that all the properties that are natural to the soul are inherent in it as parts of its substance and they are born and develop with it from the moment it comes into existence. Seneca here as so often agrees, when he says: 'The seeds of all arts and ages are implanted in us and God, our Master, secretly produces the qualities of our mind,' that is, through the seeds planted within us in infancy; mainly, our intellect. From this our mental qualities develop.

"There is a specific form for each seed of each plant, and each plant has its own mode of growth. Some come easily to full maturity, while others wither or thrive according to the conditions of sun and soil, the amount of care they receive, the variations of the weather, and the vicissitudes of chance. Thus, while souls may all come from one kind of seed, individuality manifests itself as soon as growth begins. For here, too, we also find environment among other relevant factors.

"They say all Thebans are born dull and stupid, while Athenians are clever in speech and understanding, and, around Colyttus, the children are so precocious that they talk before they are a month old. Plato in the Timaeus tells us that Minerva, when building her beloved city, paid most attention to this quality of the climate which would favor mental development. Hence, in the Laws, he commands Megillus and Clinias to take pains as to the site of their city. On the other hand, Empedocles felt that the source of genius or stupidity lay in the character of the blood, and that any progress or perfection was due to learning and training. National characteristics of this type, however, have become proverbial. The comic poets always joke about the cowardice of the Phrygians; Sallust reproaches the Moors as fickle and the Dalmatians as cruel; and even St. Paul brands all Cretans as liars.

"It is likely, too, that bodily health has something to do with intellectual development. Obesity is not conducive to wisdom which thrives in the thin man; the mind wastes away in paralysis, while consumption sharpens it. Besides, there are many extrinsic conditions besides obesity and strength which in the arts, experimental knowledge, business, and sustained study have a way of developing the mind, while it loses its sharpness if allowed to wallow in ignorance, laziness, lust, idleness, and vice. To all of which may be added the influence of higher powers." – A Treatise on the Soul, in Ante-Nicene Fathers 3, pg. 20

"Now it is by the departure of the spirit, which is generated with [the body,] that the living being dies; therefore the spirit which is generated with [the body] is a corporeal substance. But this spirit which is generated with [the body] is the soul: it follows, then, that the soul is a corporeal substance. Cleanthes, too, will have it that family likeness passes from parents to their children not merely in bodily features, but in characteristics of the soul; as if it were out of a mirror of [a man's] manners, and faculties, and affections, that bodily likeness and unlikeness are caught and reflected by the soul also. It is therefore as being corporeal that it is susceptible of likeness and unlikeness." – A Treatise on the Soul, in Ante-Nicene Fathers 3, pg. 5

"All the natural properties of the soul which relate to sense and intelligence are inherent in its very substance, and spring from its native constitution, but that they advance by a gradual growth through the stages of life and develope themselves in different ways by accidental circumstances, according to men's means and arts, their manners and customs their local situations, and the influences of the Supreme Powers…" – *A Treatise on the Soul*, in *Ante-Nicene Fathers* 3, pg. 38

Speaking strictly of man's immaterial soul:
"Among all the nations man is one and the same, though the name varies; there is one soul, though many tongues; one spirit, though many sounds." – *The Soul's Testimony*, in *Apologetic Works*, pg. 143

"We are indeed said to be the 'third race' of men. What, a dog-faced race? Or broadly shadow-footed? Or some subterranean Antipodes? If you attach any meaning to these names, pray tell us what are the first and the second race, that so we may know something of this 'third.' . . . Granted, then, that the Phrygians were the earliest race, it does not follow that the Christians are the third. For how many other nations come regularly after the Phrygians? Take care, however, lest those whom you call the third race should obtain the first rank, since there is no nation indeed which is not Christian. Whatever nation, therefore, was the first, is nevertheless Christian now. It is ridiculous folly which makes you say we are the latest race, and then specifically call us the third. But it is in respect of our religion, not of our nation, that we are supposed to be the third; the series being the Romans, the Jews, and the Christians after them." – *Ad Nationes*, in *Ante-Nicene Christian Library*, vol. 1, pg. 464 [85]

"Every thing which is against nature deserves to be noted as a monstrous thing among all men; but among us (Christians) is to be styled also sacrilege against God, the Lord and Author of nature." – *Apologetic And Practical Treatises, The Crown, Ante-Nicene, Its Founder*, vol. 1, pg. 96

"In like manner, the soul may well be uniform in its seminal origin, although multi form by the process of nativity…
"However great, too, at present is the variety of men's manners, it was not so in Adam, the founder of their race. But all these discorances ought to have existed in him as the fountain-

head, and thence to have descended to us in an unimpaired variety, if the variety had been due to nature." – *Ante-Nicene, Its Founder*, vol. 1, pg. 201

— TERTULLIAN —

"This instances, therefore, will make it sufficiently plain that you can vindicate the keeping of even unwritten tradition established by custom; the proper witness for tradition when demonstrated by long-continued observance. But even in civil matters custom is accepted as law, when positive legal enactment is wanting; and it is the same thing whether it depends on writing or on reason, since reason is, in fact, the basis of law…Earnestly now inquire of this teacher [divine reason], keeping intact your regard for tradition, from whomsoever it originally sprang; nor have regard to the author, but to the authority, and especially that of custom itself, which on this very account we should revere, that we may not want an interpreter; so that if reason too is God's gift, you may then learn, not whether custom has to be followed by you, but why." – *Apologetic And Practical Treatises, The Crown, Ante-Nicene, Its Founder*, vol. 1, pg. 95 [86]

---

85 Tertullian contends that all nations can (and presumably will) become Christian, as Christianity is fundamentally a religious category, not a racial one. To speak of Christianity as an independent "race" is not appropriate.
86 Tertullian was addressing women veiling themselves, saying it was a custom, but custom from tradition, tradition from reason, reason a law of nature, nature of God.

Theocritus

Speaking of Ptolemy II Philadelphus prince from Macedonia who governed Egypt:

"..of such noble sort is the flaxen-haired prince that is throned in these level plains... farewell, Lord Ptolemy; and I will speak of thee as of other demi-gods.." – *The Greek Bucolic Poets*, pg. 219

"I was halfway o' the road, beside Lycon's, when lo! I espied walking together Delphis and Eudamippus, the hair o' their chins as golden as cassidony, and the breasts of them, for they were on their way from their pretty labour at the school, shone full as fair as thou, great Moon." – *The Greek Bucolic Poets*, pg. 33

Theodoret of Cyrus

"Some of the strength of the iron will be in it in the way you saw the iron mixed with potting clay. And the toes of the feet were partly iron and partly clay (vv. 41–42). This does not call for comment from us: the prophet himself gives the interpretation in saying A part of the kingdom will be strong, and will be crushed by it. After this he proceeds, As you saw the iron mixed with potter's clay, they will be mixed in human offspring (v. 43). This it is in particular that brings out that this is no different kingdom from the iron one, only the same one in a weaker condition, part of it being strong and part of it weak; a bond of kinship will connect the weak part with the strong, suggested by the phrase they will be mixed in human offspring. He is saying, There will be a mingling and intermarriage of the one and the other, but discord will spoil the rights of kinship: the one will not be attached to the other (he is saying), just as iron does not mix with clay... as soon as he pointed out the weakness of the iron kingdom's clay extremity, he went on, And in the days of those kingdoms, namely, the clay and iron ones that intermingled and contracted a relationship with each other without this resulting in harmony." – *Commentary on Daniel*, ch. 2, pg. 57

A.C. Thiselton

"God's decree was made in the light of the purpose or role which he assigned 'to each' of his creatures. A broad comparison with examples in BAGD but more especially a comparison with the issue of how God apportions gifts to believers within the body of Christ's church καθὼς ἠθέλησεν (12:18) will corroborate this point (see above on 12:18). Differentiation in accordance with God's sovereign decree in relation to his future purposes remains a fundamental principle of the 'ordering' (15:24–28; 14:40; 12:4–11), whether of the old creation or the new...

"The key phrase remains 'God gives to it a body just as he purposed,' but the second principle is that of contrast, differentiation, and variety which simultaneously promotes a continuity of identity. This is one reason why 'order' becomes so important for chs. 12, 14, and 15: genuine differentiation and variety reflects the will of God, provided that it does not collapse into sheer confusion and the loss of the very identity which preserves the otherness of the other as other and not a mere replication or projection of 'the strong' within any group." – *New International Greek Testament Commentary. The First Epistle to the Corinthians: a commentary on the Greek text*, pg. 1265. 1 Corinthians 15:38.

Henry David Thoreau

On The influence of place:

"Is it some influence, as a vapour which exhales from the ground, or something in the gales which blow there, or in all things there brought agreeably to my spirit. . ."
– Journal 21 July 1851; *Writing Nature: Henry Thoreau's Journal*, pg. 8

James Henley Thornwell

"That the division into national Churches – that is, Churches bounded by national lines – is, in the present condition of human nature, a benefit, seems to us too obvious for proof. It realizes to the Church Catholic all the advantages of a division of labor. It makes a Church organization homogeneous and compact – it stimulates holy rivalry and zeal – it removes all grounds or suspicion and jealousy on the part of the State. What is lost in expansion is gained in energy. The Church Catholic, as thus divided, and yet spiritually one; divided, but not rent, is a beautiful illustration of the great philosophical principle which pervades all nature – the co-existence of the one with the many...

"The Church Catholic is one in Christ, but it is not necessarily one visible, all-absorbing organization upon the earth. There is no schism where there is no breach of charity. Churches may be perfectly at one in every principle of faith and order, and yet geographically distinct, and mutually independent. As the unity of the human race is not disturbed by its division into countries and nations, so the unity of the spiritual seed of Christ is neither broken nor impaired by separation and division into various Church constitutions. Accordingly, in the Protestant countries, Church organizations have followed national lines." – Joint Address of the First General Assembly of the Presbyterian Church in the Confederate States of America, in *Schaff's American Church History Series*, pg. 395

"As every legislator is bound to be a Christian man, he has no right to vote for any laws which are inconsistent with the teachings of the Scriptures. He must carry his Christian conscience into the halls of legislation." – *Sermon on National Sins*, in *Fast-Day Sermons*, pg. 18

"The inception and successful progress of this enterprise encourage the hope that we mean to maintain our moderation. It is a public testimony to our faith that the Negro is of one blood with ourselves that he has sinned as we have and that he has an equal interest with us in the great redemption. Science falsely so called may attempt to exclude him from the brotherhood of humanity. Men may be seeking eminence and distinction by arguments which link him with the brute but the instinctive impulses of our nature combined with the plainest declarations of the Word of God lead us to recognize in his form and lineaments in his moral religious and intellectual nature the same humanity in which we glory as the image of God. We are not ashamed to call him our brother. The subjugation of the fears and jealousy which a systematic misrepresentation of religion, on the part of our inveterate opposers, has had a tendency to produce, is a publick declaration to the world, that, in our philosophy, right is the highest expediency, and obedience to God the firmest security of communities as well as individuals." – *The Christian Doctrine of Slavery*, in *Religions of the United States in Practice*, vol. 1, pg. 472

Alexis de Tocqueville

"The principle of equality begets two tendencies: the one leads men straight to independence and may suddenly drive them into anarchy; the other conducts them by a longer, more secret, but more certain road to servitude. Nations readily discern the former tendency and are prepared to resist it; they are led away by the latter, without perceiving its drift; hence it is peculiarly important to point it out." – *Democracy in America*, bk. 1, ch. 1

"It would seem as if every step they make towards equality brings them nearer to despotism." – *Democracy in America*, bk. 1, ch. 1

"I have visited the two nations in which the system of provincial liberty has been most perfectly established, and I have listened to the opinions of different parties in those countries. In America I met with men who secretly aspired to destroy the democratic institutions of the Union; in England I found others who attacked the aristocracy openly, but I know of no one who does not regard provincial independence as a great benefit. In both countries I have heard a thousand different causes assigned for the evils of the State, but the local system was never mentioned amongst them. I have heard citizens attribute the power and prosperity of their country to a multitude of reasons, but they all placed the advantages of local institutions in the foremost rank. Am I to suppose that when men who are naturally so divided on religious opinions and on political theories agree on one point (and that one of which they have daily experience), they are all in error? The only nations which deny the utility of provincial liberties are those which have fewest of them; in other words, those who are unacquainted with the institution are the only persons who pass a censure upon it." – *Democracy In America*, Book 1, ch. 5

"There is one sort of patriotic attachment which principally arises from that instinctive, disinterested, and undefinable feeling which connects the affections of man with his birthplace. This natural fondness is united to a taste for ancient customs, and to a reverence for ancestral traditions of the past; those who cherish it love their country as they love the mansions of their fathers. They enjoy the tranquillity which it affords them; they cling to the peaceful habits which they have contracted within its bosom; they are attached to the reminiscences which it awakens, and they are even pleased by the state of obedience in which they are placed. This patriotism is sometimes stimulated by religious enthusiasm, and then it is capable of making the most prodigious efforts." – *Democracy In America*, Book 1, ch. 14

— ALEXIS DE TOCQUEVILLE —

"The Americans have no neighbors, and consequently they have no great wars..." – *Democracy In America*, Book 1, ch. 17

"As long as family feeling was kept alive, the antagonist of oppression was never alone; he looked about him, and found his clients, his hereditary friends, and his kinsfolk. If this support was wanting, he was sustained by his ancestors and animated by his posterity. But when patrimonial estates are divided, and when a few years suffice to confound the distinctions of a race, where can family feeling be found? What force can there be in the customs of a country which has changed and is still perpetually changing, its aspect; in which every act of tyranny has a precedent, and every crime an example; in which there is nothing so old that its antiquity can save it from destruction, and nothing so unparalleled that its novelty can prevent it from being done? What resistance can be offered by manners of so pliant a make that

they have already often yielded? What strength can even public opinion have retained, when no twenty persons are connected by a common tie; when not a man, nor a family, nor chartered corporation, nor class, nor free institution, has the power of representing or exerting that opinion; and when every citizen—being equally weak, equally poor, and equally dependent—has only his personal impotence to oppose the organized force of the government?" – *Democracy In America*, Book 1, ch. 17

"Civilization is the result of a long social process which takes place in the same spot, and is handed down from one generation to another, each one profiting by the experience of the last." – *Democracy In America*, Book 1, ch. 18

"Among democratic nations new families are constantly springing up, others are constantly falling away, and all that remain change their condition; the woof of time is every instant broken and the track of generations effaced. Those who went before are soon forgotten; of those who will come after, no one has any idea: the interest of man is confined to those in close propinquity to himself. As each class gradually approaches others and mingles with them, its members become undifferentiated and lose their class identity for each other. Aristocracy had made a chain of all the members of the community, from the peasant to the king; democracy breaks that chain and severs every link of it. As social conditions become more equal, the number of persons increases who, although they are neither rich nor powerful enough to exercise any great influence over their fellows, have nevertheless acquired or retained sufficient education and fortune to satisfy their own wants. They owe nothing to any man, they expect nothing from any man; they acquire the habit of always considering themselves as standing alone, and they are apt to imagine that their whole destiny is in their own hands. Thus not only does democracy make every man forget his ancestors, but it hides his descendants and separates his contemporaries from him; it throws him back forever upon himself alone and threatens in the end to confine him entirely within the solitude of his own heart." – *Democracy In America*, Book 2, ch. 2

"True dignity in manners consists in always taking one's proper station, neither too high nor too low, and this is as much within the reach of a peasant as of a prince. In democracies all stations appear doubtful; hence it is that the manners of democracies, though often full of arrogance, are commonly wanting in dignity, and, moreover, they are never either well trained or accomplished." – *Democracy in America*, Book 3, ch. 14

"When men live more for the remembrance of what has been than for the care of what is, and when they are more given to attend to what their ancestors thought than to think themselves, the father is the natural and necessary tie between the past and the present, the link by which the ends of these two chains are connected. In aristocracies, then, the father is not only the civil head of the family, but the organ of its traditions, the expounder of its customs, the arbiter of its manners. He is listened to with deference, he is addressed with respect, and the love that is felt for him is always tempered with fear. When the condition of society becomes democratic and men adopt as their general principle that it is good and lawful to judge of all things for oneself, using former points of belief not as a rule of faith, but simply as a means of information, the power which the opinions of a father exercise over those of his sons diminishes as well as his legal power." – *Democracy In America*, Book 8, ch. 3

"The foremost or indeed the sole condition required in order to succeed in centralizing the supreme power in a democratic community is to love equality or to get men to believe you love it. Thus, the science of despotism, which was once so complex, has been simplified and reduced, as it were, to a single principle." – *Democracy in America*, Book 4, ch. 4

"The very next notion to that of a single and central power which presents itself to the minds of men in the ages of equality is the notion of uniformity of legislation. As every man sees that he differs but little from those about him, he cannot understand why a rule that is applicable to one man should not be equally applicable to all others. Hence the slightest privileges are repugnant to his reason; the faintest dissimilarities in the political institutions of the same

people offend him, and uniformity of legislation appears to him to be the first condition of good government. I find, on the contrary, that this notion of a uniform rule equally binding on all the members of the community was almost unknown to the human mind in aristocratic ages; either it was never broached, or it was rejected...As the conditions of men become equal among a people, individuals seem of less and society of greater importance; or rather every citizen, being assimilated to all the rest, is lost in the crowd, and nothing stands conspicuous but the great and imposing image of the people at large. This naturally gives the men of democratic periods a lofty opinion of the privileges of society and a very humble notion of the rights of individuals; they are ready to admit that the interests of the former are everything and those of the latter nothing. They are willing to acknowledge that the power which represents the community has far more information and wisdom than any of the members of that community; and that it is the duty, as well as the right, of that power to guide as well as govern each private citizen. The Americans hold that in every state the supreme power ought to emanate from the people; but when once that power is constituted, they can conceive, as it were, no limits to it, and they are ready to admit that it has the right to do whatever it pleases. They have not the slightest notion of peculiar privileges granted to cities, families, or persons; their minds appear never to have foreseen that it might be possible not to apply with strict uniformity the same laws to every part of the state and to all its inhabitants." – *Democracy in America*, Book 4, ch. 2

"In that part of the Union where the Negroes are no longer slaves, have they become closer to the whites? Everyone who has lived in the United States will have noticed just the opposite. Race prejudice seems stronger in those states that have abolished slavery than in those where it still exists, and nowhere more intolerant than in those states where slavery was never known. In the South, where slavery still exists, less trouble is taken to keep the Negro apart: they sometimes share the labors and the pleasures of the white men; people are prepared to mix with them to some extent; legislation is more harsh against them, but customs are more tolerant and gentle." – *Democracy in America*, pg. 339

"Indeed, we should be ill advised to belittle our ancestors; and would do better to regain, even if it meant inheriting their prejudices and their failings, something of their nobility of mind." – *The Old Regime and the French Revolution*, pg. 119

J.R.R. Tolkien

"Hump, well! I wonder (if we survive this war) if there will be any niche, even of sufferance, left for reactionary back numbers like me (and you). The bigger things get the smaller and duller or flatter the globe gets. It is getting to be all one blasted little provincial suburb. When they have introduced American sanitation, morale-pep, feminism, and mass production throughout the Near East, Middle East, Far East, U.S.S.R., Hither Further and Inner Mumbo-land, Gondhwanaland, Lhasa, and the villages of darkest Berkshire, how happy we shall be. At any rate it ought to cut down on travel. There will be nowhere to go. So people will (I opine) go all the faster. Collie Knox says 1/8 of the world's population speaks 'English', and that is the biggest language group. If true, damn shame—say I. May the curse of Babel strike all their tongues till they can only say 'baa baa'. It would mean much the same. I think I shall have to refuse to speak anything but Old Mercian." – letter to Milton Waldman, 9 December 1943, pg. 131

"I was from early days grieved by the poverty of my own beloved country: it had no stories of its own (bound up with its tongue and soil)... There was Greek, and Celtic, and Romance, Germanic, Scandinavian, and Finnish... but nothing English, save impoverished chap-book stuff. Of course there was and is the Arthurian world, but powerful as it is, it is imperfectly naturalized, associated with the soil of Britain but not with English; and does not replace what I felt to be missing... Do not laugh! But once upon a time... I had in mind to make a body of more or less connected legend, ranging from the large and cosmogonic, to the level of romantic fairy-story... which I would dedicate simply to: to England; to my country. It should possess the tone and quality that I desired, somewhat cool and clear, be redolent of our 'air' (the clime and soil of the North West, meaning Britain and the hither parts of Europe: not Italy or the Aegean, still less the East), and, while possessing (if I could achieve it) the fair elusive beauty that some call Celtic (though it is rarely found in genuine ancient Celtic things), it should be 'high', purged of the gross, and fit for the more adult mind of a land long now steeped in poetry. I would draw some of the great tales in fullness, and leave many only placed in the scheme, and sketched. The cycle should be linked to a majestic whole, and yet leave scope for other minds and hands, wielding paint and music and drama." – *The Letters of J.R.R. Tolkien: A Selection*, pg. 141

Pippin and Merry when upon the heights of Minas Tirith:

"Pippin remained behind. 'Was there ever anyone like him [Aragorn]?' he said. 'Except Gandalf, of course. I think they must be related. My dear ass, your pack is lying by your bed, and you had it on your back when I met you. He saw it all the time, of course. And anyway I have some stuff of my own. Come on now! Longbottom Leaf it is. Fill up while I run and see about some food. And then let's be easy for a bit. Dear me! We Tooks and Brandybucks, we can't live long on the heights.'

"'No,' said Merry. 'I can't. Not yet, at any rate. But at least, Pippin, we can now see them, and honour them. It is best to love first what you are fitted to love, I suppose: you must start somewhere and have some roots, and the soil of the Shire is deep. Still there are things deeper and higher; and not a gaffer could tend his garden in what he calls peace but for them, whether he knows about them or not. I am glad that I know about them, a little. But I don't know why I am talking like this. Where is that leaf? And get my pipe out of my pack, if it isn't broken.'" – *Lord Of The Rings, The Return Of The King*, pg. 149

"In these days came to pass the fulfillment of the time of the desire of the Valar and the hope of the Eldalië, for in great love Idril bore to Tuor a son and he was called Eärendel...

"Now this babe was of greatest beauty; his skin of a shining white and his eyes of a blue surpassing that of the sky in southern lands – bluer than the sapphires of the raiment of Manwë; and the envy of Meglin[87] was deep at his

---

87 Meglin was shorter of stature than the elves of Gondolin and was said to be half elf and mixed with orc blood. He

birth, but the joy of Turgon and all the people very great indeed." – *The Fall Of Gondolin; The Book of Lost Tales: Part Two*, pg. 221

"I know what you have come to say, Frodo: you wish to return to your own home. Well, dearest friend, the tree grows best in the land of its sires; but for you in all the lands of the West there will ever be a welcome." – *The Lord of the Rings, The Return of the King*, pg. 292

— J.R.R. TOLKIEN —

"I sit beside the fire and think
Of all that I have seen
Of meadow flowers and butterflies
In summers that have been
Of yellow leaves and gossamer
In autumns that there were
With morning mist and silver sun
And wind upon my hair
I sit beside the fire and think
Of how the world will be
When winter comes without a spring
That I shall ever see
For still there are so many things
That I have never seen
In every wood in every spring
There is a different green
I sit beside the fire and think
Of people long ago
And people that will see a world
That I shall never know

But all the while I sit and think
Of times there were before
I listen for returning feet
And voices at the door"
– A song by Bilbo, *The Fellowship of the Ring*

Far over the misty mountains cold
To dungeons deep and caverns old
We must away ere break of day
To seek the pale enchanted gold.
The dwarves of yore made mighty spells,
While hammers fell like ringing bells
In places deep, where dark things sleep,
In hollow halls beneath the fells
For ancient king and elvish lord
There many a gleaming golden hoard
They shaped and wrought,
    and light they caught
To hide in gems on hilt of sword.
On silver necklaces they strung
The flowering stars, on crowns they hung
The dragon-fire, in twisted wire
They meshed the light of moon and sun.
Far over the misty mountains cold
To dungeons deep and caverns old
We must away, ere break of day,
To claim our long-forgotten gold.
Goblets they carved there for themselves
And harps of gold; where no man delves
There lay they long, and many a song
Was sung unheard by men or elves.
The pines were roaring on the height,
The wind was moaning in the night.
The fire was red, it flaming spread;
The trees like torches blazed with light.
The bells were ringing in the dale
And men looked up with faces pale;
The dragon's ire more fierce than fire
Laid low their towers and houses frail.
The mountain smoked beneath the moon;
The dwarves, they heard the tramp of doom.
They fled their hall to dying fall
Beneath his feet, beneath the moon.
Far over the misty mountains grim
To dungeons deep and caverns dim
We must away, ere break of day,
To win our harps and gold from him!
– Dwarves' Song, *The Hobbit*

lusted after Idril but was "thrust aside" by Tuor, tall and fair-haired.

Leo Tolstoy

"Are you always in the country?" he inquired. "I should think it must be dull in the winter."

"It's not dull if one has work to do; besides, one's not dull by oneself," Levin replied abruptly.

"I am fond of the country," said Vronsky, noticing, and affecting not to notice, Levin's tone.

"But I hope, count, you would not consent to live in the country always," said Countess Nordston.

"I don't know; I have never tried for long. I experienced a queer feeling once," he went on. "I never longed so for the country, Russian country, with bast shoes and peasants, as when I was spending a winter with my mother in Nice. Nice itself is dull enough, you know. And indeed, Naples and Sorrento are only pleasant for a short time. And it's just there that Russia comes back to me most vividly, and especially the country. It's as though...." – *Anna Karenina*

— LEO TOLSTOY —

"Sergey Ivanovitch Koznishev wanted a rest from mental work, and instead of going abroad as he usually did, he came towards the end of May to stay in the country with his brother. In his judgment the best sort of life was a country life. He had come now to enjoy such a life at his brother's. Konstantin Levin was very glad to have him, especially as he did not expect his brother Nikolay that summer. But in spite of his affection and respect for Sergey Ivanovitch, Konstantin Levin was uncomfortable with his brother in the country. It made him uncomfortable, and it positively annoyed him to see his brother's attitude to the country. To Konstantin Levin the country was the background of life, that is of pleasures, endeavors, labor. To Sergey Ivanovitch the country meant on one hand rest from work, on the other a valuable antidote to the corrupt influences of town, which he took with satisfaction and a sense of its utility. To Konstantin Levin the country was good first because it afforded a field for labor, of the usefulness of which there could be no doubt. To Sergey Ivanovitch the country was particularly good, because there it was possible and fitting to do nothing. Moreover, Sergey Ivanovitch's attitude to the peasants rather piqued Konstantin. Sergey Ivanovitch used to say that he knew and liked the peasantry, and he often talked to the peasants, which he knew how to do without affectation or condescension, and from every such conversation he would deduce general conclusions in favor of the peasantry and in confirmation of his knowing them. Konstantin Levin did not like such an attitude to the peasants. To Konstantin the peasant was simply the chief partner in their common labor, and in spite of all the respect and the love, almost like that of kinship, he had for the peasant—sucked in probably, as he said himself, with the milk of his peasant nurse—still as a fellow-worker with him, while sometimes enthusiastic over the vigor, gentleness, and justice of these men, he was very often, when their common labors called for other qualities, exasperated with the peasant for his carelessness, lack of method, drunkenness, and lying. If he had been asked whether he liked or didn't like the peasants, Konstantin Levin would have been absolutely at a loss what to reply. He liked and did not like the peasants, just as he liked and did not like men in general. Of course, being a good-hearted man, he liked men rather than he disliked them, and so too with the peasants. But like or dislike 'the people' as something apart he could not, not only because he lived with 'the people,' and all his interests were bound up with theirs, but also because he regarded himself as a part of 'the people,' did not see any special qualities or failings distinguishing himself and 'the people,' and could not contrast himself with them. Moreover, although he had lived so long in the closest relations with the peasants, as farmer and arbitrator, and what was more, as adviser (the peasants trusted him, and for thirty miles round they would come to ask his advice), he had no definite views of 'the people,' and would have been as much at a loss to answer the question whether he knew 'the people' as the question whether he liked them. For him to say he knew the peasantry would have been the same as to say he knew men. He was continually watching and getting to know people of all sorts, and among them peasants, whom he regarded as good and interesting people, and he was continually observing new points in them, altering his former views of them and forming new ones. With Sergey Ivanovitch it was quite the contrary. Just as he liked and praised a country life in comparison with the life he did not like, so too he liked the peasantry in contradistinction to the class of men he did not like, and so too he knew the peasantry as something distinct from and opposed to men generally. In his methodical brain there were distinctly formulated certain aspects of peasant life, deduced partly from that life itself, but chiefly from contrast with other modes of life. He never changed his opinion of the peasantry and his sympathetic attitude towards them." – *Anna Karenina*, vol. 1, pg. 269

Theobald Wolfe Tone

"To break the connection with England, the never-failing source of all our political evils, and to assert the independence of my country – these were my objects. To unite the whole people of Ireland, to abolish the memory of all past dissensions, and to substitute the common name of Irishman in the place of the denominations of Protestant, Catholic and Dissenter – these were my means." – *Wolfe Tone: Collected Writings*, pg. 300

"I mean not to give you the trouble of bringing judicial proof to convict me, legally, of having acted in hostility to the Government of his Britannic Majesty in Ireland. I admit the fact. From my earliest youth I have regarded the connection between Ireland and Great Britain as the curse of the Irish nation, and felt convinced that, whilst it lasted, this country could never be free nor happy. My mind has been confirmed in this opinion by the experience of every succeeding year, and the conclusions which I have drawn from every fact before my eyes. In consequence, I determined to apply all the powers which my individual efforts could move in order to separate the two countries." – *The Life of Theobald Wolfe Tone*, vol. 19, pg. 302

"I believe in the history of man there is not to be found an instance, wherein of two nations, equal in all natural advantages, equal in intelligence, in spirit, in courage, one has yet been for centuries content to remain in a state of subordination, unknown and unregarded, drawing her Government, and the maxims of her Government from the other, though demonstratively injurious to her pride, her interest, her commerce, and her Constitution, and receiving not one advantage in return for such a complete surrender of her imperial and independent rights. When I consider the situation of Ireland at this day, I confess I am utterly at a loss to account for her submission to such degrading inferiority. Old prejudices will do much, but can they do all this? Or has the wisdom of the Almighty framed some kingdoms as He has some animals, only for the convenience and service of others?" – *The Life of Theobald Wolfe Tone*, vol. 1, pg. 548

James Townsend

"For the majority [of the middle ages Chinese population, culturalism] . . . would have been less important than their primary ethnic identification. It seems likely that most Chinese thought of their cultural and political community – their nation – as a Chinese one, and that culturalism, to the extent that they understood it, reinforced their sense that the empire was properly Chinese." – in J. Unger (ed.), *Chinese Nationalism*, pgs. 1-30

A.W. Tozer

"You can't change my mind about God having made us the way we are. The yellow man and the white man and the black man. God made our races. I know the Marxists and the bubble-heads say: 'Oh, that's old-fashioned baloney! Everybody should get together and intermarry and pretty soon there won't be races, and where there are no races there won't be any hate, and if there's no hate, there won't be any war.' Oh, for cotton batting to stuff in the mouths of people who don't know better than that!

"Many of you have taken a good look at history. Did you happen to notice that since the beginning of the world there never has been worse hatred between nations than today, and that hatred rarely crosses the color line? It is within the race itself.

"The presence of specific races is not the source of our trouble – it is the disease of sin within our own hearts. Twice within twenty-five years the white Germans tried to kill and destroy the white Englishmen. Occasionally there are flare-ups between races, but mostly it is within races.

"It is not race, brethren. It is sin, sin, sin, sin, sin! In place of having love for our fellowmen, we have quarreling, lying, and exploiting and competing to a shocking degree. Most people don't want to be reminded that the Bible says we should love the Lord our God and our neighbor as our self.

"Let me remind you of the warbler, almost universally distributed in this country, and will you believe that there are 120 species of this bird called the warbler in the United States? One hundred and twenty varieties, with only the slightest differences of feather, or wing, or stripe or spot. In these 120 varieties, we are told, there is no crossing the line, they mate within their own racial strain, hatch and have little ones. Nobody puts them through college, but when they get big enough to hop out on the edge of the nest and begin looking for another warbler, they always pick one like themselves, and stay within their own strain.

"Now, you get a Communist or a starry-eyed American fellow traveler working on that, and he will say: 'That's an evidence of race hate, and it's a proof those warblers hate each other!' Hate each other – your grandmother's nightcap! They don't quarrel, they never fight, they just

go on living and warbling. They've got sense enough to know that God made 120 kinds of warblers just for fun to show what He could do, and He doesn't mean for them to cross over and make one warbler out of 120!

"I think it is a most amazing thing in our day that the godless who have sowed the seed of discontent among the nations try to tell us that racial lines are artificial and an evidence of 'wickedness' – and they don't even believe in the Word and won't allow it to be used in any other way!" – *Tozer Speaks: vol. 1, ch. 46*

H.A. Scott Trask

"There is no real difference between a patriot and a nationalist. The patria (Latin) is the land that belongs to one's fathers, and the nation is one's father's people. The Latin word natio meant a people or race, and it was derived from the verb nasci (to be born). Here is the definition of the English equivalent given by the O.E.D. (2nd ed., 1989): 'An extensive aggregate of persons, so closely associated together by common descent, language, or history, as to form a distinct race or people, usually organized as a separate political state and occupying a definite territory.' The English equivalent for the Latin patria and the Greek patris is father-land; the German is Vaterland. So a patriot is one who loves and is devoted to the land of his fathers." – *Fatherland and Nation*

Carl Trueman

"I am in an important sense constituted by the social relationships that I have with other people and the ways in which they have shaped my experience of the world and my understanding of my own history…

"…human beings also act in dialogue with their surroundings. To put it very simply, we do not make these intentional decisions in a vacuum. Rather, we make them in the context of the societies we inhabit, and their wider histories in which we are placed—societies whose framework provides the means by which our actions have meaning." – *Strange New World*, pg. 112-113

"Nations almost by definition involve so vast an area of geographical space, such large populations, and so many individual communities—villages, towns, cities—that it is impossible for everyone to know everyone else. This means that, for a nation to exist, its members must imagine that they hold things in common that give them a coherent identity as a body of people...

"What binds them together, of course, is in part a strong national narrative, something that gives them a sense of history, a sense of belonging, a sense of pride—in short, a sense of identity...In short, even though few of them actually knew each other in their real, daily lives, they still saw themselves as all belonging to a community whose cause they saw as greater than themselves. That, we might note, is true belonging." – *Strange New World*, pg. 117-118

Tryphiodorus

A woman laments the taking of Ilios:

"Alas! for my woes, alas! for thee, city of my fathers, soon shalt thou be fine dust: gone is the handiwork of the immortals, gone utterly the foundations of Laomedon. And for thee, my father, and for thee, my mother, I weep to think what manner of things ye both shall suffer. Thou, my father, piteously fallen shalt lie beside the altar of mighty Zeus of the Court. Mother of the best of children, thee from human shape the gods shall turn into a hound maddened over thy children. Fair Polyxena, for thee lying low near to thy fatherland I shall weep but little: would that someone of the Argives had slain me too with thy lamented fate! For what profit have I in life any more, if life but keep me for a most pitiful death, and an alien soil shall cover me?" [88] – *Taking Of Ilios*, pg. 609

"Then they prayed unto the grey-eyed daughter of Zeus and hasted into their vessel of the horse." – *Oppian, The Taking of Ilios*, pg. 595

Francis Turretin

"Afterwards a distinction and ownership of goods was justly introduced with the authority of God, to prevent controversies, to restrain external violence and to afford certainty to inheritances and make a distinction in conditions (without which human society could not exist) ... Nor if the law of nature makes all men equal with regard to nature does it follow that they are equal with regard to qualities and exter-

nal condition." – *Institutes of Elenctic Theology*, 11.2.18, pg. 12

"Hence it is evident that the distinction of visible and invisible [church] is not a division of genus into species, as if we formed two churches in species opposed to each other (as our opponents slander us); but is only a limitation of the subject according to its various relations. As the same man numerically can be said to be invisible and visible in different respects . Thus the same church is rightly said to be visible as to external form and invisible as to internal ...

"Earthly republics and kingdoms differ from the church because Christ's kingdom is not of this world (Jn. 18:36). Hence it does not follow that if republics are always visible or consist in an external and visible government, that therefore the church must also. Although the internal affection by which citizens are united to each other contributes greatly to the tranquility of a republic, yet the essential form of the republic does not consist in this, but in the bond of an external fellowship, by an external observance of the laws (which can be kept without internal affection). But it is different with the church. Since its formal reason is in the mystical union of believers with Christ and with each other, the external union alone with him does not make anyone a member of the church; nay, without the latter union, true believers who dwell in separated places are members both of Christ and of his church. The contrary of this is the case in a republic, where those absent for a long time lose their rights of citizenship or at least do not enjoy them." – *Institutes of Elenctic Theology*, 18.7.22

"Fifth, the dignity of man himself [Hominis ipsius dignitas] demands the same thing [that the promise given to Adam was not only of a happy life to be continued in paradise, but of a heavenly and eternal life]. Since his noblest part is spirit (even of heavenly origin) touched with a vehement desire of heavenly goods (by which alone its infinite appetite for the highest good can be satisfied), he could not obtain on earth his full felicity, but must be gifted with it at length in heaven where he can enjoy the fullest and most perfect communion with God, in whom his highest good resides. For although on earth he could in some measure give himself

---

88   Because she will be taken captive away from her homeland, etc.

to be enjoyed, it is certain that the immediate and absolute fruition of God is not to be sought apart from the beatific vision which can be looked for only in heaven." – *Institutes of Elenctic Theology*, 8.6.3, pg. 583

"Although the body of Adam was in origin earthy (and as composed, so also resolvable, through the indisposition of matter), yet it could have been immortal through the dignity of original righteousness [originalis justitiae dignitatem] and the power of God's special grace." – *Institutes of Elenctic Theology*, 5.12.9, pg. 476

"We maintain that the loss of the divine image (or of original righteousness) followed the fall of Adam doubly—both meritoriously and morally (on account of the divine ordination) and efficiently and really (on account of the heaviness of that sin)." – *Institutes of Elenctic Theology*, 9.9.3 pg. 613

"Although every truth cannot be demonstrated by reason (the boundaries of truth being much more widely extended than those of reason), yet no lie against the truth can be sheltered under the protection of true reason, nor can one truth be destroyed by another (although one may transcend and surpass the other) because whatever the one may be—whether below, according to or above reason, and apprehended by the senses, the intellect or faith—it has come from no other source than God, the parent of truth. So grace does not destroy nature, but makes it perfect. Nor does supernatural revelation abrogate the natural, but makes it sure." – *Institutes* 1.13.3, pg. 44

Steve Turley

"While economic nationalism may involve protectionism, it can't be reduced to protectionism. Instead, as the name implies, scholars see economic nationalism as an economic approach that is intentionally pursued for the benefit of the culture, custom, and tradition that collectively comprise the nation. Economic nationalism is a facet of national identity, where certain kinds of cultures, traditions, religions, and ethnicities forge distinctive economic policies in accordance with specific national traits. What this means is that economic nationalism can certainly involve protectionist measures, but it can also involve free-trade measures, or subsidies, or controlled markets, or free markets; indeed, economic nationalism can actually be all of the above! It can be very libertarian in some national contexts and highly regulatory in others; the important point here is that the purpose of the economy is for the protection and perpetuation of a nation's culture, customs, and traditions, not the other way around. The economy is not seen as sovereign in an economic nationalist view; the economy is not some scientifically rationalist system that's superimposed on nations and cultures, which in turn ends up belittling and relativizing their customs, religions, and traditions. Instead, the economy here is rightly seen as an extension of national and religious identity." – *New Nationalism*, pgs. 24-25

Turoldus

Roland upon the sardine stone
  a mighty stroke let
Grided the steel but broke not,
  nor was it notched at all.
And when he had beheld it that
  the sword he could not break,
Unto himself a bitter moan he then
  began to make:
"O Durendal, how art thou
  so beautiful and white!
Flashing and flaming in the sun
  thou scatterest the light.
What time Charlemagne had halted
  in the Vale of Maurienne,
God out of Heaven an angel
  sent down unto him then,
And bade him to a noble count
  a gift to make of thee.
And the gentle King and mighty
  girded thee there on me.
For him I won all Brittany,
  Anjou, Poitou, and Maine,
And the free land of Normandy,
  Provence and Aquitain.
The Roman March and Lombardy
  I conquered to his hand,
I won beside Bavaria
  and all the Flemish land.
Bulgaria and Poland
  by me were overthrown,
Also Constantinople that Charles
  for king did own.

All Saxony, moreover,
  his whole behest hath done. —
And Ireland, Wales and Scotland
  for Charlemagne I won.
And the English island likewise,
  that he took of his own right.
A many lands and nations
  I conquered in the fight.
That now are the possession
  of white-bearded Charlemagne.
Wherefore I suffer for this sword
  great pity and great pain.
I had rather die than a pagan
  should win it by ill chance.
Fair God! let such dishonor
  fall never upon France."
 – *Song Of Roland*, 134 and following, pg. 75

What help is that?
Though fled be Marsilies,
He's left behind his uncle, the alcaliph
Who holds Alferne, Carthage, Garmalie,
And Ethiopia, a cursed land and vile;
The Negro trie from there are in his keep,
Broad in the nose they are and flat in the ear,
Fifty thousand and more in company.
These canter forth with arrogance and heat,
Then they cry out the pagans' rallying-cheer;
And Roland says: "Martyrdom we'll receive;
Not long to live, I know it well, have we;
Let him be accurse that sells his body cheap!
Strike on, my lords,
  with burnished swords and keen;
Contest each inch your life and death between,
That gentle France be not brought to shame.
When Charles my lord
  shall come into this field,
Such discipline of Saracens he'll see,
For one of ours he'll find them dead fifteen;
He will not fail, but bless us all in peace."
When Roland sees those accursed race,
Who are more black than ink is on the pen
With no part white, only their teeth except,
Then says that count: "I know now very well
That here to die we're bound, as I can tell.
Strike on, the Franks! For so I recommend."
Says Oliver: "Who holds back, is condemned!"
Upon those words, the Franks to strike again.
 – *Song Of Roland*, lines 145 and following

In the tenth [column] the men of Occiant,
  the waste deserted land.
They were indeed a nation

who never served the Lord —
Never was race of villains
  yet heard of more abhorred.
Their hides are hard as iron;
  hauberk and helm therefore
They need not. They are cruel
  and desperate in war.
 – *Song Of Roland*, lines 234-238

Petre Țuțea

"Although the nation should not be identified with the human race as a whole, it should behave concretely and spiritually as if it were. The idea of equality applied to the community of peoples confers on every people the right to comprehensive development on both levels. Every nation within its own borders aspires to develop as a whole, with all its material resources, and tends to reflect in its essential being the characteristics of the universal order… Economic power can be acquired peacefully at a global level, on the basis of the principle of economic competition, when the equality of all peoples is respected. [But] the autocratic tendencies of the great powers transform spheres of economic dominance violently or imperceptibly into Lebensraum for themselves." – *Between Sacrifice and Suicide*, pg. 31

"I belong to the Romanian people, to its time and space, and participate in the eternity of the Christian order lived out by that people, with all the vigour or its Latin spirit. And because my people is, therefore I am. The soul of the whole human race (as incarnate in the Saviour) is experienced by every Romanian who is aware of existing, both spiritually and iconographically, in a way specific to our nation. Valorile neautohtonizate ('non-autochthonous values') are ficitions." – *Between Sacrifice and Suicide*, pg. 32

"To believe that nations eventually disappear shows either irresponsibility or weariness, or alternatively sheer selfishness and greed. The desire of certain nations for expansion and dominance cannot be satisfied without the destruction of others. Realisation of the individual and of the corporate must begin from the present, historically determined state of things. Ethnicity constitutes the premise of any human activity." – *Philosophia Perennis*, pg. 187

William Tyndale

"Since the world began, wheresoever repentance was offered and not received, there God took cruel vengeance immediately: as ye see in the flood of Noah, in the overthrowing of Sodom and Gomorrah and all the country about: and as ye see of Egypt, of the Amorites, Canaanites and afterward of the very Israelites, and then at the last of the Jews too, and of the Assyrians and Babylonians and so throughout all the empires of the world.

"Gildas preached repentance unto the old Britons that inhabited England: they repented not, and therefore God sent in their enemies upon them on every side and destroyed them up and gave the land unto other nations. And great vengeance hath been taken in that land for sin since that time.

"Wycliffe preached repentance unto our fathers not long since: they repented not for their hearts were indurate and their eyes blinded..."
– *The Prologue to the Prophet Jonas, Works*, pg. 64

Fyodor Tyutchev

Be silent, hide away and let
Your thoughts and longings rise and set
In the deep places of your heart.
Let dreams move silently as stars,
In wonder more than you can tell.
– *Silentium!* (st. 1) [89]

Streaming over with the waters
In their rush to meet the vale,
Winter's chill and snows of yester
Down the mountains softly sail.
– *Spring Waters* (st. 1)

Nature is a Sphinx. And her ordeal
Is built upon the ashes of the dead;
She breathes the riddles of the dread
Into the heart and mind of every soul.
– *Nature is a Sphinx* (st. 1)

Those heights, those oaks, those hills –
I loved them all, I loved them dearly!
I'm happy that the Russian land
Will lie upon my heart so near.
– *Last Love* (st. 4)

---

89 Tyutchev was a Russian Romantic poet who wrote about the beauty of the Russian landscape and the connection between the people and their environment.

U

The United States Constitution

To "secure the Blessings of Liberty to ourselves and our Posterity."

United States Commission on Civil Rights

"Illegal immigration to the United States in recent decades has tended to depress both wages and employment rates for low-skilled American citizens, a disproportionate number of whom are black men. Expert economic opinions concerning the negative effects range from modest to significant." – *The Impact of Illegal Immigration on the Wages and Employment Opportunities of Black Workers*, 2008, pg. 3

J.D. Unwin

"When a desire is compelled to remain unsatisfied, strong mental tension occurs; the emotional energy is compressed. According to Dr. Rivers, 'the energy arising out of the conflict is diverted from some channel which leads in an asocial direction and turned into one leading to an end connected with the higher ideals of society. . . . Many lines of evidence are converging to show that all great accomplishments in human endeavour depend on processes which go on outside those regions of the mind of the activity of which we are clearly conscious.' To this diversion Dr. Freud applied a word which has been translated 'sublimation'. It is not a satisfactory word; indeed it has almost disappeared from technical literature; but I shall retain it, for it occurs in the simple text-books from which I am quoting. Dr. Rivers defines it thus: 'By sublimation is meant a process in which an instinctive tendency, more or less fostered by experience, which would normally find expression in some kind of undesirable conduct, has its energy diverted into a channel in which it comes to have a positive social value.' Dr. Freud says: 'We believe that civilization has been built up by sacrifices in gratification of the primitive impulses, and that it is to a great extent for ever being recreated as each individual repeats the sacrifice of his instinctive pleasures for the common good. The sexual are amongst the most important of the instinctive forces thus utilized: they are in this way sublimated, that is to say, their energy is turned aside from its sexual goal and diverted towards other ends, no longer sexual and socially more valuable.'" – *Sex And Culture*, pg. 313

"In other words, psychological researches reveal that the placing of a compulsory check upon the sexual impulses, that is, a limitation of sexual opportunity, produces thought, reflection, and energy.

"Now the evidence is that a cultural advance has been caused by a factor which produces thought, reflection, and social energy and that it occurs only when the sexual opportunity has been limited. I submit, therefore, that the limitation of the sexual opportunity must be regarded as the cause of the cultural advance." – *Sex And Culture*, pg. 317

"...compulsory continence must be regarded as the immediate cause of a cultural advance. Any extension of sexual opportunity must always be the immediate cause of a cultural decline... a) the extension or limitation of sexual opportunity, either in society as a whole or in a class within the society, cannot have its full cultural effect for a hundred years; b) that culturally the sexual opportunity of the females is a more important factor than that of the males; c) that scientifically an individual cannot be considered apart from the society of which he is a member, the dominating Unconscious being of a social character." – *Sex And Culture*, pg. 326

"…the cultural condition of any society in any geographical environment is conditioned by its past and present methods of regulating the relations between the sexes. This is the first primary law which operates in all human societies." – *Sex And Culture*, pg. 326

—J.D. Unwin—

"Generally speaking, in the past when they began to display great energy (as opposed to the lesser energy of uncivilized peoples), human societies were absolutely monogamous. There is only one example of a polygamous society displaying productive social energy, that of the Moors; but in their case the women whom the men took to wife had been reared in an absolutely monogamous tradition. The energy of the Moors faded away when the mothers spent their early childhood in a less rigorous tradition. With this exception, the energy of the most developed civilized societies, or that of any group within them, was exhibited for so long as they preserved their austere regulations. Their energy faded away as soon as a modified monogamy became part of the inherited tradition of the whole society." – *Sex And Culture*, pg. 343

"Any society in which complete pre-nuptial sexual freedom (outside the exogamic regulations and prohibited degrees) has been permitted for at least three generations will be in the zoistic cultural condition (the lowest social state). It

will also be at a dead level of conception if previously it has not been in a higher cultural condition." – *Sex And Culture*, pg. 347

"Thus it seems to be true that, just as a decrease of sexual opportunity produces a cultural advance, so an increase results in a cultural decline." – *Sex And Culture*, pg. 365

"In the records of history, indeed, there is no example of a society displaying great energy for any appreciable period unless it has been absolutely monogamous. Moreover, I do not know of a case in which an absolutely monogamous society has failed to display great energy. In the past different societies have risen up in different parts of the earth, flourished greatly, and then declined. In every case the society started its historical career in a state of absolute monogamy, manifested great energy while it preserved its austere regulations, and relaxed after a less rigorous tradition had been inherited by a complete new generation." – *Sex And Culture*, pg. 369

"We must always remember that the social energy which is displayed at any time by any society depends not only upon the sexual opportunity it enjoys but also upon that enjoyed by the two preceding generations. It takes at least three generations for an extension or a limitation of sexual opportunity to have its full cultural effect; and if we happen to observe a society which is beginning, or has just begun, to extend its sexual opportunity, the full effects of the change have not yet been felt. The society still displays an energy which corresponds in some part to its old regulations." – *Sex And Culture*, pg. 370

"Now in the past, as I have said, sexual opportunity has been reduced to a minimum only by the adoption of absolute monogamy; a complete reduction of sexual opportunity has never taken place unless the females have been subjected to the domination of their husbands." – *Sex And Culture*, pg. 374

"Paul spent his early years in a Romano-Jewish environment; the ideas he absorbed from contact with the dominating Roman element in his native town were confirmed by what he learnt from Gamaliel. In each case the ideas were those of absolute monogamy; and in this manner some implications of absolute monogamy have been petrified in a Christian ideal." – *Sex And Culture*, pg. 375

"When labour and heirs of his blood. A wife and her children are under the domination of her husband; in the eyes of the law he alone is an entity. The wife is taught to submit to her husband in all things; it is her duty to serve him and to obey him. No woman may have sexual relations with any other man than with him whom she marries as a virgin. When she is married, she is not permitted to withhold conjugal rights. In an absolutely monogamous society female chastity becomes desirable for its own sake, for after a while the women accept as a point of honour the restraint imposed upon them by their lords. Over his children also a man has complete power." – *Sex And Culture*, pg. 379

"In my survey of the facts the points I wish to make are: 1. that when they began to display great social energy the societies had reduced their sexual opportunity by the adoption of absolute monogamy; 2. that in each case the society was dominated by the group which displayed the greatest relative energy; 3. that as soon as the sexual opportunity of the society, or of a group within the society, was extended, the energy of the society, or of the group within it, decreased and finally disappeared; 4. that whatever the racial extraction of the people, and whatever the geographical environment in which they lived, the manner in which they modified their absolute monogamy was the same in every case." – *Sex And Culture*, pg. 382

"In each case they reduced their sexual opportunity to a minimum by the adoption of absolute monogamy; in each case the ensuing compulsory continence produced great social energy. The group within the society which suffered the greatest continence displayed the greatest energy, and dominated the society. When absolute monogamy was preserved only for a short time, the energy was only expansive, but when the rigorous tradition was inherited by a number of generations the energy became productive. As soon as the institution of modified monogamy, that is, marriage and divorce by mutual consent, became part of the inherited tradition of a complete new generation, the energy, either of the whole society or of a group within the

society, decreased, and then disappeared." – *Sex And Culture*, pg. 411

"Now I can formulate the second primary law which operates on all human societies. ... It is this:

"No society can display productive social energy unless a new generation inherits a social system under which sexual opportunity is reduced to a minimum. If such a system be preserved, a richer and yet richer tradition will be created, refined by human entropy.

"There is no need for the whole society to suffer the same continence. So long as the sexual opportunity of one social stratum is maintained at a minimum, the society will display productive energy." – *Sex And Culture*, pg. 414

"Now let us return to the experimental society with which we began. We left it energized to such an extent as to bring it into the deistic cultural condition. If we wish to energize it to a greater extent, we must reduce its post-nuptial sexual opportunity, thereby introducing some post-nuptial dissatisfaction. If we merely give it a modified form of polygamy, it simply exists as a deistic unit while it retains its demand for pre-nuptial chastity; but if the male as well as the female is compelled to confine himself to one sexual partner the society begins to display some expansive energy. It bursts over the boundaries of its habitat, explores new countries, and conquers less energetic peoples. Such energy does not create a cultural change; expansive energy is the form of behaviour adopted by societies which have reduced their sexual opportunity to a minimum." – *Sex And Culture*, pg. 428

"So far we have energized it by a complete reduction of its pre-nuptial opportunity, first in two stages, then in one stage, and by placing varying limitations on its post-nuptial opportunity. In order to make it display expansive energy, we reduced its sexual opportunity to a minimum. Now let us retain that opportunity at a minimum for at least three generations. The society now begins to display such energy as the world has seldom seen. Indeed, among the societies we have discussed, there are only three indisputable instances of such behaviour. I refer to the Athenians, Romans, and English." – *Sex And Culture*, pg. 430

"We begin with a number of individuals locked together by their uniform ideas and behaviour. The first energizing, painful though it is, produces few cultural results; with subsequent energizings cultural effects become more noticeable; under the influence of still greater sexual checks, the society bursts its boundaries, conquers, slays, subdues, and explores; but, if this intense continence remains part of the inherited tradition for two generations, the energy increases abundantly, changes its form, and displays attributes which up to now remained hidden. The energy increases, indeed, in what seems to be geometrical progression. The society expands in all its multifarious activities, exhibits a terrific mental energy that is manifest in the arts and sciences, refines its craftsmanship, changes its opinions on every conceivable subject, exerts considerable control over its environment, and manifests its potential powers in the loftiest forms yet known. Its inherited tradition is augmented by the products of its abundant energy, and refined by human entropy. A rationalistic stratum separates itself from the main body and forms another belt outside the deistic one. The cultural state of such a society can also be represented by a cone, with a rationalistic top, a deistic centre, perhaps a manistic stratum too, and a zoistic base." – *Sex And Culture*, pg. 431

"In the past, too, the greatest energy has been displayed only by those societies which have reduced their sexual opportunity to a minimum by the adoption of absolute monogamy. In every case the women and children were reduced to the level of legal nonentities, sometimes also to the level of chattels, always to the level of mere appendages of the male estate. Eventually they were freed from their disadvantages, but at the same time the sexual opportunity of the society was extended. Sexual desires could then be satisfied in a direct or perverted manner; no dissatisfaction demanded an outlet; no emotional stress arose. So the energy of the society decreased, and then disappeared." – *Sex And Culture*, pg. 431

James Ussher

On the 5th Commandment:

"The meaning (of the fifth commandment is) Civil, or Ecclesiastical, and with whatever relations, be duly acknowledged and respected. For it requires the performance of all such Duties as (are fittingly) owed unto another, by some particular bond in regard of special callings and differences, which God made between special Persons. "

(These special persons are) "Superiors and Inferiors, or Equals."

(In the name of Honor is contained) "every particular Duty according to their particular Estates. (The word Honor confers) ornament and Dignity unto them."

(We owe them) "reverence of heart, word, and behavior…because reverence of mind is to be declared by some civil behavior."

(Superiors are those whom) "God has by some supernatural gifts lifted above others, whether they be of Body, as Strength and Beauty, or of the Mind, as Wit and Learning, or of outward State, as Wealth and Nobility."

(Inferiors are) "those who are younger, and of meaner gifts, whether of Nature or of Grace, or of such as are gotten by Exercise. (Our duty towards such Superiors is) to acknowledge the things wherein God hath preferred them before us, and to respect and regard them according to their Graces and Gifts."

(The duty of such as are our Superiors is) "to use their skill and other Graces so as others may be benefitted by them….To protect and support such as are committed unto them, to provide good things for the body and soul, to common things that are good and profitable for the Inferiors, governing them prudently, and after a holy manner."

(Obedience is) "a voluntary and hearty doing of that which the Superiors command or patient suffering of that they shall inflict upon them…."

(The duty of Superiors in a family are) "to provide for the household the things belonging to their Soul…the Householder being therein to be the Mouth of his Family."

(The wife's duties to her husband are) "She must represent in all godly and commendable matters, his Image in her behavior, that in her a man may see the wisdom and uprightness of her Husband."

(The duties of parents to children are) "to lay up and provide for them, that they may live honestly afterward. And therefore they are to distribute their goods among their children; and what they have received from their ancestors, to leave the same to their posterity." – *Body of Divinity*, pg. 231

—JAMES USSHER—

On the Image of God:

Q. How did God make man at the beginning ?

A. According to his own likeness and image.

Q. Wherein was the Image of God principally seen ?

A. In the perfection of the understanding and the freedom and holiness of the Will. ...

Q. What followed upon this sin [first sin in the garden]?

A. The loss of the perfection of the Image of God, and the corruption of nature, in Man. ...

"They were dead in sin, which is more fearful than the Death of the Body, as that which is a Separation from the Favour of God. For there came upon them the Decay of God's glorious Image in all the Faculties of their Soul, and also a Corruption of the Powers of their Body from being fo fit instruments to serve the Soul as God made them; And this in them is signified by nakedness Gen. 3. 7. and in their Children

called Original Sin." ...

The benefits of salvation, communion, justification, etc:

"It is the renewing of our Nature according to the Image of God, righteousness, and true Holiness: Which is but begun in this life, and is called sanctification and is perfected in the Life to come, which therefore is called Glorification." – *Body of Divinity*, pg. 406, 110

V

William Vaile

"They came to this country because it was already made as an Anglo-Saxon commonwealth. They added to it, they often enriched it, but they did not make it, and they have not yet greatly changed it. We are determined that they shall not. It is a good country. It suits us. And what we assert is that we are not going to surrender it to somebody else or allow other people no matter their merits to make it something different. If there is any changing to be done, we will do it ourselves."– Speech on the Immigration Act of 1924; *Genetics and American Society*, pg. 110

Adrianus Valerius

"Almighty God! Dear, merciful Heavenly Father, Thou who art the support of the puny, the comfort of the oppressed, the source and font of all goodness and blessings. We poor sinners acknowledge before you what is merely the truth: that in our own beloved Fatherland we have time and again felt and beheld your all-mighty power and the blessings of your inscrutable wisdom, and have received succor and favor when stricken by ferocious tyrants even as we were thrown into great poverty and forced to leave our Fatherland, lock and stock, our house, our friends and our trades and so as to escape the bloody claws of our enemies, to go sojourn in strange lands, and, even as from the force of Spanish Edicts so much blood of the pious has been spilled that together we were reduced to a motley rabble and sunk into the pit of the world, O Lord when all was ill with you You brought us up into a land wherein we were enriched through trade and commerce and have dealt kindly with us, even as you have led the Children of Israel from their Babylonian prison; the waters receded before us and you brought us dry-footed even as the people of yore, with Moses and with Joshua, were brought to their Promised Land. O Lord Your Fatherly blessings and the bounties you have bestowed upon us have been great and prodigious…you have made the golden liberty and olden laws of the Netherlands renowned throughout the world…" – *Nederlandtsche gedenck-clanck*, 1626; *The Embarrassment of Riches An Interpretation of Dutch Culture in the Golden Age*, pgs. 98-99

Dominique Venner

"To live is to struggle against that which seeks to negate your existence. Being a dissident does not mean collecting forbidden books, dreaming up fantastical plots, or taking to the hills. It means remaining true to yourself, out of a higher fidelity and in defiance of the herd if necessary; it demands that you never outgrow your youth and that you would sooner take on the entire world than bend yor knee to it. In the face of adversity, it means never questioning the purpose of the struggle. You act because it would be unworthy no to, and it is preferable to go down fighting than to surrender." – *A Handbook For Dissidents*, pg. 36

"Tradition is not the past. It is that which never passes." – *A Handbook For Dissidents*, pg. 17

Jules Verne

Captain Nemo had somewhat rallied from the prostration which had overcome him, and his eyes shone with their wonted fire. A faint smile even curled his lips.

The colonists drew around him.

"Gentlemen," said the captain, "you are brave and honest men. You have devoted yourselves to the common weal. Often have I observed your conduct. I have esteemed you—I esteem you still! Your hand, Mr. Harding."

Cyrus Harding gave his hand to the captain,

who clasped it affectionately.

"It is well!" he murmured.

He resumed,—

"But enough of myself. I have to speak concerning yourselves, and this Lincoln Island, upon which you have taken refuge. You now desire to leave it?"

"To return, captain!" answered Pencroft quickly.

"To return, Pencroft?" said the captain, with a smile. "I know, it is true, your love for this island. You have helped to make it what it now is, and it seems to you a paradise!"

"Our project, captain," interposed Cyrus Harding, "is to annex it to the United States, and to establish for our shipping a port so fortunately situated in this part of the Pacific."

"Your thoughts are with your country, gentlemen," continued the captain; "your toils are for her prosperity and glory. You are right. One's native land!—there should one live! there die! And I die far from all I loved!"

"You have some last wish to transmit," said the engineer with emotion, "some souvenir to send to those friends you have left in the mountains of India?"

"No, Captain Harding; no friends remain to me! I am the last of my race, and to all whom I have known I have long been as are the dead.—But to return to yourselves. Solitude, isolation, are painful things, and beyond human endurance. I die of having thought it possible to live alone! You should, therefore, dare all in the attempt to leave Lincoln Island, and see once more the land of your birth. I am aware that those wretches have destroyed the vessel you have built."

"We propose to construct a vessel," said Gideon Spilett, "sufficiently large to convey us to the nearest land; but if we should succeed, sooner or later we shall return to Lincoln Island. We are attached to it by too many recollections ever to forget it."

"It is here that we have known Captain Nemo," said Cyrus Harding.

"It is here only that we can make our home!" added Herbert. – *The Secret of the Island*, pg. 188

Carlo Maria Viganò

"We must understand that our rulers are traitors of our Nation who are devoted to the elimination of populations, and that all of their actions are carried out in order to cause the greatest amount of harm to citizens. It is not a problem of inexperience or inability but rather of an intentio nocendi – a deliberate intention to harm. Honest citizens find it inconceivable that those who govern them could do it with the perverse intention of undermining and destroying them, so much so that they find it very hard to believe." – interview with Steve Bannon, July 30th, 2022

John Vinson

"Nationhood is not an arbitrary human arrangement, but a principle of divine order." – *The Bible and Borders*

Marvin Vincent

"Marriage was regarded as a duty among the Jews, so that a man was considered to have sinned if he had reached the age of twenty without marrying. The Mishna fixed the age of marriage at seventeen or eighteen, and the Babylonish Jews as early as fourteen. A rabbinical precept declared that a Jew who has no wife is not a man." – *Word studies in the New Testament*, vol. 3, pg. 217

Vuk Vinaver

"The whole [Serbian] land has rebelled, six hundred villages arose, everybody pointed his gun against the [Ottoman] emperor." – cited in *Прве устаничке борбе против Турака (The first insurgent fights against the Turks)*, pg. 17 [90]

Pierre Viret

"There is such a union between the father and his children and those who are of the same flesh and blood and of the same covenant that the punishments can scarcely be separated in such a way that the ones can refrain from in some way sharing in that of the others." – *Nothing Like God*, pg. 62

"I say that we are bound to love as ourselves, all those whom we must hold as our neighbors. But it does not follow that I am equally bound to everybody. For the husband is more bound to

---

90   In reference to the Serbian revolt (Uprising in Banat) from Ottoman rule in 1596.

his wife, and the wife to her husband, and the fathers and mothers to their children, and the children to them, and the brothers and sisters to each other, than to strangers. For this reason St. Paul says, 'Do good to all, but especially to those of your own household.' If, therefore, it is a question of a Christian, a Turk and a Jew, I am more bound to the Christian than to the other two; and must let the others help themselves, if I cannot help them at all. Similarly, in the law of God, many things were permitted to the people of Israel towards foreigners, which were not permitted to them in their own nation; such as usury and other things." – *Instruction Chrétienne II*, pg. 768-769

Virgil

Strong from the cradle, of a sturdy brood, We bear our newborn infants to the flood;
There bathed amid the streams our boys we hold, With winter hardened and inured to cold.
They wake before the day to range the wood, Kill ere they eat, nor taste unconquered food.
No sports but what belong to war they know: To break the stubborn colt, to bend the bow
Our youth of labor patient earn their bread; Hardly they work, with frugal diet fed.
From plows and harrows sent to seek renown, They fight in fields and storm the shaken town.
No part of life from toils of war is free, No change in age or difference in degree.
Even time, that changes all, yet changes us in vain-The body, not the mind–nor can control
The immortal vigor, or abate the soul.
Our helms defend the young, disguise the gray; We live by plunder and delight in prey.
– *The Aeneid*, Dryden trans., 9.590

Describing a god (Mercury) as having blonde hair:
    "Now that everything was ready, and he was resolved on going, Aeneas was snatching some sleep, on the ship's high stern. That vision appeared again in dream admonishing him, similar to Mercury in every way, voice and colouring, blonde hair, and youth's graceful limbs." – *Aeneid, Virgil, with an English Translation*, pg. 433

Describing a Queen Dido of Carthage in North Africa has having blonde hair:
    "As soon as the queen saw the day whiten,

from her tower, and the fleet sailing off under full canvas, and realised the shore and harbour were empty of oarsmen, she struck her lovely breast three or four times with her hand, and tearing at her blonde hair..." – *The Aeneid of Virgil*, pg. 88

— VIRGIL —

Describing the Gauls, from N. Italy/S. France:
    "The Gauls were there in the gorse, taking the Citadel, protected by the dark, the gift of shadowy night. Their hair was gold, and their clothes were gold, they shone in striped cloaks, their white necks torqued with gold, each waving two Alpine javelins in his hand, long shields defending their bodies..." – *Aeneid*, Ruden trans., pg. 225

Describing the youthful beauty of Ascanius, divine Aeneas' son (these people are offspring of the gods, whom we can assume are similar in appearance):
    "See, the Trojan boy, himself, in their midst, Venus's special care, his handsome head uncovered, sparkling like a jewel set in yellow gold adorning neck or forehead, gleaming like ivory, inlaid skillfully in boxwood or Orician terebinth: his milk-white neck, and the circle of soft gold clasping it, received his flowing hair..." – *Aeneid*, Kline trans., pg. 248

Describing Lavinia, princess of Latium (modern day Rome, Italy):

"As soon as the wretched Latin women knew of the disaster, first her daughter Lavinia fell into a frenzy, tearing at her yellow tresses and rosy cheeks with her hands, then all the crowd around her..." – *Aeneid*, Kline trans., pg. 316

Walther von der Vogelweide

I have visited many lands
and always gaily seen the bapolosdest ones.
But woe is me
if I were ever able to convince my heart
to like foreign customs.
What would I get if I told lies?
German manner are preferable to all the others.
From the Elbe to the Rhine
and back to Hungary,
there are the best people
I have ever seen.
If I am able to
evaluate good demeanour and looks,
by God, I would like to swear that
    in this country women
are better than ladies anywhere else.
German men are well accomplished,
and the women look like angels.
He who chides them lies to himself;
otherwise I cannot fathom him.
If someone seeks virtue
and pure love,
he must come to our country:
    here delight dwells.
I would like to live here a long time!
– *Ir sult sprechen willekomen*, see further *Dichter und Konvention*

Fain (could it be) would I a home obtain,
And warm me by a hearth-side of my own.
Then, then, I'd sing about
    the sweet birds' strain,
And fields and flowers, as I have whilome done;
And paint in song the lily and the rose
That dwell upon her cheek who smiles on me.
But lone I stray – no home its comfort shows:
Ah, luckless man! still doom'd a guest to be!
– *Address to Emperor Frederic II*

Vǫluspǫ́

Hearing I ask from the holy races,
From Heimdall's sons, both high and low;
Thou wilt, Valfather, that well I relate
Old tales I remember of men long ago.
I remember yet the giants of yore,
Who gave me bread in the days gone by;
Nine worlds I knew, the nine in the tree
With mighty roots beneath the mold.
– *Poetic Edda, Lays of the Gods*, pg. 3

At the end of the world:
Brothers shall fight and fell each other,
And sisters' sons shall kinship stain
– *Poetic Edda, Lays of the Gods*, pg. 19

Abbott Vonier

"There seems to be no contradiction in supposing that spiritual souls may differ widely in qualities, God forming them according to the differences of hereditary dispositions. . . . Saint Thomas Aquinas distinctly inclines towards the view that Almighty God fashions the soul He creates according to the body into which He infuses it. As long as the soul's spirituality is safeguarded, there is no reason why the body, with its qualities, should not be to God the occasion for creating a soul with corresponding qualities.

[Man's physical make-up] has its qualities and its defects, which the soul cannot change. . . the soul's office is . . . to tune all the strings of nature to the highest pitch; but all the tuning in the world will never change the make of the instrument." – *The Human Soul*, pgs. 45-47

Geerhardus Vos

"Nationalism, within proper limits, has the divine sanction; an imperialism that would, in the interest of one people, obliterate all lines of distinction is everywhere condemned as contrary to the divine will. Later prophecy raises its voice against the attempt at world-power, and that not only, as is sometimes assumed, because it threatens Israel, but for the far more principal reason, that the whole idea is pagan and immoral.

"Now it is through maintaining the national diversities, as these express themselves in the difference of language, and are in turn upheld by this difference, that God prevents realization of the attempted scheme… [In this] was a positive intent that concerned the natural life of humanity. Under the providence of God each race or nation has a positive purpose to serve, fulfillment of which depends on relative seclusion from others." – *Biblical Theology*, pg. 60

"God shall enlarge Japheth, and he shall dwell in the tents of Shem" — Gen. 9:27.

"The German scholar Delitzsch remarked that we are all Japhethites dwelling in the tents of Shem. The prophecy uttered by Noah was that God would enlarge Japheth, and Japheth would dwell in the tents of Shem. In the Hebrew idiom, to dwell in the tents of someone means to be the inheritor of that person's wealth and estate.

"Noah's prophecy concerns the broad lines of the future development of the various branches of the human race. God would enlarge Japheth. Japheth was the ancestor of the Indo-European peoples, to which we ourselves belong. It is a fact of history that for the last 2500 years the Indo-European peoples have been dominant in world affairs, not only in material and scientific progress, but in political control of the major part of the civilized world…

"We are now concerned especially with the prediction that Japheth should dwell in the tents of Shem. It is particularly in the matter of religion that the Christian people of Europe and America dwell in the tents of Shem. Our religion is an inheritance from the descendants of Shem. It has come down to us, in the providence of God, from Semitic sources." – *Wrong Tendencies in the Use of the Psalms*, in *Blue Banner Faith and Life*, vol. 7, pg. 123

W

Nicholas Wade

"Human sociability is two-edged. The trust extended to members of one's own group is mirrored by the suspicion and potential mistrust shown toward strangers. Willingness to defend one's own people is the counterpart of readiness to kill the enemy. Human morality is not universal, as philosophers have argued: it is strictly local, at least in its instinctual form. Reflections of this ambivalence are now apparent from the level of the genes." – *A Troublesome Inheritance: Genes, Race and Human History*, pg. 50

Richard Wagner

"The word 'deutsch,' according to the latest and most profound researches, is not a definite Folk's name in history there has been no people that could claim the original title 'Deutsche.' Jacob Grimm, on the contrary, has proved that 'diutisk' or 'deutsch' means nothing more than what is homelike to ourselves, 'ourselves' being those who parley in a language mutually intelligible. It was early set in contrast with the 'walsch,' whereby the Germanic races signify the 'proper to the Gaels and Kelts.' The word 'deutsch' reappears in the verb 'deuten' [to 'point, indicate, or explain']: thus 'deutsch' is what is plain (deutlich) to us, the familiar, the wonted, inherited from our fathers, racy of our soil. Now it is a striking fact, that the peoples remaining on this side of the Rhine and Alps began to call themselves by the name of 'Deutsche' only after the Goths, Vandals, Franks and Lombards had established their dominion in the rest of Europe. Whilst the 'Franks' spread their name over the whole great conquered land of Gaul, but the races left on the hither side of the Rhine consolidated themselves into Saxons, Bavarians, Swabians and East-Franks, it is at the division of the empire of Karl the Great [Charlemagne] that the name 'Deutschland' makes its first appearance; and that as collective-name for all the races who had stayed this side the Rhine. Consequently it denotes those peoples who, remaining in their ancestral seat, continued to speak their ure-mother-tongue, whereas the races ruling in Romanic lands gave up that mother-tongue. It is to the speech and the ure-homeland, then, that the idea of 'deutsch' is knit; and there came a time when these 'Deutschen' could reap the advantage of fidelity to their homeland and their speech, for from the bosom of that home there sprang for centuries the ceaseless renovation and freshening of the soon decaying outland races." – *What Is German?*; *Richard Wagner's Prose Works*, vol. 4, pg. 152

Lew Wallace

"There is no law by which to determine the superiority of nations; hence the vanity of the claim, and the idleness of disputes about it. A people risen, run their race, and die either of themselves or at the hands of another, who, succeeding to their power, take possession of their place, and upon their monuments write new names; such is history. If I were called upon to symbolize God and man in the simplest form, I would draw a straight line and a circle, and of the line I would say, 'This is God, for he alone moves forever straightforward,' and of the circle, 'This is man–such is his progress.' I do not mean that there is no difference between the careers of nations; no two are alike. The difference, however, is not, as some say, in the extent of the circle they describe or the space of earth they cover, but in the sphere of their movement, the highest being nearest God." – *Ben Hur*, pg. 107

Michael Walzer

"Most political theorists, from the time of the Greek onward, have assumed the national or ethnic homogeneity of the communities about which they wrote. Prior to the work of Rousseau, theory was never explicitly nationalist, but the assumption of a common language, history, or religion underlay most of what was said about political practices and institutions." – *Pluralism in Political Perspective*, in M. Walzer, E. Kantowicz, J. Higham, and M. Harrington (eds.), *The Politics of Ethnicity*, pg. 1

John Wanamaker

"They heartily welcomed to their little State all men of other sects, or of no sects, who adhered to the essentials of Christianity and were ready to conform to the local laws and customs. Naturally they did not welcome zealots who came for the avowed purpose of overthrowing their Church, and when such intruders became troublesome they did not hesitate to drive them out." – *Reviews: The Pilgrim Republic*, in *Book News: A Monthly Survey of General Literature*: vol. VI: September 1887 to August 1888 (Philadelphia, PA: John Wanamaker, 1888), pg. 498

Wang Fuzhi

"The barbarians are a different species from us, like animals; it is the Chinese who should stay in this land, and the barbarians who should be driven out." – quoted in Jonathan Spence, *Treason by the Book*, New York: Penguin, 2012, pg. 7.

"There are two great barriers in the empire: [the first is the barrier between] Chinese (hua-xia) and barbarians (yi-di), [and the second is that between] superior people (junzi) and petty-minded people (xiaoren) .... The barbarians, with respect to the Chinese, are born in alien lands. As their lands are alien, their customs are alien, and as their customs are alien, so their behavior is entirely alien." – Cited in John D. Langlois, Jr., *Chinese Culturalism and the Yuan Analogy: Seventeenth-Century Perspectives*, Harvard Journal of Asiatic Studies 40 (1980), 3 64.

B.B. Warfield

"Scripture goes further in teaching that God weaves his purposes of grace and judgment within the threads of an individual's family life. The family is not the sole instrumentality of the divine purpose, of course, but it is of vast importance. ... the family ... is the New Testament basis of the Church of God. ... [God] does, indeed, require individual faith for salvation; but He organizes His people in families first; and then into churches, recognizing in their very warp and woof the family constitution. His promises are all the more precious that they are to us and our children. And though this may not fit in with the growing individualism of the day, it is God's ordinance." – *The Works of Benjamin B. Warfield*, vol. IX, New York, 1932, pgs. 405-406.

"The difference in conclusions between (the Apostle Paul) and the feminist movement of today is rooted in a fundamental difference in their points of view relative to the constitution of the human race. To Paul, the human race is made up of families...To the feminist movement the human race is made up of individuals; a woman is just another individual by the side of man and is can see no reason for any differences in dealing with the two." – *Paul On Women Speaking In Church*, *The Presbyterian* (October 30, 1919)

George Washington

"The General has great Reason [to be]; and is highly displeased, with the Negligence and Inattention of those Officers, who have placed as Centries, at the outposts, Men with whose Characters they are not acquainted. He therefore orders, that for the future, no Man shall be appointed to those important Stations, who is not a Native of this Country, or has a Wife, or Family in it, to whom he is known to be attached. This order is to be consider'd as a standing one and the Officers are to pay obedience to it at their peril." – *General Order to the Army*, 7th July, 1775; *The Writings of George Washington from the Original Manuscript Sources, 1745-1799*, pg. 316

"On 10 July [1775] General Gates issued an order to be observed by the recruiting officers, who were immediately sent upon that service: 'You are not to enlist any person who is not an American born, unless such person has a wife and family, and is a settled resident in this country.'" – In the *Gaines Mercury* of July 24th, 1775; *The Writings of George Washington*, vol. 3, pg. 16

"I want to form a company for my guard. In doing this I wish to be extremely cautious, because it is more than probable, that, in the course of the campaign, my baggage, papers, and other matters of great public import, may be committed to the sole care of these men. This being premised, in order to impress you with proper attention in the choice, I have to request, that you will immediately furnish me with four men of your regiments...I think it [fidelity] most likely to be found in those, who have family connexions in the country. You will therefore send me none but natives, and men of some property, if you have them." – In a letter to Col. Alexander Spotswood, written from Morristown, 30 April, 1777; *Recollections and Private Memoirs of Washington* Part 1, pg. 258

"I would only observe, without insinuating the most distant shadow of distrust of Monsieur Ducoudray's honor, candor, or integrity, that, on the general maxims of prudence and policy, it may be questioned with much propriety, whether so important a command as that of the artillery should be vested in any but a native, or one attached by the ties of interest to these States." – In a letter to the President of Congress written from Middlebrook, 31st May, 1777; *The Writings of George Washington*, vol. 4, pg. 445

"You should be extremely cautious in your enquiries into the character of those who are not natives who offer to enlist. Desertions among men of that class have been so frequent that unless you find 'em on examination to be of good & unsuspicious conduct, they should not be taken by any means. Otherwise, most probably, they will deceive you— add no strength to our arms, but much expence to the Public account and upon first opportunity will join the Enemy." – In a letter to Colonel Baylor, written 19th June, 1777; *The Writings of George Washington, vol. 5*, pg. 441

"I will further add, that we have already a full proportion of foreign officers in our general councils; and, should their number be increased, it may happen upon many occasions, that their voices may be equal if not exceed the rest. I trust you think me so much a citizen of the world, as to believe I am not easily warped or led away by attachments merely local or American; yet I confess I am not entirely without ' em, nor does it appear to me that they are unwarrantable, if confined within proper limits. Fewer promotions in the foreign line would have been productive of more harmony, and made our warfare more agreeable to all parties. The frequency of them is the source of jealousy and of disunion." – In a letter to Henry Laurens, written from Camp, near White Plains, 24th July, 1778; *The Writings of George Washington*, vol. 6, pg. 18

"Baron Steuben, I now find, is wanting to quit his inspectorship for a command in the line. This will be productive of much discontent to the brigadiers. In a word, although I think the Baron an excellent officer, I do most devoutly wish, that we had not a single foreigner among us, except the Marquis de Lafayette, who acts upon very different principles from those which govern the rest." – In a letter to Gouverneur Morris, written from White Plains, 24 July, 1778; *History of the George Washington Bicentennial*, vol. 3, pg. 446

"The nation which indulges towards another an habitual hatred or an habitual fondness is in some degree a slave. It is a slave to its animosity or to its affection, either of which is sufficient to lead it astray from its duty and its interest." – *Farewell Address, The Writings of George Washington*, vol. 13, pg. 312

"But I will take the liberty of advising such as are not ' thoroughly convinced,' and whose minds are yet open to conviction, to read the pieces and hear the arguments, which have been adduced in favor of as well as those against, the constitutionality and expediency of those laws (Alien And Sedition), before they decide; and consider to what lengths a certain description of men in our country have already driven, and seem resolved further to drive matters, and then ask themselves if it is not time and expedient, to resort to protecting laws against aliens (for citizens you certainly know are not affected by that law), who acknowledge no allegiance to this country, and in many instances are sent among us (as there is the

— GEORGE WASHINGTON —

best circumstantial evidence to prove) for the express purpose of poisoning the minds of our people, and to sow dissensions among them, in order to alienate their affections from the government of their choice, thereby endeavoring to dissolve the Union, and of course the fair and happy prospects, which were unfolding to our view from the revolution." – In a letter to Alexander Spotswood, written from Philadelphia, 22nd November, 1789; *The Writings of George Washington*, vol. 14, pg. 122

"The policy or advantage of [immigration] taking place in a body (I mean the settling of them in a body) may be much questioned; for, by so doing, they retain the language, habits, and principles (good or bad) which they bring with them. Whereas by an intermixture with our people, they, or their descendants, get assimilated to our customs, measures, and laws: in a word, soon become one people." – Letter to John Adams, November 15, 1794, in *Relative to the Further Restriction of Immigration*, pg. 5

"The unity of government which constitutes you one people is also now dear to you. It is justly so, for it is a main pillar in the edifice of your real independence, the support of your tranquility at home, your peace abroad; of your safety; of your prosperity; of that very liberty which you so highly prize…it is of infinite moment that you should properly estimate the immense value of your national union to your collective and individual happiness; that you

should cherish a cordial, habitual, and immovable attachment to it; accustoming yourselves to think and speak of it as of the palladium of your political safety and prosperity; watching for its preservation with jealous anxiety; discountenancing whatever may suggest even a suspicion that it can in any event be abandoned; and indignantly frowning upon the first dawning of every attempt to alienate any portion of our country from the rest." – *Farewell Address, The Writings of George Washington*, vol. 13, pg. 286

"A free people should promote such manufactures as tend to render them independent on others for essentials, especially military supplies." – *First Message to Congress*

"The great rule of conduct for us in regard to foreign nations is, in extending our commercial relations, to have with them as little political connection as possible. So far as we have already formed engagements, let them be fulfilled with perfect good faith. Here let us stop. Europe has a set of primary interests which to us have none, or a very remote relation. Hence, she must be engaged in frequent controversies, the causes of which are essentially foreign to our concerns. Hence, therefore, it must be unwise in us to implicate ourselves, by artificial ties, in the ordinary vicissitudes of her politics, or the ordinary combinations and collisions of her friendships or enmities. Our detached and distant situation invites and enables us to pursue a different course. If we remain one people, under an efficient government, the period is not far off when we may defy material injury from external annoyance; when we may take such an attitude as will cause the neutrality we may at any time resolve upon to be scrupulously respected; when belligerent nations, under the impossibility of making acquisitions upon us, will not lightly hazard the giving us provocation; when we may choose peace or war, as our interest, guided by justice, shall counsel. Why forego the advantages of so peculiar a situation? Why quit our own to stand upon foreign ground? Why, by interweaving our destiny with that of any part of Europe, entangle our peace and prosperity in the toils of European ambition, rivalship, interest, humor, or caprice? It is our true policy to steer clear of permanent alliances with any portion of the foreign world; so far, I mean, as we are now at liberty to do it; for let me not be understood as capable of patronizing infidelity to existing engagements. I hold the maxim no less applicable to public than to private affairs, that honesty is always the best policy. I repeat it; therefore, let those engagements be observed in their genuine sense; but in my opinion it is unnecessary, and would be unwise, to extend them. Taking care always to keep ourselves, by suitable establishments, in a respectable defensive posture, we may safely trust to temporary alliances for extraordinary emergencies." – *Farewell Address*, pgs. 21-23

"Twenty years peace, with such an increase of population and resources as we have a right to expect; added to our remote situation from the jarring powers, will in all probability enable us in a just cause to bid defiance to any power on earth." – Letter to Charles Carroll, 1 May 1796; *The Political Writings of George Washington*, pg. 1,799

"Free people ought not only to be armed but disciplined; . . . and their safety and interest require that they should promote such manufactories as tend to render them independent of others for essential, particularly military, supplies." – *First Annual Message to Congress*, 1790; Richardson, Messages, 1:57

"To demonstrate the sincerity of my opinion . . . by the uniformity of my practice, in giving a decided preference to the produce and fabrics of America, whensoever it may be done without involving unreasonable expenses, or very great Inconveniences." – *Addressing the Delaware Society for Promoting Domestic Manufacturers*, April, 1789; Abbott, Washington, 1:261-64, 2:78-79

James L. Watson

"Earlier attempts to explain China's remarkable record of unity focused, inevitably perhaps, on the super elite of scholar-bureaucrats . . . One must consider the role of ordinary people: farmers, artisans, shopkeepers, midwives, silk reelers, and laborers . . . who were engaged in the construction of a unified culture . . . In this view, peasants are not, as some have claimed, 'easy material for ideological molding'; they are leading actors in the performance that we have come to call Chinese culture." – "Rites or Be-

liefs? The Construction of a Unified Culture in Late Imperial China" in Dittmer, *China's Quest for National Identity*, pg. 82

John Waters

"I am an authority on the destruction of my country. I can parse, plumb, dice and slice the catalogue of disaster that has been inflicted upon her by those we trusted to be her husbanders, but who turned out to be villains, cowards, traitors and batterers. I can tell you how they do it, blow by blow, descending on her baffled face like rain. I can describe the involutions of their guile and underhandedness. I can show how it impacts on each of us who are forced to watch and wait as they prate on concerning their 'compassion' and 'humanity', while we, her children, stand paralysed and muted by several centuries of demoralisation and bad religion. I know it all inside out. I feel it all, though I cannot always find the exact words corresponding to my feelings, and so the sentences burst out of me and trip each other up, and yet are understood sufficiently by others to surprise and puzzle me, though I hear in them only the spaces in which the missing parts might have been.

"I am an authority on the destruction of my country. I stand before audiences and tell them why their souls are dying and their grandchildren may never be born. I watch them nod as though understanding for the first time. I see tears trickle down their cheeks and briefly worry that I have caused this to occur, though I am but the midhusband, and innocent of the conception.

"I am an authority on the destruction of my country. For the first 64 years of my life, I did not anticipate that my country would fall into the hands of pimps who would sell her into prostitution, who would banish her children to wander in the world without a place to rest their heads, a home to call their own. I thought they had felt at least the essence of what they had preached about her long struggle for Independence, and the importance of her freedoms, and the sacrifices of her martyrs, and now they act as if this was all but bewitchment and foolishness.

"I am an authority on the destruction of my country. I did not expect to be such, not knowing there would arise a vacancy. Little did

I know, as I walked to school with the words of Pearse rattling around my head that, in studying the writings and deeds of my country's heroes, the ultimate use to which I would put this knowledge would be to underline its resonances in a present that lay ahead as though a misplaced stretch of the past. I had thought of these stories as a kind of adornment on a finished history, an emblem of patriotic sincerity, the luxury of a people whose trials were over, their problems resolved.

"I am an authority on the destruction of my country, but a Bachelor of Destruction only. I am studying for my Masters and writing here my thesis, in which I hope finally to overcome what I believe is my total inability to express what I feel, what needs to be said, and what is to be imagined in order to prevent this cycle recurring.

"I am an authority on the destruction of my country. I wish I weren't. I wish I were an expert in building boats, or growing butternut squash. I wish I were not an amateur specialist in psychopathy and ponerology, or an eyewitness authority on authoritarianism. I wish I were a better accordionist or crosswordist instead.

"I wish I were not an authority on the destruction of my country. I wish I could take her for granted as I did for most of my life, walking on tiptoe across her blood-soaked fields, with a heart as light as my step. Oh, days of innocence and naïveté, how we pay for them now, and how we pray to have them back! How we rummage in our heads and memories for some formula or formulation that would enable us to rest, if only for an hour, without thoughts of her obliteration haunting our dreams." – Introduction, *The Abolition of Reality*

Thomas Watson

Commentary on the 5th Commandment:
    FATHER is of different kinds; as the political, the ancient, the spiritual, the domestic, and the natural....The POLITICAL father, the magistrate. He is the father of his country....God has set these political fathers to preserve order and harmony in a nation, and to prevent those state convulsions which otherwise might ensue....

"There is the grave ANCIENT father, who is venerable for old age; whose grey hairs are resembled to the white flowers of the almond-tree. Eccl 12:5. There are fathers for seniority, on whose wrinkled brows, and in the furrows of whose cheeks is pictured the map of old age...

"There are SPIRITUAL fathers, as pastors and ministers. These are instruments of the new birth....The spiritual fathers are to be honored, in respect of their office. Whatever their persons are, their office is honorable; they are the messengers of the Lord Almighty. Mal 2:7. They represent no less than God himself....

"There is the DOMESTIC father, that is, the master. He is 'the father of the family'; therefore Naaman's servants called their master, father. 2 Kings 5:13. The centurion calls his servant, son. Matt 8:6. (Greek.) The servant is to honor his master, as the father of the family. Though the master is not so qualified as he should be— yet the servant must not neglect his duty—but show some kind of honor to him.

"In OBEYING his master, 'in things which are lawful and honest.' 'Servants, be subject to your masters; not only to the good and gentle— but also to the froward.' 1 Pet 2:18. God has nowhere given a charter of exemption to free you from your duty. You cannot disobey your earthly master—but you are disobeying your master in heaven. Think not that birth, or great abilities, no, nor even grace, will exempt you from obedience to your master. To obey him is an ordinance of God; and an apostle says, 'Those who resist the ordinance, shall receive to themselves damnation. Rom 13:2.' ...

"The NATURAL father, the father of the flesh. Heb 12:9. Honor your natural father. This is so necessary a duty....Children are to show honor to their parents, by a reverential esteem of their persons. They must 'give them a civil veneration.'" – *Body of Divinity, Ten Commandments, 5th commandment*

Evelyn Waugh

"Something quite remote from anything the builders intended has come out of their work, and out of the fierce little human tragedy in which I played; something none of us thought about at the time: a small red flame—a beaten-copper lamp of deplorable design, relit before the beaten-copper doors of a tabernacle; the flame which the old knights saw from their tombs, which they saw put out; that flame burns again for other soldiers, far from home, farther, in heart, than Acre and Jerusalem. It could not have been lit but for the builders

and the tragedians, and there I found it this morning, burning anew among the old stones."
– *Brideshead Revisited*, pg. 331

John Weaver

"I believe it should be obvious to anyone who believes the Bible that God created the races. Had God desired only one race, He would not have created the other races. And if God had desired that we intermarry and amalgamate and become one, why would He have begun the other races to begin with? Very obviously it was not His desire that we intermarry. Because when you intermarry what you do then is basically destroy the races. You cannot maintain the differences.

"One of the principles that is laid down very plainly in the book of Genesis, what God created is that everything was to bring forth fruit after its kind. Now that's very simple. Now how in the world can you bring forth fruit after your kind if you intermarry? The answer is you can't. You produce a different kind. Now let me just make a statement and then I want to show it to you from the Bible. You see the amalgamation of races is a form of adultery. You say 'What?', yes the amalgamation of the races is a form of adultery.

"The eighth commandment is 'Thou shalt not commit adultery'. I want you to understand that adultery is far more than a sexual sin. It is that. But it is also a watering down, and a dissolution and destruction of a bond and/or a substance. Certainly, physical adultery involves sexual sin. But what is the great calamity of that sexual sin? It is destroying and dissolving the bond that exists between the husband and the wife. It also destroys the bond that exists between the parents and the children. It also destroys the bond that exists between the families. Do you see what I'm saying? So what happens is, it is a watering down. Now, listen carefully to what our Founding Fathers said. 'To secure the blessings of liberty for ourselves and out posterity.' The question must be asked, How many Mexicans? How many Orientals? How many blacks and other races were present and participating in the execution of that document. What is the answer? None. Not one. Yes, there were blacks in the country, but they were slaves. Yes, there were Mexicans and there were Indians out in the Western frontier that had not yet been conquered or purchased, but none were at the founding of this nation.

"Now I'm not trying to sound racist, nor am I being racist. I'm simply, pointing out a fact, and here is the fact, this country was founded by White European Christians who wanted to establish a Christian culture. Not an African culture. Not a Oriental culture. Not a Muslim culture. Not a Mexican culture. But a Christian culture. And it was this Christian culture that was to be passed down to our posterity. Now what is happening in America? Are you listening? The exact same thing that happened in Israel. Interracial marriage, idolatry, and multi-culturalism." – *God Created Races*

Richard Weaver

"When we come to analyze the real nature of time, we are forced to see that the present does not really exist, or that, at the utmost concession, it has an infinitesimal existence. The man who pretends to exist in this alone would cut himself off from almost everything. There is a past, and there is a future, but the present is being translated into the past so rapidly that no one can actually say what is the present. If we say that everything should be for the present, we must quickly divorce ourselves from each past moment and at the same time not attend to those subjective feelings, born of past experience, which are our picture of the future. The richness of any moment or period comes through the interweaving of what has been with what may be. If every moment past is to be sloughed off like dead skin and a curtain is to be drawn upon future probabilities, which are also furnished by the mind, the possibilities of living and of enjoyment are reduced to virtually nothing." – *The Attack on Memory; Visions Of Order*, pg. 48

"When we affirm that philosophy begins with wonder, we are affirming in effect that sentiment is anterior to reason. We do not undertake to reason about anything until we have been drawn to it by an affective interest. In the cultural life of man, therefore, the fact of paramount importance about anyone is his attitude toward the world. How frequently it is brought to our attention that nothing good can be done if the will is wrong! Reason alone fails to justify Itself. Not without cause has the devil been called the prince of lawyers, and not by accident are Shakespeare's villains good reasoners. If the disposition is wrong, reason increases maleficence; if it is right, reason orders and furthers the good. We have no authority to argue anything of a social or political nature unless we have shown by our primary volition that we approve some aspects of the existing world. The position is arbitrary in the sense that here is a proposition behind which there stands no prior. We begin our other affirmations after a categorical statement that life and the world are to be cherished." – *Ideas Have Consequences*, pg. 18

— RICHARD WEAVER —

"An election, is after all, a highly undemocratic proceeding; the very term means discrimination. How is it possible to choose the best man when by definition there is no best? If a society wishes to be its natural self, that is to say, if it wishes to flourish wild, unshaped by anything superior to itself, it should make a perfectly random choice of administrators. Let youth and age, wisdom and folly, courage and cowardice, self-control and dissoluteness, sit together on the bench. This will be representative; this is a cross-section, and there seems no room to question that it would create that society 'filled with wonderful variety and disorder' which Plato called democracy." – *Ideas Have Consequences*, pg. 42

"Amnesia as a goal is a social emergent of

unique significance. I do not find any other period in which men have felt to an equal degree that the past either is uninteresting or is a reproach to them. When we realize the extent to which one's memory is oneself, we are made to wonder whether there is not some element of suicidal impulse in this mood, or at least an impulse of self-hatred." – *The Attack Upon Memory; Visions Of Order: Cultural Crisis Of Our Time*, pg. 41

"For the success of our restoration it cannot be too often said that society and mass are contradictory terms and that those who seek to do things in the name of mass are the destroyers in our midst. If society is something which can be understood, it must have structure; if it has structure, it must have hierarchy; against this metaphysical truth the declamations of the Jacobins break in vain." – *Ideas Have Consequences*, pg. 32

"The comity of peoples in groups large or small rests not upon this chimerical notion of equality but upon fraternity, a concept which long antedates it in history because it goes immeasurably deeper in human sentiment. The ancient feeling of brotherhood carries obligations of which equality knows nothing. It calls for respect and protection, for brotherhood is status in family, and family is by nature hierarchical. It demands patience with little brother, and it may sternly exact duty of big brother. It places people in a network of sentiment, not of rights—that hortus siccus of modem vainglory.

"Equality is a disorganizing concept in so far as human relationships mean order. It is order without a design; it attempts a meaningless and profitless regimentation of what has been ordered from time immemorial by the scheme of things. No society can rightly offer less than equality before the law; but there can be no equality of condition between youth and age or between the sexes; there cannot be equality even between friends. The rule is that each shall act where he is strong; the assignment of identical roles produces first confusion and then alienation, as we have increasing opportunity to observe. Not only is this disorganizing heresy busily confounding the most natural social groupings, it is also creating a reservoir of poisonous envy. How much of the frustration of the modern world proceeds from starting with the assumption that all are equal, finding that this cannot be so, and then having to realize that one can no longer fall back on the bond of fraternity!

"However paradoxical it may seem, fraternity has existed in the most hierarchical organizations; it exists, as we have just noted, in that archetype of hierarchy, the family. The essence of cooperation is congeniality, the feeling of having been 'born together.' Fraternity directs attention to others, equality to self; and the passion for equality is simultaneous with the growth of egotism. The frame of duty which fraternity erects is itself the source of ideal conduct. Where men feel that society means station, the highest and the lowest see their endeavors contributing to a common end, and they are in harmony rather than in competition. It will be found as a general rule that those parts of the world which have talked least of equality have in the solid fact of their social life exhibited the greatest fraternity. Such was true of feudal Europe before people succumbed to various forms of the proposal that every man should be king. Nothing is more manifest than that as this social distance has diminished and all groups have moved nearer equality, suspicion and hostility have increased. In the present world there is little of trust and less of loyalty. People do not know what to expect of one another. Leaders will not lead, and servants will not serve." – *Ideas Have Consequences*, pg. 39

"If it promises equality of condition, it promises injustice, because one law for the ox and the lion is tyranny." – *Ideas Have Consequences*, pg. 44

"Those who have no concern for their ancestors will, by simple application of the same rule, have none for their descendants. The decision of modern man to live in the here and now is reflected in the neglect of aging parents, whom proper sentiment once kept in positions of honor and authority. There was a time when the elder generation was cherished because it represented the past; now it is avoided and thrust out of sight for the same reason. Children are liabilities. As man becomes more immersed in time and material gratifications, belief in the continuum of race fades, and not all the tinkering of sociologists can put homes together again." – *Ideas Have Consequences*, pg. 28

"Forms and conventions are the ladder of ascent. And hence the speechlessness of the man of culture when he beholds the barbarian tearing aside some veil which is half adornment, half concealment. He understands what is being done, but he cannot convey the understanding because he cannot convey the idea of sacrilege. His cries of abejti profani are not heard by those who in the exhilaration of breaking some restraint feel that they are extending the boundaries of power or of knowledge." – *Ideas Have Consequences*, pg. 24

"That it does not matter what a man believes is a statement heard on every side today. The statement carries a fearful implication. If a man is a philosopher in the sense with which we started, what he believes tells him what the world is for. How can men who disagree about what the world is for agree about any of the minutiae of daily conduct? The statement really means that it doesn't matter what a man believes so long as he does not take his beliefs seriously. Anyone can observe that this is the status to which religious belief has been reduced for many years. But suppose he does take his beliefs seriously? Then what he believes places a stamp upon his experience, and he belongs to a culture, which is a league founded on exclusive principles. To become eligible, one must be able to say the right words about the right things, which signifies in turn that one must be a man of correct sentiments. This phrase, so dear to the eighteenth century, carries us back to the last age that saw sentiment and reason in a proper partnership." – *Ideas Have Consequences*, pg. 22

"Rational society is a mirror of the logos, and this means that it has a formal structure which enables apprehension. The preservation of society is therefore directly linked with the recovery of true knowledge. For the success of our restoration it cannot be too often said that society and mass are contradictory terms and that those who seek to do things in the name of mass are the destroyers in our midst. If society is something which can be understood, it must have structure; if it has structure, it must have hierarchy; against this metaphysical truth the declamations of the Jacobins break in vain." – *Ideas Have Consequences*, pg. 32

"In our contemporary setting the young man stands for science and technology, and the father for the order of nature. For centuries now, we have been told that our happiness requires an unrelenting assault upon this order; dominion, conquest, triumph—all these names have been used as if it were a military campaign. Somehow the notion has been loosed that nature is hostile to man or that her ways are offensive or slovenly, so that every step of progress is measured by how far we have altered these. Nothing short of a recovery of the ancient virtue of pietas can absolve man from this sin" – *Ideas Have Consequences*, pg. 154

Daniel Webster

"Protection of our own labor against the cheaper, ill-paid, half-fed, and pauper labor of Europe is…a duty which the country owes to its own citizens." – Speech, March 15, 1837; *Speeches and Forensic Arguments*, vol. 3, pg. 141

Noah Webster

"PAT'RIOT, noun [Latin patria, one's native country, form pater, father.]

A person who loves his country, and zealously supports and defends it and its interests. Such tears as patriots shed for dying laws. PAT'RIOT, adjective Patriotic; devoted to the welfare of one's country; as patriot zeal.

"NATION, noun [to be born]

1. A body of people inhabiting the same country, or united under the same sovereign or government; as the English nation; the French nation It often happens that many nations are subject to one government; in which case, the word nation usually denotes a body of people speaking the same language, or a body that has formerly been under a distinct government, but has been conquered, or incorporated with a larger nation Thus the empire of Russia comprehends many nations, as did formerly the Roman and Persian empires. Nation as its etymology imports, originally denoted a family or race of men descended from a common progenitor, like tribe, but by emigration, conquest and intermixture of men of different families, this distinction is in most countries lost." – *Webster Dictionary 1828*

Max Weber

"Only the occident knows the state in the modern sense with a professional administration, specialized officialdom, and law based on the concept of citizenship…Only the occident knows rational law, made by jurists and rationally interpreted and applied, and only in the occident is found the concept of citizen (civis Romanus, citizen, bourgeois) because only in the occident again are there cities in the specific sense. Furthermore, only the occident possesses science in the present-day sense of the word. Finally, western civilization is further distinguished from every other by the presence of men with a rational ethic for the conduct of life." – *General Economic History*

H.G. Wells

"The stresses that arose from the unscientific map-making of the diplomatists gathered force more deliberately, but they were even more dangerous to the peace of mankind. It is extraordinarily inconvenient to administer together the affairs of peoples speaking different languages and so reading different literatures and having different general ideas, especially if those differences are exacerbated by religious disputes. Only some strong mutual interest, such as the common defensive needs of the Swiss mountaineers, can justify a close linking of peoples of dissimilar languages and faiths; and even in Switzerland there is the utmost local autonomy. Ultimately, when the Great Power tradition is dead and buried, those Swiss populations may gravitate towards their natural affinities in Germany, France and Italy. When as in Macedonia, populations are mixed in a patchwork of villages and districts, the cantonal system is imperatively needed. But if the reader will look at the map of Europe as the Congress of Vienna drew it, he will see that this gathering seems almost as if it had planned the maximum of local exasperation. It destroyed the Dutch Republic, quite needlessly it lumped together the Protestant Dutch with the French-speaking Catholics of the old Spanish (Austrian) Netherlands, and set up a kingdom of the Netherlands. It handed over not merely the old republic of Venice but all of North Italy as far as Milan to the German-speaking Austrians, French-speaking Savoy it combined with pieces of Italy to restore the kingdom of Sardinia. Austria and Hungary, already a sufficiently explosive mixture of discordant nationalities, Germans, Hungarians, Czecho-Slovaks, Jugo-Slavs, Romanians, and now Italians, was made still more impossible by 1772 and 1795. The Catholic and republican-spirited Polish people were chiefly given over to the less civilized rule of the Greek-Orthodox Tsar, but important districts went to Protestant Prussia. The Tsar was also confirmed in his acquisition of the entirely alien Finns. The very dissimilar Norwegian and Swedish peoples were bound together under one king. Germany, the reader will see, was left in a particularly dangerous state of muddle. Prussia and Austria were both partly in and partly out of a German confederation which included a multitude of minor states. The King of Denmark came into the German confederation by virtue of certain German-speaking possessions in Holstein. Luxembourg was included in the German confederation, though its ruler was also king of the Netherlands, and though many of its peoples talked French. Here was a complete disregard of the fact that the people who talk German and base their ideas on German literature, the people who talk Italian and base their ideas on Italian literature, and the people who talk Polish and base their ideas on Polish literature, will all be far better off and most helpful and least obnoxious to the rest of mankind if they conduct their own affairs in their own idiom within the ring-fence of their own speech. Is it any wonder that one of the most popular songs in Germany during this period declared that wherever the German tongue was spoken there was the German Fatherland?

"Even today men are still reluctant to recognize that areas of government are not matters for the bargaining and interplay of tsars and kings and foreign offices. There is a natural and necessary political map of the world which transcends these things. There is a best way possible of dividing any part of the world into administrative areas, and a best possible kind of government for every area, having regard to the speech and race of its inhabitants, and it is our common concern to secure those divisions and establish those forms of government quite irrespective of diplomacies and flags, 'claims' and melodramatic 'loyalties,' and the existing political map of the world. The natural political map of the world insists upon itself. It heaves and frets beneath the artificial political map like some misfitted giant." – *Outline of History*, pgs. 943-944

Franz Werfel

"For many people it is depressing even to move house. A lost fragment of life always remains. To move to another town, settle in a foreign country, is for everyone a major decision. But, to be suddenly driven forth, within twenty-four hours, from one's home, one's work, the reward of years of steady industry. To become a helpless prey of help. To be sent defenceless out to Asiatic highroads, with several thousand miles of dust, stones, and morass before one. To know that one will never again find a decently human habitation, never again sit down to a proper table. Yet this is all nothing. To be more shackled than any convict. To be counted as outside the law, a vagabond, whom anyone has the right to kill unpunished." – *The Forty Days of Musa Dagh*, pg. 93

Aage Westenholz

When Sargon of Akkad invaded Sumer, the people of the region resisted because:
"…Sumerians considered Sargon and his 'sons of Akkade' to be foreigners; another, that the cities had lost their relative autonomy." After Sargon's death, the cities "revolted in a victory-or-death rebellion" against his successor, Rimush. – *Six City-State Cultures*, pg. 39

Edward Westermarck

"Kinship certainly gives rise to special rights and duties, but when unsupported by local proximity it loses much of its social force." – *The Origin and Development of the Moral Ideas*, pg. 202

John Wesley

"God is the first object of our love: Its next office is, to bear the defects of others. And we should begin the practice of this amidst our own household." – *A Plain Account of Christian Perfection*, pg. 42

Westminster Shorter Catechism

"The fifth commandment requireth the preserving the honour, and performing the duties, belonging to everyone in their several places and relations, as superiors, inferiors, or equals." – *Answer 64*

Edmund Burke Whitman

"That Nation which respects and honors its dead, shall ever be respected and honored itself. [1868]" – Brevet Lieut.-Col. Edmund B. Whitman, National Cemetery Administration, *Memorial Day*

Walt Whitman

"The proof of a poet is that his country absorbs him as affectionately as he has absorbed it." – *Leaves Of Grass*

Chilton Williamson

"The bedrock of populist discontent lies deeper, and stretches far more extensively, than concerns about national pride, national sovereignty, and economic distress...it has to do with the perpetual unsettledness of everything today... Human beings are constitutionally incapable of feeling comfortable in modern liberal societies...The free-market, free-trade system that subsumes all of human society is inhumane, humanly intolerable, and finally unworkable, since in the end society as a whole will naturally rebel against it." – *Loss of the Familiar*

Samuel Willard

"The Wellfare of Humane Society is very much Concerned in this matter. Man is made a sociable Creature, and the Comfort of Mankind is maintained by mutual Entercourse and Communion: Man is a Dependent Creature, and not only have all men their absolute Dependence upon God; but one man hath a great deal of Dependence upon another, without which the Affairs of this life cannot be carried on for the support of our Livelyhood, there are many things man wants, and there are many Vocations are needful for the supply of them, one man cannot Carry on all by himself; and hence it comes to pass, that there is mutual Traffick between men and Transactions among them in the Management of it: nor can all things be carried so, as that there should be no more but Present commutation, but men must trust one another; and therefore Covenants and Promises must pass between them for the future doing this or that, which may Answer the ends of each: & that which makes these promises to pass for currant between man & man, is truth in the promiser; it is the Opinion of that which gives him Credit with the other party; but for which Opinion he would refuse to take his word or credit him on the value of it: if therefore there be a failure upon this account, mankind is disappointed; & if it should grow to be a common thing, the Ligament of Humane society is dissolved and Communities must be disbanded: if Truth fail all is put to a rout: if once a man cannot be believed, what should any others have any more to do with him? by this means secrets come to be revealed to men's great detriment; expectations are hereby frustrated, businesses of greatest moment disappointed and humane traffick wofully entangled; hence arise quarrellings, tedious lawsuits, yea Contention & every evil work: whereas on the other hand were men but True & faithful, how happily might they live together? what helps and Comforts might they be mutually one to another? it is indeed the Ligature of all societies & if it be broken they will fall in pieces: & when all those things are put together, It will tell us what reason the Apostle had to be so Careful in defending his credit in this Respect." – *Promise-Keeping*, pgs. 19-21

"There are diverse Degrees of Neighborhood. The Word Neighbor is very [comprehensive]; it comprehends in it all with whom we may have any civil (Communion) and so the greatest Strangest, and (all) of Men. And it involves all the several (Nations) and Religions. So in this respect, some may be our nearer Neighbours than others. A Brother is nearer than a Stranger, Etc. Hence, there (are) necessary degrees of the Law.

"That hence there do necessarily flow diverse degrees of this Love. That we are to Love all equally alike, is in vain asserted by some, and flows from the ignorance of the Relations which God hath fixed among Men; unto which he hath annexed those special Duties, which are to be discharged by a special Love one to another. There are some to whom we own only a love of Benevolence, which commands our Beneficence; but others deserve our love of Complacency. Hence that in Psalm 16:3, 'But to the saints that are in the earth, and to the excellent in whom is all my delight.' There are some whom we ought to be more concern for than others.

"Every Man owes the first and principal of this Love to himself. Every Man is his own next Neighbor. The Rule laid down doth not require a parity, but only a similitude. I owe Charity to others, but it must begin at home. I may not suffer my self to starve, to keep another alive. I ought to do all I can for the Salvation of others, but my first care is the Salvation of my own Soul, and if others will perish, I must flee to save my self.

"Yet it is the same Love for kind, that a Man owe to himself and to his Neighbor. And that in all respects. Tho' there is a difference in the extensiveness, yet they are not two sorts of Love but one." – *Body Of Divinity*, pg. 585-586

"Had man abode in his primitive state, there would have been always some naturally superior to others." – *Body Of Divinity*, pg. 619

"...as the world had began to be peopled, there would necessarily have been a multiplying of civil societies, and these distinct, for the up-holding of civil commerce and amity. They are therefore in a great error who tell us that so many kingdoms or commonwealths as there are in the world, so many testimonies of divine displeasure." – *Body Of Divinity*, pg. 619

Douglas Wilson

"A godly husband is tribal, which means he thinks in terms of his ancestors and his descendants. The first commandment promises blessings to a thousand generations: 'Thou shalt not bow down thyself to them, nor serve them: for I the Lord thy God am a jealous God, visiting the iniquity of the fathers upon the children unto the third and fourth generation of them that hate me and shewing mercy unto thousands of them that love me, and keep my commandments' (Exod. 20:5-6). If people are faithful to God, then God gives mercy to them-to a thousand generations. Therefore, a godly husband thinks of his great-grandparents and of his great-grandchildren." – *The Covenant Household*

"Quantity [of people] also has to breed distrust. Trust is the bond of community, and if we lack personal knowledge we can't trust. Without trust, our neighbors become constant threats of some sort. The modern city is simply too dangerous for familiarity. It demands distrust and protective aloofness to survive. Its people simultaneously complain about loneliness and yet desire anonymity.

"Quantity not only breeds impersonality and distrust, it forces the city to place people into convenient types and categories. Since there is no time to know individuals, it's most convenient to throw out the distinguishing marks and lob everyone into general categories – black, Latino, Asian, white. It is no surprise that race conflict finds its origins in the city. It is the natural culmination of mass impersonality and distrust. ...

"And all together we present such an intriguing diversity that 'multiculturalists' haven't even begun to recognize. Such relativists are only concerned with abstract people; they hate real people." – *Angels In The Architecture*, pg. 134

"Reformers are conservatives, which means they must prefer the concrete to the abstract. The past is concrete, just like the future is going to be. The goal is to preserve and defend everything the Spirit has done in history in such a way as to carry it forward into what the Spirit is going to do. Given our time-bound nature, we must conserve some things, and we must progress toward certain things. But what do we conserve, and what do we seek to build? Our duties are always in the present, but we must read the past, as well as the future (albeit more dimly), and we must do so by the performance of concrete duties. Love your neighbor, not mankind. Build an actual school for your children, and do not love the notion of educational 'great concepts' in some Euclidean eschaton." – *Rules for Reformers*, pg. 3

"A number of people have wanted to say that 'America is dedicated to a proposition,' and that we are not bound together by those common ties that bind other nations—mundane things like language, culture, music, food, and common descent. Because of this assumption, believing or not believing in America becomes a choice, like a religious choice, and that means you can fault people for not making it." – *Empires of Dirt*, pg. 11

"My natural affection for my people and place—which every Christian must cultivate in his place, for his people—does not interfere with my ability to challenge the regnant follies, insanities, and cruelties. That natural affection, that patriotism, is actually one of my qualifications for doing so. We have plots currently afoot in Washington that George III would not have countenanced in his nightmares. And if I go to a big rally dedicated to telling the federal government to stop acting like a colony of Mordor, I am willing to bet you that, as I make my way through the parking area, I will spot an awful lot of the pick-up trucks with American flags on them." – *Empires of Dirt*, pg. 27

"American exceptionalism is the idea that America is more of a creed than a nation. This kind of American exceptionalism makes a certain kind of civic religion possible, a quasi-sacramental approach which all consistent Christians reject as, in equal turns, blasphemous and silly. American exceptionalism in this sense is currently the high church form of secularism. American exceptionalism should not be defined as the grateful recognition that we live in a nation that has been enormously blessed in many ways. What might be called normal patriotism is not idolatrous, but is simply natural affection." – *Empires of Dirt*, pg. 10

"Hard libertarianism or anarchy is a function of what might be called civic fatherlessness. Just as the antitheist regards the eternality of the Father as tyrannical on the face of it, so also the hard libertarian regards any civic authority whatever as something to chafe the soul.

"Within this paradigm, all political authority is based on coercion, straight up, and since coercion is (obviously) bad, then at best we should regard political authority as a necessary evil, and at worst a tyranny to be thrown off. Those who are more eschatologically minded long for the day when the state withers, or blows up, or something, and then every man can sit fatherless under his own fig tree. This view assumes that the only possible justification for civil authority is pragmatic, and when we grow past the need for such pragmatic expedients, then we will no longer have any presidents or kings. We will have grown out of our need for civil fathers, or so the pipe dream goes." – *Empires of Dirt*, pg. 187

"Christian patriots are the ones best suited to help America in her current idolatrous impasse.

In my experience, those who are most ambivalent or cynical about patriotic pieties—flags, fireworks, and fun—are most likely to support the abuses of statist power when the state is attempting to become some jitney god in the lives of its citizens. But those who wave the flag at the parade and eat their hot dogs afterward are most likely to recognize that the government has gotten itself way out of line. Take a couple big E on the eye chart issues—homosexual marriage and abortion. Take a poll of a thousand people at a Fourth of July parade, where flags are everywhere, and then poll the same number of people who would not dream of attending such a cheesy event. Which group is most likely to support the oppressive tyranny, right or wrong, and which group is most likely, overwhelmingly, to oppose it? Right." – *Empires of Dirt*, pg. 28

Edmund Wilson

"The Northerner is sure to be shocked when the Southerner speaks frankly of the Negroes as creatures—an inferior race— for whom political or social equality is utterly and forever unthinkable. But the position of the Northerner himself depends upon human exploitation. He may, of course, be entirely unaware of it, not know who makes the clothes he wears, prepares the food he eats, digs the fuel that heats him or pours the steel for the building he lives in—he may not even know where the money comes from that enables him to buy all these things; but though his consciousness may be more innocent, he is none the better off for that. And the Southerner, on his side, becomes suspicious of the Northerner's pretensions—smelling hypocrisy in his humane anxieties, mania in his moral idealism, and in his eternal insistence on 'service' an attempt to make up for, to palliate, the savageries of a mechanized society self-seeking and rapacious in the highest degree." – *American Earthquake*, pg. 332

Henry Wilson

"Men who see not God in our history have surely lost sight of the fact that, from the landing of the Mayflower to this hour, the great men whose names are indissolubly associated with the colonization, rise, and progress of the Republic have borne testimony to the vital truths of Christianity...

"Young men of this Christian association, remember, ever and always, that your country was founded, not by 'the most superficial, the lightest, the most unreflective of all the European races,' but by the stern old Puritans, who made the deck of The Mayflower an altar of the living God, and whose first act, on touching the soil of the New World, was to offer on bended knees thanksgiving and prayer to Almighty God. Remember, too, that the great men of your country — Washington, Franklin, Jefferson, the Adamses, Hamilton, Jay, Marshall, Kent, Webster, and their illustrious compeers — possessed the intellectual force and severity necessary to carry far and long the greatest conception of the human understanding, the idea of God. Never forgetting the religious character of our national origin..." – Vice President under Grant, *Speech Founding the Free Soil Party*; *The Life and Public Services of Henry Wilson*, pg. 879

James Wilson

"Whether we consult the soundest deductions of reason, or resort to the best information conveyed to us by history, or listen to the undoubted intelligence communicated in holy writ, we shall find, that to the institution of marriage the true origin of society must be traced.... To that institution, more than to any other, have mankind been indebted for the share of peace and harmony which has been distributed among them. 'Prima societas in ipso conjugio est,' ['The first bond of society is marriage'] says Cicero in his book of offices; a work which does honor to the human understanding and the human heart." – *Lectures on Law*; *The Works of James Wilson* vol. 2, pg. 31

"In civil society, previously to the institution of civil government, all men are equal. Of one blood all nations are made; from one source the whole human race has sprung.

"When we say, that all men are equal; we mean not to apply this equality to their virtues, their talents, their dispositions, or their acquirements. In all these respects, there is, and it is fit for the great purposes of society that there should be, great inequality among men. In the moral and political as well as in the natural world, diversity forms an important part of

beauty; and as of beauty, so of utility likewise. That social happiness, which arises from the friendly intercourse of good offices, could not be enjoyed, unless men were so framed and so disposed, as mutually to afford and to stand in need of service and assistance. Hence the necessity not only of great variety, but even of great inequality in the talents of men, bodily as well as mentally. Society supposes mutual dependence: mutual dependence supposes mutual wants: all the social exercises and enjoyments may be reduced to two heads – that of giving, and that of receiving: but these imply different aptitudes to give and to receive.

"Many are the degrees, many are the varieties of human genius, human dispositions, and human characters. One man has a turn for mechanicks; another, for architecture; one paints; a second makes poems: this excels in the arts of a military; the other, in those of civil life. To account for these varieties of taste and character, is not easy; is, perhaps, impossible. But though their efficient cause it may be difficult to explain; their final cause, that is, the intention of Providence in appointing them, we can see and admire. These varieties of taste and character induce different persons to choose different professions and employments in life: these varieties render mankind mutually beneficial to each other, and prevent too violent oppositions of interest in the same pursuit. Hence we enjoy a variety of conveniences; hence the numerous arts and sciences have been invented and improved; hence the sources of commerce and friendly intercourse between different nations have been opened; hence the circulation of truth has been quickened and promoted; hence the operations of social virtue have been multiplied and enlarged." – *Lectures on Law*; *The Works of James Wilson* vol. 3, pgs. 306-307

"...within the range of our commercial intercourse whole continents and islands, on which the light of civilization has scarce yet dawned..." At home, "ignorance, depravity, immorality and irreligion, abounding to an extent disgraceful to a civilized country... We seriously believe will do more than any other visible agent to extend civilization and morality — yes, to extinguish slavery itself." – *Liberalism at Large*, pg. 37

Thomas Wilson

"What do ye call natural affections?

"Such as be among them of one blood and kindred, as between parents and children, husbands and wives, kindred, country, heathens, yea Christians also void of these.

"(How) does it differ from human and Christian affection?

"Human affection is that whereby we embrace all men as men; natural affection is that where by we embrace them which are nearer unto us by blood; Christian affection is that whereby we love good men because they belong to Christ."
– *A Commentary on the Most Divine Epistle of St. Paul to the Romans*, pg. 54

Wilhelmus of Nassouwen

Remains our song of joy!
The God in which we placed our trust
Will not leave Holland.
The blood of our fathers
Has not turned 'French' inside us.
It runs through our veins
Where it shines Orange! ...
Keep following in your loyal fathers'
    glorious footsteps,
Orange will lead you, loyal heroes.
The French pride is mortified
While glory triumphs
Through loyalty, loyalty, loyalty!
– *Wilhelmus*, pgs. 320-321

William of Malmesbury

Lamenting a "French England":

"England is become the residence of foreigners and the property of strangers...they prey upon the riches and vitals of England; nor is there any hope of a termination of this misery."
– quoted in *National Life and Character in the Mirror of Early English Literature*, pg, 191

"For what is more agreeable than to go back over the grace accorded to our ancestors, so that the reader may learn the deeds of those who accorded him both the first principles of the faith and the motivation it provides him to live well?" – *Gesta*, pg. 3

Woodrow Wilson

"Immigrants poured in as before, but...now there came multitudes of men of lowest class from the south of Italy and men of the meanest sort out of Hungary and Poland, men out of the ranks where there was neither skill nor energy nor any initiative of quick intelligence; and they came in numbers which increased from year to year, as if the countries of the south of Europe were disburdening themselves of the more sordid and hapless elements of their population." – quoted in *Making and Remaking America*, pg. 5

Christian Winter

"...when the ancestral is good – as it generally is in America – then it is problematic when the ancestral is degraded by 'foreign customs' that uproot the individual from his religion, his people, and his place." – *Why We Remain In Flyover Country, American Reformer*, April 10, 2023

John Winthrop

"God Almighty in his most holy and wise providence, hath so disposed of the condition of mankind, as in all times some must be rich, some poor, some high and eminent in power and dignity; others mean and in submission.

"1st Reason. First to hold conformity with the rest of his world, being delighted to show forth the glory of his wisdom in the variety and difference of the creatures, and the glory of his power in ordering all these differences for the preservation and good of the whole; and the glory of his greatness. ...

"3rd Reason. Thirdly, that every man might have need of others, and from hence they might be all knit more nearly together in the Bonds of brotherly affection." – *A Model of Christian Charity, Writing New England*, pg. 4

"The intent of the [immigration] law is to preserve the 'welfare of the body' and for this end to have none received into any fellowship with it who are likely to disturb the same, and this intent (I am sure) is lawful and good." – *A Declaration In Defence Of An Order Of Court Made In May, 1637, Life and Letters of John Winthrop* pg. 184

"The churches take liberty (as lawfully they may) to receive or reject at their discretion; yea particular towns make orders to the like effect;

why then should the common weale be denied the like liberty, and the whole more restrained than any part?" – *A Declaration In Defence Of An Order Of Court Made In May, 1637, Life and Letters of John Winthrop*, pg. 183

"If strangers have right to our houses or lands etc., then it is either of justice or of mercy; if of justice let them plead it, and we shall know what to answer: but if it be only in way of mercy, or by the rule of hospitality etc., then I answer 1st a man is not a fit object of mercy except he be in misery. 2d. We are not bound to exercise mercy to others to the ruin of ourselves. 3d. There are few that stand in need of mercy at their first coming hither. As for hospitality, that rule doth not bind further than for some present occasion, not for continual residence." – *A Declaration In Defence Of An Order Of Court Made In May, 1637, Life and Letters of John Winthrop*, pg. 183

"The rule of the Apostle, John 2. 10. [2 John 1:10] is, that such as come and bring not the true doctrine with them should not be received to house, and by the same reason not into the common weale." – *A Declaration In Defence Of An Order Of Court Made In May, 1637, Life and Letters of John Winthrop*, pg. 184

"1. If we here be a corporation established by free consent, if the place of our cohabitation be our own, then no man hath right to come into us etc. without our consent.

"2. If no man hath right to our lands, our government privileges etc., but by our consent, then it is reason we should take notice of before we confer any such upon them.

"3. If we are bound to keep off whatsoever appears to tend to our ruin or damage, then we may lawfully refuse to receive such whose dispositions suit not with ours and whose society (we know) will be hurtful to us, and therefore it is lawful to take knowledge of all men before we receive them. ...

"7. A family is a little common wealth, and a common wealth is a great family. Now as a family is not bound to entertain all comers, no not every good man (otherwise than by way of hospitality) no more is a common wealth." – *A Declaration In Defence Of An Order Of Court Made In May, 1637, Life and Letters of John Winthrop*, pg. 183

Hermann Witsius

"God has made our country another Jerusalem, from where the Word of God proceeds to other nations. . . . We are God's nation, drawn close by God, and specially elected to be his property – therefore he also expects more from us than the rest." – quoted by G. Groenhuis in *De Predikanten*, pg. 77

"Here certainly appears the extraordinary love of our God, in that as soon as we are born, and just as we come from our mother, he hath commanded us to be solemnly brought from her bosom as it were into his own arms, that he should bestow upon us, in the very cradle, the tokens of our dignity and future kingdom; that he should put that song into our mouth, 'Thou didst make me hope, when I was upon my mother's breast: I was cast upon thee from the womb: thou art my God from my mother's belly,' Ps. xxii. 9, 10, that, in a word, he should join us to himself in the most solemn covenant from our most tender years: the remembrance of which, as it is glorious and full of consolation to us, so in like manner it tends to promote Christian virtues, and the strictest holiness, through the whole course of our lives. Nothing ought to be dearer to us than to keep sacred and inviolable that covenant of our youth, that first and most solemn engagement, that was made to God in our name." – *The Economy of the Divine Covenants*, pg. 414

William G. Witt

"Historically, there is a single argument that was used in the church against the ordaining of women: women could not be ordained to the ministry (whether understood as Catholic priesthood or Protestant pastorate) because of an inherent ontological defect. Because of a lack of intelligence, or a tendency to irrationality or emotional instability, a greater susceptibility to temptation, or an inherent incapacity to lead, women were held to be inferior to men, and thus were not eligible for ordination. Moreover, this argument was used to exclude women not only from clerical ministry, but from all positions of leadership over men, and largely to confine women to the domestic sphere....
The point of this somewhat lengthy summary, including numerous quotations, is to provide documentation of the claim made earlier. It

should be clear from the above that the church has indeed had a historic position against the ordination of women. From a variety of sources – eastern, western, patristic, medieval, Reformation, Catholic and Protestant – the following has been the key argument: women cannot be ordained or indeed exercise any positions of leadership in the church because of an inherent ontological incapacity. Women were characterized as less intelligent, more sinful, more susceptible to temptation, emotionally unstable, incapable of exercising leadership. In addition, it needs to be recognized that (with the exception of Aquinas) this disqualification was not merely a disqualification from clerical ordination, but from any position of leadership or of exercising authority over men, whether in or out of the church. An extreme position, perhaps, but Knox's essay shows that male theologians were willing to expand the disqualification beyond the clerical sphere to the secular. A fortiori, if women could not exercise leadership in the church, they certainly could not do so elsewhere." – *Icons of Christ: A Biblical and Systematic Theology for Women's Ordination*

Stephen Wolfe

"The particularity of people and place is a necessary good for living well, for it is the ground of robust civil fellowship. Being a necessary good, it is worthy of conservation, and civil authority ought to conserve it. It also creates conditions for true religion to flourish, serving as the ethno-cultural substructure for cultural Christianity, Christian civil law, and strong civil rulers. Thus, the Christian religion, though itself universal, flourishes in particularity. Christianity flourishes in nations. It would seem, then, that too much immigration and bad immigration policies damage the people, even striking at fundamental goods. Therefore, such policies, though not absolutely and universally unjust, can be tyrannical and can create tyrannical conditions." – *The Case For Christian Nationalism*, pg. 343

"A disordered body politic is not conducive to a well-ordered soul." – *The Case For Christian Nationalism*, pg. 201

"The instinct to love the familiar more than the foreign is good and remains operative in all spiritual states of man." – *The Case For Christian Nationalism*, pg. 118

"The stability of a community requires that the people have a common relation to the space they inhabit." – *The Case For Christian Nationalism*, pg. 124

"Nations today are not built around bloodlines stretching back to arch-patriarchs. But blood relations remain relevant to nations when referring to one's ancestral connection to a people and place back to time immemorial. The originating source for one's affection of people and place is his natural relations–those of his kin. But the ties of blood do not directly establish the boundaries of one's ethnicity. Rather, one has ethnic ties of affection because one's kin conducted life with other kind in the same place...Blood relations matter for your ethnicity, because your kin have belonged to this people on this land–to this nation and this place–and so they bind you to that people and place, creating a common voltgeist.

"We should not, however, disregard the work of intermarriage over time in creating bonds of affection, as Aristotle argues. Out of marriage form various brotherhoods and tribes and shared or public pastimes. 'This sort of thing.' writes Artistotle, 'the work of affection,' making possible the highest civic virtues. The same people living in the same place for many generations can see each other as cousins of a sort, since all are connected by a core ancestry.

"My intent is here is not to discount or dismiss the importance of blood ties in ethno-genesis–a dismissal that is fashionable, politically correct, and could save me some trouble. It simply is the case that a 'community of blood' is crucial to ethnicity. But this should not lead us to conclude that blood ties are the sole determinate of ethnicity." – *The Case For Christian Nationalism*, pg. 142

"The human instinct to socialize and dwell with similar people is universal, though for many today, especially Westerners, this instinct is understood as evil or pathological. Of course, such people typically denounce this 'evil' when found among Westerners, while celebrating the ethno-centrism of others. But this instinct in itself is good actually, even universally good. Your instinct to conduct everyday life among similar people is natural and, being natural, it is for your good…Hence, the preference for those who are similar s natural and arises not necessarily from maliciousness toward those who are dissimilar. Similarity enables you to exercise the highest love to fellow man and to receive love in return." – *The Case For Christian Nationalism*, pg. 142

"People of different ethnic groups can exercise respect for difference, conduct some routine business with each other, join in inter-ethnic alliances for mutual good, and exercise humanity (e.g., the good Samaritan), but they cannot have a life together that goes beyond mutual alliance." – *The Case For Christian Nationalism*, pg. 148

— STEPHEN WOLFE —

"…a community of similar people provides the best social conditions for the communication of gifts and achieving collective goals. Dissimilar people together can achieve the basic goods of humanity, but not the complete good. Similarity is a necessary prerequisite to well-functioning symbiosis in and by which a people come to live well. The common good is a bounded common good, and the whole is best served by individuals preferring the common good to which they are bound. One ought to give his people priority in his heart and action." – *The Case For Christian Nationalism*, pgs. 150-151

"…ethnicity is largely a product of sharing particulars–the sharing of customs, pastimes, and traditions; and the union of someone in

relation to his fellow countrymen is based on those particulars." – *The Case For Christian Nationalism*, pg. 156

"By nature we have an instinct to prefer some over others and we are rarely conscious of it. This instinct is not arbitrary, nor is it a product of the fall, nor is it a holdover from millions of years of evolution; rather, it is fundamental to our natural constitution, drawing us to form and sustain the necessary social organization in which man can achieve his complet good, according to nature." – *The Case For Christian Nationalism*, pg. 161

"The nation is not a people united around propositions alone; no nation can be so disembodied and dis-embedded from concrete things…The people and place are one, for the adorned meaning of space depends on the people, and the people, taken as a whole, are the place. This people-place symbiosis is held together by ties of affection, based fundamentally on natural affection toward kin. One loves a particular people in a particular place because his family did so too, and through his connection with his family did so too, and through his connection with his family and their activity with others, he has a home-land and a people." – *The Case For Christian Nationalism*, pg. 162

"…the nation, properly understood, is a particular people with ties of affection that bind them to each other and place of dwelling; and thus nationalism is the nation acting for their national good, which includes conservation of those ties of affection." – *The Case For Christian Nationalism*, pg. 165

"Western man is enamoured with his ideology of universality; it is the chief and only ground of his self-regard. His in-group is all people–it is a universal in-group. Everyone is an object of his beneficence. But in perverse fashion he is his ow in-group's out-group. The object of his regard is the non-Westerner at the Westerner's expense–a bizarre self-denigration rooted in guilt and malaise. Loss and humiliation is the point…

"Ultimately, the modern Westerner resides in another's land. This is true not because he stole it centuries earlier, but because he keeps and maintains it for the taking of outsiders, whom he invites and who ultimately dispossess him." – *The Case For Christian Nationalism*, pgs. 168-169

"The in-group/out-group distinction, which prioritizes concern for one's own people and native soil, troubles many in the West, at least when Western ethnic-groups begin to distinguish themselves in this way. Christians will ask, aren't we called to love all equally?, assuming the affirmative answer is obvious. But despite modern Christian sentiment, a quick glance at the Christian tradition (and mile reflection of one's own relationships) reveals the almost ubiquity of the opposite view--that the intensity of love varies by degree according to similarity and the extent that another is bound to you." – *The Case For Christian Nationalism*, pg. 149

"...the foreigner has a duty not to disrupt the host people's way of life, and the hosts have every right to hold such people to these duties, even to the point of deportation." – *The Case For Christian Nationalism*, p.168

Thomas Wolfe

"I had found out during all these years of wandering that the way to discover one's own country was to leave it; that the way to find America was to find it in one's heart, one's mind, one's memory, and one's spirit, and in a foreign land. So it had been with me. Around me day by day in all these months and years and voyages to Europe I had seen the million forms and shapes and patterns of an alien life. My life had been enriched and quickened immeasurably by contemplating and experiencing them, and always when I saw them I had the profit of a vast, fertile, inestimable comparison. All of my powers of memory and experience were constantly brought to bear as I compared the life of which I was a part, the country from which I came, with this new and alien life in which I lived and wandered as a stranger.

"I think I may say that I discovered America during these years abroad out of my very need for her. I found her because I had left her. The huge gain of this discovery seemed to come directly from my sense of loss. I had been to Europe five times now; each time I had come with longing, delight, with maddening eagerness to

return, and each time how, where, and in what way I did not know, I had felt the bitter ache of homelessness, a desperate need and longing for America, an overwhelming desire to return.

"Now during that summer in Paris, I think I felt this great homesickness more than ever before, and I really believe that from this emotion, this constant and almost intolerable effort of memory and desire, this thing that would not let me rest, this memory of home that could not be appeased, that would not stop or vanish even when I slept—from this huge and hopeless memory of home, I say, I think the material and the structure of the books I now began to write were derived." – *The Autobiography of an American Novelist*, pgs. 28-29

Colin Woodard

"As Americans sort themselves into like-minded communities, they're also sorting themselves into like-minded nations." – *American Nations*, pg. 17

"The event we call the American Revolution wasn't really revolutionary, at least while it was underway. The military struggle of 1775-1782 wasn't fought by an 'American people' seeking to create a united, continent-spanning republic where all men were created equal and guaranteed freedom of speech, religion, and the press. On the contrary, it was a profoundly conservative action fought by a loose military alliance of nations, each of which was most concerned with preserving or reasserting control of its respective culture, character, and power structure. The rebelling nations certainly didn't wish to be bonded together into a single republic. They were joined in a temporary partnership against a common threat: the British establishment's ham-fisted attempt to assimilate them into a homogeneous empire centrally controlled from London. Some nations—the Midlands, New Netherland, and New France—didn't rebel at all. Those that did weren't fighting a revolution; they were fighting separate wars of colonial liberation." – *American Nations*, pg. 115

"Political scientists investigating voting patterns have probed electoral records dating back to the early nineteenth century, matching polling place returns with demographic information about each precinct. The results have been startling. Previous assumptions about class or occupation being the key factors influencing voter choices have turned out to be completely wrong, with the nineteenth-century Midwest providing some of the most intriguing evidence that ethnographic origins trumped all other considerations from 1850 onward. Poor white German Catholic miners in northern Wisconsin tended to vote entirely differently from poor white English Methodist miners in the same area. English Congregationalists tended to vote alike regardless of whether they lived in cities or on farms. Scandinavian immigrants voted with native-born Yankees in opposition to candidates and policies preferred by immigrant Irish Catholics or native-born Southern Baptists of Appalachian origin." – *American Nations*, pg. 179

"The Germans [of the 1800s American Mid-West] set the tone, generally buying land with the intent to build lasting family homesteads rather than as speculative investments. They sought a permanent, organic connection to their land, taking unusual care to ensure its long-term productivity through soil and forest conservation measures first perfected on the tiny farm plots of central Europe. Whether arriving from Europe or Pennsylvania, they built their homes from stone whenever possible, as it was more durable than the wood used by the Yankees or Appalachian people...

"The Germans avoided assimilating, using their language in schools and newspapers and almost exclusively marrying other Germans as late as the 1880s. In a country rushing madly toward the frontier, the Germans distinguished themselves by their emphasis on stable, permanent, rooted communities, where families would work the same piece of land for generations. This rootedness would be perhaps their most lasting contribution to the culture of the Midlands and, by extension, the American Midwest." – *American Nations*, pg. 186

William Wordsworth

"Nature then
(The coarser pleasures of my boyish days
And their glad animal movements all gone by)
To me was all in all.—I cannot paint
What then I was. The sounding cataract
Haunted me like a passion: the tall rock,
The mountain, and the deep and gloomy wood,
Their colours and their forms, were then to me
An appetite; a feeling and a love,
That had no need of a remoter charm,
By thought supplied, nor any interest
Unborrowed from the eye."
– *Tintern Abbey* (lines 74-85)

"And I have felt
A presence that disturbs me with the joy
Of elevated thoughts; a sense sublime
Of something far more deeply interfused,
Whose dwelling is the light of setting suns,
And the round ocean and the living air,
And the blue sky, and in the mind of man:
A motion and a spirit, that impels
All thinking things, all objects of all thought,
And rolls through all things."
– *Tintern Abbey* (lines 93-102)

"I wandered lonely as a cloud
That floats on high o'er vales and hills,
When all at once I saw a crowd,
A host, of golden daffodils;
Beside the lake, beneath the trees,
Fluttering and dancing in the breeze."
– *I Wandered Lonely as a Cloud* also known as *Daffodils* (lines 1-6)

"For oft, when on my couch I lie
In vacant or in pensive mood,
They flash upon that inward eye
Which is the bliss of solitude;
And then my heart with pleasure fills,
And dances with the daffodils."
– *I Wandered Lonely as a Cloud* also known as *Daffodils* (lines 19-24)

Pyotr Wrangel

"History, which knows no favoritism, will tell the importance of our struggle, the capacity of our sacrifices. It will know that the fight we carried on for the love of our country, for the resurrection of Russia as a nation, was indeed at the same time to safeguard the culture of

Europe, the struggle for an age-long civilization, for the defence of Europe against the Red terror." – *Always With Honor: The Memoirs of General Wrangel*

"The next morning my aide-de-camp came and told me that the Soldiers' Committee of my 3rd Cossack division was sitting, presided over by a demagogue priest (a Bolshevik / communist sympathizer) whom I had tried to get removed many times.

"I went down, and found General Odintzov, the commander of the division, there too. As I entered I saluted the men, as I always do: 'Good morning, Cossacks.'

"The Cossacks answered me as usual. Then the priest-president said: 'Will you please note, General, that the members here assembled are not Cossacks, as you call them, but citizens.'

"'You are quite right, Father; we are all citizens. But that does not prevent my being a General, your being a priest, and their being brave Cossacks. That they are brave I know very well, because I have seen them in battle more than once. That they are Cossacks I also know, for I myself have worn their uniform for years, and am proud of it.'

"And turning to the assembly, 'Once more, good morning, Cossacks.'

"'Greetings, Your Excellency,' they shouted as one man." – *Always With Honor: The Memoirs of General Wrangel*

Christopher J. H. Wright

"That the land should be held in the form of patrimonies which should not pass out of the family was a cherished ideal in Israel that was protected by legislation and theologically justified and sanctioned." – *God's People In God's Land*, pgs. 55-56

"What was ruled out here was the kind of inter-marrying that involved the social bonding of families and joint religious rituals." – Deut. 7:3, *Deuteronomy (Understanding the Bible Commentary Series)*, pg. 170

G. Ernest Wright

"Bêt-ʾāb ('Father's House'). This was the third level of the kinship structure of Israel, and the one in which the individual Israelite felt the strongest sense of inclusion, identity, protection, and responsibility. The 'father's house' was an extended family, comprising all the descendants of a single living ancestor (the head, rō̌ʾš-bêt-ʾāb) in a single lineage...Many studies have shown that it was within the smaller kinship units, especially the bêt-ʾāb and the mišpāḥâ, that the individual found his or her identity as a member of the covenant people of Israel, and learned his or her obligations to the society and the God of Israel." – *Anchor Yale Bible Dictionary*, vol. 2, pgs. 762-763

Walter Wriston

"When a system of national economies linked by government-regulated trade is replaced... by an increasingly integrated global economy beyond the reach of national regulation, power changes hands." – *Twilight of Sovereignty*, pg. 4

Wilbur Wright

"If I were giving a young man advice as to how he might succeed in life, I would say to him, pick out a good father and mother, and begin life in Ohio." – quoted in David McCulloch's *The Wright Brothers*, pg. 1

John Wycliffe

"The English nation . . . ought to be one body, the clergy and the commonality being alike members thereof. . . . [O]ur kingdom may justly detain its treasure for the defense of itself, in every case where necessity shall appear to require it." – *The Life and Opinions of John Wycliffe*, pg. 344

Martin Wyngaarden

"More than a dozen excellent commentaries (on Isaiah 44:5) could be mentioned that all interpret Israel as thus inclusive of Jew and Gentile, in this verse, — the Gentile adherents thus being merged with the covenant people of Israel, though each nationality remains distinct.

"This abiding distinction of the nationalities is also clearly implied by Isaiah. For, though Israel is frequently called Jehovah's People, the work of his hands, his inheritance, yet these three epithets severally are applied not only to Israel, but also to Assyria and to Egypt: 'Blessed be Egypt, my people, and Assyria, the work of my hands, and Israel, mine inheritance.' More than a dozen excellent commentaries could be mentioned that all interpret Israel as thus inclusive of Jew and Gentile, in this verse... Thus the highest description of Jehovah's covenant people is applied to Egypt, — 'my people' — showing that the Gentiles will share the covenant blessings, not less than Israel. Yet the several nationalities are here kept distinct, even when Gentiles share, in the covenant blessing, on a level of equality with Israel. Egypt, Assyria, and Israel are not nationally merged. And the same principles, that nationalities are not obliterated, by membership in the covenant, applies, of course, also in the New Testament dispensation." – *The Future of the Kingdom in Prophecy and Fulfillment*, pgs. 101-102

Stefan Wyszyński

"Do not look to the wider world. We should not wish to feed the world, we should not wish to save all mankind. We should wish to help our brothers, to feed Polish children, to serve them here and to do our duty rather than succumb to the temptation to 'save the world' at the cost of our own fatherland." – *Patriotism, Poland, and Cardinal Sarah, Catholic World Report*

"The bond with the homeland is a mystery that we can define as a law of nature, the most fundamental and most sacred of all laws." – *Patriotism*, pgs. 78-79

"There is a specific, biological community and bond between the family and the nation and their mutual service to each other. The family is ... not only a creative and biological force but also a moral, educational, social, and civic force....Experience teaches us that the lack of this bond causes the perversion of either the family or the nation." – *Patriotism*, pg. 100

"It is a great wisdom to learn from past experiences ... However, it requires vigilance, great sensitivity to the matters and spirit of the Nation, great reverence for the land that accumulates the ashes of ancestors, full readiness to serve...in the spirit of Christian love for the homeland." – *Patriotism*, pg. 80

"This is an indication for us – to persevere, live

for the homeland, gain confidence in it and the readiness to give it everything of ourselves. It is the most important duty to the homeland. We need a powerful will to organize our native forces, not to look left and right, and not to succumb to the temptation of the new Targowica, wherever it might come from. We are at home, in our homeland, we host the enormous goods that the nation has; we trust them, we want them to pay off in our land." – *Patriotism*, pgs. 110-111

"True love for the homeland is based on deep attachment and love for what is native, regardless of time and space. ... The creative force of true patriotism is, therefore, the noblest love. ... And although man sets pure values very high, he knows that God is above nations, who alone has the right to establish the highest moral norms regardless of individual countries. ... Hence, Christian love for the homeland is not the only concern for its highest economic, social, and cultural development, but also its spiritual and religious growth." – *Patriotism*, pg. 109

"A nation properly brought up and educating the young generation knows that without love it will not prepare the young generation to fulfill future tasks. Love for the homeland as an educational value teaches generosity and gives the spirit for difficult times to forget about yourself. As an educational value, love for the homeland also teaches generosity and gives spiritual strength for difficult times when you have to forget about yourself. Love for the homeland teaches us to look far into the future of the homeland and wishes for its existence and prosperity – not only today but also in the future." – *Patriotism*, pg. 108

X

Xenophanes of Colophon

"...Ethiopians are black and snub-nosed, those of the Thracians have blue eyes and red hair." – Fragments, 16. Quoted in *Greek Philosophy* by John Burnet, pg. 35

Xenophon

A woman tries to paint and dress herself up to attract her husband:

"Thereupon Ischomachus took up his parable. 'Well, one day, Socrates, I noticed that her face was made up: she had rubbed in white lead in order to look even whiter than she is, and alkanet juice to heighten the rosy colour of her cheeks; and she was wearing boots with thick soles to increase her height.'" – *Memorabilia and Oeconomicus*, pg. 447

"Nations naturally have a king of their own people: The Scythian king, for instance, would never be able to extend his rule over any other nation besides his own, although the Scythians are very numerous, but he would be well content if he could maintain himself in power over his own people; so the Thracian king with his Thracians, the Illyrian with his Illyrians, and so also all other nations, we are told. Those in Europe, at any rate, are said to be free and independent of one another even to this day." – *Cyropedia*, pg. 11

Y

William Butler Yeats

"I will arise and go now, and go to Innisfree,
And a small cabin build there,
  of clay and wattles made;
Nine bean-rows will I have there,
  a hive for the honey-bee,
And live alone in the bee-loud glade."
– *The Lake Isle of Innisfree* (lines 1-4)

"All changed, changed utterly:
A terrible beauty is born."
– *Easter, 1916* (lines 15-16)

"Turning and turning in the widening gyre
The falcon cannot hear the falconer;
Things fall apart; the centre cannot hold;
Mere anarchy is loosed upon the world,"
– *The Second Coming* (lines 1-4)

"For the good are always the merry,
Save by an evil chance,
And the merry love the fiddle,
And the merry love to dance."
– *The Celtic Twilight* (lines 1-4)

Know, that I would accounted be
True brother of a company
That sang, to sweeten Ireland's wrong,
Ballad and story, rann and song;
Nor be I any less of them,
Because the red-rose-bordered hem
Of her, whose history began
Before God made the angelic clan,
Trails all about the written page.
When Time began to rant and rage
The measure of her flying feet
Made Ireland's heart begin to beat;
And Time bade all his candles flare
To light a measure here and there;
And may the thoughts of Ireland brood
Upon a measured quietude.

Nor may I less be counted one
With Davis, Mangan, Ferguson,
Because, to him who ponders well,
My rhymes more than their rhyming tell
Of things discovered in the deep,
Where only body's laid asleep.
For the elemental creatures go
About my table to and fro,
That hurry from unmeasured mind
To rant and rage in flood and wind;
Yet he who treads in measured ways
May surely barter gaze for gaze.
Man ever journeys on with them
After the red-rose-bordered hem.
Ah, faeries, dancing under the moon,
A Druid land, a Druid tune!
While still I may, I write for you
The love I lived, the dream I knew.
From our birthday, until we die,
Is but the winking of an eye;
And we, our singing and our love,
What measurer Time has lit above,
And all benighted things that go
About my table to and fro,
Are passing on to where may be,
In truth's consuming ecstasy,
No place for love and dream at all;
For God goes by with white footfall.
I cast my heart into my rhymes,
That you, in the dim coming times,
May know how my heart went with them
After the red-rose-bordered hem.
– *To Ireland in the Coming Times*

Sergei Yesenin

In the white fields of the homeland
In the world I will remember
How the graceful, lone birch tree
Stands among the quiet marsh.
  – *The Birch Tree* (st. 1, lines 1-4) [91]

---

91 Yesenin was a Russian lyric poet known for his deep connection to the traditions of the Russian people.

I love you, slender beauty,
I love your leaves' soft sound,
I love your silver branches,
Your trunk so black and round.
– *The Birch Tree* (st. 3, lines 1-4)

I'm not sad, I'm not complaining,
In my life I've known no fears.
I've been taught the art of living
By the peasants' humble tears.
– *To the Stars* (st. 2, lines 1-4)

In this life of storm and chaos
I've found peace and quietude,
And the joys of country labor
I have learned to love and brood.
– *To the Stars* (st. 4, lines 1-4)

Lee Kuan Yew

"In multiracial societies, you don't vote in accordance with your economic interests and social interests, you vote in accordance with race and religion." – Interview with *Der Spiegel*, August 14th, 2005

E.J. Young

"In our desire to make all men welcome in the church there is one fact that must not be overlooked. Men are not equal. There is danger of embracing the modern political doctrine of egalitarianism, a doctrine which is thoroughly unscriptural. Whether we like it or not, it is a fact that men do associate with their own kind of people. Surely we should welcome and embrace in Christian love all of God's people, whatever their race or nationality, who wish to worship in our churches. But they on their part must want to worship with us and they too must want to associate with us. The past history of our Glenside Church shows what a blessed thing it can be when Negro and White Christians wish to worship voluntarily together.

"Unless, however, there is true love and desire for fellowship on the part of both we shall have a forced relationship. Hence, I question very much the wisdom of any attempts to 'integrate' the church. Making our Negro brethren in Christ welcome when they voluntarily come to worship with us is one thing; seeking to attempt integration for the sake of a witness may do more harm than good.

"... Lastly, I am troubled by the great amount of space devoted to the question of civil rights and race relations in the latest issue of the *Guardian*. These are not the paramount issues before the church today. In the dense fog of obfuscation which the liberal press has succeeded in raising even true Christians may lose sight of the church's central purpose. That central purpose is the preaching of the everlasting gospel of Jesus Christ. Scripture makes clear that a Christian should do good unto all men, especially to those who are of the household of faith. He who preaches the gospel in its fulness (including the obligations of Christians to others) is doing more for Negro and White than can possibly be accomplished by any method which in giving rights to one may take them away from another." – *The Presbyterian Guardian*, pgs. 129-130

Z

Carl Zimmermann

"In our culture the parental unit has no real backing or workable public support in law. Parents must now try to rear a family under a social and legal system adjusted to those couples who do not want the paraphenalia of familism – common income, expenses, children, union for perpetuity, or serious familistic obligations. In our modern Western society the forgotten person is the man or woman who honestly and sincerely wants to be a parent. This affects our whole social system; it affects all the practicalities of life, from renting a house to economic advancement under different forms of bureaucracy. If there are children, renting a house is difficult, changing jobs is difficult, social activities are difficult. In the words of Bacon, to have children is to give hostages to fortune, and one is no longer a free bargaining agent...Under any assumptions, the implications will be far-reaching for the future not only of the family but of our civilization as well. The question is no longer a moral one; it is social. It is no longer familistic; it is cultural. The very continuation of our culture seems to be inextricably associated with this nihilism in family behavior." – *Family and Civilization*, pg. 272

"...children are the fundamental basis of familism. A decay in familism is a decay in the social system of biological reproduction. Consequently those societies in which familism has decayed are those that are themselves decaying—and very rapidly." – *Family and Civilization*, pg. 198

"In one sense there are no such things as separate Greek, Roman, and Western civilizations; there are merely the Greek, Roman, and modern versions of the same Western, or European, civilization which in the past few centuries has spread from the old to the new worlds. From the beginning and until the end of the ancient world, the Greek and Roman civilizations were fundamentally of the same people. In the Greek world, the Romans constituted the invading barbarians. The north European peoples were the invading barbarians in the Graeco-Roman world. We are, therefore, a combined civilization...

"The Greek world was encompassed by the Roman, the Roman by the north European barbarian. These groups successively took up the challenge of European society. Plato, Aristotle, and Homer are as much a part of our inheritance and culture as they were of the Roman. From the beginning through all of Western history, the influence of these Graeco-Roman ideas has been carried over from one 'bulge' of civilization to the next...

"Modern Western civilization is based immediately on Roman and Greek society, transmitted through the agency of Christianity...When a modern European or American reads the Greek and Roman writers – from Homer through Procopius – he sees his own forefathers in the picture at all times." – *Family and Civilization*, pgs. 56-58

Walter D. Zorn

"The RSV translates Heb. noḵrî 'foreign' eleven times in connection with women. INTERMARRIAGE with foreigners was forbidden due to the negative spiritual influences that would result (Dt. 7:1–5). As mentioned above, Solomon succumbed to the worship of foreign gods through seeking to please his foreign wives (1 K. 11:1–8). Ezra was very distressed about Israel's unfaithfulness in marrying foreign women during the Exile (Ezr. 9:2f, 10-15). In order to turn aside God's anger (10:14) the whole assembly made a covenant with Him to send away all their foreign wives (ch. 10). Nehemiah also condemned foreign marriages, insisting that they

were treachery against God (Neh. 13:23–27)."
– "Foreign" in *The International Standard Bible Encyclopedia*, vol. 4, pg. 635

Zuo Zhuan

"If he be not of our kind, he is sure to have a different mind." – *The Chinese Classics*, trans. James Legge, 5: 3 54-55 (bk. 8, yr. 5)

Ehud Ben Zvi

"The world that is imagined in vv. 3b–4a to represent divine rulership is characterized in relation to polities and individuals. Thus the nations will live in eternal peace; war will be forgotten. YHWH as a just ruler and judge (cf. Ps 99:4, among many others) will fulfill one of the sovereign's main responsibilities, namely, to bring peace, tranquillity, or rest to the kingdom (cf. 1 Kgs 5:5; Isa 9:6 [NRSV 7]; 11:1–9; Jer 23:5–6; 33:15–16; see also Isa 16:5; 32:16–18). The motif of peace among the nations is then interwoven with a snapshot of the life of a person at that time (see 1 Kgs 5:5; cf. Zech 3:10). The text brings an agrarian image of security and stability: people will be able to sit and enjoy the produce of their vines and fig trees without anyone making them afraid. The reference to vines and fig trees, as opposed to grain crops, for instance, points to long-term stability and peace. It conveys also a sense of prosperity (cf. 1 Kgs 5:5 and notice its context). Additionally, it implies an image of 'a person' ('îš) as one who 'owns' a vine and a fig tree (2:2; see 1 Kgs 5:5; cf. also Zech 3:10). The image of lack of fear is reinforced by the conclusion of v. 4a: 'ên maḥărîd ('no one shall make them afraid'; cf. Jer 30:10; 46:27; Ezek 34:28; Zeph 3:13)." – *The Forms Of Old Testament Literature*, Micah, vol. 21B, pg. 99

Ulrich Zwingli

"What was the need of accusing me, a Swiss professing Christ among the Swiss, of raising this disturbance, since you say that it is taking place only in Germany, and the Swiss are not reckoned among the Germans? Yet, meanwhile, though I have been watching almost a whole month, I have been unable to discover that you have sent a like admonition to anybody anywhere in Germany. Why do ye not apply your remedy to the diseased part? Know ye not that Christ said: 'They that are whole need not a physician, but they that are sick'? (Luke 5:31) It becomes apparent, therefore, that it is I to whom ye are singing your little song; for I fancy you have more sense than to be applying a remedy to a limb that you do not consider diseased." – *The Latin Works and the Correspondence of Ulrich Zwingli*, pg. 217

SOCIOLOGY

This section will seem to some out of place in this anthology. Its material is not ancient wisdom from the venerated past but the latest scientific and sociological findings upon a given range of topics. Why should science be included with ancient wit? Let this brief essay serve as an apologia for the inclusion of the material that follows.

> "So it is that gods do not give all men the gifts of grace...neither good looks nor intelligence nor eloquence." – Homer, *The Odyssey*

> "There's many a man has more hair than wit." – Shakespeare, *Comedy of Errors*, act 2, scene 3

Our forebearers recognized a biological diversity among humans, both individually and across populations. Not all men are "given" the same intelligence, said Homer as well as Shakespeare. Some men are not like others, in intelligence, ability, or character. Often this truth is given passing acknowledgement in some piece of literature and then the story, scene, or characters move on. In the modern period, however, the reality of human inequalities has become its own topic for study. A large and growing field of scientific research now exists which records, in painstaking detail, human biological diversity. However, many people are accidentally or purposefully ignorant of this data. Others are hostile to it. Azar Gat, in *Nations: The Long History And Deep Roots Of Political Ethnicity And Nationalism*, observed:

> "There are various reasons for this neglect, rejection, and even down-right hostility. Early, crude attempts to extend the Darwinian revolution to the understanding of human behavior and society, carried out in the late nineteenth and early twentieth centuries and known as social Darwinism, leaned toward racism and class bias. In reaction, the social sciences and humanities completely moved away from anything that suggested a biological basis for human behavior.

> "Massively reinforced after the horrors of Nazism and with the dismantling of public racism in the West, this tendency reached its apogee in the 1960s and 1970s."

The tendency here of which Gat speaks is to downplay genetic studies and the relation of genetics to society. Gat continues:

> "Thus, scholars from the above fields have found themselves totally unprepared as revolutionary breakthroughs in the decipherment of the genome coupled with a great revival of evolutionary theory generated one of the most significant scientific developments of the era. Nothing in their professional training enabled them to relate to the new perspective and insights."

In brief, in the late 1800s and early 1900s, there were forays into genetic studies made by then-leading experts such as Madison Grant, Lothrop Stoddard, and others, who attempted to write racial histories or natural histories of mankind. But in the middle-1900s people began to reject these ideas in favor of a deracinated, egalitarian, liberal anthropology. This anthropology became dominant while the racialist science waned, and for over 80 years now we have been repeatedly told that "Race is only skin deep," or that "There is only one race – the human race," and that anyone who thinks race is real or meaningful is a "racist" or probably a supremacist. We have been instructed that, since race isn't real, there are therefore no "white" people either. Furthermore, Jews, Africans, Mexicans, Asians, Europeans – anyone can be an "American." Even now, Europeans are being told anyone – an African, say – can be "German" or "Irish" as well. Also, science supposedly tells us, anyone can be brought to behave and think similarly if given equal educational, cultural, and economic opportunities. "Diversity is our strength," we are told by the leading experts of the day. As such, racial and genetic sciences since the middle 1900s have largely been ignored in favor of these sorts of liberal-egalitarian platitudes.

However, science in these particular fields (genetics, biodiversity) did not stop progressing because we have chosen, around 1940 or so, no longer to listen to them or not to look at their findings. As such, the actual data on human biological diversity, on racial realities, on genetic inheritance is approximately 80 years ahead of public opinion – the opinions of the school textbook, the slogans of media talking heads, the policies of learned leaders presiding over your local business, church, or government. Rather than proving the early thinkers wrong, genetic science has shown them to be closer to the reality of things than our mythical beliefs on these topics. As Gat said above, "Nothing in their professional training enabled them to relate to the new perspective and insights."

People, ignorant of reality, are repeating mid-20th century myths, tales, or outright lies about genetics and their relation to human social behavior, which have been disproven now for decades. For instance, one pastor recently wrote a series of articles defending "Christian Race Realism." He used both scripture and data that reflects the reality of human racial makeup in order to support his point. Another pastor responded to this. One of this dissenting pastor's main points in his response was that, which you've probably heard, race is not real or meaningful because we have more genetically in common with members of other "races" than with members of our own supposed "race." Put differently, the claim is that there is more genetic variation within a given "race" than between two "races." So, a white person and a black person, so goes this rebuttal, have more genes in common than two white people. Thus, race is genetically fictitious.

Now, this pastor offered this idea with some sincerity. However, this idea has for the last two decades been considered by all in this field of science a fallacy. It even has been given its own title and its own Wikipedia entry. The reader may lookup "Lewontin's Fallacy" for verification. I repeat that this idea has been disproven for over 20 years as of 2024. And yet, this learned pastor – a man with more than two dozen published works under him, who preaches and teaches

weekly to countless thousands, and who oversees a distinguished college and graduate program – marshaled this renowned fallacy which can be found to have been long disproven via conducting a simple internet search. This illustrates Gat's point that the leading intellectuals of our day have no idea of the state of things. They are living in the mid-1900s, scientifically. (Lewontin's original thesis dates from the 1970s, the high-water mark, according to Gat, of the attempt to "dismantle public racism." Thus, those who repeat Lewontin's Fallacy reveal that their knowledge on the topic of race has not been updated for over 50 years.) Now, this pastor ignorantly repeated this disproven bit of science, ironically, in order to argue that those who believe in "race realism" hold to outdated, disproven science!

So, let's say that the reader peruses all of the ancient wisdom found in this book, from Homer to Augustine, Calvin to Dabney, Washington to Scruton. The discerning reader may then conclude, "Well, these all, too, were part of an unscientific, racist past. They have not lived in the modern era of advanced science and enlightenment, as have I, and cannot understand that we are better informed today on the nature of humanity, ancestry, belonging, and peoplehood. They couldn't know what we do – that race isn't real, that people between 'races' have more in common than people within them, that 'diversity is our strength.'" The lengthy selection of scientific data that follows this essay was included for those people or for answering them. Facts corresponding to reality can be ignored only at one's peril or at the peril of society.

Gat continues to explain these genetic science-deniers:

"For in their reaction against social Darwinism, the social sciences and humanities veered too sharply in the opposite direction. With a few exceptions, they rejected the idea that anything like human nature existed or was meaningful to the understanding of society. Instead, they adopted the view that people and human societies were wholly determined by culture and history."

This is whence come books such as "Guns, Germs, And Steel" and many others which attempt to explain Western development completely apart from human biological realities.

If the reader is at leisure to investigate for himself, he will find that nearly every Middle Ages textbook or Western Civ textbook in schools or universities today strenuously argue that the West's development had to do with oppression, bigotry, exclusion, authoritarianism, supremacy, exploitation – anything but nature. Christians, likewise, argue that the West's rise is due to its religion which raised Europeans from savage brutes to civilized citizens. Consider Tom Woods' thesis in his book "How The Catholic Church Built Western Civilization" or Rodney Stark's "How The West Won". Nevermind that Europeans had built a civilization (Rome) prior to Christianity, or that many other civilizations existed apart from Christianity (Chinese, Persian, Egyptian Aztec, etc.) And so, a host of theories have arisen as to why Europeans became so powerful, advanced, or aesthetic. It was because of guns, germs, steel, the taming of horses, navigable waterways, ocean-going ships; it was because of the phalanx or the longbow, monotheism, Christianity, free market competition; the "curse of Ham" or the "blessing of Japheth"; some even claim it was because we plundered other, more advanced cultures through colonialism and imperialism – any reason is offered among these tired speculations except human nature and biology. That is one factor that cannot have any relevance at all.

Whatever the reason for the consistent rise or decline of one people in human history, Westerners today have been trained to detest that it has something to do with those people's nature on a material level, since "human nature" is constrictive, limiting, determinative, oppressive. We must transcend our own biology. This idea taken to its end is transhumanism, the nearest corollary of which is transgenderism – the notion that a woman is not a woman due to biology or nature, since nature has nothing whatsoever to do with one's actions, thoughts, beliefs, habits, social or relational roles. These, rather, are solely due to abstract choice. Nature will be altered to fit the ideas of the individual. Transhumanism is the mere idea that biology and nature do not determine in any way at all what we make of ourselves. There is no Jew or Greek (no races), no slave or free (no social order), no male or female (no gender), for we have transcended nature and nature's God and have set ourselves free.

Gat's last comment is salient:

"This, however, was just another false either/ or dichotomy. It meant turning a blind eye to a whole side of reality, for it is both nature and nurture, indeed, precisely the interaction between them that has always shaped people and human societies. Genes are not everything, of course, but they are hardly irrelevant, or disconnected from culture." – Azar Gat, *Nations: The Long History And Deep Roots Of Political Ethnicity And Nationalism*, pg. 28

Likewise, J. Philippe Rushton remarks:

"Deconstructing the concept of race not only goes against the tendency of virtually every known culture to classify and build family histories according to some measure of common descent, it also ignores the work of biologists studying non-human species...

"Regardless of the extent to which the media promote 'politically correct,' but scientifically wrong, resolutions from professional societies such as the American Anthropological Association, facts remain facts and require appropriate scientific, not political or ideological, explanation. None of this should be construed as meaning that environmental factors play no part in individual and group differences. But with each passing year and each new study, the evidence for the genetic contribution to these differences becomes more firmly established than ever." – J. Philippe Rushton, *Mankind Quarterly*, Winter 1998, vol. 39, iss. 2, pg. 231

The future of natural social relations and of political life will be influenced, in part, by the scientific study of genetics, race, and human biodiversity. Those who neglect these fields of research divest themselves of great tools at their disposal and severely impoverish their accumulated wisdom, their ability to reason toward sound decisions, and the efficacy of their actions. Truth is that which corresponds to reality. Nature does not conflict with true ideas or systems of ideas (i.e., ideologies, religions, philosophies). Those who remain ignorant on this topic make themselves irrelevant to the future and to the influence of the masses.

A curious but prescient voice confirming this observation comes from the mysterious persona of Constin Alamariu, whose doctoral thesis illuminates the growing interest in these ideas among the youth of today. It is worth quoting and interacting with at length:

What the Youth Have Found

"(Today's right-leaning youth), who seem to be racially and culturally diverse, and relatively well-educated, have done what youth always love to do, which is to shock and epater la bourgeoisie. And the establishment "bourgeois" culture and education of our time is "liberal," or rather, anti-racist, feminist, anti-nationalist. These young people have loved nothing more than to offend journalists and pundits, who are the most vocal gatekeepers of this establishment "bourgeois" morality of our time."

Not a few perceptive minds have noted that those of us who align ourselves with nature, truth, and order are in rebellion against today's anti-naturalist, "anti-racist", "anti-nationalist" classes. Thus, we have the double joy of rebellion against authority combined with the strength of nature. Cutting with the grain, so to speak. The youth have always been given to a little rebellion. So much the better if that rebellion, today, is not against the church or morality but against degeneracy, ugliness, weakness, and death.

"To be sure, the provocations here in question haven't been driven only by a spirit of contrarianism. Young people, and certain kinds of young people, are excited and seduced by all "forbidden knowledge," and have a positive and keen interest in this forbidden knowledge."

If Christians don't talk about sex or don't allow dancing, the kids will rebel and go find out and engage in these forbidden Dionysian rituals outside of the church's matriarchal halls. If the dominant social order doesn't allow public recognition of male virility, female beauty, natural distinction, peoplehood, or national belonging, then the rebellious youth will seek them – pushed along by Nature – elsewhere.

"Through its demonization not only of "Nazism," but actually of frank discussions about human nature, about group differenc-

es, about the role heritability and genetics play in human behavior and societies, the elite of our time have made such knowledge and such ideas irresistible to the young."

If the thought-leaders in your locale tell people not to look into the chest of forbidden knowledge, the old and worn out may refrain, but the young and vigorous will eagerly devour this knowledge, no matter how many re-education classes or schoolmarmy blog posts or lectures or books people belch out for the "safety" of the young. Institutional attempts to excommunicate, fire, or otherwise unperson those who ride off with these ideas only render them more alluring. It is actually in their own self-interest for the "concerned" despisers of nature to face it squarely and openly.

Alamariu explains how this situation developed, relevant to the above discussion on the growing mass of scientific data on genetics, behavior, society, ethnicities, and races:

"Several things have happened since the early 1990's to intensify this interest and also to "weaponize" it against the current establishment...The second great change is a revolution in the field of the biological sciences that took place over two decades starting in the 1970s, and which has gone almost completely unreported. It came about from the convergence of two explosive empirical findings. The first is that not only all human behavior, no matter how complex, has a genetic basis, but that genetic differences are directly linked to behavioral differences: In other words, whether it be individuals, families, ethnicities, or races, the farther apart they are genetically, the more different they are across all behaviors. This is as well-established and uncontested a fact now as gravity, but it is unknown or outright denied outside genetics departments.

"The second finding came thanks to the very rapid development of human population genetics, in large part due to new DNA sequencing techniques that were not available before. Here, the titanic work of Cavalli-Sforza above all definitively killed Lewontin's Lie: the mendacious cliché that there is more genetic variation within races than between them. We now have a very minute understanding of the considerable genetic diversity between historical population groups. Black Africans, in particular, are so divergent from the rest of humanity that they exceed the threshold commonly used in other species to draw sub-species boundaries. A revelation as shocking as it is by now indisputable...

"Sforza's 1994 magnum opus, 'The History and Geography of Human Genes,' will likely prove to be a watershed work. Together with the discovery of the genetic correlation of behavior, this represents the most thorough and unanswerable vindication of the idea of nature produced by modern science.

B

The Genetic Reality of Race

"Since then, further studies have fleshed out the minutiae of heritability of intelligence and complex behaviors such as political preferences. New and major books are appearing and about to appear on these subjects. Intimidation and other coercive tactics will not succeed for much longer in confining knowledge of this revolution to scientists. It will become increasingly untenable to deny the reality of human nature and particularly of heritability of qualities, behaviors, and even modes of thought. Holdouts are no doubt going to remain in some academic departments and at some publications, but young people will ignore them. For the most part it will not be possible to ignore these

findings; for those on all sides, it will be necessary to engage them..."

The change in the sciences is so obvious and clear in the mass of collected data we have available to us at the mere click of a computer button. It is likewise so clear due to the era in which we live where disparate peoples are artificially thrust side-by-side, cameras record every interaction, and social media broadcasts and records the difference in lifestyle, behavior, actions, words, dress, and appearances. Biological realism is everywhere coming down upon us and the deniers can only hide their heads in the sand and repeat withered liberal platitudes with waning vigor. It is impossible to ignore these findings, says Alamariu, and we must engage with them.

Yet, more salient to the purposes of this anthology are the following comments:

"So a change occurred since the 1990's where the idea of nature was now no longer defended simply by pointing to examples from classical literature or philosophy, or from common sense, but to the biological sciences as such, to scientific studies showing natural differences between groups."

It is now insufficient for the majority of those not already convinced merely to be pointed to the majority of ancient voices who disagree with our outrageous anti-natural world today. Most people, at least in the West, have been duped by propaganda and must be approached with something other than Aristotle or other "dead white men". However, the biological, genetic, sociological and other sciences prove the wisdom of our ancestors on this topic. And the modern mind readily trusts these technical experts of ancient wisdom. Therefore, it is necessary as a support for us and as a foundation for others to acknowledge this growing body of material which says in the language of the expert what others say in prose, poetry, or prophecy.

In this last section, Alamariu notes that the world is turning today in the direction of nature, reality, and a venerated past. If we are shrewd, we will sense this change in the winds of the age and position ourselves to receive, inform, and pass on to the coming generations the ideas of our and of their own ancestors.

"The disaffected and rebellious youth that journalists have confused for the "alt-right" have predictably been excited by such new findings that seem to make a mockery of the orthodoxy of our time, with which they were hectored and aggressively indoctrinated. No one will say that an average seventeen- or even twenty-year-old will have a deep understanding either of genetics, population genetics, or of human nature, but they have used some of the most striking findings or studies to step on the toes of both liberal and conservative journalists, who seem to know even less. This has alarmed academic, educational and literary authorities. They have at times denied the new science, and tried to second-guess and historicize its assumptions. Or, finally, seeing that none of this works, some have lately attempted to "correct" people's opinions about the new findings in genetic "epigenetics," of which they have no knowledge nor expertise. It's not even right to say that the new findings in question are going to "chip away" at assumptions made by modern Western intellectual elites. There is an avalanche or torrent of knowledge that will very soon entirely do away with the social-constructionist paradigm that liberalism has adopted as the basis for the education of the young...

"The nascent youth rebellion is international, remarkably broad-based among high-school students and others somewhat older, and it is, like all youth rebellions, contrarian and nihilistic. But it has genuine, substantial criticisms of the egalitarian world-view. These young people are attracted in general to knowledge of human nature that was made "forbidden" to them by the educational and moral establishment of our time. Without engaging or being able to engage the new scientific body of knowledge that is coming out at an increasingly rapid pace, readers, of whatever moral or political conviction, will simply lose the plot." – Constin Alamariu, *Selective Breeding and the Birth of Philosophy*, pgs. 43-47

We cannot deny reality but must live in the light of creation and providence. If we neglect what is before and even within us, we fight against nature and merely make such knowledge forbidden and irresistible while we ourselves become irrelevant. Liberal egalitarianism is an anomaly. Science will, in the end, uncover the facts of what is. As it turns out, we are fortunate enough to live in a time where science is catching back up with what humans have universally recognized as true about natural order, affections, and social relations.

— HUMAN BIO-DIVERSITY —

"So it is that gods do not give all men the gifts of grace...neither good looks nor intelligence nor eloquence." – Homer, *The Odyssey*

"There's many a man has more hair than wit." – Shakespeare, *Comedy of Errors*, act 2, scene 3

"There are various reasons for this neglect, rejection, and even down-right hostility. Early, crude attempts to extend the Darwinian revolution to the understanding of human behavior and society, carried out in the late nineteenth and early twentieth centuries and known as social Darwinism, leaned toward racism and class bias. In reaction, the social sciences and humanities completely moved away from anything that suggested a biological basis for human behavior. Massively reinforced after the horrors of Nazism and with the dismantling of public racism in the West, this tendency reached its apogee in the 1960s and 1970s. Thus, scholars from the above fields have found themselves totally unprepared as revolutionary breakthroughs in the decipherment of the genome coupled with a great revival of evolutionary theory generated one of the most significant scientific developments of the era. Nothing in their professional training enabled them to relate to the new perspective and insights. Indeed, everything they had learned served to predispose them against it. For in their reaction against social Darwinism, the social sciences and humanities veered too sharply in the opposite direction. With a few exceptions, they rejected the idea that anything like human nature existed or was meaningful to the understanding of society. Instead, they adopted the view that people and human societies were wholly determined by culture and history. This, however, was just another false either/or dichotomy. It meant turning a blind eye to a whole side of reality, for it is both nature and nurture, indeed, precisely the interaction between them that has always shaped people and human societies.

Genes are not everything, of course, but they are hardly irrelevant, or disconnected from culture." – Azar Gat, *Nations: The Long History And Deep Roots Of Political Ethnicity And Nationalism*, pg. 28

"Deconstructing the concept of race not only goes against the tendency of virtually every known culture to classify and build family histories according to some measure of common descent, it also ignores the work of biologists studying non-human species...

"Regardless of the extent to which the media promote 'politically correct,' but scientifically wrong, resolutions from professional societies such as the American Anthropological Association, facts remain facts and require appropriate scientific, not political or ideological, explanation. None of this should be construed as meaning that environmental factors play no part in individual and group differences. But with each passing year and each new study, the evidence for the genetic contribution to these differences becomes more firmly established than ever." – J. Philippe Rushton, *Mankind Quarterly*, Winter 1998, vol. 39, iss. 2, pg. 231

— Biological Realism —

Summary Of Findings

Thuletide, *The Genetic Validity of Race*, 12/29/2020. Read this article for a readable summary of the detailed information contained in this section.

Genetics In Social Science

Using Genetics for Social Science

Harden, K.P., Koellinger, P.D. *Natural Human Behavior* 4, 567–576 (2020).

"Social science genetics is concerned with understanding whether, how and why genetic differences between human beings are linked to differences in behaviours and socioeconomic outcomes. Our review discusses the goals, methods, challenges and implications of this research endeavour. We survey how the recent developments in genetics are beginning to provide social scientists with a powerful new tool-box they can use to better understand environmental effects, and we illustrate this with several substantive examples. Furthermore, we examine how medical research can benefit from genetic insights into social-scientific outcomes and vice versa. Finally, we discuss the ethical challenges of this work and clarify several common misunderstandings and misinterpretations of genetic research on individual differences."

Genetics And Psychology

Genetic and Environmental Influences on Human Psychological Differences

Thomas J. Bouchard, Jr., Matt McGue. Department of Psychology, University of Minnesota, Minneapolis, Minnesota 55455

"There is a strong consensus within psychology that g [1] can be measured objectively using appropriate methods of factor analysis... g is a universally found statistical regularity."

"Advances in genomics and statistical modeling now offer scientists an opportunity to begin to directly find 'g' at a genetic level — that is, identify an underlying reality, at a genetic level, between general ['g'] and specific aspects of cognitive ability." – Paolo Shirasi

Bad Science

The Natural Selection of Bad Science

Smaldino, Paul & McElreath, Richard. (2016). *Royal Society Open Science*.

"Poor research design and data analysis encourage false-positive findings. Such poor methods persist despite perennial calls for improvement, suggesting that they result from something more than just misunderstanding. The persistence of poor methods results partly from incentives that favour them, leading to the natural selection of bad science. This dynamic requires no conscious strategizing—no deliberate cheating nor loafing—by scientists, only that publication is a principal factor for career advancement. Some normative methods of analysis have almost certainly been selected to further publication instead of discovery."

---

1   In genetics, "G" represents the nucleotide base Guanine, one of the four building blocks of DNA, alongside Adenine (A), Cytosine (C), and Thymine (T).

Shifting Debates

Carl, N. How Stifling Debate Around Race, Genes and IQ Can Do Harm

Noah Carl. Evolutionary Psychological Science 4, 399–407 (2018).

"It is often asserted that, when it comes to taboo topics like race, genes and IQ, scholars should be held to higher evidentiary standards or even censored entirely because of the harm that might result if their findings became widely known. There is held to be an asymmetry whereby the societal costs of discussing certain topics inevitably outweigh any benefits from doing so. This paper argues that no such asymmetry has been empirically demonstrated, and that stifling debate around taboo topics can itself do active harm."

Quoted in the paper: "To suppress free speech is a double wrong. It violates the rights of the hearer as well as those of the speaker." —Frederick Douglas, 1860, A *Plea for Free Speech in Boston*

Race Understanding Is Changing

How Genetics Is Changing Our Understanding of 'Race'

New York Times, March 3, 2018

"I have deep sympathy for the concern that genetic discoveries could be misused to justify racism. But as a geneticist I also know that it is simply no longer possible to ignore average genetic differences among 'races.'

"Groundbreaking advances in DNA sequencing technology have been made over the last two decades. These advances enable us to measure with exquisite accuracy what fraction of an individual's genetic ancestry traces back to, say, West Africa 500 years ago — before the mixing in the Americas of the West African and European gene pools that were almost completely isolated for the last 70,000 years. With the help of these tools, we are learning that while race may be a social construct, differences in genetic ancestry that happen to correlate to many of today's racial constructs are real.

"Recent genetic studies have demonstrated differences across populations not just in the genetic determinants of simple traits such as skin color, but also in more complex traits like bodily dimensions and susceptibility to diseases. For example, we now know that genetic factors help explain why northern Europeans are taller on average than southern Europeans, why multiple sclerosis is more common in European-Americans than in African-Americans, and why the reverse is true for end-stage kidney disease. I am worried that well-meaning people who deny the possibility of substantial biological differences among human populations are digging themselves into an indefensible position, one that will not survive the onslaught of science…

"While most people will agree that finding a genetic explanation for an elevated rate of disease is important, they often draw the line there. Finding genetic influences on a propensity for disease is one thing, they argue, but looking for such influences on behavior and cognition is another. But whether we like it or not, that line has already been crossed. A recent study led by the economist Daniel Benjamin compiled information on the number of years of education from more than 400,000 people, almost all of whom were of European ancestry. After controlling for differences in socioeconomic background, he and his colleagues identified 74 genetic variations that are over-represented in genes known to be important in neurological development, each of which is incontrovertibly more common in Europeans with more years of education than in Europeans with fewer years of education…

"This is why knowledgeable scientists must speak out. If we abstain from laying out a rational framework for discussing differences among populations, we risk losing the trust of the public and we actively contribute to the distrust of expertise that is now so prevalent. We leave a vacuum that gets filled by pseudoscience, an outcome that is far worse than anything we could achieve by talking openly."

Genetic Psychological Traits

Genetic Influence on Human Psychological Traits: A Survey

Thomas J. Bouchard, Jr., University of Minnesota, Minneapolis

"There is now a large body of evidence that supports the conclusion that individual differences in most, if not all, reliably measured psychological traits, normal and abnormal, are substantively influenced by genetic factors. This fact has important implications for research and theory building in psychology, as evidence of genetic influence unleashes a cascade of questions regarding the sources of variance in such traits. A brief list of those questions is provided, and representative findings regarding genetic and environmental influences are presented for the domains of personality, intelligence, psychological interests, psychiatric illnesses, and social attitudes. These findings are consistent with those reported for the traits of other species and for many human physical traits, suggesting that they may represent a general biological phenomenon.

"Among knowledgeable researchers, discussions regarding genetic influences on psychological traits are not about whether there is genetic influence, but rather about how much influence there is, and how genes work to shape the mind. As Rutter (2002) noted, 'Any dispassionate reading of the evidence leads to the inescapable conclusion that genetic factors play a substantial role in the origins of individual differences with respect to all psychological traits, both normal and abnormal' (pg. 2). Put concisely, all psychological traits are heritable."

Genetic Code Harvard Research

Zip Code or Genetic Code?

Ekaterina Pesheva, The Harvard Gazette, January 14, 2019

A team of researchers from Harvard University and Massachusetts General Hospital has developed a new method to quantify the effects of genes and environment on 560 common diseases and conditions. Using data from UK Biobank, the researchers analyzed genetic information and electronic health records of over 300,000 individuals, which allowed them to measure the role of genetics and environmental factors in the development of common conditions.

The researchers found that most conditions, including heart disease, high blood pressure, and diabetes, have a substantial genetic component. They also discovered that the interplay between genes and environment varies between individuals, which could lead to a more personalized approach to disease prevention and treatment in the future.

This study represents a significant advancement in understanding the role of genetics and environment in human health and disease, paving the way for more targeted therapies and preventative measures based on individual genetic makeup.

Skin Color Adaptation

Adaptation of human skin color in various populations

Deng, L., Xu, S. Hereditas 155, 1 (2018).

"Previous studies generally indicated a complex genetic mechanism underlying the skin color variation, expanding our understanding of the role of population demographic history and natural selection in shaping genetic and phenotypic diversity in humans. Future work is needed to dissect the genetic architecture of skin color adaptation in numerous ethnic minority groups around the world, which remains relatively obscure compared with that of major continental groups, and to unravel the exact genetic basis of skin color adaptation."

Ancestry Estimation

Ancestry Estimation Using Cranial and Postcranial Macromorphoscopic Traits

Micayla C. Spiros M.Sc., Joseph T. Hefner Ph.D. *Journal of Forensic Science*, vol. 65, iss. 3 May 2020, pgs. 921-929. Presented in part at the 71st Annual Scientific Meeting of American Academy of Forensic Sciences, February 18–23, 2019, in Baltimore, MD.

"Study identified the genetic ancestry (European or African) of a skeleton with up to 92% accuracy using a variety of machine learning classification models.

"Large-scale multi-ethnic cohorts offer unprecedented opportunities to elucidate the genetic factors influencing complex traits related to health and disease among minority populations. At the same time, the genetic diversity in these cohorts presents new challenges for analysis and interpretation. We consider the utility of race and / or ethnicity categories in genome-wide association studies (GWASs) of multi-ethnic cohorts. We demonstrate that race / ethnicity information enhances the ability to understand population-specific genetic architecture."

Social Race And Genetic Ancestry Match

GENETIC ANCESTRY AND SOCIAL RACE ARE NEARLY INTERCHANGEABLE

Emil O. W. Kirkegaard, Ulster Institute for Social Research, December 2021

"Using cross-validated multinomial regression to predict social race from 6 genetic ancestry variables, we find that the AUC is .89. Using Dirichlet regression to predict ancestries from social race, we find an overall correlation of .94 (R2 = 88.4%). Further analyses using more sophisticated methods (random forest, support vector machine) found similar results. In conclusion, social race and genetic ancestry are nearly interchangeable."

Social Status Inheritance

THE INHERITANCE OF SOCIAL STATUS: ENGLAND, 1600 TO 2022

Greg Clark. Edited by Dalton Conley, Princeton University, Princeton, NJ; received January 17, 2023; accepted May 17, 2023. *Proceedings Of The National Academy Of Sciences* vol. 120 | No. 27 July 4, 2023 PubMed: 37364122

In PNAS today, Greg Clark documents the inheritance of social status in an impressive dataset on 422,374 people born in England between 1600 to 2022.

Clark finds a strong persistence in social status going from close to distant relatives, which fits a model dating back to RA Fisher's 1918 work on correlations between relatives due to additive genetic effects and assortative mating.

Clark's modeling implies a very high (0.57) correlation between spouses' underlying genetic components affecting social status.

The high correlation between spouses' social status (and underlying genetic components) implies that social status has greater persistence across generations than if spouses were not correlated in their social status.

It is possible that more complicated models may turn out to explain Clark's and other data better. However, Clark shows that a simple model of additive genetic effects and assortative mating (with limited non-genetic inheritance effects, except for wealth) can fit correlations between relatives' social status over a long time period — a time period in which dramatic social changes have occurred in education and employment.

Generational Inequality

THE SHADOW OF PEASANT PAST: SEVEN GENERATIONS OF INEQUALITY PERSISTENCE IN NORTHERN SWEDEN

Martin Hällsten and Martin Kolk. *American Journal of Sociology* vol. 128, no. 6 May 2023

"...we find 7 generations of inequality persistence (or social mobility) in education, wealth, and occupation. We use data from 18th-century northern Sweden until today in our new study in American Journal of Sociology. We use digitized parish records from Skellefteå and Umeå (≈1700-1970) linked to nationwide administrative data (1960-2017). Our data covers mobility in a rapidly changing society: from agricultural, via sawmill and mining, and into contemporary society. Using historical kinship networks, we measure multigenerational persistence with two methods: higher-order cousin correlations and dynastic correlations (where ancestors' social class is averaged generation by generation, and correlated with index generation's outcomes). We find multigenerational persistence in up to six (or five) generations in education, occupations, and wealth. Past generations structure life chances many generations later, even though mobility is high (4th cousin correlations around 0.011)."

MRI Tells Ancestry

EVIDENCE FOR BIAS OF GENETIC ANCESTRY IN RESTING STATE FUNCTIONAL MRI

Altman, Andrew and Janaina Mourão-Miranda. IEEE 16th International Symposium on Biomedical Imaging (ISBI 2019), 8-11 April 2019, Venice, Italy, vol.: 16.

You can determine someone's race by an MRI scan.

"...we demonstrated that genetic ancestry is encoded in the functional connectivity pattern of the brain at rest. We hypothesize that these observed differences are a result of known ethnicity-related variations in head and brain morphology, which may be carried forward through the rs-fMRI processing pipeline, rather than true neuronal differences. In any case, genetic ancestry constitutes a bias that should be accounted for in the analysis of rs-fMRI data."

Race And Cancer

The Race for Ancestral Genetics in Clinical Trials

Beckman, Mary. Journal of the National Cancer Institute 98 (2006).

"A seasoned cancer researcher would never set up a study in which all the ill patients were, say, Canadian, and all the healthy controls were Japanese. And yet cancer researchers risk making a similar mistake if they overlook genetic information that fleshes out what many of us like to think of as race or ethnicity, some experts say.

"Fortunately, awareness of how ancestral genetics might contribute to risk of disease and drug response in people has risen over the last several years. Studies that look directly at the problem are on the rapid rise, and this increased interest has biotechnology companies lowering the cost of tests that determine genetic ancestry, thanks to a little competition."

Social Construct Challenged

Contrary to much of the racial identity debate, race is far from a social construct

Berezow, Alex & Razib Khan. USA Today, June 28, 2015.

"...the history of human evolution, including race, is real, genetically traceable, and cannot be denied. Race, therefore, is a reflection of our history and geography. It is scientifically inaccurate to reduce human populations to mere social constructions and arbitrary crystallizations of power relations. Rather, genetics compels us to view race and ethnicity as part of a larger journey that started with our first ancestors who evolved over the course of tens of thousands of years into the riotous colors and shapes that we recognize as human."

Geneticist On HBD

Unequal by nature: a geneticist's perspective on human differences

Crow, James F., Daedalus, Winter 2002.

"The magnificent advances in molecular biology will bring new depths of understanding of human differences, normal and pathological, and the extent to which these are genetic or environmental – or, as usually will be the case,

both. Whether society will accept this knowledge willingly and use it wisely I don't know. My hope is that gradual progress, starting with small beginnings, can lead to rational individual behavior and thoughtful, humanitarian social policies. ...

"I believe that knowledge, even unpleasant knowledge, is far preferable to ignorance. I hope that American society can be less fearful of learning the truth about biological inequalities and more courageous in using discoveries in ways that are humanitarian and promote human welfare."

The Nature Of Race

Natural Division, Race and Biology

Fuerst, John., Open Behavioral Genetics, June, 2015.

"In this paper, an onto-epistemology of biology is developed. What it is, by this, to be 'biological real' and 'biologically meaningful' and to represent a 'biological natural division' is explained. Early 18th century race concepts are discussed in detail and are shown to be both sensible and not greatly dissimilar to modern concepts. A general biological race concept (GBRC) is developed...The sense in which races are both real and natural is explained. Racial essentialism of the relational sort is shown to be coherent...Traditional human racial classifications are defended from common criticisms: historical incoherence, arbitrariness, cluster discordance, etc....Further, it is pointed out that some species concepts potentially allow certain human populations to be designated as species. It is explained why, by conventional population genetic and statistical standards, genetic differences between major human racial groups are at least moderate. Behavioral genetic differences associated with human races are discussed in general and in specific. The matter of race differences in cognitive ability is briefly considered. Finally, the race concept is defended from various criticisms. First, logical and empirical critiques are dissected. These include: biological scientific, sociological, ontological, onto-epistemological, semantic, and teleological arguments. None are found to have any merit. Second, moral-based arguments are investigated in context to a general ethical frame and are counter-critiqued. Racial inequality, racial nepotism, and the 'Racial Worldview' are discussed. What is dubbed the Anti-Racial Worldview is rejected on both empirical and moral grounds. Finally, an area of future investigation – the politics of the destruction of the race concept – is pointed to."

Faster Evolution

FASTER EVOLUTION MEANS MORE RACIAL DIFFERENCES

Haidt, Jonathan., *Edge*, 2009.

"A wall has long protected respectable evolutionary inquiry from accusations of aiding and abetting racism. That wall is the belief that genetic change happens at such a glacial pace that there simply was not time, in the 50,000 years since humans spread out from Africa, for selection pressures to have altered the genome in anything but the most trivial way (e.g., changes in skin color and nose shape were adaptive responses to cold climates). Evolutionary psychology has therefore focused on the Pleistocene era – the period from about 1.8 million years ago to the dawn of agriculture — during which our common humanity was forged for the hunter-gatherer lifestyle. ...

"The protective 'wall' is about to come crashing down, and all sorts of uncomfortable claims are going to pour in. ...

"...the ways in which we now think about genes, groups, evolution and ethnicity will be radically changed by the unstoppable progress of the human genome project."

Rare Variants

RARE VARIANTS AND HUMAN GENETIC DIVERSITY

Hsu, Steve., *Information Processing*, July 8, 2012.

"You may have read that there is more genetic variation within major ethnic groups than between ethnic groups. That this precludes the possibility of group differences is Lewontin's Fallacy. Deep sequencing of the human genome, which reveals rare variants (here, defined as those found in fewer than 0.5 percent of the population), shows that there is actually more variation between groups than within groups."

Rediscovering Genetic Science

LEARNING CAN HURT

Hsu, Steve., *Information Processing*, May 1, 2013.

"In this paper I investigate the recent re-emergence of genetic race in more detail, and endeavour to ascertain how, after a half-century hiatus, a young team of population geneticists could casually rediscover race in 2002. Was it happenstance? Or was it opportune timing? My tentative conclusions are: (a) the flipside of serendipity is sociopolitical context; and (b) in the first few years of the new millennium, on the face of it, the time was indeed ripe for genetic race to re-emerge within the scientific mainstream."

JayMan FAQ

RACE, INHERITANCE, AND IQ F.A.Q. (F.R.B.)

JayMan., JayMan's Blog, May 4, 2014.

"Well, yes, race is a social construct. But race does exist. Saying something is a 'social construct' can be true and still yet not be really meaningful. Think of it, the periodic table of chemical elements is a social construct. Do chemical elements then not exist? Or, much more relevant – in fact, exactly like race – Linnaean taxonomy is a social construct. Do kingdoms, classes, species not exist? Race is merely an extension of this. In reality, genetic analysis can separate human populations into distinct groups. This works at the level of continental groups or even ethnic groups within a continent (or even groups within an ethnicity). At times the progression is smooth, with each group gradually giving way to the next, and at other times, the transition is abrupt."

The Race Question

THE RACE QUESTION: ARE BONOBOS HUMAN?

Khan, Razib., Discover Magazine, Feb. 23, 2012.

"There's a big difference between revealed preferences and avowed preferences. For example, most Americans espouse a love of diversity. But they sure don't love diversity when it comes to who they date. These include many people who I know personally, who are diversity loving progressives, but who seem to fall into the trap of disaggregation. Since I don't love diversity and don't care about that issue I don't bring it up with them often. But it's what I call a revealed preference. Or, to give an amusing example, I said something offensive in one of my posts apparently a few years back, which prompted one outraged reader to leave a long shocked rant about my racism. The comment was trashed, and the reader banned. Nevertheless, I traced their Facebook account. The individual was a young white professional resident in San Francisco. And, their friends list was visible. I did a quick spot check, and estimated that ~90 percent of their San Francisco friends were white. In contrast, about ~50 percent of San Francisco's population is white. I'm not going to accuse anyone of racism, but there are quite interesting revealed preferences in the world (I saw this when I lived in Berkeley, where a few times I was the only non-white at a party where people were trashing how little diversity there was in Oregon when they found out that that was where I was from). Most people like to associate with 'their own kind,' however that is defined."

A Biological Construct

WHY RACE AS A BIOLOGICAL CONSTRUCT MATTERS

Khan, Razib., *Discover Magazine*, May 16, 2013.

"Few moderns agree with Lothrop Stoddard's The Rising Tide of Color Against White World-Supremacy, but many implicitly accept the framework of whites and a coalition of 'people of color.'"

A Brief Review

RACE DIFFERENCES: A VERY BRIEF REVIEW

Kierkegaard, Emil O.W., *Mankind Quarterly* (2019).

"…human races are distinctive phenotypically and genotypically, the latter with regard to the frequencies of a very large number (millions) of alleles. Distributions of these traits are clinal rather than discrete, and human races are subject to continuous change across evolutionary time…

"The most popular view in the West currently among social scientists is that race denotes a concept of discrete/typological populations in an ancient Greek sense (Platonic/essentialist), and that genomic data shows that such discrete populations do not exist. Hence human races

do not exist in any biological sense, but only as (at least somewhat) arbitrary social categories. The contrary minority view is that race denotes a subspecies, breeding population, genetic cluster, extended family (or some other biologically-based idea along those lines), and that genomic data shows that these exist, and have or might have important relationships to socially valued phenotypic traits among humans. In line with standard terminology in philosophy, the first view will be denoted the social constructivist view (or sometimes, anti-realist), and the second the realist view ('race realism')."

Celebrating (Genetic) Diversity

LET'S CELEBRATE HUMAN GENETIC DIVERSITY

Lahn, Bruce & Lanny Ebenstein., *Nature* 461, no. 35 (2009).

Summary: Enough human genetic science is now overturning "biological egalitarianism" and people must not only change their minds to account for this but provide moral frameworks for living in light of this reality.

"A growing body of data is revealing the nature of human genetic diversity at increasingly finer resolution. It is now recognized that despite the high degree of genetic similarities that bind humanity together as a species, considerable diversity exists at both individual and group levels. … enough evidence has come to the fore to warrant the question: what if scientific data ultimately demonstrate that genetically based biological variation exists at non-trivial levels not only among individuals but also among groups?"

Biology and Equality

THE BIOLOGY OF RACE AND THE CONCEPT OF EQUALITY

Mayr, Ernst, *Daedalus*, vol. 131, No. 1, *On Inequality* (Winter, 2002), pgs. 89-94

"No matter what the cause of the racial difference might be, the fact that species of organisms may have geographic races has been demonstrated so frequently that it can no longer be denied. And the geographic races of the human races – established before the voyages of European discovery and subsequent rise of a global economy – agree in most characteristics with the geographic races of animals. Recognizing race of animals. Recognizing races is only recognizing a biological fact."

Recent Evolutionary Developments

OUR SPECIES—AND INDIVIDUAL RACES—HAVE RECENTLY MADE BIG EVOLUTIONARY CHANGES

McAuliffe, Kathleen. *Discover Magazine*, Feb. 2, 2009.

"…to suggest that humans have undergone an evolutionary makeover from Stone Age times to the present is nothing short of blasphemous. Yet a team of researchers has done just that. They find an abundance of recent adaptive mutations etched in the human genome; even more shocking, these mutations seem to be piling up faster and ever faster, like an avalanche. Over the past 10,000 years, their data show, human evolution has occurred a hundred times more quickly than in any other period in our species' history.

"The new genetic adaptations, some 2,000 in total, are not limited to the well-recognized differences among ethnic groups in superficial traits such as skin and eye color. The mutations relate to the brain, the digestive system, life span, immunity to pathogens, sperm production, and bones—in short, virtually every aspect of our functioning."

A Quiet Crisis In Knowledge

THE LOOMING CRISIS IN HUMAN GENETICS

Miller, Geoffrey. *The Economist*, Nov 13, 2009.

"Once enough DNA is analysed around the world, science will have a panoramic view of human genetic variation across races, ethnicities and regions. We will start reconstructing a detailed family tree that links all living humans, discovering many surprises about mis-attributed paternity and covert mating between classes, castes, regions and ethnicities. We will also identify the many genes that create physical and mental differences across populations, and we will be able to estimate when those genes arose. Some of those differences probably occurred very recently, within recorded history."

Genetics and Race in Health

ASSESSING GENOMIC CONTRIBUTIONS TO PHENOTYPIC DIFFERENCES AMONG RACIAL AND ETHNIC GROUPS

Mountain, Joanna L. & Neil Risch. *Nature Genetics* 36, no. 11 (2004).

Summary: Over the past three decades, significant data on human genetic and phenotypic diversity have emerged, revealing clusters aligning with social or geographic groups. While genetic factors could influence group-based phenotypic distinctions, caution is needed in drawing conclusions. The lack of comprehensive understanding has two implications: Firstly, stringent criteria are essential for attributing genetic contributions to group differences, emphasizing responsible discourse in genetics and group disparities. Secondly, despite concerns of perpetuating racism, racial and ethnic labels remain necessary for epidemiological and clinical purposes due to health disparities. Such labels serve as proxies for various factors, genetic and non-genetic, with some labels more predictive than others. In the future, improved databases and individualized analyses may reduce the reliance on such categorizations, but their utility persists as long as they explain variation beyond other factors.

DNA Testing Reveals Race

A NEW DNA TEST CAN ID A SUSPECT'S RACE, BUT POLICE WON'T TOUCH IT

Newsome, Melba. *Wired*, Dec. 20, 2007.

An article written in 2007 discussing then-new technology that allows one to determine a person's race based upon DNA. The technology has so progressed since 2007, that now millions of people sign up for ancestry services which use DNA to report to people their genetic ancestry going back hundreds, sometimes thousands of years.

Changing Our Understanding

HOW GENETICS IS CHANGING OUR UNDERSTANDING OF 'RACE'

Reich, David. *New York Times*, March 23, 2018.

Summary: In 1942, Ashley Montagu's book, "Man's Most Dangerous Myth: The Fallacy of Race," challenged the concept of race as a social construct with no genetic basis. This perspective gained momentum in 1972 when geneticist Richard Lewontin's study found that around 85% of genetic variation could be attributed to differences within populations and only 15%

across populations. This led to the belief that human genetic variation was so minimal that it supported the idea that race is purely a social construct that changes over time.

However, recent advancements in DNA sequencing technology have enabled researchers to measure genetic ancestry accurately. This has revealed that, while race is a social construct, genetic differences correlating with racial categories do exist. For instance, genetic studies have identified variations in genes associated with diseases and intelligence that differ across populations. These findings challenge the idea that genetic differences among populations are negligible.

The reluctance to openly discuss these genetic differences has allowed individuals like James Watson and Nicholas Wade to make unsubstantiated claims, blending factual observations of academic reluctance with unsupported conclusions about genetic differences and stereotypes. This situation has left geneticists like David Reich in a dilemma, torn between acknowledging genetic differences and countering potential misuse of this information. It underscores the complexity of navigating the intersection of genetics, race, and society.

Categorizing From Biomedical Research

CATEGORIZATION OF HUMANS IN BIOMEDICAL RESEARCH: GENES, RACE AND DISEASE

Risch, Neil, et al. Genome Biology, July 1, 2002.

Summary: The discussion provides insights into the genetic categorization of humans for biomedical research. It emphasizes the goal of genetic research in identifying specific genes and variants influencing disease risk and drug response, aiming for individualized therapy. While few such genes have been identified, the authors argue that genetic structure exists in the human population, leading to potential categorization based on genetic clusters.

Human evolution is discussed as a factor influencing genetic differentiation, with populations outside Africa originating from migration events in the last 100,000 years. Genetic studies consistently show continental-based racial categorization, including African, Caucasian, Asian, Pacific Islander, and Native American groups.

The terms race, ethnicity, and ancestry are defined, and the impact of migrations and admixture is highlighted, particularly in the United

States. The article notes that despite admixture, genetic differentiation persists among racial groups, suggesting that self-reported ancestry can be genetically informative.

The article also discusses the number of genetic markers required for accurate clustering, indicating that a modest number of markers can distinguish major racial groups but more are needed for closely related populations. It concludes that self-defined ethnicity may be more genetically informative than genetic clustering based on a limited set of markers.

In summary, the article provides a perspective on genetic categorization for biomedical research, emphasizing genetic differentiation among human populations based on continental ancestry and the potential utility of self-reported ethnicity in research studies.

GENETIC STRUCTURE, SELF-IDENTIFIED RACE/ETHNICITY, AND CONFOUNDING IN CASE-CONTROL ASSOCIATION STUDIES

Risch, Neil, et al. American Journal of Human Genetics 76 (2005).

Summary: The article delves into the genetic categorization of humans for biomedical research, focusing on the primary objective of genetic research: identifying specific genes and variants responsible for disease risk and drug response to enable personalized therapies. While the identification of such genes is still limited, the authors argue that a fundamental genetic structure exists within the human population, which could potentially facilitate categorization based on genetic clusters. Human evolution is discussed as a significant driver of genetic differentiation, with populations outside Africa stemming from migration events within the past 100,000 years. Genetic studies consistently reveal the existence of continental-based racial categories, including African, Caucasian, Asian, Pacific Islander, and Native American groups.

The article also outlines the distinctions between race, ethnicity, and ancestry, emphasizing the impact of migrations and admixture, particularly in the United States. Despite varying degrees of admixture, the article underscores that genetic differentiation remains evident among racial groups. This observation suggests that self-reported ancestry can serve as a valuable genetic indicator. Moreover, the article addresses the number of genetic markers required for precise clustering, noting that while a modest number of markers can effectively distinguish major racial groups, more markers are necessary for closely related populations. Ultimately, the article concludes that self-defined ethnicity might offer greater genetic insight than genetic clustering based on a limited set of markers, providing a perspective on genetic categorization for biomedical research.

Six Clusters Observed

GENETIC STRUCTURE OF HUMAN POPULATIONS

Rosenberg, Noah A. et al. Science 298, no. 5602 (2002).

"We studied human population structure using genotypes at 377 autosomal microsatellite loci in 1056 individuals from 52 populations. Within-population differences among individuals account for 93 to 95% of genetic variation; differences among major groups constitute only 3 to 5%. Nevertheless, without using prior information about the origins of individuals, we identified six main genetic clusters, five of which correspond to major geographic regions, and subclusters that often correspond to individual populations. General agreement of genetic and predefined populations suggests that self-reported ancestry can facilitate assessments of epidemiological risks but does not obviate the need to use genetic information in genetic association studies."

See also:

Rosenberg, Noah A. Clines, Clusters, and the Effect of Study Design on the Inference of Human Population Structure, PLOS Genetics, 2005.

A Social Construct?

RACE: A SOCIAL DESTRUCTION OF A BIOLOGICAL CONCEPT

Sesardic, Neven. Biology and Philosophy, 2010.

"It is nowadays a dominant opinion in a number of disciplines (anthropology, genetics, psychology, philosophy of science) that the taxonomy of human races does not make much biological sense. My aim is to challenge the arguments that are usually thought to invalidate the biological concept of race. I will try to show that the way 'race' was defined by biologists several decades ago (by Dobzhansky and others) is in no way discredited by conceptual criticisms that are now fashionable and widely regarded as cogent. These criticisms often arbitrarily burden the biological category of race with some implausible connotations, which then opens the path for a quick eliminative move. However, when properly understood, the biological notion of race proves remarkably resistant to these deconstructive attempts. Moreover, by analyzing statements of some leading contemporary scholars who support social constructivism about race, I hope to demonstrate that their eliminativist views are actually in conflict with what the best contemporary science tells us about human genetic variation."

See Also:

Sesardic, Neven. Confusions about race: A new installment, Studies in History and Philosophy of Biological and Biomedical Sciences, 2013.

SIRE Correlations

GENETIC STRUCTURE, SELF-IDENTIFIED RACE/ ETHNICITY, AND CONFOUNDING IN CASE-CONTROL ASSOCIATION STUDIES

Tang, H. et al. The American Journal of Human Genetics 76 (2005).

"We have analyzed genetic data for 326 microsatellite markers that were typed uniformly in a large multiethnic population-based sample of individuals as part of a study of the genetics of hypertension (Family Blood Pressure Program). Subjects identified themselves as belonging to one of four major racial/ethnic groups (white, African American, East Asian, and Hispanic) and were recruited from 15 different geographic locales within the United States and Taiwan. Genetic cluster analysis of the microsatellite markers produced four major clusters, which showed near-perfect correspondence with the four self-reported race/ethnicity categories. Of 3,636 subjects of varying race/ethnicity, only 5 (0.14%) showed genetic cluster membership different from their self-identified race/ethnicity. On the other hand, we detected only modest genetic differentiation between different current geographic locales within each race/ethnicity group. Thus, ancient geographic ancestry, which is highly correlated with self-identified race/ethnicity—as opposed to current residence—is the major determinant of genetic structure in the U.S. population. Implications of this genetic structure for case-control association studies are discussed."

A Troublesome Inheritance

GENES, RACE, AND HUMAN HISTORY

Wade, Nicholas. *A Troublesome Inheritance.* Penguin Press, 2014.

Summary: Nicholas Wade discusses various studies using genetic tools like tandem DNA repeats and single nucleotide polymorphisms (SNPs) that reveal distinct genetic differences among human populations. These genetic variations influence both physical and mental traits. Some of these genes have been subject to selection in the last 5,000 years, challenging the idea that human evolution has ceased since the advent of agriculture. Computer algorithms, when used to cluster genes without bias, consistently identify five major continental races: Caucasian, East Asian, African, Native American, and Australian Aboriginal. This suggests that there are clear genetic underpinnings for traits like skin color and height, and these differences are not solely explained by one or two genes but rather by combinations of genes.

Mr. Wade criticizes the views of prominent thinkers like Stephen Jay Gould and Richard Lewontin, who downplayed genetic differences among human populations. The author argues that even minor differences in gene frequencies can lead to significant variations in physical, mental, and social characteristics. The book also delves into the more speculative realm of genetics' potential influence on cognitive, social, and personality traits. While evidence in this area is limited, the author suggests that genes may play a role in complex differences between races. The author emphasizes that acknowledging genetic differences does not imply superiority or inferiority but rather serves as a basis for understanding human diversity. Overall, the book advocates for the open exploration of scientific topics, even if they have the potential to be socially or politically controversial, and underscores the importance of separating scientific findings from their political implications.

See also:

Wade, Nicholas. *Race Is Seen as Real Guide To Track Roots of Disease, New York Times,* July 30, 2002.

Wade, Nicholas. *Gene Study Identifies 5 Main Human Populations, Linking Them to Geography, New York Times,* Dec. 20, 2002.

Wade, Nicholas. *Humans Have Spread Globally, and Evolved Locally, New York Times,* June 26, 2007.

Wade, Nicholas. *What Science Says About Race and Genetics, Time Magazine,* May 9, 2014.

Wade, Nicholas. *Did humans really stop evolving thousands of years ago? DNA explains more than you think, Spectator,* May 17, 2014.

ON THE REALITY OF RACE AND THE ABHORRENCE OF RACISM

Winegard, Bo with Ben Winegard & Brian Boutwell., *Quillette,* June 23, 2016.

"Most people believe that there are human races. They believe this not because they have a sophisticated understanding of genetic variation or human evolution, but because they see and categorize perspicuous phenotypic (and possibly behavioral) differences. Although many intellectuals have contended that these differences are largely superficial and distort underlying genetic realities, most research suggests that there are meaningful genetic differences among racial groups and that these differences are largely consistent with common racial classifications. Race is as real and useful as other constructs in the social sciences such as neuroticism, self-esteem, and intelligence. Therefore, with appropriate care and caution, scientists can and should study racial variation. This argument may appear alarming to people concerned about racial justice. But it doesn't need to be. Tolerance and cosmopolitanism don't require the leveling of diversity; they require the celebration of it. Race exists, but racism does not have to."

SNP Genotypes

FINE-SCALED HUMAN GENETIC STRUCTURE REVEALED BY SNP MICROARRAYS

Xing, Jinchuan et al., *Genome Research* 19 (2009).

"...principal components analyses reveal discernible genetic differentiation among almost all identified populations in our sample, and in most cases, individuals can be clearly assigned to defined populations on the basis of SNP genotypes. All individuals are accurately classified into continental groups using a model-based clustering algorithm…Our results emphasize the correlation of genetic and geographic distances and highlight other elements, including social factors that have contributed to population structure."

Cold Winter Theory

Kierkegaard, E. O. W. "Cold winters theory: a summary of the evidence and replies to objections". Just Emil Kirkegaard Things on Substack, Dec. 8, 2022.

The Cold Winters Theory (CWT) posits that colder climates have selected for higher intelligence in human populations over time. In the above essay, Emil Kirkegaard reviews the evidence supporting the theory, drawing from various studies and data sources.

1. Geographic distribution of intelligence: There is a clear correlation between latitude and intelligence, with populations residing at higher latitudes generally displaying higher average intelligence. This pattern holds true even when controlling for factors such as GDP and educational attainment.
1. Evolutionary mechanisms: The CWT is grounded in the idea that colder environments are more cognitively demanding, as they require more complex planning, problem-solving, and innovation to ensure survival. This selective pressure has led to the evolution of higher intelligence in colder climates.
2. Genetic evidence: Studies have identified genes associated with intelligence that show higher frequency in populations from colder climates. This supports the notion that there has been a genetic selection for higher cognitive abilities in colder regions.
3. Migration patterns: Populations that migrated from colder regions to warmer ones generally maintain higher average intelligence levels than native populations in those warmer regions. This suggests that the higher intelligence levels seen in colder climates are not solely due to environmental factors but also have a genetic basis.
4. Brain size: Colder climates have been associated with larger brain sizes in both humans and animals. Larger brains are believed to be an adaptive response to the cognitive demands of cold environments and are correlated with higher intelligence.
5. Criticisms and alternative explanations: Critics argue that other factors, such as disease prevalence, may account for the observed patterns in intelligence. However, Kirkegaard contends that the evidence supporting the CWT is robust and that alternative explanations do not sufficiently account for the observed correlations.

— HBD [2] AND INTELLIGENCE —

Intelligence Research

EFFECT SIZES, POWER, AND BIASES IN INTELLIGENCE RESEARCH: A META-META-ANALYSIS

Nuijten MB, van Assen MALM, Augusteijn HEM, Crompvoets EAV, Wicherts JM. J Intell. 2020 Oct 2;8(4):36.

"We concluded that intelligence research does show signs of low power and publication bias, but that these problems seem less severe than in many other scientific fields."

Intelligence research has problems but is more reliable in predictive power than other fields of sociological research. Successful replication studies in Intelligence sciences is much higher than in other fields.

Mainstream Science On Intelligence

MAINSTREAM SCIENCE ON INTELLIGENCE: AN EDITORIAL WITH 52 SIGNATORIES, HISTORY, AND BIBLIOGRAPHY

Linda S. Gottfredson, University of Delaware, *The Wall Street Journal*, December 13, 1994

"Since the publication of 'The Bell Curve,' many commentators have offered opinions about human intelligence that misstate current scientific evidence. Some conclusions dismissed in the media as discredited are actually firmly supported.

"This statement outlines conclusions regarded as mainstream among researchers on intelligence, in particular, on the nature, origins, and practical consequences of individual and

---

2 Human bio-diversity speaks of distinct populations, a similar concept to "race."

group differences in intelligence. Its aim is to promote more reasoned discussion of the vexing phenomenon that the research has revealed in recent decades. The following conclusions are fully described in the major textbooks, professional journals and encyclopedias in intelligence."

1. Intelligence is a very general mental capability that, among other things, involves the ability to reason, plan, solve problems, think abstractly, comprehend complex ideas, learn quickly and learn from experience.

2. Intelligence, so defined, can be measured, and intelligence tests measure it well. They are among the most accurate (in technical terms, reliable and valid) of all psychological tests and assessments.

3. While there are different types of intelligence tests, they all measure the same intelligence.

4. The spread of people along the IQ continuum, from low to high, can be represented well by the bell curve.

5. Intelligence tests are not culturally biased against American blacks or other native-born, English-speaking peoples in the U.S.

6. The brain processes underlying intelligence are still little understood.

7. Members of all racial-ethnic groups can be found at every IQ level.

8. The bell curve for whites is centered roughly around IQ 100; the bell curve for American blacks roughly around 85; and those for different subgroups of Hispanics roughly midway between those for whites and blacks.

9. IQ is strongly related, probably more so than any other single measurable human trait, to many important educational, occupational, economic, and social outcomes.

10. A high IQ is an advantage in life because virtually all activities require some reasoning and decision-making.

11. The practical advantages of having a higher IQ increase as life settings become more complex (novel, ambiguous, changing, unpredictable, or multifaceted).

12. Differences in intelligence certainly are not the only factor affecting performance in education, training, and highly complex jobs (no one claims they are), but intelligence is often the most important.

13. Certain personality traits, special talents, aptitudes, physical capabilities, experience, and the like are important (sometimes essential) for successful performance in many jobs, but they have narrower (or unknown) applicability or "transferability" across tasks and settings compared with general intelligence.

14. Individuals differ in intelligence due to differences in both their environments and genetic heritage. Heritability estimates range from 0.4 to 0.8 (on a scale from 0 to 1), most thereby indicating that genetics plays a bigger role than does environment in creating IQ differences among individuals.

15. Members of the same family also tend to differ substantially in intelligence (by an average of about 12 IQ points) for both genetic and environmental reasons.

16. That IQ may be highly heritable does not mean that it is not affected by the environment.

17. Although the environment is important in creating IQ differences, we do not know yet how to manipulate it to raise low IQs permanently.

18. Genetically caused differences are not necessarily irremediable (consider diabetes, poor vision, and phenylketonuria), nor are environmentally caused ones necessarily remediable (consider injuries, poisons, severe neglect, and some diseases).

19. There is no persuasive evidence that the IQ bell curves for different racial-ethnic groups are converging.

20. Racial-ethnic differences in IQ bell curves are essentially the same when youngsters leave high school as when they enter first grade.

21. The reasons that blacks differ among themselves in intelligence appear to be basically the same as those for why whites (or Asians or Hispanics) differ among themselves.

22. There is no definitive answer to why IQ bell curves differ across racial-ethnic groups.

23. Racial-ethnic differences are somewhat smaller but still substantial for individuals from the same socioeconomic backgrounds.

24. Almost all Americans who identify themselves as black have white ancestors the white admixture is about 20%, on average-and many self-designated whites,

Hispanics, and others likewise have mixed ancestry

25. The research findings neither dictate nor preclude any particular social policy, because they can never determine our goals.

"…The lesson here is that what have often been caricatured in the public press as discredited, fringe ideas actually represent the solid scientific center in the serious study of intelligence. As Snyderman and Rothman's (1988) survey of IQ experts and journalists revealed, the media, among others, have been turning the truth on its head. Many of the conclusions outlined in 'Mainstream' are ones that many scholars have reached only recently and reluctantly (Gottfredson, 1996). The mainstream shifted slowly but steadily in recent decades as accumulating research evidence changed our understanding of the nature, measurement, origins, and consequence of differences of intelligence. The press and public have yet to catch up to the new mainstream."

Survey of g Consensus

SURVEY OF OPINIONS ON THE PRIMACY OF G AND SOCIAL CONSEQUENCES OF ABILITY TESTING: A COMPARISON OF EXPERT AND NON-EXPERT VIEWS

Charlie L. Reeve, Jennifer E. Charles. *Intelligence* vol. 36, iss. 6, November–December 2008, pgs. 681-688

"The current study examines the views of experts in the science of mental abilities about the primacy and uniqueness of g and the social implications of ability testing, and compares their responses to the views of a group of non-expert psychologists. Results indicate expert consensus that g is an important, non-trivial determinant (or at least predictor) of important real world outcomes for which there is no substitute, and that tests of g are valid and generally free from racial bias."

Gaps Not Changing

TRENDS IN GRE SCORES AND GRADUATE ENROLLMENTS BY GENDER AND ETHNICITY

April Bleske-Rechek, Kingsley Browne. *Intelligence*, vol. 46, September–October 2014, pgs. 25-34

"First, we found that the gap between men's and women's GRE quantitative reasoning scores has changed little since the 1980s,

although female representation in science, technology, engineering, and math (STEM) graduate programs has increased substantially. Second, ethnic gaps on the GRE persist, especially in quantitative reasoning, although representation of historically disadvantaged ethnic groups in graduate programs has increased. Enrollment gaps have narrowed despite ethnic and gender GRE gaps persisting, so it appears that continued use of the GRE for admissions decisions has not blocked efforts toward equalizing representation in higher education."

Scholastic-Cognitive Relation

THE RELATIONSHIP BETWEEN THE SCHOLASTIC ASSESSMENT TEST AND GENERAL COGNITIVE ABILITY

Meredith C. Frey and Douglas K. Detterman, Case Western Reserve University

Summary: The outcomes of standardized academic and university entrance exams exhibit similar racial disparities as those observed in IQ tests, encompassing the approximate one standard deviation discrepancy in performance between black and white individuals in the United States.

Widening Scoring Gaps

THE WIDENING RACIAL SCORING GAP ON THE SAT COLLEGE ADMISSIONS TEST

Summary: The article points out that in recent years, there has been growing debate and criticism regarding the use of standardized tests in college admissions, with some suggesting that these tests are not a fair or accurate measure of an individual's academic potential. Critics argue that the tests are biased towards certain racial and socio-economic groups, and that they do not take into account other factors that contribute to a student's success in college, such as motivation, perseverance, and the ability to overcome adversity.

In response to these concerns, a number of colleges and universities have implemented test-optional or test-flexible admissions policies. These policies allow applicants to choose whether or not to submit their test scores as part of their application, or in some cases, to submit alternative forms of assessment, such as AP exam scores or graded high school work. The goal of these policies is to level the playing field for students from underrepresented or disadvantaged backgrounds and to promote a more holistic approach to evaluating applicants.

However, despite these changes in admissions policies, the article highlights that the race gap in test scores remains a significant issue. Research has shown that the average black student scores around one standard deviation below the average white student on both the SAT and ACT exams. This gap persists even after controlling for socio-economic factors, suggesting that there may be other underlying causes contributing to the discrepancy.

Expert Opinion On Racial *g* Disparity

SURVEY OF EXPERT OPINION ON INTELLIGENCE: CAUSES OF INTERNATIONAL DIFFERENCES IN COGNITIVE ABILITY TESTS

Rindermann H, Becker D, and Coyle TR (2016), *Frontiers In Psychology* 7:399

Summary: Over 60% of intelligence researchers believe genes account for more than half of intelligence gaps between races:

"Following Snyderman and Rothman (1987, 1988), we surveyed expert opinions on the current state of intelligence research. This report examines expert opinions on causes of international differences in student assessment and psychometric IQ test results. Experts were surveyed about the importance of culture, genes, education (quantity and quality), wealth, health, geography, climate, politics, modernization, sampling error, test knowledge, discrimination, test bias, and migration. The importance of these factors was evaluated for diverse countries, regions, and groups including Finland, East Asia, sub-Saharan Africa, Southern Europe, the Arabian-Muslim world, Latin America, Israel, Jews in the West, Roma (gypsies), and Muslim immigrants. Education was rated by N = 71 experts as the most important cause of international ability differences. Genes were rated as the second most relevant factor but also had the highest variability in ratings. Culture, health, wealth, modernization, and politics were the next most important factors, whereas other factors such as geography, climate, test bias, and sampling error were less important."

Psychology and Neuroscience Research Unreliable

EMPIRICAL ASSESSMENT OF PUBLISHED EFFECT SIZES AND POWER IN THE RECENT COGNITIVE NEUROSCIENCE AND PSYCHOLOGY LITERATURE

Szucs D, Ioannidis JPA (2017), PLoS Biol 15(3): e2000797.

"With some reasonable assumptions about how often researchers come up with correct hypotheses, we conclude that more than 50% of published findings deemed to be statistically significant are likely to be false."

Genetics and Intelligence

GENETICS AND INTELLIGENCE DIFFERENCES: FIVE SPECIAL FINDINGS

Plomin, R., Deary, I., *Molecular Psychiatry* 20, 98–108 (2015).

"…the core of this general intelligence factor is 'the ability to reason, plan, solve problems, think abstractly, comprehend complex ideas, learn quickly, and learn from experience'. Intelligence is at the pinnacle of the hierarchical model of cognitive abilities…"

Ancestry Cognitive Scores

ROBUSTNESS ANALYSIS OF AFRICAN GENETIC ANCESTRY IN ADMIXTURE REGRESSION MODELS OF COGNITIVE TEST SCORES

John G.R. Fuerst, Ulster Institute for Social Research, *The Mankind Quarterly*, December 2021, 62(2):396-413

Study points to the role of genes in the black-white IQ gap: "Several recent admixture regression studies find that proportion of African genetic ancestry has strong explanatory power for cognitive ability test scores."

Life, Death, and Intelligence

LIFE, DEATH, AND INTELLIGENCE

Linda S. Gottfredson, *Journal of Cognitive Education and Psychology* [online], 4, 1, 23-46.

"General intelligence (g) is a highly practical ability that affects personal well-being in many aspects of life. This article reviews five key facts documenting its pervasive utility, and then illustrates how higher levels of intelligence enhance an individual's performance and well-being in four realms of daily life: work, daily self-mainte-nance, chronic illness, and accidents. The first key fact is that people who do well on one men-tal test tend to perform well on all of them; that is, all mental tests correlate with one another. All measure mostly the same underlying ability factor, no matter what their manifest content or purpose. Mental abilities differ in their gener-ality-specificity, and the general mental ability factor, g, is the most general of all. Second, high intelligence is expressed as a set of generic thinking skills that includes learning efficiently, reasoning well, thinking abstractly, and solving novel problems. These information-processing skills can be applied to virtually any kind of content in any context."

Race Differences In Intelligence

Between-group mean differences in intelligence in the United States are > 0% genetically caused: five converging lines of evidence

R.T. Warne, 2021, *The American Journal of Psychology*, 134(4), 480-501.

"The past 30 years of research in intelligence has produced a wealth of knowledge about the causes and consequences of differences in intelligence between individuals, and today mainstream opinion is that individual differenc-es in intelligence are caused by both genetic and environmental influences. Much more conten-tious is the discussion over the cause of mean intelligence differences between racial or ethnic groups. In contrast to the general consensus that interindividual differences are both genetic and environmental in origin, some claim that mean intelligence differences between racial groups are completely environmental in origin, whereas others postulate a mix of genetic and environ-mental causes. In this article I discuss 5 lines of research that provide evidence that mean differences in intelligence between racial and ethnic groups are partially genetic. These lines of evidence are findings in support of Spear-man's hypothesis, consistent results from tests of measurement invariance across American racial groups, the mathematical relationship that exists for between-group and within-group sources of heritability, genomic data derived from ge-nome-wide association studies of intelligence and polygenic scores applied to diverse samples, and

admixture studies. I also discuss future potential lines of evidence regarding the causes of average group differences across racial groups. However, the data are not fully conclusive, and the exact degree to which genes influence intergroup mean differences in intelligence is not known. This discussion applies only to native English speak-ers born in the United States and not necessarily to any other human populations."

Thirty Years Research Summary

Thirty Years of Research on Race Differences in Cognitive Ability

J. Philippe Rushton, Arthur R. Jensen, *Psychology, Public Policy, and Law 2005*, vol. 11, No. 2, 235-294

"The culture-only (0% genetic–100% environ-mental) and the hereditarian (50% genetic–50% environmental) models of the causes of mean Black–White differences in cognitive ability are compared and contrasted across 10 categories of evidence: the worldwide distribution of test scores, g factor of mental ability, heritability, brain size and cognitive ability, transracial adoption, racial admixture, regression, related life-history traits, human origins research, and hypothesized environmental variables. The new evidence reviewed here points to some genetic component in Black–White differences in mean IQ. The implication for public policy is that the discrimination model (i.e., Black-White differ-ences in socially valued outcomes will be equal barring discrimination) must be tempered by a distributional model (i.e., Black-White outcomes reflect underlying group characteristics)."

Genetics And Intelligence

Genetics and intelligence differences: five special findings

Plomin R, Deary IJ, *Mol Psychiatry*. 2015 Feb; 20(1): 98–108.

"Here, we highlight five genetic findings that are special to intelligence differences and that have important implications for its genetic architec-ture and for gene-hunting expeditions. (i) The heritability of intelligence increases from about 20% in infancy to perhaps 80% in later adult-hood. (ii) Intelligence captures genetic effects on diverse cognitive and learning abilities, which correlate phenotypically about 0.30 on average but correlate genetically about 0.60 or higher… [These findings] are being confirmed by the first new quantitative genetic technique in a century—Genome-wide Complex Trait Analysis (GCTA)—which estimates genetic influence using genome-wide genotypes in large samples of unrelated individuals. Comparing GCTA results to the results of twin studies reveals important insights into the genetic architecture of intelligence that are relevant to attempts to narrow the 'missing heritability' gap."

Heritable Psychology

Genetic and environmental influences on human psychological differences

Bouchard TJ Jr, McGue M., *Journal of Neurobiology* 2003 Jan; 54(1):4-45.

"Psychological researchers typically distinguish five major domains of individual differences in human behavior: cognitive abilities, personality, social attitudes, psychological interests, and psychopathology. In this article we: discuss a number of methodological errors commonly found in research on human individual differences; introduce a broad framework for interpreting findings from contemporary behavioral genetic studies; briefly outline the basic quantitative methods used in human behavioral genetic research; review the major criticisms of behavior genetic designs, with particular emphasis on the twin and adoption methods; describe the major or dominant theoretical scheme in each domain; and review behavioral genetic findings in all five domains. We conclude that there is now strong evidence that virtually all individual psychological differences, when reliably measured, are moderately to substantially heritable."

Brain Size Functioning

A Multimodal MRI-based Predictor of Intelligence and Its Relation to Race/ Ethnicity

Fuerst, J. G. R., Mankind Quarterly, 63(3), Article 2. (2023)

- Using a large modern dataset with top tier neurological data from MRI, we were able to confirm existing hereditarian-minded research on the relationship between brain measures and intelligence.
- The accuracy of this model was surprisingly

high, but some of this was related to ancestry confounding that had also previously been explored by other researchers. Using the White subsample of the data is sufficient to remove this, but beware of variance differences in test samples.

- Race gaps show up on these modern predictions of intelligence based on brain data where the model has never seen a non-White person, and they are quite large.
- The MRI-model can account for about a third of the observed intelligence gaps (36% for Black-White).
- The extended Spearman's hypothesis was seen whereby g-loadings (of the MRI predictors) relates positively to group differences (Black-White, Hispanic-White gaps), and polygenic score validities (heritabilities).
- The hereditarian research paradigm keeps being productive, generating new and interesting results in modern data.

Imaging Correlations

Brain imaging correlates of general intelligence in UK Biobank

SR Cox, SJ Ritchie, C Fawns-Ritchie, EM Tucker-Drob, IJ Deary, BioRxiv 599472, April 04, 2019

A massive 2018 study using UK Biobank data from 13,608 adults, which was controlled for sex, age, height, socioeconomic status and race found a "robust association between total brain volume and fluid intelligence… consistent with previous findings."

Volume Studies

Are bigger brains smarter? Evidence from a large-scale preregistered study

Nave, Gideon; University of Pennsylvania Wharton School, Marketing, Jung, Wi Hoon; Korea University, Psychology, Linnér, Richard; Vrije Universiteit, Amsterdam Faculteit Economische wetenschappen en Bedrijfskunde, Economics, Kable, Joseph; University of Pennsylvania, Psychology, Koellinger, Philipp; Vrije Universiteit Amsterdam Faculteit Economische wetenschappen en Bedrijfskunde, Economics, Psychological Science, PSCI-17-1601.R1, 24 July 2018

This very large study of 29,004 individuals found an association between total brain volume and general intelligence: "We find a robust association between total brain volume and fluid intelligence (r=0.19), which is consistent with previous findings in the literature after controlling for measurement quality of intelligence in our data. We also find a positive relationship with educational attainment (r=0.12). These relationships are mainly driven by grey matter (rather than white matter or fluid volume) and effect sizes are similar for both sexes and across age groups."

Brain Volume and Intelligence

Big-brained people are smarter: A meta-analysis of the relationship between in vivo brain volume and intelligence

Michael A. McDaniel, *Intelligence* 33 (2005) 337 – 346

"The relationship between brain volume and intelligence has been a topic of a scientific debate since at least the 1830s. To address the debate, a meta-analysis of the relationship between in vivo brain volume and intelligence was conducted. Based on 37 samples across 1530 people, the population correlation was estimated at 0.33. The correlation is higher for females than males. It is also higher for adults than children. For all age and sex groups, it is clear that brain volume is positively correlated with intelligence."

The causal influence of brain size on human intelligence: Evidence from within-family phenotypic associations and GWAS modeling

James J. Leea, Matt McGue, William G. Iacono, Andrew M. Michaelb, Christopher F. Chabris, Intelligence 75 (2019), July–August 2019, pgs. 48-58

This 2019 GWAS meta-analysis, one of the largest ever conducted (involving over 50,000 individuals), identified 346 new genes associated in the overlap between brain volume and intelligence. Modern brain studies use advanced imaging and scanning technologies to accurately measure brain size, and study sample sizes can be dozens or even hundreds of times larger than in studies conducted only decades ago. Many of the specific genes associated with brain size have now been identified in a large genome-wide association study (GWAS). "[M]any specific brain structures [are] strongly heritable (i.e., 80% or more)... [there is] a strong heritability for brain volume (greater than 80%)."

Cognitive Ability and Crime

Is the Association between General Cognitive Ability and Violent Crime Caused by Family-Level Confounders?

Thomas Frisell, Yudi Pawitan, Niklas Långström

"Research has consistently found lower cognitive ability to be related to increased risk for violent and other antisocial behaviour."
Since the association remains after adjusting for parental SES and other variables, it is often assumed to be causal.

Smart Fraction Theory Vindicated

Smart Fraction Theory: A Comprehensive Re-evaluation

Kirkegaard, E. O. W., & Carl, N. (2022). *Comparative Sociology*, 21(6), 677-699.

The Smart Fraction Theory (SFT) suggests that a nation's economic growth and prosperity are highly dependent on the cognitive abilities of its most intelligent individuals, known as the smart fraction. In his article, Emil Kirkegaard discusses a recent study which provides empirical support for the SFT.
The study, conducted by researchers at the London School of Economics (LSE), analyzed PISA and TIMSS data from 85 countries and demonstrated a strong correlation between the cognitive abilities of the top 5% of the population and economic growth. According to the study, a 1-point increase in the cognitive ability of the smart fraction leads to a 0.35-point increase in annual GDP per capita growth.

Hypothesis For *g* via ABCD Database

A Genetic Hypothesis for American Race/Ethnic Differences in Mean g: A Reply to Warne (2021) with Fifteen New Empirical Tests Using the ABCD Dataset.

Fuerst, J. & Shibaev, V. & Kirkegaard, E. O. W. (2023)., *Mankind Quarterly*, 2023 June

The study discusses a research conducted using the Adolescent Brain Cognitive Development (ABCD) dataset, which is a large-scale project focused on brain development in children.
The study aimed to examine the relationship between genetic ancestry, intelligence, and brain size, particularly across different racial and

ethnic groups.

The findings of the study indicate that there are genetic influences on general intelligence (referred to as "g") and brain size. The heritability of intelligence and brain volume was found to be moderate to high within both White and non-White groups. Shared environmental factors were found to have a low impact on these traits.

The study also explored the role of genetic ancestry in intelligence and brain size. The results suggest that genetic ancestry, rather than self-reported or social race, is a better predictor of intelligence. The study observed that individuals with higher proportions of European ancestry tended to have higher intelligence and larger brain sizes.

Additionally, the study examined the use of polygenic scores (PGS) to predict intelligence based on genetic variants. It was found that PGS worked better for individuals with European ancestry compared to other racial and ethnic groups. The validity of brain size as a predictor of intelligence was also observed within each group.

The study also analyzed the influence of parental socioeconomic status (SES) on intelligence and brain size. The findings indicated that parental SES had a limited impact on intelligence among adopted children, suggesting that the association between SES and intelligence may not be solely mediated by the parental environment.

Overall, the study provides evidence supporting the partial genetic basis of intelligence and brain size, with genetic ancestry playing a significant role. The findings suggest that genetic factors contribute to differences in intelligence and brain size across different racial and ethnic groups.

Intelligence Inheritability

GENOME-WIDE ASSOCIATION STUDIES ESTABLISH THAT HUMAN INTELLIGENCE IS HIGHLY HERITABLE AND POLYGENIC

Davies, Gail., Molecular Psychiatry (2011). *Mol Psychiatry*. 2011 Oct; 16(10): 996–1005.

"Our results unequivocally confirm that a substantial proportion of individual differences in human intelligence is due to genetic variation, and are consistent with many genes of small effects underlying the additive genetic influences on intelligence."

The Ancestor Effect

THE ANCESTOR EFFECT: THINKING ABOUT OUR GENETIC ORIGIN ENHANCES INTELLECTUAL PERFORMANCE

Fischer, Peter et al. European Journal of Social Psychology 41 (2011).

"The present research hypothesizes that thinking about one's genetic origin (i.e. ancestors) provides people with a positive psychological resource that increases their intellectual performance. To test this line of reasoning, we manipulated whether participants thought about their ancestors or not (manipulation of ancestor salience), and measured their expected as well as actual intellectual performance in a variety of intelligence tasks. Four studies supported our assumptions: participants show higher expected (Study 1) and actual intellectual performance (Studies 2-4) when they are reminded about their ancestors. We also have initial evidence that this effect may be fueled by increased levels of perceived control and promotion orientation. Theoretical and practical implications are discussed."

Egalitarian Fiction

EGALITARIAN FICTION AND COLLECTIVE FRAUD

Gottfredson, Linda S., *Society* 31, no. 3 (1994).

The current state of social science is criticized for perpetuating a falsehood known as the "egalitarian fiction," which asserts that racial-ethnic groups have no average differences in developed intelligence (general mental ability). Despite substantial evidence supporting the existence of intelligence differences among groups, this misconception persists in social policy. The text questions why and how this falsehood is maintained, whether social scientists inadvertently contribute to it, and if they engage in a form of "collective fraud" by collectively distorting or evading the truth. While individual scholars may not be guilty of fraud, their cumulative actions contribute to sustaining this untruth, prompting an examination of the social process behind this phenomenon.

G Matters

Why g matters: The Complexity of Everyday Life

Gottfredson, Linda S., Intelligence 24 (1997).

"Personnel selection research provides much evidence that intelligence (g) is an important predictor of performance in training and on the job, especially in higher level work. This article provides evidence that g has pervasive utility in work settings because it is essentially the ability to deal with cognitive complexity, in particular, with complex information processing. The more complex a work task, the greater the advantages that higher g confers in performing it well. Everyday tasks, like job duties, also differ in their level of complexity. The importance of intelligence therefore differs systematically across different arenas of social life as well as economic endeavor. Data from the National Adult Literacy Survey are used to show how higher levels of cognitive ability systematically improve individuals' odds of dealing successfully with the ordinary demands of modern life (such as banking, using maps and transportation schedules, reading and understanding forms, interpreting news articles). These and other data are summarized to illustrate how the advantages of higher g, even when they are small, cumulate to affect the overall life chances of individuals at different ranges of the IQ bell curve. The article concludes by suggesting ways to reduce the risks for low-IQ individuals of being left behind by an increasingly complex postindustrial economy."

The Failure of Compensatory Education

How Much Can We Boost IQ and Scholastic Achievement?

Jensen, Authur R., Harvard Educational Review 39 (1969).

Arthur Jensen questions the effectiveness of compensatory education programs in improving children's IQ and academic achievement. He challenges the prevailing idea that IQ differences are mainly due to environmental factors and cultural biases in IQ tests. Jensen defines IQ as a common factor in all mental ability tests and uses an analysis of variance model to separate genetic and environmental influences on IQ. He argues that genetic factors play a sig-nificant role in determining IQ, with environmental factors, particularly prenatal influences, having a lesser impact.

Jensen suggests that social class and racial differences in intelligence cannot be solely attributed to environmental factors but involve genetic factors as well. He explains that environmental factors act as a "threshold variable," limiting a child's performance to their genetic potential, and enriched educational programs cannot surpass this potential.

Additionally, Jensen discusses the limitations of educational programs aimed at increasing IQ and proposes a shift towards teaching specific skills instead. He believes that educational methods should be based on a broader range of mental abilities beyond IQ to be more effective.

See also:

Jensen, Authur R. *The g Factor: The Science of Mental Ability*, Praeger Publishers, 1998.

Jensen, Authur R. *Clocking the Mind: Mental Chronometry and Individual Differences*, Elsevier Science, 2006.

Global Bell Curve

The work of Richard Lynn illustrates a wide array of consequences and possibilities related to populations with low or high IQ. His study on the Jews is of particular interest.

Lynn, Richard. *Dysgenics: Genetic Deterioration in Modern Populations*, Praeger Publishers, 1996.

Lynn, Richard. *Eugenics: A Reassessment*, Praeger Publishers, 2001.

Lynn, Richard. *Race Differences in Intelligence: An Evolutionary Analysis*, Washington Summit Publishers, 2006.

Lynn, Richard. *The Global Bell Curve*, Washington Summit Publishers, 2008.

Lynn, Richard. *The Chosen People: A Study of Jewish Intelligence and Achievement*, Washington Summit Publishers, 2011.

Lynn, Richard. *IQ and the Wealth of Nations: Richard Lynn Replies to Ron Unz*, VDare, August 2, 2012.

Lynn, Richard & Tatu Vanhanen. *IQ and the Wealth of Nations*, Praeger Publishers, 2002.

Lynn, Richard & Tatu Vanhanen. *Intelligence: A Unifying Construct for the Social Sciences*, Ulster Institute for Social Research, 2011.

Fraudulent Science in the 20th C.

THE GREATEST COLLECTIVE SCIENTIFIC FRAUD OF THE 20TH CENTURY: THE DEMOLITION OF DIFFERENTIAL PSYCHOLOGY AND EUGENICS

Nyborg, Helmuth. *Mankind Quarterly* 60, no. 3 (2011).

"Supporters of differential psychology and eugenics were allowed to freely reflect on the importance of individual differences, on how to avoid dysgenic development, and even on how to improve the human condition. This basic proviso for meaningful scientific inquiries changed radically around 1950 when the topics were banned and their adherents demonized, despite supportive evidence. The present paper provides examples of typical attacks and analyzes the reasons for this bizarre deviation from normal science. It points to some of the people and institutions responsible, discusses the unfair tools they use, and illustrates how damaging their inexcusable intellectual corruption has been for the academic life at many modern universities. It remains an important future task to find ways of breaking the spell and return differential psychology and eugenics to normal science again."

DNA Markers Effective

COMMON DNA MARKERS CAN ACCOUNT FOR MORE THAN HALF OF THE GENETIC INFLUENCE ON COGNITIVE ABILITIES

Plomin, Robert et al. *Psychological Science*, March 15, 2013.

"For nearly a century, twin and adoption studies have yielded substantial estimates of heritability for cognitive abilities, although it has proved difficult for genomewide-association studies to identify the genetic variants that account for this heritability (i.e., the missing-heritability problem). However, a new approach, genomewide complex-trait analysis (GCTA), forgoes the identification of individual variants to estimate the total heritability captured by common DNA markers on genotyping arrays. In the same sample of 3,154 pairs of 12-year-old twins, we directly compared twin-study heritability estimates for cognitive abilities (language, verbal, nonverbal, and general) with GCTA estimates captured by 1.7 million DNA markers. We found that DNA markers tagged by the array accounted for .66 of the estimated heritability, reaffirming that cognitive abilities are heritable. Larger sample sizes alone will be sufficient to identify many of the genetic variants that influence cognitive abilities."

Cognitive Capitalism

INTELLECTUAL CLASSES, TECHNOLOGICAL PROGRESS AND ECONOMIC DEVELOPMENT: THE RISE OF COGNITIVE CAPITALISM

Rindermann, Heiner. *Personality and Individual Differences* 53 (2012).

"Cognitive ability theory claims that peoples' competences are decisive for economic wealth. For a large number of countries Lynn and Vanhanen (2002) have published data on mean intelligence levels and compared them to wealth and productivity indicators. The correlation between intelligence and wealth was supported by studies done by different authors using different countries and controls. Based on their pioneering research two research questions were developed: does intelligence lead to wealth or does wealth lead to intelligence or are other determinants involved? If a nation's intelligence increases wealth, how does intelligence achieve this? To answer them we need longitudinal studies and theoretical attempts, investigating cognitive ability effects at the levels of individuals, institutions and societies and examining factors which lie between intelligence and growth. Two studies, using a cross-lagged panel design or latent variables and measuring economic liberty, shares of intellectual classes and indicators of scientific-technological accomplishment, show that cognitive ability leads to higher wealth and that for this process the achievement of high ability groups is important, stimulating growth through scientific-technological progress and by influencing the quality of economic institutions. In modernity, wealth depends on cognitive resources enabling the evolution of cognitive capitalism."

The Moralistic Fallacy

James Watson's most inconvenient truth: Race realism and the moralistic fallacy

Rushton, J. Philippe & Arthur R. Jensen. *Medical Hypotheses* 71 (2008).

"Recent editorials in this journal have defended the right of eminent biologist James Watson to raise the unpopular hypothesis that people of sub-Saharan African descent score lower, on average, than people of European or East Asian descent on tests of general intelligence. As those editorials imply, the scientific evidence is substantial in showing a genetic contribution to these differences. The unjustified ill treatment meted out to Watson therefore requires setting the record straight about the current state of the evidence on intelligence, race, and genetics. In this paper, we summarize our own previous reviews based on 10 categories of evidence: The worldwide distribution of test scores; the g factor of mental ability; heritability differences; brain size differences; trans-racial adoption studies; racial admixture studies; regression-to-the-mean effects; related life-history traits; human origins research; and the poverty of predictions from culture-only explanations. The preponderance of evidence demonstrates that in intelligence, brain size, and other life-history variables, East Asians average a higher IQ and larger brain than Europeans who average a higher IQ and larger brain than Africans. Further, these group differences are 50–80% heritable. These are facts, not opinions and science must be governed by data. There is no place for the 'moralistic fallacy' that reality must conform to our social, political, or ethical desires."

More Than Skin-Deep

Color May Be More than Skin Deep

Rushton, J. Philippe. *VDare*, July 17, 2012.

The text discusses the relationship between pigmentation [skin color], aggression, sexuality, and intelligence in humans and animals. It references studies and data showing correlations between darker skin pigmentation and higher levels of aggression and sexuality, as well as lower intelligence scores. These correlations are observed in various countries and across different racial groups, with darker-skinned pop-

ulations generally exhibiting these traits more prominently.

The text also points out that these correlations can have real-life consequences, such as higher rates of sexually transmitted diseases in populations with darker skin. It suggests that genetic factors may play a role in these correlations, alongside cultural and environmental factors often cited as explanations for differences in behavior and outcomes.

See further:

Rushton, J. Philippe and Donald I Templer. *Do pigmentation and the melanocortin system modulate aggression and sexuality in humans as they do in other animals?*, *Personality and Individual Differences* 53 (2012).

Ability Differentials

Ability differentials between nations are unlikely to disappear

Woodley, M. A., & G. Meisenberg. American Psychologist, Sept. 2012.

The article challenges Nisbett et al.'s optimistic view that the Flynn effect (increased IQ scores over generations) will eliminate cross-national IQ inequalities by the end of the 21st century and disprove the idea that some nations lack the intelligence to industrialize. The authors argue that this optimism is not supported by the evidence.

They point out that in Europe and the United States, Flynn effects are rare in cohorts born after about 1980. They also emphasize the need to distinguish between accelerated childhood development and higher adult intelligence. For example, while British children showed improved performance on IQ tests between 1980 and 2008, adolescents aged 14 and 15 experienced a decline in IQ scores.

The article also discusses findings from developing countries, highlighting that gains in IQ are not uniform across age groups and that even children enrolled in selective private schools may not achieve high average IQ scores. They note that only a few studies in developing countries found significant Flynn effects.

The authors suggest that cultural amplifier effects and the heritability of intelligence contribute to incomplete convergence between high-IQ and low-IQ countries. They argue that the basic pattern of IQ differences between countries is likely to persist, although the magnitude of these differences may decrease.

Additionally, they mention the phenomenon of "dysgenic" differential fertility, where individuals with lower IQ and education tend to have more children. This pattern, they assert, suggests that "genetic g" (genotypic IQ) is declining globally, counteracting the Flynn effect's impact on IQ scores.

In conclusion, the authors argue that these empirical observations should inform any discussions about the future of human intelligence differentials, casting doubt on the idea that such disparities will be eliminated entirely in the coming decades.

— Ethnic Genetic Interests —

EGI Overview

Why Was the Understanding of Ethnic Genetic Interests Delayed for 30 Years?

Sallis, Ted. Occidental Observer, June 17, 2009

Summary: The article discusses the concept of Ethnic Genetic Interests (EGI) and its relevance in understanding issues related to ethnic and racial nationalism. EGI is the idea that individuals share more genetic similarity with members of their ethnic or racial group than with individuals from different groups. This genetic relatedness creates a biological interest in preserving and promoting the well-being of one's ethnic or racial group.

The article traces the development of the EGI concept, starting with the work of evolutionary biologist W.D. Hamilton, who introduced the idea of kin selection, where individuals are more likely to help their close relatives because they share genes. Later, Henry Harpending quantified how helping one's ethnic group could be adaptive in the context of group competition.

The article also addresses the obstacles and resistance faced by scholars advocating for EGI as a legitimate concept. It points out that some academics, particularly those on the political left, have been reluctant to accept EGI due to its potential implications for ethnic and racial issues. The article suggests that political preferences have played a significant role in hindering the acceptance of EGI in academic discourse.

Pharmacogenomic Risk Stratification

Population structure and pharmacogenomic risk stratification in the United States

Shashwat Deepali Nagar, Andrew B. Conley, I.K. Jordan

"Background: Pharmacogenomic (PGx) variants mediate how individuals respond to medication, and response differences among racial / ethnic groups have been attributed to patterns of PGx diversity. We hypothesized that genetic ancestry (GA) would provide higher resolution for stratifying PGx risk, since it serves as a more reliable surrogate for genetic diversity than self-identified race / ethnicity (SIRE), which includes a substantial social component...

"Results: Whole genome genotypes were used to characterize individuals' continental ancestry fractions – European, African, and Native American – and individuals were grouped according to their GA profiles. SIRE and GA groups were found to be highly concordant. Continental ancestry predicts individuals' SIRE with > 96% accuracy, and accordingly, GA provides only a marginal increase in resolution for PGx risk stratification. In light of the concordance between SIRE and GA, taken together with the fact that information on SIRE is readily available to clinicians, we evaluated PGx variation between SIRE groups to explore the potential clinical utility of race and ethnicity."

Ethnic Density Health

Health Advantages of Ethnic Density for African American and Mexican American Elderly Individuals

Alvarez, Kimberly et al. *American Journal of Public Health* (2012).

Greater ethnic density reduces health risks and correlates with increased health in young and old populations of African America and Mexican American groups.

Ethnocentric Behavior Theories

The Evolution of Ethnocentric Behavior

Axelrod, Robert, & R. A. Hammond. *Midwest Political Science Convention*, April 16, 2003.

"Ethnocentrism is a nearly universal syndrome of attitudes and behaviors. Behaviors associated with ethnocentrism include cooperation with members of the in-group, but not out-groups. We show that ethnocentric behavior can emerge from a simple evolutionary model of local competition between individuals...Results from the model demonstrate that ethnocentric behavior can evolve even when direct reciprocity is impossible, opportunities for 'cheating' exist, and agents have minimal cognitive ability. When cooperating is relatively costly, ethnocentric behavior can even be necessary to sustain cooperation."

See also:

Axelrod, Robert, R. A. Hammond & A. Grafen. *Altruism via kin-selection strategies that rely on arbitrary tags with which they coevolve, Evolution* 58, no. 8 (2004).

Pain Resonance

RACIAL BIAS REDUCES EMPATHIC SENSORIMOTOR RESONANCE WITH OTHER-RACE PAIN

Avenanti, Alessio. *Current Biology* 20 (2010).

"Although social psychology studies suggest that racism often manifests itself as a lack of empathy, i.e., the ability to share and comprehend others' feelings and intentions, evidence for differential empathic reactivity to the pain of same- or different-race individuals is meager. Using transcranial magnetic stimulation, we explored sensorimotor empathic brain responses in black and white individuals who exhibited implicit but not explicit ingroup preference and race-specific autonomic reactivity. We found that observing the pain of ingroup models inhibited the onlookers' corticospinal system as if they were feeling the pain. Both black and white individuals exhibited empathic reactivity also when viewing the pain of stranger, very unfamiliar, violet-hand models. By contrast, no vicarious mapping of the pain of individuals culturally marked as outgroup members on the basis of their skin color was found. Importantly, group-specific lack of empathic reactivity was higher in the onlookers who exhibited stronger implicit racial bias. These results indicate that human beings react empathically to the pain of stranger individuals. However, racial bias and stereotypes may change this reactivity into a group-specific lack of sensorimotor resonance."

Ethnic Density Buffers

ETHNIC DENSITY AS A BUFFER FOR PSYCHOTIC EXPERIENCES: FINDINGS FROM A NATIONAL SURVEY

Das-Munshi, Jayati et al. *British Journal of Psychiatry*, July 26, 2012.

"For every ten percentage point reduction in own-group density, the relative odds of reporting psychotic experiences increased 1.07 times (95% CI 1.01–1.14, P = 0.03 (trend)) for the total minority ethnic sample. In general, people living in areas of lower own-group density experienced greater social adversity that was in turn associated with reporting psychotic experiences.

"Conclusions: People resident in neighbourhoods of higher own-group density experience 'buffering' effects from the social risk factors for psychosis."

Civic Identity vs Euro Ethnicity

THE GREEK-ROMAN INVENTION OF CIVIC IDENTITY VERSUS THE CURRENT DEMOTION OF EUROPEAN ETHNICITY

Duchesne, Ricardo., *Occidental Quarterly* 15, no. 3 (2015).

"...the historical research validates the idea that European nation-states were founded around a strong ethnic core even if there were minorities coexisting with majorities. The states of Western Europe developed liberal civic institutions within the framework of this ethnic core. Sociobiological research further supports the natural inclination of humans to have a preference for their own kin. This biologically based research demonstrates that humans cannot be abstracted from an ethnic collective. The claim that such a preference is an irrational disposition imposed from above by regressive elites is false. Ethnocentrism is a rationally driven disposition consistent with civic freedoms. Civic freedoms are consistent with a collective sense of kin-culture. What is not consistent with rationally based research, with individual rational decision making, and with our collective kin-dispositions, are the claims that Western nations were civic in origins, and the current enforcement of mass immigration without allowance of open rational debate."

Hamilton's Gene-Sharing Theory

Kinship and Population Subdivision

Harpending, Henry., *Population and Environment* 24, no. 2 (2002).

Summary: Gene-sharing correlates and/or causes in-group affinity at the parent-child relation but also (and perhaps) beyond to ethnic groups.

See also:

Harpending, Henry. *Giving Bigotry a Chance, West Hunter*, March 1, 2012.

Multi-Pronged Strategies to Ethnicity

An Integrative Evolutionary Perspective on Ethnicity

MacDonald, Kevin., *Politics and the Life Sciences* 20, no. 1 (2001).

"This paper integrates several different but mutually consistent evolutionary approaches to ethnicity: genetic similarity theory, social identity theory, individualism/collectivism, an evolved racial/ethnic human kinds module, and rational choice mechanisms relying on domain general cognitive mechanisms. These theories are consistent with each other, and together they illustrate the interplay of evolved cognitive and motivational systems with mechanisms of rational choice that are able to choose adaptive strategies in uncertain, novel environments."

Psychology and White Ethnocentrism

Evolutionary Roots of Ethnocentrism

MacDonald, Kevin., *Occidental Quarterly* 6, no. 4 (2006).

"I think that evolutionists have not been properly sensitive to the enormous gulf between humans and animals resulting from human general intelligence and the Conscientiousness system. At a very broad level, the Conscientiousness system allows our behavior to come under the control of the surrounding culture. We make complex appraisals of how our behavior will affect us given the current cultural milieu. Potential murderers may think about the possibility of leaving DNA evidence and what types of plea bargains might be possible if they are caught. Potential thought criminals must assess the risks to their livelihood and their reputation in their face-to-face world.

"But it gets more complicated than that. Modern humans are exposed to an often bewildering array of cultural messages that affect how they see the world. These messages are often directed at the explicit processing system and they may be influenced by a wide range of competing interests. For example, it is a commonplace that media images have important effects on behavior even though people are often unaware that their behavior is influenced by the images. These images are often engineered by advertisers who are consciously attempting to influence the recipients of the messages in ways that conform to the advertisers' interests, not those of the audience.

"More important, media messages shape the discussion of issues related to white identity and interests. The culture of critique has become the explicit culture of the West, endlessly repeated in media messages but packaged differently for people of different levels of intelligence and education, and for people with different interests and from different subcultures. The message of this paper is that by programming the higher areas of the brain, this explicit culture is able to control the implicit ethnocentric tendencies of white people.

"In attempting to find a way out of this morass, therefore, changing the explicit culture is critical. To paraphrase Bill Clinton's presidential campaign slogan, it's the explicit culture, stupid. Changing the explicit culture won't be easy, but I suggest that the first step is a psychological one: Proud and confident explicit assertions of ethnic identity and interests among white people, and the creation of communities where such explicit assertions are considered normal and natural rather than a reason for ostracism. The fact that such assertions appeal to our implicit psychology is certainly an asset. It's always easier to go with a natural tendency than to oppose it. And in this case, opposing our natural ethnocentric tendencies by using our quintessentially human prefrontal inhibitory control against our own ethnic interests is nothing less than a death sentence."

See further:

MacDonald, Kevin. *The Utter Normality Of Ethnonationalism — Except For Whites, VDare*, March 27, 2008.

MacDonald, Kevin. *Evolution, Psychology, and a Conflict Theory of Culture, Evolutionary Psychology* 7 (2009).

The Homophily Principle

Birds of a Feather: Homophily in Social Networks

McPherson, Miller et al., *Annual Review of Sociology* 27 (2001).

"Similarity breeds connection. This principle—the homophily principle—structures network ties of every type, including marriage, friendship, work, advice, support, information transfer, exchange, comembership, and other types of relationship. The result is that people's personal networks are homogeneous with regard to many sociodemographic, behavioral, and intrapersonal characteristics. Homophily limits people's social worlds in a way that has powerful implications for the information they receive, the attitudes they form, and the interactions they experience. Homophily in race and ethnicity creates the strongest divides in our personal environments, with age, religion, education, occupation, and gender following in roughly that order. Geographic propinquity, families, organizations, and isomorphic positions in social systems all create contexts in which homophilous relations form. Ties between nonsimilar individuals also dissolve at a higher rate, which sets the stage for the formation of niches (localized positions) within social space. We argue for more research on: (a) the basic ecological processes that link organizations, associations, cultural communities, social movements, and many other social forms; (b) the impact of multiplex ties on the patterns of homophily; and (c) the dynamics of network change over time through which networks and other social entities co-evolve."

Genetic Affinity In Marriage

Married couples have more DNA in common than random pairs of people

Morin, Monte., *LA Times*, May 19, 2014.

"We provide evidence for genetic assortative mating in this population but the strength of this association is substantially smaller than the strength of educational assortative mating in the same sample. Furthermore, genetic similarity explains at most 10% of the assortative mating by education levels. Results are replicated using comparable data from the Framingham Heart Study."

Pathological Altruism

Negative aspects of altruism and empathy

Oakley, Barbara A. ed. *Pathological Altruism*. Oxford University Press, 2011.

The book discusses the concept of "pathological altruism" (PA), a relatively new term referring to the sincere attempt to help others that, instead of benefiting them, harms them or oneself. PA involves an unhealthy focus on others at the detriment of one's own needs. Several contributors to the book provide definitions and examples of PA, such as people falsely believing they caused others' problems or believing that their own success harms others. The book also highlights the addictive nature of self-righteousness and the pleasure of feeling morally superior.

The book points out that some forms of PA may be related to excessive agreeableness or an excessively female brain, and it can lead to co-dependency, self-sacrifice, or enabling harmful behavior in others. It suggests that PA can be observed in various contexts, including foreign aid, and discusses how individuals may seek the pleasure of altruism for their own sake.

The book also briefly touches on group differences in altruism and mentions "parochial altruism," where individuals may harm themselves or their group to benefit their own group. It acknowledges that in-group loyalty is part of human nature but expresses concerns about it leading to the persecution of outsiders.

Natural Selection of Friends

Friendship and natural selection

Nicholas A. Christakis and James H. Fowler, University of California, 111 (supplement_3) 10796-10801

"More than any other species, humans form social ties to individuals who are neither kin nor mates, and these ties tend to be with similar people. Here, we show that this similarity extends to genotypes. Across the whole genome, friends' genotypes at the single nucleotide polymorphism level tend to be positively correlated (homophilic). In fact, the increase in similarity relative to strangers is at the level of fourth cousins. However, certain genotypes are also negatively correlated (heterophilic) in friends. And the degree of correlation in genotypes can be used to create a 'friendship score' that predicts the existence of friendship ties in a hold-out sample. A focused gene-set analysis indicates that some of the overall correlation in genotypes can be explained by specific systems; for example, an olfactory gene set is homophilic and an immune system gene set is heterophilic, suggesting that these systems may play a role in the formation or maintenance of friendship ties. Friends may be a kind of 'functional kin.' Finally, homophilic genotypes exhibit significantly higher measures of positive selection, suggesting that, on average, they may yield a synergistic fitness advantage that has been helping to drive recent human evolution."

Kin Preference Genetic Theories

GENETIC SIMILARITY, HUMAN ALTRUISM, AND GROUP SELECTION

Rushton, J. Phillipe., Behavioral and Brain Sciences 12 (1989).

"A new theory of attraction and liking based on kin selection suggests that people detect genetic similarity in others in order to give preferential treatment to those who are most similar to themselves. There are many sources of empirical and theoretical support for this view, including (1) the inclusive fitness theory of altruism, (2) kin recognition studies of animals raised apart, (3) assortative mating studies, (4) favoritism in families, (5) selective similarity among friends, and (6) ethnocentrism. Specific tests of the theory show that (1) sexually interacting couples who produce a child are genetically more similar to each other in blood antigens than they are either to sexually interacting couples who fail to produce a child or to randomly paired couples from the same sample; (2) similarity between marriage partners is most marked in the more genetically influenced of sets of anthropometric, cognitive, and personality characteristics; (3) after the death of a child, parental grief intensity is correlated with the child's similarity to the parent; (4) long-term male friendship pairs are more similar to each other in blood antigens than they are to random dyads from the same sample; and (5) similarity among best friends is most marked in the more genetically influenced of sets of attitudinal, personality, and anthropometric characteristics. The mechanisms underlying these findings may constitute a biological substrate of ethnocentrism, enabling group selection to occur."

See also:

Rushton, J. Phillipe. *Ethnic nationalism, evolutionary psychology and Genetic Similarity Theory, Nations and Nationalism* 11, no. 4 (2005).

Rushton, J. Phillipe. *Inclusive fitness in human relationships, Biological Journal of the Linnean Society* 96 (2009).

Rushton, J. Phillipe. *Shared Genes: The Evolution of Ethnonationalism, VDare,* Aug. 20, 2009.

Good Fences Create Good Neighbors

GOOD FENCES: THE IMPORTANCE OF SETTING BOUNDARIES FOR PEACEFUL COEXISTENCE

Rutherford, Alex et al., *New England Complex Systems Institute,* Oct. 6, 2011.

"We consider the conditions of peace and violence among ethnic groups, testing a theory designed to predict the locations of violence and interventions that can promote peace. Characterizing the model's success in predicting peace requires examples where peace prevails despite diversity. Switzerland is recognized as a country of peace, stability and prosperity. This is surprising because of its linguistic and religious diversity that in other parts of the world lead to conflict and violence. Here we analyze how peaceful stability is maintained. Our analysis shows that peace does not depend on integrated coexistence, but rather on well defined topographical and political boundaries separating groups, allowing for partial autonomy within a single country. In Switzerland, mountains and lakes are an important part of the boundaries between sharply defined linguistic areas. Political canton and circle (sub-canton) boundaries often separate religious groups. Where such boundaries do not appear to be sufficient, we find that specific aspects of the population distribution guarantee either sufficient separation or sufficient mixing to inhibit intergroup violence according to the quantitative theory of conflict. In exactly one region, a porous mountain range does not adequately separate linguistic groups and that region has experienced significant violent conflict, leading to the recent creation of the canton of Jura. Our analysis supports the hypothesis that violence between groups can be inhibited by physical and political boundaries. A similar analysis of the area of the former Yugoslavia shows that during widespread ethnic violence existing political boundaries did not coincide with the boundaries of distinct groups, but peace prevailed in specific areas where they did coincide. The success of peace in Switzerland may serve as a model to resolve conflict in other ethnically diverse countries and regions of the world."

Adaptive EGI

ESTIMATING ETHNIC GENETIC INTERESTS: IS IT ADAPTIVE TO RESIST REPLACEMENT MIGRATION?

Salter, Frank., *Population & Environment* 24, no. 2 (2002).

"Analyses of the costs and benefits of immigration have not considered the dependence of an ethny's reproductive fitness on its monopoly of a demarcated territory. Global assays of human genetic variation allow estimation of the genetic losses incurred by a member of a population when random fellow ethnics are replaced by immigrants from different ethnies. This potential loss defines an individual's ethnic genetic interest as a quantity that varies with the genetic distance of potential immigrants. W. D. Hamilton showed that self-sacrificial altruism is adaptive when it preserves the genetic interests of a population of genetically similar individuals. Ethnic genetic interest can be so large that altruism on behalf of one's ethny—'ethnic nepotism'—can be adaptive when it prevents replacement. It follows that ethnies usually have an interest in securing and maintaining a monopoly over a demarcated territory, an idea consonant with the universal nationalism of Bismarck and Woodrow Wilson. ...

"Population-genetic data show that great genetic diversity still exists between ethnic groups. Modern ethnies are less homogeneous than their ancestral tribal forebears due to improvements in transport and the increasing size of administrative and economic units. But the same developments have widened the competitive realm from neighboring tribes to encompass all human populations. Populations that have not been in contact for many tens of millennia are now able to migrate to each other's lands in large numbers. Enculturation of immigrants does not necessarily eliminate ethnic competition. The genetic distance between modern ethnies is often so great that it is visible in racial differences of skin color, physiognomy, and body proportions. These differences are reliable markers of significant ethnic kinship distance, as predicted by Hamilton (1975, pg. 144): 'At

about the point where the colony members are related to each other like outbred sibs it should become relatively easy for individuals to detect a fairly clear difference in appearance when comparing fellow colony members with outsiders.... [This] should make possible fairly accurate separation of "us" and "them"...' This is not the "green beard" effect in which the same gene causes altruism and some visible characteristic, since Hamilton is referring to 'several traits which are independently inherited'. He is thus referring to the same kind of broad-based genetic similarities that characterize genealogical kin. Citizens in multi-ethnic societies, especially multi-racial ones, are faced with an invidious choice. They can do what comes naturally and practice ethnic nepotism, which is adaptive by promoting relative fitness but, especially when exhibited by the majority, engenders social conflict and can make the economy less productive. Alternatively, citizens can adopt the discipline of non-discriminatory behavior which, when they are in the majority might raise the carrying capacity of society as a whole but sacrifices relative fitness. Eliminating majority discrimination only worsens the problem if minority discrimination is not also eliminated, since asymmetrical mobilization is likely to give minorities disproportionate influence, hastening the majority's decline. For historical reasons this asymmetry is commonly accepted as multiculturalism that is 'working.' Until about 1965 Western multi-ethnic societies gave the ethnic majority precedence, disadvantaging minorities. Majority free-riding on minority labor was commonplace, for example in the institution of slavery and the post-emancipation importation of low-cost labor. However, since the 1960s and the broad acceptance of civil rights claims a new modus operandi developed. Majority ethnic groups restrained their own discrimination towards minorities more than the reverse, a formula known as multiculturalism. This unilateral withdrawal from ethnic competition arguably benefited the economy as a whole and certainly benefited minorities. But this formula was risky for a majority when minorities were genetically distant, since it turned minorities into potential free-riders on majority altruism. In several Western societies, including the United States, Canada, and Australia, the new approach coincided with the lifting of controls on non-European immigration and consequent rapid changes to those countries' ethnic make-up. From the majority perspective, it would seem that the only thing more maladaptive than multiculturalism that does not 'work' is multiculturalism that does 'work.' Minority free-riding occurs in a number of ways. When there is ethnic stratification, a characteristic of all multicultural societies, minority free-riding can occur at the bottom of the class structure in the form of social welfare and other benefits conferred by public goods. A redistributive system thus entails majority-ethnic taxpayers paying for their own loss of relative fitness by financing reproduction by families belonging to other ethnies. Ethnic majorities can also find themselves economically or culturally dominated by a highly competitive minority, when minority free-riding is liable to take top-down forms such as steering cultural, immigration, and foreign policies towards minority goals with collateral harm to majority interests. Multi-ethnic societies thus tend to be maladaptive for majorities under multicultural regimes and maladaptive, or at least inequitable, for minorities under traditional regimes. Confirmation of the large scale of ethnic genetic interests will warrant a reconsideration of the essential nature of national interests as well as the meaning of a just world system. The present analysis reaffirms the value of national sovereignty. From a Darwinian perspective, a sovereign polity is one that controls immigration to its territory, both in times of war and peace. A biologically just world order might be something like the universal nationalism advocated in the nineteenth century by Otto von Bismarck and in the early twentieth century by Woodrow Wilson. In a growingly integrated world, one people's disaffection is liable to reduce everyone's interests, so that all stand to benefit from a formula that acknowledges both the need for autonomy and the reality of interdependence by respecting the most basic interest, genetic continuity. The same formula would make stabilization of the world's population evolutionarily sustainable by protecting the genetic interests of the most restrained populations. Universal nationalism means thinking again about ethnic states where the state unambiguously serves the ethnic interests of the majority. By ethnic state I mean something closer to the traditional German than the French model of the nation. The German model adopts ethnicity as shared

descent as a criterion of citizenship and thus offers a constitutional barrier to replacement migration. In the second half of the twentieth century this barrier collapsed in wealthy states that adopted the French model. The main risk appears to be the substitution of a set of abstract concepts as the defining symbols of the nation in place of ethnicity. The 'constitutional patriotism' espoused by anti-nationalists such as J. Habermas (1998) is a formula for reconciling ethnic majorities to their own demise while serving the sectional interests of minorities and free-riding elites. Every state currently managing the replacement of its founding ethnic group (e.g., Australia, Britain, Canada, France, USA) has adopted constitutional patriotism of one form or another. This is usually linked to the doctrine of multiculturalism, which encourages minority ethnocentrism while directing majority patriotic feelings towards universalistic ideals. According to this formula a country would lose nothing if the founding ethnic group were peacefully replaced so long as some set of values—democracy, equality, non-discrimination, minority rights—were retained. The combination of constitutional patriotism and multiculturalism is, as one would expect, subversive of the ethnic interests of the majority. The revival of ethnic nationalism would run counter to current liberal democratic opinion. However, from the original liberal perspective such a substitution would be warranted since it would salvage majority interests from precipitous decline. Minority interests could be partly served in an evolutionarily stable manner through federalism, in an evolutionarily uncertain manner through assimilation, as well as in a preventative manner through restrictive immigration combined with a foreign policy that adopted an informed and even-handed version of nineteenth century nationalist doctrine."

See also:

Salter, Frank. *Is Ethnic Globalism Adaptive for Americans? Population and Environment* 25, no. 5 (2004).

Salter, Frank. *Welfare, Ethnicity and Altruism: New Data and Evolutionary Theory.* Routledge, 2005.

Salter, Frank. *On Genetic Interests.* Transaction Publishers, 2006.

Salter, Frank. *Ethnicity and Indoctrination for Violence: The Efficiency of Producing Terrorists.* In Ibrahim A. Karawan (ed.), *Values and Violence: Intangible Aspects of Terrorism.* Springer, 2008.

Salter, Frank. *Evolutionary Analyses of Ethnic Solidarity: An Overview.* People and Places 16, no. 2 (2008).

Salter, Frank. *Genes and homogeneous trading groups.* Journal of BioEconomics 10, no. 3 (2008).

Salter, Frank. *Misunderstandings of Kin Selection and the Delay in Quantifying Ethnic Kinship.* Mankind Quarterly 48, no. 3 (2008).

Salter, Frank. *The War Against Human Nature: Race and the Nation in the Media.* Quadrant 56, no. 10 (2012).

Salter, Frank and Henry Harpending. *Rushton's theory of ethnic nepotism.* Personality and Individual Differences (2012).

— DIVERSITY AND PROXIMITY —

"...the pursuit of free-market democracy becomes an engine of potentially catastrophic ethnonationalism, pitting a frustrated 'indigenous' majority, easily aroused by opportunistic vote-seeking politicians, against a resented wealthy ethnic minority. This confrontation is playing out in country after country, from Indonesia to Sierra Leone, from Zimbabwe to Venezuela, from Russia to the Middle East." – Amy Chua, *A World On Edge*, pg. 6

"The importance of ethnic conflict, as a force shaping human affairs, as a phenomenon to be understood, as a threat to be controlled, can no longer be denied. By one reckoning, ethnic violence since World War II has claimed more than ten million lives, and in the last two decades ethnic conflict has become especially widespread. Ethnicity is at the center of politics in country after country, a potent source of challenges to the cohesion of states and of international tension. Connections among Biafra, Bangladesh, and Burundi, Beirut, Brussels, and Belfast were at first hesitantly made – isn't one 'tribal,' one 'linguistic,' another 'religious'? – but that is true no longer. Ethnicity has fought and bled and burned its way into public and scholarly consciousness. As the rediscovery of ethnicity has proceeded apace, so has the availability of information about it. What has emerged is a plethora of more or less parochial material on ethnic conflict in scores of countries." – David Horowitz, *Ethnic Groups In Conflict*, pg. xi

The most obvious feature of diversity is that it causes problems – problems which the most powerful nations and technology in human history cannot combat. "Racism" has a strange tendency to increase in proportion to the number of races present in a given milieu, regardless of the specific races present, the social arrangements, civil laws, local customs, religion, or historical epoch. For instance, it is not clear how diversity benefitted West Africans in the 1500s, or American Natives around the same time.

Admitting this is difficult for Western peoples to do, being naturally high-trusting, altruistic, and historically insular. The following brief essay is included, therefore, by way of historical illustration of the sociological data findings; namely, that diverse societies tend to experience heightened out-group animosities as different ethnic factions sharpen, stratify, and compete for physical and cultural space.

The idea that groups within ethnically diverse societies will remain indifferent to demographic fluctuations is utopian. In reality, "diverse" states are held together by force, limiting political freedom and in-group cultural expression. In short, "diversity" requires, and gives way to, uniformity or carefully permitted forms of unique expression. Factors such as ethnicity, religion, and language can also clash and compound these issues, furthering the likelihood of conflict. While policies aimed at promoting inter-group dialogue and understanding have heralded a new era of ethnic unity, they have not addressed the underlying sources of tension. Thus, understanding the historical and natural realities of ethnic identity and the disruption of diversity is crucial to develop effective strategies for promoting social cohesion and peaceful existence.

Lebanon

Lebanon is a stark example of how demographic changes can destabilize political and economic prosperity in a given country. Prior to the arrival of Palestinian refugees in the country, Lebanon was one of the wealthiest nations in the Middle East due, in part, to the nation's emphasis on representative government. However, an influx of refugees in the mid-1900s caused great demographic shifts, with Palestinians comprising a suddenly large proportion of the population. Afterward, tensions between different groups within the country arose, ultimately leading to a devastating civil war that lasted for 15 years.

Today, Lebanon still suffers the consequences of this conflict, with corruption, hyperinflation, and frequent blackouts where once these were unknown. These troubles are further compounded by ongoing political strife, as different groups continue to vie for power and influence within the country. Racial egalitarians will merely conclude that the experience of Lebanon underscores the importance of carefully managing demographic shifts and ensuring that all groups within society are adequately represented and empowered. It serves as a failed social experiment, they surmise, on the road to great unity – some day. However, for those with better sense Lebanon highlights the long-lasting negative effects that come with mass fluctuations in demographics.

Tibet

The Chinese government's policies towards Tibet, Xinjiang, and Hong Kong have caused fiery controversy and debate in recent years. In the case of Tibet, the Chinese government has tried to bring the region into the "Chinese Whole," including the forced migration of ethnic Han settlers into traditionally Tibetan areas. This has all but destroyed the region's original ethnic demographics and culture. Once a largely ethnically homogenous region, Tibetan now see their people, traditions, and life-ways fragmenting among large numbers of Chinese peasant migrants, Tibetans are now powerless "majority-minorities" in their own (former) lands.

The mass migration of Han settlers has also deteriorated the environment and the economy. Traditional Tibetan land use practices and livelihoods are squeezed to the margins by large-scale development projects and commercial enterprises – much like the small farmer, homesteader, and "trad" movements experience in America. The Chinese government's policies have been met with natural resistance from Tibetans, who protest (and even engage in self-immolation). In response, the Chinese government has sought to suppress dissent by means of greater tyranny, including forceful coercion and widespread surveillance. It seems diversity and economic progress require the gun.

The situation in Tibet is part of a broader pattern of top-down authoritarianism in China aimed at promoting political "unity" and economic development, often at the expense of actual ethnic and cultural diversity. The communist government's policies towards Tibet and other regions are also tied to broader geopolitical ambitions, including designs to root out "ethnic separatism" and external influence. These issues are likely to continue to shape China's approach to eradicate or homogenize ethnic and cultural diversity in the years to come. Globalists in the West imagine that resistance
to immigration and the destruction of a simpler way of life are latent features of white racists. But the same phenomenon is seen in nonwhite (and non-Christian) countries.

Indonesia

Indonesia is a land with over 300 distinct ethnic groups, each with their own culture, language, and traditions. Has the dream of the West – for "Diversity is our strength" – come true for this multiculturally rich region? In fact, one of the primary social features of Indonesia is discrimination and marginalization of minority ethnic groups. This is particularly true for indigenous groups, such as the Dayak, who have faced displacement and discrimination due to government policies and development projects forcing integration. Discrimination is also prevalent in the job market, where non-Javanese ethnic groups often face hiring biases and are underrepresented in higher-level positions.

Ethnic and religious conflicts flare up in Indonesia continually, the more so in areas with a high level of diversity. For example, in some regions of Indonesia, such as Ambon and Poso, there have been violent conflicts between Christian and Muslim groups. The government has tried to address these issues, such as through the establishment of interfaith dialogue forums and policies promoting diversity and tolerance. Ultimately, these have been band-aids over a gushing wound.

Additionally, there is a challenge in promoting a common national identity in a multiethnic society, as many ethnic groups fragment into strong cultural identities and prioritize their group identity over a singular national identity. This has led in Indonesia to feelings of exclusion and marginalization, particularly among minority groups, who further spiral the outward away from national unity. Without white people to blame, Western academics and media pundits largely ignore such problems, acting as though religious or ethnic clashes are unique challenges in European countries. Thomas Sowell's studies on culture and diversity highlight issues in this region.

The Balkans

The Balkans, a region in southeastern Europe, has a complicated history of ethnic and cultural diversity that has led to significant political instability and conflict. In fact, the word "balkanize" is now a proverb for the breakup of national unity into ethnic-oriented nation-states. In the late 19th and early 20th centuries, the Balkans were part of the Ottoman Empire, which ruled over a wide range of ethnic and religious peoples. As nationalism spread across Europe, many nationalist movements arose in the Balkans region seeking greater autonomy for their respective ethnic groups.

During World War I, the Ottoman Empire collapsed, leading to the emergence of several new states in the Balkans, including Yugoslavia, Albania, and Bulgaria, each of which included various ethnic peoples all smashed together under the rule of one dominant tribe of people favored by the more powerful "allied" nations. Hence, these new states remained deeply divided along ethnic and religious lines, which led to ongoing friction and even war.

In the 1990s, the Balkans experienced a series of devastating conflicts that resulted in the breakup of Yugoslavia. Following the death of the Yugoslav leader Josip Broz Tito in 1980, nationalist and separatist movements promoting the self-determination of a particular people gained momentum, and Yugoslavia began to unravel. In 1991, Slovenia and Croatia also declared independence, followed by Bosnia and Herzegovina in 1992.

As Yugoslavia fell apart, a series of hot conflicts developed in which various ethnic groups fought for control of territories and resources. In Bosnia and Herzegovina, Bosnian Serb forces conducted a campaign of ethnic cleansing against Bosniak Muslims, resulting in the deaths of tens of thousands of people and the displacement of millions.

The conflicts in the Balkans ended with the in-tervention of the international powers, including the UN and NATO. Again, the historical lesson is that diversity and proximity lead to war, which can only be solved by either separation of various groups or suppression of the same by external imperial/international power.

Croatia and Serbia

It is important to make a further note about the Croats and Serbs, two of the largest ethnic groups in the above-discussed Balkans, since they share a common Slavic ancestry and language and yet still have a history of mutual violence and dissociation. It need not be, say, white people and black people living side-by-side to make for social disharmony. Here are two related groups whose history shows cannot live together long in peace.

Indeed, the roots of the conflict between Croats and Serbs go back centuries. In the Middle Ages, the Croats were under the rule of the Hungarian Kingdom, while the Serbs were part of the Ottoman Empire. But then in the 19th century, both Croatia and Serbia became part of the Austrian Empire. During World War II, Croatia became an independent state under the rule of the Ustasha regime, which collaborated with Nazi Germany against Serbs, Jews, and Romani people. This led to mistrust between the two groups. After World War II, Croatia and Serbia became part of the Socialist Federal Republic of Yugoslavia, which was led by the Communist Party.

In short, two historically disparate nations were thrown together during and after WWII, with one group given power over the other. Thus, many Croats felt at this time that they were being dominated by the more populous Serbs. This led to the rise of Croatian nationalism in the 1980s, which culminated in the declaration of independence from Yugoslavia in 1991.

Serbia, under the leadership of Slobodan Milošević, opposed Croatian independence and supported ethnic Serbs living in Croatia. Consequently, Croatian forces and Serb forces in Croatia fought each other in what is known as the Croatian War of Independence.

This war lasted until 1995 and resulted in the deaths of tens of thousands of people and the displacement of hundreds of thousands more. In addition to the conflict in Croatia, there was also a war in Bosnia and Herzegovina, which was fought along ethnic lines between Croats,

Serbs, and Bosniaks.

Today, the relationship between Croats and Serbs remains strained. While there have been efforts to improve relations, there is still resentment on both sides. Has diversity been their strength? Western leaders seem to move forward with their plans without addressing raw reality and historical examples such as these. Furthermore, such ethnic strife and war arose between two peoples historically neighboring one another, sharing more things in common than the mass migrations seen today from Africa into Europe or South America in the United States. If decades-long animosities and war can arise from neighbors, what from foreigners?

Ireland

Irish nationalism arose from a long history of English overrule dating back to the 12th century. During the 16th and 17th centuries England imposed a colonial presence in Ireland, controlling the island and its resources and suppressing Irish culture, language, and religion.

Thus, the 19th century saw the emergence of Irish nationalism as a political movement, which aimed to secure autonomy and independence from English rule. This movement was driven by economic grievances, cultural and religious differences, and the desire for ethno-national self-determination.

The 19th century also saw the emergence of cultural nationalism in Ireland, as artists, writers, and intellectuals sought to revive and celebrate Irish language, literature, and traditions. This cultural revival played an important role for national identity among the Irish people. Consequently, Irish poetry, song, and writing during and after this period is rich in ethnic consciousness and national themes.

Political nationalism also gained momentum in the late 19th and early 20th centuries, as Irish politicians and activists organized around the goal of Irish self-determination. The Irish Republican Brotherhood, founded in 1858, sought to use force to end English rule in Ireland, while other groups such as the Home Rule Party pursued a pacifist path towards greater Irish autonomy.

Ultimately, the rise of Irish nationalism was connected to the conflict arising from forced ethnic proximity, particularly English colonial rule and the injustices and grievances it inflicted upon the Irish people. The movement for Irish independence led to the Irish War of Independence, which lasted from 1919 to 1921, and ultimately to the establishment of the Irish Free State in 1922, which later became the Republic of Ireland. Diversity in this centuries-long tale of two nations was no one's strength. Rather, separation provided freedom, liberty, and social health.

The Boers

The Boer War was fought from 1899 to 1902 between the British Empire and the two independent Boer states, the South African Republic (Transvaal) and the Orange Free State. The conflict arose out of long-standing tensions and disputes between the British, Boers, and indigenous populations over control of land, resources, and political power.

The Boers were descendants of Dutch settlers who had established two independent republics in southern Africa, the above-mentioned South African Republic and the Orange Free State. They were predominantly farmers and sought to maintain their ethnic independence and traditional way of life. However, the discovery of gold and diamonds in the region had led to an influx of British settlers and capital, leading to tensions between the two groups.

The British, seeking to consolidate their power and control over the region, annexed the South African Republic and attempted to annex the Orange Free State. This led to a conflict between the Boers and the British, who had superior military and technological capabilities. The Boers, seeing themselves as freedom fighters for home, hearth, God, and country, employed guerrilla tactics and were initially successful, but the British eventually prevailed and established control over the entire region.

The conflict also had a significant impact on the black populations of southern Africa, who were often caught in the crossfire between Boers and the British. Additionally, the war had lasting impacts on South African society, contributing to the development of apartheid policies and segregation between different ethnic groups.

Much like how the North treated the South after the U.S. Civil War, the British treated the Boers after this war – by overturning their political order, giving black people more political power, and "reconstructing" their society. The Boers responded similarly with its apartheid laws as did the U.S. South's "black codes" and later "Jim Crow". There is a pattern of two groups of whites coming into proximity and then conflict, with the victor imposing still another ethnic group upon the defeated as a means of social control.

South Africa

South Africa has a high diversity of 10-15 major ethnic groups. Despite being a historically prosperous country, the end of apartheid regime saw a significant decline in the economy and a worsening – not an improving – of the political order. The power vacuum created after apartheid led to the rise of mostly incompetent and corrupt officials who not only failed to address problems but also excused their failures on the grounds of legacy inequalities. Consequently, crime and dysfunctionality have been on the rise in the country, such as the violent murder of white farmers and land seizures. Many farmers have been driven off their land, leading many others to flee the country to seek refuge, particularly those of European descent, further destabilizing the country. Additionally, theft of vital infrastructure, such as railroad tracks, has caused damage to the economy. The country's obsession with race has led to a deepening of ethnic animosities, further complicating the already existing ethnic diversity. The future of South Africa remains uncertain as the country continues to grapple with the exact opposite of the supposed "strength" of ethnic diversity.

Iraq

Iraq, as a post-Empire creation, encompasses three major and disparate ethnic groups: Sunni Arabs, Shia Arabs, and Kurds. The British colonial government stitched these groups together to create a new country in the aftermath of World War I. The lack of a shared national identity and the inability to reconcile sectarian differences meant that group animosities were almost inevitable. Under Ba'athist rule, with one group ruling over the others, western promises of social harmony collapsed, nepotism grew, power was monopolized, and every man had concern each for his own ethnic and religious group. For example, during the Iran-Iraq war, the Sunni-led government of Saddam Hussein used chemical weapons against the Shia population in south-

ern Iraq. While Saddam Hussein might have concealed these divisions during his reign, as had been the case with the Ottoman Empire, the fragmentation of centralized power led to the intensification and strengthening of sectarian differences. The subsequent U.S. invasion in 2003 and the toppling of Saddam's regime further exposed these ethnic divisions, leading to a surge in ethnic violence and instability that still plagues Iraq today. The U.S. military spent its longest military campaign in American history in Iraq toppling a dictator and making the land safe for a liberal, diverse democracy, only to watch it all collapse literally overnight once its imperial power was withdrawn during Obama's presidency. Diverse ethnic groups in close proximity breed war, which can only be partially suppressed by a dictator like Saddam, a terrorist organization like the Taliban, or the full might of the strongest military in the world.

Papua New Guinea

Papua New Guinea has an extremely diverse population, both linguistically and culturally. The country is home to over 840 different languages, making it the most linguistically varied country on the planet. Is this diversity a source of strength, unity, and prosperity? Quite the contrary, the country has experienced low-level tribal warfare since time immemorial and a lack of infrastructure due to rampant corruption in governance. This has resulted in the failure to build roads between major cities, which has contributed to a higher crime rate in urban areas. For instance, the capital city of Port Moresby is known for its high rates of crime, including carjacking and robbery. Gangs with ethnic, linguistic, and in-group markers roam about with guns and machetes, defending patches of tribal turf. Despite its challenges, Papua New Guinea is home to many unique and beautiful cultures, such as the Huli tribe in the Tari Valley, who have maintained their traditional customs for centuries. However, this cultural richness is often overshadowed by multicultural instability and violence. In either case, multiple cultures and peoples living side-by-side has not seen them melting into one pot but standing distinct and growing more so.

Israel

The conflict between Israelis and Palestinians is a long-standing dispute over territory, land, and religion. It dates back to the late 19th century when Zionism, a Jewish nationalist movement, began to advocate for the establishment of a Jewish homeland in Palestine. This led to an influx of Jewish immigrants and tension with the Arab population in the region, who saw the immigration as a threat to their own claim to the land.

In 1947, the United Nations approved a partition plan that would divide the land into separate Jewish and Arab states, but this was rejected by Arab leaders who believed it was unfair. The following year, Israel declared its independence and war broke out between Israel and its Arab neighbors, including Palestinians. This resulted in the displacement of hundreds of thousands of Palestinians, who became refugees in neighboring countries.

The conflict has continued over the decades, with both Israelis and Palestinians claiming the same land as their own. The status of Jerusalem, which both Israelis and Palestinians claim as their capital, has been a particularly contentious issue. The ongoing Israeli occupation of the West Bank and Gaza Strip, which began in 1967, has also been a major point of conflict, with Palestinians seeking independence and a state of their own.

Religion has also played a significant role in the conflict, with both Israelis and Palestinians claiming a religious connection to the land. Jews view Israel as the biblical homeland of their ancestors, while Muslims consider Jerusalem a holy city and believe that the Prophet Muhammad ascended to heaven from that city.

The conflict has led to multiple wars and countless acts of violence and terrorism, some would say nigh genocide. Many attempts have been made to negotiate a peace agreement, but so far, a lasting solution has not been reached. If you ask Jews whether diversity would be a strength for Israel, whether open borders, religious pluralism, and welcoming immigrants would improve their nation, you might be called antisemitic.

Brazil

Brazil is one of the world's most culturally and racially diverse nations, and so it is not without its share of social and economic problems. Notorious corruption, crime, partisan politics, and inequality are some of the significant common themes of the country for years. Unsurprisingly, Brazil's divisions fall nearly perfectly along racial fault lines on nearly every public, moral, religious, economic, or cultural issue. Internal migrations of ethnic groups has led to racial stratification, exacerbating crime, poverty, drugs, and social collapse in various areas – while others excel in prosperity, productivity, technology, art, education, and more. More biased readers would gleefully point out which ethnicities pertain to which locales. In fact, Brazil has become a proverb for demographic problems, serving as a model for Western nations to avoid or ignore. Seemingly unresolvable, at least by the methods and tools available to liberal democratic regimes, these issues are leading to sub-First World standards of living.

Zimbabwe

The case of Zimbabwe illustrates how moral concerns surrounding racial disharmony, particularly those related to ethnic rights, can lead to the collapse of basic social codes of conduct necessary for running a functional country. Once known as the British-governed flourishing country of Rhodesia, Zimbabwe received aid from Western countries and won independence after a terrible war. However, as some 200,000 whites left (including white governors and rulers) and "diversity" increased in politics, the country fell into hyperinflation, corruption, and failed land reform. The government's anti-white racist decision to take land from white farmers and redistribute it to black citizens fueled ethnic tribalism and led to a collapse in agricultural output. It was only after repeated failures to produce enough food for the nation that Mugabe's government had to plead with white farmers to return to the lands taken from them.

The government's policies have had long-term consequences, as the economy has stagnated, and the country has become one of the poorest in the world. Citizens regularly go without fuel, food, and energy, standing in lines for days at times to await air-dropped supplies from functional first-world countries. What was once a beautiful, thriving country is now a dilapidated, impoverished, post-apocalypse level wastescape.

Zanzibar

Zanzibar was home to East Africa's largest slave trade. It was dominated by Arabs who ruled over Africans in a very clearly delineated racial caste system. Although slavery here was abolished in the 19th century by the British, the racial caste system persisted. Black communist groups emerged in the 1960s, seeking to dismantle the racial hierarchy and establish a socialist government.

In 1964, a revolution took place, leading to the overthrow of the Arab-dominated government and the establishment of an independent Zanzibar. Members of the predominantly African political party, the Afro-Shirazi Party, began attacking Arabs and South Asians living on the island. Thousands of people were massacred along ethnic lines, with some estimates suggesting as many as 20,000 deaths.

The violence continued for several months, and many Arabs and South Asians were forced to flee the island. The new government of Zanzibar, led by the Afro-Shirazi Party, declared the island a socialist state and aligned itself with communist countries like China and the Soviet Union. Here is an example of Africans, Arabs, and Asians – no whites, no Christians, no Westerners – who engaged in ethnic-racial slavery, caste systems, and bloody revolution. Was diversity their strength?

Liberia

The idea of creating a homeland for freed African-American slaves in Africa was first promoted by white American abolitionists, who saw this plan as a solution to the "Negro problem" in America. The American Colonization Society was formed in 1816 to promote the recolonization of freed slaves back to Africa, and by the mid-19th century, thousands of African Americans had migrated to Liberia on U.S. government largesse. Leading figures such as James Madison and Abraham Lincoln were among the movement's foremost champions. The assumption was that freedom for all men was good, but social equality was not possible. Furthermore, true freedom entailed political and geographic self-rule, which entails segregation. The notion that English colonists or enslaved Africans wanted freedom from the British Empire or white slaver-owners, respectively, but still wished to live under the rule of their overlords is a contradiction. To be free for both meant freedom from overlords and independence of political rule.

Thus, many African slaves were freed and sent back to Africa to be colonized in a new nation called Liberia. However, rather than finding common cause with native Africans, former African American slaves-now-settlers in Liberia established their own ethnic caste system that placed them above the indigenous population. They segregated themselves from the natives and discriminated against them, much as they had experienced in America – and indeed as was the practice in all of Africa. This created resentment that persisted for a century and contributed to a Liberian civil war and the violent overthrow of the Americo-Liberian ruling class in the 1980s.

The establishment of Liberia as a homeland for freed African-American slaves was supposed to bring ethnic harmony, being modeled after the white man's U.S. constitution which tied together Swedes, British, Irish, Germans, Frenchmen, and other European ethnicities. However, it did not lead to greater empathy between former African-Americans and native Africans. Instead, it led to the establishment of an ethnic hierarchy that perpetuated group discrimination against the indigenous population and contributed to the violent overthrow of the ruling class. The legacy of ethnic-settler diversity in Liberia continues to shape the country's politics and society today. Westerners imagine that what happened once here can and should happen all over the world again and again. But time after time we see the same project failing and causing great violent eruptions to the human social fabric.

Myanmar

Burma, also known as Myanmar, is a country that has been marked by conflict and political consequences resulting from anxieties about demographic and cultural displacement. Contrary to popular ideas in the West, "replacement" theories are not unique to white people. This Eastern-Pacific country has a long history as a predominantly Buddhist society, but in recent years, there has been a significant influx of non-ethnic Burmese Rohingya Muslims – diversity and proximity which have fueled tensions and conflict.

Burmese nationalists claim these Muslim foreigners are being forced upon them, bringing crime, Islamization, and high birth rates that threaten displacement upon the native people. The Rohingya have been subject to brutal violence and discrimination, with many forced to flee the country as refugees. The United Nations and other international organizations have called for Burma to become a more pluralistic power-sharing democracy that respects the rights of all its citizens, including the Rohingya.

However, these calls have been met with resistance from Burmese society, which rightly sees that the influx of Rohingya and other minority groups will lead to cultural displacement and the loss of Burmese identity. In 2021, the Burmese military led a coup against the liberal-democratic government destroying its country, seized control of it, and proclaimed "Myanmar's Sovereignty."

In short, Burma's long history of colonization and foreign influence has created a deep-seated sense of national identity and the desire for autonomy. Past diversity gave the nation a strengthened sense of national consciousness which fuels its resistance to liberal-democracy's enforced diversity agendas.

Sri Lanka

Sri Lanka is a multi-ethnic country with a long record of ethnic strife and faction. The two major ethnic groups in Sri Lanka are the Sinhalese, who make up the majority of the population, and the Tamils, who are concentrated in the northern and eastern parts of the country.

Historically, the relationship between these two groups has been marked by strain and occasional violence. The Tamils feel marginalized and discriminated against by the Sinhalese-dominated government. The modern origins of this conflict are usually traced back to British colonialism, which created an artificial system of governance that conflated historically disparate ethnic groups under one political border and power, favoring the Sinhalese majority and excluding Tamils from positions of power. Ethnic groups unable to rule themselves, and being ruled by other ethnic groups, always leads to faction, dissension, and violence. When let free, ethnic groups naturally segregate to rule and govern themselves.

Thus, the post-independence period saw the emergence of Tamil nationalist movements, which sought greater autonomy and self-deter-

mination for the Tamil regions. This led to a violent conflict between the Sri Lankan government and Tamil separatist groups, most notably the Liberation Tigers of Tamil Eelam (LTTE), which waged a brutal insurgency for over two decades. The conflict ended in 2009 with the defeat of the LTTE, but friction between the Sinhalese and Tamil communities has not abated.

In addition to the Sinhalese and Tamil communities, Sri Lanka is also home to a number of other ethnic groups, including Muslims, Burghers, and Malays. These groups have faced discrimination and marginalization, particularly in the context of the Sinhalese-Tamil conflict. Muslims, in particular, have been targeted by "extremist" Buddhist groups in recent years. Those natural ethnic in-group forces, which a strong governing colonial power could keep sequestered, have under less total authority erupted in strife and aggression. Diversity is not a strength. Rather, it requires strength to be regulated.

Kashmir

Kashmir is a region in South Asia that has been a source of conflict between India and Pakistan for decades. The region is home to many ethnic and religious groups, including Kashmiri Muslims, Kashmiri Hindus, and various other minority communities. The historical and political problems of diverse ethnic groups in Kashmir are convoluted and have contributed to ongoing troubles in the region.

Historically, Kashmir has been a site of contestation between different empires and ruling dynasties. The land has been ruled by various Hindu and Muslim kingdoms throughout its history and was incorporated into British India in the 19th century. At the time of partition in 1947, Kashmir was a Muslim-majority state ruled by a Hindu Maharaja, and the decision of the Maharaja to accede to India rather than Pakistan has caused conflict ever since. In short, unlike above examples where one group ruled unequally over another, Kashmir was a diverse society which the British tried to setup such that everyone had equal representation. But what ends up happening in such scenarios is that one group feels that the imperialists have put a puppet ethnic-diversity hire over them. And they grow to hate it.

The conflict between Indians and Pakistanis over Kashmir has led to a range of human rights abuses, particularly against the ethno-religious

Kashmiri Muslim population. The Indian government has deployed tens of thousands of troops to the region to dispel separatist movements and maintain control, leading to extrajudicial killings, torture, and enforced disappearances. The situation has been exacerbated by the rise of militant nationalist groups that seek to establish an independent Kashmir, some of which have engaged in acts labeled by the government as "terrorism."

The political problems of diverse ethnic groups in Kashmir are also related to issues of representation and self-determination. The Kashmiri Muslim population has long sought greater independence, arguing that they have been marginalized and oppressed by Indian rule. However, the Indian government has resisted these demands, claiming that Kashmir is an integral part of India and that separatist movements pose a threat to national security. Once again, diversity and proximity within one political or geographic region has disproved the liberal-democratic dream of multicultural harmony.

Fiji

Fiji is a Pacific Island country with an artificially diverse ethnic population that includes indigenous Fijians, Indo-Fijians, and other minority groups. The historical and political problems of diverse ethnic groups in Fiji have contributed to a centuries-long strife between these different communities, with no amount of western-liberal solutions affecting change. Historically, Fiji was colonized by the British in the late 19th century, and the colonial government introduced indentured labor that brought Indian foreigners by the masses into the country. The indigenous Fijians view these Indo-Fijians as aliens and a threat to their cultural and political dominance. Thus, Fiji is another example of international powers forcing diversity upon a local people via mass migration; with local population gaining ethnic consciousness and reacting to protect itself and its historical rootedness.

Furthermore, the political problems of diverse ethnic groups in Fiji have grown since the country gained independence in 1970. Indigenous Fijians have dominated politics and held great amounts of power, which they used to discriminate against Indo-Fijians and other minorities. This has included policies such as affirmative action for indigenous Fijians (the opposite of what the majority ethnic group in America did), restrictions on land ownership and political representation for Indo-Fijians, and discriminatory practices in employment and education.

The divisions between different ethnic groups in Fiji have led to political upheaval and coups. In 1987, a coup spearheaded by indigenous Fijians deposed the government, leading to the establishment of an interim government that was dominated by the indigenous Fijians. In 2000, there was another coup, again led by a group of indigenous Fijian nationalists who opposed the government's tolerant policies towards Indo-Fijians.

In recent years, there have been efforts to address the historical and political problems

of diverse ethnic groups in Fiji, including the adoption of a new, globalist-inspired constitution in 2013 that aimed to promote greater equality and inclusion. However, historical and natural realities persist where diversity is found, and asymmetrical power relations remain between the various groups who hold fast to their various identities.

Sudan

Sudan has over 500 ethnic groups, with the largest being the Arab, Nubian, and Beja. By the western utopian logic of "Diversity Is Our Strength", Sudan is a country that should be brimming full with strong political and cultural vibrancy. However, these diverse ethnic groups in Sudan have wrought such horrific violence and devastation upon one another as to avert western attention altogether.

Sudan, like Fiji above, was also colonized by the British in the late 1800s. The colonial government exacerbated ethnic tribalism by forcing diverse groups – historically segregated – together under one imperial rule, favoring some groups over others. Forcing naturally divided groups together and then giving one group power, privileges, and/or rights over the others is always a disaster. Thus, after independence in 1956, various ethnic groups struggled for political power and economic resources. This story by now should be a familiar pattern.

After the strong ruling power is removed, groups re-stratify and begin warring once more. And so, the tribally partisan government of Sudan has been accused of neglecting some regions of the country where out-group peoples dwell, leading to economic disparities and a sense of marginalization among some ethnic groups. The equivalent in America would be the U.S. government and mainstream media outlets caring and acting on behalf of black Americans or immigrants but neglecting the social maladies and crimes against white Americans. In Sudan, such tribal-political partisanship has contributed to a range of conflicts, including ethnic and religious violence, as well as militancy and insurgency in some parts of the country.

One of the most significant political issues in Sudan has been the struggle for power and resources between the dominant Arab ethnic group and smaller minority groups. The Darfur region, for example, is home to a number of minority peoples who have been marginalized by the government and the dominant Arab groups. This has led to the rise of insurgent factions such as the Sudan Liberation Army (SLA) and the Justice and Equality Movement (JEM), both of which have used violence to demand greater political autonomy and control over resources.

Recently, the government of Sudan introduced policies to promote national unity and inclusivity, such as the Comprehensive Peace Agreement, which ended the civil war between the North and South of the country. There have also been calls for constitutional reforms that would decentralize power and give greater autonomy to the regions. While it is not clear that decentralized power heals ethnic animosities, racial or ethnic identity and self-determination are certainly what fuel resistance to enforced group subjugation by an out-group.

Rwanda

Rwanda has an explosively hostile history between the Hutu and Tutsi ethnic peoples, which has contributed to one of the worst genocides in modern history, as well as continued warring conflicts.

Historically, the Hutu and Tutsi peoples have lived in Rwanda for centuries, with fluid yet strongly delineated social and economic relations. However, during colonial rule in the late 19th and early 20th centuries, the Belgian colonizers introduced a strict ethnic classification system, exacerbating tensions between the Hutu and Tutsi. The Tutsi were favored by the colonizers, leading to resentment and marginalization of the Hutu.

After independence in 1962, political power in Rwanda was largely controlled by a brutal Tutsi minority (majorities are not what always dominate in politics), leading to further resentment among the Hutu majority. This culminated in the 1994 genocide, in which an estimated 800,000 Tutsis and moderate Hutus were killed by militant Hutus. The genocide was a result of a longstanding culture of ethnic hatred and violence, stoked by political propaganda and agitating speeches. In the aftermath of the genocide, Rwanda has made efforts to promote national unity and reconciliation – not unlike that between the North and the South after the U.S. nation slaughtered some 600,000+ of its own people. However, there are still ongoing divisions in Rwanda, particularly around issues of power-sharing and representation. The current government, led by President Paul Kagame, is dominated once again by the Tutsi ethnic group, with claims still heard of prejudice against the Hutu.

But The West Is Different!

White people, according to liberal westerners, are the exception to this record of human experience. Racial egalitarians point beyond empirical history to a few utopian experiments which pose continual contradictions to the idea. According to this theory, all peoples and nations may have failed, but we in America, we in the West will achieve what they did not. In 2020, the former president Barack Obama affirmed this vision when he said, "...America is the first real experiment in building a large, multiethnic, multicultural democracy. And we don't know yet if that can hold. There haven't been enough of them around for long enough to say for certain that it's going to work." (Why Obama Fears Our Democracy, The Atlantic, Nov 15, 2020) Likewise, in a speech given at the Mackinac Policy Conference on 30 May 2024, Democrat politician Pete Buttigieg said, "The world has never actually seen a large-scale, fully-functioning, fully-inclusive, multi-ethnic, multi-racial, democratic republic that represented everybody. We've never actually had that all the way, but we could." It's never happened, but it could! Hopes and dreams!

Yet, has America's diversity experiment of the past 400 years been wonderful for black people? Native tribes-peoples? Obama and Buttigieg seem to think that after four centuries the jury is still out on the question. How much longer will we be made to wait to draw conclusions? The Israelites, too, were in Egypt for 400 years and never became Egyptian. Is it so strange that this happens again in our day and time? Readers who balk at this language should consider the location they have chosen to live and work, their friendships and networks, the locales they frequent, the marriages they have contracted, or the places where they spend quantities of money to buy their children a seat. People love diversity, in opinion polls and from afar. The wife of the 2024 vice presidential candidate, Tim Walz, said that during the BLM protests she opened her window to smell the burning fumes in order to feel connected to the event. Yes, she opened her window, but she didn't go out to join the vibrantly diverse "mostly peaceful protests."

Other examples of supposed harmonious diversity bandied about include Switzerland, Canada, France, the UK, or Germany. In reality, however, diversity has been a great disaster even in these countries so far and is only in its beginning stages of eating away the centuries – often millennia – of social capital and good-will so long built up. It is a testament to the altruism and high trust of western peoples that their institutional stability has held up under the influx of tens of millions of non-westerners over the last decades of liberal-democratic politics. Daily we hear fresh hells of the effects of diversity in once idyllic European towns or famous places. Entire cities become swallowed up by foreigners, aflame with diversity, and then abandoned by retreating western natives. And the newcomers boldly declare victory at the takeover while the media ignores it all! It is Camp Of The Saints in real life.

A nonwestern example of diversity seemingly working is Singapore. But this tiny island-country is heavily authoritarian, which, in the eyes of freedom-loving westerners, would compare with more totalitarian regimes. Yet, such strong-willed, top-down control is what it takes to enforce harmony amid naturally stratifying elements. It is possible to keep oil and water blended if you keep shaking them – destabilizing their norms. This was indeed the policy of Singapore's first prime minister, Lee Kuan Yew, who, in a Der Spiegel interview, said, "In multiracial societies, you don't vote in accordance with your economic interests and social interests, you vote in accordance with race and religion." Yew elsewhere noted that diversity is not a strength; rather, ethnic unity produces greater social results: "I have said openly that if we were 100 percent Chinese, we would do better. But we are not and never will be, so we live with what we have." Ever the realist, and shorn of white guilt or global do-goodism toward the world's less fortunate groups, former Prime Minister Yew was able to articulate a policy for Singapore that runs roughshod over liberal democracy and yet achieves that harmony amid diversity so coveted by liberal-democratic proponents.

Overall, while it is possible to have different types of diversity, in general, the more diverse a society is in terms of factors such as ethnicity, religion, intelligence, historical attachments, etc., the more authoritarian interventions are required to maintain a high level of functionality. Diversity and harmonious liberty are, by historical record, incompatible. The following studies prove this historical experience true.

Ethnicity And War

ETHNICITY AND CIVIL WAR

Elaine K Denny, Department of Political Science And School Of International Relations And Pacific Studies, University Of California, San Diego. Barbara F Walter, Graduate School Of International Relations And Pacific Studies, University Of California, San Diego, *Journal Of Peace Research* col. 51, iss. 2

"If a civil war begins, it is more likely to be initiated by an ethnic group than any other type of group. We argue that ethnic groups, on average, are likely to have more grievances against the state, are likely to have an easier time organizing support and mobilizing a movement, and are more likely to face difficult-to-resolve bargaining problems." ...

"Since 1964, 64% of all civil wars have divided along ethnic lines. Ethnic identity played an influential role in civil wars in Iraq, Lebanon, Congo, Burundi, Syria, Sudan, Uganda, Pakistan, Rwanda, Georgia, and Nigeria (to name a few). This large ratio of ethnic to non-ethnic civil wars is intriguing for two reasons. First, societies organize themselves along many different line – class, geography, political ideology, religion, and ethnicity, for example – yet when societies go to war it is usually between groups defined by ethnicity."

Income Inequality

HOW DOES RACIAL DIVERSITY RAISE INCOME INEQUALITY

Meisenberg, Gerhard., *The Journal of social, political, and economic studies* 33 (2008).

"In international comparisons, a high level of racial diversity is associated with a high level of income inequality. One hypothesis proposes that racial diversity leads to increased variance in intellectual ability, which leads to increased income inequality presumably through the action of market forces. A second hypothesis proposes that racially diverse societies are more unequal because they have less social solidarity and less redistribution of wealth from the rich to the poor...

"If racial diversity favors income inequality, and if advanced postindustrial nations are becoming more diverse in the wake of replacement migration, we can predict a continuing trend towards greater income inequality."

Individualism and Diversity

DOES DIVERSITY FOSTER INDIVIDUALISM? THE RELATION OF RACIAL-ETHNIC DIVERSITY TO INDIVIDUALISM-COLLECTIVISM ACROSS THE 50 AMERICAN STATES

Stewart J. H. McCann, The Journal of Social Psychology, 06 Jun 2022

"Contrary to the earlier longitudinal findings, the current results show that states with higher racial-ethnic diversity are less individualistic and more collectivistic."

Electoral Integrity and Diversity

ETHNICITY AND ELECTORAL FRAUD IN BRITAIN

Noah Carl, *Electoral Studies*, vol. 53, June 2018, pg. 150

"Several reports have highlighted that, within Britain, allegations of electoral fraud tend to be more common in areas with large Pakistani and Bangladeshi communities. However, the extent of this association has not yet been quantified. Using data at the local authority level, this paper shows that percentage Pakistani and Bangladeshi (logged) is a robust predictor of two measures of electoral fraud allegations: one based on designations by the Electoral Commission, and one based on police enquiries. Indeed, the association persists after controlling for other minority shares, demographic characteristics, socio-economic deprivation, and anti-immigration attitudes. I interpret this finding with reference to the growing literature on consanguinity (cousin marriage) and corruption. Rates of cousin marriage tend to be high in countries such as Pakistan and Bangladesh, which may have fostered norms of nepotism and in-group favoritism that persist over time. To bolster my interpretation, I use individual level survey data to show that, within Europe, migrants from countries with high rates of cousin marriage are more likely to say that family should be one's main priority in life, and are less likely to say it is wrong for a public official to request a bribe."

Evolution and Human Behavior

KIN SELECTION AND ETHNIC GROUP SELECTION

Doug Jones, vol. 39, iss. 1, January 2018, pgs. 9-18

"Ethnicity looks something like kinship on a larger scale. The same math can be used to measure genetic similarity within ethnic / racial groups and relatedness within families. For example, members of the same continental race are about as related (r = 0.18–0.26) as half-siblings (r = 0.25). However (contrary to some claims) the theory of kin selection does not apply straightforwardly to ethnicity, because inclusive fitness calculations based on Hamilton's rule break down when there are complicated social interactions within groups, and / or groups are large and long-lasting. A more promising approach is a theory of ethnic group selection, a special case of cultural group selection. An elementary model shows that the genetic assimilation of a socially enforced cultural regime can promote group solidarity and lead to the regulation of recruitment to groups, and to altruism between groups, based on genetic similarity – in short, to ethnic nepotism. Several lines of evidence, from historical population genetics and political psychology, are relevant here."

Diversity, Proximity, and Social Breakdown

E PLURIBUS UNUM: DIVERSITY AND COMMUNITY IN THE TWENTY-FIRST CENTURY

Johan Skytte Prize Lecture Robert D. Putnam (2007) [3]

Diversity reduces social solidarity, general trust, trust in media, trust in local government, trust in political leaders, social capital, voter registration, political efficacy, charity, life satisfaction, happiness, co-operation, number of friendships, workplace effectiveness, general health. Diversity increases social isolation, military desertion rates, workforce turnover.

"Trust (even of one's own race) is lower, altruism and community cooperation rarer, friends fewer ... in ethnically diverse neighborhoods residents of all races tend to 'hunker down'."

Diversity is inversely correlated to trust levels:
"Inter-racial trust is relatively high in homogeneous South Dakota and relatively low in heterogeneous San Francisco or Los Angeles. The more ethnically diverse the people we live around, the less we trust them. ... the more we are brought into physical proximity with people of another race or ethnic background, the more we stick to 'our own' and the less we trust the 'other'."

Individuals who live in diverse communities are poorer and less educated than individuals who live in homogenous communities:
"Moreover, individuals who live in ethnically diverse places are different in many ways from people who live in homogeneous areas. They tend to be poorer, less educated, less likely to own their home, less likely to speak English and so on."

Less trusting individuals are most likely to tolerate diversity:
"...the first whites to flee (or the most reluctant to move in) would be the most trusting, and the last to flee would be the least trusting; or alternatively, that ethnic minorities and immigrants would selectively choose to move into neighborhoods in which the majority residents are most irascible and misanthropic."

Asians, Africans, Hispanics all trust their neighbors less than Whites. Diverse communities harbor more criminality: "Diverse communities tend to be larger, more mobile, less egalitarian, more crime-ridden"

Diversity of any sort makes people more likely to defect and cheat in game-theoretic scenarios.
"Within experimental game settings such as prisoners-dilemma or ultimatum games, players who are more different from one another (regardless of whether or not they actually know one another) are more likely to defect (or 'cheat')."

Ending immigration will not end "diversity":
"...because immigrant groups typically have higher fertility rates than native-born groups, ethnic diversity in virtually all of these countries would still increase in the years ahead, even if all new immigration were somehow halted"

3　Putnam is vehemently pro-diversity and dedicates at least half of his paper to his own anecdotal and entirely speculative arguments on why "while diversity is immediately extremely harmful, it may be beneficial in the future." Putnam also uses "good for GDP, good for the "economy'" as one of his primary pro-diversity arguments, despite the state of the "economy" being completely unrelated to individual citizen's happiness and life satisfaction levels. This is evident when comparing, for example, Hong Kong's high suicide and mental illness rates, to the high happiness and social cohesion levels in the "tribal" parts of the undeveloped Third World, in which the concept of an economy doesn't even exist.

Context: "What happens when a liberal scholar unearths an inconvenient truth?"

Police and Community

THEME AND VARIATION IN COMMUNITY POLICING

Jerome H. Skolnick and David H. Bayley *Crime and Justice* vol. 10 (1988), pgs. 1-37 (37 pages)

"Police-community reciprocity can be achieved only when there is a genuine bonding of interests between the police and the served citizenry.... That may turn out to be progressively difficult to accomplish in demographically complex urban areas, with their increasing ethnic diversity."

Diversity and Sense of Community

THE (IN)COMPATIBILITY OF DIVERSITY AND SENSE OF COMMUNITY

Zachary P. Neal, Jennifer Watling Neal (2013), American Journal of Community Psycholgy (2014) 53:1–12

Diversity is incompatible with strong communities.

"Community psychologists are interested in creating contexts that promote both respect for diversity and sense of community. However, recent theoretical and empirical work has uncovered a community-diversity dialectic wherein the contextual conditions that foster respect for diversity often run in opposition to those that foster sense of community. ... integration provides opportunities for intergroup contact that are necessary to promote respect for diversity but may prevent the formation of dense inter-personal networks that are necessary to promote sense of community."

Diversity is inversely correlated to social cohesion.

"The most cohesive neighborhoods are almost never the most diverse ones. ... these findings show it may not be possible to simultaneously create communities that are both fully integrated and fully cohesive, in essence, when it comes to neighborhood desegregation and social cohesion, you can't have your cake and eat it too."

These trends are so strong that it is unlikely that policy can change them.

"It's not that local leaders and policymakers aren't trying hard enough, rather, we now think it's because the goals of integration and cohe-sion are just not compatible with each other."

States with little diversity have more democracy, less corruption, and less inequality.

Homogeneous polities have less crime, less civil war, and more altruism.

Group Evolutionary Strategy

JEWISH GROUP EVOLUTIONARY STRATEGY IS THE MOST PLAUSIBLE HYPOTHESIS: A RESPONSE TO NATHAN COFNAS' CRITICAL ANALYSIS OF KEVIN MACDONALD'S THEORY OF JEWISH INVOLVEMENT IN TWENTIETH CENTURY IDEOLOGICAL MOVEMENTS

Edward Dutton

"Kevin MacDonald (1998) has argued that a series of twentieth century ideologies which have challenged European traditions should be understood as part of a Jewish evolutionary strategy to promote Jewish interests in the West, as evidenced by Jewish leadership of and disproportionate involvement in these movements. Cofnas Human Nature 29, 134–156 (Cofnas 2018a) has critiqued this model and countered that the evidence can be more parsimoniously explained by the high average intelligence and urban location of Jews in Western countries. This, he avers, should be the 'default hypothesis.' In this response, I argue that it is MacDonald's model that is the more plausible hypothesis due to evidence that people tend to act in their ethnic group interest and that group selectedness among Jews is particularly strong, meaning that they are particularly likely to do so."

Diversity and Neighborhoods

STATISTICAL AND PERCEIVED DIVERSITY AND THEIR IMPACTS ON NEIGHBORHOOD SOCIAL COHESION IN GERMANY, FRANCE AND THE NETHERLANDS

Ruud Koopmans, Merlin Schaeffer (2015), Social Indicators Research vol. 125, pgs. 853–883 (2016)

Immigration-related diversity negatively impacts natives and immigrants alike.

"In line with the majority of previous studies, we find negative effects of statistical ethnic diversity on each of our five measures of neighborhood social cohesion: trust, collective efficacy, connectedness, reported social problems, and overall satisfaction with neighborhood life. With few exceptions these effects are statistically significant in all three countries and apply to natives and persons of immigrant origin very much alike."

Contact Hypothesis Research Reviewed

THE CONTACT HYPOTHESIS RE-EVALUATED

Elizabeth Paluck, Seth Green, Donald Green (2018), *Behavioural Public Policy*, vol. 3, iss. 2, November 2019, pgs. 129-158

"This paper evaluates the state of contact hypothesis research from a policy perspective. Building on Pettigrew and Tropp's (2006) influential meta-analysis, we assemble all intergroup contact studies that feature random assignment and delayed outcome measures, of which there are 27 in total, nearly two-thirds of which were published following the original review. We find the evidence from this updated dataset to be consistent with Pettigrew and Tropp's (2006) conclusion that contact 'typically reduces prejudice.' At the same time, our meta-analysis suggests that contact's effects vary, with interventions directed at ethnic or racial prejudice generating substantially weaker effects. Moreover, our inventory of relevant studies reveals important gaps, most notably the absence of studies addressing adults' racial or ethnic prejudices, an important limitation for both theory and policy. We also call attention to the lack of research that systematically investigates the scope conditions suggested by Allport (1954) under which contact is most influential. We conclude that these gaps in contact research must be addressed empirically before this hypothesis can reliably guide policy."

Demographic and Ethnocentric Attitudes

DEMOGRAPHIC, ECONOMIC, AND GENETIC FACTORS RELATED TO NATIONAL DIFFERENCES IN ETHNOCENTRIC ATTITUDES

Edward Dutton, Guy MadisonRichard Lynn, October 2016, Personality and Individual Differences 101:137-143

"Religiousness is positively associated with positive ethnocentrism (the belief that your society is superior and a desire to make sacrifices for your society) …

"We can make numerous testable predictions, beyond those proposed and tested by Kanazawa (2012), that religiousness may be associated with

many 'instinctive' forms of behavior: forms of behavior which would have been 'normal' under preindustrial conditions of Natural Selection. In this regard, it makes sense that religiousness predicts ethnocentrism (see Dutton et al. 2016b), and a desire to have a large family (Swenson 2008, p.73), when intelligence predicts the opposite (Kanazawa 2012)."

Ethnic Diversity and Social Trust

ETHNIC DIVERSITY AND SOCIAL TRUST: A NARRATIVE AND META-ANALYTICAL REVIEW

Peter Thisted Dinesen University of Copenhagen, Merlin Schaeffer University of Copenhagen, Kim Mannemar Sønderskov Aarhus University (2019)

Ethnic diversity breeds social distrust

There is a "statistically significant negative relationship between ethnic diversity and social trust across all studies…Extant studies have relatively consistently reported a significant negative relationship between neighborhood-level ethnic diversity and various forms of social trust."

"To be clear, the overall negative relationship between residential ethnic diversity and social trust is statistically significant and holds up when conditioning on a range of potential confounders and moderators.

The professor of politics at Birkbeck University of London, Eric Kaufmann, has also backed the study's findings, saying: "Higher diversity is significantly associated with lower trust in communities, even when controlling for deprivation."

Social Capital in Homogenous States

STRIKING A BALANCE BETWEEN QUALITY OF LIFE AND SOCIAL CAPITAL (2017)

Benjamin Schultz, Balkan University in Skopje, Macedonia

Analysis of publicly available data and social science research finds that smaller, homogeneous cities have more social capital than larger, diverse cities.

Ethnic Diversity and Attitudes

Does Ethnic Diversity Have a Negative Effect on Attitudes towards the Community? A Longitudinal Analysis of the Causal Claims within the Ethnic Diversity and Social Cohesion Debate

James Laurence, Lee Bentley (2015), *European Sociological Review*, vol. 32, iss. 1, February 2016, pgs. 54–67

Community cohesion and individual connection to community is inversely correlated to diversity (1). (A UK-based replication of Putnam's study).

"…the findings suggest that changes in community diversity do lead to changes in attitudes towards the community. However, this effect differs by whether the change in diversity stems from a community increasing in diversity around individuals who do not move (stayers) or individuals moving into more or less diverse communities (movers). Increasing diversity undermines attitudes among stayers. Individuals who move from a diverse to a homogeneous community report improved attitudes. However, there is no effect among individuals who move from a homogeneous to a diverse community. … The most robust test is conducted among stayers. For those who remain in the same area for two or more consecutive waves, increasing community diversity is related to a decline in attachment. Among movers, there is heterogeneity in diversity's effect based on moves into/out of diverse environments. For individuals relocating to less diverse communities, the more homogeneous the destination the more likely their attachment will increase."

Ethnic Diversity and Trust

Ethnic diversity in neighborhoods and individual trust of immigrants and natives: A replication of Putnam (2007) in a West-European country.

Bram Lancee, Jaap Dronkers (2008), European University Institute, Department of Social and Political Sciences

Community cohesion and individual connection to community is inversely correlated to diversity (2). (A Netherlands-based replication of Putnam's study).

"…we confirm Putnam's claim and find that both for immigrants and native residents

1) neighborhoods' ethnic diversity reduces individual trust in neighborhoods; 2) those with neighbors of a different ethnicity have less trust in neighborhoods and neighbors 3) a substantial part of the effect of neighborhoods' ethnic diversity can be explained by the higher propensity of having neighbors of a different ethnicity. "

Attachment to Place

Community social and place predictors of sense of community: A multilevel and longitudinal analysis

D. Adam Long, Douglas D. Perkins (2007), *Journal Of Community Psychology*, vol. 35, iss. 5 July 2007 pgs. 563-581

Attachment to location of an individual's community is as important for their levels of happiness as the level of social cohesion within their community.

"Sense of Community (SOC) is intimately related to social capital (neighboring, citizen participation, collective efficacy, informal social control), communitarianism, place attachment, community confidence, and community satisfaction. … Being attached to one's community as a place may make feelings of social isolation or difference from one's neighbors all the more stark and disappointing."

80 Meters Diversity

Ethnic Diversity and Social Trust: Evidence from the Micro-Context

Peter Thisted Dinesen and Kim Mannemar Sønderskov (2015), *American Sociological Review*, 80(3), 550-573.

Diversity within 80 meters of a person reduces their social trust.

"The results show that ethnic diversity of the micro-context–measured within a radius of 80 meters of a person–has a statistically significant negative impact on social trust, controlling for a large number of potentially confounding variables. "

Diversity and Trust

DEMOGRAPHIC STRUCTURE AND THE POLITICAL
ECONOMY OF PUBLIC EDUCATION

James M. Poterba (1996), National Bureau Of Economic
Research, Working Paper 5677

Diversity reduces social trust.

"...an increase in the fraction of elderly
residents in a jurisdiction is associated with a
significant reduction in per child educational
spending. This reduction is particularly large
when the elderly residents and school-age population are from different racial groups."

Inverse Diversity and Trust

ETHNIC DIVERSITY, TRUST, AND THE MEDIATING
ROLE OF POSITIVE AND NEGATIVE INTERETHNIC
CONTACT: A PRIMING EXPERIMENT

Susanne Veit, Ruud Koopmans (2014), *September Social
Science Research* 47

Greater diversity causes greater mistrust among
communities, both native and immigrant. Close,
positive interpersonal experiences with other
races or ethnicities can increase trust, but the
frequency that these occur is inversely correlated to amount of diversity, thus creating a
paradox.

"This study not only shows that the empirically well-established negative relationship between
residential diversity and trust in neighbors holds
for the case of Germany, but goes beyond existing research by providing experimental evidence
on the causal nature of the diversity effect. ...
When people come to perceive their neighborhood in terms of religious or ethnic differences,
something is triggered that makes them less
trusting of their neighbors."

In-Group Bias

PATTERNS OF IMPLICIT AND EXPLICIT ATTITUDES:
IV. CHANGE AND STABILITY FROM 2007 TO 2020

Tessa E S Charlesworth, Mahzarin R Banaji,
Psychol Sci . 2022 Sep;33(9):1347-1371. doi:
10.1177/09567976221084257. Epub 2022 Jul 27.

Huge study involving over 7 million individuals
finds that the ingroup bias (preference for one's
own group) of black Americans is approximately 5 times stronger than the ingroup bias of
whites.

Immigration and Trust

ETHNIC DIVERSITY, ECONOMIC AND CULTURAL
CONTEXTS, AND SOCIAL TRUST: CROSS-SECTIONAL
AND LONGITUDINAL EVIDENCE FROM EUROPEAN
REGIONS, 2002–2010

Conrad Ziller (2014), *Social Forces*, vol. 93, iss. 3, March
2015, pgs. 1211–1240

Immigration-related diversity strongly decreases
social trust.

"The results show that across European
regions, different aspects of immigration-related
diversity are negatively related to social trust. In
longitudinal perspective, an increase in immigration is related to a decrease in social trust.
... Immigration growth is particularly strongly
associated with a decrease in social trust."

International Evidence on Trust and Diversity

PREDICTING CROSS-NATIONAL LEVELS OF
SOCIAL TRUST: GLOBAL PATTERN OR NORDIC
EXCEPTIONALISM?

Jan Delhey, Kenneth Newton (2005), *European
Sociological Review*, vol. 21, iss. 4, September 2005, pgs.
311–327

Ethnic and religious homogeneity have a direct
impact on trust.

"This analysis of variations in the level of
generalized social trust (defined here as the belief that others will not deliberately or knowingly do us harm, if they can avoid it, and will look
after our interests, if this is possible) in 60 nations of the world shows that trust is an integral
part of a tight syndrome of social, political and
economic conditions. High trust countries are
characterized by ethnic homogeneity, Protestant
religious traditions, good government, wealth
(gross domestic product per capita), and income
equality."

Localized Study on Trust

TRUST IN A TIME OF INCREASING DIVERSITY:
ON THE RELATIONSHIP BETWEEN ETHNIC
HETEROGENEITY AND SOCIAL TRUST IN DENMARK
FROM 1979 UNTIL TODAY

Peter Thisted Dinesen, Kim Mannemar Sønderskov
(2012), *Scandinavian Political Studies*, vol. 35, iss. 4,
December 2012, pgs. 273-294

Diversity decreases trust on local levels, even if general societal trust has increased in average on a country-wide scale.

"The results show that while trust at the national level has increased to very high levels over this period of increased ethnic diversity in the country, ethnic diversity at the municipality level in fact has a negative impact on social trust when taking into account the overall national trend and unobserved time-invariant characteristics of the municipalities analyzed."

Putnam's Theory Replicated

ETHNIC DIVERSITY AND ITS IMPACT ON COMMUNITY SOCIAL COHESION AND NEIGHBORLY EXCHANGE

Rebecca Wickes, Renee Zahnow, Gentry White, Lorraine Mazerolle (2013), *Journal Of Urban Affairs*, vol. 36, iss. 1 February 2014 pgs. 51-78

Putnam's "Hunker Down" theory is replicated in Australia, though findings show that immigrant populations are less affected than White Australians.

"Our findings indicate that social cohesion and neighborly exchange are attenuated in ethnically diverse suburbs. However, diversity is less consequential for neighborly exchange among immigrants when compared to the general population. Our results provide at least partial support for Putnam's thesis."

Ethnic Diversity and Theft

MEASURING TRUST

Edward L. Glaeser David I. Laibson José A. Scheinkman Christine L. Soutter (2000)

In an economic "game," 92% of the cases in which money was "stolen" was between racially diverse (heterogeneous) pairs of participants.

"Most strikingly, 92 percent of the cases where the recipient sent back nothing occurred when the individuals were of different races, while only 59 percent of the pairings were racially diverse"

Borders and Violence

GOOD FENCES: THE IMPORTANCE OF SETTING BOUNDARIES FOR PEACEFUL COEXISTENCE

Alex Rutherford, Dion Harmon, Justin Werfel, Shlomiya Bar-Yam, Alexander Gard-Murray, Andreas Gros, and Yaneer Bar-Yam (2011)

Strong borders between separate ethnic groups reduces violence between them, meaning that diversity causes fractionalization and conflict. "Our analysis shows that peace does not depend on integrated coexistence, but rather on well defined topographical and political boundaries separating groups. Mountains and lakes are an important part of the boundaries between sharply defined linguistic areas. Political canton and circle (sub-canton) boundaries often separate religious groups. Where such boundaries do not appear to be sufficient, we find that specific aspects of the population distribution either guarantee sufficient separation or sufficient mixing to inhibit intergroup violence according to the quantitative theory of conflict."

Pregnancy and Criminality

MORE PREGNANCY, LESS CRIME 2019, WITH 2023 UPDATE

Massenkoff, Maxim: Naval Postgraduate School; Rose, Even K.: University of Chicago and NBER. "Family Formation and Crime". Nov. 11, 2019, rev. Apr. 2023

"...pregnancy triggers sharp declines in crime rivaling any known intervention. For mothers, criminal offending drops precipitously in the first few months of pregnancy, stabilizing at half of pre-pregnancy levels three years after the birth. Men show a smaller, but still important, 25 percent decline beginning at the onset of pregnancy, although domestic violence arrests spike for fathers immediately after the birth. A design using stillbirths as counterfactuals suggests a causal role for children. In contrast, marriage is a stopping point, marking the completion of a roughly 50 percent decline in offending for both men and women. The data present a unique opportunity to test the implications of a dynamic rational addiction model, which suggests forward-looking behavior among married and unmarried mothers."

Homogenous Military and Combat Effectiveness

COWARDS AND HEROES: GROUP LOYALTY IN THE AMERICAN CIVIL WAR

Dora L. Costa, Matthew E. Kahn (2001)

Homogeneous military units have lower desertion rates than diverse units.

"We find that individual and company socio-economic and demographic characteristics, ideology, and morale were important predictors of group loyalty in the Union Army. Company characteristics were more important than ideology or morale. Soldiers in companies that were more homogeneous in ethnicity, occupation, and age were less likely to shirk."

Diversity Impacts on Conflict

DIVERSITY AND CONFLICT

Cemal Eren Arbatli, Quamrul H. Ashraf, Oded Galor, Marc Klemp (201)

Over the last half-century, diversity has contributed significantly to frequency of ethnic civil conflict, the intensity of social unrest, growth of unshared policy preferences, and economic inequality.

"This research advances the hypothesis and establishes empirically that interpersonal population diversity has contributed significantly to the emergence, prevalence, recurrence, and severity of intrasocietal conflicts. ... The findings arguably reflect the adverse effect of population diversity on interpersonal trust, its contribution to divergence in preferences for public goods and redistributive policies, and its impact on the degree of fractionalization and polarization across ethnic, linguistic, and religious groups."

Diversity and Violence

IS COLLECTIVE VIOLENCE CORRELATED WITH SOCIAL PLURALISM?

Rudolph J. Rummel (1997)

Ethnic pluralism (diversity) is correlated with collective violence.

"The more ethnic groups in a state, the more likely it will have a high rate of guerrilla and revolutionary warfare. And the more religious groups in a society, the more intense the general violence. This is largely moderated by the size of a state. Thus, the larger and older (counting from 1932) a state in addition to the more religious groups, the more the general violence."

Nepotism and Diversity

ETHNIC CONFLICTS: THEIR BIOLOGICAL ROOTS IN ETHNIC NEPOTISM.

Tatu Vanhanen (2012)

Conflict will always arise within diverse societies due to ethnic nepotism.

"Ethnic heterogeneity [diversity] explains 55% of the variation in the scale of ethnic conflicts, and the results of regression analysis disclosed that the same relationship more or less applies to all 187 countries. These results led to the conclusion that ethnic nepotism is the common cross-cultural background factor which supports the persistence of ethnic conflicts in the world as long as there are ethnically divided societies."

Segregation and Violence

THE GEOGRAPHY OF ETHNIC VIOLENCE

Alex Rutherford, May Lim, Richard Metzler, Dion Harmon, Justin Werfel, Shlomiya Bar-Yam, Alexander Gard-Murray, Andreas Gros, Yaneer Bar-Yam (2015)

Segregation decreases violence between ethnic groups.

"Our analysis supports the hypothesis that violence between groups can be inhibited by both physical and political boundaries."

Borders and Conflict

SWISS-IFICATION: SYRIA'S BEST CHANCE FOR PEACE

Yaneer Bar-Yam and Casey Friedman (2013)

Poorly defined boundaries between ethnically or racially diverse/disparate communities lead to conflict.

"...conflict arises when groups are neither well integrated nor well separated. In highly mixed regions, groups either don't develop strong collective identities or don't lay claim to public spaces. ... Well-separated groups don't engage in conflict. However, partial separation with poorly defined boundaries fosters conflict."

Diversity and Trust

Ethnic Diversity and Trust

Oguzhan C. Dincer (2011)

Diversity causes social conflict.

"Using data from U.S. states, I investigate the relationship between ethnic diversity and trust. I find a negative relationship between ethnic polarization and trust ... The main channel through which ethnic diversity is hypothesized to affect trust is social conflict."

Antagonism and Diversity

Culture, Ethnicity, and Diversity

Desmet, Klaus, Ignacio Ortuño-Ortín, and Romain Wacziarg. 2017. *Culture, Ethnicity, and Diversity. American Economic Review*, 107 (9): 2479-2513.

A 2017 paper concludes that in societies where individuals differ from each other in both ethnicity and culture, social antagonism is greater, and political economy outcomes are worse.

"We investigate the empirical relationship between ethnicity and culture, defined as a vector of traits reflecting norms, values, and attitudes. Using survey data for 76 countries, we find that ethnic identity is a significant predictor of cultural values, yet that within-group variation in culture trumps between-group variation. Thus, in contrast to a commonly held view, ethnic and cultural diversity are unrelated. Although only a small portion of a country's overall cultural heterogeneity occurs between groups, we find that various political economy outcomes (such as civil conflict and public goods provision) worsen when there is greater overlap between ethnicity and culture."

Minorities and Self-Segregation

Melting pot or salad bowl: the formation of heterogeneous communities

Arun Advani, Bryony Reich (2015), Institute for Fiscal Studies, 7 October 2015

Minority groups within a diverse population will begin to self-segregate from the majority when they reach a certain population size, moving towards division and away from co-operation.

"We find that a small minority group will adopt majority cultural practices and integrate.

In contrast, minority groups above a certain critical mass, may retain diverse practices and may also segregate from the majority. The size of this critical mass depends on the cultural distance between groups, the importance of culture in day to day life, and the costs of forming a social tie."

Most Diverse Cities

The Most Diverse Cities Are Often The Most Segregated

Nate Silver (2015)

"It is all too common to live in a city with a wide variety of ethnic and racial groups — including Chicago, New York, and Baltimore — and yet remain isolated from those groups in a racially homogenous neighborhood. ... the exceptions are cities like Sacramento that have large Hispanic or Asian populations. Cities with substantial black populations tend to be highly segregated. Of the top 100 U.S. cities by population, 35 are at least one-quarter black, and only 6 of those cities have positive integration scores."

Diversity and Economic Growth

Fractionalization

Alesina, Alberto, Arnaud Devleeschauwer, William Easterly, Sergio Kurlat, and Romain Wacziarg (2003), *Journal of Economic Growth* 8(2): 155-194

Diversity is correlated with slow economic growth.

"We concluded that ethnic and linguistic diversity fractionalization variables, but not religious ones, are likely to be important determinants of economic success, both in terms of output (GDP growth), the quality of policies, and the quality of institutions."

Diversity's Impact on Economics

Ethnic Diversity and Economic Performance

Alesina, Alberto, and Eliana La Ferrara (2005), *Journal of Economic Literature* 43(3): 762-800

Diversity is negatively associated with economic growth, even after controlling for wealth over time.

Meta-Study on Diversity and Group Functioning

Demography and Diversity in Organizations: A review of 40 years of research

Katherine Y. Williams, Charles A. O'Reilly (1998), *Research In Organizational Behavior*, vol. 20

A review of 80 studies spanning 40 years concludes that diversity impedes group functioning and is most likely to cause negative effects.

"Simply having more diversity in a group is no guarantee that the group will make better decisions or function effectively. ... empirical evidence suggests that diversity is most likely to impede group functioning. ... diversity by itself is more likely to have a negative than positive effects on group performance. ... There is substantial evidence from both laboratory and field studies conducted over the past four decades that variations in group composition can have important effects on group functioning. These studies show that increased diversity, especially in terms of age, tenure, and ethnicity, typically have negative effects on social integration, communication, and conflict."

Diversity and Innovation

Negative Effects on Innovation

Bala Ramasamy, Matthew C. H. Yeung (2016), *Applied Economics Letters*, vol. 23, 2016 – iss. 14

Ethnic diversity has a negative effect on innovation, "values diversity" has the opposite effect, but only as long as ethnic diversity is low.

"...ethnic diversity or fractionalization and values diversity are distinct and while the former has a negative effect on innovation, the latter contributes positively. ... countries that are ethnically homogenous but diverse in values orientation are the best innovators."

Workplace Cohesion

What Makes Teams Work: Group Effectiveness Research from the Shop Floor to the Executive Suite

Susan G. Cohen, Diane E. Bailey (1997), *Journal of Management*, vol. 23, iss. 3

Ethnically diverse workplaces have lower cohesion, lower satisfaction and higher turnover.

"Group cohesiveness is positively related to

performance. Three metaanalyses and several empirical studies found a slight to moderate positive relationship between cohesiveness and performance. This is a robust finding in an area that has long been studied."

Immigration and Inequality

Imported Inequality? Immigration and Income Inequality in the American States

Ping Xu, James C. Garand, Ling Zhu (2015), *State Politics & Policy Quarterly*, vol. 16, iss. 2

Immigration into the United States has increased income inequality.

"Empirical evidence from both static and dynamic models shows that the foreign-born population has a strong positive effect on state-level income inequality, even when we control for a range of federal and state political and economic contextual variables. We also find that the positive relationship between immigration and state income inequality is driven primarily by low-skill immigrants (rather than high-skill immigrants) ... immigration—particularly low-skilled immigration—has an important effect on income inequality in the American states."

Group Cooperation

Effects of Heterogeneity and Homophily on Cooperation

Ozan Aksoy (2015), *Social Psychology Quarterly*, vol. 78, iss. 4

Diversity negatively impacts group cooperation.

"The results show that heterogeneity hampers between-group cooperation at the dyadic level. In addition, endogenous sorting mitigates this negative effect of heterogeneity on cooperation." (Diversity hinders between-group cooperation at both one-on-one and group levels).

Negative impact of diversity upon group cooperation is exacerbated if group participants belong to racial or ethnic groups with negative history or conflict.

"Heterogeneity hampers cooperation at the tetradic level most substantially if there is a commonly known negative history between groups."

Neighborhood Cooperation

COOPERATION IN ETHNICALLY DIVERSE
NEIGHBORHOODS: A LOST-LETTER EXPERIMENT

Susanne Veit, Ruud Koopmans (2014), June
2014Political Psychology 35(3)

Diversity reduces neighborhood co-operation.

"We find strong support for the negative effect
of ethnic diversity on cooperation. We find no
evidence, however, of in-group favoritism. Letters from Turkish or Muslim organizations were
as often returned as those from German and
Christian organizations, and the ethnic diversity effect was the same for all types of letters."

Lowers GDP

HARVARD INSTITUTE OF ECONOMIC
RESEARCH, DISCUSSION PAPER NUMBER 1959:
FRACTIONALIZATION

Alberto Alesina, Arnaud Devleeschauwer, William
Easterly, Sergio Kurlat and Romain Wacziarg (2002)

"...ethnic variable is highly correlated with GDP
per capita growth, schooling and telephones per
capita ... Ethnic fractionalization is also closely
correlated with GDP per capita and geographic
variables, like latitude. More ethnic fragmentation is more common in poorer countries which
are closer to the equator."

Ethnic homogeneity correlates with strong
democracy.

"The democracy index is inversely related to
ethnic fractionalization (when latitude is not
controlled for). This result is consistent with
theory and evidence presented in Aghion, Alesina and Trebbi (2002). The idea is that in more
fragmented societies a group imposes restrictions on political liberty to impose control..."

More [ethnic] fractionalization leads to lower
quality of government.

"It seems that governments have a much
more difficult task achieving consensus for
redistribution to the needy in a fractionalized
society. ... conflict among groups brings about
more difficult policy and inefficient policymaking."

Diversity and Poverty

THIS MODEL OF WEALTHY SUBURBAN LIVING IS
STARTING TO FRAY

Antonio Olivo (2016), *Washington Post*

Rapid diversification of a wealthy Virginia
county coincides with increasing poverty and
decreasing social cohesion.

"For decades, Fairfax County has been a
national model for suburban living, a place of
good governance and elite schools that educate
children from some of the country's richest
neighborhoods. But Virginia's largest municipality is fraying around the edges. A population
that is growing older, poorer and more diverse
is sharpening the need for basic services in what
is still the nation's second-wealthiest county,
even as a sluggish local economy maintains a
chokehold on the revenue stream. Since the
2008 recession, local officials have whittled
away at programs to the tune of $300 million.
They now say that there is no fat left to trim.
Instead, they are searching for ways to raise
taxes, draw new businesses and revitalize worn
neighborhoods."

Institutional Quality

CAN INSTITUTIONS RESOLVE ETHNIC CONFLICT?

W. Easterly (2001)

Diversity decreases institution quality. Within a
nation with poor institutions, diversity strongly
predicts low economic growth.

Easterly's measurement of institutional
quality includes the following: "(a) freedom
from government repudiation of contracts, (b)
freedom from expropriation, (c) rule of law, and
(d) bureaucratic quality into an overall index
of institutional quality." It is highly correlated
with other measures of corruption and quality
of business environment. Easterly showed that
diversity more strongly predicted low economic
growth the poorer a nation's institutions were.

Segregated Neighborhoods Affluence

NEIGHBORHOOD GAP FOR BLACKS, HISPANICS AND
ASIANS IN METROPOLITAN AMERICA

John R. Logan (2011)

Segregated minority (non-White) neighborhoods are less affluent than White neighbor-

hoods, with worse infrastructure and lower institution quality.

"Racial segregation itself is the prime predictor of which metropolitan regions are the ones where minorities live in the least desirable neighborhoods. ... neighborhood poverty is associated with inequalities in public schools, safety, environmental quality, and public health. ... The average affluent black or Hispanic household lives in a poorer neighborhood than the average lower-income white resident."

Cognitive Diversity

TEAM-LEVEL PREDICTORS OF INNOVATION AT WORK: A COMPREHENSIVE META-ANALYSIS SPANNING THREE DECADES OF RESEARCH.

Hülsheger UR, Anderson N, Salgado JF (2009)

Ethnic diversity does not improve cognitive diversity within groups and interferes with innovative endeavors.

"Unlike job-relevant diversity, background diversity does not evoke cognitive resource diversity. Instead, it may entail a number of consequences that interfere with innovative endeavors. Background diversity may lead to communication problems and difficulties in resolving opposing ideas and reaching consensus within the team. However, the ability to discuss opposing ideas, integrate divergent viewpoints, and reach consensus is vital for the creation and implementation of new ideas. ... background diversity correlated at -.133 (95% CI: -.318:+.052) with innovation."

Happiness and Diversity

HAPPINESS IN MODERN SOCIETY: WHY INTELLIGENCE AND ETHNIC COMPOSITION MATTER

Satoshi Kanazawa The London School of Economics and Political Science, Norman P Li Singapore Management University (2015)

Data from the National Longitudinal Study of Adolescent Health showed that multiethnic diversity decreases happiness among all groups, and most markedly for the downscale and economically dispossessed.

"Recent developments in evolutionary psychology suggest that living among others of the same ethnicity might make individuals happier and further that such an effect of the ethnic composition on life satisfaction may be stronger among less intelligent individuals. Data from the National Longitudinal Study of Adolescent Health showed that White Americans had significantly greater life satisfaction than all other ethnic groups in the US and this was largely due to the fact that they were the majority ethnic group; minority Americans who lived in counties where they were the numerical majority had just as much life satisfaction as White Americans did. Further, the association between ethnic composition and life satisfaction was significantly stronger among less intelligent individuals. The results suggest two important factors underlying life satisfaction and highlight the utility of integrating happiness research and evolutionary psychology."

Biracial Mental Health Disparity

STUDY FINDS DISPARITY IN MENTAL HEALTH OF BIRACIAL ASIAN AMERICANS

Lauren Berger 2008

A study at the University of California-Davis recently found that bi-racial Asian Americans are twice as likely to suffer from depression as their monoracial counterparts.

"Biracial Americans of Asian and white descent are twice as likely to be diagnosed with a psychological disorder compared to monoracial Asian Americans, according to a new study from the Asian American Center on Disparities Research at UC Davis."

Mixed-Race Pregnancy

ASIAN-WHITE COUPLES FACE DISTINCT PREGNANCY RISKS

Yasser El-Sayed 2008

"The Stanford University School of Medicine recently found that pregnant women of mixed white/Asian couples were more likely to develop gestational diabetes, a complication of pregnancy with severe consequences if untreated. Racial distinctions in the genes controlling bone marrow production have made it difficult for mixed race individuals to find matching donors for bone marrow transplants, according to the National Marrow Donor Program."

Mixed-Race and Obesity

The Prevalence of Obesity in Ethnic Admixture Adults

Obesity (Silver Spring). 2008 May; 16(5): 1138–1143.

The Cancer Research Center at the University of Hawaii released a study showing that individuals of five ethnic admixtures were significantly more likely to be overweight or obese than their component ethnic groups.

Diversity and Psychosis

Ethnic density as a buffer for psychotic experiences: findings from a national survey (EMPIRIC)

Jayati Das-Munshi, Laia Bécares, Jane E. Boydell, Michael E. Dewey, Craig Morgan, Stephen A. Stansfeld, and Martin J. Prince (2012)

Diversity increases psychotic experiences.
"People resident in neighborhoods of higher own-group density experience 'buffering' effects from the social risk factors for psychosis."
A 10% increase in diversity doubles the chance of psychotic episodes.
"For every ten percentage point reduction in own-group density, the relative odds of reporting psychotic experiences increased 1.07 times (95% CI 1.01–1.14, P = 0.03 (trend)) for the total minority ethnic sample."
Diversity increases social adversity.
"people living in areas of lower own-group density experienced greater social adversity."

Diversity and Minority Health

Health Advantages of Ethnic Density for African American and Mexican American Elderly Individuals

Kimberly J. Alvarez MPH, and Becca R. Levy PhD (2012)

Diversity harms the health of African Americans and Mexican Americans, ethnically homogeneous neighborhoods are beneficial for health.
"...ethnic density predicted lower rates of cardiovascular disease and cancer, adjusting for covariates, showing that the health benefits of ethnic density apply to both minority communities."
– Study finds lower rates of heart disease and cancer than for those living in more mixed areas.

Diversity and Environmentalism

Environmental Performance in Socially Fragmented Countries

Elissaios Papyrakis (2012)

Diversity reduces concern for the environment.
"...this is the first study to our knowledge that makes use of a large panel dataset of several environmental indicators to explore links between ethnic/religious diversity and the environment. We find that all indices of social fragmentation are negatively linked to measures of environmental quality."

Immigration and Schizophrenia

UK life blamed for ethnic schizophrenia

Institute of Psychiatry (via BBC *Health News*, 2000)

In the UK, African-Caribbean people are six times more likely than whites to be diagnosed as schizophrenic.
"UK life blamed for ethnic schizophrenia. ... A study by the Institute of Psychiatry has found that poor social conditions are causing black people to develop the symptoms of mental illness. We find that all indices of social fragmentation are negatively linked to measures of environmental quality ... Researchers from the Institute of Psychiatry investigated whether black people were somehow genetically more prone to schizophrenia. The answer was no."

Migration and Schizophrenia

Schizophrenia in black Caribbeans living in the UK: an exploration of underlying causes of the high incidence rate

Rebecca Pinto, BA (Hons), MSc, Research Associate, Mark Ashworth, DM, MRCP, MRCGP, Clinical Senior Lecturer, and Roger Jones, DM, MA, FRCP, FRCGP, FMedSci, FFPHM, Wolfson Professor of General Practice (2008)

Higher rates of schizophrenia are found among migrants globally, even among White migrants moving to societies of another White ethnic group.
"In 1932, Ødegård found that Norwegians emigrating to the US were twice as likely to be

admitted to hospital with first-onset schizophrenia as native-born Americans or Norwegians residing in Norway. Subsequent studies have confirmed the high incidence in migrants, demonstrating an overall relative risk of 2.7 in first-generation migrants and 4.5 in second-generation migrants."

Minorities living in majority neighborhoods appear to be more susceptible to schizophrenia.

"African-Caribbeans living in predominantly white neighbourhoods have been found to have a higher incidence of schizophrenia.

Second generation immigrants are more likely to suffer schizophrenia than first.

"...studies report higher rates in second-generation African-Caribbeans and other migrant groups."

Low "social capital" is correlated to higher rates of schizophrenia.

"Social capital has variously been described as the investment that people make to life within the local community, or 'the glue that holds society together'. Measures of social capital (voter turnout) and social cohesion (ethnic fragmentation) have been linked with schizophrenia incidence, and may therefore contribute to the raised rates in black Caribbeans. Evidence is accumulating that the most socially disorganised neighbourhoods, rather than the poorest neighbourhoods, have the highest incidence of schizophrenia, and these may be the areas where black Caribbeans are more likely to live."

Majority Connection and Well-Being

EMOTIONAL FIT WITH CULTURE: A PREDICTOR OF INDIVIDUAL DIFFERENCES IN RELATIONAL WELL-BEING.

De Leersnyder J, Mesquita B, Kim H, Eom K, Choi H (2014)

Emotional connection to majority culture improves well-being.

"Using an implicit measure of cultural fit of emotions, we found across 3 different cultural contexts (United States, Belgium, and Korea) that (1) individuals' emotional fit is associated with their level of relational well-being, and that (2) the link between emotional fit and relational well-being is particularly strong when emotional fit is measured for situations pertaining to relationships (rather than for situations that are self-focused). Together, the current studies suggest that people may benefit from emotionally 'fitting in' to their culture."

Traditionalist Societies and Suicide

ON THE PICTURE OF DEPRESSION AND SUICIDE IN TRADITIONAL SOCIETIES.

Jacobsson L (1988)

Traditional societies have 'very low' rates of suicide.

"...the incidence of suicide in a society has no clear correlation with the prevalence of mental disorders and no clear correlation with different forms of mental disorders ... The suicide rate is generally very low in traditional societies."

Diversity And IQ

THE DECAY OF WESTERN CIVILIZATION: DOUBLE RELAXED DARWINIAN SELECTION

Helmuth Nyborg (2015)

"The reverse Lynn–Flynn effect has also been observed in Norway (Sundet, Barlaug, & Torjussen, 2004), but continue elsewhere in- and out side Europe. Still worse, the large birth differentials will over time drive the future population expansion, and low-IQ immigrants (IQs < 90) consistently display higher birth rates than better endowed immigrants (IQ > 90). Average population IQ is sure to decline. ... Gifted immigrant women may lower their fertility when engaged in higher education, but their relatively low number will not affect the overall picture."

Lower IQ migrants will outbreed natives within 40 years.

"Sixth, in terms of total population growth, mainly non-Western citizens with IQ 70–85 can be expected to numerically surpass the mainly Western group with IQs 90–104 at about 2065. ... Gifted immigrant women may lower their fertility when engaged in higher education, but their relatively low number will not affect the overall picture."

Biracial Identity Development

BIRACIAL IDENTITY DEVELOPMENT AND RECOMMENDATIONS IN THERAPY

Raushanah Hud-Aleem, DO and Jacqueline Countryman, MD Paulette M. Gillig, PhD, MD, series editor. *Psychiatry* (Edgmont). 2008 Nov; 5(11): 37–44. Published online 2008 Nov. PMCID: PMC2695719 PMID: 19724716

"It is believed that all people, regardless of race, go through a process of developing racial consciousness." ...

"Studies have also shown that biracial children are at risk to develop racial identification issues, lowered self esteem, violence, substance abuse, and feeling marginal in two cultures"

Multiracial Adolescent Risks

ARE MULTIRACIAL ADOLESCENTS AT GREATER RISK? COMPARISONS OF RATES, PATTERNS, AND CORRELATES OF SUBSTANCE USE AND VIOLENCE BETWEEN MONORACIAL AND MULTIRACIAL ADOLESCENTS

Yoonsun Choi, PhD, Tracy W. Harachi, PhD, Mary Rogers Gillmore, PhD, and Richard F. Catalano, PhD, Am J Orthopsychiatry. 2006 Jan; 76(1): 86–97. doi: 10.1037/0002-9432.76.1.86 PMCID: PMC3292211 NIHMSID: NIHMS293848 PMID: 16569131

"Rates and patterns of substance use and violent behaviors among multiracial adolescents were examined and compared with 3 monoracial groups, European, African, and Asian Americans. The relationships between ethnic identity and the subjective experience of racial discrimination, substance use, and violent behavior were also examined. The authors found multiracial adolescents reporting higher rates of problem behaviors." ...

"Scholars argue that multiracial adolescents are likely to be at higher risk than monoracial European American or ethnic minority youths, as issues related to their multiracial background become more salient during the already challenging developmental period of adolescence. For example, peer acceptance may be a particularly pervasive problem for multiracial youths due to their ambiguous racial status, and it may lead to higher levels of behavioral and psychosocial problems, including a higher incidence of social isolation and involvement in delinquent behaviors." ...

"Both majority and ethnic minority groups may reject multiracial youths, and such social marginality can place multiracial youths at higher risk for delinquent behavior and substance use..." ...

"We hypothesize that multiracial adolescents who experience racial discrimination are more likely to initiate substance use and violent behaviors and to report higher frequency of these behaviors and that the relationships between ra-cial discrimination and problem behaviors will be stronger among multiracial than monoracial ethnic minority youths." ...

"The results of this study, overall, support the hypothesis of higher rates of problem behaviors among multiracial adolescents relative to monoracial adolescents (i.e., European, African, and Asian Americans). Multiracial adolescents reported higher rates of initiation than monoracial groups for several substances and violent behaviors. There were fewer statistically significant differences between multiracial and African American youths, but the overall patterns were similar in that multiracial youths reported higher rates of problem behaviors. The differences were quite large at times. Unlike the majority of studies on multiracial adolescents, this study used nonclinical samples, but the pattern of higher rates of problems among multiracial youths, particularly compared to European and Asian American youths, was evident. It is often suggested that racial/ethnic group differences are an artifact of socioeconomic status differences. However, these differences remained after socioeconomic status was controlled. In addition, findings from multiracial subgroup analyses suggest some differences in the level of risk among subgroups of multiracial youths but more strongly indicate that multiracial youths as a group are at heightened risk of problem behaviors." ...

"The findings of this study provide empirical evidence that multiracial youths are at greater risk for problem behaviors such as substance use and engaging in violence than monoracial youths and that perceived racial discrimination may be an added risk factor for multiracial youths. The findings also suggest that a stronger, positive ethnic identity may serve as a protective factor, particularly for the frequency of substance use and violence."

Mixed-Race Health/Mental Risk

HEALTH AND BEHAVIOR RISKS OF ADOLESCENTS WITH MIXED-RACE IDENTITY

J. Richard Udry

A University of North Carolina study found that children of mixed race were more likely to manifest higher risk behaviors includng a 50% greater risk of depression, 24% increased risk of smoking, 20% increased risk of drinking, 34% greater likelihood to have serious thoughts of suicide, 50% more likely to be sexually active in high school, and 94% more likely to be suspended from school compare to children of white ancestry alone. In fact, mixed race children had higher risk factors across nearly all categories compared to single race children, including the most disadvantaged single race group, African-Americans. This suggests that racial mixing could lead to social problems greater in severity to those currently present in our predominantly African-American inner cities.

Diversity and Student Education

IMMIGRANTS IN THE CLASSROOM AND EFFECTS ON NATIVE CHILDREN

Peter Jensen (2015)

Diverse classrooms, or presence of immigrant students, harms educational outcomes of native students in most countries, causing higher dropout rates and increase in exam failure.

"In most countries, a high share of immigrant children in schools leads to lower test scores of native children. ... A high share of immigrant students can lead to higher dropout rates from high school and lower chances of passing exams."

Diverse classrooms, or presence of immigrant students, causes higher rates of bullying towards native children and "native flight" from diverse schools.

"Native children tend to experience more incidents of bullying when there are more immigrant children in the same classroom. ... Native flight from schools that have many immigrant children can amplify negative effects on native children, as native parents move their children to schools with fewer immigrant children."

Diversity and Student Suicide Risk

Race, social networks, and school bullying

Faris, Robert (2019)

Diverse schools significantly increase students' probability of committing suicide.

"Being bullied decreases popularity and increases depression and the likelihood of suicide attempts. With one exception, the effect of bullying on mental health and school attachment does not vary by race. Minority students who bully others make larger gains in popularity than whites, suggesting one possible

explanation for their higher perpetration rates. ... Racial diversity of the school increases the prevalence of bullying."

School Bullying

ETHNICITY AND BULLYING INVOLVEMENT IN A NATIONAL UK YOUTH SAMPLE.

Tippett Neil, Wolke D, Platt L. (2013). *The Roles of Ethnicity and School Context in Predicting Children's Victimization* by Peers Laura D. Hanish, Nancy G. Guerra (2000)

Non-Whites are significantly more likely to bully Whites than vice versa, are more likely to bully in general, regardless of socio-economic factors, and are significantly less likely to be victims of bullying than Whites.

"Overall, ethnic minority youths were not more likely to be victims; African boys and girls were significantly less likely to be victimised than same sex White youths. Pakistani and Caribbean girls were significantly more likely to have bullied others compared to White girls."

"Hispanic children had lower victimization scores than did either African-American or White children. These findings, however, were moderated by school context, such that attending ethnically integrated schools was associated with a significantly higher risk of victimization for White children and a slightly lower risk of victimization for African-American children and did not affect the risk of victimization for Hispanic children. In addition, African-American children were less likely than Hispanic and White children to be repeatedly victimized by peers over time."

"None of the variables mediate the higher perpetration rates of African-Americans and Latinos."

Diversity and School Withdrawal

SCHOOL CHOICE, UNIVERSAL VOUCHERS AND NATIVE FLIGHT FROM LOCAL SCHOOLS

Beatrice Schindler Rangvid (2009)

Native Danes opt-out of public schools with immigrant populations above 35%.

"The results suggest that, when a rich set of covariates at student, school, and neighbourhood levels is controlled for, up to an immigrant concentration of about 35 per cent in the local school, opting out decisions of Danes are not affected. But, Danes are far more likely to opt out as soon as the concentration exceeds 35 per cent."

Diverse Schools and Trust

SCHOOL ETHNIC DIVERSITY AND WHITE STUDENTS' CIVIC ATTITUDES IN ENGLAND

Jan Germen Janmaat (2015)

Diverse schools do not increase positive attitudes towards immigrants among White British students, but do reduce trust in people of one's own age.

"In agreement with contact theory, the paper initially finds a positive relation between diversity and inclusive attitudes on immigrants. However, this link disappears once controls for social background, gender and prior levels of the outcome are included in the model. This indicates that students with particular pre-enrollment characteristics have self-selected in diverse schools and that inclusive attitudes have stabilized before secondary education. Diversity further appears to have a negative impact on trust, irrespective of the number of controls added to the model."

Asian Influx and White Flight

THE NEW WHITE FLIGHT

Suein Hwang (2015). *The New Separate But Equal.* James Chen (2005)

Asian migration into liberal San Francisco and surrounding suburbs causes White parents to pull children out of public schools.

"...in a continuous arc of high—performing public school districts ringing San Francisco Bay, Asian student enrollments have climbed sharply over the past decade as white enrollments plummeted. These include middle—class neighborhoods in cities throughout the most liberal region in the United States. Suburban cities in the area with both rapidly—growing Asian student populations and steadily—diminishing numbers of white students include Alameda, Albany, Fremont (Kerry by 51%) Cupertino, San Jose (Kerry by 29%) and San Mateo (Kerry by 40%)."

Diversity and Tension, Disorder, Abuse, Gangs, Cults

Indicators of School Crime and Safety: 2011. National Center for Education Statistics (2011)

Diversity within schools increases: racial tensions, verbal abuse of teachers, classroom disorder, student disrespect for teachers, gang activity, cult or extremist groups on campus, quantity of serious violent incidents.

Serious violent incidents include: rape, robbery, and actual or threatened attack with a weapon. Hierarchy of student races from most to least violent is as follows: Black, Hispanic, White, Asian.

Integration and Achievement Gap

IN SEARCH OF THE KEY TO CLOSING ACHIEVEMENT GAPS

Michael Hansen (2016)

School "integration" (forced proximate diversity) does not close race achievement gaps.

"New research indicates that integrating schools to equalize access to teachers will not significantly close student achievement gaps."

Despite massive government investment and long-time policy interests, schools are becoming more segregated, not less.

"American schools have had an unremarkable track record in achieving greater levels of school integration, in spite of long-time policy interests to do so. ... schools did show an increasing trend towards integration in the decades immediately following the 1954 Brown v. Board of Education decision, that trend has reversed over the last 20 years, and schools in many states are now only slightly less segregated than they were before the decision."

Desegregation and Black Education

AFRICAN AMERICAN STUDENTS IN EAST BATON ROUGE PARISH: HOW HAVE THEY FARED IN DESEGREGATED SCHOOLS?

Fossey, Richard (1996)

Baton Rouge desegregation led to lower graduation rates among black students, resulted in a white enrollment collapse, and tracked SED student increases. The nominal budget went from $40 to $250 million dollars to implement a smooth transition to a school population the remained unchanged in quantity. 40% of students classified as Trainable Mentally Retarded, and most new funds went to special ed. 50% students get suspended.

"Three generations of children have passed through the Baton Rouge (Louisiana) school system since the 'Brown' decision (1954) and one generation since the federal court's 1981 desegregation order. The impact of school desegregation on African American children was studied in the East Baton Rouge School District. For the student body as a whole, graduation rates have declined slightly, stabilizing at about 60%. African American graduation rates have ranged from 50 to 65% over the time period. African American students have been, and remain, far more likely to be suspended than any other race. About half the African American students attending district middle schools in 1992-93 received at least one suspension. African American students are disproportionately represented in district special education programs. Racial isolation is increasing in the schools, with predominantly white gifted and talented students in one set of classes and the general school population, largely African American, in another set of classes. Increasing amounts of human and financial resources are being poured into the district, but it is evident that conditions have not improved for African American students in Baton Rouge. Findings suggest that now is the time to reexamine the way African American students are being educated in Baton Rouge."

Liberals Avoid Diverse Schools

WHERE CIVILITY IS A MOTTO, A SCHOOL INTEGRATION FIGHT TURNS BITTER

Liberals love diversity but won't send their kids to diverse schools.

"Democratic presidential candidates have embraced school desegregation. But in this heavily Democratic suburb, parents are fighting an integration proposal, showing such efforts remain deeply divisive when it comes to liberals' own children." ...

"A plan to desegregate schools in a liberal Maryland suburb founded on values of tolerance has met with stiff resistance."

Self-Identified Race

GENETIC STRUCTURE, SELF-IDENTIFIED RACE/ ETHNICITY, AND CONFOUNDING IN CASE-CONTROL ASSOCIATION STUDIES

Hua Tang, Tom Quertermous, Beatriz Rodriguez, Sharon L. R. Kardia, Xiaofeng Zhu, Andrew Brown, James S. Pankow, Michael A. Province, Steven C. Hunt, Eric Boerwinkle, Nicholas J. Schork, and Neil J. Risch

Of 3,636 subjects of varying race/ethnicity, only 5 (0.14%) showed genetic cluster membership different from their self-identified race/ethnicity. On the other hand, we detected only modest genetic differentiation between different current geographic locales within each race/ethnicity group. Thus, ancient geographic ancestry, which is highly correlated with self-identified race/ethnicity—as opposed to current residence—is the major determinant of genetic structure in the U.S. population. Implications of this genetic structure for case-control association studies are discussed.

Genetic Similarity Preferences

ETHNIC NATIONALISM, EVOLUTIONARY PSYCHOLOGY AND GENETIC SIMILARITY THEORY

J. Philippe Rushton (2005)

There is extensive evidence people prefer others who are genetically similar to themselves.

"Altruism toward kin and similar others evolved in order to help replicate shared genes. Since ethnic groups are repositories of shared genes, xenophobia is the dark side of human altruism. A review of the literature demonstrates the pull of genetic similarity in dyads such as marriage partners and friendships, and even large groups, both national and international. The evidence that genes incline people to prefer others who are genetically similar to themselves comes from studies of social assortment, differential heritabilities, the comparison of identical and fraternal twins, blood tests, and family bereavements. DNA sequencing studies confirm some origin myths and disconfirm others; they also show that in comparison to the total genetic variance around the world, random co-ethnics are related to each other on the order of first cousins."

Ethnocentrism and Biology

The Evolutionary Dominance of Ethnocentric Cooperation

Max Hartshorn, Artem Kaznatcheev, and Thomas Shultz (2013)

Ethnocentrism is biological, genetic in origin, and an evolutionary strategy that dominates all other evolutionary strategies.

"From a random start, ethnocentric strategies dominate other possible strategies (selfish, traitorous, and humanitarian) based on cooperation or non-cooperation with in-group and out-group agents. Here we show that ethnocentrism eventually overcomes its closest competitor, humanitarianism, by exploiting humanitarian cooperation across group boundaries as world population saturates. Selfish and traitorous strategies are self-limiting because such agents do not cooperate with agents sharing the same genes. Traitorous strategies fare even worse than selfish ones because traitors are exploited by ethnocentrics across group boundaries in the same manner as humanitarians are, via unreciprocated cooperation. By tracking evolution across time, we find individual differences between evolving worlds in terms of early humanitarian competition with ethnocentrism, including early stages of humanitarian dominance. Our evidence indicates that such variation, in terms of differences between humanitarian and ethnocentric agents, is normally distributed and due to early, rather than later, stochastic differences in immigrant strategies."

Ethnocentrism Is Universal

The Evolution of Ethnocentric Behavior

Robert Axelrod and Ross A. Hammond (2003)

Ethnocentrism is universal:

"Ethnocentrism is a nearly universal syndrome of attitudes and behaviors. The attitudes include seeing one's own group (the in-group) as virtuous and superior and an out-group as contemptible and inferior. The attitudes also include seeing ones own standards of value as universal. The behaviors associated with ethnocentrism are cooperative relations with the in-group and absence of cooperative relations with the out-group. ... the ability to discriminate can support the evolution of cooperation based on ethnocentric behavior. "

Altruism Ties To Relatedness

Kinship and altruism: a cross-cultural experimental study

Madsen EA1, Tunney RJ, Fieldman G, Plotkin HC, Dunbar RI, Richardson JM, McFarland D (2007)

Humans are more altruistic towards individuals to whom they are more closely related

"...humans titrate their willingness to incur costs for the direct benefit of others as a direct function of biological relatedness. ... Irrespective of the intentions that motivate human behaviour, these results demonstrate that humans behave in such a way as to maximize inclusive fitness: they are more willing to benefit closer relatives than more distantly related individuals. Demonstrating the effect in two different cultures (including a population relatively isolated from mainstream contemporary Western economics and culture) suggests that this phenomenon has broad applicability beyond post-industrial European society."

Genetic Similarity Attraction

Genetic similarity, human altruism, and group selection

J. Philippe Rushton (1989)

People subconsciously prefer those who are genetically similar to themselves for biological reasons.

"A new theory of attraction and liking based on kin selection suggests that people detect genetic similarity in others in order to give preferential treatment to those who are most similar to themselves. There are many sources of empirical and theoretical support for this view, including (1) the inclusive fitness theory of altruism, (2) kin recognition studies of animals raised apart, (3) assortative mating studies, (4) favoritism in families, (5) selective similarity among friends, and (6) ethnocentrism."

Race and Extended Family

The Ethnic Phenomenon

Pierre Van Den Berghe (1987)

Races are extended families, ethnocentrism is genetically rational.

"While social classes are grouped according to common material interests, ethnic groups are organized by real or punitive common descent—ultimately on the basis of common interests. ...

"Ethnic nepotism is, at its very foundation, biological."

Ethnic Kinship

Misunderstandings of Kin Selection and the Delay in Quantifying Ethnic Kinship

Frank Salter, Max Planck Society (2008)

Kinship between members of an ethnic group is greater than expected.

"Recent population-genetic research has quantified the genetic similarity between random members of an ethnic group as up to three orders of magnitude greater than that computed from genealogies. The kinship between random co-ethnics can exceed that between grandparent and grandchild. Quantifying ethnic kinship, whether within bands, tribes or modern ethnicities, is theoretically significant because it is essential for developing and testing evolutionary theories of ethnic altruism, just as understanding the evolution of nepotism began with the quantification of kinship within families. It is now clear that ethnicities do generally have genetic identities, that despite blurred boundaries they are in fact, not only in myth, descent groups. The significance of ethnic group similarity can only be apprehended through the lens of theory, not through naïve evaluation of data. If the kinship found within extended families is significant, then probably so too is that found between members of ethnic groups."

DNA and Friendship

Friends Have More DNA in Common than Strangers

Jillian Rose Lim (2014)

Friends share more common DNA than strangers.

"The study was published (July 14, 2014) in the journal Proceedings of the National Academy of Sciences. ... Researchers compared gene variations between nearly 2,000 people who were not biologically related, and found that friends had more gene variations in common than strangers. ... Why do we make friends? Not only that, we prefer the company of people we resemble."

Friends are as genetically related to each oth-er as any individual is to their great-great-great-grandfather or fourth cousin.

"After analyzing almost 1.5 million markers of gene variations, the researchers found that pairs of friends had the same level of genetic relation as people did with a fourth cousin, or a great-great-great grandfather, which translates to about 1 percent of the human genome. ... Most people don't even know who their fourth cousins are, yet we are somehow, among a myriad of possibilities, managing to select as friends the people who resemble our kin."

Race and Friendship

Race, Religion, and Political Affiliation of Americans' Core Social Networks

Daniel Cox, Juhem Navarro-Rivera, Robert P. Jones (2016)

Race and ethnicity have a strong influence on friendship groups; the average White American has 91% White friends, the average Black American has 83% Black friends.

"Among white Americans, 91% of people comprising their social networks are also white, while five percent are identified as some other race. Among black Americans, 83% of people in their social networks are composed of people who are also black, while eight percent are white and six percent are some other race."

Majority Friendships Same-Race

Race and Social Connections—Friends, Family and Neighborhoods

Kim Parker, Juliana Menasce Horowitz, Rich Morin and Mark Hugo Lopez (2015)

A supermajority percentage among ethnic/racial groups claim that all of their closest friends belong to their own ethnic group.

"Among adults who are white with no other race in their background, fully 81% say that all or most of their close friends are white. Among single-race blacks, 70% say that all or most of their close friends are black. And among single-race Asians, 54% say all or most of their close friends are Asian."

Interracial Friendships

Best Friends Forever? Race and the Stabiliy of Adolescent Friendships

Jesse Rude, Daniel Hera (2010)

Interracial friendships are far more likely to fail relative to monoracial friendships.

"We find the following: First, interracial friendships are less stable than same-race friendships, even after controlling for a variety of contextual and dyadic characteristics, such as school racial composition and friends' similarities in attitudes and behaviors. Second, measures of dyadic similarity (aside from race) are weak predictors of friendship stability. Third, measures of reciprocity and closeness are strong predictors of friendship stability and appear to dampen the effects of racial difference. These results indicate that race is of continuing significance in structuring the social lives of American adolescents. "

Oxytocin Effect: Ethnocentrism

OXYTOCIN PROMOTES HUMAN ETHNOCENTRISM

Carsten K. W. De Dreu, Lindred L. Greer, Gerben A. Van Kleef, Shaul Shalvi, and Michel J. J. Handgraaf (2011)

Oxytocin (the 'love chemical') promotes ethnocentrism and in-group preference while also promoting out-group derogation and hostility (xenophobia).

"Human ethnocentrism—the tendency to view one's group as centrally important and superior to other groups—creates intergroup bias that fuels prejudice, xenophobia, and intergroup violence. Grounded in the idea that ethnocentrism also facilitates within-group trust, cooperation, and coordination, we conjecture that ethnocentrism may be modulated by brain oxytocin, a peptide shown to promote cooperation among in-group members. ... Results show that oxytocin creates intergroup bias because oxytocin motivates in-group favoritism and, to a lesser extent, out-group derogation."

Ethnocentrics and Welfare

DISENTANGLING THE 'NEW LIBERAL DILEMMA': ON THE RELATION BETWEEN GENERAL WELFARE REDISTRIBUTION PREFERENCES AND WELFARE CHAUVINISM

Tim Reeskens, Wim van Oorschot (2012)

Those most in favor of welfare for the needy are the most ethnocentric and xenophobic with regards to immigrant welfare usage.

"...those who favor that welfare benefits should in the first place target the neediest, place the highest restrictions on welfare provisions for immigrants. In addition, the relationship between preferences for welfare redistribution and opinions about immigrants' access to social welfare is moderated by a national context of cultural heterogeneity."

Genetic Similarity, Social Application

J.P. RUSHTON'S THEORY OF ETHNIC NEPOTISM

Frank Salter, Henry Harpending (2013)

Genetic Similarity Theory could explain why diverse groups in close proximity increases both ethnic conflict and ethnic nepotism.

"...humans give preferential treatment to others in whom they detect genetic resemblance and that such behavior enhances genetic fitness. ... Genomics confirms the theory for interactions within populations with sufficient genetic diversity, such as ethnically mixed societies. GST applied to ethnicity is promising for further research in evolutionary social science because it unifies evolutionary and behavioral mechanisms in a single theory."

Biological Friend Limit

ROBIN DUNBAR: WE CAN ONLY EVER HAVE 150 FRIENDS AT MOST

Aleks Krotoski (2010)

Dunbar's Number: a biologically-programmed cognitive limit to the number of people (150) an individual can maintain stable social relationships with.

"...community sizes were designed for hunter-gatherer-type societies where people weren't living on top of one another. Your 150 were scattered over a wide area, but everybody shared the same 150. This made for a very densely interconnected community, and this means the community polices itself. You don't need lawyers and policemen. If you step out of line, granny will wag her finger at you. ...]Our problem now is the sheer density of folk – our networks aren't compact. You have clumps of friends scattered around the world who don't know one another: now you don't have an interwoven network. It leads to a less well integrated society. How to re-create that old sense of community in these new circumstances?"

Patients and Same-Race Doctors

IS DOCTOR-PATIENT RACE CONCORDANCE ASSOCIATED WITH GREATER SATISFACTION WITH CARE?

Thomas A LaVeist (2002)

Patients report greater satisfaction when treated by doctors of their own race.

"Study finds more satisfaction in same-race doctor-patient relationships"

THE PREDICTORS OF PATIENT–PHYSICIAN RACE AND ETHNIC CONCORDANCE: A MEDICAL FACILITY FIXED-EFFECTS APPROACH

Ana H Traylor, Julie A Schmittdiel, Connie S Uratsu, Carol M Mangione, and Usha Subramanian (2010)

Patients choose doctors of their own race 95+% of the time.

"[In a study of 109,745 patients, it was found that] patients who chose their physicians were more likely to have a same race/ethnicity physician [as themselves 95-98% of the time]"

PATIENTS' BELIEFS ABOUT RACISM, PREFERENCES FOR PHYSICIAN RACE, AND SATISFACTION WITH CARE

Frederick M. Chen, George E. Fryer, Robert L. Phillips, Elisabeth Wilson, Donald E. Pathman (2005)

Patients with racial preferences (which is almost all of them – over 95%) report much higher satisfaction with care when these preferences are matched.

"African Americans who have [racial] preferences are more often satisfied with their care when their own physicians match their preferences."

Diverse Churches Study

RACE, BELONGING, AND PARTICIPATION IN RELIGIOUS CONGREGATIONS

Brandon C. Martinez, Kevin D. Dougherty (2013)

Diverse churches have difficulty maintaining their multiracial composition, regardless of the size of congregation.

"...uniting worshippers of different races remains a challenging endeavor. ... congregations that successfully attract worshippers of different races often have difficulty sustaining their multiracial composition. ... differences in belonging and participation by racial group persist regard-less of group size."

Churchgoers who belong to the church's dominant racial group report greater sense of belonging and participation than other races.

"...those who are a part of a congregation's largest racial group possess a stronger sense of belonging and participate at a deeper level than congregants of other races."

Customers and Same-Race Servers

SHARED ETHNICITY EFFECTS ON SERVICE ENCOUNTERS: A STUDY ACROSS THREE U.S. SUBCULTURES

Detra Y. Montoya, Elten Briggs (2013)

Customers prefer being served by individuals of their own race.

"...shared ethnicity affects customers' expectations of exchanging particularistic resources and receiving preferential treatment benefits. Qualitative data on customer service experiences from three different ethnic subcultures (i.e., Hispanics, Asians, and Caucasians) extend the experimental findings. Under conditions of shared ethnicity, high levels of ethnic identification appear to promote in-group favoritism."

Same-Race Educators

THE BENEFITS OF MINORITY TEACHERS IN THE CLASSROOM

Anna Egalite, Brian Kisida (2015)

All students benefit by being taught by members of their own race.

"...we follow the trajectories of 2.9 million public school students in Florida over a seven-year time period ... Black, White, and Asian students benefit from being assigned to a teacher that looks like them. Their test scores go up in years when their teacher shares their ethnicity, compared to years when their teacher has a different ethnicity. ... Elementary-aged Black students seem to particularly benefit from demographically-similar teachers."

Ethnic Identity and Happiness

ETHNIC IDENTITY GIVES TEENS DAILY HAPPINESS BOOST

Wake Forest University, via John M. Grohol (2009) National Institute of Mental Health, via "MadameNoire" (2011)

A strong ethnic and racial identity increases an individual's happiness.

"Ethnic pride can help teenagers maintain happiness when faced with stress, according to a new study ... The study, involving 415 ninth-graders from Chinese and Mexican backgrounds, shows the protective effects of ethnic identity on daily psychological well-being ... having positive feelings about one's ethnic group appeared to provide an extra boost of positivity in individuals' daily lives"

"For the study, the researchers surveyed black adults in Michigan. The results suggest the more the participants identified with being black – or the more being black was an important part of who they are – the more happy they were with life as a whole"

Babies Racial Preferences

Babies Prefer Individuals Who Harm Those That Aren't Like Them

Kiley Hamlin (2013)

Babies prefer individuals who harm those who are not like themselves:

"Infants as young as nine months old prefer individuals who are nice to people like them and mean to people who aren't like them, according to a new study published in *Psychological Science*, a journal of the Association for Psychological Science.

Humans Memory of Other-Race Faces

Why Faces of Other Races Look Alike

Remy Melina (2011)

Humans are iologically programmed to forget or not recognize the facial features of "other-race faces."

"The brain works differently when memorizing the face of a person from one's own race than when attempting to remember the face of someone of another race, new biological evidence suggests. ... The well-documented 'other-race effect' finds that people are less likely to remember a face from a racial group different from their own. "

Babies Same-Race Bias

Racist Babies? Nine-Month-Olds Show Bias When Looking At Faces, Study Shows

Lisa Scott/University of Massachusetts, via Wynne Parry (2012)

By the age of 9 months, babies are shown to be biased towards their own race.

"...by the time they are 9 months old, babies are better able to recognize faces and emotional expressions of people who belong to the group they interact with most, than they are those of people who belong to another race. ... biases in face recognition and perception begin in pre-verbal infants, well before concepts about race are formed. It is important for us to understand the nature of these biases in order to reduce or eliminate [the biases]"[4]

Children Prefer Same-Race Play

Child's Play? 3-Year-Olds Fancy Their Own Ethnic Group

European Journal of Developmental Psychology, via Stephanie Pappas (2011)

When given the choice, children naturally play with members of their own race or ethnic group.

"...when given the choice, children of the same ethnicity preferred to play with one another rather than with kids from different ethnic groups. Unless a child has the rare genetic disorder Williams syndrome, these preferences emerge by age 3 or so."

Same-ethnicity pairs also socialize for longer than mixed-ethnicity pairs.

"As it turned out, the kids interacted with one another for longer stints when in the same-ethnicity pairs than when playing with a child of another ethnicity. Same-ethnicity partners spent about 58 percent of their time playing together during their session, compared with 44 percent in mixed-ethnicity pairs."

Intergroup Empathy

Intergroup Empathy: How Does Race Affect Empathic Neural Responses?

Joan Y. Chiao, Vani A. Mathur (2010)

---

4 "We must understand nature in order to undo nature and achieve our ideological goals" appears to be a common belief held by many of the authors of these studies.

Individuals feel less empathy towards people who are not of their own race.

"The results of all of these studies indicate that empathic neural response is heightened for members of the same race, but not those of other races."

Ethnicity Correlates Voting Patterns

THE PERSISTENCE OF WHITE ETHNICITY IN NEW ENGLAND POLITICS

James G. Gimpel, Wendy K. Tam Cho (2004)

Ethnicity is a greater predictor of voting behavior than economic status.

"Contrary to earlier predictions, ethnic origin does retain some explanatory power in models of recent voting behavior, and ethnic cleavages have not been entirely replaced by economic divisions in the electorate."

Ethnic groups do not politically "assimilate" over time.

"...the political salience of white ethnicity persists, suggesting that ethnic groups do not simply dealing or politically 'assimilate' over time. Some groups maintain a strong identity in spite of upward mobility because movement from city to suburbs is selected not just on housing, income or school characteristics, as is usually the case, but on ethnicity too."

"There is a distinct divide between White (or 'native') non-White (immigrant or 'minority') political alignments, with non-Whites (immigrants) leaning 'Left' or 'Progressive' and Whites (natives) leaning 'Right' or 'Conservative.'"

"Towns with significant concentrations of specific European ancestry groups lean Republican, even after we have accounted for the presence of other sources of political leaning and past voting tendencies, while Democratic attachments are undeniably strong in towns where the newer immigrant groups have settled. The 'new ethnicity' (i.e. racial minorities) and the 'old ethnicity' (i.e. white ethnics) clearly carry distinct political implications for this region's presidential politics."

Diversity Increases Tribal Politics

RACIAL IDENTITY, AND ITS HOSTILITIES, ARE ON THE RISE IN AMERICAN POLITICS

Eduardo Porter (2016)

As diversity increases, politics becomes more tribalistic.

"In Europe, voters are increasingly drawn to xenophobic politics, driven ... by fear 'based on the instinctive realization that the 'white man's world' is in terminal decline.' ... Americans are moving in the same direction. Racial identity and its attendant hostilities appear to be jumping from their longstanding place in the background of American politics to the very center of the stage."

Ideal Government Size

The Rise of Asian Americans, Pew Research, June 19, 2012

On political issues, the USA is divided strictly down racial lines. Non-Whites almost unanimously vote Left-Wing, support larger government, increased restriction on personal freedoms, decreased immigration restrictions, increased government spending, increased state interference in economic matters. Whites vote majority Right-Wing, and consistently either directly oppose these views, or support them to a much lower degree. See sources below:

"Would you like a bigger government?"
(Bigger Smaller)

Hispanic	African	Asian	European
73% 23%	64% 36%	55% 36%	27% 62%

Proximity and Racial Awareness

HOW TECHNOLOGY CREATED A GLOBAL VILLAGE AND PUT US AT EACH OTHER'S THROATS

Nicholas Carr

Globalization and the internet are increasing the proximity of human diversity and consequently increasing mutual animosity as well. "The scholars traced the phenomenon to what they called 'environmental spoiling.' The nearer we get to others, the harder it becomes to avoid evidence of their irritating habits. Proximity makes differences stand out." how-technology-created-global-village-and-put-each-other-throats

Diversity Correlates with More White Nationalism

COMPETITIVE THREAT, INTERGROUP CONTACT, OR BOTH? IMMIGRATION AND THE DYNAMICS OF FRONT NATIONAL VOTING IN FRANCE

Daniel J. Della Posta

Diversity is associated with more White support for nationalist parties, except at the local level where large immigrant populations cut into vote totals for nationalist parties.

Neighborhood Integration Viability Study

Is A 'Better World' Possible?

Zachary Neal

Using social science data and computer modeling, researchers found that policies that attempt to create neighborhoods that are both integrated and socially cohesive are "a lost cause".

"Is a better world possible? Unfortunately, these findings show it may not be possible to simultaneously create communities that are both fully integrated and fully cohesive," Neal said. "In essence, when it comes to neighborhood desegregation and social cohesion, you can't have your cake and eat it too."

Genetic Intelligence Research

Research on group differences in intelligence: A defense of free inquiry

Nathan Cofnas

"In a very short time, it is likely that we will identify many of the genetic variants underlying individual differences in intelligence. We should be prepared for the possibility that these variants are not distributed identically among all geographic populations, and that this explains some of the phenotypic differences in measured intelligence among groups. However, some philosophers and scientists believe that we should refrain from conducting research that might demonstrate the (partly) genetic origin of group differences in IQ. Many scholars view academic interest in this topic as inherently morally suspect or even racist. The majority of philosophers and social scientists take it for granted that all population differences in intelligence are due to environmental factors. The present paper argues that the widespread practice of ignoring or rejecting research on intelligence differences can have unintended negative consequences. Social policies predicated on environmentalist theories of group differences may fail to achieve their aims. Large swaths of academic work in both the humanities and social sciences assume the truth of environmentalism and are vulnerable to being undermined. We have failed to work through the moral implications of group differences to prepare for the possibility that they will be shown to exist."

Racial Diversity Correlates with Dating Exclusion

Patterns of Racial-Ethnic Exclusion by Internet Daters

Belinda Robnett, Cynthia Feliciano. *Social Forces*, vol. 89, iss. 3, March 2011, pgs. 807–828,

Exclusionary dating is a natural consequence of racial diversity.

"Using data from 6070 U.S. heterosexual internet dating profiles, this study examines how racial and gender exclusions are revealed in the preferences of black, Latino, Asian and white online daters. Consistent with social exchange and group positions theories, the study finds that whites are least open to out-dating and that, unlike blacks, Asians and Latinos have patterns of racial exclusion similar to those of whites. Like blacks, higher earning groups including Asian Indians, Middle Easterners and Asian men are highly excluded, suggesting that economic incorporation may not mirror acceptance in intimate settings. Finally, racial exclusion in dating is gendered; Asian males and black females are more highly excluded than their opposite-sex counterparts, suggesting that existing theories of race relations need to be expanded to account for gendered racial acceptance."

Diversity and School In-Group Preference

The Impact of Adolescents' Classroom and Neighborhood Ethnic Diversity on Same- and Cross-Ethnic Friendships Within Classrooms

Anke Munniksma, Peer Scheepers, Tobias H. Stark, Jochem Tolsma

"...students were more likely to engage in same-ethnic rather than cross-ethnic friendships. In line with conflict theory, greater classroom and neighborhood diversity were related to stronger tendencies to choose same-ethnic rather than cross-ethnic friends, among both ethnic majority and minority students."

Diversity Inverse Aid To Nonwhites/Females

DIVERSITY POLICIES RARELY MAKE COMPANIES FAIRER, AND THEY FEEL THREATENING TO WHITE MEN

Tessa L. Dover, Brenda Major, Cheryl R. Kaiser

Company diversity policies don't help minorities or women, and they psychologically discriminate against White men.

Diversity Correlation with Unhappiness

DOES ETHNIC DIVERSITY HAVE A NEGATIVE EFFECT ON ATTITUDES TOWARDS THE COMMUNITY? A LONGITUDINAL ANALYSIS OF THE CAUSAL CLAIMS WITHIN THE ETHNIC DIVERSITY AND SOCIAL COHESION DEBATE

James Laurence and Lee Bentley

"A longitudinal test of the impact of diversity finds that it makes existing residents feel unhappier and more socially isolated."

Diversity and Dissension

INTERNAL DISSENSION CITED AS REASON FOR CAHOKIA'S DISSOLUTION

Dr. Thomas E. Emerson and Dr. Kristin M. Hedma

Internal dissension stoked by ethnic, social, political, and religious diversity, rather than environmental degradation, caused the collapse of the urbanized Cahokia Indian Tribe.

Cohesion: People And Place

COMMUNITY SOCIAL AND PLACE PREDICTORS OF SENSE OF COMMUNITY: A MULTILEVEL AND LONGITUDINAL ANALYSIS

D. Adam Long and Douglas D. Perkins

A sense of social cohesion with the people who live around us is as happiness-inducing as love for the place itself.

Desire For Like-Minded

SIMILARITY IN RELATIONSHIPS AS NICHE CONSTRUCTION: CHOICE, STABILITY, AND

INFLUENCE WITHIN DYADS IN A FREE CHOICE ENVIRONMENT

Angela Bahns and Chris Crandall

Our desire for 'like-minded others' is hardwired.

Reporting Biases

BLACK AND WHITE DISCRIMINATION IN THE UNITED STATES: EVIDENCE FROM AN ARCHIVE OF SURVEY EXPERIMENT STUDIES

L.J. Zigerell

"This study reports results from a new analysis of 17 survey experiment studies that permitted assessment of racial discrimination, drawn from the archives of the Time-sharing Experiments for the Social Sciences. For White participants (n=10 435), pooled results did not detect a net discrimination for or against White targets, but, for Black participants (n=2781), pooled results indicated the presence of a small-to-moderate net discrimination in favor of Black targets; inferences were the same for the subset of studies that had a political candidate target and the subset of studies that had a worker or job applicant target."

Immigration Not Net Economic Benefit

THE BORDERLESS WELFARE STATE

Jan van de Beek, Hans Roodenburg, Joop Hartog and Gerrit Kreffer, 2021, Amsterdam School of Economics.

"The net costs of immigration to the government are considerable, and projections show they will consume a steadily increasing portion of the annual government budget. These costs are mainly due to redistribution through the welfare state. Continuation of the current level of immigration and current arrangements of the welfare state increases pressure on public finances. Downsizing the welfare state and/or curtailment of immigration will then be inevitable.

"Immigration does not appear to be a solution to the ageing population either. In essence, ageing is mainly dejuvenation due to a low fertility rate. The only structural solution for that is an increase in the average number of children per woman in the Netherlands to approximately 2.1

Identify and Drive To Succeed

Is Secessionism Mostly About Income Or Identity? A Global Analysis of 3,003 Subnational Regions

Klaus Desmet, Ignacio Ortuño-Ortín, Ömer Özak, National Bureau Of Economic Success, Working Paper 30428

What most sparks a region's desire to seek independence from their country—income or identity?

A new study from SMU (Southern Methodist University, Dallas) and UC3M (Universidad Carlos III de Madrid, Spain) found that the group people identify with tends to play a bigger factor in secession than differences in per capita income between regions.

Identity was shown to be a larger factor than income for many real-life examples of pro-independence movements in recent years—such as Tibet in China and Tigray and other Southern Nations in Ethiopia. Researchers looked at a total of 173 countries with 3,003 subnational regions, like Texas and California in the United States or Canadian provinces in Quebec and Ontario.

Race-Mixing Impact on Family Therapy

Monica McGoldrick and Joe Giordano, *Overview: Ethnicity and Family Therapy. In Ethnicity and Family Therapy*, pgs. 1-30

"We may ignore our ethnicity or deny it, but we do so to the detriment of our well-being.

"Intermarriage greatly complicates those issues that partners from a single ethnic group face ... The more different the partners' cultures are, the more trouble they will have in adjusting to marriage."

Steven Silbiger, *The Jewish Phenomenon: Seven Keys to the Enduring Wealth of a People*, pg. 34

"Teach your own family history and teach about your family's ancestral homeland. If your family has many branches, try to concentrate on the two most prevalent so the identity is not diffused. Give your children an international view. Use a globe or maps to show them the world and where they fit into it. For Jews, one of the most profound cultural experiences is visiting Israel, much like Muslims who make their pilgrimage to Mecca.

"Having a background and a heritage helps immunize children from negative influences. Those who believe that they live in a huge, chaotic world where they have no real place or purpose tend to be less focused and more susceptible to distractions."

Trust in Diverse Societies

Trust in a Time of Increasing Diversity: On the Relationship between Ethnic Heterogeneity and Social Trust in Denmark from 1979 until Today

Trust in a Time of Increasing Diversity: On the Relationship between Ethnic Heterogeneity and Social Trust in Denmark from 1979 until Today – Dinesen – 2012 – Scandinavian Political Studies

"This article examines the impact of ethnic diversity in Danish municipalities on citizens' social trust over the last three decades. During this period, Danish society has grown increasingly ethnically diverse, and this begs the question whether this has influenced trust in others negatively. Existing evidence from the Anglo-Saxon countries would suggest that this is the case, whereas evidence from the European continent mainly suggests that no link exists between ethnic diversity and social trust. The empirical analysis uses individual-level data on social trust from several surveys in Denmark in the period from 1979 to 2009 coupled with diversity at the municipality level. Individual-level measures of trust over time enable estimation of the impact of changes in ethnic diversity within municipalities on social trust and, it is argued, thereby a more precise estimate of the effect of ethnic diversity on trust. The results suggest that social trust is negatively affected by ethnic diversity. The article concludes by discussing this result and suggest avenues for further research."

Cooperation and Testosterone

Testosterone is associated with cooperation during intergroup competition by enhancing parochial altruism

Reimers L, Diekhof EK. Testosterone is associated with cooperation during intergroup competition by enhancing parochial altruism. Front Neurosci. 2015

"The steroid hormone testosterone is widely

associated with negative behavioral effects, such as aggression or dominance. However, recent studies applying economic exchange tasks revealed conflicting results. While some point to a prosocial effect of testosterone by increasing altruistic behavior, others report that testosterone promotes antisocial tendencies. Taking into account additional factors such as parochial altruism (i.e., ingroup favoritism and outgroup hostility) might help to explain this contradiction. First evidence for a link between testosterone and parochial altruism comes from recently reported data of male soccer fans playing the ultimatum game. In this study high levels of endogenous testosterone predicted increased altruistic punishment during outgroup interactions and at the same time heightened ingroup generosity. Here, we report findings of another experimental task, the prisoner's dilemma, applied in the same context to examine the role of testosterone on parochial tendencies in terms of cooperation. In this task, 50 male soccer fans were asked to decide whether or not they wanted to cooperate with partners marked as either fans of the subject's own favorite team (ingroup) or fans of other teams (outgroups). Our results show that high testosterone levels were associated with increased ingroup cooperation during intergroup competition. In addition, subjects displaying a high degree of parochialism during intergroup competition had significantly higher levels of testosterone than subjects who did not differentiate much between the different groups.

"In sum, the present data demonstrate that the behavioral effects of testosterone are not limited to aggressive and selfish tendencies but may imply prosocial aspects depending on the context. By this means, our results support the previously reported findings on testosterone-dependent intergroup bias and indicate that this social hormone might be an important factor driving parochial altruism."

Productivity and Diversity

LABOR DIVERSITY AND FIRM PRODUCTIVITY

Pierpaolo Parrotta, Dario Pozzoli, Mariola Pytlikova. Department of Economics, School of Business and Economics, Maastricht University, 6200 MD Maastricht, Netherlands. The Danish Institute for Regional Government Research (KORA), Denmark. VSB-Technical University of Ostrava, Czech Republic

"Using a matched employer–employee data-set, we analyze how workforce diversity associates with the productivity of firms in Denmark, following two main econometric routes. In the first one, we estimate a standard Cobb–Douglas function, calculate the implied total factor productivity and relate the latter to diversity statistics in a second stage. This reduced-form approach allows us to identify which types of labor heterogeneity appear to descriptively matter. In the second approach, we move toward a richer production function specification, which takes different types of labor as inputs and that allows for flexible substitution patterns, and possible quality differences between types. Both methods show that workforce diversity in ethnicity is negatively associated with firm productivity. The evidence regarding diversity in education is mixed."

Birth Rates and Diversity

E PLURIBUS, PAUCIORES (OUT OF MANY, FEWER): DIVERSITY AND BIRTH RATES

Gurun, Umit G. and Solomon, David H., E Pluribus, Pauciores (Out of Many, Fewer): Diversity and Birth Rates. 2024

"In the United States, local measures of racial and ethnic diversity are robustly associated with lower birth rates. A one standard deviation decrease in racial concentration (having people of many different races nearby) or increase in racial isolation (being from a numerically smaller race in that area) is associated with 0.064 and 0.044 fewer children, respectively, after controlling for many other drivers of birth rates. Racial isolation effects hold within an area and year, suggesting that they are not just proxies for omitted local characteristics. This pattern holds across racial groups, is present in different vintages of the US census data (including before the Civil War), and holds internationally. Diversity is associated with lower marriage rates and marrying later. These patterns are related to homophily (the tendency to marry people of the same race), as the effects are stronger in races that intermarry less and vary with sex differences in intermarriage. The rise in racial diversity in the US since 1970 explains 44% of the decline in birth rates during that period, and 89% of the drop since 2006."

Mental Health and Diversity

Mental health and Multiracial/ethnic adults in the United States: a mixed methods participatory action investigation

Shaff J, Wang X, Cubbage J, Bandara S, Wilcox HC. Mental health and Multiracial/ethnic adults in the United States: a mixed methods participatory action investigation.

"Findings indicate over half of the participants endorsed at least one mental health concern with prevalence of anxiety, depression, post-traumatic stress disorder, and suicidal thoughts and behaviors surpassing available national estimates. Exposure to trauma, discrimination, and microaggressions were found to play a significant role in these outcomes. Conversely, strong social support and strong ethnic identity emerged as protective factors. Qualitative insights brought forward the challenges faced by individuals in navigating bias and stigma, especially in the context of mental health care. Despite these barriers, emerging themes highlighted resilience, the importance of secure identity formation, and the critical role of community and cultural support.

"The marked prevalence of mental health concerns among Multiracial and multiethnic populations emphasizes the pressing need for tailored interventions and inclusive research methodologies. Recognizing and addressing the unique challenges faced by these communities is imperative in driving mental health equity in the U.S. The findings advocate for community-engaged practices, interdisciplinary collaborations, and the importance of addressing mental health challenges with cultural sensitivity, particularly in historically oppressed and marginalized groups. Future efforts must focus on refining these practices, ensuring that public health initiatives are genuinely inclusive and equitable."

Mental Health in Youth with Diversity

The Relationship Between Mixed Race/Ethnicity, Developmental Assets, and Mental Health Among Youth

Garcia GM, Hedwig T, Hanson BL, Rivera M, Smith CA. The Relationship Between Mixed Race/Ethnicity, Developmental Assets, and Mental Health Among Youth. J Racial Ethn Health Disparities. 2019

"This study assessed whether high school youth with mixed race/ethnicity are at greater risk for poor mental health conditions compared to their single race/ethnic counterparts and whether this mental health risk can be mitigated by youth developmental assets regardless of one's race/ethnicity. Methods involved secondary data analysis of the 2009-2013 Youth Risk Behavioral Survey-Anchorage, Alaska subsample. Difference in rates of mental health conditions and mean number of developmental assets (protective factors) were assessed among three racial/ethnic groups. Logistic regression models tested whether race/ethnicity has an independent association with mental health conditions and whether there is an interaction effect between race/ethnicity and protective factors. Results show that, compared to white students, mixed race/ethnic students have significantly higher rates of poor mental health condition and significantly fewer protective factors. A significant interaction effect between race/ethnicity and protective factors was also found, showing decreasing likelihood of poor mental health condition with increasing number of protective factors among all racial/ethnic groups. However, this effect was more pronounced among white students compared to both mixed and single race/ethnicity minority students. Study findings indicate that youth of mixed race/ethnicity are more likely to be at risk for poor mental health outcomes, yet less likely to mitigate this risk even with similar number of external developmental assets as their single race/ethnic counterparts. More research is needed to further understand the differential effect of certain developmental assets among different racial/ethnic groups."

Identity Development and Diversity

Examining multiracial youth in context: ethnic identity development and mental health outcomes

Fisher S, Reynolds JL, Hsu WW, Barnes J, Tyler K. Examining multiracial youth in context: ethnic identity development and mental health outcomes. J Youth Adolesc. 2014

"Although multiracial individuals are the fastest growing population in the United States, research on the identity development of multiracial adolescents remains scant. This study explores the relationship between ethnic identity, its components (affirmation, exploration), and mental health outcomes (anxiety, depressive symptoms) within the contexts of schools for multiracial adolescents. The participants were multiracial and monoracial minority and majority high school students (n = 4,766; 54.6% female). Among the participants, 88.1% were Caucasian, 7.4% were African American, and 4.5% were multiracial. The research questions examined the relationship between ethnic identity exploration and affirmation on mental health outcomes and explored the role school context plays in this relationship. The findings suggested that multiracial youth experience more exploration and less affirmation than African Americans, but more than Caucasians. In addition, multiracial youth were found to have higher levels of mental health issues than their monoracial minority and majority peers. Specifically, multiracial youth had higher levels of depressive symptoms than their African American and Caucasian counterparts. Multiracial and Caucasian youth had similar levels of anxiety but these levels were significantly higher than African Americans. School diversity did not influence mental health outcomes for multiracial youth. These findings provide insight into the experiences of multiracial youth and underscore the importance of further investigating factors that contribute to their mental health outcomes."

Mental Health and Diversity Review

MENTAL HEALTH OUTCOMES OF MULTIRACIAL INDIVIDUALS: A SYSTEMATIC REVIEW BETWEEN THE YEARS 2016 AND 2022

Hans Oh, Jade G. Winn, Juliann Li Verdugo, Ronna Bañada, Corinne E. Zachry, Gloria Chan, Lucinda Okine, Juyoung Park, Marco Formigoni, Edouard Leaune, Mental health outcomes of multiracial individuals: A systematic review between the years 2016 and 2022, *Journal of Affective Disorders*, Volume 347, 2024

"Studies were mainly from the United States, with one study from the United Kingdom and one from the Netherlands. Sample sizes ranged from 57 to 393,681. Findings revealed a complicated picture between multiracial identity and mental health, which may be a function of how multiracial identity is defined and empirically examined. Among studies comparing multiracial individuals with monoracial groups, multi-

racial individuals tended to have worse mental health, with notable exceptions depending on the multiracial subgroup, the mental health outcome, and the reference group. Among studies that only examined multiracial individuals, discrimination and ethno-racial identity emerged as complex explanatory factors that can shape mental health, though each of these constructs can be explored more deeply across social milieu.

"Multiracial individuals tended to have worse mental health outcomes compared to their monoracial counterparts, with variations depending on the outcomes, populations / subgroups, contexts, and reference groups. Racial discrimination and ethno-racial identity may shape mental health trajectories of multiracial people, calling for more research to inform targeted interventions."

A Gene for Rioting?

ARE GENETIC TRAITS ASSOCIATED WITH RIOTS? THE POLITICAL LEGACY OF PREHISTORICALLY DETERMINED GENETIC DIVERSITY

Vu, T.V. (2021) Are genetic traits associated with riots? The political legacy of prehistorically determined genetic diversity. Kyklos

"This paper establishes that the worldwide distribution of political instability has its deep historical roots in genetic diversity, predetermined over the prehistoric course of the exodus of Homo sapiens from East Africa tens of thousands of years ago. It proposes that the relationship between prehistorically determined genetic diversity and contemporary political instability follows a U-shaped pattern. More specifically, genetic diversity at first reduces the persistence of political instability by increasing the opportunity cost of engaging in riots and revolts. However, genetically fragmented societies tend to suffer from interpersonal mistrust and the under-provision of public goods, which plausibly undermine the establishment of politically stable regimes.

"Using an ancestry-adjusted index of predicted genetic diversity, this paper consistently finds precise estimates that genetic diversity imparts a U-shaped influence on different measures of political instability and the probability of observing the occurrence of riots and revolts across 141 countries. Furthermore, the contribution of genetic diversity to political instability is at least partially mediated through income/productivity levels, the provision of public goods, income inequality and social trust."

Effects on Mixed Race Adolescents

THE PLIGHT OF MIXED RACE ADOLESCENTS

Roland G. Fryer, Jr, Lisa Kahn, Steven D. Levitt, and Jörg L. Spenkuch, NBER Working Paper

"The number of mixed-race children has increased dramatically. Sociologists have theorized about the challenges facing these individuals since early in the 20th century, but little systematic empirical research has explored their outcomes. Using the Add Health data set, we find high rates of risky/anti-social behavior on the part of mixed race adolescents on virtually every dimension we are able to measure. Formalizing the existing sociological theories using a Roy model, we conclude that the observed pattern of behaviors appears consistent with such a model. While the predictions of the Roy model and a conformity model are generally similar, the Roy model alone can reconcile the observation that when mixed race adolescents are in environments where their peers are predominately black, they are no more likely to adopt black behaviors than when they have peers who are predominately white."

In-Group Bias Compared by Race

PATTERNS OF IMPLICIT AND EXPLICIT ATTITUDES: IV. CHANGE AND STABILITY FROM 2007 TO 2020

Charlesworth TES, Banaji MR. Patterns of Implicit and Explicit Attitudes: IV. Change and Stability From 2007 to 2020.

"Huge study involving over 7 million individuals finds that the ingroup bias (preference for one's own group) of black Americans is approximately 5 times stronger than the ingroup bias of whites.

"Using more than 7.1 million implicit and explicit attitude tests drawn from U.S. participants to the Project Implicit website, we examined long-term trends across 14 years (2007-2020). Despite tumultuous sociopolitical events, trends from 2017 to 2020 persisted largely as forecasted from past data (2007-2016). Since 2007, all explicit attitudes decreased in

bias between 22% (age attitudes) and 98% (race attitudes). Implicit sexuality, race, and skin-tone attitudes also continued to decrease in bias, by 65%, 26%, and 25%, respectively. Implicit age, disability, and body-weight attitudes, however, continued to show little to no long-term change. Patterns of change and stability were generally consistent across demographic groups (e.g., men and women), indicating widespread, macrolevel change. Ultimately, the data magnify evidence that (some) implicit attitudes reveal persistent, long-term change toward neutrality. The data also newly reveal the potential for short-term influence from sociopolitical events that temporarily disrupt progress toward neutrality, although attitudes eventually return to long-term homeostasis in trends."

ECONOMICS

To complete our study of natural social relations, we included material on economics. "Economics" derives from the Greek words meaning "household management." For our ancestors, the purpose of economic life was not merely the production and consumption of material goods but the support of families as the fundamental units of social life and human action, from which broader social institutions and identities evolve.

Economic nationalism is broader than questions about tariffs and trade protection. It is an economic approach that seeks to benefit the nation and sustain the culture and people that define it. It takes account of different regions seeking to balance the needs of rural and urban, capital and labor, farmers, manufacturers, and small businesses. It is a facet of national identity and not a mere expression of material interests.

In particular we include discussions of the philosophy of free trade. For, the topic is more than policy but theory as well. Free Trade is more than the mere cold calculations of Ricardo's comparative advantage but a full religious dogma that prophecies of deracinating given peoples, undoing nationhood and domestic cohesion, and globalizing macro- and micro-economics until no particular culture or trade is left. Hence, our inclusion of sources that highlight the economics, moral, and politics problems with free trade. This observation is not unique. Figures from George Washington to Karl Marx have realized the deleterious effects free trade economics has upon a nation, both economically, morally, and culturally. Indeed, Hamilton's Report On Manufactures explicitly advocated for a national economy that coheres internally as the basis for political freedom. If a nation cannot sustain itself economically but relies upon other nations for its food, medicine, or defense goods, then that nation is neither free nor sovereign.

— Studies —

Estimated Foreign Births

Stephen Camarota. *There Are an Estimated 39,000 Births Annually to Foreign Students, Guestworkers, and Other Long-Term Temporary Visitors.* Center For Immigration Studies, December 11, 2019

"We estimate that in 2016 there were about 39,000 births in the United States to a mother on a non-immigrant visa. We further estimate that 90 percent of the fathers of these children were non-citizens themselves, making it very likely that the fathers were either on non-immigrant visas like the mothers or were possibility illegal immigrants. This means that in 2016, about 35,000 children were born to a non-immigrant mother and were awarded U.S. citizenship at birth solely because they were born on U.S. soil and not because of their parents' citizenship. While nowhere near as large as the number born to illegal immigrants, it still means that each decade some 350,000 people are given automatic U.S. citizenship because their parents came to the United States to study or work temporarily."

Births to Legal and Illegal Immigrants in the U.S.

Stephen Camarota, Karen Zeigler, and Jason Richwine. *Births to Legal and Illegal Immigrants in the U. S.* Center For Immigration Studies, October, 2018

"In 2014, one in five births (791,000) in the United States was to an immigrant mother (legal or illegal). Our best estimate is that legal immigrants accounted for 12.4 percent (494,000) of all births, and illegal immigrants accounted for 7.5 percent (297,000)."

Immigration Shifts Political Power

Stephen Camarota and Karen Zeigler. *The Impact of Legal and Illegal Immigration on the Apportionment of Seats in the U.S. House of Representatives in 2020.* Center For Immigration Studies, December, 2019.

The presence of all immigrants (naturalized citizens, legal residents, and illegal aliens) and their U.S.-born minor children will redistribute 26 seats in the House in 2020.

Ohio will have three fewer seats in 2020 than it otherwise would have had but for the presence of all immigrants and their minor children in other states. Michigan and Pennsylvania will have two fewer; and Alabama, Arkansas, Georgia, Idaho, Indiana, Iowa, Kentucky, Louisiana, Minnesota, Mississippi, Missouri, North Carolina, Oklahoma, Rhode Island, South Carolina, Tennessee, Utah, West Virginia, and Wisconsin will each have one fewer seat. California will have 11 more seats in 2020 than it otherwise would have; New York and Texas will have four more seats each; Florida will have three more seats; New Jersey will have two more seats; and Illinois and Massachusetts will each have one additional seat.

Open Borders Affects Income

Garett Jones. *Measuring the Sacrifice of Open Borders.* November, 2019

"How would Open Borders – a policy of unlimited immigration – change the wages of current residents of the United States? To answer this question, I begin by running the same quantitative experiment that Caplan runs on page 131 of his graphic novel *Open Borders: The Science and Ethics of Immigration*. This experiment presumes that the only two drivers of national income per capita are national average IQ and an unexplained productivity residual. I use the same constant returns to scale framework as Caplan, in which the migration of every human being to the United States would increase global output per capita by about 80%. I then estimate that in the benchmark model, where IQ's social return is much larger than its private return, the per-capita income of current U.S. residents would permanently fall by about 40%. This is not an arithmetic fallacy: this is the average causal effect of Open Borders on the incomes of ex-ante Americans. This income decline occurs because cognitive skills matter mostly through

externalities: because your nation's IQ matters so much more than your own, as I claim in 2015's *Hive Mind*. Therefore, a decline in a nation's set of average cognitive skills will tend to reduce the productivity of the nation's ex-ante citizens."

Smart Fraction Theory

Smart Fraction Theory II: Why Asians Lag, La Griffe du Lion. vol. 6 no. 2, May, 2004.

Smart Wealth Fraction Theory of IQ and Wealth of Nations. The Smart Fraction Theory is essentially the idea that in modern information-based economies, data shows that national IQ averages correlate strongly with economic success. If a certain percentage of the populace isn't above a certain threshold of intelligence, modern economies cannot function. Not everyone needs to be a genius. But a large portion of the workforce needs to be at least smart enough to use a computer and do basic arithmetic, etc. Individual IQ is a strong predictor of individual success, but the same holds true at the population level. National IQ averages are strong predictors of national economic success.

Trade With China Cost Several Million Jobs

David Autor, David Dorn, and Gordon Hanson David. *When Work Disappears: Manufacturing Decline and the Falling Marriage-Market Value of Young Men.* American Economic Review: Insights, September, 2019.

"We estimate that import competition from China, which surged after 2000, was a major force behind both recent reductions in US manufacturing employment and—through input-output linkages and other general equilibrium channels—weak overall US job growth. Our central estimates suggest job losses from rising Chinese import competition over 1999–2011 in the range of 2.0–2.4 million."

China Trade, Outsourcing and Jobs

Robert E. Scott and Will Kimball. *China Trade, Outstanding and Jobs. EPI Briefing Paper,* Dec., 11, 2014.

"Since China entered the World Trade Organization in 2001, the massive growth of trade between China and the United States has had a dramatic and negative effect on U.S. workers and the domestic economy. Specifically, a growing U.S. goods trade deficit with China has the United States piling up foreign debt, losing export capacity, and losing jobs, especially in the vital but under-siege manufacturing sector. Growth in the U.S. goods trade deficit with China between 2001 and 2013 eliminated or displaced 3.2 million U.S. jobs, 2.4 million (three-fourths) of which were in manufacturing. These lost manufacturing jobs account for about two-thirds of all U.S. manufacturing jobs lost or displaced between December, 2001 and December 2013."

The Economic Impact of the 1965 Immigration Act

Rubenstein, Edwin. *The Economic Impact of the 1965 Immigration Act. Social Contact Journal*, Fall 2015.

"Mass immigration lowered the wages of native-born workers, especially those with low skills who compete directly with the new entrants. It benefited native-born workers who do not compete with the foreign arrivals in the labor force...The bottom line is that immigration exacerbates the gap between America's haves and have-nots."

Free Trade Means More Deaths

Adam Dean and Simeon Kimmel. *Free Trade and Opioid Overdose Death in the United States.* SSS Population Health, December, 2020.

"Opioid overdose deaths in the U.S. rose dramatically after 1999, but also exhibited substantial geographic variation. This has largely been explained by differential availability of prescription and non-prescription opioids, including heroin and fentanyl. Recent studies explore the underlying role of socioeconomic factors, but overlook the influence of job loss due to international trade, an economic phenomenon that disproportionately harms the same regions and demographic groups at the heart of the opioid epidemic. We used OLS regression and county-year level data from the Centers for Disease Controls and the Department of Labor to test the association between trade-related job loss and opioid-related overdose death between 1999 and 2015. We find that the loss of 1000 trade-related jobs was associated with a 2.7

percent increase in opioid-related deaths. When fentanyl was present in the heroin supply, the same number of job losses was associated with a 11.3 percent increase in opioid-related deaths."

Immigration and the American Worker

George Borjas. *Immigration and the American Worker: A Review of the Academic Literature.* Center For Immigration Studies Backgrounder, April 9, 2013.

"For American workers, immigration is primarily a redistributive policy. Economic theory predicts that immigration will redistribute income by lowering the wages of competing American workers and increasing the wages of complementary American workers as well as profits for business owners and other 'users' of immigrant labor. Although the overall net impact on the native-born is small, the loss or gain for particular groups of the population can be substantial."

Immigration Dramatically Increases the Size of the Labor Force

Rubenstein, Edwin S. "The Economic Impact of the 1965 Immigration Act". The Social Contract Press. Vol. 26, No 1 (Fall 2015)

"Immigrants account for a disproportionate share of U.S. labor force growth. Immigrants accounted for nearly 50 percent of the total labor force increase between 1996 and 2000, and as much as 60 percent of the increase between 2000 and 2004. Assuming net immigration of about 1 million per year, new immigrants and their children will account for all of the growth in the U.S. labor force between 2010 and 2030."

Open Immigration Decreases Opportunities For Black Men

George Borjas., Jeffrey Grogger, Gordon Harrison. *Immigration and the Economic Status of African-American Men, Economica,* vol. 77, iss. 306

"The employment rate of black men, and particularly of low-skilled black men, fell precipitously between 1960 and 2000. At the same time, their incarceration rate rose. This paper examines the relation between immigration and these trends in employment and incarceration. Using data from the 1960–2000 US censuses, we find that a 10% immigration-induced increase in the supply of workers in a particular skill group reduced the black wage of that group by 2.5%, lowered the employment rate by 5.9 percentage points, and increased the incarceration rate by 1.3 percentage points."

"The large-scale immigration of unskilled labor does impact the wages of the native-born unskilled. Since the labor pool of the unskilled is heavily structured by race, the main 'loser' would appear to be unskilled African-American male labor; though unskilled white labor is equally vulnerable, as are 'the contingent of previous immigrants, who compete for much more similar jobs and occupations with new immigrants.'"

David Coates. *The Economic Impact of Immigration.*

"How big a loss is hard to quantify, because the general demand for labor remains high and growing over time, and because the available supply of African-American labor has been significantly reduced of late by unprecedented levels of black incarceration."

Stephen Camarota, *The Labor Market Impact of Immigration: A Review of Studies.* Center For Immigration Studies, May 1, 1998

"The study focused primarily on workers employed in occupations that generally require only a high school degree or less — about 25 million workers. The results indicate that a 1 percent increase in the immigration composition of an occupation reduces the wages of natives in that occupation by 0.8 percent...

"Not surprisingly, the study also found that, because native born minorities, especially African Americans, are heavily concentrated in the adversely affected occupations, a much higher percentage of them are negatively affected by immigration. Additionally, the wage loss resulting from immigration is likely to represent a more significant reduction in material prosperity for minorities because their wages are lower than those of white natives."

The Effect of Immigration on Domestic Wages: Evidence From Longitudnal Data (unpublished)

"Overall, he [Bratsberg] found that young, less-skilled African-Americans and Hispanics are harmed by immigrant competition. Increasingly,

his results suggest that there is an 'optimal' level of immigration. That is, as long as the level of immigration is not too high in a country (around 2 or 3 percent of the total population), immigrants either have no effect on wages or a positive effect."

David R. Howell and Elizabeth J. Mueller, *The Effects of Immigrants on African-American Earnings: A Job-Level Analysis of the New York City Labor Market, 1979-1989*

"Overall, the findings of this study suggest that the wage effects of immigration on native-born African-American men in New York City are substantial"

Ethnic Diversity May Inhibit Productivity and Group Function

Jonas Hjort. *Ethnic Divisions and Production in Firms, Quarterly Journal of Economics* 129, no. 4 (2014): 1899.

"A body of literature suggests that ethnic heterogeneity limits economic growth...My findings suggest that inter-ethnic rivalries lower allocative efficiency in the private sector, that the economic costs of ethnic diversity vary with the political environment, and that in high-cost environments firms are forced to adopt "second best" policies to limit discrimination distortions."

Katherine Y. Williams and Charles A. O'Reilly III, *Demography and Diversity in Organizations: A Review of 40 Years of Research, Research in Organizational Behavior* 8 (1998): 70–140.

"The preponderance of the empirical evidence suggests that diversity is most likely to impede group functioning. Unless steps are taken to actively counteract these effects, the evidence suggests that, by itself, diversity is more likely to have negative than positive effects on group performance... Simply having more diversity in a group is no guarantee that the group will make better decisions or function effectively... Much of the literature that supports the claim that diversity is beneficial is often based on variation in individual attributes such as personality, ability, and functional backgrounds, and not on ascriptive attributes such as ethnicity and sex."

Susan E. Jackson, Aparna Joshi, and Niclas L. Erhardt, *Recent Research on Team and Organizational Diversity: SWOT Analysis and Implications, Journal of Management* 29, no. 6 (2003): 810

"The evidence that supports the often-made claim that racio-ethnic diversity improves performance is limited. One study found no significant relationship. . . . Some studies reported negative effects of racio-ethnic diversity on performance."

Elizabeth Mannix and Margaret A. Neale, *What Differences Make a Difference? The Promise and Reality of Diverse Teams in Organizations, Psychological Science in the Public Interest* 6, no. 2 (2005): 31

"The preponderance of the evidence favors a more pessimistic view: that diversity creates social divisions, which in turn create negative performance outcomes for the group. Why is the reality of diversity less than the promise? ... Racial diversity tended to have negative effects on team process."

Karsten Jonsen, Susan C. Schneider, and Martha L. Maznevski, *Diversity—A Strategic Issue?* In *Diversity in the Workplace*, ed. Stefan Gröschl (London and New York: Routledge, 2016): 29.

"Research and practice has found the business case for diversity to be elusive... [showing] no overall relationship between diversity and performance or a very small negative effect."

Peter Thisted Dinesen, Merlin Schaeffer, and Kim Mannemar Sønderskov, *Ethnic Diversity and Social Trust: A Narrative and Meta-Analytical Review. Annual Review of Political Science* 23 (2020): 441–65.

"We find a . . . negative relationship between ethnic diversity and social trust across all studies. The relationship is stronger for trust in neighbors, and when studied in more local contexts."

IMMIGRATION

"The opposition to (early-1800s immigration) restriction was from the steamship companies, whose interest was obvious, and from the large employers of cheap labor, who were likewise not at all disinterested. It also arose among alien groups in the United States, that wished to get more of their own people into this country. The most active forces in its favor were, primarily, organized labor, which wished no more competition from floating aliens with a wholly un-American standard of living and, most of all, the native American groups, eugenists and others who were far-sighted and unwilling to see the racial character and national unity of America destroyed and republican ideals endangered and undermined." – Madison Grant, *Conquest Of A Continent*, pg. 269

The 1965 Immigration Act

Perhaps few pieces of legislation have more altered the American nation than the 1965 Immigration Act. It is from this moment that numerous changes – economic, demographic, domestic, moral, religious, academic, health, criminal, and more – are measured and dated. Christopher Caldwell calls this period generally the time in which a second American Constitution was written. Thomas Sowell marks this decade as that moment at which African-American quality of life began to decline. Lawrence Auster specifically points to the Immigration Act itself as undoing the fabric of Old America. In Our Borders, Ourselves, Auster says, "Even when they begin to recognize the unprecedented scale of the ethnic changes taking place in our country, they take it for granted that those changes are inevitable. It is as though the 'browning of America,' as newsmagazines and minority spokesmen have cheerfully dubbed it, where a kind of vast natural phenomenon, as far outside of human control as continental drift. There seems to be almost no awareness of the fact that this alteration of our society has been the result not of

an act of God but of an act of Congress, not of some inviolable provision in the Constitution but of a law passed in 1965." He goes on to note that demographic alteration was never the intent, at least the stated intent. But, once the borders were thrown open, they may not so easily be shut again.

The Act, signed by LBJ, removed the national origins quotas installed in the immigration acts of the 1920s. These quotas restricted the immigration to the ethnic makeup of Americans at the time – most of which were European, and north-western European to be specific. William Vaile spoke of the intent of the 1924 Immigration Act,

"Let me emphasize here that the restrictionists of Congress do not claim that the 'Nordic' race, or even the Anglo-Saxon race, is the best race in the world. Let us concede, in all fairness that the Czech is a more sturdy laborer, with a very low percentage of crime and insanity... and that the Italian has a spiritual grasp and an artistic sense which have greatly enriched the world and which have, indeed, enriched us, a spiritual exaltation and an artistic creative sense which the Nordic rarely attains. Nordics need not be vain about their own qualifications. It well behooves them to be humble. What we do claim is that the northern European, and particularly Anglo-Saxons made this country. Oh, yes; the others helped. But that is the full statement of the case. They came to this country because it was already made as an Anglo-Saxon commonwealth. They added to it, they often enriched, but they did not make it, and they have not yet greatly changed it. We are determined that they shall not. It is a good country. It suits us. And what we assert is that we are not going to surrender it to somebody else or allow other people, no matter what their merits, to make it something different. If there is any changing to be done, we will do it ourselves." (William N. Vaile, CO. U.S. Rep., in Cong. Rec. April 8, 1924, 5922.)

All of this would change, however, with the

advent of the Civil Rights Movement. Indeed, Auster notes that the "the Immigration Act of 1965 can be best understood as a civil rights bill applied to the world at large." And yet, debate on the Senate floor and elsewhere over this 1965 bill centered on its not affecting the then-current ethnic makeup of our country. This was in response to opponents of the bill who argued that it would alter the original stock and eventually deprive its inheritors of the land of their fathers.

However, great changes did occur in just a few decades. In 1988 Scott McConnell wrote in Fortune magazine, "What no legislator voting on the 1965 act envisioned was how quickly family reunification would produce chain immigration. Imagine one immigrant, say an engineering student, who was studying in the U.S. during the 1960s. If he found a job after graduation, he could then bring over his wife [as the spouse of a resident alien], and six years later, after being naturalized, his brothers and sisters [as siblings of a citizen]. They, in turn, could bring their wives, husbands, and children. Within a dozen years, one immigrant entering as a skilled worker could easily generate 25 visas for in-laws, nieces, and nephews." ("The New Battle over Immigration," Fortune, May 1988, 98).

As you read the following refutations of the notion that the ethnic makeup of the country would change due to this bill, ask yourself if these predictions were accurate? Further, has this gesture toward healing racial animus achieved its end? Have race relations healed since 1965? Rather, it is our thesis that today's disintegrated society, noted by Robert Putnam among others, is tied to this act of Congress. Indeed, the country has changed so much that their own words, recorded below, could not even be spoken in public settings in the America that those very words helped to reshape. The political principle to be drawn is that one should not listen to pacifying rhetoric, be it left- or right-leaning, but to what the effect of that rhetoric, those sentiments, and the policies born of them lead to. [5]

— EXPECTATION —

Lyndon Boyd Johnson

"This bill we sign today is not a revolutionary bill. It does not affect the lives of millions. It will not restructure the shape of our daily lives."

Rep. Emanuel Celler (D-NY)

"With the end of discrimination due to place of birth, there will be shifts in countries other than those of northern and western Europe. Immigrants from Asia and Africa will have to compete and qualify in order to get in, quantitatively and qualitatively, which, itself will hold the numbers down. There will not be, comparatively, many Asians or Africans entering this country. .. .Since the people of Africa and Asia have very few relatives here, comparatively few could immigrate from those countries because they have no family ties in the U.S." – *Congressional Record*, Aug. 25, 1965, pg. 21812.

Attorney General Robert Kennedy

"I would say for the Asia-Pacific Triangle it [immigration] would be approximately 5,000, Mr. Chairman, after which immigration from that source would virtually disappear; 5,000 immigrants would come the first year, but we do not expect that there would be any great influx after that." – U.S. Congress, House, 1964 hearings, pg. 418.

"The time has come for us to insist that the quota system be replaced by the merit system... It deprives us of able immigrants whose contributions we need...It would increase the amount of authorized immigration by only a fraction." – *The New York Times*, Aug. 24, 1964, pg. 26. Senate immigration subcommittee chairman Edward Kennedy (D-MA.)

"First, our cities will not be flooded with a million immigrants annually. Under the proposed bill, the present level of immigration remains substantially the same ... Secondly, the ethnic mix of this country will not be upset ... Contrary to the charges in some quarters, [the bill] will not inundate America with immigrants from any one country or area, or the most

---

5 All quotations in this section sourced from CIS entry in the bibliography.

populated and deprived nations of Africa and Asia ... In the final analysis, the ethnic pattern of immigration under the proposed measure is not expected to change as sharply as the critics seem to think.

"The bill will not flood our cities with immigrants. It will not upset the ethnic mix of our society. It will not relax the standards of admission. It will not cause American workers to lose their jobs." – U.S. Senate, Subcommittee on Immigration and Naturalization of the Committee on the Judiciary, Washington, D.C., Feb. 10, 1965. pgs. 1-3.

Attorney General Nicholas Katzenbach

"This bill is not designed to increase or accelerate the numbers of newcomers permitted to come to America. Indeed, this measure provides for an increase of only a small fraction in permissible immigration." – U.S. Senate, Subcommittee on Immigration and Naturalization of the Committee on the Judiciary, Washington, D.C., Feb. 10, 1965, pg. 8.

Secretary of State Dean Rusk

"The present estimate, based upon the best information we can get, is that there might be, say, 8,000 immigrants from India in the next five years ... I don't think we have a particular picture of a world situation where everybody is just straining to move to the United States ... There is not a general move toward the United States." – U.S. Senate, Subcommittee on Immigration and Naturalization of the Committee on the Judiciary, Washington D.C., Feb. 10, 1965, pg. 65.

Senator Hiram Fong (R-HI)

"Asians represent six-tenths of 1 percent of the population of the United States ... with respect to Japan, we estimate that there will be a total for the first 5 years of some 5,391 ... the people from that part of the world will never reach 1 percent of the population ... Our cultural pattern will never be changed as far as America is concerned." – U.S. Senate, Subcommittee on Immigration and Naturalization of the Committee on the Judiciary, Washington, D.C., Feb. 10, 1965, pgs. 71, 119.

Rep. Sidney Yates (D-IL)

"I am aware that this bill is more concerned with the equality of immigrants than with their numbers. It is obvious in any event that the great days of immigration have long since run their course. World population trends have changed, and changing economic and social conditions at home and abroad dictate a changing migratory pattern." – Congressional Record, August 25, 1965, pg. 21793.

Sen. Claiborne Pell (D-RI)

"Contrary to the opinions of some of the misinformed, this legislation does not open the floodgates." – Congressional Record, Sept. 20, 1965, pg. 24480.

Washington Post

"The most important change, in fact, was in direction, shuffling the preference categories to give first consideration to relatives of American citizens instead of to specially skilled persons. This had more emotional appeal and, perhaps more to the point, insured that the new immigration pattern would not stray radically from the old one." – The Washington Post, Oct. 4, 1965, pg. 16.

Sen. Strom Thurmond (R-SC)

"The preferences which would be established by this proposal are based, I believe, on sound reasoning and meritorious considerations, not entirely dissimilar in effect from those which underlie the national origins quotas of existing law." – Congressional Record, Sept. 17, 1965, pg. 24237.

Rep. William Miller of New York

"We estimate that if the President gets his way, and the current immigration laws are repealed, the number of immigrants next year will increase threefold and in subsequent years will increase even more ... shall we, instead, look at this situation realistically and begin solving our own unemployment problems before we start tackling the world's?" – The New York Times, Sept. 8, 1964, pg. 14.

Sen. Spessard Holland (D-FL)

"What I object to is imposing no limitation insofar as areas of the earth are concerned, but saying that we are throwing the doors open and equally inviting people from the Orient, from the islands of the Pacific, from the subcontinent of Asia, from the Near East, from all of Africa, all of Europe, and all of the Western Hemisphere on exactly the same basis. I am inviting attention to the fact that this is a complete and radical departure from what has always heretofore been regarded as sound principles of immigration." – *Congressional Record*, Sept. 22, 1965, pg. 24779.

Myra C. Hacker, Vice President of the New Jersey Coalition

"In light of our 5 percent unemployment rate, our worries over the so called population explosion, and our menacingly mounting welfare costs, are we prepared to embrace so great a horde of the world's unfortunates? At the very least, the hidden mathematics of the bill should be made clear to the public so that they may tell their Congressmen how they feel about providing jobs, schools, homes, security against want, citizen education, and a brotherly welcome ... for an indeterminately enormous number of aliens from underprivileged lands.

"We should remember that people accustomed to such marginal existence in their own land will tend to live fully here, to hoard our bounteous minimum wages and our humanitarian welfare handouts ... lower our wage and living standards, disrupt our cultural patterns ...

"Whatever may be our benevolent intent toward many people, [the bill] fails to give due consideration to the economic needs, the cultural traditions, and the public sentiment of the citizens of the United States." – U.S. Senate, Subcommittee on Immigration and Naturalization of the Committee on the Judiciary, Washington, D.C., Feb. 10, 1965.

Sen. Sam Ervin, N Carolina

One senator, Sam Ervin from North Carolina, pointed out that the 1965 Immigration Act did not remove discrimination but reallocated positive discrimination to new groups of people, from new countries. Thus, he argued, if America is going to discriminate between immigrants based upon race, ethnicity, and country of origin, then it should do so in favor of its current national people and composition:

"Ervin: That racial and national origin discrimination, I think, is a very important thing for us to pursue... The fact that the McCarran-Walter Act gives a preference... to those ethnic groups I have mentioned [northern Europeans], is the objection to it, isn't it?

Secretary of State Rusk: Yes; as opposed to the others all over the world.

Ervin: Mr. Secretary... do you know of any people in the world that have contributed more to making America than those particular groups?... In other words, you take the English-speaking people, they gave us our language, they gave us our common law, they gave us a large part of our political philosophy...The reason I say this bill is discriminatory against those people is because it puts them on exactly the same plane as the people of Ethiopia are put, where the people of Ethiopia have the same right to come to the United States under this bill as the people from England, the people of France, the people of Germany, the people of Holland, and I don't think... I don't know of any contributions that Ethiopia has made to the making of America.

The point I am making is, we discriminate every day in every phase of life, we make discriminations in law, we make them in our personal actions, we discriminate in our opinions... we discriminate by the girls we marry, choose one and object to the choice of another, or they object to us.

The only possible charge of discrimination in the McCarran-Walter Act is that it discriminates in favor of the people who made the greatest contribution to America, and this bill puts them on the same plane as everybody else on earth....

I do not think you could draft an immigration bill in which you do not discriminate. I think discrimination is ordinarily the exercise of intelligence to make conscious choices... we always discriminate, only the basis of it is different, each of us think[s] our own way is wise and right....I think there is a rational basis and a reasonable basis to give a preference to Holland over Afghanistan, and I hope I am not entertaining a very iniquitous thought when I entertain that honest opinion." – Senate Committee on the Judiciary, Subcommittee on

Immigration, Hearings on Immigration Reform Act of 1965, February 10, 1965 to March 11, 1965.

— AFTERMATH —

Bill Clinton

"Our nation is rightly disturbed by the large numbers of illegal aliens entering our country… [who] take jobs from citizens… [and] impose burdens on our taxpayers… It is wrong…to permit this kind of abuse of our immigration laws." – State of the Union, 1995

Henry Kissinger

"It was a grave mistake to let in so many people of totally different culture and religion and concepts, because it creates a pressure group inside each country that does that." – *Politico*, Commenting on the scenes of Arab migrants in Germany celebrating Hamas' attack on Israel in October of 2023

— VIEW FROM ENGLAND —

Enoch Powell

The supreme function of statesmanship is to provide against preventable evils. In seeking to do so, it encounters obstacles which are deeply rooted in human nature …

A week or two ago I fell into conversation with a constituent, a middle-aged, quite ordinary working man employed in one of our nationalised industries.

After a sentence or two about the weather, he suddenly said: "If I had the money to go, I wouldn't stay in this country. … I have three children, all of them been through grammar school and two of them married now, with family. I shan't be satisfied till I have seen them all settled overseas. In this country in 15 or 20 years' time the black man will have the whip hand over the white man." …

Here is a decent, ordinary fellow Englishman, who in broad daylight in my own town says to me, his Member of Parliament, that his country will not be worth living in for his children.

I simply do not have the right to shrug my shoulders and think about something else.

What he is saying, thousands and hundreds of thousands are saying and thinking – not throughout Great Britain, perhaps, but in the areas that are already undergoing the total transformation to which there is no parallel in a thousand years of English history.

In 15 or 20 years, on present trends, there will be in this country three and a half million Commonwealth immigrants and their descendants. That is not my figure. That is the official figure given to parliament by the spokesman of the Registrar General's Office.

There is no comparable official figure for the year 2000, but it must be in the region of five to seven million, approximately one-tenth of the whole population, and approaching that of Greater London. Of course, it will not be evenly distributed from Margate to Aberystwyth and from Penzance to Aberdeen. Whole areas, towns and parts of towns across England will be occupied by sections of the immigrant and immigrant-descended population.

As time goes on, the proportion of this total who are immigrant descendants, those born in England, who arrived here by exactly the same route as the rest of us, will rapidly increase. Already by 1985 the native-born would constitute the majority. It is this fact which creates the extreme urgency of action now, of just that kind of action which is hardest for politicians to take, action where the difficulties lie in the present but the evils to be prevented or minimised lie several parliaments ahead.

The natural and rational first question with a nation confronted by such a prospect is to ask: "How can its dimensions be reduced?" Granted it be not wholly preventable, can it be limited, bearing in mind that numbers are of the essence: the significance and consequences of an alien element introduced into a country or population are profoundly different according to whether that element is 1 per cent or 10 per cent.

The answers to the simple and rational question are equally simple and rational: by stopping, or virtually stopping, further inflow, and by promoting the maximum outflow. Both answers are part of the official policy of the Conservative Party.

It almost passes belief that at this moment 20 or 30 additional immigrant children are arriving from overseas in Wolverhampton alone every week – and that means 15 or 20 additional families a decade or two hence. Those whom the gods wish to destroy, they first make mad. We must be mad, literally mad, as a nation to be permitting the annual inflow of some 50,000 dependants, who are for the most part the material of the future growth of the immigrant-descended population. It is like watching a nation busily engaged in heaping up its own funeral pyre. So insane are we that we actually permit unmarried persons to immigrate for the purpose of founding a family with spouses and fiancés whom they have never seen.

Let no one suppose that the flow of dependants will automatically tail off. On the contrary, even at the present admission rate of only 5,000 a year by voucher, there is sufficient for a further 25,000 dependants per annum ad infinitum, without taking into account the huge reservoir of existing relations in this country – and I am making no allowance at all for fraudulent entry. In these circumstances nothing will suffice but that the total inflow for settlement should be reduced at once to negligible proportions, and that the necessary legislative and administrative measures be taken without delay. ...

Hence the urgency of implementing now the second element of the Conservative Party's policy: the encouragement of re-emigration.

Nobody can make an estimate of the numbers which, with generous assistance, would choose either to return to their countries of origin or to go to other countries anxious to receive the manpower and the skills they represent. ...

Nothing is more misleading than comparison between the Commonwealth immigrant in Britain and the American Negro. The Negro population of the United States, which was already in existence before the United States became a nation, started literally as slaves and were later given the franchise and other rights of citizenship, to the exercise of which they have only gradually and still incompletely come. The Commonwealth immigrant came to Britain as a full citizen, to a country which knew no discrimination between one citizen and another, and he entered instantly into the possession of the rights of every citizen, from the vote to free treatment under the National Health Service.

Whatever drawbacks attended the immigrants arose not from the law or from public policy or from administration, but from those personal circumstances and accidents which

cause, and always will cause, the fortunes and experience of one man to be different from another's.

But while, to the immigrant, entry to this country was admission to privileges and opportunities eagerly sought, the impact upon the existing population was very different. For reasons which they could not comprehend, and in pursuance of a decision by default, on which they were never consulted, they found themselves made strangers in their own country.

They found their wives unable to obtain hospital beds in childbirth, their children unable to obtain school places, their homes and neighbourhoods changed beyond recognition, their plans and prospects for the future defeated; at work they found that employers hesitated to apply to the immigrant worker the standards of discipline and competence required of the native-born worker; they began to hear, as time went by, more and more voices which told them that they were now the unwanted. ...

In the hundreds upon hundreds of letters I received when I last spoke on this subject two or three months ago, there was one striking feature which was largely new and which I find ominous. All Members of Parliament are used to the typical anonymous correspondent; but what surprised and alarmed me was the high proportion of ordinary, decent, sensible people, writing a rational and often well-educated letter, who believed that they had to omit their address because it was dangerous to have committed themselves to paper to a Member of Parliament agreeing with the views I had expressed, and that they would risk penalties or reprisals if they were known to have done so. The sense of being a persecuted minority which is growing among ordinary English people in the areas of the country which are affected is something that those without direct experience can hardly imagine. ...

The other dangerous delusion from which those who are wilfully or otherwise blind to realities suffer, is summed up in the word "integration." To be integrated into a population means to become for all practical purposes indistinguishable from its other members.

Now, at all times, where there are marked physical differences, especially of colour, integration is difficult though, over a period, not impossible. There are among the Commonwealth immigrants who have come to live here in the last fifteen years or so, many thousands whose wish and purpose is to be integrated and whose every thought and endeavour is bent in that direction.

But to imagine that such a thing enters the heads of a great and growing majority of immigrants and their descendants is a ludicrous misconception, and a dangerous one.

We are on the verge here of a change. Hitherto it has been force of circumstance and of background which has rendered the very idea of integration inaccessible to the greater part of the immigrant population – that they never conceived or intended such a thing, and that their numbers and physical concentration meant the pressures towards integration which normally bear upon any small minority did not operate.

Now we are seeing the growth of positive forces acting against integration, of vested interests in the preservation and sharpening of racial and religious differences, with a view to the exercise of actual domination, first over fellow-immigrants and then over the rest of the population. The cloud no bigger than a man's hand, that can so rapidly overcast the sky, has been visible recently in Wolverhampton and has shown signs of spreading quickly. ...

For these dangerous and divisive elements the legislation proposed in the Race Relations Bill is the very pabulum they need to flourish. Here is the means of showing that the immigrant communities can organise to consolidate their members, to agitate and campaign against their fellow citizens, and to overawe and dominate the rest with the legal weapons which the ignorant and the ill-informed have provided. As I look ahead, I am filled with foreboding; like the Roman, I seem to see "the River Tiber foaming with much blood."

That tragic and intractable phenomenon which we watch with horror on the other side of the Atlantic but which there is interwoven with the history and existence of the States itself, is coming upon us here by our own volition and our own neglect. Indeed, it has all but come. In numerical terms, it will be of American proportions long before the end of the century.

Only resolute and urgent action will avert it even now. Whether there will be the public will to demand and obtain that action, I do not know. All I know is that to see, and not to speak, would be the great betrayal.[6]

---

6   Delivered to a Conservative Association meeting in Birmingham on April 20 1968. Came to be known as the "Rivers of Blood" speech

"Mankind? It is an abstraction. There are, always have been, and always will be, men and only men."
– Goethe, in *Spengler* pg. 464

"My principles are only those that, before the French Revolution, every well-born person considered sane and normal."
– Julius Evola, *A Traditionalist*, pg. xxiii

BIBLIOGRAPHY

Abbott, W. W. 1987. The Papers of George Washington: Presidential Series. Charlottesville: University Press of Virginia.

Abernathy, John. 1748. Sermons On Various Subjects. Vol. 2. London: D. Browne.

Abinski, Nan Browman, ed. 2021. Routledge Library Editions: Utopias: 6 Volume Set. Routledge.

Adams, Charles F. 1850. The Works of John Adams. Charles C. Little and James Brown.

Adams, John. 1851. The Works of John Adams, Second President of the United States: With a Life of the Author, Notes and Illustrations. Little, Brown.

———. 1977. Papers of John Adams: September 1755 - October 1773. Belknap Press of Harvard University Press.

Adams, John, and Charles Francis Adams. 1851. The Works of John Adams, Second President of the United States: With a Life of the Author, Notes and Illustrations. Little, Brown.

———. 1852. The Works of John Adams, Second President of the United States: With a Life of the Author, Notes and Illustrations. Little, Brown.

———. 1853. The Works of John Adams, Second President of the United States: With a Life of the Author, Notes and Illustrations. Little, Brown.

Adams, John Quincy. 1837. An Oration Delivered Before the Inhabitants of the Town of Newburyport, at Their Request, on the Sixty-First Anniversary of the Declaration of Independence, July 4th, 1837. Morss and Brewster.

Aelian, Claudius. 1665. Claudius Ælianus His Various History. Translated by Thomas Stanley. The British Library.

Aeschylus. 1926. Aeschylus, with an English Translation, Vol I, Seven Against Thebes. Translated by Herbert Smyth. London: W. Heinemann.

———. 2009. The Persians. Translated by Robert Potter. Dodo Pr.

———. 2012. Persians. Translated by Ian Johnston. Nanaimo, British Columbia: Vancouver Island University. https://johnstoniatexts.x10host.com/aeschylus/persianshtml.html.

———. n.d. "Agamemnon." Translated by E. D. A. Morshead. MIT Classics Archive. Accessed January 4, 2024. https://classics.mit.edu/Aeschylus/agamemnon.html.

Ainsworth, Henry. n.d. "The Communion Of Saints, 1628." Accessed January 18, 2024. https://ebooks.regent-college.edu/Ainsworth-Commvnion-Saincts/6/.

Ajeyaseelan, Michael. 2022. "The Forest." Collection at Bartleby.Com. September 13, 2022. https://www.bartleby.com/lit-hub/poems-of-places-an-anthology-in-31-volumes/the-forest.

Alamariu, Costin. 2023. Selective Breeding and the Birth of Philosophy. Costin Alamariu.

Alexander, Christopher. 2018. A Pattern Language: Towns, Buildings, Construction. Oxford University Press.

Alexander, T. Desmond, and David Weston Baker. 2003. Dictionary of the Old Testament: Pentateuch. InterVarsity Press.

Alexander, T. Desmond, and Brian S. Rosner. 2020. New Dictionary of Biblical Theology. Inter-Varsity Press.

Alexandria, Clement of. 2010. Stromateis, Books 1–3 (The Fathers of the Church, Volume 85). CUA Press.

Alighieri, Dante. 1990. Banquet. Garland.

Allestree, Richard. 1660. The Gentlemans Calling. Printed for T. Garthwait at the Little North-doore of S. Pauls. https://quod.lib.umich.edu/e/eebo/A23718.0001.001/1:1?rgn=div1;view=fulltext.

———. n.d. The Government of the Thoughts a Prefatory Discourse to The Government of the Tongue / by the Author of The Whole Duty of Man. London: rinted by R. Smith for Richard Cumberland, at the Angel in St. Paul's Church-Yard. M DC XC IV. Accessed February 3, 2024. https://quod.lib.umich.edu/e/eebo/A23734.0001.001?view=toc.

Alois Kircher. 1973. Dichter Und Konvention. Zum Gesellschaftlichen Realitätsproblem Der Deutschen Lyrik Um 1200 (Literatur in Der Gesellschaft 18. Düsseldorf.

Althoen, David. 2003. "Natione Polonus and the Naród Szlachecki. Two Myths of National Identity and Noble Solidarity." Zeitschrift für Ostmitteleuropa-Forschung 52 (4): 475–508. https://doi.org/10.25627/20035248118.

Althusius, Johannes. 1964. The Politics of Johannes Althusius. Translated by Frederick Smith Carney. University of Michigan: Beacon Press. https://oll.libertyfund.org/title/althusius-politica.

Ames, Fisher. 1983. Works of Fisher Ames. Liberty Classics.

Ames, Fisher, and Seth Amers. 1854. Works of Fisher Ames: Memoir, by J. T. Kirkland. Letters. Little, Brown.

Andersen, Francis I., and David Noel Freedman. 2006. Micah: A New Translation with Introduction and Commentary. Yale University Press.

Andrews, Helen. 2021. Boomers: The Men and Women Who Promised Freedom and Delivered Disaster. Penguin.

Andrews, Lancelot. 1675. The Pattern Of Catechetical Doctrine. London. https://ebooks.regent-college.edu/Andrewes-Pattern-Catechistical/4/.

Anthony, David W. 2010. The Horse, the Wheel, and Language: How Bronze-Age Riders from the Eurasian Steppes Shaped the Modern World. Princeton University Press.

Apollonius (Rhodius). 1919. The Argonautica. Translated by Robert Cooper Seaton. Harvard University Press.

Appelbaum, Diana Muir. 2013. "Biblical Nationalism and the Sixteenth-Century States." National Identities 15 (4): 317–32. https://doi.org/10.1080/14608944.2013.814624.

Aquinas. 1874. Catena Aurea: Commentary on the Four Gospels. J. Parker.

———. 1924. Summa Contra Gentiles. Vol. 3. Fathers of the English Dominican Province. London: Burns Oates & Washbourne.

———. 1966. Commentary On Saint Paul's Epistle To the Galatians. Translated by F.R. Larcher, O.P. Albany, NY: Magi Books, Inc.

———. 2010. Commentary on the Gospel of John: Chapters 13-21. CUA Press.

———. n.d. Summa Theologica. Fathers of the English Dominican Province. London: Burns Oates & Washbourne.

Aristides, Aelius. 2017. Orations. Translated by Michael Trapp. Vol. 1. Cambridge, Massachusetts ; London, England : Harvard University Press.

Aristophanes. 1938. Birds, The Complete Greek Drama. Translated by Eugene O'Neill. Vol. 2. New York: Random House.

Aristotle. 1925. The Works of Aristotle. Edited by W. D. Ross. Oxford: The Clarendon Press.

Armagh.), John BRAMHALL (successively Bishop of Derry and Archbishop of. 1677. The Works of the Most Reverend Father in God, John Bramhall ... Collected into One Volume. In Four Tomes. To Which Is Prefixt the Authour's Life; and in the End Is Added ... an Exact Copy of the Records, Touching Archbishop Parker's Consecration ... as Also the Copy of an Old Manuscript in Corpus Chr: Colledge in Cambridge, of the Same Subject. Edited by John Vesey, Archbishop of Tuam. Benjamin Tooke.

Arnold, Sir Edwin. 2021. Bhagavad Gita. Beyond Books Hub.

Arrowsmith, John. 1659. Armilla Catechetica: A Chain Of Principles. Cambridge University Press. https://ebooks.regent-college.edu/Arrowsmith-Armilla-Catechetica/4/.

Assac, Philippe Ploncard d'. 2000. Le Nationalisme Français. Société de Philosophie Politique édition. La Garde: Société de Philosophie Politique.

Assembly, Presbyterian Church in the U. S. General. 1861. Minutes. Presbyterian Committee of Publication.

Atkinson, Joseph C. 2014. Biblical and Theological Foundations of the Family: The Domestic Church. Washington, D.C: The Catholic University of America Press.

Augoustakis, Antony, and Neil W. Bernstein. 2023. Silius Italicus' Punica: Rome's War with Hannibal. 1st edition. Abingdon (GB): Routledge.

Augustine. 1847. Seventeen Short Treatises. Translated by John Henry Parker. London: Oxford University Press.

———. 1849. Expositions on the Book of Psalms ... Translated, with Notes and Indices [by J. Tweed, T. Scratton, H. M. Wilkins and Others]. J. H. Parker.

———. 1873. The Works of Aurelius Augustine: The Sermon on the Mount Expounded ; and, The Harmony of the Evangelists. T. & T. Clark.

———. 1880. Homilies on the Gospel According to S. John: And His First Epistle. W. Smith.

———. 1887. St. Augustin's City of God and Christian Doctrine. Edited by ed. Philip Schaff, trans. J. F. Shaw. Vol. 2. Select Library of the Nicene and Post-Nicene Fathers of the Christian Church, First Series. Buffalo, NY: Christian Literature Company.

———. 1947. The Fathers of the Church. University of Michigan: Cima Publishing Company.

———. 1950. Saint Augustine's De Fide Rerum Quae Non Videntur: A Critical Text and Translaton [Sic] with Introduction and Commentary. Catholic University of America Press.

———. 1952. The City of God, Books VIII–XVI. Edited by Hermigild Dressler, trans. Gerald G. Walsh and Grace Monahan. Vol. 14. The Fathers of the Church. Washington, DC: The Catholic University of America Press.

———. 1954. The City of God, Books XVII–XXII. Edited by Hermigild Dressler, trans. Gerald G. Walsh and Daniel J. Honan. Vol. 24. The Fathers of the Church. Washington, DC: The Catholic University of America Press.

———. 1955a. Letters (165–203),. Edited by Hermigild Dressler, trans. Wilfrid Parsons. Vol. 30. The Fathers of the Church. Washington, DC: The Catholic University of America Press.

———. 1955b. Treatises on Marriage and Other Subjects. Edited by Roy Joseph Deferrari, trans. Charles T. Wilcox. Vol. 27. The Fathers of the Church. Washington, DC: The Catholic University of America Press.

———. 1956. Letters (204–270),. Edited by Hermigild Dressler, trans. Wilfrid Parsons. Vol. 32. The Fathers of the Church. Washington, D. C: The Catholic University of America Press.

———. 1968. The Retractations. Edited by ed. Roy Joseph Deferrari, trans. Mary Inez Bogan. Vol. 60. The Fathers of the Church. Washington, D.C: The Catholic University of America Press.

———. 2010a. Confessions (The Fathers of the Church, Volume 21). CUA Press.

———. 2010b. On Genesis: Two Books on Genesis Against the Manichees and On the Literal Interpretation of Genesis: An Unfinished Book (The Fathers of the Church, Volume 84). CUA Press.

Augustine, Mark J. Edwards, and Thomas C. Oden. 2014. Galatians, Ephesians, Philippians. InterVarsity Press.

Aurelius, Marcus. n.d. "The Meditations." Translated by George Long. MIT Classics Archive. Accessed January 5, 2024. https://classics.mit.edu/Antoninus/meditations.1.one.html.

Auster, Lawrence. 2009. "A Real Islam Policy for a Real America." In . Baltimore, Maryland. http://www.amnation.com/vfr/archives/012935.html.

———. Our Borders, Ourselves: America in the Age of Multiculturalism. Vdare.

———. "What Is European America?" AmNation. Accessed February 13, 2024. http://www.amnation.com/vfr/archives/001631.html.

Bacchylides. 1991. "Epinicians." Translated by Diane Arnson Svarlien. Perseus Tufts Edu. 1991. https://catalog.perseus.org/catalog/urn:cts:greekLit:tlg0199.tlg001.perseus-eng1.

Bacon, Leonard, ed. 2002. The Song of Roland. Dover Publications.

Bainton, Roland. 2014. Here I Stand - A Life Of Martin Luther. Read Books Ltd.

———. 2008. Christian Attitudes toward War and Peace: A Historical Survey and Critical Re-Evaluation. Wipf and Stock Publishers.

Bak, János M., and Béla K. Király. 1982. From Hunyadi to Rákóczi: War and Society in Late Medieval and Early Modern Hungary. Social Science Monographs.

Barford, Paul M. 2001. The Early Slavs: Culture and Society in Early Medieval Eastern Europe. Cornell University Press.

Barnes, Albert. 1840. Notes on the Epistles to the Thessalonians, to Timothy, Titus and Philemon, Explanatory and Practical. Gall & Inglis.

———. 1852. Notes, Explanatory and Practical, on the Second Epistle to Corinthians and the Epistle to the Galatians. By Rev. Albert Barnes ... Edited ... by Rev. Ingram Cobbin. Knight and Son.

Barney, Stephen A., ed. 2006. The Etymologies of Isidore of Seville. Cambridge University Press.

Baroja, Pío. 1920. Youth and Egolatry. A. A. Knopf.

Bartholomew, Craig G. 2011. Where Mortals Dwell: A Christian View of Place for Today. Baker Academic.

Barton, George A. 1920. Archaeology and The Bible, 3rd Ed. Philadelphia: American Sunday School.

Basil, Saint. 2010. Exegetic Homilies (The Fathers of the Church, Volume 46). CUA Press.

Bastiat, Frédéric. 1964. Economic Sophisms. D. Van Nostrand.

Baucham, Voddie T. 2021. Fault Lines: The Social Justice Movement and Evangelicalism's Looming Catastrophe. Simon and Schuster.

Bavinck, Herman. 2003. Reformed Dogmatics: Prolegomena. Edited by John Bolt and John Vriend. Baker Academic.

———. 2008. Reformed Dogmatics : Volume 4: Holy Spirit, Church, and New Creation. Baker Books.

———. 2012. The Christian Family. Acton Institute for the Study of Religion & Liberty.

Baxter, Richard. 1830. The Practical Works of the Rev. Richard Baxter. Edited by William Orme. 23 vols. London: James Duncan.

Baxter, Richard. 1838. The Practical Works of Richard Baxter: With a Preface, Giving Some Account of the Author, and of This Edition of His Practical Works : An Essay on His Genius, Works and Times : And a Portrait. Vol. 1. Harvard University: G. Virtue.

BBC, dir. 1989. In the Highest Tradition. Digital. Vol. 1. 6 vols. BBC. https://www.bbc.co.uk/programmes/p00j9vk2.

Beaune, Colette. 1991. The Birth of an Ideology: Myths and Symbols of Nation in Late-Medieval France. University of California Press.

Bede, St. 2007. The Ecclesiastical History of the English Nation. Cosimo, Inc.

Belloc, Hilaire. 1927. This and That and the Other. Purdue University: Methuen.

———. 1937. The Crisis of Civilization. Fordham University Press.

Bellows, Henry Adams. 1923. The Poetic Edda. American-Scandinavian Foundation.

Benczédi, László. 1986. "Hungarian National Consciousness as Reflected in the Anti-Habsburg and Anti-Ottoman Struggles of the Late Seventeenth Century." Harvard Ukrainian Studies 10 (3/4): 424–37.

Benedict XVI, Pope. 2012. "Message for the 99th World Day of Migrants and Refugee." Vatican. October 12, 2012. https://www.vatican.va/content/benedict-xvi/en/messages/migration/documents/hf_ben-xvi_mes_20121012_world-migrants-day.html.

Bengel, John A. 2016. Gnomon of the New Testament, Volume 4. Wipf and Stock Publishers.

Benton, Josiah Henry. 1911. Warning Out in New England. W. B. Clarke Company.

Berkhof, Louis. 1933. Manual of Christian Doctrine. Grand Rapids, MI: Eerdmans. https://www.logos.com/product/6695/manual-of-christian-doctrine.

Berkouwer, G.C. 1962. Studies in DogmaticsL Man: The Image of God. Grand Rapids, MI: Eerdmans.

Berman, Bruce, Dickson Eyoh, and Will Kymlicka. 2004. Ethnicity and Democracy in Africa. Ohio University Press.

Berry, Wendell. 1971. The Unforeseen Wilderness: An Essay on Kentucky's Red River Gorge. University Press of Kentucky.

———. 1993. Sex, Economy, Freedom & Community: Eight Essays. Pantheon Books.

———. 2003. Life Is a Miracle: An Essay Against Modern Superstition. Catapult.

———. 2007. Conversations with Wendell Berry. Univ. Press of Mississippi.

———. 2010. The Way of Ignorance: And Other Essays. ReadHowYouWant.com.

———. 2012. The Long-Legged House. Catapult.

———. 2015. The Unsettling of America: Culture & Agriculture. Catapult.

Berthoud, Jean-Marc. 2011. Le Règne terrestre de Dieu : du gouvernement de notre s…. L'Age d'homme.

Black, Henry Campbell. 1910. Handbook of American Constitutional Law. West publishing Company.

Block, Daniel I. 2012. Deuteronomy. Zondervan Academic.

Bloxham, Donald, and A. Dirk Moses. 2010. The Oxford Handbook of Genocide Studies. OUP Oxford.

Blundell, Mary Whitlock, and Ruby Blondell. 1991. Helping Friends and Harming Enemies: A Study in Sophocles and Greek Ethics. Cambridge University Press.

Bock, Darrell L. 1996. Luke : 2 Volumes (Baker Exegetical Commentary on the New Testament). Baker Academic.

———. 2007. Acts. Baker Academic.

———. 2009. Luke. Zondervan Academic.

Bonhoeffer, Dietrich. 1996. Berlin: 1932-1933: Dietrich Bonhoeffer Works, Volume 12. Fortress Press.

Borjas, George. 2011. Heaven's Door: Immigration Policy and the American Economy. Princeton University Press.

———. 2017. "Opinion | The Immigration Debate We Need." The New York Times, February 27, 2017, sec. Opinion. https://www.nytimes.com/2017/02/27/opinion/the-immigration-debate-we-need.html.

Borza, Eugene N. 2020. In the Shadow of Olympus: The Emergence of Macedon. Princeton University Press.

Botterweck, G. Johannes, Helmer Ringgren, and Heinz-Josef Fabry. 1998. Theological Dictionary of the Old Testament, Volume IX. William B. Eerdmans Publishing Company.

Boxer, Charles Ralph. 1965. The Dutch Seaborne Empire, 1600-1800. Knopf.

Bradford, M. E. 2017. A Better Guide Than Reason: Federalists and Anti-Federalists. Routledge.

Brand, Chad, Eric Mitchell, and Holman Reference Editorial Staff. 2015. Holman Illustrated Bible Dictionary. B&H Publishing Group.

Braybrooke, Neville. 1970. T.S. Eliot: A Symposium for His Seventieth Birthday. Garnstone Press.

Bremmer, Jan. 2020. The Early Greek Concept of the Soul. Princeton University Press.

Briggs, Vernon M. 1996. Mass Immigration and the National Interest. M.E. Sharpe.

Brigham, William. 1836. The Compact with the Charter and Laws of the Colony of New Plymouth: Together with the Charter of the Council at Plymouth, and an Appendix. Boston: Dutton And Wentworth.

Brimelow, Peter. 1993. "Does the Nation-State Exist?" The Social Contract, 1993.

———. 2024. "Time to Rethink Immigration?" VDARE.Com. 2024. https://vdare.com/articles/vdare-time-to-rethink-immigration-part-2.

Britain, National Book League of Great. 2017. Book News, Vol. 7: A Monthly Survey of General Literature; September 1888 to August 1889 (Classic Reprint). 1kg Limited.

Bromiley, Geoffrey W. 1979. International Standard Bible Encyclopedia, Volume III: K-P. Wm. B. Eerdmans Publishing.

Bromiley, Geoffrey William. 1979. The International Standard Bible Encyclopedia. Wm. B. Eerdmans Publishing.

Brown, William P. 1996. Obadiah Through Malachi. Westminster John Knox Press.

Brubaker, Rogers. 2009. Citizenship and Nationhood in France and Germany. Harvard University Press.

Bruce, F. F. 1988. The Book of Acts. Wm. B. Eerdmans Publishing.

Bruce, William Cabell. 1922. John Randolph of Roanoke, 1773-1833: A Biography Based Largely on New Material. G.P. Putnam's Sons.

Brunner, Emil. 2014. The Christian Doctrine of Creation and Redemption: Dogmatics: Vol. II. Wipf and Stock Publishers.

Bryan, William Jennings, and Mary Baird Bryan. 1925. The Memoirs of William Jennings Bryan. John C. Winston Company.

Buchanan, Patrick J. 1998. The Great Betrayal: How American Sovereignty and Social Justice Are Being Sacrificed To.. First Edition. Boston: Little, Brown.

———. 2007. Day of Reckoning: How Hubris, Ideology, and Greed Are Tearing America Apart. Macmillan.

———. 2009. Day of Reckoning: How Hubris, Ideology, and Greed Are Tearing America Apart. Macmillan.

———. 2011. Suicide of a Superpower: Will America Survive to 2025? Macmillan.

———. 2018. "Tariffs Made America Great." The American Conservative. July 27, 2018. https://www.theamericanconservative.com/tariffs-made-america-great/.

Buckley (Jr.), William F. 1959. Up from Liberalism: By William F. Buckley, Jr.; Foreword by John Dos Passos. McDowell, Obolensky.

Bullinger, Heinrich. 1849. The Decades of Henry Bullinger. Edited by Thomas Harding. Harvard University Press.

Bunyan, John, and George Offor. 1867. The Whole Works. Vol. 3. Glasgow And Edinburgh: Blackie And Son, Paternoster Row.

Burckhardt, Jacob. 2013. History of Greek Culture. Courier Corporation.

Burke, Edmund. 1812. The Works of ... Edmund Burke. F. & C. Rivington.

———. 1814. Reflections on the Revolution in France. Apollo Press.

Burnet, Gilbert. 1710. An exposition of the church catechism, for the use of the diocese of Sarum. By the Right Reverend Father in God, Gilbert, Lord Bishop of Sarum. 1710. London: Joseph Downing. http://archive.org/details/bim_eighteenth-century_an-exposition-of-the-chu_burnet-gilbert_1710.

Burnet, John. 1914. Greek Philosophy. Part I, Thales to Plato. Macmillan and Company, limited.

Burnham, James. 1967. The War We Are in: The Last Decade and the Next. Arlington House.

Burns, Robert. 1870. The Poetical Works of Robert Burns: Complete. J. Dicks.

"Busing of Schoolchildren : Hearing before the Committee on the Judiciary, United States Senate, Ninety-Fifth Congress, First Session, on S. 1651." n.d. Accessed February 14, 2024. https://hdl.handle.net/2027/uiug.30112104078842?urlappend=%3Bseq=1.

Buxton, Dudley. 1920. "The Inhabitants of the Eastern Mediterranean." Biometrika 13 (1): 92–112.

Byron, George Gordon Byron Baron. 1831. Don Juan, in Sixteen Cantos, with Notes. booksellers.

———. 1872. The Poetical Works of Lord Byron. Edited, with a Critical Memoir, by William Michael Rossetti. Illustrated by Ford Madox Brown.

Cahill, Edward. 1926. The Irish Ecclesiastical Record. Browne and Nolan.

Cai, Zong-qi, ed. 2007. How to Read Chinese Poetry: A Guided Anthology. Illustrated edition. New York: Columbia University Press.

Caldwell, Calhoun, John. 1851. Works of John C. Calhoun Volume 4. Best Books on.

Calhoun, John Caldwell. 1959a. The Papers of John C. Calhoun. Univ of South Carolina Press.

———. 1959b. The Papers of John C. Calhoun. Univ of South Carolina Press.

———. 2003. John C. Calhoun: Selected Writings and Speeches. Regnery Gateway.

Calvin, John. 1844. Commentary Upon the Acts of the Apostles. By John Calvin. Edited from the Original English Translation of Christopher Fetherstone ... by Henry Beveridge. [With the Text.]. Calvin Translation Society.

———. 1845. Commentary on a Harmony of the Evangelists, Matthew, Mark, and Luke. By John Calvin. Translated from the Original Latin, and Collated with the Author's French Version, by the Rev. William Pringle. [With the Text.]. Edited by Rev. William Pringle. Calvin Translation Society.

———. 1846. Commentaries on the Twelve Minor Prophets. Calvin Translation Society.

———. 1850a. Commentaries on Romans. Calvin Translation Society.

———. 1850. Commentaries on the Book of the Prophet Jeremiah and the Lamentations. By John Calvin. Translated from the Latin, and Edited by the Rev. John Owen. [With the Text.]. Calvin Translation Society.

———. 1850b. Commentary on the Book of the Prophet Isaiah. Calvin Translation Society.

———. 1853. Commenaaries on the Four Last Books of Moses, Arranged in the Form of a Harmony. 1852-55. Calvin translation society.

———. 1856. Commentaries on the Epistles to Timothy, Titus and Philemon. By John Calvin. Translated from the Original Latin, by the Rev. William Pringle. [With the Text in Latin and English.]. The British Library. Calvin Translation Society.

———. 1960. Calvin: Institutes of the Christian Religion. Edited by John T. McNeill. Westminster John Knox Press.

———. 1992. Men, Women and Order in the Church: Three Sermons. Translated by Seth Skolnitsky. 1st ed edition. Presbyterian Heritage Publications.

———. 1996. The Epistles of Paul the Apostle to the Galatians, Ephesians, Philippians and Colossians. Wm. B. Eerdmans Publishing.

Cameron, Sharon. 1989. Writing Nature: Henry Thoreau's Journal. University of Chicago Press.

Camões, Luís de. 1880. The Lusiads (Tr. Burton). Translated by Richard Francis Burton. 2 vols. London: Wyman And Sons.

Campbell, Phillip. 2016. The Catholic Middle Ages: A Primary Document Catholic Study Guide. Lulu.com.

Capes, David B., and J. Daryl Charles. 2011. Thriving in Babylon: Essays in Honor of A. J. Conyers. Wipf and Stock Publishers.

Caput, Charles, Archibishop O.F.M. Cap. n.d. "Piety and Patriotism." Catholic Philly. Accessed January 28, 2024. https://catholicphilly.com/2017/06/archbishop-chaput-column/piety-and-patriotism/.

Carchedi, Guglielmo. 2010. Behind the Crisis: Marx's Dialectics of Value and Knowledge. BRILL.

Carroll, Lewis. 1897. Alice's Adventures in Wonderland: And Through the Looking-Glass. Macmillan.

Casey, Edward S. 1993. Getting Back Into Place: Toward a Renewed Understanding of the Place-World. Indiana University Press.

Catallus. 1940. Acta Orientalia. Vol. 18–19. University of Michigan: E. J. Brill.

Chang, Chun-shu. 2007. The Rise of the Chinese Empire: Nation, State, & Imperialism in Early China, ca. 1600 B.C.-A.D. 8. University of Michigan Press.

Chang, Ha-Joon. 2010. Bad Samaritans: The Myth of Free Trade and the Secret History of Capitalism. Bloomsbury Publishing USA.

Charles, Robert Henry. 1913. The Apocrypha and Pseudepigrapha of the Old Testament in English: With Introductions and Critical and Explanatory Notes to the Several Books. The Ohio State University: Clarendon Press.

Charlesworth, James H. 2007. The Old Testament Pseudepigrapha and the New Testament: Expansions of the "Old Testament" and Legends, Wisdom, and Philosophical Literature, Prayers, Psalms and Odes, Fragments of Lost Judeo-Hellenistic Works. Vol. 2. Yale University Press.

Chesterton, Gilbert Keith. 1901. The Defendant. J.M. Dent & Sons Limited.

———. 1903. Varied Types. Dodd, Mead.

———. 2025. What's Wrong with the World. Western Front Books.

———. 1911. Appreciations and Criticisms of the Works of Charles Dickens. J. M. Dent & sons, Limited.

———. 1918. The Illustrated London News. William Little.

———. 1925. The Everlasting Man. Dodd, Mead.

———. 1928. The Illustrated London News. International News Company.

———. 1983. "Puritan and Anglican." The Chesterton Review 9 (4). https://doi.org/10.5840/chesterton19839456.

———. 1986a. The Collected Works of G.K. Chesterton. Vol. 1. Ignatius Press.

———. 1986b. The Collected Works of G.K. Chesterton. Vol. 29. Ignatius Press.

———. 1986c. The Collected Works of G.K. Chesterton. Vol. 20. Ignatius Press.

———. 1986d. The Collected Works of G.K. Chesterton. Vol. 3. Ignatius Press.

———. 1989. The Collected Works of G.K. Chesterton. Vol. 31. Ignatius Press.

———. 1991. The Collected Works of G.K. Chesterton. Vol. 34. Ignatius Press.

Cheung, Vincent. 2007. "Commentary on Galatians." https://www.vincentcheung.com/books/Commentary%20on%20Galatians.pdf.

Chilton, David. 2018. Paradise Restored: A Biblical Theology of Dominion. American Vision, Incorporated.

Chodakiewicz, Marek Jan, and John Radzilowski. n.d. Spanish Carlism and Polish Nationalism: The Borderlands of Europe in the 19th and 20th Centuries. Transaction Publishers.

Christopher Dawson. 1956. The Dynamics Of World History. Sheed And Ward. http://archive.org/details/dynamicsofworldh0088899mbp.

Chrysostom, John. 1840. Commentary on the Epistle to the Galatians: And Homilies on the Epistle to the Ephesians, of S. John Chrysostom ... J.H. Parker.

———. 1842. The Homilies of S. John Chrysostom, Archbishop of Constantinople, on the Statues, or to the People of Antioch, A Library of Fathers of the Holy Catholic Church. London: Oxford University Press.

———. 1843. The Homilies of S. John Chrysostom on the Epistles of St. Paul the Apostle to Timothy, Titus, and Philemon. Parker.

———. 1986. On Marriage and Family Life. St Vladimir's Seminary Press.

———. 2010a. Discourses Against Judaizing Christians (The Fathers of the Church, Volume 68). Vol. 68. CUA Press.

———. 2010b. Homilies on Genesis 18–45 (The Fathers of the Church, Volume 82). CUA Press.

Chua, Amy. 2004. World on Fire: How Exporting Free Market Democracy Breeds Ethnic Hatred and Global Instability. Knopf Doubleday Publishing Group.

Churchill, Winston. 1920. "Zionism Versus Bolshevism." Llustrated Sunday Herald, February 8, 1920. Wikisource.

———. 2013. Never Give In!: Winston Churchill's Speeches. A&C Black.

Cicero, Marcus Tullius. 1829. The Somnium Scipionis of Cicero. Translated by William Danby. Exeter, Printed by E. Woolmer, Gazette-office.

———. 1853. The Treatises of M.T. Cicero on the Nature of the Gods [Tr. by T.Francklin]; on Divination; on Fate; on the Republic; on the Laws; and on Standing for the Consulship, Tr. Chiefly by the Ed. C.D.Yonge [and F.Barham]. Edited by Charles Duke Yonge. Oxford University: Henry Bohn.

————. 1921. De Officiis. University of California: W. Heinemann.

CIS. 1995. "The Legacy of the 1965 Immigration Act," September. https://cis.org/Report/Legacy-1965-Immigration-Act.

Clark, David J., and Norm Mundhenk. 1982. A Translator's Handbook on the Books of Obadiah and Micah. United Bible Societies.

Clark, H. B. 2011. Biblical Law. Lawbook Exchange, Limited.

Clay, Henry. 1959. The Papers of Henry Clay. Edited by James F. Hopkins. University of Kentucky Press.

————. 2015. The Papers of Henry Clay: The Rising Statesman 1815–1820. University Press of Kentucky.

Cochrane, Peter. 2018. Best We Forget: The War for White Australia, 1914–18. Text Publishing.

Codreanu, Corneliu Zelea. 1990. For My Legionaries: The Iron Guard. Liberty Bell Pub.

Commission, United States George Washington Bicentennial. 1932. History of the George Washington Bicentennial Celebration ...: Literature Series. United States George Washington Bicentennial Commission.

Commission, United States Revenue. 2022. Report of a Commission Appointed for a Revision of the Revenue System of the United States 1865-'66. BoD – Books on Demand.

Confucius. 1885. The Sacred Books of China: The Lî Kî, I-X. Translated by James Legge. Clarendon Press.

————. 2002. The Ethics of Confucius. Edited by Miles Menander Dawson. University Press of the Pacific.

————. 1915. The Basic Thoughts of Confucius: The Conduct of Life. Garden City publishing Company, Incorporated.

Confucius, and William Edward Soothill. 1910. The Analects of Confucius.

Congress, United States. 1834. The Congressional Globe. Blair & Rives.

————. 1928. Congressional Record: Proceedings and Debates of the ... Congress. U.S. Government Printing Office.

————. 1945. Congressional Record: Proceedings and Debates of the ... Congress. U.S. Government Printing Office.

————. 1967. Congressional Record: Proceedings and Debates of the ... Congress. U.S. Government Printing Office.

————. 1970. Congressional Record: Proceedings and Debates of the ... Congress. U.S. Government Printing Office.

————. n.d. Reports and Documents.

Congress, United States, and Thomas Hart Benton. 1858. Abridgment of the Debates of Congress, from 1789 to 1856: Nov. 13, 1820-April 14, 1824. D. Appleton.

Connolly, R. Hugh. 2010. Didascalia Apostolorum: The Syriac Version Translated and Accompanied by the Verona Latin Fragments. Wipf and Stock Publishers.

Conzelmann, Hans. n.d. Acts of the Apostles.

Coolidge, Calvin. 1921. "Whose Country Is This?" Good Housekeeping, February 1921.

Coolidge, Calvin. 1923. "First Annual Message." The American Presidency Project. December 6, 1923. https://www.presidency.ucsb.edu/documents/first-annual-message-20.

————. 1926. Foundations of the Republic: Speeches and Addresses. C. Scribner's Sons.

Cooper, James. 1902. The Testament of Our Lord: Translated Into English from the Syriac. T. & T. Clark.

————. 2010. The American Democrat: The Social and Civic Relations of the United States of America. Transaction Publishers.

Copeland, Lewis, Lawrence W. Lamm, and Stephen J. McKenna. 2012. The World's Great Speeches: Fourth Enlarged (1999) Edition. Courier Corporation.

Corse, Taylor. 1991. Dryden's Aeneid: The English Virgil. University of Delaware Press.

Courthial, Pierre, and Matthew S. Miller. 2015. A New Day of Small Beginnings. Zurich Publishing.

Cowper, William. 1806. The Task: A Poem in Six Books. Benjamin Johnson, Jacob Johnson, and Robert Johnson.

Cregan, John P. 1991. America Asleep: The Free Trade Syndrome and the Global Economic Challenge : A Conservative Foreign Economic Policy for America. United States Industrial Council Educational Foundation.

Crèvecoeur, J. Hector St John. 2007. Letters from an American Farmer. Applewood Books.

Creveld, Martin Van. 2016. Equality: The Impossible Quest. Castalia House.

Curtis, Rebekah. n.d. "Emancipated Surf." Touchstone: A Journal of Mere Christianity. Accessed February 13, 2024. https://www.touchstonemag.com/archives/article.php?id=29-02-025-v.

Custis, George Washington Parke. 1860. Recollections and Private Memoirs of Washington. Derby & Jackson.

Cyrrhus, Theodoret (Bishop of. 2006. Commentary on Daniel. Society of Biblical Lit.

Dabney, Robert Lewis. 1885. Syllabus and Notes of the Course of Systematic and Polemic Theology Taught in Union Theological Seminary, Virginia. Presbyterian Committee of Publication.

———. 1890. Discussions. Edited by Clement Read Vaughan. Vol. 1. Presbyterian Committee of Publication.

———. 1891. Discussions. Edited by Clement Read Vaughan. Vol. 2. Presbyterian Committee of Publication.

———. 1897. The Practical Philosophy: Being the Philosophy of the Feelings, of the Will, and of the Conscience, with the Ascertainment of Particular Rights and Duties. Hudson, Kimberly Publishing Company.

Dagg, John Leadley. 1859. Manual of Theology. Vol. 1. Southern Baptist Publication Society.

———. 1860. The Elements of Moral Science. Sheldon.

Dale, Edmund. 1907. National Life and Character in the Mirror of Early English Literature. University Press.

Dandrieu, Laurent. 2019. "The Church Is Plunged Into The Darkness Of Good Friday." Culture à Valeurs Actuelles. March 27, 2019. https://www.valeursactuelles.com/clubvaleurs/societe/cardinal-sarah-leglise-est-plongee-dans-lobscurite-du-vendredi-saint.

Dante. 2013. Paradise. Random House Publishing Group.

Darwin, Charles. 2003. On the Origin of Species. Broadview Press.

Davies, Kristian. 2005. The Orientalists: Western Artists in Arabia, the Sahara, Persia & India. University of Michigan: Laynfaroh.

Davies, Samuel. 1832. Memoir of the Rev. Samuel Davies: Formerly President of the College of New Jersey. Massachusetts Sabbath School Society.

Davis, Christopher A. 2000. Revelation. College Press.

Dawson, Christopher. 1962. Dynamics of World History. New York: New American Library.

———. 2009a. Understanding Europe (The Works of Christopher Dawson). CUA Press.

———. 2009b. Religion and the Rise of Western Culture: The Classic Study of Medieval Civilization. Crown Publishing Group.

———. 2011. The Judgment of the Nations. CUA Press.

———. 2012a. Medieval Essays (The Works of Christopher Dawson). CUA Press.

———. 2012b. Progress and Religion: An Historical Inquiry (The Works of Christopher Dawson). CUA Press.

———. "Library : The Patriarchal Family in History." Accessed January 19, 2024. https://www.catholicculture.org/culture/library/view.cfm?recnum=860.

Dawson, William Harbutt. 1927. Richard Cobden and Foreign Policy: A Critical Exposition, with Special Reference to Our Day and Its Problems. G. Allen & Unwin, Limited.

Day, Vox. 2017. "Don't Resist the Truth." Vox Popoli (blog). January 26, 2017. https://voxday.net/2017/01/26/dont-resist-tru/.

D.D, Loraine Boettner. 2017. The Reformed Doctrine Of Predestination. Lulu.com.

Delbanco, Andrew. 2001. Writing New England: An Anthology from the Puritans to the Present. Harvard University Press.

Dessain, C.S. 1953. The Acts of the Apostles. Edited by B. Orchard & E. F. Sutcliffe. A Catholic Commentary on Holy Scripture.

Devlin, F. Roger. 2023. "At The Scandza Forum: Looking Ahead to 2050." The Unz Review. May 24, 2023. https://www.unz.com/article/at-the-scandza-forum-looking-ahead-to-2050/.

Dibdin, Michael. 2012. Dead Lagoon: An Aurelio Zen Mystery. Knopf Doubleday Publishing Group.

Disraeli, Benjamin. 1881. Endymion. Belford, Clarke.

Dittmer, Lowell, and Samuel S. Kim. 2018. China's Quest for National Identity. Cornell University Press.

Dix, John. 1831. The African Repository. American Colonization Society.

Dostoyevsky, Fyodor. 1916. The Possessed: A Novel in Three Parts. Macmillan.

———. 2020. The Brothers Karamazov. BoD – Books on Demand.

Dow, James R. 2006. German Folklore: A Handbook. Bloomsbury Academic.

Downame, John. 1652. Annotations upon All the Books of the Old and New Testament Wherein the Text Is Explained, Doubts Resolved, Scriptures Parallelled and Various Readings Observed / by the Joynt-Labour of Certain Learned Divines, Thereunto Appointed, and Therein Employed, as Is Expressed in the Preface. London: John Legatt and John Raworth. https://quod.lib.umich.edu/e/eebo2/A36467.0001.001.

Dryden, John. 1966. Absalom and Achitophel. Oxford University Press.

Dudley Buxton. 1920. "The Inhabitants of the Eastern Mediterranean,." Biometrika 13 (1): 111.

Duffy, Seán. 2001. Robert the Bruce's Irish Wars: The Invasions of Ireland 1306-1329. Tempus.

Duguid, Iain M., James M. Hamilton Jr, Jay Sklar, Dennis E. Johnson, Robert L. Plummer, Sam Storms, Matthew S. Harmon, Ray Van Neste, and Thomas R. Schreiner. 2018. ESV Expository Commentary: Hebrews–Revelation. Wheaton, Illinois: Crossway.

Duncan, Archibald Alexander McBeth. 1970. The Nation of Scots and the Declaration of Arbroath (1320). Historical Association.

Dupanloup, Felix. 1879. The Monitor: An Illustrated Dublin Magazine. Dublin: Joseph Dollard.

Durant, Will, and Ariel Durant. 2012. The Lessons of History. Simon and Schuster.

Durha, James. 1658. A Commentarie upon the Book of the Revelation Wherein the Text Is Explained. Edinburgh: Christopher Higgins, Harts Close. http://name.umdl.umich.edu/A37035.0001.001.

Durham, Dr John I. 2018. Exodus, Volume 3. Zondervan Academic.

Dwight, Timothy. 1845. Fisher's National Magazine and Industrial Record. Edited and published by Redwood Fisher.

Earp, Frank Russell. 1971. The Way of the Greeks. AMS Press.

Eckes, Alfred E. 1993. Trade Policy Outlook: Past as Prologue. Economic Strategy Institute.

———. 2000. Opening America's Market: U.S. Foreign Trade Policy Since 1776. Univ of North Carolina Press.

Edgar, William. 2016. Created and Creating: A Biblical Theology of Culture. InterVarsity Press.

Edmonds, J. M. n.d. "Lyra Gaeca, Fragments, Alcman." Theoi.Com. Accessed January 5, 2024. https://www.theoi.com/Text/LyraGraeca1B.html.

Edwards, James R. 2002. The Gospel According to Mark. Wm. B. Eerdmans Publishing.

Edwards, Jonathan. 1832. A Narrative of Many Surprising Conversions in Northampton and Vicinity. Harvard University: Moses W. Grout.

———. 2002. The Miscellanies: (Entry Nos. 833–1152). Edited by Harry S. Stout, Amy Plantinga Pauw, and Perry Miller. Vol. 20. The Works Of Jonathan Edwards. New Haven: Yale University Press.

Eliot, George. 1906. Daniel Deronda. T. Nelson.

Eliot, Thomas Stearns. 1960. Christianity and Culture: The Idea of a Christian Society and Notes Towards the Definition of Culture. Houghton Mifflin Harcourt.

Elliott, E. N., David Christy, Albert Taylor Bledsoe, Thornton Stringfellow, Robert Goodloe Harper, James Henry Hammond, Samuel Adolphus Cartwright, and Charles Hodge. 1860. Cotton Is King, and Pro-Slavery Arguments: Comprising the Writings of Hammond, Harper, Christy, Stringfellow, Hodge, Bledsoe, and Cartwright, on This Important Subject. Pritchard, Abbott & Loomis.

Elliott, J. H. 1984. The Revolt of the Catalans. Cambridge University Press.

Elliott, Marianne. 2012. Wolfe Tone. Liverpool University Press.

Elliott, Mark C. 2001a. The Manchu Way: The Eight Banners and Ethnic Identity in Late Imperial China. Stanford University Press.

———. 2001b. The Manchu Way: The Eight Banners and Ethnic Identity in Late Imperial China. Stanford University Press.

Elwell, Walter A. 1988. Baker Encyclopedia of the Bible. Baker Book House.

Emerson, Ralph Waldo. 1976. Journals and Miscellaneous Notebooks of Ralph Waldo Emerson, Volume XII: 1835-1862. Harvard University Press.

Eminescu, Mihai. 1999. Opera politică. București: Editura Eminescu.

England, Church of. 1887. The Book of Common Prayer, A.D. 1886: Compared with the First Prayer Book of King Edward the Sixth, A.D. 1549. Griffith, Farran, Okeden and Welsh.

———. 2011. The Book of Common Prayer: The Texts of 1549, 1559, and 1662. OUP Oxford.

Epictetus. 1925. Discourses as Reported by Arrian, the Manual, and Fragments. Translated by W.A. Oldfather. Vol. 1. 2 vols. Cambridge, MA: Harvard University Press.

Erasmus. 1917. The Complaint of Peace. Translated from the Querela Pacis (A.D. 1521) of Erasmus. Chicago: Open Court.

Esolen, Anthony. 2014. Ten Ways to Destroy the Imagination of Your Child. Open Road Media.

Essays On Segregation. 1960. Houston : St. Thomas Press.

Essen, Jantje Lubbegiena van, and Herbert Donald Morton. 1990. Guillaume Groen Van Prinsterer: Selected Studies. Wedge Publishing Foundation.

Euripides. 1904. The Plays of Euripides. Translated by Edward Philip Coleridge. 2 vols. Indinana University: G. Bell and sons, Limited.

———. 1997. Medea: Hippolytus ; Electra ; Helen. Clarendon Press.

———. 2013. Euripides IV: Helen, The Phoenician Women, Orestes. University of Chicago Press.

———. 2020. Trojan Women and Two Other Plays: Orestes and Rhesus. Translated by George Theodoridis. Independently published.

———. forthcoming. Euripides, with an English Translation by David Kovacs. Cambridge, MA: Harvard University Press.

Evelyn-White, H. G. n.d. "Hesiod, Catalogues of Women." Theoi.Com. Accessed January 5, 2024. https://www.theoi.com/Text/HesiodCatalogues.html.

Evola, Julius. 2015. A Traditionalist Confronts Fascism. Arktos.

Fahey, Denis. 2010. The Rulers of Russia and the Russian Farmers. Loreto Publications.

Faye, Guillaume. 2011. Why We Fight: Manifesto of the European Resistance. Arktos.

Fee, Gordon D. 2011. 1 & 2 Timothy, Titus (Understanding the Bible Commentary Series). Baker Books.

Fichte, Johann Gottlieb. 1922. Addresses to the German Nation. Open Court Publishing Company.

Finance, United States Congress Senate Committee on. 1911. Reciprocity with Canada: Compilation of 1911. U.S. Government Printing Office.

Fingleton, Eamonn. n.d. "Nobel Laureate: The U.S. Is The 'Naked Woman' Of The World Economy." Forbes. Accessed February 15, 2024. https://www.forbes.com/sites/eamonnfingleton/2013/05/26/americas-open-economy-is-a-naked-woman-says-nobel-laureate-mundell/.

Fischer, David Hackett. 1991. Albion's Seed: Four British Folkways in America. Oxford University Press.

Fishman, Joshua A. 2001. Handbook of Language & Ethnic Identity. Oxford University Press.

———. 2007a. Romans: A New Translation with Introduction and Commentary. Yale University Press.

———. 2007b. The Acts of the Apostles: A New Translation with Introduction and Commentary. Yale University Press.

Flaccus, Gaius Valerius. 1936. The Argonautica of Valerius Flaccus. Harvard University Press.

Flavel, John. 1820. The Whole Works of John Flavel: Late Minister of the Gospel at Dartmouth, Devon. W. Baynes and son.

———. 2016. "AN EXPOSITION OF THE ASSEMBLY'S CATECHISM With Practical Inferences from Each Question:" Reformed Presbyterian Church (Covenanted) - "Steelite" Covenanters. May 4, 2016. https://www.covenanter.org/reformed/2016/5/4/an-exposition-of-the-assemblys-catechism-with-practical-inferences-from-each-question.

Fleming, Thomas. 2004. The Morality of Everyday Life: Rediscovering an Ancient Alternative to the Liberal Tradition. University of Missouri Press.

———. 2014. "The Death Throes of an Imperial Nation - Chronicles." July 25, 2014. https://chroniclesmagazine.org/web/the-death-throes-of-an-imperial-nation/, https://chroniclesmagazine.org/web/the-death-throes-of-an-imperial-nation/.

———. 2015a. "Aliens and Strangers - Chronicles." January 1, 2015. https://chroniclesmagazine.org/columns/perspective/aliens-and-strangers/, https://chroniclesmagazine.org/columns/perspective/aliens-and-strangers/.

———. 2015b. "Family Tradition - Chronicles." May 1, 2015. https://chroniclesmagazine.org/columns/perspective/family-tradition/, https://chroniclesmagazine.org/columns/perspective/family-tradition/.

———. 2017. "City-States Rights, Part I A (FREE)." The Fleming Foundation (blog). November 25, 2017. https://fleming.foundation/2017/11/city-states-rights-part-i-free/.

———. 2022. Properties of Blood: The Reign of Love. Fleming Foundation.

Fletcher, Ian. 2011. Free Trade Doesn't Work: What Should Replace It and Why. Coalition for a Prosperous America.

Flood, Anthony T. 2018. The Metaphysical Foundations of Love: Aquinas on Participation, Unity, and Union. CUA Press.

Ford, Paul Leicester. 1888. Pamphlets on the Constitution of the United States: Published During Its Discussion by the People, 1787-1788. s.l.

Fortescue, Sir John. 1869. The Works of Sir John Fortescue, Knight, Chief Justice of England and Lord Chancellor to King Henry the Sixth. Edited by Thomas Fortescue, Baron Clermont. University of Colorado Boulder.

Foster, Michael, and Dominic Bnonn Tennant. 2022. It's Good to Be a Man: A Handbook for Godly Masculinity. Canon Press.

Foundation, Poetry. 2024. "Wendell Berry." Text/html. Poetry Foundation. January 23, 2024. https://www.poetryfoundation.org/poets/wendell-berry.

Frame, John. 2012. "Racisms, Sexisms, and Other Isms." Frame-Poythress.Org. May 22, 2012. https://frame-poythress.org/racisms-sexisms-and-other-isms/.

———. n.d. "Toward a Theology of the State." Accessed January 26, 2024. https://www.the-highway.com/theonomy_Frame.html.

France, R. T. 2013. Luke (Teach the Text Commentary Series). Baker Books.

———. 2017. "Why Race Matters." American Renaissance. April 30, 2017. https://www.amren.com/news/2017/04/why-race-matters-white-identity-sam-t-francis/.

———. 2019. "The Return of the Repressed." American Renaissance. July 6, 2019. https://www.amren.com/news/2019/07/race-and-the-american-prospect-sam-francis/.

———. 1991. "The Phrase 'America First' - Chronicles." December 1, 1991. https://chroniclesmagazine.org/columns/principalities-powers/the-phrase-america-first/, https://chroniclesmagazine.org/columns/principalities-powers/the-phrase-america-first/.

———. 1994. Beautiful Losers: Essays on the Failure of American Conservatism. University of Missouri Press.

———. 2017. "Burnham Agonistes - Chronicles." November 2, 2017. https://chroniclesmagazine.org/web/burnham-agonistes/, https://chroniclesmagazine.org/web/burnham-agonistes/.

———. 2021. Leviathan and Its Enemies. Washington Summit Publishers.

Francis, Samuel T., and Jared Taylor. 2007. Essential Writings on Race. New Century Foundation.

Frank, Andre Gunder. 1970. Latin America and Underdevelopment. NYU Press.

Franklin, Benjamin. 1819. Memoirs of the Life and Writings of Benjamin Franklin ... Written by Himself to a Late Period, and Continued to the Time of His Death, by ... W. T. Franklin. Now First Published from the Original MSS., Comprising the Private Correspondence and Public Negociations of Dr. Franklin; and a Selection from His Political, Philosophical, and Miscellaneous Works.

———. 1904. The Works of Benjamin Franklin: Including the Private as Well as the Official and Scientific Correspondence Together with the Unmutilated and Correct Version of the Autobiography. G.P. Putnam's Sons, The Knickerbocker Press.

———. 1918. Observations Concerning the Increase of Mankind, Peopling of Countries, &c. Reprinted, W. Abbatt.

Freedman, David Noel. 1992. The Anchor Bible Dictionary. Yale University Press.

———. 2019. Eerdmans Dictionary of the Bible. Wm. B. Eerdmans Publishing.

Freudenberg, Graham. 2008. Churchill and Australia. Macmillan Publishers Aus.

Friedman, Milton. 1988. Why Liberalism Is Now ObsoleteCollected Works of Milton Friedman Project records. https://miltonfriedman.hoover.org/objects/57401/why-liberalism-is-now-obsolete.

Fudge, Thomas A. 2017. Jan Hus: Religious Reform and Social Revolution in Bohemia. Bloomsbury Publishing.

Fukuyama, Francis. 1996. Trust: The Social Virtues and the Creation of Prosperity. Simon and Schuster.

Fuzhi, Wang. 1981. "Index to The Harvard Journal of Asiatic Studies Volume 36 (1976)--Volume 40 (1980)." Harvard Journal of Asiatic Studies 40 (3): 699–711.

Gangulee, N. 2013. Giuseppe Mazzini -Selected Writings. Read Books Ltd.

Gardels, Nathan. 1991. "Two Concepts of Nationalism: An Interview with Isaiah Berlin." The New York Review of Books, November 21, 1991. https://www.nybooks.com/articles/1991/11/21/two-concepts-of-nationalism-an-interview-with-isai/.

Gat, Azar, and Alexander Yakobson. 2013. Nations: The Long History and Deep Roots of Political Ethnicity and Nationalism. Cambridge University Press.

Gaulle, Charles de. 1999. Mémoires d'espoir, Suivis Des Allocutions et Messages (1946– 1969),. Paris: Plon.

Gibbon, Edward. 1879. The History of the Decline and Fall of the Roman Empire. Harper Bros.

Gilder, George F. 1986. Men and Marriage. Pelican Publishing Company.

Giles, John Allen, and Gildas. 1848. Six Old English Chronicles: Of Which Two Are Now First Translated from the Monkish Latin Originals. Henry G. Bohn.

Giles, William. 1827. Political Miscellanies. Vol. 1. Richmond: Thomas W. White.

Gill, John. 1852. An Exposition of the Old Testament. W. H. Collingridge.

———. 1853. An Exposition of the New Testament. W. H. Collingridge.

Glazer, Nathan. 1983. Ethnic Dilemmas, 1964-1982. Harvard University Press.

Glubb, Sir John Bagot. 1978. The Fate of Empires and Search for Survival. Blackwood.

Goldberg, Jeffrey. 2020. "Why Obama Fears for Our Democracy." The Atlantic (blog). November 16, 2020. https://www.theatlantic.com/ideas/archive/2020/11/why-obama-fears-for-our-democracy/617087/.

Goldberg, Jonah. 2008. Liberal Fascism: The Secret History of the American Left, From Mussolini to the Politics of Meaning. Crown Publishing Group.

Gollin, Alfred M. 1964. Proconsul in Politics: A Study of Lord Milner in Opposition and in Power. Macmillan.

Goodman, Ellen. 1995. The Origins of the Western Legal Tradition: From Thales to the Tudors. Federation Press.

Gore, Bishop. 1908. "The Churchman, Bishop Gore On The Church In India," June 27, 1908.

Gottfried, Paul. 2016. Fascism: The Career of a Concept. Cornell University Press.

———. 2004. Multiculturalism and the Politics of Guilt: Toward a Secular Theocracy. University of Missouri Press.

Goyau, Georges. 1911. "Councils of Orléans." The Catholic Encyclopedia. Vol. 11. New York: Robert Appleton Company.

Grant, Madison. 1922. Immigration and Other Interests of Prescott Fransworth Hall. Knickerbocker Press.

Grant, Madison, and Charles Stewart Davison. 1928. The Founders of the Republic on Immigration, Naturalization and Aliens ... C. Scribner's Sons.

Grattan, Henry. 1823. Galignani's Literary Gazette. Paris: Galignani.

Green, Joel B. 1997. The Gospel of Luke. Wm. B. Eerdmans Publishing.

Greene, George Washington. 1867. The Life of Nathanael Greene, Major-General in the Army of the Revolution. Books for Libraries Press.

Greene, Jack P. 1975. Settlements to Society, 1607 [Ie. 1584]-1763: A Documentary History of Colonial America. Norton.

Greenfeld, Liah. 1992. Nationalism: Five Roads to Modernity. Harvard University Press.

Groenhuis, G. 1977. De Predikanten. De Sociale Positie van de Gereformeerde Predikanten in de Republiek Der Verenigde Nederlanden Voor ± 1700. Groningen: Wolters-Noordhoff,. https://www.dbnl.org/tekst/groe023predo1_01/groe023predo1_01_0006.php#392.

Grosby, Steven. 2002. Biblical Ideas of Nationality, Ancient and Modern. Penn State Press.

Grudem, Wayne A. 2010. Politics According to the Bible: A Comprehensive Resource for Understanding Modern Political Issues in Light of Scripture. Zondervan.

Grund, Francis Joseph. 1837. The Americans, in Their Moral, Social, and Political Relations. Marsh, Capen and Lyon.

Guanzhong, Luo. 2014. The Three Kingdoms, Volume 1: The Sacred Oath: The Epic Chinese Tale of Loyalty and War in a Dynamic New Translation. Edited by Ronald C. Iverson. Translated by Yu Sumei. 1st edition. Tokyo ; Rutland, Vermont: Tuttle Publishing.

Günther, H. F. K. 1927. The Racial Elements of European History. Translated by G. C. Wheeler. London: Methuen.

Haag, Ernest van den. 1965. "More Immigration?" National Review, September 21, 1965.

Habermas, Jürgen. 2018. The Postnational Constellation: Political Essays. John Wiley & Sons.

Hálfdanarson, Guðmundur. 1999. "Hver á sér fegra föðurland. Staða náttúrunnar í íslenskri þjóðernisvitund." Skírnir, Blöð og tímarit frá Íslandi, , no. 173 (January): 304–36.

Hall, David. 2005. The Genevan Reformation and the American Founding. Lexington Books.

Hall, Thomas. 1658. A Practical and Polemical Commentary Or, Exposition Upon the Third and Fourth Chapters of the Latter Epistle of Saint Paul to Timothy: Wherein the Text Is Explained, Some Controversies Discussed, Sundry Cases of Conscience Are Cleared, Many Common Places Are Succinctly Handled, and Divers Usefull, and Seasonable Observations Raised,. E. Tyler.

Halleck, Fitz-Greene. 1888. Poems. Hurst & Company.

Hamilton, Alexander. 1810. The Works of Alexander Hamilton: Comprising His Most Important Official Reports; an Improved Edition of the Federalist, on the New Constitution, Written in 1788; and Pacificus, on the Proclamation of Neutrality, Written in 1793. Williams and Whiting, at their Theological and Classical Book-store, No. 118 Pearl-street. Printed by J. Seymour.

———. 1904. The Works of Alexander Hamilton. Edited by Henry Cabot Lodge. G.P. Putnam's Sons.

———. 1928. Hamiltonian Principles: Extracts from the Writings of Alexander Hamilton. Little, Brown.

———. 2006. Citizen Hamilton: The Wit and Wisdom of an American Founder. Rowman & Littlefield.

———. 2017a. The Political Writings of Alexander Hamilton: Volume 1, 1769–1789. Cambridge University Press.

———. 2017b. The Political Writings of Alexander Hamilton: Volume 1, 1769–1789. Cambridge University Press.

Hamilton, Victor P. 2011. Exodus: An Exegetical Commentary. Baker Academic.

Hammond, Peter. 2018a. "The Christian Case for Intra-Racial Marriage." https://generation5.files.wordpress.com/2010/05/intraracialmarriage.pdf.

———. 2018b. "Peter Hammond Responds to Joel McDurmon." April 5, 2018. https://www.christrules.com/peter-hammond-responds-to-joel-mcdurmon/.

Hampel, Walter. 2002. "Ashland Theological Journal. Vol. 34 (2002)." http://archive.org/details/ashlandtheologicooooounse.

Hansen, Mogens Herman. 2002. A Comparative Study of Six City-State Cultures: An Investigation. Kgl. Danske Videnskabernes Selskab.

Harper, William Rainey, Ernest DeWitt Burton, and Shailer Mathews. 1919. The Biblical World. University of Chicago Press.

Hastings, Adrian. 1997. The Construction of Nationhood: Ethnicity, Religion and Nationalism. Cambridge University Press.

Hauerwas, Stanley, and Bishop William H. Willimon. 2014. Resident Aliens: Life in the Christian Colony (Expanded 25th Anniversary Edition). Abingdon Press.

Hawley, Ellis Wayne. 1981. Herbert Hoover As Secretary of Commerce: Studies in New Era Thought and Practice. University of Iowa Press.

Hayek, F. A. 1958. "Freedom, Reason, and Tradition." Ethics 68 (4): 229–45. https://doi.org/10.1086/291177.

———. 2013. Law, Legislation and Liberty: A New Statement of the Liberal Principles of Justice and Political Economy. Routledge.

———. 2014. The Road to Serfdom: Text and Documents: The Definitive Edition. Routledge.

———. 2020. The Constitution of Liberty: The Definitive Edition. Routledge.

Hazony, Yoram. 2018. The Virtue of Nationalism. Basic Books.

———. 2022. Conservatism: A Rediscovery. Simon and Schuster.

———. "Https://Twitter.Com/Yhazony/Status/1124801954276937728?S=21." X (Formerly Twitter). Accessed January 23, 2024. https://twitter.com/yhazony/status/1124801954276937728?s=21.

Hegel, G. W. F. 1998. Aesthetics: Volume 1. Clarendon Press.

———. 2012. Philosophy of Right. Courier Corporation.

———. 1902. Lectures on the Philosophy of History. G. Bell and Sons.

———. 1971. Philosophy of Mind: Being Part Three of the "Encyclopaedia of the Philosophical Sciences" (1830). Clarendon Press.

Heidegger, Johann Heinrich. 2021. Concise Marrow of Theology. Reformation Heritage Books.

Heidegger, Martin. 2008. Being and Time. Harper Collins.

Henderson, Alexander. 1641. The Government and Order of the Church of Scotland. James Bryson.

Henry, Matthew. 1790a. An Exposition of the Old and New Testament. In Six Volumes ... By Mattew Henry ... Vol. 1. [-6.]: Volume 2. Containing Joshua, Judges, Ruth, 1. Samuel, 2. Samuel ... 2. Bell and Bradfute, J. Dickson, and J. McCliesh.

———. 1790b. An Exposition of the Old and New Testament. In Six Volumes ... By Mattew Henry ... Vol. 1. [-6.]: Volume 2. Containing Joshua, Judges, Ruth, 1. Samuel, 2. Samuel ... 2. Bell and Bradfute, J. Dickson, and J. McCliesh.

———. 2017. Matthew Henry's Commentary on the Whole Bible: Volume I-II - Leviticus to Deuteronomy. Lulu.com.

Henry, Matthew, and William Jenks. 1839. The Comprehensive Commentary on the Holy Bible: Acts-Revelation. Fessenden & Company.

Henry, Matthew, and Noah Webster. 2018. Matthew Henry Study Bible - Revised King James Version. Importantia Publishing.

Herbert, Frank. 2019. Dune: Deluxe Edition. Penguin.

Herbert Helbig and Lorenz Weinrich, eds, ed. 1970. "Urkunden und erzählende Quellen zur deutschen Ostsiedlung im Mittelalter." Wissenschaftliche Buchgesellschaft 2 (26): 352–56.

Herder, Johan Gottfried. 1969. Herder on Social and Political Culture a Selection of Texts Translated, Edited and with an Introduction by F. M. Barnard. Translated by F. M. Barnard. CUP Archive.

Hermans, Felicia. 1839. The Works of Mrs. Hermans, with a Memoir of Her Life, by Her Sister. Vol. 2. 7 vols. Edinburgh: William Blackwood.

Herodotus. 1920. Herodotus, with an English Translation by A. D. Godley. Translated by D.A. Godley. Cambridge University Press.

Herriot, Trevor. 2012. Grass, Sky, Song: Promise and Peril in the World of Grassland Birds. Harper Collins.

Herzl, Theodor. 1917. A Jewish State: An Attempt at a Modern Solution of the Jewish Question. Federation of American Zionists.

Hesiod. 1932. Homeric Hymns And Homerica. Translated by H. G. Evelyn-White. Loeb Classical Library. Cambridge, MA: Harvard University Press.

Hess, Moses. 1918. Rome and Jerusalem: A Study in Jewish Nationalism. Bloch Publishing Company.

Hess, Richard S. 2005. Song of Songs (Baker Commentary on the Old Testament Wisdom and Psalms). Baker Books.

Hiebert, Theodore. 1996. The Yahwist's Landscape: Nature and Religion in Early Israel. Oxford University Press.

Hildebrand, Stephen M. 2011. On the Holy Spirit: St. Basil the Great. Yonkers, N.Y: St Vladimirs Seminary Pr.

Hill, D.H. 1866. The Land We Love. Vol. 1. 1. Charlotte, N.C.: Jas. P. Irwin & D.H. Hill.

Hillerbrand, Hans H. 2017. The Annotated Luther, Volume 5: Christian Life in the World. Fortress Press.

Hinwood (o.f.m), Bonaventure, and Edward Victor Hinwood. 1964. Race: The Reflections of a Theologian. Herder.

Hippocrates. 1923. Hippocrates. Edited by Paul Potter, William Henry Samuel Jones. Translated by Edward Theodore Withington. Vol. 1. Cambridge, MA: Harvard University Press.

Hirst, Francis Wrigley. 1903. Free Trade and Other Fundamental Doctrines of the Manchester School: Set Forth in Selections from the Speeches and Writings of Its Founders and Followers. Harper & brothers.

Hirst, Margaret Esther. 1909. Life of Friedrich List and Selections from His Writings. C. Scribner's sons.

Hobsbawm, E. J. 2012. Nations and Nationalism since 1780: Programme, Myth, Reality. Cambridge University Press.

Hodge, Charles. 1857. Essays and Reviews. R. Carter.

———. 1872. Systematic Theology. Vol. 2. Scribner's.

———. 1993. Commentary on the Epistle to the Romans. Wm. B. Eerdmans Publishing.

Hoekema, Anthony A. 1994. Created in God's Image. Wm. B. Eerdmans Publishing.

Hoffmeier, James K. 2009. The Immigration Crisis: Immigrants, Aliens, and the Bible. Crossway Books.

Homer. 1919. The Odyssey. Translated by A. T. Murray. Cambridge, MA: Harvard University Press.

———. 1924. Iliad. Translated by A. T. Murray. Loeb Classical Library. Harvard University Press.

———. 1942. The Iliad. Translated by Samuel Butler. Roslyn, NY: Walter J. Black INC.

———. 1944. The Odyssey. Translated by Samuel Butler. Roslyn, NY: Walter J. Black INC.

———. 1997. The Odyssey. Translated by Robert Fagles. Penguin.

———. 2016a. The Iliad. Translated by A.S. Kline. Poetry In Translation.

———. 2016b. The Odyssey. Translated by A.S. Kline. Poetry In Translation.

Hooker, Richard. 1825. Of the Laws of Ecclesiastical Polity. Book V-VIII. A Supplication Made to the Council by Master Walter Travers. Master Hooker's Answer to the Supplication That Master Travers Made to the Council. A Learned Discourse of Justification, Works, and How the Foundation of Faith Is Overthrown. A Learned Sermon of the Nature of Pride. A Remedy against Sorrow and Fear, Delivered in a Funeral Sermon. Of the Certainty and Perpetuity of Faith in the Elect: ... Two Sermons upon Part of St. Jude's Epistle. A Sermon upon Matt. Vii. 7,8. G. Cowie and Company ... Baynes and Son, ... Hatchard and Son, ... Smith, Elder, and Company ... R. Baynes, ... Deighton and Sons, Cambridge; J. Cumming, M. Keene, and R.M. Tims, Dublin; and H.S. Baynes, Edinburgh.

Hopkins, John Henry. 1864. A Scriptural, Ecclesiastical, and Historical View of Slavery.

Hoppe, Hans-Hermann. 2018. Democracy – The God That Failed: The Economics and Politics of Monarchy, Democracy and Natural Order. Routledge.

Hoppe, Hans-Hermann. n.d. "Books / Digital Text." Text. Mises Institute. Accessed January 21, 2024. https://mises.org/library/getting-libertarianism-right/html/c/689.

Horace. 1872. The Odes and Carmen Saeculare of Horace. Translated by John Conington. 5th ed. London: Bell And Daldy.

———. 1929. Horace: Satires, Epistles and Ars Poetica. Translated by H. Rushton Fairclough. Revised edition. Cambridge, Mass.: Harvard University Press.

Hornberger, Richard M. Ebeling and Jacob G. 1995. The Case for Free Trade and Open Immigration. The Future of Freedom Foundation.

Horowitz, Donald L., Horowitz Donald L, and Professor Donald L. Horowitz. 1985. Ethnic Groups in Conflict. University of California Press.

House, Concordia Publishing. 2004. The Lord Will Answer: A Daily Prayer Catechism. Concordia Publishing House.

Howting, John. 2019. "Protectionism as a Path to Piety - Chronicles." May 1, 2019. https://chroniclesmagazine.org/view/protectionism-as-a-path-to-piety/, https://chroniclesmagazine.org/view/protectionism-as-a-path-to-piety/.

Hughes, R. Kent. 2014. Acts (ESV Edition): The Church Afire. Crossway.

Hughes, R. Kent, and Bryan Chapell. 2012. 1–2 Timothy and Titus (ESV Edition): To Guard the Deposit. Crossway.

Hugo, Victor. n.d. Les Misérables, Volume 1. Jazzybee Verlag.

Huizinga, Johan. 2014. Men and Ideas: History, the Middle Ages, the Renaissance. Princeton University Press.

Hull, Cordell. 1948. The Memoirs of Cordell Hull: Tennessee and Congress (1871-1933). Macmillan Company.

Hull, Ernest R. 1909. The Formation of Character. Examiner Press.

Hume, David. 1822. Essays and Treatises on Several Subjects. James Walker.

———. 1888. A Treatise of Human Nature. Clarendon Press.

———. 1902. Enquiries Concerning the Human Understanding and Concerning the Principles of Morals. Clarendon Press.

———. 1994. Hume: Political Essays. Cambridge University Press.

Hussey, Andrew. 2014. The French Intifada: The Long War Between France and Its Arabs. Granta Books.

Hutchinson, John, and Anthony D. Smith. 1994. Nationalism. Oxford University Press.

Hyde, Douglas. 1967. A Literary History of Ireland from Earliest Times to the Present Day. New Ed. with Introduction. Benn.

Ibrahim, Raymond. 2022. Defenders of the West: The Christian Heroes Who Stood Against Islam. Simon and Schuster.

Ilyin, Ivan. 2019. Foundations of Christian Culture. Waystone Press.

Irenaeus. 2019. Against Heresies Revised. Devoted Publishing.

Irwin, Douglas A. 2020. Against the Tide: An Intellectual History of Free Trade. Princeton University Press.

Isidore. 2006. The Etymologies of Isidore of Seville. Edited by Stephen A. Barney. Cambridge University Press.

Italicus, Tiberius Catius Silius. 1950. Punica. Translated by James Duff. Harvard University Press.

Jackman, William James, Jacob Harris Patton, and Rossiter Johnson. 1920. History of the American Nation. Western Press Association.

Jackson, Andrew. 1926. Correspondence of Andrew Jackson. Edited by John Spencer Bassett. Carnegie institution of Washington.

Jacob, Anthony. 2017. White Man. Think Again! Blurb, Incorporated.

Jacqueline A. Laing, Russell Wilcox. 2013. The Natural Law Reader. Wiley.

James, John Angell. 1853. Female Piety, Or, The Young Woman's Friend and Guide Through Life to Immortality. Robert Carter & Bros.

James Legge. n.d. The Shû King, Shih King and Hsiâo King. Accessed January 8, 2024. https://sacred-texts.com/cfu/sbe03/index.htm.

Jamieson, Robert, Fausset, A.R., and Brown, David. 1997. Commentary Critical and Explanatory on the Whole Bible. Vol. 2. Oak Harbor, WA: Logos Research Systems, Inc.

Jeffers, James S. 2009. The Greco-Roman World of the New Testament Era: Exploring the Background of Early Christianity. InterVarsity Press.

Jefferson, Thomas. 1832. Notes on the State of Virginia. Lilly and Wait.

———. 1861. Correspondence. H. W. Derby.

———. 1950a. The Papers of Thomas Jefferson. Princeton University Press.

———. 1950b. The Papers of Thomas Jefferson, Volume 2: January 1777 to June 1779. Princeton University Press.

———. 1999. Jefferson: Political Writings. Cambridge University Press.

———. 2018. The Papers of Thomas Jefferson, Volume 20: April 1791 to August 1791. Princeton University Press.

Jeffrey, David Lyle. 2012. Luke (Brazos Theological Commentary on the Bible). Baker Books.

Jensen, Lotte. 2016. The Roots of Nationalism: National Identity Formation in Early Modern Europe, 1600-1815. Amsterdam University Press.

Jeske, Diane, and Richard Fumerton. 2011. Readings in Political Philosophy: Theory and Applications. Broadview Press.

John Bostock. 1855. The Natural History. Pliny the Elder. London: Red Lion Court. https://www.perseus.tufts.edu/hopper/text?doc=Perseus%3Atext%3A1999.02.0137%3Abook%3D26%3Achapter%3D93.

John McDowell, Martin Davie, Stephen R. Holmes, Thomas Noble, Tim Grass, ed. 2016. New Dictionary of Theology: Historical and Systematic (Second Edition). Inter-Varsity Press.

John Nichols. 1838. The Gentleman's Magazine. Indiana University: W. Pickering.

John, P. 2017. Mater Et Magistra: Encyclical Letter of Pope John XXIII, on Christianity and Social Progress, May 15, 1961. CreateSpace Independent Publishing Platform.

John Paul II, Pope. n.d. "Dilecti Amici." March 31, 1985. Vatican. Accessed January 27, 2024. https://www.vatican.va/content/john-paul-ii/en/apost_letters/1985/documents/hf_jp-ii_apl_31031985_dilecti-amici.html.

Johnson, Donald Bruce. 1978. National Party Platforms: 1960-1976. University of Illinois Press.

Johnston, Ian. "Homer's Iliad Book 1 (English Text)." Accessed January 5, 2024. https://johnstoniatexts.x10host.com/homer/iliad1html.html.

Jones, Douglas, and Douglas Wilson. 1998. Angels in the Architecture: A Protestant Vision for Middle Earth. Canon Press & Book Service.

Jordan, James B. 1999. Through New Eyes: Developing a Biblical View of the World. Wipf and Stock Publishers.

———. 2019. Christendom and the Nations. Theopolis Books.

Judicature, New Hampshire Superior Court of, and Jeremiah Smith. 1879. Decisions of the Superior and Supreme Courts of New Hampshire: From 1802 to 1809, and from 1813 to 1816. Selected from the Manuscript Reports of the Late Jeremiah Smith, Chief Justice of Those Courts. With Extracts from Judge Smith's Manuscript Treatise on Probate Law, and from His Other Legal Manuscripts. Little, Brown,.

Jun, Moses Y. Lee, Thabiti Anyabwile, Alexander. 2021. "Why Ethnic-Specific Churches Are Still Important: An Interview with Pastor Thabiti Anyabwile and Dr. Alexander Jun." SOLA Network (blog). January 25, 2021. https://sola.network/article/why-ethnic-specific-churches-still-important-interview/.

Jung, Carl G. 2011. Memories, Dreams, Reflections. Knopf Doubleday Publishing Group.

Junger, Ernst. 2016. Storm of Steel: (Penguin Classics Deluxe Edition). Penguin Publishing Group.

Jusdanis, Gregory. 2011. The Necessary Nation. Princeton University Press.

Kaminsky, Howard. 1967. A History of the Hussite Revolution, Berkeley. Berkeley, CA: University of California Press.

Kari Ellen Gade, Theodore M. Andersson, ed. 2012. Morkinskinna: The Earliest Icelandic Chronicle of the Norwegian

Kings (1030–1157). Cornell University Press.

Karlsson, Gunnar. 1999. "Tímarit.Is." Skírnir, Blöð og tímarit frá Íslandi, , no. Vor (January). https://timarit.is/geg-nir/991004531109706886.

Kass, Leon. 2003. The Beginning of Wisdom: Reading Genesis. Simon and Schuster.

Keener, Craig S. 2014. Acts: An Exegetical Commentary : Volume 3: 15:1-23:35. Baker Academic.

Kerr, James, C. Matthew McMahon, and Samuel Rutherford. 2009. The Covenanted Reformation. Puritan Publications.

Keyes, Professor Emeritus Charles F., and Washington State University School of International Studies. 1981. Ethnic Change. University of Washington Press.

Keynes, John Maynard. 1978. The Collected Writings of John Maynard Keynes. Cambridge University Press.

Kharkhordin, Oleg. 2005. Main Concepts of Russian Politics. University Press of America.

King, Rufus. 1895. The Life and Correspondence of Rufus King: 1795-1799. G. P. Putnam's sons.

Kirill (Gundyaev), Patriarch. 2000. "Religious Faith as the Source of Social Norms. Correlating Traditional and Liberal Values in Individual and Societal Choices (Address to the Theological Conference of the Russian Orthodox Church 'Orthodox Theology at the Turn of the Third Millennium.'" February 7, 2000. http://www.odinblago.ru/freedom_n_responsibility/3?http://www.odinblago.ru/freedom_n_responsibility/3?

———. 2016. 'Western laws now clash with moral nature of man' – Russian Orthodox Patriarch Kirill. https://www.rt.com/news/367599-patriarch-kirill-rt-interview/.

Kirk, Russell. 1982. The Portable Conservative Reader. Viking Press.

———. 2019. Russell Kirk's Concise Guide to Conservatism. Simon and Schuster.

Kirschke, James J. 2005. Gouverneur Morris: Author, Statesman, and Man of the World. Macmillan.

Kissinger, Henry. n.d. "Henry Kissinger on Hamas Attacks Fallout: Germany Let in Too Many Foreigners." Politico. Accessed January 5, 2024. https://www.politico.eu/article/henry-kissinger-germany-let-in-way-too-many-foreigners/.

Klages, Ludwig. 2015. Cosmogonic Reflections: Selected Aphorisms from Ludwig Klages. Arktos.

Knox, John. 1687. The First Blast of the Trumpet against the Monstrous Regiment of Women ... By John Knox. M.D.LVIII. The British Library.

———. 1846a. The Works of John Knox. Edited by David Lain. Vol. 4. Edinburgh : Printed for the Wodrow Society.

———. 1846b. The Works of John Knox. Edited by David Lain. Vol. 1. Edinburgh : Printed for the Wodrow Society.

———. 1846c. The Works of John Knox. Edited by David Lain. Vol. 3. Edinburgh : Printed for the Wodrow Society.

———. 1850. Select Practical Writings of John Knox [Edited, with a Memoir, by T. Thomson].

———. 2021. The Collected Prayers of John Knox. Edited by Brian G. Najapfour. Grand Rapids, Michigan: Reformation Heritage Books.

———. n.d. The Works of John Knox. Vol. 2. Oxford: Printed for the Bannatyne Society, 1848. Accessed January 20, 2024.

Kockelmans, J. J. 2012. Heidegger on Art and Art Works. Springer Science & Business Media.

Koenig, Harry Corcoran. 1943. Principles for Peace: Selections from Papal Documents, Leo XIII to Pius XII. National Catholic Welfare Conference.

Kotesky, R.L. 1981. "Growing up Too Late, Too Soon." ChristianityToday.Com. March 13, 1981. https://www.christianity-today.com/ct/1981/march-13/growing-up-too-late-too-soon.html.

Kragt, Paul Earl. 2023. Deuteronomy: A Concise Theological Commentary. Independently published.

Kramer, Lloyd S. 2011a. Nationalism in Europe and America: Politics, Cultures, and Identities since 1775. UNC Press Books.

———. 2011b. Nationalism in Europe and America: Politics, Cultures, and Identities since 1775. UNC Press Books.

Kundera, Milan. 2000. The Book of Laughter and Forgetting. Faber and Faber.

Kunstler, James Howard. 1996. "Home From Nowhere." The Atlantic, September 1, 1996. https://www.theatlantic.com/magazine/archive/1996/09/home-from-nowhere/376664/.

Kuyper, Abraham. 1900. Cavinism: Six Lectures Delivered in the Theological Seminary at Princeton. Fleming H. Revell Company.

———. 1998. Abraham Kuyper: A Centennial Reader. Wm. B. Eerdmans Publishing.

———. 2016a. Common Grace: God's Gifts for a Fallen World, Volume 1. Lexham Press.

———. 2016b. On the Church. Bellingham, WA: Lexham Press.

Labor, American Federation of, Samuel Gompers, and Herman Gutstadt. 1908. Meat Vs. Rice: American Manhhod Against Asiatic Coolieism, Which Shall Survive? American Federation of Labor and printed as Senate document 137 (1902); reprinted with intro. and appendices by Asiatic Exclusion League.

Lactantius. 2008. The Divine Institutes, Books I–VII. CUA Press.

Ladd, Geroge Eldon. 1972. A Commentary on the Revelation of John. Eerdmans.

L'Amour, Louis. 2003. Sackett's Land. Random House Publishing Group.

Lange, John Peter. 2008. A Commentary on the Holy Scriptures: Revelation. Translated by E.R. Craven. Vol. 10. Lange's Commentary. Logos Research Edition.

Langella, Julien. 2020. Catholic & Identitarian: From Protest to Reconquest. Arktos.

Lasch, Christopher. 1991. The True and Only Heaven: Progress and Its Critics. W. W. Norton & Company.

Lee, Francis Nigel. n.d. The Christian Afrikaners: A Brief History of Calvinist Afrikanerdom from 1652 to 1980. Lectures Presented to Geneva Divinity School. Tyler, Texas. https://www.originofnations.org/books,%20papers/afrikaners. pdf.

Legge, James, Confucius, Mencius, Confucius. Chun qiu, and Ming Zuo zhuan Zuoqiu. 1893. The Chinese Classics. Oxford, Clarendon Press.

Legutko, Ryszard. 2016. The Demon in Democracy: Totalitarian Temptations in Free Societies. Encounter Books.

Leithart, Peter J. 2007. The Baptized Body. Canon Press & Book Service.

Leo XIII, Pope. 1890. "Sapientiae Christianae." Vatican. January 10, 1890. https://www.vatican.va/content/leo-xiii/en/ encyclicals/documents/hf_l-xiii_enc_10011890_sapientiae-christianae.html.

———. 1891. "Rerum Novarum." Vatican. May 15, 1891. https://www.vatican.va/content/leo-xiii/en/encyclicals/ documents/hf_l-xiii_enc_15051891_rerum-novarum.html.

———. 1895. "Immortale Dei." Vatican. November 1, 1895. https://www.vatican.va/content/leo-xiii/en/encycli-cals/documents/hf_l-xiii_enc_01111885_immortale-dei.html.

Lewis, C. S. 2001. Weight of Glory. Zondervan.

———. 2004. The Collected Letters of C.S. Lewis, Volume 3: Narnia, Cambridge, and Joy, 1950 - 1963. Zondervan.

———. 2009. The Collected Letters of C.S. Lewis, Volume 1: Family Letters, 1905-1931. Zondervan.

———. 2014. God in the Dock. Wm. B. Eerdmans Publishing.

———. 1991. The Four Loves. Houghton Mifflin Harcourt.

———. 2002. Present Concerns. Houghton Mifflin Harcourt.

———. 2017. The Abolition of Man: C.S. Lewis's Classic Essay on Objective Morality: A Critical Edition by Michael Ward. Lulu.com.

Lienhard, Joseph T., and Thomas C. Oden. 2014. Exodus, Leviticus, Numbers, Deuteronomy. InterVarsity Press.

Lincoln, Abraham. 1894a. Abraham Lincoln. Century Company.

———. 1894b. Speeches & Letters of Abraham Lincoln, 1832-1865. J.M. Dent & Company.

———. 1907. Life and Works of Abraham Lincoln. Current Literature Publishing Company.

———. 1989. Abraham Lincoln: Speeches and Writings Vol. 1 1832-1858 (LOA #45). Library of America.

———. 2008a. The Collected Works of Abraham Lincoln. Wildside Press LLC.

———. 2008b. The Collected Works of Abraham Lincoln. Wildside Press LLC.

List, Friedrich. 1916. The National System of Political Economy. Longmans, Green.

———. 2016. The Natural System of Political Economy. Routledge.

Littell, E. 1892. The Living Age. E. Littell & Company.

Livy. 1919. The History Of Rome, Books I and II With An English Translation. Translated by William Heinemann. Cambridge, MA: Harvard University Press.

———. 2005. The Early History of Rome, Books I-V. Translated by Aubrey de Sélincourt. Penguin Classics.

Lodge, Henry Cabot. 1902. A Fighting Frigate, and Other Essays and Addresses. C. Scribner's Sons.

———. 1906. A Frontier Town, and Other Essays. C. Scribner.

Longfellow, Henry Wadsworth. 1884. Twenty Poems from Henry Wadsworth Longfellow. Houghton, Mifflin.

———. 1901. Poems. T.Y. Crowell.

Longman, Tremper. 2001. Song of Songs. Wm. B. Eerdmans Publishing.

Loomis, Louis. 1964. Change in Medieval Society. Edited by S. Thrupp. New York: Appleton.

Lotter, Chas. 1999. Echoes of an African War. Covos-Day Books.

Lovecraft, H. P. 2016. The Lovecraft Compendium. Arcturus Publishing.

———. 1965. Selected Letters: 1932-1934. Arkham House.

———. 1968. Selected Letters. Arkham House.

Lowry, Rich. 2019. The Case for Nationalism. HarperCollins.

Luby, Thomas Clarke. 1863. "'82 And '29." The Irish People, November 1, 1863.

Lucian. 1905. The Works of Lucian of Samosata: Complete with Exceptions Specified in the Preface. Translated by Francis George Fowler, Henry Watson Fowler. At the Clarendon Press.

Ludmerer, Kenneth M. 1972. Genetics and American Society: A Historical Appraisal. Johns Hopkins University Press.

Lukacs, John. 1986. Immigration and Migration: A Historical Perspective. American Immigration Control Foundation.

Luther, Martin. 1883. First Principles of the Reformation: Or, the Ninety-Five Theses and the Three Primary Works of Dr. Martin Luther. John Murray.

———. 1955. Lectures on Genesis. Concordia Publishing House.

———. 1959. Large Catechism. Muhlenberg Press.

———. 1967. Luther's Works, Vol 46. Concordia Publishing House.

———. 1971. Luther's Works, Vol 47. Concordia Publishing House.

———. "Martin Luther (1483-1546): Address To The Nobility of the German Nation, 1520." Accessed January 15, 2024. https://sourcebooks.fordham.edu/mod/luther-nobility.asp.

Lytle, Andrew Nelson. 1992. A Wake for the Living. J.S. Sanders Books.

MacArthur, John. 1995. 1 Timothy. Moody Publishers.

———. 1996. Acts 13-28 MacArthur New Testament Commentary. Moody Publishers.

———. 2011. Luke 6-10 MacArthur New Testament Commentary. Moody Publishers.

Macatangay, Francis M. 2011. The Wisdom Instructions in the Book of Tobit. Walter de Gruyter.

MacCrie, Thomas. 1807. Statement of the Difference between the Profession of the Reformed Church of Scotland, as Adopted by Seceders, and the Profession Contained in the New Testimony ... to Which Are Added Reasons by the Ministers Who Protested against Acts of Synod, for Constituting Themselves into a Separate Presbytery, Etc. G. Caw.

MacCulloch, Diarmaid. 2010. Christianity: The First Three Thousand Years. Penguin.

Machen, J. Gresham. 2002. "Mountains and Why We Love Them." Edited by John Gresham Machen. Committee for the Historian of the Orthodox Presbyterian Church, 8.

———. 2009. Christianity and Liberalism, New Ed. Wm. B. Eerdmans Publishing.

———. 1915. The Literature and History of New Testament Times. Philadelphia : Presbyterian Board of Publication and Sabbath School Work.

Machen, John Gresham. 1951. What Is Christianity?: And Other Addresses. Eerdmans.

Machiavelli, Niccolò. 2005. The Prince. OUP Oxford.

———. 2009. Discourses on Livy. Edited by Julia Conaway Bondanella and Peter Bondanella. Reissue edition. Oxford New York: Oxford University Press.

MacIntyre, Alasdair. 2013. After Virtue. A&C Black.

Macpherson, John. 1883. Presbyterianism. Edinburgh: T. & T. Clark.

Madison, James. 1900. The Writings of James Madison: 1769-1783. Edited by Gaillard Hunt. G.P. Putnam's Sons ; New York.

———. 1904. The Writings of James Madison: 1787-1790. G.P. Putnam's Sons.

———. 1908. The Writings of James Madison: 1808-1819. G.P. Putnam's Sons.

Maistre, Joseph de. 1994. Maistre: Considerations on France. Cambridge University Press.

———. 1996. *Against Rousseau: On the State of Nature and On the Sovereignty of the People*. McGill-Queen's Press - MQUP.

Malory, Sir Thomas. 1899. *Le Morte Darthur : Sir Thomas Malory's Book of King Arthur and of His Noble Knights of the Round Table. : The Text of Caxton*. Macmillan.

Manser, Martin H. 1999. *Zondervan Dictionary of Bible Themes: The Accessible and Comprehensive Tool for Topical Studies*. ZondervanPublishingHouse.

Mansi, J. D., ed. 1936. *Sacrorum Conciliorum Nova et Amplissima Collectio. A Source Book for Medieval Economic History*. Milwaukee: The Bruce Publishing Co.

Martin, George R. R. 2013. *A Dance with Dragons: A Song of Ice and Fire: Book Five*. Random House Publishing Group.

Martin, Philip. n.d. *Making and Remaking America: Immigration into the United States*. Hoover Press.

Martin, Ralph P., and Peter H. Davids. 2010. *Dictionary of the Later New Testament & Its Developments: A Compendium of Contemporary Biblical Scholarship*. InterVarsity Press.

Marx, Karl. 1888. *Free Trade: A Speech Delivered Before the Democratic Club, Brussels, Belgium, Jan. 9, 1848. With Extract from La Misère de La Philosophie*. Lee & Shepard.

Marx, Karl, and Friedrich Engels. 2009. *The Communist Manifesto*. The Floating Press.

Massachusetts. 1814a. *The Charters and General Laws of the Colony and Province of Massachusetts Bay: Carefully Collected from the Publick Records and Ancient Printed Books. To Which Is Added an Appendix, Tending to Explain the Spirit, Progress and History of the Jurisprudence of the State; Especially in a Moral and Political View. Published by Order of the General Court*. T.B. Wait and Company.

———. 1814b. *The Charters and General Laws of the Colony and Province of Massachusetts Bay: Carefully Collected from the Publick Records and Ancient Printed Books. To Which Is Added an Appendix, Tending to Explain the Spirit, Progress and History of the Jurisprudence of the State; Especially in a Moral and Political View. Published by Order of the General Court*. T.B. Wait and Company.

McCarthy, Daniel. 2018. "Opinion | The Case for Trump's Tariffs and 'America First' Economics." The New York Times, March 9, 2018, sec. Opinion. https://www.nytimes.com/2018/03/08/opinion/trump-tariffs-economics.html.

———. 2019. "A New Conservative Agenda | Daniel McCarthy." First Things. March 1, 2019. https://www.firstthings.com/article/2019/03/a-new-conservative-agenda.

McClay, Wilfred M. 2020. *Land of Hope: An Invitation to the Great American Story*. Encounter Books.

McClintock, John, and James Strong. 1878. *Cyclopædia of Biblical, Theological, and Ecclesiastical Literature*. Harper.

McCormick, James. 1844. *The "Irish Rebellion of 1798," with Numerous Historical Sketches, Etc*. Dublin: James McCormick.

McCullough, David. 2015. *The Wright Brothers*. Simon and Schuster.

McDannell, Colleen. 2018. *Religions of the United States in Practice, Volume 1*. Princeton University Press.

McKay, John P., Bennett D. Hill, John Buckler, Clare Haru Crowston, Merry E. Wiesner-Hanks, and Joe Perry. 2010. *A History of Western Society, Volume 1: From Antiquity to the Enlightenment*. Macmillan.

McKinley, William. 1893. *Speeches and Addresses of William McKinley: From His Election to Congress to the Present Time*. D. Appleton.

———. 1894. *Speeches and Addresses from His Election to Congress to the Present Time*. Appleton.

Mcknight, Scot. n.d. "The (so-Called) 'Traditional' Argument Is Not Traditional." Jesus Creed | A Blog by Scot McKnight. Accessed January 27, 2024. https://christianitytoday.com/scot-mcknight/2020/december/so-called-traditional-argument-is-not-traditional.html.

McWhiney, Grady. 1988. *Cracker Culture: Celtic Ways in the Old South*. University of Alabama Press.

Meilaender, Gilbert. 2005. *Bioethics: A Primer for Christians*. Wm. B. Eerdmans Publishing.

"Memorandum of Discussion at the 409th NSC Meeting." 1959. https://history.state.gov/historicaldocuments/frus1958-60v03mSupp/d161.

Mettinger, Tryggve N. D. 1971. *Solomonic State Officials: A Study of the Civil Government Officials of the Israelite Monarchy*. Gleerup.

Michelet, Jules. 1846. *The Life of Luther Gathered from His Own Writings*. Whittaker and Company.

Mill, John Stuart. 1861. *Considerations on Representative Government*. Parker, Son, and Bourn.

———. 1866. *Principles of Political Economy: With Some of Their Applications to Social Philosophy*. Longmans,

Green, Reader, and Dyer.

———. 1905. A System of Logic, Ratiocinative and Inductive: Being a Connected View of the Principles of Evidence and the Methods of Scientific Investigation. G. Routledge.

Miller, Marion Mills. 1913. Great Debates in American History: Economic and Social Questions, Part 2; with an Introduction by C. R. Van Hise. Current literature publishing Company.

Milson, Andrew J., Chara Haeussler Bohan, Perry L. Glanzer, and J. Wesley Null. 2010. American Educational Thought - 2nd Ed.: Essays from 1640-1940. IAP.

Milton, John. 1961. Areopagitica. Oxford University Press.

Mises, Ludwig Von. 1944. Omnipotent Government: The Rise of the Total State and Total War. Yale University Press.

Mohler, Dr R. Albert. 2008. Desire and Deceit: The Real Cost of the New Sexual Tolerance. Crown Publishing Group.

———. 2018. "Report in Slavery and Racism in the History of the Southern Baptist Theological Seminary." The Southern Baptist Theological Seminary. December 12, 2018. https://www.sbts.edu/history/southern-project/.

Montaigne, Michel de. 1965. The Complete Essays of Montaigne. Stanford University Press.

Montesquieu, Charles de Secondat baron de. 1989. Montesquieu: The Spirit of the Laws. Cambridge University Press.

Moore, Frank. 1871. American Eloquence: A Collection of Speeches and Addresses by the Most Eminent Orators of America. D. Appleton and Company.

Morrill, James. 1857. The Congressional Globe: Containing the Debates and Proceedings of the ... Session of the ... Congress ; Also of the Special Session of the Senate.

Morris, Dr Henry M. 1991. The Beginning of the World: A Scientific Study of Genesis 1 - 11. New Leaf Publishing Group.

Morris, Gouverneur. 2012. To Secure the Blessings of Liberty: Selected Writings. Edited by J. Jackson Barlow. Indianapolis: Liberty Fund,.

Morris, Henry Madison. 1976. The Genesis Record: A Scientific and Devotional Commentary on the Book of Beginnings. Baker Book House.

Morris, Leon. 1988. The Epistle to the Romans,. Edited by Carson, D.A. The Pillar New Testament Commentary. Grand Rapids: Eerdmans.

Morris, Leon L. 2008. 1 Corinthians. Tyndale New Testament Commentary. InterVarsity Press.

Moscow Patriarchate. 2016. "Economy in the Conditions of Globalization (Orthodox Ethical View)." May 23, 2016. https://katehon.com/ru/article/ekonomika-v-usloviyah-globalizacii-pravoslavnyy-eticheskiy-vzglyad.

MS, Robert W. Malone MD. 2022. "Interview with ARCHBISHOP CARLO MARIA VIGANÒ APOSTOLIC NUNCIO." Substack newsletter. Who Is Robert Malone (blog). June 30, 2022. https://rwmalonemd.substack.com/p/interview-with-archbishop-carlo-maria.

Muller, James W. 1999. Churchill's "Iron Curtain" Speech Fifty Years Later. University of Missouri Press.

Muller, Jerry Z. 2008. "Us and Them." Foreign Affairs, March 2, 2008. https://www.foreignaffairs.com/articles/europe/2008-03-02/us-and-them.

Muss-Arnolt, William. 1904. Assyrian and Babylonian Literature: Selected Transactions, With a Critical Introduction by Robert Francis Harper. New York: D. Appleton & Company.

NA, NA. 2016. Creating An American Culture: 1775-1800. Springer.

Nason, Elias, and Thomas Russell. 1876. The Life and Public Services of Henry Wilson: Late Vice-President of the United States. B.B. Russell.

Naturalization, United States Congress House Committee on Immigration and. 1912. Relative to the Further Restriction of Immigration: Hearings Before the Committee on Immigration and Naturalization, House of Representatives, Sixty-Second Congress, Second Session. U.S. Government Printing Office.

Nester, William R. 2019. Theodore Roosevelt and the Art of American Power: An American for All Time. Rowman & Littlefield.

Network, Alexander Jun, SOLA. 2022. "The Journey and Value of Asian American Churches: An Interview with Dr. Alexander Jun." SOLA Network (blog). September 22, 2022. https://sola.network/article/journey-value-of-asian-american-churches-interview/.

Newman, James R. 2000. The World of Mathematics. Рипол Классик.

Nichols, James. 1981. Puritan Sermons 1659–1689 (6 Vols.). 6 vols. Wheaton, IL: Richard Owen Roberts.

Niles, John D. 2007. Beowulf: An Illustrated Edition. Translated by Seamus Heaney. First Edition. New York: W. W. Norton & Company.

Nisbet, Robert A. 1976a. The Social Philosophers. Paladin.

———. 1976b. Twilight of Authority. Heinemann.

Noll, Mark A. 2016. In the Beginning Was the Word: The Bible in American Public Life, 1492-1783. Oxford University Press.

Obama, Barack. 2006. The Audacity of Hope: Thoughts on Reclaiming the American Dream. Crown.

Ólason, Páll Eggert. 1919. Menn Og Menntir Siðskiptaaldarinnar á Íslandi v. 1. https://hdl.handle.net/2027/umn.319510012707352?urlappend=%3Bseq=21.

O'Leary, Brendan. 2019. A Treatise on Northern Ireland, Volume I: Colonialism. Oxford University Press.

Olson, Carl E. n.d. "Cardinal Sarah: 'I Believe That We Are at a Turning Point in the History of the Church.'" Accessed January 28, 2024. https://www.catholicworldreport.com/2019/09/23/cardinal-sarah-i-believe-that-we-are-at-a-turning-point-in-the-history-of-the-church/.

Oppian, Colluthus, and Tryphiodorus. 1963. Oppian, Colluthus, Tryphiodorus. W. Heinemann.

Origen. 1869. Ante-Nicene Christian Library: The Writings of Origen. Translations of the Writings of the Fathers Down to A.D. 325 · Volume 12. T. and T. Clark.

———. 1957. The Song of Songs: Commentary and Homilies. Paulist Press.

———. 1982. Homilies on Genesis and Exodus. Edited by Hermigild Dressler. Translated by Ronald E. Heine. Vol. 71. The Fathers of the Church. Washington, DC: The Catholic University of America Press.

———. 2006. Commentary on the Gospel According to John, Books 13-32. CUA Press.

Origen, Alexander Roberts, and Sir James Donaldson. 1872. Ante-Nicene Christian Library: Origen Contra Celsum. T. and T. Clark.

Orr, William F. and Walther, James Arthur. 1976. The Yale Anchor Bible, 1 Corinthians: A New Translation. Vol. 32. New Haven: Yale University Press.

Outhwaite, William, and Luke Martell. 1998. The Sociology of Politics: Political Ideologies and Movements. E. Elgar.

Ovid. 1709. Ovid's Art of Love. In Three Books. Together with His Remedy of Love. Translated by Dryden. The British Library. J. Tonson.

———. 1922. Metamorphoses. Translated by Brookes More. Boston: Cornhill Publishing Co.

———. 1933. Ovid's Metamorphoses. Translated by Brookes More. University of California: Cornhill Publishing Company.

———. 2014. The Metamorphoses. Translated by A.S. Kline. Poetry In Translation.

———. "The Heroides: VIII to XV." Translated by A.S. Kline. Poetry In Translation. Accessed January 8, 2024. https://www.poetryintranslation.com/PITBR/Latin/Heroides8-15.php.

Owsley, Frank Lawrence. 2008. Plain Folk of the Old South. LSU Press.

Palgrave, Francis Turner, ed. 1861. The Golden Treasury of The Best Songs and Lyrical Poems in the English Language. Cambridge: Macmillan.

Palmer, B. M. 2018. The Family in Its Civil and Churchly Aspects: An Essay, in Two Parts (Classic Reprint). Fb&c Limited.

Paul VI, Pope. 1964. "Lumen Gentium." Vatican. November 21, 1964. https://www.vatican.va/archive/hist_councils/ii_vatican_council/documents/vat-ii_const_19641121_lumen-gentium_en.html.

———. 1965. "Dei Verbum." Vatican. November 18, 1965. https://www.vatican.va/archive/hist_councils/ii_vatican_council/documents/vat-ii_const_19651118_dei-verbum_en.html.

Peabody, Selim Hobart. 1885. American Patriotism: Speeches, Letters and Other Papers Which Illustrate the Foundation, the Development, the Preservation of the United States of America. Millar.

Peace, Catholic Association for International. 1935. Pamphlet.

Pentin, Edward. 2019. "Cardinal Sarah's Cri de Coeur: The Catholic Church Has Lost Its Sense of the Sacred." NCR. September 23, 2019. https://www.ncregister.com/interview/cardinal-sarah-s-cri-de-coeur-the-catholic-church-has-lost-its-sense-of-the-sacred.

Percy, Walker. 2011. Lost in the Cosmos: The Last Self-Help Book. Open Road Media.

Perkins, William. 2015. The Works of William Perkins, Volume 2. Reformation Heritage Books.

Pesch, Heinrich. 2002a. Lehrbuch Der Nationalökonomie: The Satisfaction of a Nation's Wants as the Purpose of the National Economy and Production. Edwin Mellen Press.

———. 2002b. Lehrbuch Der Nationalökonomie: The Satisfaction of a Nation's Wants as the Purpose of the National Economy and Production. Edwin Mellen Press.

Peter, Lange, John. n.d. Lange's Commentary on the Holy Scripture, Volume 6: Matthew to John. Delmarva Publications, Inc.

Petersen, Rodney L. 2014. Divinings: Religion at Harvard: From Its Origins in New England Ecclesiastical History to the 175th Anniversary of The Harvard Divinity School, 1636–1992. Vandenhoeck & Ruprecht.

Peterson, David. 2009. The Acts of the Apostles. Wm. B. Eerdmans Publishing.

Pfizer, Gustav. 1840. The Life of Luther with Notices and Extracts of His Popular Writings. Society for the promotion of popular instruction.

Philo. 1995. The Works of Philo: Complete and Unabridged. Translated by Yonge, Charles Duke. Peabody, MA: Hendrickson Academic.

Phrygius, Dares. 2017. History of the Fall of Troy. Translated by R. M. Frazer. Independently Published. https://www.theoi.com/Text/DaresPhrygius.html.

Pindar. 1990. "Pythian Odes." Translated by Diane Svarlien. Perseus Tufts Edu. 1990.

Pius XI. 1937. "Mit Brennender Sorge." Vatican. March 14, 1937. https://www.vatican.va/content/pius-xi/en/encyclicals/documents/hf_p-xi_enc_14031937_mit-brennender-sorge.html.

Pius XII. 1958. "Ad Apostolorum Principis." Vatican. June 29, 1958. https://www.vatican.va/content/pius-xii/en/encyclicals/documents/hf_p-xii_enc_29061958_ad-apostolorum-principis.html.

———. n.d. "Summi Pontificatus (October 20, 1939) | PIUS XII." Accessed February 25, 2024. https://www.vatican.va/content/pius-xii/en/encyclicals/documents/hf_p-xii_enc_20101939_summi-pontificatus.html.

Plato. 1924. The Dialogues of Plato. Oxford University Press, American branch.

———. 1941. Plato's Republic. Modern Library.

———. 1953. Dialogues. Clarendon Press.

———. 1961. Plato: With an English Translation. Heineman.

———. n.d.-a. "Crtio." Translated by Benjamin Jowett. MIT Classics Archive. Accessed January 4, 2024. https://classics.mit.edu/Plato/crito.html.

———. n.d.-b. "Laws." Translated by Benjamin Jowett. MIT Classics Archive. Accessed January 4, 2024. https://classics.mit.edu/Plato/laws.4.iv.html.

———. n.d.-c. "Lysis, Plato in Twelve Volumes, Vol. 8 Translated by W.R.M. Lamb. Cambridge, MA, Harvard University Press; London, William Heinemann Ltd." Accessed January 8, 2024. http://data.perseus.org/catalog/urn:cts:greekLit:tlg0059.tlg020.perseus-eng1.

———. n.d.-d. "The Republic." Translated by Benjamin Jowett. MIT Classics Archive. Accessed January 4, 2024. https://classics.mit.edu/Plato/republic.7.vi.html.

Pliny, the Elder. 1855. The Natural History of Pliny, Vol. 5. U.S. National Library of Medicine. London: Henry G. Bohn. http://archive.org/details/57011150RX5.nlm.nih.gov.

Plummer, Joseph. 2014. Tragedy and Hope 101: The Illusion of Justice, Freedom, and Democracy. Brushfire Publishing.

Plutarch. 1865. Lives. Translated by John Dryden. Vol. 1. 5 vols. Boston: Little, Brown, and Company.

———. 1919. Plutarch's Lives. Translated by Bernadotte Perrin. Vol. 7. W. Heinemann.

Point, Editors of Rock. 2022. The Constitution of the United States of America and Other Writings of the Founding Fathers. Rock Point.

Politico. 2023. "Henry Kissinger on Hamas Attacks Fallout: Germany Let in Too Many Foreigners." POLITICO (blog). October 11, 2023. https://www.politico.eu/article/henry-kissinger-germany-let-in-way-too-many-foreigners/.

Poole, Matthew. 1853. Annotations Upon the Holy Bible: Wherein the Sacred Text Is Inserted, and Various Readings Annexed, Together with the Parallel Scriptures; the More Difficult Terms in Each Verse Are Explained, Seeming Contradictions Reconciled, Questions and Doubts Resolved, and the Whole Text Opened. J. Nisbet.

Pope John Paul. 2005. Memory and Identity: Conversations at the Dawn of a Millennium. Random House.

Popescu, Alexandru. 2018. Petre Tutea: Between Sacrifice and Suicide. Routledge.

Porter, Stanley E. 2023. The Pastoral Epistles: A Commentary on the Greek Text. Baker Books.

President, United States. 1837. The Addresses and Messages of the Presidents of the United States, to Congress: Comprising All the Inaugural, Annual, Special, and Farewell Addresses and Messages. C. Lohman.

Pringle, Nicholas. 2012. The Unknown Warriors. Lulu.

Prinsterer, G. Groen van. 2022. Liberty, Equality, Fraternity: A Refutation of Liberalism. RefCon Press.

Pritchard, James B. 2016. Ancient Near Eastern Texts Relating to the Old Testament with Supplement. Princeton University Press.

Proper, Emberson Edward. 1900. Colonial Immigration Laws: A Study of the Regulation of Immigration by the English Colonies in America. Columbia University Press.

Provan, Iain. 2011. Ecclesiastes, Song of Songs. Zondervan Academic.

Quasten, J. and Plumpe, J.C., eds. 1948. The Didache, The Epistle of Barnabas, The Epistles and the Martyrdom of St. Polycarp, The Fragments of Papias and The Epistle to Diognetus. 6th ed. New York: Newman Press.

Raimondo, Justin. 1998. "Buchananism: Two Opinions - Chronicles." July 1, 1998. https://chroniclesmagazine.org/reviews/buchananism-two-opinions/, https://chroniclesmagazine.org/reviews/buchananism-two-opinions/.

Ramelli, Ilaria. 2009. Hierocles the Stoic: Elements of Ethics, Fragments and Excerpts. Society of Biblical Lit.

Randall, Henry Stephens. 1858. The Life of Thomas Jefferson: In 3 Volumes. Derby & Jackson.

Ranum, Orest A. 1975. National Consciousness, History, and Political Culture in Early-Modern Europe. Johns Hopkins University Press.

Raymond, Daniel. 1823. The Elements of Political Economy. F. Lucas jun. and E. J. Coale.

Renan, Ernest. 1996. Qu'est-Ce Qu'une Nation? Tapir Press.

———. 2018. What Is a Nation? And Other Political Writings. Columbia University Press.

Reynolds, Gerald A. n.d. "The Impact of Illegal Immigration on the Wages and Employment Opportunities of Black Workers | U.S. Commission on Civil Rights." Accessed February 15, 2024. https://www.usccr.gov/reports/2010/impact-illegal-immigration-wages-and-employment-opportunities-black-workers.

Reynolds, Susan. 1997. Kingdoms and Communities in Western Europe, 900-1300. Clarendon Press.

Richards, Greg. n.d. "Why Is Trump Fighting the Trade War?" Accessed January 22, 2024. https://www.americanthinker.com/articles/2018/08/why_is_trump_fighting_the_trade_war.html.

Richardson, James D. 1917. A Compilation of the Messages and Papers of the Presidents. 20 vols. New York: Bureau of National literature and art.

Ridderbos, Herman N. 1977. Paul, an Outline of His Theology. S.P.C.K.

Riddle, John. 2012. Acts of the Apostles. John Ritchie Limited.

Rix, Robert. 2014. The Barbarian North in Medieval Imagination: Ethnicity, Legend, and Literature. Routledge.

Roberts, Alastair. 2017. "President Trump's Executive Order and the Moral Confusion of the Immigration Debate." Alastair's Adversaria (blog). January 30, 2017. https://alastairadversaria.com/2017/01/30/president-trumps-executive-order-and-the-moral-confusion-of-the-immigration-debate/.

———. n.d. "Brexit and the Moral Vision of Nationhood | Mere Orthodoxy." Accessed January 22, 2024. https://mereorthodoxy.com/political-social-earthquake-brexit-future-britain.

———. "The Refugee Crisis and Christian Hope." Accessed January 22, 2024. https://www.reformation21.org/articles/over-the-past-week-the.php.

———. "Welcoming the Stranger: A Final Immigration Response." Theopolis Institute (blog). Accessed January 22, 2024. https://theopolisinstitute.com/conversations/welcoming-the-stranger-a-final-immigration-response/.

Roberts, Alexander, Sir James Donaldson, Arthur Cleveland Coxe, and Allan Menzies. 1885. The Ante-Nicene Fathers: Tertullian, Pt. 4th; Minucius Felix; Commodian; Origen, Pts. 1st and 2d. C. Scribner's Sons.

———. 1886. The Ante-Nicene Fathers: Hippolytus, Cyprian, Caius, Novatian, Appendix. Christian Literature Company.

Roberts, Reverend Alexander. 2007. The Ante-Nicene Fathers: The Writings of the Fathers Down to A. D. 325, Volume VII Fathers of the Third and Fourth Century - Lactantius, Venantius, Ast. Cosimo, Inc.

Robinson, J. Armitage. 1916. Texts and Studies: Contributions to Biblical and Patristic Literature. Cambridge University Press.

Roosevelt, Teddy. 1905. Tariff League Bulletin. Vol. 35. American Protective Tariff League.

Roosevelt, Theodore. 1921. Roosevelt in the Kansas City Star: War-Time Editorials. Houghton Mifflin.

———. 1925. The Foes of Our Own Household; The Great Adventure; Letters to His Children. C. Scribner's sons.

———. 1951. The Letters of Theodore Roosevelt. Edited by Elting Elmore Morison. Mass.

Röpke, Wilhelm. 1960. A Humane Economy: The Social Framework of the Free Market. H. Regnery Company.

Ross, Edward Alsworth. 1914. The Old World in the New: The Significance of Past and Present Immigration to the American People. Johnson Reprint Corporation.

Rothbard, Murray Newton. 2000. Egalitarianism as a Revolt Against Nature and Other Essays. Ludwig von Mises Institute.

Rousseau, Jean Jacques. 2016. The Social Contract & Discourses. Lulu.com.

———. 2018. Rousseau: The Social Contract and Other Later Political Writings. Cambridge University Press.

Rousseau, Richard. 2001. Human Dignity and the Common Good: The Great Papal Social Encyclicals from Leo XIII to John Paul II. Bloomsbury Publishing USA.

Rozwenc, Edwin Charles. 1972. Reconstruction in the South. Heath.

Rumburg, H. Rondel. 2020. One Blood--Many Races. Independently Published.

Rushdoony, R. J. 1993. RR187AV87 - Justice and World Law. https://pocketcollege.com/transcript/RR187AV87.html.

———. 1994a. RR161DD198 - War. Easy Chair Number 308. https://pocketcollege.com/transcript/RR161DD198.html.

———. 1994b. RR161DL209 - Immigration. Easy Chair Number 321. https://pocketcollege.com/transcript/RR161DL209.html.

———. 2009a. The Biblical Philosophy of History. Chalcedon Foundation.

———. 2009b. The Institutes of Biblical Law Vol. 1. Chalcedon Foundation.

———. 2009c. Numbers: Volume IV of Commentaries on the Pentateuch. Chalcedon Foundation.

———. 2010. Tents of Shem. Audio Sermon. Studies In Early Genesis. https://chalcedon.edu/resources/audio/tents-of-shem.

———. 2014. The One and the Many: Studies in the Philosophy of Order and Ultimacy. Chalcedon Foundation.

———. 2018. The Easy Chair: Envy. https://soundcloud.com/rushdoonyradio/191-envy-2?utm_source=clipboard&utm_campaign=wtshare&utm_medium=widget&utm_content=https%253A%252F%252Fsoundcloud.com%252Frushdoonyradio%252F191-envy-2.

———. 2019. This Independent Republic. Chalcedon Foundation.

———. n.d. God's Plan For Victory: The Meaning of Postmillennialism.

———. RR130AT83 - The Virgin Birth & Property. Digital. Restitution & Forgiveness. Accessed January 27, 2024. https://pocketcollege.com/transcript/RR130AT83.html.

———. n.d.-b. RR171G13 - Calling Versus Presumption. Accessed January 27, 2024. https://pocketcollege.com/transcript/RR171G13.html.

———. n.d.-c. RR197T35 - Enemies In and Out of the Church. Accessed January 27, 2024. https://pocketcollege.com/transcript/RR197T35.html.

———. n.d.-d. "RR4114b - The Eschatology of Covenant Man." Accessed January 27, 2024. https://pocketcollege.com/transcript/RR4114b.html.

Rushdoony, Rousas John. 1991. The Roots of Reconstruction. Vallecito, Calif: Ross House Books.

———. 1995. Politics of Guilt and Pity. Vallecito, Calif: Ross House Books.

———. 2005. Leviticus: Volume III of Commentaries on the Pentateuch. Ross House Books.

———. "RR161DL209 - Immigration." Accessed January 15, 2024. https://pocketcollege.com/transcript/RR161DL209.html.

Rushton, J. Philippe. 1998. "Race Is More Than Just Skin Deep: A Psychologist's View." Mankind Quarterly 39 (2). https://doi.org/10.46469/mq.1998.39.2.6.

Ruskin, John. 1862. "Unto This Last": Four Essays on the First Principles of Political Economy. Smith, Elder and Company.

Russell, Bertrand. 2017. The Scientific Outlook. Routledge.

Russell, James C. 1996. The Germanization of Early Medieval Christianity: A Sociohistorical Approach to Religious Transformation. Oxford University Press.

Rutherford, Samuel. 1843. Lex, Rex: The Law and the Prince, a Dispute for the Just Prerogative of King and People, Containing the Reasons and Causes of the Defensive Wars of the Kingdom of Scotland, and of Their Expedition for the Ayd and Help of Their Brethren of England. In Which a Full Answer Is given to a Seditious Pamphlet, Intituled, Sacro-Sancta Regum Majestas, Penned by J. Maxwell. By S. Rutherford. [Followed by] De Jure Regni apud Scotos; a Dialogue, Tr. by R. Macfarlan (Repr. from the Ed. of 1799).

Ryan, M.J. 1908. The Catholic Encyclopedia. 3 vols. New York: Robert Appleton Company.

Ryken, Philip Graham. 2012. Exodus: Saved for God's Glory. Crossway Books.

Sacred Bishops' Council of the Russian Orthodox Church. 2000. "The Basis of the Social Concept, Church And Nation." Jubilee Bishop's Council of the Russian Orthodox Church. https://mospatusa.com/files/THE-BASIS-OF-THE-SO-CIAL-CONCEPT.pdf.

Salmond, Charles Adamson. 1888. Princetoniana: Charles & A. A. Hodge: With Class and Table Talk of Hodge the Younger. Scribner & Welford.

Salyer, Jerry. 2020. "Patriotism, Poland, and Cardinal Sarah." February 16, 2020. https://www.catholicworldreport.com/2020/02/16/patriotism-poland-and-cardinal-sarah/.

Samuelson, Paul Anthony. 1980. Economics: To Accompany Samuelson: Economics, Eleventh Ed. Study Guide. McGraw-Hill.

Santvoord, George Van. 1851. Life of Algernon Sidney: With Sketches of Some of His Contemporaries and Extracts from His Correspondence and Political Writings. Scribner.

Sappho. n.d. "Sappho (630 BC–570 BC) - Poems and Fragments." Translated by A.S. Kline. Poetry In Translation. Accessed January 5, 2024. https://www.poetryintranslation.com/PITBR/Greek/Sappho.php.

Sarah, Robert, and Nicolas Diat. 2019. The Day Is Now Far Spent. Ignatius Press.

Sargent, Epes. 1854. The Life and Public Services of Henry Clay, Down to 1848. Miller, Orton & Mulligan.

Saunders, Frederick. 1893. Addresses, Historical and Patriotic, Centennial and Quadrennial, Delivered in the Several States of the Union: July 4th, 1876-1883. E.B. Treat.

Saxo (Grammaticus). 1894. The First Nine Books of the Danish History. Edited by Oliver Elton. London: University Library Basel.

Schaff, Philip. 1881. A Dictionary of the Bible: Including Biography, Natural History, Geography, Topography, Archaeology, and Literature. American Sunday-School Union.

———. 1895. The American Church History Series: A History of the Presbyterian Churches, by R.E. Thompson. Christian literature Company.

———. 1988. A Select Library of Nicene and Post-Nicene Fathers of the Christian Church: Second Series. T & T Clark.

———. 2007a. Nicene and Post-Nicene Fathers First Series, St. Augustine: Gospel of John, First Epistle of John, Soliloquies. Cosimo, Inc.

———. 2007b. Nicene and Post-Nicene Fathers: Second Series, Volume VII Cyril of Jerusalem, Gregory Nazianzen. Cosimo, Inc.

———. 1912. A Select Library of Nicene and Post-Nicene Fathers of the Christian Church: St. Jerome: Letters and Select Works. 1912. Christian Literature Company.

Schall, James V. n.d. "15 Lies at the Basis of Our Culture." Accessed February 12, 2024. https://www.catholicworldreport.com/2014/01/31/15-lies-at-the-basis-of-our-culture/.

Schama, Simon. 1988. The Embarrassment of Riches: An Interpretation of Dutch Culture in the Golden Age. University of California Press.

Schlesinger, Arthur Meier. 1998. Disuniting of America Revised and Enlarged: Reflections On A Multicultural Society. W. W. Norton & Company.

Schlossberg, Herbert. 1993. Idols for Destruction: The Conflict of Christian Faith and American Culture. Crossway.

Scott, Joan Wallach. 2010. The Politics of the Veil. Princeton University Press.

Scott, Walter. 1805. The Lay of the Last Minstrel: A Poem. Longman, Hurst, Rees, and Orme, Paternoster-row, and A. Constable and Company Edinburgh.

————. 1872. Rob Roy. J.R. Osgood and Company.

Scruton, Roger. 1991. Conservative Texts: An Anthology. Macmillan.

————. 2006a. England and the Need for Nations. Civitas.

————. 2006b. England: An Elegy. A&C Black.

————. 2014a. Our Church: A Personal History of the Church of England. Atlantic Books.

————. 2014b. How to Be a Conservative. A&C Black.

————. 2014c. How to Think Seriously about the Planet: The Case for an Environmental Conservatism. Oxford University Press.

————. 2015. Fools, Frauds and Firebrands: Thinkers of the New Left. Bloomsbury Publishing.

————. 2018. Conservatism: An Invitation to the Great Tradition. St. Martin's Publishing Group.

————. 2021. Confessions of a Heretic, Revised Edition. New York Review of Books.

Seland, Torrey. 2014. Reading Philo: A Handbook to Philo of Alexandria. Wm. B. Eerdmans Publishing.

Seldon, John. 1652. Of the Dominion, Or, Ownership of the Sea Two Books ... Written at First in Latin, and Entituled, Mare Clausum ... Translated ... with Som Additional Evidences and Discourses by Marchamont Nedham. (Dominium Maris, Or, the Dominion of the Sea. Expressing the Title, Which the Venetians Pretend Unto the Sole Dominion, and Absolute Sovereigntie of the Adriatick Sea. Translated Out of Italian. [The Preface Signed: Κλαρεαμοντος.]). William Du-Gard. https://quod.lib.umich.edu/e/eebo/A59088.0001.001/1:7.1.4?rgn=div3;view=toc.

Seneca, Jeffrey. n.d. Epistles, Volume I. Translated by Richard Gummere. Vol. 1. 3 vols. Loeb Classical Library. Accessed January 5, 2024.

Shain, Barry Alan. 2014. The Declaration of Independence in Historical Context: American State Papers, Petitions, Proclamations, and Letters of the Delegates to the First National Congresses. Yale University Press.

Shaw, Carl A. 2018. Euripides: Cyclops: A Satyr Play. Bloomsbury Publishing.

Shepard, Thomas. 1853. The Parable of the Ten Virgins Opened and Applied: Being the Substance of Divers Sermons on Matth. 25. 1-13. ... Published from the Authours Own Notes ... by J. Mitchell, ... T. Shepard, Son to the ... Author. Aberdeen: George And Robert King.

Sherrow, Victoria. 2006. Encyclopedia of Hair: A Cultural History. Bloomsbury Academic.

Shipler, David K., and Special To the New York Times. 1982. "ISRAEL BURIES BONES OF ANCIENT WARRIORS." The New York Times, May 12, 1982, sec. World. https://www.nytimes.com/1982/05/12/world/israel-buries-bones-of-ancient-warriors.html.

Sidney, Algernon. 1750. Discourses Concerning Government. Vol. 1. G. Hamilton and J. Balfour.

————. 1805. Discourses Concerning Government. Vol. 2. C. P. Wayne, for the Rev. M. L. Weems.

Siedentop, Larry. 2014. Inventing the Individual: The Origins of Western Liberalism. Harvard University Press.

Sienkiewicz, Henryk. 1925. Quo Vadis: A Tale of the Time of Nero. Grosset & Dunlap.

Silas Von Lindt, dir. 2010. Poythress on Babel [Christianity For Kinism]. https://www.youtube.com/watch?v=A9VCkVz-doIw.

Silberner, Edmund. 2015. The Problem of War. Princeton University Press.

Simeon, Charles, and Jean Claude. 1832a. Horae Homileticae. London, Holdsworth. http://archive.org/details/horae-homileticae21simeuoft.

————. 1832b. Horae Homileticae, or Discourses, Now First Digested into One Continued Series, and Forming a Commentary upon Every Book of the Old and New Testament, to Which Is Annexed an Improved Edition of a Translation of Claude's Essay on the Composition of a Sermon. London, Holdsworth. http://archive.org/details/horaehomileticae21simeuoft.

Sismondi, Jean-Charles-Léonard Simonde. 1847. Political Economy, and the Philosophy of Government: A Series of Essays Selected from the Works of M. de Sismondi : With an Historical Notice of His Life and Writings by M. Mignet. J. Chapman.

Skinner, Thomas Harvey. 1851. Love of Country: A Discourse, Delivered on Thanksgiving Day, December 12th, 1850, in the Bleecker Street Church. E. French.

Smith, Adam. 1880. Essays Philosophical and Literary. Ward, Lock.

————. 2012. The Theory of Moral Sentiments. Courier Corporation.

———. 1843. An Inquiry Into the Nature and Causes of the Wealth of Nations. C. Knight ; J. Cornish.

Smith, Anthony D. 1986. The Ethnic Origins of Nations. Basil Blackwell.

———. 1999. "Gastronomy or Geology? The Role of Nationalism in the Reconstruction of Nations." In Myths and Memories of the Nation, by Anthony D Smith, 163–86. Oxford University PressOxford. https://doi.org/10.1093/oso/9780198295341.003.0007.

———. 2003. Chosen Peoples. Oxford University Press.

———. 2008. The Cultural Foundations of Nations: Hierarchy, Covenant, and Republic. John Wiley & Sons.

Smith, Morton. 1964. "The Racial Problem Facing America." The Presbyterian Guardian 33 (October). https://opc.org/cfh/guardian/Volume_33/1964-10.pdf.

Solzhenitsyn, Alexander. n.d. "The Nobel Prize in Literature 1970." NobelPrize.Org. Accessed February 17, 2024. https://www.nobelprize.org/prizes/literature/1970/solzhenitsyn/lecture/.

Sophocles. 2020. The Theban Plays: Oedipus Rex, Oedipus at Colonus and Antigone. Translated by George Theodoridis. Independently published.

South Africa. Archives Commission. n.d. "Suid-Afrikaanse Argiefstukke. Transvaal" Vol. 1 (1949)-v. 7.

Sowell, Thomas. 2010. Black Rednecks and White Liberals. Basic Books.

———. 2019. Discrimination and Disparities. Basic Books.

Sparks, Jared, Edward Everett, James Russell Lowell, and Henry Cabot Lodge. 1911. The North American Review. O. Everett.

Speer, Robert E. 1910. Christianity and the Nations. Fleming H. Revell Company.

Spence, Jonathan. 2012. Treason By The Book: Traitors, Conspirators and Guardians of an Emperor. Penguin UK.

Spengler, Oswald. 2021. The Decline of the West: Form and Actuality. Arktos 2021 ed. edition. London: Arktos Media Ltd.

Spengler, Oswald, Arthur Helps, and Charles Francis Atkinson. 1991. The Decline of the West. Oxford University Press.

Sproul, R.C. 1990. "Parables: Kernels Of Truth." Tabletalk Magazine, August 1990.

Spurgeon, Charles. 2011. The New Park Street Pulpit, Volume 1. Passmore And Alabaster.

———. 1879. The Metropolitan Tabernacle Pulpit: Sermons Preached and Revised. Passmore & Alabaster. https://www.spurgeon.org/resource-library/sermons/to-those-who-are-angry-with-their-godly-friends/.

———. 1965. Men of the New Testament. Marshall, Morgan & Scott.

———. 2017. Spurgeon's Sermons Volume 10: 1864. Lulu.com.

———. n.d. Spurgeon's Sermons Volume 14: 1868. Lulu.com.

St. Herman of Alaska Brotherhood, ed. 2014. The Royal Passion-Bearers of Russia: Their Life and Service. St. Herman of Alaska Brotherhood.

Stăniloae, Dumitru. 1939. Ortodoxie şi românism. Tiparul Tipografiei Arhidiecezane.

Statius, Publius Papinius. 1955. Statius: Silvae. Thebaid I-IV. Translated by John Henry Mozley. Harvard University Press.

Stedman, Edmund Clarence, and Ellen Mackay Hutchinson. 1888. A Library of American Literature: Literature of the Revolutionary Period, 1765-1787. C.L. Webster.

Stephensen, Percy Reginald. 1962. "Colonialism In Our Literature." The Bulletin, June 6, 1962, sec. Vol. 84 No. 4296.

Stoker, Hendrik Gerhardus. 2010. Philosophy Of Creation Idea. Potchefstroom, South Africa. http://archive.org/details/HGStokerPhilosophyOfCreationIdea2010.

Strickler, G.R. and Barnett, D.D., eds. 1888. "The Presbyterian Quarterly" 2 (1).

———, eds. 1894. "The Presbyterian Quarterly" 8 (1–4).

Stuart, Joseph T. 2022. Christopher Dawson: A Cultural Mind in the Age of the Great War. CUA Press.

Sturluson, Snorri. 1916. The Prose Edda. Translated by Arthur Gilchrist Brodeur. American-Scandinavian Foundation.

Suetonius. 1920. Suetonius. Translated by John Carew Rolfe. Vol. 1. W. Heinemann.

———. 2008. Lives of the Caesars. Translated by Catharine Edwards. OUP Oxford.

Sullivan, Andrew. 2020. "Why Is Wokeness Winning?" Substack newsletter. The Weekly Dish (blog). October 16, 2020. https://andrewsullivan.substack.com/p/why-is-wokeness-winning.

Sydney Morning Herald. 1842. "Australianism." Sydney Morning Herald, November 14, 1842. http://nla.gov.au/nla.

news-article12414674.

Symons, Julian. 1974. Buller's Campaign. 2nd edition. London [Etc.] : White Lion Publishers.

Tacitus, R. M. Ogilvie, Eric Herbert Warmington, and Michael Winterbottom. 1914. Agricola. Germania. Dialogus. Translated by M. Hutton and W. Peterson. Revised edition. Cambridge, Mass: Harvard University Press.

Taft, George S., and United States Congress Senate Committee on Privileges and Elections. 1893. Compilation of Senate Election Cases from 1789 to 1885. U.S. Government Printing Office.

Talbot, Winthrop. 1917. Americanization: Principles of Americanism, Essentials of Americanization, Technic of Race-Assimilation, Annotated Bibliography. H. W. Wilson Company.

Taleb, Nassim Nicholas. 2018. Skin in the Game: Hidden Asymmetries in Daily Life. Random House Publishing Group.

Tattam, Henry, ed. 1848. The Apostolical Constitutions: Or, Canons of the Apostles, in Coptic. Oriental translation fund of Great Britain and Ireland.

Taylor, Charles. 1886. The Teaching of the Twelve Apostles: With Illustrations from the Talmud : Two Lectures on an Ancient Church Manual Discovered at Constantinople, Given at the Royal Institution of Great Britain on May 29th and June 6th, 1885. Deighton Bell.

———. 1992. Sources of the Self: The Making of the Modern Identity. Cambridge University Press.

Tertullian. 1870. The Writings. Bavarian State Library. Clark.

———. 1885. Ante-Nicene Fathers 3: Latin Christianity: Its Founder, Tertullian. Vol. 3. Buffalo, NY: Christian Literature Comapny.

———. 1903. The Ante-Nicene Fathers: Latin Christianity: Its Founder, Tertullian. I. Apologetic; II. Anti-Marcion; III. Ethical. C. Scribner's Sons.

———. 1959. Treatises on Penance: On Penitence and On Purity. Paulist Press.

———. 2020. Ante-Nicene Christian Library: Volume XI: The Writings of Tertullian. Edited by Alexander Donaldson Roberts James. BoD – Books on Demand.

Tertullian, and Minucius Felix. 1950. Apologetical Works; Octavius. Washington, D.C.: CUA Press.

Tertullian, Alexander Roberts, and Sir James Donaldson. 1869. Ante-Nicene Christian Library: The Writings of Tertullian, v. 1 (1872). T. and T. Clark.

The Southern Magazine. 1871. Vol. 8. Murdoch, Browne & Hill.

The Spirit of the Nation: By the Writers of The Nation Newspaper. 1844. Duffy.

Theocritus. 1912. The Greek Bucolic Poets. Loeb Classical Library 28. University of Chicago: W. Heinemann.

Thielman, Frank. 2010. Ephesians (Baker Exegetical Commentary on the New Testament). Baker Books.

Thiselton, Anthony C. 2000. The First Epistle to the Corinthians: A Commentary on the Greek Text. Wm. B. Eerdmans Publishing.

Tho. 2017. "Nations by Consent." Text. Mises Institute. October 3, 2017. https://mises.org/library/nations-consent.

Times, Christopher Lydon Special to The New York. 1976. "CARTER DEFENDS ALL WHITE AREAS." The New York Times, April 7, 1976, sec. Archives. https://www.nytimes.com/1976/04/07/archives/carter-defends-allwhite-areas-says-government-shouldnt-try-to-end.html.

Tocqueville, Alexis de. 2003. Democracy in America. The Lawbook Exchange, Ltd.

Tocqueville, Alexis De. 2010. The Old Regime and the French Revolution. Knopf Doubleday Publishing Group.

Tolkien, J. R. R. 1986. The Return of the King: The Lord of the Rings: Part Three. Random House Worlds.

———. 1992. The Book of Lost Tales: Part Two. Random House Worlds.

———. 2012. The Letters of J. R. R. Tolkien. HarperCollins UK.

Tolkien, John Ronald Reuel. 2000. The Letters of J.R.R. Tolkien: A Selection. Houghton Mifflin Company.

Tolstoy, graf Leo. 1916. Anna Karenin: A Novel by Leo Tolstoy. Heinemann.

Tone, Theobald Wolfe. 1828. The Life of Theobald Wolfe Tone. Hunt and Clarke.

Tone, Theobald Wolfe, and William Theobald Wolfe Tone. 1826. Life of Theobald Wolfe Tone ... Gales & Seaton.

Totten, Silas, ed. 1861. Fast Day Sermons: Or, The Pulpit on the State of the Country. Rudd & Carleton.

Tours), Saint Gregory (Bishop of. 1927. The History of the Franks. Clarendon Press.

Toye, Richard. 2010. Churchill's Empire: The World That Made Him and the World He Made. Henry Holt and Company.

Tozer, A. W. 2010. Tozer Speaks: Volume One: 128 Compelling & Authoritative Teachings of A.W. Tozer. Moody Publishers.

Tranquillus, Suetonius. n.d. "The Lives of the Twelve Caesars." Translated by Alexander Thomson. Gutenberg. Accessed January 5, 2024. https://www.gutenberg.org/files/6400/6400-h/6400-h.htm.

Trask, H. A. Scott. 2019. "The Fatherland and the Nation - Chronicles." February 1, 2019. https://chroniclesmagazine.org/view/the-fatherland-and-the-nation/, https://chroniclesmagazine.org/view/the-fatherland-and-the-nation/.

Treasury, United States Department of the, and Alexander Hamilton. 1892. Alexander Hamilton's Famous Report on Manufactures: Made to Congress December 5, 1791 : In His Capacity as Secretary of the Treasury. Potter publishing Company.

Trueman, Carl R. 2022. Strange New World: How Thinkers and Activists Redefined Identity and Sparked the Sexual Revolution. Crossway.

Tryphiodorus. 1928. Tryphiodorus, Oppian, Colluthus. Translated by Mair, A. W. Vol. 219. Loeb Classical Library. London: William Heinemann Ltd. https://www.theoi.com/Text/Tryphiodorus.html.

Tuininga, Matthew J. 2017. Calvin's Political Theology and the Public Engagement of the Church: Christ's Two Kingdoms. Cambridge University Press.

Turley, Steve. 2018. The New Nationalism: How the Populist Right Is Defeating Globalism and Awakening a New Political Order. CreateSpace Independent Publishing Platform.

Turretin, Francis. 1997. Institutes of Elenctic Theology. P & R Publishing.

Tyler, Moses Coit. 1887a. Patrick Henry. Houghton, Mifflin.

———. 1887b. Patrick Henry. Houghton, Mifflin.

Tyndale, William. 1831. The Works of Tyndale. Edited by Thomas Russell. Ebenezer Palmer.

Tzu, Lao. 1879. The Texts of Taoism, Part I. Oxford University Press. https://oll.libertyfund.org/title/tzu-the-texts-of-taoism-part-i.

Unger, Jonathan. 2016. Chinese Nationalism. Routledge.

University of North Carolina (1793-1962) Bureau of. 1921. "The League of Nations." Extension Bulletin 1 (8).

Unwin, Joseph Daniel. 1934. Sex and Culture. Oxford University Press, H. Milford.

Ussher, James. 1702. A Body of Divinity,or, The Sum and Substance of Christian Religion .. London, Robinson. http://archive.org/details/bodyofdivinityyorooussh.

Valerius, Catallus. 1894. Carmina. Translated by Sir Richard Francis Burton. London. https://www.perseus.tufts.edu/hopper/text?doc=Perseus%3Atext%3A1999.02.0005%3Apoem%3D34.

VanDrunen, David. 2010. Natural Law and the Two Kingdoms: A Study in the Development of Reformed Social Thought. Wm. B. Eerdmans Publishing.

Various. 1987. "Harvard Ukrainian Studies." Ukranian Research Institute XI (1/2).

———. 2006. I'll Take My Stand: The South and the Agrarian Tradition. LSU Press.

Vaughan, Alden T. 1972. The Puritan Tradition in America, 1620-1730. UPNE.

Vaughan, Robert, and John Wycliffe. 1828. The Life and Opinions of John de Wycliffe: Illus. Principally from His Unpublished Manuscripts; with a Preliminary View of the Papal System, and of the State of the Protestant Doctrine in Europe, to the Commencement of the Fourteenth Century. B.J. Holdsworth, Hatchard and Son.

Venerable), Saint Bede (the, and A. M. Sellar. 1907. Bede's Ecclesiastical History of England. G. Bell.

Vergil. 2021. The Aeneid. Translated by Sarah Ruden. Yale University Press.

Vermes, Geza. 1995. The Dead Sea Scrolls in English, Revised and Exetnded 4th Edition. Sheffield Academic Press.

Vincent, Marvin Richardson. 7. Word Studies in the New Testament. Vol. 3. C. Scribner's Sons.

Vinson, John. 1995. "The Social Contract - The Bible and Borders." The Social Contract Press. Volume , Number 3 (Spring 1995. https://www.thesocialcontract.com/artman2/publish/tsc0503/article_453.shtml.

Viret, Pierre. 2004. Instruction chrétienne. Edited by Arthur-L. Hofer. L'Âge d'homme.

Viret, Pierre, and John Calvin. 2018. Nothing Like God: A Penetrating Application of the Second Commandment. Psalm 78 Ministries.

Virgil. 1920. The Aeneid of Virgil. Translated by John William Mackail. University of California Irvine: Macmillan.

———. 2014. The Aeneid. Translated by A. S. Kline. Poetry In Translation.

———. n.d. "The Aeneid." Translated by John Dryden. Perseus Tufts Edu. Accessed January 4, 2024.

Viroli, Maurizio. 1995. For Love of Country: An Essay on Patriotism and Nationalism. Oxford University Press.

Vonier, Anscar. 1913. The Human Soul and Its Relations with Other Spirits. B. Herder.

Vos, Geerhardus. 2003. Biblical Theology: Old and New Testaments. Wipf and Stock Publishers.

Vos, Johannes Geerhardus. 1980. Blue Banner Faith and Life: Topical Index. All Thirty-Four Volumes, 1945-1979. Reformed Presbyterian Church of North America, Board of Education and Publication. https://bluebanner.com/download/faithandlife.

Wade, Nicholas. 2015. A Troublesome Inheritance: Genes, Race and Human History. Penguin.

Wagner, John A. 2018. Documents of the Reformation. Bloomsbury Publishing USA.

Wagner, Richard. 1912. Richard Wagner's Prose Works. K. Paul, Trench, Trübner.

Walker, George. 1827. Select Specimens of English Prose, from the Reign of Elizabeth to the Present Time, Etc. Bohn.

Walker, William. 2011. The Islands of Destiny. Trafford Publishing.

Wallace, Lew. 1908. Ben-Hur: A Tale of the Christ. Harper.

Walther, C.F.W. 1863. Lehre Und Wehre, Volume 09, 1863 (Doctrine and Defense; in English). Vol. 2. St. Louis, MO: Synodal Printing House of Augsberg. http://www.lutherquest.org/walther/articles/cfw00002.htm#:~:text=He%20can%20be%20a%20bondman,for%20the%20sake%20of%20peace.

Walzer, Michael, Edward T. Kantowicz, John Higham, and Mona Harrington. 1980. The Politics of Ethnicity. Cambridge, Mass u.a: Belknap Press: An Imprint of Harvard University Press.

Warfield, Benjamin B. n.d. The Works of Benjamin B. Warfield, Vol. 9: Studies in Theology. Vol. 9. Accessed January 23, 2024. https://www.logos.com/product/7048/the-works-of-benjamin-b-warfield-vol-9-studies-in-theology.

Warfield, Benjamin Breckinridge. 1919. Paul on Women Speaking in Church .. http://archive.org/details/paulonwomen-speakoowarf.

Washburn, Charles Grenfill. 1925. Henry Cabot Lodge. Massachusetts Historical Society.

Washington, George. 1889. The Writings of George Washington. G.P. Putnam' Sons.

———. 1892. The Writings of George Washington: 1794-1798. G. P. Putnam's sons.

———. 1913. Washington's Farewell Address to the People of the United States, 1796. Houghton, Mifflin.

———. 1931. The Writings of George Washington from the Original Manuscript Sources, 1745-1799. U.S. Government Printing Office.

———. 2023. The Political Writings of George Washington: Volume 2, 1788–1799: Volume II: 1788–1799. Cambridge University Press.

Washington, H. A. 2018. The Writings of Thomas Jefferson: Volume VII. BoD – Books on Demand.

Waszink, Jan. 2023. Hugo Grotius, Annals of the War in the Low Countries: Edition, Translation, and Introduction. Leuven University Press.

Watson, Thomas. 1653. A Commentary on the Most Divine Epistle of St Paul to the Romans. 3rd ed. London: E. Cotes. https://ebooks.regent-college.edu/Wilson-Commentary-1653/4/.

Waugh, Evelyn. 1968. Brideshead Revisited. Penguin.

Weaver, Richard. 1995. Visions Of Order: Cultural Crisis Of Our Time. Bryn Mawr, Penn: Intercollegiate Studies Institute.

Weaver, Richard M. 2013. Ideas Have Consequences. University of Chicago Press.

Weber, Max. 2023. General Economic History. Taylor & Francis.

Webster, Daniel. 1843. Speeches and Forensic Arguments. Tappan & Dennet.

Wehner, Peter. 2019. "The Moral Universe of Timothy Keller." The Atlantic (blog). December 5, 2019. https://www.theatlantic.com/ideas/archive/2019/12/timothy-kellers-moral-universe/603001/.

Welfare, National Conference on Social. 1885. The Social Welfare Forum: Official Proceedings [of The] Annual Meeting.

———. 1886. Proceedings of the National Conference of Social Work. University Of Chicago Press.

Wells, H. G. 1921. The Outline of History.

Werfel, Franz. 1934. The Forty Days of Musa Dagh. Modern Library.

Wesley, John. 1821. Plain Account of Christian Perfection. McDonald, Gill & Company.

———. 1906. Wesley's Revision of the Shorter Catechism. Jennings and Graham.

Wessels, Hannes. 2015. A Handful of Hard Men: The SAS and the Battle for Rhodesia. Casemate.

Westermarck, Edward. 2022. The Origin and Development of the Moral Ideas. DigiCat.

Wheeler, Henry G. 1848. History of Congress: Biographical and Political ; Comprising Memoirs of Members of the Congress of the United States, Drawn from Authentic Sources ; Embracing the Prominent Events of Their Lives, and Their Connection with the Political History of the Times. Harper & Brothers.

White, Christopher. 2013. "The Decline of the Family and the Death of Faith." August 5, 2013. https://www.catholicworldreport.com/2013/08/05/the-decline-of-the-family-and-the-death-of-faith/.

White, Heather. 1989. New Studies in Greek Poetry. University of Michigan: J.C. Gieben.

Whitford, David Mark. 2001. Tyranny and Resistance: The Magdeburg Confession and the Lutheran Tradition. Concordia Publishing House.

Willard, Samuel. 1691. Promise-Keeping a Great Duty. Boston: Benjamin Harris, and John Allen, at the London-Coffee-House. http://name.umdl.umich.edu/N00461.0001.001.

———. 1726. A Complete Body Of Divinity, In Two Hundred And Fifty Expository Lectures. Edited by Sewall, Joseph and Prince, Thomas. Boston: B. Green and S. Kneeland for B. Eliot and D. Henchman.

William of Malmesbury. n.d. Gesta Pontificum Anglorum: The History of the English Bishops. Edited by M. Winterbottom. Translated by R.M. Thomson. Vol. 1. Oxford: Clarendon Press.

Williams, Daniel K. 2020. The Election of the Evangelical: Jimmy Carter, Gerald Ford, and the Presidential Contest of 1976. University Press of Kansas.

Williamson, Chilton. 2018. "The Loss of the Familiar - Chronicles." March 1, 2018. https://chroniclesmagazine.org/web/the-loss-of-the-familiar/, https://chroniclesmagazine.org/web/the-loss-of-the-familiar/.

Wilson, Douglas. 2014. Rules for Reformers. Canon Press & Book Service.

———. 2016. Empires of Dirt: Secularism, Radical Islam, and the Mere Christendom Alternative. Canon Press & Book Service.

———. 2022. The Covenant Household. Canon Press.

Wilson, Edmund. 1996. The American Earthquake. Farrar, Straus and Giroux.

Wilson, James. 1804. The Works of the Honourable James Wilson, L.L.D. Vol. 3. At the Lorenzo Press, printed for Bronson and Chauncey.

———. 1896. The Works of James Wilson, Associate Justice of the Supreme Court of the United States ...: Being His Public Discourses Upon Jurisprudence and the Political Science, Including Lectures as Professor of Law, 1790-2. Callaghan.

Winter, Christian. 2023. "Why We Remain in Flyover Country | Christian Winter." American Reformer (blog). April 10, 2023. https://americanreformer.org/2023/04/why-we-remain-in-flyover-country/.

Winthrop, Robert Charles. 1895. Life and Letters of John Winthrop: Governor of the Massachusetts-Bay Company at Their Emigration to New England, 1630. Ticknor and Fields.

Witsius, Herman. 1804. The Economy of the Covenants, Between God and Man: Comprehending a Complete Body of Divinity. Thomas Kirk, no. 94, Water-street.

Witt, William G. 2021. Icons of Christ: A Biblical and Systematic Theology for Women's Ordination. Baylor University Press. https://www.christianitytoday.com/scot-mcknight/2020/december/so-called-traditional-argument-is-not-traditional.html.

Wolfe, Thomas. 1983. The Autobiography of an American Novelist. Harvard University Press.

Woodard, Colin. 2012. American Nations: A History of the Eleven Rival Regional Cultures of North America. Penguin.

Wordsworth, Christopher. 1853. Eclesiatical Biography Connected with the History of Religion in England. Rivington.

Wrangel, Pyotr. 2020. Always with Honor: The Memoirs of General Wrangel. Translated by Sophie Goulston. Independently published.

Wright, Christopher J. H. 1990. God's People in God's Land: Family, Land, and Property in the Old Testament. Wm. B. Eerdmans Publishing.

Wriston, Walter B. 1992. The Twilight of Sovereignty: How the Information Revolution Is Transforming Our World. Scribner.

Wyngaarden, Martin J. 2008. The Future of the Kingdom in Prophecy and Fulfillment: A Study of the Scope of "Spiritualization" in Scripture. Wipf and Stock Publishers.

Xenophon. 1914. Cyropaedia, Volume I: Books 1-4. Translated by Walter Miller. Loeb Classical Library 51. Cambridge, MA: Harvard University Press.

———. 1923. Memorabilia and Oeconomicus. W. Heinemann.

XI, Pope Pius. 2018. Mit Brennender Sorge: (With Burning Concern). CreateSpace Independent Publishing Platform.

XII, Catholic Church Pope (1939-1958 : Pius. 1939. Summi Pontificatus: Encyclical Letter of Pope Pius XII on the Function of the State in the Modern World (Official Vatican English Translation with Discussion Study Club Outline). National Catholic welfare conference.

XIII, Catholic Church Pope (1878-1903 : Leo. 1941. Immortale Dei, the Christian Constitution of State: Encyclical Letter [of] Pope Leo XIII. Paulist Press.

XIII, Catholic Church Pope (1878-1903 : Leo, and Pope Leo XII. 2002. Rerum Novarum: Encyclical on the Rights and Duties of Capital and Labour. Catholic Truth Society.

XVI, Pope Benedict, and Joseph Ratzinger. 2007. Europe Today and Tomorrow: Addressing the Fundamental Issues. Ignatius Press.

Young, E.J. 1964. "Letters on the Racial Question." The Presbyterian Guardian 33 (8): 128–30.

Zevin, Alexander. 2021. Liberalism at Large: The World According to the Economist. Verso Books.

Zimmerman, Carle C. 2014. Family and Civilization. Open Road Media.

Zinn, Howard, and Anthony Arnove. 2011. Voices of a People's History of the United States. Seven Stories Press.

Zondervan. 2010. The Zondervan Encyclopedia of the Bible, Volume 2: Revised Full-Color Edition. Zondervan Academic.

Zvi, Ehud Ben. 2000. Micah. Wm. B. Eerdmans Publishing.

Zwingli, Ulrich. 2010. The Latin Works and The Correspondence of Hulderich Zwingli: Together With Selections from His German Works 1510 - 1522. Wipf and Stock Publishers.

ALPHABETICAL INDEX

including alternate names when known

TOPICAL INDEX

ANCIENT GRECO-ROMANS

ANCIENT GRECO-ROMANS: AESTHETICS

Botticelli's famous painting of the Birth of Venus casts high ideals of human beauty during the European Renaissance. But is this an accurate depiction of the ancient mediterranean world? Not a few voices in our present day claim that Western civilization is no such thing. Rather, it is a confluence of many non-Westerners, non-Europeans, and, most importantly for these detractors, non-whites. Any standard textbook on the Middle Ages now portrays the ancient-to-medieval time period as a global network of proto-multiculturalism. Modern film retells both the medieval and ancient worlds as one of cosmopolitan diversity. But is this accurate? Is there a substantial Western continuity of people, place, language, religion, invention, architecture, song, and even aesthetic?

ANCIENT NON-WESTERN

Although we have sourced some material which admits of natural social relations, we have found that these ideas were expressed indirectly through a devotion to king, for instance, or in a loyalty to nature itself. The selection below represents a very small amount of material available. Further work is needed in this area, as Jewish, Indian, and Chinese cultures have vast resources in philosophy, theology, and history. Indeed, some areas are still being uncovered and categorized by contemporary scholars.

BIBLE COMMENTARY

BIBLICAL SCHOLARSHIP

The vast resources of biblical scholarship expounding upon the views of people, place, country, lineage, and so on, reveal a wide chasm between the state of theological research and what leaves the pulpit and reaches the pews. While in seminary, this editor researched every dictionary, encyclopedia, and commentary on select themes and passages of Scripture that dealt with socially complex issues, such as slavery, divorce, homosexuals, nationhood, race or ethnicity, and more. The conclusion from such research vindicates an observation once made by Don Carson, to the effect that there's a problem with bible-believing Christians that the theologically liberal "Christian" need not confront. That is the problem of holding as true and explaining to today's world those political incorrect passages we find in Scripture. One often finds conservative scholarship multiplying words or evading the topic altogether, while the liberal scholar straightforwardly explains the issue

at hand. The material below contains only what is germane to the themes of this study. A wide field of scholarship remains open to those wanting further inquiry.

BIBLICAL SCHOLARSHIP: IMAGE OF GOD

The image of God is employed today in order to support the claim that, as all humans are equal in essence (being), they are therefore equal in existence (nature, habit, society). However, theologians have always distinguished between the imago essentialis and the imago conformitas. Humans are all equal in being as God's image – the aspect not lost in the fall; but we are not equal in our confor-

mity to God's likeness – the aspect marred, perverted, or lost in the fall. Internally, we are all equal in essence. Externally, we are unequal in existence.

CHURCH FATHERS

The early church fathers combatted Roman accusations from atheism to immorality while also providing comfort to the Christians scattered about the empire. To prove that Christianity was not a new sect of atheists, these writers defended the antiquity of Christian religion and often justified breaking with the cultural norms of their pagan fathers in order to join this more ancient way. This included social ostracization and persecution. One famous story is of Perpetua whose allegiance to Christ caused her to resist the pleas of her own aged father and the cries of her nursing infant as she was led to her execution.

It is all the more noteworthy, therefore, when the Christians of this same period affirm the goodness and continuity of familial affection, domestic circumspection, and civic identity. Christians today who look back on the church during this time as a pure, spiritual community set apart from the hostile world, should note well the permanence of natural relations.

EARLY CHURCH ON SLAVERY

The purpose of this work is not to promote slavery but to provide insight into natural social relations in the past, particularly in an area that is weakly considered today. The index here is included as a small sample of the divergence between modern evangelical views of slavery and those of the spiritual ancestors of the same.

One explanation for the acceptance of slavery among ancient Christians is that "it was different" during the ancient world. Such claims are general and lack precision. Beyond specifics, the following selection provides valuable hermeneutical clarity concerning social hierarchy. Elsewhere in this work, hierarchy is a natural good, one that God himself created for the purposes of man's benefit and for His glory. Social inequality was a feature of an ordered universe. The moral fabric of Christianity, therefore, did not disrupt this order but instructed Christians to act righteously within it.

ECONOMIC NATIONALISM

Middle Ages

Modern Politics

Poets

The poets often sing of national characters and common life. It is from the countryside that popular material is drawn. This is true in our own day as well as ancient times.

Political Philosophy

SCRIPTURAL INDEX

including deuterocanonical books

Hebrews

4:7 –(237)
7:13-14 –(123)
11:2-9 –(284, 357, 436)
13:1 –(326)

James

3:9 –(55)

1 Peter

2:18 –(436)
3 –(97)
4:10 –(26)

2 Peter

1:7 –(326)

2 John

1:10 –(447)

Revelation

2:26 –(141)
5:9 –(50, 68, 130, 141, 250, 357)
7:9 –(68, 130, 357)
11:9-19 –(140, 357)
12-22 –(258)
12:5 –(68, 119, 141, 258)
13:7 –(141)
14:6 –(68, 141, 357)
15:3-4 –(68, 119, 141)
20:3-8 –(141, 357)
21:1-24 –(50, 69, 119, 130, 141, 252, 253, 357, 373)
22:2-3 –(46, 50, 69, 141)

CHRONOLOGICAL INDEX

some dates are estimates

ETHNIC INDEX

AFRICAN

AMERICAN

English Ancestry

German Ancestry

Dutch Ancestry

Irish Ancestry

Scottish Ancestry

Other American

ＡＵＳＴＲＡＬＩＡＮ

ＡＵＳＴＲＩＡＮ

ＢＲＩＴＩＳＨ

DENOMINATIONAL INDEX

Christian religious affiliation only, not a judgement
on orthodoxy | unknowns and other religions excluded

Lutheran

Methodist

Orthodox

Presbyterian